# ... Thurston Genealogies

1635—1880

# THURSTON GENEALOGIES

COMPILED BY

BROWN THURSTON, PORTLAND, MAINE.

. . . . . "Si quid novisti rectius istis,
Candidus imperti: si non, his utere mecum."—*Hor.*

PUBLISHED BY
BROWN THURSTON,
AND HOYT, FOGG & DONHAM,
PORTLAND, MAINE,
1880.

6

# CONTENTS.

# LIST OF PORTRAITS.

# TO THE READER.

GENEALOGICAL researches are comparatively recent in this country. It doubtless seems to many that questions of birth and lineage are of little consequence under republican institutions, where all men are free and equal, and where laws of primogeniture and hereditary distinctions have no place. The attempt to trace out the lines of family descent and history is too often frustrated by the indifference of those who might impart the desired information ; and the compiler is met at the threshold of his inquiries with the question *Cui bono?* — of what use will it be?

Many are unable to give their ancestry back of their parents, and one writes, "Socrates was once reproached for want of knowledge of his ancestry, and he replied 'So much the better, for my race begins with myself.'" This is not good doctrine ; for I think experience has proved that the influence of genealogy has been elevating and refining, imparting a desire to be useful in society, and to hold a respectable place in history. Socrates himself, probably, would have been glad to be remembered.

It would be difficult for the compiler to enumerate the obstacles he has had to encounter in getting the annals of the Thurstons in this country into their present shape ; and he must crave the indulgence of his readers for many errors and omissions, by far the larger part of which are fairly chargeable to imperfect reports received. At the same time, it should be stated, there are those who have taken a hearty interest, and worked right royally, to have their families placed with proper fullness and accuracy upon these pages. Several of them

are persons who have come into the family by marriage, and by their faithful and painstaking endeavors, have proved their appreciation of the name and their desire to perpetuate its history.

If the most distinguished genealogist this country has ever produced, the late James Savage of Boston, found it necessary to add to his four volumes one hundred and fifty pages of "additions and corrections," the author of these pages ought to be accorded the privilege of fifty. Having already detected many errors, he expects to find more; and what he fails to find he hopes will be pointed out to him by correspondents, so that he may leave behind him a corrected copy for some future gleaner in the field.

I have not limited these researches to the descendants of a single branch of the Thurston family, but have included all of the name in the United States. The leading feature of the work, however, comprises those who sprung from the first three of the name who came to New England, Daniel, John, and Edward. I have no knowledge that these were kindred to each other, though there seems to be some probability that such was the fact. In pursuit of the required information for this volume, I have sent out over 5000 circulars and letters, and received about 1500 letters and postals in reply. Nearly a hundred city, town, and church records have been consulted; old Bibles containing family records sought out, and their treasures of genealogy rescued from oblivion; the memories of aged people have been brought into requisition, and valuable information has been put upon the printed page to be handed down to posterity, which, but for this effort, would have perished with the lives of those from whom it was obtained.

Some of the communications received should rightly have a place in the book as *addenda*, as epistolary curiosities worthy of preservation. I have admitted a few which some, it is true, may think puerile; but which others will probably read with interest and pleasure.

The extended search for our ancestors in England has utterly failed

of satisfactory results. I have the record of nearly a hundred Thurstons of Challock, county of Kent, England, coming down to 1638, after which date the name became extinct in that locality. The scribe imagines he has in this list the name of ·Daniel Thurston, who settled in Newbury, Mass., and married Anne Pell, a name which he says is very common in Kent; but it is evident to me that it is mere conjecture. I have the outline of thirty-eight wills, recorded in the Kent registry, but no trace of our English ancestors can be derived from them. The result of a search in the College of Arms in London, where the pedigrees or arms of sixty-one Thurstons are recorded, reveals nothing more tangible than the fact that the arms of Thurstons of Kent have been perpetuated by three families recorded in these pages.

Genealogy is defined by an encyclopedist to be "an account or history of the origin, lineage and relationships of a distinguished family." So far as relates to the twelve or thirteen thousand names that fill these pages, the word "distinguished" may as well be omitted, as it is appropriate to but very few of them; yet without high or wide distinction, it is an amiable and fruitful sentiment which cherishes the family life, characteristically pure, patriotic, and beneficial to the world. Riches, honor, and attainments in literature and the arts have not, as a rule, been the heritage of the descendants of the name in this country. There are, however, exceptions. The great majority have had a competency, and have been seemingly happy to adopt the language of Queen Anne in the play.

> . . . " 'Tis better to be lowly born,
> And range with humble livers in content,
>    Than to be perked up in a glistering grief,
> And wear a golden sorrow."

Nearly all the Thurstons have moved in the middle walks of life— not so elevated as to be dazed by splendor, nor so poor as to be pinched by want. Very many it will be seen have been christian ministers, and a very large proportion connected otherwise with church-

es as members or church officers. An unusual majority were pious, God-fearing men and women.

Upon the whole, the writer is quite satisfied with the character of his ancestors, and the book is as perfect as he could make it under the circumstances. Time and again he has been surprised by receiving important corrections and additions a day or two after the pages were printed. All these, however, will be found in the appendix, under "corrections and additions," and at the end of the index. He gives it to the public as it is, and hopes those who have the curiosity to peruse its pages will do so in a spirit of candor, and an appreciative sense of the impossibility of putting in a form entirely correct the statistics of any family running back through a period of two hundred and fifty years.

The statistics of names in the volume are as follows:

Names of Thurstons . . . . . . . . . . . . . . . . 5,390
Descendants having other names . . . . . . . . . . 4,008
Persons who have married Thurstons or their descendants . 4,115
Persons incidentally mentioned . . . . . . . . . . . 1,846
The pedigrees of 23 families who have married Thurstons are given.

# EXPLANATIONS.

The names of Thurstons and their descendants are numbered consecutively from the beginning to the end of the book; so that there can be no difficulty in finding the person looked for, by following the numbers in the index.

The indexes at the end of the volume are full and complete, giving every name and the number attached to it. They are given in four distinct families; so that any person in either family may be more readily found. Let every one examine the arrangement of these indexes carefully when you first get the volume, and when you have learned their order and scope, you will be able readily to ascertain where any name wanted is to be found.

The generation of every Thurston is given in the first lines of every name introduced; the small figures after the name denoting the generation. For example, take my own name on page 171. Brown,[6] i.e., the sixth generation, son of David,[5] the fifth generation, son of David,[4] the fourth generation, son of Richard,[3] the third generation, son of Daniel,[2] the second generation, son of Daniel,[1] the first generation, who came to this country about 1635, and settled in Newbury, Mass.

This + character placed before any name, denotes that further on in the book the same number will be found, in larger figures, and placed in the middle of the line, so as to strike the eye at a glance. Under these figures the history and children of the person named are given.

The grand-children, when introduced after the first appearance of the name, are set a little further in from the margin than the children, and printed in italic letters ; so also the great-grand-children, are placed still further in from the margin. By taking heed to these suggestions, you need have no confusion in tracing out the families.

## ARMS OF THURSTONS IN ENGLAND.

THURSTON of Hoxne Abbey, Suffolk, where monuments exist tracing the family back to the reign of James I. (1603), sa. three bugle-horns stringed, or, garnished az. Crest: A stork, ar. Motto: Esse quam videri.

THURSTON, Lancashire, sa. three bugle-horns stringed, ar. two and one.

THURSTON, Cranbrook, Kent, sa. a chev. betw. three bugle-horns stringed, or. Crest: Out of a plume of five ostrich feathers, a demi-griffin, segreant. Motto: Thrust-on.

THURSTON, sa. three bugle-horns ar. stringed or. Crest: A woodpecker proper.

THURSTON. Crest: A thrush ppr.

THURSTON, ar. three bars, sa.; on the first, a lion pass. guard. betw. two martlets, or; on the second, three cinquefoils of the last; on the third, three escallops of the third; on a canton gu. a bird, with wings expanded, of the first.

THURSTONE, Elston, Co. Huntingdon. Or, on a canton, az. a falcon volant, with jesses and bells of the first. Crest: a wolf's head or, pierced through the neck with an arrow gu. headed and feathered ar., vulned of the second.

# READ THIS EVERY ONE.

It has been my aim from the start, to make a full and perfect record. I have never expected to gain anything pecuniarily by my labor upon this work.

THEREFORE, let any one who discovers an omission or an error, *immediately* communicate the same to me, and I will leave a corrected copy of the book for some one to enlarge upon, as the generations to follow shall have come upon the stage of life. Direct to

BROWN THURSTON, *Portland, Me.*

# IMPORTANT NOTICE.

Let every one who wishes to get the full benefit of the contents of this book, turn to page 493, and note the corrections and additions, which came to the compiler after the pages alluded to were printed. They are so numerous and so important that he wishes he could afford to print the book over again.

Take the first case, mentioned on page 493 : p. 30, no. 27, 3d line. Turn to page 30, and after the word Seaver, make a + with a pen, and note on the margin, see p. 493.

Go through with all the corrections and additions, found all along to the very *end* of the index, in the same way, and the book will be prepared to give you all the information it contains.

Without this labor, you may miss some very important facts.

# IN GENERAL.

THE name of THURSTON is said to be derived from the Saxon, Danish, and Runic *troest*, meaning *trusty* or *faithful*.

Lower's Patronymica says, "in some cases, perhaps, from the Teutonic name *Turstin*, which is found in Domesday as the designation of persons of both Norman and Saxon. One *Turstanus* is there described as *machinator*, probably a military engineer. *Ton*, a common termination for names of places, and consequently for those of persons."

Ferguson says, "THURSTON and others from the god Thor, son of Odin."

Arthur, in his work on the derivation of family names, says, "Thurston—local—the hill or town where the Saxon god Thor was worshiped."

In Horstred's work on the Danes in England, Scotland, and Ireland, THURSTON is found as a Scandinavian name.

F. H. Thurston of Oconto, Wis., says, "I have no question that the name Thurston is of Scandinavian origin, and was originally Thor-sten — Thor's stone — freely, 'God's Rock.' In the Swedish poem of Fridthof's Saga, by Bishop Tegnér, Thorsten, although the friend of the king, and the father of the mighty Fridthof, was still a yeoman."

Prof. Longfellow, in a letter dated Cambridge, May 11, 1877, says, "I have no doubt that you are of Scandinavian descent. Thorston, Thorsten, and Thurston must be one and the same. The Stone of Thor—the god of thunder. That is rather portentous, but you cannot escape this divine genealogy. Yours, very truly, Henry W. Longfellow."

Extract from a letter received from Rev. Henry Blodget,* missionary in China, under the auspices of the American Board:

PEKING, Aug. 4, 1877.

*My Dear Cousin:*—I am interested to know that you are preparing an account of the genealogy of the Thurston family. In these days when so much is made of the science of etymology, and when fanciful derivations of words are not unfrequently suggested, you may be excused if you trace back the name Thurston to the times of heathen mythology, and find, even in paganism, a religious idea in the combination of the two words by which the name is formed.

You will naturally find in "Thurs" the god Thor, and in "ton" you might at first be disposed to find "town," and thus judge that "Thurston" was at first the name of a town in which worship was paid to the god "Thor." But we find the

* Son of Mrs. Mary (Thurston) Blodget, Bucksport, Me.

2

name Thurs*tan*, which can hardly be other than Thurs*ton*, as early as the twelfth century. Sir Walter Scott, in his "History of Scotland," vol. i, chap. 3, p. 28, writes, "Thurstan, archbishop of York, a prelate of equal prudence and spirit, summoned a convention of the English northern barons, and exhorted them to a determined resistance." This form of the name, ending in "*tan*," suggests *thane*, a "minister, servant, soldier, officer, master," lord of manor, baron, as the original of "ton." In that case the Thurstons were originally the servants or ministers of Thor, and, when converted, we may hope they became the no less zealous servants of the living and true God. At all events it is pleasing to find that one of the family in the early part of the twelfth century had attained to the dignity of being archbishop of York. And it may be excusable in a son, if in reading of the "blessing of the aged Thurstan," spoken of by Sir Walter Scott, he is reminded of the benedictions which but a few years since in the state of Maine so often fell upon waiting congregations from the lips of his own sire, "the venerable Father Thurston." *

Thorstein (son of Erik the Red) in 1005 made an unsuccessful visit to Vineland (New England, called Vineland from its abundance of vines) and died on the expedition, showing that America was surely discovered by the Northmen long before Columbus.

### THE NAME IN ENGLAND.

THURSTON, a parish in Suffolk county.

THURSTONLAND, a town in York county.

THURSTON, a Danish monk, lived in the Abbey of Croyland A.D. 800.

THURSTON, a Dane, rebuilt Ely.

THURSTON, another Danish monk, is mentioned in history A.D. 879.

THURSTON, a Thane, lived in 1014, under King Canute.

THURSTON was a coiner under King Edward in 870.

THURSTON at York was coiner under King Ethelred in 917 and to 1013.

THURSTON, a knight in King Edward's suite in 1048.

THURSTON of Thetford, Norfolk county, and his son Ralph were mint-masters at the time of the conquest under William the conqueror in 1066, and had the same arms as borne at the present day by their descendants.

THURSTON in Norwich, 1066.

THURSTON under King Henry II., 1109.

THURSTAN, the Abbot of Glastonbury, retired in 1084 to Caen, Normandy, from whence he came. He was afterward restored, in the time of King William Rufus.

THURSTAN was elected the twenty-eighth archbishop of York, chaplain and secretary to Henry II. in 1100. In 1132 he founded Fountain Abbey, and upon its ruins still remains his device, "a thrush upon a tun." He is described as a "man of lofty stomach, but yet of notable learning." As an interesting scrap of ancient history and practice we copy from "The Early English Church," by Edward Churton, M.A., rector of Crayke, Durham, England:

In this reign of confusion and blood, there is yet one name which cannot be remembered by Englishmen without respect,—the name of Thurstan, archbishop of York. He was elected by the clergy, as it appears by the wish of King Henry (II.), whose chaplain he was. He went abroad a few years after, to be invested by Pope

---

* Rev. David Thurston, D.D., of Winthrop, Me.

Calixtus, who in A.D. 1119 was holding a council or synod at Rheims. This act gave great offense to Henry, who banished him for a year or more; but he was afterward restored, and gained from the pope the privilege that his See should be independent of and equal to that of Canterbury. This was one of many points of contention in those times, and changes were often made. York was sometimes subject to Canterbury and sometimes independent, the popes favoring either, as they liked them best; but at length Canterbury prevailed. These contests of Norman pride helped on the popes' usurpations. Thurstan himself was a compound of the Norman baron with the christian bishop, and his character may serve as a specimen of many of the great churchmen of his day; but there were in him great and good qualities mixed with the darkness and superstition of his time. When he was fixed in his exalted station, he was remarkable for the strictness of his life and the firm uprightness of his conduct. His mode of living was frugal, and yet as generous as became a bishop, who ought to be "given to hospitality." He was abundant in alms-deeds and instant in prayer. In the celebration of the holy communion he was often moved to tears. He promoted men of good life and learning; was gentle to the obedient and unbending, though without harshness, to the opponents of good discipline. He was as severe to himself as he was to others, and was remarked for the severity of his penances, going on fast days attired in sackcloth and, what was then a common practice, afflicting his body with a scourge.

He was at an advanced age when, in the third year of Stephen's reign, A.D. 1138, David, king of Scotland, having declared in favor of his niece, the empress Matilda, collected his forces and made a dreadful inroad into the northern counties, turning his pretext of opposing a usurper into a plea for plundering and massacring the inhabitants of a country at peace with him. There was neither counsel nor conduct among the barons of the north! Some who dwelt nearest the border had joined the invading army that they might partake the spoils, when Thurstan invited them to a conference for the defense of the country. He represented to them the disgrace that was brought upon the realm of the Norman conquerors if they, who had overcome a people often victorious over the Scots, were now to quail before such less worthy antagonists. He showed them that the nature of the inroad made it no longer a question whether the Scots came as allies of the empress or enemies of England, and that whoever might be the rightful sovereign, it was their duty to protect the soil and the people against such wanton injury and destruction. The barons, Walter l'Espec of Cleveland, Roger Mowbray, William Percy, and other large landed proprietors in Yorkshire, assembled an army, with which they encamped at North Allerton. To impress on the people the conviction that they were to fight, not for a doubtful title, but for the cause of religion, their churches and their homes, there was no royal banner carried to the field; but a tall shipmast, erected on a wagon, bore a sacred ensign, such as was used in the processions of the church, representing our Saviour on the cross, pierced with his five wounds. Round this the Norman barons, with their retainers, vowed to stand or fall. Ralph, bishop of Orkney, a suffragan of Thurstan (Thurstan being too infirm to come in person), mounted the wagon, and encouraged the soldiers to fight with the confidence that it was a holy war. The Scots, after a stubborn conflict, were completely routed and fled in disorder; and thus an end was put to the most successful attempt they ever made on the borders, and one which, but for Thurstan's devout energy, would in all probability have given them possession of the whole country north of the Humber.

Within two years after the battle of the standard, as it was called, the aged Thurstan felt his vital vigor to decay, and prepared for a more solemn hour of conflict. He set his house in order, and assembling the priests of the cathedral of York in his own chapel, made his last confession before them; and lying with bared body on the ground before the altar of St. Andrew, received from some of their hands the discipline of the scourge, with tears bursting from his contrite heart. And remembering a vow made in his youth at Clugny, the famous monastery in Burgundy, he went to Pontefract, to a newly founded house of Cluniac monks, followed by an honorable procession of the priests of the church of York and a great number of laymen. There, on the festival of the conversion of St. Paul, he took the habit of a monk in the regular way, received the abbot's blessing, and for the remainder of his life gave himself entirely to the care of the salvation of his soul.

On the 6th of February, A.D. 1140, twenty-six years and a half after his accession to the archbishopric, the canons of the church of York and other religious persons standing round, the hour of his departure being at hand, he celebrated the vigils in commemoration of the dead in Christ, read the lesson himself (probably Job, chap.

x.), and with a clear voice, pausing and sometimes groaning in spirit, chanted the solemn verses of the hymn *Dies iræ:*

Day of wrath, the dreadful day,
Shall the bannered cross display,
Earth in ashes melt away.

Who can paint the agony,
When his coming shall be nigh,
Who shall all things judge and try?

When the trumpet's thrilling tone,
Through the tombs of ages gone,
Summons all before the throne,

Death and time shall stand aghast,
And creation at the blast
Rise to answer for the past.

Then the volume shall be spread,
And the writing shall be read
Which shall judge the quick and dead.

Then the Judge shall sit; oh, then
All that's hid shall be made plain,
Unrequited nought remain.

Woe is me! what shall I plead?
Who for me shall intercede,
When the righteous scarce is freed?

King of dreadful majesty,
Saving souls in mercy free,
Fount of pity, save thou me.

Weary, seeking me, wast thou,
And for me in death didst bow,
Let thy pain avail me now.

Thou didst set the adultress free,
Heardst the thief upon the tree,
Hope vouchsafing e'en to me.

Nought of thee my prayers can claim,
Save in thy free mercy's name,
Save me from the undying flame!

With thy sheep my place assign,
Separate from the accursed line,
Set me on thy right with thine!

When the lost, to silence driven,
To devouring flames are given,
Call me with the blest to heaven!

Suppliant, lo! to earth I bend,
My bruised heart to ashes rend,
Care thou, Lord, for my last end!

At the end of this solemn service of humiliation he sank to the earth, and while the monks gathered around and prayed for him, breathed his last.

The beautiful Cistercian Abbey of Fountains was founded by the charity of this remarkable christian bishop. He was also the founder of the See of Carlisle, A.D. 1133.

THURSTON was one of the archbishops of Fife, Scotland, in the twelfth century.

JOHN THURSTON and Margaret his wife were imprisoned in Colchester castle, where he died in May, 1557, and his wife, on Sept. 17th following, was burned.

WALTER THURSTON, vicar of Mettingham, Suffolk county, 1349.

JOHN THURSTON, rector of Flixton, Suffolk county, 1562.

THURSTONS of Challock, resident there as early as the reign of Edward IV., 1461, extinct since 1622.

Pedigrees of the following families are contained in manuscripts in the British Museum:

Kent county—Thurston of Challock.
Lancashire—Thurston of Anderton.
London—Thurston of Hunts.
London—Thurston.
Suffolk—Thurston of Hoxne.

### EARLY SETTLERS IN NEW ENGLAND.

DANIEL THURSTON, probably from Cranbrook, Kent county, in the south-east portion of England, had a grant of "an house lott" in Newbury, Mass., Nov. 6, 1638. He married Anne Lightfoot, Aug. 29, 1648, and died without issue Feb. 16, 1666.

DANIEL THURSTON, probably a nephew of the above, as he gave him all his property by will, married Anne Pell, Oct. 20, 1655, and lived and died in Newbury; is the germ from which all the Newbury Thurstons came, as will be seen further on in this book.

There is a tradition that three brothers of the name came together from England, and landed in Newbury, in 1638. Of these, the two Daniels settled in Newbury. Farmer mentions a John Thurston of Newbury in 1641, who may have been of the number. It is possible that Edward Thurston of Newport, R. I., was one, whose descendants are largely delineated in this work.

RICHARD THURSTON had a ten acre lot granted him in Salem, Mass., Jan. 29, 1636–7 ; was a mariner. He married Martha Stanley, daughter of Christopher Stanley, moved to Boston and had a son, Samuel, born there July 11, 1652.

CHARLES THURSTON, in Plymouth, Mass., was able to bear arms in August, 1643.

JOHN THURSTON had a grant of twenty acres of land in Salem, Mass., Jan. 21, 1638–9, and appears on record in Salem till 1655, in which year we find a John in Newport, R. I., on the list of freemen, which very likely was the same man.

JOHN THURSTON of Wrentham, Suffolk county, Eng., aged thirty, and his wife Margaret, aged thirty-two, were passengers for New England in the "Mary Anne" of Yarmouth, Eng., May 10, 1637. They are traced down to the present time further on in the volume.

RICHARD THURSTON, commander of the "John Adventure" of New England, by order of the council of state, had license to go to Maryland with his ship June 9, 1651. By another order of June 11th, a petition from him was referred to the committee of the admiralty. July 29, 1652, he was granted permission by the English authorities to carry one ton of shot and fifty-six barrels of powder to New England, and was instructed to declare the Dutch enemies to the commonwealth ; war having just been declared against Holland.

THOMAS THURSTON, a Quaker, aged thirty-four, was a passenger in the "Speedwell," from London, May 30, 1656, and landed at Boston Aug. 27, 1656. He, with three other passengers, after being examined, were committed to prison, "there to remain until the return of the ship that brought them," and then to be carried back to England, "lest the purity of the religion professed in the churches of New England should be defiled with error."

THOMAS THURSTON resided at Southold, L. I., 1670 to 1692. He married Priscilla, daughter of Richard Benjamin. He died October, 1697. She died October, 1722. They had:

John, married Mary, daughter of Jonathan Moore.
Thomas, born 1680; died Feb. 6, 1736.
Robert, married Martha Horton.

# THURSTON GENEALOGIES.

DANIEL THURSTON, senior, came from England to Newbury, in the county of Essex, state of Massachusetts, at a very early day, as upon the records of Newbury there is an entry of a grant to him in these words : "24 November, 1638, there was granted unto Daniell Thurston an house lot on the Neck, over the great river, of four acres, next to John Osgood." As Newbury was incorporated in 1635, he must have come to America between 1635 and 1638.

Thus far, it has been impossible to ascertain for a certainty from

what county in England this Daniel came.    There was at the time an
immense emigration from England to this country.    And among the
names collected by Drake while in England, no name of Thurston
appears among the early emigrants except that of John Thurston,
who was from Wrentham, in the county of Suffolk, and came over in
the "Mary Anne" of Yarmouth, and settled in Dedham in 1637, at
the age of thirty-six.

Upon this subject of the place of nativity of the elder Daniel,
James Savage, the historian, of Boston, in a letter to Hon. A. S.
Thurston of Elmira, N. Y., dated Sept. 16, 1858, says:

> As yet nobody can answer your two points as to the *place* in England from which
> your progenitor came, or the *ship* which brought him.   That all the Thurstons in
> America did *not* spring from the Newbury family, the highest probability appears.
> One John Thurston had a grant of land [twenty acres] at Salem in 1638 [records
> say, 21, 11 month, 1639], but he may be a different John, I think, from him whose
> baptism at Wrentham, Eng., 13 January, 1601, I have certified to me.   He came in
> the Mary Anne from Great Yarmouth in Norfolk, the nearest port for that part of
> Suffolk in which Wrentham lies, about fifteen miles distant, 1637, bringing two
> sons, Thomas, baptized 4 August, 1633, and John, baptized 13 September, 1635.
> Here he lived at Dedham and owned estate in that part which became Medfield. . .
> A Charles, too, I find at Plymouth, 1643, and Edward at Newport, who married,
> 1647, and had plenty of children.   As none of these give me their whereabouts in
> England, or tell in what ship any one came, we are left quite at large to conjecture.
> Still it must be a good point to know so exactly about John, and it is a fair infer-
> ence that one or more of the next came from the county of Suffolk.   Many of the
> substantial yeomen and prosperous mechanics of that shire were, no doubt, attract-
> ed to our side of the water by the success of their neighbor, our first governor,
> Winthrop.

Joshua Coffin of Newbury, who was somewhat of a historian, writes
to A. S. Thurston, under date of April 15, 1859:

> I find in the county records the names of two hundred and thirty-six persons of
> Newbury who took the oath of allegiance in September, 1678.   The list is in the
> elegant hand writing of Rev. John Woodbridge, who affixed the age to every name.
> Thus he says, "Daniel Thurston, forty."   Now if the age and date of his marriage
> are correct, he was only seventeen when he was married to Anne Pell, who, I
> think, came from Salem.   There were Pells in Salem but none in Newbury.
> Whether the age of Daniel is or is not correct, he was a boy when he came to
> Newbury with his uncle Daniel, who was one of the original grantees of Newbury,
> and of course came between 1635 and 1638.   Again, the Newbury troubles about
> the militia happened, if I remember rightly, about 1655.   It is therefore very prop-
> erly said, "young Daniel Thurston is under his uncle."   Of the two hundred and
> thirty-six who took the oath of fidelity the ages are from sixteen to sixty.   Young
> Daniel to be under his uncle must have been less than twenty-one.   He probably
> had taken the oath of allegiance and signed the petition.   Nothing satisfactory can
> be ascertained from the witnesses of the two wills.   John Poor was Daniel Thurs-
> ton's next door neighbor in Newbury.   He came from Wiltshire, 1635.   John
> Cheney came to Roxbury in 1635, thence to Newbury.   Richard Dole, son of Wil-
> liam, was born in Thornbury, Eng., 1624; was a clerk in Mr. Lowell's store in
> Bristol, 1639.   Thomas Hale came from some other part of England, and all of
> them, Poor, Cheney, Dole, and Hale, were Thurston's near neighbors in Newbury.

In the History of Kent, by Edward Hasted, published at Canterbury in 1798, vol. vii., and in the Kent Genealogies, published by
William Bowry in 1830, will be found something relating to the history
and genealogy of families of the name of Thurston, but the only
ground for supposing our Newbury family sprung from them is the
frequent occurrence of "Richard" and "Daniel," family names.
The books above referred to will be found in the Astor Library.

The elder Daniel is stated by Savage to have lost his first wife May 25, 1648, and to have married for his second, Aug. 29, 1648, ANN LIGHTFOOT, who without doubt was the widow of Francis Lightfoot of Lynn, who came from London and died in 1646. Daniel Thurston died Feb. 16, 1666, having on the 25th day of June, 1665, made his last will and testament. On March 27, 1666, Richard Dole testified to the making of the will, and on the 10th of April, 1666, John Cheney, senior, before William Gerrish and Nich. Noyes, certified to its authenticity. Those taking the proof are styled "commissioners." The following is a copy of his will:

JUNE ye 20th, 1655. I, Daniell Thurston of Newberry in New England, being weake in body but in parfect memorie, doe make and appoynt this as my last will and Testamunt. Wherein ffirst I doe give and bequeathe my now dwelling house and Barne and all my lands both up land and meadow with all ye privileges and appurtainences thereunto belonging unto Daniell Thurston my kinsman of ye same town of Newberry before mentioned: save only what I shall except: And also I doe give unto ye same Daniel all my goods and chattels.

I give unto Ann my wife my fetherbeds with bolster and pillow: and all appurtaining thereto, and her chest and her box, with all her clothing, her own brass kettle and an iron pot: and ten pounds by ye yeare in good pay namely, in corn, butter, cheese and porke: or her thirds of ye lande: All this above mentioned concarning my wife: during her natural life I do give it unto her. But in case my wife chuse rather to live with my kinsman Daniell Thurston then he shall comfortably mayntain her with meat, drink and clothes: and give her twenty shillings by ye yeare ye one half in money, ye other half in cheese and butter.

And I doe ordayne and apoiynt my kinsman Daniell Thurston above mentioned to be my soall and alone executor. The mark for D. T., Daniell Thurston. Seal.

Signed and sealed in ye presence of us, John Cheney, Sen$^r$, Richard Dole.

Ye court held at Ipswich the 27 of March, 1666, Richard Dole upon oath testified that this is the last will and Testament of Daniel Thurston to the best of his knowledge. As attest Robert Lord, Clerk.

John Cheney, Sen$^r$, certified on oath that this will is the Last of Daniell Thurston to the best of his knowledge this 10th day of April, 1666. Before us, Wm. Gerrish, Nich$^s$ Noyes, Com$^m$.

The "kinsman," Daniel Thurston, the devisee in the foregoing will, was undoubtedly a nephew of the testator, as in a paper entitled "Newbury troubles,"[*] it is there stated, as a ground of the disability of some of the signers, that "young Daniell Thurston is under his *uncle*." Though this paper is without date, Coffin in his letter to me says it was about 1655. If this were so, and young Daniel were then a *minor*, he must have been almost an infant in arms when his uncle came to Newbury.

In 1678 there was a list of two hundred and thirty-six names of those who took the oath of allegiance.[†] In this is the name Daniel *Thompson*, forty, which should undoubtedly be Daniel *Thurston*, as this printed list contains many mistakes.[‡] There is also in the list the name of "Daniel Thurston, jun$^r$, seventeen," and this makes the year of this Daniel's birth 1661, which agrees with the record.

*Genealogical Register, vol. viii., page 274.
† Genealogical Register, vol. vii., page 349
‡ Coffin's letter, Genealogical Register, vol. viii., page 72.

# POSTERITY OF DANIEL THURSTON.

## First Generation.

### 1

DANIEL THURSTON,[1] the "kinsman," and probable ancestor of all the Newbury Thurstons, married,* Oct. 20, 1655, ANNE PELL, a daughter, as Savage supposes, of Joseph Pell of Lynn, the same town whence came Ann Lightfoot, the wife of the elder Thurston, a circumstance adding probability to Savage's conjecture. He died Feb. 19, 1693. The following is a copy of his will:

Be it known to all men by these presents that I, Daniel Thurston, Sen[r], of Newberry in the county of Essex in New England, being weak of body but of perfect memory, doe hereby make my last will and testament.

Commending my soul to God and my body when it shall depart this life to decent buriall in an assured hope of a blessed resurrection. And for my worldly goods which God of his mercy hath given me I dispose of as followeth, viz.:

I have by deed of gift under my hand and seale made over to my sonne Daniel Thurston one-half of my lands and meadow that I have in the town of Newberry known by the name of Rake Lott, which was done upon his marriage, with all priviledges and appurtenances yerto belonging, and I doe now make over to my sonne Daniel Thurstain All my buildings with the other half of all my lands and meadows with priviledges and appurtenances yrto belonging on conditions as follows:

First. That he, my said sonne Daniel, and his heirs Doth take care of and provide comfortably for his mother soe long as She shall remain my widow.

Secondly. I do oblidge my son Daniel to pay to my daughter Sarah the sum of thirty pounds in Cattell within two years after my decease.

Thirdly. I doe oblidge my sonne Daniel to pay to my sonne Joseph the sum of thirty pounds in Cattell within fower yeares after my decease.

Fourthly. I doe oblidge my sone Daniel to pay to my sonne Steven the sum of thirty pounds in Cattell Five years after my decease.

Fifthly. I oblidge my sonne Daniel to pay to my daughter Abigail the sum of thirty pounds in cattell within eight years after my decease.

Item. I give and bequeath to my sonne James a parcel of land lying in Newberry known by the name of my Rake Lott with my pistolls and houlsters, which is held in full of his portion.

Item. I also give to my sonne Joseph a p[r] of loomms with the tackling belonging to them and also a cowe and a gun.

Item. I give to my son Stephen a pair of loomms and my carbine.

Item. I doe also give to my daughter Hannah five shillings which is to be with what I have before given her in full of her portion.

Item. I give to my daughter Sarah fiveteen pounds which she shall have out of my household goods which is to be in full of her portion.

Item. I doe also leave all the rest of my moveable estate in my sonne Daniel's hands, except a fether bed and furniture belonging to it and to the value of. other five pounds in other household stuff, which I do leave to my beloved wife to make use of during her life.

And I give my son Daniel full power as administrator to receive all my debts due to me by bills or otherwise. And I doe also order him, my said sonne Daniel, to

---

* Coffin's History of Newbury.

pay for my funerall expenses and also to pay all my lawful debts which he is to do out of my movable estate. And if there be any overplus the rest of it is to be divided amongst four of my children, viz., Joseph, Stephen, Sarah and Abigail. But if it soe fall y[t] yer be not enough of my movable estate to pay all my lawfull debts then I order that my son Daniel shall be abated so much of the hundred and twenty pounds which he was to pay to his brothers and sisters above mentioned as will discharge the remainder of my debts, and my four children, Joseph, Steven, Sarah, and Abigail, shall beare it equally among them, and I doe desire my loving friends John Poore, Henry Poore, to be the overseers of this my last will and testament. I hereby revoking all former wills of myne. In confirmation of what is before written as my last will and testat., I have hereunto set my hand and seale the 17 day of January, 1692-3. The mark of Daniel Thurston.

Signed, sealed, and declared in ye presence of John Poor, Thomas Hale. The mark of Stephen Thurston.

NOTE. I have inspected the original document in the probate office in Salem, and it is scorched as though it had been thrown in the fire and rescued from the flames before being consumed. It is mere conjecture that this was done, and that the addendum following, dated the same day, was made to appease somebody who was dissatisfied with the first part of the will. A. S. THURSTON.

For some addition to what is above written, Whereas it is expected that my beloved wife shall haive a feather bed and furniture and five pound more out of the house during life and also that my daughter Sarah shall have fourteen pound out of the household stuff, And whereas I left the rest of my movables within doors to my son Daniel, My will now is that after my daughter Sarah have had her fiveteen and my beloved wife her bed with furniture and her five pounds that then what is left of my movable estate within doors shall be equally divided between my daughters Sarah and Abigail and prized to them as part of their thirty pounds apeace, and so much as it amounts to shall be taken off from the sixty pounds in Cattell which my son Daniel was to pay them. And my will is that my son Daniel shall pay all the abatement of said sixty pounds to my two sons Joseph and Stephen. And Whereas it is above provided that if my movable estate without doors will not pay all my lawfull debts, that then my son Daniel shall be abated so much of the hundred and twenty pound which he was to pay his brothers and sisters as would discharge the remainder of my debt, and that my two sons Joseph and Stephen and my two daughters Sarah and Abigail should bear it equally between them, My will now is y[t] if my movable estate without doors will not discharge all my lawfull debts, that then my said Daniel shall take out of what I ordered him to pay my two sons Joseph and Stephen Soe much as will discharge the remainder of my debts and with the same pay the remainder of my engagements.

And whereas I have given to my beloved wife a bed with furnitur and five pounds more out of the house which she is to have during her life, my will is that at her decease it shall be equally divided between my two daughters Sarah and Abigail. My will further is that whereas I did order my son Daniel to pay his brothers and sisters portions in Cattell, my will is that it shall be paid in neat Cattell under Seaven years old.

As witness my hand the 17 January, 1692-3. The mark and seal of Daniel Thurston.

Signed, sealed, and delivered in the presence of us, John Poore, Thomas Hale. The mark of Stephen Thurston.

## Their children were:

2    Daniel,[2] b. July 2, 1657; d. Nov. 3, 1657.
+ 3  Hannah,[2] b. Jan. 20, 1659; m. Benjamin Pearson.
4    A daughter, b. Nov. 22, 1660; d. Dec. 16, 1660.
+ 5  Daniel,[2] b. Dec. 18, 1661; m. Mary Dresser.
6    Sarah,[2] b. Jan. 8, 1664: m. ———.
7    Stephen,[2] b. Oct. 25, 1665; d. soon.
+ 8  Joseph,[2] b. Sept. 14, 1667; m. Mehitable Kimball.
9    Anne,[2] b. Sept. 6, 1669; d. soon.
+10  James,[2] b. Sept. 24, 1670; m. Mary Pearson.
11   Stephen,[2] b. Oct. 25, 1672; d. soon.
+12  Stephen,[2] b. Feb. 5, 1674; m. Mary ——.
+13  Abigail,[2] b. March 17, 1678; m. Joseph Chase.

## Second Generation.

### 3

HANNAH THURSTON[2] (*Daniel*[1]), second child of the "kinsman" Daniel and Anne (Pell) Thurston of Newbury, Mass., born in Rowley Jan. 20, 1659; married, Jan. 20, 1679–80, BENJAMIN PEARSON,* son of John and Dorcas Pearson of Rowley, Mass., born Feb. 1, 1658. He died June 16, 1731, aged 73. She died June 26, 1731, aged 72. He had a mill at Byfield, Mass., which he bought of Mr. Cheney.

#### Their children were:

14  Hannah (Pearson), b. April 5, 1681.
15  Phebe (Pearson), b. July 14, 1682.
16  Daniel (Pearson), b. Dec. 25, 1684.
17  Ruth (Pearson), b. Aug. 2, 1687.
18  Abigail (Pearson), b. March 1, 1689.
19  Benjamin (Pearson), b. Aug. 12, 1690.
20  Sarah (Pearson), b. Dec. 10, 1691.
21  Jedediah (Pearson), b. April, 1694.
22  Mehitable (Pearson), b. May 18, 1695.
23  Jonathan (Pearson), b. Dec. 14, 1699.
24  David (Pearson), b. Jan. 18, 1702.
25  Oliver (Pearson), b. Aug. 14, 1704; died aged 16 years.
26  Bartholomew (Pearson).

### 5

DANIEL THURSTON[2] (*Daniel*[1]), brother of the preceding, and son of the "kinsman" Daniel and Anne (Pell) Thurston of Newbury, Mass.; born there Dec. 18, 1661; married MARY DRESSER, born Dec. 24, 1667, daughter of Lieut. John Dresser of Rowley, Mass., who

---

*The PEARSON FAMILY.

I. DEA. JOHN PEARSON came from England to Ipswich, then to Rowley, Mass., in 1643, bringing with him machinery for a fulling-mill, which was the first in this country. Supposing America had no wood that would stand water, he brought cedar posts also. Some of these posts were taken up about 1800 and found in a good state of preservation. He leased a grist-mill of P. Nelson, which his son John subsequently bought. He was sent to the general court in 1678 and seven times after; was also selectman. In 1660 his tax was £1 5s. 7d. and in 1691 it was £7 15s., the highest but one in Rowley. He married Dorcas ——; had thirteen children, and died 1693; his wife died 1703. Their son Samuel, born 1648, married, in 1670, Mary Poor, and lived in Haverhill, Mass., till the place was burned by the Indians, after which they lived in Newbury, Mass. She died at the birth of their daughter Mary, who married James Thurston [see no. 10]. Their son Benjamin, born 1658, married Hannah Thurston [see no. 3].

II. CAPT. JOHN PEARSON, eldest son of John, born Dec. 22, 1644, married, 1671, Mary Pickard; had the mill, and had six children. Joseph, born 1656, was killed at Bloody brook, in Deerfield, Mass., 1675, where seven hundred Indians attacked one hundred men, the flower of Essex county, and killed seventy-five of them.

III. JOSEPH PEARSON, son of Capt. John, born 1677, married Sarah Walker; had the Pearson homestead and a large landed property; lived in a garrison house, the walls filled in with brick; died 1753.

IV. CAPT. JOHN PEARSON, son of Joseph, born May 13, 1702, married Ruth Hale, born Nov. 17, 1706. They had eight children. He died Mar. 18, 1784, and she in 1788. Their son Joseph, born 1737, married a Boston lady, had no children, graduated from Harvard 1758, and was the first secretary of state of New Hampshire, which office he held twenty-eight years, resigning at the age of seventy. He lived in Exeter, N. H.

V. CAPT. JOHN PEARSON, son of Capt. John, born October, 1746, married, June 13, 1775, Sarah Thurston [see no. 37]. They had seven children.

VI. JOHN PEARSON, son of John, last of the male line, born March 4, 1791, Friday, two o'clock A.M.; died October, 1819. His sister Mehitable, born Jan. 1, 1783, married, 1805, James Webster. She died Sept. 15, 1818. Among her last words were these, "I know God will take care of my children," of whom they had five.

VII. CAROLINE MEHITABLE WEBSTER, daughter of James Webster, born Nov. 15, 1808, on the old Pearson place in Rowley, married, September, 1839 (at the house of Col. John Mills of Marietta, Ohio, who married his sister Dorothy), Rev. J. R. Barnes of New Haven, Ct., then pastor of Presbyterian church in Evansville, Ind. Mrs. Barnes has rendered valuable service in this work.

was sent to the general court 1691 and four times after. She died
Dec. 7, 1735, very suddenly, aged 69. She was "standing and
dropped down and was not perceived to breathe after." The same
month Mary Jewett, Thomas, son of Daniel Thurston,[3] and Daniel
Thurston, died at their house. We are unable to tell who this Daniel
was. Daniel Thurston[2] died Feb. 18, 1738, aged 77.

Daniel Thurston,[2] with one hundred and nineteen other persons, received a grant of land called Narragansett, No. 1, now Buxton, Me.,
range of lots known by the letter D, on the right of his father Daniel,[1]
for services in the Narragansett war. His will is as follows:

The last will and testament of Daniel Thurston of Newberry, in ye province of
Massachusetts Bay, New England, husbandman, which is as followeth:

First. In God's appointed time I resign my soul into ye hands of GOD that
gave it and my body to ye dust until ye day of ye reserection of ye just according
to ye gracious promise of ye and trust in Christ Jesus. And as for my temporal
goods that GOD have given me I dispose of as followeth:

Imp[s]. I give to my son Benj[n] Thurston and his heirs and assigns one-third *
part of my right, propriety, or share of land and meadows in ye township of Lunenburgh in ye county of Middlesex in ye Province aforesaid. And also my two thatch
islands lying in the great creek between Newbury and Rowley, and also half an acre
of thatch bank at ye south-west corner of that piece of my meadow commonly
called Biships meadow, and this with what I have before given him is in full of his
portion.

Item. I have given my son Jonathan Thurston a deed of the land on which he
now dwells. I also give to my s[d] son Jonathan and his heirs and assigns one-third *
part of my right, propriety, and share of land and meadow in ye township of Lunenburgh aforesaid, and also one-half of my lot of marsh called by ye name of my
lower lott, and also one-halfe of my lott of mead that I bought of my brother
Nathaniel Dresser, lying in the township of Rowley in ye county aforesaid and on
the North side of Nelsons Island (so called), and also one lott of land lying below
Pen Brook in ye township of Rowley aforesaid, and it is the fifth lott on a range of
lotts known by ye letter G, and also a convenient driftway through to my F lotts in
the three thousand acres in ye township of Rowley aforesaid in full of his portion.

Item. I give to my son Richard Thurston his heirs and assigns seventeen lots of
land lying in ye township of Rowley aforesaid, in that part of said Rowley that is
commonly called the thousand acres. Said lotts were laid out by ye proprietors of
ye common land in said Rowley, and also a house which standeth on part of said
lotts (only I reserve the liberty of a driftway for my son Jonathan through ye F lotts
as aforesaid). Also I give to my said son Richard and his heirs and assigns one-
third * part of my right, propriety, or share of land and meadow in the township of
Lunenburgh aforesaid, and also one-half of my lott of marsh called by ye name of
my lower lott in ye township of Newbury aforesaid, and also one-half of my lot
of meadow that I bought of my brother Nathaniel Dresser, lying in ye township of

---

*In the register's office at Worcester, Mass., there is the record of three deeds, as follows:
Richard Thurston of Rowley. gentleman, to Ebenezer Thurston of Fitchburgh, house-wright.
Deed dated Aug. 21, 1769; witnessed by William Spofford and William Chandler; acknowledged before Aaron Wood, J. P. Conveys two lots of land in Fitchburgh, being one-third
part of two lots laid out for Mr. Daniel Thurston. The first lot laid out December, 1729, containing one hundred and thirty-five acres; the second lot November, 1731, containing eighty-
six acres, as per plan. Consideration, £34 7s.
John Thurston of Fitchburgh, yeoman, to Ebenezer Thurston. Deed the same as above in
date and description. Consideration, £35.
Daniel Thurston, gentleman, of Bradford, to Ebenezer Thurston. Deed same as above in
all respects.
John Thurston undoubtedly derived title to one-third of the Fitchburgh lots above granted
as the heir of his father Jonathan, who, as we shall see hereafter died intestate Sept. 28, 1738.
Daniel Thurston derived his title under the will of his father Benjamin, which was admitted
to probate Oct. 13, 1746.
There is on record in Worcester registry office, vol. vii., page 77, a deed as follows: Benjamin Thurston of Bradford, Jonathan Thurston of Rowley, Richard Thurston of Rowley,
husbandmen, to Benjamin Foster of Bradford, convey lot 50, Lunenburgh, which seems to be
referred to in deeds hereafter made to Ebenezer Thurston. This deed is dated June 1, 1731,
before the date of their father's will. Deed acknowledged before John Dummer, J. P., Oct.
25, 1734; recorded Aug. 13, 1735; witnessed by Samuel Filar and Hilkiah Boynton. This
Ebenezer Thurston was a son of John, who went from Rowley to Fitchburgh, 1766.

Rowley aforesaid and on ye North side of Nelsons Island (so called) in full of his portion.

Item. I give to my daughter Mary Chute twenty and six pounds to be paid within one year after my decease and also one-third part of my household goods, which is (with what she already had) in full of her portion.

Item. I give to my daughter Hannah Frazer twenty-six pounds and twelve shillings to be paid within two years after my decease and also one-third part of my household goods, which is (with what shee have already had) in full of her portion.

Item. I give to my daughter Martha Jewett twenty and nine pounds to be paid within three years after my decease and also one-third part of my household goods, which is (with what she have already had) in full of her portion.

Item. I give to my granddaughter Sarah Thurston twenty pounds to be paid within four years after my decease in full of her portion.

Lastly. I give to my son John Thurston and his heirs and assigns, whom I likewise constitute, make, and ordain my whole and sole Ex$^r$ of this my last will and testament, all my land and meadow housing goods and chattels that I have not disposed of in this my will. Also I give him all the debts that is due to me. And I order him to pay all the debts that I do owe and legacies that I have given in this my will and also to pay my funeral charges. And this is my last will and testament having my perfect memory and understanding.

As witness my hand and seal this sixth day of July anno domini one thousand seven hundred and thirty-six. Daniel Thurston. Seal.

Signed, sealed, and declared in the presence of us, the Subscribers, Jonathan Plumer, Jno. Poor, Daniel Hale.

Essex probate office. A true copy as of record in said office, approved May 27, 1737. Attest James Ropes, Reg$^r$.

### Their children were:

+27   Daniel,$^8$ b. June 26, 1690; m. Lydia Seaver.
 28   Son and daughter, twins, b. May 7, 1691, and died in two weeks.
+29   John,$^8$ b. June 12, 1692; m. Dorothy Woodman.
+30   Mary,$^8$ b. Jan. 7, 1694; m. James Chute.
+31   Benjamin,$^8$ b. May 4, 1695; m. Mary Gage.
 32   Hannah,$^8$  } twins, born  } m. Jan. 9, 1718, Gersham Frazer, b. Aug. 8, 1697,
 33   Lydia,$^8$   } Jan. 20, 1698; } son of Colin Frazer of Rowley. She died
             Sept. 18, 1770. Lydia m. May 11, 1723, Robert Rogers of Gloucester.
             She died Sept. 4. 1727.
 34   Martha,$^8$ b. Nov. 27, 1699; m. Jan. 9, 1718 (same day as her sister Hannah),
             Ezekiel Jewett.
+35   Jonathan,$^8$ b. March 16. 1701; m. Lydia Spofford.
 36   Stephen,$^8$ b. 1704; d. Sept. 18, 1727.
 37   Sarah,$^8$ b. Dec. 30, 1706; m. Capt. John Pearson.
+38   Richard,$^8$ b. Oct. 16, 1710; m. Mehitable Jewett.

## 8

JOSEPH THURSTON $^2$ (*Daniel*$^1$), brother of the preceding, and son of the "kinsman" Daniel and Anne (Pell) Thurston of Newbury, Mass.; born there Sept. 14, 1667; married, first, 1695, MEHITABLE KIMBALL; second, Aug. 25, 1707, ELIZABETH WOODBURY, daughter of John Woodbury of Beverly, Mass.

Mr. Thurston was a weaver in Newbury and after in Rowley, Mass.

### Children, by first wife, Mehitable:

 39   Mehitable,$^8$ m. Oct. 15, 1718, Joseph Russell of Newbury.
+40   Joseph,$^8$   } twins, born  { m. Mary Jane Finson.
 41   Benjamin,$^8$ } Jan. 23, 1698–9; { d. June 30, 1699.
 42   Abigail,$^8$ b. October or December, 1700.
 43   Hannah,$^8$ b. Feb. 27, 1702–3.
+44   Benjamin,$^8$ m. Elizabeth ——.

## 10

JAMES THURSTON $^2$ (*Daniel*$^1$), brother of the preceding, and son of the "kinsman" Daniel and Anne (Pell) Thurston of Newbury, Mass.;

born there Sept. 24, 1670; married, Jan. 24, 1693, MARY PEARSON of Rowley, Mass. He probably settled in Exeter, N. H.

### Their children were:

45 Hannah,[8] b. Nov. 15, 1694; d. Nov. 8, 1701.
46 Dorcas,[8] b. Oct. 20, 1696.
+47 Abner,[8] b. Feb. 28, 1699.
48 Phebe,[8] b. June 20, 1702.

## 12

STEPHEN THURSTON [2] (*Daniel*[1]), brother of the preceding, and son of the " kinsman " Daniel and Anne (Pell) Thurston of Newbury, Mass.; born there Feb. 5, 1674; married, first, MARY ——; second, SARAH ——.

His estate was probated 1728, Moses, administrator. In the register of deeds office at Exeter, N. H., under date of 1725, is a deed to Stephen Thurston of Stratham, N. H. Estate appraised Sept. 9, 1728, at £536 12s. 3d. In September, 1732, the widow Sarah leased her dower to Moses for £5 a year.

### Their children were:

+49 Moses,[8] b. July 19, 1707; m. Sarah ——.
+50 John,[8] b. Aug. 29, 1709; m. 1st, Mrs. Phebe Wiggin; 2d, Elizabeth ——.
+51 Robert,[8] b. Feb. 25, 1712; m. ——.
52 Daniel,[8] b. Aug. 27, 1714; d. Feb. 16, 1737.
53 Mary,[8] b. June 3, 1716; m. Sept. 23, 1756, Jeremiah Searle.
+54 Nathaniel,[8] b. July 12, 1718; m. Miner Chase.
+55 Stephen,[8] b. 1720; m. Mary St. Clare.
56 Mehitable,[8] m. Capt. Jonathan Jewett; his second wife.
57 Rebecca.[8]
58 Abigail,[8] spinster; May 10, 1748, she relinquished her right in the estate of her father to her brother Moses for £92 10s.
These children were quite large land owners, as the registry of deeds office contains very numerous deeds to and from them.

## 13

ABIGAIL THURSTON [2] (*Daniel*[1]), sister of the preceding, and daughter of the " kinsman " Daniel and Anne (Pell) Thurston of Newbury, Mass.; born there March 17, 1678; married, Nov. 28, 1699, JOSEPH CHASE, born March 25, 1677, son of Aquila and Esther Chase of Newbury, ancestor of Hon. Salmon P. Chase, former secretary of the United States treasury and chief justice of the United States. They removed to Littleton, Mass., in 1726, and it is thought died there.

### Their children were:

59 Nathan (Chase), b. Aug. 2, 1701; m. Ruth Peaslee.
60 George (Chase), b. Feb. 17, 1702-3; m. 1st, Elizabeth ——; 2d, Lucy Wood.
61 Stephen (Chase), b. Oct. 26, 1705; m. 1732, Jane Wingate.
62 Anne (Chase), b. Feb. 11, 1707; m. Joseph Webster.
63 Abigail (Chase), b. March 27, 1709; m. Simon Tuttle, jr.
64 Hannah (Chase), b. Feb. 25, 1711.
65 Rebecca (Chase), b. Nov. 16, 1714; m. March 6, 1734, Thomas Warren.
66 Benjamin (Chase), b. June 21, 1717; m. 1st, June 17, 1740, Widow Rachel Hartwell; 2d, May 15, 1766, Mary Dayton.
67 Joseph (Chase), b. Dec. 8, 1719; m. Sarah Wood.

## Third Generation.

### 27

DANIEL THURSTON[3] (*Daniel,*[2] *Daniel*[1]), eldest son of Daniel[2] and Mary (Dresser) Thurston of Newbury, Mass.; born there June 26, 1690; married, Nov. 14, 1715, LYDIA SEAVER of Rowley. He died March 10, 1720, and his widow married Stephen Jewett.

Their children were:

68 Gideon,[4] b. Nov. 12, 1716; m. Abigail ——; lived in Exeter, N. H., till about 1744, as March 24, 1744, he was admitted to the church in Rowley by letter from church in Exeter. He had a son *Oliver*, b. April 8, 1735, who died before Sept. 18, 1755, as his will, made that date, makes no mention of any children, but gives his wife Abigail all his personal estate and use of his dwelling-house in Rowley so long as she shall remain his widow. His land in Munson, N. H., and all his estate after his widow dies to his cousin Daniel Thurston, son of Capt. Richard Thurston. This will was approved Dec. 2, 1776, in which year he died. The will was witnessed by James Chandler, Samuel Plumer, Edner Plumer; A. C. Goodell, register.

69 Thomas,[4] d. at his grandfather's Dec., 1735.

70 Sarah,[4] b. May 13, 1719; m. Dec. 17, 1741, Joseph Kilburn and had:
  71 *Daniel* (Kilburn), b. Oct. 6, 1742.

72 Mehitable,[4] m. Capt. Jonathan Wiggin as his second wife; he married first, Molly Little. Mehitable died Nov. 14, 1784. He died 1810. They had:
  73 *Edmund* (Wiggin), b. 1772, Thomaston, Me.
  74 *Mehitable* (Wiggin), b. 1773; m. Samuel Marble.
  75 *Abigail* (Wiggin), b. 1775; m. Thomas Chase.
  76 *William H.* (Wiggin), b. 1776, Thomaston, Me.
  77 *Sally* (Wiggin), b. 1778; m. —— Sincler.
  78 *Clarissa* (Wiggin), b. 1780; m. Stephen Boardman.
  79 *Augusta* (Wiggin), b. 1782.
Capt. Wiggin married a third wife, who survived him.

### 29

JOHN THURSTON[3] (*Daniel,*[2] *Daniel*[1]), second son of Daniel[2] and Mary (Dresser) Thurston of Newbury, Mass.; born there June 12, 1692; married when he was forty years of age, May 17, 1732, DOROTHY WOODMAN, born 1705, daughter of Joshua Woodman of Newburyport, Mass. He died May 27, 1751, aged 59 [grave-stone at Newbury]. She died Oct. 27, 1773, aged 68.

His will bears date twenty-three days before his death. We get the names of his children from his will. They were all minors, as there was an interval of only nineteen years between his marriage and death. The following is a copy of his will:

· The last will and testament of John Thurston of Newbury, in the county of Essex in the province of yᵉ Massachᵗᵗˢ Bay in New England, which is as followeth:

First. In God's appointed time I resign my soul into the hands of God that gave it, and my body to the dust untill the day of the resurrection of the just, with assured hope at that day to receive it according to the gracious promise of the GOD of grace and trust in Christ Jesus: and for my temporal goods that God hath given me I dispose of as followeth:

Item. I give to my daughter Mehitable Thurston and her heirs and assigns one acre of wood land at the nearest end of my wood lott in Newbury near to ye Danford's and Pearson's mills. Also I give to my said daughter Mehitable one hundred and sixty ounces of silver, one-halfe to be paid to her at marriage or at the age of twenty and one, whichever comes first, the other half to be paid her when shee shall arrive at yᵉ age of twenty-five years. Also I give to my said daughter a privillege in my East chamber and in my cellar and oven and well so long as she shall live unmarried, in full of her portion.

Item. I give to my daughter Mary Thurston and her heirs and assigns one acre of wood land towards the Norwest end of my wood land in Newbury, adjoyning to yᵉ acre that I have given to my daughter Mehitable. Also I give to my daughter Mary one hundred and sixty ounces of silver, one-halfe to be paid to her at marriage or at the age of twenty-one, whichever comes first, the other halfe when shee shall arrive to the age of twenty-five years. Also I give to my said daughter a privillege in my east chamber and a privillege in my cellar and oven and well so long as shee live unmarried, in full of her portion.

Item. I give to my daughter Judeth Thurston and her heirs and assigns one acre of wood land toward ye norwest end of my wood lott in Newbury, adjoining to the acre I gave to my daughter Mary. Also I give to my daughter Judeth one hundred and sixty ounces of silver, one-halfe to be paid to her at marriage or at yᵉ age of twenty and one, whichever comes first, the other halfe to be paid to her when shee shall arrive at the age of twenty and five years. Also I give to my said daughter a privillege in my east chamber and a privillege in my cellar, oven and well so long as shee shall live unmarried, in full of her portion.

Item. I give to my daughter Patience Thurston her heirs and assigns one acre of wood land toward yᵉ norwest end of my wood lott in Newbury, adjoining to the acre that I gave to my daughter Judeth. Also I give to my daughter Patience one hundred and sixty ounces of silver, one halfe to be paid to her at marriage or at the age of twenty and one, whichever comes first, the other halfe to be paid to her when shee shall arrive to the age of twenty and five years. Also I give to my said daughter a privillege in my east chamber and a privillege in my cellar, oven and well so long as she shall live unmarried, in full of her portion.

Item. I give to my daughter Hannah Thurston and her heirs and assigns one acre of wood land laying toward the norwest end of my wood land in Newbury, adjoyning to yᵉ acre I gave to my daughter Patience. Also I give to my said daughter Hannah one hundred and sixty ounces of silver, one-halfe to be paid to her at marriage or at the age of twenty and one, whichever comes first, the other halfe to be paid to her when shee shall arrive to the age of twenty-five years. Also I give to my said daughter a privillege in my east chamber and a privillege in my cellar and oven and well so long as she shall live unmarried, in full of her portion.

Item. I give to my son John Thurston and to his heirs and assigns six acres of wood land laying in Newbury and adjoyning to Thurlo's land. Also I give to my said son John my clock, my gun and my sword.

Item. I give to my two sons John Thurston and Benjⁿ Thurston and to their heirs and assigns all and every part and parcel of my lands and meadow or marsh land that I have within the townships of Newbury and Rowley and my right of land in Narragansett Township* number one lying on Sawco River. Also I give to my two sons John and Benjamin all my buildings excepting the privilleges that I have already reserved for my daughters or hereafter may reserve in my house. I also give to my said sons all my utensels for husbandry, all of which lands, buildings and utensels equally to be divided between my two sons John and Benjⁿ (excepted yᵉ six acres of land, my clock, gun and sword which I first gave to my son John), and this my will is that if either of my two sons should die before they arrive to the age of twenty and one years my surviving son shall have all I have given unto them both (excepting my Narragansett right on Sawco river), and if either of them should die before that he arrive to the age of twenty and one years as aforesaid, then my Sawco right to return to my five daughters, equally to be divided betwixt them. Furthermore this my will is that my two sons John and Benjamin pay to my daughter Hannah the last payment of her portion equally betwixt them if living, or if but one of them be alive when said payment be due he shall pay yᵉ whole and to have the possession of the premises at yᵉ end of twelve years from yᵉ day of yᵉ date hereof.

Lastly. I give to my beloved wife Dorothy (whom I likewise constitute, make

---

* Narragansett No. 1. now called Buxton. This land John Thurston must have derived title to as the residuary devisee under his father's will, and his father derived his title to it from Daniel the kinsman. Genealogical Register, vol. xxii., pp. 27ⁿ, 279.

Richard Thurston also had land there. So also had Rev. Jonathan Jewett, who was Richard Thurston's wife's father. Also James Chute.

These lands were given to those who were in the Narragansett expedition against the Indians in 1675. The kinsman was therefore without doubt in that expedition and received land for his services, which went in the manner above stated. Gen. Reg., vol. xvi., pp. 143, 216.

By the will of the "kinsman" he was a fighting man, as he gives pistols, holsters, and carbine. If he was born in 1628, according to the English will, he was forty-seven in 1675.

and ordain executrix of this my last will and testament) all my household goods and moveable estate within doors forever. I also give to my said wife all my stock of creatures and all y$^e$ money due and debts owing to me, and my chaise, wheeles and harness to enable her to pay my legacies. I also give to my executrix the improvement and income of all my estate, real and personal, for and during the term of twelve years from the day of the date hereof, that she may be enabled to bring up my children and support my family, said income and profits to be used and put to said ends at the discretion of my executrix unless shee see cause to marry, and if so then at the time of her marriage to acquitt the improvement of all my real estate, her right of dower or power of thirds excepted, which right of dower or power of thirds this my will is that my said wife enjoy during y$^e$ term of her natural life (excepting her right in my wood lotts in Newbury, which right this my will is that shee acquitt on y$^e$ time of her marriage). And furthermore this my will is that my executrix pay all the debts that I do owe and all the legacies that I have given excepting the legacy that I have ordered my two sons to pay to my daughter Hannah and to pay my funeral charges. And this is my will and testament having my perfect memory and understanding. As witness my hand and seal this fourth day of May, One thousand seven hundred and fifty-one. John Thurston. Seal.

Signed, sealed, and declared in the presence of us y$^e$ Subscribers, Jno. Plumer, Ju$^n$., Jn$^o$. Poore, Jonathan Plumer.

Essex, s.s. Probate office. A true copy as of record in said office (approved June 24, 1751). Attest A. C. Goodell, Register.

The will of Dorothy, the widow of the foregoing John Thurston, is as follows:

In the name of God, Amen: the third day of September, 1770. I, Dorothy Thurston of Newbury, in the county of Essex and Province of the Massachusetts Bay in New England, widow, being of perfect mind and memory, thanks be given unto God, therefore calling unto mind the mortality of the body and knowing that it is appointed for all men once to die, do make and ordain this my last will and testament, that is to say, Principally, and first of all, I give and recommend my soul into the hands of God that gave it, and my body I recommend to the earth to be buried at the discretion of my executor, nothing doubting, but at the general Resurrection I shall receive the same again by the mighty power of God, and as touching such worldly estate wherewith it has pleased God to bless me in this life, I give, devise and dispose of the same in the following manner and form:

First. I give to my beloved son John Thurston about three acres of salt marsh land be the same more or less, laying on Newbury Neck, in partnership and was formerly owned by my Hon$^{ble}$ Father dec$^d$ and descended to me from him, and to his heirs and assigns forever.

Secondly. I give to my beloved son Benjamin Thurston eight pounds lawful money

Thirdly. I give to my beloved daughter Judith Thurston six pound thirteen shilling and four pence lawful money and all my weavers geers of all sorts, and one hundred weight of pork.

Fourthly. I give to my granddaughter Patience Adams twenty shillings lawful money, to be kept for her by her father till she arrive to the age of twenty and one years or till her marriage day, that which comes first, and then to be paid to her with the interest by her father.

Fifthly. I give to my four daughters, viz., Mehitable Coats, Mary Stickney, Hannah Adams, and Judith Thurston, all the rest of my estate, that I have not already disposed of in this my will, viz., all my stock of creatures of all sorts, and all my household goods and personal estate of every sort and all my wearing apparel, and all the just debts that are due to me and all the money I have by me or security for, to them my said four daughters, equally to be divided between them and by them freely to be enjoyed.

Sixthly. And finally, I do hereby constitute, make and ordain my well beloved son-in-law Edmund Adams, of the town and county aforesaid, yeoman, my sole executor of this my last will and testament, and I do hereby disallow and revoke all other former testament or wills and executors, by me any ways before made or named, ratifying this and no other to be my last will and testament.

In witness whereof, I have hereto set my hand and seal the day and year above written. Dorothy Thurston. Seal.

Signed, sealed, published, pronounced and declared by the said Dorothy Thurston

as her last will and testament in presence of us the subscribers. Bitfield Plummer, Mark Plummer, Joseph Willet.

Essex, ss. Probate office. A true copy of record in said office (approved Dec. 1, 1773). Attest A. C. Goodell, Register.

### Children :

80   Mehitable,[4] b. about 1733; m. David Coats.
81   Mary,[4] b. 1737; m. Oct. 17, 1759, Wm. Stickney; d. May 18, 1790, aged 53.
82   Judith,[4] m. March 24, 1784, Daniel Balch.
+83  Hannah,[4] b. about 1740; m. Edmund Adams.
84   John,[4] b. 1744; m. Eunice ——. She died July 23, 1818, aged 75. He died
        Nov. 29, 1820, aged 76; buried in Newbury Oldtown. They had :
    85   Stephen,[5] b. 1765; d. April 10, 1789, aged 24.
    86   Daniel,[5] b. Oct. 1, 1774; d. Aug. 4, 1775.
    87   Amos,[5] b. Sept. 10, 1776; d. Nov. 6, 1776.
88   Benjamin,[4] b. 1746; m. Jan. 20, 1785, Jane Knight. He was assessor in
        Newbury 1807, and died Dec. 11, 1807, aged 62. She died April 8, 1820,
        aged 65; both buried in Newbury Oldtown. They had :
    89   June,[5] b. 1789; d. Oct. 6, 1795.
    90   Sarah,[5] b. Nov., 1793; d. May 18, 1795.
91   Patience,[4] d. without issue.

## 30.

MARY THURSTON[3] (Daniel,[2] Daniel[1]), sister of the preceding, and daughter of Daniel[2] and Mary (Dresser) Thurston of Newbury, Mass.; born there Jan. 7, 1694; married, Jan. 26, 1715, DEA. JAMES CHUTE * of Byfield, Mass., born June 14, 1686, son of James and Mary (Wood) Chute. She died Aug. 12, 1760, aged 66. He married, second, March 30, 1761, Mrs. Sarah Pearson of Rowley, and died Jan. 31, 1769.

### Their children were :

92   Mary (Chute), b. Nov. 8, 1716; m. Mark Jewett of Rowley and had twelve
        children.
93   Ruth (Chute), b. Aug. 27, 1720; m. Joseph Searle of Rowley and had thir-
        teen children.
94   Daniel (Chute) (Capt., so called), b. May 6, 1722; m. Hannah Adams of
        Newbury, Mass., a very remarkable woman for her time. Dr. Elijah
        Parish is reported to have said "that next to George Washington he
        knew of no one more fit to govern this nation than she." He died Jan.
        6, 1805, and she died April 12, 1812, aged 90, having had:
    95   Judith (Chute), b. Jan. 20, 1743; m Daniel Thurston [see no. 163].
    96   James (Chute), b. Jan. 6, 1745; d. 1749.

*The CHUTE FAMILY.

I. LIONEL CHUTE, the sixteenth generation from Alexander Chewte or Chute, who was lord of the manor of Taunton, Somersetshire, Eng , in 1268, married Rose Symonds, daughter of Samuel Symonds, lieutenant governor of Massachusetts, and had one son, James. Lionel came to America in 1635, and settled in Ipswich, Mass. He taught a grammar school there in 1636. and died in June, 1645.

II. JAMES CHUTE, son of Lionel, married the daughter of William Epps of Ipswich and had one son, James. He was register of deeds in Ipswich in 1650. and died in 1690.

III. JAMES CHUTE, son of James. born 1649, married, Nov. 10, 1673, Mary Wood, daughter of William Wood. and had Mary, Elizabeth, Ann, Lionel, James, Thomas, Martha, Ruth, Hannah. He removed to Byfield, Mass. (Rowley side) in 1681, and commenced the settlement of the old Chute place, near the meeting-house, where Rev. Ariel Parish Chute, who furnished this history, was born.

IV. DEA. JAMES CHUTE, son of James, was born June 14, 1686; married, Jan. 26. 1715, Mary Thurston, born 1694, daughter of Daniel Thurston of Newbury, Mass. [see no. 30].

V. CAPT. DANIEL CHUTE. son of James, married, 1742, Hannah Adams of Newbury, and had Judith, born Jan. 20, 1748, married Daniel Thurston of Rowley [see no. 163], and Dea. James, born Feb. 16, 1751.

VI. DEA. JAMES CHUTE, son of Capt. Daniel, born Feb. 16, 1751, married Mehitable Thurston, and had a son Richard [see no. 166].

VII. RICHARD CHUTE, son of Dea. James, married Dorothy Pearson, and had Rev. Ariel Parish Chute, who furnished this history [see no. ——].

3

97   *David* (Chute), b. Dec. 28, 1747; d. Jan. 25, 1749.
98   *Susannah* (Chute), b. and d. in 1749.
99   *James* (Chute) (Dea.), b. Feb. 16, 1751; m. Mehitable Thurston [see no.
       166], and d. April 8, 1825.
100  *David* (Chute), b. 1753; d. 1756.
101  *Daniel* (Chute), b. July 21, 1754; d. November following.
102  *David* (Chute), b. Aug. 19, 1756; d. 1843.
103  *Richard* (Chute), b. Aug. 4, 1758; d. Aug. 3, 1760.
104  *Daniel* (Chute), b. Sept. 28, 1760; d. March, 1843; no issue.
105  *Mary* (Chute), b. Dec. 28, 1762; m. Dea. Benj. Colman, and d. 1851.
106  *Hannah* (Chute), b. April, 1765; m. Rev. Ariel Parish July 7, 1792.
107  James (Chute), b. May 12, 1725; d. in childhood.
108  David (Chute), b. 1727; d. in childhood.
       Three other daughters who died early.

## 31.

BENJAMIN THURSTON [3] (*Daniel,* [2] *Daniel* [1]), brother of the preceding, and son of Daniel [2] and Mary (Dresser) Thurston of Newbury,
Mass.; born there May 4, 1695; married, Oct. 15, 1718, MARY GAGE
of Bradford, Mass.  He died Sept. 6, 1746, aged 51.  His wife died
March 5, 1778.

Mr. Thurston was a joiner in Bradford, Mass.  The following is a
copy of his will:

In the name of God, Amen.  This first day of May, 1746, I, Benjamin Thurston
of Bradford, in the county of Essex and Province of the Massachusetts Bay in New
England, Joyner, calling to mind the certainty of death and that it is appointed unto
men once to die and being of a disposing mind and memory, do make and ordain
this my last will and testament: that is to say, Principally and first of all I give and
recommend my soul into the hands of God that gave it trusting in his mercy
through Jesus Christ, and my body I commit to the earth to be decently buried at
the discretion of my Exec[rs] hereafter named.

And as touching such worldly estate wherewith it has pleased God to bless me in
this life I demise, give and dispose of the same in the following manner, Viz[t].

Imp[m] I will that all my just debts I owe to any person or persons be well and
truly paid by my executors hereafter named.

Item.  I will unto my beloved wife Mary Thurston ye use and improvem[t] of ye
one-halfe of my Homestead, the one-third part of my dwelling house with one cellar which she shall choose, whilst shee shall continue my widow, with sufficient fire
wood cutt and brought to her door in equal halfe by my Executors hereafter named.

Item.  I give and bequeath unto my beloved wife Mary Thurston the one-third
part of the moveables in the house, two cows which shee shall choose, five sheep,
and my rideing horse, for her own forever.  As also the one-fifth part of the provisions in the house, and the rest of the provisions to be equally divided between my
four daughters.

Item.  I give and bequeath unto my son Dan[ll] Thurston the place I bought of
John Green, which he now lives on, with the buildings thereon, as also my right * I
have in the township of Lunenburgh and the one-halfe of my pasture lying by Jonathan Chadwick's for quantity and quallity, as also the Thatch Banks I had of my
father Daniel Thurston.  I also give him my best suit of wearing apparrill, my best
saddle and bridle, silver hilted sword, pistols and holsters, and a pair of steers of
two years old, as also the one-halfe of the money I shall leave in my house with ye
one-halfe of what is due to me that I have not before disposed of.

Item.  I give and bequeath unto my son Nath[ll] Thurston my homestead with all
the buildings thereon, to come into the possession of one-halfe of the lands and
two-thirds of the buildings at my decease and the whole at the expiration of my
wife's continuing my widow, and the one-halfe of my pasture lying by Jon[a] Chadwick's both for quantity and quallity, as also the wood lott I bought of Abraham Haseltine lying in a place called Dismall Hole, and the thatch island I bought
of Philip Atwood's Heirs lying in Plumb Island River, with all my stock of every
kind (except what I have before disposed of), and my wearing apparrill of all sorts

* This from his father.  See will, page 27.

(except what I have before disposed of), with my husbandry utensills and one-halfe of my joyners and carpenter's tools; my desk and clock with one-halfe of the money I shall leave in the house and halfe of all my just debts that are due to me (which I have not before disposed of).

Item. I give and bequeath unto my daughter Mary Thurston one hundred and fifty pounds old tenor, at the rate of silver at thirty and four shillings per ounce, to be paid by my Exec'' hereafter named in equal halfes when shee arrives to the age of twenty and one years or marriage, which shall happen first, with the one-quarter part of the two-thirds of the moveables in my house (which I have not before disposed of).

Item. I give and bequeath unto my daughter Sarah Thurston one hundred and fifty pounds old tenor. after the rate of silver money, at thirty and four shillings per ounce, to be paid by my executors hereafter named in equal halfes when shee shall arrive unto the age of twenty and one years or at marriage, which shall happen first, with the one-quarter part of the two-thirds of the moveables in my house (which I have not before disposed off).

Item. I give and bequeath unto my daughter Hannah Thurston the sum of one hundred and fifty pounds old tenor, after the rate of silver at thirty and four shillings per ounce, to be paid by my executors hereafter named in equal halfes when shee arrives to the age of twenty and one years or at marriage, which shall happen first, with the one-quarter part of ye two-thirds of the moveables in my house (which I have not before disposed of).

Item. I give and bequeath unto my daughter Elizabeth Thurston the sum of one hundred and fifty pounds old tenor, after the rate of silver at thirty and four shillings per ounce, to be paid by my executors hereafter named in equal halfes when shee arrives to the age of twenty and one years or marriage, which shall happen first, with the one-quarter part of the two-thirds of the moveables in my house (which I have not before disposed off).

Item. I do constitute, make, and ordain my two sons Dan[ll] Thurston and Nath[ll] Thurston sole executors of this my last will and testam[t], disallowing all others, rattifying and confirming this and no other, my last will and testam[t].

In witness whereof I have hereunto sett my hand and seal ye day and year above written.   Benj[a] Thurston.   Seal.

Signed, sealed, delivered, published, and declared by y[e] sd Benj[a] Thurston to be his last will and testam[t] in presence of us subscribers.   John Cogswell. Solomon Springe, Stephen Huse.   Approved Oct. 13, 1746.   Attest, A. C. Goodell, register.

NOTE.   Deed in Worcester registry office.   Daniel Thurston of Bradford, "house joiner," to Jacob Gould, Lunenburgh.   Dated in 174-.   Acknowledged before Thomas Kimball.   Witnesses, Richard Adams and Nathaniel Gould.   Conveys one-third of house lot.   This deed was made by Daniel the year after his father died.

### They had the following children :

+119   Daniel,[4] b. March, 1720; m. 1st, Hannah Parker; 2d, Judith Gerrish; 3d, Mrs. Elizabeth Rolf.
120   Nathaniel,[4] b. 1722; m. Feb. 19, 1744, Sarah Kimball; d. Dec. 7, 1746. They had:
121   *Mehitable*,[5] b. Oct. 14, 1746.
122   Sarah,[4] b. 1731; d. in infancy.
123   Sarah,[4] b. Oct. 14, 1734; m. Dec. 14, 1748. James Head.
124   Elizabeth,[4] b. May 6, 1740.
125   Mary,[4] m. May 21, 1771, Edward Walker of Bradford.
126   Hannah.[4]

## 35.

JONATHAN THURSTON [3] (*Daniel,[2] Daniel[1]*), brother of the preceding. and son of Daniel[2] and Mary (Dresser) Thurston of Newbury, Mass.; born there March 16, 1701; married, Dec. 10, 1722, LYDIA SPOFFORD, born 1700, baptized July 7th.   He died intestate Sept. 28, 1738, aged 37.   His grave-stone in Georgetown, Mass., is the oldest bearing the name of Thurston and about the oldest there, and has this inscription upon it:  "Here lies buried the body of Mr. Jonathan

Thoston, died Sept. 28, 1738, in the 38th year of his age." Lydia, his widow, married, March 15, 1744, Dea. William Fish.

Mr. Thurston was one of the original members of the second church in Rowley, now Georgetown, at its organization, Oct. 4, 1732. He was also one of the collectors in the parish at its incorporation, 1731.*

Their children were:

+137   John,[4] b. Aug. 19, 1723; m. 1st, Hepzibah Burpee; 2d, Lydia Kimball.
138   Sarah,[4] b May 26, 1725.
+139   Samuel,[4] b. June 7, 1727; m. Priscilla Burpee.
140   Lydia,[4] b. April 1, 1730.
141   Mary,[4] b. Feb. 27, 1731-2; m. April 2, 1751, Timothy Jackman.
142   Benjamin,[4] b. Feb. 10, 1733-4; d. Oct. 31, 1736.
+143   David,[4] b. July 9, 1736; m. Eunice Whitney.
144   Martha,[4] b. April 3, 1737; m. Oct. 18, 1753, Joseph Thurlow, b. May 30, 1734, son of Thomas and Joanna Thurlow of Newbury, Mass., where the new family lived.
145   Jonathan,[4] b. Sept. 10, 1738.

## 38.

Dea. Richard Thurston [3] (*Daniel*,[2] *Daniel*[1]), brother of the preceding, and youngest child of Daniel [2] and Mary (Dresser) Thurston of Newbury, Mass.; born there Oct. 16, 1710; married, May 5, 1731, Mehitable Jewett, born July 19, 1710, daughter of Jonathan Jewett, who was grandson of Joseph, who came from England in 1638.†

* By a letter received from James Ropes, the assistant register of Essex county, it appears that Lydia Thurston was the widow and administratrix of the estate of Jonathan, and that there is a receipt on file from John, son of Jonathan, to his guardian Richard, of "the whole real and personal estate." This receipt is dated Nov. 5, 1744. Deduct 21 form 44 would make John born in 1723. The inscription upon the grave-stone of John the elder, at Fitchburgh, Mass., is. "In memory of Dea. John Thurston, who died Aug. 5, 1807, aged 83 years. The sweet remembrance of the just Shall flourish when they sleep in dust." Being 83 years of age in 1807 would make him born in 1724; so there is no doubt, in my mind, but that he was *the* John mentioned as the son of Jonathan. Mr. Cyrus Thurston of Fitchburgh informed me that John Thurston removed from Rowley in 1766, when 43 years of age. In the register's office at Worcester is the record of a deed, Ephraim Whitney of Fitchburgh to John Thurston of Rowley, dated Aug. 16, 1765. This purchase was the fall before he moved from Rowley, as above. His wife's name was Lydia. Fitchburgh was formed from Lunenburgh, and all the Thurstons had land there, as is seen by their wills.    A. S. Thurston.

† The Jewett Family.
Edward Jewett, clothier (manufacturer of cloth), in Bradford, West Riding, Yorkshire county, Eng , married, Oct. 1, 1604, Mary Taylor, daughter of William Taylor. They had William, baptized Sept. 15, 1605, Maximilian, baptized Oct. 4, 1607, Joseph, baptized Dec. 31, 1609, and Sarah.
I. Maximilian Jewett and Joseph, brothers, and Joseph's son Joseph came to this country in 1638, in company with Rev. Ezekiel Rogers of Rowley, Yorkshire county, Eng., and twenty "householders" (sixty persons), and settled in Rowley, Mass. A church was organized there Dec. 3, 1639, and Mr. Rogers was chosen their first pastor. He died 1661, aged 70. The new settlement was named Rowley from the place where he was minister in England. Maximilian married first Ann ——; she died Nov. 9, 1667; second, Aug. 30, 1671, Mrs. Elinor Boynton; he died Oct. 19, 1684. Their children were Ezekiel, b. Feb. 1, 1643, d. Sept. 2, 1723; m. Feb. 21, 1663 Faith Parrot; she died Oct. 15, 1715; Ann, b. Dec. 12, 1644; Mary, b Dec. 16, 1646; Elizabeth, b. March 22, 1650; Faith, b. Oct.. 1652; Joseph; Sarah, b. March 17, 1657, d. June 19, 1660; Sarah, b. 1660, m. Jeremiah Ellsworth of Rowley; Priscilla, b. May 19, 1664, d. Sept. 5, 1664.
II. Joseph Jewett, died Oct. 29, 1724. He married, March 2, 1676, Rebecca Law, and had Jonathan, b. March 11, 1678; Aquilla, b. Sept. 4, 1681, m. Oct. 23, 1704, Ann Tenney; Priscilla, b. Aug. 9, 1687, m. July 12, 1708, Stephen Jewett, son of Ezekiel; Rebecca, b. July 24, 1693, m. Jeremiah Burpee.
III. Jonathan Jewett, born March 11, 1678; married, Jan. 29, 1700, Mary Wicom, and had Joseph, b. Dec. 31, 1700, a farmer in company with Rev. Ezekiel Rogers of Stratham, N. H., m. Ann Wiggin; he d. May, 1765; Benjamin, b. April 1, 1703, a farmer in Stratham and Hopkinton, N. H., m. Dorothy Rogers of Rowley; Jedediah, b. Jan. 1, 1705, m. Elizabeth Dummer; he was the fifth pastor of the Congregational church in the first parish of Rowley from 1729 to 1774, when he died; Jacob, b. Jan. 28, 1708-9, m. Bethiah Boynton, a tanner in Rowley; Mehitable, b. July 19, 1710, m. Dea. Richard Thurston; Mark, b. Jan. 15, 1712-13, m. Mary ——, and lived in Hopkinton, Mass.; Moses, b. Nov. 15, 1715, m. Nov. 17, 1737, Martha Hale, lived in Exeter, N. H.; James, b. Jan. 29, 1718; Sarah, b. 1720, m. Joseph Hoyt of Stratham, N. H.

Upon the stones which mark their graves in Georgetown, Mass., is inscribed, " Memento Mori. Erected in memory of Dea. Richard Thurston, who departed this life July the 12th, 1782, in the 72d year of his age." " Memento Mori. In memory of Mrs. Mehitable Thurston, relict of Dea. Richard Thurston, who died May the 18th, 1789, ætat 78 yrs., 9 mo., 10 d." In a memorandum of deaths left by him he says, " my venerable grandfather Dresser died March 14, 1724, in his 85th year. My honored mother [i. e. his wife's mother], Mary Jewett, died Jan. 22, 1742, in the 63d year of her age. My honored father, Jonathan Jewett, died July 25, 1745, in his 67th year."

Dea. Richard Thurston* was a farmer in Rowley, now Georgetown, Mass.; was chosen deacon of the second church at its organization, Oct. 4, 1732. In his family devotions he was accustomed to use this petition, " that the Lord would be a God to him and his descendants to the latest generation, as long as the sun and moon endure." Rev. David Thurston, D.D., a great grandson of Richard, settled over the Congregational church in Winthrop, Me., for over forty years, not long before he died in 1865, said concerning these prayers, " they have been greatly blessed as regards their spiritual interests; quite a number are or have been deacons and deacons' wives, and ministers and ministers' wives." He was a captain of the " second foot company " of Rowley June, 1757, and in that company were John Thurston and Stephen Thurston as privates. Benjamin Thurston was on Capt. Thurston's alarm list. The following is his will:

In the name of GOD, Amen. I, Richard Thurston of Rowley, in the county of Essex and commonwealth of the Massachusetts in New England, gentleman, being sound of body and perfect in mind and memory, but calling to mind the cartainty of death and the uncartainty of the time when it will come, do make and ordain this to be my last will and testament, in manner and form following:

In the first place I recommend my soul to GOD who gave it and my body to the earth to be buried in a decent christian manner as my executors hereafter named shall think fit and proper, and as touching the distribution of my worldly goods and estate, I dispose of the same as followeth:

Imprimis. I give to my beloved wife Mehitable Thurston the improvement of one-third part of all my real estate in Rowley or elsewhere, with the one-half my dwelling house and one-third of my barns, viz., the westerly end of my house that

---

IV. JAMES JEWETT, born Jan. 29, 1718, married Martha Scott; was a merchant in Newburyport, Mass., and had Joseph, b. 1749, a merchant in Portland, Me.; Rev. Caleb, ordained in Gorham, Me., Nov. 5. 1783, m. Nov., 1783, Elizabeth Bacon; James, b. May 28, 1758, came to Portland, Me., 1784, d. Sept. 16, 1843.

Ezekiel Jewett[2] and Faith Parrot had Stephen,[3] b. Feb 23, 1682-3; m. 1st, July 12, 1708, Priscilla Jewett,[3] 2d, Nov. 23, 1725, Lydia Rogers, and had among other children Eliphalet,[4] b. Jan. 22, 1711, m Feb 27, 1734, Ruth Pickard, daughter of Jonathan and Joanna Pickard; she died Sept. 18, 1750. Their sixth child was David,[5] b. May 31, 1746, m. Oct. 31, 1771, Phebe Thurston [see l. o. 160].

JOSEPH JEWETT,[1] emigrant, married first, Oct. 1, 1634, Mary Mallinson; she died May 12, 1652; second, May, 1653, Mrs. Ann Allen, widow of Bozonne Allen, one of the first settlers of Hingham, Mass. Joseph Jewett died in Rowley Feb. 26, 1630, having had Jeremiah, b. 1637, m. March 4, 1661, Sarah Dickinson, d. May 20, 1714; Hannah, b. 1639, m. John Carleton; Nehemiah, b. 1643, m. Experience Pearce; Faith and Patience, b. 1645, Patience m. Shubael Walker; Mary, b. Feb. 4, 1654; Joseph, b. Feb. 1, 1656, m. Jan. 16, 1680, Ruth Wood.

* Extract from the works of John Adams by his grandson, vol. ii., page 290. 1771, Nov. 5, Tensday At Salem; fine weather. Deacon Thurston of Rowley came in last night; a venerable old man with his snowy, hoary locks. Kent and the deacon soon clashed upon religion. " Don't you think, sir," says the deacon, " we are here probationers for eternity?" " No, by no means," says Kent. " We are here probationers for the next state, and in the next we shall be probationers for the next that is to follow, and so on through as many states as there are stars or sands to all eternity. You have gone through several states already before this." " Ay," says the deacon, " where do you get this; don't you believe the Scriptures?" I put in my oar. " He made it, deacon, out of whole cloth; it never existed out of his imagination." Kent. " I get it from analogy." It is the delight of this Kent's heart to tease a minister or deacon with his wild conceits about religion.

I do now improve; also, the improvement of all my household goods with the youce of my clock during her natural life. I also give my beloved wife to be at her disposal forever my riding horse and the one-half my stock of Catel and sheep and swin, with what provision I shall leive in my house.

Item. I give to my son Daniel Thurston and his heirs and assigns my dwelling house and barn and the land on which they stand, being about forty-two acres and being the four first lots on the letter B and three on a range known by the letter A, viz., the first and second and eighth on said range, also another tract of land laying north of my house, it being land I purchased of Eleazer Spafford, formerly Nathan Boynton's, and bounded according as the deed of said land describes them with a peaice of woodland at the north of said land, which I purchased of Stephen Hardy, junᵣ, for bounds I refer to the deed I had of said Hardy, also a piece of meadow and upland about seven acres, known by the name of Barrit meadow, also a piece of salt marsh laying north of Nelson Island (so called) and laying in partnership with Thomas Gage, esqᵣ, also a piece of salt marsh laying in Ipswich, which marsh I purchased of the widow of Colº Berry, deceased.

Item. I give to my son David Thurston and his heirs and assigns a tract of land in the township of Rowley containing about fifty-five acres, with a barn and orchard on the same and known by the name of the F lots, and it being thirteen lots on that rainge of lots, also an orchard I purchased of Eleazer Spafford and known by the name of the Boynton orchard, and bounded as may appear by the deed I had of sᵈ Spafford, also a wood lot on a rainge of lots known by the letter D, and being the tenth lot on that rainge of lots; also a piece of Meadow and upland known by the name of Pleasant Hill meadow, and laying in partnership with John Smith; also a piece of Salt marsh laying in Rowley and known by the name of Shepard's marsh, and contains about six acres; also a wood lot in the township of Boxford containing ten acres, which I purchased of John Hale, for bounds I refer to the deed I had of said land.

Item. I give to my daughter Mary Searl and her heirs and assigns twenty-eight pounds, four shillings, lawful silver money, to be paid by my executors hereafter named in one year after my decease, with one-fifth part of my household goods after my wife's decease, with what I have before given her in full of her portion.

Item. I give to my daughter Phebe Jewett and her heirs and assigns twenty-four pounds, eighteen shillings, lawful silver money, to be paid by my executors hereafter named within two years after my decease, with one-fifth part of my household goods after my wife's decease, with what I had before given her in full of her portion.

Item. I give to my daughter Sarah Pearson and her heirs and assigns twenty-three pounds, sixteen shillings, lawful silver money, to be paid by my executors hereafter named within three years after my decease, with one-fifth part of my household goods after my wife's decease, with what I have given her before in full of her portion.

Item. I give to my daughter Mehitabel Chute and her heirs and assigns twenty-three pounds, sixteen shillings, lawful silver money, to be paid by my executors hereafter named within four years after my decease, with one-fifth part of my household goods after my wife's decease, with what I have given her before in full of her portion.

Item. I give to my granddaughter Mary Harris and her heirs and assigns eight pounds, sixteen shillings, lawful silver money, to be paid by my executors hereafter named within five years after my decease, with one-tenth part of my household goods after my wife's decease, with what I had before given to her mother in full of her portion.

Item. I give to my granddaughter Phebe Harris and her heirs and assigns eight pounds, sixteen shillings, lawful silver money, to be paid by my executors hereafter named within six years after my decease, with one-tenth part of my household goods after my wife's decease, with what I had before given to her mother in full of her portion.

Lastly. I give to my two sons above named all my land in Lunenburgh and Fitchburgh, also all my land in Hollis and Amherst in Newhampshire, also all my remaining stock of cattle, horses, sheep and swine, wearing apparel, guns, sword and clock, and every other thing not given away before, except my books of Piety, them, my will is, should be equally divided to my wife and all my children and my two grandchildren heretofore mentioned one share. My will is that my two sons, viz., Daniel Thurston and David Thurston, whom I constitute and appoint my soul executors of this my last will and testament, shall receive all the debts that are now due to me, and pay all the debts I justly owe and all the legacies I have given in

this my will,—renouncing all other wills, I do declare this to be my last will and testament, and do now set to my hand and seal, this eleventh day of May, one thousand seven hundred and eighty-two, and in the six year of the Independency of the Younited States of America. Richard Thurston.   Seal.

Signed, sealed and delivered in presence of David Chute, Daniel Chute, jr, Daniel Chute.

Their children were:

155   Stephen,[4] b. Mar. 4, 1733; at the age of 29, May 13, 1762, he was shipwrecked on Cape Ann bar, near Squam harbor, and the body was not found till June 21st, following, at the lower end of Marble Head, thirty miles from the place of disaster.   It was taken to Rowley and buried.
+156   Mary,[4] b. Oct. 26, 1734; m. Dea. Jeremiah Searle.
+157   Eunice,[4] b. Oct. 4, 1736; m. John Harris.
158   Hannah,[4] b. May 16. 1738; d. Nov. 9, 1739.
159   Jonathan,[4] b. Sept. 26, 1739; d. Jan. 23, 1740.
+160   Phebe,[4] b. Dec. 14, 1741; m. 1st, Rev. David Jewett; 2d, Dea. Daniel Spofford.
161   Hannah,[4] b. Jan. 4, 1744; m. June 24, 1773, John Adams of Andover, Mass.; d. Jan. 22, 1775, aged 31, leaving
162   *Joseph* (Adams), d. June 22, 1776, aged 2 years, 1 month.
+163   Daniel,[4] b. Dec. 14, 1745; m. 1st, Judith Chute; 2d, Mrs. Margaret Kinsman.
+164   Sarah,[4] b. April 14, 1748; m. John Pearson.
+165   David,[4] b. March 19, 1751; m. 1st, Mary Bacon; 2d, Chloe Redington.
+166   Mehitable,[4] b. Sept. 25, 1753; m. Dea. James Chute.

## 40

JOSEPH THURSTON [3] (*Joseph,*[2] *Daniel*[1]), eldest son of Joseph [2] and Elizabeth (Woodbury) Thurston of Rowley, Mass.; born there Jan. 23, 1698–9; married, March 9, 1725, MRS. MARY (LANE) FINSON, born Aug. 8, 1697, daughter of John Lane.  Her first husband, Thomas Finson, was killed at Fox island, Me., by the Indians, with five others, in June, 1724.  She had four children by this marriage. She died 1792.

Mr. Thurston was the first of the name who settled in Gloucester, Mass.   He afterward removed to (Sandy Bay) Rockport, Mass., and followed fishing.   He died May 29, 1780.

This record was taken from a bible which contains this memorandum: "Joseph Thurston and my son William bought this bible 1756. Feb. 16, 1779, my son William being lost at sea, I have sold this bible to my son Joseph for twelve pounds, lawful money.  Witness my hand, Joseph Thurston.  A true copy, Mary Thurston."

### Children:

177   Sarah,[4] b. Dec. 2, 1726; m. Thomas Finson, and d. 1795.
+178   Joseph,[4] b. Feb. 15, 1729; m. Agnes Davis.
179   Elizabeth,[4] b. Nov. 8, 1731; m. Henry Clark.
+180   Daniel,[4] b. Feb. 16, 1735; m. Anna Tarr.
+181   John,[4] b. June 30, 1737; m. Eunice Stockbridge.
182   Dorcas,[4] b. in Haverhill, Mass., Jan. 22, 1740; m. Thomas Robbins (or Roberts), and d. April 28, 1825.
+183   William,[4] b. Nov. 27, 1742; m. Martha Pool.

## 44

BENJAMIN THURSTON [3] of Uxbridge, Mass. (*Joseph,*[2] *Daniel*[1]), brother of the preceding, and second son of Joseph [2] and Elizabeth (Woodbury) Thurston of Newbury, Mass.; born there Jan. 23, 1698; married ELIZABETH ——.

Their children were:

194 John,[4] b. March 20, 1741.
195 Elizabeth,[4] b. June 26, 1743; d. Feb. 24, 1745.
196 Peter,[4] b. Sept. 17, 1745.
197 Benjamin,[4] b. Jan. 2, 1748.
198 Levi,[4] b. July 30, 1751.

## 47

ABNER THURSTON[3] (*James,[2] Daniel[1]*), son of James[2] and Mary (Pearson) Thurston of Newbury, Mass.; born Feb. 28, 1699; married ———.

Mr. Thurston may have been born in Newbury, Mass., and come to Exeter, N. H., with his father. The records show that he bought land in Exeter in 1728 and sold land to Moses of Stratham in 1734 and 1735. He was corporal in the company of Capt. Daniel Ladd in the "march after the enemy toward Winnipiseogee pond," May 17, 1724.

Their children were:

+209 Abner,[4] b. 1729; m. Martha Piper.
+210 Ichabod,[4] b. about 1731; m. Betty Filbrick.
+211 James,[4] b. Sept. 8, 1733; m. 1st, Mary Jones; 2d, Elizabeth Peabody.
 212 Susan,[4] n.m.; lived to be over 90 in Exeter, N. H.
+213 Caleb,[4] b. 1737; m. Hannah Dudley.
+214 Peter,[4] b. 1739; m. Dorothy Gates.
 215 Elizabeth,[4] n.m; d. in Exeter.
+216 Timothy,[4] b. 1742; m. Susan Wheeler.

## 49

MOSES THURSTON[3] (*Stephen,[2] Daniel[1]*), eldest son of Stephen[2] and Mary Thurston of Stratham, N. H.; born there July 19, 1707; married SARAH ———. He died Oct. 12, 1756; his son Stephen appointed administrator Nov. 24, 1756.

Estate appraised at £213. Jan. 20, 1757, sworn to by said Stephen to be correct. April 26, 1757, the widow Sarah's dower was set off. 1731, deed recorded in Exeter, N. H., Moses to John of Stratham, probably his brother. 1787, deed from Sarah, widow of Moses, to son Josiah. He was sergeant in company C of Col. Nathaniel Meserve's regiment in an expedition against Crown Point in 1756; enlisted May 1st, discharged Oct. 2d.

Children:

 228 Josiah.[4]
+229 Moses,[4] b. June 10, 1730; m. Elizabeth Clifford.
+230 Ezekiel,[4] m. ———.
 231 Sarah,[4] d. April 8, 1752.
+232 Stephen,[4] m. ———.
+233 Oliver,[4] b. about 1738; m. Sarah French.
 234 John.[4]
 235 Benjamin.[4]
  The three last were under twenty-one Jan. 10, 1757, as letters of guardianship were issued to John Thurston, probably their uncle [see no. 50].

## 50

JOHN THURSTON[3] (*Stephen,[2] Daniel[1]*), second son of Stephen[2] and Mary Thurston of Stratham, N. H.; born there Aug. 29, 1709; married, first, MRS. PHEBE WIGGIN, who had a daughter Hannah (Wiggin). She died April 24, 1750. Second, ELIZABETH ———. He died Dec. 28, 1773.

He was probably a farmer in Stratham, N. H., as his will, probated 1774, gives his "wife Elizabeth 20 bush. good corn, 6 bush. rye, 200 lbs. good pork, 80 lbs. beef, and 10 lbs. flax." His granddaughter, Mrs. Nourse, says he gave the land to build the Congregational church upon in Stratham.

His children were:

+246 John,[4] m. Elsie Leavitt.
+247 Paul,[4] m. Margaret ——.
  248 Hannah,[4] } m. —— Stockbridge.
  249 Phebe,[4] }

## 51

ROBERT THURSTON [3] (*Stephen,*[2] *Daniel*[1]), brother of the preceding, and son of Stephen [2] and Mary Thurston of Stratham, N. H.; born there Feb. 25, 1712; married ——. He died at his brother John's Feb. 16, 1752.

Mr. Thurston deeded land in township of Bow, N. H., "said land having belonged to my honored father Stephen of Stratham, N. H." He was in a company "guarding and scouting at Canterbury," under command of Capt. Jeremiah Clough, from July 4 to ~~July 4~~, 1746.

Their children were:

  260 Robert,[4] mariner; was in the revolutionary war and died in Stratham, intestate, 1788.
+261 Samuel,[4] m. Mary ——.
+262 James,[4] b. 1744; m. ——.

## 54

NATHANIEL THURSTON [3] (*Stephen,*[2] *Daniel*[1]), brother of the preceding, and son of Stephen [2] and Mary Thurston of Stratham, N. H.; born there July 12, 1718; married MINER CHASE, born Nov. 17, 1721, daughter of Stephen Chase of Nottingham, N. H. He died Oct. 12, 1775, aged 57. She died April 9, 1815, aged 93.

Mr. Thurston was a tailor in Newbury, Mass., and after marriage took his wife on horseback to Plaistow, N. H., to reside; deeded land in Chester, N. H., 1747, and in Bakerstown, 1771; was a member of the Congregational church. Mrs. Thurston used to walk nearly a mile and a half to meeting, down a long and steep hill, till after ninety years old. The following is a copy of his will:

In the name of GOD, amen. This twenty-seventh day of September, Anno Domini one thousand seven hundred and seventy-five, I, Nath[l] Thurston of Newbury, in the county of Essex and Province of the Massachusetts Bay in New England, taylor, calling to mind the uncertain state of this life, do make and declare this my last will and testament in the manner and form following:

First. I commend my soul to GOD who gave it, and my body I commit to the earth to be decently buried at the discretion of my executrix; and for the settling of my estate as it hath pleased GOD to bestow upon me, I do give and dispose of the same in the manner and form following:

Firstly. I give to my beloved wife Miner all my estate both real and personal of what name or nature soever, to use and dispose of as she shall se fit, she paying to my children six shillings apiece, also six shillings apiece to four of my grandchildren, viz., my son Paul Thurston's three children and my daughter Sarah Moulton's child.

Secondly. I give to my son Enoch six shillings in money, to be paid to him in ten years after my decease by my executrix.

Thirdly. I give to my son Jonathan six shillings in money, to be paid to him in ten years after my decease by my executrix.

Fourthly. I give to my son Stephen six shillings in money, to be paid to him in ten years after my decease by my executrix.

Fifthly. I give to my son Daniel six shillings in money, to be paid to him in ten years after my decease by my executrix.

Sixthly. I give to my daughter Minor six shillings in money, to be paid to her when she arrives to the age of twenty-one years by my executrix.

Seventhly. I give to my daughter Susanna six shillings in money, to be paid to her by my executrix when she arrives to the age of twenty-one years.

Eighthly. I give to my daughter Lydia six shillings in money, to be paid to her by my executrix when she arrives to the age of twenty-one years.

Ninthly. I give to my daughter Rhoda six shillings in money, to be paid to her by my executrix when she arrives to the age of twenty-one years.

Tenthly. I give to my grandson John Thurston six shillings in money, to be paid to him by my executrix when he arrives to the age of twenty-one years.

Eleventhly. I give to my granddaughter Anne Thurston six shillings in money, to be paid her by my executrix when she arrives to the age of twenty-one years.

Twelfthly. I give to my granddaughter Sarah Thurston six shillings in money, to be paid to her by my executrix when she arrives to the age of twenty-one years.

Thirteenthly. I give to my grandson Silas Moulton six shillings in money, to be paid to him by my executrix when he arrives to the age of twenty-one years.

Fourteenthly. I appoint my beloved wife my sole executrix of this my last will and testament, to pay my just debts and funeral charges ; also to receive my just dues.

I do hereby revoke, disannul and make void all former wills and testaments by me made, declaring this only to be my last will and testament.

In confirmation hereof I have hereto set my hand and seal the day and year above written. Nathaniel Thurston. Seal.

Signed, sealed, pronounced and declared in the presence of these witnesses. Moody Follansbe. Joseph Bartlet, Joseph Bartlet, jun,.

Essex, ss. Probate office. Approved May 7, 1776. A. C. Goodell, register.

### Their children were :

+273 Enoch,[4] b. July 29, 1741; m. 1st, Lucy McIntyre; 2d, Elizabeth Chase.
+274 Paul,[4] b. Nov. 22, 1743; m. Hannah Rawson.
+275 Jonathan,[4] b. Dec. 21, 1745; m. Elizabeth Hovey.
276 Sarah,[4] b. Nov. 27, 1747; m. —— Moulton of West Newbury, Mass.; d. Sept. 20, 1769, having had:
   277  *Silas* (Moulton).
+278 Stephen,[4] b. Jan. 24, 1750; m. 1st, Keziah Cheney; 2d, Mrs. Pettingall.
279 Daniel,[4] b. Aug. 24, 1752; lived in Beverly, Mass., and had *John*,[5] *Anne*,[5] *Sarah*,[5] all minors Sept. 7, 1775.
283 Miner,[4] b. Dec. 1, 1754; m. Jan. 29, 1785, Benjamin Carleton, a farmer and basket weaver in Plaistow, N. H.; a member of the Congregational church in Haverhill, Mass. She d. 1831; he d. Nov.. 1833. They had :
   284  *David* (Carleton), b. Dec. 13, 1785; m. Mary Mitchell of Plaistow; served in the war of 1812 and received a bounty of one hundred and sixty acres of land; was deacon and one of the founders of the Baptist church in Plaistow; sang in the choir till he was over sixty years old.
   285  *Hannah* (Carleton), b. Feb. 2, 1787; m. Saml Farrington of Newton, N.H.
   286  *Miner* (Carleton), b. Sept. 16, 1788; m. Wm. J. Chase of Newbury, Mass.
   287  *Benjamin* (Carleton), b. Jan. 4, 1790; went to sea, and died in a hospital in Asia, 1814.
   288  *Paul Thurston* (Carleton), b. Jan. 10, 1792; m. Ruth Harriman of Derry, N. H.; was in the war of 1812, and died soon after.
   289  *John* (Carleton), b. Aug. 18, 1794; n.m.; d. in Plaistow, 1866, aged 72.
   290  *Tappan* (Carleton), b. Sept. 2, 1796; d. Sept. 2, 1797.
291 Silas,[4] b. March 2, 1757; d. April 12, 1758.
292 Lydia,[4] b. Dec. 4, 1759; m. May 23, 1779, Peterson Roby; d. Mar. 15, 1780.
+293 Susannah,[4] b. May 7, 1763; m. Josiah Chase.
294 Ruth,[4] } twins, born { d. Sept. 7, 1775.
295 Rhoda,[4] } Jan. 14, 1766; { m. —— Thurlow of Newburyport, Mass., where they lived and died.

The above is taken from an old bible in hands of J. H. Noyes, Webster, N. H.

## 55

STEPHEN THURSTON[3] (*Stephen*,[2] *Daniel*[1]), brother of the preceding, and son of Stephen[2] and Mary Thurston of Stratham, N. H.;

born there about 1720; married MARY ST. CLAIRE. He died Nov. 27, 1782. She married again and had one child. She died Sept. 10, 1811, aged 83.

Mr. Thurston lived in Stratham, N. H.; was in Capt. Ezekiel Worthen's company, Col. Nathaniel Meserve's regiment, in the expedition against Crown Point, 1756. He enlisted April 17, 1758, in Capt. Somerbee Gilman's company, Col. John Hart's regiment, in the expedition against Lewisborough, N. Y., and was discharged Oct. 30, 1758. He next enlisted, April 24, 1760, in Capt. Jeremiah Marston's company, Col. John Goff's regiment, for the invasion of Canada, and deserted June 2d.

### Children:

+306    Stephen,[4] b. April 8, 1760; m. Betsey Wiggin.
   307    Mehitable,[4] m. Zebulon Ring of Deerfield, N. H., and had:
     308    *Abijah* (Ring),   } twins.
     309    *Iphaliah* (Ring), }
     310    *Rebecca* (Ring).
     311    *Sally* (Ring).
     312    *Stephen* (Ring).
     313    *Daniel* (Ring). All dead 1877.
+314    Daniel,[4] b. July 29, 1763; m. Hannah Dutch.
   315    Ruth,[4] m. —— Wiggin of New Market, N. H.
   316    A daughter,[4] m. —— St. Claire.
   317    Sarah,[4] b. 1752; m. Col. Joseph Hilton of Deerfield, N. H.; d. May 15, 1813, aged 61. They had:
     318    *Betsey* (Hilton).
     319    *Sally* (Hilton).
     320    *Hannah* (Hilton), d. young.
     321    *Mehitable* (Hilton).
     322    *Hannah* (Hilton).
     323    *Stephen* (Hilton).
     324    *Joseph* (Hilton).
     325    *Daniel* (Hilton).
     326    *Theodore* (Hilton).
     327    *Nathaniel* (Hilton).
     328    *Winthrop* (Hilton). All dead 1877.
   329    Deborah (half-sister), m. Richard Bartlett of Deerfield, N. H., and had:
     *John* (Bartlett).
     *Stephen* (Bartlett).
     *Richard* (Bartlett).
     *Deborah* (Bartlett).

Stephen Thurston is said to have had fourteen daughters.

---

## Fourth Generation.

### 83

HANNAH THURSTON [4] (*John,*[3] *Daniel,*[2] *Daniel*[1]), fourth daughter of John [3] and Dorothy (Woodman) Thurston of Newbury, Mass.; born about 1740; married, Nov. 22, 1764, EDMUND ADAMS, an energetic and thrifty farmer in Londonderry, N. H. The following is an abstract of Mr. Adams' will:

March 17, 1823, Edmund Adams made his will, in which he gives his wife Hannah all those goods she brought to me when she became my wife, also one cow, six of my best chairs, a suit of mourning apparel, fifty dollars, and directs his executor to furnish her with provisions sufficient for herself and my daughter Susannah for six months from the time of my decease; the sole use of the west room and west

bedroom, together with the use of the well, cellar, oven, gar len, and fruit from my farm, as much as she may want for her own use, and the use of my chaise, and so long as she shall remain my widow to have her cow kept on the farm. and to be furnished with firewood sufficient to keep one fire, cut and placed convenient for her use, and also to have delivered to her annually in six months after my decease 12 bush. good Indian corn, 3 bush. good rye, 2 bush. good wheat, 120 lbs. good mess beef, 200 lbs. good pork, 10 bush. potatoes, 15 lbs. beef tallow, 8 lbs. good sheep's wool, and 15 lbs. of good flax.

To his son James the farm on which I now live with all the privileges and appurtenances thereto belonging, except what I have bequeathed my wife, also half the stock on my homestead farm, half my farming utensils and casks, together with all my blacksmith tools, half my wearing apparel.

To his son Edmund his farm in the town of Salem on which he now lives and my McKeen lot in Londonderry near Leverett's meadow, containing about twenty-seven acres; my mill farm, saw-mill and mill privileges, with the buildings situated in Londonderry; a wood lot in the town of Chester, about thirty acres; also half the live stock on my homestead farm and half my farming utensils and casks and half my wearing apparel.

To my daughter Jane Marsh two large silver spoons, three silver teaspoons, and $1,000.

To my daughter Susannah Pike my best bed and bedding, two large silver spoons, three silver teaspoons, best brass kettle, a desk which was my son Amos', a suit of mourning apparel, $1,000 to be paid her at age of twenty-one, or when she is married, and interest annually, also $50 in one and two years after my decease.

To my granddaughter Mary Moor two large silver spoons, two silver teaspoons, and one cow or the value of one.

To my grandsons Edmund Adams, Edmund Marsh, and John Adams, $100 equally between them.

To my four children before named and granddaughter Mary Moor, equally between them, my books, watches, clocks, beds and bedding and household furniture not already disposed of.

To my executor $300, in trust for my granddaughter Mary Moor.

To first parish church in Londonderry $100, for a permanent fund.

I will and order that my pew in the East meeting-house in Londonderry be kept for the use of my children and heirs.

That my farm in Chester and land in Rumney and all other lands not disposed of at my decease be sold, and the proceeds with all the residue of my estate, after paying all debts, to be given to my sons James and Edmund equally, and I appoint Capt. John Clark of Londonderry my executor. The will was witnessed by John Burnham, William Choate, John Burnham, jr. Thomas Leavitt, register of probate.

### Their children were :

340 James (Adams), b. May 5, 1765; m. Ann Griffin Jan. 24, 1793. She died in 1807. He died Jan. 18, 1825, aged 85.
341 Jane (Adams), b. Jan. 2, 1767; m. Daniel Marsh Dec. 31, 1794.
342 Amos (Adams), b. May 10, 1768; killed in a saw-mill Nov. 13, 1813.
343 Patience (Adams), b. July 16, 1770; d. July 20, 1806.
344 Hannah (Adams), b. Feb. 8, 1775; d. June 5, 1795.
345 Edmund (Adams), b. May 14, 1777; m. Elizabeth Carr 1808; was a farmer in Salem, N. H.
346 Richard (Adams), b. Nov. 14, 1779; d. soon.
347 Benjamin (Adams), b. May 31, 1782; d. in Havana Sept. 21, 1811.
348 Jacob (Adams), b. Jan. 14, 1785; d. unmarried, Aug. 10, 1823, having endowed by his will the "Adams Female Academy" at Londonderry, N. H.
349 Susannah Pike (Adams).

## 119

COL. DANIEL THURSTON [4] (*Benjamin,*[3] *Daniel,*[2] *Daniel*[1]), eldest son of Benjamin [3] and Mary (Gage) Thurston of Newbury, Mass.; born there March, 1720; married, first, Sept. 3, 1741, HANNAH PARKER; she died Jan. 11, 1759. Second, Sept. 10, 1761, JUDITH GERRISH; she died August, 1765. Third, MRS. ELIZABETH ROLF of Newburyport, Mass. He died July 14, 1805, aged 85. She died 1819, aged 97.

Mr. Thurston was an architect and house carpenter\* in Bradford, Mass. He was a "noted man in his day;" was a member of the Massachusetts Provincial Congress and enlisted in the revolutionary war. He and his son Nathaniel were representative and senator for thirty years in succession, one and sometimes both at the same time in the legislature of Massachusetts. He held many responsible offices in town and state; was colonel of a regiment, one of the framers of the constitution of Massachusetts, and a deacon in the Congregational church. The following is a copy of his will :

In the name of God, amen. The twenty-ninth day of October eighteen hundred and one. I, Daniel Thurston, of Bradford in the County of Essex, and Commonwealth of Massachusetts, Esquire, being of sound mind and memory, and considering the uncertainty of Life, think it best to settle my estate, which I now undertake to do in the following manner, viz.:

First and principally, I commit my soul into the hands of God who gave it, and my body to the earth from whence it was taken, to be buried at the discretion of my executor hereafter named.

Imprimis. I will that all my just debts and funeral charges be paid by my executor herein hereafter named.

Item. I will that Elizabeth my loving wife take one-third part of my real estate according to Law, and also I give her one-third of the household furniture, and the other two-thirds of said furniture I give to my three daughters, to be equally divided between them or their desendants. I also order that my executor pay my said wife yearly the sum of ten dollars, so long as it pleases God to continue her life, and that my executor shall provide firewood for my said wife ready cut at the door; also that he find her an horse and chaise to ride to meeting and elsewhere, as she shall have occation.

Item. I give to my son Benjamin Thurston ten dollars, which is his part of my estate, including what he hath already had.

Item. I give to my son Nathaniel Thurston, Esquire, all my real estate lying in the town of Bradford, and also a piece of salt meadow in the Town of Rowley; together with all my quick stock of every discription, except what is otherwise disposed of.

Item. I give to my son Daniel Thurston the sum of five hundred dollars, to be paid him in three months after my decease, and also I give him my share in Bradford Social Library.

Item. I give to Capt[n] Peter Kimball, who married my daughter Betty, the sum of twenty-six dollars, to be paid him in three months after my decease.

Item. I give to Deacon Richard Walker, who married my daughter Mary, the sum of twenty-six dollars and one cow, to be paid him in three months after my decease.

Item. I give to the children of my daughter Hannah, who was the wife of Timothy Gage, the sum of twenty-six dollars, to be paid them in three months after my decease.

I likewise make and ordain my son Nathaniel Thurston, esquire, sole executor of this my last will and testament, ratifying this and no other to be such. Daniel Thurston. Seal.

---

\* When a young man he built a meeting-house in New Hampshire. Tea and coffee were not much used in those days, and he took several cakes of chocolate to the lady with whom he boarded and requested her to make some chocolate for breakfast. She put it into a large kettle and hung it over the fire, and when she came to take it up she exclaimed. "O. Mr. Thurston, it has all come to pieces, what shall I do!" He told her to pass a bowl of it and a pitcher of hot water and he would make it all right. They had a good laugh over it and a fine dish of chocolate. He had two front teeth come after he was seventy years old.

Mr. Thurston was a man who commanded the respect of every one. He was usually made moderator of their town meetings. A gentleman says, "they had a town meeting one day, and Col. Thurston was detained for a short time, and they put a vote which divided the house and made great noise and confusion. Just at this time Mr. Thurston stepped in, and every hat was off and every man in his seat in a moment, and so still that the slightest noise was perceptible." Mr. Thurston remarked afterward that he never was in a more orderly meeting.

He was a man of great strength. His son Daniel went to his house for a barrel of cider, and went to the barn to get a man to help him get it out of the cellar and into his cart, and when returning met his father carrying the barrel by the chimes out of the yard, over the gate-way, and placing it in the cart said, "you may drive off Daniel."

Signed, sealed, published, pronounced, and declared by the said Daniel Thurston as his last will and testament, in presence of us witnesses. Eliot Payson, David Marble, Joseph Marble.
Essex Probate Office. Proved Aug. 5, 1805. James Ropes, Asst. Regr.

### His children were :

350 Hattie,[5] b. 1742.
351 Betty,[5] b. Oct. 25, 1744; m. Capt. Peter Kimball.
352 Mary,[6] b. July 24, 1746; m. May 21, 1771. Dea. Richard Walker, a farmer and tanner in Bradford, Mass. They had :
   353 *Mehitable* (Walker), b. 1773.
   354 *Hannah* (Walker), b. 1775; m. Samuel Gardner, a shoe manufacturer of Haverhill, Mass.
   355 *David* (Walker), b. 1778; m. Sarah Thurston [see no.*1300*].
   356 *Betsey* (Walker), b. 1782; m. Samuel Gardner, above.
   357 *Richard* (Walker), b. 1786; m. Catherine Trickey of Bradford; was a farmer in Hanover, N. H.
358 Hannah,[6] m. March 14, 1771, Timothy Gage, a farmer in Bradford. They had :
   359 *Daniel* (Gage), m. Hannah Curtis.
   360 *Betsey* (Gage), m. Thomas Webster.
   361 *Hannah* (Gage), m. Samuel Chadwick of Bradford.
+362 Benjamin,[6] b. Sept. 25, 1753: m. Sarah Phillips.
+363 Nathaniel,[6] b. Jan. 17, 1755; m. 1st, Betsey Webster and six others.
+364 Daniel,[6] b. June 12, 1757; m. Susannah Crombie.
365 Judith,[6] b. Aug. 14, 1765; d. Sept. 4. 1765.

### 137

DEA. JOHN THURSTON[4] (*Jonathan,[3] Daniel,[2] Daniel[1]*), son of Jonathan[3] and Lydia (Spofford) Thurston of Rowley, now Georgetown, Mass.; born there Aug. 19, 1723; married, first, March 15, 1743-4, HEPZIBAH BURPEE; second, April 28, 1768, LYDIA KIMBALL of Bradford, Mass. He died August, 1807.

Mr. Thurston purchased a farm in the westerly part of Lunenburgh, before the town of Fitchburgh was incorporated, Aug. 6, 1765, and moved there in the spring of 1766. He was a soldier in the French and Indian wars, and several relics captured by him from the enemy are still in possession of his descendants. He was deacon of the Congregational church, and a man much respected in town.

The inscription upon the head-stone of his wife in the grave-yard at Fitchburgh is "In memory of Lydia Thurston, died Feb. 3, 1805, aged 70 years."

> "Now my last charge to you I give,
> That you repent, believe, and live.
> Remember what I've said to you,
> And so I bid you all adieu."

### His children, all born in Rowley, were :

366 Ebenezer,[5] b. 1749; published Oct. 27, 1770; m. Lydia Flagg of Worcester. He was a farmer, deacon of the Congregational church many years. No family; d. June, 1822, aged 73. She died Nov., 1831, aged 78.
367 Priscilla,[5] published July 11, 1770; m. Abram Farwell, b. Aug. 18, 1743, a farmer, son of Gen. Samuel Farwell of Fitchburgh. She died Dec. 30, 1837. They had :
   368 *Hepzibah* (Farwell), b. Oct. 15, 1770; m. May 23, 1793, Simeon Farwell.
   369 *Samuel* (Farwell), b. Nov. 10, 1772.
   370 *Abram* (Farwell), b. Aug. 16, 1774.
   371 *Josiah* (Farwell), b. Feb. 9, 1777.
   372 *Abel* (Farwell), b. Feb. 11, 1780.
   373 *Merriam* (Farwell), b. May 9, 1782.
   374 *Levi* (Farwell), b. Oct. 19, 1784.

375 *Joseph* (Farwell), b. Jan. 22, 1787; m. Dec. 6, 1804, Polly Kimball.
376 Hepzibah,[5] published July 6, 1786; m. John Osborn, a farmer in Fitch-
    burgh. She died Nov. 29, 1808. They had :
377   *Hepzibah B.* (Osborn), b. Sept. 30, 1787.
378   *Lydia K.* (Osborn), b. July 19, 1790.
379   *John* (Osborn), b. April 6, 1792.
380   *Ephraim* (Osborn), b. May 2, 1794.
381   *Miriam* (Osborn), b July 13, 1801.
382   *Abram* (Osborn), b. May 5, 1804.
383 Daniel,[5] published March 30, 1780; m. April, 1780, Hannah Hilton of
    Fitchburgh, and had *Enoch*,[6] b. Aug. 24, 1780; probably removed from
    Fitchburgh soon after.
+384 Thomas,[5] m. 1st, Lydia Davis; 2d, Mehitable Upton.
+385 John,[5] b. 1757; m. Esther Wood.
+386 Stephen,[5] m. Mary Osgood.

## 139

SAMUEL THURSTON [4] (*Jonathan,[3] Daniel,[2] Daniel[1]*), son of Jona-
than [3] and Lydia (Spofford) Thurston of Rowley, now Georgetown,
Mass.; born there June 7, 1727; married, by Rev. James Chandler,
April 18, 1751, PRISCILLA BURPEE of Rowley, born Jan. 20, 1727.
He died March, 1806. She died November, 1811.

Mr. Thurston was a farmer in Lancaster, Mass.

### Their children were:

395 Priscilla,[5] b. March 24, 1752; d. May 29, 1812.
396 John,[5] b. Sept. 15, 1753; d. Jan. 1, 1754.
397 John,[5] b. Nov. 15, 1754; a farmer in Lancaster.
398 Judith,[5] b. Jan. 9, 1757; d. June 20, 1774.
399 Silas,[5] b. Dec. 12, 1758; a farmer in Lancaster.
400 Mary,[5] b. Oct. 17, 1761; m. —— Richards.
+401 Pearson,[5] b. Dec. 9, 1763; m. Jerusha Greenleaf.
402 Sally,[5] b. June 14, 1767; d. June 16, 1801.
403 Susanna,[5] b. April 7, 1769; m. June 9, 1790, Dr. Silas Allen of Leominster,
    Mass., where he was a physician of standing and repute. She died Sept.
    13, 1824. He died Sept. 5, 1841. They had :
404   *Julia* (Allen), b. Sept. 14, 1791; d. June 6, 1857.
405   *Henry* (Allen), b. Oct. 5, 1793; m. twice; was a merchant in Leominster
    many years, and after a member of the firm of Hallet & Davis, piano
    makers in Boston, where he died, 1874.
406   *Susan* (Allen), b. Sept. 15, 1795; d. July 15, 1799.
407   *Mira* (Allen), b. Sept. 11, 1797; m. L. Burrage.
408   *Susan* (Allen), b. Dec. 27, 1800; d. Nov. 2, 1801.
409   *Silas* (Allen), b. May 18, 1802; connected with the firm of Hallet & Da-
    vis, Boston; was organist of Park street church many years, where he
    died, about 1873.
410   *William Thurston* (Allen), b. Oct. 12, 1811; d. June 6, 1842.
411 Hepzibah,[5] b. Aug. 1, 1771; m. June 16, 1805, —— Kendall, a carpenter of
    Sterling, Mass.; d. July 31, 1814.
412 Lydia,[5] b. Jan. 24, 1774; d. Nov. 25, 1803.

## 143

DAVID THURSTON [4]* (*Jonathan,[3] Daniel,[2] Daniel[1]*), brother of the
preceding, and son of Jonathan [3] and Lydia (Spofford) Thurston of
Rowley, Mass.; born July 9, 1736; married EUNICE WHITNEY. She
died Jan. 5, 1802, aged 63. He died Aug. 6, 1826, aged 90 y. 28 d.

David Thurston lived in Leominster, Mass., several years, when he
left and was one of the first settlers in Marlborough, N. H., as early

---

* It is proper to say that the parentage of David is not *positively* proved, but extensive correspondence and wide search for evidence all point to Jonathan of Rowley.

as 1775, near the Monadnoc mountains, when the township was almost an unbroken forest, subjecting them to great hardships. The catamounts, wolves, bears, and wild turkeys were very numerous and troublesome, disturbing the slumbers of the night by their noise and search after sheep and fowls. It is said of Mrs. Thurston that she was particularly tough and smart, oftentimes walking long distances on snow shoes in the care of her family. By a letter from his son David written to his sister Eunice (found 1878), he records that David Thurston (his father) went to live with him in Oswego, N. Y., some years before his death, and that "he died sitting in his great chair, the place chosen by himself to die a few minutes before, and closing his own eyes passed away like one going into a gentle sleep." He was a member of the Presbyterian church and to all appearances a sincere christian.

### Children, born in Leominster, Mass.:

423 Benjamin,[5] b. Dec. 26, 1766; m. Sally —— and had:
    424 *Ginnet*,[6] b. in Marlborough Aug. 30, 1792.
    425 *Sally*,[6] b. in Marlborough March 9, 1794.
+426 David,[5] b. Oct. 17, 1768; m. Fanny Darling.
+427 Levi,[5] b. June 1, 1770; m. Abigail Newton.
+428 John,[5] b. Jan. 21, 1772; m. Lydia Ball.

### Born in Marlborough, N. H.:

+429 Samuel.[5] b. Aug. 16, 1775; m. Sally French.
+430 Jason,[6] b. Jan. 23, 1777; m. Mrs. Lydia (Palmer) Rollins.
431 Eunice.[5] b. June 25, 1780; m. in Marlborough, N. H., Oct. 6, 1805, Abraham Garfield, b. 1779, son of John and Lucy (Smith) Garfield of Lincoln, Mass. He was a farmer, living in Troy and Londonderry, N. H., and in Landgrove, Vt. He died in Jaffrey, N. H., Sept. 24, 1865. She died in Marlborough Feb. 23, 1841. They had:
    432 *Eunice* (Garfield), b. July 27, 1806.
    433 *Maria* (Garfield), b. May 19, 1808.
    434 *Abraham* (Garfield), b. April 24, 1810.
    435 *John* (Garfield), b. Feb. 27, 1812.
    436 *Fanny* (Garfield), b. Sept. 18, 1814.
    437 *David* (Garfield), b. March 2, 1817.
    438 *Solomon* (Garfield), b. Jan. 2, 1819.
    439 *Andrew Jackson* (Garfield), b. June 18, 1821; d. Sept. 24, 1848.
    440 *Daniel Jackson* (Garfield), b. Aug. 9, 1824.
441 Stephen,[5] b. March 18, 1783; d. Jan. 25, 1784.

## 156

MARY THURSTON[4] (*Richard*,[3] *Daniel*,[2] *Daniel*[1]), eldest daughter of Richard[3] and Mehitable (Jewett) Thurston of Rowley, now Georgetown, Mass.; born there Oct. 26, 1734; married, Sept. 23, 1756, DEA. JEREMIAH SEARLE, born 1723, son of William and Jane (Nelson) Searle. She died Aug. 20, 1804, aged 70.

### Their children were:

449 Jeremiah (Searle); b. 1761; n.m.
450 Stephen (Searle), m. about 1790 Mary Jewett and had:
    451 *Jeremiah* (Searle), b. 1794.
    452 *Jacob* (Searle), b. 1798.
    453 *Stephen* (Searle), b. 1803; m. Sally Stickney and had Stephen (Searle), b. 1830.
    454 *Benjamin Gardner* (Searle), b. 1809.
    455 *Richard* (Searle), b. 1814.
456 Betsey (Searle), n.m.
457 Martha (Searle), n.m.
458 Jonathan (Searle), n.m.

459 Mehitable (Searle), m. March 1, 1793, Rev. Samuel Toombs, b. in Wallkill, N. Y., Jan. 1, 1776; installed Feb. 19, 1806, as pastor of a Presbyterian church in Salem, Washington county, N. Y., where he labored very successfully twenty-six years, and died March 28, 1832. It is recorded of him that "few equaled him in profoundness and solidity of intellect. His mind was clear, vigorous, and comprehensive, and while expounding the great doctrines and principles of christianity, in which his whole heart and soul were engaged, he gave utterance to thoughts that were eloquent and impressive."

## 157

EUNICE THURSTON[4] (*Richard,*[3] *Daniel,*[2] *Daniel*[1]), sister of the preceding, and daughter of Richard[3] and Mehitable (Jewett) Thurston of Rowley, now Georgetown, Mass.; born there Oct. 4, 1736; married JOHN HARRIS, grandson of Dea. Timothy Harris. She died Sept. 21, 1775. He died Sept. 20, 1808, aged 78.

Their children were:

470 Mary (Harris), d. in youth.
471 Phebe (Harris), b. Dec. 23, 1769; m. June 14, 1793, Dr. Joshua Jewett of Rowley. She died Oct. 12, 1854, aged 85, leaving no living issue. In a letter written by Dr. Jewett Nov. 21, 1852, he says he is in his eighty-fifth year, and that his wife has two silver table spoons made from silver money found in the pocket of Stephen Thurston after he was shipwrecked, marked S. T. [see no. 155].
472 Eunice (Harris), m. Dea. Joshua Jewett and had:
   473 *Henry C.* (Jewett), pastor of a church in Winslow, Me., at one time; m. but had no children.
   474 *Mary* (Jewett), d. in youth, and a son d. n.m.

## 160

PHEBE THURSTON[4] (*Richard,*[3] *Daniel,*[2] *Daniel*[1]), sister of the preceding, and daughter of Richard[3] and Mehitable (Jewett) Thurston of Rowley, now Georgetown, Mass.; born there Dec. 14, 1741; married, first, Oct. 31, 1771, REV. DAVID JEWETT, born May 31, 1746, graduated from Harvard 1769, and settled as a Congregational minister in Candia, N. H., in 1771; dismissed in 1780, and settled as the first pastor of the Congregational church in Winthrop, Me., Jan. 2, 1782, having preached several months preceding, where he died March, 1783, aged 37. Second, DEA. DANIEL SPOFFORD of Rowley, Mass.; his third wife. He died April 26, 1803. She died Aug. 15, 1811, aged 70.

Her children were:

485 Phebe (Jewett), m. —— Adams of Newbury, Mass.
486 David (Jewett), m. Mrs. Judkins; a farmer of Monmouth, Me., where he lived and died.
487 Sarah (Jewett), d. in Rowley, young.
488 Eunice (Jewett), m. Rev. Randall Noyes; d. in Atkinson, Me. One of their sons married a daughter of his uncle David Jewett, and became a Baptist preacher.
489 John (Jewett).

## 163

DANIEL THURSTON[4] (*Richard,*[3] *Daniel,*[2] *Daniel*[1]), brother of the preceding, and son of Richard[3] and Mehitable (Jewett) Thurston of Rowley, now Georgetown, Mass.; born there Dec. 14, 1745; married, first, Feb. 4, 1768, JUDITH CHUTE, born Jan. 20, 1743, daughter of Capt. Daniel and Hannah (Adams) Chute of Newbury, Mass. She

4

died Dec. 3, 1788. Second, Nov. 5, 1789, MRS. MARGARET KINS-
MAN of Ipswich, Mass. She was a sister of James Chute, who married Daniel Thurston's sister Mehitable. She died Feb. 27, 1822,
aged 75. He died at Ipswich April 30, 1817. The following is a
copy of his will:

In the name of GOD, amen. I, Daniel Thurston of Ipswich, in the county of
Essex and commonwealth of Massachusetts, yeoman, being sound in body and
mind, but considering the shortness of life and the certainty of death, do make and
ordain this my last will and testament in manner following, viz.:

After recommending my soul to GOD who gave it, and my body to the earth to
be decently buried as my executor hereafter named shall judge proper, I make the
following distribution of the worldly goods and estate with which it hath pleased
GOD to bless me.

Imprimis. I give to my wife Margaret Thurston the use and improvement of the
one-third part of my real estate during her natural life; also one cow, all the swine,
and all the provisions, of whatever kind, shall be in the house at the time of my
decease.

Item. I give to my son Stephen Thurston the whole of the wearing apparel
which I shall have at the time of my decease, which, with the money and notes of
hand I have heretofore given him, shall be his full portion out of my estate.

Item. I give and devise to my grandchildren, Daniel Thurston Colman, Hannah
Colman, Judith Colman, Dorothy Colman, Sumner Colman, Lucy Colman, and
Mary Colman, the one-half of the real estate I may die possessed of, as also the
one-half of my personal estate, excepting so much as I have before disposed of,
which shall be their full portion out of my estate.

Item. I give and devise to my daughter Judith Pearson the other half of my real
estate, as also the one-half of the personal estate I may die seized of, excepting so
much as I have before disposed of, which, with what I have before given her, shall
be her full share out of my estate.

Item. I constitute and appoint my brother-in-law, Benjamin Colman of Newbury,
to be sole executor of this my last will and testament, hereby revoking and annull-
ing all former wills by me made.

In witness whereof I have hereunto set my hand and seal, and declared it to be
my last will and testament, this fifteenth day of August, in the year of our Lord
one thousand eight hundred and fourteen. Daniel Thurston. Seal.

Thomas Burnham, Daniel Ross, Lemuel Pearson. D. A. White, judge of probate. James Ropes, register.

### His children, by first wife, were:

+500 Susannah,[5] b. Nov. 1, 1768; m. William Colman.
+501 Stephen,[6] b. Jan. 2, 1770; m. 1st, Philomela Parish; 2d, Sarah Burge; 3d,
    Hannah Worcester.
502 Judith,[6] b. Dec. 31, 1771; m. Oct. 10, 1793, Samuel Pearson, a cotton mer-
    chant of Providence, R. I., and had:
   503 *Luther* (Pearson), b. Sept. 21, 1794; m. and had Phebe, Louisa, and
       Sarah; he d. June 24, 1871.
   504 *Daniel* (Pearson, m. —— Williams.
   505 *William* (Pearson), m. —— Earle, and had William and Henry.
   506 *Harriet* (Pearson), m. Capt. William Comstock, a popular steamboat
       captain, running from Providence to New York, and had Richard and
       a daughter who m. —— Sprague; Anna, who m. —— Balch.
   507 *Samuel* (Pearson), m. and had Samuel.
   508 *Susan Thurston* (Pearson), resided in New York; n.m.
   509 *Henry* (Pearson), m. and d. childless in 1836.
510 Daniel,[5] b. Dec. 18, 1772; d. unmarried April 19, 1792.
511 Hannah,[6] d. in childhood.

## 164

SARAH THURSTON [4] (*Richard,*[8] *Daniel,*[2] *Daniel*[1]), sister of the preceding, and daughter of Richard [8] and Mehitable (Jewett) Thurston
of Rowley, Mass.; born there April 14, 1748; married, June 13,

1775, CAPT. JOHN PEARSON, born October, 1746 [see Pearson family, p. 26]. He died Sept. 15, 1807 ; she died April 28, 1818, aged 70.

Sarah Thurston and her sister Mehitable were married at the same time, Tuesday before the battle of Bunker Hill, which was fought Saturday, June 17, 1775. She was evidently fond of music, as she copied tunes which formed a thick book, and bound it in tin covers, which is now, 1879, in possession of H. Webster, Milton, Mass. She was "lame thirty years and suffered divers trials with patience."

Their children were :

522   Ruth (Pearson), b. Dec. 9, 1776; d. May 27, 1777.
523   Sarah (Pearson), b. March 22, 1778; m. Rev. Moses Elliot of Concord, N. H. After marriage he became a preacher, and after that went through college. They had thirteen children, two of whom are living, 1877 :
    524   *Elijah Parish* (Elliot), b. March, 1809, and lives at Amesbury Mills, Mass.
    525   *Matthew Pearson* (Elliot), b. Dec., 1817; m. Abby Adams, and lives at Somerville, Mass., business 77 Court street, Boston.
526   Elizabeth (Pearson), b. Feb. 5, 1780; d. Dec. 5, 1786. One still born Oct. 27, 1781.
527   Mehitable (Pearson), b. Jan. 1, 1783; m. James Webster and had five children, three now living [see Pearson family, p. 26] :
    528   *Horatio* (Webster), of Milton, Mass.
    529   *Caroline M.* (Webster), m. Sept. 19, 1839, Jeremiah R. Barnes and had three children.
    530   *Dorothy* (Webster), m. John Mills and had two children.
531   Hannah (Pearson), b. Oct. 9, 1785; d. Aug. 10, 1814, aged 29.
532   John (Pearson), b. March 4, 1791; last of the male line; d. Oct. 5, 1819; n.m.

## 165

DAVID THURSTON [4] of North Sedgwick, Me. (*Richard,*[3] *Daniel,*[2] *Daniel*[1]), brother of the preceding, and son of Dea. Richard [3] and Mehitable (Jewett) Thurston of Rowley, now Georgetown, Mass. ; born there March 19, 1751 ; married, first, MARY BACON, born Aug. 18, 1750, only daughter of Rev. Jacob and Mary (Wood) Bacon * of

---

*The BACON FAMILY.

I. THOMAS BACON, born 1636, married Hannah Fales; she died April, 1711; he died April 11, 1749, aged 83. They had Thomas, d. 1784, aged 92; James, d. 1785, aged 86; JACOB; and Hannah, m. Nathaniel Wright and d. Oct. 8, 1764; Mr. Wright d. April 3, 1755.

II. REV. JACOB BACON, born in Rowley, Mass., 1706, married, first, June 22, 1749, Mary Wood, born 1717; she died Nov. 17, 1772. Second, Mary Whitney. He died Aug. 14, 1787, aged 81; she died at David Thurston's in Sedgwick, Me., March 6, 1815, aged 87. He graduated from Harvard 1731, and was the first minister of the township of Upper Ashuelot, now Keene, N. H. It is not known at what date he went there, but in October, 1737, it was voted that "the worthy Mr. Jacob Bacon draw lots for the whole property;" this was at the second division of meadow land. In the course of that year he was appointed proprietors' clerk. He received a call to settle as their minister May 5, 1738, gave an affirmative answer Aug. 5th, and was ordained to the work of the ministry Oct. 18, 1738. when a church of nineteen members was organized. The council consisted of pastors and delegates from the churches in Wrentham, Sunderland, Northfield, and Medway, viz., Rev. Messrs. Rand, Doolittle, and Buckman, with the delegates from each church. He was much beloved by his church and people. In the language of the proprietors, he was "the worthy and reverend Mr. Bacon." Some persons were added to the church under his ministry, but it no record has come down to us. He was excused from all obligations to his church and people by an informal vote of the proprietors just before they abandoned the town when it was burned by the Indians in 1747. He became the pastor of the third church in Plymouth, Mass., 1749, and continued there till 1776, when the society became so greatly diminished by the war that they ceased to maintain public worship in their house, and in 1784 were united to the first church. His children were MARY, b. Aug. 18, 1750, m. David Thurston, d. Oct. 21, 1790; Jacob, b. Aug. 25, 1751, who had one child, Sally, b. Jan. 27, 1785, and lived in Salem, Mass.; Jacob d. July 27, 1816; Thomas, b. Feb. 5, 1753, d. Aug. 6, 1753; David, b. Aug. 24, 1754, d. in Templeton, Mass., Nov. 30, 1849, aged 95 years, 3 months; Oliver, b. Oct. 25, 1755, d. at Jaffrey, N. H.; Samuel, b. June 3, 1757, d. in Templeton, Mass., Oct., 1838, aged 81; Charles, b. April 8, 1759, d. Sept. 16, 1759. Rev. Jacob Bacon made this record, "May the 19, 1780 On fryday was such a Darkness as I Never saw in the Daytime before—the morning was cloudy and something hasey. at 9 O'clock there was a yalow Capp on the clouds and the Darkness increased till 12 o'clock When I put out my Candle and it appeared as Dark as the star Lite Nite then the Light Came on Gradually till about 5 after Noon and it is sayed by some Persons that the Night far exceeded the Day for Darkness."

Rowley. She died Oct. 21, 1790. Second, CHLOE REDINGTON, born May 11, 1767. She was a daughter of —— and Sarah (Hook) Redington. Mr. Redington was a farmer in Boxford, Mass. When Chloe was quite young he sold his farm and purchased a trading vessel. On the morning of his departure in this vessel he took his family, wife and six small children, into the front room, drew the shutters, and commended them all to God. He left and was never heard from after. Chloe's mother died in Newburyport Sept. 28, 1823, aged 86 years, 9 months. While yet an infant Chloe was given by her mother to her aunt, Mrs. Rev. Jacob Bacon. After Mrs. Bacon's death, and when Mr. Thurston married her daughter, he took Chloe with his wife to their new home, which became her life home. Mr. Thurston often said "I brought my two wives home at once."

David Thurston died in Sedgwick, Me., Aug. 26, 1821, aged 70; his wife died in Bucksport, where she spent the last few years of her life in the family of her daughter, Mrs. Blodget, Oct. 12, 1862, at the ripe old age of 95 years, 5 months, and was buried in Sedgwick.

David Thurston was a farmer in New Rowley* till June, 1796, when he removed to Sedgwick, following the same occupation. He made the journey on horseback, stopping at many places to see what advantages they offered, but with the resolution that he would not locate where there was no orthodox minister. In conversation with a gentleman in Bangor he said, "I have money in my pocket to buy this land, which included all that is now Bangor city, but I will not settle where my family cannot have the gospel." So he went on forty miles to Sedgwick, where Rev. Daniel Merrill, a pupil of Dr. Spring, senior, was pastor of a Congregational church. Very soon there was a great revival and his two older sons were converted; his seven sons were all christians.

The family came in a sloop from Newburyport to Bluehill Falls. There with four children, the oldest four years old, they were put into a boat and rowed four miles to the old saw-mill in the dead of night. Here they waited for the dawn. David and Richard came with an

---

*Among the papers of Rev. David Thurston, D.D., of Winthrop, was found the following interesting record: "In New Rowley they were a long time destitute of a pastor, though they generally had preaching on the Sabbath. Some sixty different ministers preached there between the time the first minister of the church, Rev. James Chandler, became unable to preach through the infirmities of age and the settlement of the second minister, Rev. Isaac Braman, in June, 1797. They extended invitations to three candidates to become pastors, who all returned a negative answer. Mr. William Bradford was, lacking one vote, unanimously invited to be their pastor. He deferred giving his answer a long time and then sent a negative. Then another and another were employed, among whom was Rev Elijah Kellogg, who negatived their call and was afterward pastor of the second church in Portland, Me. After him, Mr. Samuel Toombs had a call, which he declined. Mr. Toombs was after that pastor of a church in West Newbury, Mass., and then pastor of a church in Salem, N. Y. Several of these ministers boarded in my father's family. So noted had the place become for employing candidates without settling them, that it became a sort of proverb among them that no one could obtain a settlement until he had preached a while in New Rowley.

"The sad result of hea ing so many, was the division of the church and society, very near equally, into two parties, distinguished by the terms Hopkinsians and moderate Calvinists. Some of the leading points upon which they differed, and about which there was much warm discussion, were 'the duty of men to exercise disinterested benevolence, the natural ability of the sinner to repent or to comply with the terms of the gospel, the doings of the unregenerate,' etc. Rev. Samuel Hopkins, D.D., of Newport, R. I., and Rev. Samuel Spring, D.D., of Newburyport were among the ablest advocates on the Hopkinsian side, and Rev. David Tappan, D.D., then of West Newbury, afterward professor of theology in Harvard University, and Rev. Joseph Dana, D.D., of Ipswich on the side of the moderate Calvinists. My father embraced the views of the Hopkinsians, and was an admirer of the writings of Drs. Hopkins and Spring, with the latter of whom he had a personal acquaintance, residing only ten miles from him."

ox-team to take them to their new home, which was rough and not very clean. Some time after, a quantity of milk having been spilled, mother called to the maid, " Patty, Patty, I have found the floor." [This incident was related by one of the children.]

He was a man of commanding presence, nearly six feet high. He held the reins of government with a strong hand ; exerted a molding influence on the character of his large family, so that not one fell into habits of vice. In his religion he was firmly orthodox, owning and studying such works as Edwards' and Hopkins.' He was constant in family worship, taught his children the Assembly's catechism, and so influenced them that they have all remained steadfast in the orthodox faith.* He was selectman of Sedgwick and justice of the peace many years.

Mrs. Chloe Thurston was a bright, sprightly woman, of great energy and endurance, and did a wonderful work in the care of a large family, for which they bless her memory.

His children, by first wife, Mary, born in Rowley, were :

+540  David,⁵ b. Feb. 6, 1779 ; m. 1st, Eunice Farley ; 2d, Prudence Brown.
+541  Richard,⁶ b. July 5, 1781 ; m. Ann Bowers.

By second wife, Chloe :

+542  Mary,⁵ b April 7, 1792 ; m. Dea. Bliss Blodget.
+543  Samuel,⁵ b. July 8, 1793 ; m. 1st, Prudence Goodale ; 2d, Mrs. Charlotte (Goodale) Greeley.
+544  John,⁵ b. Nov. 26, 1794 ; m. Abigail King Lawrence.
+545  Sarah,⁶ b. April 1, 1796 ; m. Dea. John Buck.

Born in Sedgwick, Me. :

+546  Stephen,⁵ b. Nov. 22, 1797 ; m. Clara Matilda Benson.
+547  Mehitable,⁶ b. Feb. 5, 1800 ; m. John Godfrey.

---

*The family were eminently social and fraternal in their feelings, and had several very interesting family gatherings and two golden weddings. The first family gathering that the writer is cognizant of was at the paternal homestead in Sedgwick, Daniel Oliver Thurston's residence, Aug. 25, 1849, where eleven brothers and sisters, with the wives and husbands of ten of them, passed the night, making twenty-seven in all.

The second, June 28, 1850, was at the house of Samuel Thurston of Bangor, at which were present the mother, Mrs. Chloe R. Thurston, 93 years old, four sons, four daughters, five children by marriage, eighteen grandchildren, ten grandchildren by marriage, seven great-grand-children, making forty-nine. The incidents transpiring are given by Rev. David Thurston as follows : " Collected to partake of refreshments, thanks being given and a blessing sought, all except mother were standing. As she was having such a green old age and all were disposed to honor her, in token of respect Mary Pond had prepared a garland of evergreen. It fell to me, as the oldest, to place it as a crown upon mother's head. Holding it up I remarked. 'this, though called an evergreen, will ultimately fade. We put it upon your head, trusting that hereafter there will be placed upon it a crown of righteousness, a crown of glory which shall never fade.' After supper John R. and Fanny desired me to administer baptism to their infant son. Having in prayer besought the God of Abraham, the father of the faithful, for his presence and blessing on the parents and the child, Walter Lawrence was baptized into the name of the Father, the Son, and the Holy Ghost. This gave variety, solemnity, and interest to the occasion. In the evening several tunes were performed on the piano, several hymns sung, cheerful conversation was had. The parting hymn, 'Blest be the tie that binds,' was sung, some parting words uttered, and prayer offered. The season has been exceedingly pleasant and I trust not without profit. We may never all expect to meet again in this world It will be marvelous grace should we all be happy as to meet in that better world where sorrowful parting will not be known. May the God of all grace grant we may there meet."

The third meeting was Aug. 2, 1861, at the house of Dea. John Buck of Orland. The mother was present, five brothers, four wives, four sisters with their husbands, and children and grandchildren to the number of eighty.

Oct. 31, 1861, at the house of Brown Thurston in Portland, the golden wedding of Rev. David and Prudence (Brown) Thurston was celebrated in an appropriate manner, thirty-one of the relatives and friends being present.

June 6, 1877, at his own house in Searsport, the golden wedding of Rev. Stephen and Clara (Benson) Thurston was happily and enthusiastically celebrated, thirty-one of their relatives and a large company of resident friends being present.

548  Hannah,⁵ b. Nov. 16, 1801; baptized by Rev. Daniel Merrill; d. Sept. 14, 1824, aged 23. She had been teaching a school in New Bedford, Mass., where, having sometime before going there thought she was a subject of renewing grace, she united with the Congregational church. About the time she closed her school she was seized with a fever and died.

+549  Elizabeth Chloe,⁵ b. June 18, 1803; m. Rev. Joseph Smith.
+550  Daniel Oliver,⁵ b. May 5, 1805; m. Aphia Hinckley.
+551  William,⁵ b. Feb. 7, 1807; m. 1st, Dorothy Pearson Colman; 2d, Caroline Elizabeth Greenleaf.
552  Phebe,⁵ b. March 15, 1809; baptized by Rev. Jonathan Fisher of Bluehill; n.m.; d. Jan. 24, 1857.

## 166

MEHITABLE THURSTON⁴ (*Richard,*³ *Daniel,*² *Daniel*¹), sister of the preceding, and youngest daughter of Richard⁸ and Mehitable (Jewett) Thurston of Rowley, now Georgetown, Mass.; born there Sept. 25, 1753; married, June 13, 1775, DEA. JAMES CHUTE, born Feb. 16, 1751, son of Capt. Daniel and Hannah (Adams) Chute of Newbury, Mass. She died in Byfield, Mass., Oct. 18, 1819, aged 66; he died in Madison, Ind., April 28, 1825, aged 74.

He was a farmer, and lived in Boxford, Mass., while his father was able to carry on the farm in Byfield, Mass., which he afterward occupied.

Their children, born in Boxford, were:

563  Betsey (Chute), b. 1776; m. Daniel Hale of Newbury, Mass.
+564  Richard (Chute), b. Sept. 3, 1778; m. Dorothy Pearson.
565  Hannah (Chute), b. 1780; m. John Poor of Rowley, Mass.
566  Mehitable (Chute), b. 1782; m. Jonathan Elliott of Concord, N. H.
567  Eunice (Chute), b. 1783; m. 1806 Joseph Hale of Newbury, Mass., b. Dec. 1, 1781. She died June 20, 1868; he died June 18, 1820. They had:
    568  *Joseph* (Hale), b. Jan. 6, 1807.
    569  *Henry* (Hale), b. Feb. 18, 1808.
    570  *Mary* (Hale), b. Aug. 14, 1809.
571  Mary (Chute), b. Jan. 7, 1786; m. Jeremiah Colman of Newbury, Mass., b. Feb. 15, 1783 and had:
    572  *Dorothy Pearson* (Colman), b. Feb. 13, 1810 [see no.    ].
    573  *Betsey Little* (Colman), b. Dec. 21, 1813.
    574  *Moses* (Colman), b. Jan. 27, 1817.
    575  *Mehitable Thurston* (Colman), b. Aug. 28, 1821.
    576  *James Chute* (Colman), b. April 28, 1826.
577  Daniel (Chute), b. 1787; m. 1st, Dec. 27, 1813, Rachel McGriffin; she died Sept. 21, 1840; 2d, Oct. 20, 1842, Mrs. Sarah Benjamin. He graduated from Dartmouth in 1810. His daughter Elizabeth is the wife of Ex-Gov. Conrad Baker of Indiana, whose name with others has just been, March, 1877, handed in to President Rutherford B. Hayes as a suitable candidate for the cabinet. He died June 20, 1859, leaving a large family, mostly settled in the West.
578  James (Chute), b. Nov. 15, 1788; m. 1st, Oct. 23, 1817, Martha Hewes Clapp of Dorchester, Mass.; 2d, 1834, at Dayton, Ohio, Mrs. Mary (Crane) Haven, daughter of Rev. Samuel Crane, one of the first missionaries to the Tuscarora Indians. He graduated from Dartmouth in 1813, and was settled over a Presbyterian church in Fort Wayne, Ind., several years, and died there Dec. 28, 1835, leaving three sons and two daughters.

## 178

JOSEPH THURSTON⁴ (*Joseph,*⁸ *Joseph,*² *Daniel*¹), son of Joseph⁸ and Mary (Finson) Thurston of Rockport, Mass.; born there Feb. 15, 1729; published July 30, 1750; married AGNES DAVIS, born Oct. 15, 1733, daughter of Capt. Samuel Davis. He died June 8, 1801; she died at age of 73.

He was a fisherman, residing at (Sandy Bay) Rockport, Mass.

### Their children were:

589   Sarah,[5] b. Nov. 27, 1751; m. Edmund Grover.
590   Joseph,[5] b. Nov. 15, 1755; m. Lydia Parsons, b. 1758. He died 1807; she died 1848, aged 90. They had:
+591   *William,*[5] b. Feb. 22, 1783; m. Nancy Parsons.
+592   *Joseph,*[5] b. Jan. 22, 1787; m. Esther Norwood.
593   *Sally,*[6] b. Aug. 21, 1790; m. 1st, William Davis; 2d, Anthony Chipman; moved to Steuben, Me.; both died, leaving William (Davis), Anthony (Chipman), Daniel (Chipman), James (Chipman), George (Chipman).
594   William,[5] b. Oct. 27, 1762; d. young.
595   Annis,[6] b. 1764; m. John Tarr.
596   Benjamin,[5] b. 1765; d. young.
597   Olive,[5] b. April 7, 1766; d. young.
598   Benjamin,[6] b. Dec. 25, 1771; d. young.
599   Hannah.[6] b. 1772.
600   Samuel Davis.[6] b. Oct. 14, 1775; m. Margaret Oakes. He joined the Congregational church in 1805, and died in the West Indies in 1808. Their children were:
601   *Ebenezer Oakes,*[6] b. Dec. 9, 1796; n.m.; drowned at sea.
602   *Peggy,*[6] b. Aug. 21, 1798; m. Winthrop Harridan; no children.
603   *Samuel Davis.*[6] b. 1802; d. 1804.
604   *Lydia Parsons,*[6] b. Aug. 25, 1804; m. July 29, 1820, Samuel Saunders, b. July, 1798. She joined the Congregational church Feb. 26, 1832. They had:
605   *Mary Ann* (Saunders), b. Aug. 13, 1821; m. Dudley G. Adams.
606   *Margaret* (Saunders), b. Sept. 3, 1823; m. Freeman Mitchell.
607   *Elizabeth* (Saunders), b. Dec. 19, 1825; m. John Woodfall.
608   *Samuel* (Saunders), b. Aug. 15, 1832; m. Ann McDonald.
609   *William E.* (Saunders), b. March 3, 1836; m. Hannah McCarthy.
610   *Henry* (Saunders), b. Oct. 8, 1840; m. Esther Robinson.
611   *Emily C.* (Saunders), b. Aug. 8, 1846; m. Henry Welch.
612   *Annis,*[6] b. Feb. 23, 1806; n.m.; d. Feb. 4, 1878.
613   *Elizabeth,*[6] b. Sept. 30, 1809; m. Dec. 6, 1827, William Bailey of North Village, b. Dec. 6, 1801, and had:
614   *Charlotte* (Bailey), b. April 20, 1828; d. Sept. 20, 1832.
615   *Annis Thurston* (Bailey), b. July 18, 1831; m. Stinson Mitchell.
616   *Elizabeth* (Bailey), b. Jan. 4, 1835; m. James McClaron.
617   *William* (Bailey), b. April 9, 1842; m. Martha Goday.

### 180

DANIEL THURSTON[4] (*Joseph,*[3] *Joseph,*[2] *Daniel*[1]), brother of the preceding, and son of Joseph[3] and Mary (Finson) Thurston of Rockport, Mass.; born there Feb. 16, 1735; married, 1756, ANNA TARR. He died in 1818, aged 83.

He was interested in fishing; built a vessel in front of his house, and was quite a land owner and farmer.

### Children:

+630   Daniel,[5] b. 1758; m. Sally Rowe.
+631   Nathaniel,[5] b. Aug. 7, 1769; m. Betsey Gee.
632   Benjamin,[5] the first sea captain who sailed out of Rockport. His ship foundered on the passage from London to Boston, and he was lost in her.

### 181

CAPT. JOHN THURSTON[4] (*Joseph,*[3] *Joseph,*[2] *Daniel*[1]), brother of the preceding, and son of Joseph[3] and Mary (Finson) Thurston of Gloucester, now Rockport, Mass.; born there June 30, 1737; married MRS. EUNICE (GOTT) STOCKBRIDGE, born April 5, 1738. She had a son Benjamin (Stockbridge), a master mariner. Mr. Thurston died June 25, 1814; she died March 7, 1832.

Mr. Thurston was a fisherman, living in Rockport, Mass., and lost his vessel by the French in 1783, when he moved to Deer Isle, Me., and pursued the same business there. He was taken prisoner by the British in the revolutionary war and confined in Dartmoor prison. He was a member of the Baptist church.

### Children, born in Rockport, Mass. :

+643    Ambrose,[6] m. Polly Gamage.
+644    Amos,[6] b. Oct. 20, 1772; m. Mary Gott.
645    Stephen,[6] m. Mrs. Pierce Carter; settled in Cape Elizabeth, Me.
+646    William,[6] b. Aug. 27, 1778; m. Nancy Foster.
+647    John,[6] b. 1781; m. Sarah Foster.

### Born in Deer Isle, Me. :

+648    Solomon,[6] b. Feb. 21, 1783; m. Sarah Gott.
649    Lovis,[6] m. 1st. —— Hooper; 2d, Charles Gott.
650    Eunice,[6] m. David Smith of Swan's Island, Me.
651    Susan,[6] m. Charles Gott of Mt. Desert, Me.; she d. and he m. Lovis, above.

### 183

WILLIAM THURSTON [4] (*Joseph*,[3] *Joseph*,[2] *Daniel*[1]), brother of the preceding, and son of Joseph [3] and Mary (Finson) Thurston of Rockport, Mass.; born there Nov. 27, 1742; married, Jan. 10, 1764, MARTHA POOL, born 1747. He was lost at sea in 1779. After the death of her husband she married Capt. Andrew Woodbury. She died August, 1821, aged 74.

Mr. Thurston was a seaman and owner of a schooner in 1779, in which he sailed for the Western Banks, and never returned.

### Their children were :

662    Martha,[5] b. Oct. 17, 1765; m. Felix Doyle and had :
663      *William* (Doyle), m. Polly Stillman.
664      *Abraham* (Doyle), m. Rhoda Blatchford.
665      *Felix* (Doyle), m. Fanny Clark.
666      *Martha* (Doyle), m. John Hunt of Newburyport.
667      *Sally* (Doyle), m. Joshua Colby of Newburyport.
+668    William,[5] b. Oct. 31, 1767; m. 1st, Polly Tarr; 2d, Lucy Seward.
669    Sally,[5] b. 1769; m. Moses Platts Clark; she joined the Congregational church Aug. 14, 1814; d. Aug. 24, 1859, aged 90 years, 1 month. They had six children, two died young:
670      *Moses* (Clark), b. 1786; m. Rhoda Tarr; d. April 3, 1835. They had Rhoda (Clark), m. Benjamin Choate; Sophia (Clark), m. Oliver Craig; Howard (Clark), Jason (Clark).
671      *William Platts* (Clark), b. July 23, 1791; m. 1815 Sally Thurston [see no.  ], and had six children. He is living, 1877.
672      *Sally* (Clark), b. 1800; m. Amos Tarr; d. April 3, 1860, aged 60.
673      *Betsey* (Clark), b. 1805; m. Oct. 5, 1825, Moses Haskins, and had six children.
674    Josiah,[5] b. 1771; m. Lydia Bradstreet, and had seven children, all daughters; moved to Boothbay, Me., and died, aged about 65. Their eldest m. Samuel Clark, Lydia m. Joseph Haycock, one m. A. Stetson of New York; others unmarried.
675    Abraham,[5] d. unmarried.

### 209

ABNER THURSTON [4] (*Abner*,[3] *James*,[2] *Daniel*[1]), eldest son of Abner [3] of Exeter, N. H.; born 1729; married MARTHA PIPER, born 1729. She died in Candia, N. H., Nov. 4, 1825, aged 96.

Mr. Thurston resided in Exeter, N. H.; enlisted in the revolutionary war March 20, 1777, in Capt. Wait's company, Col. John Stark's

regiment, and was paid state bounty of £20. Jan. 22, 1778, was in Capt. Farwell's company, Col. Joseph Cilley's regiment; became a corporal, and is reported to have been killed in action.*

Their children were:

686. Thomas,[5] b. Jan. 19, 1752; m. Lucy Fenderson.
+687 Suah,[5] m. Aaron Brown.
+688 David,[5] b. July 31, 1775; m. Sally Eaton.
689 A daughter.

## 210

ICHABOD THURSTON[4] (*Abner,[3] James,[2] Daniel[1]*), brother of the preceding, and son of Abner[3] of Exeter, N. H.; born about 1731; married BETTY FILBROOK.

Mr. Thurston with "his wife Betty, formerly Betty Filbrook," deeded land in Epping 1748, and in Exeter 1753. He was in the military company of Capt. John Parsons, regiment of Col. Peter Gilman of Exeter, in an expedition to Albany in 1755; he enlisted Sept. 19th, and was discharged Dec. 28th. April 7, 1760, he was in Capt. George Marsh's company, Col. John Goff's regiment; was left sick at No. 4 (Charlestown), N. H., and went home Oct. 10th.

Their children were:

700 Betty,[6] n.m.
701 Anna.[6] m. 1st, Dec. 4, 1777, James Underwood; 2d, —— Nutter of Pittsfield, N. H.
702 Patty,[6] m. —— Chase.
703 Dolly,[6] m. —— Babcock.
704 Debby,[6] lived with father and with Capens.

## 211

CAPT. JAMES THURSTON[4] (*Abner,[3] James,[2] Daniel[1]*), brother of the preceding, and son of Abner[3] of Exeter, N. H.; born Sept. 8, 1733; married, first, Aug. 26, 1756, MARY JONES of Newmarket, N. H.; she died Oct. 29, 1787. Second, May, 1789, MRS. ELIZABETH PEABODY, widow of Dr. Thomas Peabody. He died July 13, 1808, aged 75.

Mr. Thurston was selectman of Exeter 1781, associated with Daniel Tilton and Ephraim Robinson. He must have been the James noted as in the revolutionary war and at the battle of New Town, Chemung county, N. Y.

Children, all by first wife, Mary:

715 Mary,[5] b. Sept. 22, 1757; d. June 6, 1759.
716 Mary,[6] b. Sept. 30, 1759; m. Caleb Johnson.
717 Abigail,[5] b. Nov. 3, 1761; m. Jonathan Powers.
718 Joanna,[5] b. Sept. 15, 1765; m. July 15, 1792, Simon Wiggin.
+719 James,[5] b. March 17, 1769; m. Elizabeth Peabody.
720 William,[5] b. Sept. 29, 1772; m. Sept. 18, 1798. Elizabeth Peck. He graduated from Dartmouth in 1792, read law with Hon. John Lowell of Boston, Mass., and practiced in Boston till his health failed, when he went to Italy, and died in Naples Aug. 25, 1822, leaving no issue. He adopted a son, *William*, who died in South Carolina June. 1846, aged 31. He also adopted a daughter, *Sarah Jane Wiggin*, b. in 1802.

---

*The names of John, Josiah, Ward, Samuel, Ambrose, and Joseph Thurston are on the rolls of men from New Hampshire in the French and Indian and revolutionary wars. We know not who these men were. There was a Moses in company of Capt. Reuben Dow of Hollis. N. H., Col. William Prescott's regiment, Nov. 20, 1775, as a private, who is thought to have been from Hollis.

## 213

CALEB THURSTON [4] (*Abner,*[3] *James,*[2] *Daniel*[1]), brother of the preceding, and son of Abner[3] of Exeter, N. H.; born 1737; married, Oct. 7, 1756, HANNAH DUDLEY of Exeter. He died Jan. 4, 1799, aged 62; she died Nov. 3, 1802, aged 66.

Mr. Thurston settled in Exeter; was a private in Capt. John Ladd's company, Thomas Tush of Durham, N. H., major of the battalion, from Aug. 19 to Sept. 24, 1757.

### Their children were:

+731 Caleb,[5] m. 1st, Mary Gilman; 2d, Anne Wiggins.
+732 John.[5]
+733 Dudley,[5] m. Betsey Thurston [see no. 1038].
+734 Trueworthy,[5] b. 1777; m. Priscilla Royal.
  735 Sarah,[5] b. Dec. 27, 1769; m. Philip Bullen of Hallowell, Me.; d. April 2, 1814. They had:
    736 *A son*, b. and d. 1804.
    737 *Hannah* (Bullen), b. Aug., 1805; m. 1829, Caleb Hunt; two daughters.
    738 *Paulina* (Bullen), b. Oct. 30, 1807; m. 1831, Moses B. Bliss; one son.
    739 *Henry Martin* (Bullen), b. May 8, 1809.
    740 *Laura* (Bullen), b. Nov. 10, 1810.
    741 *Samuel* (Bullen), b. Jan. 2, 1812.
  742 Hannah,[5] b. April 17, 1765; m. Samuel Hopkinson, b. Nov. 22, 1769, son of Noyes and Dolly (Scribner) Hopkinson of Exeter, N. H. He was a hatter in Exeter, and d. May 23, 1853. She was a member of the Baptist church, as were all her children. She died at her daughter's, Hannah Miles, in Brooklyn, N. Y., Jan. 28, 1859. They had:
    743 *Samuel* (Hopkinson).
    744 *Noyes* (Hopkinson), b. 1795; d. May 28, 1850.
    745 *Joseph* (Hopkinson), d. in infancy.
    746 *Hannah* (Hopkinson), b. Feb. 25, 1799; m. —— Miles.
    747 *Dolly Scribner* (Hopkinson), b. Oct. 3, 1800; m. —— Harris.
    748 *Sarah Thurston* (Hopkinson), b. June 1, 1802; d. Feb. 24, 1875.
    749 *Harriet* (Hopkinson), b. March 22, 1804; m. —— Smith.
    750 *Deborah Thurston* (Hopkinson), b. March 1, 1806; m. —— Baldwin.
    751 *Lucy Dana* (Hopkinson), b. Nov. 2, 1807; d. April 2, 1819.
+752 Daniel,[5] b. Aug. 6, 1776; m. Deborah Folsom.

## 214

PETER THURSTON [4] (*Abner,*[3] *James,*[2] *Daniel*[1]), brother of the preceding, and son of Abner[3] of Exeter, N. H.; born there 1739; married DOROTHY GATES, daughter of Hezekiah,[4] John,[3] Thomas,[2] Stephen Gates,[1] who came from Norwich, Norfolk county, Eng., and settled in Hingham, Mass., in 1642. He died Dec. 22, 1812,; she died Feb. 16, 1831, aged 92.

Mr. Thurston was a farmer in New Boston, now South Lancaster, Mass.; was engaged in the revolutionary war.

### Children:

  755 Rebecca.[5] m. Amos Allen of Lancaster; moved into state of New York; had two or three sons, one a physician in Philadelphia. She died at Kingsbury, N. Y., May 27, 1827, aged 65.
+756 Gates,[5] b. 1760; m. Elizabeth Pollard.
  757 Dorothy or Dolly,[5] b. Nov. 6, 1766; m. June 12, 1789, Josiah Flagg, b. Nov. 12, 1760, son of William and Sarah (Mecom) Flagg of Boston, Mass. He was a merchant and town clerk in Lancaster; a member of the Unitarian church. She died June 1, 1835; he died Feb. 11, 1840. They had:
    758 *William* (Flagg), b. July 29, 1790; d. at sea Feb. 7, 1806.
    759 *Sally* (Flagg), b. Nov. 19, 1791.

760 *Dolly* (Flagg), b. July 25, 1793.
761 *Rebecca* (Flagg), b. May 8, 1795.
762 *George Washington* (Flagg), b. July 31, 1797; d. Oct. 17, 1819, in Boston.
763 *Samuel Ward* (Flagg), b. April 22, 1803.
+764 Peter,[6] b. Sept. 23, 1768; m. Sally Sweetser.

## 229

Moses Thurston [4] (*Moses,*[3] *Stephen,*[2] *Daniel*[1]), son of Moses [3] and Sarah Thurston; born June 10, 1730; married, 1755, Elizabeth Clifford, born Aug. 12, 1735. He died Aug. 23, 1812, aged 82 y. 2 m. 2 d.; she died Dec. 24, 1817, aged 82 y. 4 m. 12 d.

In 1769 Moses Thurston, with John Ladd, commenced the settlement of Unity, N. H., as a farmer, having six children. Soon after they were destitute of food, and he went to Walpole barefoot, guided by spotted trees, bought two bushels of corn, had it ground, and carried it home, twenty-five miles, on his back. He said he never felt happier than when his family sat down to that meal of pudding and maple molasses. He was a man of iron frame and iron will. He officiated in all the town offices at different times. In the French and Indian war he was in Capt. John Allcock's company, Col. Peter Gilman's regiment, from Sept. 22 to Nov. 14, 1755. He was sergeant in a company of which Lieut. Col. John Hart was captain, in Col. Nathaniel Meserve's regiment, from May 1 to Oct. 12, 1756. In an account of the sums paid by Capt. Samuel Leavitt, muster-master and paymaster of the forces raised out of Col. Atkinson's regiment for the Canada expedition, 1759, he enlisted March 25th, and received 3£ 7s. 6d. He was in Capt. Jacob Tilton's company, Col. John Goffe's regiment, from April 26 to Nov. 27, 1760. We cannot ascertain how long he served as a private in the revolutionary army, but he was second lieutenant in company 5, Col. Benjamin Bellows' regiment, raised for the relief of Ticonderoga, the last of June, 1777; but as that fortress surrendered July 7th, they arrived only in time to swell the army on its retreat. It appears from the "Report" that this regiment was not at the battle of Bennington, although another one under the same colonel was there. War with France being anticipated, Gen. John Sullivan, then "president" of New Hampshire, gave Moses Thurston a commission as colonel March 9, 1787.

### Their children were:

765 Sally,[6] b. in Stratham, N. H., Feb. 6, 1756; m. Sept. 13, 1774 or 5, Jesse Bailey of Dracut, Mass. He was a farmer and settled in Corinth, Vt., where he died, Sept. 5, 1837; she died Sept. 12, 1853, aged 97 y. 7 m. 7 d. They had:
766 *Mary* (Bailey), b. Feb. 12, 1776.
767 *Amanda* (Bailey), b. March 25, 1777.
768 *Jesse* (Bailey), b. Feb. 9, 1779.
769 *Elizabeth* (Bailey), b. March 12, 1781.
770 *Phinehas* (Bailey), b. July 13, 1783.
771 *Rhoda* (Bailey), b. Sept. 26, 1785; m. in Corinth Jan. 26, 1804, Capt. John Ford. She lived with her husband on the farm where she died sixty-three years and was the mother of sixteen children; she died Sept. 7, 1869.
772 *Dolly* (Bailey), b. April 5, 1788.
773 *Alotty* (Bailey), b. May 26, 1790.
774 *Polly* (Bailey), b. Aug. 8, 1792.
775 *Sarah* (Bailey), b. Dec. 27, 1794.

776  *Abial* (Bailey), b. Feb. 11, 1798.
777  *Permelia* (Bailey), b. Aug. 12, 1801.
+778  Phinehas,[5] b. in Epping, N. H., Jan. 7, 175?; m. Polly Wood.
+779  Moses,[5] b. Jan. 18, 1760; m. 1st, Jane Spaulding; 2d. Polly Cross.
780  Anna,[5] b. in Nottingham, N. H., Jan. 25, 1762; m. May 1, 1782, Samuel
      Hurd, b. in Killingworth, Ct., Nov. 12, 1758, son of Samuel and Lydia
      (Wilcox) Hurd of Newport, N. H.  He was a farmer in Newport; dea-
      con in the Congregational church, and died March 8, 1826; she died May,
      1835.  They had:
781  *Lydia* (Hurd), b. Feb. 16, 1783; 'd. Jan. 30, 1793.
782  *Anna* (Hurd), b. Oct. 23, 1786; m. Zadoc Bowman; she died 1832; had
      seven children, who all emigrated to Illinois 1843.
783  *Asenath* (Hurd), b. Aug. 27, 1787; d. Nov. 8, 1787.
784  *A daughter*, b. and d. Aug. 26. 1788.
785  *Samuel* (Hurd), b. Sept. 29, 1789; d. Jan. 17, 1793.
786  *Parmenas* (Hurd), b. Sept. 3, 1790; m. Sophia Dean; d. June, 1877;
      three children.
787  *Samuel* (Hurd), b. Nov. 30, 1792; m. Mary Ann Corbin; d. Aug. 5,
      1826; one child.
788  *Lydia* (Hurd), b. Sept. 13, 1795; m. Moses Chapin; died; ten children.
789  *Ruel* (Hurd),  } twins, born  { d. Dec. 2, 1803.
790  *Rua* (Hurd),   } Feb. 4, 1798; { m. Parmenas Whitcomb; d. 1864; three
      children.
791  *Paulina* (Hurd), b. July 23, 1801; m. David S. Newell of Lebanon, N.
      H.; no children living.
792  Elizabeth,[5] b. in Deerfield, N. H., March 23, 1764; m. about 1785, John •
      Ayer of Corinth, Vt.  They had:
793  *Elisha* (Ayer), a soldier in the war of 1812.
794  *Warren* (Ayer), b. July 25, 1788; 'm. Esther Moody of Vermont.  They
      had:
795  *Elizabeth* (Ayer), b. March 2, 1808; m. —— Merrill, and living in
       Ulysses, Penn.
796  *Warren* (Ayer), b. May 28, 1810; m. Polly Laytan; living in Apala-
       chin. N. Y.
797  *Isaac* (Ayer), b. April 11, 1814.
798  *Esther* (Ayer), b. April 9, 1824.
799  *John* (Ayer), d. in 1832.
800  *John* (Ayer), b. July 1, 1790; m. July 6, 1814, Mary George of West
      Fairlee, Vt.; a farmer; Free Baptist.  He died in Pike, Bradford
      county, Pa., July 7, 1852; she died at the same place Sept. 25, 1850.
      They had:
801  *Micah George* (Ayer), b. Jan. 23,'1816; m. June, 1843, Lydia Ann Al-
       len; d. in Chicago July 12, 1849.
802  *John* (Ayer), b. June 25, 1818; m. Oct., 1844, Harriet Wood.
803  *Lucy Ring* (Ayer), b. Sept. 3, 1819; m. Jan. 15, 1839, Geo. W.Wells.
804  *Elbridge Nelson* (Ayer), b. Nov. 13, 1820; d. at Chicago July 14, 1849.
805  *Mary* (Ayer), b. Feb. 16, 1822; m. Oct. 29, 1846, Homer Wells; liv-
       ing in Le Raysville, Pa.
806  *Elizabeth Thurston* (Ayer), b. Sept. 16, 1823; d. Jan. 12, 1825.
807  *Martha* (Ayer), b. Feb. 22, 1825; m. July 15, 1854, Alonzo White-
       head; he served in the army two years.
808  *Samuel* (Ayer), b. July 26, 1826; d. Aug. 15, 1828.
809  *Warren* (Ayer), b. Aug. 4, 1828; m. July, 1858, Ann Eliza Wood;
       enlisted in 1864 and served till the close of the war; lives in Alba-
       ny, Pa.
810  *Lucinda* (Ayer), m. John Burke.
811  *Isaac* (Ayer), a soldier of 1812; d. in Ohio.
812  *Mary* (Ayer), m. Amasa Wells.
813  *David* (Ayer), d. young.
814  *Elizabeth* (Ayer), d. young.
815  Mary,[5] b. in Deerfield Jan. 14, 1767; m. Thomas Smith of Unity, N. H., b.
      Sept. 4, 1752, d. July 31, 1830; she died Aug. 26, 1850.  They had:
816  *Sally* (Smith), b. March 26, 1786; m. Sept. 2, 1804, Noah Ladd of Unity;
      d. Jan. 31, 1861.  They had:
817  *Lorenda* (Ladd), b. July 26, 1805; d. Nov. 4, 1809.

818 *Caroline* (Ladd), b. March 14, 1807; m. 1827, John Sleeper; d. in Oneida, Ill., Feb. 5, 1857; three children.
819 *Lorenda* (Ladd), b. May 23, 1810; m. Wilson Bartlett of Unity; d. Jan. 4, 1843; two children.
820 *Washington Thurston* (Ladd), b. July 4, 1812; d. April 22, 1820.
821 *Adeline* (Ladd), b. Jan. 25, 1815; m. Stephen Glidden of Unity.
822 *James Monroe* (Ladd), b. June 1, 1818; m. Sarah Graves; living in Oneida, Ill.; three children.
823 *Harriet* (Ladd), b. April 12, 1820; m. Alvin Roundy; two children.
824 *Washington Thurston* (Ladd), b. Nov. 10, 1822; m. Frances Neal; d. in Oneida, Ill., March 31, 1862.
825 *Noah Jefferson* (Ladd), b. Sept. 14, 1825; m. Hannah Frost; d. in Claremont, N. H., June 1, 1849.
826 *Wallace Wingate* (Ladd), b. April 22, 1827; m. Ann Jones; d. in Springfield, Vt., July 10, 1852.
827 *Asenath* (Smith), b. April 8, 1790; m. Edward Sleeper of Unity; d. Sept. 14, 1873; was a member of the Baptist church; seven children.
828 *Thomas* (Smith), b. Dec. 15, 1791; d. young.
829 *Thomas* (Smith), b. March 14, 1794; m. 1st, Hannah Huntoon of Unity; 2d, Hepsy Newton of Dalton, N. H. He was a soldier of the war of 1812; a member of the New Hampshire legislature; a farmer, and belonged to the Methodist church. He died in Dalton Oct. 24, 1876; nine children.
830 *Josiah* (Smith), b. Jan. 8, 1796; m. Cynthia Farwell of Unity; was drummer in the war of 1812, for which service he receives a pension. He is living in Claremont, N. H.; is a shoemaker, and belongs to the Methodist church; four children. One son, Curtis, was in the war against the rebellion.
831 *John* (Smith), b. Jan. 27, 1798; m. Delia Cram of Unity; d. in Jonesville, Mich., Jan. 17, 1873; a farmer; three children.
832 *Betsey* (Smith), b. Dec. 22, 1799; m. Ichabod Farrington of Claremont; is a member of the Baptist church; no children.
833 *Hiram* (Smith), b. April 1, 1802; m. Lucinda Marshall of Lempster, N. H.; is a farmer in Unity; has been town representative; three children.
834 *Moses* (Smith), b. July 28, 1804; d. young.
835 *Hannah* (Smith), b. May 3, 1807; m. Jesse Cram of Unity; d. in Ohio 1830; one child.
836 *Moses Thurston* (Smith), b. Oct. 8, 1809; m. Eunice Blake of Rockingham, Vt.; d. Sept., 1860, in Springfield, Vt.; a mechanic, and member of the Baptist church; three children.
837 *Alvah Chase* (Smith), b. Dec. 7, 1811; m. Phebe Ann Faulkner of Hamilton, Mass.; is a physician in Reading, Mass., and member of the Congregational church; two children.
838 *Frederic Plummer* (Smith), b. July 30, 1814; m. Locia Morris of Lisbon, N. H.; is a farmer, living in Claremont; seven children.

### Born in Unity:

839 Dorothy,[5] b. Nov. 14, 1769; m. Jan. 1, 1789, Nathaniel Hunton,[*] b. Jan. 21, 1764, son of Charles and Maria (Smith) Hunton of Kingston, after of Unity, N. H.; a farmer. She died Feb. 10, 1828; he died Dec. 29, 1857. They had, all born in Unity:
840 *Ariel* (Hunton), b. July 5, 1789; m. March 18, 1809, Polly Pingry, b. Sept. 6, 1791, daughter of William and Mary (Morrill) Pingry of Rowley, Mass., after of Salisbury, N. H. She died in Bethel, Vt., April 29, 1874; he died in Hyde Park, Vt., Nov. 25, 1857. He commenced the practice of medicine in Groton, N. H., in 1814; July, 1818, he removed to Hyde Park, where he was the village doctor for thirty-nine years. They had:
841 *Parmenas* (Hunton), b. in Salisbury Nov. 30, 1809; m. May 22, 1838, Laura Pearson of Randolph, Vt., b. in Roxbury, Vt., Mar. 17,

---

* This family all originally spelled their name Hunton, but about 1825 a part of them changed it to Huntoon.

1815, daughter of John T. and Mary (Fowler) Pearson; after his death she married again, and is living in Wheatland, N. J., 1878. He studied law and was admitted to the bar at Hyde Park in 1838, and died in Charleston, S. C., Aug. 4, 1839; no children.

842 *Sylvanus* (Hunton), b. in Salisbury June 2, 1811; m. Sept. 5, 1841, Clarissa M. Bailey, b. in Weare, N. H., Sept. 29, 1811, daughter of Bradbury and Agnes (Marshall) Bailey of Unity; she died in Unity Dec. 21, 1842. He graduated from the Vermont Academy of Medicine at Castleton in 1836; went to South Carolina on account of ill health in Oct., 1839, and engaged in teaching; was at Gaillard's plantation on the great southern bend of the Santee, at Sumterville, Charleston, and Aiken; and in Nov., 1846, he went to Carrollton, Ga., to take charge of a school, where he died, Feb. 25, 1847, at the house of Dr. W. P. Parker; no children.

843 *Eudosia Dorothy* (Hunton), b. in Salisbury May 1, 1813; d. single at Hyde Park Aug. 3, 1844.

844 *Augustus Pingry* (Hunton), b. in Groton, N. H., Feb. 23, 1816; m. April 29, 1849, Caroline Paige, b. Feb. 14, 1817, daughter of Dr. Alfred and Sarah (Bigelow) Paige of Bethel, Vt. He was admitted to the bar in Montpelier, Vt., April, 1837; commenced practice in Warren, Vt.; removed to Bethel in 1838, where he still resides, 1878; has been several times representative to the legislature; was speaker of the house 1860-1; has been state senator, and was presidential elector in 1864. They have :

845 *Mary* (Hunton), b. in Bethel, Vt., April 25, 1851; m. Feb. 1, 1877, Wm. Brunswick Curry Stickney [no. 1405 in Stickney family], b. in Marblehead, Mass., Jan. 16, 1845, son of Rev. Moses Parsons [no. 1405 in Stickney family] and Jane Frances (Curry) Stickney of Bethel. Mr. Stickney is a partner in the law firm of Hunton & Stickney, Bethel. They have William (Stickney), b. March 6, 1878.

846 *Albert* (Hunton), b. in Bethel June 20, 1853; d. July 18, 1864.

847 *Tryphena Ruth* (Hunton), b. in Hyde Park Jan. 10, 1827; d. single Nov. 11, 1843.

848 *William Philo* (Hunton), } b. in Hyde Park } d. single Feb. 22, 1856.

849 *Mary Augusta* (Hunton), } Nov. 24, 1832; } m. July 8, 1860, Rev. Sylvester Ames Parker, b. June 10, 1834. son of William Bateman and Malvina (Miner) Parker of Lempster, N. H.; has been pastor of the Universalist church in Stowe, and in Bethel, Vt., where he still is, 1879; no children.

850 *Tryphena* (Hunton), b. March 22, 1791; m. Oct. 1, 1820, Moody Gilman of Goshen, N. H.; she died Nov. 15, 1821; no children.

851 *Reuel* (Hunton), b. July 22, 1794; d. in Unity May 2, 1823; n.m.

852 *Harvey* (Huntoon), b. Nov. 10, 1800; m. July 5, 1831, Maria P. Morse, daughter of Ichabod and Polly (Bailey) Morse of Newport, N. H., b. April 25, 1813; she died Feb. 1, 1871. He is a farmer on the homestead in Unity, 1879; was appointed first railroad commissioner in 1844; high sheriff for Sullivan county from 1850 to 1855; been justice of the peace fifty years. They have :

853 *Reuel* (Huntoon), b. July 1, 1832; m. Nov. 21, 1861, Susie E. Russell, b. Sept. 10, 1837, daughter of Phileman and Mary (Wilkins) Russell of Cambridge, Mass. She died at Somerville, Mass., May 30, 1875. He enlisted in the 16th New Hampshire regiment Nov. 4, 1862, as corporal, and was promoted to first sergeant; was mustered out Aug. 20, 1863, and died Sept. 17, 1863, three weeks after reaching home; one child.

854 *Ransom* (Huntoon), b. April 25, 1836; m. Sept. 12, 1859, Elizabeth L. Thorp of Wataga, Ill.; is a farmer in Newport, N. H.; four children.

855 *Ora Morse* (Huntoon), b. May 1, 1839; m. Nov. 30, 1871, Mary Vilona Curtice of Contoocook, N. H.; was representative to legislature 1868-9; is a farmer in Contoocook; two children.

856 *Ira McLaughlin* (Huntoon), b. June 1, 1843; m. July 3, 1867, Jennie S. Lowell of Lempster, N. H.; is a farmer in Unity; four children.

857 *Lemira Jennett* (Huntoon), b. Feb. 22, 1847; m. May 26, 1874, Joel A. Jillson of Bellows Falls, Vt.; one child.

858 *Ariel Augustus* (Huntoon), b. Sept. 29, 1851; m. June 1, 1874, Carrie
    F. Kenerson of Newport; is a grocer in Newport; three children.
859 *Roxana* (Hunton), b. July 15, 1805; d. Oct. 22, 1827; n.m.
860 *Ransom* (Huntoon), b. Aug. 10, 1810; entered the military academy at
    West Point 1830, and died in Unity Feb. 18, 1834; n.m.
+861 Josiah,[5] b. May 7, 1772; m. 1st, Polly (Wood) Thurston; 2d, Martha March.
862 Hannah,[5] b. Sept. 13, 1774; m. March 19, 1793, Jedediah Philbrick, b. Nov.
    5, 1767, son of Samuel and Sarah (Sanborn) Philbrick of Kingston, N. H.
    He was a farmer in Springfield, N. H., where he died, Aug. 19, 1820; he
    was a member of the Methodist church. She died in Croyden, N. H.,
    Oct. 5, 1850. They had:
863 *Betsey Eliza* (Philbrick), b. Dec. 7, 1794; m. April 4, 1814, Moses Bean;
    d. in Petersburgh, Ill., Feb. 12, 1869.
864 *Samuel* (Philbrick), b. July 22, 1796; m. June 24, 1822, Aurelia Clement;
    d. in Havana, Ill., Dec. 31, 1873.
865 *Dorothy* (Philbrick), b. Aug. 10, 1798; d. March, 1800.
866 *Lua* (Philbrick), b. Dec. 27, 1801; m. 1822, Winn Gilman of Springfield, d.
867 *Anna McKensiry* (Philbrick), b. Jan. 8, 1806; m. Nov. 23, 1826, Ezra
    Pillsbury of Springfield, where she is now living, 1879.
868 *Diah* (Philbrick), b. May 23, 1811; m. in Derry, N. H., March 4, 1835,
    Sarah Gibson; d. in Derry Oct. 23, 1838.
869 *Emily Bingham* (Philbrick), b. Aug. 10, 1816; m. Aug. 21, 1841, James
    Colby; is living, 1879, in Kewanee, Ill.
870 John,[5] } twins, born { m. Betsey Ladd. He was a farmer in Unity; d.
871 Joanna,[5] } Dec. 14, 1776; } Oct. 5, 1839; she d. Jan. 19, 1860; no children.
    Joanna m. Nov. 26, 1795, Jonathan Fitts, b. May 9, 1772, son of Jonathan
    and Susannah (Pike) Fitts of South Hampton, N. H. He was a farmer
    in Unity till 1807, when they moved to Smithville, N. Y.; both members
    of the Baptist church. He died Oct. 9, 1847; she died in McDonough,
    N. Y., April 29, 1855. They had:
872 *Jonathan* (Fitts), b. Oct. 24, 1796; m. 1st, in Smithville, N. Y., Jan. 4,
    1820, Martha Chamberlain of that place, b. Jan. 7, 1794; she died in
    Harrisville, Ohio, July 19, 1839; 2d, in Elyria, Ohio, June 3, 1841,
    Nancy DeWitt, b. in Vermont Aug. 22, 1816; she died in Elyria Feb.
    4, 1859. He was a farmer in Harrisville, afterward Lodi, Ohio, in 1820;
    member of the Congregational church; d. June 1, 1850. They had:
873 *Hiram Lewis* (Fitts), b. Feb. 22, 1821; n.m.; d. April 26, 1838.
874 *Sylvia* (Fitts), b. July 11, 1822; n.m.; d. July 7, 1838.
875 *Celinda* (Fitts), b. May 13, 1824; m. Feb. 12, 1845, George Burr of
    Harrisville; living, 1878, in Lodi.
876 *Sophia* (Fitts), b. Sept. 15, 1825; m. May 5, 1846, John T. Wells of
    Lodi; moved to Coral, Ill., where she died, Feb. 5, 1847.
877 *Sophronia* (Fitts), b. Dec. 22, 1827; d. June 29, 1849.
878 *Julia De Francey* (Fitts), b. Jan. 21, 1832; d. July 19, 1843.
879 *Wealthy* (Fitts), } twins, born { d. Nov. 13, 1838.
880 *Welton* (Fitts), } Mar. 9, 1834; } enlisted, 1861, in the 2d regiment of
    U. S. sharp-shooters; remained in camp Instruction near Washing-
    ton, D. C., till May, 1862, when his regiment was ordered to march;
    was carried to the hospital at Fredericksburgh with typhoid fever,
    where he died, June, 17, 1862. He lies buried in the soldiers' bury-
    ing-ground at Falmouth Village, Virginia.
881 *Rollin Jonathan* (Fitts), b. Feb. 5, 1843; m. March 8, 1862, Cornelia
    J. Nevins of Elvria; d. May 6, 1877.
882 *Harvey Edmund* (Fitts), b. Oct. 6, 1844; m. March 3, 1868, Lizzie
    Spurriss of Tennessee. He entered the army in the spring of 1862,
    belonging first to the infantry, then the cavalry, and served till the
    close of the war in 1865; living, 1878, in Aberdeen, Miss.
883 *Virgil* (Fitts), b. Oct. 12, 1847; d. Oct. 5, 1850.
884 *Anna* (Fitts), b. March 13, 1798; m. Dec. 31, 1818, Seth Curtis of Mc-
    Donough, N. Y.; d. May 19, 1876. She was a member of the Baptist
    church, as were all her children, as follows:
885 *James Harvey* (Curtis), b. Nov. 29, 1819; m. Feb. 1, 1846, Fanny
    Coville of McDonough; d. April 29, 1869.
886 *Palmyra Leach* (Curtis), b. Oct. 15, 1821; m. 1st, Sept. 4, 1840, George
    McIntyre of Cincinnatus, N. Y., who died Aug. 8, 1841; 2d, May

19, 1844, Merrit Daniels of McDonough. In Nov., 1878, they went to Nebraska.

887 *Sally* (Curtis), b. Jan. 2, 1823; d. July 17, 1839.

888 *John Thurston* (Curtis), b. Aug. 5, 1824; m. Oct., 1851, Julia Ackley of McDonough; lived on the old homestead for several years, then was overseer on railroads in different towns till a few years since they moved to Kentucky, where they reside, 1878.

889 *Edmund Bostwick* (Curtis), b. March 9, 1826; m. Oct., 1851, Mary Moore of McDonough; was clerk in the treasury department for sixteen years; 1878 is a dealer in eggs, butter, and cheese; is deacon of the Baptist church and Sunday-school superintendent in Washington, D. C.

890 *Adelaide Elizabeth* (Curtis), b. July 13, 1828; m. Aug. 27, 1856, Nelson Coville of McDonough; d. Sept. 3, 1872.

891 *Charles Edgar* (Curtis), b. May 24, 1830; m. Oct., 1852, Maria Gibson of McDonough; enlisted Sept, 1864, in the 90th New York regiment; was taken prisoner at the battle of Cedar Creek Oct. 19, and died from starvation in prison hospital at Salisbury, N. C., Feb. 8, 1865.

892 *Louisa Rebecca* (Curtis), b. May 9, 1832; d. March 17, 1861.

893 *Lorena Allen* (Curtis), b. Feb. 23, 1834; m. Sept., 1853, Asa McDaniels of McDonough. In 1868 they moved to Norwich, N. Y., and in 1878 to Garnett, Kansas.

894 *William Henry* (Curtis), b. Dec. 10, 1838; d. Jan. 10, 1839.

895 *Hattie Adoresta* (Curtis), b. June 11, 1840; n.m.; living in McDonough, 1878.

896 *Betsey* (Fitts), b. Oct. 12, 1800; went with her parents to Smithville, N. Y., in 1807; was for many years a teacher of district school and of Baptist Sunday-school; m. 1st, May 21, 1844, Elder Bennett Hart, Baptist, of Smithville, who was killed by lightning June 12, 1845; 2d, Dea. Silas Betts of Greene, N. Y.; he died Feb. 8, 1878; she is living at Brisbin, N. Y., 1878; no children.

897 *Sally Bartlett* (Fitts), b. Oct. 1, 1802; m. April 5, 1826, Isaac Tichinor Towslee of Pownal, Vt.; d. Sept. 3, 1870; was a Baptist; had, all b. in Smithville:

898 *Henry Lafayette* (Towslee), b. Jan. 6, 1827; m. Louisa Van Tassel of Oxford, N. Y.; she died May 8, 1864. He was a boatman at Greene, N. Y., where he died, April 2, 1874.

899 *Clarrenda Jane* (Towslee), b. Feb. 17, 1828; d. June 1, 1832.

900 *Lavorian Thurston* (Towslee), b. Feb. 7, 1830; m. 1st, Jane Knickerbocker of Smithville; she died Dec. 31, 1857; 2d, Diantha Congdon of Scipio, N. Y.; is a grocer and butcher in Locke, Cayuga county, N. Y., 1878.

901 *Francis Chase* (Towslee), b. May 1, 1831; m. Sarah Caukins of Hadley, Mass.; is a farmer in Smithville, 1878.

902 *Delos Hiram* (Towslee), b. May 20, 1833; m. Jan. 1, 1861, Hannah Thackry of Leeds, Eng.; is a farmer and blacksmith in Greene, 1878; both members of the Baptist church.

903 *Clarrenda Jane* (Towslee), b. May 21, 1835; m. Sept. 1, 1861, Harvey Symonds of Oxford, N. Y.; live in Greene, 1878; Baptists.

904 *Lovina* (Fitts), b. Nov. 2, 1808; m. Sept. 19, 1849, John Carpenter of Ohio; he died in McDonough May 2, 1864; both members of the Baptist church. She lives in McDonough, 1878; no children.

905 *Hiram Lewis* (Fitts), b. May 2, 1812; m. Jan. 5, 1842, Almeida Ward Beardsley of McDonough, where he resides, 1878. They have, born in Smithville:

906 *George Harvey* (Fitts), b. Nov. 13, 1842; m. Hattie Alvard; live in Iowa, 1878; Methodist.

907 *Ellen Douglas* (Fitts), b. Feb. 22, 1844; n.m.; d. at Oxford, N. Y., April 9, 1872; Baptist.

908 *Alice* (Fitts), b. May 14, 1845; d. April 29, 1853.

909 *Adelaide Elizabeth* (Fitts), b. April 14, 1848; m. in 1869 Hadlai Fish Pendleton of Norwich, N.Y., where they now reside, 1878; Baptist.

910 *Martha Minerva* (Fitts), b. in McDonough Jan. 9, 1851; d. in Oxford Nov. 12, 1871.

911 *Mary Ida* (Fitts), b. March 30, 1853; m. Nov. 9, 1872, George Burr of Lodi, Ohio, where they reside; member Congregational church.
912 *Frank* (Fitts). b. in Maine, N. Y., March 4, 1859; lives in McDonough; is studying to be a teacher.

NOTE. The descendants and relatives of Moses Thurston, no. 229, page 59, are under lasting obligation to Mary Augusta Hunton, no. 849, wife of Rev. Sylvester Ames Parker of Bethel, Vt., for her untiring labors in research and preparation of the materials for the history of these families as given in these pages.

## 230

EZEKIEL THURSTON [4] (*Moses,*[8] *Stephen,*[2] *Daniel*[1]), brother of the preceding, and son of Moses [8] and Sarah Thurston; married ———.
Mr. Thurston was a resident of Exeter, N. H., in 1775, as he was enlisted from that place in the revolutionary war under Col. Joseph Cilley; was in the battle at Saratoga Oct. 7, 1777.

Their children, born in Epping, N. H., were:

+923 Jonathan,[5] b. May 7, 1761; m. 1st, Sarah ———; 2d, Mary Ardway.
+924 Ezekiel,[5] b. May 28, 1765; m. Mrs. Bray.

## 232

STEPHEN THURSTON [4] of Stratham, N. H. (*Moses,*[8] *Stephen,*[2] *Daniel*[1]), brother of the preceding, and son of Moses [8] and Sarah Thurston; married ———.

Child:

+935 Moses,[5] m. Betsey Wiggin.

## 233

OLIVER THURSTON [4] (*Moses,*[8] *Stephen,*[2] *Daniel*[1]), brother of the preceding, and son of Moses [8] and Sarah Thurston; born about 1738; married SARAH FRENCH. She died in Eaton, N. H., 1814; he died in Shapleigh, Me., or Wakefield, N. H.

Mr. Thurston was a butcher in Brentwood, N. H., a very large and athletic man. He was in Capt. George March's company, Col. John Goff's regiment, in an expedition for the invasion of Canada, from March 6 to Nov. 27, 1760. He next enlisted in Capt. Rowell's company, Col. Nathan Hale's regiment, Feb. 11, 1778. In the battle of New Town, Chemung county, N. Y., fought Sunday, Aug. 29, 1779 (a very large and enthusiastic centennial celebration of this battle was held on the spot Aug. 29, 1879), he was sergeant in the 8th company of Col. Reed's regiment, shot through the thigh, and suffered much for many years before the ball could be removed. Discharged Feb. 26, 1781; examined and commenced garrison duty Feb. 26, 1783. Received a pension of two dollars per month.

Children:

946 Thomas,[5] m. twice; was a shoemaker, living in Shapleigh, Me., Freedom and Eaton, N. H., where he died between 1835 and 1840; no children.
+947 Moses,[5] b. about 1770; m. Sarah or Sally Moses.
+948 Oliver,[5] b. May 10, 1773; m. Anstress Cross.
+949 Reuben,[5] b. 1775; m. Sally Cross.
+950 William,[5] b. Oct. 19, 1777; m. Mary Robinson.
+951 John,[5] b. July 5, 1782; m. Alice S. Hutchins.
952 Ann,[5] lived and died in Brentwood.

5

## 246

JOHN THURSTON [4] (*John,*[3] *Stephen,*[2] *Daniel*[1]), son of John [3] and Elizabeth Thurston of Stratham, N. H.; married ELSIE LEAVITT. Mr. Thurston was a farmer in Stratham. He was in the revolutionary war.

### Their children were:

+966    John,[5] b. 1780; m. 1st, Hannah Mason; 2d, Jane Smith.
 967    Phebe,[5] b. 1784; m. James Cram of Newmarket, N. H.; d. 1871. They had:
      968   *Benjamin Franklin, Joseph, Mary,* and *Ann* (Cram).
 972    Sally,[5] b. 1791; n.m.; d. in Exeter, N. H., 1867, aged 76.
 973    Betsey,[5] n.m.; d. young.
 974    Dolly,[5] m. Theophilus Jones of Exeter; d. 1843; five children.
 980    David,[5] b. about 1798; m. Lydia Drew of Wakefield, N. H.; d. about 1858.
 981    Hannah,[5] b. March 31, 1803; m. John Lyford Conner, a carpenter of Exeter. He died Jan. 22, 1848, aged 43; she died July 26, 1872. They had:
      982   *John* (Conner).
      983   *Sarah E.* (Conner).
      984   *Enoch J.* (Conner).
      985   *Margaret B.* (Conner).
      986   *Carrie Frances* (Conner), b. July 1, 1837; m. Sept. 2, 1860, Geo. Washington Wiggin, b. Feb. 22, 1831, son of Andrew N. and Sarah B. (Messer) Wiggin of Northampton, N. H., a manufacturer of drain tile in Exeter; a member and clerk of the Baptist church. Children:
        987   *Emma Adell* (Wiggin), b. Jan. 18, 1862.
        988   *Perley Olive* (Wiggin), b. Nov. 30, 1864.
        989   *Amy Floretta* (Wiggin), b. July 27, 1868.
      990   *William H.* (Conner).
 991    Mary Carr,[5] b. Nov. 9, 1804; m. March, 1831, John I. Nourse, a farmer of Andover, Mass., b. Sept. 1, 1808, son of John and Elizabeth (Ingalls) Nourse of Lynn, Mass. He died Aug. 1, 1857. She resides in Lawrence, Mass. They had:
      992   *Nathaniel Thurston* (Nourse), b. Dec. 3, 1832; d. May 4, 1855.
      993   *Mary Susan* (Nourse), b. April 3, 1843; m. A. B. Cutler of Andover.
      994   *Sarah Elizab-th* (Nourse), b. Jan. 15, 1847; d. April 27, 1856.
+995    Nathaniel,[5] m. Hannah Dutch.

## 247

PAUL THURSTON [4] (*John,*[3] *Stephen,*[2] *Daniel*[1]), brother of the preceding, and son of John [3] and Elizabeth Thurston of Stratham, N. H.; married MARGARET ——.

### Their children were:

1006    Paul,[5] was a tax-payer in Belchertown, now Pelham, Mass., in 1769; served six months in the revolutionary war; was elected to a town office in 1775, and constable in 1780; became deranged and froze to death in Hardwick, Mass.
1007    Samuel,[5] was a tax-payer in Belchertown in 1767.
1008    Pagy,[5] m. —— Norton.
+1009   Thomas,[5] m. Elizabeth Larmon.

## 261

SAMUEL THURSTON [4] (*Robert,*[3] *Stephen,*[2] *Daniel*[1]), son of Robert [3] of Stratham, N. H.; married MARY ——. Mr. Thurston was a joiner in Exeter, N. H., and died, intestate, 1765. April 28, 1766, dower was set off from his estate to Mary, his widow.

### Their children were:

+1020   Samuel,[5] m. Elizabeth Gilman.
+1021   Ephraim,[5] b. March 25, 1753; m. Annie Marsh.

## 262

JAMES THURSTON[4] of Nottingham, N. H. (*Robert,[3] Stephen,[2] Daniel[1]*), brother of the preceding, and son of Robert[3] of Stratham, N. H.; born 1744; married ———. He died Nov. 20, 1816, aged 72. Mr. Thurston was a farmer and wealthy land owner in Nottingham and New Sandwich, N. H.

His children, said to have been born in New Sandwich, were:

+1032 Ebenezer,[5] m. 1st, Betsey Doughty; 2d, Jane ———.
1033 Jonathan,[5] a farmer in Nottingham, and had *Helpy.*[6]
+1034 Peter,[5] b. March 6, 1770; m. Rachel Doughty.
1035 Joseph,[5] went to New Orleans and died there.
+1036 Moses,[5] m. Nancy Harvey.
+1037 Polly,[5] b. Feb. 5, 1776; m. Freeman Dexter.
1038 Betsey,[5] m. Dudley Thurston [see no. 733].
1039 Hannah,[5] lived and died single in Nottingham.
1040 Dudley.[5]
1041 Sally,[5] b. 1786; m. March 12, 1853, Eben Harvey of Nottingham. She died Dec. 20, 1858; he died Feb. 26, 1860, aged 84.

## 273

ENOCH THURSTON[4] of Beverly, Mass. (*Nathaniel,[3] Stephen,[2] Daniel[1]*), eldest son of Nathaniel[3] and Miner (Chase) Thurston of Plaistow, N. H.; born there Aug. 9, 1741; married, first, April 14, 1763, ELIZABETH CHASE, born Jan. 21, 1746, daughter of Aquila and Mary (Bowley) Chase; second, Feb. 24, 1774, LUCY McINTYRE of Danvers, Mass.; third, BETSEY SHELDON of Beverly. He was a butcher in Beverly, and died March, 1828.

His children, by second wife, Lucy, were:

1052 Enoch.[5]    1053 Eben.[5]    1054 Lucy.[5]    1055 Lydia.[5]
1056 Ruth,[5] m. 1801, Jonathan Cressey of Beverly. They had:
   1057 *Sally* (Cressey), b. June 5, 1802.
   1058 *Aaron* (Cressey), b. Sept. 4, 1804; in Beverly.
   1059 *Lucy McIntyre* (Cressey), b. June 9, 1809.
   1060 *Rebecca* (Cressey), b. Feb. 18, 1814.
   1061 *Enoch* (Cressey), b. Aug. 28, 1817; in Danvers.
   1062 *Rebecca L.* (Cressey), b. Nov. 28, 1819.
   1063 *Solomon* (Cressey), b. Nov. 3, 1824.

By third wife, Betsey:
+1064 James,[5] b. June 16, 1795; m. 1st, Nabby Black; 2d, Louisa Ray.

## 274

PAUL THURSTON[4] (*Nathaniel,[3] Stephen,[2] Daniel[1]*), brother of the preceding, and son of Nathaniel[3] and Miner (Chase) Thurston of Plaistow, N. H.; born Nov. 22, 1743; married ———. Mr. Thurston was a farmer in West Newbury, Mass.

Children:

1075 John.[5]    1076 Anne.[5]    1077 Miner.[5]
1078 Sarah.[5] John, Anne, and Sarah named in their grandfather's will.

## 275

JONATHAN THURSTON[4] (*Nathaniel,[3] Stephen,[2] Daniel[1]*), brother of the preceding, and son of Nathaniel[3] and Miner (Chase) Thurston of Plaistow, N. H.; born there Dec. 21, 1745; married, October, 1769, ELIZABETH HOVEY, born Sept. 23, 1741, daughter of Samuel and Eliz-

abeth Hovey of Newbury, Mass.   She died Aug. 14, 1823, aged 82 ;
he died June 8, 1832, aged 87.

Mr. Thurston was a farmer in Boscawen, N. H.; was in the revolutionary war, remained till the close, and was honorably discharged.
Owing to the loss of the muster roll of his company, he failed to receive a pension.   In 1860 the town was divided and Webster formed,
the division bringing the homestead into the new town, where all the
family lived except Nathaniel, who bought a farm in the eastern part
of the town, which is still Boscawen.

### Their children were :

1089  Mary,[5] b. Aug. 18, 1770; m. 1794, Ephraim Noyes, b. 1765, son of James
and Jane Noyes of Newbury (Old Town), Mass.   He was a shoemaker
in Boscawen, a soldier in the war of 1812, and a member of the Congregational church.   He died May 11, 1856; she died Sept. 5, 1857, aged
87.   They had :
1090  *James* (Noyes), b. 1795; was in the war of 1812, and supposed to have
been lost at sea.
1091  *Jane* (Noyes), b. 1797; n.m.; d. 1819.
1092  *Elizabeth Wyatt* (Noyes), b. 1799; n.m.; d. 1870.
1093  *Edna Adams* (Noyes), b. May 13, 1801; n.m.
1094  *Judith Stickney Whittier* (Noyes), lives in Rowley, Mass.
1095  *Nicholas Moody* (Noyes), b. Oct. 24, 1806.
+1096  Nathaniel,[5] b. Dec. 29, 1771; m. Susanna Jackman.
1097  Moses,[5] b. Sept. 27, 1773; teacher; n.m.; d. March 14, 1861.
1098  Ruth,[5] b. Oct. 12, 1775; n.m.; d. July 19, 1843.
1099  Phebe,[5] b. May 30, 1778; teacher; n.m.; d. March 27, 1867, aged 89.

### 278

STEPHEN THURSTON[4] (*Nathaniel,[3] Stephen,[2] Daniel[1]*), brother of
the preceding, and son of Nathaniel[3] and Miner (Chase) Thurston of
Plaistow, N. H.; born in Newburyport, Mass., Jan. 24, 1750; married, first, KEZIAH CHENEY, born in 1749 at Newburyport; she died
Sept. 25, 1814, aged 65.   Second, in 1816, MRS. PETTINGALL of Newport, N. H., born 1791, having had three children, Jefferson (Pettingall), Phebe (Pettingall), and Rev. Erastus (Pettingall), who was a
Methodist minister; she died in 1873 in Barnard, Vt.

Stephen Thurston was a farmer and joiner, and lived in Rowley,
now Georgetown, Mass., Boscawen and Orford, N. H., and Fairlee,
Vt., where he died, May 26, 1846, aged 96 years and 4 months.   He
was in the revolutionary war under Washington at Valley Forge.
His daughter Jane writes : " They were Congregationalists till late in
life when he joined the Methodists ; an exemplary member ; an honest and upright man.   They were very industrious people.   As soon
as the girls were old enough to work we were taught to knit, sew,
spin flax, card tow, wool, and cotton, and spin and weave material for
the principal part of our clothing and that of the family.   The order
of the day with my brothers was, work ; with the motto, whatever you
do, do well."

### His children, all by first wife, born in Rowley, were :

+1110  Eunice Smith,[5] b. June 9, 1774; m. Porter Estabrook.
1111  Keziah,[5] b. May 21, 1779; m. Oct. 15, 1795, Abel Gillet, a joiner and farmer of Norwich, Vt.   She died May 1, and he May 15, 1852.   They had :
1112  *Sarah, Abel, Otis, Hannah, Franklin, Lova,* and *Harriet* (Gillet).

1119   *Fannie* (Gillet), m. 1844, Nahala Davis and had Sarah Keziah (Davis), m. June 4, 1864, A. E. Wardwell, Congregationalists and live in Norwich; Anna Isadore (Davis), m. Nov. 26, 1870, A. H. Trescott; she is a Methodist and they live in Norwich; George Ransom (Davis), lives in Centerville, La.

+1120   Stephen,[5] } twins, born { m. Philena Pamelia Dunham.
1121   Patty,[5]   } April, 1781; { m. Lewis Churchill; lived in Cornish, N. H., where they died. They had :

1122   *Barker Brewster* (Churchill), m. and had Edgar (Churchill); both father and son were in the war against the rebellion; Lydia (Churchill), m. —— Nelson.

1123   Sally,[5] b. Nov. 25, 1782; m. John Terry, a farmer of Hanover, N. H.; d. leaving :

1124   *Caroline* (Terry), m. and lives in Kansas.
1125   *Julius* (Terry), m. and lives in Claremont, N. H.

1126   Dolly,[5] b. Oct. 4, 1784; m. Dec. 25, 1807, Ithamar Watson, b. Sept. 7, 1784, son of Caleb and Lydia (Houlet) Watson of Weare and Salisbury, N. H., a machinist and later in life a farmer of Salisbury, where he died Nov. 2, 1855; she died June 6, 1859. He was captain of militia, justice of the peace, and many years master of Warner lodge of Masons. They were members of the Baptist church. They had :

1127   *A child* who did not survive its birth.
1128   *Henry Lyman* (Watson), b. Feb. 10, 1811; m. June 4, 1840, Roxana Hughes. He graduated from Vermont medical college 1838, and practiced medicine successfully over twenty years in Guildhall, Vt.
1129   *Melinda Cheney* (Watson), b. June 8, 1816; m. Jan. 1, 1838, Tenney Hardy, b. March 26, 1808, son of Thaddeus Hardy of Warner, N. H., where he died Feb. 23, 1873.
1130   *Joseph Warren* (Watson), b. June 10, 1823; d. Oct. 10, 1824.
1131   *Porter Baldwin* (Watson), b. July 13, 1825; m. Oct. 17, 1848, Luvia Ellen Ladd. He was a farmer, but is now, 1878, overseer of a glove-leather tannery in Littleton, N. H.; was representative in the legislature in 1863 and 1864.

1132   Jane,[5] b. June 27, 1788; m. 1806, Stephen Stanley, a farmer of Salisbury, where they lived till after their children were born, and after in Warner. He died June 11, 1853. Mrs. Stanley has been very helpful in collecting these facts, 1877. They had :

1133   *Eunice* (Stanley), b. Mar. 21, 1810; lives with her mother, unmarried.
1134   *Stephen Thurston* (Stanley), } twins, born { m. 1840, Sarah Emerson
1135   *Phinehas* (Stanley),      } Dec. 28, 1812; { of South Reading, now Wakefield, Mass.; live in Warner. Phinehas m. 1st, 1842, Virtue Jones of Rumney, N. H.; 2d, in 1850, Mary Wiggin of Moultonborough, N. H., and live in Lowell, Mass.

1136   *Benjamin* (Stanley), b. April 14, 1815; m. 1851, Elizabeth Cutting of Concord, N. H., and live with his mother.

1137   *Charles* (Stanley), b. May 31, 1820; d. 1843.

1138   John,[5] b. Oct. 1, 1790; m. and went West about 1812, and was never heard from.

+1139   Nathaniel,[5] b. April 22, 1795; m. 1st, Martha Hall; 2d, Jane Fellows.

## 293

Susannah Thurston[4] (*Nathaniel,*[3] *Stephen,*[2] *Daniel*[1]), sister of the preceding, and daughter of Nathaniel[3] and Miner (Chase) Thurston of Plaistow, N. H.; born there May 7, 1763; married, Oct. 11, 1781, Josiah Chase, born April or Aug. 2, 1762, son of Aquila and Mary (Bowley) Chase of Newbury, Mass. She died Oct. 6, 1813.

Their children were :

1150   Moses (Chase), b. March 2, 1782; m. Feb. 29, 1820, Sally Lewis.
1151   Josiah (Chase), b. Jan. 12, 1784; m. 1st, Nov. 25, 1809, Sarah Woodward; 2d, Feb. 5, 1817, Esther S. Fernald.
1152   Rebecca (Chase), m. Jonas Lewis.
1153   Nathaniel (Chase), n.m.; d. in Newbury.

1154  Mary (Chase), m. Sept. 25, 1814, Eliphalet Randall.
1155  Charles Aquila (Chase), n.m.; d. in Newbury.
1156  Susan (Chase), n.m.; d. in Newbury.
1157  Lydia F. (Chase), n.m.; d. in Newbury.
1158  Nancy (Chase), m. May 12, 1818, Richard Hawes.
1159  William (Chase), n.m.; d. in Newbury.
1160  Hannah Sawyer (Chase), m. Charles Crocket.
1161  Lydia Thurston (Chase), b. Nov. 30, 1806; m. Nov. 10, 1832, Job Tapley.
1162  Elizabeth (Chase), b. May 18, 1808; m. in Brooksville, Me., Job Tapley;
      d. Dec. 16, 1830.

## 306

STEPHEN THURSTON[4] (*Stephen,*[3] *Stephen,*[2] *Daniel*[1]), son of Stephen[3] and Mary (St. Claire) Thurston of Stratham, N. H.; born there April 8, 1760; married 1784, BETSEY WIGGIN, born Oct. 10, 1762, daughter of Capt. Jonathan and Molly (Little) Wiggin of Stratham, and her grandmother was Molly Jaquith of Newbury, Mass. [see no. 72.] He died Jan. 23, 1861, aged 100 y. 9 m.; she died May 8, 1859, aged 97.

Mr. Thurston was a farmer in Stratham. In 1806 moved to Cornish, Me., where he remained one year, and removed to West Madison, Me. He entered the army of the revolution at an early age, and was at West Point when Arnold left there so precipitately; was there when Washington arrived and saw him frequently. At the time of the death of his wife, it was said that they had six children, fifty-four grandchildren, sixty great-grandchildren, and three great-great-grandchildren. They lived with their son Col. William, from whom they had never been separated more than a few days at a time since his birth.

Their children were:

+1173  William,[5] b. Jan. 11, 1786; m. Charity Eames.
1174  Mary,[5] b. March 15, 1792; m. March 23, 1815, Dea. Daniel Hobart of Solon, Me.; d. May 1, 1857. They lived in Skowhegan, Me., and had:
    1175  *Huldah* (Hobart), b. Feb. 23, 1818; m. 1st, Oct. 6, 1840, Luther Jewett; he died March 16, 1854; 2d, James Malbon of Skowhegan. She is a member of the Congregational church.
    1176  *Warren* (Hobart), b. June 30, 1819; m. Oct. 22, 1857, Mary Ann Lincoln; d. Nov. 6, 1861, leaving one son, who died Feb., 1878.
    1177  *Elizabeth* (Hobart), b. May 31, 1821; d. Feb. 24, 1863.
    1178  *Mary* (Hobart), b. Oct. 9, 1822; m. June 6, 1844, Daniel Paul, a farmer in South Solon; seven children.
    1179  *Martha Jane* (Hobart), b. July 1, 1824; d. Nov. 16, 1847.
    1180  *Daniel Franklin* (Hobart), b. Feb. 6, 1826; m. Feb., 1855, Martha Jenkins and reside in East Madison; one son.
    1181  *Sextus* (Hobart), b. March 31, 1828; m. Nov. 7, 1856, Sibel Rowell of Solon; live in Boston, Mass.; one son.
    1182  *George Fargo* (Hobart), b. Nov. 4, 1829; drowned April 3, 1845.
    1183  *Hannah Wright* (Hobart), b. Dec. 30, 1831; d. Jan. 24, 1854.
    1184  *Joel Williams* (Hobart), b. July 21, 1833; m. Jan. 30, 1855, Hannah Norton of Solon. They live in East Madison; two sons.
1185  Betsey,[5] b. May 12, 1795; m. April 12, 1817, David Baker; d. Nov. 12, 1856. They resided in South Solon. She was a member of the Congregational church. They had:
    1186  *Phebe Hazzleton* (Baker), b. April 11, 1819; lives in Portland, Me.; is a member of the Baptist church.
    1187  *Elizabeth Thurston* (Baker), b. May 19, 1828; m. Feb., 1867; d. June 4, 1875, in Solon.
    1188  *David* (Baker), b. March 27, 1831; a farmer and teacher in Nebraska; enlisted in the Union army 1861 in 1st Nebraska Cavalry; d. in the hospital in Cincinnati, Ohio, April 8, 1862; was a member of the Congregational church.

1189  *Jesse* (Baker), b. Oct. 14, 1835; enlisted in 21st Maine regiment in 1862; badly wounded before Port Hudson May, 1863. He was a spar maker in Bath; m. March 26, 1865, Susan W. Brownson; resides in Solon; three children. She is a member of the Baptist church.

1190  *Mary Hobart* (Baker), b. April 18, 1838; n.m.

1191  Mehitable,[5] b. in Meredith, N. H., Nov. 8, 1797; m. May 18, 1817, Reuben Martin, a farmer and lumberman. They had:

    1192  *Mary Elizabeth* (Martin), b. Nov. 15, 1819; m. May 31, 1842, Edward Hobart, b. April 11, 1817, son of Caleb and Hannah (Paul) Hobart of Solon. They resided in Madison till 1846, when they moved to Maine Settlement in Wisconsin, and in 1850 to Hingham, Wis., where he owned and operated saw and grist-mills till 1866, when he moved to Sheboygan Falls, and in 1868 to Rockford, Ill., where he now resides, 1879. They have, b. in Hingham:

        1193  *Adah Maria* (Hobart), b. March 7, 1852; graduated in music from Rockford female seminary 1871; m. Jan. 1, 1872, Fred James Whiffin from Sheboygan county, Wis., and had Mary (Whiffin), b. in Rockford Nov. 14, 1872.

        1194  *Sarah Alma* (Hobart), b. Feb. 6, 1855; graduated from Rockford high school 1874; m. April 23, 1876, Melville Adelbert Calkins of Rockford.

1195  *Ripley* (Martin), b. Sept. 22, 1822; d. April 25, 1862.

1196  *Maria* (Martin), b. Sept. 29, 1824; m. Dec. 11, 1843, Hiram Hobart; had two children, b. in Sheboygan; d. Sept. 27, 1849.

1197  *Mark* (Martin), b. Nov. 1, 1826.

1198  *Asher* (Martin), b. Sept. 23, 1828; d. July 8, 1837.

1199  *Alonzo* (Martin), b. Nov. 23, 1831.

1200  *Sarah* (Martin), b. Feb. 25, 1833; d. June 2, 1856.

1201  *Reuben* (Martin), b. March 28, 1837.

+1202  Jonathan,[5] b. 1801; m. Lucinda Emerson.

## 314

DANIEL THURSTON[4] of North Parsonsfield, Me. (*Stephen,*[3] *Stephen,*[2] *Daniel*[1]), brother of the preceding, and son of Stephen[3] and Mary (St. Claire) Thurston of Stratham, N. H.; born there July 29, 1763; married, 1794, HANNAH DUTCH, born in Lee, N. H., Dec. 8, 1764. She died Feb. 28, 1839; he was a farmer and died 1845.

Their children were:

1213  Sally,[5] b. Feb. 27, 1795; m. Dec. 26, 1816, by Rev. John Buzzell, Ephraim Thompson, a farmer of Brownfield, Me., after of Eaton and Conway, N. H., b. in Buxton, Me., Oct. 8, 1790. She died Dec. 15, 1866; he died Dec. 13, 1863. They had:

    1214  *Mary Ann* (Thompson), b. Dec. 23, 1817; m. Ephraim Hatch of Conway, N. H.

    1215  *Hannah Smith* (Thompson), b. Nov. 14, 1819; m. July 15, 1860, Isaac Meader.

    1216  *Daniel Thurston* (Thompson), b. Oct. 23, 1820; n.m.; a farmer in Minnesota.

    1217  *Lorenzo Dow* (Thompson), b. July 15, 1822; a farmer of Eaton.

    1218  *Jane Dutch* (Thompson), b. Feb. 10, 1824; m. May 19, 1842, Jonathan Leavitt, a farmer in Chatham, N. H.

    1219  *Stephen Thurston* (Thompson), b. Jan. 25, 1826; m. March 8, 1860, and is a farmer in Minnesota.

    1220  *Artemas Richardson* (Thompson), b. Feb. 29, 1828; d. June, 1829.

    1221  *Rebecca Hall* (Thompson), b. Nov. 15, 1830; m. Dec. 5, 1857, George N. Merrill, a farmer in Danvers, Mass.

Born in Conway, N. H.:

    1222  *Thaddeus Broad* (Thompson), b. Dec. 15, 1833; m. March 7, 1861, by Rev. King Atkinson, Susan M. Stuart of Eaton.

1223  *Samuel Dutch* (Thompson), b. Dec. 31, 1836; m. Feb. 25, 1864, Mary
      Estell; is a farmer in Minnesota.
1224  George,[6] b. Nov. 23, 1797; m. Jane Thompson; was a carpenter in Great
      Falls and Somersworth, N. H.  He died 1842; she died 1872; had two
      sons who died in infancy.
1225  Mittee,[6] b. Dec. 22, 1798; m. William Thurston [see no. 1447].
1226  Stephen,[6] b. June 10, 1802; a farmer; n.m.; d. of lock-jaw, caused by a
      slight wound, Feb. 18, 1823.
1227  Mary,[6] b. April 29, 1806; n.m.; d. Oct. 10, 1836.
1228  Betsey,[6] b. July 30, 1808; n.m.; d. July 14, 1834.
1229  Hannah,[6] b. July 23, 1811; n.m.; d. Dec. 4, 1835.
1230  Daniel,[6] b. March 15, 1814; n.m.; d. Dec. 11, 1835.

---

## Fifth Generation.

### 362

REV. BENJAMIN THURSTON[5] (*Col. Daniel,[4] Benjamin,[3] Daniel,[2]
Daniel[1]*), son of Col. Daniel[4] and Hannah (Parker) Thurston of
Bradford, Mass.; born there Sept. 25, 1753; married, 1778, SARAH
PHILLIPS, born Dec. 25, 1755, daughter of John Phillips of Boston,
formerly governor of Massachusetts.  She died May 22, 1789; he
died near Raleigh, N. C., in 1804.

Rev. Benjamin Thurston graduated from Harvard 1774; settled at
Northampton, N. H., Nov. 2, 1784; resigned Oct. 27, 1800.  He had
rare talent, pleasing address, and was an efficient preacher.  Feb. 22,
1797, he gave the right hand at the ordination of Rev. Jesse Appleton at Hampton, N. H.  Dr. Phillips, the founder of Phillips academy, Exeter, procured the charter of the legislature of New Hampshire April 3, 1781.  The inaugural ceremonies took place in 1783.
They were performed by Rev. Benjamin Thurston, a gentleman of
the trust, with a particular address and charge to the preceptor.  In
the solemn charge, delivered in the presence of the founder, to the
first preceptor of the academy, this sentence occurs:  "You will
therefore, sir, make no discrimination in favor of any particular
state, town, or family, on account of parentage, age, wealth, sentiments of religion, etc.,—the institution is founded upon principles of
the most extensive liberality."  Mr. Thurston's charge and the response by Mr. William Woodbridge exist in manuscript in the library
of Harvard college.  Mr. Thurston was a trustee for twenty years,
from 1781 to 1801.

Their children were:

+1250  John Phillips,[6] b. 1781; m. Mary Tucker.
 1251  Sarah,[6] b. Feb. 12, 1783; m. July 12, 1803, Joel Hall; d. Oct. 23, 1806.
       They had:
       1252  *Sarah Thurston Phillips* (Hall), b. 1804; m. Nov. 4, 1835, James
             Merrill Cummings, b. July 27, 1810, graduated from Bowdoin, M.D.,
             1834; a practicing physician in Portland, Me.  They had:
             1253  *Elizabeth W.* (Cummings), b. Sept. 27, 1836.
             1254  *James Abbott* (Cummings), b. Feb. 12, 1840.
       1255  *Jane* (Hall), b. 1806; m. 1827, John K. Hale, lawyer; d. 1857; had:
             1256  *Mary* (Hale), m. Dr. Guild and had Jeannie Thurston (Guild).
             1257  *Sarah* (Hale), m. Rev. J. M. Robinson.
             1258  *Matthew* (Hale).

1259 Benjamin,[6] b. June 17, 1785; attended Phillips academy at the age of 13; n.m.; d. July 30, 1803, at St. Georges, Granada.
1260 Betsey,[6] b. June 6, 1787; m. Nov. 25, 1804, James Milk Ingraham of Portland; d. 1858. They had:
   1261 *James Milk* (Ingraham), b. Oct. 13, 1805.
   1262 *Elizabeth Thurston* (Ingraham), b. March 8, 1807; m. D. B. Holbrook, and had Caroline (Holbrook).
   1263 *Joseph Holt* (Ingraham), b. Jan. 26, 1809; m. Mary Brooks, and had Josephine (Ingraham), Sargent P. (Ingraham), Louisa (Ingraham), Caroline (Ingraham).
   1264 *Benjamin* (Ingraham), m. Laura Brooks, and had William (Ingraham), Henry (Ingraham).
   1265 *Caroline* (Ingraham).
   1266 *John Phillips Thurston* (Ingraham), m. and had three children.
   1267 *Charles* (Ingraham).
   1268 *Julia* (Ingraham).
1269 Daniel,[6] b. May 7, 1789; n.m.; d. at Northampton, N. H., Nov., 1816.

## 363

HON. NATHANIEL THURSTON[5] (*Col. Daniel,[4] Benjamin,[3] Daniel,[2] Daniel[1]*), brother of the preceding, and son of Col. Daniel[4] and Hannah (Parker) Thurston of Bradford, Mass.; born there Jan. 17, 1755; married, first, Jan. 30, 1780, BETSEY WEBSTER of Bradford; second, MARTHA BRIDGES of Andover, Mass.; third, HULDAH PERKINS of Portsmouth, N. H.; fourth, CLARISSA TUCKER of Newburyport, Mass.; fifth, MARTHA B. LOVEJOY of Andover; sixth, Sept. 22, 1807, MARY CHADWICK, daughter of Joshua Chadwick of Rindge, N. H.; seventh, FRANCES FLETCHER of Boston, Mass. This last marriage we found recorded in the Williamsburgh, Va., Gazette of 1809, with the following quotation in connection, "counsel our counselors and give our senators wisdom," "Virginia State Library."

He was a farmer in Bradford, and exporter of beef; for many years a member of the legislature of Massachusetts; was distinguished for his benevolence and greatly lamented by his friends. He died in Lansingburgh, N. Y., Oct. 21, 1811, aged 56, after which his widow married an ex-governor of Massachusetts, and went to the South. The following epitaphs are copied from the stones in the old burying-ground in Bradford:

Here lies interred the remains of Mrs. Betsey Thurston, consort of Capt. Nathaniel Thurston, who departed this life Dec. 10, 1790, aged 34.

> Let mourning friends and husband dear
> Lament the dead, repent, and fear;
> Let youthful children read this stone,
> Feel they must die and soon be gone.

Mrs. Martha Thurston, consort of Nathaniel Thurston, Esq., died May 12, 1799, aged 32.

> See there, all pale and dead she lies,
> Forever flow my streaming eyes;
> There dwells the fairest, loveliest mind,
> Faith sweetens it, together joined,
> Dwelt faith and wit and sweetness there,
> O view the change and drop a tear.

Mrs. Huldah Thurston, consort, etc., died Sept. 8, 1801, aged 24.
Mrs. Clarissa Thurston, consort, etc., died Nov. 14, 1803, aged 36.
Mrs. Martha B. Thurston, consort, etc., died July 27, 1804, aged 25.
Mrs. Mary Thurston, consort, etc., died March 30, 1808, aged 27.

His children were:

+1279 Daniel,[6] b. Jan. 12, 1796; m. Abbie Stephens.
+1280 Nathaniel Bridges,[6] b. 1797; m. Ruby Gage.

1281  Benjamin,[6] b. July, 1800; d. March 11, 1801, aged 8 months.
1282  Benjamin,[6] m.; no children.
1283  Betsey,[6] m. Benjamin Kimball, a shoe manufacturer of Bradford, and had :
    1284  *Eliza* (Kimball), m. Stephen Mansur, mayor of the city and merchant in Lowell, Mass.; had three daughters and four sons; all dead 1878.
    1285  *Thurston* (Kimball), m. Harriet Griffin of Bradford.
    1286  *Ellen* (Kimball), m. William Gage, a shoe manufacturer of Londonderry, N. H.
    1287  *Leonard* (Kimball), d. young.
    1288  *Benjamin* (Kimball), d. young.

## 364

DANIEL THURSTON [5] (*Col. Daniel,*[4] *Benjamin,*[3] *Daniel,*[2] *Daniel*[1]), brother of the preceding, and son of Col. Daniel[4] and Hannah (Parker) Thurston of Bradford, Mass.; born there June 12, 1757; married, Nov. 5, 1781, SUSANNAH CROMBIE, born Nov. 11, 1764, daughter of James and Sarah (Poor) Crombie, of Andover, Mass. He died at his son's in Methuen, Mass., June 11, 1831, and was buried in Bradford. She died Dec. 10, 1844.

Mr. Thurston was a farmer in Bradford; assessor, treasurer, and collector of the town. He was in the revolutionary and 1812 wars. They were professors of religion but not members of the church.

Their children were:

+1299  Daniel,[6] b. Oct. 11, 1782; m. Mary Stacy.
1300  Sarah,[6] b. Nov. 20, 1786; m. David Walker of Bradford, a tanner and inspector of beef; lived thirty years in Troy, N. Y. She died Jan., 1831; he died in Hanover, Mass., 1836; no children.
1301  Nathaniel Parker,[6] b. June 25, 1790; in the United States service as drummer for five years, and was stationed at Marblehead and Fort Independence, Boston. May 6, 1811, had orders to march to Pittsburgh, Pa. His sister Clarissa writes, 1878, at the age of 75, "next we heard from him at Vincennes, Fort Harrison, March 20, 1812, after the battle of Tippecanoe; he says, 'but through the goodness of God the bullets fell harmless at my feet. The number killed and wounded was 188, the Indians 224.' He was in all the principal battles of the war, and when Gen. Hull surrendered to the English, said he could have taken the English flag if Hull would have let him, but he chose to surrender, and every true-hearted soldier's blood boiled with indignation and shame at the consummate, self-willed blunder. They were marched through the streets to the tune of 'Yankee Doodle' to the prison; and as they marched the old ladies came to their doors with light in hand (it was evening), holding up their glasses and crying out, 'have you got all the rebels now?' That was more than my brother could bear, and his drumsticks would not beat. They were thrust into a filthy prison and given rations of horse flesh and wormy bread. When the prisoners were exchanged they were put on board a vessel, and the English put copperas into the casks of water; but fortunately before they were out of the harbor the trick was discovered, and they were saved from being poisoned. He after enlisted for the war, and then for five years more, which he served as drum-major at West Point military academy as teacher. He was drowned in June, 1820, in Lake Erie. Thirty ladies and gentlemen, out sailing on a pleasure party, were overtaken by a violent squall, so common on the lake, which capsized the boat, and all but two or three were drowned. My brother was a splendid swimmer, but was lost. He was a dear brother."
1302  Susan,[6] b. March 28, 1793; m. George Ellis of Bradford, who was station agent on the Boston and Maine railroad at North Andover, Mass., till he died, June, 1837. They had:
    1303  *Susan Martin* (Ellis), m. Daniel Smith of Haverhill, Mass., a box manufacturer. He enlisted in the war against the rebellion as first lieutenant, and was at the first battle of Bull Run. They have four sons and one daughter.

1304 *George* (Ellis), m. Caroline Allen of Andover; is an engineer and box manufacturer in Haverhill; captain of steam fire department. They have four sons and one daughter.

1305 *Julia Ann* (Ellis), m. 1st, Chandler Smith, a machinist in Andover, who died 1856; two daughters; 2d, Henry Wilson, a shoe manufacturer in Lynn, Mass.; no children.

1306 *Clara Spofford* (Ellis), d. in infancy.

1307 *Clara Thurston* (Ellis), m. Charles Foster of Andover, a manufacturer of all kinds of cutlery and needles used in shoe making; is alderman of the city and enlisted in the war against the rebellion; reside in Lynn and have two sons.

1308 Martha Bridges,[6] b. Oct. 25, 1797; m. Dec. 8, 1817, Seth Clark,* b. Jan. 14, 1783, a merchant tailor in Portland, Me., a man of character and influence. Mr. Clark m. 1st, March 18, 1808, Nabby Tucker, b. Feb. 18, 1789, d. Dec. 27, 1816, having had George Howe (Clark), b. Dec. 24, 1808, m. Nov. 1, 1836, Maria L. Smith of Hadley, Mass; Francis Tukey (Clark), b. May 16, 1811, d. Dec. 16, 1813; Isaac Towle (Clark), b. June 5, 1814, m. 1st, June, 1837, Louisa A. Marston, 2d, June 24, 1864, Julia C. Winslow; Nabby Tucker (Clark), b. May 27, 1816, m. Sept. 9, 1834, William Goold. Seth Clark died Aug. 13, 1871, leaving his second wife, Martha B., who from eight years of age was reared in the family of her cousin, John Phillips Thurston, an eminent merchant of Portland, who moved to New York in 1819, and became one of the leading commission merchants of that city. She was several years a scholar at the Portland academy, commencing under the tuition of Edward Payson, afterward D.D. She lived to a good old age, respected and loved by all who knew her, and died Jan. 16, 1879. She had:

1309 *A son*, b. Oct. 4, 1818; d. in infancy.

1310 *Stephen Tukey* (Clark), b. Oct. 29, 1819; m. April 22, 1847, Charlotte A. Ilsley of Westbrook, Me. He was interested in the New York Express and after on the editorial staff of the New York Tribune; died in Italy 1869; family reside in New York.

1311 *Thurston* (Clark), b. Jan. 14, 1822.

1312 *Henry Thurston* (Clark), b. Feb. 15, 1823; m. Oct. 12, 1852, Louisa Stinchfield of Clinton, Me; is connected with railroading and resides at Cumberland, Mills, Me.

1313 *Ezra* (Clark), b. April 7, 1825; m. May 11, 1848, Elizabeth Durgan.; was a tinsmith in Portland and in Titusville, Pa., where he died, 1868.

1314 *Seth* (Clark), b. Jan. 7, 1827; m. June 19, 1853, Sarah L. Lambert of Port Jervis, N. Y.; is in the boot and shoe business in Clinton, Iowa.

1315 *Edward* (Clark), b. Dec. 2, 1833; is on the editorial staff of the New York Tribune.

---

* The CLARK FAMILY.

I. WILLIAM CLARK came from England and settled in Dorchester, Mass., May 30, 1630. He and his wife Sarah were members of the Dorchester church before 1639. He removed to North Hampton, Mass., in 1650 or 1660, and was many years a leading man and a deputy to the general court. He died July 18, 1690, aged 83. They had Nathaniel, b. Jan. 27, 1641; Rebeckah, b. about 1649; JOHN, b. about 1651; Samuel, bap Oct. 2, 1653; William, b. July 8, 1656; Sarah, b. March 19, 1659.

II. JOHN CLARK, born about 1651; married, first, July 12, 1677, at Springfield, Mass., Rebeckah Cooper; she died May 8, 1678. Second, March 20, 1679, Mary Strong, daughter of Elder John Strong. John Clark was deacon, deputy to general court, and died Sept. 3, 1704. Children, all by second wife: Sarah, b. April 20, 1678; John. b. Dec. 28, 1679; Nathaniel, b. May 13, 1681; EBENEZER, b. Oct. 18, 1682; Increase, b. April 8, 1684; Mary, b. Dec. 27, 1685; Rebecca, b. Nov. 22, 1687; Experience, b. Oct. 30, 1689; Abigail, b. Mar.. 1692; Noah, b. Mar. 28, 1694; Thankful, b. Feb. 18, 1696, d. May 9, 1696; Josiah, b. June 11, 1697.

III. EBENEZER CLARK, born Oct. 18, 1682; married, Dec. 10, 1712, Abigail Pearson; he was a substantial man; died Feb. 27, 1781, aged 98. They had Ebenezer, b. Aug. 16, 1714; EZRA, b. April 4, 1716; Abigail, b. Nov. 29, 1718; William, b. Jan. 2, 1721; Sarah, b. April 23, 1723; Jedediah, b. March 25, 1726; Israel, b. March 15, 1729; Elihu, b. Sept. 30, 1731.

IV. EZRA CLARK, born April 4, 1716; married, 1739, Martha Phelps. They had Martha, b. Sept. 4, 1740; Abigail, b. March 6, 1742; Hannah, b. Sept. 15, 1743; EZRA, b. Feb. 26, 1745; Martin, b. Dec. 23, 1746; Mary, b. July 17, 1748, d. young; Phebe, b. about 1750; Jonas, b. about 1751; Naomi, b. Oct. 4, 1753; Job, b. Nov. 30, 1755; Zenas, b. Sept. 23, 1757; Dorothy, bap. Feb. 7, 1760.

V. EZRA CLARK, born Feb. 26, 1745; married, Jan. 20, 1775, Sarah Howe, born Aug. 14, 1758. He died Aug. 14, 1818. They had Anna, b. March 14, 1776; James, b. Sept. 30, 1780; SETH, b. Jan. 14, 1783, m. Martha Bridges Thurston; Samuel, b. Aug. 26, 1784; George, b. Feb. 27, 1787; Sarah, b. Sept. 16, 1797; Jonas, b. June 14, 1799.

1316 Mary Walker,[6] b. July 13, 1800; m. Joseph C. Pearson of Bradford; had:
 1317 *Sarah W.* (Pearson), b. March 6, 1820; m. 1st, Joseph H. Delaware; 2d, Daniel N. Poor; two children.
 1318 *Laburton* (Pearson), b. June 18, 1822; m. Susan Buswell, and had Gertrude and Ida (Pearson).
 1319 *William Henry* (Pearson), b. June 13, 1825; m. Elizabeth Ann Austin, and had William, Nydra, Louise, Daniel, Grace, and Charles (Pearson).
 1320 *Daniel Thurston* (Pearson), b. May 6, 1830; n.m.; d. in Happy Valley, Cal., about 1848.
 1321 *Charles S.* (Pearson), b. Sept. 16, 1832; n.m.; engaged in the war against the rebellion, and died in Bradford.
 1322 *Mary Thurston* (Pearson), b. Aug. 19, 1834; m. Henry P. Morse; three children.
 1323 *Martha A. C.* (Pearson), b. Aug. 16, 1838; m. Geo. H. B. Howe; no children.
1324 Clarissa Tucker,[6] b. Dec. 7, 1802; m. March 25, 1819, George Spofford of Georgetown, Mass., b. Feb. 2, 1797; a merchant, then express to Boston thirteen years, then station agent on Georgetown and Newburyport railroad, and parish clerk; was once appointed postmaster but did not accept; he died Feb. 18, 1873. They had:
 1325 *Amos* (Spofford), b. June 23, 1822; was named for his grandfather, Dr. Amos Spofford, who purchased the old Thurston farm on Spofford's hill in Georgetown for $1,800, which he paid in silver dollars, making half a bushel. Amos entered West Point 1837, but from a naturally weak constitution could not stand the discipline; he resigned, became a civil engineer, and assisted in locating the Saratoga and Sacketts Harbor railroad, which runs near Raquett lake and the Adirondac mountains. Game was so plenty in those days that he sent home to his friends at one time six carcasses of deer; the lake was literally full of beautiful trout. In 1862 he enlisted in the war against the rebellion; had his knee badly injured by a railway accident; suffered much from lack of treatment, but went to New Orleans, barely escaping shipwreck on a condemned steamer; did service in the 50th Massachusetts regiment hospital at Baton Rouge, where he died, June 23, 1863. and his remains were brought home in 1865 and placed beside those of his father and two of his children. In 1845 he married Sophia Savary of Georgetown and had:
  1326 *Clara Tucker* (Spofford), b. in Georgetown Feb. 10, 1846; m. 1872, Harry Stetson, a printer in New York; d. April 30, 1875.
  1327 *Martha Savary* (Spofford), b. in Epsom, N. H., Oct. 24, 1849; d. in Georgetown Oct. 17, 1863.
  1328 *Judith Follansbee* (Spofford), b. in Georgetown Sept. 28, 1851; m. Chandler L. Parker of Boxford, Mass., a musician, teacher of all kinds of wind instruments, and composer of music; live in Groveland, Mass. They have:
   1329 *George Gilman* (Parker), b. Dec. 2, 1875.
   1330 *Herbert Chandler* (Parker), b. Dec. 13, 1877.
  1331 *Amos Little* (Spofford), b. in Lowville, N. Y., April 11, 1856; graduated from Massachusetts Agricultural college 1878, and is studying medicine in Harvard university.
  1332 *Jennie Smith* (Spofford). b. in Lowville April 8, 1858; m. David Mighill Winter Morrill, a mechanic of Georgetown. They have:
   1333 *Luther Edward* (Morrill), b. May 2, 1878.
  1334 *George John* (Spofford), b. at Lyons Falls, N. Y., Nov. 29, 1859; a shoemaker.
+1335 Benjamin,[6] b. Aug. 7, 1805; m. 1st, Eliza Gage; 2d, Lydia Carlton.

## 384

THOMAS THURSTON[5] (*Dea. John,[4] Jonathan,[3] Daniel,[2] Daniel[1]*), son of Dea. John and Hepzibah (Burpee) Thurston of Rowley, now Georgetown, Mass.; married, first (published March 30, 1780), LYDIA DAVIS of Concord, Mass.; she died Jan. 19, 1806. Second, Jan. 1,

1807, MEHITABLE UPTON, born Nov. 6, 1763, daughter of William and Hannah (Stanley) Upton of North Reading, Mass.

He was a farmer in Fitchburgh, Mass., and member of the Congregational church.

Capt. Tom, as he was afterward familiarly called, was a musical genius. He inherited superior talent, which, with some cultivation, made him the leading musician in town, in fact in all this region. He had a good voice, a fine ear for music, and was leader of the church choir for over thirty years. His father, though himself a good singer, had no idea of allowing his son to depend upon his musical talent for a living, so he determined that Thomas should learn a trade, as was the custom in those days. Accordingly he apprenticed him to a shoemaker by the name of Brown in Concord, Mass. The trade was not adapted to his tastes; but he was remarkably successful teaching singing-schools, and he won a reputation in all the surrounding towns.

There is a bit of romance connected with his early life, which has never been written, which may account for the musical talent of this branch of the Thurston family. We have said he was a singing master and during the winter traveled about the country teaching singing-schools. One winter, in the town of Concord, he saw and fell in love with a charming-faced, rich-voiced maiden—one, in his eyes, the fairest of the fair. His heart was devoted to music then more than ever, and the cooling shades of old Concord lured him, out of singing-school season, to sundry rehearsals of which no public notice was given. It was a mutual love, and very soon it was whispered around that Singing Master Thurston and Miss Lydia Davis were "courting." They were duly published and married. What wonder that children born in such wedlock should be musicians? What wonder that Uncle Cyrus is so often called "to lead the old folks?" What wonder that Grandpa Ebenezer, at eighty years of age, could beat the bass drum with unerring precision and whistle Yankee Doodle like a boy? Nay, more, what wonder, with Emerson, Alcott, Hawthorne, Thoreau—celebrities Concord has produced—that the intellectual basis of an able missionary should be brought forth in such a union?

Rev. Dr. Ripley, for many years a pastor of Concord, officiated at the wedding. Mr. Thurston took his young bride to his new home in Fitchburgh, and commenced in earnest to fell the giant forest pines that covered the Turkey hills. He used to say he could stand on one spot and touch with his axe every inch of ground he could clear in one day, so thick was the growth of trees. After he had succeeded in clearing a small patch, his wife became so homesick that he was obliged to pack up and move to her father's in Concord, where he engaged at his trade as a shoemaker. In a year and a half they came back to Fitchburgh to find the cleared patch grown up with briars, and everything looked discouraging in the extreme. But they went to work with a will, and there was a happy home on the hill, with music in doors and out.

The autumn of 1787, seven years after the nuptials at Concord, found Thomas and Lydia Thurston with a family of three children— one son and two daughters. On the twelfth day of October came a

little stranger to the hillside home to share with his brother and sisters the joys and sorrows of childhood, and fill the parents' hearts with gratitude.

That was a gladsome day, was it not? Who would have dreamed that in the far-off islands of the Pacific was a kingdom awaiting the advent of this child, upon which his character should be stamped. While he slept so peacefully in his cradle, that nation was groaning under the burdens of heathenism and wasting its blood in ghastly conflicts. What uninspired seer would have been bold enough to announce the workman and his work? There was no unwonted melody in the sighing of the breezes that swept the brow of old Watatic, or bent the waving fields of corn on the hills and in the valleys of Fitchburgh. Nor did the birds, as they winged their way southward, sing sweeter farewell songs when this child was born whose maturer life was in such harmony with God. Perhaps the sun shone benignly on richly-laden orchards and fields white with the frosts of autumn, as the news spread from farm to farm that a child had been born and a household had been blessed. For those were days when children were welcomed. There was room for them then. No edict of fashion forbade them. No stingy selfishness begrudged them a living. No fear of present poverty or coming want debarred them, but with a trust in God that was hearty, the sturdy pioneers greeted their new-born children.

The winter of 1803 found them with ten children. Theirs was a happy household of gay, rollicking children as ever clustered round a fireside. Thomas, the eldest son, had just passed his majority and was intending to enter the ministry. Asa had been boarding two years at Joseph Farwell's, learning his trade at Farwell's scythe shop on West street. He was a strong and robust fellow, and his frequent visits home "to see mother" were jovial seasons as such natures might make them. While Mrs. Thurston lived, her house was a favorite resort for all the young people of the neighborhood. The Eaton family, who lived where Daniel Eaton now resides, were particular friends. The two families were alike in many respects. Both of buoyant spirits, fond of music, companionable, and ranging about equal ages, there grew a bond of sympathy and friendship between them which ripened and deepened with the years.

There were playmates from other households, boys for the boys to visit, and girls for the girls to visit, and we may be pardoned, perhaps, for guessing that laughing blue eyes and black had mutual attractions, sometimes unspoken. It is convenient often for brothers to have sisters, and sisters to have brothers, else the bashful minority of humankind might fare worse than it does. Many a trembling fellow has been enabled to carry on the first half of his courting successfully under the excuse of going to see "her brother;" and likewise a diffident, shrinking girl is made bolder because "his sister" gave the invitation.

Mr. Thurston apprenticed Asa and Cyrus, for seven years, as soon as the youths reached fourteen, to learn the scythe-maker's trade of John and Joseph Farwell.

The house seen to-day on the Thurston farm bears but slight re-

semblance to the original. Instead of the contracted dwelling that sheltered the family of twelve within its clapboardless sides and around its enormous fireplace, an addition has enlarged it to nearly twice its former size. The old-fashioned glass still remains in the windows and two generous chimneys peer above the roof. The front door has been moved to the west, but the ancient door rock, around which the children played eighty years ago, still marks the place of its former usefulness.

That rural simplicity which characterized the early homes of New England was found in Thomas Thurston's humble domicile. It is true there were singing books and a violin, but the Bible and Pilgrim's Progress were usually the extent of literature, and, indeed, the singing books and violin might be called as much a luxury then as a piano is to-day. But the home was brightened by the advent of little ones, and merry voices cheered what otherwise would have been a less attractive fireside. Lydia presided in the house with true womanly dignity, and her cares and duties grew and multiplied as the years rolled on.

Rev. John Payson, the minister, in his usual round of visits, found a welcome to their hospitality, and when he called, the old-fashioned courtesy of a mug of the best flip was ready for his lips. The conversation often turned, with his choir leader, upon church music, and sometimes upon the innovations which were sought to be introduced, in singing, in the house of the Lord. It was during the year 1787 that the decision, considered so important as to convulse the town, in regard to deaconing the hymns, was settled in town meeting by compromise. A committee chosen for the purpose reported, and the town accepted the report, "that there shall be singing five times in the worshiping on the Lord's day, and three times the hymn shall be sung without reading." As we look back upon the petty differences which caused such bitter animosities, we little think the questions with which we grapple, and over which we quarrel, will seem as childish to those who come after us. In the light of intervening years they doubtless will. Children:

1343  Thomas,[6] b. Aug. 23, 1781; n.m.; d. Feb. 15, 1806.
1344  Hannah,[6] b. Sept. 27, 1782; m. Jan. 7, 1802, Dea. John Farwell of Fitchburgh, b. March 23, 1775, son of Dea. John and Sarah (Hovey) Farwell of Groton, Mass. They were both members of the Congregational church. He was a scythe manufacturer in Fitchburgh, and died Dec. 24, 1855; she died Oct. 8, 1856. Children:
1345  *John Thurston* (Farwell), b. Jan. 22, 1803; m. 1st, Aug., 1823, Elizabeth H. Holden, b. March 15, 1800, d. Nov. 28, 1828; 2d, Feb. 18, 1830, Mersilvia Todd, b. Nov. 14, 1800. John T. Farwell was a scythe manufacturer in Fitchburgh; chosen deacon of the Congregational church Nov. 9, 1833, and held the office until his death; town clerk several years; a man of sterling integrity. His children:
1346  *Elizabeth Hannah* (Farwell), b. Dec., 1825; d. Jan. 25, 1831.
1347  *Elizabeth Mersilvia* (Farwell), b. July 2, 1831; m. Sept. 24, 1857, Charles H. Merrill of Cambridge, Mass., a farmer in Fitchburgh.
1348  *John A.* (Farwell), b. Sept. 3, 1833; m. Oct. 28, 1869, Ava M. Chambers; is now, 1877, comptroller of Chicago, Ill.
1349  *Sarah C.* (Farwell), b. May 31, 1836; m. Oct. 4, 1855, Joseph M. Barney of Brimfield, Ill., a farmer in Erie, Kansas.
1350  *Maria Thurston* (Farwell), b. July 11, 1838; m. Oct. 27, 1859, Charles A. Sullivan, a lawyer in Starkville, Oktibbeha Co., Miss.
1351  *Mary Jane* (Farwell), b. July 12, 1840; d. Aug. 29, 1841.

1352    *Edward P.* (Farwell), b. Oct. 24, 1843; enlisted in the Union
        army, and died at Port Hudson, La., July 19, 1863.
1353    *Jane Todd* (Farwell), b. Dec. 4, 1846; m. Nov. 26, 1873, Edward
        P. Downs, secretary Mutual Insurance Company of Fitchburgh.
1354    *Stephen Thurston* (Farwell), b. June 21, 1805; m. 1834, Elizabeth Carle-
        ton Todd of Rindge, N. H.  He was a merchant in Cambridge,
        Mass. ; in 1837 chosen deacon of the Shepard Congregational church,
        Cambridge, and continued thirty-five years, till his death, Oct. 20,
        1872.  He was a man greatly beloved, and held important trusts of
        a public and private nature; was member of the legislature several
        years.
1355    *Lydia Elizabeth Thurston* (Farwell), b. Nov. 15, 1807.
1356    *Thomas Thurston* (Farwell), b. Sept. 11, 1809.
1357    *Hannah* (Farwell), b. Dec. 24, 1812.
1358    *Sarah* (Farwell), b. Jan. 13, 1814; d. May 25, 1823.
1359    *Matilda B.* (Farwell), b. May 3, 1816.
1360    *Asa Thurston* (Farwell), b. May 13, 1818.
1361    *Mehitable W.* (Farwell), b. Aug. 21, 1820; d. June 19, 1821.
1362    Elizabeth,[6] b. Sept. 16, 1785; n.m.; d. Feb. 28, 1806.
+1363   Asa,[6] b. Oct. 12, 1787; m. Lucy Goodale.
+1364   Ebenezer,[6] b. Nov. 25, 1789; m. Lydia Sawyer.
1365    Polly,[6] b. May 16, 1792; n.m.; d. Nov. 1, 1818.
+1366   Cyrus,[6] b. May 20, 1796; m. Caroline Boutelle.
1367    Sylvania,[6] b. Feb. 13, 1798; m. Oct. 2, 1823, George S. Messenger of
        Chelmsford, Mass., a farmer in Fitchburgh.  They had :
    1368    *Elizabeth* (Messenger).
    1369    *Caroline* (Messenger).
1370    Mahala,[6] b. June 5, 1801; m. April 16, 1823, Thomas Hale, a wheelwright
        in Fitchburgh.  They had:
    1371    *Elizabeth Thurston* (Hale), b. Nov. 1, 1825.
    1372    *Thomas Thurston* (Hale), b. March 4, 1828.
    1373    *Augustus S.* (Hale), b. Feb. 12, 1839; d. Nov. 8, 1840.
1374    Maria,[6] b. Sept. 9, 1803; m. Oct. 2, 1823, Augustus H. Searle of Westford,
        Mass., a scythe maker in Fitchburgh; she d. July 19, 1831.  They had :
    1375    *Augusta Maria* (Searle), b. July 22, 1824; d. Oct. 12, 1825.
    1376    *Augusta Maria* (Searle), b. Oct. 20, 1825; d. Sept. 26, 1828.
    1377    *Ellen Eliza* (Searle), b. July 17, 1827.

## 385

DEA. JOHN THURSTON [5] (*Dea. John,*[4] *Jonathan,*[8] *Daniel,*[2] *Daniel*[1]),
brother of the preceding, and son of John [4] and Hepzibah (Burpee)
Thurston of Rowley, now Georgetown, Mass. ; born there 1757; married, Aug. 2, 1782, ESTHER WOOD of Fitchburgh, Mass.  She died
July 22, 1801, aged 44; he died April 28, 1814, aged 57.

Mr. Thurston came to Fitchburgh with his father and succeeded
him in carrying on the place.  He was a deacon in the Congregational church, as was his father before him.  He was a man of
considerable influence in church and town affairs, and his name frequently appears in ecclesiastical and political records; was selectman
several years.  Their children were :

1384    Sally,[6] b. Apr. 5, 1783; m. Samuel Philips, a farmer in Fitchburgh, and had :
    1385    *Sally* (Philips), m. Charles Russell and had three children.
    1386    *Ivers* (Philips), became a colonel, a prominent business man, and dep-
            uty sheriff of Worcester county.  He had a family of five children,
            some of them holding offices of trust in the city and influential
            members of the church.
+1387   Jonathan,[6] b. May 8, 1785; m. Abigail Allen.
+1388   Susan,[6] b. Aug. 4, 1787; m. Joseph Upton.
1389    John,[6] b. July 6, 1789; m. April 4, 1815, Roxa Gerould, b. March 17, 1791,
        daughter of Samuel and Arubah (Thompson) Gerould of Stoddard, N.
        H., and sister of Rev. Moses Gerould of Goffstown, N. H., 1878.  Mr.

Thurston was a farmer and resided in Fitchburgh, Mass., Walpole and Gilsum, N. H., where he engaged in a woolen manufactory with his brother-in-law, Lyman Gerould. He died Nov. 17, 1838. They had five children, all of whom died in infancy. She afterward married and moved to Northampton, Mass., where she died, Feb. 20, 1870.

+1390 Abel,[6] b. Dec. 24, 1791; m. 1st, Eunice Allen; 2d, Deborah Butler.
1391 Clarissa,[6] b. Oct. 10, 1794; m. Joseph Low, a farmer in Fitchburgh; had:
    1392 *Caroline* (Low).
    1393 *Frances* (Low).
1394 Nancy,[6] b. Aug. 10, 1797; m. Asa Sawyer and had a daughter.
1395 Martha,[6] } twins, born } d. in infancy.
1396 Mary,[6]    } July 8, 1801; } m. John Coleman, a farmer in Ashby, Mass., and had *Mary, John, Edward, Samuel* (Coleman), and one other child.
1397 Daniel,[6] b. March 10, 1804; d. in infancy.

## 386

STEPHEN THURSTON[5] (*Dea. John,[4] Jonathan,[3] Daniel,[2] Daniel[1]*), brother of the preceding, and son of Dea. John[4] and Hepzibah (Burpee) Thurston of Rowley, Mass.; married (published Aug. 10, 1787) MARY OSGOOD of Lancaster, Mass. He died March 15, 1805; she died June 17, 1811.

Mr. Thurston was a farmer in Fitchburgh, Mass. He was a soldier in the revolutionary war, and in 1781 the town voted to give his father one hundred and six bushels of corn for his son's services in the continental army. While laboring under temporary insanity he hung himself in the woods near his house.

### Children, all born in Fitchburgh:

+1409 John,[6] b. Sept. 24, 1788; m. Elizabeth Dascomb.
1410 Susanna Osgood,[6] b. Dec. 2, 1789; m. Jabez Sawyer, a shoemaker in Fitchburgh; d. March 18, 1858. Children:
    1411 *Samuel Thurston* (Sawyer), b. Dec. 22, 1819; n.m.; d. Jan. 6, 1843.
    1412 *Mary Osgood* (Sawyer), b. Dec. 3, 1821; m. George Litchfield; d. Oct. 9, 1846, in Fitchburgh.
    1413 *John* (Sawyer), b. Oct. 5, 1824; n.m.; d. March 16, 1852.
1414 Samuel,[6] b. Dec. 4, 1791; n.m.; d. Jan. 11, 1815, in Fitchburgh.
1415 Mary,[6] b. Sept. 27, 1794; d. Sept. 7, 1796, in Fitchburgh.
1416 Nathiel.[6] b. June 23, 1797; m. March 31, 1847, Mrs. Sarah R. (King) Brown, b. in Wilton, N. H., Feb. 4, 1797. He was a carpenter, worked at farming summers and taught school winters; lived in Fitchburgh, Mass., Mt. Morris, N. Y., Lowell, Mass., where he was deacon of a church, and in Wilton, N. H., where he died, April 3, 1874.

## 401

REV. PEARSON THURSTON[5] (*Samuel,[4] Jonathan,[3] Daniel,[2] Daniel[1]*), son of Samuel[4] and Priscilla (Burpee) Thurston of Lancaster, Mass.; born there Dec. 9, 1763; married, 1794, JERUSHA GREENLEAF, born 1765, daughter of Samuel and Ann (Bradbury) Greenleaf (who were married May 17, 1749, she being eighteen years old) of Newburyport, Mass. Jerusha was a member of the Congregational church under the pastoral care of Rev. Samuel Spring, D.D., the father of Rev. Gardiner Spring, D.D., of New York city. She was an active christian, and retained her mental faculties and usefulness to the day of her death, which occurred suddenly at Amherst, Mass., Dec. 10, 1834, to which place she removed three years previously. He died in Leominster, Mass., Aug. 15, 1819.

Pearson Thurston graduated at Dartmouth 1787, and studied theology with Rev. Nathaniel Emmons, D.D., the celebrated Hopkinsian

theologian of Franklin, Mass., and with Rev. Samuel Spring, D.D., of Newburyport, Mass.  He was ordained in Somersworth, N. H., Feb. 1, 1792, with a salary of $400 a year.  He built a house there, thinking, as most Congregational clergymen of that day did, that he was settled for life ; but in the extremely severe winter of 1812, in the absence of his wife, his house, out-buildings, furniture, and everything was burned, the family not even saving a suit of clothes each.  The night was so cold that not a bucket of water could be obtained in the village.  He always regarded it as a wonderfully kind providence that not a life was lost.  The people were too poor to assist him to rebuild, and he was commissioned by the Massachusetts Home Missionary Society a missionary, with his field of labor first at Norway and then at Limerick, the then district of Maine.  He obtained a temporary home for his family and removed them there, his wife preferring to share his privations and toils as a missionary rather than to remain in comfort among her friends.  After laboring in Maine about three years he was assigned to St. Johnsbury, Vt., where he went, leaving his family in Limerick.  Here was extended to him a unanimous call from the first Congregational church in St. Johnsbury, and then the only one in the region, to become their pastor, which he accepted, removing his family again, hoping for a permanent place of rest and of labor for the Master.  He continued there, and doing missionary work for miles around, until his health utterly failed on account of the extra labor required by the scattered population, the scarcity of co-laborers, and the loss of his library and all the sermons accumulated during his former ministry.  He then took his son William from his medical studies, which he had pursued for a year, to travel with him on account of his health ; went to Boston and consulted eminent physicians, but to very little purpose.  Their universal advice was to leave both preaching and study, purchase a small farm, and without labor be out upon it as much as possible.  To this end he purchased a farm in Leominster, Mass., in connection with his son, and moved his family again, to be near his relatives.  He failed gradually and survived less than two years.  A contemporary says, " He was a faithful minister of the gospel for twenty-seven years and was taken from his labors by distressing illness.  Blessed are the dead that die in the Lord."  An obituary notice of Mrs. Jerusha Thurston, by one of the officers of Amherst college, says, " Dropsy on the chest is supposed to have caused a spasm of the heart, which extinguished life almost instantly and without warning.  Thus suddenly have four of the family been cut down by the angel of death.  She apprehended such a termination of her life, and frequently spoke of it to her family with a manifestation of feeling which indicated a happy preparation for the promised Canaan above.  She had in health and in youth devoted herself to the Saviour, and had long been an active laborer in his vineyard.  Faith had disarmed the king of terrors.  A most affectionate disposition, sanctified by holy love, made her a kind and beloved parent, an amiable and valued friend, and commended her to all."

Their children, born in Somersworth, N. H., were:

+1424   William Parsons,[6] b. 1795; m. Mary Gardner.
1424a  Elizabeth Parsons,[6] b. 1797; d. Sept. 3, 1803.
425    Anna Mary,[6] b. 1798; d. Sept. 5, 1803.

1426　Judith Sawyer,[6] b. Sept. 4, 1800; n.m.
1427　Eunice Greenleaf,[6] b. Oct. 9, 1805; n.m.; d. in Virginia Sept. 28, 1862, and was buried in Leominster.
1428　Elizabeth Ann,[6] b. May 3, 1810; n.m.; she and her sisters Judith and Eunice were educated for teachers, and continued with their mother till her death, when they went to Virginia and established a school for young ladies, where they continued more than twenty-five years, burying one of their number in the meantime, and returned to North Leominster about three months before the close of the war in 1865, losing every dollar of their savings except the avails of furniture sold on leaving.
There were three other children, died in infancy.

## 426

DAVID THURSTON [5] (*David,*[4] *Jonathan,*[3] *Daniel,*[2] *Daniel*[1]), second son of David [4] and Eunice (Whitney) Thurston of Marlborough, N. H.; born in Leominster, Mass., Oct. 17, 1768; married, 1808, FANNY DARLING, born Dec. 27, 1788, daughter of Rev. David and Esther (Metcalf) Darling of Keene, N. H. David Darling was born in Wrentham, Mass., Sept. 14, 1753. He pursued a collegiate course in Brown university, Providence, R. I. His class was ready to graduate when the British took the place and used the college buildings for barracks. The president of Yale invited the president of Brown to graduate his class there, which invitation was accepted. He afterward became the pastor of the Congregational church in Keene. Esther Metcalf, born Nov. 3, 1761, was a highly educated woman. Being associated with the college faculty she took the college course, and was prepared and ought to have graduated with the class, but was debarred from doing so by the customs of the times.

Mr. Thurston moved to Owego, N. Y., about 1812. He was a farmer, and died there Jan. 6, 1858; she died June 3, 1860. His daughter Mary Almeda says, "my father was a man of more than ordinary intelligence, a great reader, in physique faultless, tall, well-built, vigorous, and in perfect health till past the age of 70. Though unfortunate financially, he was an honest man, a good father, and a christian. He and my mother were among the seven who united to form the first Methodist church in Owego. My mother was a superior woman, endowed with a superior mind; and though her early advantages were limited, yet amid all her cares she never ceased her efforts for improvement, by reading, writing, etc., and her poetry has frequently graced the village papers. Her days were filled with usefulness, and she died respected by all who knew her. The children are all good looking, good sized, wide awake, and it may be with aim in life too high to hit, but we are trying to make our mark."

Their children, born in Marlborough, N. H., were:

1439　Fanny,[6] b. June 27, 1809; m. 1828, Prentice Ransom, and reside in Iowa City, Iowa.
1440　Nancy,[6] b. Dec. 4, 1812; d. May 9, 1814.

Born in Owego, N. Y.:

1441　Nancy Darling,[6] b. March 24, 1814; a graduate of Cazenovia seminary. N. Y.; taught school many years in New York, Mississippi. and Mobile, Ala., where she married, Feb. 6, 1864, Drury Thompson, b. in Augusta, Ga., a grandson of Gen. Elijah Clark of revolutionary history. He took part in the war of the rebellion, though he had emancipated his slaves long before. He died July 12, 1873.

+1442  George Waldo,[6] b. April 19, 1816; m. Mary Ann Collins.
+1443  David Whitney,[6] b. April 8, 1818; m. Elizabeth S. Bowen.
 1444  John Metcalf,[6] b. Oct. 16, 1820; m. 1st, 1850, Sarah Wood; 2d, Persis
        Wight; had one child by each, who died in infancy. He resides in
        Utica, N. Y.
 1445  Mary Almeda,[6] b. Feb. 10, 1823; m. 1st, Jan. 5, 1843, Anson Garrison of
        Cold Spring, N. Y. He was foreman in an iron foundry in Owego;
        died by the hand of an assassin Feb. 2, 1850; 2d, Jan. 28, 1878, Rev.
        Benjamin Pomeroy, b. in Williamsburgh, Mass., April 27, 1808; of the
        Troy (N. Y.) Conference, a speaker and writer of originality and power,
        who has published many of his thoughts in book and pamphlet form.
        After the death of her first husband she taught school in Utica, N. Y.,
        and from there took charge of the art department in the Cazenovia sem-
        inary for several years; then opened a painting studio in Syracuse, giv-
        ing instruction, etc., till 1871, when she commenced the study of medicine.
        In 1872 she entered the college for women in New York, taking a three
        years' course, spending two years there and one in the medical universi-
        ty in Boston, from which she graduated in 1875. She practiced medi-
        cine in Syracuse for a while, and is now, 1879, practicing in Albany, N.
        Y. She had:
 1446   *Fanny Elizabeth* (Garrison), b. Jan. 24, 1845; m. Jan. 28, 1861, Mel-
        ville E. Dayton of Clinton, N. Y., a graduate of Hamilton universi-
        ty; he is practicing in Chicago, Ill., as a solicitor of patents and
        expert in patent suits: three children.
 1447  James Sidney,[6] b. Oct. 14, 1825; m. Sept. 3, 1850, Phebe Ann Van Ben-
        schoten, b. May 9, 1829. He was a merchant till 1862, then quarter-
        master of the 107th New York regiment in the war against the rebellion
        one year; promoted to paymaster in 1863, till some months after the
        war; then banker and manufacturer till 1875, since which time has been
        business manager of the Binghamton (N. Y.) Publishing Company;
        votes the republican ticket straight, and attends the Methodist church.
        They have:
 1448   *Mary Elizabeth*,[7] b. Oct. 31, 1852; m. June 26, 1878, Edward Morris
        Ames, b. Oct. 17, 1855, son of George and Lucy A. Ames of South
        Killingly, Ct.
 1449   *Emma Louise*,[7] b. Feb. 11, 1857.
 1450   *James Sidney*,[7] b. Nov. 8, 1861; d. July 29, 1862.
 1451   *Charles Whitney*,[7] b. Oct. 15, 1865; d. Nov. 7, 1875.

## 427

LEVI THURSTON [5] (*David*,[4] *Jonathan*,[3] *Daniel*,[2] *Daniel*[1]), brother of
the preceding, and son of David [4] and Eunice (Whitney) Thurston of
Marlborough, N. H.; born in Leominster, Mass., June 1, 1770; married ABIGAIL NEWTON, born in Brookfield, Mass., Oct. 11, 1777. She
died March 11, 1861, aged 83; he died Aug. 20, 1861, aged 91.

He was a farmer in Keene, N. H., Binghamton, N. Y., and Nichols, Tioga county, N. Y., where he was crippled by rheumatism for
many years and found a home and care with his daughter Maria. He
was a member of the Methodist church.

Their children were:

 1462  Maria,[6] b. in Keene, N. H., May 19, 1797; m. Nov. 24, 1818, in Owego,
        N. Y., Daniel McDaniel Shoemaker, b. in Stroudsburgh, Pa., Feb. 24,
        1795. He was a farmer in Nichols, N. Y., and died Nov. 26, 1873; she
        died Dec. 26, 1874. They were both earnest and efficient workers in the
        Methodist church. He was steward and clerk of the board of trustees
        of the Asbury Methodist church forty years, whose meeting-house he
        was the chief mover in building in 1824. His daughter Elizabeth writes,
        "this was the Methodist itinerants' home. The first quarterly-meeting
        was held in their corn-house, where sixty dined and forty staid the night.
        Going thirty miles in a big wagon or on horseback to attend such meet-
        ings was common in those days. With the hard work of spinning for

the manufacture of all sheets and wearing apparel, the scouring of floors, etc., it is no wonder our mother became an invalid. With right care she might have lived a hundred years." They had:

1463　*Hiram W.* (Shoemaker), b. Feb. 5, 1819; m. Oct. 25, 1850, Ellen H. Schott; was sheriff of Tioga county four years, and has been express messenger and mail agent, gaining credit to himself in all positions he has held.

1464　*Elizabeth N.* (Shoemaker), b. June 21, 1821; been a teacher twenty years in various places, and now, 1878, lives on a part of the old farm in Nichols, where "she will at any time be pleased to see any branch of the Thurston family."

1465　*Horace Agard* (Shoemaker), b. Feb. 22, 1831; a farmer in Nichols; m. and has two sons and one daughter.

1466　*Lyman Thurston* (Shoemaker), b. Jan. 22, 1833; a railroad engineer; lived in Port Jervis, N. Y., and died Feb. 13, 1875; two daughters.

1467　Hubbard,[6] b. in Surry, N. H., Feb. 20, 1800; m. and d. in Indiana, where his daughter Anna resides; daughters Maria and Amy live near Williamsport, Pa.

1468　Hartwell,[6] b. in Alstead, N. H., Feb. 16, 1802; d. in Wyoming, Ill., Nov. 17, 1845.

1469　Luman,[6] b. in Orange, N. H., April 6, 1804; lived in Wyoming, Ill., and after went to Minnesota with his family.

1470　David,[6] b. in Canaan, N. H.; is a carpenter in Waverly, N. Y.; m. March, 1827, Mary B. Smith, b. in Smithburgh, N. J., March 3, 1800, daughter of James and Betsey (Bowman) Smith; she died in Bradford county, Pa., 1842. They had:

1471　*Daniel Wallace,*[7] b. in Bradford county, Pa., Sept. 28, 1842.

1472　Clark,[6] b. in Canaan, N. H., Feb. 10, 1810; went to Pennsylvania and has not been heard from.

1473　Malvina,[6] b. in Canaan, N. H., Oct. 14, 1813; d. March 3, 1815.

1474　Eliza,[6] b. in Owego, N. Y., Dec. 19, 1815; m. and had two children; all dead.

1475　Hannah,[6] b. in Berkshire, N. Y., May 28, 1818; m.

## 428

JOHN THURSTON[5] (*David,*[4] *Jonathan,*[3] *Daniel,*[2] *Daniel*[1]), brother of the preceding, and son of David[4] and Eunice (Whitney) Thurston of Marlborough, N. H.; born in Leominster, Mass., Jan. 21, 1772; married, Nov. 4, 1801, LYDIA BALL, born in Holden, Mass., Dec. 26, 1775, daughter of Daniel and Lydia (Smith) Ball of Princeton, Mass. He died July 31, 1843; she died in Hinsdale, N. H., April 29, 1847. Mr. Thurston was a farmer in Keene, N. H.; was in the war of 1812.

Children:

+1487　Leland,[6] b. in Windham, Vt., May 29, 1803; m. Margaret Hutchins.
+1488　Roswell,[6] b. in Marlborough, N. H., Oct. 22, 1807; m. Frances Cummings.
+1489　Emily,[6] b. in Marlborough March 8, 1810; m. Melvin Starkey.
1490　Miranda,[6] b. in Northfield, Mass., Sept. 19, 1813; m. E. Marsh of Montague, Mass.; lived with him a few months; had one child, which died at the age of two years; she had her name changed back to Thurston and is living, a single woman, in Hinsdale, N. H.
+1491　Wesson,[6] b. in Northfield Nov. 4, 1816; m. Harriet Scott.

## 429

SAMUEL THURSTON[5] (*David,*[4] *Jonathan,*[3] *Daniel,*[2] *Daniel*[1]), brother of the preceding, and son of David[4] and Eunice (Whitney) Thurston of Marlborough, N. H.; born there Aug. 16, 1775; married, Jan. 1, 1800, SALLY FRENCH, born in Chelmsford, Mass., March 9, 1776, daughter of Joseph and Bridget (Farrar) French of Jaffrey, N. H. She died March 2, 1839, aged 63; he died Dec. 23, 1873, aged 98 years, 4 months, 7 days.

He was a farmer and school teacher in New Alstead, N. H. He taught eighteen terms of school, eight in one district. When he was a boy he says he has lain in bed and heard the yelling of the cata-mounts and the howling of the wolves, and in the morning, after a light snow, has tracked the wolves all about the house and barn, even to looking into the windows of the sheep hovel.

### Children :

1502   Louisa,[6] b. Dec. 16, 1800; m. Timothy Dort; d. Nov. 6, 1835.   They had:
   1503   *Sarah French* (Dort), b. March 23, 1819; m. March 20, 1842, Levi Mansfield, a farmer in Gilsum, N. H.; four children.
   1504   *Hattie Maria* (Dort), m. Edward Elisha Roundy; live in Fitzwilliam, N. H.; three children.
   1505   *Helen Louisa* (Dort), m. John Isham; live in Gilsum.
   1506   *Ausian Mansfield* (Dort), m. Jennie Knight; live in Fitzwilliam; one child.
   1507   *Joseph Hartley* (Dort), b. Jan. 14, 1828; m. May, 1851, Sabrina H. Mack Hay; four children.
   1508   *Mary Louisa* (Dort), b. Oct. 4, 1831; m. May 27, 1850, Claudius B. Hayward, a farmer in Gilsum; six children.
1509   James Gilman,[6] b. Oct. 8, 1802; d. April 17, 1804.
+1510   Joseph,[6] b. May 30, 1804; m. Betsey Brown.
+1511   Hartley,[6] b. March 3, 1806; m. Arminda Robinson.
+1512   Alden Spooner,[6] b. Sept. 12, 1809; m. Esther Adeline Miller.
+1513   Franklin Robinson,[6] b. Jan. 22, 1815; m. Fanny Louisa Holman.

## 430

JASON THURSTON [5] (*David,*[4] *Jonathan,*[3] *Daniel,*[2] *Daniel*[1]), brother of the preceding, and son of David[4] and Eunice (Whitney) Thurston of Marlborough, N. H.; born there Jan. 23, 1777; married MRS. LYDIA (PALMER) ROLLINS, born Sept. 9, 1778. He died March 7, 1862, aged 85; she died July, 1870, aged 92.

Mr. Thurston was a ship carpenter, and went to Damariscotta, then called Nobleborough, Me., in 1804 or 1805. He was a very faithful member of the Alna lodge of Free Masons.

### Their children were :

1525   Elizabeth Palmer,[6] b. Nov. 18, 1810; m. March 15, 1835, Tilden Hall, a blacksmith in Damariscotta, b. Sept. 16, 1806, son of Thomas and Anna (Vannah) Hall of Nobleborough.   They had:
   1526   *Augustus* (Hall), b. March 30, 1841; enlisted in the 21st Maine regiment against the rebellion; went to New Orleans, was taken sick, and died in the hospital at Baton Rouge, La., July 20, 1863; a noble young man, the idol of the family.
   1527   *Anna Elizabeth* (Hall), b. Sept. 13, 1844.
1528   Jerusha Rollins,[6] b. in Newcastle, Me., June 1, 1813; m. Feb. 15, 1838, Joseph Teague, a ship ironer of Damariscotta, b. July 23, 1812, son of Joseph and Eleanor (Hussey) Teague of Newcastle.   They had:
   1529   *Orlando* (Teague), b. Dec. 10, 1838; d. Sept. 21, 1846.
   1530   *Lizzie Hall* (Teague), b. April 8, 1842; m. Sept. 3, 1867, Capt. W. A. Woodard.
   1531   *Georgie Day* (Teague), b. Feb. 4, 1848; m. July 12, 1870, Horace N. Hatch, a merchant in South Boston, Mass.
   1532   *Ida Eudora* (Teague), b. May 18, 1850.
   1533   *Joseph* (Teague), b. Sept. 9, 1856; a merchant in Damariscotta.

## 500

SUSANNAH THURSTON [5] (*Daniel,*[4] *Richard,*[3] *Daniel,*[2] *Daniel*[1]), daughter of Daniel[4] and Judith (Chute) Thurston of Ipswich, Mass.; born Nov. 1, 1768; married, May 17, 1792, WILLIAM COLMAN, born Oct.

26, 1768. She died Oct. 8, 1808. He married, second, April 15, 1809, Zeruiah Temple; she died July 25, 1815; third, Jan. 12, 1816, Hannah Brown; she died August, 1843. He died May 23, 1820. Mr. Colman was a wheelwright in Byfield, Mass.

Her children were:

1544 Daniel Thurston (Colman), twin, b. March 5, 1793; m. Feb. 3, 1818, Nancy Harris; she died Sept. 13, 1872. They had:
    1545 *Charles Harris* (Colman), b. Feb. 8, 1819; m. Oct. 19, 1846, Deborah Long Dinsmore and had:
        1546 *Arthur Dinsmore* (Colman), b. May 8, 1849.
        1547 *Nellie Thurston* (Colman), b. July 2, 1853.
        1548 *Charles E.* (Colman), b. Feb. 1, 1856.
        1549 *Hattie B.* (Colman), b. Oct., 1862.
        1550 *Clara L.* (Colman).
    1551 *Ann Maria* (Colman), b. May 29, 1821.
    1552 *William Thurston* (Colman), b. Aug. 4, 1823; m. Sept. 26, 1848, Hannah B. Dinsmore: she died May 3, 1868. They had:
        1553 *Alice M.* (Colman), b. Aug. 7, 1850.
        1554 *Mary H.* (Colman), b. Aug. 20, 1856.
        1555 *George W.* (Colman), b. June 12, 1860.
        1556 *Hannah B.* (Colman), b. April 24, 1868.
    1557 *Daniel Thurston* (Colman), b. April 7, 1827; d. Dec. 6, 1832.
    1558 *Margaret Toppan* (Colman), b. Sept. 7, 1829; m. Sept. 3, 1855, Arthur Dinsmore and had:
        1559 *George S.* (Dinsmore), b. Jan. 28, 1857.
        1560 *Lucy Colman* (Dinsmore), b. Nov. 25, 1860.
        1561 *Frank Thurston* (Dinsmore), b. Jan. 18, 1862.
        1562 *Robert* (Dinsmore), b. Jan. 5, 1863; d. Feb., 1863.
        1563 *Louis* (Dinsmore), b. July 6, 1874.
    1564 *Lucy* (Colman), b. Oct. 26, 1831.
1565 Hannah Thurston (Colman), twin, b. March 5, 1793; m. 1814, Marshall French and had:
    1566 *Marshall* (French), b. 1815; d. aged 6 months.
    1567 *Susannah Thurston* (French), d.
    1568 *Sumner* (French), m. Eliza Faville and had:
        1569 *A daughter*, d. young.
        1570 *Sumner Faville* (French), b. 1854.
1571 Judith (Colman), b. March 7, 1795; m. 1824, Erastus Dean, b. in Bristol, Vt., May 13, 1798; d. at Dubuque, Iowa, March 3, 1852. They had:
    1572 *Sarah* (Dean), d. aged 2 years.
    1573 *James William* (Dean), b. in Lyons, N. Y., July 12, 1830; m. Oct. 7, 1861, Susan Brown and had:
        1574 *Chester Colman* (Dean), b. July 25, 1863.
        1575 *James Sumner* (Dean), b. Nov. 23, 1864.
        1576 *William Allen* (Dean), b. Sept. 26, 1867.
        1577 *Elmore Williams* (Dean), b. Sept. 24, 1869.
        1578 *Carrol Edward* (Dean), b. Jan. 17, 1874; d. Sept. 28, 1874.
        1579 *Susan Clara* (Dean), b. Dec. 18, 1876.
    1580 *Sarah Colman* (Dean), b. in Westfield, N. Y., April 20, 1832; m. April 7, 1852, N. M. Kelsey and had:
        1581 *James Munroe* (Kelsey), b. Aug. 16, 1854.
        1582 *Frank Chester* (Kelsey), b. May 23, 1858.
        1583 *Archibald Rodell* (Kelsey), b. June 16, 1862.
        1584 *Alice Cornelia* (Kelsey), b. April 28, 1866.
        1585 *Clara Dean* (Kelsey), b. Feb. 4, 1870.
        1586 *Sarah Malvina* (Kelsey), b. Sept. 24, 1873.
    1587 *Clarissa Thurston* (Dean), b. in Westfield Oct. 22, 1834; m. Oct. 12, 1853, Orville Wright and had:
        1588 *Clara Isabella* (Wright), b. Oct. 22, 1854.
        1589 *Sarah Ethilinda* (Wright), b. July 19, 1857; m. Feb. 14, 1877, George Wills.
1590 Dorothy (Colman), b. Jan. 29, 1797; m. in Providence, R. I., 1819, Phi-

lander Wilmarth, b. in Richmond, Vt., May 19, 1796, son of Rev. Ezra
and Mehitable (Cooper) Wilmarth of Georgetown, Mass. She died in
Brooklyn, N. Y., May 4, 1850; he died in New York March 4, 1861.
They had:

1591   *William Colman* (Wilmarth), b. Nov. 23, 1820; d. May 30, 1823.
1592   *Abel* (Wilmarth), d. soon.
1593   *Abel Cooper* (Wilmarth), b. July 25, 1822; m. Jane Dias; no children.
1594   *William Colman* (Wilmarth), b. July 26, 1825; m. Ann Brown and
       had William, d.; Rebecca; Ida, d.; Sumner (Wilmarth), d., and
       another son, d.
1595   *Susannah Thurston* (Wilmarth), b. May 12, 1827; m. June 13, 1849,
       Edwin Alexander Brooks, and had Emma, b. May 20, 1850; Ada, d.
       1873; Bell, d. 1864; Edwin (Brooks), b. Feb. 10, 1852.
1596   *Alonzo Henry* (Wilmarth), b. Oct. 8, 1837; drowned July 4, 1856, 18
       years of age.
1597 Sumner (Colman), b. Aug. 11, 1799; m. Oct. 26, 1826, Sophronia L. Hinck-
       ley; d. Dec. 12, 1864. They had:
1598   *Sumner O. Thurston* (Colman), b. Aug. 13, 1832; m. Sept. 10. 1855,
       Ann Newman, and had Harry Hudson, b. Nov. 14, 1859; Edwin
       Sumner, b. Nov. 4, 1863; Blanche Hinckley (Colman), b. March 11,
       1869; all living 1877.
1599 Betsey (Colman), b. June 18, 1801; d. April 29, 1803.
1600 Lucy (Colman), b. April 2, 1803; d. unmarried.
1601 Betsey (Colman), b. Sept. 26, 1805; d. Oct. 26, 1809.
1602 Mary (Colman), b. Feb. 16, 1807; m. Aug. 11, 1829, Stillman Moores, b.
       Dec. 20, 1805; he died May 16, 1865.   They had:
1603   *Mary B.* (Moores), b. Dec. 7, 1830; m. Dec. 24, 1874, Leonard Rog-
       ers, and had Hester Ann and Mary Jane (Rogers).
1604   *Jeremiah Colman* (Moores), b. Dec. 8, 1832; m. June, 1870, Hester
       Ann Alloway, and had William Henry, b. April 1, 1871, and Mary
       (Moores), b. Sept. 25, 1878.
1605   *Henry Martyn* (Moores), b. Sept. 25, 1834; d. April 11, 1869.
1606   *William Colman* (Moores), b. June 19, 1836; m. March 12, 1865, and
       had Mary Ellen, b. Jan. 9, 1866, d. June, 1866; William Henry, b.
       July 12, 1867; Mary Emma, b. March 13, 1871; a son, who died
       1875, and Benjamin Franklin (Moores), b. June 20, 1878.
1607   *Edward Payson* (Moores), b. June 7, 1838; d. Oct. 10, 1862.
1608   *Lucy Colman* (Moores), b. Oct. 5, 1840; m. June 5, 1856, John A.
       Kimble, and had :
1609     *Fanny Colman* (Kimble), b. Aug. 23, 1857; m. Sept. 10, 1875,
         Francis Hoyer, and had Francis and Martin (Hoyer), twins, b.
         Nov. 23, 1876.
1610     *Mary L.* (Kimble), b. Nov. 21, 1858; m. Dec. 25, 1874, Frederick
         Chapman, and had William (Chapman), b. Jan. 25, 1876.
1611     *Ellen M.* (Kimble), b. May 22, 1859; John E., b. March 12, 1861,
         d. July, 1874; William Colman, b. March 5, 1864; Lulu, b. Jan.
         5, 1867, d. 1867; a son, b. March 3, 1869, d. same day; Frank
         S., b. Aug. 5, 1871; Flora May, b. May 14, 1874; Lucy (Kimble),
         b. April 28, 1877.
1612   *Samuel Stillman* (Moores), b. Feb. 20, 1843; m. Jan., 1868, Mrs. Emma
       J. Williams, and had Eddie Lincoln, b. Nov. 3, 1868, and Emma
       (Moores), b. Sept. 23, 1873.
1613   *Hannah Thurston* (Moores), b. Aug. 15, 1845.
1614   *Daniel Thurston* (Moores), b. March 28, 1847; m. March 28, 1869,
       Mary Voadicie Clark, and had William Colman, b. March 23, 1870;
       Stella Winnifred, b. Aug. 25, 1874; Hattie (Moores), b. July 2, 1878,
       d. Jan. 19, 1879.

By second wife, Zeruiah:

1615 Luther (Colman), b. Feb. 1, 1810; d. March 21, 1854.
1616 Calvin (Colman), b. April 17, 1812; name changed to William; d. Feb. 20
       1864.
1617 David (Colman), b. July 3, 1814.

David Thurston

## 501

DEA. STEPHEN THURSTON [5] (*Daniel*,[4] *Richard*,[3] *Daniel*,[2] *Daniel*[1]), brother of the preceding, and son of Daniel [4] and Judith (Chute) Thurston of Ipswich, Mass.; born Jan. 2, 1770; married, first, June 26, 1794, PHILOMELA PARISH, born in Windham, Ct., Dec. 4, 1768. Her maternal grandmother was Hannah Foster, née Standish. Mrs. Thurston was only sister of Rev. Elijah Parish, D.D., of Byfield, Mass. Hannah Foster was great-granddaughter of Capt. Miles Standish of Plymouth colony. She died at Bedford, N. H., July 24, 1818. Second, April 14, 1821, SARAH BURGE, born at Hollis, N. H., May 20, 1777, and died in September, 1825. Third, Jan. 19, 1826, HANNAH WORCESTER,* born in Hollis March 17, 1783, daughter of Capt. Noah Worcester; she died at Elmira, N. Y., Dec. 28, 1871. He died of cholera at Bedford, N. H., Sept. 13, 1833.

Mr. Thurston was a farmer in Andover and Bedford, Mass., Goffstown and Bedford, N. H.; deacon and elder in the Presbyterian church, the organizer of the first Sunday-school in Bedford, as well as the first temperance society; a strictly conscientious man.

His children, by first wife, Philomela, were:

+1624    Philomela,[6] b. in Rowley, Mass., April 11, 1795; m. Rev. Samuel Newell.
1625    Delia,[6] b. in Rowley Dec. 21, 1796; n.m.; d. at Bedford, N. H., Sept. 24, 1823.
1626    Clarissa,[6] b. in Andover, Mass., Feb. 26, 1801; has been a teacher of repute for over forty years; has taught in six different states; beside being an author.
1627    Lucinda,[6] b. in Bedford, Mass., July 21, 1805; d. in Bedford March 23, 1806.
1628    Mary Colman,[6] b. in Bedford Sept. 23, 1806; d. in Putnam county, Ga., July 23, 1825.
+1629    Ariel Standish,[6] b. in Goffstown, N. H., June 11, 1810; m. 1st, Julia Clark Hart; 2d, Cornelia Sophia Hull; 3d, Georgiana Gibson.

By third wife, Hannah:

1630    Mary Delia,[6] b. at Bedford Feb. 28, 1827; n.m.; d. at Elmira, N. Y., Aug. 23, 1866. She was beloved by all who knew her.

## 540

REV. DAVID THURSTON [5] of Winthrop, Me. (*David*,[4] *Richard*,[3] *Daniel*,[2] *Daniel*[1]), eldest son of David [4] and Mary (Bacon) Thurston of Sedgwick, Me.; born in New Rowley, Mass., Feb. 6, 1779; baptized by Rev. James Chandler; married, first, Dec., 26, 1808, EUNICE FAR-

* She was the last survivor of seventeen children of Noah Worcester, who died at Hollis, N. H., in 1817, at the age of eighty-two. She sprung from a stern Puritan ancestry, being the sixth in descent from William Worcester, who emigrated from England to Essex county, Mass., about the year 1638, and among whose descendants are enrolled some of the most eminent names that have graced the annals of American biography. Noah Worcester, the father, was a captain in the revolutionary army and marched at the head of a company in the winter of 1775-6 to reinforce Washington at Cambridge. For forty years he was a magistrate in his native town of Hollis, and was a member of the convention which formed the constitution of New Hampshire. Her two elder brothers enlisted in the continental army at the ages respectively of fifteen and sixteen years. The elder participated in the battles of Bennington and Bunker Hill, and the younger accompanied the expedition to Ticonderoga. Upon the return of peace one of these brothers became a farmer at the paternal homestead in Hollis—still held by one of his descendants—and the elder of the two and three more became, and for long years were, pastors of churches in New Hampshire, and were men eminent in letters and distinguished for learning and piety.

Mrs. Ireland having lost two husbands, the former Stephen Thurston of Bedford, N. H., and the latter Jonathan Ireland of Dunbarton, N. H., made Elmira her permanent place of residence in the fall of 1855, residing with her only child and her step-children, Clara and Ariel S. Thurston, with the latter of whom she was living at the time of her decease.

Naturally of a retiring disposition, she was only known to her intimate friends. They can bear testimony to her shining character as a woman and a christian. No poor encomiums that we can pass upon her life can come up to the full and complete measure of her worth. What her hand found to do in acts of christian benevolence and kindness she did.

LEY, born Feb. 15, 1787, daughter of Hon. John Farley of Newcastle, Me. They were married by Rev. Kiah Bailey, the Congregational clergyman of Newcastle. She was a lady of great beauty of person and refinement of character. She died April 21, 1809, only four months after marriage, aged 22 y. 2 m. 5 d. Her father was a tanner and large farmer, a man of social standing and influence. He was town treasurer thirty-one years, twice chosen county treasurer, fourteen times elected representative to Massachusetts legislature, one term in the senate of Maine, presidential elector in 1804, postmaster until his death in 1812. Second, Oct. 31, 1811, PRUDENCE BROWN, born April 3, 1786, daughter of Benjamin and Prudence (Kelley) Brown * of Chester, N. H. She died at her daughter's in West Springfield, Mass., May 28, 1871, aged 85 years. Rev. David Thurston died at Litchfield Corner, Me., May 7, 1865, aged 86 years.

Mrs. Thurston was a lady of great efficiency and decision of character; possessing energy, fervent piety, and a wonderful equability of temper. Her administrative qualities were marked by an undefinable quiet influence, which created an enthusiasm in all with whom she labored. She did very much to promote thrift and forethought in the members of her household, and also a self-sacrificing spirit of benevolence in them and in the parish. She acted upon the principle, and inculcated it in others, that what is given without sacrifice is hardly true benevolence, and therefore, to make up a purse for some benevolent or missionary object, she would interest the members of her family to go without tea, sugar or coffee, and thus save the cost of such articles for the object in hand. In this way the true spirit of benevolence was implanted, which grew into a habit, to be practiced through life in many cases.

---

* BROWN FAMILY.

I. THOMAS BROWNE, weaver, of Malford, Eng., and his wife Mary sailed in the "James" of London, 300 tons, about April 6, 1635, and came to Newbury, Mass. He died Jan. 8, 1687, aged 80. They had FRANCIS; Mary, b. 1636, the first white child born in Newbury; Isaac, b. 1638.

II. FRANCIS BROWNE, born 1632; married, first, Mary Johnson; second, Mary Rogers. He had, by first wife, Elizabeth, Mary, Hannah, Sarah, JOHN, Thomas, Joseph, Francis; by second wife, Benjamin.

III. JOHN BROWNE, born 1665; married Ruth Huse and had John, Isaac, THOMAS, Joseph, Ruth, Abel.

IV. THOMAS BROWNE, born Jan. 1, 1689; married Ann Cheney and had FRANCIS, Anne, died young, John, Anne, Daniel, Ruth.

V. FRANCIS BROWNE, born Nov. 14, 1716; married, May 5, 1741, Mercy Lowell, and had Anne, Molly, Thomas, Ruth, Mercy, BENJAMIN, Francis, John.

VI. BENJAMIN BROWN, born Oct. 14, 1755; married, first, Feb. 2, 1776, Prudence Kelley, born April 17, 1753; she died Sept. 9, 1798; second, Mary Lunt, born July 27, 1753; she died March 13, 1838. Mr. Brown was a merchant of high standing in Chester, N. H., and died April 13, 1818. He had, all by first wife, Nancy, b. Oct. 26, 1776, m. —— Sweetser, d. April 27, 1799; Mercy, b. April 18, 1778, m. Daniel French, d. March 8, 1802, having had Benjamin Brown French, b. Sept. 4, 1800, a man of considerable prominence and influence in Washington, D. C., for many years till his death, 1863; Lydia, b. Feb. 6, 1782, m. Hon. Toppan Robie, a gentleman of property and standing in Gorham, Me., and d. Feb. 23, 1811, having had Harriet Robie and Francis Brown Robie; Hannah, b. Feb. 5, 1780, m. Dea. Jacob Mitchell, a tanner and farmer in Yarmouth, Me., and d. May 13, 1863, having had Benjamin Francis, Samuel Woodbury, Asa Cummings, and Mary Elizabeth Mitchell; FRANCIS; PRUDENCE [see no. 540], who m. Rev. David Thurston.

VII. FRANCIS BROWN, born Jan. 11, 1784; married, Feb. 11, 1811, Elizabeth Gilman, daughter of Rev. Tristram Gilman of Yarmouth, Me., a lady of fine intellectual powers and devoted christian character. He died July 27, 1820 [see page 102]; she died Sept., 1851. They had SAMUEL GILMAN, Mary Elizabeth and Francis, who died in infancy.

VIII. SAMUEL GILMAN BROWN, born in North Yarmouth, now Yarmouth, Me., Jan. 4, 1813; graduated from Dartmouth 1831; finished professional studies in Andover, Mass., 1837; professor in Dartmouth, first of rhetoric and English literature, then of intellectual philosophy and political economy, from 1840 to 1867; president of Hamilton college 1867; married, 1846, Sarah Savage, daughter of Rev. Jacob Van Veghten, D.D., of Schenectady, N. Y.; seven children; three daughters and two sons living 1879.

In her day, the minister's house was a sort of hotel, and often de-volved great burdens upon the wife.  She was always in readiness for these emergencies; in such a quiet way, too, that it was often a won-der how she sustained the strain, and maintained the cheerful, unruf-fled demeanor, which marked her life.  It was no uncommon occur-rence for eight or ten persons to arrive at the house without any notice, to be fed and lodged; but it made no visible change or distraction in her manner—she was equal to the occasion.  All clergymen, and many other classes of educated men of the various professions, agents for benevolent objects, in the early part of this century, used to go to the minister's, as a matter of course.

She was foremost in every good work, of education, of habits, or of reform, and always accomplished something, if not all that was aimed at.  The last years of her life were clouded by an aberration of mind which destroyed her own happiness, though she retained for her hus-band, her children, and her friends, all the love and watchful interest that characterized her previous life.

Among her husband's papers was found the following estimate he put upon her character: "Having uncommon soundness of judgment, she was a very discreet and judicious counselor.  Her moral princi-ples were elevated and pure; her integrity scrupulously exact; her conscientiousness strict and extensive.  She was eminently peaceable and contented, patient in sufferings and submissive under afflictive and trying dispensations.  My income was very limited; yet such was her economical skill in the arrangement of her domestic concerns, that the family—she was the mother of eight children—always had a com-fortable supply of wholesome, well prepared food, and of decent ap-parel.  She was benevolent to her fellow-men, and took a lively inter-est in all the benevolent enterprises of the day; she was not ashamed to plead the cause of the oppressed and fallen, and was ready to every good work.  Her piety was not superficial, but deep and controlling; not fitful, but uniform.  She was humble and decided in regard to all the fundamental truths and duties of the bible.  She was harmless and blameless without rebuke.  The heart of her husband safely trusted in her.  Her children arise up and call her blessed."

Rev. David Thurston was in childhood devoted to God in baptism; from his earliest recollection he was accustomed to hear the Scrip-tures read, and prayer offered in the family, and early commenced committing to memory what he styled "that invaluable manual of christian doctrine and duty, the Westminster Assembly's Shorter Cat-echism."  Through the influence of strict family discipline and relig-ious instruction, he was kept back from presumptuous sins, and was what was called a decently behaved moral boy.

He has left in manuscript a pleasant account of his childhood days. "He was a 'spindling boy,' subject to frequent ill turns.  He attend-ed school winter and summer; the only branches studied were read-ing, spelling, arithmetic, and writing.  His teacher was disposed to flatter him for his good spelling.  Classed with those who were twice his height, he was required to stand on a low seat to bring him nearer to an equality.  He loved play like other boys, but was not inclined to be mischievous; was never feruled or whipped at school.

"When seventeen years old, he procured a Latin grammar, and his

teacher told him to commit it to memory, so that he could repeat it all at once, which he did, and had most of it in his memory when eighty-four years old. He then took Corderius. At recitation he was required to cover the translation, read the Latin, and translate it into English. Of what use his grammar was he knew not, as his teacher made no allusion to it. In this style he went through Corderius and Æsop's Fables. In arithmetic he became a 'mighty cipherer,' filling several large books with his operations; but had he been asked why he carried one for every ten, more than for seven or eight, he could not have told. He was taught the *how*, but not the *why*. His teacher was a graduate of Harvard.

"About this time his father removed to Sedgwick, in the then district of Maine, where he was put under the tuition of Rev. Daniel Merrill, pastor of the Congregational church. Mr. Merrill set him to parsing, and this 'brought him up very short.' But he soon abandoned his Latin and went to work on the farm."

In the autumn of 1798 some of his youthful associates became interested in the subject of religion. "With shame," he says, "I have to confess that I felt sorry, and hoped they would relapse, that our seasons of youthful pleasure might not be interrupted. But, Oh! the boundlessness of God's forgiving love! that I was not utterly given up to walk in my own ways to endless perdition. God awakened my own mind to feel, in some measure, my need of a part in the salvation of the gospel. As a transgressor of God's law I felt that I was justly condemned. For several days a sense of my condition bowed me down. As one night I was attempting to pray, I thought I was willing to renounce my sinful ways, and submit myself to God. The passage, 'Whoso confesseth and forsaketh his sins shall find mercy,' came to my mind, and afforded me some relief. I had a calmness and peace of mind such as I had never before experienced. I was encouraged to think that my heart had been renewed. From time to time I have cherished the hope that, through the riches of divine grace in Christ Jesus, I shall finally be saved." He was admitted a member of the Congregational church in Sedgwick two days after he was twenty years old.

The momentous question then came up, in what way he could most honor God, and be useful to his fellow men. The result was, a determination to resume his studies, with a view to the ministry.

In September, 1802, he entered the junior class in Dartmouth college, having pursued all his previous studies under the tuition of his pastor. The standard of qualifications for entering college at that time was low, and he considered himself poorly qualified for that. Of his college life, his classmate, Rev. G. T. Chapman, D.D., furnished the following testimony:

He came to Dartmouth in the junior year, and his regular, mild, and sedate manner first attracted my attention. He sustained the character of a truly religious man to the close of his college life without spot or wrinkle. With such feelings, it is not surprising that he was a close, diligent, and conscientious student, and that the bloom of his youth fully indicated the ripened fruits of his manhood and age. His standing as a scholar was good, and on commencement day he had a part in the Hebrew dialogue. Within the last few years I have met him several times at Newburyport, and the more I saw of him, the more I had reason to love him as a christian, and be proud of him as a son of Dartmouth.

Hè graduated in August, 1804, and immediately after entered on a course of theological study, under the Rev. Dr. Burton, at Thetford, Vt. His estimate of the character of his instructor is given as follows in the American Quarterly Register for May, 1838, page 333:

As an instructor in systematic theology, I give him a higher place than any other man I have ever known. He had studied more intensely the operations of the human mind than any other man in the circle of my acquaintance. The subject of moral agency was a theme on which he had bestowed immense thought. This gave a clearness, a depth, and comprehensiveness to his views which were very uncommon, and qualified him, in an eminent degree, to be an interesting and profitable instructor in divinity. His great excellency as a teacher of systematic divinity consisted in his talent to present divine truth in a manner unusually lucid, rational, comprehensive, convincing. His pupils never had occasion to inquire what he meant in any instruction which he communicated. Other men might have views as profound, but rarely so distinct. He had followed so many minds, of such various structure, that he had become exceedingly familiar with the whole circle of truths comprised in a system of divinity, with the arguments, objections, answers, bearings, relations, etc., with the whole and with each particular part. The course of his instructions was admirably suited to develop the faculties of his pupils. He would make suggestions which would lead them to investigate for themselves; they must depend upon their own resources. In this way the ideas and views which his pupils obtained were very much their own. Hence few, if any, who ever pursued a regular course of study under his instruction, ever changed materially the sentiments which they embraced under his care. I have never known one.

In June, 1805, he was "approbated" by the Orange Association, and preached his first sermon July 4, 1805, as a preparatory lecture for Rev. Sylvester Dana of Orford, N. H. He continued his studies with Dr. Burton till October, usually preaching somewhere on the Sabbath.

He says of himself at this time: "I had written but one sermon. As the association met only once in three months, the doctor advised me to present myself for examination at this time. The sermon which I read before the meeting was founded on John iii. 7. I find notes in my journal of this day, 'had some solemn reflections on the greatness of the work of the ministry. My own wickedness and ignorance appeared so great that I felt almost ready to sink. How can such a stupid mortal be instrumental of good to the cause of Zion! O that God would give me strength for the work; felt somewhat dejected.' July 4th, at the earnest solicitation of Rev. Sylvester Dana of Orford, N. H., preached my first sermon at his preparatory lecture. Was somewhat intimidated in reading the first Psalm and in the first prayer; delivered my discourse without much embarrassment. I have great reason to be humbled for my pride and stupidity. May God bless the seed sown. The Sabbath following, P.M., I preached the same sermon to the doctor's people in Thetford. Rev. Roswell Shurtleff, professor and preacher at Dartmouth college, insisted upon my preaching a Sabbath for him. Perhaps very imprudently, I consented. I wrote a discourse from Titus ii. 6, and on Lord's day, July 14th, preached my two sermons before the president, professors, tutors, and three classes with whom I had been a fellow-student. Presumptuous as this was, I lived through it.

"I returned, after purchasing a horse, saddle, and bridle in East Hanover, for which I gave my note for $80, and pursued my studies with Dr. Burton. The next Sabbath I preached at West Fairlee my two sermons, where there was some special interest in religion, par-

ticularly among the young people.  Here I passed several days with interest and profit.  The next Sabbath I preached all day for the doctor; the next Lord's day I preached for Rev. Eden Burroughs, D.D., East Hanover, in whose family I had passed some months while connected with the college.  The latter part of the week, in company with Mrs. Burton, who was in feeble health, commenced a journey across the Green mountains.  Mrs. Burton being unable to travel on Saturday, we passed the Sabbath at Vershire, with Rev. Stephen Fuller, for whom I preached.  On Monday we rode to Berlin.  The doctor and Mr. Fuller overtook us; passed the night at Rev. James Hobart's, Berlin; Tuesday night we tarried at Waterbury.  The next day at Essex an ecclesiastical council convened, and examined Mr. Asaph Morgan, who had been a fellow-student with me at Dr. Burton's for a season.  He had been a preacher before he came to the doctor's; but not being satisfied with the 'exercise scheme' in which he had been instructed, and desiring to know more of the 'taste scheme,' he came, and having examined it, entered fully into it.

"The next day, Thursday, Aug. 15th, the exercises of ordination were performed as follows:  introductory prayer, Rev. Mr. Parker of Underhill, Dr. Burton preached from 2 Tim. iv. 2, Rev. S. Fuller of Vershire led in the consecrating prayer, Rev. Benjamin Wooster of Fairfield gave the charge, Rev. J. Hovey of Waterbury the right hand of fellowship, Rev. Mr. Kingsbury of Jericho offered the prayer by which Dea. Buel, who had been examined by the council, was ordained to that office, Rev. Silas L. Bingham of New Haven gave the deacon his charge, Rev. Leonard Worcester of Peacham offered the concluding prayer.  The next day went to Burlington, called on President Saunders of the Vermont university.  It had been said that the morals of this place were exceedingly corrupt.  The president seemed very desirous to convince us that the morality of the place and of the college was rapidly improving.  There was one college building, four stories high of brick, 160 by 75 feet.  It stands about one mile from the margin of Burlington bay in Lake Champlain.  The land rises gradually from the shore to the site of this edifice, which has 'an elevation of 330 feet above the surface of the water.'  The view, from this building, of the lake, its islands, the lofty hills on its western shore in the state of New York, and the country in Canada, is very extensive, beautiful, and grand.  It was delightful beyond all the scenery I had ever before seen.  The following Sabbath I preached in Williston, eight miles from Burlington.  Monday eve I preached a lecture at New Haven and tarried with the minister, Rev. S. L. Bingham.  Tuesday, at Middlebury, was kindly entertained at Judge Painter's.  The people about the college made provision, in their hospitality, to entertain all preachers of the gospel.  Attended an exhibition of the Freshman class.  Evening heard a genuine revival sermon from Rev. Mr. Preston of Rupert, from Isa. xxxiii. 14.  Wednesday attended the exercises of commencement.  The performances were creditable to the students and their instructors.  In the evening Rev. Martin Fuller of Royalton preached from 2 Tim. iii. 15.  Thursday, A.M., Rev. Mr. Fuller of Vershire preached from Matt. xi. 28.  Here was an atmosphere of piety.  This college was not patronized by the state; but God blessed it by frequent outpour-

ings of his spirit and the conversion of many of the students. For a number of years no class passed through its whole course without a revival of religion.

"The following three Sabbaths I preached in Sharon, Vt. I attended commencement at my *Alma Mater*, saw and visited many friends. For the first time saw and got upon the back of an elephant. On the 4th of September, 1805, preached my first funeral sermon at the funeral of Isaac Latham, in Sharon, text 1 Cor. vii. 29. Sept. 11th attended the meeting of the Orange Association at Rev. Mr. Lambert's, Newbury, Vt. Present, Hon. N. Niles, Rev. Messrs. Burton, Fuller, Kellogg, Fitch, Carpenter, Sutherland, Smith, Bliss, Dana, and Messrs. Calvin, Noble, and Jewell, students in theology; passed the night in Haverhill, N. H. 13th, visited some friends in West Fairlee and preached a lecture. The next two Sabbaths preached in Windsor, for Rev. Bancroft Fowler, who was ordained there last May; he was now absent on a journey. While here I formed some very pleasant acquaintances; was present at a wedding; Judge Hunter administered the marriage covenant and called on me to make the prayers. Here I formed acquaintance with Rev. Andrew Law, a teacher and writer of music, a godly man, of whom Dr. Burton said, 'he was the only teacher of music I ever knew who *thought.*' His health failed while a preacher. 25th, was present with an ecclesiastical council called to ordain Mr. Ignatius Thompson over the Congregational church in Pomfret, Vt. They continued the examination about five hours, and were then about two hours by themselves. They decided, with one exception, that they could not conscientiously proceed to ordain him. He was, in regard to doctrines, both ignorant and heretical.

"Preached the next Sabbath in Sharon, and the following one in Royalton, Oct. 6, 1805. The next day visited friends in Thetford. Wednesday I took leave of Dr. Burton's family, and especially of dear Mrs. B., who is apparently on the verge of heaven in consumption. After calling on some friends in Hanover, I made my way down to Jaffrey, N. H., and visited my uncle Oliver Bacon's family. On the Sabbath A.M. heard Rev. Laban Ainsworth preach from Jonah iv. 10, 11; P.M. I preached for him. Tuesday and Wednesday visited uncle Samuel Bacon's family, in company with cousin Mary Bacon, in Templeton, Mass. Returned with cousin Mary to Jaffrey. Friday rode to Hollis, N. H., and called on Capt. William Tenney, a very estimable and beloved friend of my father. On my way to Boxford, Mass., the next day, took tea with my classmate, Samuel Gile, at Rev. Jonathan French's, Andover, with whom Mr. G. was studying theology. Lord's day at Rowley, in my native parish; A.M. heard Rev. Mr. Williams of Linebrook preach from Ps. cxix. 45; P.M. I preached, and afterward attended the funeral of the wife of Mr. Asa Pingree. Passed the night with cousin Stephen Searle. Monday visited uncle Dr. Jacob Bacon's family, Salem. Called on Rev. Samuel Worcester. Wednesday called on Rev. Jonathan Strong, Randolph, and passed the night with Rev. Samuel Niles, Abington. Next day visited uncle David Bacon's family, Plymouth, my mother's native place. Uncle being absent, concluded to remain over the Sabbath, contrary to my plan.

The next day called on Rev. Adoniram Judson, then pastor of a Congregational church there, and father of the celebrated Dr. Judson of the Burman mission. I preached for him three times. In the evening had an interview with my friend and classmate, Gile, who had preached to the other church. Monday rode out with cousin Lucy Bacon to Manomet pond and returned. My uncle is an irreligious man, and aunt is very melancholy. I passed Tuesday night with Rev. Ezra Weld, Braintree, of whom it has been said that he would have his cud and his pipe in his mouth, and his snuff in his nose at the same time. Next day called on my classmates, Ezekiel Webster and O. Fifield, in Boston, and passed through Cambridge to Salem. The next day was introduced to Rev. Eli Smith of Hollis, who insisted I should go and preach three Sabbaths at Dunstable, N. H. I was intending to pursue my journey to Sedgwick, as I had not visited my father's family for two years.

"Went with Mr. Worcester, was introduced to Rev. Abiel Abbot and wife. Mr. W. preached a preparatory lecture for Mr. A., from Col. iii. 1. This was the first ministerial intercourse they had had. Was then introduced to Rev. Joseph Emerson and wife and the famous Miss Hannah Adams. Evening I preached for Mr. W. in the tabernacle, Salem. The next day called on uncle Daniel Thurston, Ipswich, and passed the night at uncle Pearson's, Rowley. Saturday, in company with Rev. Caleb Jewett Tenney of Newport, R. I., and Dr. Muzzey, rode to Pelham, N. H. Went over to Dunstable on the Sabbath and preached twice. Monday Mr. Tenney called, and we rode to his father's, Capt. Wm. Tenney's, Hollis. The next day I preached in Hollis P.M. and evening. Thursday, returned to Mr. Israel Hunt's, my boarding place. I preached here five Sabbaths and Thanksgiving. I preached also a preparatory lecture for Rev. Joshua Heywood, Dunstable, Mass., where I had an interview with Rev. Mr. Bullard of Pepperell, Mass. Rev. Joseph Kidder, former minister where I was preaching, gave me a very full account of his trials with the people, which was not suited to raise them in my estimation. But during the five Sabbaths I spent there, the congregation enlarged and there was increasing solemnity. They would have me remain, but I 'longed after my father's house.' Whether I did right to leave them is an undecided question. Dec. 2d I passed the night at Bradford at Mr. Hasseltine's with my friend and classmate, Abraham Burnham, preceptor of the academy. I spent about two weeks in Rowley and Byfield, visiting friends, preached eight times and left for Sedgwick. Passed a night with Rev. S. Toombs of Newtown, whose wife was cousin Mehitable Searle—another with my friend and classmate, Seaver, at Berwick, Me.; called on Rev. Pearson Thurston, Somersworth. The following Sabbath was at Brunswick with Prof. Cleaveland. Pres. McKeen requested me to preach, but I did not dare to; heard him all day and passed a night with him. Called on Rev. Eliphalet Gillet at Hallowell; and reached uncle Samuel Redington's, Vassalborough, Dec. 25th. I met here Rev. Alexander McLean, who, on being told I was a preacher, says to me: 'And do you preach the gospel?' I replied that I preached what I understood to be the gospel; preached in the evening. The next day rode with him to Paler-

mo and heard him preach from Zech. xii. 10. Saturday 28th reached Frankfort and passed the Sabbath with my dear brother Richard. It was so rainy I preached but once. Wednesday, Jan. 1, 1806, brother and I went to father's at Sedgwick. I had not visited my father's family before since September, 1803. A great change had taken place in the minister, Rev. Daniel Merrill, and in the church of which I was a member. The pastor had been immersed and re-ordained by a council of close communion Baptists, and a large majority of the church had gone with him. Nor is it owing to any want of earnest, persevering labors on his part that I am not a Baptist. He deemed it inconsistent to ask me to preach, but he came and heard me preach at several lectures. I remained at my father's about four weeks. Visited many of my former acquaintances in Sedgwick, who received me cordially, though I did not become a Baptist. I preached about a dozen times in different neighborhoods. I then spent four weeks in the eastern part of Hancock and Washington counties, and preached twenty sermons. James Campbell, Esq., gave me a dollar, which was all I received for my labors, except some thanks. I passed a night at the house of a Mr. Archer, on the Narraguagus river, where he and his wife had become the parents of twenty-one children. She was truly 'a fruitful vine.'

"On arriving at my father's, I found a letter from uncle Asa Redington of Waterville, inviting me to go there and preach. Saturday, March 1, 1806, I reached Waterville at uncle Asa Redington's, father of Hon. Asa Redington of Augusta, and after of Lewiston, Me., and brother of my step-mother. · The next day preached twice in a school-house to small audiences. My letter informing them that I designed to be there had not been received. The audience appeared very cold and dead. I preached the next Sabbath at West Waterville. Here and at the settlement on the river I preached alternately for nine Sabbaths and the annual fast. The religion, if there was any in the settlement on the river, was hidden. There was not a house in which family prayer was attended, nor a man who professed to be a regenerated follower of the Lord Jesus. Nor did I find a woman among them who seemed like Mary, sitting at the feet of Jesus. I felt as though I had neither Aaron nor Hur to hold up my hands. In the west part of the town were a few pious Baptists. I may never forget my emotions as I was leaving the house of God an aged female took my hand and said, 'I trust I have got a few crumbs from my Master's table to-day.' Who or what she was I knew not ; afterward I was told she was a godly woman in the Baptist church. Her remark encouraged and strengthened my poor heart. Well, I thought, if by preaching I could feed one of God's dear children with a few crumbs of the bread of life, I did not live in vain. I preached twenty-eight sermons in Waterville, two in Fairfield, and two in Clinton. I visited but little in the settlement on the river ; the greater part of my time was required to write my sermons.

"At my last lecture in Clinton, April 29th, I met Rev. Jotham Sewall, of whom I had heard, but never before seen. I had agreed, with the divine permission, to be at Winthrop to preach the next Sabbath. Mr. Sewall rather urged me to go with him ; so the next day we rode

7

to Canaan; in the evening I preached again. The next day we rode to Starks, where I was glad to meet Rev. Alexander McLean again. Here was a council called to settle some difficulties. Next day accompanied Mr. Sewall to his home in Chesterville and preached in the evening.

"Having preached nine Sabbaths in Waterville in March and April, 1806, having been invited to preach in Winthrop, went there in May, and preached most of the time till Feb. 18, 1807, when I was ordained pastor of the Congregational church."

He was appointed by the Massachusetts Missionary Society, "a missionary for one year in the district of Maine." As the people in Winthrop seemed inclined to retain his services, by advice of neighboring ministers, he relinquished his mission. Nov. 3d he was presented with a call from the church to become their pastor. This had been preceded by a day of fasting and prayer. The following day he was presented with a vote of concurrence by the town; and on the 18th of February, 1807, he was ordained. The officiating ministers were the Rev. Messrs. Asa Lyman of Bath; Elijah Parish of Byfield, Mass. (who preached); Jonathan Powers of Penobscot; Eliphalet Gillet of Hallowell; Mighill Blood of Bucksport; and Kiah Bailey of Newcastle. The council hesitated somewhat on account of the inadequacy of support, which was four hundred dollars a year, and four hundred dollars "settlement," in accordance with a custom formerly prevailing in New England. But this was to be paid in annual installments; in other words he was to receive five hundred dollars a year for four years, and four hundred dollars afterward. But having encouragement from the committees of the church and town that further provision should be made, they proceeded to ordain him.

On Jan. 1st, 1805, while with Dr. Burton, he commenced a journal, in which he made a daily entry of his situation and employments, and this he continued, without intermission, till seventeen days before his death. In his journal, as well as in his sermons, he used a system of stenography, invented by the Rev. Jonathan Fisher of Bluehill.

For several years he was accustomed to sum up, at the end of every month, the labors of the month; and at the end of the year the labors of the year. The following summing up of the year 1812 may serve as a specimen:

"During this year I have attended two meetings of associations, two of societies, three councils, three ordinations, two schools, four town meetings, four days of fasting and prayer, seven meetings of trustees, eight marriages, ten funerals, thirteen singing schools, forty-seven conferences, heard nineteen sermons, and preached one hundred and forty-seven; administered six baptisms, made eighty-three pastoral and fifty-two friendly visits, and three hundred and thirty calls; have received ninety-three companies, and one hundred and forty-nine calls; have written twenty-two letters, and ridden fourteen hundred and sixty-four miles out of town."

It will be recollected that the *riding* in those days was not done by *railroad*.

In 1819 Mr. Thurston was unanimously elected professor of theology, by the trustees of the "Maine Charity School," then located in

Hampden, now better known as the Bangor theological seminary. He yielded to the unanimous wish of the church, and declined the appointment.

His logical mind was early brought to a firm conviction of the inherent sinfulness of slave-holding; and he was a member of the convention at Philadelphia, at which the American Anti-slavery society was organized; and though he mourned over the aberrations of some prominent men in the cause, he firmly adhered to the principles of anti-slavery, and spent one year in advocating them, by lecturing through the state—his pulpit being supplied by the Rev. Daniel D. Tappan.

In 1850 he went as delegate from Maine to the Peace Congress at Frankfort, Germany, and visited a part of Wales, England, France, Switzerland, Germany, Prussia, and Belgium.

He kept the records of the church himself, and made a careful entry, not only of every business meeting, but every conference, specifying the topics that were discussed.

In 1853 the trustees of Dartmouth college conferred on him the degree of doctor of divinity.

He was an efficient member of most of the benevolent societies, and in 1859 was elected president of the American Missionary Association, and was annually re-elected till his death. He was a member of the board of overseers of Bowdoin college, a trustee of the Bangor theological seminary, of Hallowell and Monmouth academies for many years, and of the Maine Missionary Society for half a century. We copy still further from his journal:

"I remained pastor of the church in Winthrop till Oct. 15th, 1851, when, in compliance with my request, with the advice of an ecclesiastical council, I was dismissed. I was induced to request a dismission, because some desired to have a younger man, and some were dissatisfied with my anti-slavery course. I had conscientiously plead the cause of the enslaved, and had endeavored to act as I believed and prayed. I removed to Vassalborough, where I preached half of the time, and the other half was divided between the North Parish in Augusta and the Union house in Sidney. The year following I preached all the time in Vassalborough.

"The next year till its close, Dec., 1854, I preached three-fourths of the time in Vassalborough, and one-fourth in Sidney.

"In Jan., 1855, I removed to the East parish in Searsport. There a Congregational church, composed of members dismissed from the 1st church in Searsport, of which my brother, Stephen Thurston, was pastor, was organized Sept. 19, 1855. In this parish are about forty families, and several young married couples who have not kept house, being much of the time absent at sea. Twenty-five captains of vessels now follow the seas.

"My wife and I removed our relation from the church in Winthrop to the second church in Searsport March 9, 1856. I continued to preach in Searsport, enjoying highly the intercourse with my brother and family. The Maine Missionary Society not being able to assist the 2d church and the church at Sandy Point, without leaving some other feeble churches destitute, proposed that these two should unite in the support of a minister. Such an arrangement was accordingly

made. Not being desirous of having the charge of two churches, I left Searsport the last of Dec., 1858, and being invited to preach a year in Litchfield, Kennebec county, Me., I began to preach there the third Sabbath in Jan., 1859, on a salary of $300. This church has few members and but little property. They are exemplary christians, large-hearted and liberal. It is doubtful whether any church in the state or country do more for the support of the gospel in proportion to their means. At the expiration of the year they extended a unanimous invitation to me to preach for them another year. With this invitation I complied.

"April 23, 1860, having entered my eighty-second year last February, my wife and I left Litchfield for Goshen, N. H., to visit our oldest and youngest daughters; May 8th returned to Portland. The 10th son Samuel and I took tickets from Portland to Chicago, Ill. I paid $60 fare for both to go and return in thirty days. We left Portland twenty minutes before nine o'clock A.M.; Saturday A.M., at eight o'clock, we were in Detroit, Mich., eight hundred and fifty-eight miles from Portland. We reached in the evening the residence of my second daughter. Tuesday, 29th, at four A.M., left Adrian, and at forty minutes past eight P.M., Wednesday, was in Portland; at nine took a steamer for Boston, and at ten Thursday morning I was presiding at a meeting of the American Missionary Association in the Music hall, Boston. Friday evening left Boston in a steamer, and Saturday, four P.M., was at Litchfield. Through the great goodness of my heavenly Father, have passed, going and returning, about two thousand, two hundred and seventy-five miles, in good health, without any harm or casualty. Preached the next day, heard my class in the Sunday school, and attended monthly concert in the evening, and felt no more fatigue than usual."

Mr. Thurston continued vigorous in body and mind, and remained in Litchfield, preaching his last sermon on the day of the National Fast, just after the assassination of President Lincoln, seventeen days before his death.

The Creator dealt most kindly with him in endowing him with an assemblage of social affections, which eminently fitted him both to enjoy and to impart an unusual amount of happiness in the various relations of life. Few appreciated more highly, or enjoyed more keenly, the blessings of the conjugal and parental relations. His house was therefore the home of quietness and serene comfort. He had great pleasure in the society of his friends. He greeted them with warm cordiality, and entertained them with sincere, though unpretentious, hospitality.

As a man of intellectual capacity, Mr. Thurston stood among the ablest men in the ministry of Maine; as a scholar, he took high rank in college; as a theologian, he acquired so much reputation, that several young men, even after theological seminaries were established, chose to receive his private instruction in the study of divinity.

As a preacher, he regarded the doctrines of the gospel as constituting its vital force, shedding light on its precepts, opening to view the path of life, unfolding the wondrous method of grace and salvation, displaying the wisdom and matchless love of God in redemption,

teaching men what they must do, and what they must be, in order to gain eternal life, enforcing duty by the sublime fact of eternal retribution both for saints and sinners.

His manners in the pulpit were characterized by simplicity, solemnity, earnestness, and an affectionate persuasiveness. He was utterly unpretentious. He stood erect in the calm simplicity of one charged with a message from God to immortal men, soon to enter upon their eternal retribution.

As a pastor, he was kind, faithful, and sympathetic. He not only visited the people from house to house, but preached lectures on week days and evenings in the various parts of his parish very frequently. Among the leading elements of his christian character were reverence, conscientiousness, devoutness, and firmness of moral principle. His reverence was developed in all his intercourse with his Maker, in all his treatment of divine truth, and religious ordinances. In conscientiousness, he would sooner have suffered the loss of all human favor than the approbation of his own conscience. For the sake of preaching the gospel, he was willing to practice the most rigid economy, and live on very humble fare. Notwithstanding his means were small, he gave a tenth of all his income in charity.

Religious devoutness was one of his most marked characteristics. He must have communed much with the Father of Spirits, with things unseen and eternal, in order to have acquired such reverent facility and holy fervor in the privilege of prayer. He often seemed near the throne, as if in the presence chamber of the Most High. In no other way, probably, did he ever make so deep an impression on the minds of men, as by the prayers he was called upon to offer on some public occasions. I will mention two.

In 1831 he met the General Assembly of the Presbyterian church in Philadelphia, as delegate from the Maine conference. It was a time of division and excitement in that church, regarding what was called new and old divinity; each party, very conscientiously no doubt, striving for the ascendency. In this meeting party spirit ran high, and discussions arose which gathered warmth. The session was stormy and tumultuous, and in the midst of one of their most excited passages, the moderator arrested the regular business, and called upon the delegate from Maine to pray. He prayed, in melting strains. and with fervent desire, that God would calm those perturbed spirits, that those christian men and ministers might not, by unhallowed strife, give occasion to the wicked exultingly to exclaim: "Aha, aha, so would we have it." The assembly was melted, the excitement was allayed. It was as if the Master had said, "peace, be still, and there was a great calm." The public prints spoke much of that prayer and its effects; and the Maine delegate was long remembered with peculiar interest.

The other occasion was at the ordination of his nephew in Newbury, the Rev. John R. Thurston. Prof. Shepard, of blessed memory, preached one of his striking and impressive sermons; the uncle offered the ordaining prayer. An intelligent hearer of that prayer gives his impression of it as follows: "The prayer was exceedingly appropriate, solemn, pathetic, comprehensive, and minute; touching every

department of labor and duty devolving upon a good minister; quoting some very beautiful and appropriate passages of Scripture. It seemed for the time that the heavens and earth were brought very near together, and a finite saint was in very deed communing with the infinite and holy God, and that he had brought all the audience up, or the Infinite down, to the blessed communion. I think the impression will never be obliterated from my mind and heart."

The question of right, of duty, having been settled, he adhered to it with oaken firmness. His quick moral discernment carried him in advance of his times in regard to the evils to be reformed. Early did he become a laborer in the cause of temperance and of the oppressed. He remembered those in bonds as bound with them. Notwithstanding all he suffered in the cause of the oppressed, whether by his brethren in the ministry, or the church, or the baser sort, I never heard of a hard or unforgiving word he ever uttered respecting them. His forgiving love, his broad charity, covered a multitude of wrongs done to himself.

Children of David and Prudence Thurston, all born in Winthrop:

+1641　Eunice Farley,[6] b. Nov. 19, 1812; m. Rev. Henry Richardson.
+1642　Brown,[6] b. Oct. 6, 1814; m. 1st, Harriet Chapman; 2d, Amanda Chapman.
　1643　Mary,[6] b. Feb. 18, 1817; d. Nov. 1, 1819.
+1644　Elizabeth,[6] b. Nov. 28, 1818; m. Charles Philbrook.
　1645　David Francis,[6] b. June 17, 1821; d. Sept. 30, 1830.
　1646　Mary Brown,[6] b. April 18, 1823; d. Jan. 18, 1835.
+1647　Samuel,[6] b. Aug. 14, 1825; m. 1st, Lucretia Harrington Bartels; 2d, Mary Louisa Waters.
+1648　Harriet Ann,[6] b. May 8, 1829; m. 1st, Melvin Gilmore Deane; 2d, Hon. Edward Southworth.

PRESIDENT FRANCIS BROWN[7] (*Benjamin,*[6] *Francis,*[5] *Thomas,*[4] *John*[3], *Francis,*[2] *Thomas*[1]), youngest son of Benjamin[6] and Prudence (Kelley) Brown of Chester, N. H.; born there Jan. 11, 1784; married, Feb. 4, 1811, ELIZABETH GILMAN. He died July 27, 1820; she died September, 1851.

From various sources we gather the following interesting history of his short but eventful life: His mother was distinguished as well for her intellectual as moral qualities; and though she died when he had only reached his tenth year, she had already done much to give permanent direction to his character. At the age of fourteen he ventured to communicate to his father his wish that he might have the advantages of a collegiate education; but his father, in consideration of his straitened worldly circumstances, felt obliged to deny his request. By a subsequent marriage, however, his circumstances were improved; and through the generosity of his new mother his desire for an education was gratified. He always retained the most grateful sense of her kindness, and delighted to think of her in connection with all the honorable usefulness to which he subsequently attained.

In his sixteenth year he became a member of Atkinson academy, then a highly respectable institution, under the care of the Hon. John Vose. Here he was a most diligent and successful student, and when his instructor wrote to Dr. Wheelock, recommending him to college, he informed him that he had sent him an Addison.

Of the commencement of his religious character the most that is

known is the following statement which he communicated to the friends who were standing around his death-bed: "During my sickness at Atkinson academy, about the time the fever formed a crisis, while in a state of partial delirium, I had a view of the happiness of heaven—I was gently led on to the portal and beheld a glory which I can never describe. I was then conducted to the gate of hell, where I had a view of the pit below. I fell asleep, and upon waking, thought I could not live. Greatly distressed in my mind, I called to my mother and asked her what I should do. When she counseled me and directed me, as my case required, I changed my position in the bed, and for the first time in my life attempted to pray. After this I had clear and impressive views of the Saviour, succeeded by great enjoyment, such as I had never experienced. I felt a desire to go to college and become a minister." He made a public profession of his faith when he was a tutor in college, and then joined the church in his native place.

He graduated from Dartmouth in 1805. The year after his graduation he spent as a private tutor in the family of Judge Paine of Williamstown, Vt., and then, at the close of 1806, he was appointed to a tutorship in the college at which he had graduated. Here he remained till 1809, and, while discharging the duties of his office, he was pursuing a course of theological study in preparation for the ministry.

Having been licensed to preach by the Grafton association, he resigned his office as tutor, with a view to give himself solely to the duties of his profession. After a short time he received a call from the church in North Yarmouth,* Me.; this call he accepted, and on his birthday, Jan. 11, 1810, he was set apart as their pastor. Scarcely had he entered on the duties of his pastorate before he was chosen professor of languages in Dartmouth college, but declined. During the five following years his influence was widely felt in favor both of learning and of religion.

After the difficulty between President Wheelock and the trustees of Dartmouth college had commenced, and the trustees, acting on a provision of the charter, had removed him from the presidency, Mr. Brown was appointed in his place, and was inaugurated Sept. 27, 1815. The controversy in the midst of which this occurred was a most agitating one, and just as it was at its height, and it seemed difficult to predict the issue, Mr. Brown was invited to the presidency of Hamilton college; but he unhesitatingly declined the invitation, determined to stand by the college with which he was then connected and to share its fortunes, whatever they might be.

The legislature passed an act enlarging the sphere of the college, adding to the number of the trustees, changing the name to Dartmouth university, and giving the appointing power of teachers and officers to the governor and council. Under this act a treasurer was appointed, President Wheelock was reinstated, the college buildings, library, and apparatus were forcibly appropriated, thus turning out the original trustees and President Brown. The students generally adhered to President Brown, and temporary quarters were secured.

---

* The present town of Yarmouth.

The trustees immediately sued the treasurer, before the superior court of New Hampshire, for the recovery of the property and were defeated, the court sustaining the doings of the legislature.   An appeal was at once made to the supreme court of the United States, and the case was argued before the full bench by Hon. Daniel Webster.   The action of the lower court was reversed, the trustees sustained, and a principle of law established, which has been recognized as the law of the land ever since, in regard to all charitable institutions, colleges, academies, corporations, etc., viz., that all such institutions are charitable and therefore private; that the legislature cannot interfere, or make any change, without the consent of the trustees, unless such power is expressly reserved by the charter.   Never has higher legal ability been brought to bear upon any question.   On the side of the trustees were Jeremiah Smith, Jeremiah Mason, Daniel Webster, and Joseph Hopkinson.   On the part of the treasurer, supported by the governor and council, were John Holmes, William Pinckney, and William Wirt.

Rev. Henry Wood, in a sketch of his life, says: "It was characteristic of President Brown that he was always equal to any emergency; no call could be made upon his resources unhonored; at a word, all the sleeping energies of his mind came up in their glowing beauty and just proportions, awakening the admiration and securing the confidence of timid friends, and overawing the presumption that already exulted in the overthrow of the college.   Reluctantly given up by his people, he had only to touch again the soil of his native state, and move amid the eyes and ears of its citizens, to be admitted as that superior mind which Providence had raised up and kept, like Moses in the desert, for this very crisis.   A certain dignity of person, altogether native and inimitable, made every one feel himself in the presence of original greatness, in honoring which he also honored himself. Such were the conciliation and command belonging to his character that, from the first moment of his reappearance in his own state, the voice of detraction was silent; whoever else was rebuked, he escaped, whom all conspired to honor.   Judgment founded upon a clear and ready perception of things was a leading characteristic of his mind. Reason presided over and kept in subjection all the inferior powers; cool, investigating, cautious, the rigid discipline he maintained over his spirit allowed little indulgence for excitement of feeling, little play for the fervor of imagination.   He so well understood the structure of our institutions, the power of legislatures, and the rights of corporate bodies secured by contract, he was so confident of success in the ultimate decision of the highest tribunal of the nation, that when others were disheartened he stood erect and fixed in his purpose. Never has a cause been litigated in our country more important from the principle to be established and the interests remotely involved; the existence not only of this, but of all seminaries for education, and of all corporate bodies whatever, was suspended upon the present decision.   The permanence of all the institutions of our country, whether charitable, literary, or religious, and indeed the very character of the nation in its future stages were connected with this adjudication upon a point of constitutional law."

President Brown's labors proved too much for his physical constitution. Beside being almost constantly occupied during the week with his duties in the college, he preached nearly every Sabbath somewhere in the neighborhood, and his vacations were generally spent in traveling for the purpose of increasing the college funds. Soon after the Commencement of 1818 it became painfully apparent that he was the subject of pulmonary disease. His last effort in the pulpit was in Thetford, Vt., on the first Sabbath in October, 1818. In the fall of 1819 he traveled south as far as South Carolina and Georgia, in the hope that he might be benefited by a milder climate; but he returned in June, 1820, only to convince his friends as soon as they met him that he had come home to die. As he was unable to appear in public, he invited the senior class, as they were about to scatter at the beginning of their last vacation, to come to his house, and there, with a voice which was manifestly soon to be hushed in death, he addressed to them the most affectionate, appropriate, and weighty counsels, which were received with the warmest gratitude and deepest veneration. He lingered, in the most serene and cheerful submission to the divine will, until July 27, 1820, and then ascended with the words, "Glorious Redeemer, take my spirit," upon his lips.

The degree of doctor of divinity was conferred upon him by both Williams and Hamilton colleges in 1819.

Dr. Brown was commanding in his person, affable in his manners, and exceedingly dignified in his whole bearing. His mind was of a very high order, profound, comprehensive, and discriminating. His habits of study were liberal, patient, and eminently philosophical. His preaching was highly evangelical, in the best taste, and always instructive and impressive. He presided over the college with great wisdom, dignity, and kindliness, and the students loved and honored him as a father. His whole character—intellectual, moral, christian—was beautiful.

He published an address on Music, delivered before the Handel society of Dartmouth college, 1809; a sermon delivered at the ordination of Allen Greeley, 1810; a sermon delivered on the occasion of the state fast appointed in consequence of the declaration of war with Great Britain, 1812; a sermon delivered before the Maine Missionary society, 1814; Calvin and Calvinism defended against certain injurious representations, contained in a pamphlet entitled "A Sketch of the Life and Doctrine of the celebrated John Calvin"—of which the Rev. Martin Ruter claims to be the author—1815; a reply to the Rev. Martin Ruter's letter relating to Calvin and Calvinism, 1815; a sermon delivered at Concord before the convention of Congregational and Presbyterian ministers of New Hampshire, 1818.

## 541

DEA. RICHARD THURSTON[5] of Bangor, Me. (*David*,[4] *Richard*,[3] *Daniel*,[2] *Daniel*[1]), brother of the preceding, and son of David[4] and Mary (Bacon) Thurston of Sedgwick, Me.; born in Rowley, Mass., July 5, 1781; baptized by Rev. James Chandler; married, by Rev. N. Whitman, Oct. 13, 1817, ANN BOWERS, born in Bilerica, Mass., Feb. 17, 1787, daughter of Samuel Bowers, a merchant in Boston. They both died in Bangor; he May 24, 1852; she June 13, 1869.

He went to Sedgwick, Me., with his father in 1796, and about 1805 settled in Frankfort, Me., as a merchant, where he remained till 1830. In 1832 removed to Bangor, and spent the remainder of his life in mercantile business. Early in life he experienced religion, and was instrumental in establishing a Congregational church in Frankfort, of which he became a deacon. He was a very hospitable man, and kept what was called in those days a "minister's tavern." Frankfort was a godless place when he settled there as a young man, and his life was so sober and correct that he was called deacon long before the office was conferred upon him.

### Children:

+1659 Richard Bowers,[6] b. at Charlestown, Mass., June 28, 1819; m. Jane Miller Pierce.
+1660 Samuel David,[6] b. at Frankfort Feb. 10, 1822; m. 1st, Susan Duncan Pierce; 2d, Jane Maria Sparhawk.
1661 Caroline Ann Parker,[6] b. at Frankfort Nov. 2, 1825; m. in Stamford, Ct., April 12, 1873, Hugh Young. b. Jan. 2, 1831, eldest son of James and Elizabeth Young, née Learmouth, of Edinburgh, Scotland. His parents afterward lived in Kilmarnock. He came to this country in 1851. He was captain of the 79th New York volunteers in the war of the rebellion. He is a manufacturer and inventor of Young's diamond saw machine, for sawing stone, and lives in New York city.

### 542

MARY THURSTON [5] (*David,*[4] *Richard,*[3] *Daniel,*[2] *Daniel*[1]), sister of the preceding, and daughter of David [4] and Chloe (Redington) Thurston of Sedgwick, Me.; born in Rowley, Mass., April 7, 1792; baptized by Rev. Joseph Dana; married, at Sedgwick, Feb. 18, 1818, by her father, who was a justice, assisted by Rev. David Thurston, her brother, DEA. BLISS BLODGET, born in Lebanon, N. H., Dec. 9, 1785, son of Daniel and Mary (Bliss) Blodget of Chelsea, Vt. He died April 29, 1857.

Dea. Blodget's parents moved to Chelsea in his early childhood, where he remained till he was twenty-one, when he went to Bucksport, Me., into a store as clerk. In this capacity he served one year, and then became a partner in the business. He continued in trade, with several changes, until his death. He was an officer in the Congregational church for many years, and always interested in all religious and educational objects. He was a public-spirited man, and helped forward, so far as he could, all matters of progress and improvement. He never spared any effort for the education and advancement of the members of his family. In all these departments he was thoroughly seconded and aided by his consort, and their lives have been filled with usefulness, as their house has always been the home of all in any way connected with the advancement of society and religion. Their son Henry has been a missionary to China since 1854.

### Their children, all born in Bucksport, were:

+1672 Mary Thurston (Blodget), b. Jan. 9, 1819; m. Rev. Enoch Pond.
+1673 Sarah Ann (Blodget), b. Aug. 24, 1820; m. John Hincks.
+1674 Elizabeth (Blodget), b. Nov. 12, 1822; m. Rev. John P. Skeele.
+1675 Henry (Blodget), b. July 13, 1825; m. Sarah Ripley.
+1676 John (Blodget), b. July 11, 1827; m. Sarah Case.
+1677 George (Blodget), b. April 6, 1831; m. Mary Sophia Pond.
1678 William Stephen (Blodget), b. Jan. 21, 1834; d. Jan. 31, 1838.
1679 Charles Howard (Blodget), b. July 5, 1836; d. Sept. 5, 1862.

## 543

SAMUEL THURSTON[5] of Bangor, Me. (*David,[4] Richard,[3] Daniel,[2] Daniel[1]*), brother of the preceding, and son of David[4] and Chloe (Redington) Thurston of Sedgwick, Me.; born in Rowley, Mass., July 8, 1793; baptized by Rev. Ebenezer Bradford; married, first, Jan. 21, 1824, PRUDENCE GOODALE, born in Worcester, Mass., March 16, 1801, daughter of Hon. Ephraim and Prudence (Willard) Goodale of Orrington, Me.; she died Dec. 19, 1838. Second, Jan. 1, 1840, MRS. CHARLOTTE (GOODALE) GREELEY, sister of his first wife, born May 13, 1809; married, first, July 16, 1832, Rev. Greenleaf Greeley, a Methodist minister of Readfield, Me., a man of deep piety and much usefulness; he died in Burke county, Ga., where he had gone for his health, Feb. 29, 1836.

Hon. Ephraim Goodale was born in Worcester, Mass., Jan. 6, 1773; died May 25, 1858, aged 85. He married, Aug. 3, 1796, Mrs. Prudence Howard Willard (widow Haven), born in Milford, April 16, 1773, died Feb. 4, 1850, aged 76. They removed to Orrington, district of Maine, in 1803. He was a deist, and brought Payne's and Voltaire's works into that country, and made a business of publishing and selling books as well as of scientific farming. He supplied the first fruit trees planted in Penobscot county. In 1809 they were converted and joined the Methodist church in Orrington, Rev. Enoch Mudge, pastor. Notwithstanding his infidelity, he and his wife went ten miles on one occasion to attend a meeting, and were both awakened and rode home in perfect silence. Before retiring, they both knelt in prayer. The next day he burnt all his infidel works, and established a family altar, which ever after was sacredly maintained. They both left an excellent record, adorning their profession by a holy life. He was for many years one of the justices of the court of sessions, and of the same court under a new name in the county of Penobscot till 1835, when he resigned.

Mr. Samuel Thurston was a merchant at Mill creek, Orrington, Me., for eleven years, till about 1831, where he accumulated a very handsome property. He then moved to Brewer, a town on the opposite side of the Penobscot river from Bangor, where he kept store, built houses, dealt in lumber, and succeeded well till 1835, when he entered into the land speculation, which swept like a destructive tornado over all the northern part of New England, and lost all the accumulations of his past life. His wife was sick with consumption, soon after died, and with five young children he commenced life anew. In 1840 he moved to Bangor and pursued the lumber business the remainder of his days. Here, too, he met with many losses by fire and flood and business indorsements, which he bore with serene patience, never bringing his troubles into his house to depress his family.

When he started in life, he determined to attain riches, and he had come almost to the realization of his wishes, when the disaster came which showed him that "it is not in man that walketh to direct his steps," but that the Lord directeth them for better ends than the mere attainment of wealth. The loss of his wife and his earthly possessions led him to consider those interests of a more enduring character, and he gave his heart to God, established a family altar, taught his

children, both by precept and example, to seek first the kingdom of God and his righteousness. He gave his children a good education, sustained the institutions of society generally, and was a decided abolitionist, when it was very unpopular to be one. He did not join the church till 1860, when he was received into the Bangor Central church, at that time under the care of Prof. Shepard of the theological seminary. Through all his life he maintained an unblemished moral character. All his children but one are members of some Congregational church.

Children, by first wife, Prudence, born in Orrington:

1690    Samuel Redington,[6] b. Feb. 4. 1825; d. in Brewer Oct. 31, 1847.
+1691   Ephraim Goodale,[6] b. July 2, 1827; m. Charlotte Margretta Darling.
1692    Helen Maria,[6] b. Sept. 1, 1830.
+1693   Emily,[6] b. in Bucksport, her mother being on a visit there, Jan. 1, 1834; m. Charles Wood.

Born in Brewer:

1694    Henry Martin,[6] b. Oct. 13, 1836; d. Aug. 3, 1841.

By second wife, Charlotte:

1695    Charlotte Greenleaf (Greeley), child of Rev. Greenleaf and Charlotte (Goodale) Greeley, b. July 4, 1836.
1696    Willard Nelson,[6] } twins, born } d. Aug. 26, 1842.
1697    Horace Page,[6]   { July 9, 1841; { d. Aug. 30, 1842.
+1698   Mary Elizabeth,[6] b. Dec. 15, 1843; m. Augustus Hall Walker.
1699    Arthur Everett,[6] b March 5, 1845; d. in Brewer Aug. 18, 1849.
1700    Isabel Redington,[6] b. Sept. 30. 1848; m. Jan. 1, 1873, Edgar Clarence Pearson, b. Jan. 9, 1850. son of Orpcalyer and Susan E. Pearson of Bangor; he is a lumber merchant in Bangor.
1701    Willis Little,[6] b. Aug. 16, 1850; m. Oct. 31, 1878, Catharine Barker, daughter of Isaac P. and Almeda W. Barker of Brookline, Mass.; is a wholesale grocer in Bangor in firm of Thurston, Patterson & Bragg.

### 544

JOHN THURSTON[5] of Bangor, Me. (*David,[4] Richard,[3] Daniel,[2] Daniel[1]*), brother of the preceding, and son of David[4] and Chloe (Redington) Thurston of Sedgwick, Me.; born in Rowley, Mass., Nov. 26, 1794; baptized by Rev. Ebenezer Dutch; married, 1826, ABIGAIL KING LAWRENCE of Brooksville, Me. She died Jan. 6, 1834; he died March 14, 1834.

Mr. Thurston was a farmer at his father's, and after he left home in Bangor, a few miles from the city; but a few years before his death sold his farm and moved into the city, where he kept the ordinary for the theological seminary.

Their children were:

Born in Sedgwick:

1712    David,[6] b. Nov. 14, 1827; drowned in Penobscot river Oct. 3, 1837.
1713    Margaret,[6] b. April 4, 1830; d. April 30, 1830.

Born in Bangor:

+1714   John Rogers,[6] b. Sept. 4, 1831; m. 1st, Frances Orilla Goodale; 2d, Caroline Augusta Wells Story.
1715    William,[6] b. Dec. 19, 1833; d. Oct. 13, 1834.

### 545

SARAH THURSTON[5] (*David,[4] Richard,[3] Daniel,[2] Daniel[1]*), sister of the preceding, and daughter of David[4] and Chloe (Redington) Thurston of Sedgwick, Me.; born in Rowley, Mass., April 1, 1796; bap-

Stephen Hurrston

tized by Rev. Humphrey C. Perley; married, Oct. 30, 1823, DEA.
JOHN BUCK, born Feb. 16, 1795, son of Benjamin and —— (Sewall)
Buck of Bucksport, Me.  He died Feb. 13, 1872.

Mr. John Buck was a man of a genial and happy nature.  The support of his father's family largely devolved upon him, quite early in life, and he engaged in school teaching and fishing, sometimes taking fifty salmon from his weir at a single tide.  He commenced business in Orland, Me., in 1823, as a trader, and increased his facilities as the place grew; bought large tracts of timber land, built and equipped fishing vessels and coasters; was successful in his business, became one of the first men in the town, and offices of honor and trust were often conferred upon him.  He was deacon of the Congregational church in Orland from the time of its organization, Sept. 25, 1850, till his death.  He was chiefly instrumental in forming the church and in building a house of worship.  He was constantly doing good things that the world never heard of.  He was a strong antislavery man and acted as conductor on the "under ground" railroad, during the years of the fugitive slave law, sheltering and helping many on their way to the Queen's dominions.  He was heartily seconded by his companion in life in all social and benevolent matters, and their house was the common resort for all progressive minds, as well as relatives, who were all made to feel at home and happy in their munificent mansion.

Their children, all born in Orland, were:

 1726  Maria (Buck), b. July 25, 1824; d. in Bradford, Mass., May 12, 1842.
+1727  John Albert (Buck), b. Aug. 15, 1825; m. Charlotte Maria Buck.
+1728  Frank (Buck), b. April 24, 1827; m. Ann Catherine Buck.
+1729  Edward (Buck), b. April 17, 1829; m. Emeline Billings Darling.
 1730  Hannah Thurston (Buck), b. May 17, 1832.
 1731  Sarah Emeline (Buck), b. April 12, 1835.
 1732  Charlotte Elizabeth (Buck), b. Feb. 27, 1837; d. Sept. 12, 1862.

## 546

REV. STEPHEN THURSTON [5] of Searsport, Me. (*David*,[4] *Richard*,[3] *Daniel*,[2] *Daniel*[1]), brother of the preceding, and son of David [4] and Chloe (Redington) Thurston of Sedgwick, Me.; born there Dec. 22, 1797; baptized by Rev. Daniel Merrill; married, at No. 67 Kingston street, Boston, Mass., June 5, 1827, CLARA MATILDA BENSON, born in Bucksport, Me., Jan. 6, 1803, daughter of John and Sarah (Buck) Benson of Boston.

Mr. Thurston joined the Congregational church in Bluehill, Me., under the pastoral charge of Rev. Jonathan Fisher, in 1816, at the age of nineteen, and had his mind turned toward the ministry.  He studied nearly two years with his brother, David Thurston of Winthrop.  By an imprudent use of his eyes there, they were so injured as to render a college course, which he had contemplated, an impossibility.  After more than a year spent in other employments, he entered Bangor theological seminary and graduated in 1825.  He was ordained as pastor of the first church in Searsport Aug. 9, 1826, and remained there until May 22, 1864, when he was elected to the office of secretary of the Maine Missionary Society, an office which he filled with great satisfaction to the churches till June, 1876, when failing

health induced him to resign. In 1856 he received the degree of doctor of divinity from Colby university. Since 1850 he has been a trustee of the Bangor theological seminary, and is now, 1879, president of the board. Since 1849 he has been a trustee of the Maine Missionary Society.

He was abundantly blessed in his labors as pastor in Searsport. During the first two years one hundred and ten members were added to the church. Several seasons of refreshing were enjoyed between the years 1830 and 1839, in connection with some special efforts in the form of protracted meetings of four days' continuance. In 1840, without any special preparatory efforts, the Holy Spirit was poured out in a remarkable manner, moving powerfully the whole community. Ninety-nine were added to his church, besides large accessions to the Methodist church. Again in 1852 another revival brought fifty into the church; and during the forty years of his ministry more than four hundred souls were gathered into the fold.

Mr. Thurston is eminently social in his nature, and his relatives and friends can recall many happy and joyful seasons spent at his own cheerful fireside and at theirs. Particularly fraternal have been the relations between himself and his brothers and sisters. Many delightful social gatherings have given expression to the good will, kindliness of heart, social gratification and affection for each other, consecrated by a manifest trust and repose in the Father above, which have bound them together as with "hooks of steel." But the climax, the grandest and best of all, was on the occasion of their golden wedding, June 5, 1877. Their children assembled at the homestead some days before, and made extensive preparations for the reception of the wide circle of relatives and friends who had been some time previously invited. The mansion was a perfect bower of flowers and evergreen, arranged with skillful taste; tables were loaded with substantial food and attractive condiments. In the afternoon the house was thronged with friends from the neighborhood coming to congratulate the happy pair on the occasion and leave their tokens of remembrance; and every one who came was pressed to the table of refreshments. The evening was devoted to a social reunion of relatives, about fifty of whom were present, several coming fifteen hundred miles to be there. The house and grounds were brilliantly illuminated and sweet music added her charm to the occasion. The blessing of Heaven was invoked; several poems written for the occasion were read; appropriate and interesting remarks were made; nearly a thousand dollars in gold and many valuable and beautiful keepsakes were presented; and the whole was of great interest, ever to be remembered with satisfactory pleasure by all who were present. Four sisters and one brother (one brother only being absent, and he seventy-two years old), were present, whose united ages were 387 years. Two brothers of Mrs. Thurston and their wives, and one sister were present, while others from New York and San Francisco were handsomely represented by generous gifts.

As a preacher, he saw the great fundamental truths of the bible in a clear light, and feeling the indispensable need that others should see them as clearly, he was forcible and direct in his expositions and

exhortations, often rising to an abandon of self, which greatly added force and power to the thoughts uttered. He was tenacious of the form of sound words, had no misgivings about preaching the *whole* truth, and never curtailed it to satisfy the timid.

Prof. Enoch Pond, D.D., of Bangor theological seminary, says: "I have been intimately acquainted with Rev. Dr. Thurston for more than forty years, nearly the whole of his long ministerial life. He has a clear head, an invincible conscience, and a warm heart. He has long been regarded as one of the most efficient and useful ministers of Maine. As a counselor, he is discreet, searching, and impartial; as a pastor, he is watchful, sympathetic, and active, not neglecting the sick and the sorrowful, and especially those who are sorrowing for their sins. All this is evinced in his eminent pastoral success. His church, originally a small one, has, years ago, become three bands.

"But it is as a preacher that I wish particularly to speak of him. He is among the early graduates of the Bangor theological seminary, which he left previous to my connection with it. His theology is strictly of the New England type, following that of Hopkins and Emmons. His sermons are lucidly planned, mostly doctrinal, and always instructive, and *impressive* because they are instructive. It is not his method to rely on a flow of words or gushes of strong feeling to make an impression, but on the point and weight of the truths he delivers. These truths, he well knows, are 'quick and powerful, and sharper than any two-edged sword, piercing even to the dividing asunder of soul and spirit, and of the joints and marrow, and is a discerner' and *revealer* 'of the thoughts and intents of the heart.' His chief reliance, so far as impression is concerned, has obviously been on this 'sword of the Spirit, which is the word of God.' Strange that the reliance of any gospel minister should be on aught else. His ministry has been fruitful in conversions and revivals of religion.

"Although he is very decided in what he believes to be the truth of God's word, he is not wanting in christian liberality—not that liberality which regards the doctrines of religion as of small importance; which tells you with a sneer that 'christianity is not a dogma, but a life'—but that true liberality which is watchful over the religious rights of others, which accords to them the same liberality of thought and opinion which he claims for himself.

"He has long sustained and honored the character of a reformer. He was an outspoken and persistent opponent of slavery during the long agitation of that subject in this country, and the same may be said of the cause of temperance, which has no firmer friend and advocate.

"The regard in which he is held by the ministers and churches of Maine is evinced in the responsibilities which they have laid upon him. He was dismissed from his people several years ago, that he might become secretary and general agent of the Maine Missionary Society. He has long been a trustee of the Bangor theological seminary and is now president of the board. He is deservedly held in high estimation by a wide circle of christian friends and associates, and long may he be spared—a blessing both to himself and them."

Rev. Luther Wiswall says: "My personal acquaintance with Dr. Thurston began in 1837. I was a member of the ministerial association of which he was the oldest and most trusted counselor. He was

a genial companion and a welcome guest in the families ·of surrounding parishes.  As a preacher he was most acceptable ; his written sermons were able, sound, pointed. easily understood, and delivered with fluency ; but, to my apprehension, he excelled in his extemporaneous efforts, some of which I have never heard equaled as to matter and manner combined.  As a pastor he was active, watchful, and very laborious.  His parish was territorially large in the first part of his ministry, as for many years past two other Congregational churches have existed in the territory which was originally embraced in his parish.  He gave many week-day lectures in the outlying districts of his parish, and was a kind of missionary to all the feeble Congregational churches in the interior of Waldo county, and personally influential in creating several of them.  The denomination in that county owes more to his labors and counsel than to those of any other man.  Of the eleven Congregational churches now reported in that county, only five were in existence when he commenced his labors there.  His pastorate was nearly forty years, but not for lack of calls to other and larger churches in the cities."  Children, all born in Searsport:

1743   Clara Benson,[6] b. April 14, 1828; m. March 15, 1850, Dr. Samuel Woodbury Blanchard, b. April 15, 1818, son of Sylvanus and Dorcas (Prince) Blanchard of Yarmouth, Me.  He graduated at Bowdoin college in 1841, attended medical lectures at Bowdoin, and finally graduated from Jefferson medical college, Philadelphia, in 1844.  He commenced the practice of medicine in Searsport, and finally settled in Yarmouth.  He died Dec. 23, 1857, aged 39.  His widow lives in Portland, Me.  They had, born in Yarmouth:
    1744   *Lucy Nichols* (Blanchard), b. June 12, 1852.
    1745   *Alice Benson* (Blanchard), b. July 22, 1855.
    1746   *Maria Woodbury* (Blanchard), b. April 20, 1857.
1747   Stephen Augustus,[6] b. Aug. 6, 1829; d. Aug. 26, 1829.
1748   Sarah Buck,[v] b. Feb. 7, 1831; d. Feb. 19, 1831.
+1749   Stephen Rollo,[6] b. July 20, 1832; m. Annie Frances Carpenter.
1750   Alfred,[6] b. Feb. 25, 1834; d. March 19, 1834.
1751   Mary,[6] b. Aug. 13, 1835; m. by Rev. Stephen Thurston, her father, in State street church, Portland, Me., Nov. 6, 1866, William Albert Rogers, born in Bristol, Me., Jan. 20, 1832, son of Josephus and Sarah (Lord) Rogers of Frankfort, Me.  He is a master mariner, having made several voyages to San Francisco, China, and Europe, his wife going with him at times.  They have, born in Searsport:
    1752   *William Thurston* (Rogers), b. June 29, 1868.
    1753   *Stephen Thurston* (Rogers), b. April 8, 1872.
1754   Sarah Buck,[6] b. Aug. 18, 1836.
1755   Hannah,[6] b. Sept. 9, 1837; m. Feb. 21, 1861, Capt. Freeman McGilvery, b. Oct., 1824, son of Robert and Elizabeth (Chase) McGilvery of Prospect, Me.  He was a ship-master in the foreign trade, and on the breaking out of the southern rebellion, in 1861, collected the 6th Maine battery and went into Virginia.  He was afterward promoted from the captaincy of this battery to be colonel, commanding a corps of artillery at his death, which took place in Petersburgh, Va., Sept. 3, 1864.  He was a brave and very efficient officer.  Mrs. McGilvery resides in Portland, Me. ; no children.
+1756   Henrietta Maria,[6] b. March 31, 1839; m. Rev. Charles Whittier.
1757   Elizabeth Homer,[6] b. Nov. 26, 1840; m. May 22, 1879, by her father, James Muir MacDougall. b. May 25, 1840, son of James and Elizabeth (Muir) MacDougall of Auburn, N. Y. ; he was appointed assistant engineer U. S. revenue marine June 20, 1864, commissioned chief engineer May 26, 1871, and is stationed, 1879, on the Pacific coast.
1758   William Colman,[6] b. April 3, 1842; d. April 10, 1843.
1759   William Redington,[6] b. Dec. 13, 1843; d. May 26, 1844.

## 547

MEHITABLE THURSTON[5] (*David*,[4] *Richard*,[3] *Daniel*,[2] *Daniel*[1]), sister of the preceding, and daughter of David[4] and Chloe (Redington) Thurston of Sedgwick, Me.; born there Feb. 5, 1800; baptized by Rev. Daniel Merrill; married, at Searsport, Me., April 24, 1838, HON. JOHN GODFREY * of Bangor, Me., born May 27, 1781, son of John and Jerusha (Hodges) Godfrey of Taunton, Mass., where his parents lived and died.

Hon. John Godfrey graduated at Brown university, Rhode Island, 1804, and studied law at Taunton. He established himself in Hampden, Me., in the practice of the law in 1805; removed to Bangor in 1821, and continued the practice till his death, May 28, 1862. He held the office of chief justice of the court of sessions for Penobscot county from 1825 till 1827, when he was appointed county attorney, which office he held seven years. He was a man of influence in his profession and a promoter of all good enterprises, both material and spiritual. He was one of the class, now nearly gone, who held to the good old custom of seeking God's blessing at the table and before the family altar, although he never made a profession of religion.

His children, all by first wife, Sophia, were,

Born in Hampden:

1765 Sophia (Godfrey), b. Feb. 18, 1808; d. May 28, 1811.
1766 John Edwards (Godfrey), b. Sept. 6, 1809; m. 1st, May 16, 1837, Elizabeth Angela Stackpole, daughter of David Stackpole of Portland, Me.; she died May 27, 1868; 2d, Sept. 19, 1876, Laura J. Schwartz, daughter of M. Schwartz of Bangor. John E. Godfrey is a member of the bar, has been in the common council of Bangor, alderman four consecutive years, on the school committee over ten years, and judge of the probate court for Penobscot county since 1856. He had two sons by first wife and a daughter by the last. His eldest son, John Franklin (Godfrey), was captain of cavalry in Louisiana under Butler and Banks, and afterward lieutenant-colonel of 2d Maine cavalry. He is now a lawyer and city attorney of Los Angeles, Cal.; is married and has a son and daughter. His second son, George F. (Godfrey), is married and has Henry Prentiss, George Herbert, Edward Rawson, named for his ancestor, the secretary of the colony of Massachusetts 40 years, and Angela (Godfrey).
1767 Charlotte (Godfrey), b. March 25, 1811; m. Rev. Alpha Morton; d. in West Auburn, Me., Sept. 4, 1871. He went to Oakham, Mass., 1872.
1768 Ann Sophia (Godfrey), b. Dec. 24, 1812; m. Rev. John Dodge of Waldoborough, Me., and after in Braintree, Mass., where he died, June 19, 1872, aged 60. Their daughter Ellen is the wife of Rev. Minot J. Savage of Boston.
1769 Emeline (Godfrey), b. Nov. 11, 1814; m. Rev. W. W. Whipple, now of Jaynesville, Iowa.
1770 Mary (Godfrey), b. March 12, 1817; m. Samuel F. Stone of Harvard, Mass.
1771 Caroline (Godfrey), b. Aug. 15, 1819; d. Aug. 19, 1819.
1772 Julia (Godfrey), b. Aug. 20, 1820; m. 1st, Robert Dutton of Bangor; he died Nov. 23, 1843; 2d, A. C. Waltman of LaGrange, Mo.

Born in Bangor:

1773 James (Godfrey), b. Oct. 8, 1822; m. Mary C. Wheelwright, daughter of George and sister of Hon. Joseph S. Wheelwright of Bangor. He graduated from Bowdoin 1844, and settled in Houlton, Me., as a lawyer, where he died, Aug. 30, 1850.

---

* RICHARD GODFREY was born in England, came to this country and was in Taunton as early as 1652. Hon. John, above, was the fifth descent from him; married, first, May 21, 1807, Sophia Dutton, born July 31, 1786, daughter of Col. Samuel Dutton of Bangor; she died 1835.

8

1774  George Godfrey), b. Oct. 22, 1824; d. Dec. 31, 1834.
1775  Arthur (Godfrey), b. Feb. 18, 1828; d. in Virginia City, Nevada.
1776  A daughter, b. Aug. 20, 1831; d. Aug. 22, 1831.

## 549

ELIZABETH CHLOE THURSTON[5] (*David*,[4] *Richard*,[3] *Daniel*,[2] *Daniel*[1]), sister of the preceding, and daughter of David[4] and Chloe (Redington) Thurston of Sedgwick, Me.; born there June 18, 1803; baptized by Rev. Daniel Merrill; married, in Sedgwick, Jan. 1, 1843, REV. JOSEPH SMITH, born in Cornish, Me., Feb. 7, 1810, son of John Pike and Nancy (Hayes) Smith, a farmer and dealer in lumber, who afterward lived in Denmark and died there; his wife Nancy died in Belvidere, Ill.   J. P. Smith was born in New Market, N. H., Dec. 6, 1785; Nancy Hayes, his wife, was born in Dover, N. H., April 27, 1786; they were married in Cornish Feb. 11, 1807.

Rev. Joseph Smith attended North Bridgton and Fryeburgh academies and studied two years with Rev. J. P. Fessenden of South Bridgton, attended the classical school at Bangor, and graduated from Bangor theological seminary in 1842.   He was ordained as an evangelist at Oldtown Nov. 10, 1842, where he preached a year.   Taken sick, he went to his father's in Denmark, and after a long illness preached a while there.   In 1845 he went to Wilton and labored four years; spent the winter of 1849–50 in Belvidere, Ill., supplying the Presbyterian church six months.   The malarial climate injuring his health, he returned to Maine and in the autumn of 1850 commenced preaching at Boothbay Harbor, and remained a year and a half, when health failing again he went to his mother's, then residing in Bridgton.   Commenced preaching at Lovell July 11, 1852, where he remained about sixteen years; spent a few months at the West and returned to supply at Buxton Center in 1868, and in Minot 1871 till July, 1876.   He was a laborious, faithful, and successful pastor, having received one hundred and sixty-one members to the church during his ministry in his various fields of labor.   No children.

## 550

DANIEL OLIVER THURSTON[5] of North Sedgwick, Me. (*David*,[4] *Richard*,[3] *Daniel*,[2] *Daniel*[1]), brother of the preceding, and son of David[4] and Chloe (Redington) Thurston of Sedgwick, Me.; born there May 5, 1805; baptized by Rev. Daniel Oliver;* married, June 1, 1843, APHIA KIMBALL HINCKLEY, daughter of Nehemiah and Phebe Peters (Kimball) Hinckley of Bluehill, Me.   She died June 2, 1878, aged 57.

Mr. Thurston has always lived on the homestead, and is a thrifty farmer and lumberman, having acquired a competence beside giving his children a good education.   His wife was a member of the Congregational church in Bluehill and was greatly beloved by all who knew her.

---

*After Rev. Mr. Merrill with a majority of the church in Sedgwick became Baptists, about thirty under the lead of David Thurston, the father of Daniel Oliver, maintained meetings under the patronage of the Massachusetts Missionary Society.   Revs. Daniel Lovejoy, Jotham Sewall, John Sawyer [who lived to be 103 years old], and Daniel Oliver of Boston [who baptized and gave the name to Daniel Oliver Thurston], labored there at different times, sent by the society.

Their children, all born in Sedgwick, were:

1787 David,[6] b. April 11, 1844; m. March 12, 1872, Elva Medora Gale; is a farmer in Sedgwick. They have:
    1788 *Harry David,*[7] b. Dec. 19, 1872.
    1789 *George Lawrence,*[7] b. Dec. 17, 1874.
    1790 *Clara Emeline,*[7] b. June 26, 1876.
    1791 *Ray Condon,*[7] b. March 21, 1878.
1792 George Henry,[6] b. Oct. 9, 1845; n.m.; in Oakland, Cal.
1793 Franklin Hinckley,[6] b. Oct. 26, 1847; d. Oct. 20, 1864.
1794 Daniel,[6] b. Dec. 1, 1849; m. Dec. 5, 1876, Delia A. Hewey; clerk in Orland, Me.
1795 Clara Maria,[6] b. Feb. 11, 1852; m. Sept. 7, 1871, Capt. Grenville Payson Clapp, a master mariner in Sedgwick. They have:
    1796 *Eugene Payson* (Clapp), b. Oct. 15, 1872.
    1797 *Rowland Grenville* (Clapp), b. March 13, 1874.
    1798 *Nellie Eliza* (Clapp), b. June 23, 1877.
1799 John,[6] b. Feb. 3, 1854.
1800 Fanny Goodale,[6] b. March 12, 1856; d. Aug. 12, 1871.
1801 Ella Mehitable,[6] b. May 16, 1858.
1802 Jennie Sparhawk,[6] b. March 20, 1861; d. June 9, 1877.
1803 Frederic Harlow,[6] b. Jan. 6, 1865.

## 551

WILLIAM THURSTON[5] of Newburyport, Mass. (*David,*[4] *Richard,*[3] *Daniel,*[2] *Daniel*[1]), brother of the preceding, and son of David[4] and Chloe (Redington) Thurston of Sedgwick, Me.; born there Feb. 7, 1807; baptized by Rev. Joseph Brown; married, first, Oct. 16, 1837, DOROTHY PEARSON COLMAN, born Feb. 13, 1810, daughter of Jeremiah and Mary (Chute) Colman of Newburyport, Mass. [see no. 571]; she died Jan. 4, 1868. Second, March 3, 1870, CAROLINE ELIZABETH GREENLEAF, born Feb. 8, 1823, daughter of George and Elizabeth (Wheelwright) Greenleaf of Newburyport.

Mr. Thurston is a lumber merchant in Newburyport. He left his father's house at the age of seventeen, and lived at South Orrington some four years, at Bucksport a year, at West Prospect, now Searsport, a year, at Bangor for five years, till 1836, then Bucksport and Orland till 1844, when he went to Newburyport, and has remained there since. He joined the Congregational church in Bucksport in 1829; removed his connection to the first church in Bangor and colonized to form the Hammond street church, Bangor, in 1833; removed to the first church in Newbury, Mass., in 1845, and Jan. 1, 1850, was, with others, dismissed to form the Whitefield Congregational church in Newburyport, and has been the senior deacon ever since its formation. Both his wives were members of this church. He has ever been an active and influential member of the church, and has been moderator of the General Conference of Massachusetts and president of the State Sunday-school Convention of all the evangelical denominations of the state, held at Newburyport, 1858.

His children, by first wife, Dorothy, were:

1814 Mary Colman,[6] b. Nov. 1, 1838.
1815 Lucy Redington,[6] b. Dec. 16, 1840.
1816 Maria Buck,[6] b. July 4, 1843.
1817 Alice Hale,[6] b. Sept. 18, 1845; m. March 12, 1872, Alvah F. Hunter.
1818 William,[6] b. Aug. 11, 1847; m. Aug. 11, 1875, Sarah Eva Eastman; no children.

1819   Elizabeth Smith,[6] b. Nov. 20, 1849.
1820   George,[6] b. Dec. 21, 1851; went down with the ship Tennyson, in the Indian ocean, Feb. 22, 1873.
1821   Sarah Dorothy,[6] b. Sept. 11, 1853.
1822   Helen Tracy,[6] b. Nov. 8, 1855; d. March 10, 1872.

## 564

RICHARD CHUTE [6] (*Mehitable Thurston*,[4] *Richard*,[8] *Daniel*,[2] *Daniel*[1]), son of Dea. James and Mehitable (Thurston) Chute of Boxford, Mass.; born there Sept. 3, 1778; married, Oct. 17, 1805, DOROTHY PEARSON, born May 8, 1784, daughter of Benjamin Pearson of Newbury, Mass., the seventh Benjamin Pearson, in a direct line, living on the same spot and in the same house, and whose grandson of the same name now, 1877, owns and occupies it. He died in St. Louis, Mo., Oct. 24, 1820, aged 42 ; she died· May 9, 1870, aged 86.
Richard Chute was a farmer in Byfield, Mass.

Their children were :

1833   Alexander (Chute), b. Sept. 27, 1806; m. Martha F. Gould of Malden, Mass., and died Oct. 11, 1841, leaving one daughter.
1834   Ariel Parish (Chute), b. May 16, 1809; m. April 25, 1836, Sarah Maria Winslow Chandler, b. Dec. 13, 1805, daughter of Peleg and Esther (Parsons) Chandler of New Gloucester, Me., then, but since of Bangor, Me. He graduated from Bowdoin in 1832, pursued theological studies at Bangor, and graduated from Andover, Mass., in 1835; ordained over the Congregational church in Oxford. Me., March 16, 1836, having commenced preaching there Jan. 1 previous, Rev. David Thurston of Winthrop, Me., preached the sermon : dismissed Dec. 31, 1838; went to Pownal, Me., in April, 1839, and left in Dec.,1841, when he was appointed preceptor of the Warren academy, where he remained nearly five years; installed at Harrison, Me., Feb. 24. 1847, dismissed Aug. 15, 1849; preached and taught school at Lynnfield, Mass., one year, when he was elected preceptor of the Dummer academy of Newbury, Mass., where he remained nearly three years ; supplied the church in Lynnfield principally till June, 1857, when he was settled over the first Congregational church in Ware, Mass., where he remained four years ; for sixteen years past he has been in the government service in connection with the United States Treasury, in post-office building in Boston, his family living in Sharon, Mass.   Children :
    1835   *Ellen Maria* (Chute), b. in Oxford May 23, 1837; m. Sept. 11, 1865. Dr. Amasa D. Bacon of Sharon, where they reside; one daughter.
    1836   *Francis Pearson* (Chute), b. in Pownal June 2, 1840.
    1837   *Richard Henry* (Chute), b. in Woburn, Mass., March 13, 1843; m. Nov. 6, 1867, Susan R. Nelson of Georgetown, Mass.; live in Eau Claire, Wis., and have three children living, one deceased.  He was in the war against the rebellion from private to captain.
    1838   *Esther Andrews* (Chute), b. in Milton, Mass., June 22, 1846; m. July 3, 1866, Edgar Mace Hixon of Sharon, and died there Dec. 31, 1866.
    1839   *Sarah Barnes* (Chute), b. in Harrison July 30, 1848.
1840   Betsey (Chute), b. June 7, 1810; d. Oct. 27, 1856.
1841   Andrew (Chute), b. April 11, 1814; m. Sept. 30, 1836, Ann Perry, daughter of Isaac Perry, Esq., of Orland, Me.  They had :
    1842   *Charles Richard* (Chute), b. Aug. 1, 1837; d. Sept., 1870, just as he was landed from the ship of which he was first officer at Queenstown, Ireland.
    1843   *Martha Elizabeth* (Chute), b. Jan. 4, 1841; d. June 24, 1868.
    1844   *George Albert* (Chute), b. Mar. 3, 1843; m. Clara Wood of Bluehill, Me.
    1845   *Sarah Buck* (Chute), b. Sept. 13, 1846.
    1846   *Kimball C.* (Chute), b. April 24, 1848; d. Sept. 3, 1850.
    1847   *James Andrew* (Chute), b. Nov. 12, 1850.
    1848   *Edward L.* (Chute), b. 1853; in theological seminary at Andover, 1877.
1849   Benjamin Pearson (Chute), b. May 13, 1816.

## 591

WILLIAM THURSTON[6] (*Joseph,*[5] *Joseph,*[4] *Joseph,*[3] *Joseph,*[2] *Daniel*[1]), son of Joseph[5] and Lydia (Parsons) Thurston of Rockport, Mass.; born there Feb. 22, 1783; married NANCY PARSONS, daughter of James and Patience Parsons of Rockport.

Mr. Thurston was a fisherman, residing in Rockport.

### Their children were:

1858  Nancy,[7] m. Washington Tarr; both dead.  They had:
    1859  *Phebe* (Tarr), m. George Blatchford of Rockport; is dead, 1877.
    1860  *Washington* (Tarr), m. Anna James of Ipswich, Mass.
    1861  *Elisa* (Tarr), m. David Smith, jr., of Rockport; is dead.
    1862  *Jane* (Tarr), m. Edwin York of Rockport.
    1863  *Howard* (Tarr), m. Sarah Elliot of Beverly, Mass.
1864  Martha,[7] m. Benjamin Andrews and had:
    1865  *Benjamin* (Andrews), m. Delia Gamage of South Bristol, Me.
    1866  *Martha* (Andrews), m. John Norwood of Rockport; is dead.
1867  William,[7] b. Sept. 6, 1816; m. Oct. 10, 1835, Emily Pool, b. April 27, 1816. He resided in Rockport, and died May 24, 1854, after which she married Benjamin Knights of Rockport.  They had:
    1868  *George William,*[8] b. March 21, 1836; m. Sally Pool.
    1869  *Levi Pool,*[8] b. Dec. 21, 1840; m. Susan Trafts.
    1870  *Samuel Davis,*[8] b. Sept. 9, 1845; m. Mary J. Allen.
    1871  *Albert F.,*[8] b. Aug. 7, 1849; m. Anna Parker of Nova Scotia.
1872  Lucy,[7] n.m.
1873  Samuel D.,[7] d. young.

## 592

JOSEPH THURSTON[6] (*Joseph,*[5] *Joseph,*[4] *Joseph,*[3] *Joseph,*[2] *Daniel*[1]), brother of the preceding, and son of Joseph[5] and Lydia (Parsons) Thurston of Rockport, Mass.; born there Jan. 22, 1787; married ESTHER NORWOOD.  He was a fisherman, living in Rockport.

### Their children were:

1884  William,[7] b. 1811; m. Margaret O. Blatchford; was a fisherman, living in Rockport.  They had:
    1885  *William E.,*[8] b. Dec. 5, 1834; m. Nov. 9, 1862, Elizabeth Denison Burnham, b. June 17, 1841; no children.
    1886  *John,*[8] b. Oct. 11, 1836; drowned in 1859, coming from Georges Banks in schooner Young America.
    1887  *Margery A.,*[8] b. 1838; m. Benjamin Wetherbee.
1888  Esther,[7] m. Andrew Griffin of Gloucester, Mass., and had:
    1889  *George* (Griffin), drowned Jan. 17, 1865, on a passage from Newfoundland to Gloucester.
    1890  *John* (Griffin), enlisted in the war against the rebellion, in 1861, and never returned.
    1891  *Andrew* (Griffin), living, 1878, with his mother; n.m.
1892  Martha,[7] m. William Goday and had:
    1893  *Martha* (Goday), m. William Bailey.
    1894  *A child,* burned in a school-house.
1895  Joseph,[7] drowned in 1851 from schooner Four Sisters, on a passage from Gloucester to St. Lawrence bay.
1896  Sally,[7] m. William Winn of Wells, Me., and had:
    1897  *Sarah Jane* (Winn), m. Edward Walton of Eastport, Me.; he was lost at sea on the Georges Banks Feb., 1879.
    1898  *Mary A.* (Winn), m. George Barron.
    1899  *Ida* (Winn), m. Albert Lane of Gloucester.
    1900  *Fostina* (Winn), m. George Billings of Kittery, Me.
    1901  *Nelly* (Winn).
    1902  *Alberta* (Winn), d.
    1903  *Hannah* (Winn), n.m.

## 630

DANIEL THURSTON[5] (*Daniel,[4] Joseph,[3] Joseph,[2] Daniel[1]*), son of Daniel[4] and Anna (Tarr) Thurston of Rockport, Mass.; born there 1758; married, Jan. 2, 1812, SALLY ROWE, born 1795. He died 1836; she died Jan. 10, 1878.

He was a fisherman, owned a vessel that was lost, loaded with fish, on Cape Negro, N. S. He said he had a peck of silver dollars when he bought the vessel.

Children:

+1914    John Rowe,[6] b. Sept. 25, 1812; m. Lucy Rowe.
   1915    Daniel,[6] b. 1817; m. Martha Harris of Rockport, and died in 1854, aged 37; no children.
   1916    Sally,[6] m. Samuel Avery Bray of West Gloucester, Mass.; three children.
+1917    Winthrop,[6] b. Nov. 9, 1820; m. 1st, Mary Fears; 2d, Sarah Eliza Burnham.
+1918    William Henry,[6] b. Sept. 24, 1823; m. Anna Sparrow.

## 631

NATHANIEL THURSTON[5] (*Daniel,[4] Joseph,[3] Joseph,[2] Daniel[1]*), brother of the preceding, and son of Daniel[4] and Anna (Tarr) Thurston of Rockport, Mass.; born there Aug. 7, 1769; married, July 10, 1801, BETSEY GEE, born July 10, 1782. He died Oct. 2, 1829; she died March 26, 1838.

Children:

   1929    Eliza,[6] b. May 3, 1802; m. Dec. 4, 1825, William Wharf.
   1930    Maria,[6] b. May 6, 1804; m. Oct. 6, 1823, Charles Ward.
+1931    Nathaniel,[6] b. Aug. 5, 1806; m. Ruth Butler.
   1932    Benjamin,[6] b. Jan. 16, 1809; d. Oct. 29, 1810.
+1933    William Gee,[6] b. Dec. 24, 1811; m. Rachel Rich Smith.
   1934    Mary Jane,[6] b. June 11, 1814; d. Nov. 10, 1825.
   1935    Fanny,[6] b. Oct. 11, 1816; m. Gerry Lane.
+1936    James Gee,[6] b. April 23, 1820; m. Lucy Harvey.
+1937    Benjamin,[6] b. Aug. 16, 1823; m. Nancy Lane.

## 643

AMBROSE THURSTON[5] (*Capt. John,[4] Joseph,[3] Joseph,[2] Daniel[1]*), eldest son of Capt. John[4] and Mrs. Eunice (Gott) (Stockbridge) Thurston of Rockport, Mass.; married POLLY GAMAGE.

He resided in Mt. Desert, Me.; was a carpenter on the United States ship Merrimac. He died in Rockport, Mass.

Their children, all born in Rockport, were:

   1948    Ambrose,[6] drowned in Rockport harbor.
   1949    Polly or Mary,[6] m. Isaac Gott of Mt. Desert, Me., and had:
      1950    *Polly* or *Mary* (Gott), m. John Verrill of Mt. Desert; eight children.
      1951    *Nancy* (Gott), m. John Gott of Mt. Desert; eight children.
      1952    *Hannah* (Gott), m. Sullivan Webster of Mt. Desert; two children.
      1953    *Serena Merrill* (Gott), m. Ambrose Thurston [see no. 2005].
      1954    *Isaac* (Gott), m. Betsey Thurston [see no.    ].
      1955    *Almira T.* (Gott), m. Ambrose Thurston [see no.    ].
      1956    *James T.* (Gott), m. Martha Small of Deer Isle, Me.
      1957    *Lydia* (Gott), d.
   1958    Betsey,[6] m. Alexander Robinson Foster of Bristol, Me. He died 1869; she died Sept. 6, 1870. They had:
      1959    *Ambrose* (Foster).
      1960    *Alexander* (Foster).
      1961    *Frederick* (Foster).
      1962    *Elijah* (Foster).
      1963    *John Jackson* (Foster).

1964　*Thomas* (Foster).
1965　*Charlotte Trumbull* (Foster), m. Wm. Cunningham of Newcastle, Me.
1966　*Belinda* (Foster).
1967　*Nancy Thurston* (Foster).
1968　*Deborah Tarr* (Foster).
1969　*Harriet Thorp* (Foster).
+1970　Nathaniel C.,[6] m. Elizabeth Robbins.
1971　Susan,[6] m. Israel Putnam; lived in Deer Isle, Mt. Desert, and Columbia, Me., where he died, insane; eight children.
+1972　John,[6] m. Nancy Gott.
1973　James,[6] m. Deborah Tarr of Bristol; she and her only child died at same time and he went to sea and was never heard from.

### 644

AMOS THURSTON [5] (*Capt. John,*[4] *Joseph,*[8] *Joseph,*[2] *Daniel*[1]), brother of the preceding, and son of Capt. John [4] and Eunice (Gott) (Stockbridge) Thurston of Rockport, Mass.; born there Oct. 20, 1772; married MARY GOTT, daughter of Daniel Gott of Gott's Island, Me. He died June 14, 1850.

Mr. Thurston was a farmer, fisherman, and fitter in Deer Isle, Me.; was captain nearly forty years. He and his wife were very devout members of the Baptist church.

### Their children were:

1984　Mary,[6] b. Jan. 26, 1798; d. 1803.
1985　Eunice,[6] b. Feb. 6, 1800; m. Edward Small, a sailor in Deer Isle. They had:
　　1986　*Mary Hatch* (Small), b. March 11, 1820; m. Joshua Gross of Orland, Me.; seven children.
　　1987　*Martha* (Small), b. 1822.
1988　Susan,[6] b. Jan. 17, 1802; m. Dec. 7, 1821, John Webster Small, b. May 12, 1799; he was a farmer in Deer Isle, and died Feb., 1875. They had:
　　1989　*Mary Ann* (Small), b. Sept. 9, 1822; m. William Allen; live in Cape Elizabeth, Me.; eight children.
　　1990　*John* (Small), b. Oct. 12, 1824; m. Elizabeth Stinson; eleven children.
　　1991　*Edward* (Small), b. March 23, 1826; m. Harriet Stinson; nine children.
　　1992　*Enoch* (Small), b. July 6, 1828; m. Mary Jane York; three children.
　　1993　*Amos T.* (Small), b. March 17, 1831; m. Sarah Robbins; ten children.
　　1994　*Walter H.* (Small), b. Sept. 8, 1833; m. 1st, Sarah E. Fifield; 2d, Ora A. Lane; two children.
　　1995　*Susan T.* (Small), b. May 5, 1836; m. Martin V. Warren; three children.
　　1996　*Elizabeth S.* (Small), b. Sept. 15, 1839; m. Avery Fifield; six children.
　　1997　*William W.* (Small), b. April 2, 1842; m. Susan Crockett.
　　1998　*Serena* (Small), b. Sept. 17, 1844.
1999　Mary,[6] b. April 6, 1804; m. Nov. 5, 1826, Nathaniel Havelock Richardson, a ship carpenter at Green's Landing, Tremont, Me., deacon of Free Baptist church; he died May 2, 1842; she died Sept. 5, 1850. They had:
　　2000　*Amos Thurston* (Richardson), b. Feb. 10, 1829.
　　2001　*William* (Richardson).
　　2002　*Frederick* (Richardson), d. 1846.
　　2003　*Mary Ann* (Richardson).
　　2004　*Clara* (Richardson), d. 1836.
+2005　Ambrose,[6] b. Aug. 24, 1806; m. Serena Merrill Gott.
+2006　Amos,[6] b. Jan. 31, 1809; m. Ann Stinson.
2007　Elizabeth,[6] b. Aug. 31, 1815; m. 1st, Walter Butler Hamblen; he died 1836; 2d, Capt. Jesse Stinson, a farmer and fisherman of Deer Isle. She had:
　　2008　*Ambrose Thurston* (Hamblen), b. Oct. 17, 1833; m. Sept. 30, 1855, Caroline Matilda Mills of Deer Isle; is member of F. Baptist church.
　　2009　*Margaret* (Hamblen), b. June 2, 1836; m. Sept. 30, 1855, Peter H. Mills, a ship carpenter, residing in West Deer Isle; both members of the Free Baptist church; he was S. S. superintendent eight years.
　　2010　*Ira* (Stinson), b. Dec. 19, 1839; m. Feb. 26, 1862, Elizabeth Barber.
　　2011　*Amos* (Stinson), b. March 8, 1842; lost, with his brother Ira, on the

Georges Banks in the gale of March 23, 1864, and a marble monument has been erected in the cemetery at West Deer Isle to their memory.

2012 *James Edwin* (Stinson), b. March 19, 1845; m. his brother Ira's widow; three children.
2013 *Walter Butler* (Stinson), b. Aug. 1, 1847; d. April 10, 1870.
2014 *Enoch Small* (Stinson), b. Sept. 25, 1850; d. Dec. 10, 1850.
2015 *Sophronia Elizabeth* (Stinson), b. Oct. 27, 1851; m. Oct. 16, 1863, Simeon Goss, and had Austin Colby Stinson (Goss).
2016 *Mary Alice* (Stinson), b. March 25, 1854; m. Dec. 28, 1875, Austin Avery Colby; had one son, d. in infancy.
2017 *Sullivan* (Stinson), b. Nov. 4, 1856; d. Dec. 15, 1871.

The mother of these children has been confined to her bed for many years. They are both members of the Free Baptist church.

2018 Hannah Ann,[6] b. April 14, 1819; d. Oct. 8, 1836.

## 646

WILLIAM THURSTON[5] (*Capt. John,[4] Joseph,[3] Joseph,[2] Daniel[1]*), brother of the preceding, and son of Capt. John[4] and Eunice (Gott) (Stockbridge) Thurston of Rockport, Mass.; born there Aug. 27, 1778; married, Dec. 24, 1800, NANCY FOSTER, born Feb. 12, 1783. He died June 11, 1852.

He was a pilot, residing in Castine, and Pemaquid, Bristol, Me.; a Congregationalist. His father moved to Deer Isle, Me., when he was very young.

Their children were:

+2029 William,[6] b. Nov. 9, 1802; m. Margaret McKay.
+2030 Solomon,[6] b. Feb. 16, 1804; m. Margaret McKay.
2031 Matilda,[6] b. May 15, 1808.
+2032 George Washington,[6] b. March 13, 1810; m. 1st, Sarah McKay; 2d, Mrs. Mary Sproul.
2033 Nancy,[6] b. May 18, 1812: m. John Blaisdel of Bristol.
2034 Susan F.,[6] b. in Pemaquid, Bristol, April 3, 1822; m. 1st, Mar. 29, 1851, Eben Trask; he died Oct. 13, 1851, at East Boston, Mass., aged 28; 2d, May 27, 1856, Capt. Charles D. Ferrin of Brunswick, Me. He sailed for Aspinwall in September, where he contracted the local fever together with all his crew. He shipped another crew and sailed for the West Indies Dec. 12th, and died when ten days out, aged 42; his mate died same day. The brig was taken into Carthagena after being out fifty-two days. 3d, 1863, John Andrews, son of John and Lucy (Coombs) Andrews of Brunswick; a farmer, residing in West Jefferson, Me.; a Methodist. She had:
2035 *Eben Austin* (Trask), b. in East Boston Jan. 29, 1852; resides in Reno, Nevada; n. m.

## 647

JOHN THURSTON[5] (*Capt. John,[4] Joseph,[3] Joseph,[2] Daniel[1]*), brother of the preceding, and son of Capt. John[4] and Eunice (Gott) (Stockbridge) Thurston of Rockport, Mass.; born there 1781; married, 1804, SARAH FOSTER, born 1781, daughter of John and Susannah (Robinson) Foster of Bristol, Me. He died Nov. 9, 1835; she died Nov. 26, 1847.

He lived at Christmas Cove, South Bristol, Me.; was a farmer and mariner; summers occupying his time between the farm and sea, and teaching school winters. He was a Baptist, and though not ordained used to preach wherever he was and the people had no supply. He was a man of great physical strength and agility. It used to be said of him that "he was one of nature's noblemen, with free and inalienable rights written all over him."

## Children:

2046 Susan Sproul,[3] b. 1805; n.m.; d. 1831.
2047 Nancy,[6] b. April 21, 1808; m. 1828, Robert Russell, a master mariner of
    Bristol, b. Feb. 6, 1804, son of George and Nancy (Hanly) Russell of
    Bristol. He died April 14, 1862; she died April 21, 1865. They had:
    2048 *Rachel Ann* (Russell), b. Aug. 23, 1829; went on board a schooner in
        Boston, Capt. Jonathan Pierce master, bound for Bristol, and on the
        morning of Nov. 24, 1854, foundered in a squall in the Sheepscot
        river, and all were drowned, and only her body was recovered,
        which was buried in the cemetery at South Bristol.
    2049 *Ellen* (Russell), b. March 22, 1831; m. Capt. Loring Thorpe of Bristol.
    2050 *Margaret Ann* (Russell), b. March 15, 1837; m. Capt. Edward Thorpe
        of Bristol.
    2051 *Mahala* (Russell), b. Aug. 23, 1841; m. Edward Marr of Southport,
        Me.; is a widow, living in Bristol.
    2052 *Mary Elizabeth* (Russell), b. April 6, 1845; m. Llewellyn Gamage of
        Bristol.
    2053 *Hannah* (Russell), b. Nov. 4, 1851; m. Albion Gamage of Bristol.
2054 Sarah,[6] b. 1809; n.m.; d. Aug. 20, 1848.
2055 Eliza,[6] b. March 13, 1812; m. Nov. 25, 1838, Loring Pierce, b. July 12,
    1812, son of Jonathan and Lydia (Rand) Pierce of Southport; he is a
    master mariner, residing in Southport. They had:
    2056 *Thomas Warren* (Pierce), b. Aug. 13, 1839; d. Aug. 20, 1845.
    2057 *Susan Elizabeth* (Pierce), b. Dec. 9, 1841; m. Dec. 7, 1852, Elisha
        Merritt Whitten of Southport; d. Dec. 7, 1863.
    2058 *Mahala Thurston* (Pierce), b. March 26, 1844; d. Oct. 7, 1845.
    2059 *Hollis Loring* (Pierce), b. Aug. 8, 1846; d. Feb. 10, 1868.
    2060 *Ida Ella* (Pierce), b. Sept. 1, 1849; m. June 21, 1874, Wilber Grover
        of Southport.
    2061 *Harvey Thomas* (Pierce), b. Oct. 1, 1851.
2062 Almira,[6] b. 1813; n.m.; d. 1831.
2063 John,[6] b. 1815; m. Mrs. Almira Given; was passenger on a vessel bound
    from Bristol to Boston, wrecked on Rye beach, N. H., Nov., 1850, and
    was the only one lost; his body was recovered and buried in the ceme-
    tery at Bristol Mills; no children.
2064 Mahala,[6] b. 1817; m. March, 1841, Capt. Daniel Cameron 2d, of South-
    port; d. Aug. 9, 1841.
+2065 Thomas Foster,[6] b. Sept. 21, 1822; m. Alice Vose Albee.
2066 Ambrose,[6] b. 1824; d. 1826.
2067 Harvey,[6] b. 1826; d. 1830.
2068 Arvilla Lyons,[6] b. June 27, 1827; m. Dec. 16, 1845, Capt. Daniel Cameron
    2d, formerly husband of her sister Mahala. He has been for years sen-
    ior member of the firm of Cameron & Orne of Southport, and is engaged
    in navigation and trade; has been selectman several years, town treas-
    urer, and has held other offices of trust. They had:
    2069 *Mahala* (Cameron), b. Dec. 22, 1846; m. Emerson McKown of South-
        port.
    2070 *Sarah Alice* (Cameron), b. Oct. 29, 1848; d. May 17, 1851.
    2071 *Charles* (Cameron), b. Oct. 27, 1849; d. Dec. 9, 1872.
    2072 *Melissa Alice* (Cameron), b. Oct. 2, 1851; d. March 24. 1863.
    2073 *John* (Cameron), b. Aug. 31, 1853; graduated at mercantile school.
    2074 *Thomas Thurston* (Cameron), b. June 15, 1855; graduated at mercan-
        tile school.
    2075 *William* (Cameron), b. Sept. 15, 1857; m. Maria Todd of Southport.
    2076 *Emma* (Cameron), b. Nov. 27, 1861; d. June 3, 1873.
    2077 *Freddie* (Cameron), b. March 14, 1863; d. April 20, 1873.
    2078 *Moses Nickerson* (Cameron), b. May 5, 1866; d. Jan. 10, 1870.

## 648

SOLOMON THURSTON[5] (*Capt. John,*[4] *Joseph,*[3] *Joseph,*[2] *Daniel*[1]),
brother of the preceding, and son of Capt. John[4] and Eunice (Gott)
(Stockbridge) Thurston of Rockport, Mass.; born in Deer Isle, Me.,
Feb. 21, 1783; married SARAH GOTT, born May 26, 1786, daughter

of Daniel and Hannah (Norwood) Gott of Mt. Desert, Me. He died
in Rockport, at his son William's, Aug. 4, 1854; she died Aug. 23,
1869.

Mr. Thurston was a sea captain, residing in Deer Isle, Rockport,
and Camden, Me. He was a member of the Baptist church since
the age of fifteen. He and his vessel were taken by the British while
getting wood and water at Seal cove, and carried to Hailfax. The
vessel was not condemned, and he returned late in the season, losing
his summer's work.

Their children were:

2089  Sarah,[6] b. Nov. 9, 1809; m. Enos Cooper of Rockport, b. in North Haven,
        Me., July 3, 1813, son of Lemuel and Margaret (McDonald) Cooper; he
        was a ship master and member of the Baptist church. She died July 23,
        1874, beloved by all who knew her, and inscribed on her tomb-stone was
        "she always made home happy." They had, born in North Haven:

2090  *Mattie* (Cooper), b. April 6, 1839; m. J. B. Arnold, a cooper in Rock-
        land, Me.

2091  *Vonia* (Cooper), b. March 17, 1842; m. Albert Snow, a pattern maker
        in Hyde Park, Mass.

2092  *Daniel Thurston* (Cooper), b. Oct. 24, 1846; m. June 26, 1870, Maggie
        L. Crockett, daughter of Dea. Samuel Y. Crockett of So. Haven.
        He is clerk for J. Bird & Co., corn and flour dealers in Rockland;
        is deacon of the Baptist church. They have Blanche May (Cooper),
        b. April 11, 1871

2122   *Lucy* (Robards), b. April 22, 1821.
2123   *George* (Robards), b. May 29, 1823.
2124   *Henry* (Robards), b. June 28, 1825.
2125   *Laura* (Robards), b. June 27, 1827.
2126   *Esther* (Robards), b. July 7, 1831.
2127   *William* (Robards), b. Sept. 30, 1836.
2128   Sally,[6] b. July 4, 1796; m. 1815, Wm. Platts Clark, b. July 23, 1791, and had :
    2129   *William Platts* (Clark), b. Oct. 27, 1815; m. Oct. 2, 1837, Judith
        Woodbury Griffin.   He died Feb. 4, 1867: she died July 4, 1875;
        four children.
    2130   *Moses* (Clark), b. March 1, 1819; n.m.; d. Dec., 1878.
    2131   *Benjamin Platts* (Clark), b. May 27, 1827.
    2132   *Eliza Ann* (Clark), b. Jan. 6, 1831; m. James Pool.
    2133   *Charles* (Clark), b. Jan. 27, 1835; m. Martha Parsons.
    2134   *George* (Clark), b. 1837; n.m.
2135   William,[6] b. about 1802; m. Margaret A. Jordan of Portland; sailed from
    there as master, and was lost in a gale when three days out, in 1831.
    They had :
    2136   *William H.,*[7] b. June 26, 1830; d. 1848, aged 18.
2137   Charlotte,[6] b. Aug. 1, 1804; m. Dec. 15, 1825, William Tarr, and had :
    2138   *William* (Tarr).
    2139   *Edward* (Tarr).
    2140   *George Washington* (Tarr).
+2141   Henry,[6] b. Dec 1, 1808; m. 1st, Rhoda Kinsman; 2d, Jane Plummer.
2142   Betsey,[6] m. David Dyer of Portland.
2143   James,[6] unmarried.

---

**686**

                                                 122½

THOMAS THURSTON[5] (*Abner,*[4] *Abner,*[3] *James,*[2] *Daniel*[1]), son of
Abner[4] and Martha (Piper) Thurston of Exeter, N. H.; born there
Jan. 19, 1752; married, April 7, 1775, LUCY FENDERSON, born Dec.
17, 1751.   He died in 1830, and was buried on his farm; she died in
1832.

    Mr. Thurston purchased a tract of land in Parsonsfield, Me., im-
proved it a little, sold and went to Scarborough, Me., and bought
land on which he lived and died.   He built a little house on what is
called the "ash swamp road," about two miles from Dunstan Corner, in which his wife lived while he was in the revolutionary war.
The wolves were numerous then and used to make night hideous with
their howling.   After the war he built the old homestead on the
"broad turn road," about the same distance from Dunstan.   This old
house was replaced by another, and within three years a more modern one still has been built in its place.   He was also an itinerant
shoemaker, as was the custom in newly settled places in those days.

### Children, all born in Scarborough :

+2149   Daniel,[6] b Oct. 17, 1776; m. Sally Merrill.
2150   Sarah,[6] b. Aug. 5, 1780; m. Dec., 1799, Ephraim Holmes of Buxton, Me.
2151   Mary,[6] b. June 6, 1782; m. Roger Edgecomb of Hollis, Me., and moved to
    New York.
+2152   Alexander,[6] b. June 10. 1784; m. Almira Fickett.
+2153   James,[6] b. Dec. 19, 1787; m. Sarah McKenney.
+2154   Thomas,[6] b. Feb. 23, 1790; m. Clarissa B. Kimball.
2155   Lucy,[6] b. Nov. 11, 1791; m. Oct. 23, 1808, by Rev. Asa Heath, Phineas
    Merrill of Scarborough Beach, and had :
    2155a   *William* (Merrill).
    2155b   *John* (Merrill).
    2155c   *Catharine* (Merrill).
+2156   William,[6] b. June 20, 1794; m. Catherine Simonton.

Their children, born in Bridgewater, N. H., were:

+2178  Asa,⁶ b. Dec. 17, 1800; m. Eliza Woodward Hartwell.
+2179  Abner,⁶ b. Oct. 13, 1802; m. Mary Worthen Huntoon.
+2180  Ebenezer,⁶ b. March 13, 1805; m. 1st, Sarah Salma Huntoon; 2d, Sarah
         Knowles Rogers.
+2181  Sally,⁶ b. Sept. 13, 1807; m. John Langford Hodgdon.

Born in Hill, N. H. :

+2182  Lydia,⁶ b. July 28, 1810; m. 1st, George M. Phelps; 2d, Hillery Knox.
 2183  Mary,⁶ b. March 8, 1813; m. Warren G. Currier of Brookline, Mass.

## 719

REV. JAMES THURSTON⁵ (*Capt. James,⁴ Abner,³ James,² Daniel¹*),
son of Capt. James⁴ and Mary (Jones) Thurston of Exeter, N. H.;
born there March 17, 1769; married, Oct. 9, 1791, ELIZABETH PEA-
BODY, daughter of Dr. Thomas and Elizabeth (Shaw) Peabody. Elizabeth Peabody's mother, Elizabeth, married Capt. James Thurston as
his second wife. Rev. James died in Exeter Dec. 12, 1835; his wife
died Oct. 15, 1845, aged 71.

In 1783, at the age of fourteen, he entered Phillips academy, Exeter, which commenced that year under the care of William Woodbridge, where he remained several years, and though very desirous of
a collegiate course relinquished it in deference to his father's wishes,
who desired to retain him nearer home.  He taught school a year or
two and then entered into business in Exeter, but soon removed to
Boston to superintend the business of a very respectable firm, one of
the partners being resident in England.  In a few years he became
interested in religion and returned to Exeter, and by the advice of
friends entered the ministry, in which his efforts were everywhere distinguished with remarkable success.  He had numerous calls to settle,
and in 1800 was ordained at Newmarket, N. H., where his labors
were greatly blessed.  The following notice we take from the Exeter
News Letter, Dec. 29, 1835:

"In 1805 he was engaged by the 'Piscataqua Missionary Society'
to go as a missionary to parts of Maine, New Hampshire, Vermont,
and Canada which were destitute of gospel instructors.  The success
which attended this mission may be learned from the 'Piscataqua
Evangelical Magazine,' in the second volume of which may be found
'Extracts from the Rev. Mr. Thurston's Journal' and other information on the subject.  Twice afterward, once in 1806 and once in 1807,
he was employed on a like mission.

"In 1808 he received a call from the church and society in Manchester, Mass., which he accepted, and was installed April 19, 1809.
The sermon was by the venerable Dr. Buckminster of Portsmouth,
N. H., charge by Rev. Mannasseh Cutler, LL.D., of Ipswich, Mass.
Here again his labors were crowned with remarkable success.  All
former disputes and animosities were settled; peace, union, and harmony prevailed throughout the whole town, and the church was very
much enlarged.  This happiness and usefulness continued for many
years; but at length some who had joined the church stirred up strife
and contention.  After ineffectual attempts to restore union, an ecclesiastical council was called, and at the request of Mr. Thurston they
recommended a separation.

"Some abusive attacks upon his personal and ministerial character

induced Mr. Thurston, at the urgent solicitation of his friends, to appeal to the laws in his defense. His cause was argued by the Hon. Daniel Webster and Hon. Leverett Saltonstall, before Judge Ward, Judge Shaw, and Hon. Samuel Hoar. The defendants' counsel were W. Prescott, D. Cummins, and B. R. Nichols, Esq'rs. The result was an award of $1500 for damages to Mr. Thurston.

"He returned with his family to Exeter in 1820 and continued to reside there until his death; but so much trouble and affliction had he been called to pass through that he gave up the intention of a resettlement. He continued, however, to preach in destitute parishes in the vicinity as long as his strength and ability would permit.

"To a sound judgment he united warmth of feeling, and to christian mildness and candor a full share of energy and decision. That he was without faults we have no intention to say. He was ardently devoted to the ministerial office, bringing to it all the energies of his mind and heart; and in his last years he lamented nothing so much as his inability to resume its duties. It was the object of his thoughts by day and by night. To his family he was devotedly attached, and willing to make any sacrifice for their good. In his pastoral office he was ready to undergo any hardship in discharge of his duties.

"In his feelings he was truly catholic. He ever maintained a friendly intercourse with other denominations of christians and all who differed from him in sentiment. When the attempt was first made to draw lines of separation between the trinitarian and unitarian Congregational ministers, he opposed it with his most strenuous efforts, though at that time his sentiments were trinitarian. The spirit of alienation and bitterness and exclusiveness he ever frowned upon. In the words of one who was many years with him in the ministerial office, 'Mr. Thurston was a man of a truly christian spirit.'

"In the latter years of his life, by an earnest, unremitted, and prayerful study of the sacred scriptures, his religious views were changed, and he became a decided unitarian. In his last sickness he was calm and happy. He wished to live longer, if God's will were so, that he might be useful again in the world."

Their children were:

2194  Mary,[6] b. Sept. 2, 1792; d. Dec. 18, 1817.
2195  Elizabeth Peabody,[6] b. Dec. 10, 1794; m. William Norwood; he died 1836; she died 1841; no children.
2196  Abigail,[6] b. March 3, 1798; d. Dec. 17, 1806.
2197  Ann Rogers,[6] b. March 28, 1801; d. Jan. 14, 1806.
2198  Henrietta Peabody,[6] b. Jan. 3, 1804; m. 1826, Charles Benjamin Abbot, b. Jan. 19, 1805, son of Benjamin Abbot, LL.D., for nearly fifty years the popular preceptor of Phillips academy, Exeter. He entered Harvard in class of 1826, but left before graduating; taught school; then settled on a farm in Glenburn, Me., and for some years was agent of the Brownville slate company. He died in Bangor, Me., March 8, 1874; she died 1874. They had:
　　　2199  *Francis Peabody* (Abbot), b. Jan. 1, 1827, a dentist to the imperial family of Germany; m. 1858, Caroline L. Fay, daughter of Theo. S. Fay, late United States minister to Switzerland; reside at No. 2 Hausvoigtei Platz, Berlin. They have Caroline Laura, b. 1860, Charles Henry, b. 1862. and Henrietta (Abbot), b. 1864.
+2200  James,[6] b. Dec. 11, 1806; m. Elizabeth Austin.
2201  John Rogers,[6] b. Jan. 2, 1810; graduated from Harvard 1829; n.m.; d. in Glenburn Nov. 23, 1843.

2202 Martha Ann,[6] b. March 26, 1813; m. Calvin Rogers Hubbard; he died 1837; she died 1867; no children.
2203 Thomas Peabody,[6] b. June 27, 1816; d. Sept. 11, 1816.

## 731

CALEB THURSTON [5] (*Caleb,[4] Abner,[3] James,[2] Daniel[1]*), eldest son of Caleb[4] and Hannah (Dudley) Thurston of Exeter, N. H.; married, first, Nov. 17, 1792, MARY GILMAN; second, Aug. 31, 1799, ANNE WIGGINS; she died May 16, 1822.

### His children were:

2214 Mary.[6]
2215 Caleb.[6]
2216 Dudley,[6] went to Oregon.
2217 Daniel.[6]
2218 Joshua.[6]
2219 Fletcher.[6]

## 733

DUDLEY THURSTON [5] of Monmouth, Me. (*Caleb,[4] Abner,[3] James,[2] Daniel[1]*), brother of the preceding, and son of Caleb[4] and Hannah (Dudley) Thurston of Exeter, N. H.; married BETSEY THURSTON, daughter of James Thurston of Nottingham, N. H. [see no. 1038.] Mr. Thurston was a farmer in Monmouth.

### Their children were:

2230 Abigail,[6] m. —— Fox.
2231 Caleb,[6] d. young.
2232 James,[6] m. 1st, —— Witham; 2d, Hannah Baker. They had *Mary J.,[7] Dudley,[7] Elizabeth,[7]* and six others.
2233 Hannah,[6] n.m.
2234 Dudley,[6] d. young.

## 734

TRUEWORTHY THURSTON [5] (*Caleb,[4] Abner,[3] James,[2] Daniel[1]*), brother of the preceding, and son of Caleb[4] and Hannah (Dudley) Thurston of Exeter, N. H.; born there June 1, 1778; married, Nov. 26, 1801, PRISCILLA ROYAL, born Oct. 13, 1779. He died in Peru, Me., July 20, 1849, aged 71; she died Oct. 16, 1865, aged 86.
He was a farmer in Monmouth, Me., and moved to Peru in 1819.

### Their children were:

2245 Levi Moody,[6] b. Dec. 2, 1802; d. Jan. 15, 1831.
2246 Clarissa,[6] b. Sept. 18, 1805; m. Feb. 23, 1840, William Paul of Peru and had:
2247 *Dealbea Osca* (Paul), b. June, 1845.
2248 *William* (Paul), b. Sept., 1849.
+2249 Daniel Adams,[6] b. July 16, 1808; m. Olive Bray.
2250 Gilman,[6] b. March 15, 1811; d. Feb. 20, 1830.
2251 Benjamin,[6] b. April 17, 1813; m. Nov., 1844, Laura A. ——; a farmer in Poland, Me.; d. Sept. 20, 1849.
+2252 Samuel Royal,[6] b. in Monmouth April 17, 1816; m. Elizabeth McLench.
+2253 Trueworthy,[6] b. in Monmouth April 15, 1819; m. Rachel Fisher Welch.
2254 Elvira Priscilla,[6] b. in Peru Aug. 25, 1822; m. July 20, 1851, John Simmons Lunt, b. Nov. 13, 1819, son of Francis and Lydia (Simmons) Lunt of Peru; he is a farmer in Dixfield, Me.; enlisted in the 56th Massachusetts regiment against the rebellion. They had:
2255 *Priscilla Clara Augusta* (Lunt), b. March 6, 1853; m. April 5, 1874, Frank E. Kidder.
2256 *George Washington* (Lunt), b. Oct. 20, 1854; d. Jan. 29, 1863.
2257 *Lilla Stanton* (Lunt), } twins, born } d. July, 1862.
2258 *Rose Standish* (Lunt), } Aug. 16, 1856; }

2259 *Emma Frances* (Lunt), b. Nov. 23, 1857.
2260 *John True* (Lunt), b. April 14, 1860; d. May 12, 1860.
2261 *John Franz Sigel* (Lunt), b. July 22, 1861.
2262 *Ulysses Grant* (Lunt), b. Oct. 26, 1863.

## 752

DANIEL THURSTON [5] (*Caleb*,[4] *Abner*,[3] *James*,[2] *Daniel*[1]), brother of the preceding and son of Caleb [4] and Hannah (Dudley) Thurston of Exeter, N. H.; born there Aug. 6, 1776; married, Aug. 4, 1798, DEBORAH FOLSOM, born April 29, 1778. He died Sept. 25, 1855; she died at her daughter's in Portsmouth, N. H., Nov. 12, 1863.

Mr. Thurston was a carpenter in Exeter and a member of the Congregational church.

Their children were:
2273 Elizabeth Gilman,[6] b. Nov. 6, 1799; d. May 22, 1820.
2274 Mary Jane,[6] b. Sept. 3, 1801; d. Aug. 4, 1803.
2275 Mary Jane,[6] b. June 15, 1804; m. Nov. 24, 1825, Samuel Kingsbury of Portsmouth, N. H., born in York, Me., Dec. 4, 1798. He was a house and ship joiner. She died May 20, 1856. They had:
2276 *Elizabeth Mary* (Kingsbury), b. May 9, 1827; d. Dec. 17, 1835.
2277 *Deborah Folsom* (Kingsbury), b. May 8, 1830; m. June 27, 1866, Michael R. Perkins; live in Portsmouth.
2278 *Samuel Henry* (Kingsbury), b. Nov. 17, 1833; m. Nov. 1, 1858, Sarah E. Rand of Portsmouth. They had:
2279 *Maude Thurston* (Kingsbury), b. Jan. 11, 1861; d. Jan. 13, 1861.
2280 *Charles Henry* (Kingsbury), b. July 16, 1862.
2281 *Samuel Lincoln* (Kingsbury), b. March 4, 1864.
2282 *John Gilman* (Kingsbury), b. Dec. 15, 1866.

## 756

GATES THURSTON [5] (*Peter*,[4] *Abner*,[3] *James*,[2] *Daniel*[1]), son of Peter [4] and Dorothy (Gates) Thurston of South Lancaster, Mass.; born 1760; married, Jan. 12, 1790, ELIZABETH POLLARD of Lancaster; her father and mother died about 1812, being about 90 years old each. He died February, 1816; she died at her son John Gates', 1849, aged 86.

Mr. Thurston was a farmer in New Boston, now South Lancaster, living in the homestead mansion.

Children:
2293 James,[6] b. Nov. 9, 1790; m. Sept. 15, 1814, Mary West; about 1835 lived in Tioga county, N. Y., as a farmer.
+2294 Henry.[6] b. Aug. 19, 1792; m. Aurelia Fox.
+2295 John Gates,[6] b. March 18, 1794; m. Harriet Patrick Lee.
2296 Nancy Elizabeth,[6] b. Jan. 31 1796; m. as his second wife, Oct. 11, 1827, Nathaniel Rand, hotel keeper, sheriff, and postmaster in Lancaster. They had:
2297 *Charles Henry* (Rand), b. 1828; m. Lucy Rand of Westfield, Mass.; d. 1868; no children.
2298 *Ellen Elizabeth* (Rand), b. 1831; d. Nov., 1835.
+2299 William,[6] b. March 6, 1798; m. 1st, Sabra Houghton, and four others.
2300 Thomas Gates,[6] b. Nov. 15, 1800; m. 1st, Aug. 18, 1825, Mary Ann Stoddard; was a blacksmith in Concord, Mass., after a merchant in Wilmington, N. C., after Louisville, Ky., and m. there; d. about 1848; several children.
2301 Abel Atherton,[6] b. Sept. 15, 1802; d. April 20, 1803.
+2302 Wilder Stoddard,[6] b. Oct. 8, 1806; m. Rosanna Meliscent Pierce.

## 764

PETER THURSTON [5] (*Peter*,[4] *Abner*,[3] *James*,[2] *Daniel*[1]), brother of the preceding, and son of Peter [4] and Dorothy (Gates) Thurston of South

Lancaster, Mass.; born there Sept. 23, 1768; married, Dec. 8, 1796, SALLY SWEETSER, born Dec. 2, 1778, daughter of Jacob and Margaret (Cooledge) Sweetser of Boston, Mass.   He died Dec. 9, 1824; she died Jan. 21, 1832.

Peter Thurston was a hatter in South Lancaster, living next door neighbor to his father, whose farm was divided between his two sons, Gates and Peter.   He was a member of the Unitarian church.

### Their children were:

2313  Caroline,[6] b. Sept. 22, 1797; n.m.; d. at South Lancaster March 1, 1878.
2314  Sarah Ann,[6] b. May 14, 1799; m. Nov. 9, 1820, Eben Sawyer, b. Feb. 2, 1798, son of Amos and Hannah (Dustin) Sawyer of Haverhill, Mass; he is a merchant in South Lancaster.  They have.
    2315  *Sarah Ann* (Sawyer), b. Sept. 3, 1821; m. Sept. 14, 1843, William H. Young; live, 1877, in Worcester, Mass.
    2316  *Mary Elizabeth* (Sawyer), b. Nov. 8, 1822; m. May 14, 1844, Herbert H. Stimpson; live in South Lancaster.
2317  George Peter,[6] b. March 28, 1801; a hatter; n.m.; d. in Worcester Oct. 7, 1859.

## 778

PHINEAS THURSTON[5] (*Moses,*[4] *Moses,*[3] *Stephen,*[2] *Daniel*[1]), son of Moses[4] and Elizabeth (Clifford) Thurston of Unity, N. H.; born in Epping, N. H., Jan. 7, 1758; married, Jan. 24, 1787, POLLY WOOD, born June 6, 1768, daughter of David and Mary Wood of Rockingham, Vt.   He died March 17, 1796.   After her husband's death she married his brother Josiah [see no. 861].

Phineas Thurston was one of the first settlers of Barnet, Vt.; took the freeman's oath there March 10, 1789.   He was a farmer and settled near that part of the town known as Passumpsicville.   He was a soldier in the revolutionary war; was taken prisoner, sent to England and nearly starved; compelled to eat the entrails of sheep broiled on coals, which he said was the sweetest meat he ever ate.   He was exchanged, and on his way home the vessel was wrecked in the bay of Biscay, and he was saved from starving again only by eating salt pork for several days with intense thirst.   After he had served his time and come home he asked his sisters to sing; they sang a new war song about the wrecked prisoners.   He heard them with great emotion, and when he could command his feelings, said, "I was one of those prisoners."   None of his family had known of his imprisonment.

### Their children were:

2328  John,[6] d. young.
2329  Mary,[6] b. in Barnet, Vt., Sept. 15, 1791; m. June 5, 1806, John Spencer, b. in Charlestown, N. H., April 15, 1787, son of Joseph and Mary Spencer. They lived on the farm in Barnet which she inherited from her father till 1828, when they removed to St. Johnsbury, Vt., where she died, April 18, 1843; he died in West Concord, Vt., Oct. 29, 1858.  They had, all born in Barnet:
    2330  *Phineas Thurston* (Spencer), b. Sept. 18, 1806; m. at St. Johnsbury Feb. 25, 1838, Atlanta W. Gage, b. there Oct. 22, 1810; was a farmer and died in St. Johnsbury May 1, 1877, where his family still reside, 1879.
    2331  *Mary Caroline* (Spencer), b. July 3, 1808; m. 1830, George Washington Gage of St. Johnsbury, where she died, Oct. 18, 1838.  Her husband removed to New York city in 1844, where he was a merchant till his death in 1874.

2332 *Loren Albert* (Spencer), b. April 23, 1812; graduated from Dartmouth 1837; was a lawyer at St. Louis, Mo., where he d. May 1, 1847; n.m.
2333 *Willard* (Spencer), b. Aug. 1, 1817. In 1841 started on a whaling voyage from which he returned in about three years, having sailed around the world. Dec. 20, 1848, he started for California, went from there to Oregon in 1850, where he established a trading post at a place called Eminence, thirty miles from the mouth of the Columbia river; remained there in trade till May, 1866, when he was thrown from a horse and killed; n.m.
2334 *Milo* (Spencer), b. March 29, 1822; m. at St. Johnsbury Feb. 27, 1850, Rosaline Eliza Hill of West Concord, b. June 22, 1818. In March, 1855, he removed to West Concord; was a farmer and drover. In Jan., 1869, he entered the Massachusetts General Hospital for the removal of a tumor under his left ear; operated upon by Dr. Bigelow Jan. 30, and he died in the hospital of phlegmon erysipelas Feb. 6, 1869. His widow and son are living at West Concord, 1879.

## 779

MOSES THURSTON [5] (*Moses,*[4] *Moses,*[3] *Stephen,*[2] *Daniel*[1]), brother of the preceding, and son of Moses[4] and Elizabeth (Clifford) Thurston of Unity, N. H.; born in Brentwood, N. H., Jan. 18, 1760; married, first, JANE SPAULDING of Unity, born 1759; she died May 31, 1799. Second, POLLY CROSS; she died April 7, 1839, aged 62 y. 8 m. 21 d.; he died 1848.

Mr. Thurston was a farmer in Corinth and Orange, Vt., Indian Stream, now Pittsburgh, Coos county, N. H., near the head of the Connecticut river, and finally came back to Orange, where he died in 1848. He was a member of the Free Baptist church and used to preach some.

His children, all by first wife, were:

+2345 John Spaulding,[6] m. Joanna Thurston [see no.     ].
+2346 Jane,[6] had a son Andrew,[7] and afterward m. —— Hurd.
+2348 Ezekiel,[6] b. Feb. 11, 1785; m. Sally Darling.
+2349 Moses,[6] m. Betsey Lovering.
+2350 Sampson,[6] b. *April* 1789; m. Hannah Payne.
+2351 William,[6] b. Oct. 4, 1791; m. 1st, Clarissa Church; 2d, Betsey M. Wiley, 3d, Mrs. Huldah Farmer.
2352 Cyrus,[6] b. Jan. 19, 1794.
2353 Tenney,[6] b. Feb. 18, 1796.
2354 David,[6] b. March 31, 1799.

## 861

JOSIAH THURSTON [5] (*Moses,*[4] *Moses,*[3] *Stephen,*[2] *Daniel*[1]), brother of the preceding, and son of Moses[4] and Elizabeth (Clifford) Thurston of Unity, N. H.; born there May 7, 1772; married, first, in Barnet, Vt., Feb. 14, 1797, POLLY (WOOD) THURSTON, the widow of his brother Phineas. In 1806 they removed to St. Johnsbury, Vt., and afterward to Campton, N. H., where she died, March 5, 1835. Second, June 1, 1835, MARTHA MARCH of Campton, born March 16, 1805. He died in Thornton, N. H., Feb. 7, 1863; his widow is living in Campton Village, 1879.

His children, by second wife, were:

2365 Franklin Josiah,[6] b. in Plymouth, N. H., May 11, 1836; m. May, 1863, Julia Merrill; she died June, 1872. He served in the war against the rebellion in the 8th regiment New Hampshire infantry; is living in Woodstock, N. H., 1879. They had:
2366 *Julia,*[7] b. 1864.

9

2367  *John*,[7] b. 1866.
2368  Martha Ellen,[6] b. in Thornton, N. H., April 13, 1838; m. in Plymouth, N. H., April 15, 1874, Drury Fairbanks Cummings of Plymouth, b. Oct. 30, 1802, son of Jonathan and Ruth (George) Cummings, a surveyor by occupation; no children.
2369  Horace Livermore,[6] b. in Thornton June 6, 1842; m. Dec. 10, 1868, Ann Gilman, b. in Thornton Nov., 1842; she died in Campton Dec., 1876; 2d, Oct. 4, 1877, Stella L. Baker, b. in Carroll, N. H., Feb. 27, 1858, daughter of Rev. William and Asenath (Scates) Baker of Campton. He enlisted Aug. 11, 1864, in Co. A, 8th regiment New Hampshire volunteers. He was at New Orleans, Natches, and Vicksburgh; was discharged Oct. 20, 1865. He is living at Campton, 1879, a member of the Baptist church; his occupation is freighting from Plymouth depot to Campton. He had, by first wife:
2370  *Lilly May*,[7] b. in Thornton Jan. 1, 1870.

## 923

JONATHAN THURSTON [5] (*Ezekiel*,[4] *Moses*,[3] *Stephen*,[2] *Daniel*[1]), eldest son of Ezekiel Thurston [4] of Epping, N. H.; born there May 7, 1761; married, first, SARAH ——; she died March, 1784; Second, MARY ARDWAY, born 1768, died July 5, 1790. He died Nov. 22, 1788, so recorded in an old bible, but probably it should be 1798.

Mr. Thurston was a seaman in Portland, Me.

His children, all born in Portland, were,

By first wife, Sarah:

2381  Asa,[6] b. Jan. 24, 1780; d. April 10, 1781.
2382  Sarah,[6] b. March 11, 1782.

By second wife, Mary:

2383  Betsey,[6] m. —— Clark.
+2384  Ezekiel,[6] b. Oct. 9, 1786; m. Hannah Moulton.
2385  Hannah Ardway,[6] b. Feb. 4, 1788; m. —— Thompson.
2386  Elizabeth,[6] b. Jan. 20, 1790.

## 924

EZEKIEL THURSTON [5] (*Ezekiel*,[4] *Moses*,[3] *Stephen*,[2] *Daniel*[1]), brother of the preceding, and son of Ezekiel Thurston [4] of Epping, N. H.; born there May 28, 1765; married WIDOW BRAY. He took the yellow fever in the West Indies and died in Savannah, Ga., on his passage home in 1809, aged 44.

Mr. Thurston was a master mariner and owner of a vessel trading with the West Indies, residing in Portland, Me. March 8, 1781, at the age of sixteen, he enlisted for three years in the 1st New Hampshire regiment, under Col. Joseph Cilley, from the town of Deerfield, N. H.

### Children:

2397  John,[6] m. Jan. 12, 1825, Susan Libby; was a seaman; killed on a wharf in Portland by being jammed between a team and pile of lumber.
2398  Gilman,[6] a seaman, and was drowned Sept. 13, 1860, by the upsetting of a boat near Portland.
+2399  Samuel,[6] m. Mary Tucker.
2400  Eliza,[6] m. Oct. 13, 1821, John Dela, a trader in Portland, and had:
2401  *Lewis* (Dela), m. April 25, 1844, Frances E. Bagley.

## 935

MOSES THURSTON [5] (*Stephen*,[4] *Moses*,[3] *Stephen*,[2] *Daniel*[1]), son of Stephen Thurston [4] of Stratham, N. H.; married BETSEY WIGGIN of Stratham. He was a farmer in Wolborough, N. H.; died about 1830.

Children:

+2411 Isaac,[6] b. Jan. 28, 1799; m. Maria Dodge.
2412 James,[6] b. Oct. 16, 1802; d. Feb. 21, 1877.

## 947

MOSES THURSTON [5] (*Oliver,*[4] *Moses,*[8] *Stephen,*[2] *Daniel*[1]), son of Oliver [4] and Sarah (French) Thurston of Brentwood, N. H.; born about 1770; married, Sept. 2, 1793, SALLY MOSES.

Mr. Thurston was a hatter in Exeter, N. H.; moved to Eaton, N. H., about 1808 and was a farmer there.

### Their children were:

+2420 Moses,[6] b. March 5, 1795; m. Phebe Forrist.
2421 Sally,[6] b. in Exeter; m. Nathaniel Thurston [see no. 2475].
+2422 Oliver,[6] b. in Exeter Sept. 23, 1800; m. Betsey Harriman.

## 948

OLIVER THURSTON [5] (*Oliver,*[4] *Moses,*[8] *Stephen,*[2] *Daniel*[1]), brother of the preceding, and son of Oliver [4] and Sarah (French) Thurston of Brentwood, N. H.; born there May 10, 1773; married, 1792, ANSTRESS CROSS, born in Exeter, N. H., Nov. 3, 1775. She died Jan. 5, 1851; he died Oct. 3, 1852. He was a farmer in Freedom, N. H.

### Their children were:

2433 Mary,[6] b. in Exeter Feb. 5, 1793; m. 1810, John Kennison, a preacher in the Free Baptist denomination, residing in Effingham, N. H. She died March 18, 1834; he died in Parsonsfield, Me., about 1845. They had:
   2434 *Asenath* (Kennison).
   2435 *Daniel* (Kennison).
   2436 *Ivory* (Kennison).
   2437 *Isaac* (Kennison).
   2438 *Susan* (Kennison).
   2439 *Melvina* (Kennison).
   2440 *John* (Kennison).
   2441 *Oliver* (Kennison).
   2442 *Henry* (Kennison).
   2443 *Mary* (Kennison).
   2444 *Elmon* (Kennison).
+2445 Oliver,[6] b. March 5, 1795; m. Amy Forrest.
2446 William,[6] b. Sept. 11, 1798; d. in infancy.
+2447 William,[6] b. May 23, 1799; m. Mittee Thurston.
2448 Sally,[6] b. July 17, 1801; d. young.
2449 Martha,[6] b. in Meredith, N. H., Dec. 1, 1803; m. by Rev. Jonathan Woodman, Jan. 12, 1823, Hale Watson, a farmer and carpenter in Freedom, where he was also selectman and member of Free Baptist church, b. Aug. 12, 1795, son of Daniel and Lydia (Hinckley) Watson of Lee, N. H. They had:
   2450 *Albert Newell* (Watson), b. Sept. 27, 1823; m. March 4, 1849, Elizabeth Ann Downes of Freedom; lives with his father on the homestead.
   2451 *Emily Ann* (Watson), b. Oct. 2, 1825; m. March 16, 1845, Erastus Ward of Freedom.
   2452 *Lydia Ruth* (Watson), b. Aug. 8, 1828; m. April 26, 1849, John Davis, a farmer in Freedom.
   2453 *Mary Jane* (Watson), b. April 14, 1835; m. Dec. 23, 1852, Ara D. Shaw, a farmer and shoemaker of Hampton, N. H.
   2454 *Martha Ann* (Watson), b. April 28, 1837; m. Oct. 30, 1857, Frederick E. Bradbury, a farmer and trader in Limerick, Me., and now in Effingham, N. H.

2455   *Sarah E.* (Watson), b. Nov. 27, 1838; m. Oct. 25, 1860, Amos F. Andrews, a farmer of Freedom.

2456   *Ann Sophia* (Watson), b. July 29, 1841; m. Feb. 16, 1867, Ira A. Clough, a farmer in Parsonsfield, Me.

2457   *Anstress Thurston* (Watson). b. Oct. 17. 1844; m. Aug. 28, 1864, Benjamin P. Philbrick, a shoemaker of Freedom.

2458   Nathaniel,[6] b. March 22, 1806; m. 1830. Martha Spaulding; studied medicine till fitted to practice, when he had a call to preach as a Free Baptist minister in Dover, N. H., and in Lowell, Mass.; 1852 went to San Francisco, Cal., and practiced medicine many years and died there; no children; adopted *Laura*, who married —— Parker of Lowell and went to California soon after her adopted father died.

2459   Josiah,[6] b. Oct. 30, 1808; d. 1812.

2460   Sally,[6] b. Feb. 17, 1812; m. Nov. 13. 1834. Samuel Stokes. a farmer in Freedom, b. March 28, 1810, son of Jeremiah and Polly (Durgin) Stokes of Northwood, N. H.   They adopted a little girl who died soon after.

2461   *Stephen A. Lary* (Stokes), m. and lives in Freedom; three children.

+2462   Josiah,[6] b. June 9, 1814; m. 1st, Mary Ann Thurston; 2d, Julia Ann Roberts Pierce.

2463   Eunice,[6] b. March 9, 1816; d. Sept., 1831.

2464   Isaac,[6] b. May 4, 1819; d. 1824.

## 949

REUBEN THURSTON[5] of Eaton, N. H. (*Oliver,*[4] *Moses,*[8] *Stephen,*[2] *Daniel*[1]), brother of the preceding, and son of Oliver[4] and Sarah (French) Thurston of Brentwood, N. H.; born there 1775; married, 1792, SALLY CROSS, born about 1772 in Exeter, N. H.   She died 1835.   He was a farmer, and died 1840.

Their children were:

+2475   Nathaniel,[6] b. 1793; m. Sally (or Nancy) Thurston.

2476   James,[6] b. 1795; d. in the East.

+2477   Oliver,[6] b. 1797; m. 1st, Rebecca Harmon; 2d, Susan Colby; 3d, Susan Hayes.

2478   Sarah,[6] b. March 27, 1799; m. Dec. 19, 1819, Jacob Allard. a farmer, son of Job and Sarah (Durgin) Allard of Eaton, N. H.; in 1854 moved to Ellison, Warren county, Ill.   She died Sept. 17, 1856; he died April 1, 1878.   They had:

2479   *Alvah C.* (Allard), b. Oct. 21, 1820; d. May 5, 1840.

2480   *Job* (Allard), b. July 12, 1822; m. Mittee Ann Thurston.

2481   *David* (Allard), b. April 6, 1824; lives in Ellison.

2482   *Eleanor Jane* (Allard), b. Sept. 14, 1826; m. March 22, 1849, David Young, jr., a farmer in Freedom, N. H.

2483   *Jacob* (Allard), b. Dec. 28, 1828; d. Feb. 11, 1846.

2484   *Martha Ann* (Allard), b. Feb. 1, 1831; m. Oct. 24, 1857, Chas. Davis.

2485   *Josiah* (Allard), b. April 13, 1837; lives in Ellison.

2486   *Eliza Ann* (Allard), b. Jan. 1, 1840; m. Bradley Davis; live in California.

2487   *Rose Ann* (Allard), b. Mar. 15, 1843; m. Henry Baldwin; live in Oregon.

2488   *Alvah Cross* (Allard), b. Oct. 17, 1845; lives in Ellison.

2489   Martha,[6] b. 1801; m. William Palmer of Eaton, N. H.

2490   Joseph,[6] b. 1803; m. Adeline Simonds; lived in Lowell, Mass.; had two or more sons; d. in Eaton about 1845.

+2491   Henry,[6] b. 1805; m. Drusilla Wedgwood.

+2492   Elias Cushman,[6] b. 1807; m. Eliza Brown.

+2493   Reuben Leavitt,[6] b. 1809; m. 1st, Lydia Welch; 2d, Mary Phillips. Three died in infancy.

## 950

WILLIAM THURSTON[5] of Eaton, N. H. (*Oliver,*[4] *Moses,*[8] *Stephen,*[2] *Daniel*[1]), brother of the preceding, and son of Oliver[4] and Sarah (French) Thurston of Brentwood, N. H.; born there Oct. 19, 1777;

married, in Exeter, N. H., 1806, MARY ROBINSON, born at Hampton Falls, N. H., March 31, 1775. She died Aug. 7, 1843; he died May 19, 1867. He was a farmer; deacon in the Free Baptist church.

Their children were:

2504 Abigail,[5] b. May 22, 1810; m. March 22, 1849, Henry Blaisdell, as his second wife. He had five children by a former marriage but none by the second wife. He is a teacher and Free Baptist preacher at Tamworth Iron Works, N. H.; was ordained by the Methodists in Jefferson City, Mo., in 1842.
+2505 William Robinson,[5] b. April 5, 1812; m. Elizabeth W. Snell.
+2506 Daniel,[5] b. July 21, 1814; m. Mary Ann Alley.
+2507 Mary Ann,[5] b. May 15, 1816; m. Josiah Thurston.

## 951

JOHN THURSTON[5] (*Oliver*,[4] *Moses*,[3] *Stephen*,[2] *Daniel*[1]), brother of the preceding, and son of Oliver[4] and Sarah (French) Thurston of Brentwood, N. H.; born there July 5, 1782; married, July 5, 1807, ALICE S. HUTCHINS, born April 5, 1787, daughter of Solomon and Hannah (Lewis) Hutchins of Wakefield, N. H. He died in Kenduskeag, Me., March 28, 1869; she died in Hartland, Me., Sept. 9, 1873.

Mr. Thurston was a farmer, cooper, and clothier in Wakefield and Freedom, N. H.; in Harmony and Kenduskeag, Me., a farmer only. In the fall of 1825 his house and barn were burnt, losing all his hay, grain, and household effects except one bed. He soon recovered himself, rebuilt, and maintained his family in a respectable manner.

Their children were:

+2508 Solomon Hutchins,[6] b. in Wakefield Sept. 10, 1808; m. Jennie Wiggin, née French.

Born in Freedom:

2509 John Lewis,[6] b. Sept. 10, 1810; d. Sept. 24, 1811.
2510 Hannah Lewis,[6] b. July 6, 1812; m. June 5, 1855, Joseph Gray, a farmer in Harmony. She was a member of the Christian church, and died Nov. 19, 1870; no children.
+2511 John Langdon Roberts,[6] b. July 16, 1814; m. Louisa Hutchins.
+2512 Asa Lewis,[6] b. Sept. 25, 1816; m. Julia Ann Corson.
+2513 Joseph Hutchins,[6] b. Sept. 17, 1818; m. Mary Jane Crosby.
+2514 Alvah Wiggin,[6] b. Oct. 24, 1820; was drafted in March, 1865, for the war against the rebellion, discharged Nov., 1865; m. Frances Ann Libbey; d. in Kenduskeag May 19, 1866. [See page 218 for further notice.]

Born in Harmony:

2515 Sarah French,[6] b. Aug. 19, 1822.
2516 Nancy Ann,[6] b. March 12, 1825; m. 1st, Nov., 1857, Rev. William Smith, b. June 12, 1813, son of Isaac Smith of Harmony; he was a minister of the Free Baptist church and farmer, and died Sept. 30, 1870; 2d, June, 1875, Robert Ludwig, a farmer in Palmyra, Me. She was a member of the Christian church. Her children, by first husband, b. in Harmony:
2517 *Alice Emma* (Smith), b. Sept. 9, 1858.
2518 *Flora Anna* (Smith), b. Feb. 15, 1860; she and her sister Alice Emma graduated with honors from Maine Central Institute, Pittsfield, June 19, 1879, and are successful teachers.
2519 *Estelle Eugenia* (Smith), b. Aug. 24, 1863.
2520 *Anson Eugene* (Smith), b. in Palmyra Sept. 6, 1868.

2521　Eugene True,[6] b. April 26, 1827; m. in Ellsworth, Me., Sept. 24, 1861, Zarissa Annie Morse, b. Feb. 6, 1841, daughter of John Thistle and Emily (Hammond) Morse of Surry, Me. He is a teacher, residing in Oakland, Cal. They have:

2522　*Eugene True,*[7] b. April 24, 1873.
2523　Mary Herrick,[6] b. April 28, 1830; m. Oct. 9, 1851, Thomas Jefferson Farrar, b. Aug. 25, 1811; he is a blacksmith in Harmony. Children, all b. in Harmony:

2524　*Grace Greenwood* (Farrar), b. Sept. 22, 1852; m. June 1, 1870, Smith Alonzo Symonds of Dexter, Me.
2525　*Alexis Walter* (Farrar), b. Jan. 5, 1854; m. Aug. 30, 1874, Etta Thombs.
2526　*Lauriston Everett* (Farrar), b March 2, 1861; d. Aug. 3, 1862.
2526a　*Estelle Etta* (Farrar), b. Nov. 23, 1862.
2526b　*Alice Eugenia* (Farrar), b. July 3, 1865.
2526c　*Liston Alverdo* (Farrar), b. March 24, 1868.
2527　Hattie Newell,[6] b. April 17, 1832; m. 1st. May 22, 1858. George Libbey, b. in Wellington, Me., March 23. 1831, d. July 10, 1864; 2d. Aug. 15, 1867. Benjamin Randall Huff, b. July 19, 1818, d. in Hartland, Me., Jan. 12, 1878. She had, by first husband:

2527a　*John Samuel* (Libbey), b. in Kenduskeag May 28, 1859.
2527b　*Eleanor* (Libbey), b. in Levant, Me., Sept. 23, 1861.

By second husband:
2527c　*George Everett* (Huff), b. in Hartland Nov. 16, 1868.

### 966

JOHN THURSTON[5] (*John,*[4] *John,*[3] *Stephen,*[2] *Daniel*[1]), eldest son of John[4] and Elsie (Leavitt) Thurston of Stratham, N. H.; born there 1780; married, first, HANNAH MASON; she died December, 1820. Second, 1822, JANE SMITH of Stratham. He died May 23, 1825. Mr. Thurston was a farmer in Stratham.

His children, by first wife, Hannah, were:

2528　George,[6] b. 1814; n.m.; d. aged about 22.
2529　Nancy Mason,[6] b. May 11, 1816; m. March 26, 1840, George Washington Horne, a brick manufacturer in Dover, N. H. They had:

2530　*Gustavus Henry* (Horne), b. Jan. 29, 1841; was cashier of a bank; d. Nov. 23, 1873.
2531　*Georgiana Emma* (Horne), b. Nov. 8, 1843; d. Oct. 21, 1872.
2532　*Charles William* (Horne), b. Nov. 7, 1845; d. March 15, 1850.
2533　*Fanny Sarah* (Horne), b. Nov. 2, 1847; d. Jan. 13, 1869.
2534　*Charles Albert* (Horne), b. Jan. 2, 1850; d. Aug 20, 1851.
2535　*George Allen* (Horne), b. Feb. 15, 1852; d. Sept. 13, 1869.
2536　*John Edwin* (Horne), b. June 29, 1855; d. April 20, 1858.
2537　*Susan Alice* (Horne), b. Nov. 30, 1861.
2538　William,[6] b. 1819; n.m.; d. in Salem, Mass., May 23, 1852.

By second wife, Jane:

2539　Hannah Jane,[6] b. 1823; m. Oct. 14, 1844, John Lambert of Kittery, Me.
2540　Nathaniel,[6] b. 1825; d. in infancy.

### 995

NATHANIEL THURSTON[5] (*John,*[4] *John,*[3] *Stephen,*[2] *Daniel*[1]), brother of the preceding, and son of John[4] and Elsie (Leavitt) Thurston of Stratham, N. H.; married HANNAH DUTCH.

Mr. Thurston was a stone worker, killed by blasting rocks in Newmarket, N. H., 1820.

Their children were:

+2541　Andrew Leavitt,[6] b. Nov. 18, 1815; m. Anna Fisher.
2542　Clarissa D.,[6] m. —— Marsh of Exeter, N. H.

## 1009

THOMAS THURSTON[5] (*Paul*,[4] *John*,[3] *Stephen*,[2] *Daniel*[1]), son of Paul[4] and Margaret Thurston, said to be of Litchfield, Ct.; married ELIZABETH LARMON of Ware, Mass.   He died 1797; she died 1821.
Mr. Thurston was a tax-payer in Belchertown, now Pelham, Mass., in 1769; served six months in the war of the revolution.   He was elected to an office in town once or twice.

Their children were:

2553  Mary.[6] m. Elias Shaw of Belchertown; they had:
    2554  *Betsey* (Shaw).
    2555  *Hannah Mary* (Shaw), d. young.
    2556  *Elias* (Shaw).
    2557  *Susan* (Shaw).
    2558  *Leonard* (Shaw), accidentally hung himself in Granby, Mass.
    2559  *Esther* (Shaw).
+2560  Paul,[6] m. Mary Moody.
2561  Betsey (or Elizabeth), b. Feb. 27, 1779; m. May 19, 1803, Caleb Tillson,*
    b. in Greenwich, now Enfield, Mass., July 27, 1780.   One of her sons
    says: "She was a woman of uncommon industry, dignity, integrity,
    and sensibility, a hater of all shams and untruths; for instance, she ob
    jected to some of the literature of the Sunday-school libraries, because
    she believed many of the stories about unnaturally holy children were
    only pious tales, and she revolted at the idea of promoting religion by
    the sacrifice of truth.   The writer of this believes she never uttered an
    untruth knowingly, and is confident he never detected her in anything
    false, even for the purpose of being polite or agreeable."   She died Aug.

* The TILLSON FAMILY.
I. —— TILLSON, the first that we have any record of, came to this country about the year 1670 and settled in Plymouth, Plymouth Co., Mass.  He had two sons, Edmund and Ephraim. From the latter came the Tillsons living in Middleborough and part of those living in Carver.
II. EDMUND TILLSON, had five wives; the last one, Deberuch Caswell of Taunton, Mass., was the mother of
III. STEPHEN TILLSON, m. Jannett Murdoch, daughter of John Murdoch, son of John Murdoch, merchant in Plymouth, and a native of Scotland.  Stephen settled in Plymouth, and had William, b. March 5, 1740, o. s., m. Mary Ransom, moved to Connecticut, thence to New Jersey, thence to Virginia or Pennsylvania; John, b. Dec 31, 1742, o s., m. Ruth Barrows, settled in Carver and had a family; STEPHEN, b. Aug. 30, 1747, o s.; Ichabod, b. April 25, 1750, o. s., m. Azuba Thomas, settled in Plympton or Carver, Mass., and had a family; two of his sons were furnace men in 1809 or 1810 in the Francouia iron works, Franconia, N. H.; Jenet, b. Feb. 10, 1753, d. in childhood.
IV. STEPHEN TILLSON, b. in Plympton, now Carver, Plymouth Co., near the town of Plymouth, about forty miles from Boston, Aug. 30, 1747, o. s.   He married Hopestill Shaw, b. in Middleborough, Mass., May 25, 1744, o.s., daughter of Moses and Mary (Darling) Shaw of Pembroke, Mass.; Moses Shaw was son of Bensoni Shaw of Carver.  Stephen Tillson was a furnace man, working most of the time at his trade in Stafford,Ct., while his family lived upon a farm in Enfield, Mass., after the birth of their second child.  She died May 3, and he May 6, 1814.  He was esteemed for his rare honesty and temperate habits; never belonged to any church.  Mrs. Tillson was a woman of great energy and executive ability.  It is said she managed the farm, in her husband's absence, with more energy and economy than most men.  Children, all but the two first born in Enfield: Elizabeth, b. in Plympton Nov. 2, 1769, at 1 o'clock A.M.; m. 1784, Isaac Green of Greenwich, Mass.; settled in Middlefield, Otsego county, N. Y., and had a family. Jonah, b. in Plympton Aug. 10, 1771, at 11 o'clock A.M.; went to Richfield, Otsego county, N. Y., cleared up a farm; m. about 1803 Ruth Lammon, and had a family.  Stephen, b. Oct. 15, 1773 at 11 o'clock A.M.; went to Richfield, cl-ared a farm; m. Azuba Noyes of Richfield, and had a family.  Cephas, b. Dec. 15, 1775, a' 6 o'clock A.M.; went to Butternutts, now M rris, Otsego county, N. Y., and settled on a farm; m. Betsey Converse of Stafford, Ct., and had a family.  Moses, b. July 6, 1778, at 4 o'clock A.M.; went to Butternutts, settled on a farm; m. Mary Young of Richfield, formerly from Rhode Island.  CALEB, b. July 27, 1780, at 1 o'clock A.M.  George, b. Nov. 25, 1782, at 12 M.; was a furnace man and manufacturer of hollow ware patterns; worked in Stafford and other places; m. Miss Barker from Maine; settled at Long Point, Canada West; in a short time moved to Dereham, Oxford county, Canada, where he founded a prosperous village called Tillsonburgh; had a family.  Hannah, b. March 20, 1785, at 7 o'clock P.M.; m. Joseph Ruggles, a farmer; went to Peru, Huron county, Ohio, where they had a family.  Thoma s, b. Feb. 11, 1788, at midnight; m. Patty Bartlett of Enfield; lived a while upon a farm owned by his father as a second farm, in Enfield, then went to Peru, Ohio; had a family.
V. CALEB TILLSON, b. July 27, 1780; m. Betsey Thurston, as above.

23, 1861, aged 82 y. 5 m. 23 d. Caleb Tillson was a farmer, an honest, industrious man, not addicted to any bad habits of intemperance in the use of intoxicating liquors or tobacco in any of their forms. He died Feb. 6, 1846, aged 65 y. 6 m. 10 d. They lived on the old Tillson homestead and were both members of the Congregational church. For their children, see Appendix.

2562   Thomas,[6] m. ———; d. in Wiscasset, Me., about 1810–15. Children:
     2563   *Betsey.*[7]
     2564   *Joseph,*[7] fell overboard and drowned at sea.
     2565   *James.*[7]
+2566   James,[6] b. Feb. 8, 1787; m. 1st, Susan Thayer; 2d, Maria Gleason.
2567   Margaret,[6] m. ——— Lane.
2568   Susanna,[6] n.m.

## 1020

SAMUEL THURSTON [5] (*Samuel,*[4] *Robert,*[3] *Stephen,*[2] *Daniel*[1]), eldest son of Samuel[4] and Mary Thurston of Exeter, N. H.; married ELIZABETH GILMAN, daughter of Moses Gilman of Exeter.

Mr. Thurston resided in Epping, N. H. His will was probated in 1783, and his widow Elizabeth was administratrix.

### Their children were:

2581   Samuel.[6]
2582   Anna.[6]
2583   Elizabeth.[6]
2584   Gilman.[6]
2585   Nathaniel.[6]
     The four last were minors Dec. 15, 1784, as the mother and Samuel Morrill of Epping were appointed guardians at that date.

## 1021

EPHRAIM THURSTON [5] (*Samuel,*[4] *Robert,*[3] *Stephen,*[2] *Daniel*[1]), brother of the preceding, and son of Samuel[4] and Mary Thurston of Exeter, N. H.; born there March 25, 1753; married, Jan. 11, 1780, ANNIE MARSH, born April 20, 1760, died in Wakefield, N. H., Nov. 10, 1789.

Mr. E. Thurston of Exeter deeded land away in 1787; was in the revolutionary war.

### Their children were:

2596   Ephraim,[6] b. Aug. 22, 1780; lived in Wakefield.
2597   Betsey,[6] b. Jan. 1, 1782; d. Jan. 6, 1782.
2598   Nancy,[6] b. April 3, 1783; m. William Pike; d. in Oxford, Me., April 12, 1859; three children, all dead.
2599   Betsey,[6] b. Oct. 27, 1785; m. ——— Hackett; lived in Wakefield.
+2600   John,[6] b. July 31, 1787; m. Mercy Hale.
2601   Dolly,[6] b. Aug. 14, 1789; d. in Wakefield Nov. 17, 1789.

## 1032

EBENEZER THURSTON [5] of Monmouth, Me. (*James,*[4] *Robert,*[3] *Stephen,*[2] *Daniel*[1]), son of James Thurston[4] of Nottingham, N. H.; born in New Sandwich, N. H.; married, first, BETSEY DOUGHTY of Lisbon, Me., born June, 1772; she died Sept. 12, 1839. Second, JANE ———. He died Oct. 17, 1847.

Mr. Thurston was a farmer in Monmouth, where he came with his sister Polly about 1795; they were professors of religion.

His children, by first wife, Betsey, were:

2612   Stephen,[6] b. Jan. 7, 1796; d. young.
2613   Nancy W.,[6] b. Aug. 28, 1797; m. May 3, 1828, Irving Dexter, carpenter
       and farmer of Winthrop, Me. She was a Methodist; he a Baptist. She
       died March 13, 1863; he died Aug. 18, 1872. They had:
   2614   *Isaiah* (Dexter), m. Mahala Mabrey of Boston, Mass. They had:
       2615   *Sarah* (Dexter), b. Feb. 26, 1856; d. Nov. 13, 1872.
       2616   *George A.* (Dexter), b. July 12, 1857.
       2617   *Hattie E.* (Dexter), b. April, 1861; d. Oct., 1861.
       2618   *Alston B.* (Dexter), b. Aug., 1869.
   2619   *Ira L. T.* (Dexter), m. Ruth Dixon of Boston. They had:
       2620   *Willard M.* (Dexter), b. Aug. 19, 1860,
       2621   *Carrie A.* (Dexter), b. Feb. 10, 1864; *d. 1873.*
       2622   *Ernest* (Dexter), b. Sept. 1, 1874; d. March 19, 1875.
       2623   *Everett Elwood* (Dexter), b. Nov. 15, 1877; *d. 1879.*
   2624   *Mary E.* (Dexter), d. in infancy.
2625   Joseph,[6] b. May 27, 1799; d. young.
2626   David M.,[6] b. March 22, 1802; m. May 25, 1834, Louisa Fairbanks Fogg
       of Monmouth; a Methodist minister; no children.
+2627  Elijah Doughty,[6] b. Aug. 28, 1803; m. Mary Dexter.
2628   Louisa,[6]            } twins, born { n.m.; d. Aug. 29, 1848.
2629   Clarissa Augusta,[6] } May 22, 1807; { m. Meshack Blake of Gardiner, Me.
       They had:
       2630   *Henry Clay* (Blake), n.m.; d.
       2631   *Ann* (Blake), m.
       2632   *Louisa* (Blake), n.m.; d.
       2633   *Samuel* (Blake), m.
       2634   *Ellen* (Blake), n.m.; d.
       2635   *Mary* (Blake), d. young.
2636   Hannah Wallace,[6] b. May 8, 1809; n.m.; d. Sept. 26, 1846.
2637   Peleg Benson,[6] b. Oct. 22, 1811; n.m.; d. April 1, 1834.
+2638  Ira Towle,[6] b. Sept. 12, 1815; m. Pamelia Fairbanks Fogg.

By second wife, Jane:

2639   Charles F.,[6] b. Nov. 12, 1847; served in the war against the rebellion.

## 1034

PETER THURSTON[5] of Nottingham, N. H. (*James,*[4] *Robert,*[3] *Stephen,*[2]
*Daniel*[1]), brother of the preceding, and son of James Thurston[4] of
Nottingham; born in New Sandwich, N. H., March 6, 1770; married
RACHEL DOUGHTY, born in Topsham, Me., Feb. 15, 1770. He died
March 8, 1840, aged 70; she died Dec. 25, 1859, aged 89.

Mr. Thurston was a farmer and builder of stone walls and wells, a
very strong and rugged man; it was said he could walk further with a
crowbar, axe, and shovel on his shoulder than without them.

Their children were:

+2640  James,[6] m. Deborah Chase.
2641   Samuel,[6] m.; went West 1820; d.; had:
       2642   *Harrison,*[7] in Raymond, N. H.
2643   Elijah,[6] b. Oct. 15, 1800; m. March 20, 1824, Abigail Merrill of Derry, N.
       H.; a farmer in Deerfield, N. H.; d. Nov. 26, 1846; she still lives in
       Deerfield, a member of the Free Baptist church; no children.
2644   Betsey,[6] d.
2645   Levi,[6] went away and was never heard from.
2646   Mercy,[6] b. Dec. 15, 1810, a housekeeper in Nottingham; n.m.; member of
       the Free Baptist church.
2647   Hannah,[6] b. 1812; n.m.; d. July 28, 1874.
+2648  Freeman Dexter,[6] b. Aug. 16, 1815; m. Nancy Ann Jones.
2649   Elizabeth,[6] b. Oct. 15, 1817; m. 1st, Oct. 31, 1847, Orin Jones; he died
       Oct. 6, 1854; 2d, Oct. 28, 1856, Washington Fogg Jones, brothers, and
       both farmers in Nottingham. She had:

2650   *Ada Helen* (Jones), m. Feb. 15, 1877, Sidney Smith French of Notting-
           ham.
2651   Mary,[6] n.m. ; d. Aug. 9, 1855.

## 1036

MOSES THURSTON[5] of Nottingham, N. H. ( *James,[4] Robert,[8] Stephen,[2]*
*Daniel[1]* ), brother of the preceding, and son of James Thurston[4] of
Nottingham; married NANCY HARVEY of Nottingham. He died 1829,
and his widow married —— Kennerson and moved to Orange, Vt.
He was a farmer.

### Children :

2662   Mehitable,[6] m. John Brown of Deerfield, now Newton, N. H.
2663   Betsey,[6] went to Orange with her mother.
2664   James,[6] m. ; lived and died in Epping, N. H.; had :
    2665   *Malvina.[7]*
2666   Samuel D.,[6] m. ; lived in Epping and died in the war against the rebellion
           of wounds received at Fredericksburgh.
2667   Delia Jane,[6] went to Orange with her mother.

## 1037

POLLY THURSTON[5] ( *James,[4] Robert,[8] Stephen,[2] Daniel[1]* ), sister of
the preceding, and daughter of James Thurston[4] of Nottingham, N.
H.; born in New Sandwich, N. H., Feb. 5, 1776; married, Nov. 20,
1794, FREEMAN DEXTER of Winthrop, Me., born Sept. 14, 1773. She
died June 15, 1839. He was a farmer in Winthrop; died Dec. 1, 1840.

### Their children were ;

2678   Nathaniel (Dexter), b. Aug. 15, 1795; m. Nov. 25, 1819, Mary Rich of
           Harpswell, Me.; was a farmer in Winthrop. They had:
    2679   *Harrison* (Dexter), m. Catherine McCormick and had:
        2680   *Clara E.* (Dexter), b. Aug. 28, 1854; m.
        2681   *George* (Dexter), b. Nov. 7, 1856.
        2682   *Nathaniel G.* (Dexter), b. May 16, 1860.
        2683   *Daniel* (Dexter), b. Nov. 1, 1864.
    2684   *Emeline Trufant* (Dexter), m. Joseph Rice King, a farmer and manu-
               facturer of Monmouth, Me., and had :
        2685   *Albertus Rice* (King), m. ~~Elora Wing~~ *Ella Romsedell.*
        2686   *Eva Arletta* (King).
        2687   *Emogene Crowell* (King).
    2688   *Amanda F.* (Dexter), m. David Irving of Boston, and had :
        2689   *Frank* (Irving), b. 1852; m.; one child.
        2690   *Edson E.* (Irving), b. March, 1854; d. 1856.
        2691   *Flora* (Irving), b. April, 1856; d. Oct., 1856.
        2692   *William* (Irving), b. Feb., 1858.
        2693   *Minnie* (Irving), b. April, 1861, *and Emma (Irving).*
2694   Irving (Dexter), b. Jan. 15, 1797; m. Nancy Thurston of Monmouth [see
           no. 2614].
2695   Freeman (Dexter), b. Dec. 12, 1798; m. Sept. 2, 1820, Abigail Harvey of
           Monmouth, where he lived, as a carpenter, till he removed to Boston,
           where he died. They had:
    2696   *Julia* (Dexter), m. Hiram Ladd, a farmer in Readfield, Me., and after
               in Winthrop; one child.
    2697   *Samuel* (Dexter), n.m. ; d.
    2698   *Abigail* (Dexter), n.m. ; d.
    2699   *Mary Jane* (Dexter), m. Geo. Merrill of Livermore, Me.; no children.
    2700   *Drusilla* (Dexter), m. Solomon Leighton of Mt. Vernon, Me.; no child.
    2701   *Reuel* (Dexter), m. Elnora C. Mank; no children.
2702   Sumner (Dexter), b. Oct. 26, 1800; m. June 12, 1834, Priscilla Getchell of
           Winthrop, and had :
    2703   *Lucilla* (Dexter), n.m. ; d. aged 19.

2704  *Emily* (Dexter), b. Jan. 28,1837 ; m. Rufus Wing, Wayne, Me. ; no child.
2705  *Ellen* (Dexter), n.m. ; d.
2706  *George Monroe* (Dexter), b. Feb. 22, 1839; m. Julia Burgess of Wayne;
  three children.
2707  *Wesley* (Dexter), b. 1851 ; n.m.
2708  Amasa (Dexter), b. Feb. 18, 1803; m. Feb. 27, 1830, Eliza Bessey of
  Wayne, and had :
  2709  *Wilbor* (Dexter), m. Anna Brooks of Boston; *2 children.*
  2710  *Scott* (Dexter), d. young and an infant d.
2711  Mary (Dexter), b. Oct. 26, 1804; m. Elijah D. Thurston of Monmouth [see
  no. 2627].
2712  Louisa (Dexter), twin, b. Nov. 2, 1806; m. 1st, Feb. 14, 1835, Capt. David
  Rich of Harpswell; 2d, William Banks, She had :
  2713  *John L.* (Rich), d. in infancy.
  2714  *John L.* (Rich), m. Anna Fraser of *Boston*; one child.
  2715  *Allura L.* (Rich), m. —— Stetson of Boston ; one child.
2716  Alonzo (Dexter), twin, b. Nov. 2, 1806; m. April 14, 1830, Lucy Woodward of Gardiner, Me., and had :
  2717  *Emma Jane* (Dexter), m. —— Lane of Boston ; one child.
  2718  *Lucy N.* (Dexter), m. —— Lane of Boston.
  2719  *Everett* (Dexter), m. ; is an attorney at law, Boston.
2720  Gideon (Dexter), b. Oct. 9, 1808; m. Sept. 16, 1834, Rebecca Getchell of
  Winthrop, and had :
  2721  *George W.* (Dexter), n.m. ; d.
  2722  *Lemuel* (Dexter).
  2723  *Charles* (Dexter); *m. Ellen Frost of Wayne.*
2724  Hannah (Dexter), b. April 23, 1810; m. 1st, Jan. 20, 1834, Aaron Palmer;
  2d, Silas Peck of Illinois. She had :
  2725  *Mary E.* (Palmer), m.
  2726  *Aaron* (Palmer), d. in infancy.
2727  Charles S. (Dexter), b. Feb. 27, 1812; m. 1st, May 1, 1837, Sylvia Pierce
  of Greene, Me.; three children, d. in infancy; m. 2d, ——, and had :
  2728  *Charles* (Dexter).
2729  Meribah (Dexter), b. May 13, 1814; m.; d. aged 32.
2730  Betsey (Dexter), b. Jan. 20, 1816; m. March 12, 1834, Capt. Isaac Rich of
  Harpswell, and had :
  2731  *David* (Rich), a master mariner; m. and has two children; reside in
   Harpswell.
  2732  *Louisa* (Rich), and perhaps others.
2733  Stephen T. (Dexter), b. April 19, 1818; m. April 26, 1843, Betsey Frost of
  Wayne, and had :
  2734  *Arianna* (Dexter), n.m.
  2735  *Roansa* (Dexter), m. C. Bacon of Boston; one child.
  2736  *Stephen Alston* (Dexter).

## 1064

JAMES THURSTON[6] of Peabody, Mass. (*Enoch,[4] Nathaniel,[3] Stephen,[2]
Daniel[1]*), youngest son of Enoch[4] and Betsey (Sheldon) Thurston of
Beverly, Mass.; born there June 16, 1795 ; married, first, Jan. 9, 1817,
NABBY BLACK, daughter of Nathaniel and Anna Black of Beverly;
she died Jan. 26, 1820. Second, Nov. 20, 1821, LOUISA RAY, daugh-
ter of Ebenezer Ray of Beverly ; she died Sept. 8, 1864, aged 67.

Mr. Thurston was a morocco dresser; attended the Unitarian church.

He had one child, by first wife, Nabby :

2745  Abbie,[6] b. Jan. 15, 1820; m. June 5, 1838, Eben Shillaber Daniels, son of
  Daniel Daniels of Peabody, a shoe dealer. They had :
  2746  *Mary Ellen* (Daniels), b. Feb. 16, 1848; m. March 16, 1869, William
   Lamson Wonson, son of Augustus Wonson of Gloucester, Mass.
   They had :
  2747  *Augustus Daniels* (Wonson), b. in Gloucester July 25, 1871.
  2748  *William Thurston* (Wonson), b. in Beverly Aug. 25, 1873.
  2749  *Ellen Lamson* (Wonson), b. in Gloucester Dec. 25, 1875.

## 1096

NATHANIEL THURSTON[5] of Boscawen, N. H. (*Jonathan,*[4] *Nathaniel,*[3] *Stephen,*[2] *Daniel*[1]), second child of Jonathan[4] and Elizabeth (Hovey) Thurston of Boscawen; born in Newbury, Mass., Dec. 29, 1771; married, May 17, 1792, SUSANNA JACKMAN of Boscawen, born May 17, 1774. She died May 8, 1842; he died July 21, 1849. He was a farmer.

### Their children were:

2760   Polly Jackman,[6] b. Nov. 20. 1792; n.m.; d. Sept., 1860.
2761   Moses,[6] b. Feb. 2, 1795; d. Nov. 9, 1798.
2762   Abel,[6] b. April 5, 1797; n.m.; d. March 20, 1873.
2763   Moses,[6] b. Oct. 20, 1799; n.m.; d. Oct. 22, 1849.
2764   Aphia Coffin,[6] b. June 15, 1802; n.m.; in Boscawen.
2765   Ruth,[6] b. Oct. 7, 1804; m. Feb. 4, 1827, Gideon Walker Huntress of Portsmouth, N. H.; he was a tailor in Boscawen and died there. They had :
    2766   *William Augustus* (Huntress), b. Nov. 14, 1827; was a member of the 2d New Hampshire cavalry in the war against the rebellion.
    2767   *John Emery* (Huntress), b. Sept. 6, 1838.
    2768   *Clara Ann* (Huntress), b. May 24, 1840; d. Sept. 11, 1870.
    2769   *Charles Walker* (Huntress), b. April 21, 1842; d. June 8, 1859.
    2770   *George Hervey* (Huntress), b. July 21, 1844; d. Nov. 14, 1864.
    2771   *Francis Edson* (Huntress), b. Oct. 21, 1846.
    2772   *Albert Bridge* (Huntress), b. April 7, 1849; d. April 27, 1864.
+2773   Enoch,[6] b. March 24, 1807; m. Caroline Blanchard.
2774   Mary Bartlett,[6] b. Sept. 19, 1809; m. May, 1838, Jeremiah Littlefield of Boscawen, b. July 21, 1816; he is a farmer in Danbury, N. H. They had :
    2775   *George* (Littlefield), b. July 13, 1838; m. Angeline Sweatt of Danbury.
    2776   *Susan Adeline* (Littlefield), b. Sept. 22, 1839; m. Luther Sawyer of Hill, N. H.; reside in Andover, N. H.
    2777   *Frances Augusta* (Littlefield), b. Feb. 8, 1841; m. Frank Tucker of Andover.
    2778   *Mary Jane* (Littlefield),  }  twins, born  } m. John Bartlett of Warner,
    2779   *Eliza Jane* (Littlefield),  } Jan. 19, 1843; }  N. H. Eliza Jane m. John E. Huntress of Boscawen; d. April 27, 1878.
    2780   *Lewis* (Littlefield), b. Nov. 20, 1844; d. Sept. 4, 1869.
    2781   *Phebe* (Littlefield), b. Aug. 9, 1846; d. Sept. 20, 1851.
    2782   *Fitz Henry* (Littlefield), b. Sept. 5, 1848; d. Oct. 11, 1851.
    2783   *Abby Hoyt* (Littlefield), b. May 11, 1850; m. George Clark of Danbury.
+2784   John Jay,[6] b. April 3, 1813; m. 1st, Eunice R. Andrews; 2d, Mrs. Orzilla Elkins.
2785   Susan Jackman,[6] b. Oct. 18, 1815; m. May 11, 1852, Capt. Bradley Atkinson, a carpenter of Boscawen. They have :
    2786   *George* (Atkinson), b. March 29, 1859; m. Sept., 1878, Hattie Annis of Boscawen.
+2787   Nathaniel,[6] b. April 6, 1820; m. Hannah Noyes.
Three other children who died young.

## 1110

EUNICE SMITH THURSTON[5] (*Stephen,*[4] *Nathaniel,*[3] *Stephen,*[2] *Daniel*[1]), daughter of Stephen*[4] and Keziah (Cheney) Thurston of Boscawen, N. H.; born in Rowley, now Georgetown, Mass., June 9, 1774; married, Dec. 31, 1795, PORTER ESTABROOK of Lebanon, N. H. She died in Junius, Senaca county, N. Y., July 31, 1811. He was a carpenter in Utica, N. Y.

---

* On page 68, under no. 278, it is said Mrs. Pettingall Thurston died in Barnard, N. H.; it should be Barnard, Vt., as we since learn she spent her last days with the widow of her son, Rev. Erastus Pettingall.

#### Children:

2798   Porter (Estabrook), b. Jan. 8. 1797; d. in Hartford, Vt., Jan. 9, 1797.
2799   Alvan (Estabrook). b. Sept. 4. 1798.
2800   John (Estabrook), b. May 24, 1800.
2801   Thesda (Estabrook), b. Jan. 16, 1803; d. Sept. 4, 1803.
2802   Thesda (Estabrook), b. April 3, 1805; d. Aug. 6, 1806.
2803   Porter (Estabrook, b. Aug. 20, 1807.
2804   Joseph (Estabrook), b. May 19, 1809; d. Dec. 19, 1810, at Westfield, Vt.

## 1120

STEPHEN THURSTON [5] (*Stephen,*[4] *Nathaniel,*[3] *Stephen,*[2] *Daniel*[1]), brother of the preceding, and son of Stephen [4] and Keziah (Cheney) Thurston of Boscawen, N. H.; born in Rowley, now Georgetown, Mass., April, 1781; married PHILENA PAMELIA DUNHAM, daughter of William and Pamelia (Dimmick) Dunham. He died Sept. 6, 1864, aged 83 y. 5 m.; she died Sept. 12, 1867, aged 87 y. 7 m. He was a carpenter and farmer in West Hartford, Vt.

#### Children:

+2805   Volney.[6] b. July 21, 1806; m. Hannah C. Barbour.
2806   Lucia Maria,[6] b. March 22, 1808; m. Darius Foster of Haverhill, N. H.; d. Dec., 1876.
2807   Valorous Morris Tillotson,[6] b. Nov. 23, 1810; n.m.; d. in New Orleans Dec., 1835.
2808   Emily Louisa,[6] b. Aug. 14, 1814; n.m.; d. Dec. 12, 1841.
+2809   John Cheney,[6] b. Oct. 18, 1816; m. Harriet Maria Snow.
+2810   Charles Henry,[6] b. Nov. 30, 1820; m. Susan Ann Miller.
2811   Philena.[6] b. March 21, 1822; m. Orris Wills; live on the homestead; no children.

## 1139

NATHANIEL THURSTON [5] (*Stephen,*[4] *Nathaniel,*[3] *Stephen,*[2] *Daniel*[1]), brother of the preceding, and son of Stephen [4] and Keziah (Cheney) Thurston of Boscawen, N. H.; born in Rowley, Mass., April 22, 1795; married, first, 1816, MARTHA HALL, born in Francistown, N. H., 1795; she died Oct. 26, 1833, and was buried at Hanover, N. H. Second, February, 1834, JANE FELLOWS, daughter of Isaac Fellows of Hanover. She died 1849; he died in Hanover Feb. 15, 1844.

Mr. Thurston lived successively in Boscawen, N. H., Hartford, Vt., Hanover and Orford, N. H.

#### His children, by first wife, Martha, were:

2822   Joel,[6] b. 1818; d. 1820.
2823   Lurena Carlton,[6] b. April 27, 1820; d. Feb. 7, 1843.
+2824   Henry Warren Lyman,[6] b. Nov. 20, 1823; m. 1st, Eliza Ann Burnham; 2d, Mary Elizabeth Charts.
2825   Nathaniel Pillsbury,[6] b. Sept. 23, 1830; d. July 4, 1846.

#### By second wife, Jane:

2826   Martha Jane,[6] b. April 9, 1835; m. 1852, R. B. Eastman of Canaan, N. H., and had one daughter; mother and child died in 1855.

## 1173

COL. WILLIAM THURSTON [5] of Madison, Me. (*Stephen,*[4] *Stephen,*[3] *Stephen,*[2] *Daniel*[1]), eldest son of Stephen [4] and Betsey (Wiggin) Thurston of Stratham, N. H.; born there Jan. 11, 1786; married, October, 1807, CHARITY EAMES, born Jan. 22, 1786.

Mr. Thurston was a farmer, a justice of the peace, member of the legislature when held in Portland, Me., and colonel of militia; held many offices of trust in town; was a Free Mason; and a man of more than ordinary natural ability, to which he was constantly adding by his studious and practical habits. This couple are still smart and living with their son Winthrop in Hartland, Wis., where four generations are living in the same house, 1879.

Their children were:

+2837 Joseph Hilton,[6] b. Aug. 31, 1808; m. Deborah Luce Remick.
2838 Maria,[6] d. in infancy.
+2839 William Wiggin,[6] b. Jan. 17, 1811; m. Eliza Nutting.
+2840 Daniel,[6] b. Dec. 6, 1812; m. Ann Burns.
2841 Alfred,[6] d. in infancy.
2842 Betsey,[6] b. Oct. 10, 1815; m. June 26, 1837, Jesse Nutting of Madison, a farmer and stone cutter; soon after moved to Parkman, Me., where he died Oct. 30, 1875. They had:

    2843 *Horatio Nelson* (Nutting), b. March 24, 1838; m. Nov., 1863, Helen L. Leighton; graduated from Colby 1863, and is a lawyer in Redwood City, Cal.
    2844 *Marcellus Albert* (Nutting), b. March 13, 1840; m. Nov., 1868, Emma Haines, and lives in Oceola, Iowa.
    2845 *Ann Jane Morrill* (Nutting), b. Sept. 10, 1842; m. July 30, 1866, G. A. Mathews of Andover, Mass.
    2846 *Frank Thurston* (Nutting), b. Oct. 23, 1846; m. July 4, 1870, Mary Page, and lives in Parkman.
    2847 *Jerome Jewett* (Nutting), b. May 6, 1848; m. June 19, 1870, Emma Macomber, and lives in Hollister, Cal.
    2848 *Mary Elizabeth* (Nutting), b. May 23, 1852; m. Sept. 23, 1876, Fred Leighton, and lives in Sangerville, Me.
2849 Mary,[6] m. Josiah Holbrook of North Madison.
2850 Stephen,[6] d. in infancy.
+2851 Winthrop Hilton,[6] b. June 23, 1821; m. Hannah Spears.
2852 Augusta Wiggin,[6] b. Feb. 16, 1823; m. Nov. 13, 1845, Andrew Jewett, b. June 23, 1816, son of Nathan and Lucy (Cook) Jewett of South Solon, Me. He is a farmer, selectman, assessor, and member of the Universalist church in South Solon. They have:

    2853 *Marcellus* (Jewett), b. Dec. 3, 1847, in Peoria, Ill.
    2854 *Maxie* (Jewett), b. May 19, 1849; m. April 8, 1875, Vandalia Carter of Iowa; is a farmer and stock raiser in Shenandoah, Page county, Iowa.
    2855 *Ansel* (Jewett), b. May 21, 1851; mining in Prescott, Arizona.
    2856 *Sumner* (Jewett), b. March 30, 1853; m. Dec. 1, 1877, Flora A. Heath of Augusta, Me.; is a cabinet maker in Augusta.
    2857 *Emma Jessie* (Jewett), b. April 23, 1855; d. Sept. 22, 1859.
    2858 *Frank Rowley* (Jewett), b. June 24, 1857.
    2859 *Howard Leslie* (Jewett), b. Sept. 11, 1864.
2860 Caroline,[6] b. Nov. 8, 1825; m. 1st, in Solon, Feb. 19, 1846, Matthew Benson, b. in Industry, Me., May 4, 1823, son of Matthew and Mary (Gray) Benson of Madison; he was a farmer in Madison and died Jan. 20, 1867; 2d, Feb. 8, 1868, Earl Marshall Norton, b. in Madison June 26, 1821, son of Earl Marshall and Sally (Weston) Norton of Solon; he was a farmer in Solon, but 1878 resides at 61 Cambridge st., Charlestown, Mass. She had:

    2861 *Hannah* (Benson), b. April 17, 1850.
2862 Aura,[6] b. 1828; m. Cyrus Holbrook, a farmer in Madison; d. Aug. 19, 1871. They had:

    2863 *Cyrus Delmont* (Holbrook).
    2864 *Abbie Jane* (Holbrook).

## 1202

JONATHAN THURSTON[5] (*Stephen,*[4] *Stephen,*[3] *Stephen,*[2] *Daniel*[1]), brother of the preceding, and son of Stephen[4] and Betsey (Wiggin)

Thurston of Stratham, N. H.; born there 1801; married, 1820, LuCINDA EMERSON. He died March 7, 1873.

Mr. Thurston was a farmer and lumberman in Madison, Me., having come with his father from Stratham when six years old. He was a Free Mason, member of the Key Stone lodge in Solon, Me. He went to Winona, Minn., a few months before his death from lingering consumption, and to the last expressed the strongest assurance of a personal interest in Christ as his Saviour.

Their children were:

2875 Sarai Cushion,[6] b. May 19, 1827; m. Feb. 13, 1851, Alden Heald, b. July 16, 1822, son of Warren and Eunice (Hilton) Heald of Solon; he is a farmer in Solon. They have:

    2876 *Eunice* (Heald), b. Nov. 6, 1852; m. Herbert Doble of West Quincy, Mass., and has Gracie (Doble).
    2877 *Delia Maria* (Heald), b. Nov. 3, 1856.
    2878 *Mary Emma* (Heald), b. Feb. 13, 1860.
    2879 *Abby Frances* (Heald), b. Oct. 2, 1861.
    2880 *Caddie Ada* (Heald), b. Oct. 22, 1863.
    2881 *Flora Elvira* (Heald), b. May 9, 1866.
    2882 *William Alden Russell* (Heald), b. May 10, 1869.

2883 Stephen,[6] b. 1829; m. Esther Weld; d. 1860.
2884 Hannah Descomb,[6] b. Aug. 13, 1831; m. Josiah Whipple.
2885 Prescott,[6] b. 1833; m. Frances Jewett; enlisted in the war against the rebellion and died in the army.
2886 Danville Clarence,[6] ⎰ twins, born ⎰
2887 Eliza P.,[6] ⎱ Feb. 9, 1838; ⎱ m. Jan. 1, 1859, Henry C. Higgins, b. in Smithfield, Me., April 16, 1838, son of Curtis and Harriet (Decker) Higgins of Augusta, Me.; he is an engineer in Winona. They have:
    2888 *Freddie Eugene* (Higgins), b. in Skowhegan, Me., May 23, 1866.
2889 Lucinda L.,[6] b. 1840; m. Charles Weld.
2890 Mary L.,[6] b. 1842; d. 1860.
2891 Leander T.,[6] b. 1844; m.; settled in Minnesota.
2892 Martha Jane,[6] b. 1846; lives in Minnesota.

## Sixth Generation.

### 1250

JOHN PHILLIPS THURSTON [6] (*Rev. Benjamin,*[5] *Col. Daniel,*[4] *Benjamin,*[3] *Daniel,*[2] *Daniel*[1]), eldest son of Rev. Benjamin [5] and Sarah (Phillips) Thurston of Exeter, N. H.; born there Feb. 22, 1781; married, March 27, 1803, MARY TUCKER of Portland, Me., born September, 1782. He died June 28, 1832; she died Sept. 1, 1839.

He studied in Phillips academy, Exeter; graduated from Dartmouth 1797; taught school at Bradford, N. H., two years, at Fryeburgh, Me., six months, and then, in 1805, was an importer of sugar and commission merchant in Portland till 1822, in which year he moved to New York city and pursued the same business there.

Their children, all born in Portland, were:

2902 Frederick George,[7] b. Sept. 3, 1808; went to New York with his father, succeeded him in the importing and commission business, acquired a handsome property, took great interest in the genealogy of the family, and with his two sisters lived in Brooklyn, N. Y., where he died in 1861; n.m. Mr. Thurston was for years a diligent inquirer after facts, names,

and dates concerning the descendants of Daniel Thurston of Newbury. He made a very elaborate chart of the families in this descent, which has been of great service to the compiler of this work. During a visit to England a few years before his death he explored, as best he could, for the connections there, but was unable to find them, though he came to the conclusion that they came from the county of Kent.

2903   Ellen.[7]
2904   Caroline,[7] b. May 21, 1811.

## 1279

DANIEL THURSTON [6] (*Hon. Nathaniel,[5] Col. Daniel,[4] Benjamin,[3] Daniel,[2] Daniel[1]*), eldest son of Hon. Nathaniel [5] and Martha (Bridges) Thurston of Bradford, Mass.; born there Jan. 12, 1796; married ABBIE STEPHENS of Haverhill, Mass. He was a farmer in Haverhill; died May 18, 1855.

### Their children were:

2915   Abigail,[7] m. Milton B. Mears of Haverhill.
+2916   John Albert,[7] b. Jan. 27, 1817; m. Eliza S. Downing.
2917   Nathaniel Kimball,[7] in Brentwood, N. H.
2918   Eliza Ann,[7] d. young.
2919   George,[7] in Gloucester, Mass.

## 1280

CAPT. NATHANIEL BRIDGES THURSTON [6] (*Hon. Nathaniel,[5] Col. Daniel,[4] Benjamin,[3] Daniel,[2] Daniel[1]*), brother of the preceding, and son of Hon. Nathaniel [5] and Martha (Bridges) Thurston of Bradford, Mass.; born there 1797; married, April, 1823, RUBY GAGE of Bradford. He died August, 1831, and his widow married John Perley.

Mr. Thurston was a merchant in Bradford, and filled the offices of selectman, overseer of the poor, and major of a regiment.

### Their children were:

2930   Aroline Amelia,[7] b. Jan. 19, 1824; m. Sept. 23, 1846, Allison Wheeler of Haverhill, Mass; divorced. She has:
    2931   *Ella Amelia* (Wheeler), m. Edward Kitfield; two daughters.
2932   William Gage,[7] b. March 10, 1825; m. 1848, Charlotte Eaton; lived in Charlestown, Mass., La Crosse and Viroqua, Wis.; was an architect and carpenter; fell from the steeple of a meeting-house and was killed June 27, 1868; she died Jan. 10, 1866. They had:
    2933   *Adelfred Adionysius,[8]* b. 1851; d. Jan. 10, 1861.
    2934   *Osric Adolphso,[8]* in parts unknown.
    2935   *Allfo Luit,[8]* b. in Charlestown Feb. 10, 1856; a painter and inventor in West Salem, Wis.
    2936   *Lara Elden,[8]* b. March 20, 1862; attending school in Waukesha, Wis.
2937   Martha Bridges,[7] b. Jan. 30, 1828; m. Sept., 1856, Chas. L. F. Atkinson; d. Aug. 2, 1871. They had:
    2938   *Frank Thurston* (Atkinson), d. in infancy.

## 1299

DANIEL THURSTON [6] (*Daniel,[5] Col. Daniel,[4] Benjamin,[3] Daniel,[2] Daniel[1]*), eldest son of Daniel [5] and Susanna (Crombie) Thurston of Bradford, Mass.; born there Oct. 11, 1783; married, Sept. 29, 1805, MARY STACY of Salem, Mass. He died Jan. 13, 1820; she died Jan. 4, 1860. He was a house carpenter in Salem.

### Their children were:

2949   Daniel,[7] b. June 28, 1806; m. Sarah Stanley of South Danvers, now Peabody, Mass.; d. April 11, 1830; no children.

2950 Mary Stacy,[7] b. May 29, 1808; n.m.; d. Jan. 7, 1828.
2951 Henry Winchester,[7] b. Dec. 8, 1818; m. 1st, April 5, 1849, Margaret Ellen MacKenzie, b. Sept. 30, 1827, daughter of Reuben and Isabella (Hutchins) (b. in Aberdeen, Scotland) MacKenzie of Salem; she died Feb. 14, 1866; 2d, April 30, 1868, Elizabeth Pingree Smith, b. Jan. 22, 1828, daughter of Aaron and Mehitable (Pingree) Smith of Salem. Mr. Thurston is a furniture dealer in Salem; was a member of the city council in 1868-9. He had, by first wife:
  2952 *William Henry*,[8] b. Feb. 3, 1850; d. March 29, 1859.
  2953 *Helen Stacy*,[8] b. Aug. 8, 1852.
  2954 *Mary Isabella*,[8] b. Dec. 2, 1857.

## 1335

BENJAMIN THURSTON [6] (*Daniel*,[5] *Col. Daniel*,[4] *Benjamin*,[3] *Daniel*,[2] *Daniel*[1]), brother of the preceding, and son of Daniel [5] and Susanna (Crombie) Thurston of Bradford, Mass.; born there Aug. 7, 1805; married, first, Jan. 1, 1827, ELIZA GAGE, born Aug. 16, 1804, daughter of Daniel and Hannah (Trask) Gage of Bradford; she died Feb. 7, 1839. Second, June 22, 1840, LYDIA CARLTON, born Aug. 18, 1818, daughter of Warren and Ludea (Mills) Carlton of Methuen, Mass. Her mother was the daughter of Gen. Mills of Lee, N. H., of revolutionary fame. Mrs. Lydia Thurston died Nov. 1, 1851; Benjamin Thurston died Dec. 7, 1874. He was landlord of the Washington House in Lowell, Mass.

His children, by first wife, Eliza, were:
2965 Nathaniel,[7] b. Feb. 7, 1829; d. Feb. 28, 1829.
2966 Annie L.,[7] b. Oct. 30, 1836; m. 1878, William Clemments; he has been city marshal of Lowell and is now, 1879, chief of the Massachusetts state detectives.

By second wife, Lydia:
2967 Benjamin Carlton,[7] b. July 1, 1846; d. June 12, 1847.

## 1363

REV. ASA THURSTON [6] (*Thomas*,[5] *Dea. John*,[4] *Jonathan*,[3] *Daniel*,[2] *Daniel*[1]), son of Thomas [5] and Lydia (Davis) Thurston of Fitchburgh, Mass.; born there Oct. 12, 1787; married, Oct. 12, 1819, LUCY GOODALE, daughter of Dea. David Goodale of Marlborough, Mass. He died in Honolulu, Sandwich Islands, March 11, 1868, aged 80 years; she died Oct. 13, 1873, lacking only sixteen days of being 81 years old.

Mr. Thurston learned the trade of scythe making and worked at it till twenty-two years of age, when he turned his mind toward the ministry, and graduated from Yale in 1816 and from Andover in 1819. He was the most athletic man in his class. In August of the same year he was ordained as a missionary to the Sandwich Islands, and sailed with his wife Oct. 23, 1819, on the brig Thaddeus; arrived March 30, 1820, and was assigned to the station at Kailua Hawaii, the old residence of the kings of the islands. He lived there more than forty years, until disabled by paralysis, when they moved to Honolulu, where he spent the few remaining years of his life, respected and esteemed, honored and beloved.

Rev. E. D. G. Prime, D.D., "Eusebius" of the New York Observer, wrote the memoir of Rev. William Goodale, D.D., his father-in-law, published 1866, in which he gives the following description of the

courtship and marriage of Rev. Asa Thurston: "Among those associated with me at Andover were Bingham and Thurston. They belonged to the class before me, and were already designated to be the pioneers of the mission to the Sandwich Islands. Early in September, 1819, the prudential committee, hearing of a good opportunity in the brig 'Thaddeus,' directed those brethren to complete all their arrangements and hold themselves in readiness to embark at the very shortest notice.

"At the last moment the mothers of the young ladies, who had engaged to accompany our brothers to the Sandwich Islands, interfered and refused to let their daughters go. It was an unexpected and severe trial to them. Something must be done and that speedily, but there seemed no time to accomplish so important a matter. That they should go unaccompanied by suitable companions was not to be thought of for a moment; for they were not expected to return, and the voyage itself was one of six months' duration. The result was, the society to which we belonged clubbed together and procured for me a fine horse, that would carry me fully ten miles an hour, and sent me, if not on a quixotic, a most delicate mission. Receiving from Mr. Thurston what was perhaps equivalent to a *carte blanche* in regard to one or two young ladies whom I had described to him, I started early one morning and 'streamed' through the country after a wife for my destitute brother, borne on by the best wishes and fervent prayers of the whole theological seminary of Andover. After a forty miles' ride, I slackened my pace and put up my horse in a stable in one of the principal towns of Massachusetts. Unsuccessful there, yet believing in the perseverance of the saints and that what is foreordained will surely come to pass, I early next day turned my horse's head and partly retraced my steps, but not by the same road, to a school-house where I knew a distant relative of mine was teaching school.

"Dismounting I bolted into the school-room and not having much time for a long conference I opened my business at once. The days of photographs had not then come, and I intimated to her that there were a thousand little matters of taste that she alone could decide and that she should have the opportunity. 'Next week,' said I, 'is the anniversary at Andover, and the next day Mr. Thurston will start to go to his ordination in Connecticut. Your father's house is on the way. I will accompany him and we will pass the night under your roof; you will thus have an opportunity of becoming acquainted. No person need know the object of our stopping, nor need you feel under any obligation to encourage his suit.'

"Had she like Priscilla asked, 'why do you not speak for yourself, John?' the natural answer would have been, 'John is already provided for.' On the day appointed I took Mr. Thurston and walked with him to the town of Marlborough. The sun was sinking in the western woods and all the windows were reflecting his glorious rays, which we took for a good omen. We knocked and were soon admitted. Before we had time to be seated, I saw the black-eyed damsel entering from a door at the other end of the room. Stepping forward and taking her hand, I said, 'How do you do, cousin,' and drawing Mr. Thurston *nolens volens* through the crowd I put his hand

in hers.   The next morning I was directed to go to the town clerk and get him to publish that 'marriage was intended between the Rev. Asa Thurston and Miss Lucy Goodale.'   As there would not be three Sabbaths before the time of their embarkation in which to publish the bans, as the law of Massachusetts required, I requested him to make use of their town-meeting, which occurring the following week fulfilled the requirement of the law.   That in this case I acted right is beyond a doubt.   It was a mode of procedure under extraordinary circumstances, and not to be judged by common rules.   The union proved a comfort and a blessing to the parties concerned."

The following sketch is condensed from the Fitchburgh Sentinel of April, 1878:  "Leaving home was a new era in the life of Asa Thurston.   In the neighborhood and at the district school he had been the champion of muscle, and was known as a wrestler who could floor any fellow of his age.   It was fun for the crowd which often gathered after singing-school to see the tussle.

"His shopmates had a severer test of strength and agility.   An open hogshead standing upon one end was kept for practice for apprentices, in jumping into and out of without touching the sides. The men who dared attempt the dangerous feat were few, but he was equal to the test.   A rail fence ran alongside West street from the house of Joseph Farwell to the scythe shop.   It was the custom of young Thurston to vault from right to left over each length of this fence, on his way between the shop and his boarding-place.   The exercise of tending a trip-hammer ten or twelve hours per day ought to satisfy an exuberant nature, but he possessed a spontaneity of life that never seemed to wane.

"Apprenticeship brought new associations.   Boyish sports gave way to maturer pleasures.   Instead of the wrestling match, his buoyant nature seized upon the ball-room and the fascinations of the dance for its gratification.   His love of music and gayety found agreeable companions in the brilliantly-lighted hall and the mazes of the dance.   He was the center of life, and a ball-room in Fitchburgh without the presence of Asa Thurston to enliven it was considered tame.   He knew no half-way, but entered into the festivities with his whole soul.

"The autumn of 1805 was a season of severe sickness in this region.   Typhoid fever was prevalent and proved fatal in many cases. The athletic form of Asa Thurston was a subject for a fever to attack and rage with exceeding violence.   Death seemed to revel over his victim for several days, but life was spared.   However, his mother, for whom he had such warm attachment and who watched over him with great tenderness, was taken sick, and died Jan. 19, 1806, of this disease.   A brother and sister followed, so that in six short weeks the family circle was sadly broken and the light of home seemed to have gone out in darkness.

"Up to this time young Thurston had been a gay fellow.   There was nothing gross or vicious about him, but he had led, 'the gayest of the gay,' to use his own words, and had never taken that interest in religious matters that afterward characterized him.   Another era marked his life.   A new impulse seized him which turned the whole

10

tenor of his existence. He became one of the most zealous advocates of the doctrines which Mr. Worcester and his successor, Rev.
Titus Theodore Barton, taught, and like Paul he 'declared with great
boldness those things which he had heard and believed.' All his former plans of life were laid aside, and he set at work to obtain an education and fit for the ministry with a special purpose of foreign
mission service.

"We do not pretend to give an analysis of the different elements
which constituted the character of Asa Thurston. Some things have
been hinted which seem essential to a correct estimation of the man
and his mission. Scientists tell us that children inherit marked traits
of character, and that there are peculiarities of mind which are often-
er impressed previous to birth than otherwise. Some children seem
to possess deep religious natures from birth. This was not the case
with Asa Thurston; there was nothing dark, shadowy, foreboding
about him in boyhood; not even a vein of solemnity, but a gay, frol-
icsome spirit, delighting in music, fun, and bold, daring feats. The
simple habits of the early settlers, the plain mode of living compell-
ing to conform to hygienic laws, gave children born under such circumstances good physical development, but that religious fervor so
prominent afterward was not apparent then.

"Mr. Thurston's convictions were the result of no sudden emotion.
For six long years his mind had been agitated and he had pondered
the teachings of Mr. Barton. Many of his most intimate friends had
announced their position and his mind grappled with grave theological questions in desperate conflict. There was no superficial view, no
hastily-formed conclusion to be recanted in the future. Like Paul,
'he knew in whom he had believed and was persuaded that he was
able to keep that which he had committed unto him unto that day.'
He was one of the men who gave Fitchburgh and that religious revival a widespread reputation.

"He had reached twenty-two years of age, had recovered health,
was in the enjoyment of vigorous manhood, and had that essential
foundation of mental stamina, 'a sound mind in a sound body.' His
intellectual faculties, heretofore but partially developed, gave promise
of strength, and the choice of the ministry was in the line of his talent as his future success proved.

"Some phases of the inner life of Asa Thurston may possibly appear, in this sketch, to be overdrawn, or wholly the product of fancy
or imagination. It may be questioned how so much should be revealed of the secret workings of the heart, especially since the records of those days are meager and more than seventy years have
elapsed. It would be impossible to establish these points but for the
existence of a curious document, written by the subject himself, a
copy of which is in possession of Dea. Alvan Simonds of Boston, an
ardent admirer of Mr. Thurston, and also a native of Fitchburgh. It
is an interesting paper, in view of recent discussions upon the dogmas
and doctrines held and taught in the early days. It has a historical
value which also makes it worthy of preservation. It was originally
presented to the examining committee of the church when he was
propounded for admission, and we give it verbatim.

## ASA THURSTON'S RELATION.

I lived almost entirely unconcerned about my precious soul till I was past sixteen years of age. I sometimes thought that religion was of importance and that I would attend to it at some future period, but I felt disposed to put off repentance to a more convenient season. I thought that after I had become old I should have nothing else to do but to attend to religion, but could not bear the thought of attending to the concerns of eternity so young. I thought that I was as good as many others and that I should fare as well. When I was about sixteen years old, it pleased God to send his Holy Spirit to convince and convict many in this place of their sins, by which I was alarmed. I began to think religion was of some importance, that I would attend to it. Seeing some of my young friends and connections embracing the Saviour and singing the wonders of redeeming love, I thought I should like to be one of the happy number. I felt somewhat anxious about being prepared for death and eternity, but I had very little if any conviction of sin by the law. I knew that I was a sinner, but I had no realizing sense of the opposition of my heart to God and holiness. I knew that I must repent of my sins or perish forever, but notwithstanding all this knowledge, I soon lost all my serious impressions and anxious thoughts about myself and became as careless as ever. But I could not go on in sin with so calm a conscience as before. Some of my friends and connections, that formerly had been my most intimate companions in sin, became faithful witnesses against me, and in particular my sister. She would often reprove me for my folly. Her friendly voice would frequently warn me in the most solemn manner: "Why will you not forsake your beloved sinful companions and go along with me? Do be entreated, my dear brother, to forsake your sins and embrace the Saviour. How can you crucify the benevolent Jesus?" But I could see no loveliness in him, so I said, "Go thy way for this time, when I have a more convenient season I will call for thee," and thus I went on in my own chosen way till at length God appeared in judgment against me, and visited me with sickness, at which time few, if any, expected I should recover; but God, being rich in mercy, saw fit to forbear, and restored me to health. I felt somewhat rejoiced, but had no heart to sing praises to God for his mercy. My spared life, which ought to have been devoted to God, was spent in the service of Satan. I expected I should have no more to trouble me, but I was soon arrested by a most solemn providence. God was pleased to take from me a most affectionate and loving mother. This, indeed, was a most solemn scene to me. To think that but a few weeks before she was in sound health and I, to all appearance, on the verge of eternity, and then to look back and behold the hand of God in restoring me to health, while she was called into the eternal world! About this time my eldest brother was taken sick, and in a short time departed this life. In his last moments I stood by the side of his dying bed to hear his last, his dying admonition. Solemn and heart-affecting were his last words. He earnestly entreated me to see first that my peace was made with God. He solemnly warned me to escape from the wrath to come. I then made some resolves that I would attend to religion. I was soon called to witness the departure of my sister. She was one of the richest of Heaven's blessings to me, and, alas! she was too precious a blessing for me to retain. God was pleased to take her from me, and thus in about the space of six weeks I was called to part with a most affectionate parent, a most faithful brother, and an affectionate and dear sister.

I thought, if all these solemn warnings and admonitions that I had been called to pass through did not excite me to attend to the concerns of my soul, that there was no means that would. But, alas! I soon forgot them and became as careless and heedless as ever and more so. That I was extremely hardened in sin by these providences is evident from this,—in about six months I was engaged in the ball-room! Who would have thought this of a rational creature? To look back on the solemn scenes that I had been called to pass through so lately, and then to see the ungrateful, stupid part I was acting! Who would have thought that my limbs, that had been so lately snatched from the grave, would have been suffered to move in the service of Satan? But I scruple not to say, there was no one there more gay and active than myself; but in the midst of these scenes of gayety and sinful pleasure, these solemn words of my deceased brother would come into my mind, viz., "Escape from the wrath to come." These words followed me for the space of about four years, until at length I was brought to feel that if I did not escape I should soon be lifting up my eyes in torment. In this solemn situation I looked back on my past life with trembling. I then saw how I had been deaf to all the solemn calls, warnings, and invitations of the gospel and the offers of mercy. I saw how I

had been fighting against God all my days, and that it was because he was God and not man that I was spared.

Twenty-two years of my precious life had been trifled away in the service of Satan! So much time gone to eternity and the deeds thereof sealed up to the judgment of the great day! In this solemn situation I bade farewell to my gay companions. I felt, indeed, that I was in a lonely and disconsolate state. In this gloomy and melancholy situation I sometimes attempted to ask for mercy, but no mercy could I find, and indeed I could see no mercy that I deserved, for saith the eternal God, " I have called but ye have refused, I have stretched out my hand and no man regarded, therefore I will laugh at your calamity, and mock when your fear cometh, when distress and anguish come upon you, then shall ye call but I will not answer." I felt that God had called so long on me to repent, and I had turned a deaf ear to his voice, that there could be no hope respecting me. I found that my heart was wholly and totally opposed to God and holiness, and that it would be just in God should he cast me off forever. All the solemn warnings that had been addressed to me in my past life from the people of God, and in particular those from my brother and sister, stared me in the face. I could almost hear them saying, " Escape from the wrath to come." But I could see no way of escape for me. I thought I had sinned against so much light and knowledge that there could be no hope respecting such an ungrateful wretch as myself. I sometimes read my long-neglected bible, but, dreadful to behold, the curses of the divine law all stood against me. I looked forward to the dreadful judgment day—there I seemed to stand trembling, expecting every moment to hear the righteous Judge pronounce the awful sentence, " Depart!" and myself saying, "Amen! it is just!" Under these solemn considerations I would frequently ask myself, " What shall I do?" and the answer would always be at hand, which was this, " Submit to God!" and at length I was brought to feel that such was the hardness of my heart and the stubbornness of my will, that nothing short of the power that raised Christ from the dead could ever subdue the heart of stone and bow the stubborn will. I then felt that I was entirely dependent on God's sovereign will and pleasure, and that he would do with and dispose of me and all his creatures for his own glory.

I was brought, as I humbly hope and trust, to feel willing to say, with my heart, to my God, " Glorify thyself with me, do with and for me that which shall be most for thine honor and glory." I thought I felt willing that God should take the throne that I had been long contending with him about, likewise I was willing to cast myself down at the foot of sovereign mercy. I then was brought to feel the way in which mercy could flow down to such a heaven-daring sinner as I had been, and to my joyful surprise I beheld, with the eyes of the mind, the Lord of life and glory suspended on the cross. I then saw how my sins had pierced his innocent hands and feet and fastened them to the accursed tree. I saw the big wound in his side that the spear of unbelief had made, and then I seemed to hear him saying to me (not with an audible voice, but by his Spirit), " Come unto me, look and live," and truly astonishing and animating was the smiling of his countenance. Oh, how cheerfully did I embrace him as the Lord my righteousness. I felt willing to trust my all, my eternal all, in his hands. Oh, how sweet was the union and communion between Christ and my soul! And what love and joy then filled my peaceful breast! Oh, how glorious was that Saviour who honored the divine law in my view! Even the Lord of glory condescended to dwell in the heart of such a self-destroying apostate. Oh, what songs of praise did my heart sing to my God and Saviour! I felt in my heart that the inhabitants of heaven were rejoicing over a repenting, returning prodigal. I went about saying to myself, " Can this be true?" Am I a subject of the love of God? Can this be the heart so lately filled with bitterest enmity against God and all goodness? But now it is melting! Melting with what? Why, with love to my God and Saviour. Who can measure the love of Christ? Surely no one. It is boundless; it cannot be fathomed. And oh, what gratitude I owe to my God for his long-suffering patience with such a vile wretch, and for the wonders he has wrought for me in the course of my past life. Once he delivered me from immediate death by the untimely discharge of a gun, and once his almighty arm brought me up from the borders of the grave. Must not this God have all my songs and all my love? He must and shall have the first share in the affections of my heart. I must count all things but loss and dross for the excellence of the blessed Immanuel. I think I now take comfort and satisfaction in religion if I am not deceived. The long-despised band of christains now appear most lovely; they have the first share in my affections below my God and Saviour. I think, if I am not deceived, I feel willing to deny myself and take up the cross and follow Christ.                                        ASA THURSTON.

"The church accepted its applicant. The American Board of Missions was then in its infancy. A great interest had been excited, throughout this country, in the benighted portions of the earth, and a few brave hearts had gone to distant lands to carry the gospel of peace and good-will to men and plant the seeds of industry and civilization. Though past his majority, he decided to give up his trade as a scythe-maker and commence studying for the ministry. Mission life was one grand idea that possessed his soul and he knew no other purpose.

"He fitted for college and was ready to enter in the summer of 1812. He selected Yale, and started on his journey from Fitchburgh. It was a time when the country was convulsed with war with England, but nothing of a political nature could keep him from his purpose. Home, country, friends, all were laid upon the altar.

"In his physical nature he was Asa Thurston still. Hazing freshmen was a pastime more frequently enjoyed than at Princeton to-day. New Haven sophs did not lack courage; they possessed discretion. There was a postponement, a consultation, a meeting in one of the rooms, and the faculty heard of it. They anticipated the deliberations and sent for Asa Thurston, and he was instructed to go up and clean out the crowd. He did it.

"He graduated from Yale in 1816, with honor, and from Andover in 1819; he was considered one of the best men that institution produced. His visits home had been few. Traveling expenses were large and means of public conveyance limited to the old-fashioned stage-coach. It took from ten to fifteen days, according to the condition of the roads, for a letter to reach New Haven from Boston.

"In the fall of 1819, after finishing his seminary course, he turned his steps homeward for the last time. His purpose to be a missionary had long been known, but his chosen field of labor, the Sandwich Islands, had just been announced. The story of the barbarous murder of Capt. Cook had sent a chill through England and America. Youth and age alike, not only in Fitchburgh, but in all the adjacent towns, were interested in the man who had courage to carry the gospel among savages. He who dared venture on such an errand, with such a people, was a curiosity. Every fireside discussed the probabilities of his fate and the majority decided he was to throw his life away; a few had him eaten up by the savages in less than a twelvemonth.

"Services were held in the church, and many a prayer ascended from family altars and pulpits for the safety of the little band who with him were about to embark. Fitchburgh was filled with a missionary spirit. The Sabbath previous to his departure he preached in Mr. Eaton's pulpit from the text, John x. 16,—'And other sheep I have which are not of this fold: them also I must bring; and they shall hear my voice; and there shall be one fold, and one shepherd.' The church was filled to overflowing. In the choir were Ebenezer, Cyrus, Sylvania, and Mahala, his brothers and sisters.

"There was a gathering of neighbors and relatives at the old homestead the morning of Mr. Thurston's departure, and right warmly was the 'God bless you!' given. The time was fixed for the vessel to

sail. It was a sorrowful day. Gray-haired men and women and little children wept, but no tear could be traced on his cheek as the little groups, talking, laughing, crying, were all anxious to shake hands. ' It was a great undertaking,' they said, and so it proved.

"His horse was saddled and brought to the door. As he mounted and drove away not a shadow crossed his brow. Longing eyes went after him as he ascended the hill, and as he entered the woods which then covered the brow of the hill he turned his horse about and sat 'for a moment surveying the scene and group before him—a last look at home, kindred, and friends—then drew his reins and galloped away. Brave soul! His goal was no visionary, flighty castle, but a sublime height reached only by patient toil that knew no rebuff of fortune or flickering of faith, and its reward is ' manifold more in this present time and in the world to come life everlasting.'

"There is a story of touching pathos, exceeding tales of fiction, connected with the establishment of the Sandwich Island mission. Henry Obookiah, a Hawaiian youth, was found one day upon the steps of the college buildings at New Haven, weeping because he thought the doors of instruction were closed to him. He was an orphan of tender sensibilities though born in a heathen land. His parents had been slain in his presence and he remained a captive until an uncle, who was a priest of the island, found him and took him to his home. He was restless and unhappy, and formed the plan of leaving the island. He secured passage, with two other youths, in a merchant vessel, commanded by Capt. Brintnal of New Haven, and bound for that port. He became converted to christianity, and was living in New Haven while Mr. Thurston was a student at Yale. Obookiah, with four other Hawaiians, was placed by christian friends at the mission school at Cornwall, Ct., where he and they made rapid advancement. His great desire was to obtain an education and go back to teach his fellow-countrymen. In this he was disappointed. A sudden fever seized him, and in February, 1818, he died. But he lived long enough to arouse a great interest, throughout America, in the Sandwich Islands. The establishment of missions upon this field was determined, and this little incident, intensified by his death, was published by newspapers in all christendom.

"The managers of the Andover Missionary Society believed Asa Thurston and Hiram Bingham, classmates at the seminary, possessed the necessary qualifications for mission service, and recommended them to the American board. This selection was made with care, as the field was deemed not only difficult, but one of unusual importance. Dr. Worcester was then corresponding secretary of the board.

"The ordination of Messrs. Thurston and Bingham took place under the auspices of the North Consociation of Litchfield county, at Goshen, Ct., on the 29th of September, 1819. The sermon was preached by Rev. Heman Humphrey, afterward president of Amherst college, from the text, Josh. xiii. 1—'There remaineth yet very much land to be possessed.' Mr. Bingham found his bride at this ordination. That morning, while walking to the church, he was met by a young lady who inquired the way to the house of worship where the services were to be performed. He volunteered to accompany her to

the church, found her an earnest, educated christian, made an offer of marriage, which was accepted, and she became his wife.

"The first company sent out by the American board to the Sandwich Islands comprised seventeen persons. Beside the two missionaries and their wives were Dr. Thomas Holman, physician, Samuel Whitney, mechanic and school-master, Samuel Ruggles, catechist and teacher, Elisha Loomis, printer and school-master, and Daniel Chamberlain, farmer. All were married and accompanied by their wives. Mr. and Mrs. Chamberlain came from Brookfield, Mass.; they were in the prime of life, and took with them a family of five children, three sons and two daughters. Mr. C. had been a well-to-do farmer and had acquired considerable property by thrift and industry. The other members of the company were young couples, who had offered themselves to the board to engage in this mission enterprise. Three native Sandwich Island youths, who had been educated at Cornwâll, Ct., were sent as interpreters; their names were Thomas Hopu, John Honoree, and William Tenoee. These persons were organized into a church, and a farewell meeting was held in Park street church, Boston, previous to the departure. The house was packed to overflowing with friends of the enterprise. Mr. Thurston made the principal farewell address. The assembly adjourned to the wharf, where a vast throng awaited their arrival. Prayer was offered and 'Coronation' sung upon the pier. If ever that grand old tune and those sublime words found fitting expression, it was on that occasion. Says an eye-witness, 'The enthusiasm kindled to its height as the last verse was sung—'Let every kindred, every tribe'—and it seemed as though the arches of heaven responded, 'Amen!'' The missionaries were pronounced foolish and fanatical, and the plan of taking ladies to live or die among the barbarians of Hawaii appeared to many, who sympathized with the object in the main, as objectionable and forbidding. It was deemed advisable to send a frame dwelling, and this was transported free through the generosity of Messrs. Sturgis & Bryant, owners of the vessel, prompted by sympathy for the ladies of the mission, for whose comfort it was thought the grass-thatched huts of Hawaii would be unsuitable. These gentlemen also gave their ship-master instructions to offer the missionaries free passage home, as it was believed they could not long remain among the vile barbarians.

"Mr. Thurston, then just passed thirty-two, and his new wife Lucy were among the most cheerful passengers. The brig was small and the quarters contracted. Nearly all the party were seasick. Fifty days out, in latitude 2° south, longitude 20° west, the brig was spoken by an East India merchantman and letters were sent home. They had encountered head winds with rain and had made slow sailing; they had a long and tempestuous voyage around Cape Horn, and reached Honolulu March 30, 1820, having been one hundred and sixty-nine days from Boston, 18,000 miles.

"The condition of the Sandwich Islanders on the arrival of Mr. and Mrs. Thurston, in 1820, was pitiable in the extreme. From a nation variously estimated, by Capt. Cook and others, at 300,000 to 400,000 people, they had been reduced by wars, bloodshed, and vices which follow evil passions to about 150,000. Disease, drunkenness,

and debauchery had so weakened and prostituted their powers as to place them in a forlorn and almost hopeless condition. To human vision there was a sickening prospect before the missionaries. Loathsome forms of disease, introduced by profligate seamen or foreign refugees from vessels which entered the harbors, were universal. The entire experience of the natives, from the first visit of white men, had been one of fraud and intrigue, and the missionaries found an innate and crafty suspicion of every motive and precept they sought to inculcate. The grossest forms of idolatry abounded. Filial affection was unknown. Cannibalism was universal, and captives taken in war were slain by thousands as sacrifices to the gods, or roasted for the feasts.

"With these filthy, naked, besotted creatures and their degraded surroundings before them, this brave band looked upon Hawaii. It is one thing to listen to tales of horror and another to endure. Revolting as the picture seemed there was a ray of light that pierced the darker background. The natural beauty was charming; the climate was delightful. But there was something better than these.

"Kamehameha I., one of the most gifted rulers of the islands, died, at the age of 66, only a few months previous to the time the mission bark sailed from Boston. Although adhering strenuously to idolatry, he modified some of its worst ceremonies. He would not permit human sacrifices to be offered during his sickness. At his death, his eldest son, Liholiho, succeeded to the kingdom. Soon after his accession to the throne, the 'tabu' system, which was a set of restrictions and prohibitions inseparably connected with idolatry, was disregarded. Among the prohibitions of the tabu were these: the wife could not eat with her husband on penalty of death; the choicest kinds of meats, fruit, and fish were forbidden women of all classes on the same penalty. The destruction of idols soon followed; this brought on a civil war, in which idol worshipers were conquered, so that upon the arrival of the missionaries the way seemed prepared before them. The first intimation they had of the new regime was upon their arrival in the harbor of Honolulu, March 31st. But they found, a few days after, on their arrival at Kailua, the place of royal habitation, that the king had not abandoned the old religion with any desire for a new one.

"Permission was first obtained for the missionaries to land. It was given with reluctance. The king was invited to dine on board ship. He came with only a 'malo' or narrow girdle around his waist, a silken scarf thrown over his shoulders, a string of beads around his neck, and a feather wreath on his head. In this scanty attire he was introduced to the first company of white ladies he ever saw.

"The band was to be divided. Mr. and Mrs. Thurston and Dr. Holman and wife were stationed at Kailua, near the royal residence. The village is on the western coast of the island of Hawaii, one hundred and forty miles from Honolulu. It contained three thousand inhabitants. Mr. Thurston was selected as teacher of the royal family. His pupils were the king and his brother (afterward Kamehameha III.), two of the king's wives, the governor of Hawaii, and a lad named John Ii, who afterward became one of the judges of the su-

preme court. Mr. and Mrs. Thurston were assigned quarters in a thatched hut three and one half feet in height at the foot of the rafters. It was without floor or ceiling, furniture or matting, and though one of the royal palaces, was filled with fleas and vermin. The frame dwelling brought from Boston was left at Honolulu. Thus they began their mission labors. There was no written language, and the first work was to construct one. It was found that twelve letters— five vowels and seven consonants—expressed every sound in the pure Hawaiian, and each syllable ended with a vowel. This rendered it easy for the natives to learn to read and write. After three months of toil amid the darkness and pollution of a heathen village, Mr. Thurston obtained an opportunity to preach to the king by the aid of Thomas Hopu as interpreter. He chose as his text, 'I have a message from God unto thee.'

"In a short time the royal family removed to Honolulu and Mr. Thurston and wife accompanied them; they remained here two years. Mr. Thurston compiled a dictionary and grammar of the native language, and translated parts of Genesis, Numbers, Deuteronomy, the whole of Samuel and 11 Kings, and portions of the New Testament into Hawaiian. He learned to speak that language with great accuracy and fluency. His influence upon the conduct and disposition of the kings, Kamehameha II. and Kamehameha III., was very great. It was a time of utmost importance to secure the good will of those highest in authority when the word of the king was law and his will absolute. Mr. Thurston was peculiarly fitted to instruct ruling minds. Possessed of sound sense, excellent judgment, a commanding presence, he won the admiration and respect alike of the chiefs and subjects; they regarded him physically as the strongest man that ever visited their island. In the early days of the mission a burly chief followed Mrs. Thurston home from another part of the village with evil intent. Mr. Thurston met him at the door and, comprehending his purpose, gave him a castigation so severe that the insult was never repeated.

"The printing press came into use on the islands in 1822, and an additional band of missionaries arrived in 1823. At the expiration of two years Mr. and Mrs. Thurston returned to Kailua, where they remained until the close of his mission service, more than forty years.

"They brought up a family of children, whom they educated with the greatest care, though surrounded by the vices of heathenism. They kept them aloof from association with the natives, and did not allow them to learn the language until after twelve years of age. The Hawaiians were accustomed to wear no clothing, and the missionaries were compelled to make a restriction that no one should attend service without some article of dress, however coarse and rude it might be. This prohibition had the effect of fashion in civilized lands. Many excused themselves because 'they had nothing to wear.'

"The severest blow that befell this noble couple was the death of a darling daughter, Lucy Goodale, who died in Brooklyn, N. Y., just after her arrival in this country, Feb. 24, 1841, aged 17 years. In company with her mother, sister, and brother, she came on a visit to America. Arriving from the southern latitude in mid-winter, she

quickly became a victim of the fell destroyer. She was attractive and lovely, a favorite with all who knew her. Mrs. Thurston was absent about two years. During her visit to Fitchburgh, the Ladies' Missionary Society made up a suit of clothes for Mr. T. Dr. Jonas A. Marshall was measured for the suit. Mr. Thurston intended to accompany his family on this trip, but postponed on account of the necessities of his station. He never afterward found opportunity. He came as far east as San Francisco for his health, in 1863, but never returned to New England. They lived to see more than fifty thousand converts to christianity upon the islands and a degree of civilization established which compares favorably with the christianized nations of the earth.

"From the lowest depths of cannibalism, they beheld a nation raised to power, influence, and respect, with a commerce stretching over seas and turning its wealth even upon the nation which produced and sent out its benefactors. They saw from the vilest idolatrous superstitions a marvelous growth of religious ideas, a degree of civilization of such marked advancement as to astonish the world, and there is no satisfactory explanation save in the power of God's Spirit and his truth thoroughly, practically, and wisely taught. We desire to place no improper emphasis upon human agencies, but if there ever has been one grand effort to elevate mankind more free from criticism than another it is the Sandwich Island mission. The details of its work were laid out and executed with excellent judgment and sound common sense, and the remarkable success that has crowned those labors is in great measure due to the wisdom and shrewdness of Asa Thurston.

"His piety was of purest mold. The dross that mingles in humankind was purged from his soul as it seldom is; and that heart which went out in such sympathy for the benighted ones of earth was closely linked with God. To declare this requires no stretch of the imagination which sometimes throws the mantle of charity over the dead, but it is a simple, honest tribute to his memory.

"Mr. Thurston's earnestness was conspicuous. He went into mission work, as in his younger days he went into the dance hall, with all his might. As in the giddy dance he was 'the gayest of the gay,' so in his after life he formed the sets and with his whole might led the procession 'marching up Zion's hill.' He had no uncertain step; he never broke time with divine music. He was ready for the prompter's first call and he anticipated the changes. His words are expressive:

We want men and women who have souls, who are crucified to the world and the world to them, who have their eyes and their hearts fixed on the glory of God in the salvation of the heathen, who will be willing to sacrifice every interest but Christ's, who will cheerfully and constantly labor to promote his cause; in a word, those who are pilgrims and strangers such as the apostle mentions in the eleventh chapter of Hebrews—men like these we want. Many such we need to complete the work which God in his providence has permitted us to commence. The request which we heard while standing on the American shores, from these islands, we reiterate with increasing emphasis: "Brethren, come over and help us."

"That life is most successful which best fits others to live. He labored not only for the direct influences of his teaching, but for the indirect. He sought to make virtue contagious, and gave to his in-

struction such cast of perfection as made it desirable, and stamped his character on that heathen people in a peculiar manner, as man has rarely done.  He made the natives feel not only his presence, but the presence of his God, and when they were converted to christianity they had thoroughly instilled into them the idea and purpose of conveying that christianity to others.  And so the Sandwich Island mission has a remarkable history.  It has been an aggressive mission. It has accepted and obeyed the command of the Great Founder of christianity, 'Go ye into all the world and preach the gospel to every creature.'  It has thrown out its arms to the Micronesian and the far-distant South Pacific islands, and said to them, 'The nation which sat in darkness has seen a great light.'  That light which glimmered from the old hill farm in Fitchburgh has shed its rays afar and its beams are yet spreading.

"With such a natural soil for positiveness as existed in him, what wonder that his views, born in a season of such religious zeal, were strong and decided to the end!  What wonder that when he 'put his hand to the plow he did not look back!'  That he never visited his native Fitchburgh because his mission to preach the gospel was so important!  Men of weaker decision and less zeal might have been excused if, in a missionary life of almost fifty years, with a great loving heart like his beating in their bosoms, the desire to see once more the home and friends of childhood had lured them from their labors. With Judson, Mills, Bingham, King, and a score of other noble spirits who were pioneers of missionary work, wherever this gospel is preached this that they have done is told as a memorial of them. He is described by Hawaiians as a man of noble physique, with broad, deep chest, a finely-shaped head, a full, clear, blue eye that beamed with love and intelligence.  He wore a long, flowing beard 'like Aaron's beard, which came down to the skirts of his garments,' and in his riper years as it turned to a snowy whiteness, with his locks, 'his hoary head was a crown of glory.'  His youthful exuberance of spirits never left him, and his rich, deep voice would ring out in Hawaiian melody as in the songs of youth.

"Asa Thurston was undoubtedly the ablest man Fitchburgh ever produced.  That he had wonderful power physically, intellectually, and morally is manifest in that scripture test which the world acknowledges correct, 'By their fruits ye shall know them.'  That he had a noble ambition, lofty purposes, and grand ideas, we have but to turn the leaves of Hawaiian history.  We claim a remarkable life such as the world has seldom known, and if in our poor vision we have caught glimpses of its origin which bear investigation, which may lead others to consider the great possibilities of life, nay, which may bring a decision by which the world will be benefited through their labors, our effort will not be lost.  We acknowledge admiration for a character so pure, noble, lovely, and manly that the more it is studied the purer and nobler and manlier it grows.  And if one purpose has prompted more than another, it has been to redeem from oblivion recollections soon to be buried in the grave, and place upon record the fact that Fitchburgh, though derelict in her duty and tardy in her recognition, produced in Asa Thurston a man who is worthy to be written among the heroic and self-sacrificing of the world."

## Children, all born at Sandwich Islands:

+2978 Persis Goodale,[7] b. Sept. 28, 1821; m. Rev. Townsend Elijah Taylor.

2979 Lucy Goodale,[7] b. April 25, 1823; d. in Brooklyn, N. Y., Feb. 24, 1841, just after her arrival in this country. A sketch of her life was written by Mrs. A. P. Cummings. The book is entitled, "The Missionary's Daughter."

+2980 Asa Goodale,[7] b. Aug. 1, 1827; m. Sarah Andrews.

+2981 Mary Howe,[7] b. June 3, 1831; m. 1st, Edwin A. Hayden; 2d, Marcus Benfield.

+2982 Thomas Gairdner,[7] b. May 9, 1836; m. 1st, Harriet Frances Richardson; 2d, Alice Gasking.

## 1364

EBENEZER THURSTON [6] (*Thomas,*[5] *Dea. John,*[4] *Jonathan,*[3] *Daniel,*[2] *Daniel*[1]), brother of the preceding, and son of Thomas [5] and Lydia (Davis) Thurston of Fitchburgh, Mass.; born there Nov. 25, 1789; married LYDIA SAWYER, daughter of Jabez and Hannah Sawyer of Fitchburgh. He was a farmer in Fitchburgh; died Oct. 2, 1871.

### Their children were:

2993 Lydia Elizabeth,[7] b. May, 1812; m. May, 1833. Samuel Melvin Caswell of Fitchburgh, and had:

2994 *Charles Melvin* (Caswell), b. March 15. 1840.

2995 *Herbert Eugene* (Caswell), b. Jan. 8, 1848.

2996 *Emma Etta Mindwell* (Caswell), b. Sept. 9, 1849.

2997 *Ellen Maria* (Caswell), b. Oct. 1, 1852.

2998 *Lottie Elizabeth* (Caswell), b. Sept. 9, 1854; d. Jan. 2, 1875.

2999 Mary Maria,[7] b. Aug. 18, 1815; d. Sept. 22, 1833.

3000 Charles Thomas,[7] b. Nov. 15, 1819; m. Sept. 27, 1843. Martha Aldrich Cousins, and had:

3001 *Nelson A.*,[8] b. Sept. 27, 1848.

3002 Susan Abigail,[7] b. Dec. 3. 1826; m. Sept., 1844, Asa W. Raymond of Gardner, Mass., and had:

3003 *Luman* (Raymond), } twins, b. Sept. 25, 1845.
3004 *Lyman* (Raymond). }

3005 *Mary Abbie* (Raymond), b. Oct., 1849.

## 1366

CYRUS THURSTON [6] (*Thomas,*[5] *Dea. John,*[4] *Jonathan,*[3] *Daniel,*[2] *Daniel*[1]), brother of the preceding, and son of Thomas [5] and Lydia (Davis) Thurston of Fitchburgh, Mass.; born there May 20, 1796; married, April 16, 1822, CAROLINE BOUTELLE, born Oct. 12, 1796, daughter of Nathaniel and Polly (Hill) Boutelle of Fitchburgh.

Cyrus Thurston was a teacher of singing thirty years, teacher of public schools several years, selectman and assessor of Fitchburgh ten years, overseer of the poor twenty-seven years, and chairman of the board in 1877 and for several years previous; has always been a faithful and efficient officer, a friend and benefactor to the poor, a helper in every good cause, and is highly respected by all. We give quite a full report of a pleasant reunion held on the occasion of Mr. Thurston's eighty-second birthday, which shows in what estimation he is held by the community in which he lives:

### BIRTHDAY REUNION.

The "Old Folks' Singing Class," which was a flourishing organization in 1857 when four concerts were given in the town hall, held a grand reunion in the Calvinistic chapel Monday evening, May 20. 1878, in honor of their director, "Uncle" Cyrus Thurston, who that day completed his eighty-second year. About three hun-

dred persons, including about thirty-five of the original members of the class, were present. Thirty-seven of the seventy-four male members of the class in 1857 are dead, and eighteen were present on Monday evening.

After the entire company had tested the bountiful collation spread upon the tables, and enjoyed an hour in reviving memories of "ye olden time," the audience was called to order in the chapel by Dea. J. C. Moulton, and the old folks, under the direction of Uncle Cyrus, with Banks Davison as organist, sang some of the old tunes, including Turner, Majesty, New Jerusalem, and others. These were all rendered with vim and were a rich treat to the younger portion of the audience. It was remarked by many that during this part of the programme Uncle Cyrus and the members of his class seemed "just as young as they used to be."

Rev. S. J. Stewart read the following appropriate reunion poem, written for the occasion by Mrs. Caroline A. Mason:

Sing the old tunes we used to sing
When life was in its May,
When time went by on gladsome wing
And hearts were young and gay.

Sweet is the music of the spheres:
To us a sweeter chime
Floats upward from the vanished years,
The happy olden time.

The strains that we together sung
Come back to us once more,
And greet us like our native tongue
Upon a foreign shore.

Again sublime old "Majesty"
Rings like a trumpet's blare!
And plaintive "Windham" and "Dundee"
Float, trembling, on the air,—

While he whose voice was wont to lead
Each mazy theme along,
Still lives, thank God, to serve our need
And guide the tuneful throng.

But some, alas, who sang with us
Have passed beyond our sight;
Perhaps their voices, emulous,
Take up these strains to-night,

And waft them, jubilant and free,
O'er all the heavenly hills,
In notes from whose grand harmony
No earthliness distills.

O shining ones, whose glad eyes view
The King, the great "I am!"
When shall we sing the song with you
Of Moses and the Lamb?

Dear Father, tune our hearts below
To that diviner lay,
That we their blessedness may know
Who serve thee night and day.

Make us to yield to thy commands
The glad obedience due:
In temples, then, not made with hands
Our praises we'll renew.

A nice easy chair was then rolled in, much to the surprise of Uncle Cyrus, who was finally persuaded to occupy it. Rev. J. T. Hewes, being called upon for a few remarks, spoke as follows:

*Honored and Aged Friend:*—One of the purposes which your friends had prominently in mind in bringing about this reunion was to show their respect and affection for you. They could think of no better way of expressing their regard for you than by remembering your eighty-second birthday. The bible says that the glory of young men is their strength, and the beauty of old men is the gray head. And it adds another word by way of qualification and amendment: "The hoary head is a crown of glory if it be found in the way of righteousness." We honor you, my friend, not only for your age, but for your character. It is gratifying to your friends that they can look back over the years that they have known you and recall so much that is pleasant and honorable in their intercourse with you. They delight to remember you as an able and enthusiastic teacher of music, as a genial companion, as a good citizen, and a high-toned, true-hearted man. Of the original members of this union I understand that nearly one-half are gone, some to other parts of the country, and some to their eternal homes. But whether present or absent, your name will never be erased from the memory of your friends.

It would not become me to enlarge upon the associations and remembrances which this occasion awakens in the minds of the older portion of this company. Before the close of this meeting they will all have an opportunity to speak of these things and to rehearse the old memories. The part which I have been asked to perform on this occasion, and which gives me great pleasure in performing, is soon told. I have been asked to present you, in behalf of your friends and fellow-members of the Old Folks' Union, this easy chair. It is a simple testimonial of their regard. They hope that you will find it pleasant to sit in, as the infirmities of age increase, and trust that it may sometimes bring to your mind the memories of old friends and pupils. May you long live to sit in and enjoy it. May the infirmities of age come gently and tenderly upon you, and may you be spared to see many another birthday in the possession of health and the capacity of usefulness, is the wish of all your friends.

Mr. Thurston, in his response, showed that this pleasant surprise had touched his tenderest feelings. After thanking his friends for so kindly meeting on the occasion, he referred to the chair as of special value to him from the circumstances which caused its presentation. He should never forget the first meeting of the class, the many pleasant hours he had spent with them, and expressed the hope that these meetings would continue to be held long after he passed away. His associations

with the class had always been pleasant. When he looked back to that portion of his life he had given to music, he had little to regret and much to be thankful for. He said he had much on his mind that he could not express, and again returned hearty thanks for so kind an expression of the love of his friends.

Revs. I. R. Wheelock, Fred Wood, and S. J. Stewart, in response to calls from Dea. Moulton, spoke briefly of the pleasing features of the evening entertainment. Each alluded to the pleasure experienced in their intercourse with their older friends and the encouragement they received from warm-hearted, high-toned gentlemen like the one all joined in honoring on this occasion. Roby R. Safford of Royalston also spoke very kindly of Mr. Thurston, his first music teacher.

Mr. Thurston then favored the company with the old song, "The Down-hill of Life," with bass viol accompaniment. Probably few persons ever heard the song rendered by an old singing master on his eighty-second birthday.

In the down-hill of life when I find I'm declining,
May my fate no less fortunate be
Than a snug elbow-chair can afford for reclining,
And a cot that o'erlooks the wide sea:
With an ambling pad pony to pace o'er the lawn
While I carol away idle sorrow,
And brisk as the lark that each day hails the morn,
Look forward with hopes for to-morrow.

With a porch at my door, both for shelter and for shade, too,
As the sunshine or the winds may prevail:
With a small spot of land for the use of my spade, too,
And a barn for the use of my flail,
A cow for my dairy and a dog for my game,
And a purse when a friend wants to borrow,
I'll envy no king his riches or fame,
Or the "honors" that await him to-morrow.

From the bleak northern blast may my cot be completely
Secured by a neighboring hill,
And at night may repose steal on me more sweetly
By the sound of a murmuring rill;
And when peace and plenty I find at my board,
I'll forget all past trouble and sorrow,
With my friends will I share what to-day may afford,
And let them spread their tables to-morrow.

And when I at last must throw off this frail covering
Which I've worn full three-score years and ten,
On the brink of the grave I'll not cease to keep hovering,
Nor my thread wish to spin o'er again:
But my face in the glass I'll serenely survey,
And with smiles count each wrinkle and furrow,
That this poor worn-out staff, which is threadbare to-day,
May become everlasting to-morrow.

During the evening Dea. Moulton read a letter from the Kimball brothers of Lawrence, Kansas, regretting their inability to join the reunion of their old singing class. Soon after ten o'clock the reunion closed by singing to "Auld Lang Syne" the following ode written for the occasion by Uncle Cyrus :

THE OLD FOLKS' SINGING CLASS.

Kind friends, we here again have met
Our union to restore,
And join in those time-honored songs
We sang in days of yore:
Those joyous songs our fathers sang,
In which we used to join,
When gathered round the household hearth
In the days of auld lang syne.

As we in retrospect survey
The scenes of former years,
And think of loved ones passed away,
How sad the thought appears:
Yet, though they meet us here no more
To join us in our song,
We trust they're only gone before
To join the angelic throng.

Now let us all, before we part,
Our hearts and voices raise
To him who gave us power to sing
These consecrated days:
We'll praise him for his mercies past
And his protecting care,
Who still has lengthened out our days
This pleasure here to share.

Should this reunion be the last
While we on earth remain,
In purer realms, when life is past,
May we all meet again:
There, with our friends now absent here,
Whose loss we all deplore,
To join in new and nobler songs,
Where parting comes no more.

Their children were :

3006 Frances Caroline,[7] b. Nov. 26, 1823; m. Jan. 11, 1845, Henry J. Lowe. b. July 15, 1822, son of Stephen and Susan Lowe of Fitchburgh. She died in Marion, N. J., Jan. 15, 1878; he died a few years previous. They had:

    3007 *Helen Frances* (Lowe), b. June 16, 1847; m. Henry F. Nason of New York, and have Fannie Elizabeth (Nason), b. in Fitchburgh Nov. 22, 1875.

    3008 *Louise Caroline* (Lowe), b. Oct. 11, 1849; m. Chauncy Mason of Jersey City, N. J., and have :

        3009 *Nellie Frances* (Mason), b. in Jersey City April 13, 1873.

        3010 *Florence* (Mason), b. in Jersey City Sept. 12, 1875.

    3011 *Jennie Maria* (Lowe), b. Jan. 19, 1857.

    3012 *Charles Henry* (Lowe), b. Nov. 3, 1858; d. Jan. 25 1861.

    3013 *Annie E.* (Lowe), b. June 27, 1860; d. Aug. 3, 1860.

    3014 *Clara E.* (Lowe), b. Jan. 8, 1862; d. Aug. 14, 1862.

    3015 *Frank Preston* (Lowe). b. Feb. 24, 1864.

    3016 *Florence Gertrude* (Lowe). b. Dec. 2, 1867; d. Feb. 24, 1875.

3017 Thomas Boutelle,[7] b. June 4, 1825; m. Nov. 9, 1850, Susan Tyler of Northfield, Vt. They had :

    3018 *Frances C.*,[8] b. in Northfield, Vt., 1851; d. young.

    3019 *Marcia M.*,[8] b. in Warren, Vt., 1853; d. young.

3020 *James Tyler*,[8] b. in Fitchburgh Aug., 1855.
3021 William Davis,[7] b. Oct. 22, 1829; m. Nov. 3, 1853, Elizabeth J. Billings, b. June 9, 1834, daughter of Silas L. and Joanna Billings of Fitchburgh; no children.
3022 Ellen Maria,[7] b. Nov. 9, 1833; m. Jan. 4, 1855, Samuel Porter Durant, b. March 25, 1828, son of Amos and Joanna Durant of Fitchburgh. They had :
    3023 *George Henry* (Durant), b. Dec. 21, 1855; d. Jan. 10, 1861.
    3024 *Freddie Martin* (Durant), b. Nov. 21, 1857; d. Oct. 15, 1858.
    3025 *Walter* (Durant), ⎱ twins, born ⎰ d. Sept. 13, 1862.
    3026 *Willie* (Durant), ⎰ April 6, 1862; ⎱ d. Sept. 17, 1862.
3027 Mary Catherine,[7] b. Feb. 6, 1836; m. Nov. 27, 1871, Justin Howard of Wakefield, Mass.; no children.

## 1387

JONATHAN THURSTON[6] (*Dea. John,*[5] *Dea. John,*[4] *Jonathan,*[3] *Daniel,*[2] *Daniel*[1]), eldest son of Dea. John[6] and Esther (Wood) Thurston of Fitchburgh, Mass.; born there May 8, 1785; married ABIGAIL ALLEN of Fitchburgh. He died at Burlington, Wis., 1855; she died 1867.

Mr. Thurston was a farmer, living with his brother Abel on the homestead in Fitchburgh till about 1825, when he sold and went to New York state.

### Their children were :

3023 Martha Wood,[7] b. 1807; m. David Battles, and had :
    3029 *David Warren* (Battles), b. 1833.
    3030 *George Thurston* (Battles), b. 1835.
    3031 *Albert Gannet* (Battles), b. 1837; d. 1872.
    3032 *Charles P.* (Battles), b. 1839; d. 1864 in New Orleans in service in the war against the rebellion.
    3033 *Abby Foster* (Battles), b. 1846; d. 1875.
3034 Samuel A.,[7] b. 1809; m. Martha Hastings; went to Smyrna, N. Y., and after a few years to Illinois; three daughters.
3035 Abigail F.,[7] b. 1811; m. Horace Dailey of New York; d. in Illinois; three children, married.
3036 Eliza Ann,[7] b. 1813; m. —— Pool of New York; d. in New York Sept., 1876; three children.
3037 Caroline,[7] d. in infancy.
3038 Charles,[7] m.; went to California and died.
3039 John L.,[7] d. in infancy.
3040 Alonzo,[7] m.; went to Illinois to live; took a trip to Ohio on business and died suddenly.
3041 Nancy,[7] d. aged 22.
3042 Warren,[7] lives in Norwich, Chenango county, N. Y.
3043 Clarissa,[7] m. Thomas Buel of Burlington, Wis.; d. 1868.

## 1388

SUSAN THURSTON[6] (*Dea. John,*[5] *Dea. John,*[4] *Jonathan,*[3] *Daniel,*[2] *Daniel*[1]), sister of the preceding, and daughter of Dea. John[5] and Esther (Wood) Thurston of Fitchburgh, Mass.; born there Aug. 4, 1787; married, Feb. 12, 1807, JOSEPH UPTON, born July 3, 1784, son of John and Abigail (Lowe) Upton of Fitchburgh. She died in Roxbury, Mass., April 28, 1873.

Mr. Upton was a carpenter in Fitchburgh; Mrs. Upton was a member of the Congregational church and a woman of excellent christian character, and brought up her children in the path of integrity.

### Their children were :

3044 Joseph (Upton), b. Oct. 15, 1807; m. 1st, Jan. 20, 1831, Betsey Messenger, b. Jan. 21, 1806; she died Dec. 25, 1864; 2d, March 28, 1866, Mrs. Amelia F. (Vose) Low. He was a farmer and military captain in Fitchburgh; a prominent member of the Congregational church and leader of

the singing for twenty years. His children were *Susan Elizabeth, Calvin, Jane Augusta, Emily M., Louisa Addine, Harrison, Mary Thurston, Daniel, Lydia H., Abby Caroline, Susan A.*, and *George N.* (Upton).

3045　Mary Thurston (Upton), b. Nov. 10, 1809; m. April 30, 1833. Jonathan Burrage, residing in Fitchburgh, afterward a manufacturer of varnish at Roxbury, Mass. She died in Fitchburgh June 22, 1841. They had :

　3046　*Thomas Fairbanks* (Burrage), b. July 4, 1834; m. Harriet L. Battis ; d. in service in the war against the rebellion. They had :

　　*Henry Thompson* (Burrage), b. Oct. 27, 1857.
　　*William Edwin* (Burrage), b July 15, 1859.
　　*Charles Albert* (Burrage), b. Sept. 20, 1860; d. Sept. 25, 1860.

　3047　*Henry Sweetser* (Burrage), b. Jan. 7, 1837; m. May 19, 1873, Caroline Champlin, daughter of Rev. James T. [and Mary (Pierce)] Champlin, D.D.. president of Colby University, Waterville, Me. ; she died Nov. 24, 1875. Mr. Burrage graduated at Brown University 1861 and entered Newton Theological Institution. Aug. 1, 1862, he enlisted against the rebellion as a private in the 36th Massachusetts regiment ; was promoted to sergeant, sergeant major, second lieutenant, first lieutenant, captain, brevet major, and acting assistant adjutant general ; was wounded at Cold Harbor, Va., June 3, 1864. prisoner in Richmond and Danville, Va., from Nov. 1, 1864, till Feb. 22, 1865. He served in Maryland, Kentucky, Mississippi, Tennessee, and Virginia, and was mustered out June 8, 1865; returned to the theological institution and graduated in 1867: prepared the memorial volume for his alma mater, entitled " Brown University in the Civil War," issued in Providence in 1867; ordained as pastor of the Baptist church in Waterville Dec. 30, 1869; resigned Oct. 1, 1873, and became proprietor and editor of the Zion's Advocate, Portland, Me.. which position he still holds, 1879. Children :

　　*Champlin* (Burrage), b. April 14, 1874.
　　*Thomas Jayne* (Burrage), b. Nov. 15, 1875.

3048　*William Upton* (Burrage), b. Dec. 22, 1838; d. Aug. 12, 1839.
3049　*Edwin Augustus* (Burrage), b. Nov. 21, 1840; d. Sept. 15, 1841.
3050　Thomas (Upton), b. 1813; m. 1836, Abigail Downe. He was an insurance agent and teacher of vocal music; held the commission of ensign during the war of the rebellion. was on the detached reserve. and quartermaster and assistant superintendent of negro affairs in Virginia. They had *Hattie Downe, Mary Emma*, m. —— Pitts, and *Charles Emerson* (Upton), b. Aug. 14, 1843; was first lieutenant 25th Massachusetts regiment and was killed in battle near Petersburgh, Va., May 9, 1864.

3051　Edwin (Upton), b. Dec. 9, 1815; m. Nov. 10, 1842, Louisa Maria Farwell of Hoosick, N. Y., and had one son, who died in infancy; adopted a daughter, who married but is now dead. He was colonel of militia for twenty years, representative in the legislature two years, selectman of Fitchburgh fourteen years, assessor five years, jailor, and a prominent member of the Congregational church. When the war of the rebellion broke out he raised the 25th Massachusetts regiment volunteers, which was in the Burnside expedition in North Carolina. He lost his sight a few years ago by a premature discharge in blasting rocks. He has rendered much service in preparing this genealogy of his family.

3052　John (Upton), b. Dec. 29, 1817; m. April 5, 1848, Louisa C. Willis, and have *Frederic Willis* and *Amy Louisa* (Upton). He was a dry goods merchant fourteen years, insurance agent and deputy collector of taxes four years, and is now, 1877, collector of internal revenue.

3053　Abigail Susan (Upton), b. July 20, 1819; m. James P. Putnam, and had *Ann Maria, Thomas Farrington, Daniel Cowdin, James Edward, Frederic Adams, Charles Benjamin, Frank Porter, Walter Herbert*, and *William Sweetser* (Putnam). Three of the boys were over six feet high. She died 1860.

3054　Charles (Upton), b. Nov. 4, 1821; m. Dec. 16, 1845, Sarah Amelia Hagar, and had *George Clinton, Charles Herbert*, and *Lillian* (Upton). He is a mechanic: has been town officer and selectman.

3055　Martha Ann (Upton), b. Feb 27, 1826; m. Sept. 18, 1845, George Curtis, and had ten children, *Henry Clifford, Martha Gertrude, Edwin Upton*, and *Nelson O.* (Curtis); the others died in infancy.

## 1390

DEA. ABEL THURSTON[6] (*Dea. John,[5] Dea. John,[4] Jonathan,[3] Daniel,[2] Daniel[1]*), brother of the preceding, and son of Dea. John[5] and Esther (Wood) Thurston of Fitchburgh, Mass.; born there Dec. 21, 1791; married, first, Dec. 14, 1815, EUNICE ALLEN, born March 18, 1790, daughter of Benjamin and Dolly (Flagg) Allen of Fitchburgh; she died Feb. 9, 1823. Second, Sept. 30, 1823, DEBORAH BUTLER, born in Townsend Nov. 22, 1797. He died July 9, 1864.

Mr. Thurston was a farmer, living on the homestead in Fitchburgh for some years in company with his brother Jonathan, building himself a house on the opposite side of the road from the homestead. Some years ago he sold this place, moved to the center of the town and engaged in the manufacture of bellows, and afterward became secretary of the Fitchburgh Mutual Fire Insurance Co., which office he held till his death. He held several offices of trust in the town; was deacon in the Congregational church for forty-one years, and superintendent of the Sunday-school for thirty years. His daughter says, "He was a truly good man, who set a most worthy example, and gained the confidence of all who knew him as few men do; he was a peace-maker in the family, church, and neighborhood, and when he died he left a host of friends and not one enemy." Rev. G. B. Wilcox, his pastor, said to his daughter, Mrs. Litchfield, "I have had some very good deacons in the churches over which I have been pastor, but I never had one like your father. I always knew where to find him." His children, by first wife, Eunice, were:

3057　Elizabeth Adams,[7] b. Oct. 3, 1816; m. James Davis Litchfield, a chair maker in Fitchburgh, and had *Carrie* (Litchfield).
3058　Dorothy Caroline,[7] b. Dec. 28, 1818; m. 1845, Ira Carlton, a miller in Fitchburgh; he became insane and hung himself 1855. They had:
　　3059　*Eliza* (Carlton), b. Oct. 30, 1846.
　　3060　*Abby E.* (Carlton), b. Oct. 29, 1848.
　　3061　*William Abel* (Carlton), b. Sept. 7, 1850.
+3062　Abel Leander,[7] b. June 21, 1821; m. Elizabeth Knapp.

By second wife, Deborah:

3063　Aaron Butler,[7] b. Dec. 29, 1824; d.
3064　Rufus Winslow,[7] b. Dec. 15, 1828; d.

## 1409

CAPT. JOHN THURSTON[6] (*Stephen,[5] Dea. John,[4] Jonathan,[3] Daniel,[2] Daniel[1]*), eldest son of Stephen[5] and Mary (Osgood) Thurston of Fitchburgh, Mass.; born there Sept. 24, 1788; married, Nov. 28, 1816, ELIZABETH DASCOMB, born Aug. 14, 1792, daughter of Jacob (who was a lieutenant in the revolutionary war) and Rachel (Dale) Dascomb of Wilton, N. H. He died June 16, 1852; she died in Lunenburgh, Mass., June 9, 1873.

Capt. John was a farmer and resided in Fitchburgh, Northampton, Northfield, Mass., and Wilton, N. H., where he died. He was captain in the war of 1812, and was selectman of Northfield.

They had twelve children, only one surviving infancy:

3067　Mary Elizabeth,[7] b. in Northfield Sept. 5, 1833. She has devoted herself mainly to teaching juvenile singing schools, seventy-six of which she taught between 1859 and 1869, closing each with a floral concert. February, 1877, she went to Brooklyn, N. Y., to assist in getting up a floral concert in one of the mission schools connected with Rev. Henry Ward Beecher's church. **11**

## 1424

WILLIAM PARSONS THURSTON [6] (*Rev. Pearson,[5] Samuel,[4] Jonathan,[3] Daniel,[2] Daniel[1]*), eldest son of Rev. Pearson[5] and Jerusha (Greenleaf) Thurston of Leominster, Mass.; born in Somersworth, N. H., 1795; married, 1821, MARY GARDNER, born about 1802, daughter of John Gardner of Leominster. He died March, 1847; she died August, 1850.

Mr. Thurston was educated at Dummer academy and commenced the study of medicine, but was compelled to leave his studies to travel with his father in an endeavor to regain his health, and did not return to it but became a farmer in Amherst, Mass.; was a member of the Congregational church, and after of the Episcopal.

### Their children were:

3069 Mary Elizabeth,[7] b. in Leominster Dec. 1, 1821; d. in Amherst Nov. 5, 1840.
3070 Sarah Greenough,[7] b. in Leominster June 4, 1823; m. by Rev. M. C. Colton, in Amherst, April 22, 1845, George Osgood, b. in Charlestown, Mass., Sept. 14, 1819, son of Benj. Binney and Clara (Call) Osgood, a successful merchant of Boston for many years; retired and now resides in Old Cambridge; a member of the Episcopal church. They had, b. in Boston:
3071     *Clara Call* (Osgood), b. March 30, 1846; d. Nov. 14, 1849.
3072     *George* (Osgood), b. Nov. 2, 1847; d. Sept. 14, 1848.
3073     *William Thurston* (Osgood), b. June 23, 1849; a merchant in Boston.
3074     *John Gardner* (Osgood), b. in Roxbury, Mass., Jan. 18, 1851; m. Elizabeth Jane Legro of Great Falls, N. H.; is in business in Boston.
3075     *Benjamin Binney* (Osgood), b. in Roxbury May 10, 1852; d. May 12, 1852.
3076     *Samuel Call* (Osgood), b. in Cambridge, Mass., Aug. 30, 1853; d. July 2, 1855.
3077     *Emily Call* (Osgood), b. in Cambridge Oct. 23, 1854; m. Oct. 23, 1878, Appleton Payson Clark Griffin, b. in Wilton, N. H., an officer in public library, Boston.
3078     *Frederick Huntington* (Osgood), b. in Newton, Mass., April 16, 1857; m. Oct. 17, 1878, Ella Ann Brown of Sunderland, Mass., b. in Toronto, Can.; graduated from Amherst agricultural college with much honor and is in Scotland, pursuing medical studies.
3079     *Walter Griffith* (Osgood), b. in Brookline, Mass., Jan. 10, 1859; is in the Traveller office, Boston.
3080     *Mary Florence* (Osgood), b. in Belmont, Mass., April 21, 1861.
3081     *Edward Tufts* (Osgood), b. in Cambridge March 1, 1864; d. Sept. 13, 1866.
+3082 William Henry,[7] b. in Nashua, N. H., March 27, 1827.

## 1442

GEORGE WALDO THURSTON [6] (*David,[5] David,[4] Jonathan,[3] Daniel,[2] Daniel[1]*), son of David[5] and Fanny (Darling) Thurston of Owego, N. Y. (formerly of Keene, N. H.); born there April 19, 1816; married, May 17, 1839, MARY ANN COLLINS, born April 19, 1818, daughter of Barnett Collins of New York city.

Mr. Thurston is a wood worker and lumber dealer in Owego. A copy of an interesting document has come to our hand concerning George W. Thurston's grandfather David [no. 143, p. 47] since that was printed, which we give place to here.

"Marlborough, N. H., July 9, 1776. We the subscribers do hereby solemnly engage and promise that we will to the utmost of our powers, at the risk of our lives and fortunes, with ARMS oppose the hostile proceedings of the British Fleets and Armies against the

United American colonies." Signed David Thurston, and forty-nine others.

Their children were :

3093 William Collins,[7] b. March 17, 1840; m. Jan. 7, 1864, Sarah Adelaide Sheldon, b. in Binghamton, N. Y., Oct. 6, 1844; is an engineer on the Erie railroad and resides in Owego. They have :
    3094  *Mary Elizabeth,*[8] b. Feb. 28, 1865.
    3095  *George Sheldon,*[9] b. June 21, 1867.
    3096  *Cora Sarah,*[8] b. June 6, 1871.
3097 Fanny Alice,[7] b. May 13, 1842; m. Nov. 27, 1861, Edward T. Haskins of Taunton, Mass.; d. Oct. 5, 1872.
3098 Chester Prentice,[7] b. Aug. 8, 1848; in company with his father.
3099 Frederick Gilman,[7] b. Sept. 16, 1853.

## 1443

REV. DAVID WHITNEY THURSTON [6] (*David,*[5] *David,*[4] *Jonathan,*[3] *Daniel,*[2] *Daniel*[1]), brother of the preceding, and son of David [5] and Fanny (Darling) Thurston of Owego, N. Y.; born there Aug. 8, 1818; married, at Sanquoit, N. Y., May 24, 1846, ELIZABETH S. BOWEN, born at Sanquoit March 3, 1826, daughter of Rev. Elias and Abigail (Birdseye) Bowen.

Mr. Thurston is a Methodist Episcopal clergyman, formerly presiding elder; delegate to General Conference of ·1860; now, 1879, an evangelist, residing in Syracuse, N. Y.; a man of influence in his profession and quite successful as an evangelist.

Their children are :

3110 Addie Catherine,[7] b. in Cincinnatus, N. Y., March 7, 1847; m. George J. Sager of Syracuse.
3111 Nellie Delphene,[7] b. in Sherburne, N. Y., July 4, 1849; m. Amasa Parker Sager of Syracuse, and has :
    3112  *Frederick Whitney* (Sager).
    3113  *Fannie Adaline* (Sager).
3114 Edward Watson,[7] b. in Utica, N. Y., June 19, 1854; m. Eva Dodge of Syracuse, and has:
    3115  *Earl Edmund.*[8]
    3116  *Harry Dodge,*[8] b. Jan. 19, 1879.
3117 Carrie Jane,[7] b. in Cortland, N. Y., March 11, 1859.

## 1487

LELAND THURSTON [6] (*John,*[5] *David,*[4] *Jonathan,*[3] *Daniel,*[2] *Daniel*[1]), eldest son of John [5] and Lydia (Ball) Thurston of Keene, N. H.; born at Windham, Vt., May 29, 1803; married, in Boston, April 22, 1827, MARGARET HUTCHINS, born in Epsom, N. H., May 29, 1806, daughter of Samuel and Betsey (Lock) Hutchins of Concord, N. H.

Mr. Thurston was a mason by trade, lives in Denver, Col., and member of the Baptist church.

Children :

+3127 Charles Currier,[7] b. in Troy, N. H., Jan. 13, 1828; m. Caroline Humphrey.
  3128 Edwin M., b. in Troy April 12, 1830.
  3129 Emily M.,[7] b. in Troy Aug. 21, 1832.
+3130 Franklin Alden,[7] b. in Keene Oct. 9, 1834; m. Annie Eliza Rapelge.
  3131 Martha J.,[7] b. in Keene Feb. 3, 1837.
  3132 Mary E.,[7] b. in Keene Aug. 20, 1839.
  3133 Catherine M.,[7] b. in Keene Nov. 6, 1841.
  3134 Henry S.,[7] b. in Boston Aug. 10, 1844.
  3135 Josephine,[7] b. in Boston April 24, 1847.

## 1488

ROSWELL THURSTON[6] (*John,[5] David,[4] Jonathan,[3] Daniel,[2] Daniel[1]*), brother of the preceding, and son of John[5] and Lydia (Ball) Thurston of Keene, N. H.; born in Marlborough, N. H., Oct. 22, 1808; married, Sept. 25, 1834, FRANCES CUMMINGS, born in Keene Sept. 15, 1814. He died in Keene April 29, 1850, and his widow married, Nov. 22, 1856, Apollos Nye, born 1795, died in Keene Mar. 22, 1864. She married a third husband, Dec. 16, 1868, Charles P. Page, and lives in Keene. Mr. Thurston was a butcher by occupation in Keene.

### His children were:

3146 Charles Henry,[7] b. in Swanzey, N. H., June 1, 1836; m. in Claremont, N. H., June 6, 1860, Elizabeth Doane Newcomb, b. in Wellfleet, Mass., Nov. 23, 1839, daughter of Jeremiah and Abigail (Harding) Newcomb of Boston Highlands. Mr. Thurston is editor and proprietor of the Westborough Chronotype, Westborough, Mass., under the firm name of Holton & Thurston; is a member of the Congregational church; no children.
3147 Francis Warren,[7] b. May 7, 1839; d. April 8, 1840.
3148 William Cummings,[7] b. June 27, 1841; d. Jan. 2, 1842.
3149 Julia Ann,[7] b. Jan. 2, 1843; d. April 13, 1845.
3150 Lyman Cummings,[7] b. Oct. 4, 1847; d. Sept. 4, 1848.
3151 George Roswell,[7] b. 1849; n.m.; a seaman, going a whaling voyage of five years when he was seventeen; then enlisted in United States marine service, and was stationed at Hong Kong and other foreign ports. His term of enlistment closed June, 1878, and he was drowned Oct. 12, 1878, by the capsizing of bark Sarah off New Bedford, Mass.

## 1489

EMILY THURSTON[6] (*John,[5] David,[4] Jonathan,[3] Daniel,[2] Daniel[1]*), sister of the preceding, and daughter of John[5] and Lydia (Ball) Thurston of Keene, N. H.; born in Marlborough, N. H., March 8, 1810; married, Nov. 17, 1834, MELVIN STARKEY, born Aug. 9, 1809, son of Benjamin and Sally (Smith) Starkey of Westminster, Mass. He died in Orange, Mass., July 29, 1870.

Mr. Starkey was a mechanic and farmer in Winchester, N. H.

### Children, born in Keene, N. H.:

3161 Sarah Harriet (Starkey), b. Dec. 27, 1835; m. July 13, 1855, Samuel Sawyer; d. in Orange Sept. 21, 1867, leaving:
3162 *Hattie Maria* (Sawyer), b. in Orange Sept. 27, 1859; m. May 20, 1875, Edwin Angel, a mechanic, and had one child, Eveline (Angel), b. May 14, 1876, d. Aug., 1876.
3163 Elizabeth Amanda (Starkey), b. Aug. 27, 1841; m. Aug. 18, 1869, Henry H. Murdock, a farmer. They have:
3164 *Frank Milton* (Murdock), b. in Orange Jan. 17, 1874.
3165 *Charles Edward* (Murdock), b. in Athol Feb. 20, 1877.

## 1491

WESSON THURSTON[6] (*John,[5] David,[4] Jonathan,[3] Daniel,[2] Daniel[1]*), brother of the preceding, and son of John[5] and Lydia (Ball) Thurston of Keene, N. H.; born in Northfield, Mass., Nov. 4, 1816; married, in Lowell, Mass., June 9, 1838, HARRIET SCOTT, daughter of James and Sally Scott of Stoddard, N. H. He died Jan. 24, 1868.

He was a machinist; worked at it winters in South Boston, Mass.; lived in Stoddard, where he owned and worked a farm summers.

Their children were:

3176 Charles Wesson,[7] b. in Stoddard Oct. 5, 1839; m. Jennie Prank of Waldoborough, Me.; was a machinist by trade; enlisted in the war against the rebellion in the 6th New Hampshire regiment; was taken prisoner Sept. 3, 1864, and confined at Salisbury, N. C., where he was put in charge of a bakery and served the union prisoners with many an extra ration and saved many lives. He finally escaped and rejoined his regiment. He went to Alabama in 1870, and died there Aug. 3, 1871; had one child, which is not living.

3177 James Edward,[7] b. in Keene Feb. 16, 1843; residing in Nelson, N. H.; is an engineer; enlisted in the 2d New Hampshire regiment against the rebellion and served during the war, after which he married, June 5, 1867, Lucy Ann Center, b. in Merrimack, N. H., June 1, 1848, daughter of Ervin H. and Almira J. (Winn) Center of Stoddard. They have:
   3178   *Addie L.*,[8] b. April 8, 1868.
   3179   *Myra F.*,[8] b. Oct. 28, 1870.
3180 Helen Maria,[7] b. in Lowell Oct. 24, 1845; m. Aug. 26, 1861, Henry H. Stevens of Stoddard, who died in the army Oct. 29, 1864, aged 23. She died Jan. 1, 1866, leaving:
   3181   *Hattie L.* (Stevens), b. 1862.
   3182   *Henry H.* (Stevens), b. July, 1864.
3183 Frank L.,[7] b. in Concord, N. H., March 6, 1848. At the age of fifteen he enlisted in the 9th New Hampshire regiment; was taken prisoner Sept. 3, 1864, and confined in Salisbury prison till exchanged in 1865; m. Dec. 15, 1870, Eleanor Bartlett of Francistown, N. H.; has been a great sufferer for the last four years [1877] from hardships and injuries received in the war and in prison. They have:
   3184   *Charles Wesson*,[8] b. Oct. 26, 1871.

## 1510

JOSEPH THURSTON [6] (*Samuel*,[5] *David*,[4] *Jonathan*,[3] *Daniel*,[2] *Daniel*[1]), son of Samuel [5] and Sally (French) Thurston of New Alstead, N. H.; born there May 30, 1804; married, June, 1828, BETSEY BROWN, born June 20, 1803. She died June 3, 1876.

Mr. Thurston was a blacksmith in Dublin, N. H., four or five years; then purchased a stand in Sullivan, N. H., and continued the business six or seven years; sold and bought a place in Dublin, where he lived twenty years, working at his trade; sold and bought in Keene, N. H.; sold and bought a farm in Belchertown, Mass.; staid six years, sold and is now, 1878, in Gardiner, Ulster county, N. Y.

Their children were:    '

3185 Joseph Edwin,[7] b. Nov. 18, 1830; d. Nov. 13, 1837.
3186 Albert Bradley,[7] b. June 20, 1837; m. Sept. 10, 1868, Hannah Bertholf Jenkins, b. in New Paltz, N. Y., May 20, 1833, daughter of Crines and Rachel (Hardenbergh) Jenkins of Gardiner, N. Y. He is a teacher of music, repairer and tuner of musical instruments in Gardiner; is highway surveyor and deacon in the Reformed Dutch church.
3187 William Henry,[7] b. July 20, 1840; d. Oct. 19, 1848.

## 1511

HARTLEY THURSTON [6] (*Samuel*,[5] *David*,[4] *Jonathan*,[3] *Daniel*,[2] *Daniel*[1]), brother of the preceding, and son of Samuel [5] and Sally (French) Thurston of New Alstead, N. H.; born there March 3, 1806; married, in Alstead, June 6, 1832, ARMINDA ROBINSON, born in Greenfield, N. H., Jan. 14, 1811, daughter of Benjamin and Esther (Greeley) Robinson.

Mr. Thurston when young had feeble health, taught school winters

and worked on the farm summers; at age of twenty-one was book-keeping in Boston, but it did not agree with his health and he went back to his former occupations. After marriage he bought a farm in New Alstead, where he resided a few years, acting as superintending school committee. After a few years he sold and purchased a farm in Gilsum, N. H., where he lived a number of years and held several town offices; then sold and bought a farm in Manchester, Wis.; sold and bought in Berlin, Green Lake county, Wis., where he still resides, retired from business.

Their children were:

+3188 Andrew Jackson,[7] b. in Alstead Dec. 6, 1835; m. Jane Delzelle.
3189 Marion Emogene,[7] b. in Gilsum Sept. 16, 1844; m. Sept. 14, 1861, in Pardeeville, Wis., Erastus Darwin Corning, a farmer in Cicero, N. Y., b. in Canaan, Columbia county, N. Y., June 16, 1834, son of Edwin and Cynthia (Babcock) Corning of Clay, N. Y. They had:
    3190 *Edwin Hartley* (Corning), b. in Clay Aug. 31, 1866; d. May 1, 1869.
    3191 *Herbert Leon* (Corning), b. in Clay June 25, 1871; d. Feb. 11, 1872.
    3192 *Clara Estelle* (Corning), b. in Berlin May 29, 1873.
    3193 *Anna M.* (Corning), b. in Cicero Sept. 1, 1875.
3194 Emma Estelle,[7] b. in Gilsum Dec. 18, 1850; m. Feb. 14, 1875, Judge Thos. Curran Ryan, b. in Utica, N. Y., July 4, 1841, son of Michael and Margaret Ryan of Ireland; he lives in Berlin; obtained his education by his own efforts and delivered a course of scientific lectures when eighteen; enlisted in the war against the rebellion, served two years, and was discharged on account of wounds received in battle; was admitted to the bar at age of twenty-four, and has held the office of district attorney or county judge nearly all the time since. They have:
    3195 *Thomas Hartley* (Ryan), b. Sept. 3, 1876.

## 1512

ALDEN SPOONER THURSTON [6] (*Samuel,*[5] *David,*[4] *Jonathan,*[3] *Daniel,*[2] *Daniel*[1]), brother of the preceding, and son of Samuel[5] and Sally (French) Thurston of New Alstead, N. H.; born there Sept. 12, 1809; married, Sept. 15, 1836, ESTHER ADELINE MILLER, born July 20, 1812, daughter of Robert and Mary (Boyce) Miller of Marlow, N. H. She died May 18, 1878.

Mr. Thurston has taught fifty-five terms of school in New Alstead and adjoining towns; been superintending school committee eight years, selectman and justice of the peace for the county of Cheshire twenty years, beside numerous other offices, and has now settled down as a farmer on two hundred acres of land.

Children:

3196 George Franklin,[7] b. Feb. 17, 1838; d. Oct. 7, 1839.
3197 Charles Samuel,[7] b. Aug. 21, 1840; taught two district schools, winters of 1861 and 1862; in the spring of 1863 went to Pesotum, Ill., took the fever and ague, and died April 18, 1864.
3198 Edwin Alden,[7] b. Nov. 5, 1843; m. May 16, 1867, Nellie Louise Reeves, dau. of David A. and Almira (Smith) Reeves of Suffield, Ct.; he worked with his uncle Franklin Robinson Thurston three years at blacksmithing and then went to Saxton River, Vt., where he worked at ironing carriages until a short time before his death, May 3, 1876, at that place. They had:
    3199 *Charles Edward,*[8] b. May 18, 1868.
    3200 *Edwin Horace,*[8] b. July 7, 1876.
3201 Lorenzo Goldsbury,[7] b. Jan. 26, 1847; n.m.; lives with his parents.
3202 Harriet Ellen,[7] b. Aug. 27, 1852; m. June 6, 1871, Edwin Emerson Roundy of Winchester, Mass., and has:
    3203 *Nellie Lillian* (Roundy), b. Dec. 14, 1872.

## 1513

FRANKLIN ROBINSON THURSTON [6] of Marlborough, N. H. (*Samuel*,[5] *David*,[4] *Jonathan*,[8] *Daniel*,[2] *Daniel*[1]), brother of the preceding, and son of Samuel [5] and Sally (French) Thurston of New Alstead, N. H.; born there Jan. 22, 1815; married, first, FANNY LOVISA HOLMAN, born in Roxbury, N. H., Aug. 31, 1816, daughter of Dea. Charles and Polly Holman of Marlborough; she died Dec. 23, 1870. Second, Nov. 28, 1878, by Rev. F. D. Ayer, MRS. HANNAH ELIZABETH (NICHOLS) HOIT of Concord, N. H., born in Boston, Mass., July 12, 1829, daughter of Luther Western and Hannah (Tompkins) Nichols; she was first married by Rev. D. D. Burrows, March 4, 1852, in Amherst, N. H., to Sewell Hoit of Concord, where she lived twenty-seven years, and has a daughter, Jennie Lizzie (Hoit), born Sept. 23, 1860.

Mr. Thurston was formerly a blacksmith; is now, 1879, manufacturing agent for the Thurston Knob Screw Company of Marlborough; was republican representative to the legislature 1877 and 1878.

His children, all by first wife, were:

+3213  Charles Holman,[7] b. June 3, 1842; m. Amanda C. Frost.
3214  Ellen Chestina,[7] b. Dec. 4, 1848; m. Aug. 20, 1872, Horatio Stilman Richardson, b. May 21, 1846, son of Thomas Hall and Hannah (Morse) Richardson of Marlborough; he is a pharmacist in Cambridgeport, Mass., of the firm of A. R. Bayley & Co., and also of the firm of Bayley & Richardson. They have:
3215  *Frank Linden* (Richardson), b. Oct. 13, 1877.

## 1624

PHILOMELA THURSTON [6] (*Stephen*,[5] *Daniel*,[4] *Richard*,[8] *Daniel*,[2] *Daniel*[1]), eldest daughter of Stephen [5] and Philomela (Parish)* Thurston of Rowley, now Georgetown, Mass.; born there April 11, 1795; Oct. 2, 1817, she embarked as a missionary for Bombay, India, and after a voyage of five months or thereabouts, married, first, March 26, 1818, REV. SAMUEL NEWELL, son of Ebenezer and Mary (Richards) Newell of Durham, Me., born there July 24, 1784. He graduated from Harvard 1808 from Andover 1810; was ordained at Salem, Mass., Feb. 6, 1812; married, Feb. 9, 1812, Harriet Atwood, and sailed Feb. 19, 1812, for Calcutta, as a missionary of the A. B. C. F. M. His wife died in the Isle of France, Nov. 30, 1812, before reaching their field of labor. He died of cholera at Bombay May 30, 1821, and his widow married, second, March, 1822, JAMES GARRETT, born in Trenton, Oneida county, N. Y. He was a printer at the Bombay mission, where he died, 1831. In 1832 she returned to this country and died at Poughkeepsie, N. Y., Sept. 16, 1849.

Her children, by first husband, Newell, were:

3226  Harriet Atwood (Newell), b. 1819; m. Smith Hart of Liberty county, Ga.; he died 1865. They had:

---

* Eunice Foster was the consort of Elijah Parish, and died Dec. 18, 1799, aged 66. She was daughter of Nathan Foster, and granddaughter of Dea. Josiah Standish, who was grandson of Capt. Miles Standish, military commander of the colony which landed at Plymouth, Mass., December, 1620. Her eldest son was Rev. Elijah Parish of Byfield, Mass. [see p. 98. preached ordination sermon of Rev. David Thurston at Winthrop]. Her second son was the Rev. Ariel Parish of Manchester, Mass., who died May 20, 1794, aged 80. Her only daughter was Mrs. Philomela, wife of Stephen Thurston, the father of Ariel Standish Thurston [no. 1629].

Hannah Standish [see no. 501, p. 89] was grandmother of Lafayette Standish Foster of Connecticut, vice-president, *ex-officio*, of the United States after the assassination of Lincoln.

3227  *Samuel Newell* (Hart), b. Dec. 6, 1856.
3228  *Clara Thurston* (Hart), d. in infancy.
3229  *Hattie Atwood* (Hart), b. Feb. 23, 1860.

By second husband, Garrett:

3230  Mary Hardy (Garrett), b. 1823; d. 1825.
3231  James (Garrett), b. 1830; was a soldier in the war against the rebellion; taken prisoner at the battle of Cold Harbor; taken from Richmond to Andersonville, and from there to Florence, S. C., where he died.

## 1629

HON. ARIEL STANDISH THURSTON[6] (*Stephen,*[5] * *Daniel,*[4] *Richard,*[3] *Daniel,*[2] *Daniel*[1]), brother of the preceding, and only son of Stephen[5] and Philomela (Parish) Thurston of Rowley, now Georgetown, Mass.; born in Goffstown, N. H., June 11, 1810; married, first, Sept. 8, 1836, JULIA CLARK HART, born July 6, 1813, daughter of Dr. Erastus Langdon Hart of Goshen, Ct.; she died April 17, 1844. Second, May 7, 1846, at Angelica, N. Y., CORNELIA SOPHIA HULL, born Dec. 20, 1820, daughter of Andrew C. Hull of Nelson, Madison county, N. Y.; she died suddenly at Brooklyn, N. Y., June 27, 1865. Third, April 15, 1867, at Elmira, N. Y., GEORGIANNA GIBSON (née CONVERSE), born in Palmer, Mass., March 16, 1827, daughter of Maxy Manning Converse of Woburn, Mass.

Mr. Thurston prepared for college at Kimball Union academy, Meriden, N. H., 1826–28; entered Amherst college September, 1828, remained during the freshman year; went to Elmira 1830, studied law, and was admitted to the supreme court May, 1835; was elected judge and surrogate in Chemung county, N. Y., which office he held five years; state assessor three years, and is a manager of the State Reformatory, 1879.

He has in his possession a bible, formerly the property of Gideon Thurston [no. 68], bought in 1756, and given by him to his cousin Daniel [no. 163]. Daniel gave it to his daughter Judith, who married Samuel Pearson [no 502], and after her death Mr. Pearson gave it to Clarissa Thurston [no. 1626], and she gave it to her brother Ariel S. On the fly leaf is written, "Gideon Thurston, his bibel, bot in 1756, cost £1 6s. lawful."

---

* Obituary of Stephen Thurston, father of A. S. Thurston, published in "The Farmer's Cabinet" Nov. 1, 1833: Died suddenly, Sept. 13, 1833, in Bedford, N. H., Dea. Stephen Thurston, aged 68. He was born in Rowley, Mass., and having resided at different periods in various places in Massachusetts and New Hampshire, the circle of his acquaintance was extensive. In early life he was married to a sister of the late Dr. Parish of Byfield, afterward to Miss Sarah Burge of Hollis, and the widow who survives him is sister of the late Dr. Samuel Worcester. Happy in the choice of his domestic connections, he was a man whose piety and benevolence qualified him to diffuse happiness to those around him, not only in his family but in society at large. Dea. Thurston was an eminent instance of what a christian in the common walks of life can accomplish. In the sphere in which he moved the influence which he exerted was of the happiest kind. He was not able to make large benefactions, but his charities were, to the extent of his ability, freely and unostentatiously bestowed. In all his intercourse with the world, and he was called to mingle much with it, he made it his great aim to be doing good. With characteristic zeal he entered into all the benevolent enterprises of the day. If a single passage of scripture were to be selected that might at once express his character it should be. "Not slothful in business, fervent in spirit, serving the Lord." The summons to depart, though unexpected, found him as we trust not unprepared. He died in active service. One Sabbath he was in attendance upon divine service, apparently in health, and the next his pastor was called upon to preach in reference to his death.

It should be mentioned as a kind and affecting providence that his eldest daughter, Mrs. Garrett, who has lately returned from Bombay, after an absence of sixteen years, and who since her return has been chiefly in the state of New York, arrived at her father's on a visit just in season to soothe his dying moments and receive his parting benediction [see no. 501, page 89].

Mr. Thurston is more entitled to the credit of laying the foundation for the history of the ·descendants of Daniel Thurston of Newbury, as contained in this genealogy, than all others put together. He not only collected the early names, records, and wills in this country, but made considerable research in England for the connections there.

His children, all born in Elmira, were,

By first wife, Julia:

3242  Theodore,[7] b. April 8, 1838; d. Sept. 14, 1839.
+3243  Mary Parmalee,[7] b. July 29, 1840; m. Curtis Crane Gardiner.
+3244  Clara Standish,[7] b. Nov. 3, 1842; m. Henry White Strang.

By second wife, Cornelia:

3245  William Hull,[7] b. March 29, 1847; d. Aug. 21, 1861.
+3246  Julia Hart,[7] b. May 16, 1849; m. George Washington Thomas.
+3247  Charles Parish,[7] b. Feb. 22, 1851; m. Mary Toll Ried.
3248  Elizabeth Morse,[7] b. Sept. 13, 1855; m. Aug. 27, 1873, Henry Bowring, ship and freight broker in Brooklyn, N. Y., son of C. T. Bowring of the Devonshire family of Bowrings, of whom was Sir John Bowring, author of many beautiful hymns, and among others the one commencing "Watchman, tell us of the night;" publisher of the works and executor of Jeremy Bentham, British Minister to Hong Kong, member of parliament, etc. C. T. Bowring is now a resident of Liverpool. Eng. They have:

3249  *Harriet Cornelia* (Bowring), b. Oct. 14, 1877.
3250  Richard Hull,[7] b. Oct. 10, 1863.

## 1641

EUNICE FARLEY THURSTON[6] (*David,*[5] *David,*[4] *Richard,*[3] *Daniel,*[2] *Daniel*[1]), eldest child of Rev. David[5] and Prudence (Brown) Thurston of Winthrop, Me.; born there Nov. 19, 1812; married, Sept. 3, 1832, REV. HENRY RICHARDSON,* born in Springfield, Mass., Nov. 28, 1799, son of John Barnard and Mabel (Wolcott) Richardson.

Henry Richardson entered Bradford academy, Mass., in 1823, and studied there three years. During this time he taught school three winters, two of them in that town. In 1826 he entered the theological seminary in Bangor, Me.

In 1829 a small Congregational church was organized in Sidney, on the Kennebec river, and Mr. Richardson was ordained its pastor Nov. 23, 1831. The people did not feel able to pay for preaching, and he was dismissed Sept. 20, 1833. Not long after he became pastor of the Congregational church in Brownville, Me. Neither the church or town had long been in existence. He was dismissed in the winter of 1838; went to Gilead, Me., the following spring,

---

* RICHARDSON FAMILY.

I. WILLIAM RICHARDSON and Edward, who is supposed to have been his brother, were in West Newbury, Mass., as early as 1647; we know not how much earlier, nor from what part of England they came. He was born about 1620; married, Aug. 23, 1654, Elizabeth Wiseman. He died March 25, 1657, and his estate consisted of "a house, foure akers of land prised at £23." They had JOSEPH, Benjamin, and Elizabeth.

II. JOSEPH RICHARDSON, born May 18, 1655; married, July 12, 1681, Margaret Godfrey; was a cordwainer in West Newbury. They had DANIEL and seven other children.

III. DANIEL RICHARDSON, born April 4, 1692; married Lydia ——. They had STEPHEN and four other children.

IV. STEPHEN RICHARDSON, married Mary Chase of West Newbury; lived in Methuen and after in Dracut, where he died in the autumn of 1813. They had JOHN BARNARD and eight other children.

V. JOHN BARNARD RICHARDSON, born in Methuen 1768; married Mabel Wolcott. He was a boot and shoemaker in Springfield, Wilbraham, and Chickopee, Mass. He died at his son William's in Hadley, Mass., April 6, 1841, aged 72. They had HENRY, who married Eunice Farley Thurston, as above.

and preached there and in the adjoining town of Shelburne, N. H., eleven years. He left Gilead in the spring of 1849, and in March, 1850, became acting pastor of the church in Goshen, Sullivan county, N. H.; went back to Gilead Sept. 1, 1861, and preached a time with failing health. He has been able to preach but little for the last seventeen years. During the last thirteen years he has been so disabled by rheumatism as to be unable to walk a step, still his mind is active and unclouded, and he maintains a lively interest in transpiring events throughout the world. He and his wife are living, 1879, with Mr. William Reade Peabody, who married their daughter Mary Elizabeth, and enjoy a pleasant and comfortable home.

He was an independent thinker and a forcible preacher, and his sermons were always characterized by vigor, closeness, and originality of thought; were framed with a logical and pointed bearing and delivered with a natural, persuasive power.

Mrs. Richardson is a woman of more than ordinary force of character, as exhibited through all her life, by maintaining in the various societies where she has been located, and in her household affairs, that influence and energy that sustains and encourages a clergyman in his ofttimes perplexing and cheerless work; and has tended to strengthen his hands and encourage his heart, while the people of his charge have been inspired by it to greater exertions and more self-denying efforts to increase religious interest and bring souls to Christ. She has always striven for the elevation and advancement of all within her influence. Though at one time suffering for several years with a disease which rendered it difficult for her to walk, and sometimes impossible, she maintained a cheerfulness and hopefulness of disposition which rendered her society very attractive and her influence charming. For some years past, since her husband's illness, she has enjoyed remarkably good health.

### Children:

3261  John Francis (Richardson), b. in Sidney Aug. 25, 1833; m. June 4, 1872, Emily Susan Hutchins of Boston. He is a designer and wood engraver of the firm of Russell & Richardson, 194 Washington street, Boston; owns a pleasant cottage and lives in Belmont, a few miles out of the city, 1879. They have:
> 3262  *Mabel Wolcott* (Richardson), b. Sept. 5, 1877.
3263  Henry Brown (Richardson), b. in Winthrop Aug. 23, 1837; m. in St. Joseph, La., June 18, 1867, Anna Howard Farrar. He is a civil engineer, and has been employed on the levee on the Mississippi river, on railroads in Texas, was chief engineer in the construction of the Natchez railroad; is assistant state engineer, appointed by Governor Nichols in 1878, with his residence in St. Joseph, La.; was in the war of the rebellion, wounded and taken prisoner at Gettysburgh. Their children, all born in St. Joseph, are:
> 3264  *Thomas Farrar* (Richardson), b. Sept. 28, 1871.
> 3265  *Mary Wolcott* (Richardson), b. Oct. 26, 1873.
> 3266  *John* (Richardson), b. March 21, 1876.
3267  Mary Elizabeth (Richardson), b. in Gilead May 2, 1841; m. Oct. 29, 1863, William Reade Peabody, b. in Gilead Jan. 31, 1837, son of Asa Peabody; he is a farmer in Gilead; has held offices in town, and is a member of the Congregational church. Children:
> 3268  *Mary Gertrude* (Peabody), b. July 29, 1864.
> 3269  *Ada Louise* (Peabody), b. Aug. 10, 1865.
> 3270  *Henry Asa* (Peabody), b. Dec. 21, 1866; d. Aug. 20, 1868.
> 3271  *William Welcome* (Peabody), b. Dec. 24, 1869.
> 3272  *Francis Richardson* (Peabody), b. April 9, 1871.

*Very Truly Yours*

*Brown Thurston*

*my J. N. Ayres*

*Prof. Thurston*

## 1642

BROWN THURSTON[6] of Portland, Me. (*David,*[5] *David,*[4] *Richard,*[3] *Daniel,*[2] *Daniel*[1]), brother of the preceding, and eldest son of Rev. David[5] and Prudence (Brown) Thurston of Winthrop, Me.; born there Oct. 6, 1814; married, first, July 19, 1842, HARRIET CHAPMAN,[*] born Sept. 8, 1813, daughter of Dea. George Whitefield and Mary (Greenwood) Chapman of Gilead, Me.; she died Feb. 23, 1858. Second, Oct. 26, 1859, AMANDA CHAPMAN, born Dec. 30, 1828, sister to his first wife.

Mrs. Harriet Thurston joined the Congregational church in Gilead in her youth, removing her church relation after marriage to High street church in Portland, and maintained a consistent christian character through all her life. She was noted for her self-sacrificing benevolence, and highly esteemed and greatly beloved by all who knew her. Miss Amanda Chapman united with the High street church by profession April 28, 1858.

Mr. Thurston, when a lad, had slender health. In 1821, when seven years of age, he lived a year with his aunt, Mrs. Mary Blodget, in Bucksport, attending school. In the summer of 1825 went nine trips from Bangor and Searsport to Boston, with Capt. David Nichols of Searsport, in a coasting schooner, in the hope of securing better health; spent the year 1830 in Dr. Hubbard's family in Winthrop, under his medical care. In 1831 he went by stage to Lowell, Mass., and learned the art of printing in the office of the Lowell Observer, owned by Allen & Shattuck. They sold to Rev. Asa Rand, and

---

*CHAPMAN FAMILY.

I. EDWARD CHAPMAN. miller, of Ipswich, Mass., is said to have come from the north-east of England, not far from Hull in Yorkshire. In 1642 he married, first, Mary, daughter of Mark Symonds; she died June 10, 1658. Second, Dorothy, daughter of Richard Swain and widow of Thomas Abbott of Rowley, Mass. He died April 18, 1678. He was an industrious, energetic, christian man; accumulated some property; was cautious, firm, and decided in his opinions. His wife Dorothy survived him and married, Nov. 13, 1678, Archelaus Woodman of Newbury, Mass. His children, by first wife, were SAMUEL, Simon, Nathaniel, and Mary. His will closes with these words: "My will is that all my children be satisfied with that I have done for them; and if any of them shall through discontent make trouble about this, my will is that then they shall forfeit and lose what I have herein bequeathed unto them or him."

II. SAMUEL CHAPMAN, born 1654; was a wheelwright and farmer, a man of influence and piety. He took the homestead and was allowed three years to settle the estate and six years to pay the heirs. He married, May 20, 1678, Ruth, daughter of Samuel Ingalls; he died Jan. 26, 1722. They had SAMUEL, John, Joseph, Ruth, Edward, Mary, Job, Edmund.

III. SAMUEL CHAPMAN. born Feb. 12, 1679; married, March 11, 1702, Phebe Balch of Manchester, N. H.; was a cordwainer in Hampton, and after a farmer in Greenland, N. H. He died April 21, 1742. They had Phebe, Paul, SAMUEL, Martha, Penuel, Joseph, Benjamin, Jonathan, Ruth. Abigail.

IV. SAMUEL CHAPMAN, born in Hampton Dec. 7, 1706; baptized in Greenland 1717; married, first, —— York; second, ——. He was taxed in Newmarket, N. H., 1782, and is supposed to have lived in Stratham. N. H. He had, by first wife, John, Mary, Samuel, Benjamin, Phebe. Edmund, Noah, Elizabeth, ELIPHAZ, Martha, David. and by second wife, Hannah.

V. ELIPHAZ CHAPMAN, born in Newmarket March 7, 1750; married, first, ——; she died soon after marriage. Second, Aug. 12, 1772. Hannah, daughter of Timothy Jackman of Newbury. He was a Congregational minister and preached in Madbury from 1770 to 1773, then in Methuen, Mass., till February, 1791, when he removed to Sudbury-Canada, now Bethel, Me. He journeyed with two two-horse teams through the towns of York, Gorham, Bridgton, Waterford, and Albany, from where there was no road, to Bethel; only a one-horse team had ever passed over the route before. There were but few families in Bethel at that time, and no traveled road within twenty miles. He selected a lot on the north side of the Androscoggin river. which his son Timothy afterward occupied and which is now, 1879, owned by his grandson Timothy Hilliard, the seventh child of Timothy. He was a very prominent and popular man in town, judging from the number of children named after him. He died Jan. 20, 1814; she died Dec. 15, 1839, aged 92. They had Hannah, Eliphaz, Elizabeth, Abigail, GEORGE WHITEFIELD, Timothy, Samuel, Edmund.

VI. GEORGE WHITEFIELD CHAPMAN, born in Methuen Dec. 25, 1780; married, first, Sept. 20, 1804, Mary Greenwood [see page 173], parents of Harriet and Amanda, who married Brown Thurston, above.

he went to New York, worked at his trade a few months, and business being dull he shipped for a whaling voyage in the ship Statira of Nantucket, Capt. Cannon, master. He was on board this ship just four years, visiting the Azores, Cape Verd Islands, sailing close under Teneriffe, around Cape Horn, landing at Valparaiso, the seaport of Santiago in Chili, Callao in Peru, Atacames, United States of Colombia, Galapagos Islands, several of the Society, Navigator, Friendly, Tonga, and Sunday Islands, arriving back at Nantucket with about half a cargo of sperm and black whale oil in 1838, having been promoted from seaman to boat-steerer for nearly half the voyage. He resumed his trade again, and worked in Brunswick, Hallowell, and Bangor till 1840, when he procured material and established an office in Augusta; moved to Portland in 1841. At one time he had associated with him Arthur H. Branscomb, Levi W. Fenley, and George F. H. Ilsley, under the firm name of Thurston, Ilsley & Co.; after this his brother Samuel, under name of Thurston & Co.; then Newell A. Foster and William H. Jerris, under the name of Thurston, Foster & Co. These firms existed for about six years, since which time he has had no partner till 1876, when he took in Stuart A. Strout and John H. Russell. He was the first job printer to introduce the power press in Portland. He also introduced stereotyping, electrotyping, and wood engraving. He stereotyped Town's full series of school books, Weld's Grammar and Parsing Book, Payson's Works in 3 vols., Pearl Bible, and many other books. In 1866, July 4, the great fire which destroyed over $10,000,000 worth of property and about one-third of the city, including his office, subjected him to a loss of over $25,000 above insurance. He soon started again and has maintained a leading position in the business since.

In 1842 he was received into the High street Congregational church; was elected deacon in 1856, and has been superintendent of the Sunday-school twelve years. He was early engaged in the temperance cause, and was one of the first to espouse the cause of the slave. During the reign of the fugitive slave law he with others did what they could to help the bondman in his flight from slavery; at one time having the care of thirty fugitives, who were dispatched to St. John, N. B., and Montreal, Canada.

His children, all by first wife, were:

3283   Charles Brown,[7] b. June 10, 1843; enlisted as private in 13th Maine regiment infantry Dec. 2, 1861; promoted to be sergeant Aug. 28, 1863; discharged at expiration of term of service, Jan. 6, 1865; with army of the gulf from March 1, 1862, to July, 1864, from Pensacola to Baton Rouge; from July, 1864, to January, 1865, in Shenandoah Valley, Va., under Gen. Sheridan; is now engaged in the scroll saw and fancy woods business in Portland, Me., 1879.

3284   Jane Mary,[7] b. Dec. 22, 1845; d. Jan. 9, 1846.

3285   Harriet Chapman,[7] b. March 11, 1847; d. March 13, 1847.

3286   George Francis,[7] b. Jan. 20, 1848; m. Sept. 7, 1871, Ella Amelia Kendall, b. in Ashby, Mass., Oct. 30, 1848, daughter of Hosea and Lydia (Taylor) Kendall of Portland. He is a banker and broker in partnership with Henry M. Payson, at 32 Exchange street, Portland. They had:

3287   *Agnes*,[8] b. March 20, 1877; d. March 24, 1877.

3288   Clara Amanda,[7] } twins, b. June 20, 1851.
3289   Mary Brown,[7] }

3290   David Frederick,[7] b. July 25, 1853; d. Dec. 7, 1857.

3291   Jessie Louise,[7] b. June 20, 1856.

GEORGE WHITEFIELD CHAPMAN [6] (*Eliphaz,[5] Samuel,[4] Samuel,[3] Samuel,[2] Edward[1]*), son of Eliphaz [5] and Hannah (Jackman) Chapman of Bethel, Me.; born in Methuen, Mass., Dec. 25, 1780; married, first, Sept. 30, 1804, MARY GREENWOOD, born 1787, daughter of Nathaniel Greenwood of Bethel; she died March 17, 1849. Second, Aug. 20, 1851, MRS. HANNAH (PRINCE) BUXTON of Bridgton, Me. She died April 18, 1863; he died June 31, 1875, aged 94 y. 6 m.

Mr. Chapman was a farmer in Gilead, Me. Coming to this new country with his father at the age of eleven years, he participated in all the privations and hardships of pioneer life, and experienced the fear which pervaded the country on account of the Indians, who had shortly before this committed depredations in that region, and some of whom were still straggling about the country.

He united with the Congregational church in Bethel, by profession of faith, in 1810, and in 1818 removed his connection to Gilead, where he had located upon a farm, when a Congregational church was established there. There had been a powerful revival of religion in Gilead, during which nearly every head of a family in town was converted; this gave the church at its outset an earnest and vigorous life. He was chosen one of the deacons, at the time of the formation of the church, and maintained the office till 1852, when he removed to Bethel. For nearly half the time they were without any shepherd, and the deacons kept up the service regularly and read sermons. He was superintendent of the Sunday-school for the first ten years. He was a man of general influence in the region, representative to the legislature one term before Maine was set off from Massachusetts, a justice of the peace, which office he honored in the eyes of his fellow citizens, who deferred to his judgment in many matters of difference in preference to going to court. For many years he was selectman of the town, and was one of the first to organize the temperance reform and practice the principle of total abstinence in haying time, at "raisings," and the like, on which occasions it was the universal custom to provide ardent spirits.

Soon after his second marriage he purchased a farm in Bethel, and in 1855 became wholly blind, when he sold and purchased a house on the hill, near the church. After his wife's death he made his home with his eldest son, Granville, on the homestead, summers, and with his daughter, Mrs. Thurston, in Portland, winters, during which time he wrote several chapters of the history of Gilead, which were printed in the Bethel Courier, and in 1867 he published a volume of poems, which he composed during his blindness.

His children, all by first wife, were:

3301　Abigail [7] (Chapman), b. Aug. 25, 1807; d. May 7, 1814.
3302　George Granville [7] (Chapman), b. Aug. 22, 1809; m. March 19, 1835, Eliza Chapman, b. March 5, 1810, daughter of Timothy and Betsey (Barker) Chapman of Bethel; is a farmer on the homestead in Gilead. They had :
　　3303　*Fordyce Granville* [8] (Chapman), b. Jan. 30, 1836; drowned Sept. 20, 1840.
　　3304　*Sarah Elizabeth* [8] (Chapman), b. June 4, 1838.
　　3305　*Abbie L.* [8] (Chapman), b. Oct. 13, 1840; d. May 26, 1858.
　　3306　*William Chalmers* [8] (Chapman), b. Nov. 13, 1841; m. Nov. 30, 1870, Martha E. Baldwin, b. in Stratford, N. H., Oct. 29, 1847; is a farmer with his father on the homestead. They have :
　　　　3307　*Hannibal Hamlin* [9] (Chapman), b. April 28, 1872.
　　　　3308　*Alger Baldwin* [9] (Chapman), b. Nov. 8, 1873.
　　　　3309　*Marion Eliza* [9] (Chapman), b. May 19, 1876.

3310 *George T.*[8] (Chapman), b. Feb. 5, 1844; d. Aug. 20, 1846.
3311 *Hannibal Hamlin*[8] (Chapman), b. Oct. 31, 1845; d. May 22, 1862.
3312 *Lamartine T.*[8] (Chapman), b. Jan. 27, 1848; d. May 5, 1849.
3313 *Augustus Faulkner*[8] (Chapman), b. Oct. 18, 1849; a clerk with his uncle Timothy Appleton Chapman in Milwaukee, Wis.
3314 Mary[7] (Chapman), b. March 18, 1811; d. Jan. 31, 1835.
3315 Harriet[7] (Chapman), b. Sept. 8, 1813; m. Brown Thurston [see no. 1642].
3316 Joseph Greenwood[7] (Chapman), b. Oct. 18, 1815; d. June 24, 1835.
3317 Albion Perry[7] (Chapman), b. Aug. 12, 1817; m. 1st, April 3, 1844, Sophronia Eames; she died April 28, 1865, aged 42; 2d, Jan. 12, 1866, Mary Ophelia Skillings; she died April 15, 1869, aged 28; 3d, Oct. 23, 1871, Mrs. Betsey (Crockett) Penley of Norway, Me.; she died Jan. 26, 1876, aged 57; 4th, Sept. 5, 1878, Susanna P. Wight of Bethel. Mr. Chapman is a farmer in Bethel, a member of the Methodist church. He had, by first wife:
3318 *Leander Thurston*[8] (Chapman), b. March 8, 1845; went west and has not been heard from for many years.
3319 *Paulina Kimball*[8] (Chapman), b. March 6, 1847; d. Jan. 15, 1869.
3320 *Ebenezer Eames*[8] (Chapman), b. Jan. 19, 1850; a farmer in Bethel.
.3321 *Hannah Prince*[8] (Chapman), b. Oct. 24, 1851; m. May 13, 1879, Nathan Newman Penley, b. in Norway, Me., Jan. 18, 1842; he is in a cotton mill at Conway Center, N. H.
3322 *Augustine Washington*[8] (Chapman), b. Aug. 20, 1853; d. in Worcester, Mass., Oct. 30, 1877.
3323 *Sophronia Hazen*[8] (Chapman), b. Feb. 6, 1856.
3324 *George Albion*[8] (Chapman), b. July 28, 1858.
3325 *Timothy Hannibal* (Chapman), b. Sept. 21, 1862.
3326 Leander Thurston[7] (Chapman), b. Sept. 18, 1819; studied medicine; was practicing dentistry in Yarmouth, Me., where he died, Dec. 23, 1845.
3327 Jarvis[7] (Chapman), b. Jan. 22, 1822; m. Oct. 17, 1849, Anna Twitchell, daughter of Col. Eli Twitchell of Bethel. He was a farmer in Gilead; enlisted in the war against the rebellion in the 13th Maine regiment and died at Fort St. Philip, below New Orleans, La., 1862; she died 1860. They had:
3328 *Fordyce Granville*[8] (Chapman), b. Sept., 1850; d. Jan., 1851.
3329 *Clarence Eugene*[8] (Chapman), b. June 27, 1851; graduated from the Michigan university, a law school at Ann Arbor, Mich., 1879.
3330 *Adelaide Josephene*[8] (Chapman), b. July 11, 1853; folder and stitcher in a book bindery in Worcester, Mass., 1879.
3331 *Harriet Amanda*[8] (Chapman), b. Oct. 13, 1857.
3332 *Annie Grace*[8] (Chapman), b. Dec. 18, 1858; m. Oct. 31, 1877, William J. Osgood of Leominster, Mass.
+3333 Timothy Appleton[7] (Chapman), b. May 23, 1824; m. Laura Bowker.
3334 Hannibal Greenwood[7] (Chapman), b. Oct. 5, 1826; a dry goods merchant in Boston, a young man of bright promise, till his health failed, when he went on to a farm in Gilead, and died Feb. 5, 1858.
3335 Amanda[7] (Chapman), b. Dec. 30, 1828; m. Brown Thurston [see no. 1642].
3336 Fordyce[7] (Chapman), b. July 31, 1831; d. May 14, 1833.

# 1644

ELIZABETH THURSTON[6] (*Rev. David,*[5] *David,*[4] *Richard,*[3] *Daniel,*[2] *Daniel*[1]), sister of the preceding, and daughter of Rev. David[5] and Prudence (Brown) Thurston of Winthrop, Me.; born there Nov. 28, 1818; married, June 20, 1839, CHARLES PHILBROOK,* born May 16,

* PHILBROOK FAMILY.
I. THOMAS PHILBROOK, came from England in one of the thirty transports that brought imigrants to this country in 1633. He had three sons, Jonathan, Samuel, and WILLIAM.
II. WILLIAM PHILBROOK, had three sons, Walter, JONATHAN, and William.
III. JONATHAN PHILBROOK, had four sons, William, JONATHAN, Joshua, and Job.
IV. JONATHAN PHILBROOK, married the daughter of Rev. Abijah Wells, D.D., pastor of the Congregational church in Attleborough, Mass., and had five sons, John, Thomas, Samuel, Robert, and CHARLES.
V. CHARLES PHILBROOK, married Betsey Johnson, settled in Winthrop, Me., and had seven children, Lucy; Samuel Johnson, living at the West, 1877; Thomas, died in West Indies; Jotham Sewall; Moses, living in Illinois; Eliza, married Henry Goodale and lives in Adrian, Mich.; and CHARLES.
VI. CHARLES PHILBROOK, married Elizabeth Thurston, as above.

1811, son of Charles and Betsey (Johnson) Philbrook of Winthrop. She died in Portland, Me., while on a visit to her brothers, Sept. 16, 1875. She was a consistent member of the Congregational church, very much esteemed by all who knew her.

Mr. Philbrook was a shoemaker by trade, working at it in Winthrop. In the spring of 1836 he settled in Adrian, Mich. He spent the winter of 1837–8 in Port au Prince, San Domingo, W. I., settling the estate of his brother, who died there. In March, 1863, they moved to Geneseo, Ill., on to a farm, he having become so deaf as to incapacitate him for the shoe business, in which he was engaged in Michigan. He is a very devout member of the Congregational church.

Their children, all born in Adrian, were:

3347 Francis Thurston (Philbrook), b. April 12, 1846.
3348 William Thomas (Philbrook), b. Feb. 22, 1848; d. March 26, 1849.
3349 Charles (Philbrook), b. Oct. 10, 1854; d. Oct. 13, 1854.
3350 Ella (Philbrook), b. Dec. 23, 1856.
3351 Harriet (Philbrook), b. March 14, 1859.

## 1647

SAMUEL THURSTON [6] (*David,*[5] *David,*[4] *Richard,*[3] *Daniel,*[2] *Daniel*[1]), brother of the preceding, and son of Rev. David[5] and Prudence (Brown) Thurston of Winthrop, Me.; born there Aug. 14, 1825; married, first, June 5, 1850, LUCRETIA HARRINGTON BARTELS, born Sept. 12, 1829, daughter of John and Sarah Bartels of Portland, Me.; she died at Steep Falls, Me., Sept. 7, 1856. Second, June 15, 1858, MARY LOUISA WATERS, born Sept. 10, 1833, daughter of Cornelius and Abigail (Irish) Waters of Gorham, Me.

Mr. Samuel Thurston spent his early days in Winthrop, working on a farm and attending school, closing his education at the Monmouth academy, then taught by Dr. N. T. True. Soon after arriving at majority he came to Portland and worked with his brother, Brown Thurston, in the stereotyping business, after which he engaged first in the apothecary and then in the grocery trade. During his early life he developed a capacity and taste for vocal music, and became a superior tenor singer. About 1855 he gave up trade and devoted his time to teaching music, being appointed teacher of vocal music in the public schools of Portland. When the war of the rebellion broke out his loyalty and martial spirit caused him to enlist, Aug. 22, 1862, as a private in the 6th Maine battery of mounted artillery. As a token of respect for their teacher, the lads of the three grammar schools presented him with an elegant revolver. The presentation was made before a large concourse of people in the city hall by Mr. Manthano Pickering, teacher of the Park street school, in behalf of the lads, who read an address which was signed by a committee of lads from each of the schools. Mr. Thurston responded in a few patriotic remarks, the boys sang "America" with a will, and gave three hearty cheers for Mr. Thurston.

Though enlisting as a private, his bravery and energy were soon recognized, and on Oct. 28, 1862, he was appointed sergeant. Dec. 1, 1862, he was appointed quartermaster sergeant of the artillery brigade, 2d division, 12th corps. He returned to the battery Feb. 28, 1863, and Jan. 15, 1864, was appointed orderly sergeant. March 1, 1864, he was commissioned second lieutenant. He was wounded

Edward Southworth

Yours very truly,
R. B. Thurston.

12

Yours very truly
R. G. Thans.

ny for thirty years, and president at the time of his death of the Hampshire Paper Company of South Hadley Falls. He was deacon of the first Congregational church in West Springfield from 1857 to 1869, an active christian and a man of deservedly great influence. He married, first, June 1, 1841, Ann Elizabeth Shepard, born in Little Compton, R. I., June 24, 1810, daughter of Rev. Mase and Deborah (Haskins) Shepard. She died Aug. 7, 1855, aged 45, having had George Champlain Shepard (Southworth) [see no. 3381], born Dec. 13, 1842; Edward Wells (Southworth), born Feb. 12, 1845, died Feb. 8, 1847; Mase Shepard (Southworth), born Sept. 23, 1847, member for three years of the class of 1868 at Yale, after which he was student of chemistry at Tübingen in Germany, where he received the degree of doctor of philosophy (Ph. D.) in 1873, and in 1876 was chosen professor of chemistry at Williams college; the degree of M. A. was conferred upon him by Yale in 1877; Charles Upham Shepard (Southworth), born June 26, 1850, died Nov. 24, 1853; Wells (Southworth), born March 6, 1852, died Feb. 22, 1854. He married, second, Dec. 4, 1856, Mary Woodbury Shepard, born in Ashfield, Mass., Oct. 10, 1827, daughter of Rev. Thomas, D.D., and Sarah Williams (Barrett) Shepard of Bristol, R. I. She died June 15, 1861, aged 33, having had Edward (Southworth), born Sept. 27, 1857, is a member of the class of 1879 at Yale; Mary Woodbury (Southworth), born Sept. 26, 1859; Thomas Shepard (Southworth), born June 7, 1861.

Mrs. Southworth has spent about three years in Europe since her husband's death with the most of her family; is a member of the Congregational church.

Her children, by first husband, Deane, were:

3380  Sarah Shepard (Deane), b. at Goshen, N. H., Oct. 30, 1850; d. at Winthrop Dec. 23, 1851.

+3381  Ada (Deane), b. March 24, 1853; m. Geo. Champlain Shepard Southworth.

By second husband, Southworth:

3382  Alice Harriet (Southworth), b. Feb. 19, 1868.

## 1659

REV. RICHARD BOWERS THURSTON[6] (*Richard*,[5] *David*,[4] *Richard*,[3] *Daniel*,[2] *Daniel*[1]), eldest son of Richard[5] and Ann (Bowers) Thurston of Bangor, Me.; born in Charlestown, Mass., June 28, 1819; married, in Friendsville, Susquehanna county, Pa., May 24, 1847, JANE MILLER PIERCE, born in Owego, Tioga county, N. Y., Sept. 14, 1823, daughter of Henry Miller and Susan (Peironnet) Pierce of Waverly, Tioga county, N. Y.

Mrs. Thurston had unusual skill as an amateur artist. Her gift was useful in promoting the culture of art in the places of her residence. In the time she could withdraw from the cares of her family, she painted many landscapes and other pictures of much beauty and merit, which adorn her home and those of some of her friends.

Mr. Thurston belonged to the first class which graduated from the Bangor city high school in 1837; graduated from Bowdoin college in 1841, and from the theological seminary, Bangor, in 1846. He was ordained over the Congregational church in Waterville Nov. 11, 1846.

12

Rev. Stephen Thurston of Searsport preached the sermon, Rev. David Thurston of Winthrop offered the ordaining prayer, Eliphalet Gillet, D.D., of Hallowell, secretary of the Maine Missionary Society, gave the charge to the pastor, Rev. Eli Thurston of Hallowell gave the right hand, and Rev. Benjamin Tappan, D.D., of Augusta gave the address to the people. He was dismissed April 27, 1855, and became acting pastor of the church at Chickopee Falls, Mass., where he remained three years. He was settled in Waltham, Mass., in 1858. Rev. Edward N. Kirk, D.D., of the Mt. Vernon church, Boston, preached the sermon, Rev. Isaac R. Worcester of Boston gave the charge, and Rev. George W. Field of the Salem street church, Boston, the right hand. He was installed over the church in Stamford, Ct., 1865, Rev. Richard S. Storrs, D.D., of Brooklyn, preaching the sermon; removed to New Haven in 1874 and preached for the second church in Fair Haven two years, and removed to Old Saybrook, Ct., Jan. 1, 1877. He is a man of more than ordinary ability, and his ministry was accompanied in all these places with satisfactory results. He was the author of the prize essay on the "Error and Duty in regard to Slavery," published in 1857, and of the resolution passed by the Jubilee Convention in Chicago, 1870, which led to the founding of the National Council of Congregational Churches in Oberlin, Ohio, in 1871.

Prof. William M. Barbour of Yale says of him, "He was held in high esteem by his ministerial brethren for his mental acumen and his scholarly attainments. Faithful in the pastorate, yet his chief place was the pulpit, where he excelled in the delivery of clear, earnest, and instructive thought. He was the sworn foe of slavery, and his preaching and writing contained weighty arguments and outspoken denunciations of the national evil. He was and is still one of the most earnest reformers of rooted wrongs. After hearing some of his weighty deliverances, some of his parishioners have been heard to say, 'Mr. Thurston is a born statesman.' To condense the estimates of him drawn from his fields of labor, let him be known as one with his family's traits, 'a strong, clear, earnest teacher, an able and fearless defender of the christian faith, a kindly and cautious counselor, an upright and spotless man of God.'"

Their children were:

3393   Florence Bowers,[7] b. in Waterville, Me., March 3, 1849; m. Mar. 7, 1870, Henry Carroll Humphrey, b. 1848, a chemist, residing in Philadelphia, Pa., 1877. They have:
    3394   *Mary* (Humphrey), b. in Dresden, Saxony, Aug. 11, 1871.
3395   Henry Stephen,[7] b. in Waterville Sept. 4, 1852; d. Sept. 27, 1852.
3396   Jennie King,[7] b. in Waterville Oct. 2, 1854; m. Rev. John Howard Hincks [see no. 3431].
3397   Marion Percy,[7] b. in Waltham, Mass., March 25, 1863.

## 1660

SAMUEL DAVID THURSTON[6] (*Richard,[5] David,[4] Richard,[3] Daniel,[2] Daniel[1]*), brother of the preceding, and son of Richard[5] and Ann (Bowers) Thurston of Bangor, Me.; born in Frankfort, now Winterport, Me., Feb. 10, 1822; married, first, May 24, 1848, in Waterville, Me., SUSAN DUNCAN PIERCE, born in Friendsville, Pa., 1832, daugh-

ter of Henry Miller and Susan (Peironnet) Pierce; she died in Bangor May, 1851. Second, June 14, 1852, JANE MARIA SPARHAWK, born 1819, daughter of Noah and Maria (Stetson) [born in Kingston, Mass., 1791] Sparhawk of Bucksport, Me. Mr. Stetson moved to Harvard, Mass., 1798, where Maria was married, Aug. 17, 1817, to Noah Sparhawk, by Rev. Warren Fay of Charlestown, Mass., afterward D.D. Mr. Sparhawk after marriage moved to Bucksport, where he died, May, 1858. Mrs. Sparhawk lives with her daughter in Bangor, 1879. Mr. Sparhawk's father was a Congregational minister in Templeton, Mass.

At the age of twenty Mr. Thurston began business in lumber and merchandise in Bangor; 1851 moved to Bridgeport, Ct., and continued the lumber business under name of Hincks & Thurston; returned to Bangor 1857, and engaged in ship chandlery and ship building in company with John L. Crosby, building some of the largest ships ever built in Bangor. Served as councilman and alderman 1861–1866; was mayor of Bangor, 1869, 1870; treasurer of Bangor and Piscataquis railroad, Bangor theological seminary, and Bangor savings bank. He united with the 1st Congregational church 1840, and has been deacon of the Hammond street Congregational church since 1860.

His children, by first wife, Susan, were:

3408  George Pierce,[7] b. March 30, 1849; m. in San Francisco, Cal., May 8, 1879, Dora M. Riversmith, daughter of W. H. Riversmith of Saco, Me. He went to San Francisco in 1868, and is secretary of mining companies and broker.

By second wife, Jane:

3409  Elliot Sparhawk,[7] b. in Bridgeport Oct. 10, 1853; went to San Francisco in 1874, and is mining engineer.
3410  Samuèl Richard,[7] b. in Bridgeport Oct. 11, 1855; d. Nov. 9, 1856.
3411  Maria Stetson,[7] b. in Bangor Sept. 10, 1858.

## 1672

MARY THURSTON BLODGET (*Mary Thurston,*[5] *David,*[4] *Richard,*[3] *Daniel,*[2] *Daniel*[1]), eldest daughter of Bliss and Mary (Thurston) Blodget of Bucksport, Me.; born there Jan. 9, 1819; married, May 25, 1843, REV. ENOCH POND, born in Ward, Mass., June 20, 1820, son of Rev. Enoch Pond, D.D., president of the Bangor theological seminary, an institution of great importance to the Congregational denomination in Maine, and in which Dr. Pond has maintained a vigorous and healthy influence for more than forty-four years.

Rev. Enoch Pond, jr., prepared for college in the Bangor classical school, and entered Bowdoin college in 1834; graduated in 1838; graduated from Bangor theological seminary in 1842. He was ordained colleague pastor with Rev. Isaac Braman, who had been sole pastor for forty-five years, in Georgetown, Mass., December, 1842. His ministry was earnest and faithful, but short, as in the spring of 1846 he had the influenza, from which he never recovered, and after nine months of wasting health finished his life at Bucksport Dec. 17, 1846. Prof. George Shepard of Bangor attended his funeral. His remains are interred in Georgetown, where his parishioners desired to have them. Shortly before his demise he expressed the following sentiments: "I am going to be with my Saviour, into his immediate

presence, free from those doubts which so harass the soul; free from sin, to be forever at rest. I think I know in whom I have believed. I rejoice in submission to God's will. I am willing to follow where the divine hand leads. The two worlds seem closely connected." His widow has resided with her mother at Bucksport since the death of her husband.

They had one child, born in Georgetown:

3421  Mary Bliss (Pond), b. Oct., 1844; d. in Bucksport Oct. 22, 1869. She was a lovely christian, as will be seen by the following transcript: "I have known nothing but love all my life and am going where all is love. It has been hard to give up life, but now I long to go. My life seems like a dream, all incomplete, but complete in Christ."

## 1673

SARAH ANN BLODGET (*Mary Thurston,*[5] *David,*[4] *Richard,*[3] *Daniel,*[2] *Daniel*[1]), sister of the preceding, and daughter of Dea. Bliss and Mary (Thurston) Blodget of Bucksport, Me.; born there Aug. 24, 1820; married, Aug. 23, 1839, JOHN WINSLOW HINCKS, born in North Bucksport Aug. 23, 1817, son of Jesse Young and Ruth Payne (Rich) Hincks. She died at Bridgeport, Ct., July 26, 1864; he died there Feb. 6, 1875.

Mr. Hincks was a merchant, and for some time before and after his marriage was connected with his father-in-law, Dea. Bliss Blodget, in the general business of a country store, ship stores, and ship building. In 1852 he moved to Bridgeport and went into the lumber trade, and subsequently, in company with his son William B., in the nursery business. Mrs. Hincks was a very spiritually minded christian lady; her friends trusted in her and "her children arise up and call her blessed."

Their children, born in Bucksport, were:

3422  Wm. Bliss (Hincks), b. Sept. 8, 1841; m. Sept. 11, 1866, Mary Louise Hart, b. Feb. 20, 1843, daughter of Dea. Baldwin and Charlotte J. (Welles) Hart of Madison, Ct. Mr. Hincks fitted for college, but after passing examination went into the army against the rebellion and was both private and commissioned officer in the 14th Connecticut regiment, taking part in most of the battles of the army of the Potomac, leaving the army with the commission of major. In 1878 the degree of A. M. was conferred upon him by Yale. He is now, 1879, treasurer of the Bridgeport Gas-light Company; is deacon and scribe in the Congregational church. Their children are:

3423  *Edward Baldwin* (Hincks), b. Jan. 4, 1869.
3424  *William Thurston* (Hincks), b. Jan. 22, 1870.
3425  *Robert Stanley* (Hincks), b. April 28, 1875.

3426  Edward Young (Hincks), b. Aug. 13, 1844; m. April 19, 1877, Elizabeth Champlin Perry, daughter of Oliver Hazard and Anne (Randolph) Perry of Andover, Mass. Mr. Hincks fitted for college in a private school; graduated from Yale 1866, and from Andover 1870. In his course of study he acquired proficiency as a writer and received the "DeForest Prize." He was ordained over the State street Congregational church in Portland, Me., Oct. 18, 1870; sermon by Rev. William McLeod Barbour, D.D., Buck professor of christian theology and lecturer on pastoral duties in Bangor theological seminary, ordaining prayer by Rev. Stephen Thurston, D.D., of Searsport, Me., right hand by Rev. Newman Smyth, professor in the theological seminary, Andover. During the nine years in which he has held this position he has aimed to preach the central truths of the gospel. They have:

3427  *Annie Perry* (Hincks), b. Feb 7, 1879.

3428   Enoch Pond (Hincks), b. Dec. 22, 1846; m. Oct. 5, 1869, Cornelia Emerine
        Hart, sister of his eldest brother's wife.   He is one of the firm of Wood
        Bros., carriage manufacturers in Bridgeport; is a member and treasurer
        of the 1st Congregational church.   They have :
    3429   *Annie Hart* (Hincks), b. May 22, 1872.
    3430   *Henry Winslow* (Hincks), b. Dec. 13, 1875.
3431   John Howard (Hincks), b. March 19, 1849; m. April 4, 1878, Jennie King
        Thurston [see no. 3396].   He graduated from Phillips academy, Andover,
        giving the valedictory, 1868; from Yale 1872, and from Yale theological
        seminary 1876.   Like his brother he gained distinction as a writer and
        won the "DeForest Prize."   He was ordained pastor of the Congrega-
        tional church, Montpelier, Vt., Sept. 27, 1877; sermon by his brother,
        Rev. E. Y. Hincks, ordaining prayer by Rev. C. B. Drake, D.D., of
        Royalton, Vt., charge to the pastor by his wife's father, Rev. R. B.
        Thurston, charge to the people by Rev. M. H. Buckham, D.D., president
        of the Vermont university, right hand by Rev. Wm. S. Hazen of North-
        field, Vt.   Rev. Mr. Hincks has a philosophical and independent mind;
        he calls no man master, but follows Christ.   In his pastorate he suc-
        ceeded an eminent man, the late Rev. Wm. H. Lord, D.D., and his min-
        istry has made its impression on the community.   They have :
    3431a   *Percy Thurston* (Hincks), b. Feb. 17, 1879.
3432   Jane Isabel (Hincks), b. in Bridgeport Jan. 6, 1856.

## 1674

ELIZABETH BLODGET (*Mary Thurston,*[5] *David,*[4] *Richard,*[3] *Daniel,*[2]
*Daniel*[1]), sister of the preceding, and third daughter of Dea. Bliss
and Mary (Thurston) Blodget of Bucksport, Me.; born there Nov.
12, 1822 ; married, Feb. 9, 1851, REV. JOHN PARKER SKEELE, son of
John and Charlotte (Fisher) Skeele of Kennebunk, Me.

Rev. Mr. Skeele graduated from Bowdoin in 1845, and from Bangor in 1850; was ordained over the Congregational church in Hallowell, Me., Oct. 9, 1850; invocation and reading scriptures, Rev. P.
F. Barnard of Richmond; introductory prayer, Rev. David Thurston,
D.D., of Winthrop; sermon, Rev. John Maltby of Bangor; ordaining
prayer, Rev. Benj. Tappan, D.D., of Augusta ; charge to pastor, Rev.
Stephen Thurston, D.D., of Searsport; right hand, Rev. W. L. Hyde
of Gardiner; address to the people, Rev. Geo. Shepard, D.D., of Bangor; concluding prayer, Rev. Albert Cole of Winslow; Dr. Benj.
Tappan was moderator and Rev. R. B. Thurston of Waterville, scribe.
He was dismissed Dec. 23, 1857 and went south to regain his health.
For a while he was agent for the A. B. C. F. M.   In July, 1873, he
became the pastor of the church in East Bloomfield, N. Y.   He is a
man of highly respectable attainments, a consecrated and useful
minister of the gospel.

### Children :

3433   Henry Blodget (Skeele), b. Aug. 21, 1852.
3434   Arthur Fessenden (Skeele), b. April 3, 1854.
3435   Charles Blodget (Skeele), b. Feb. 7, 1857; d. Oct. 12, 1863.
3436   Walter Fisher (Skeele), b. Sept. 26, 1865.

## 1675

REV. HENRY BLODGET (*Mary Thurston,*[5] *David,*[4] *Richard,*[3] *Daniel,*[2]
*Daniel*[1]), brother of the preceding, and eldest son of Dea. Bliss and
Mary (Thurston) Blodget of Bucksport, Me.; born there July 13,
1825 ; married, December, 1846, SARAH RIPLEY, born March, 1822,
daughter of Franklin and Charlotte (Barrett) Ripley of Greenfield,
Mass.

Henry Blodget was received to the Congregational church in Bucksport 1837; graduated from Yale 1848, and received the honorary title of D.D. from his Alma Mater 1872; removed his church relation to the college church 1844, and was deacon till 1848; 1870 he transferred his church relation back to Bucksport. Studied in Bangor theological seminary till the autumn of 1850, when he was appointed tutor in Yale; resigned 1853; was ordained as a missionary to China at Bucksport Jan. 25, 1854; sailed for China April, 1854. He resided at Shanghai until 1860, when he went to Teintsin, being the first protestant missionary in the province of Chihli. In 1864 went to Peking, where he has resided to this time, 1879. He says, "It was my privilege to baptize the first convert among protestant christians in the province." He was one of the committee to translate the new testament into the Mandarin, and he prepared a hymn book for the use of the native christians. He has been a faithful and self-denying laborer in this field, being separated from his wife for several years. The climate of the low country not being suited to her, she came back to this country and remained till he removed to Peking, which is more elevated and salubrious.

Rev. N. George Clark, D.D., secretary A. B. C. F. M., says: "Rev. Henry Blodget, D.D., is a man of superior intellectual gifts, of great singleness of purpose, and thoroughly consecrated to the cause of Christ. By his labors as a translator of the new testament into the Mandarin colloquial, in connection with missionaries of other societies, he has helped lay the foundation of a christian literature for nearly half the population of the Chinese empire. His self-denial and devotion to the cause of missions have been a worthy example and an inspiration to younger men."

Their children are:

3437   Henry (Blodget), b. in Greenfield Oct. 22, 1854; graduated from Yale 1877
       and has nearly completed studies for the medical profession, 1879.
3438   Charlotte Ripley (Blodget), b. in Shanghai, China, Feb. 24, 1857; gradu-
       ated from Abbott Female seminary, Andover, 1878.

## 1676

JOHN BLODGET (*Mary Thurston,*[5] *David,*[4] *Richard,*[3] *Daniel,*[2] *Daniel*[1]), brother of the preceding, and second son of Dea. Bliss and Mary (Thurston) Blodget of Bucksport, Me.; born there July 11, 1827; married, in Bangor, Me., Feb. 3, 1852, SARAH PAGE CASE, born Sept. 8, 1830, daughter of Isaac and Abigail (Page) Case of Kenduskeag, Me. She died in Lemars, Iowa, May 6, 1871.

John Blodget was a merchant in Bucksport, in company with his father, from October, 1854, till February, 1869, when he went to Lemars and established a life and fire insurance agency. He says, "When I came here there was no store in the county, and no railroad nearer than Sioux City, twenty-five miles west, and Fort Dodge, one hundred miles east; now [1877] we have two railroads. There was only one house where our town now stands and contains fifteen hundred inhabitants. I started a Sabbath-school in 1869, from which has grown two schools, each of about one hundred and fifty members, a Congregational church of sixty-five members, and a Methodist church of about one hundred, and some work has been done at out

stations." He was a member of the Congregational church in Bucksport, and was chosen deacon after his father's death to fill his place. At Lemars he was the only deacon until a grandson of Rev. Samuel Spring, D.D., of Newburyport, Mass., was chosen as his associate.

Children, all born in Bucksport:

3439 Julia Case (Blodget), b. Dec. 19, 1853.
3440 Albert Morrill (Blodget), b. July 17, 1855.
3441 Grace Howard (Blodget), b. April 8, 1864.

## 1677

GEORGE BLODGET[6] (*Mary Thurston*,[5] *David*,[4] *Richard*,[8] *Daniel*,[2] *Daniel*[1]), brother of the preceding, and third son of Bliss and Mary (Thurston) Blodget of Bucksport, Me.; born there April 6, 1831; married, Sept. 20, 1859, MARY SOPHIA POND, born July 19, 1834, daughter of Rev. Enoch, D.D., and Julia Ann (Maltby) Pond of Bangor, Me.

Mr. Blodget graduated from Williams college 1857, and is engaged in the manufacture of leather in Bucksport. He is a deacon in the Congregational church.

Children:

3442 Benjamin Pond (Blodget), b. Aug. 7, 1860.
3443 George Redington (Blodget), b. Sept. 17, 1862.
3444 Annie Maltby (Blodget), b. Feb. 8, 1864; d. in Bangor Feb. 17, 1876.
3445 Frederic Swazey (Blodget), b. May 26, 1876.
3446a *Sarah Elizabeth* " *b. Feb. 28, 1879.*

## 1691

EPHRAIM GOODALE THURSTON[6] (*Samuel*,[5] *David*,[4] *Richard*,[8] *Daniel*,[2] *Daniel*[1]), second son of Samuel[5] and Prudence (Goodale) Thurston of Mill creek, South Orrington, Me.; born there July 2, 1827; married, Sept. 25, 1852, CHARLOTTE MARGRETTA DARLING, daughter of Henry and Eliza (Cobb) Darling of Bucksport, Me., born there June 2, 1830.

Mr. Thurston was a lumber merchant of great energy, carrying on business in Bangor, Me., and Boston, Mass., at one time, till his health failed him and he was compelled to relinquish the Boston branch. He spent the winter of 1866 in Florida, with his family, for his health, and in the summer went in a sailing vessel to the East Indies, and after starting from Rangoon for home was never heard from; all on board are supposed to have been lost. He was a member of the Congregational church.

Their children were:

3446 Harry Darling,[7] b. in Bucksport May 25, 1854; lumber dealer in Bangor.
3447 Helen Foster,[7] b. in Bangor Oct. 3, 1860.

## 1693

EMILY THURSTON[6] (*Samuel*,[5] *David*,[4] *Richard*,[8] *Daniel*,[2] *Daniel*[1]), sister of the preceding, and second daughter of Samuel[5] and Prudence (Goodale) Thurston of Brewer, Me.; born in Bucksport, Me., Jan. 1, 1834; married, Oct. 31, 1855, CHARLES WOOD, born in Burlington, Mass., July 9, 1808. He died Jan. 16, 1875.

Mr. Wood was a merchant in Boston, Mass., till 1840, when he went to Lovell, Me., to reside. He owned considerable real estate in Lovell and his later years were occupied mostly in the care of it.

Their children, born in Lovell, are:

3450   Charles Thurston (Wood),b. Aug. 25, 1859; studying medicine, Portland,Me.
3451   Harold Blanchard (Wood), b. July 23, 1864.

## 1698

MARY ELIZABETH THURSTON [6] (*Samuel,*[5] *David,*[4] *Richard,*[3] *Daniel,*[2] *Daniel*[1]), sister of the preceding, and daughter of Samuel [6] and Charlotte (Greeley, née Goodale) Thurston of Brewer, Me.; born there Dec. 15, 1843; married, Oct. 1, 1863, AUGUSTUS HALL WALKER, born in Fryeburg, Me., Dec. 22, 1833. She died, after a lingering illness of several years, during which her christian character shone out with beautiful luster, Feb. 16, 1873, aged 30. He is a practicing lawyer in Lovell, Me.; judge of the probate court.

They had one child:

3452   Alice Thurston (Walker), b. Oct. 14, 1865; d. Aug. 29, 1876, aged 11.

## 1714

REV. JOHN ROGERS THURSTON [6] ( *John,*[5] *David,*[4] *Richard,*[3] *Daniel,*[2] *Daniel*[1]), son of John [6] and Abigail King (Lawrence) Thurston of Bangor, Me.; born there Sept. 4, 1831; married, first, Sept. 4, 1858, FRANCES ORELLA E. GOODALE, daughter of Walter and Elizabeth (Hincks) Goodale of Orrington, Me., born Feb. 4, 1831; she died in Newburyport, Mass., Feb. 21, 1868. Second, March 16, 1871, in New York city, CAROLINE AUGUSTA WELLS STOREY, daughter of Charles William and Elizabeth (Burnham) Storey of Newburyport, born Sept. 7, 1835.

Mr. Thurston being quite young when his parents died, he lived with his aunt, Mehitable Godfrey, and always looked upon her house as his home. He fitted in the Bangor high school, and graduated from Yale college in 1851; taught in a boarding-school in Stamford, Ct., until 1855, proving an able, successful teacher and a good manager of boys; graduated from Bangor theological seminary in 1858. He was ordained pastor of the Congregational church in Newbury, Mass., Jan. 20, 1859, as the colleague of Rev. L. Withington, D.D. The sermon was by Prof. George Shepard, D.D., of Bangor, Me.; ordaining prayer by Rev. David Thurston, D.D., of Winthrop, Me.; charge to the pastor by L. Withington, D.D., senior pastor of the church; right hand of fellowship by Rev. J. L. Jenkins of Lowell, Mass. This was a successful pastorate till March 28, 1870, when he was dismissed. April 20, 1871, he was installed pastor of the Congregational church in Whitinsville (Northbridge), Mass. Sermon by Rev. Richard B. Thurston of Stamford, Ct.; charge by Rev. D. T. Fiske of Newburyport. He is still acceptably filling this place. He has been a laborious and watchful minister. His preaching is honest, earnest, sound, and instructive. He is fond of original study and careful investigation of a subject. In Associations he vigorously upholds the standard of ministerial scholarship; in all relations a practical, diligent, faithful, fraternal man.

Children, by first wife, Frances, born in Newburyport:

3453   Walter Lawrence,[7] b. May 2, 1860; d. Dec. 31, 1860.
3454   Margaret Mead,[7] b. April 21, 1862.
3455   Elizabeth Goodale,[7] b. Sept. 24, 1865.

By second wife, Augusta, born in Whitinsville:

3456    Charles Storey,[7] b. April 17, 1872.
3457    John Lawrence,[7] b. Aug. 4, 1874.
3458    Caroline Burnham,[7] b. Aug. 21, 1876; d. Aug. 18, 1877.
3459    Helen,[7] b. Dec. 19, 1877.

## 1727

JOHN ALBERT BUCK [6] (*Sarah Thurston,[5] David,[4] Richard,[3] Daniel,[2] Daniel*[1]), eldest son of Dea. John and Sarah (Thurston) Buck of Orland, Me.; born there Aug. 15, 1825; married, Nov. 5, 1846, CHARLOTTE MARIA BUCK, daughter of Joseph and Abby (Hill) Buck of Bucksport, Me., born there May 18, 1828. She joined the Congregational church in 1865.

Mr. Buck is a successful merchant, ship builder, and ship owner; was a member of the house of representatives in the legislature of 1868, and of the senate in 1869 and 1870, and of the house again in 1875.

Their children, all born in Orland, were:

3464    Albert Redington (Buck), b. Nov. 20, 1847; m. May 14, 1876, May Louise Saunders. They have:
    3465    *John Dudley* (Buck), b. Sept. 25, 1878.
3466    Maria (Buck), b. Sept. 7, 1849; d. March 11, 1850.
3467    Harry Hill (Buck), b. Feb. 21, 1851.
3468    Harriet Elizabeth (Buck), b. April 5, 1853; d. May 30, 1853.
3469    Frank Swazey (Buck), b. June 19, 1855; d. Oct. 21, 1856.
3470    Joseph (Buck), b. July 24, 1857; d. Nov. 15, 1858.
3471    Lottie Linwood (Buck), b. May 5, 1860.
3472    Lizzie Lane (Buck), b. Oct. 11, 1861; d. Feb. 26, 1862.
3473    Walter Darling (Buck), b. June 8, 1865.

## 1728

FRANK BUCK [6] (*Sarah Thurston,[5] David,[4] Richard,[3] Daniel,[2] Daniel*[1]), brother of the preceding, and second son of Dea. John and Sarah (Thurston) Buck of Orland, Me.; born there April 24, 1827; married, in Boston, Mass., Oct. 13, 1847, ANN CATHERINE BUCK, daughter of James and Lydia (Treat) Buck of Bucksport, Me., born there March 1, 1826. Mr. James Buck was born in Frankfort, Me., April 29, 1795, and died in Bucksport March 31, 1867. Mrs. James Buck died Dec. 17, 1872.

Frank Buck is a farmer in Orland, and is much interested in the improvement of stock. They are both members of the Congregational church in Orland.

Their children, all born in Orland, were:

3474    Waldo Pierce (Buck), b. Feb. 27, 1849; d. Aug. 12, 1849.
3475    Julia Florence (Buck), b. July 31, 1850; d. April 8, 1862.
3476    Willis Frank (Buck), b. Nov. 18, 1851; m. Sept. 29, 1873, Helen Sweetser Soper, b. May 13, 1853, daughter of Elisha and Charlotte (Eldridge) Soper of Bucksport. They reside in Orland, and have:
    3476a    *Belle Pearson* (Buck), b. Oct. 3, 1878.
3477    Lucilla Pierce (Buck), b. July 8, 1853; d. Sept. 1, 1857.
3478    Jennie Nelson (Buck), b. Dec. 29, 1854.
3479    George Alfred (Buck), b. Sept. 22, 1857.
3480    Augustus Walker (Buck), b. May 29, 1859; d. Oct. 19, 1859.
3481    James Herbert (Buck), b. July 19, 1860; d. Aug. 3, 1864.
3482    Fred (Buck), b. Oct. 27, 1862.
3483    Lizzie Rice (Buck), b. May 17, 1864.
3484    Carrie Maria (Buck), b. June 10, 1866.
3485    Kitty Clover (Buck), b. Dec. 15, 1868; d. Sept. 10, 1870.

## 1729

EDWARD BUCK [6] (*Sarah Thurston,*[5] *David,*[4] *Richard,*[8] *Daniel,*[2] *Daniel*[1]), brother of the preceding, and son of Dea. John and Sarah (Thurston) Buck of Orland, Me.; born there April 17, 1829; married, June 3, 1853, EMELINE BILLINGS DARLING, born June, 1832, daughter of Dea. Henry and Ruth (Cobb) Darling of Bucksport, Me.

Mr. Buck graduated from Yale 1852, and from Bangor theological seminary 1855; preached in Orland, Sedgwick, Brooksville, and Union from 1858 to 1866. He stood high as a scholar and preached with much ability; but circumstances led him to enter into business, which he carries on in Orland, residing in Bucksport.

They have one child:

3486   Carl Darling (Buck), b. Oct. 2, 1856.

## 1749

STEPHEN ROLLO THURSTON [6] (*Rev. Stephen,*[5] *David,*[4] *Richard,*[8] *Daniel,*[2] *Daniel*[1]), son of Rev. Stephen[5] and Clara Matilda (Benson) Thurston of Searsport, Me.; born there July 20, 1832; married, Jan. 13, 1859, ANNIE FRANCES CARPENTER, born Sept. 17, 1836, daughter of George and Frances (Spaulding) Carpenter of Augusta, Me.

Mr. Thurston graduated from Colby university in 1853; went into the ship chandlery business, in Portland, Me., with McGilvery, Ryan & Davis; after, into the general insurance business, under the firm name of Loring & Thurston. In January, 1873, he went to Chicago, Ill., and is now, 1879, in the law and land brokerage business, under the firm name of Isaac Claflin & Co., residing in Lombard, a few miles out of the city. While in Portland, he was a deacon in State street Congregational church.

Their children, born in Portland, are:

3487   George Carpenter,[7] b. Dec. 8, 1861.
3488   Grace Carpenter,[7] b. Sept. 10, 1864.

## 1756

HENRIETTA MARIA THURSTON [6] of Dennysville, Me. (*Rev. Stephen,*[5] *David,*[4] *Richard,*[8] *Daniel,*[2] *Daniel*[1]), sister of the preceding, and daughter of Rev. Stephen[5] and Clara Matilda (Benson) Thurston of Searsport, Me.; born there March 31, 1839; married, Oct. 3, 1861, REV. CHARLES WHITTIER, born Aug. 3, 1830, son of Edmund and Anna (Patten) Whittier of Merrimac, Mass.

Mr. Whittier graduated from Williams college 1856, and from Bangor theological seminary 1860; was ordained pastor of the Congregational church in Dennysville Nov. 13, 1860; Rev. Henry F. Harding of Hallowell, moderator of council; Rev. Seth H. Keeler, D.D., of Calais preached the sermon; Rev. Wm. Warren, D.D., of Gorham, Me., offered the ordaining prayer. Mr. Whittier is a man of excellent judgment and wields a strong influence for good in the county where he is settled; has been very successful as a pastor, uniting and enlarging his church. It is said there is scarcely a family in town which has not felt the reviving influences of religion.

Children:
3493  Charles Thurston (Whittier), b. Dec. 20, 1862.
3494  Stephen Thurston (Whittier), b. March 16, 1864.
3495  John Kilby (Whittier), b. Feb. 2, 1867.
3496  Arthur Benson (Whittier), b. Aug. 9, 1868.
3497  Clarence Patten (Whittier), b. June 6, 1876.

## 1914

JOHN ROWE THURSTON [6] (*Daniel,*[5] *Daniel,*[4] *Joseph,*[3] *Joseph,*[2] *Daniel*[1]), eldest son of Daniel [5] and Sally (Rowe) Thurston of Rockport, Mass.; born there Sept. 25, 1812; married, 1840, LUCY ROWE of Portland, Me., born in Rockport 1817.

Mr. Thurston was a mariner, and the first person to send a petition to congress against slavery, and the first one to engage actively in the temperance reform in Rockport.

Children:
3507  Arethusa,[7] b. April, 1847; d. July 5, 1847.
3508  Frederick William,[7] b. 1854; d. in Portland April 1, 1862.

## 1917

WINTHROP THURSTON [6] (*Daniel,*[5] *Daniel,*[4] *Joseph,*[3] *Joseph,*[2] *Daniel*[1]), brother of the preceding, and son of Daniel [5] and Sally (Rowe) Thurston of Rockport, Mass.; born there Nov. 9, 1820; married, first, MARY FEARS, born April, 1823, daughter of John and Hannah Fears, of Rockport; she died Sept. 12, 1872. Second, in Boston, Mass., April, 1873, SARAH ELIZA BURNHAM, daughter of Abraham and Catherine (Belmore) Burnham of Grand Menan, N. B. He died Oct. 14, 1878.

Mr. Thurston was a grocer and curer of fish, in which he dealt. He was the first man to introduce the system of buying from the fishermen to cure; the fishermen previously curing their own fish. He was inspector of customs for Rockport from 1855 to 1859, a director of the Rockport railroad, and a member and officer of the Universalist church.

Children, by first wife, Mary:
3509  John Winthrop Hale,[7] b. Dec. 31, 1848; lives in Topeka, Kansas, clerk in a bank.
3510  Henry,[7] b. Sept. 7, 1853; was with his father in business.

## 1918

WILLIAM HENRY THURSTON [6] (*Daniel,*[5] *Daniel,*[4] *Joseph,*[3] *Joseph,*[2] *Daniel*[1]), brother of the preceding, and son of Daniel [5] and Sally (Rowe) Thurston of Rockport, Mass.; born there Sept. 24, 1823; married, June 22, 1855, ANNA SPARROW.

Children:
3520  Annette,[7] b. July 26, 1857.
3521  Daniel,[7] b. July 30, 1859.
3522  John Ellis,[7] b. July 16, 1861.
3523  Mary Olive,[7] b. Sept. 14, 1866.

## 1931

NATHANIEL THURSTON [6] of Gloucester, Mass. (*Nathaniel,*[5] *Daniel,*[4] *Joseph,*[3] *Joseph,*[2] *Daniel*[1]), eldest son of Nathaniel [5] and Betsey (Gee) Thurston of Rockport, Mass.; born there Aug. 5, 1806; married RUTH BUTLER.

* Children, all born in Gloucester:

3530  Nathaniel,[7] m.
3531  Melisse,[7] m. and lives in Southport, Me.
3532  George,[7] m.
3533  William H.,[7] m.; lost on Georges Banks; had children.
3534  James,[7] m.

## 1933

WILLIAM GEE THURSTON [6] (*Nathaniel,[5] Daniel,[4] Joseph,[3] Joseph,[2] Daniel [1]*), brother of the preceding, and son of Nathaniel [5] and Betsey (Gee) Thurston of Rockport, Mass.; born there Dec. 24, 1811; married, Dec. 10, 1832, RACHEL RICH SMITH, born Oct. 17, 1809, daughter of Thomas and Rachel (Rich) Smith of Riverdale, Mass.
Mr. Thurston is a mariner and resides in Riverdale.

### Children:

3543   Betsey Jane,[7] b. May 22, 1834; d. May 23, 1838.
+3544  William,[7] b. Aug. 14, 1836; m. Caroline Elwell.
3545   Betsey Jane,[7] b. Oct. 14, 1837; m. Dec. 13, 1856, Eli Gott, b. Oct. 7, 1831; d. March 19, 1875.  They had:
    3546  *Castillo Doddridge* (Gott), b. Dec. 14, 1857.
    3547  *Lizzie Jane* (Gott), b. Feb 12, 1859.
    3548  *Eva Florence* (Gott), b. July 6, 1861.
    3549  *Frank Eli* (Gott), b. Aug. 30, 1867.
    3550  *Effie May* (Gott), b. Dec. 20, 1869.
+3551  James,[7] b. Sept. 9, 1839; m. Martha Hood.
3552   Lewis,[7] b. Sept. 18, 1841; d. Dec. 31, 1845.
3553   Mary F.,[7] b. Dec. 5, 1842; d. Dec. 26, 1845.
3554   Rachel,[7] b. May 25, 1845; d. Jan. 2, 1846.
3555   Lewis,[7] b. Oct. 5, 1846.
3556   Rachel,[7] b. Jan. 9, 1849; m. Jan. 20, 1874, Daniel Brewton, b. Nov. 17, 1850; d. May 16, 1875.
3557   Elias Howard,[7] b. Nov. 4, 1850.
3558   Mary Fuller,[7] b. Oct. 4, 1853; m. Jan. 1, 1872, Frank Sawyer Day, and had:
    3559  *Frank Sawyer* (Day), b. Nov. 19, 1872; d. Nov. 2, 1874.
    3560  *Mabel Dennison* (Day), b. April 23, 1874.
    3561  *Annie Gertrude* (Day), b. Nov. 7, 1875.

## 1936

CAPT. JAMES GEE THURSTON [6] (*Nathaniel,[5] Daniel,[4] Joseph,[3] Joseph,[2] Daniel [1]*), brother of the preceding, and son of Nathaniel [5] and Betsey (Gee) Thurston of Rockport, Mass.; born there April 23, 1820; married, first, Nov. 18, 1841, LUCY L. HARVEY; she died March 10, 1852.  Second, March 23, 1853, DEBORAH PARSONS.

### Children, by first wife, Lucy:

3562   Charles L.,[7] b. Oct. 10, 1842; d. Feb. 11, 1846.
3563   Lucy E.,[7] b. Sept. 28, 1845; d. Jan. 30, 1846.
3564   Charles L.,[7] b. March 15, 1847; m. Jan. 1, 1874, Justine Hicks; d. Sept. 1, 1876.
3565   Alfred,[7] b. April 23, 1849; m. Jan. 1, 1874, Mary Ingersol, b. Aug. 30, 1847, daughter of Samuel and Mary (Haddock) Ingersol of Riverdale, Mass.

### By second wife, Deborah:

3566   Julia F.,[7] b. Oct. 29, 1856.
3567   Emma,[7] b. Feb. 19, 1859.
3568   Marillia,[7] b. Oct. 25, 1862; d. Jan. 28, 1864.
3569   Marillia,[7] b. March 24, 1866.

## 1937

BENJAMIN THURSTON[6] (*Nathaniel*,[5] *Daniel*,[4] *Joseph*,[3] *Joseph*,[2] *Daniel*[1]), brother of the preceding, and son of Nathaniel[5] and Betsey (Gee) Thurston of Rockport, Mass.; born there Aug. 16, 1823; married, Nov. 26, 1846, NANCY LANE, born June 13, 1825, daughter of James and Judith (Lane) Lane of Annisquam, Mass.

He is a mariner, residing at Riverdale, Mass. Capt. Ezekiel Call was lost in the severe gale of April 2, 1871, and Mrs. Nancy Thurston showed her christian beneficence by collecting the means to build a house for the widow and five small children left by this casualty.

Children:

3578 Judith Merrima,[7] b. June 23, 1848.
3579 Benjamin Albert,[7] b. July 4, 1850; d. Sept. 9, 1875.
3580 Sidney Lane,[7] b. June 23, 1853; d. April 9, 1870, by the accidental discharge of his gun.
3581 Edith Rosalind,[7] b. Aug. 4, 1856.
3582 Etta Florence,[7] b. Nov. 27, 1859.
3583 Sherman Horace,[7] b. Jan. 28, 1865.

## 1970

NATHANIEL GAMAGE THURSTON[6] (*Ambrose*,[5] *Capt. John*,[4] *Joseph*,[3] *Joseph*,[2] *Daniel*[1]), son of Ambrose[5] and Polly (Gamage) Thurston of Mt. Desert, Me.; born in Rockport, Mass., May 2, 1790; married, June 11, 1811, ELIZABETH ROBBINS, born Nov. 25, 1790, daughter of Nathan and Elizabeth (Colby) Robbins of Cambridge, Mass. He died May 1, 1856.

Mr. Thurston was a farmer and master mariner in Deer Isle, Me.; member of the Methodist church.

Their children were:

3593 Sarah Robbins,[7] b. Mar. 17, 1812; m. Jan. 2, 1834, Ignatius Small, b. June 5, 1810. He is a farmer in So. Deer Isle; has been representative to the legislature, selectman, and held various other town offices. They have :
    3594 *Elizabeth Thurston* (Small), b. Sept. 24, 1835; m. 1852, Benjamin N. Sylvester of Jefferson, Me.; two children.
    3595 *Edward Fairfield* (Small), b. Mar. 19, 1838; m. Nov. 26, 1865, Susan S. Robbins of Deer Isle; three children.
    3596 *Hannah Ann* (Small), b. July 16, 1839; m. Nov. 14, 1862, Joseph K. Buckminster of Deer Isle; four children.
    3597 *Matilda* (Small), b. Mar. 15, 1843; m. Dec. 25, 1871, Jonathan Knowles of Belfast, Me., and live in South Deer Isle.
    3598 *Sylvia* (Small), b. Nov. 11, 1845; m. Feb. 20, 1865, Amaziah Billings of Sedgwick, Me.; reside in Salem, Mass.; three children.
    3599 *Stephen Thurston* (Small), b. July 2, 1848; a captain in Deer Isle.
    3600 *Maggie Helen Thurston* (Small), b. March 10, 1850; m. June, 1872, Capt. Wallace Turner of Isle au Haute, Me.; one child.
    3601 *Pauline Ackley* (Small), b. Aug. 23, 1853.
    3602 *Frances Abbie McKay* (Small), b. Nov. 8, 1855.
    3603 *Mary Evelyn* (Small), b. Feb. 4, 1859; d. Feb. 14, 1860.
3604 Ambrose,[7] m. Almira Gott, daughter of Polly Gott; lives in Tremont, Me.; six children.
3605 Betsey,[7] m. Isaac Gott of Mt. Desert; seven children.
3606 Serena,[7] m. 1851, John Knight of South Deer Isle. They have :
    3607 *John Edward* (Knight), m. and has two children.
3608 William Snow,[7] last heard of was in New Orleans or Mexico, and supposed to be dead; n.m.
+3609 Stephen,[7] b. Jan. 13, 1825; m. Margaret B. Sylvester.
+3610 Thomas,[7] b. Aug. 24, 1828; m. Caroline Stinson.
+3611 James Robbins,[7] b. Sept. 6, 1832; m. Pauline Ackley.

## 1972

JOHN THURSTON[6] (*Ambrose,*[5] *Capt. John,*[4] *Joseph,*[3] *Joseph,*[2] *Daniel*[1]), brother of the preceding, and son of Ambrose[5] and Polly (Gamage) Thurston of Mt. Desert, Me.; married NANCY GOTT.

Mr. Thurston was a seaman till a few years before his death, when he tended a lighthouse at Tremont, Me.; lived in Mt. Desert, P. O., Tremont.

### Their children were :

3619  James,[7] m. Eliza Benson.
3620  John,[7] m. Delia Putnam.
3621  Solomon,[7] m. Mary Webster of Mt. Desert.
+3622  Charles,[7] m. Hannah Ann Thurston.
3623  Fannie,[7] m. William Stockbridge of Swan's Island, Me.; live in Gloucester, Mass.
3624  Lydia,[7] m. James Wilson of Mt. Desert.
3625  Louie,[7] m. Morris Rich of Mt. Desert.
3626  Daniel,[7] m. Katie Gott.
3627  Susan,[7] d. at age of 17.

## 2005

AMBROSE THURSTON[6] (*Amos,*[5] *John,*[4] *Joseph,*[3] *Joseph,*[2] *Daniel*[1]), son of Amos[5] and Mary (Gott) Thurston of Deer Isle, Me.; born there Aug. 24, 1806; married, 1835, SERENA MERRILL GOTT, daughter of Capt. Isaac and Mary (Thurston) Gott.

Mr. Thurston has been master of a fishing vessel for many years, residing in Deer Isle, Me., and brought the first fare of mackerel from the Gulf of St. Lawrence to this place.

### Their children were :

3637  Hannah Ann,[7] b. Aug. 22, 1836; m. Charles Thurston [see no. 3622].
3638  John,[7] b. Feb. 16,.1839; incompetent; lives with his father.
3639  Eunice,[7] b. July 19, 1844; m. Dec. 27, 1860, Henry Banks, b. in Holland, Sept. 30, 1835. They had:
    3640  *Henry G.* (Banks), b. Dec. 18, 1861.
    3641  *Mina S.* (Banks), b. Sept. 17, 1863.
    3642  *Ezra* (Banks), b. July 24, 1867.
    3643  *Phineas M.* (Banks), b. Jan. 14, 1869.
    3644  *A son,* b. Jan. 6, 1873; d. Jan. 9, 1873.
    3645  *Hattie G.* (Banks), b. March 27, 1875.
3646  Nancy,[7] b. April 3, 1846; m. Roland Lunt of Tremont, Me.; one son.
3647  Harriet,[7] b. Feb. 1, 1848; m. Ezra Gott, b. April 28, 1841; d. Nov. 5, 1872. They had:
    3648  *Joseph* (Gott), b. Sept. 23, 1871.
3649  Ambrose,[7] b. Sept. 23, 1852; m. Jan. 27, 1877, Mary Kenney, b. Nov. 1, 1852; she died Dec. 22, 1877.
3650  Watson,[7] b. Oct. 5, 1855; d. six months of age.

## 2006

AMOS THURSTON[6] (*Amos,*[5] *John,*[4] *Joseph,*[3] *Joseph,*[2] *Daniel*[1]), brother of the preceding, and son of Amos[5] and Mary (Gott) Thurston of Deer Isle, Me.; born there Jan. 31, 1809; married ANN STINSON. She died July 7, 1860; he died March 27, 1870.

Mr. Thurston was a farmer and fisherman, living in Deer Isle.

### Their children were :

3661  Mary Abigail,[7] b. March, 1839; d. March 27, 1867.
3662  Serena Ann,[7] b. Aug. 15, 1842; d. Oct. 5, 1866.
3663  Susan E.,[7] b. Jan. 4, 1844; m. July 9, 1861, Josiah Webb Stinson, b. Jan. 4, 1842. They had:

3664   *William Edmund* (Stinson), b. Jan. 15, 1863.
3665   *Ira S.* (Stinson), b. May 13, 1866; d. June 30, 1869.
3666   *Anna Lillian* (Stinson), b. April 23, 1869.
3667   *Alden Turner* (Stinson), b. April 2, 1872; d. Jan. 26, 1878.
3668   *Lyman Haskell* (Stinson), b. April 28, 1874.
3669   *Maggie Hamblen* (Stinson), b. Dec. 6, 1877.
3670   Jesse,[7] b. June 25, 1847; m. April 12, 1868, Olive Stinson, b. March 23,
          1849; two children.
3671   Louisa,[7] b. Nov. 19, 1851; d. Nov. 25, 1869.
3672   Nellie,[7] b. Nov. 5, 1856.

## 2029

WILLIAM THURSTON [6] (*William,*[5] *John,*[4] *Joseph,*[3] *Joseph,*[2] *Daniel*[1]), eldest son of William [5] and Nancy (Foster) Thurston of South Bristol, Me.; born there Nov. 9, 1802; married, in Pemaquid, Me., April 17, 1834, MARGARET McKAY, born Nov. 25, 1806, daughter of Gilbert and Rebecca (Berry) McKay of Shelburne, N. S.

Mr. Thurston was a master mariner, residing in South Bristol.

### Their children were:

3682   George Edward,[7] b. April 1, 1835; m. Oct. 7, 1864, Elizabeth Sargent.
          He was a seaman, and was lost at sea March 8, 1870; she lives at Booth-
          bay, Me.   They had:
   3683   *James Edward,*[8] b. Nov. 20, 1865.
   3684   *Hiram Sargent,*[8] b. Sept. 2, 1867.
   3685   *Mabel,*[8] b. April 17, 1870.
3686   Albert,[7] b. Sept. 10, 1837; m. May 11, 1862, Martha Eliza Poole, b. Dec.
          28, 1837, daughter of Eben C. and Martha (Plummer) Poole of South
          Bristol.   He is a seaman, residing in Bristol.   They had:
   3687   *Willard S.,*[8] b. Feb. 8, 1866.
   3688   *Laura Etta,*[8] b. Jan. 13, 1868.
   3689   *Franklin,*[8] b. Aug. 26, 1869.
   3690   *Albert M.,*[8] b. Sept. 19, 1871.
   3691   *Elmer McKay,*[8] b. Aug. 2, 1873.
   3692   *Warren,*[8] b. Oct. 28, 1875; d. June 28, 1876.
3693   James,[7] b. April 20, 1839; fisherman, lost at sea July 18, 1859.
3694   Mary Ellen,[7] b. Dec. 4, 1842; tailoress in Oakland, Cal.; n.m.
3695   William,[7] b. Jan. 23, 1847; master mariner; served one year in the 14th
          Maine regiment in the war against the rebellion; n.m.
3696   Nancy,[7] b. April 17, 1850; is a seamstress in Bristol.

## 2030

SOLOMON THURSTON [6] (*William,*[5] *John,*[4] *Joseph,*[3] *Joseph,*[2] *Daniel*[1]), brother of the preceding, and son of William [5] and Nancy (Foster) Thurston of Bristol, Me.; born there Feb. 16, 1804; married, 1834, MARGARET McKAY, born March 3, 1814, daughter of Hugh and Anne (McPherson) McKay of Shelburne, N. S., and after of East Boston, Mass.   He was drowned in Boston harbor in 1847.

Mr. Thurston was a sea captain, engaged in the coasting trade, residing in Bristol, and after in East Boston.

### Their children, born in Bristol, were:

3706   Ann Elizabeth,[7] b. 1836; m. 1st, Montague Burk; 2d, April 29, 1872, Jo-
          seph Francis Taylor, b. Jan. 15, 1837, son of Davis and Hannah (Cros-
          by) Taylor of Biddeford, Me.   Mr. Taylor is a boot maker in East
          Weymouth, Mass.; was a soldier in the war against the rebellion.
          They have:
   3707   *Fannie May* (Taylor), b. Jan. 29, 1873.
   3708   *Frank Thurston* (Taylor), b. Aug. 6, 1874.
   3709   *Annie Gertrude* (Taylor), b. Feb. 13, 1876.

3710 Benjamin Franklin,[7] b. 1838; went to school in East Boston after his parents moved there; worked at painting, but was not satisfied, and went to a commercial college, after which he shipped in the "Great Republic," and she was burned in New York harbor.   He then sailed in the "Sea Flower," came back second mate; went to England and sailed as first mate of the large and beautiful ship "Bolingbroke" to India.   After returning from this voyage he sailed as master of the "British Lyon" two voyages to India.   After an absence of nine years, he returned home and married Mary Major of East Boston, and sailed for England as master of the bark "Edna" with his wife on board, and was lost off the coast of Ireland in a terrific storm.   Their bodies were found and buried in one grave on that island.

3711 Eugene,[7] b. 1842; a seaman in the merchant service till the rebellion broke out, when he shipped on board the U. S. flag ship "Brooklyn," which fought many severe and successful battles, and he was not wounded.   He is now, 1878, in the U. S. flag ship "Tennessee" on the coast of Japan.

3712 Judith,[7] d. aged 14.

3713 Albenia,[7] m. George A. Wadleigh of Boston; now, 1878, in New York. They have:

    3714  *Jennie* (Wadleigh), b. 1866.

3715 Oscar,[7] b. in East Boston July 14, 1846; enlisted in 3d Massachusetts cavalry and served three years under Gen. Banks; is now, 1878, a boot maker in East Weymouth; m. Nov. 23, 1868, Addie Milici White of East Weymouth b. Feb. 1, 1850.   They had:

    3716  *Albenia,*[8] b. April 7, 1872.
    3717  *Eugene,*[8] b. March 10, 1875; d. Dec. 25, 1875.
    3718  *Ernest,*[8] b. Aug. 4, 1876.

## 2032

GEORGE WASHINGTON THURSTON[6] (*William,*[5] *John,*[4] *Joseph,*[3] *Joseph,*[2] *Daniel*[1]), brother of the preceding, and son of William[5] and Nancy (Foster) Thurston of Bristol, Me.; born there March 13, 1810; married, first, SARAH MCKAY, daughter of Hugh and Anne (McPherson) McKay of Shelburne, N. S.; she died Sept. 20, 1868.   Second, May 27, 1869, MRS. MARY E. SPROUL of Bristol.   He died Nov. 5, 1870.   He was a master mariner, residing in Bristol.

### His children, all by first wife, were:

3728 Emma Louisa,[7] b. Jan. 19, 1842; m. in San Francisco, Cal., June 23, 1868, John Major, b. April 11, 1840, son of Robert and Catherine (Magee) Major of Boston, Mass.; he is a rancher at Wheatland, East Bear River township, Yuba county, Cal.; both members of the Baptist church. They have:

    3729  *Lizzie Lucretia* (Major), b. June 22, 1869.
    3730  *Ralph Thurston* (Major), b. Dec. 14, 1873.
    3731  *Sarah Theresa* (Major), b. Sept. 22, 1875.
    3732  *Reginald Erving* (Major). b. Nov. 12, 1877.

3733 Susan Alice,[7] b. Oct. 3, 1843; d. Jan. 1, 1866.
3734 Donald McKay,[7] ⎫ twins, born ⎰ d. Sept. 3, 1862.
3735 Henry William,[7] ⎭          ⎱ m. in Boston Oct. 9, 1867, Margaretta Gilmore, b. in South Boston July 17, 1843, daughter of John T. and Sarah (Burgess) Gilmore.   Mr. Thurston is a machinist, having learned his trade with his uncle Donald McKay of East Boston, and is now, 1878, foreman of the American Net and Twine Co. of East Cambridge, Mass.   They had:

    3736  *Donald Henry,*[8] b. Oct. 13, 1868; d. May 27, 1869.
    3737  *Lottie Elizabeth,*[8] b. March 24, 1869; d. May 14, 1876.
    3738  *Alice Emma,*[8] b. April 4, 1872; d. April 3, 1876.
    3739  *Ida May,*[8] b. Sept. 17, 1874.
    3740  *Lottie Alice,*[8] b. April 17, 1877.

3741 Lucretia McClure,[7] b. March 1, 1848; d. April 17, 1869.
3742 Margaret,[7] b. Nov. 30, 1850; d. Dec. 25, 1870.
3743 Annie,[7] b. Aug. 12, 1853; d. Jan. 19, 1868.
3744 Harriet Ellen,[7] b. Jan. 20, 1858; d. March 13, 1871.

## 2065

THOMAS FOSTER THURSTON [6] (*John,*[5] *John,*[4] *Joseph,*[3] *Joseph,*[2] *Daniel*[1]), son of John [5] and Sarah (Foster) Thurston of South Bristol, Me.; born there Sept. 21, 1822; married, at Monhegan Isle, Me., March 12, 1848, ALICE VOSE ALBEE, born in Thomaston, Me., Jan. 29, 1828, daughter of Rev. Samuel and Jane R. (Fales) Albee of Rockland, Me.

Mr. Thurston is a master mariner, member of the Episcopal church, and resides in Rockland.

Their children were:

3754   Flora,[7] b. May 17, 1849; d. June 14, 1849.
3755   Samuel Albee,[7] b. June 9, 1850; d. Sept. 10, 1850.
3756   Eliza Peirce,[7] b. March 7, 1854; a compositor.
3757   Edwin Alberti,[7] b. Dec. 11, 1856; is an artist aud photographer, residing in Pittsburgh, Pa., and a member of the Episcopal church.
3758   Russell,[7] b. Oct. 5, 1861; d. Oct. 29, 1863.
7359   Paulina Jane,[7] b. April 2, 1863; d. Aug. 4, 1864.

## 2094

SOLOMON THURSTON [6] (*Solomon,*[5] *Capt. John,*[4] *Joseph,*[3] *Joseph,*[2] *Daniel*[1]), eldest son of Solomon [5] and Sarah (Gott) Thurston of Camden, Me.; born in Deer Isle, Me., Oct. 6, 1811; married, first, Nov. 21, 1833, MARY ANNIS, born 1814, daughter of Simon and Mercy (Brimhall) Annis of North Haven, Me.; she died March 22, 1841. Second, April 6, 1843, CALISTA CALDERWOOD, born Oct. 11, 1816.

Mr. Thurston is a sea captain, residing in Camden.

His children, by first wife, Mary, were:

3765   Mercy,[7] b. Jan. 2, 1834; d. 1835.
3766   Mary Ann,[7] b. Dec. 25, 1836; m. Wm. Frye, a sea captain in Beverly, Mass.
3767   David B.,[7] b. Jan. 19, 1841; a sea captain; n.m.

By second wife, Calista:

3768   Roscoe,[7] b. Aug. 24, 1844; m. Dec. 11, 1865, Mary N. Philbrook, b. Oct. 21, 1846, daughter of James B. and Mary E. (Proale) Philbrook of Rockport, Me. He is captain of a schooner. July 5, 1877, he and two others, between Owls Head and Indian island, fastened to a sword fish with a harpoon, and the fish took the boat and all in it down instantly; neither could swim much, but he with difficulty cleared himself from one of the men who grasped him, and rose to the surface and saved himself by the help of two oars, while the others were drowned. They had:
3769   *Daniel E.,*[8] b. Jan. 1, 1868; d. Nov. 14, 1875.
3770   *Alden C.,*[8] b. March 30, 1872.
3771   *Georgia Eva,*[8] b. March 27, 1875.
3772   Almeda,[7] b. Nov. 20, 1845; d. Dec. 16, 1862.
3773   Susan C.,[7] b. April 18, 1847; m. Frank P. Webster of North Haven; reside in Camden.
3774   Daniel,[7] b. Oct. 30, 1848; m. Nov. 7, 1877, Mrs. Ella A. (Carver) Weatherspoon; a sea captain in Camden.
3775   Calista Jane,[7] b. Jan. 16, 1850; d. Jan. 7, 1863.
3776   Henry,[7] b. May 1, 1852; d. Feb. 17, 1856.

## 2141

CAPT. HENRY THURSTON [6] (*Capt. William,*[5] *William,*[4] *Joseph,*[3] *Joseph,*[2] *Daniel*[1]), son of Capt. William [5] and Polly (Tarr) Thurston of Gloucester, now Rockport, Mass.; born there Dec. 1, 1808; married, first, RHODA KINSMAN; she died May 11, 1845. Second, June 14, 1846, by Rev. J. S. Eaton, JANE PLUMMER, born Aug. 15, 1814,

13

daughter of Moses and Abigail (Smith) Plummer of Portland, Me. He died Feb. 9, 1860.

Capt. Thurston was an enterprising ship master, residing in Portland. He sailed from this port for more than thirty years, having the charge of a vessel at the age of nineteen. He traversed the ocean to foreign ports some portion of every year during that time. He was a skillful navigator, never having run his vessel ashore or carried away a spar or yard. He was endowed with the finest and warmest sensibilities; with a keen, penetrating eye he observed at a glance a deficiency in the character of his officers and crew; and with an indomitable resolution and courage, that governed and conquered and won for him their highest esteem. Few persons of his age have seen so much or so severe service. He never shrank from any duty; was brave, manly, courteous, open-hearted, and was highly esteemed for his sincerity and honesty. In the domestic relations he possessed those warm affections of the heart which adorn and beautify home. During the last year of his life he felt very sensibly that nothing but religion can fully satisfy the mind of man, and his heart was softened and his affections drawn to holy objects. While at Marseilles, France, Sept. 17, 1859, he was attacked by apoplexy; partially recovered, and as his wife and family were with him he set sail for New York on Oct. 24; had a second attack while in the Mediterranean, and some days later a third, from which he never recovered, though able to reach home. His widow is a woman of great energy of character, mentally and physically; and having no doubt been wronged in regard to some property left by her husband, has for several years past been infatuated with the idea that she was the owner of the United States and Great Britain, and has taken all the legal measures to gain possession, visiting the president at Washington and several governors of Maine and justices of the United States court, and has actually issued paper money, which she considers legal tender.

His children, by first wife, Rhoda, were:

3786  Henrietta Maria,[7] b. Aug. 28, 1836; d. Sept. 10, 1849.
3787  George Henry,[7] b. July 28, 1838.
3788  William Edward,[7] b. May 29, 1840; d. at sea Nov. 30, 1858.
3789  Charles Augustus,[7] b. March 15, 1842.

By second wife, Jane:

3790  Henrietta,[7] b. July 10, 1848; d. Sept. 28, 1870.
3791  Abbie Jane,[7] b. July 30, 1851; d. Feb. 5, 1862.
3792  Henry,[7] b. Nov. 20, 1854; d. Aug. 20, 1859.

## 2149

DANIEL THURSTON [6] (*Thomas,*[5] *Abner,*[4] *Abner,*[3] *James,*[2] *Daniel*[1]), eldest son of Thomas [5] and Lucy (Fenderson) Thurston of Scarborough, Me.; born there Oct. 17, 1776; married, 1800, SALLY MERRILL,* born July 18, 1778. He died Dec. 6, 1849; she died Dec. 6, 1852.

---

* Sally Merrill was a descendant of Charles Pine, who was an early settler of Scarborough, Me., and from whom "Pine Point" was named. Pine married Grace ——, and their daughter Mary married William Deering (son of Roger Deering), who killed her in a fit of passion. Pine's daughter Grace married, first, —— Runnels; second, —— Moulton. A child of theirs married Daniel Merrill, the father of Sally Merrill above. We subjoin an extract from Wm. S. Southgate's History of Scarborough, as found in Me. His. Soc. Col.:

The first settlers of Scarborough, after the evacuation of 1690, were a band of seven persons, who came from Lynn in a sloop. They anchored their little vessel in the bay at Black

Mr. Thurston was a teamster and farmer, and lived in Biddeford and Portland, Me., and last in Scarborough on the homestead. He was a worthy and industrious man, and member of the Free Baptist church in Scarborough. He served in the war of 1812.

### Children:

+3800    Daniel Merrill,[7] b. Oct. 31, 1801; m. Jane Tibbetts.
+3801    Lucy,[7] b. April 24, 1803; m. Nathaniel Googins.
+3802    Henry Rice,[7] b. May, 14, 1805; m. Mary Richards.
3803     Polly,[7] b. Nov. 10, 1807; n.m.; member of Free Baptist church; d. Nov. 20, 1872.
3804     Thomas,[7]     } twins, born { d. May, 1809.
3805     Hannah Merrill,[7] { Jan. 19, 1809; { a tailoress; m. Jan. 12, 1853, Jonathan Taylor, a farmer and stone cutter of Biddeford, Me., b. April 14, 1802. She died 1861; he died Dec. 25, 1874; no children.

## 2152

ALEXANDER THURSTON [6] (*Thomas,*[5] *Abner,*[4] *Abner,*[3] *James,*[2] *Daniel*[1]), brother of the preceding, and son of Thomas [6] and Lucy (Fenderson) Thurston of 'Scarborough, Me.; born there June 10, 1784; married, April 15, 1809, ALMIRA FICKETT of Gorham, Me., born Jan. 2, 1792.

---

Point, and used it as a shelter by night until they had put up a sufficient garrison on land. The names of these emigrants are known to us only by tradition, which is in this case entirely reliable. They were John Larrabee, Henry Libby and three sons, —— Pine,† and —— Blood. These resided on the Neck, in the garrison they had built, and were, at least for a,year, the only inhabitants of the town. . . . Pine Point received its name from Charles Pine, a famous hunter, whose residence was there. He was celebrated for very many brave exploits with the Indians. . . . During the eleven years of Queen Anne's war, the townsmen, or at least two of them, encountered parties of Indians, and usually came off unharmed. The two referred to were Charles Pine and Richard Hunniwell, who earned the epithet of "Indian Killer." Both of these were distinguished in their day as bitter enemies of the Indians, and often found occasion to show their hostility with terrible effect. One or two well authenticated traditions will serve to illustrate their peculiar mode of warfare and its consequences. At the time of the second settlement, an unfinished house, which had remained since the desertion of 1690, stood on Winnock's (Plummer's) Neck. This house became a sort of rendezvous for the Indians, where they would occasionally meet and amuse themselves with howling and dancing. One spring, soon after the return of the inhabitants, Mr. Pine discovered that the savages were holding in this shell a series of nightly "powwows," and at once he determined to improve the occasion for a trial of his skill as a marksman. It was his rule to hunt Indians without any companions but two guns, which he was wont to discharge, one immediately after the other, when he fired from a covert. Taking his two guns he went out alone from the garrison early one afternoon, paddled his boat up the Nonsuch till he came near the house, and then, having hid it near the bank of the river, went into the deserted dwelling, got up amongst the beams, and silently awaited the result of his adventure. Soon after dark he heard the expected Indian whistle in the woods around him, and peeping out he saw nearly a score of savages coming toward the place of his concealment, which was at least three miles from the garrison, where the nearest aid was, in case the Indians should attack him. Pine, however, was not easily frightened, and probably did not expect any more unfavorable result than that which happened. As the two foremost Indians were entering the doorway, he fired and killed them both, but before he could get ready his other gun, for a second discharge, the remaining savages were beyond danger from it. They did not even stop to see if their companions were killed. In an hour's time Pine was back in the garrison, examining the guns and ammunition of the victims. Such an occurrence was hardly out of the ordinary course of his life. But the anecdote of Pine, which used to be narrated with the greatest relish by the veterans of the past generation, is the following: The Indians were in the habit of showing themselves on the beach, between the Ferry and the Neck, and amusing themselves by insulting and provoking the garrison, with the aid of certain significant attitudes and gestures. Pine, with his wonted readiness for such employment, volunteered to put a stop to this recreation. Charging the garrison not to allow the Indians to cut off his retreat, he went out on the beach one morning before day, and covered himself with rockweed, near the usual scene of the Indians' sport. After waiting patiently until the morning was well advanced, the Indians at length appeared and began their sport. Presently an enormous fellow stepped out from the crowd that he might be fairly seen, and, turning his back toward the garrison, exposed a part of his huge body, which, in the words of Pine, "shone like a glass bottle." The hunter immediately sent his bullet to the precise spot indicated by the Indian's hand. The astounded savages seized their falling comrade and rushed headlong into the woods, while Pine walked leisurely back to the garrison, confident that there would be no more such exhibitions within sight of it.

† Mr. Southgate thinks that this was Charles Pine without doubt, but cannot prove it, who made the second settlement of Scarborough in 1702.

He died April 15, 1857; she died April 9, 1870.   He was a farmer in Poland, Me.

### Their children were:

3814  Sally Fickett,[7] b. Feb. 2, 1812; m. Jasper Haskell; lived in Poland and Auburn; d. Aug. 18, 1871.
3815  Lorenzo Swett,[7] b. Oct. 16, 1815; m. Sylvina ——.
+3816  George Fickett,[7] b. Aug. 13, 1817; m. 1st, Hannah Gorham Waterhouse; 2d, Betsey Reed Libby.
+3817  Edward McLellan,[7] b. Oct. 9, 1820; m. Flora Record.
3818  Martha Fickett,[7] b. Aug. 3, 1822; m. Philander Haines of Biddeford, Me.

## 2153

JAMES THURSTON[6] (*Thomas,[5] Abner,[4] Abner,[3] James,[2] Daniel[1]*), brother of the preceding, and son of Thomas[5] and Lucy (Fenderson) Thurston of Scarborough, Me.; born there Dec. 19, 1787; married, Sept. 4, 1808, by Rev. Asa Heath, SARAH McKENNEY, born Sept. 5, 1787.   She died Nov. 9, 1857; he died Oct. 3, 1860, aged 73.

Mr. Thurston lived in Buxton, Scarborough, Cape Elizabeth, and Danville, Me., and for more than fifty years was a member, and most of the time an officer, of the Methodist Episcopal church in Danville, now Auburn.

### Their children were:

3825  Lucy,[7] b. Jan. 20, 1810; m. June 7, 1835, William Peables McKenney. They had:
3826  *William A.* (McKenney), b. in Brunswick, Me., June 28, 1836; n.m.; d. in the army of the Potomac May 25, 1865.
3827  *Lucy Jane* (McKenney), b. in Brunswick Feb. 14, 1838; m. June 7, 1868, Albee C. May; live in Indianapolis, Ind.  They have:
3828   *Grace L.* (May), b. Aug. 10, 1874.
3829   *Gertrude* (May), b. July 21, 1876.
3830  *Annie Maria* (McKenney), m. Jan. 31, 1857, Albert Reed of Danville, Me.  They have:
3831   *Ida M.* (Reed), b. Aug. 18, 1862.
3832   *Helen* (Reed), b. Dec. 5, 1871.
3833  *Charles J.* (McKenney), b. in Brunswick Sept. 3, 1843; d. in the army of the Cumberland Oct. 5, 1863.
3834  *Clara E.* (McKenney), m. June 11, 1867, Billings P. Sibley of Manka-to, Minn., now, 1877, in Erie, Pa.  They have:
3835   *Hattie May* (Sibley), b. Dec. 8, 1868.
3836   *James Thurston* (Sibley), b. March 12, 1872.
3837   *Sadie* (Sibley), b. May 8, 1877.
3838  *Ida E.* (McKenney), b. in Portland, Me., June 18, 1853.
3839  *Sarah J.* (McKenney), b. in Danville Dec. 2, 1856.
+3840  Charles,[7] b. Jan. 20, 1812; m. Catherine Falkington.
+3841  Moses Waterhouse,[7] b. March 9, 1814; m. Eunice Hunnewell.
3842  James,[7] b. in Buxton, Me., March 12, 1816; m. Nov. 8, 1840, in Eastport, Me., Mrs. Clara Anna (Chase) Flint, daughter of William and Ruth (Lowell) Chase of Lubec, Me.  He was educated at the Maine Wesleyan seminary in Readfield, and became a minister of the Methodist Episcopal church in 1838 in the Maine conference; was presiding elder two terms in the New Hampshire conference, and in 1871, on account of poor health, became a " supernumerary," and resides in Dover, N. H., 1877.  No children.  Adopted:
3843  *Lucia Frances*, b. Nov. 21, 1856.
3844  Merabah Ann,[7] b. in Scarborough April 4, 1818; m. Dec. 8, 1841, Burton Fales of Thomaston, Me.; d. June 12, 1848.  They had:
3845  *Nathaniel* (Fales), b. 1843; lives in California.
3846  *Sarah Ozetta* (Fales), b. 1845; m. April 22, 1863, William H. Hardin of Rockland, Me., and moved to California.
3847  *Mary* (Fales), b. 1847; m., lived, and d. in Rockland.

3848 Everline,[7] b. Nov. 20, 1820; m. Aug. 28, 1844, William S. Marston, b. in North Yarmouth, Me., Aug. 14. 1814; resided in Adrian, Wis.; 1876 removed to Owatonna, Minn. They had:

    3849 *Kate* (Marston), b. in Danville June 29, 1845; m. June 19, 1868, Jacob Beag, and has:

        3850 *Florence A.* (Beag), b. in Owatonna June 25, 1869.
        3851 *Charles M.* (Beag), b. in Aurora, Minn.. Nov. 9, 1871.
        3852 *Jane G.* (Beag). b. in Aurora May 22, 1873.
    3853 *Cyrus Crafts* (Marston). b. in Danville Oct. 24, 1847; lives in Owatonna.
    3854 *Mary* (Marston), b. in Danville Dec. 12, 1849; m. Jan. 1, 1872, Geo. B. Hallock; reside, 1877, in Owatonna, and have:

        3855 *Ethelyn* (Hallock), b. in Aurora May 1, 1873.
    3856 *Evelyn* (Marston), b. in Danville July 12, 1852; m. June 30, 1874, Dennison J. Woodard, and has:

        3857 *Edith J.* (Woodard), b. in Adrian, Wis., May 8, 1875.
    3858 *Howard Abbott* (Marston), b. in Danville Dec. 24, 1854; lives in Aurora.
    3859 *Willie M.* (Marston), b. in Danville April 1, 1857; lives in Aurora.
    3860 *Dora F.* (Marston), b. in Garden City, Minn., June 18, 1861; resides, 1877, in Owatonna.

3861 Mary Edgecomb,[7] b. April 20, 1823; m. Dec. 30. 1851, Charles Robinson Whitney, b. Jan. 16. 1820, son of Haynes and Jane (Robinson) Whitney of Thomaston; he is a manufacturer of lime in Rockland. They have:

    3862 *Mary Frances* (Whitney), b. July 11, 1855; m. Nov. 6, 1875, Thomas S. Rich of Chelsea, Mass.

    3863 *Lizzie Ella* (Whitney), b. Dec. 19, 1856.
3864 Francis,[7] b. April 9, 1826; captain in the East India trade; d. at sea 1869.

## 2154

THOMAS THURSTON [6] of Readfield, Me. (*Thomas,*[5] *Abner,*[4] *Abner,*[3] *James,*[7] *Daniel*[1]), brother of the preceding, son of Thomas [5] and Lucy (Fenderson) Thurston of Scarborough, Me.; born there Feb. 23, 1790; married CLARISSA B. KIMBALL, born in Ipswich, Mass., daughter of Nathaniel and Sally (Stickney) Kimball of Winthrop, Me. He died March 28, 1851; she died July 21, 1871. He was a carpenter and farmer.

Their children were:

3870 Clorinda,[7] b. May 3, 1817; m. July 4, 1837, Simon Trueworthy, b. in Bucksport, Me., 1815; he was a seaman, residing in Thomaston, Me. They had, b. in Thomaston:

    3871 *Bernett Thurston* (Trueworthy), b. Nov. 16, 1837; enlisted in the war against the rebellion, in a Maine regiment, and served honorably to the close of the war; m. and resides in Washington, D. C.
    3872 *Orson Augustus* (Trueworthy), b. Nov. 16, 1839; m. in Auburn, Me.; d. in Washington, D. C., Sept. 27, 1865, leaving some property; two children.
    3873 *Albina Delia* (Trueworthy), b. in Readfield, Me., Dec. 22, 1842; m. in New York and is now a widow.
    3874 *Albert H.* (Trueworthy), b. in Thomaston Nov. 8, 1845; d. June, 1876.
    3875 *Lizzie Clarinda* (Trueworthy), b. in Thomaston, 1846; m. Jabez Barrett of Brookfield, Mass., where they now reside.
3876 Snell,[7] b. Oct. 10, 1819; m. Feb. 16, 1865, Anna C. Bacon, daughter of Jabez and Sally (Kimball) Bacon of Winthrop, Me. He is a farmer in Readfield; no children.
+3877 Hiram,[7] b. Oct. 1, 1820; m. Harriet Newell Hayward.
+3878 William Henry,[7] b. March 31, 1823; m. Sarah E. Waterhouse.

## 2156

WILLIAM THURSTON [6] (*Thomas,*[5] *Abner,*[4] *Abner,*[3] *James,*[2] *Daniel*[1]), brother of the preceding, and son of Thomas [5] and Lucy (Fenderson) Thurston of Scarborough, Me.; born there June 20, 1794; married,

Dec. 27, 1818, CATHERINE SIMONTON, born June 5, 1797, daughter of Ebenezer and Betsey (Maxfield) Simonton of Cape Elizabeth, Me. He died Aug. 27, 1869.

Mr. Thurston was a shoemaker in Portland, Me.; member of the Congregational church.

Their children were:

3883 Elizabeth Simonton,[7] b. March 23, 1820; m. Jan. 26, 1842, George S. Chandler of Nashua, N. H.; in business at 9 Pembroke street, Boston, 1878. They have:
    3884 *Charles Bradford* (Chandler), lives in Wilmington, Del.
    3885 *Luther Gross* (Chandler), M.D.; m. Dora Hurd; is resident physician at Deer island, Boston harbor.
    3886 *George Frank* (Chandler), n.m.; a photographer in Philadelphia, Pa.
    3887 *Lillian* (Chandler), n.m.; lives in Boston.
3888 Janette,[7] b. May 23, 1824; m. June 4, 1861, Edmund C. Merrill of Portland; d. Dec. 14, 1866. They had:
    3889 *Catherine Brabrook* (Merrill), residing at Alfred, Me.
3890 William Thomas,[7] b. May 17, 1827; n.m.; a ship carpenter in Portland.
3891 George Soule,[7] b. Feb. 4, 1831; n.m.
3892 Catherine Simonton,[7] b. June 30, 1834; m. in Dorchester, Mass., May 23, 1858, Albert A. Brabrook, a furniture dealer in Boston, residing in Somerville, Mass.; no children.
● 3893 Emily Abby,[7] b. Dec. 26, 1836; n.m.; resides in Somerville.

## 2178

ASA THURSTON [6] of Lyme, N. H. (*David,*[5] *Abner,*[4] *Abner,*[3] *James,*[2] *Daniel*[1]), eldest son of David [5] and Sally (Eaton) Thurston of Candia, N. H.; born in Bridgewater, N. H., Dec. 17, 1800; married, in Wentworth, N. H., July 22, 1840, ELIZA WOODWARD HARTWELL, born in Rumney, N. H., March 6, 1810, daughter of John and Louisa (Kimball) Hartwell of Haverhill, N. H. He died May 28, 1877.

Mr. Thurston was a merchant; representative in the legislature in 1863-4, town clerk twelve years, and a member of the Congregational church fifty-eight years.

Their children, all born in Warren, N. H., were:

3900 Ellen Eliza,[7] b. July 27, 1845; d. Aug. 12, 1845.
3901 Charles Edward,[7] b. Aug. 31, 1847; m. Sept. 27, 1873, in Concord, N. H., Minnie Ella Knox, b. Aug. 27, 1850, daughter of Crosby and Abbie (Carr) Knox of Pembroke, N. H. He is a clerk in a dry goods store in Concord, and is a member of the Congregational church.
3902 Ellen Louisa,[7] b. Jan. 26, 1849; m. Nov. 3, 1874, Leander D. Warren, and lives in Lyme, N. H. They have:
    3903 *Maude Louisa* (Warren), b. Feb. 20, 1876.
    3904 *Harry Hartwell* (Warren), b. Jan. 12, 1878.

## 2179

ABNER THURSTON [6] (*David,*[5] *Abner,*[4] *Abner,*[3] *James,*[2] *Daniel*[1]), brother of the preceding, and son of David [5] and Sally (Eaton) Thurston of Candia, N. H.; born in Bridgewater, N. H., Oct. 13, 1802; married in Charlestown, Mass., Feb. 3, 1828, MARY WORTHEN HUNTOON, born June 11, 1803, daughter of Elisha and Hannah (Worthen) Huntoon of Candia.

He was a cooper in Franklin, N. H., and belonged to the Christian denomination.

Their children, born in Charlestown, were:

+3913 David Benjamin,[7] b. July 24, 1829; m. Almira Yeaton Howard.
3914 Hannah Eliza,[7] b. March 1, 1831.

3915   Asa Josephus,[7] b. Dec. 13, 1833; is a butcher by trade, and was representative in the legislature from Franklin, N. H., 1876, 1877.
3916   Sarah Eaton,[7] b. July 13, 1836; m. in Concord, N. H., March 10, 1867, Frank Kendrick Jones; d. Oct. 11, 1872.
3917   Charlotte Rebecca,[7] b. in Hebron, N. H., May 17, 1844; d. in Franklin Dec. 16, 1848.

## 2180

EBENEZER THURSTON[6] (*David,[5] Abner,[4] Abner,[3] James,[2] Daniel[1]*), brother of the preceding, and son of David[5] and Sally (Eaton) Thurston of Candia, N. H.; born in Bridgewater, N. H., March 13, 1805; married, first, November, 1836, SARAH SALINA HUNTOON of Salisbury, N. H., born April 26, 1808; she died June 4, 1839. Second, Dec. 27, 1842, SARAH KNOWLES ROGERS, born March 24, 1815, daughter of Benjamin and Lucy (Hoagg) Rogers of Northfield, N. H.; she died April 8, 1866.

Mr. Thurston is a farmer in Northfield, but P. O. address is Tilton, N. H., on the farm where his last wife was born.

His children, by second wife, were:

3927   Lena Lucy,[7] b. in Hill, N. H., March 24, 1849; m. Sept. 29, 1877, Joseph James Prescott, a farmer in Northfield, P. O. address Tilton, b. in Pittsfield, N. H., Nov. 24, 1853, son of Ebenezer J., and Ruhama (Mason) Prescott of Loudon, N. H.
3928   Leanna Marr,[7] b. in Tilton July 8, 1853.

## 2181

SALLY THURSTON[6] (*David,[5] Abner,[4] Abner,[3] James,[2] Daniel[1]*), sister of the preceding, and daughter of David[5] and Sally (Eaton) Thurston of Candia, N. H.; born in Bridgewater, N. H., Sept. 13, 1807; married in Hill, N. H., Dec. 5, 1830, JOHN LANGFORD HODGDON, born Dec. 19, 1805, son of Israel and Comfort (Sandborn) Hodgdon of Northfield, N. H. He died Aug. 8, 1874. He was a farmer in Ashland, N. H., and member of the Methodist church.

Their children were:

3930   Hiram (Hodgdon), b. in Ashland Oct. 21, 1832; m. June 10, 1858, Martha Thurston Webster of Dunville, N. H.; a merchant in Ashland; no children.
3931   George Morey (Hodgdon), b. Aug. 13, 1835; m. Sept. 15, 1857, Pamelia A. Plaisted, b. Jan. 20, 1838, daughter of B. Eaton and Nancy Barker (Merrill) Plaisted of Ashland. They have:
3932     *Charlie Merrill* (Hodgdon), b. Oct. 24, 1860.
3933   Sarah Eaton (Hodgdon), b. in Northfield Oct. 27, 1838.

## 2182

LYDIA THURSTON[6] (*David,[5] Abner,[4] Abner,[3] James,[2] Daniel[1]*), sister of the preceding, and daughter of David[5] and Sally (Eaton) Thurston of Candia, N. H.; born in Hill, N. H., July 28, 1810; married, first, April 27, 1834, GEORGE M. PHELPS, born Jan. 27, 1788, a lawyer, who was several times representative in the New Hampshire legislature; he died in Hill Aug. 27, 1845. Second, Aug. 8, 1850, HILLERY KNOX, a farmer of Sanbornton, N. H., born in Pembroke, N. H., Feb. 17, 1798; he died June 6, 1876.

Her children, by first husband, Phelps, were:

3940   Edward Douglass (Phelps), b. in Hill Aug. 19, 1837.

By second husband, Knox:

3941   George Peabody (Knox), b. in Sanbornton Sept. 7, 1851; d. Aug. 28, 1863.

## 2200

Rev. James Thurston [6] (*Rev. James,*[5] *Capt. James,*[4] *Abner,*[3] *James,*[2] *Daniel*[1]), eldest son of Rev. James [5] and Elizabeth (Peabody) Thurston of Exeter, N. H.; born in Newmarket, N. H., Dec. 11, 1806; married, Sept. 11, 1844, Elizabeth Austin, daughter of Hon. William and Charlotte (Williams) Austin of Charlestown, Mass.   He died Jan. 13, 1872, aged 66.

Mr. Thurston fitted for college at Phillips academy, Exeter, and graduated at Harvard 1829.   He taught three years in the English high school in Boston, and graduated at the Divinity school at Cambridge in 1835.   He went west one year, and returned and was ordained over the Unitarian society in Windsor, Vt., in 1838.   In 1844 he took charge of the first Congregational society in Billerica, Mass., and remained six years; in South Natick two years.   In 1853 he was installed over the Allen street church in Cambridge, Mass., and resigned the following year.   From 1855 he was stated supply in Lunenburgh, Mass., till 1859, after which he was two years at Leicester, Mass.   The state of his health unfitting him for ministerial duties, he became agent of the Massachusetts Temperance Society.

After the war of the rebellion, he was sent by the Memorial Society to Wilmington, N. C., and for some months took charge of a school for freedmen.   At a meeting of the Historical Society held at Boston Sept. 4, 1867, he read a paper on the condition of the south since the war of the rebellion, giving his own experience of seven months in Virginia, North and South Carolina.   The last eight years of his life he spent in West Newton, Mass.   At his funeral eight classmates walked in front of the coffin, as it was taken to the church, among them Rev. Samuel F. Smith, Rev. James Freeman Clarke, and Samuel May, jr.   The entire population were sincere mourners, as he had endeared himself to all by his upright life, steadfast friendship, and amiable disposition.

Their children, born in Billerica, were:

3950   James Peabody,[7] b. March 8, 1847.
3951   William Austin,[7] b. July 9, 1848.
3952   Elizabeth Peabody,[7] b. Jan. 10, 1850.

Born in Natick, Mass.:

3953   Charles Abbot,[7] b. June 25, 1851; is in the storage business, Union wharf, Boston.

Born in Cambridge, Mass.:

3954   Charlotte Williams,[7] b. Feb. 7, 1854.

## 2249

Daniel Adams Thurston [6] (*Trueworthy,*[5] *Caleb,*[4] *Abner,*[3] *James,*[2] *Daniel*[1]), son of Trueworthy [5] and Priscilla (Royal) Thurston of Peru, Me.; born in Monmouth, Me., July 16, 1808; married, December, 1832, Olive Bray, daughter of Benjamin and Susannah (Royal) Bray of Poland, Me.   She died April 10, 1875.

Mr. Thurston is a farmer in Poland.   In 1842 he drove an ox team from Hannibal, Mo., to Oregon, being gone two years.

Their children were:

3960   Levi Moody,[7] b. June 7, 1834; d.
3961   Susanna B.,[7] b. June 22, 1836; m. March 16, 1874, Almon Andrews; no children.

3962   Gilman,[7] b. Oct. 29, 1838; m. Jan. 23, 1863, Miriam Marble.   They have :
   3963   *Frederick William*,[8] b. May 17, 1864.
   3964   *Edwin Aldo*,[8] b. Feb. 17, 1867.
   3965   *Rose*,[8] b. Dec. 29, 1870.
   3966   *Lydia Maybelle*,[8] b. July 5, 1874.

## 2252

SAMUEL ROYAL THURSTON [6] (*Trueworthy*,[5] *Caleb*,[4] *Abner*,[3] *James*,[2] *Daniel* [1]), brother of the preceding, and son of Trueworthy [5] and Priscilla (Royal) Thurston of Peru, Me. ; born in Monmouth, Me., April 17, 1816 ; married, July, 1844, ELIZABETH McLENCH, daughter of John McLench of Fayette, Me.   He died April 9, 1851.

Mr. Thurston was with his father in Peru on the farm till seventeen years of age, when an injury changed his plans for life.   He fitted for college at the Maine Wesleyan seminary, Readfield, Me. ; entered Dartmouth college in the Freshman class, and in 1840 left there and entered Bowdoin as a Sophomore, and graduated in 1843.   He read law with Hon. P. Dunlap of Brunswick, Me., and practiced there till 1845, when he went to Burlington, then the territory of Iowa, and practiced law and edited the Iowa Gazette, a leading democratic paper.   The climate did not agree with him, and in the spring of 1847 he bought a team of five yokes of oxen, two cows, and a horse, took his wife and child three months old in a wagon, and with goad in hand drove that team two thousand four hundred miles, arriving in Salem, in the valley of the Willamette river, Oregon, Sept. 12, 1847. He established himself in the practice of law ; was elected the first representative to congress, from the territory of Oregon, in June, 1849, and on the 4th of August started for Washington, D. C., in a boat propelled by Indians on the Columbia river, and arrived in San Francisco on the 18th ; left San Francisco Oct. 1st, Panama 25th, and Chagres 29th, in the steamship Empire City, bound to New York, where he arrived Nov. 11th.   He paid a flying visit to his relatives in Maine, and arrived in Washington on the last day of November. His course in congress was marked by fidelity to his adopted state and the country and with honor to himself.   He died April 9, 1851, on board the steamer California, on his way home, and was buried in Acapulco, Mexico.   His remains were subsequently removed to Salem, Oregon, and honored with a monument to his memory by the state.

He was in all relations ambitious, resolute, and determined, fond of debate and vigorous in defense of his points.   His 4th of July address of 1849 will be long remembered by those who heard it.   He was kind to his friends and magnanimous to all ; a sincere christian, humble and earnest in the prayer-meeting as he was bold and defiant in debate.   He made his way by hard and faithful work, attained success, and left an honored memory.

His widow has since married the Hon. William H. Odell, who was one of the presidential electors of 1876.

### His children were :

3970   George Henry,[7] b. in Burlington, Iowa, Dec. 2, 1846.
3971   Elizabeth Blandena,[7] b. in Salem, Oregon, 1849.

## 2253

TRUE WORTHY THURSTON[6] (*Trueworthy,*[5] *Caleb,*[4] *Abner,*[3] *James,*[2] *Daniel*[1]), brother of the preceding, and son of Trueworthy[5] and Priscilla (Royal) Thurston of Peru, Me. ; born in Monmouth, Me., April 15, 1819 ; married, March 4, 1846, RACHEL FISHER WELCH, born Sept. 3, 1823, daughter of Robert and Lois (Titus) Welch of Monmouth. He is a farmer in Rumford, Me.

### Their children, all born in Peru, are:

3975　Samuel Royal,[7] b. July 2, 1847 ; m. Jan. 2, 1871, Carrie A. Whitmarsh of Boston, Mass. ; reside in Chicago, Ill. ; he is traveling salesman for a safe and lock company of Chicago. They have :

　　3976　*Samuel Royal,*[8] b. March 12, 1875.

3977　William Henry,[7] b. Dec. 12, 1848 ; m. July 23, 1871, Salome F. Glover of Rumford, where they reside. He is a farmer; lost his right hand in a hay cutter Nov. 12, 1865. They had :

　　3978　*Willie Howard,*[8] b. Feb. 7, 1872 ; d. Dec. 28, 1874.
　　3979　*Ethel May,*[8] b. Nov. 23, 1875.
　　3980　*George Henry,*[8] b. Jan. 30, 1878.

3981　Granville True,[7] b. Oct. 13, 1850 ; m. Dec. 4, 1875, Ada E. Lufkin of Rumford, where they reside; he is a farmer. They have :

　　3982　*Carl Granville,*[8] b. June 23, 1877.

3983　Robert Lamont,[7] b. Feb. 28, 1852 ; m. April 13, 1879, Anna O'Conner of Chicago, Ill. ; is teaming in Chicago.

3984　Lydia May,[7] b. May 24, 1854 ; m. July 17, 1875, John E. Goggin of Lewiston, Me. ; he is a blacksmith in Livermore, Me. They have :

　　3985　*Bertha Lois* (Goggin), b. May 8, 1877.
　　3986　*Everett Lamont* (Goggin), b. April 26, 1879.

3987　Lizzie Odell,[7] b. Jan. 1, 1857.
3988　Daniel Adams,[7] b. Dec. 16, 1859.
3989　Franklin Marston,[7] b. Jan. 7, 1861.

## 2294

HENRY THURSTON[6] (*Gates,*[5] *Peter,*[4] *Abner,*[3] *James,*[2] *Daniel*[1]), son of Gates[5] and Elizabeth (Pollard) Thurston of Lancaster, Mass. ; born there Aug. 19, 1790 ; married, July 17, 1815, AURELIA WARREN, born in Amenia, Dutchess county, N. Y., April 12, 1794. Her father, James Warren, purchased a large tract of land near Lake George, N. Y., and removed to it in 1804. He died in early life, and his friends, in respect to him, gave the name of Warrensburgh to the place of his residence and of Warren to the county. Mr. Thurston died at Lancaster, while on a visit there, Sept. 30, 1842 ; his widow died at Troy, N. Y., Jan. 26, 1847. Previous to his marriage he resided in western New York, but after that was a farmer at Harlem, Winnebago county, Ill.

### Their children were:

3990　Sarah Maria,[7] b. at Warrensburgh May 2, 1818 ; m. at Harlem July 6, 1840, Henry George Raleigh Dearborn, b. in Salem, Mass., June 22, 1809, eldest son of Gen. H. A. S. Dearborn of Roxbury, Mass. He is a civil engineer, residing in Boston, Roxbury district, Mass. They had :

　　3991　*Henry* (Dearborn), b. Oct. 12, 1841 ; d. Sept. 5, 1842.
　　3992　*Sarah Ellen* (Dearborn), b. March 2, 1847.

### Born at Lake George:

3993　Elizabeth Melinda,[7] b. Feb. 16, 1821 ; m. June 28, 1855, Stephen Clary, b. in Montgomery county, N. Y., Sept. 25, 1814; she died April 20, 1879; he is a prominent commission merchant in Chicago; president of the Chicago Board of Trade; no children.

+3994　John Henry,[7] b. March 8, 1824 ; m. Mary Ann Barrett.

3995 William Peirce,[7] b. at Troy, N. Y., Sept. 19, 1828; m. Jan. 21, 1857, Elizabeth Harris Hooper, b. Nov. 12, 1832, daughter of Henry N. Hooper of Boston. He died Aug. 15, 1872; his widow resides in Beverly, Mass. They had :

3996 *Margaret Aurelia*,[8] b. Feb. 10, 1859.
3997 *Agnes Greenwood*,[8] b. March 4, 1860.

## 2295

JOHN GATES THURSTON [6] (*Gates,*[5] *Peter,*[4] *Abner,*[3] *James,*[2] *Daniel*[1]), brother of the preceding, and son of Gates [5] and Elizabeth (Pollard) Thurston of South Lancaster, Mass.; born there March 18, 1794; married, June 5, 1828, HARRIET PATRICK LEE, daughter of Seth Lee, a lawyer of Barre, Mass. He died March 27, 1873; she died March 6, 1878.

Mr. Thurston spent nearly all his life in his native town, though he had traveled extensively in the United States, and visited Europe in 1869. He was in Italy during Louis Napoleon's Franco-Austrian campaign, and visited the battle field of Magenta shortly after the battle; after which he accompanied a portion of the French army to Milan, the soldiers treating him and his companion (Edward A. Raymond of Boston) with great courtesy, and carrying their valises for them. He was so exhausted by the tramp that Raymond said he slept forty hours. He held many positions of public trust and responsibility; was an "old line whig" and an earnest politician; sat many terms in the legislature (both houses); was town clerk for fifteen consecutive years; bank director for many years. He was in mercantile life for more than forty years. They celebrated their silver wedding in 1853, at the same time as the celebration of the bicentennial anniversary of the incorporation of the town of Lancaster.

Children :

4000 Harriet Elizabeth,[7] b. March 31, 1829; m. Harry Peck.
+4001 George Lee,[7] b. June 16, 1831; m. Mary Baldwin Whitney.
4002 Josephene,[7] b. Sept. 9, 1832; d. Oct. 15, 1832.
4003 Francis Henry,[7] b. Dec. 21, 1833; m. in Paxton, Ill., March 4, 1863, Elizabeth Amelia Crandall, b. in Cambria, Niagara county, N. Y., Oct. 1, 1836, daughter of David Sprague, formerly editor of Niagara Courier, and Eliza (McBride) Crandall, of Lockport, N. Y. Mr. Thurston has been a merchant many years, residing in Oconto, Wis., and other places, but a trouble with his eyes has caused varied changes in his life. He has now, May, 1879, purchased a farm at Central Lake, Antrim county, Mich., where he intends to locate permanently, as he prefers that for an occupation.

## 2299

WILLIAM THURSTON [6] (*Gates,*[5] *Peter,*[4] *Abner,*[3] *James,*[2] *Daniel*[1]), brother of the preceding, and son of Gates [5] and Elizabeth (Pollard) Thurston of South Lancaster, Mass.; born there March 6, 1798; married, first, June 9, 1824, SABRA HOUGHTON of Bolton, Mass.; second, MARY MOFFAT of Vanderburgh county, Ind.; third, MRS. SARAH CARPENTER of Princeton, Ind.; fourth, JANE L. THOMAS of Luzerne county, Pa.; fifth, MRS. ISABEL M. BANNAN of Luzerne county.

Mr. Thurston lived in Scott township, Vanderburgh county, Ind.; built and kept a hotel on the state road from Evansville to Vincennes, and owned a large farm.

His children, by first wife, Sabra, were:

4010 Mary Greenleaf,[7] b. Nov. 19, 1824; m. June 15, 1844, Moses Barnes. They had:

    4011 *Sabra Elizabeth* (Barnes), b. June 29, 1845; m. Nov. 2, 1862, Frank Green; d. Jan. 24, 1872. They had:
        4012 *Moses* (Green), b. Dec. 29, 1864.
        4013 *Lottie M.* (Green), b. Sept., 1866.
        4014 *Frank H.* (Green), b. Nov. 2, 1871; d. July 8, 1872.
    4015 *Sarah Isabel* (Barnes), b. June 7, 1847; m. March 27, 1864, John Barton. They had:
        4016 *William J.* (Barton), b. Dec. 29, 1864.
        4017 *Ranie E.* (Barton), b. Aug. 2, 1868.
        4018 *Sabra A.* (Barton), b. Sept. 9, 1872.
        4019 *Herbert A.* (Barton), b. April 15, 1874.
        4020 *Ira M.* (Barton), } twins, b. April 5, 1876.
        4021 *Ida M.* (Barton), }
    4022 *William Edwin* (Barnes), b. Dec. 27, 1849.
    4023 *Clara Susanna* (Barnes), b. Oct. 13, 1851; m. Oct. 26, 1871, John Wheeler. They had:
        4024 *Mary A.* (Wheeler), b. March 26, 1873.
        4025 *Lucy B.* (Wheeler), b. Sept. 4, 1874; d. Feb. 14, 1875.
        4026 *Frank H.* (Wheeler), b. Aug. 20, 1878.
    4027 *Herbert Brinsley* (Barnes), b. June 20, 1854; m. Oct. 16, 1877, Alice M. Grant.
    4028 *Mary Ellen* (Barnes), b. Jan. 29, 1856.
    4029 *Eunice Jane* (Barnes), b. May 4, 1858.
    4030 *Charles Rufus* (Barnes), b. April 18, 1861.
    4031 *Ruth Christina* (Barnes), b. June 30, 1863.
    4032 *Louis M.* (Barnes), b. Sept. 14, 1869.
4033 Eliza Blackman,[7] b. Sept. 10, 1825; d. May 13, 1828.
4034 William Gates,[7] b. May 19, 1830; d. May 23, 1830.

By second wife, Mary:

4035 John Henry,[7] b. July, 1853; m. 1874, and had:
    4036 *Eva.*[8]

By third wife, Sarah:

4037 Emma,[7] b. Dec., 1855; m. about 1873 Charles Schmall of Princeton, Ind. They had:
    4038 *Lizzie* (Schmall).
    4039 *Annie* (Schmall).
    4040 *Augustus* (Schmall).

## 2302

WILDER STODDARD THURSTON[6] (*Gates,*[5] *Peter,*[4] *Abner,*[3] *James,*[2] *Daniel*[1]), brother of the preceding, and son of Gates[5] and Elizabeth (Pollard) Thurston of South Lancaster, Mass.; born there Oct. 8, 1806; married, Oct. 27, 1836, ROSANNA MILISCENT PEIRCE, born 1817, daughter of Jacob Peirce, a farmer of Woburn, Mass.

Mr. Thurston was baptized by the name of Sampson Wilder Thurston, named for the somewhat noted Sampson Vining Stoddard Wilder, who was once a resident of Bolton, Mass. The name was afterward changed to its present form by act of legislature. He was a merchant in Boston from 1825 for fifteen years, when he returned to Lancaster, 1840; moved to Lynn, Mass., 1857, and continued his mercantile life till 1872, when, having become largely interested in real estate, he retired from mercantile life. He was a man of influence in his native place, having been selectman, postmaster, and justice of the peace. From 1845 to 1855 he took a deep interest in political matters connected with the "American" party. He was nominated for congress by them, and was a member of their state and national conventions.

Their children were:

4050 Clara Wilder,[7] b. in Boston June 19, 1838; was educated for a teacher, graduating at the State Normal school in Framingham, Mass.; m. in Lynn Oct. 30, 1862, to Thomas E. Frye of Bolton. They lived for three years in Brooklyn, N. Y., and then removed to Chicago, Ill., where they still reside, 1878, and where they were completely stripped of all their household possessions by the great fire of Oct. 8–9, 1871. They have:

  4051 *Thomas Wilder* (Frye), b. in New York city Sept. 25, 1863.

Born in Lancaster:

4052 Russell Gates,[7] b. May 29, 1840; d. April 17, 1841.
4053 Louise Meliscent,[7] b. Sept. 19, 1842; is assistant in one of the Boston High schools.
4054 Ellen Elizabeth,[7] b. March 31, 1845; went to Chicago with her sister, Mrs. Frye, in 1865, and was employed as cashier and corresponding secretary in the music store of Root & Cady; m. in Lynn Aug. 27, 1868, Myron Leonard of Middletown, Vt.; reside in Chicago, 1878. They had:

  4055 *Frederick Thurston* (Leonard), b. June 26, 1869; d. Sept. 16, 1869.
  4056 *Elsie* (Leonard), b. Aug. 16, 1872.
  4057 *Earnest Wilder* (Leonard), b. May 3, 1874; d. Aug., 1874.
  4058 *Lois Russell* (Leonard), b. Nov. 11, 1875; d. Dec. 22, 1875.

All three of the daughters have been somewhat given to writing for various publications, mostly juvenile, and the two older have published some books for children. It was an amusing coincidence that the two having written, unknown to each other, the one in Chicago, the other in Lynn, story books in answer to an offer of three prizes for suitable Sunday-school books, by the American Unitarian Association, two of the prizes fell to them. Their names and residences being different, the awarders had little suspicion that two prizes went to the same family.

## 2345

JOHN SPAULDING THURSTON[6] (*Moses,[5] Moses,[4] Moses,[3] Stephen,[2] Daniel[1]*), eldest son of Moses[5] and Jane (Spaulding) Thurston of Orange, Vt.; married JOANNA THURSTON, born Nov. 10, 1771. He died 1850; she died Sept. 9, 1862, aged 90 years, 11 months.

Mr. Thurston was a farmer in Orange.

Their children were:

4065 Sally,[7] m. Nathan Knapp of Bradford, Vt. They had:
  4066 *John B.* (Knapp).
  4067 *Orrin C.* (Knapp), killed in the battle of Williamsburgh.
4068 John,[7] b. Oct. 1, 1801; m. in Plattsburgh, N. Y., Dec. 6, 1829, Sally Parkhurst, b. May 3, 1810, daughter of Reuben and Lydia (Powell) Parkhurst of Highgate, Vt. He is a farmer in Pottsdam, N. Y., where he went in March, 1830; no children.
4069 Eliza,[7] m. Robert Ford; reside in Corinth, Vt.; had three daughters; all d.
4070 Hiram,[7] m. Dec. 8, 1829, Jane Works; was a carpenter in Canton, N. Y., where he died, May 14, 1833. They had:
  4071 *Lucy J.,*[8] m. —— Marston of Fillmore, Minn.
4072 Ezekiel,[7] b. May 16, 1808; n.m.; a ship carpenter; d. in Pottsdam Nov. 17, 1862.
4073 Huldah,[7] b. in Plattsburgh Feb. 18, 1813; m. 1st, Joseph Colby; 2d, Dea. Benson Aldrich. He died Oct. 5, 1862; she died Nov. 1, 1877. She had, by first husband:
  4074 *Huldah* (Colby), b. in Washington, Vt., May 5, 1846; m. Hiram Richardson Thurston [see no. ].
  4075 *Joseph Benson* (Colby), lives in California.
  4076 *Louise Caroline* (Colby), m. —— Leavitt; live in Bradford, Vt.
4077 Moses,[7] m.; no children.

## 2346

JANE THURSTON[6] (*Moses,[5] Moses,[4] Moses,[3] Stephen,[2] Daniel[1]*), sister of the preceding, and daughter of Moses[5] and Jane (Spaulding) Thurston of Orange, Vt.; married —— HURD.

Child:

+4078 Andrew,[7] b. Oct. 18, 1804; m. Lovina Richardson.

## 2348

EZEKIEL THURSTON [6] (*Moses*,[5] *Moses*,[4] *Moses*,[3] *Stephen*,[2] *Daniel*[1]), brother of the preceding, and son of Moses [5] and Jane (Spaulding) Thurston of Orange, Vt.; born there Feb. 11, 1785; married, 1807, SALLY DARLING, born Nov. 2, 1792, daughter of Peter and Rebecca (Burbank) Darling of Corinth, Vt. He died Feb. 19, 1851. She married again, Samuel Darling; he died March 10, 1856, and she died in Groton, Vt., Oct. 8, 1866. Mr. Thurston was a farmer in Orange and a member of the Christian church.

Their children were:

4080 Joseph,[7] b. Oct. 10, 1808; d. in Orange 1844.
4081 Elizabeth,[7] b. April 23, 1811; d. in Orange Feb. 15, 1827.
4082 Betsey,[7] b. May 15, 1813; d. in Orange July, 1832.
4083 Moses,[7] b. April 4, 1815; enlisted in a New York regiment against the rebellion, and died Sept. 7, 1874, in Massachusetts.
4084 Sarah,[7] b. July 4, 1817; d. in Orange Sept., 1836.
4085 Lucetta,[7] b. July 27, 1820; m. Hiram Richardson; live in Rockford, Ill.
4086 Peter,[7] b. May 4, 1822.
4087 Rebecca,[7] b. June 19, 1824; m. May 26, 1841, Jeremy Paul Welch, b. Oct. 30, 1817, son of Forriss and Huldah (Paul) Welch of Orange; he is a farmer in Groton, Vt. They have:
    4088 *Joanna Elizabeth* (Welch), b. Feb. 2, 1842; m. Lewis Dimick of Lyme, N. H.
    4089 *Lucetta Abigail* (Welch), b. Apr. 29, 1844; m. Joab Hunt of Peacham, Vt.
    4090 *George Gilman* (Welch), b. Sept. 22, 1846; resides in Helena, Montana.
    4091 *James Monroe* (Welch), b. July 12, 1849; resides in Groton, Vt.
    4092 *Elsie Alvira* (Welch), b. March 11, 1852; m. Frank Davis of Groton.
    4093 *Rebecca Jane* (Welch), b. June 14, 1854; m. Sidney Cameron of Wells River, Vt.
4094 Anna,[7] b. April 15, 1827; d. in Groton July 25, 1857.

## 2349

MOSES THURSTON [6] (*Moses*,[5] *Moses*,[4] *Moses*,[3] *Stephen*,[2] *Daniel*[1]), brother of the preceding, and son of Moses [5] and Jane (Spaulding) Thurston of Orange, Vt.; born at Indian Stream, now Pittsburgh, N. H.; married BETSEY LOVERING, daughter of Simeon and Sarah (Sanborn) Lovering of West Corinth, Vt. He died Jan. 27, 1815, and she married Samuel Clifford of Duxbury, Vt., and died Jan. 24, 1844.

Mr. Thurston was a carpenter in Corinth, Vt., and was killed by being run over by a sled loaded with wood; was a member of the Free Baptist church.

Their children were:

4100 Simeon Lovering,[7] b. Aug. 3, 1804; m. 1st, Fandira Richardson; she died without issue; 2d, Sept. 20, 1854, Luvia Foster. He was a farmer in Washington, Vt.; d. Nov. 13, 1867, leaving:
    4101 *Foster Simeon*,[8] b. Sept. 27, 1855.
+4102 Moses,[7] b. Oct. 16, 1806; m. Julia Richmond.
4103 Sarah Frost,[7] b. April 25, 1808; m Capt. John Locke, b. Oct. 21, 1799, a farmer in Chelsea, Vt.; she died March 4, 1864. He is still living, 1878. They had:
    Born in Corinth:
    4104 *Lucy Maria* (Locke), b. Nov. 11, 1824.
    4105 *Nancy* (Locke), b. Feb. 27, 1827; m. Levi Grant of Washington, Vt.
    4106 *John Lovering* (Locke), b. Feb. 19, 1829; a farmer in Hatton, Kansas.
    4107 *Susan Collins* (Locke), b. April 19, 1831; m. Alpheus Heminway of Worcester, Mass.

4108   *Charles Collins* (Locke), b. Nov. 26, 1832; d. Sept. 25, 1835.
4109   *Dewit Clinton* (Locke), b. Dec. 26, 1834; a farmer in Hatton.
4110   *Charles Collins* (Locke), b. Jan. 11, 1837; a farmer in Chelsea.
4111   *Victoria Richardson* (Locke), b. Feb. 18, 1839; d. Dec. 18, 1870.
4112   *Eliot S.* (Locke), b. Jan. 3, 1841; a farmer in Hatton.
4113   *Hannah Merrill* (Locke), b. Oct. 21, 1842; m. Augustus E. Carr of Worcester.
4114   *Carrie* (Locke), b. July 18, 1844; m. James P. Richardson of West Medfield, Mass.
4115   *Sarah Julia* (Locke), b. Feb. 12, 1846; d.

Born in Chelsea:
4116   *Diantha Dickey* (Locke), b. April 10, 1848; d.
4117   *George Eugene* (Locke), b. Dec. 30, 1849; studying medicine in Montpelier, Vt.
4118   *Henry Eustace* (Locke), b. Dec. 22, 1851; d. Oct. 14, 1876.
4119   Mary Lovering,[7] b. Dec. 15, 1810; n.m.; d. July 20, 1841, in Chelsea.
4120   Huldah Spaulding,[7] b. Sept. 1, 1812; m. 1st, Dec. 7, 1829, Elijah Sabin Clark, a farmer in Landaff, N. H.; he died in Groton, Vt., May 16, 1852, aged 51 y. 9 m. 16 d.  2d, Feb. 1, 1855, Charles Huntoon Burnham, b. in Corinth Oct. 8, 1808, son of Josiah and Ruth (Huntoon) Burnham of Chelsea; he was a farmer and postmaster in Corinth.  She had, by first husband :
4121   *Jane Hibbard* (Clark), b. in Landaff May 12, 1830; m. Oct. 8, 1847, Rev. Joseph Warren Healey, D.D., graduate of Burlington, Vt.; preached in Walpole, Mass., Milwaukee, Wis., Chicago, Ill., New Orleans, La.; was two years in England as agent of the Freedmens' Mission, went to the Holy Land, and after returning preached in Iowa City, Iowa, and 1878 in Ottumwa, Kansas.
4122   *John* (Clark), b. July 25, 1831; dealer in agricultural implements in Keota, Iowa.
4123   *Meroa Kimball* (Clark), b. Oct. 7, 1833; m. M. Renfrew; reside in Groton.
4124   *Charles Lovering* (Clark), b. April 14, 1835; d. in Grinnell, Iowa, Mar. 10, 1858.
4125   *Hallis Sampson* (Clark), b. March 8, 1838; a Congregational clergyman at Genoa Bluffs, Iowa, where he d. May 26, 1873; no children.

Born in Groton:
4126   *Emma Maria* (Clark), b. Feb. 12, 1845; m. Amasa M. Converse of Springfield, Ill.  They have traveled in Italy, France, England, Germany, Palestine, and 1878 are in Oakland, Cal.
4127   *Henry Healy* (Clark), b. Aug. 14, 1846; lives in Somerville, Mass.; n.m.
4128   Hannah Lomantha,[7] b. Oct. 25, 1814; m. Sept. 24, 1835, Calvin Merrill, a farmer of East Haverhill, N. H., b. Nov. 21, 1812, son of Benjamin and Mary (Hyde) Merrill of Corinth; he has held several town offices. They have :
4129   *Julia Carpenter* (Merrill), b. Oct. 25, 1836; m. Nathan Hanson.
4130   *Fannie Thurston* (Merrill), b. Feb. 19, 1840; m. Alonzo Wasson Smith.
4131   *Simeon Thurston* (Merrill), b. June 14, 1845; m. Mary Lovina Richardson.
4132   *Lucia Mehitable* (Merrill), b. May 13, 1849; m. John Wesley Fitts.
4133   *Flora Maria* (Merrill), b. June 16, 1851; m. Frank Peaslee Cutting.

## 2350

SAMPSON THURSTON [6] (*Moses,*[5] *Moses,*[4] *Moses,*[3] *Stephen,*[2] *Daniel*[1]), brother of the preceding, and son of Moses [5] and Jane (Spaulding) Thurston of Orange, Vt. ; born there April, 1789 ; married HANNAH PAYNE, born Aug. 12, 1790.  They both died in Avon, Me., she Nov. 6, 1858, and he Dec. 14, 1860.

Mr. Thurston was a farmer and mechanic in Washington, Vt. ; moved to Danville, Vt., and from there to Indian Stream, now Pittsburgh, Coos county, in northern New Hampshire, and then to Avon,

Me., in 1835.  The wolves were very numerous and troublesome at
Indian Stream, killing many sheep and frightening the people.  As he
and his wife were coming home from a visit to a neighbor's one evening, on an ox sled, he made a noise like a wolf and a whole pack
came running after them into the very door-yard.  Moose and deer
were plenty there in those days.  He came very near being drowned
twice in Lake Champlain, by breaking through the ice, once when
walking, and once with a two horse team and his wife.  He was in
the war of 1812, a very brave and efficient soldier; was a member of
the Free Baptist church, and after of the Methodist.  Mrs. Thurston
had great power of endurance, and brought up her children to be patient and strictly honest in all things.

Their children were:

4140  Mary,[7] b. in Orange Sept. 1, 1810; m. 1st, in Washington, Vt., Jan., 1830,
       James Dailey, b. 1809, a farmer of Woodbury, Vt.; 2d, May 27, 1840,
       William Phillips, a farmer, b. in Avon, Me., March, 1799.  She now
       lives, 1878, in Grand Haven, Mich.  She had, by first husband:
   4141  *Amanda Malvina* (Dailey), b. in Woodbury Nov. 10, 1830; living in
          Lowell, Mass.; n.m.
   4142  *Julietta Walker* (Dailey), b. in Boston, Mass., May 8, 1833; m. Oct.
          30, 1864, Enoch Page Cummings, b. in Groton, N. H., Sept. 30,
          1837, a physician and dentist in Grand Haven.  They have:
       4143  *Edward Page* (Cummings), b. June 28, 1871.
       4144  *Herbert Thurston* (Cummings), b. March 10, 1874.
4145  Charlotte,[7] b. Oct, 16, 1812.
4146  Melissa,[7] b. March 19, 1815; m. Otis H. Wheeler of South Hadley, Mass.
+4147  Sampson,[7] b. Jan. 25, 1817; m. Elsie Ann Clifford.
+4148  Joshua Tenney,[7] b. July 19, 1818; m. Sally Vining.
4149  Alonzo,[7] b. Sept. 25, 1820; went west and not heard from since.
4150  Maria,[7] b. Sept. 5, 1824; d. 1827.
+4151  Willard,[7] b. May 19, 1826; m. Hester Ann Sylvester.
+4152  Dennis,[7] b. Jan. 17, 1828; m. 1st, Sarah Simpson; 2d, —— Smith.
4153  Rosanna,[7] b. Dec. 17, 1829; m. in Temple Mills, Me., Oct. 19, 1862, Silas
       Goodin, a farmer in Avon, P. O. Phillips, Me.  They have:
   4154  *Elsie Orrena* (Goodin), b. in Avon June 3, 1864.
   4155  *Edwin Alonzo Thurston* (Goodin), b. in Farmington, Me., May 31, 1866.
   4156  *Elizabeth Janett* (Goodin), b. in Farmington Dec. 19, 1867.
   4157  *Edmond Alphonzo* (Goodin), b. in Avon Aug. 3, 1871.
4158  George Washington,[7] b. Dec. 13, 1832; m. 1st, Lavina Dill of Avon; 2d,
       Rebecca Gordon Lawn of Pasely, Scotland; worked in an oil carpet
       mill in Winthrop, Me., and in a woolen mill in Springfield, Mass.; d. in
       Lowell, Mass., June 14, 1875, of sun-stroke.  He had, by first wife:
   4159  *Georgia Emma*,[8] b. Oct. 13, 1855; was adopted by her aunt, Mary
          Phillips, and lives with her in Grand Haven, 1878.
              By second wife:
   4160  *John Edwin*,[8] d. in infancy.
   4161  *Mary Etta*,[8] b. March 2, 1867.
4162  Edwin,[7] b. in Pittsburgh, N. H., Nov. 19, 1834; m. Oct. 9, 1865, Sarah
       Martha Gould, b. in Temple, Me., July 18, 1845, daughter of Joseph and
       Polly (Woodbury) Gould of Farmington, Me.  He is a carpenter, resid-
       ing in Farmington, and has saw-mills in Temple.  They have:
   4163  *Lilla Belle*,[8] b. Dec. 25, 1869.
   4164  *Edith Althea*,[8] b. Feb. 18, 1873.

## 2351

WILLIAM THURSTON[6] (*Moses*,[5] *Moses*,[4] *Moses*,[3] *Stephen*,[2] *Daniel*[1]),
brother of the preceding, and son of Moses[5] and Jane (Spaulding)
Thurston of Orange, Vt.; born in Unity, N. H., Oct. 4, 1791; married, first, Dec. 4, 1810, CLARISSA CHURCH, born in Unity Jan. 29,

1793; she died in Gaysville, Vt., Aug. 3, 1847. Second, in Roxbury, Vt., July 19, 1848, BETSEY M. WILEY, born 1832; she died in South Royalton, Vt., Aug. 4, 1851. Third, March 26, 1852, MRS. HULDAH FARMER, of South Royalton. He died in Woodstock, Vt., July 6, 1876, and his widow is living there still. He was fife-major in the war of 1812, and received for his services bounty land and a pension.

### His children, by first wife, Clarissa, were:

4170  Clarissa,[7] b. in Orange June 12, 1811; m. John Walbridge, b. 1803; d. May 1, 1869. They had:

    4171  *John* (Walbridge), b. in Roxbury, Vt.
    4172  *Louisa Clarissa* (Walbridge), b. in Roxbury.
    4173  *Clifton* (Walbridge), b. in Roxbury.
    4174  *Lurinda* (Walbridge), b. in Northfield, Vt.
    4175  *Charles* (Walbridge), b. in Northfield.
    4176  *Frankie* (Walbridge).

4177  Tryphena T.,[7] b. in Waterford, Vt., April 22, 1814; m. Leonard Chaffee of Rochester, Vt., b. 1813, and died Sept. 3, 1855; she lived with her son, Dr. Chaffee, at Chicago, Ill., till she died, July 6, 1879, and her remains were brought to Rochester for burial. They had, all born in Rochester:

    4178  *Elvira Clarissa* (Chaffee), b. May 3, 1832; d.
    4179  *Emily* (Chaffee), d.
    4180  *Esther Emily* (Chaffee), d.
    4181  *Charles William* (Chaffee), m. in Rochester Sept., 1869, Diana Mosher; graduated at Ann Arbor, Mich., and is a successful physician and surgeon in Chicago. They have:

        4182  *Charles Francis* (Chaffee), b. Jan. 3, 1878.

4183  William,[7] b. at St. Johnsbury, Vt., Oct. 7, 1817. He served in the Florida war, the Mexican war, and the war against the rebellion; was wounded in the two last; n.m.

+4184  Uzziel Tinny,[7] b. in Sharon, Vt., July 8, 1819; m. Mary Chase.
+4185  Erastus Henry,[7] b. in Sharon Aug. 23, 1827; m. Harriet Clough.
4186  Andrew Jackson,[7] b. in Sharon March 2, 1829; m. Emily Burnham; d. in St. Albans, Vt., June 23, 1866; no children.
4187  Cyrus Lorenzo,[7] b. in Hancock, Vt., Feb. 15, 1832; m. Ann Livermore; served in the war against the rebellion, and died at Brattleborough, Vt., Aug. 7, 1863, from wounds received in battle; one son.
4188  Mary Luvinna,[7] b. in Rochester Jan. 24, 1835; m. July 4, 1852, William Wallace Wills, b. in Chelsea, Vt., June 18, 1829; he is a machinist and inventor of several patents, the most noticeable of which is the "single center spring" for vehicles; living in Janesville, Wis. They have:

    4189  *Ella Luvinna* (Wills), b. in Lebanon, N. H., Oct. 16, 1854.
    4190  *George Mills* (Wills), b. in Palatine, Ill., Sept. 8, 1856; m. at Janesville Feb. 14, 1877, Ethelinda Wright, b. in Emerald Grove, Wis., July 19, 1858, daughter of Orville and Clara Thurston (Dean) Wright; living at Janesville, and is shop clerk and telegraph operator for the Chicago & N. W. R. R. They have:

        4191  *Xula Ethel* (Wills), b. in Janesville Oct. 4, 1877.

4192  Charles Albert,[7] b. in Gaysville, Vt., Oct. 28, 1838; d. there July 26, 1842.

### By second wife, Betsey:

4193  Sophia Louisa,[7] b. in Roxbury, Vt., April 11, 1849; m. in Bridgewater, Vt., Sept. 15, 1867, Charles Denison Dean, b. in Barnard, Vt., April 2, 1841, son of Paul D. and Maria A. (Topliff) Dean of Barnard; he is a farmer in Barnard. They have, b. in Bridgewater:

    4194  *William Denison* (Dean), b. June 30, 1868.
    4195  *Minora May* (Dean), b. May 1, 1872.
    4196  *Edwin Leroy* (Dean), b. March 3, 1875.
    4197  *Walter Harrison* (Dean), b. Jan. 15, 1877.

4198  Betsey M.,[7] b. in South Royalton, Vt., June 27, 1851; d. Sept., 1851.

14

## 2384

EZEKIEL THURSTON[6] (*Jonathan,[5] Ezekiel,[4] Moses,[3] Stephen,[2] Daniel[1]*), son of Jonathan[5] and Mary (Ardway) Thurston of Portland, Me.; born in Epping, N. H.. Oct. 9, 1786; married, April 10, 1810, HANNAH MOULTON, born April 20, 1788, daughter of John and Ann (Cornish) Moulton of Lisbon, Me. He died Dec. 3, 1859. She is living, 1879, in Portland.

His parents died when he was quite young and he was brought up by his uncle Ezekiel, who adopted him. He was a ship builder in Portland and was a soldier in the war of 1812.

### Their children, all born in Portland, were:

```
     4208  William Moulton,⁷ b. Feb. 7, 1811; d. Aug. 30, 1811.
   +4209  John,⁷ b. Nov. 5, 1812; m. Harriet Snow.
   +4210  Edward,⁷ b. Jan. 17, 1815; m. Mary Ann Carter.
   +4211  Eliza Moulton,⁷ b. Sept. 4, 1816; m. William Goold.
     4212  Gilman,⁷ b. Oct. 20, 1819; d. Sept. 21, 1821.
     4213  Sarah Ann Card,⁷ b. Oct. 15, 1821; m. Dr. John Heald; no children; d.
              June 28, 1863.
   +4214  Charles Plummer,⁷ b. Oct. 15, 1823; m. Athena Blake Littlefield.
```

## 2399

SAMUEL THURSTON[6] (*Ezekiel,[5] Ezekiel,[4] Moses,[3] Stephen,[2] Daniel[1]*), son of Ezekiel[5] and (Mrs. Bray) Thurston of Portland, Me.; married, May 6, 1824, MARY TUCKER, daughter of Jonathan and Mary Elizabeth Tucker of Cape Elizabeth, Me. He died March 12, 1841, aged 39; she died Aug. 9, 1876. He was a calker, residing in Portland.

### Their children were:

```
     4220  Adeline H., b. July 30, 1825: drowned in Portland harbor, with several
              others, on a sailing excursion, in 1840.
     4221  Gilman,⁷ b. Nov. 17, 1827; m.; d. March 13, 1873.
     4222  Margaretta,⁷ b. May 4, 1829; d. Jan. 28, 1835.
     4223  Mary Jane,⁷ b. June 7, 1830; d. April 14, 1831.
   +4224  John Thomas,⁷ b. Jan. 4, 1832; m. Sept. 2, 1855, Mary A. Strong.
     4225  Samuel,⁷ b. Jan. 16, 1834; n.m.; teamster in Portland, and an officer in
              the fire department.
     4226  Mary,⁷ b. Dec. 14, 1835; d. March 7, 1836.
     4227  Margaret Knights,⁷ b. March 21, 1837; m. Jan. 9, 1853, in Portland, Jason
              Howard Shaw, b. Dec. 28, 1830, son of Reuel and Hannah (Crabtree)
              Shaw of Portland. He is a railroad clerk and deacon of the West Con-
              gregational church, Portland. They had:
           4228  Anna Howard (Shaw), b. Oct. 12, 1854; m. James C. Stott, a com-
                    mercial traveler, residing in Portland.
           4229  Frank Lewis (Shaw), b. March 18, 1857.
           4230  Mary Adelaide (Shaw), b. April 18, 1860.
           4231  Carrie Louise (Shaw), b. Oct. 16, 1863.
           4232  Margaret Ellen (Shaw), b. Dec. 31, 1867; d. Feb. 17, 1869.
   +4233  Lewis Lincoln,⁷ b. July 29, 1839; m. Susan Matilda Winship.
     4234  Adeline M.,⁷ b. March 12, 1841; m. Nov. 22, 1872, George J. Hodgdon, of
              Portland; no children.
```

## 2411

ISAAC THURSTON[6] of Ossipee, N. H. (*Moses,[5] Stephen,[4] Moses,[3] Stephen,[2] Daniel[1]*), eldest son of Moses[5] and Betsey (Wiggin) Thurston of Wolfborough, N. H.; born there Jan. 28, 1799; married MARIA DODGE, daughter of Jonathan and Mehitable (Trask) Dodge of Wenham, Mass.; she died Jan. 26, 1875.

Mr. Thurston was a merchant in Ossipee; he worked for John Wingate of Wakefield, N. H., for three years, and for Samuel Wiggin in North Wolfborough two years, and one year in Union, N. H., before commencing for himself at Ossipee as a country trader. He carried on business for forty years, and was ever noted for honesty and integrity. He joined the Morning Star Lodge of Masons at Wolfborough in 1826, and is now its oldest member, 1879. He never sought office or position, but when thrust upon him the duties involved were performed in such a manner as to reflect credit upon himself and the community he served.

### Children:

4235   Charles Henry,[7] b. May 2, 1832; d. Feb. 21, 1871.
+4236  George Carter,[7] b. Oct. 28, 1837; m. 1st, Lauretta Goldsmith; 2d, Delia Hanley.
4237   Ann Eliza,[7] b. April 15, 1841; d. June 7, 1863.
4238   Pamelia Stillings,[7] b. April 20, 1847; m. Jan. 21, 1864, John C. Bickford, b. in Wolfborough Dec. 18, 1842, a lawyer of Manchester, N. H.; she died at Manchester Nov. 29, 1878. They had:
4239     *Charles Wilmot* (Bickford), b. in Ossipee Dec. 20, 1865.

### 2420

MOSES THURSTON[6] (*Moses,[5] Oliver,[4] Moses,[8] Stephen,[2] Daniel[1]*), eldest son of Moses[5] and Sally (Moses) Thurston of Exeter, N. H.; born there March 5, 1795; married, March 5, 1816, PHEBE FOREST of Eaton, N. H., born 1795. She died April 5, 1849; he died Dec. 1, 1870.

Mr. Thurston was a farmer in Errol, N. H.; had been selectman, town treasurer, representative in the legislature in 1851, and was a member of the Constitutional Convention of New Hampshire in 1850.

### Their children, all born in Eaton, were:

4245   Sophronia,[7] b. Aug. 23, 1817; m. May 6, 1834, Leonard Harriman of Eaton; resides in Biddeford, Me.
+4246  David Howard,[7] b. Oct. 24, 1821; m. Mary Jane Norton.
4247   Thomas,[7] b. Oct. 24, 1824; m. Sarah Bemas; lives in Errol.
4248   Lavina,[7] b. July 19, 1828; m. in Lowell, Mass., 1853, Nathan Hackett; lives in Portland, Oregon.
+4249  William Moses,[7] b. Feb. 15, 1832; m. Emma Rose.
4250   Phebe Ann,[7] b. June 5, 1835; m John Harden of Lawrence, Kansas.
4251   Amanda F.,[7] b. June 4, 1839; m. Charles H. Demrite; lives in Bethel, Me.

### 2422

OLIVER THURSTON[6] (*Moses,[5] Oliver,[4] Moses,[8] Stephen,[2] Daniel[1]*), brother of the preceding, and son of Moses[5] and Sally (Moses) Thurston of Exeter, N. H.; born there Sept. 23, 1800; married, June, 1823, BETSEY ANN HARRIMAN, born May 30, 1805. He died Oct. 12, 1877.

Mr. Thurston was a farmer and cooper in Eaton, N. H.; a member of the Free Baptist church, of that branch termed Bullockite.

### Their children, all born in Eaton, were:

4254   Sarah Ann,[7] b. Oct. 6, 1825; d. Aug. 7, 1830.
+4255  Daniel Hobbs,[7] b. June 26. 1827; m. Mary Littlefield; a farmer in Eaton.
+4256  Benjamin Moses,[7] b. March 13, 1829; m. Mary Ann Lary.

4257 Eliza Ann,[7] b. March 29, 1831; m. 1st, April 19, 1849, Thomas Ellis; he died May 11, 1864; 2d, Sept. 8, 1868, Lucien Danforth of Eaton. Mr. Danforth was a house carpenter and shoemaker; justice of the peace, town clerk, and representative to the legislature. She had, by 1st husband:

    4258  *Amanda Jane* (Ellis), b. Dec. 15, 1849; m. March, 1868, Loren L. Drew of Eaton.

    4259  *Ellen Frances* (Ellis), b. Dec. 30, 1852; m. Oct., 1872, John M. Giles of Eaton.

    4260  *Charles Sumner* (Ellis), b. Sept. 25, 1855; m. Nov., 1874, Ella A. Thompson of Eaton.

    4261  *Abbie Ann* (Ellis), b. Aug. 2, 1860.

    4262  *Thomas* (Ellis), b. May 10, 1863.

4263 Thomas Hobbs,[7] b. June 6, 1833; m. Dec., 1857, Sophia Downes, b. June 16, 1834, daughter of Nathaniel and Fanny (Haines) Downes of Madison, N. H. He was a farmer in Eaton, and was killed by the falling of a limb from a tree in Conway, N. H., June 22, 1870. Mrs. Thurston moved to Great Falls, N. H., 1874, and to Berwick, Me., 1879, where she died, June 5, 1879. Children:

    4264  *Ellen Frances,*[8] b. Oct. 28, 1858.

    4265  *Bradley,*[8] b. June 13, 1860.

    4266  *Thomas Lincoln,*[8] b. Dec. 4, 1861.

    4267  *Fanny,*[8] b. Dec. 8, 1863.

    4268  *Ida,*[8] b. Aug. 30, 1867.

4269 Abigail,[7] b. Feb. 22, 1836; m. 1st, Ely Thompson; 2d, Thomas Shackford of Center Conway, N. H. She had, by first husband:

    4270  *Horace M.* (Thompson), b. about 1853.

+4271 Cyrus,[7] b. Aug. 22, 1839; m.

4272 Mary Jane,[7] b. March 6, 1842; m. Jan. 1, 1873, James Oliver Libby, a farmer and lumberman of Conway, N. H., b. March 12, 1841, son of Phinehas and Mary (Hanson) Libby of Bridgton, Me.; no children.

+4273 Charles Pleaman,[7] b. May 18, 1844; m. Harriet Downs.

4274 Franklin,[7] b. Feb. 22, 1850; n.m.; a farmer in Eaton.

## 2445

OLIVER THURSTON[6] (*Oliver,*[5] *Oliver,*[4] *Moses,*[3] *Stephen,*[2] *Daniel*[1]), eldest son of Oliver[6] and Anstress (Cross) Thurston of Freedom, N. H.; born in Exeter, N. H., March 5, 1795; married, by John Marsh, Esq., April 4, 1819, AMY FOREST, born in Eaton, N. H., Oct. 4, 1799. He died Feb. 5, 1852; she died Nov. 29, 1875.

Mr. Thurston was a farmer in Freedom.

### Their children were:

4275 Nathaniel Cross,[7] b. May 16, 1820; m. 1st, by Rev. A. Butler, Feb. 4, 1849, Hannah Durgin, b. in Eaton March 14, 1821; she died Oct. 6, 1856; 2d, 1860, Mrs. Mary (Moses) Huntress of Effingham, N. H. He was a farmer in Freedom, and a member of the Free Baptist church in Eaton. He died Nov. 26, 1875; she resides in Freedom. He had, by first wife:

    4276  *Mary Ellen,*[8] b. March 27, 1851; m. in Salem, Mass., April 28, 1871, John Garney, a police officer of Lynn, Mass., b. June 10, 1833, son of Ambrose and Waitstill (Norton) Garney of Lynn. They have:

        4277  *Annie Cross* (Garney), b. Nov. 20, 1871.

        4278  *John Ambrose* (Garney), b. Aug. 19, 1873.

        4279  *Amos Franklin* (Garney), b. June 27, 1876.

        4280  *Sumner Parker* (Garney), b. May 19, 1878.

    4281  *John Moore,*[8] b. May 17, 1853; a farmer and hunter in Freedom; n.m.

    4282  *Nathaniel Cross,*[8] b. May 16, 1855; d. Nov. 25, 1875.

4283 Sarah,[7] b. Oct. 24, 1822; d. Dec. 23, 1827.

4284 Abigail,[7] b. March 9, 1825; d. Oct. 3, 1827.

4285 Catharine Melissa,[7] b. Feb. 12, 1827; m. Jan., 1856, Carr Leavitt Taylor, a carpenter in Lynn. He went to the California gold mines, and after to Nevada, lost his health, and came home shortly before his death, May 18, 1868; she died April 16, 1871. They had:

    4286  *Addie Frances* (Taylor), b. Sept., 1857; d. June 21, 1875.

4287 *Joseph Carr* (Taylor), b. Aug., 1858; d. July 30, 1863.
4288 *Emma Kate* (Taylor), b. 1860; m. Aug. 8, 1875, Frank Bryant of Effingham Falls, N. H.; d. April 30, 1876.
4289 Isaac Taylor,[7] b. March 19, 1828; m. Fannie Downes of Madison, N. H., six weeks before his death, April 10, 1858; was a merchant in Freedom.
4290 Eunice Ann,[7] b. Aug. 18, 1831; m. Dec. 27, 1851, Samuel P. Bryant, b. Sept. 28, 1826, son of Levi and Elsie (Daniels) Bryant of Effingham Falls; he is a farmer and surveyor of highways. They had:
4291  *Frank* (Bryant), b. April 27, 1853; m. Emma Taylor of Lynn; she d. 1876.
4292  *Emma* (Bryant), b. Dec. 28, 1854; m. Frank Kennett of Effingham.
4293  *Laura A.* (Bryant), b. Nov., 1857; m. Lewis Young of Manchester, N. H.
4294  *Mary* (Bryant), b. Feb. 8, 1860; m. Albert Thompson of Ossipee, N. H.
4295  *Etta* (Bryant), b. Nov. 29, 1862; d. March 31, 1878.
4296  *Clara* (Bryant), b. Aug. 4, 1866.
4297  *Herman* (Bryant), b. May 21, 1871.
4298  *Almon* (Bryant), b. Sept. 5, 1873.
4299 Amy,[7] b. April 8, 1833; d. May 13, 1853.
4300 Oliver,[7] b. Dec. 9, 1835; m. by Rev. N. Foss, June 25, 1856, Martha Ann Hurd, daughter of Aaron Hurd of Effingham; is a farmer in Freedom, living on the old homestead. They had:
4301  *Adelbert*,[8] } twins, b. Sept. 21, 1857.
4302  *Oliver*,[8] }
4303  *Alvin Oliver*,[8] b. Sept. 29, 1858.
4304  *Nathaniel Cross*,[8] b. Dec. 1, 1875; d. Aug. 5, 1877.
4305 Samuel Stokes,[7] b. Nov. 4, 1843; m. Sept. 6, 1870, Kittie Iantha Dunklee, b. in Rutland, Vt., Oct. 8, 1845, daughter of Nathan Sargent and Martha Elmira (Warner) Dunklee of Charlestown, Mass. He went to Boston in 1859; has lived in Charlestown since 1869, in the grocery business, under firm name of Thurston & Rollins; a member of the Baptist church. They had:
4306  *Martha Antoinette*,[8] b. Aug. 28, 1872; d. Dec. 4, 1872.
4307  *Nathan Samuel*,[8] b. Nov. 13, 1873.

## 2447

WILLIAM THURSTON[6] (*Oliver*,[5] *Oliver*,[4] *Moses*,[3] *Stephen*,[2] *Daniel*[1]), brother of the preceding, and son of Oliver[5] and Anstress (Cross) Thurston of Freedom, N. H.; born there March 23, 1799; married, first, by Rev. H. Lord, Oct. 18, 1818, MITTIE THURSTON, born in Parsonsfield, Me., Dec. 22, 1798, daughter of Daniel and Hannah (Dutch) Thurston [see no. 1225]; she died of cancer on the face, Aug. 13, 1867. Second, Feb. 16, 1870, ABIGAIL ALLARD (HAM) (TYLER) BLAKE, born April 23, 1807, daughter of James and Betsey (Kennett) Allard of Albany N. H.

Mr. Thurston is a farmer at Effingham Falls, N. H., formerly a merchant in Freedom and Parsonsfield.

Their children, born in Freedom, were:

4312 Sally,[7] b. April 19, 1819; member Free Baptist church in Parsonsfield; d. Sept. 17, 1839.
4313 Anna Wiggin,[7] b. Nov. 10, 1820; member Free Baptist church in Parsonsfield; d. Aug. 13, 1841.
4314 Anstress Cross,[7] b. March 23, 1822; member Free Baptist church in Parsonsfield; d. Jan. 22, 1845.
+4315 Stephen Daniel,[7] b. March 5, 1824; m. Hannah Hubbard Whitten.
4316 Hannah Dutch,[7] b. Jan. 10, 1826; m. Oct. 22, 1846, Alonzo Alley, b. Nov. 22, 1825, son of Daniel and Hannah (Leavitt) Alley of Eaton, N. H., a farmer, cooper, and deputy sheriff of Carroll county for fifteen years; they reside in Madison, N. H.; she is a member of the Free Baptist church. They had:

4317   *Arbba Eugene* (Alley), b. in Eaton April 6, 1848; m. March 27, 1872, Sarah Tibbetts of Madison; a carpenter; one child.

4318   *Alwilda Margrette* (Alley), b. May 13, 1849.

4319   *Ella Rose* (Alley), b. in Freedom Sept. 1, 1853; m. Feb. 24, 1873, Alvin Emson Philbrick, in the ice business in Wakefield, Mass.; three children.

4320   *John C. Freemont* (Alley), b. in Eaton July 14, 1856; d. Oct. 31, 1856.

4321   *Hannah Delora* (Alley), b. July 14, 1859; d. Nov. 29, 1860.

4322   *Otis Owen* (Alley), b. April 14, 1861.

4323   William Otis,[7] b. Dec. 20, 1827; n.m.; a trader of influence and character; d. Oct. 31, 1846.

4324   Mittee Ann,[7] b. Sept. 30, 1829; m. June 25, 1845, Job Allard [see no. 2480], b. July 12, 1822, son of Jacob and Sarah (Thurston) Allard of Eaton; d. Dec. 22, 1851; he was a carpenter and farmer, and after a merchant in Freedom. They had:

4325   *William Otis* (Allard), b. Sept. 29, 1846; enlisted in the war against the rebellion, and died in New Orleans April 18, 1865.

4326   *Daniel Austin* (Allard), b. July 12, 1848; lives in Wisconsin.

4327   Mary Elizabeth,[7] b. May 31, 1832; m. in Lowell, Mass., Aug. 2, 1851, Albion Keith Paris Lougee, a brick mason, farmer, and trader, formerly of Parsonsfield, now in Holden, Mass., son of Gilman and Mary (Buzzell) Lougee of Parsonsfield. They had:

4328   *Mittee* (Lougee), b. in Parsonsfield May 5, 1852; d. Aug. 15, 1852.

4329   *Grace Anna* (Lougee), b. in Parsonsfield Sept. 28, 1853; d. in Limerick, Me., Aug. 13, 1869.

4330   *Mabel* (Lougee), b. in Cambridge, Mass., Dec. 15, 1855; m. May 15, 1878, Albert Newell of Holden.

4331   Martha Elvira,[7] b. Dec. 9, 1835; m. 1851, Shephard Franklin Demeritt, a teamster and trader in Effingham, N. H., b. 1827, son of John and Betsey (Leavitt) Demeritt of Effingham. They have:

4332   *Edgar Frank* (Demeritt), b. Aug. 2, 1852; m. Jan., 1876; two children.

4333   Rozilla Jane,[7] b. June 17, 1837; m. in Plaistow, N. H., June 2, 1871, John F. Canney, a farmer in Effingham, b. in Tuftonborough, N. H., July 9, 1848, son of Cyrus and Sabra (Nute) Canney of Effingham. They have:

4334   *Etta Belle* (Canney), b. Nov. 13, 1878.

### Born in Parsonsfield:

4335   Daniel Wedgwood,[7] b. Feb. 16, 1840; d. Feb. 7, 1841.

+4336   Josiah Wedgwood,[7] b. May 21, 1842; m. Arvilla Frances Chick.

## 2462, 2507

JOSIAH THURSTON [6] (*Oliver,*[5] *Oliver,*[4] *Moses,*[3] *Stephen,*[2] *Daniel*[1]), brother of the preceding, and son of Oliver [5] and Anstress (Cross) Thurston of Freedom, N. H.; born there June 9, 1814; married, first, Sept. 10, 1840, MARY ANN THURSTON [see no. 2507], born May 15, 1816, daughter of William and Mary (Robinson) Thurston of Eaton, N. H.; she died Nov. 16, 1875. Second, April 23, 1877, JULIA ANNA ROBERTS PIERCE, born Feb. 3, 1843, daughter of Daniel and Abigail Pierce of Wyman, Me.

Mr. Thurston is a farmer, on the homestead where he was born, and lumber dealer in Freedom; president of the Ossipee Savings Bank of Freedom.

### His children, both adopted:

4340   Nathaniel Henry,[7] son of Joseph and Adeline (Simonds) Thurston [see no. 2490], b. Nov. 8, 1839; m. April 30, 1863, Georgia Anna Sias, b. Aug. 4, 1843, daughter of William Putnam and Belinda B. (Evans) Sias of Ossipee, N. H. He was a teacher and after a clerk in Boston, Mass. He died in Freedom April 28, 1875; she resides in Boston. They had, b. in Ossipee:

4341   *Maybell,*[8] b. Sept. 8, 1864.

4342  *Addie*,[8] b. Aug. 26, 1866.  4343  *Winfield Oliver*,[8] b. May 28, 1871.
4344  Sarah Ann,[7] b. Sept. 7, 1851; m. July 4, 1869, Edwin Towle. b. April 7,
     1848, a farmer; lived with her father till she died, Nov. 4, 1876.  Chil.:
4345  *Amos Calvin* (Towle), b. Oct., 1870; d. May, 1871.
4346  *Josiah Thurston* (Towle), b. Oct., 1873.

## 2475

NATHANIEL THURSTON[6] of Eaton, N. H. (*Reuben*,[5] *Oliver*,[4] *Moses*,[3]
*Stephen*,[2] *Daniel*[1]), eldest son of Reuben[5] and Sally (Cross) Thurston
of Eaton; born there 1793; married SALLY (or NANCY) THURSTON
[see no. 2421], born in Exeter, N. H., daughter of Moses and Sally
(Moses) Thurston of Eaton.  He was a farmer.  Children:
4350  Margaret,[7] b. ab. 1825; m. Ambrose Wilkinson of Eaton; d. ab. 1850; 2 chil.
4351  Ann,[7] b. Jan. 5, 1826; m. Nov. 1, 1850, James Munroe Durgin, a farmer
     and stone worker of Freedom, N. H., b. April 9, 1824, son of Dudley L.
     and Sophia (Milliken) Durgin of Freedom.  They had:
4352    *Martha Francenia* (Durgin), b. Oct. 24, 1852.
4353    *Alonzo* (Durgin), b. Jan. 16, 1856.
4354    *Edwin* (Durgin), b. March 22, 1859.
4355    *Emma Jane* (Durgin), b. Jan. 5, 1862.
4356    *Alonzo Edwin* (Durgin), b. Oct. 24, 1866.
4357  Alvah,[7] ⎫ twins; ⎱ lived in Brownfield, Me.
4358  Ansel,[7] ⎭        ⎰ thought to have been in last war.
4359  Martin,[7] d. young.   4360  Sarah Jane,[7] d.        4361  Munroe,[7] d.
4362  Nathaniel,[7] thought to have been in last war.

## 2477

OLIVER THURSTON[6] of Eaton, N. H. (*Reuben*,[5] *Oliver*,[4] *Moses*,[3]
*Stephen*,[2] *Daniel*[1]), brother of the preceding, and son of Reuben[5]
and Sally (Cross) Thurston of Eaton; born there 1797; married, first,
REBECCA HARMON; second, SUSAN COLBY; third, SUSAN HAYES.
Mr. Thurston was a farmer.  Children, by first wife, Rebecca·
+4367  James Harvey,[7] b. Nov. 4, 1826; m. Mary Jane Towle.
4368  Andrew,[7] b. 1828; m. 1st, Mahala Eaton; 2d, Priscilla Tibbetts; lived in
     Biddeford, Me., Freedom and Effingham, N. H.; d. in the war against
     the rebellion.  He had, by first wife:
4369    *Orrin*,[8] b. in Biddeford 1852; m. in Boston, Mass., Nov. 5, 1873,
         Annie E. Henlon, b. in England 1852; is tollman in Chelsea, Mass.
4370  Joseph,[7] b. 1834; m. Mary Kennison; a truckman in Boston; one son.
4371  John,[7] b. 1836; a teamster in Boston; n.m.; d. 1857.

## 2491

HENRY THURSTON[6] of Eaton, N. H. (*Reuben*,[5] *Oliver*,[4] *Moses*,[3]
*Stephen*,[2] *Daniel*[1]), brother of the preceding, and son of Reuben[5] and
Sally (Cross) Thurston of Eaton; born there 1809; married DRUSILLA
E. WEDGWOOD of Parsonsfield, Me., born 1811, died Dec. 27, 1871.
He was a farmer; died Feb. 2, 1874.  Children:
4372  Thaddeus Henry,[7] b. 1835; a farmer in Bartlett, N. H.; m. 1862, Rowena
     Seavey of Limerick, Me.; two children.
4373  Adaline Simonds,[7] b. 1838; m. 1861, Norman M. Macomber of Boston; he
     is a machinist at Beaver Falls, Penn.  Children:
4374    *William M.* (Macomber), b. April 16, 1867.
4375    *Norman B.* (Macomber), b. Nov. 30, 1878.
4376  Harrison Franklin,[7] b. 1840; a tinsmith in Bartlett; m. 1st, Mary Brown
     of Brownfield, Me.; 2d, Sarah L. Sawyer of Eaton; 3 chil. by second wife.
4377  Mary Ann,[7] b. 1842; m. 1st, 1862, Nathaniel Seavey, a tinsmith of Limer-
     ick; 2d, 1869, Alex. J. Merserve, a farmer in Brownfield Center.  Chil.:
4378    *Carrie Emma* (Seavey), b. April 17, 1864.
4379    *Frank R.* (Meserve), b. Dec. 14, 1869; d. in infancy.
4380    *Wilbor M.* (Meserve), b. March 14, 1872.
4381    *Ida M.* (Meserve), b. April 4, 1878.
4382  Almon Dana,[7] b. 1846; d. April 20, 1865, in the army at Washington.
4383  Susan Vyrene,[7] b. 1848; m. 1871, Henry S. Foster, a stationer in Boston,
     resides in Medford, Mass.

4384  Quincy Adams,[7] b. 1850; a farmer in Eaton; m. 1872, Georgie Anna
     Stewart of Eaton: one child.
4385  Warren Violin,[7] b. 1852; farmer in Eaton; m. 1873, Ella Tripp of Porter, Me.
4386  James Lorenzo,[7] b. 1853; d. in infancy.
4387  Elijah Hanson,[7] b. 1855; farmer in Eaton; m. 1875, Mary Davis of Conway.

## 2492

ELIAS CUSHMAN THURSTON[6] of Eaton, N. H. (*Reuben*,[5] *Oliver*,[4]
*Moses*,[3] *Stephen*,[2] *Daniel*[1]), brother of the preceding, and son of Reuben[5] and Sally (Cross) Thurston of Eaton; born there Jan. 20, 1812;
married, April 15, 1833, ELIZA A. BROWN.   He was a farmer; died
Dec. 20, 1868.                    Children:
4388  Sarah Ann,[7] b. March 3, 1835; m. April 25, 1855, John F. Adjutant, a
     farmer in Brownfield, Me.   Children:
    4389  *Elias F.* (Adjutant), b. March 24. 1856; m. July, 1876, Etta Hanson.
    4390  *Eliza E.* (Adjutant), b. June 14, 1859; m. July 4, 1877, Herbert Clay.
    4391  *George P.* (Adjutant), b. Aug. 24, 1862.
    4392  *Sarah C.* (Adjutant), b. Aug. 14, 1865.
4393  Charles E.,[7] b. Sept. 5, 1838; m. March 1, 1859, Caroline A. Drew; a
     farmer in Alfred, Me.   Children:
    4394  *Nellie A.*,[8] b. Sept. 14, 1860; m. Nov., 1877. E. Douglas.
    4395  *George E.*,[8] b. March 24, 1863.    4396  *Minnie G.*,[8] b. Feb. 15, 1867.
    4397  *Alice*,[8] and *Alta*,[8] twins, b. May 9, 1874.
4398  Martha F.,[7] b. Feb. 15, 1840; m. May 7, 1858, Timothy Day, a farmer in
     Brownfield.   Children:    4399  *Sumner A.* (Day), b. April 30, 1859.
    4400  *Emma C.* (Day), b. July 22, 1861.
4401  George W.,[7] b. Aug. 15, 1841; enlisted in the war against the rebellion Oct.
     29, 1861; wounded at Fair Oaks May 31, 1862: d. June 12, 1862.
4402  Hannah D.,[7] b. Jan. 15, 1842; m. April 27, 1859, Ivory Day of Windham,
     Me.   Children:
    4402a  *Mary E.* (Day), b. May 26, 1860.    4402b  *Melvina* (Day), b. June, 1863.
    4402c  *Eva* (Day), b. May, 1868.      4402d  *Grace* (Day), b. June. 1870.
4403  James R.,[7] b. May 26, 1844; m. Oct. 29, 1865, Lydia F. Adjutant. Children:
    4404  *Nettie M.*,[8] b. Aug., 1866.    4405  *Fred*,[8] b. May, 1872.
4406  Amanda T.,[7] b. June 11, 1849; m. April 28, 1868, Lorenzo D. Mills, a
     farmer and blacksmith in Conway Center, N. H.

## 2493

REUBEN LEAVITT THURSTON,[6] farmer and cooper in Madison, N. H.
(*Reuben*,[5] *Oliver*,[4] *Moses*,[3] *Stephen*,[2] *Daniel*[1]), brother of the preceding,
and son of Reuben[5] and Sally (Cross) Thurston of Eaton, N. H.;
born there 1809; married, first, LYDIA WELCH; second, MARY PHIL-
LIPS, daughter of Metiphore and Susan Phillips of Effingham, N. H.
Children, by first wife, Lydia:
4407  Albion,[7] b. 1842; killed in battle in the war against the rebellion.
4408  Nahum,[7] b. 1844.
4409  Arvilla Jane,[7] b. 1847; m. Charles Andrews of Madison.

## 2505

WILLIAM ROBINSON THURSTON[6] (*William*,[5] *Oliver*,[4] *Moses*,[3] *Stephen*,[2]
*Daniel*[1]), second child of William[5] and Mary (Robinson) Thurston
of Eaton, N. H.; born there April 5, 1812; married, Oct., 1838, ELIZ-
ABETH WALKER SNELL, born about 1812, daughter of William Snell
of Eaton.   He was a farmer in Eaton, adjoining the homestead, till
1864, when he moved to a farm in Madison, N. H.   Chil., b. in Eaton:
4410  William Paris,[7] b. June 13, 1846; n.m.; was in the war against the rebel-
     lion; d. in New York 1874.
4411  Alphonzo Walker,[7] b. July 5, 1848; n.m.; d. in Madison 1872.
4412  Elmera C.,[7] b. May 5, 1850; m. James Odell Gerry of Madison; d. Nov., 1874.
4413  Jerome,[7] b. Sept., 1852; m. Agnes ——; a farmer with his father in Madison.
4414  Laura Ellen,[7] b. April, 1855.

## 2506

DANIEL THURSTON[6] of Eaton, N. H. (*William,*[5] *Oliver,*[4] *Moses,*[3] *Stephen,*[2] *Daniel*[1]), brother of the preceding, and son of William[5] and Mary (Robinson) Thurston of Eaton; born there July 21, 1814; married, Jan. 10, 1839, MARY ANN ALLEY, born Feb. 27, 1815, daughter of Daniel and Hannah (Leavitt) Alley of Eaton. He died Sept. 30, 1854. Mr. Thurston was a farmer and cooper; a deacon in the Free Baptist church.

Their children were:

4415  Mary Ellen,[7] b. Sept. 14, 1846; m. July 24, 1871, Burleigh Monroe Taylor, a farmer of Bridgton, Me.
4416  David Marks,[7] b. June 11, 1848; m. Jan. 20, 1878, Rose Abby Allard, b. in Boston, Mass., Dec. 26, 1858, daughter of Benjamin and Elizabeth Ann (Harmon) Allard of Eaton; is a farmer on the homestead in Eaton.
4417  Daniel Lorin,[7] b. Feb. 18, 1852; is in Massachusetts.

## 2508

SOLOMON HUTCHINS THURSTON[6] of Kenduskeag, Me. (*John,*[5] *Oliver,*[4] *Moses,*[3] *Stephen,*[2] *Daniel*[1]), eldest son of John[5] and Alice (Hutchins) Thurston of Wakefield, N. H.; born there Sept. 10, 1808; married, in Harmony, Me., Jan. 16, 1856, JENNIE WIGGIN née FRENCH, daughter of Moses and Olive Hutchins (née French) French of Orneville, Me.

Mr. Thurston is a teacher, farmer, justice of the peace, and a member of the Baptist church.

Children:

4418  Florence Lillian, b. in Levant, Me., Feb. 2, 1857.
4419  Annie Myra,[7] b. in Kenduskeag Sept. 3, 1861.

## 2511

JOHN LANGDON ROBERTS THURSTON[6] (*John,*[5] *Oliver,*[4] *Moses,*[3] *Stephen,*[2] *Daniel*[1]), brother of the preceding, and son of John[5] and Alice (Hutchins) Thurston of Freedom, N. H.; born there July 16, 1814; married, Dec. 7, 1843, LOUISA HUTCHINS, daughter of Isaac and Betsey (Davis) Hutchins of Wellington, Me. She died Oct. 12, 1873; he died Sept. 23, 1875. He was a farmer, first in Levant and afterward in Kenduskeag, Me., where they both died.

Their children, born in Harmony, Me., were:

4425  Maria Hutchins,[7] b. Nov. 29, 1844; m. Feb. 9, 1868, Ephraim Frederic Nason of Kenduskeag. They have:
4426   *Ella* (Nason), b. 1870.
4427   *Albert* (Nason), b. 1872.
4428  John Langdon,[7] b. June 28, 1847; d. in Kenduskeag Aug. 7, 1857.
4429  Edwin Lewis,[7] b. in Levant Sept. 11, 1849.

Born in Kenduskeag:

4430  Frank Benjamin,[7] b. Feb. 3, 1852; m. May 19, 1874, Martha Ann Eells of Stetson, Me.; is a farmer in Kenduskeag; she died Feb. 29, 1879, leaving:
4431   *Louisa Doratha,*[8] b. March 2, 1875.
4432   *Eva Martha,*[8] b. Nov. 12, 1876.
4433  Isaac Hutchins,[7] b. July 12, 1854.
4434  Fred Walter,[7] b. April 19, 1857.
4435  Elmer Ernest,[7] b. Sept. 17, 1861; d. May 19, 1872.

## 2512

ASA LEWIS THURSTON [6] ( *John*,[5] *Oliver*,[4] *Moses*,[3] *Stephen*,[2] *Daniel*[1]), brother of the preceding, and son of John [5] and Alice (Hutchins) Thurston of Freedom, N. H.; born there Sept. 25, 1816; married, in Athens, Me., Sept. 24, 1846, JULIA ANN CARSON, born Feb. 19, 1829, daughter of Benjamin and Bathsheba (Thayer) Carson of Waterville, Me.   She died in Carmel, Me., May 16, 1866.

Mr. Thurston is a carpenter and builder, residing in Athens, Kenduskeag, Waterville, Carmel, and 1879 in Lagrange, Me.; has been town clerk and supervisor of schools; a member of the Universalist church and later in life a Spiritualist.

Their children, born in Athens, were:

+4440  Winfield Scott,[7] b. Oct. 5, 1849; m. Ellen Eliza Trafton.
 4441  Ella May,[7] b. April 7, 1854; graduated from the Eaton Family and Day
        school in Norridgewock, Me., June 22, 1871; taught school in different
        places; from Aug., 1873, to April, 1879, was principal of 2d grammar
        school in Skowhegan, Me.; is now 1880 teaching in Lagrange; a mem-

Their children, born in Harmony, were:

4465  Eliza Ann,[7] b. Oct. 9, 1849; m. George Gross.
4466  Riley Gray,[7] m. Elby Bean.

Born in Bangor, Me.:

4467  Oscar.[7]
4468  Abbie,[7] m. Leslie Withee.

Born in Kenduskeag:

4469  Eunice.[7]
4470  Elmer.[7]

## 2541

ANDREW LEAVITT THURSTON [6] of Newmarket, N. H. (*Nathaniel,*[5] *John,*[4] *John,*[3] *Stephen,*[2] *Daniel*[1]), eldest son of Nathaniel [5] and Hannah (Dutch) Thurston of Stratham, N. H.; born there Nov. 18, 1815; married, Jan. 4, 1842, ANNA FISHER, born Nov. 4, 1820, daughter of Capt. John and Catherine (Bell) Fisher of Portsmouth, N. H.  She died at Exeter, N. H., Feb. 26, 1869.

Mr. Thurston is a pattern maker; a man of standing in the community, as he is entrusted with the collection of the taxes.

Children:

4475  Harriet Ellen,[7] b. Feb. 6, 1844; m. Charles B. Chapman, and has:
    4476  *Arthur B.* (Chapman), b. Aug. 23, 1878.
4477  Charles Edwin,[7] b. Jan. 30, 1848; m. Elizabeth Varney of Melrose, Mass.; no children.

## 2566

JAMES THURSTON [6] (*Thomas,*[5] *Paul,*[4] *John,*[3] *Stephen,*[2] *Daniel*[1]), son of Thomas [5] and Elizabeth (Larmon) Thurston of Pelham, Mass.; born there Feb. 8, 1787; married, first, April 3, 1817, SUSANNA THAYER of Belchertown, Mass., born there Feb. 15, 1792; she died in Pelham Aug. 22, 1825.  Second, Dec. 5, 1827, MARIA GLEASON, born June 19, 1798, daughter of Jason and Maria (Draper) Gleason of Brimfield, Mass.  She died April 6, 1866, and he died only six hours after, April 7, 1866.

He was a farmer in Pelham and Enfield, Mass., and accumulated quite a fortune; was selectman, representative to the legislature in 1842–3, and held most of the minor offices in his native town of Pelham.  "He was a man of strict integrity, his promise being as sure as his written note, which was as good as coin.  He left a clear record of his life-work, and died without an enemy."

His children were,

By first wife, Susanna, born in Pelham:

4482  John Thayer,[7] b. Jan. 11, 1818; m. 1st, Betsey Jepson of Ashfield; she died Oct. 5, 1860; 2d, Oct. 25, 1865, Lucretia Jepson.  He died May 21, 1867.  He had, by first wife: a son who died at 3 or 4 years of age.
4483  *Cora F*,[8] b. in Belchertown July 23, 1857.
4484  *Kirk John,*[8] b. in Belchertown April 4, 1860.
4485  James,[7] b. April 29, 1820; n.m.; d. in Greenwich, Mass., Oct. 4, 1851.
4486  Susan Maria,[7] b. Dec. 22, 1822; m. May 17, 1843, Oliver Hill; live in Agawam, Mass.  They had, b. in Shutesbury, Mass.:
    4487  *Henry Newell* (Hill), b. Aug. 28, 1844; m.
    4488  *Jason Abbott* (Hill), b. Feb. 10, 1846; m.; d. Sept. 6, 1872.
    4489  *Susan Ellen* (Hill), b. Feb. 5, 1850.

4490  *Jane Eliza* (Hill), b. Nov. 3, 1851; m. W. P. Gleason of Springfield, Mass.
4491  *James Thurston* (Hill), b. Feb. 11, 1854.

By second wife, Maria:

4492  Olive Thurston,[7] b. Nov. 22, 1828; m. Dec. 27, 1853, George Chandler; he died in Monson, Mass., April 22, 1874; no children.
4493  Almira,[7] b. Jan. 21, 1832; n.m.; has been an invalid since the death of her parents. She and her widowed sister Olive live together in Warren, Mass., upon their own place.
4494  Royal Gleason,[7] b. Sept. 27, 1834; m. May 21, 1867, Helen Carey; had:
4495  *Willie Ezra*,[8] d. eight months of age.
+4496  Philander,[7] } twins, born }
4497  Lysander,[7] } May 25, 1837; } held most of the town offices in Enfield and taught school winters from 1857 to 1867 very successfully; is a farmer in Enfield; n.m.
4498  Jason.[7] b. April 5, 1840; n.m. Lysander and Jason own the homestead in Enfield, where they live and carry on the large and valuable farm in company.

## 2600

JOHN THURSTON [6] (*Ephraim*,[5] *Samuel*,[4] *Robert*,[8] *Stephen*,[2] *Daniel*[1]), son of Ephraim [5] and Annie (Marsh) Thurston of Exeter, N. H.; born there July 31, 1787; married, June 7, 1812, MERCY HALE, born Dec. 27, 1789, daughter of Israel and Esther (Taylor) Hale of Waterford, Me. She died in Oxford, Me., June 18, 1858; he died in Sherburne, Mass., 1872.

Mr. Thurston was a farmer in Norway and Oxford, Me., and was a member of the Methodist church; served in the war of 1812.

Their children, born in Norway, were:

+4503  Daniel Holt,[7] b. Jan. 24, 1813; m. 1st, Jane Drown Shackley; 2d, Mrs. Esther (Shackley) Battles.
4504  Esther Hale,[7] b. Oct. 18, 1814; d. Nov. 2, 1815.

Born in Oxford:

4505  Lorenda Holt,[7] b. March 19, 1816; m. May 28, 1845, George N. Davis of Virginia; now lives with her son, George Henry Davis, Peabody, Mass.
4506  Mary Holt,[7] b. April 1, 1818; m. George Washington Day, b. Dec. 16, 1809, a seafaring man, Methodist, living in Freeport, Me.; no children.
4507  Nancy Marsh,[7] b. June 15, 1820; m. in Oxford, Willard O. Haynes of Natick, Mass., a farmer in Sherborn, Mass. They had *Ella*, d. young, *Willard Augustus*, *Franklin Wallace*, and *Lizzie Emma* (Haynes).
4508  Harriet How,[7] b. April 24, 1822; m. Nov. 10, 1851, Joshua Haynes; d. in Cambridge, 1871. They had:
4509  *Lelia Emma* (Haynes), b. Aug. 31, 1853.
4510  *Homer Dana* (Haynes), b. April 1, 1856.
4511  *John Thurston* (Haynes), b. Nov. 19, 1857.
4512  *Annie Mary* (Haynes), b. Aug. 24, 1861.
4513  Mercy Jane,[7] b. May 1, 1824; d. in Oxford 1841.
+4514  John Colby,[7] b. Dec. 5, 1825; m. Mary Elizabeth Murphy.
4515  Hiram Leonard,[7] b. Aug. 7, 1828; learned the shoemaking trade in Natick, Mass.; m. Sept. 3, 1852, Eleanora Collins, and moved to Cochituate; enlisted Aug. 1, 1862, in the 38th Massachusetts; was in the Red river expedition; was called to reinforce Grant, and died in Washington, D. C., Aug. 21, 1864, and was buried in Natick. They had:
4516  *A son*,[8] d. young.
4517  *Melissa Jane*,[8] b. Oct. 8, 1854; m. —— Argravy of Saxonville, Mass.; two children.
4518  *Franklin Waldo*,[8] b. July 15, 1856.
4519  *Hiram Leonard*,[8] b. March, 1859.

4520 Augustus Aurelius,[7] b. Feb. 4, 1831; learned the shoemaking business in Natick; enlisted in the 3d Massachusetts April 2, 1861; re-enlisted Aug. 1, 1862, in the 38th Massachusetts; went to New Orleans, where he was taken sick, and was sent to Brashear City, La., where he died, May 21, 1863.

## 2627

ELIJAH DOUGHTY THURSTON [6] of Winthrop, Me. (*Ebenezer,*[5] *James,*[4] *Robert,*[3] *Stephen,*[2] *Daniel*[1]), fifth child of Ebenezer [5] and Betsey (Doughty) Thurston of Monmouth, Me.; born there Aug. 28, 1803; married, Feb. 5, 1828, MARY DEXTER, born Oct. 26, 1804, daughter of Freeman and Polly (Thurston) Dexter of Winthrop. She died September, 1851; he died March, 1865.

Mr. Thurston was a farmer, and deacon in the Methodist church.

### Their children were:

+4525 Aaron Sanderson,[7] b. Aug. 15, 1828; m. Adeline Phinney.

4526 Mary Elizabeth,[7] b. April 15, 1830; d. in infancy.

4527 Mary Elizabeth,[7] b. June 29, 1831; m. William Russell Cummings of Winthrop, now a farmer in Rome, Me., P. O. address Mt.Vernon, Me. She is a member of the Methodist church. They had:

    4528 *Freeman Franklin* (Cummings), b. Jan. 6, 1869; d. Jan. 13, 1870.

4529 Joseph Dexter,[7] b. July 27, 1833; m. Catherine N. Chandler of Winthrop; was a mechanic and farmer in Winthrop, a member of the Methodist church; d. May, 1861. Children:

    4530 *Mary Victoria,*[8] b. April 3, 1858; d.

    4531 *Fred Alston,*[8] b. Sept. 2, 1859.

4532 Peleg Benson,[7] b. Aug. 9, 1835; m. Feb. 25, 1858, Rachel Gave Page of North Weare, N. H., where he resides, a carpenter and cabinet maker; enlisted in the 14th New Hampshire; was at Winchester,Va., with Sheridan, taken prisoner and carried to Belle Isle, but was soon exchanged and rejoined his regiment, and served to the close of the war. Children:

    4533 *Mary Anna,*[8] b. Dec. 8, 1858; d. Dec. 6, 1862.

    4534 *Abby Maria,*[8] b. April 26, 1867.

    4535 *Mabel Isadore,*[8] b. Oct. 25, 1873.

4536 Ada Meribah,[7] b. June 10, 1837; m. 1st, Thomas Daniels of Winthrop; 2d, George Norcross, a farmer of Winthop; she was a member of the Methodist church; d. 1869. She had, by first husband:

    4537 *Edson Eugene* (Daniels), b. Feb. 28, 1859; name changed to Thurston.

4538 Cyrus Freeman,[7] b. April 7, 1839; d. April 3, 1842.

4539 Stephen Atwell,[7] b. April 19, 1841; m. 1st, Jan. 1, 1864, Mary Jane Buswell of Stetson, Me.; 2d, Sept. 2, 1871, Emma Adeline Crosby of Augusta, Me.; she died Feb. 20, 1873; 3d, Sept. 14, 1873, Mary Ann Cummings of Winthrop. He enlisted April 3, 1861, in the 3d Maine, and participated in the battles of 1st Bull Run, Yorktown, Williamsburgh, Fair Oaks, seven days before Richmond, 2d Bull Run, Chantilly, Monocacy, and Fredericksburgh, and was discharged on account of sickness Feb. 14, 1863; recovered and re-enlisted Nov. 25, 1863, in the 2d Maine cavalry, and participated in the battles of Pollard, Mariana, Spanish Fort, and Fort Blakeley, and was raised to a corporal. He was one of Gen. A. P. Spurling's scouts. At one time the general, disguised in rebel uniform, went into the rebel camp at Milton, Fla., as an inspector of military posts, had a thorough inspection of the post, comprising about one hundred men, slept with the captain in his tent, and left next morning to return soon after with a union force and capture the entire company and all the supplies. He was discharged Sept. 18, 1865. He is a stage driver and mail contractor between Augusta and Chelsea, Me., where there is a Soldiers Home, sustained by the United States. He had, by last wife, Mary A.:

    4540 *Earnest Linwood,*[8] b. Jan. 29, 1874.

    4541 *Bertha Emma,*[8] b. Feb. 5, 1875.

    4542 *Frank Freeman,*[8] b. July 18, 1877; d. June 20, 1879.

4543   Cryus Freeman,[7] b. May 13, 1844; enlisted in the 14th Maine regiment against the rebellion, and died in New Orleans in 1863, aged 19; was a christian.

4544   Isadore Alice,[7] b. Dec. 4, 1846; m. April 24, 1867, Martin Luther Clark, a carpenter of Manchester, N. H.; she is a member of the Methodist church.   Children:

    4545   *Florence Mabel* (Clark), b. March 28, 1868.
    4546   *Arthur Lincoln* (Clark), b. March 11, 1871.
    4547   *Bertha Maude* (Clark), b. May 26, d. Aug. 28, 1872.
    4548   *Junius Henri* (Clark), b. Sept. 1, 1878.

4549   Hannah Louisa,[7] b. Oct. 25, 1849; m. Nahum Addison Goodwin of Lawrence, Mass.; he was in the United States army, but is now a painter in Lawrence, 1879.   They have:

    4550   *Charles Addison* (Goodwin), b. July 2, 1868.

## 2638

Rev. IRA TOWLE THURSTON[6] of Monmouth, Me. (*Ebenezer,*[5] *James,*[4] *Robert,*[3] *Stephen,*[2] *Daniel*[1]), brother of the preceding, and son of Ebenezer[5] and Betsey (Doughty) Thurston of Monmouth; born there Sept. 12, 1812; married, June 13, 1837, PAMELIA FAIRBANKS FOGG of Monmouth.   Mr. Thurston gained his early education in the common school and Monmouth academy, teaching school winters.   He learned the trade of carpenter of Nathaniel Dexter in Winthrop, Me.; was converted, and feeling it his duty to preach the gospel, applied himself to further study at home, and attended the Maine Wesleyan seminary at Readfield.   In 1837 he joined the Maine Methodist Conference, and labored in Dixfield circuit one year, 1838 Phillips circuit, 1839 Byron circuit, 1840 in Livermore, 1841 and 1842 in Fayette, superanuated in 1843, but in 1844 took a charge in Vienna, 1845 in Unity, and 1846 in Mercer.   At the close of this year his health failed, he purchased a farm in Monmouth and labored what he could till he died, Jan. 7, 1852.

### Children:

4556   Juliette,[7] b. in Byron, Me., Jan. 8, 1839; m. Nov. 1, 1858, Alfred W. House of Monmouth; d. Dec. 7, 1873, leaving:

    4557   *Elwood Morris* (House), b. Aug. 16, 1871.

4558   Henry Clark,[7] b. in Livermore, Me., June 22, 1841; m. Dec. 25, 1862, Harriet E. Hilton.   He was a seaman in the navy one year; enlisted in the 10th New York cavalry against the rebellion and served three years; settled in Pepperell, Mass., as a paper manufacturer.   They have:

    4559   *Arlie,*[8] b. April, 1868.

4560   Octavia Fogg,[7] b. July 13, 1843; m. May 4, 1866, James Wardwell of Winthrop; died July 28, 1871, having had:

    4561   *Louisa* (Wardwell), b. April 9, 1867; d. April 9, 1869.
    4562   *Hattie E.* (Wardwell), b. Nov. 29, 1870.

4563   Emily Ann,[7] b. Oct. 26, 1845; d. Oct. 27, 1846.

4564   Ira Morris,[7] b. in Monmouth June 15, 1849; a mason, working in Pepperell, Mass., 1879.

## 2640

JAMES THURSTON[6] of Nottingham, N. H. (*Peter,*[5] *James,*[4] *Robert,*[3] *Stephen,*[2] *Daniel*[1]), eldest son of Peter[5] and Rachel (Doughty) Thurston of Nottingham; born there 1797; married DEBORAH CHASE, born 1799, daughter of Josiah and Susan (Weeks) Chase of Stratham, N. H.   He died Dec. 20, 1826, and his widow married, in Deerfield, N. H., June 2, 1829, Benjamin Noyes, a farmer of Nottingham.

Mr. Thurston was a boot and shoe maker in Nottingham, and after in Raymond, Me.

Their children were:

4570  Lucretia,[7] d. 1823, aged ten months.
+4571  Elijah Chase,[7] b. in Epping, N. H., May 16, 1824; m. Maria Lois Lucy.
4572  Lucretia,[7] b. July 11, 1825; m. Benjamin Harvey; lived in Nottingham, and died there Oct. 30, 1857.

Child of Benjamin Noyes:

4573  Huldah H. (Noyes), b. 1832; m. 1st, Leonard O. Witham; 2d, Warren S. Rollins of Lee, N. H.

## 2648

FREEMAN DEXTER THURSTON[6] of Nottingham, N. H. (*Peter*,[5] *James*,[4] *Robert*,[3] *Stephen*,[2] *Daniel*[1]), brother of the preceding, and son of Peter[5] and Rachel (Doughty) Thurston of Nottingham; born there Aug. 16, 1815; married, Nov. 9, 1838, NANCY ANN JONES, born Aug. 4, 1808, daughter of Jonathan and Comfort (Knight) Jones of Nottingham. Mr. Thurston is a farmer.

Children:

4580  Melissa Ann,[7] b. Aug. 6, 1840; m. Oct. 3, 1862, William Henry Noble, a dealer in boots and shoes in Stoneham, Mass. They have:
    4581  *Walter Herbert* (Noble), b. April 14, 1864.
4582  Frances Ann,[7] b. Nov. 4, 1841; m. May 17, 1858, Moses Bowton Neally, a farmer in Nottingham; d. April 20, 1859, leaving:
    4583  *Sarah Frances* (Neally), b. April 17, 1859; m. June 1, 1877, George Leroy Bartlett, a farmer in Deerfield, N. H., and has Naomi Myrtle (Bartlett), b. 1877.
4584  Henrietta Butler,[7] b. April 1, 1843; m. Dec. 17, 1866, Frank Greenleaf Rundlett of Epping, N. H., now a letter carrier in Lowell, Mass.; has:
    4585  *Maud Noble* (Rundlett), b. May 21, 1870.
4586  Freeman Elijah,[7] b. Dec. 9, 1848; m. March 6, 1871, Rose F. Durgin, a shoemaker of Nottingham. They have:
    4587  *Blanche Mary*,[8] b. Nov. 1, 1874.

## 2773

ENOCH THURSTON[6] of Bow, N. H. (*Nathaniel*,[5] *Jonathan*,[4] *Nathaniel*,[3] *Stephen*,[2] *Daniel*[1]), son of Nathaniel[5] and Susanna (Jackman) Thurston of Boscawen, N. H.; born there March 24, 1807; married, Sept. 27, 1843, CAROLINE BLANCHARD of Boscawen. He is a farmer.

Children:

4593  Mary Ann.[7]
4594  Oscar.[7]
4595  Amos.[7]
4596  Nancy.[7]
4597  Polly Jane.[7]
4598  Josephene.[7]

## 2784

JOHN JAY THURSTON[6] of Boscawen, N. H. (*Nathaniel*,[5] *Jonathan*,[4] *Nathaniel*,[3] *Stephen*,[2] *Daniel*[1]), brother of the preceding, and son of Nathaniel[5] and Susanna (Jackman) Thurston of Boscawen; born there April 3, 1813; married, first, December, 1841, EUNICE RANDALL ANDREWS of Somersworth, N. H., born April 11, 1817; she died Aug. 29, 1858. Second, Jan. 1, 1861, MRS. ORZILLA (BEAN) ELKINS, widow of John Elkins of Salisbury, N. H. Mr. Thurston is a carpenter.

His children, by first wife, Eunice, were:

4603  John Peacock,[7] b. Oct. 25, 1843; m. July 3, 1867, Mary Isabel Stott of Newmarket, N. H., b. April 29, 1853. He served three years in the war against the rebellion in Co. F, 4th New Hampshire regiment, and was wounded in the battle of Pocatalago, S. C.; is a shoemaker at Derry Depot, N. H.; no children.

4604  Samuel Hovey,[7] b. Sept. 29, 1845; m. June 17, 1874, Annie Davis of Boscawen; is a shoemaker in Ipswich, Mass.; no children.

4605  Phebe Jane,[7] b. Jan. 18, 1848; m. Feb 1, 1872, Charles Henry Smith of Laconia, N. H. They reside in Concord, N. H., and have:
    4606  *Lillie Bell* (Smith), b. July 18, 1873.
    4607  *Henry Arthur* (Smith), b. April, 1876.

4608  Susan Webster,[7] b. March 1, 1850; is in Concord, N. H.; n.m.

4609  Ida Ann,[7] b. March 6, 1856; is in Washington, D. C.; n.m.

## 2787

CAPT. NATHANIEL THURSTON [6] of South Boston, Mass. (*Nathaniel,[5] Jonathan,[4] Nathaniel,[3] Stephen,[2] Daniel[1]*), brother of the preceding, and son of Nathaniel [5] and Susanna (Jackman) Thurston of Boscawen, N. H.; born there April 6, 1820; married, July 9, 1851, HANNAH CLOUGH NOYES, born Jan. 19, 1831, daughter of Charles Glidden and Hannah (Haines) Noyes of Boscawen.

Mr. Thurston is a fret sawyer; was captain of artillery and a member of Berdan's sharp shooters in the war against the rebellion; participated in the battles of the Peninsular campaign under McClellan, was on picket thirteen times at the seige of Yorktown, at Hanover Court-house, Mechanicsville, Gains' Mills and Malvern Hill; was discharged for double hernia, at Crany Island hospital, Oct. 24, 1862. He says, "I have seen hard times in my country's service, but don't regret it, and if there is a call for its defence again I am ready and willing to go."

### Children:

4615  Hannah Adelaide,[7] b. May 30, 1852; d. Aug. 30, 1852.

4616  Addie May,[7] b. in Boscawen, May 1, 1854; m. in Boston, Mass., Dec. 11, 1871, Granville Otis Waltz, b. Mar. 12, 1850, son of Samuel Otis and Harriet (Genther) Waltz of Waldoborough, Me.; he is a cabinet maker and builder in Waldoborough, member of the Baptist church. They have:
    4617  *Granville Ernest* (Waltz), b. Feb. 10, 1872.
    4618  *Clarence Brown* (Waltz), b. Aug. 5, 1874.
    4619  *Guy Irving* (Waltz), b. June 23, 1875.
    4620  *Estella May* (Waltz), b. Oct. 5, 1876.
    4621  *Roland Thurston* (Waltz), b. Feb. 23, 1878.

4622  Florette Haines,[7] b. Aug. 4, 1856; m. George A. White of Gardiner, Me., and lives with her parents.

4623  John Charles Fremont,[7] b. Dec. 29, 1858; d. July 11, 1860.

4624  Charles Otis,[7] b. Oct. 20, 1863; d. Nov. 26, 1869.

4625  Hattie Maria,[7] b. April 20, 1868.

## 2805

VOLNEY THURSTON [6] (*Stephen,[5] Stephen,[4] Nathaniel,[3] Stephen,[2] Daniel[1]*), eldest son of Stephen [5] and Philena Pamelia (Dunham) Thurston of West Hartford, Vt.; born there July 21, 1806; married, first, HANNAH C. BARBOUR; second, P. M. B. WOOD, who survives him and resides in West Hartford.

Children, born in Barnard, Vt.:

4630 Edgar,[7] b. May 13, 1835; m. in Houghton, Mich.. Oct. 31, 1865, Mary Jane Selley, b. Nov. 3, 1845. daughter of Samuel and Lucinda (Fox) Selley of Waterville, N. Y. He is a farmer in Sciola, Iowa, justice of the peace, and member of the Congregational church. They have:
    4631 *Lillie Ellen*,[8] b. in Ypsilanti. Mich., Aug. 22, 1870.
4632 Vallorous,[7] b. April 19, 1838; m. in Wayne township, Ind., Nov. 5, 1871, Emma L. Farnsworth, b. in Wentworth, N. H., April 25, 1851, daughter of Hiram M. and Mira J. (Phelps) Farnsworth of Rumney, N. H. He is a carpenter in Indianapolis, Ind.; enlisted in the war against the rebellion Sept. 25, 1861, in the 1st Vermont cavalry; was a prisoner three months in Lynchburgh and Belle Isle, Va., and a second time six months in Belle Isle; no children.

## 2809

JOHN CHENEY THURSTON [6] (*Stephen*,[5] *Stephen*,[4] *Nathaniel*,[3] *Stephen*,[2] *Daniel*[1]), brother of the preceding, and son of Stephen [5] and Philena Pamelia (Dunham) Thurston of Hartford, Vt.; born there Oct. 18, 1816; married, Aug. 17, 1842, HARRIET MARIA SNOW, born Oct. 12, 1815, daughter of Martin and Lydia (Hayes) Snow of Pomfret, Vt.

Mr. Thurston is a notary public in Cambridge, Mass., and a member of the Unitarian society.

Their children, born in Cambridge, are:

+4637 James Melvin,[7] b. April 13. 1844: m. Nellie Florence Mann.
4638 Mary Emma,[7] b. Jan. 3, 1846: n.m.
4639 John Henry,[7] b. March 5, 1852; n.m.; a bookseller in Cambridge.

## 2810

CHARLES HENRY THURSTON [6] (*Stephen*,[5] *Stephen*,[4] *Nathaniel*,[3] *Stephen*,[2] *Daniel*[1]), brother of the preceding, and son of Stephen [5] and Philena Pamelia (Dunham) Thurston of Hartford, Vt.; born there Nov. 30, 1820; married SUSAN ANN MILLER, daughter of Ansel and Lucy (Wood) Miller of Orange, N. H.

Mr. Thurston is a carpenter in West Canaan, Grafton county, N. H.; also a notary public, and a member of the Congregational church in Hartford.

Their children, born at West Hartford, were:

4645 Ellen Philena,[7] b. Jan. 19, 1849; d. June 2. 1862.
4646 Charles Stephen,[7] b. April 9, 1854; m. April 28, 1875, Emma Frances Crafts of Lowell, Vt.. b. Dec. 1, 1856. They have:
    4647 *Willie Allen*,[8] b. March 17, 1876.

## 2824

REV. HENRY WARREN LYMAN THURSTON [6] (*Nathaniel*,[5] *Stephen*,[4] *Nathaniel*,[3] *Stephen*,[2] *Daniel*[1]), son of Nathaniel [5] and Martha (Hall) Thurston of Hanover, N. H.; born in Hartford, Vt., Nov. 20, 1823; married, first, April 12, 1848, ELIZA ANN BURNHAM, born Aug. 12, 1824. daughter of Joseph and Nancy (Sawyer) Burnham of Hanover, N. H.; she died April 2, 1857. Second, Nov. 20, 1858, MARY ELIZABETH CHOATE, born Dec. 25, 1836, daughter of Benjamin and Eliza A. (Whittemore) Choate of Enfield, N. H.

Mr. Thurston spent the first fifty years of his life in farming, trade, and as a mechanic. On May 1, 1875, he was called to the ministry in the Congregational denomination, and preached in Goshen, N. H., two years, having been ordained Aug. 25, 1875; in Harrisville, N. H., from May 1, 1877, to May 1, 1879, when he went to Sullivan, N. H.

15

His children, by first wife, Eliza Ann, were:

4653   Charles Henry,[7] b. March 9, 1850; d. Nov. 12, 1868.
4654   Elzina Maria,[7] b. Sept. 13, 1854; m. March 16, 1871, Alman Walker, son
       of Haskel and Irene (Lang) Walker of Goshen. They live at West
       Lebanon, N. H., and have:
   4655   *Nellie Grant* (Walker), b. Nov. 5, 1872.
   4656   *Henry Haskel* (Walker), b. May 10, 1874.
   4657   *Irene* (Walker), b. Feb. 18, 1876.
   4658   *Edna Marriel* (Walker), b. Dec. 24, 1877.

## 2837

JOSEPH HILTON THURSTON[6] of Ellsworth, Wis. (*William,[5] Stephen,[4]
Stephen,[8] Stephen,[2] Daniel[1]*), eldest son of Col. William[5] and Charity
(Eames) Thurston of Madison, Me.; born there Aug. 31, 1808; mar-
ried, March 4, 1831, DEBORAH LUCE REMICK, born in Industry, Me.,
Oct. 31, 1813, daughter of True and Catherine (Luce) Remick of
Madison. He is a farmer.

### Children, born in Madison:

4660   Mary Ann,[7] b. June 18, 1826; m. Ripley Martin [see no. 1195].
4661   Elvira,[7] b. Nov. 15, 1833; d. Oct. 9, 1860.
4662   Betsey,[7] b. Jan. 23, 1835; d. July 3, 1856.
4663   True Remick,[7] b. Dec. 30, 1836; m. in Madison Sept. 18, 1861, Nancy Ann
       Chapman; is a farmer in Cornville, Me. They have :
   4664   *Helen A.,[8]* b. Jan. 29, 1864.
4665   William,[7] b. Dec. 4, 1839; m. at Beldenville, Wis., Sept. 5, 1869, Sophia R.
       Weston; was a farmer in Trim Belle, Wis. ; d. Apr. 26, 1872. They had :
   4666   *William,[8]* b. April 10, 1871; d. March 8, 1872.
4667   Gilbert Remick,[7] b. July 28, 1841; served three years in the 30th Wiscon-
       sin regiment against the rebellion.
4668   Catherine Remick,[7] b. July 6, 1845; m. Nov. 26, 1865, Isaac Franklin
       Weston, a lumberman in Motley, Minn.; served three years in the 30th
       Wisconsin regiment against the rebellion.   Children :
   4669   *John H.* (Weston), b. June 24, 1867.
   4670   *Charles M.* (Weston), b. May 11, 1869.
   4671   *Adah Thurston* (Weston), b. Jan. 12, 1872.
   4672   *Eddie W.* (Weston), b. Aug. 31, d. Oct. 31, 1875.
   4673   *Ruemma S.* (Weston), b. Aug. 18, 1877.
4674   Mary Adelaide,[7] b. May 22, 1847; m. Dec. 25, 1866, Frank T. Williams, a
       farmer and lumberman in Lorane, Wis.; he served two years in the
       38th Wisconsin regiment against the rebellion; was one of the first men
       who went into Fort Hell at Petersburgh, Va.   Children :
   4675   *Julia Dell* (Williams), b. Dec. 15, 1867.
   4676   *Dora Alona* (Williams), b. Oct. 12, 1869.
   4677   *Myrtle Blanch* (Williams), b. Sept. 10, 1874.
4678   Ruema Norton,[7] b. Nov. 16, 1850; m. in Kinnick Kinnick, Wis., Jan. 1,
       1870, Harry S. Sawyer; he served two years in the war against the re-
       bellion in a Pennsylvania regiment of infantry; is a contractor and build-
       er at River Falls, Wis.   Children :
   4679   *Addie Belle* (Sawyer), b. Oct. 7, 1871.
   4680   *Hattie* (Sawyer), b. Jan. 31, 1873.
   4681   *Will T.* (Sawyer), b. Aug. 12, 1878.

### Born in Solon, Me. :

4682   Clementine Remick,[7] b. Nov. 15, 1852; m. Nov. 8, 1869, Levi R. Stafford,
       a farmer in Trim Belle.   Children :
   4683   *Vinna R.* (Stafford), b. June 22, 1871.
   4684   *True Thurston* (Stafford), b. Nov. 14, 1874.
   4685   *Levi R.* (Stafford), b. April 4, 1879.
4686   Adah,[7] b. Jan. 20, 1855; d. July 6, 1855.
4687   Charles,[7] b. Aug. 29, 1857; d. April 13, 1860.

## 2839

WILLIAM WIGGIN THURSTON[6] of Trim Belle, Wis. (*William,*[5] *Stephen,*[4] *Stephen,*[3] *Stephen,*[2] *Daniel*[1]), brother of the preceding, and son of Col. William[5] and Charity (Eames) Thurston of Madison, Me.; born there Jan. 17, 1811; married, Jan. 1, 1834, ELIZA NUTTING, daughter of Abel and Sally (Moore) Nutting of Madison. She died March 2, 1851; he died March 8, 1862.

Mr. Thurston was a small capitalist, loaning money and laboring.

Child:

4690   Ansel Ganselo,[7] b. Nov. 20, 1834; m. Nov., 1853, Helen Moore. He was lieutenant-colonel of state militia; d. June 7, 1855; no children.

## 2840

DANIEL THURSTON[6] (*William,*[5] *Stephen,*[4] *Stephen,*[3] *Stephen,*[2] *Daniel*[1]), brother of the preceding, and son of Col. William[5] and Charity (Eames) Thurston of Madison, Me.; born there Dec. 6, 1812; married, Aug. 15, 1842, ANN BURNS, born Sept. 17, 1817, daughter of Samuel S. and Anna (Weston) Burns of Madison.

Mr. Thurston was educated mostly at the Wesleyan seminary, Readfield, and Waterville college, Me., but finally graduated at the Asbury university, Ind., through the influence of his friend, Prof. Wm. C. Larrabee. He followed teaching in Maine and was principal of some of the largest and best schools and academies of the state; was employed for some time by the Appletons of New York to lecture on reading and general education, holding institutes in connection with the same; has been an ordained minister over thirty years of the Methodist Episcopal church. He had an attack of paralysis and physicians advised him in the fall of 1855 to go to Beldenville, Wis., since which time he has followed farming and teaching combined. He has held the office of town and county superintendent for some years and also the office of justice of the peace most of the time. Sept., 1879, moved to Round Spring, Mitchell county, Kansas.

Child:

4691   Helen Augusta,[7] b. Sept. 10, 1855; m. Dec. 12, 1876, Moses Thomas Pickard, a farmer in Mitchell county, Kansas, since 1878; no children.

## 2851

WINTHROP HILTON THURSTON[6] (*William,*[5] *Stephen,*[4] *Stephen,*[3] *Stephen,*[2] *Daniel*[1]), brother of the preceding, and son of Col. William[5] and Charity (Eames) Thurston of Madison, Me.; born there June 23, 1821; married, in Anson, Me., HANNAH SPEAR, born July 22, 1823, daughter of James and Susan (Merrill) Spear of New Portland, Me.

Mr. Thurston was a farmer in Madison, and removed to Hartland, Pierce county, Wis.

Children, all born in Madison:

4692   Ledru Rollin,[7] b. April 3, 1848; m. Nov. 8, 1877, Anna Caroline Anderson.
4693   Susan Spear,[7] b. Oct. 11, 1850; m. March 7, 1874, Ben Owen Beavins.
4694   Ann,[7] b. Sept. 23, 1852; d. March 7, 1873.
4695   James Frank,[7] b. March 8, 1854; d. April 29, 1855.
4696   Jane,[7] b. March 6, 1857; d. Aug. 23, 1859.
4697   Frank,[7] b. Oct. 24, 1860.
4698   Jane,[7] b. Jan. 2, 1862.
4699   Emma Stella,[7] b. March 28, 1866.

## Seventh Generation.
### 2916

JOHN ALBERT THURSTON[7] (*Daniel,*[6] *Hon. Nathaniel,*[5] *Col. Daniel,*[4] *Benjamin,*[3] *Daniel,*[2] *Daniel*[1]), eldest son of Daniel[6] and Abigail (Stevens) Thurston of Haverhill, Mass.; born in Bradford, Mass., Jan. 27, 1817; married, in Lynn, Mass., ELIZA SPARROW DOWNING, born in Boston, Mass., May, 1810, daughter of Smith and Hannah (Jacobs) Downing of Charlestown, Mass. She died September, 1871.

Mr. Thurston is captain of police in Lynn, Mass.; has been on the police force thirty-six years; seven years city marshal; two years assistant marshal; two years chief engineer; six years captain of police; many years constable; member of the Methodist church.    Children:

   4700  Eliza Ann,[8] b. Dec. 8, 1836; d. 1853.
   4701  Albert Adams,[8] b. 1838; d. 1840.
   4702  Mary Pool,[8] b. Dec. 19, 1840; m. Nov. 24, 1859, John Aspinwall, b. Sept. 15, 1832, son of John and Esther (Reed) Aspinwall of Charlestown. Mr. Aspinwall is a dentist in Lynn, having graduated from the Philadelphia dental college. In 1861 he entered the navy as a common sailor; was promoted to master, and then to ensign, which position he held till 1866, when he received an honorable discharge.   Children :
       4703  *Minnie Ida* (Aspinwall), b. Oct. 23, 1861.
       4704  *Carrie Isabel* (Aspinwall), b. Oct. 8, 1868.
       4705  *Annie Mabel* (Aspinwall), b. May 25, 1870.
       4706  *Lucy Gertrude* (Aspinwall), b. April, 1872; d. Sept., 1872.
       4707  *Etta Thurston* (Aspinwall), b. Sept. 16, 1873.
       4708  *Ralph Waldo* (Aspinwall), b. June 6, 1875; d. July 2, 1875.
+4709  Albert Theodore,[8] b. Dec. 23, 1842; m. Eliza Jane Howard.
   4710  Margaret Helen,[8] b. Sept. 8, 1845; m. Nov. 24, 1868, John Hobart Lincoln, a gravel roofer in Chelsea, Mass., b. March 15, 1840, son of Isaac and Sarah (Barter) Lincoln of Chelsea. They have :
       4711  *Hattie Maria* (Lincoln), b. Sept. 5, 1869.
   4712  Benjamin Stevens.[8]           4713  George Breed.[8]
   4714  Etta H.[8]

### 2978

PERSIS GOODALE THURSTON[7] (*Rev. Asa,*[6] *Thomas,*[5] *Dea. John,*[4] *Jonathan,*[3] *Daniel,*[2] *Daniel*[1]), eldest child of Rev. Asa[6] and Lucy (Goodale) Thurston of the Sandwich Islands; born there Sept. 28, 1821; married, in Dr. Cox's church, Brooklyn, N. Y., Aug. 12, 1847, REV. TOWNSEND ELIJAH TAYLOR, born July 18, 1818, son of Eleazer and Phebe (Townsend) Taylor of La Grange, N. Y.

Mr. Taylor graduated from Middlebury, Vt., July, 1844; from Union theological seminary, New York city, June, 1847, and sailed for the Hawaiian Islands, under appointment from the Seaman's Friend Society, in October, 1847.   After laboring for seamen at Lahaina and Honolulu, he was called, in 1851, to organize and take charge of the Fort street church, Honolulu.   In 1860 removed to California on account of ill health.   In 1864 was appointed delegate from California to the Christian Commission, and spent several weeks with the sick and wounded soldiers in Washington and at City Point. Since then has been pastor of churches in different parts of California and Nevada.   For two years was district missionary for home missions on the Pacific coast.   For the last few years has been laboring in southern California under the auspices of the Presbyterian Board of Home Missions, and is now, 1879, the pastor of the Presbyterian church in Nordhoff, Ventura county, Cal., presbytery of Los Angeles, synod of California.

Miss Thurston went to New England in 1840, and graduated from the Mt. Holyoke seminary 1845 ; taught in that seminary two years.

Children :

4720　Lucy (Taylor). b. in Honolulu May 28, 1849; m. in San Rafael, Cal., Aug. 19, 1874, Jacob Percy Winnie, general business man of Carson City, Nevada, where they now reside.　They have :

4721　*Lucy* (Winnie), b. Aug. 5. 1875.
4722　*Mary* (Winnie), b. Oct. 28, 1876.

4723　Mary (Taylor), b. in Lahaina Dec. 26, 1850; m. in San Rafael June 24, 1874, Charles Henry Kluegel, civil engineer and surveyor of Oakland, Cal., where they now reside.　They have :

4724　*George Taylor* (Kluegel), b. Jan. 20, 1876.

4725　George Brainerd (Taylor), b. in Honolulu March 22, 1853; d. in Oakland, Cal., Jan. 7, 1869.
4726　Henry Thurston (Taylor), b. in Kailua, H. I., May 20, 1856.
4727　James Townsend (Taylor), b. in Kailua March 19, 1858.
4728　Edward Sanford (Taylor), b. in Columbia, Cal., Sept. 18, 1862.

## 2980

ASA GOODALE THURSTON [7] (*Rev. Asa,*[6] *Thomas,*[5] *Dea. John,*[4] *Jonathan,*[3] *Daniel,*[2] *Daniel*[1]), brother of the preceding, and eldest son of Rev. Asa[6] and Lucy (Goodale) Thurston of the Sandwich Islands; born in Kailua, Hawaii, Aug. 1, 1827 ; married at Honolulu, Oct. 23, 1853, SARAH ANDREWS, born in Lahainaluna, Island of Maui, Oct. 10, 1832, daughter of Lorrin and Mary (Wilson) Andrews, missionaries of 1827 to those islands.　Mr. Andrews was the founder and for eleven years the principal of the Lahainaluna seminary for young men; for a number of years judge of the supreme court, and author of the Hawaiian dictionary and grammar.　Mary Wilson, Mrs. Andrews, was from Washington, Mason county, Ky., and is now, 1877, living in Honolulu.　Mrs. Asa Goodale Thurston, since the death of her husband. has been matron of the Haleakala government boarding school, which is situated within nine miles of the crater of Haleakala, the largest crater in the world, but now extinct.

Mr. Thurston graduated from Williams college, Williamstown, Mass., in 1848.　He returned to the Sandwich Islands and was a surveyor ; chief clerk for the minister of the interior two or three years; speaker of the house of representatives two years, and a member of the Fort street church in Honolulu, where he died, Dec. 17, 1859.

Children :

4730　Robert Taylor,[8] b. Nov. 26, 1854; d. April 17, 1874.
4731　Lorrin Andrews,[8] b. July 31, 1858; is clerk for the attorney general of the Sandwich Islands.
4732　Helen Goodale,[8] b. Aug. 28, 1860.

## 2981

MARY HOWE THURSTON [7] (*Rev. Asa,*[6] *Thomas,*[5] *Dea. John,*[4] *Jonathan,*[3] *Daniel,*[2] *Daniel*[1]), sister of the preceding, and daughter of Rev. Asa[6] and Lucy (Goodale) Thurston of the Sandwich Islands; born on board vessel, near the islands, June 3, 1831; married, first, April 5, 1859, EDWIN A. HAYDEN ; he died April 1, 1864.　Second, July 9, 1867, MARCUS BENFIELD ; he died September, 1874.　She graduated from the normal school at Westfield, Mass.

Her children, by first husband, Hayden, were :

4733　Edwin (Hayden). b. Nov. 23, 1860; d. March 24, 1866.
4734　Asa Thurston (Hayden), b. April 12, 1862.

4735   Mary (Hayden), b. June 29, 1864; d. April 25, 1866.
               By second husband, Benfield:
4736   Lilly (Benfield), b. April 20, 1868.
4737   Eric Lex (Benfield), b. Dec. 17, 1869; d. Nov. 22, 1874.
4738   Clara (Benfield), b. Sept. 18, 1871
4739   Ida (Benfield), b. June 22, 1874; d. Nov. 22, 1874.

## 2982

REV. THOMAS GAIRDNER THURSTON[7] (*Rev. Asa,[6] Thomas,[5] Dea. John,[4] Jonathan,[3] Daniel,[2] Daniel[1]*), brother of the preceding, and son of Rev. Asa[6] and Lucy (Goodale) Thurston of the Sandwich Islands; born there May 9, 1836; married, first, at the Hawaiian Islands, Oct. 25, 1866, HARRIET FRANCES RICHARDSON, born Aug. 31, 1838, daughter of Samuel and Hannah (Towle) Richardson of Maine; she died at Grass Valley, Cal., May 25, 1872.  Second, in Albany, N. Y., May 13, 1875, ALICE GASKING, born June 7, 1846, daughter of George and Alice (Black) Gasking of Rhinebeck, N. Y.

Rev. Mr. Thurston graduated from Yale 1862, and from Union theological seminary in 1865; ordained by presbytery in Hawaiian Islands in 1866.  Now, 1879, preaching in Taylorville, N. C., where he, as principal, and his wife, as assistant, are teaching an academy for boys and girls.
               Child, by first wife, born at Hawaiian Islands:
4742   Alice,[8] b. July 21, 1867.

## 3062

ABEL LEANDER THURSTON[7] (*Dea. Abel,[6] Dea. John,[5] Dea. John,[4] Jonathan,[3] Daniel,[2] Daniel[1]*), son of Dea. Abel[6] and Eunice (Allen) Thurston of Fitchburgh, Mass.; born there June 21, 1821; married, in Leominster, Mass., Oct. 3, 1843, ELIZABETH KNAPP, born Mar. 31, 1822, daughter of Elijah and Rhoda (Swallow) Knapp of Mason, N. H.

Mr. Thurston is assistant superintendent of the Cambridge (Mass.) cemetery, and a member of the Congregational church in Fitchburgh.
               Children, all born in Fitchburgh:
4750   Henry Melville,[8] b. Jan. 25, 1846; d. April 10, 1846.
4751   Rufus Leander,[8] b. Aug. 7, 1850; n.m.; in music store, firm of Goodnough
             & Thurston, 240 Farrell street, San Francisco, Cal.
4752   George Abel,[8] b. Nov. 28, 1852; n.m.; with his brother Rufus as clerk.
4753   Allen Lewis,[8] b. Dec. 28, 1855; m. July 15, 1877, Martha Elizabeth Skel-
             ton, b. in Cambridge March 1, 1848; is a stone-mason in Cambridge.

## 3082

COL. WILLIAM HENRY THURSTON[7] (*William Parsons,[6] Rev. Pearson,[5] Samuel,[4] Jonathan,[3] Daniel,[2] Daniel[1]*), son of William Parsons[6] and Mary (Gardner) Thurston of Leominster, Mass.; born in Nashua, N. H., March 27, 1827; married, first, in Elizabeth, N. J., 1854, MARY JANE WOODRUFF; divorced.  Second, in Memphis, Tenn., March 11, 1865, MAGGIE FISHER, born in Carson Armagh, north of Ireland, daughter of Alexander and Mary (Thomson) Fisher of Luzerne, N. Y.  Her father was a lawyer of some note in Ireland, and had a brother, Rev. John Fisher, deceased some years ago, who was pastor of the Presbyterian church in Rochester, N. Y.  Col. Wm. H. Thurston died in Cincinnati, Ohio, May 17, 1877, and was buried in Leominster.  His widow lives in Luzerne, 1879.

Col. Thurston was in the railroad service for seventeen years; went to Cincinnati in 1860, and for a time was agent of the Merchants Dispatch Company.  At the breaking out of the war of the rebellion,

he entered the army as captain in an Indiana regiment, and was soon promoted to be a staff officer of Gen. Lew Wallace; and served as inspector general for Gen. S. A. Hurlburt, gaining much distinction; breveted brigadier general, but would not consent to be called anything but colonel; was once wounded in battle. After the close of the war he was connected with the internal revenue service in Cincinnati. In politics he was an ardent republican and a man of much influence. In social life he was a kind, tender, and loving husband and father, and had a host of friends warmly attached to him.

His children, by first wife, Mary, were:

4760    Sarah Fannie,[8] b. about 1855.
4761    John Clute,[8] b. about 1857.

By second wife, Maggie :

4762    Sadie Blanche,[8] b. 1871.

## 3127

CHARLES CURRIER THURSTON[7] (*Leland,*[6] *John,*[5] *David,*[4] *Jonathan,*[3] *Daniel,*[2] *Daniel*[1]), eldest son of Leland[6] and Margaret (Hutchins) Thurston of Denver, Col.; born in Troy, N. H., Jan. 13, 1828; married, in Boston, Mass., CAROLINE HUMPHREY, born April 11, 1827, daughter of Charles Haden and Jane Frost (Higgins) Humphrey of Gray, Me. He is a builder in Elizabeth, N. J. Children:

4770    Lillie Maria,[8] b. Nov. 4, 1849.
4771    Mary Elizabeth,[8] b. May 31, 1851.
4772    Carrie Josephine,[8] b. April 4, 1854.
4773    George Humphrey,[8] b. Sept. 8, 1855.
4774    Fanny Humphrey,[8] b. March 27, 1857; d. March 4, 1860.
4775    Charles Clement,[8] b. Feb. 18, 1863; d. Feb. 3, 1864.

## 3130

FRANKLIN ALDEN THURSTON[7] (*Leland,*[6] *John,*[5] *David,*[4] *Jonathan,*[3] *Daniel,*[2] *Daniel*[1]), brother of the preceding, and son of Leland[6] and Margaret (Hutchins) Thurston of Denver, Col.; born in Keene, N. H., Oct. 9, 1834; married, Nov. 27, 1860, ANNIE ELIZA RAPELYE, daughter of George and Margaret (Calyer) Rapelye of Newtown, Long Island. Mr. Thurston is a master builder in New York city, and a local preacher in the Methodist Episcopal church.

Children:

4780    Minnie Jane,[8] b. in Troy, N. Y., April 4, 1863.
4781    Bertha Eliza,[8] b. in New York March 2, 1869.
4782    Frank Leland,[8] b. in New York Oct. 27, 1870.

## 3188

ANDREW JACKSON THURSTON[7] (*Hartley,*[6] *Samuel,*[5] *David,*[4] *Jonathan,*[3] *Daniel,*[2] *Daniel*[1]), eldest son of Hartley[6] and Arminda (Robinson) Thurston of Berlin, Wis.; born in New Alstead, N. H., Dec. 6, 1835; married, May 28, 1859, JANE DELZELLE. He died in Nashville, Tenn., Nov. 10, 1864.

Mr. Thurston lived in Wisconsin till the war of the rebellion, when he went to Tennessee and was in government service till his death. His widow was several years matron at the soldiers orphans home in Davenport, Iowa; her health failed, she went to her friends in Kansas, and soon died. Children:

4787    Nellie Adelle,[8] b. Jan. 28, 1861; d. Feb. 14, 1866.
4788    Orvis Greeley,[8] b. Feb. 6, 1862; d. March 21, 1863.
4789    Effie May,[8] b. Jan. 30, 1864; d. Nov. 14, 1865.

## 3213

CHARLES HOLMAN THURSTON[7] (*Franklin Robinson*,[6] *Samuel*,[5] *David*,[4] *Jonathan*,[3] *Daniel*,[2] *Daniel*[1]), eldest son of Franklin Robinson[6] and Fanny L. (Holman) Thurston of Marlborough, N. H.; born there June 3, 1842; married, Nov. 23, 1864, AMANDA CAROLINE FROST, born April 14, 1842, daughter of Col. Cyrus and Caroline (Richardson (Frost) of Marlborough.

Mr. Thurston is one of the firm of Thurston Knob Screw Co. of Marlborough, with agency offices in Boston and New York. He was the inventor of this Screw and of the machinery for the manufacture of them. He also invented the "Companion Sewing Machine," put into the market in 1879.

Children :

4795  Frank Watson,[8] b. Sept. 7, 1865.
4796  Clarence Frost,[8] b. April 1, 1870; d. Sept. 28, 1870.
4797  Charles Willis,[8] b. May 18, 1872.
4798  Arthur Clemons,[8] b. Oct. 8, 1873; d. Feb. 22, 1874.

## 3243

MARY PARMALEE THURSTON[7] (*Ariel Standish*,[6] *Stephen*,[5] *Daniel*,[4] *Richard*,[3] *Daniel*,[2] *Daniel*[1]), eldest daughter of Hon. Ariel Standish[6] and Julia Clark (Hart) Thurston of Elmira, N. Y.; born there July 29, 1840; married, Nov. 19, 1862, CURTISS CRANE GARDINER,* born Dec. 1, 1822, son of Lyman Gardiner of Sherburne, N. Y.

Mr. Gardiner was a resident of Angelica and raised the first company of volunteers in Allegany county, N. Y., in 1861, and entered the service as captain and retired as brevet colonel of the 27th New York regiment volunteers, in the war against the rebellion; was appointed United States assessor of internal revenue of twenty-seventh district New York in 1867; he became a resident of St. Louis, Mo., in 1873.

ARMS OF GARDINER.

*The GARDINER FAMILY.

Lion Gardiner, the first settler of this family, was an Englishman. He served under Gen. Fairfax, in the Low Countries, as engineer and master of works of fortification, during the reign of Charles I. Himself, wife, servant, with others, sailed from London, and arrived in Boston Nov. 28, 1635. Early the next spring he proceeded to the mouth of the Connecticut river and built Fort Saybrook and commanded it four years, under the direction of Gov. John Winthrop jr., after which he removed to an island in Long Island sound, which he had purchased of the Indians, and called it Gardiner's Island.

GENERATIONS FROM FIRST SETTLERS.

I.  LION GARDINER, born in England 1599; married Mary Wilemson in Holland 1635; died in East Hampton, L. I., 1663.
II.  DAVID GARDINER, born in Saybrook, Ct., April 29, 1636; married Mary Leringham, June 4, 1657; died in Hartford, Ct., July 10, 1689.
III.  JOHN GARDINER, born at Gardiner's Island April 19, 1661; married, in Southold. L. I., Mary King; died in New London. Ct., June 25, 1738.
IV.  JOSEPH GARDINER, born at Gardiner's Island April 22, 1697; married Sarah Grant, Oct. 1, 1729; died in Groton. Ct , May 15, 1752.
V.  WILLIAM GARDINER, born in Groton, Ct., Sept. 5, 1741; married Esther Denison, April 16, 1761; died at Chenango Forks, N. Y., March 31 1800.
VI.  DANIEL DENISON GARDINER. born in Groton, Ct., March 28, 1773; married Eunice Otis, Feb. 18, 1794; died in Eaton, N. Y., July 17, 1817.
VII.  LYMAN GARDINER, born in Sherburne, N. Y., July 25, 1798; married Mary Crane, Jan. 22, 1822; died in Nunda, N. Y., Dec. 7, 1846.
VIII.  CURTISS CRANE GARDINER, born in Eaton, N. Y., Dec. 1, 1822; married MARY PARMALEE THURSTON, as above.

T. A. Chapman

Children:

Children:
4805  Julia Thurston (Gardiner), b. Nov. 13, 1864.
4806  Clara Standish (Gardiner), b. May 1, 1867.
4807  Curtiss Crane (Gardiner), b. May 19, 1874.

## 3244

CLARA STANDISH THURSTON [7] (*Ariel Standish,[6] Stephen,[5] Daniel,[4] Richard,[3] Daniel,[2] Daniel [1]*), sister of the preceding, and daughter of Hon. Ariel Standish [6] and Julia Clark (Hart) Thurston of Elmira, N. Y.; born there Nov. 3, 1842; married, Oct. 9, 1867, HENRY WHITE STRANG, born Jan. 2, 1844, son of Samuel Bartow Strang of Elmira, born Oct. 4, 1805, son of Major Strang of the revolutionary army. Mr. Strang is a jeweler in Elmira.   Child:
4810  Catharine Malvina (Strang). b. Aug. 25, 1868.

## 3246

JULIA HART THURSTON [7] (*Ariel Standish,[6] Stephen,[6] Daniel,[4] Richard,[3] Daniel,[2] Daniel [1]*), sister of the preceding, and daughter of Hon. Ariel Standish [6] and Cornelia Sophia (Hull) Thurston of Elmira, N. Y.; born there May 16, 1849; married, June 7, 1871, GEORGE WASHINGTON THOMAS, born May 25, 1825, son of Vial Thomas of Rhode Island.   Mr. Thomas is a druggist and stationer in Angelica, N. Y.
Children:
4812  William Standish (Thomas), b. July 5, 1873.
4813  Cornelia Thurston (Thomas), b. April 29, 1875.

## 3247

CHARLES PARISH THURSTON [7] (*Ariel Standish,[6] Stephen,[5] Daniel,[4] Richard,[3] Daniel,[2] Daniel [1]*), brother of the preceding, and son of Hon. Ariel Standish [6] and Cornelia Sophia (Hull) Thurston of Elmira, N. Y.; born there Feb. 22, 1851; married, Oct. 14, 1874, MARY TOLL RIED, born Feb. 28, 1849, daughter of James and Jane (DeGraff) Ried of Amsterdam, N. Y.   Mr. Thurston is a lawyer in Elmira.
Children:
4818  Ariel Standish,[8] b. July 31, 1875.
4819  James Ried,[8] b. 1877.

## 3333

TIMOTHY APPLETON CHAPMAN [7] of Milwaukee, Wis. (*Dea. George Whitefield,[6] Eliphaz,[5] Samuel,[4] Samuel,[3] Samuel,[2] Edward [1]*), son of Dea. George Whitefield [6] and Mary (Greenwood) Chapman of Gilead, Me.; born there May 23, 1824; married, in Boston, Mass., April 16, 1850, LAURA BOWKER, born 1828, daughter of David and Eunice (Clapp) Bowker of Scituate, Mass.

During his boyhood he assisted his father upon the farm; was educated at the district school of his native town and at the academies of Bethel and Yarmouth, Me., and engaged in teaching.  He was an ambitious boy and would never allow himself to be outdone, as an anecdote best illustrates.  His brother far excelled him in singing, do what he might, so at the age of fifteen he procured a violin and in six weeks' time was drawing the bow in the village choir to the admiration of the audience, and, as we imagine, somewhat to the astonishment of the staid adviser who told him in the beginning that if he could play psalm tunes in church in two years' time he would do well. This characteristic has followed him through all his pursuits to the present time and is one of the elements of his success.

At the age of twenty, with less than ten dollars in his purse, he went to Boston and met a dry goods merchant, who gave him employment as clerk in his store. He served in that capacity for six years, to the entire satisfaction and confidence of his employers, as was evinced on more than one occasion, when he was sent into the country with a large stock of goods to be disposed of in his own fashion.

Through the encouragement of James M. Beebe, he with his brother opened a dry goods store on Hanover street, Boston, under the firm name of T. A. & H. G. Chapman. For seven years, here and on Tremont street, they prosecuted this business with but little success, except to establish a reputation for capacity and integrity; for with the commencement of their business they established the principle, and conscientiously carried it out, of truthful representation. Observing the power of capital invested in the dry goods business in the East, he determined to make his future experiments in the West.

In 1857 he went to Milwaukee, Wis., and with the assistance of C. F. Hovey & Co. of Boston established himself in business on East Water street, under the name of Hasset & Chapman. Mr. Hasset retired at the end of five years, and was succeeded by Mr. Charles Endicott, who remained three years, since which time Mr. Chapman has been alone. Having goods of good quality, selected with refined and educated taste, with system and good order in his establishment, never allowing the quality of his wares to be misrepresented, with the rule of one price, his patronage very soon exceeded his expectations. The city grew and rival houses rose, but he maintained his supremacy.

In 1872 he built one of the largest dry goods houses in the northwest, on the corner of Wisconsin and Milwaukee streets, 50 by 240 feet, four stories, airy, cheerful, and perfect in every detail, affording every convenience to employe and patron. In 1878, finding his business still increasing and needing more room, he added another store of the same frontage as the one he built and connected it with the original structure, thus nearly doubling the business area. Although giving employment in his establishment to more persons, including their familes, than the entire population of his native town, the character of its head is felt in every member, and order and system prevail throughout.

Mr. Chapman is a man who does his own thinking, is original and not a copyist, a man of positive convictions, despising cant in religion or anything else, and shows his character and ability more by what he does than by what he professes. He is sharp in trade when dealing with his peers, but was never known to take advantage of or oppress the poor or unfortunate. In his pursuit of wealth he has not been unmindful of the comfort and happiness of his employes and members of his family who have been less successful than himself, nor has he been wanting in public spirit. He contributes liberally to whatever measures are calculated to promote the public welfare, whether physical, moral, or intellectual, recognizing no distinction of creed or opinion, being broad and liberal in his views. He is attracted by the discussion of great themes, and studies with enthusiasm the works of God in nature; logical in mind and in reason acute, not content with superficial knowledge of any subject, he goes to the root of the matter. His present influential position was not attained

by chance or luck, but is the immediate and direct result of this same principle carried out in his business.

System and good judgment characterize all his work, and his sterling integrity renders his credit "gilt edged," not only in this country, but in Europe. Other men may be worth more money, but no man stands higher as to reliability and promptness. His life illustrates the success an ambitious man of high moral aims may achieve in a good field by self-reliance, sound judgment, persevering industry, strict integrity, and a determination to know the reason of things. He is no politician, desires no office, has always voted the republican ticket; was loyal during the rebellion and sent a substitute into the army; has accumulated a handsome competency; is highly respected by his fellow citizens, and if the moral and business sentiment of Milwaukee is marked by a higher and purer practice than the average of large cities, it is due as much to the example and influence of T. A. Chapman as to any other man in their midst.

Mrs. Chapman is a woman of education, culture, refinement, and the highest social qualities. She is deservedly esteemed by the purest and best people in the city, and maintains a position of rare elevation by natural dignity of character, intelligence, and true moral worth.

The Milwaukee Sentinel of June 18, 1879, says: "Yesterday Mr. T. A. Chapman, the dry goods prince, left with his family for New York, whence they will sail on Saturday for Europe. Mr. Chapman will remain two months abroad, while his family will spend two years there. A large number of citizens wished the family a pleasant journey. Mr. Chapman is one of the pioneers of enterprising business in Milwaukee. For more than twenty years he has been engaged in the dry goods business here, and in all that time has been known as the leading merchant of the city, notable for his honesty, kindness of heart, and for the credit he has made his establishment to Milwaukee. He has now the largest dry goods establishment in the northwest outside of Chicago, and even that city has no establishment which surpasses 'Chapman's' in any important respect. There are few men as generous as Mr. Chapman, few in his line as successful, and none who have done more to elevate the name of their city. His friends all over the northwest will unite in wishing him a delightful trip and a safe return."   •

Children:

4825   Alice Greenwood[8] (Chapman), b. in Boston Nov. 9, 1853.
4826   Laura Appleton[8] (Chapman), b. in Milwaukee March 20, 1866.

## 3381

ADA DEANE (*Harriet Ann Thurston,*[6] *David,*[5] *David,*[4] *Richard,*[3] *Daniel,*[2] *Daniel*[1]), daughter of Melville Gilmore and Harriet Ann (Thurston) Deane; born in Winthrop, Me., March 24, 1853; married, in Rome, Italy, April 30, 1874, GEORGE CHAMPLAIN SHEPARD SOUTHWORTH of West Springfield, Mass., born Dec. 13, 1842, son of Hon. Edward and Ann Elizabeth (Shepard) Southworth.

Mr. Southworth graduated from Yale 1863, and from the Harvard law school 1865; was representative in the Massachusetts legislature in 1871. He was administrator of his father's estate; spent two

years or more in traveling in Europe, making a circuit of the world, and stopping at Rome to be married. After coming home he settled up his father's estate and in 1877 went to Europe with his family, for the benefit of his health, where he remains, 1880.

Children :

4830 Mary (Southworth), b. at West Springfield. Mass., April 14, 1875.
4831 Constant (Southworth), b. at Gilead, Me., Sept. 21, 1876.
4832 Rufus (Southworth), b. at St. Jean de Luz, France, June 20, 1878.

## 3544

WILLIAM THURSTON[7] ( *William Gee,*[6] *Nathaniel,*[5] *Daniel,*[4] *Joseph,*[3] *Joseph,*[2] *Daniel*[1]), son of William Gee[6] and Rachel Rich (Smith) Thurston of Riverdale, Mass.; born there Aug. 14, 1836; married, March 31, 1857, CAROLINE ELWELL, born July 30, 1832.

Mr. Thurston enlisted in the 32d Massachusetts regiment Nov. 4, 1861, and was engaged in the following battles : Malvern Hill, Gainsville, second Bull Run, Chantilly, Antietam, Fredericksburgh, Chancellorsville, Gettysburgh, Rappahannock Station, Mine Run, Spottsylvania, and the Wilderness, at which he received a ball in the neck, from which he suffered for a full year and underwent several operations before the ball could be extracted, which was finally accomplished May 19, 1865.

Children :

4836 Caroline Elizabeth,[8] b. Nov. 22, 1857; d. Feb. 3, 1864.
4837 James William,[8] b. Sept. 16, 1859; d. Sept. 10, 1864.
4838 Anna Jane,[8] b. May 16. 1861.
4839 Wilbert,[8] b. June 4. 1865.
4840 Margetta,[8] b. Feb. 16, 1867.
4841 James William,[8] b. Aug. 22, 1869.
4842 Blanche,[8] b. Jan. 28, 1874.
4843 George,[8] b. July 22, 1876; d. Oct. 4, 1876.

## 3551

JAMES THURSTON[7] ( *William Gee,*[6] *Nathaniel,*[5] *Daniel,*[4] *Joseph,*[3] *Joseph,*[2] *Daniel*[1]), brother of the preceding, and son of William Gee[6] and Rachel Rich (Smith) Thurston of Riverdale, Mass.; born there Sept. 9, 1839; married, July 17, 1862, MARTHA HOOD, born Sept. 30, 1843.

Children :

4850 Martha Lenora,[8] b. Sept. 13, 1863.
4851 Rachel Frances,[8] b. Sept. 18, 1865.
4852 Flora May,[8] b. Nov. 8, 1867.
4853 Grace,[8] b. Aug. 3, 1869.
4854 Howard Lewis,[8] b. Jan. 11, 1870.
4855 Mary Fuller,[8] b. July 2, 1874.

## 3609

STEPHEN THURSTON[7] ( *Nathaniel,*[6] *Ambrose,*[5] *Capt. John,*[4] *Joseph,*[3] *Joseph,*[2] *Daniel*[1]), son of Nathaniel[6] and Elizabeth (Robbins) Thurston of Deer Isle, Me.; born there Jan. 13, 1825; married, Jan. 18, 1848, MARGARET BABBIDGE SYLVESTER, born May 15, 1827, daughter of Joseph and Mary (Staples) Sylvester of Deer Isle.

Mr. Thurston is a master mariner, residing in Deer Isle.

Children :

4860 Joseph William Sylvester,[8] b. June 13, 1849; m. Aug. 9, 1874, Bernice Babbidge Warren, b. Dec. 2, 1853, daughter of Benjamin F. and Pauline

B. (Babbidge) Warren of Deer Isle.   He is a master mariner of South Deer Isle.   They have :

4861   *Merton Franklin*,[9] b. March 25, 1877.
4862   Orville Herbert,[8] b. Aug. 17, 1856.
4863   Ernest Vernley,[8] b May 26, 1859; d. Sept. 12, 1863.
4864   Percy Sylvester,[8] b. Nov. 25, 1862.

## 3610

CAPT. THOMAS THURSTON [7] (*Nathaniel*,[6] *Ambrose*,[5] *Capt. John*,[4] *Joseph*,[8] *Joseph*,[2] *Daniel*[1]), brother of the preceding, and son of Nathaniel [6] and Elizabeth (Robbins) Thurston of Deer Isle, Me.; born there Aug. 24, 1828; married, June 18, 1849, CAROLINE STINSON, born March 28, 1831, daughter of Joseph C. and Mary (Dow) Stinson of Deer Isle.

Mr. Thurston is a master mariner, residing in South Deer Isle.

### Children :

4870   Almira,[8] b. Sept. 12, 1850; d. Feb. 8, 1854.
4871   Clarence,[8] b. Dec. 8, 1852; a seaman.
4872   Wallace,[8] b. Sept. 30, 1855; a seaman, sailing from Gloucester, Mass.

## 3611

JAMES ROBBINS THURSTON [7] (*Nathaniel*,[6] *Ambrose*,[5] *Capt. John*,[4] *Joseph*,[8] *Joseph*,[2] *Daniel*[1]), brother of the preceding, and son of Nathaniel [6] and Elizabeth (Robbins) Thurston of Deer Isle, Me.; born there Sept. 6, 1832; married, April 2, 1854, PAULINE ACKLEY, born in Machias, Me., Jan. 2, 1835.

Mr. Thurston is a sea captain, residing in Rockport, Me.; a member of the Methodist church.

### Children, born in Deer Isle :

4876   Everett,[8] b. Nov. 21, 1855; d. March 15, 1858.
4877   Lillian Isaphene,[8] b. Oct. 23, 1859.
4878   George Everett,[8] b. Nov. 21, 1860.

### Born in Rockport :

4879   Lizzie Bell,[8] b. Sept. 12, 1864.
4880   Frank,[8] b. Dec. 30, 1869.

## 3622

CHARLES THURSTON [7] (*John*,[6] *Ambrose*,[5] *Capt. John*,[4] *Joseph*,[8] *Joseph*,[2] *Daniel*[1]), son of John [6] and Nancy (Gott) Thurston of Tremont, Me.; married, May, 1868, HANNAH ANN THURSTON [see no. 3637].

Mr. Thurston is a fisherman in Tremont.

### Children :

4885   A son, d. in infancy.
4886   Edward Watson.[8]
4887   A daughter, d. in infancy.
4888   Fanny Evelyn,[8] d. in infancy.
4889   William Caspar.[8]
4890   Fanny Evelyn.[8]
4891   Charles Ray.[8]

## 3800

DANIEL MERRILL THURSTON [7] (*Daniel*,[6] *Thomas*,[5] *Abner*,[4] *Abner*,[8] *James*,[2] *Daniel*[1]), eldest son of Daniel [6] and Sally (Merrill) Thurston of Scarborough, Me.; born Oct. 31, 1801; married, September, 1826, in Portland, Me., JANE MOORE TIBBETTS, born July 11, 1805, daughter of John and Mary (Moore) Tibbetts of Newfield, Me.   She died in Minneapolis, Minn., August, 1860.

Mr. Thurston worked on the farm summers and went to school

winters till seventeen, when he went to sea, sailing to the West Indies and South America. In 1823 or 1824 he was shipwrecked in the schooner Mt. Vernon, Capt. Howell of Portland, in the port of St. Pierre, Martinique. He was then put on board the schooner Rambler, Capt. Andrews of Providence, R. I., by the American consul. She being short one man, he shipped as one of the crew at St. Bartholomews, went to Charleston, S. C., and from there to Havana. When within about twelve hours' sail of the Moro castle at Havana, they saw a sail in the mouth of a creek, which they suspected to be a pirate; not a very pleasant discovery, as the motto of the pirates of those days was, "Dead men tell no tales," and whole crews were murdered or made to walk a plank. They very soon found that their suspicions were well founded, as they saw that she was aiming to head them off. All sail was crowded on the Rambler, and the sails were wet to make them hold more wind, in order to escape. But the pirate was a fast sailer, a long, low, black craft, with one large gun amidships, and full of men. She kept gaining on the Rambler. It was a race for life. The mate went below and brought up several rusty old muskets, determined to sell his life as dearly as he could, but the captain, seeing the utter uselessness of resistance, laughed at him. There was a schooner ahead of them that they saw in the morning, and being a much poorer sailer than the Rambler, the latter had been gaining on her very much. The wake of this schooner was filled with the lumber that had composed her deck-load, and which was thrown over to lighten her. The pirate gained on the Rambler, till the crew of the latter could see the men on her decks, when a flash was seen, and a ball from her gun came whizzing over the deck, carrying terror to their hearts. They thought their time had come, and gave up all hope. The shot did no harm to the Rambler, falling in the sea beyond, but the charge set fire to one of the sails of the pirate, making a large hole in it and impeding her progress very much. As they were now nearing the castle, the pirate, probably fearing that some man of war might be in the harbor, did not keep up the chase much longer, but hauled on the wind. Their deliverance seemed to them almost miraculous.

He resided in Portland, Me., and went mate of the brig "Fountain," under Capt. Samuel Waterhouse; left the sea at the age of twenty-four and worked three or four years rigging vessels. From 1830 to 1840 was employed by Daniel Winslow in packing meats and in the retail trade, having the charge of the latter several years, till he went into the retail meat trade for himself. He at one time kept an eating house in company with Daniel Gill; was a member of the common council one term. In 1855 he went to Lakeville, Minn., and took one hundred and sixty acres of wild prairie, from which, although on the top of a high ridge, and commanding a view of from two to forty miles, not a single house, fence, or building could be seen. In 1868 he sold his farm, and has since lived with his eldest son in Farmington, Minn., assisting him in the drug business. He has been warden of the Episcopal church there since its organization; has lived to see the prairie subdued and dotted over with comfortable houses, fine barns, thriving villages, and railroads, and is now, 1880, active, capable of business, and enjoys life.

Children, all born in Portland:

4895 Mary Jane,[8] b. June 23, 1827; d. Sept. 6, 1829.
4896 Frances Ellen,[8] b. Aug. 9, 1829; d. Sept. 26, 1831.
+4897 John Henry,[8] b. Jan. 25, 1832; m. 1st, Ellen Matilda Brimhall; 2d, Louise Mosbaugh.
4898 Sumner Cummings,[8] b. April, 1834; d. Jan., 1836.
4899 Sumner Cummings,[8] b. April 29, 1836; m. April, 1856, Martha Jane Webb; learned the art of printing, and in 1855 went to Lakeville and took a farm, where in October, 1861, he enlisted as sergeant in the 4th Minnesota infantry; was in Corinth, Memphis, and Vicksburgh campaigns; was orderly sergeant U. S. colored infantry, and was appointed second lieutenant on the day of his death, which occurred while on a furlough, caused by congestive chills contracted in the army, Nov. 5, 1863. He was intending to be confirmed in the Episcopal church. His widow resides in Winona, Minn. They had:
    4900  *Kate*,[9] b. 1857.
    4901  *Grace*,[9] b. 1862.
4902 William Francis Hayes,[8] b. Sept. 9, 1838; d. March 20, 1844.
4903 Lorenzo Dow,[8] b. Feb. 1, 1840; d. July 31, 1844.
4904 Helen Jane,[8] b. March 5, 1842; d. Sept. 5, 1847.
4905 Sarah Frances,[8] b. June 15, 1844; d. Sept. 19, 1847.
4906 Albert,[8] b. 1846; d. 1847.
4907 Charles Clifton,[8] b. July 8, 1849; watchmaker in Baldwin, St. Croix county, Wis.; n.m.

## 3801

LUCY THURSTON[7] (*Daniel*,[6] *Thomas*,[5] *Abner*,[4] *Abner*,[3] *James*,[2] *Daniel*[1]), sister of the preceding, and daughter of Daniel[6] and Sally (Merrill) Thurston of Scarborough, Me.; born in Saco, Me., April 24, 1803; married, Sept. 4, 1824, NATHANIEL GOOGINS of Saco, born May 27, 1798, and is now, 1880, living in Lyman, Me. She died in Saco Nov. 7, 1870.

Children:

4915 Louisa Maria (Googins), b. May 9, 1825.
4916 Albion Keith Paris (Googins), b. Dec. 29, 1827; m. in Saco March 12, 1856, Ruth Healy Bensley, b. in Scarborough July 29, 1833. daughter of George Angell and Rachel Weston (Bowe) Bensley of Cape Elizabeth, Me. Mr. Googins went to sea eight years, then became a farmer in East Hiram, Me.; has been town clerk, and is a member of the Universalist church. They have:
    4917  *Mary Louisa* (Googins), b. Nov. 27, 1857.
    4918  *Edith Cressey* (Googins), b. Feb. 2, 1865.
    4919  *Fred Carlton* (Googins), b. Feb. 27, 1868.
4920 Francis Byron (Googins), b. Aug. 26, 1829.
4921 Ellen Hannah (Googins), b. Sept. 1, 1831.
4922 Christiana Plummer (Googins), b. Sept. 13, 1833.
4923 Daniel Thurston (Googins), b. Dec. 7, 1835; d. Aug. 6, 1837.
4924 William Hayes (Googins), b. Aug. 20, 1838.
4925 Lydia Ann (Googins), b. Dec. 4, 1840.
4926 Lucy Abby (Googins), b. Aug. 13, 1843.
4927 Charles Sumner (Googins), b. Feb. 24, 1846.

## 3802

HENRY RICE THURSTON[7] (*Daniel*,[6] *Thomas*,[5] *Abner*,[4] *Abner*,[3] *James*,[2] *Daniel*[1]), brother of the preceding, and son of Daniel[6] and Sally (Merrill) Thurston of Scarborough, Me.; born there May 14, 1805; married, 1828, MARY RICHARDS. He settled on the homestead, and carried on farming and teaming between Scarborough and Portland. He was a member of the Free Baptist church since 1842; died Oct. 25, 1876; she died Oct. 15, 1878.

### Children :

4930  Andrew Jackson,⁸ b. Jan. 23, 1829; d. young.
+4931  Ansyl Augustus,⁵ b. April 20. 1830; m. Hannah Meserve.
4932  Oren Crawford,⁸ b. Nov. 2, 1831; m. Lydia Taylor of Biddeford; a carpenter.
4933  Miranda Moses,⁸ b. March 28, 1833; m. Granville Moulton of Scarborough, where they reside.
4934  Sarah Augusta,⁸ b. Feb. 23, 1835; resides with her sister Miranda.
4935  James Meserve,⁸ b. Sept. 6, 1836; a carpenter and farmer, lives on the homestead.
4936  Jennie Hannah,⁸ b. Sept. 14, 1840; lives on the homestead.
4937  George Boothby,⁸ b. Sept. 14, 1842; m. March 26, 1866, Sarah Ann Libbey of Scarborough; is a carpenter and lives at Dunston's Corner.
4938  Nellie Frances,⁵ b. Nov. 6, 1847; m. Charles O. Roberts; lives at Dunston's Corner.
4939  Sophronia Baker,⁸ b. June 1, 1851; lives on the homestead.

## 3816

GEORGE FICKETT THURSTON⁷ (*Alexander,⁶ Thomas,⁵ Abner,⁴ Abner,⁸ James,² Daniel¹*), son of Alexander⁶ and Almira (Fickett) Thurston of Poland, Me.; born there Aug. 13, 1817; married, first, April 4, 1846, HANNAH GORHAM WATERHOUSE, born Nov. 6, 1822, daughter of Daniel and Abigail (Gorham) Waterhouse of Poland; she died Jan. 9, 1855.   Second, June 14, 1857, BETSEY REED LIBBY, born Feb. 8, 1828, daughter of Jedediah Cobb and Hannah (Prince) Libby of Gray, Me.   He died suddenly at Mechanic Falls Sept. 22, 1879.

Mr. Thurston was a farmer in Poland, a member and clerk of the Free Baptist church.

### Children, by first wife, Hannah :

4945  Edward Franklin,⁸ b. March 12, 1847; m Nov. 6, 1863, Sarah A. Pillsbury of Biddeford, Me., where she died, July 26, 1876; he died Sept. 15, 1876.
4946  Otis Waterhouse,⁸ b. Oct. 19, 1848; m. at Windham, Me., Aug. 25, 1877, Abbie Susan Brown, b. in Raymond Feb. 8, 1856.  They reside in Poland, 1878.
4947  Abby Hannah,⁸ b. April 14, 1852; d. April 9, 1870.
4948  William Lewis,⁸ b. June 13, 1854.

## 3817

EDWARD McLELLAN THURSTON⁷ (*Alexander,⁶ Thomas,⁵ Abner,⁴ Abner,⁸ James,² Daniel¹*), brother of the preceding, and son of Alexander⁶ and Almira (Fickett) Thurston of Poland, Me.; born there Oct. 9, 1820; married, in Auburn, Me., June 25, 1856, FLORA RECORD, born Feb. 21, 1831, daughter of Baruck and Sally (Dresser) Record of Greene, Me.

Mr. Thurston is a merchant at Mechanic Falls, Me., and a member of the Universalist church.

### Child :

4950  Herbert Elroy,⁸ b. Dec. 20, 1862.

## 3840

CHARLES THURSTON⁷ (*James,⁶ Thomas,⁵ Abner,⁴ Abner,⁸ James,² Daniel¹*), eldest son of James⁶ and Sarah (McKenney) Thurston of

Danville, Me.; born in Scarborough, Me., Jan. 20, 1812; married, in Liverpool, Eng., Aug. 13, 1844, CATHERINE TALKINGTON, born Jan. 28, 1828, daughter of Samuel and Sarah Newman (Hill) Talkington of Liverpool. He died at his son's house in East Boston, Mass., June 1, 1877, aged 65

Mr. Thurston was a master mariner in the merchant service between this country and China and India. They resided in Salisbury, Mass., and attended the Unitarian church.

They had one adopted child:

4955 Charles Samuel,[8] b. in Boston Dec. 20, 1842; m. 1st, Aug. 13, 1868, Addie Lomi Pratt of Winchester, Mass.; she died Aug. 13, 1869; 2d, Dec. 25, 1871, Clara Minora Jackson, b. in Randolph, Vt., daughter of Edwin Samuel and Minora (Fitz) Jackson of Bethel, Vt. Mr. Thurston was a seaman twelve years; was in the war of the rebellion in the expedition against New Orleans under Gen. Butler; on the gunboat Annacosta of the Potomac flotilla, and ensign on the United States steamers "Fort Morgan," "Penobscot," and "Kanawha." He is now, 1879, a grocer in East Boston, and is a member of the Unitarian church. Children, by second wife:

4956 *Clara Louise*,[9] b. Aug. 23, 1873.
4957 *Charles Edwin*,[9] b. Sept. 7, 1875.

## 3841

MOSES WATERHOUSE THURSTON[7] (*James*,[6] *Thomas*,[5] *Abner*,[4] *Abner*,[3] *James*,[2] *Daniel*[1]), brother of the preceding, and son of James[6] and Sarah (McKenney) Thurston of Danville, Me.; born in Cape Elizabeth, Me., March 9, 1814; married, April 13, 1834, EUNICE HUNNEWELL, born May 9, 1814, daughter of Robert and Susan (Roberts) Hunnewell of Danville. He is a farmer, and a member of the Methodist church in Danville.

Children, all born in Danville:

+4965 Charles,[8] b. Feb. 2, 1835; m. Lydia S. Goss.
4966 William Melville,[8] b. April 16, 1837; d. July, 1857.
4967 George Greely,[8] b. April 11, 1839; d. April 4, 1845.
+4968 James Henry,[8] b. Oct. 2, 1841; m. Aura Volevia Sylvester.

## 3877

HIRAM THURSTON[7] (*Thomas*,[6] *Thomas*,[5] *Abner*,[4] *Abner*,[3] *James*,[2] *Daniel*[1]), son of Thomas[6] and Clarissa B. (Kimball) Thurston of Readfield, Me.; born there Oct. 1, 1820; married, in Boston, Mass., June 16, 1844, HARRIET NEWELL HAYWARD, born in Troy, Vt., May 3, 1826, daughter of Harry and Lucy (Sterling) Hayward.

Mr. Thurston is a carpenter, millwright, and stationary engineer, living in Oberlin, Lorain county, Ohio; was in California from 1851 till 1853; enlisted in the army against the rebellion and served three years in the 2d Ohio cavalry; is a member of the Episcopal church.

Children:

4975 Ella Harriet,[8] b. in Cambridge, Mass., June 18, 1845; m. Jan. 28, 1862, Reuben Maynard Gorham of Sullivan, Ashland county, Ohio. They reside at Grand Rapids, Mich., and have:
4976 *Mary Hayward* (Gorham), b. in Sullivan Feb. 20, 1866.
4977 *Edwin Thurston* (Gorham), b. in Oberlin April 15, 1867.
4978 *Clarence Maynard* (Gorham), b. in Oberlin June 2, 1873.
4979 *Lewis Clayton* (Gorham), b. at Grand Rapids Dec. 8, 1875.
4980 *Fanny* (Gorham), b. at Grand Rapids Oct. 5, 1877.

16

4981   Edward Hiram,⁸ b. in Readfield May 5, 1847; m. Sept. 3, 1867, Agnes Maria Dorsey, b. in Malone, N. Y., Sept. 3, 1846, daughter of Richard and Sarah (Wentworth) Dorsey of Oberlin. Mr. Thurston is a manufacturer of cheese boxes, barrel hoops and headings, etc. Dec. 10, 1863, enlisted in the 128th Ohio regiment and was stationed at Johnson's Island, as guard to rebel prisoners, mostly officers, and was discharged at Camp Chase July 13, 1865. "The never changing two hours on and four hours off every other day became monotonous to the last degree, and the attempt of Cole and his confederates to capture the steamer Michigan, lying just off the island, and release the prisoners, and an occasional 'break' over the stockade by the rebs, were really enjoyed by the majority. Spent from September, 1875, to April, 1877, in Alabama and Mississippi, mostly at Quitman, Miss., with my family, and enjoyed ourselves very much." They have :
4982     *Lottie Eugenie,*⁹ b. in Oberlin June 2, 1869.
4983   Lucy Adaline,⁸ b. April 25, 1850; d. in Bath, Me., March 1, 1851.

### 3878

WILLIAM HENRY THURSTON⁷ (*Thomas,*⁶ *Thomas,*⁵ *Abner,*⁴ *Abner,*³ *James,*² *Daniel*¹), brother of the preceding, and son of Thomas⁶ and Clarissa B. (Kimball) Thurston of Readfield, Me.; born there March 31, 1823; married, first, —— ——, a noble christian lady, by whom he had one son, who died early. Second, in Charlestown, Mass., Sept. 28, 1854, SARAH E. WATERHOUSE, born May 13, 1829, daughter of John P. and Sarah (McLellan) Waterhouse of Portland, Me. He died Oct. 26, 1877.

He was a saddler, firm of Bojel & Son in Boston, for nearly thirty years, residing in Chelsea, Mass.

Children, by second wife, Sarah :
4985   Annie Jane,⁸ b. in Boston, Mass., June 27, 1855.
4986   William Kimball,⁸ b. in Boston March 28, 1857.
4987   Sarah Minnie,⁸ b. in Readfield July 5, 1859.

### 3913

DAVID BENJAMIN THURSTON⁷ (*Abner,*⁶ *David,*⁵ *Abner,*⁴ *Abner,*³ *James,*² *Daniel*¹), son of Abner⁶ and Mary Worthen (Huntoon) Thurston of Franklin, N. H.; born in Charlestown, Mass., July 24, 1829; married, in Natick, Mass., by Rev. James Thurston [no. 2200], Feb. 14, 1852, ALMIRA YEATON HOWARD, born in Strafford, N. H., Aug. 10, 1834, daughter of Paul and Sarah Yeaton (Hobbs) Howard of Wakefield, N. H. He is a farmer in Franklin.

Their children are :
4990   Louis Buchanan,⁸ b. in Natick Sept. 27, 1857.
4991   Fred Howard,⁸ b. in Natick Oct. 13, 1860
4992   Harry Lee,⁸ b. in Andover, N. H., Jan. 6, 1866.

### 3994

JOHN HENRY THURSTON⁷ (*Henry,*⁶ *Gates,*⁵ *Peter,*⁴ *Abner,*³ *James,*² *Daniel*¹), eldest son of Henry⁶ and Aurelia (Warren) Thurston of Harlem, Winnebago county, Ill.; born at Glen's Falls, N. Y., Mar. 8, 1824; married, at Harlem, Feb. 16, 1846, MARY ANN BARRETT, born in Essex, Vt., Jan. 6, 1823, daughter of Reuben and Zilpha (Simons) Barrett of Harlem.

Mr. Thurston is a butter dealer in Rockford, Winnebago county, Ill., where he has resided since March 12, 1837.

Children:

4997  William Henry,[8] b. in Harlem Dec. 9, 1846; grocer in Bismarck, Dakota.

Born in Rockford:

4998  Reuben Barrett,[8] b. Dec. 25, 1849; a grocer in Chicago, Ill.
4999  James Warren,[8] b. July 2, 1851; a tin worker in Rockford; m. June 24, 1875, Ida Elizabeth Marsh, and had:
  5000  *Louise*,[9] b. Aug. 31, 1877.
5001  Mary Elizabeth,[8] b. Feb. 17, 1859; d. July 4, 1861.

## 4001

GEORGE LEE THURSTON[7] (*John Gates*,[6] *Gates*,[5] *Peter*,[4] *Abner*,[3] *James*,[2] *Daniel*[1]), eldest son of John Gates[6] and Harriet Patrick (Lee) Thurston of Lancaster, Mass.; born there Jan. 16, 1831; married, in Boston, Mass., June 15, 1859, MARY BALDWIN WHITNEY of Brighton, Mass., born in Cambridge, Mass., Nov. 14, 1834.

Mr. Thurston was a merchant in Boston, Mass., from the age of eighteen; after which for several years a merchant in Ogdensburgh, N. Y.; then in Chicago, Ill., four or five years; after which he carried on business some four years in Lancaster, previous to the breaking out of the war of the rebellion. At different periods of his life had been a member of several military and civic organizations in Ogdensburgh, N. Y.; of the state militia and of the Light Guards (Tigers) in Boston; of the Light Guards in Chicago. He was active in reviving Trinity Lodge of Masons in Clinton, formerly Lancaster, as his father had been in his younger days. He entered the union army and was captain of company B, 55th regiment Illinois volunteers, and died at his father's, Dec. 15, 1862, from disease contracted in the army while at Corinth, Miss. He was buried at Lancaster, with Masonic honors, a large concourse of friends attending. Mrs. Thurston resides in Lancaster.

Their children were:

5005  William Lee,[8] b. May 3, 1860; grad. from Phillips academy, Exeter, 1879.
5006  Alice Clary,[8] d. in infancy.

## 4078

ANDREW THURSTON[7] (*Jane*,[6] *Moses*,[5] *Moses*,[4] *Moses*,[3] *Stephen*,[2] *Daniel*[1]), son of Jane Thurston,[6] daughter of Moses of East Orange, Vt.; born there Oct. 18, 1804; married, March 22, 1827, LOVINA RICHARDSON, daughter of Andrew and Polly (Payne) Richardson of East Orange. He died 1854.

Mr. Thurston was a farmer in East Orange, and a member of the Free Baptist church.

Their children, born in Orange, were:

5010  Diadama,[8] b. Oct. 25, 1828; m. in Orange Jan. 1, 1849, Ora Slayton Cutler, b. in Orange Aug. 16, 1826, son of John and Bethiah (Stetson) Cutler of Barre, Vt.; he is a brick mason in Barre, and member of the Universalist church. They have:
  5011  *Fayette Tower* (Cutler), b. Sept. 23, 1850; m. May 5, 1872, Nora Warren.
  5012  *Flora Emma* (Cutler), b. Sept. 25, 1853; m. Nov. 20, 1873, Horatio Nelson Parkhurst.
  5013  *Addie Ellen* (Cutler), b. Jan. 25, 1856; m. July 18, 1875, Eddie Enos Fuller.
  5014  *Edna Carrie* (Cutler), b. Oct. 3, 1858; m. Oct. 9, 1876, Otis Dennis Shurtleff, a shoemaker.
+5015  Almond Richardson,[8] b. March 3, 1830; m. Diana Wilds Jackson.
+5016  Wilson,[8] b. March 20, 1832; m. Frances Louise Kenney.

5017   Hiram Richardson,[8] b. Nov. 29, 1834; m. in Hardwick, Vt., Sept. 13, 1866, Huldah Colby, b. in Washington, Vt., May 5, 1846, daughter of Joseph and Huldah (Thurston) Colby [see no. 4074]; is a farmer in East Orange; no children.

Born in Lawrence, N. Y.:

5018   Andrew Jackson,[8] b. Nov. 1, 1836; m. Oct. 4, 1863, Eva B. Bagley, b. July 28, 1845, daughter of William A. and Ann T. (Mittson) Bagley of West Topsham, Vt., where he is an operative and speculative mason. They have:

5019   *General Wellington*,[9] b. July 2, 1865.
5020   *Alice Dell*,[9] b. June 9, 1868.
       *Daughter*, b. July 7, 1879.

5021   Lucius Hurlbert,[8] b. Jan. 13, 1842; m. April, 1862, Angelyn Cutler, b. Aug. 9, 1842, daughter of Nathan S. and Phebe (Newton) Cutler of Orange. He is a farmer in Barre; served in the war against the rebellion in the 15th Vermont regiment; is captain of state militia. Children:

5022   *Willie H.*,[9] b. in Topsham Jan. 29, 1865.
5023   *Minnie A.*,[9] b. in Topsham Sept. 18, 1866.
5024   *Lillian B*,[9] b. in Barre Oct. 31, 1870.
5025   *Walter S.*,[9] b. in Roxbury, Vt., Feb. 8, 1874.

# 4102

MOSES THURSTON[7] of Northfield, Vt. (*Moses*,[6] *Moses*,[5] *Moses*,[4] *Moses*,[3] *Stephen*,[2] *Daniel*[1]), son of Moses[6] and Betsey (Lovering) Thurston of Corinth, Vt.; born in Hartford, Vt., Oct. 16, 1806; married, Sept. 22, 1832, JULIA RICHMOND, born in Barnard, Vt., Oct. 28, 1812, daughter of Paul and Mercy (Udall) Richmond of Barnard and Northfield, Vt.   He died July 20, 1849; she died Oct. 4, 1873.

Mr. Thurston was an enterprising farmer in Hartford and Northfield, Vt., energetic and upright in business, devoted to his family, a most excellent neighbor; school committee and treasurer of the town, and attended the Congregational church. [See Appendix.]

Their children were:

5030   Charles Richmond,[8] b. Sept. 6, 1834; m. in New Hartford, N. Y., Oct. 22, 1866, Mrs. Orissa Jane (Case) Owen, b. Feb. 4, 1834, daughter of Abel and Sarah (Dutton) Case of Penfield, N. Y.; her first husband was Henry B. Owen of Penfield, m. Feb. 4, 1852; he was killed in battle May 10, 1864.   Mr. Thurston was connected with the Montpelier Manufacturing Company in Montpelier, Vt., for several years in the construction of cabs, till the autumn of 1877, when he purchased a fruit farm in West Webster, Monroe county, N. Y., about eight miles from Rochester. He is a member of the Methodist church, teacher in the Sunday-school, and a man of sterling worth; no children.

5031   An infant,[8] b. Dec. 6, 1835; d. Dec. 8, 1835.
5032   Cornelia Mason,[8] b. March 28, 1839; is a graduate, educated at Topsfield and Boston; has been preceptress in West Randolph and St. Johnsbury academies, in Blairstown and Newton collegiate institute, N. J., in the high schools of Illinois. She taught seven years in the college preparatory department of Mrs. Marr's boarding and day school in Clinton, N. Y. Her influence is felt for good wherever she goes; is a teacher of high order, and a christian lady in the Presbyterian church in Clinton.

5033   Henry Elliott,[8] b. Oct. 9, 1839; m. Oct. 9, 1861, Eliza M. Heywood; had a son, b. Aug. 4, 1864, d. Aug. 4, 1867.   He served in the commissary department of the 9th Massachusetts regiment at New Orleans under Gen. Banks; has been in the dry goods and lumber business in New England and Chicago, but is now deputy sheriff in Portland, Oregon; a smart business man.

5034   Caroline Annette,[8] d. Sept. 8, 1844, aged 11 m. 26 d.
5035   Alexander Bowman Richmond,[8] b. Sept. 4, 1845; d. April 5, 1846.
5035   A Son,[8] b. July 20, d. July 21, 1848.

## 4147

SAMPSON THURSTON[7] (*Sampson,[6] Moses,[5] Moses,[4] Moses,[3] Stephen,[2] Daniel[1]*), eldest son of Sampson[6] and Hannah (Payne) Thurston of Avon, Me.; born in Orange, Vt., Jan. 25, 1817; married, in Bradford, Vt., April 16, 1848, ELSIE ANN CLIFFORD, born there April 23, 1831, daughter of Ambrose and Lydia (Baldwin) Clifford of North Haverhill, N. H.   He is a farmer in Bradford.

### Children:

5040  George Kimball,[8] b. Sept. 6, 1849; m. Oct. 27, 1874, Ellen Frances Smith of Lyman, N. H.; is a mechanic, residing in Bradford.   They have:
    5041  *Charles Eugene,[9]* b. April 29, 1875.
    5042  *George Kimball,[9]* b. Dec. 4, 1877.
5043  Hannah Jane,[8] b. Oct. 26, 1850; m. Aug. 20, 1870, Norman Edward Small of Windsor, Vt., now living in Columbus, Platte county, Neb., agent for sewing machines.   They had:
    5044  *Freddie Harry* (Small), b. April 18, 1876; d. June 23, 1876.
5045  Martin Daniel,[8] b. Oct. 10, 1857; n.m.; a dentist in Grand Haven, Mich.
5046  John Edson,[8] b. March 20, 1860.
5047  Charles Eugene,[8] b. May 12, 1864.
5048  Mary Emma[8] b. Aug. 21, 1865.

## 4148

JOSHUA TENNEY THURSTON[7] (*Sampson,[6] Moses,[5] Moses,[4] Moses,[3] Stephen,[2] Daniel[1]*), brother of the preceding, and son of Sampson[6] and Hannah (Payne) Thurston of Avon, Me.; born in Orange, Vt., July 19, 1818; married, in Avon, May 5, 1842, SALLY VINING, born in Lewiston, Me., Sept. 8, 1814.

Mr. Thurston is a farmer and stock raiser in Ord, Valley county, Nebraska, 1878.  He says he traveled from the north-east coast of Labrador to the Columbia river, and is now settled down for life. They are both members of the Methodist church.  He resided about twenty years in Richford, Wis., and did much toward building up that place, mostly supporting· the preaching and Sunday-school; was a class leader and steward of the church.  He owned a large farm, well fenced with cedar, large barn, and good house with all conveniences and comforts, and taking the "western fever" sold it for half what it was worth, and went to Nebraska to help build them up.

### Their children, born in Avon, were:

5053  Charles,[8] b. March 1, 1843; entered the war against the rebellion and was killed in the battle of the Wilderness, May 5, 1864.
5054  Maria,[8] b. Jan. 5, 1845; m. Frank Gifford of Rome, Jefferson county, Wis. They have:
    5055  *Mittee Marion* (Gifford).
    5056  *Ernest Conrad* (Gifford).
5057  Eugene,[8] b. June 16, 1848.
5058  Herbert,[8] b. Aug. 14, 1849; m. Almena Holcomb; is a blacksmith in Ord, Neb.   They have:
    5059  *May.[9]*
    5060  *Ray.[9]*
5061  Amanda Malvina,[8] b. Oct. 23, 1850; m. Warren G. Collins.   They have:
    5062  *Oscar Ernest* (Collins).
    5063  *Carrie Marion* (Collins).
    5064  *Helen* (Collins).
5065  Dennis Eugene,[8] b. Sept. 5, 1859.

## 4151

WILLARD THURSTON[7] (*Sampson,[6] Moses,[5] Moses,[4] Moses,[3] Stephen,[2] Daniel[1]*), brother of the preceding and son of Sampson,[6] and Hannah (Payne) Thurston of Avon, Me.; born in Danville, Vt., May 19, 1826; married, Nov. 17, 1850, HESTER ANN ROGERS SYLVESTER, born Jan. 7, 1831, daughter of Maj. John and Esther (Collier) Sylvester of Avon.

Mr. Thurston is a farmer in Otsego, Columbia Co., Wis. He enlisted in the Wisconsin cavalry against the rebellion and was injured by a fall from his horse, from which he never recovered ; but came to his death finally by an apothecary putting up a poison instead of the medicine ordered. When too late to remedy the error, the apothecary came to see him, full of alarm, Mr. Thurston said, "don't hurt him, it was a mistake." He was very liberal in his religious views ; loyal to his country, and was honored by his fellow citizens, being appointed to several offices of trust.

### Their children, born in Avon, were :

5070 Eudora Geneva,[8] b. Aug. 4, 1851; d. in Macfarland, Wis., July 15, 1865.
5071 Wilson Elma,[8] b. Apr. 6,1855; d. in Otsego Feb. 12, 1873.
5072 Georgia Lou Emma,[8] b. in Macfarland May 23, 1857.
5073 Willard Sylvester,[8] b. in Macfarland July 23, 1864; d. Aug. 19, 1864.
5074 Albert Wallace,[8] b. in Otsego Nov. 2, 1866.
5075 Abbie Geneva,[8] b. in Otsego Dec. 10, 1870.

## 4152

DENNIS THURSTON[7] (*Sampson,[6] Moses,[5] Moses,[4] Moses,[3] Stephen,[2] Daniel[1]*), brother of the preceding and son of Sampson[6] and Hannah (Payne) Thurston of Avon, Me.; born in Pittsburgh, N. H., Jan. 17, 1828; married, first, SARAH SIMPSON of Phillips ; second, —— SMITH.

Mr. Thurston is a farmer and gardener in East Livermore, Maine. They are both members of the Methodist church.

### His children are :

5080 Emma,[8] m. T. S. Clough of Chesterville, Me.
5081 Elsie.[8] m. —— Wilbur of East Livermore, Maine.
5082 Jane,[8] m. Charles Josselyn of Fayette, Maine.

## 4184

UZZIEL TINNEY THURSTON[7] of Palatine, Cook Co., Ill., (*William,[6] Moses,[5] Moses,[4] Moses,[3] Stephen,[2] Daniel[1]*), son of William and Clarissa (Church) Thurston of Woodstock,Vt.; born in Sharon,Vt., July 8, 1819 ; married MARY CHASE.

### Their children were :

5087 George Elbridge,[8] m. and has six children.
5088 Julius Walbridge,[8] m.
5089 Wallace,[8] m. Emeline Lytle. He is an engineer, residing in Janesville, Wisconsin. They have :
    5090 *Cora.[9]* b. in Palatine, Ill., June 29, 1867.
    5091 *Minnie Maude,[9]* b. in Janesville, June 19, 1874.
5092 Ellen,[8] m. —— Patrick, and had one child who d. ; she is d.
5093 Clara.[8]
5094 Fannie.[8]

## 4185

ERASTUS HENRY THURSTON[7] (*William,[6] Moses,[5] Moses,[4] Moses,[3] Stephen,[2] Daniel[1]*), brother of the preceding and son of William and Clarissa (Church) Thurston of Woodstock, Vt.; born in Sharon, Vt.,

Aug. 23, 1827; married, in Chelsea, Vt., Jan. 11, 1852, HARRIET CLOUGH, born in Strafford, Vt., 1828, daughter of Anson and Sarah (Campbell) Clough of Washington, Vt.

Mr. Thurston is a lumber manufacturer in Braintree.

Their children were:

5100 Ella Betsey,[8] b. in Washington, Oct. 21, 1852; m. April 26, 1871, Thomas Aldrich of Newark, Vt.; she d. Jan. 1878; no children.
5101 Emma Luvinna,[8] b. in Canaan, N. H., Nov. 3, 1854; m. Nov. 29, 1871; Arthur Charles Campbell, b. in Lempster, N. H., Aug. 26, 1850, son of Arthur and Sibera (Scott) Campbell. Reside in Granville, Vt. and have:
   5102 *Frank Arthur* (Campbell), b. in Braintree, Vt., May 26, 1872.
   5103 *William Henry* (Campbell), b. in Braintree, June 7, 1874.
   5104 *Son*, b. Jan. 27, 1876; d. in Granville, Vt. March 11, 1876.
   5105 *Eda Maude* (Campbell), b. in Granville, Sept. 6, 1878.
5106 Harriet Elvira,[8] b. in Lyme, N. H., July 8, 1857; m. Oct. 30, 1872, Henry Seymour Hazen, b. in Hartford. Vt., Dec. 24, 1849, son of Seymour and Rebecca (Russ) Hazen; live in Braintree, Vt., and have:
   5107 *Carrie Mabel* (Hazen), b. in Braintree, Nov. 26, 1877.
5108 Ida Louisa,[8] b. in Granville, Feb. 5, 1860.
5109 Clara Bell,[8] b. in Granville, April 22, 1864.
5110 Charles Lorenzo,[8] b. in Granville, March 16, 1866.
5111 George Frank,[8] b. in Granville, Aug. 9, 1869.
5112 Phena May,[8] b. in Braintree, Oct. 22, 1874.

## 4209

JOHN THURSTON[7] (*Ezekiel,*[6] *Jonathan,*[5] *Ezekiel,*[4] *Moses,*[3] *Stephen,*[2] *Daniel*[1]), eldest son of Ezekiel[6] and Hannah (Moulton) Thurston of Portland, Me.; born there Nov. 5, 1812; married, June 13, 1838, HARRIET SNOW, born Nov. 4, 1814, daughter of Nathaniel and Sarah (Maberry) Snow of Portland. He died April 10, 1869.

Mr. Thurston was a ship builder and surveyor in Portland. He frequently told the story of a journey he took to New Hampshire with his father, when he was about twelve years of age. Much of the way was wilderness, and they would go a distance of twenty miles without seeing a house; the bears were numerous and so little disturbed that they would go to the very doors of the houses. Wolves, and snakes a yard long, were plenty. The father of Mrs. Thurston enlisted in the privateer Dash, which sailed from Portland in January, 1815, and neither he or the vessel were ever heard of after.

Their children were:

5117 Nathaniel Snow,[8] b. Nov. 21, 1839; d. April 29, 1842.
5118 Henry Irving,[8] b. April 20, 1843; enlisted in the 17th Maine reg. in the war against the rebellion and was killed by a railroad collision near Portland, July 26, 1864.
5119 Nathaniel Snow,[8] b. Feb. 17, 1848; d. Oct. 12, 1853.

## 4210

EDWARD THURSTON[7] (*Ezekiel,*[6] *Jonathan,*[5] *Ezekiel,*[4] *Moses,*[3] *Stephen,*[2] *Daniel*[1]), brother of the preceding and son of Ezekiel[6] and Hannah (Moulton) Thurston of Portland, Maine; born there January 17, 1815; married, June 5, 1845, MARY ANN CARTER, born Dec. 11. 1815, daughter of Benjamin and Betsey (Blake) Carter of Portland.

Mr. Thurston was junk dealer in Portland, a member of the common council and one of the overseers of the poor, for several years previous, and at the time of his death; a member of the Methodist church; died Feb. 3, 1875.

Their children were:
5125   Elizabeth Carter,[8] b. April 16, 1846; d. May 17, 1853.
5126   Ella Carter,[8] b. June 26, 1854.
5127   Hattie Edda,[8] b. Oct. 10, 1856.

## 4211

ELIZA MOULTON THURSTON [7] (*Ezekiel,*[6] *Jonathan,*[5] *Ezekiel,*[4] *Moses,*[3] *Stephen,*[2] *Daniel*[1]), sister of the preceding and daughter of Ezekiel[6] and Hannah (Moulton) Thurston of Portland, Me. ; born there Sept. 4, 1816 ; married, Aug. 22, 1839, WILLIAM GOOLD, born in 1807, son of Dr. John and Martha (Hinton) Goold of Portland.

Mr. Goold is a sailmaker in Portland; has been alderman, and is a member of the Congregational church.

Children:
5130   Harriet Eliza (Goold), b. Feb. 28, 1841 ; d. May 25, 1846.
5131   William Dwight (Goold), b. Jan. 9, 1843.
5132   Frank Eugene (Goold), b. Aug. 22, 1848; m. Harriet L. Howe, and resides
          in Portland.
5133   Eleanor Walker (Goold), b. Feb. 18, 1852.
5134   Milbury Green (Goold), b. June 18, 1856; d. Sept. 2, 1856.

## 4214

CHARLES PLUMMER THURSTON [7] (*Ezekiel,*[6] *Jonathan,*[5] *Ezekiel,*[4] *Moses,*[3] *Stephen,*[2] *Daniel*[1]), brother of the preceding and son of Ezekiel[6] and Hannah (Moulton) Thurston of Portland, Maine; born there Oct. 15, 1823 ; married, Dec. 15, 1847, ATHENA BLAKE LITTLEFIELD, born in Kennebunkport, Me., Feb. 10, 1826, daughter of John and Betsey (Coes) Littlefield of Chelsea, Mass.

Mr. Thurston was a naval architect, and resided in Portland, Me., Chelsea and Maplewood, Mass., where he died Nov. 13, 1875.

Their children were :
5140   Charles Plummer,[8] b. in Portland Jan. 26, 1849.
5141   Anna Elizabeth,[8] b. in Chelsea Nov. 19, 1850; d. Mar. 21, 1856.
5142   Floie Evelyn,[8] b. in Portland Dec. 24, 1856.
5143   George Quincey,[8] b. in Portland Sept. 24, 1859.

## 4224

JOHN TUCKER THURSTON [7] (*Samuel,*[6] *Ezekiel,*[5] *Ezekiel,*[4] *Moses,*[3] *Stephen,*[2] *Daniel*[1]), son of Samuel[6] and Mary (Tucker) Thurston of Portland, Me. ; born there Jan. 4, 1833 ; married, Sept. 2, 1855, MARY ANN STRONG, born Oct. 14, 1832, daughter of Daniel and Jane (Warwick) Strong of Portland.

Mr. Thurston is engineer on the Grand Trunk Railway, residing at Island Pond, Vt. In his boyhood was in the revenue service three years, on board the revenue cutter Morris, Capt. Green Walden. While cruising in the Gulf of Mexico, during the Mexican war, they experienced a hurricane Oct. 11, 1847, in the harbor of Key West, Fla., which wrecked the vessel, and the seamen went into the soldiers' barracks, where they stayed six months. Jan. 3, 1850, he sailed from Portland for Cuba in the brig G. W. Knights, Capt. Joseph Munroe. The next day, his birthday, the vessel capsized, and they all came near freezing to death, but were taken off from the wreck by Capt. Colby, of the schooner Pilot of Gloucester, Mass., all more or

less frost-bitten.   Since June 2, 1854, has been in the employ of the
G. T. Railway, four years as fireman, and since engineer.   Moved his
family to Island Pond 1860, and in 1861 built a house in which they
now live, 1879.

### Children :

5148   John Warren,[8] b. in Portland, Nov. 10, 1859; has been clerk in the G. T.
        Railway office at Island Pond, since 1875.
5149   Frank Melvin,[8] b. at Island Pond, Oct. 28, 1862.
5150   Charles Dyer,[8] b. at Island Pond, Jan. 28, 1866.
5151   Jennie Isabelle,[8] b. at Island Pond, July 7, 1872; d. Feb. 27, 1876.

## 4233

LEWIS LINCOLN THURSTON[7] (*Samuel,*[6] *Ezekiel,*[5] *Ezekiel,*[4] *Moses,*[3]
*Stephen,*[2] *Daniel*[1]), brother of the preceding, and son of Samuel[6] and
Mary (Tucker) Thurston of Portland, Me.; born there July 29, 1839 ;
married, in Poland, Me., Nov. 24, 1862, SUSAN MATILDA WINSHIP,
born Dec. 11, 1842, daughter of Amos and Elizabeth J. (Massey)
Winship.

Mr. Thurston is in the lumber business in Portland, under the firm
name of Rumery, Bernie & Co.   He enlisted in the 1st Maine Regiment in 1861, and afterward served three years in the 7th Maine.
He was severely wounded in the battle of the Wilderness, Va., May
5, 1864; was a prisoner of war at Belle Isle, Richmond, and after
being paroled, was carried to the Naval Hospital at Annapolis, where
he was under the care of Miss Adelaide Walker, daughter of Moody
Walker of Portland, Me.   She was so true and faithful a nurse that
he named his first daughter after her, and says, " she was one of
Portland's most noble offerings on the altar of liberty in behalf of the
sick and wounded soldiers of the war to suppress the late rebellion."

### Their children are :

5156   Frederick Lewis,[8] b. April 23, 1863.
5157   Adelaide Walker,[8] b. May 6, 1868.
5158   Harriet Emily,[8] b. Oct. 18, 1871.

## 4236

GEORGE CARTER THURSTON[7] of Boston, Mass. (*Isaac,*[6] *Moses,*[5] *Ste-
phen,*[4] *Moses,*[3] *Stephen,*[2] *Daniel*[1]), son of Isaac[6] and Mary (Dodge)
Thurston of Ossipee, N. H.; born there Oct. 28, 1837 ; married, first,
Nov. 16, 1861, by Rev. John Walker, LAURETTA GOLDSMITH, born
May 18, 1834, daughter of Daniel Goldsmith of Ossipee.   She died
May 6, 1878.   Second, in Boston, Mass., May 1, 1879, by Rev. Mr.
Seymour, DELIA F. HANLEY, born Dec. 11, 1839, daughter of Mar-
tin and Catherine Hanley of Halifax, N. S.

Mr. Thurston studied in Phillips academy, Exeter, N. H., 1855.
Has been engaged in railroading for quite a number of years, residing
in Boston.

### His child, by first wife :

5160   Annie Bell,[8] b. Nov. 17, 1869.

## 4246

DAVID HOWARD THURSTON[7] (*Moses,*[6] *Moses,*[5] *Oliver,*[4] *Moses,*[3] *Stephen,*[2] *Daniel*[1]), son of Moses[6] and Phebe (Forest) Thurston of Errol,
N. H.; born in Eaton, N. H., Oct. 21, 1821 ; married, in Eaton, Feb.

16, 1843, MARY JANE NORTON, born Jan. 11, 1821, daughter of Nathaniel and Hannah (Davis) Norton of Nottingham, N. H.

Mr. Thurston is a farmer and lumberman ; was selectman of Errol, N. H., ten years, town clerk four years, treasurer several years, superintending school committee twenty years, and representative in the legislature 1858, 1859, 1870 and 1872.

Their children, all born in Errol except first, were:

5165   Jacob Almon,[8] b. in Eaton Nov. 15, 1843; n.m.; resides in Errol, is justice of the peace, has been selectman five years, and town clerk two years.
5166   Annette Castelman,[8] b. Jan. 18, 1846; d. May 18, 1877; n.m.
+5167  Ernest David,[8] b. Dec. 11, 1847; m. Oct. 27, 1874, Mary Etta Bragg; reside in Errol; is a farmer.
5168   Mattier Lafayette,[8] b. Jan. 11, 1850.
5169   Mary Lavina,[8] b. Dec. 7, 1851; m. June, 1873.
5170   Young America,[8] b. May 30, 1854.
5171   Remember Baker,[8] b. March 24, 1856.
5172   Howard Forrist,[8] b. May 18, 1859.
5173   Lily Arabella,[8] b. March 17, 1861.
5174   Guy Linley,[8] b. Feb. 9, 1865.

## 4249

WILLIAM MOSES THURSTON[7] (*Moses,*[6] *Moses,*[5] *Oliver,*[4] *Moses,*[3] *Stephen,*[2] *Daniel*[1]), brother of the preceding, and son of Moses[6] and Phebe (Forest) Thurston of Errol, N. H.; born in Eaton, N. H., Feb. 15, 1832 ; married, Dec. 17, 1857, EMMA ROSE, born in Voluntown, Windham Co., Conn., April 29, 1837, daughter of Duane and Celia Maria (Clark) Rose of Bethel, Me.

Mr. Thurston is a farmer in Errol, N. H.; has been selectman, collector and school committee.

Their children, born in Bethel, were :

5184   Celia Maria,[8] b. March 3, 1859; m. Oct. 15, 1877, A. Eugene Bennett, a farmer in Errol. N. H.
5185   William Duane,[8] b. Feb. 26, 1861.
5186   Abby Clinton,[8] b. Jan. 3, 1864.

Born in Errol :

5187   Ralph Dayton,[8] b. Dec. 5, 1865.
5188   Archie Moses,[8] b. March 2, 1870.
5189   Phebe Rose,[8] b. Jan. 28, 1872.
5190   David Forest,[8] b. May 2, 1874.
5191   Dwight Clark,[8] b. Nov. 16, 1877.

## 4255

DANIEL HOBBS THURSTON[7] (*Oliver,*[6] *Moses,*[5] *Oliver,*[4] *Moses,*[3] *Stephen,*[2] *Daniel*[1]) second child of Oliver[6] and Betsey Ann (Harriman) Thurston of Eaton, N. H.; born there June 26, 1827 ; married, March 18, 1849, MARY LITTLEFIELD, born May 11, 1830, daughter of Otis and Polly (Quint) Littlefield of Eaton. He is a farmer in Eaton ; enlisted in the war against the rebellion, Sept. 1, 1864, in the 1st N. H. heavy artillery.

### Children:

5195   Elvira,[8] b. Oct. 31, 1850; m. John Hall.
5196   Fanny,[8] b. Aug. 18, 1851; m. George G. Philbrook.
5197   Georgia Anna,[8] } twins, born } m. B. P. Judkins.
5198   Rosanna,[8]          } Nov. 8, 1854; } m. Frank Fifield.
5199   Mary Augusta,[8] b. July 5, 1859; m. David Hurd.
5200   Harriet Emma,[8] b. Jan. 18, 1862.
5201   Daniel S.,[8] b. March 6, 1863.
5202   Isaac,[8] b. March 7, 1868.
5203   Cora Lena,[8] b. Feb. 1, 1872.

## 4258

BENJAMIN MOSES THURSTON[7] (*Oliver,*[6] *Moses,*[5] *Oliver,*[4] *Moses,*[3] *Stephen,*[2] *Daniel*[1]), brother of the preceding, and son of Oliver[6] and Betsey Ann (Harriman) Thurston of Eaton, N. H.; born there March 13, 1829; married, Oct. 10, 1852, MARY ANN LEARY, born June 27, 1833, daughter of James and Mary (Towle) Leary, of Eaton. He died Jan. 18, 1875.

Mr. Thurston was a farmer and carpenter in Eaton Center, N. H.

Their children, born in Eaton, were:

5208  James Alphonso,[8] b. Aug. 5, 1853; n.m.; a carriage maker in Eaton.
5209  Betsey Anna,[8] b. Feb. 25, 1855; m. Aug. 12, 1876, Horatio Sewall Nute, of Conway, N. H. They have:
    5210  *Lillian Alice* (Nute) b. April 22, 1878.
5211  George Washington,[8] b. Nov. 11, 1856; m. Jan. 22, 1876, Nelly May Abbott, b. in Bartlett, N. H., Oct. 23, 1862. He is a farmer in Eaton Center, N. H. They have:
    5212  *Sadie,*[9] b. June 22, 1878.
5213  Benjamin William,[8] b. Feb. 17. 1858; n.m.; a farmer in Eaton.
5214  Sarah Jane,[8] b. in Madison, N. H., July 4, 1860.
5215  Abraham Lincoln,[8] b. June 8, 1865; n.m.; a miner in Eaton.
5216  Nellie Etta,[8] b. April 12, 1873.

## 4271

CYRUS THURSTON[7] (*Oliver,*[6] *Moses,*[5] *Oliver,*[4] *Moses,*[3] *Stephen,*[2] *Daniel*[1]), brother of the preceding, and son of Oliver[6] and Betsey Ann (Harriman) Thurston of Eaton, N. H.; born there Aug. 22, 1839; married, in Effingham, N. H., July 4, 1865, MARY LIZZIE SHACKFORD, born Dec. 19, 1850, daughter of Thomas and Rachel (Marston) Shackford of Eaton. He is a farmer in Eaton, N. H.

Children:

5220  Sarah Ann,[8] b. May 23, 1867.
5221  Moses Edwin,[8] b. Dec. 9, 1868.
5222  Jerry Albert,[8] b. April 22, 1871.
5223  Cyrus Walter,[8] b. Feb. 6, 1875.
5224  Mary Ina,[8] b. Sept. 30, 1878.

## 4273

CHARLES PLEAMAN THURSTON[7] of Eaton, N. H. (*Oliver,*[6] *Moses,*[5] *Oliver,*[4] *Moses,*[3] *Stephen,*[2] *Daniel*[1]), brother of the preceding and son of Oliver[6] and Betsey Ann (Harriman) Thurston of Eaton; born there May 18, 1844; married, Dec. 8, 1868, HARRIET DOWNS, born Dec. 23, 1849, daughter of Nathaniel and Fanny (Haines) Downs of Madison, N. H. He is a farmer in Eaton.

Their children are:

5230  Fred W.,[8] b. March 28, 1871.
5231  Charles H.,[8] b. March 8, 1874.
5232  Benjamin M.,[8] b. April 17, 1875.
5233  Leroy,[8] b. April 11, 1878.

## 4315

STEPHEN DANIEL THURSTON[7] of Sanbornton, N. H. (*William,*[6] *Oliver,*[5] *Oliver,*[4] *Moses,*[3] *Stephen,*[2] *Daniel*[1]), fourth child of William[6] and Mittee (Thurston) Thurston of Effingham Falls, N. H.; born in Freedom, N. H., March 5, 1824; married, Nov. 5, 1846, HANNAH

HUBBARD WHITTEN, born Jan. 15, 1824, daughter of Simon J. and Mary B. (Pike) Whitten of Parsonsfield, Me.

Mr. Thurston is a farmer living in Parsonsfield, Me., Freedom, Eaton, Meredith, and now, 1879, in North Sanbornton, N. H. Was constable and collector of taxes in Parsonsfield in 1850; attends Free Baptist church.

Their children were:

5238 Adelah,[8] b. in Parsonsfield. Sept. 15, 1847; d. Oct. 16, 1847.
5239 Ada Idellah,[8] b. in Freedom, N. H., Oct. 5, 1855; d. Feb. 4, 1856.
5240 Georgie Adah,[8] b. in Freedom, Jan. 2, 1857; m. Dec. 23, 1873, Frank L. Moulton, a barber in Laconia, N. H.; no children.
5241 John Henry,[8] b. in Freedom, June 5, 1862.

## 4336

JOSIAH WEDGWOOD THURSTON [7] of Effingham Falls, N. H. (*William,[6] Oliver,[5] Oliver,[4] Moses,[3] Stephen,[2] Daniel[1]*), brother of the preceding, and son of William and Mittee (Thurston) Thurston of Effingham Falls, N. H.; born in Parsonsfield, Me., May 21, 1842; married, Feb. 3, 1867, by Rev. E. C. Page, ARVILLA FRANCES CHICK, born Aug. 22, 1849, daughter of John G. and Eliza (Hyde) Chick of Parsonsfield, Me.

Mr. Thurston is a farmer in Effingham, N. H., has been town clerk, justice of the peace, teacher of music, and deputy grand patriarch of the Sons of Temperance.

Their children are:

5246 Willie Manson,[8] b. Nov. 1, 1867.
5247 John Edwin,[8] b. Feb. 26, 1870.
5248 Eva Bell,[8] b. May 28, 1872.
5249 Delphi May,[8] b. April 11, 1876.
5250 Ethel Eliza,[8] b. Oct. 27, 1877.

## 4367

JAMES HARVEY THURSTON [7] of Freedom, N. H. (*Oliver,[6] Reuben,[5] Oliver,[4] Moses,[3] Stephen,[2] Daniel[1]*), eldest child of Oliver [6] and Rebecca (Harmon) Thurston of Eaton, N. H.; born there Nov. 4, 1826; married, April 8, 1849, MARY JANE TOWLE, born Jan. 21, 1819, daughter of Stephen and Abigail (Woodman) Towle of Parsonsfield, Me. He is a blacksmith and farmer.

Children:

5255 Edwin Augustus,[8] b. in Eaton, N. H., Sept. 2, 1851; m. Nov. 9, 1873, Ada Everline Huckins, b. Jan. 23, 1853, daughter of Simon and Cordelia D. (Noble) Huckins of Freedom. Mr. Thurston is a truckman in Boston, Mass. They have:
5256 *Jennie Cordelia,*[9] b. April 10, 1876.
5257 *Simon Harvey,*[9] b. Sept. 23, 1877.
5258 Stephen Laroy,[8] b. in Madison, N. H., July 20, 1853; m. 1875, Loanna Frances Nickerson, b. Nov., 1853, daughter of Luke and Lydia Ann (Tuttle) Nickerson of Madison, N. H.
5259 Susan Abby,[8] b. in Eaton, Jan. 13, 1857; m. June 17, 1877, Clarence Hanson of Conway, N. H.

## 4440

WINFIELD SCOTT THURSTON [7] (*Asa Lewis,[6] John,[5] Oliver,[4] Moses,[3] Stephen,[2] Daniel[1]*), eldest son of Asa Lewis [6] and Julia Ann (Carson) Thurston of La Grange, Me.; born in Athens, Me., Oct. 5, 1849; married, in Kenduskeag, Me., June 22, 1878, ELLEN ELIZA TRAFTON,

Daniel H. Thurston.

born in Carmel, Me., Feb. 14, 1851, daughter of Charles and Mary Eliza (Le Greaux) Trafton of Carmel, Me.

Mr. Thurston is a farmer and lumberman in La Grange, Me.; no children.

## 4496.

REV. PHILANDER. THURSTON [7] (*James*,[6] *Thomas*,[5] *Paul*,[4] *John*,[3] *Stephen*,[2] *Daniel*[1]), son of James and Maria (Gleason) Thurston of Pelham, Mass.; born there May 25, 1837; n.m.

Mr. Thurston worked on his father's farm in Pelham and Enfield during most of his minority, attended the Monson academy to prepare himself for teaching, and taught winters from 1856 to 1865, in Palmer, Belchertown, Amherst grammar school and Sunderland high school. While thus engaged in Palmer, in January, 1858, he says: "At midnight, without any previous serious thoughts, I was instantly convicted of sin against God, and after a struggle of three long hours, asked him, for Christ's sake, to pardon and use me as he pleased. In the morning, my first conviction was, I must preach the gospel, though previously always opposed to it." He commenced preparation, in the face of many difficulties, at Williston seminary, East Hampton, Mass.; entered Amherst college in September, 1861, graduated 1865; entered Bangor theological seminary, October, 1865, and left for Andover theological seminary, May 6, 1867, and graduated in 1868. Not wishing to settle at once, he preached in East Machias, Me., from Oct., 1868, to Dec., 1869. Was installed in Sudbury, Mass., July 1, 1870, Rev. J. M. Manning, D.D., of Boston, preaching the sermon; resigned and was dismissed in Oct., 1874, and was installed over the "Village Church" in Boston, Dorchester district, Jan. 21, 1875, having commenced preaching there Jan. 1; and still continues in successful labor, Aug., 1879.

## 4503.

DANIEL HOLT THURSTON [7] (*John*,[6] *Ephraim*,[5] *Samuel*,[4] *Robert*,[3] *Stephen*,[2] *Daniel*[1]), son of John and Mercy (Hale) Thurston of Oxford, Me.; born in Norway, Me., Jan. 24, 1813; married, in Charlestown, Mass., Feb., 1839, JANE DROWN SHACKLEY, born Oct. 3, 1816, daughter of Edmund and Mehitable (Drown) Shackley, of Kennebunk, Me. She died Nov. 23, 1866. Second, MRS. ESTHER BATTLES, sister of his first wife.

Mr. Thurston is a cracker baker in Cambridgeport, Mass., in firm of Thurston, Hall & Co., and has a store in Boston. Has served in both branches of the city government, was representative to the General Court in 1874 and 1875. Is a member of the Universalist church.

Their children are:

5264 Sarah Frances,[8] b. April 20, 1840; m. Sept. 1, 1864, Benjamin Franklin Fletcher, of Cambridge. He d. Jan. 12, 1872. They had:
5265 *Charles Walter* (Fletcher), b. Nov. 22, 1865; d. Oct. 9, 1877.
5266 Helen Jane Elizabeth,[8] b. Mar. 15, 1842; m. 1st, Mar. 15, 1866, Oliver Augustus Kelley, of Boston. He d. June 6, 1868; 2d, Oct. 22, 1871, Wm. H. Hubbard, a painter in Cambridge. She had by 1st husband:
5267 *Grace Gertrude* (Kelley), b. April 9, 1867.

By second husband:

5268 *Alice Jeanette* (Hubbard), b. Feb. 17, 1873.

5269  *Amy Louise* (Hubbard), b. April 26, 1875.
+5270  Charles Frederick,[8] b. Aug. 28, 1844; m. Annette Maria Holden.
5271  Eldora Mehitable,[8] b. Aug. 18, 1846; m. Oct. 26, 1868, Charles W.
    Mead, a printer, of Cambridge, and had :
    5272  *Ida Frances* (Mead), b. July 12, 1871.
    5273  *Olive Josephene* (Mead), b. Nov. 22, 1874.
5274  Harriet Emma,[8] b. in Kennebunk, Me., Apl. 23, 1849; m. Dec. 7, 1869,
    Charles Emery Pierce, a can manufacturer, of Boston, and have :
    5275  *James Wilson* (Pierce), b. Aug. 28, 1870.
5276  John Edmund,[8] b. in Cambridge, May 1, 1853; m. Nov., 1874, Josephene
    Cora Bowker, of Cambridge.  She d. Jan. 15, 1875.  They had :
    5277  *Winslow,*[9] b. Jan. 15, 1875.

## 4514

JOHN COLBY THURSTON [7] (*John,*[6] *Ephraim,*[5] *Samuel,*[4] *Robert,*[8] *Stephen,*[2] *Daniel*[1]), brother of the preceding, and son of John[6] and Mercy (Hale) Thurston of Oxford, Me.; born there Dec. 5, 1825; married, April 16, 1856, MARY ELIZABETH MURPHY, born in Providence, R. I., Oct. 18. 1836, daughter of John and Ona (Smith) Thurben of Madison, Wis.

Mr. Thurston is a conductor on a railroad, residence Black River Falls, Wis.

### Their children are :

5283  Clara L.,[8] b. at Lone Rock, Wis., Mar. 7, 1858.
5284  Mary E.,[8] b. at Lone Rock, Wis., June 24, 1859.
5285  Charles H.,[8] b. at Lone Rock, Wis., April 14, 1861.
5286  Nellie A.,[8] b. at Mazo Manie, Wis., Sept. 7, 1866.
5287  George E.,[8] b. at Mazo Manie, Wis., Dec. 15, 1868.
5288  Nettie Eldora,[8] b. at Mazo Manie, Wis., March 27, 1871.
5289  Alice,[8] b. at Black River Falls, Wis., Nov. 19, 1874.
5290  Jennie C.,[8] b. at Black River Falls, Wis., May 25, 1877.

## 4525

AARON SANDERSON THURSTON [7] of Rome, Me. (*Elijah Doughty,*[6] *Ebenezer,*[5] *James,*[4] *Robert,*[8] *Stephen,*[2] *Daniel*[1]), eldest son of Elijah Doughty[6] and Mary (Dexter) Thurston of Winthrop, Me.; born there Aug. 15, 1828; married ADELINE PHINNEY, of Wayne, Me.

Mr. Thurston is a farmer, post office address, Mt. Vernon, Me. Enlisted in the 6th Maine battery against the rebellion, was in the battle of the wilderness, siege of Petersburgh, and served to the close of the war.

### Children :

5295  William Chandler,[8] b. Oct. 24, 1854; m. Mary Frances Nicholas of
    Livermore, Me.
5296  Frank Alston,[8] b. Feb. 7, 1858.
5297  Joseph Washington,[8] b. Aug. 28, 1861.
5298  Linda May,[8] b. Mar. 27, 1866.
5299  John Phinney,[8] b. Oct. 9, 1868.
5300  Lizzie Mabel,[8] b. June 14, 1876.

## 4571.

ELIJAH CHASE THURSTON [7] of Lowell, Mass.(*James,*[6] *Peter,*[5] *James,*[4] *Robert,*[8] *Stephen,*[2] *Daniel*[1]), eldest son of James and Deborah (Chase) Thurston of Nottingham, N. H.; born in Epping, N. H., March 16, 1824; married MARIA LOIS LUCY, born Nov. 23, 1827, daughter of Thomas and Drusilla (Witham) Lucy of Nottingham.

Mr. Thurston is a tin and sheet iron worker; a member of the Universalist church.

Their children were:

5305  Edwin Ossian,[8] b. in New Market, N. H., Nov. 10, 1850.  He was clerk in an insurance office in Lowell, and d. July 20, 1877.

5306  Albert Eugene,[8] b. in Lowell, Sept. 6, 1853; clerk in the gas office in Lowell; m. May 8, 1879, Helen Augusta Ball, b. May 31, 1860, daughter of Charles Carroll and Ellen R. (Peirce) Ball of Lowell.

5307  Ida May,[8] b. in Lowell, June 15, 1868; d. May 23, 1869.

5308  Arthur,[8] b. in Lowell, July 18, 1873.

## 4637.

JAMES MELVIN THURSTON [7] (*John Cheney,*[6] *Stephen,*[5] *Stephen,*[4] *Nathaniel,*[3] *Stephen,*[2] *Daniel*[1]), eldest son of John Cheney[6] and Harriet Maria (Snow) Thurston of Cambridge, Mass.; born there April 13, 1844 ; married, June 1, 1874, NELLIE FLORENCE MANN, born in Lowell, Mass., Sept. 18, 1856, daughter of Rufus and Charlotte (Reed) Mann of Cambridge.  Mrs. Mann died Oct. 11, 1874.

James M. Thurston is treasurer of the Cambridge savings bank at Cambridge, Mass.  He enlisted in the 52d Illinois regiment, in the war against the rebellion, in 1861, and continued in it until the close of the war.  Was under Grant at the battle of Pittsburgh Landing (or Shiloh) Tenn. ; with Rosecrans at the battle of Corinth, Miss. ; and took part in the various engagements and marches in the siege of Atlanta, Ga., under Sherman.  Was also with Sherman in his famous "march to the sea."  He enlisted as private, but served afterward as adjutant's clerk, and general's private secretary ; also as secretary for the surgeon-in-chief at Corps field-hospital.  At the reorganization of the regiment after the expiration of the three years' term of service, he was appointed quartermaster-sergeant, and served as such until the mustering out of the regiment at the close of the war.

Their children are :

5313  Herbert Melvin,[8] b. July 8, 1875; d. July 20, 1875.

5314  Gertrude Addie,[8] b. May 25, 1877.

## Eighth Generation.

## 4709

ALBERT THEODORE THURSTON [8] (*John Albert,*[7] *Daniel,*[6] Hon. *Nathaniel,*[5] Col. *Daniel,*[4] *Benjamin,*[3] *Daniel,*[2] *Daniel*[1]), son of John Albert[7] and Eliza Sparrow (Downing) Thurston of Lynn, Mass.; born there Dec. 14, 1842 ; married, May 25, 1862, ELIZA JANE HOWARD, born in Melrose, Mass., March 25, 1843, daughter of Joseph A. and Sarah J. (Penney) Howard.

Mr. Thurston is a mason, contractor, and jobber in Lynn, Mass., a member of the special police and of the Methodist church.  He enlisted in the war against the rebellion, in the 18th company of unattached infantry, and was soon transferred to the 4th heavy artillery, and served during the war.  In 1877 he went to the Black Hills in Dakotah, took a squatter's claim, paid seven dollars per bushel for potatoes to plant, cared for them with much labor and anxiety, being compelled

to take his rifle into the field to protect himself against the Indians, and then the whole crop was devoured by grasshoppers and the potato bug, after which he returned home, having had enough of the "wild west."

Children:

5319    William Albert. b. Jan. 1, 1863.
5320    Ida Adelaide, b. Sept. 6, 1864; d. March 18, 1871.
5321    Lillia Adelaide, b. Aug. 6, 1870; adopted March 1, 1876.

## 4897

JOHN HENRY THURSTON [8] (*Daniel Merrill,*[7] *Daniel,*[6] *Thomas,*[5] *Abner,*[4] *Abner,*[3] *James,*[2] *Daniel*[1]), eldest son of Daniel Merrill and Jane Moore (Tibbetts) Thurston of Portland, Me.; born there Jan. 25, 1832 ; married, first, Nov. 1, 1858, ELLEN MATILDA BRIMHALL, born in Petersham, Mass., Oct. 21, 1837, daughter of Nathaniel and Abigail (Eaton) Brimhall, of Eureka township, Dakota county, Minn., formerly of Worcester, Mass. She died in Lakeville, Minn., Nov. 11, 1865. Second, July 18, 1866, LOUISE MOSBAUGH,* born in Cambridge City,

* MOSBAUGH FAMILY.
I.  PIERRE (or PETER) DE BEAUFORT, father of
II.  BERNARD DE BEAUFORT, married Levina Boet van Vrybergen. They had:
III.  LIEVEN FERDINAND DE BEAUFORT (pensionaris van Tholin), writer of the lives of the Princes of Orange, born Oct. 8, 1675; died Nov. 9, 1730; married first, Cornelia van Vrybergen; second, Maria de Beaufort, his niece. He had by second wife:
IV.  PIETER or PIERRE, BERNARD DE BEAUFORT, deputy councilor and delegate to the college of Admiralty of Zealand, Holland, born in the city of Tholen; married Johanna (or Anna) Catherine Schorer, born at Middlebourg, Zealand, and had:
V.  JOHANNA PETRONELLA D BEAUFORT, born May 22, 1749, at Middlebourg; married Jean van Kruyne, born at Brielle; vice admiral under the orders of the college of Admiralty in Zealand; he died at Bergen-op-Zoom, in 1787, having had:
VI.  HELENE BERNARDINA VAN KROYNE, born at Middlebourg; married Carl Freiherr von Bauer, an officer under the Prince of Nassau, highly educated, very handsome, and said to have been seven feet high. He died about 1796. They had: Pieter Bernard van Kruyne, chief of the island of Timor, East Indies; Johan Anthony van Kruyne, commander of Paramaribo, Dutch Guiana, South America, married Celia Verbrug, who died at Veeeendaal, Holland, in 1852; Johanna Petronella van Kruyne, married Hendrick Vos, formerly burgomaster of Amerongen, Holland; Adrianna Petronella van Kruyne; and
VII.  GEORGE CHRISTIAN VON BAUER,† born in Goelheim, Bavaria, Feb. 24, 1792, a gentleman and a scholar, speaking seven languages. He was in Napoleon's army through the Russian campaign, and witnessed the burning of Moscow; married Louise Marx, of his native place, and came to the United States in 1838, and died Feb. 18, 1878. Their daughter:
VIII.  LOUISE VON BAUER, born in Goelheim about 1812; married Franz Mosbaugh, born near the same place 1809. They came to the United States in 1838, and settled in Cambridge City, Ind., a pioneer, and died 1854. Their daughter:
IX.  LOUISE MOSBAUGH, born in Cambridge City, March 26, 1843, married John Henry Thurston, above.
† The grandfather of George Christian von Bauer was the owner of extensive quicksilver mines, which, under some pretext or other, were taken from him by the Prince of Nassau, and for which he gave him as a partial recompense, a position in the army as an officer. His father, Carl, was also an officer, well educated, and a very handsome man. His son avers that he was, at least, seven feet in height. The Prince of Nassau was required to send to the King of Holland a certain number of the finest looking officers and soldiers in the realm. Carl von Bauer was chosen as one of these officers. He went to Holland, and in his official capacity frequently went to the Castle at Hague, to carry orders to the Admiral, Jean van Kruyne. It was when he was on one of these errands that he first saw the Admiral's beautiful daughter, Helene Bernardina. It was said that she was so fair and delicate that the blood could be seen coursing in the veins underneath her skin. When their eyes first met, it was a case of love at first sight, mutual, deep and strong. But there were obstacles in the way of a full and free expression of it. His position, that of a minor officer in the army, prohibited his approaching her on her own level in society. However, they contrived to open a correspondence, which was carried on by means of a long cord, to which the letters were secured, let down from the window in the apartments of the castle, occupied by the fair Helene. It would have been very difficult for him to have succeeded, but from the fact of his being an officer having enabled him to make friends with the guards about the castle. This state of things continued for some time, but the lovers longed for a closer companionship, and as no other way seemed to present itself, an elopement was decided upon.
Arrangements were made with this end in view, colleagues were secured, and a rope ladder provided. Everything was in readiness at the time appointed, and the brave Carl and his assistants assembled under the window of the fair one. She let down the cord that had served

Ind., March 28, 1843, daughter of Franz and Louise (Bauer) Mosbaugh, from Germany.

Mr. Thurston received a common school education, learned the trade of a machinist in Portland, went to Lakeville, Minn., in 1855, took land adjoining that of his father's, made a farm of it, and carried it on until the war of the rebellion broke out; enlisted Oct., 1861, in the 4th Minnesota infantry, was at the front at Iuka, Miss., the second battle at Corinth, following the troops in the other battles of that campaign in the quartermaster's department. Was after quartermaster-sergeant, 1st lieutenant, and adjutant of the 49th U. S. colored infantry. Resigning this, was chief head clerk of quartermaster's department in 4th division, 17th army corps, on the march from "Atlanta to the sea." Sold his farm in 1868, and went into the drug business in Farmington, Minn., where he still continues, 1879. He barely escaped death in a railway accident in Dec., 1876. Is a communicant in the church of the Advent, Episcopal, and clerk of the vestry.

His children by first wife, Ellen Matilda, born in Lakeville, were:

5326  Mary Louise,[9] b. Sept. 30, 1859; d. Nov. 20, 1869.
5327  Daniel Merrill,[9] b. May 6, 1861; d. Aug. 17, 1865.
5328  Albert Henry,[9] b. Jan. 29, 1865; d. Oct. 1865.

By second wife Louise, born in Farmington:

5329  Walter Merrill,[9] b. Aug. 6, 1876.

## 4931

ANSYL AUGUSTUS THURSTON[8] (*Henry Rice,*[7] *Daniel,*[6] *Thomas,*[5] *Abner,*[4] *Abner,*[3] *James,*[2] *Daniel*[1]), son of Henry Rice[7] and Mary (Richards) Thurston of Scarborough, Me.; born there April 20, 1830; married, first, Jan. 22, 1852, HANNAH MESERVE, of Scarborough; she died Sept., 1862. Second, June 14, 1864, AUGUSTA LOWELL LIBBEY.

Mr. Thurston learned the carpenter's trade of Horace B. Richards of Portland, Me., and labored in Portland and other places; but now, 1879, is owner and operator of a lumber mill in North Saco, Me.

---

her so well before; this was fastened to the ladder, which was drawn up and secured, but found to be too short. Here was a dilemma, but love overcomes the greatest obstacles, and something was procured, from the top of which von Bauer could reach the ladder, which he then ascended. As Helene was about to join her lover, a little sister, with whom she slept, awoke, and began to cry. She was quieted, however, by the gift of a pear by Helene, and was soon asleep again. A last, long look, and a farewell kiss, and then Helene placed herself in her lover's arms, who was waiting for her at the window. Then commenced the long and perilous descent, which was safely accomplished, and the precious burden safely landed on terra firma.

Their troubles were not at an end here, however, as pursuit would be certain, as soon as the flight was discovered, and Carl's life would be of little value if overtaken before he reached the river Rhine, eight miles distant, after crossing which he would be comparatively safe for a while. They had to cross a canal, and here the rope ladder again served them a good turn. As it would not be safe for them to travel with horses, they walked, following unfrequented paths. While resting in a clump of bushes, they heard their pursuers coming, and saw them pass, without being discovered. They finally reached their destination, and the nuptials were performed. The King issued a decree, commanding whoever should discover von Bauer in his realm, to deliver him dead or alive, to him. Now he was discovered by the Prince of Nassau, who, instead of delivering him to the King, advised him to become a recruiting officer for Prussia (he may have remembered the quicksilver mines), which advice was taken and acted upon, thereby securing him from further molestation, as any interference after this might have made trouble between Prussia and Holland.

Of course Helene was disowned by her relatives, but her son George, and his sister, visited, after the death of their mother, their aunt (she to whom the pear was given), at Hague, who frequently took them into the King's castle, which was on the opposite side of the street from her residence, where on one occasion they dined with Queen Victoria, who was visiting there, and which circumstance the old gentleman took great pride in relating.

Carl died in 1796, when George was but four years old.

17

### His children, by first wife, Hannah :

5335  Charles Lincoln,[9] b. May 10, 1854; m. Hannah Cleaves of Saco, where he
         is a miller.   Children :
    5336  *Eben Cressey*,[10] b. March 12, 1874; d. July 6, 1875.
    5337  *Alton Lincoln*,[10] b. Feb. 22, 1876.
    5338  *Annie Mary*,[10] b. March 3, 1878.
5339  Benjamin Franklin,[9] b. April 4, 1856; d. Sept. 30, 1857.
5340  Ida Estella,[9] b. Jan. 26, 1858; m. Sept. 27, 1876, Charles Henry Magrath
         of Saco, a market gardener and dealer in stock and meats.   They have :
    5341  *Gertrude Estella* (Magrath), b. Dec. 31, 1878.
5342  Olivia Ann,[9] b. Sept. 12, 1861.
5343  Hannah E.,[8] b. Aug. 27, 1862; d. Dec. 5, 1863.

### By second wife, Augusta :

5344  Elmina Augusta,[9] b. June 24, 1865.
5345  Mary Ellen,[9] b. Aug. 6, 1866.
5346  Albert Augustus,[9] b. April 20, 1871.

## 4965

CHARLES THURSTON [8] (*Moses Waterhouse*,[7] *James*,[6] *Thomas*,[5] *Abner*,[4]
*Abner*,[3] *James*,[2] *Daniel*[1]), eldest son of Moses Waterhouse [7] and
Eunice (Hunnewell) Thurston, of Danville, Me.; born there Feb. 2,
1835 ; married, first, Dec. 31, 1858, LYDIA S. Goss, born Jan. 9, 1834,
daughter of Thomas and Sally (Jordan) Goss, of Danville; she
died April 21, 1864.   Second, in South Paris, Me., June 3, 1865, SA-
RAH E. Goss, sister of first wife.

Mr. Thurston has been baggage master at the Grand Trunk Railway depot at Danville junction for twenty-five years, 1879.   Was
1st lieutenant in the 23d regiment Maine volunteers, against the rebellion ; and is a member of the Congregational church.

### His children, by first wife, Lydia, were :

5347  Ernest Rinaldo,[9] b. Sept. 10, 1859.
5348  Charles Elmer,[9] b. April 6, 1864; d. July 3, 1864.

### By second wife, Sarah :

5349  Almon Roscoe,[9] b. March 20, 1872.

## 4968

JAMES HENRY THURSTON [8] (*Moses Waterhouse*,[7] *James*,[6] *Thomas*,[5]
*Abner*,[4] *Abner*,[3] *James*,[2] *Daniel*[1]), brother of the preceding, and son
of Moses Waterhouse [7] and Eunice (Hunnewell) Thurston of Danville, Me.; born there Oct. 2, 1840 ; married, Oct. 13, 1870, AURA
VOLEVIA SYLVESTER, born in Unity, Me., March 11, 1852, daughter
of James Whitton and Eliza Farrinton (Richardson) Sylvester, of
Freedom, Me.

Mr. Thurston is a farmer and lime burner in Freedom, Me.   He
was a soldier in the 10th and 29th regiments Maine volunteers, till
the close of the war against the rebellion.

### Their child :

5353  Frank Hale,[9] b. Aug. 13, 1876.

## 5015

ALMOND RICHARDSON THURSTON [8] (*Andrew*,[7] *Jane*,[6] *Moses*,[5] *Moses*,[4] *Moses*,[3] *Stephen*,[2] *Daniel*[1]), son of Andrew [7] and Lovina (Richardson) Thurston of Barre, Vt.; born in Orange, Vt., March 3, 1830;

married, in Orange, Vt., Nov. 19, 1850, DIANA WILDS JACKSON, born
Dec. 3, 1831, daughter of Lyman and Polly (Peak) Jackson of Manchester, N. H.

Mr. Thurston is a mechanic and wheelwright in Barre, Vt.; was
drafted for the army against the rebellion, and paid for a substitute
while living in West Topsham, Vt.; belongs to the Methodist church.

### Their children were :

5358    Emma Lovina,[9] b. in Orange, Oct. 16, 1857; m. June 4, 1876, Frank Simons Snow, b. in Williamstown, Vt., Jan. 25, 1856, son of Henry Jacob
and Philenda (Simons) Snow of Montpelier, Vt. He is a farmer in
Barre, Vt. They had a daughter, b. Aug. 29, 1877; d. same day.

5359    Clara Belle,[9] b. in Topsham, Vt., June 28, 1859; m. in Somerville, Dec. 31,
1876, Walter Charles Mentzer, b. at Brady's Bend, Penn., Oct. 26, 1852,
son of Charles Lewis and Lucy Jane (Brewer) Mentzer of Washington,
N. H. He is a butcher and wholesale dealer in beef, doing business in
Boston; they reside in Somerville, Mass. They have :

5360    *Charles Almond* (Mentzer), b. Nov. 5, 1877.

5361    Flora Angelia,[9] b. in West Topsham, Vt., Dec. 9, 1862.

### 5016

WILSON THURSTON[8] (*Andrew*,[7] *Jane*,[6] *Moses*,[5] *Moses*,[4] *Moses*,[3] *Stephen*,[2] *Daniel*[1]), brother of the preceding, and son of Andrew[7] and
Lovina (Richardson) Thurston of Barre, Vt.; born in Orange, Vt.,
March 20, 1832 ; married, March 23, 1856, FRANCES LOUISE KINNEY,
born July 10, 1831.

Mr. Thurston is a farmer in Barre, Vt.

### Children :

5366    Charles Orren,[9] b. Feb. 23, 1857.
5367    Herbert Elon,[9] b. Nov. 12, 1858; d. Feb. 23, 1864.
5368    Henry Winfred,[9] b. Feb. 28, 1861.
5369    Justus Kinney,[9] b. June 27, 1865.
5370    Della May,[9] b. May 26, 1867.
5371    Alice Ellen,[9] b. July 4, 1869.
5372    Inez Lydia,[9] b. Jan. 15, 1872.
5373    Nellie Louise,[9] b. Feb. 17, 1875.

### 5167

ERNEST DAVID THURSTON[8] (*David Howard*,[7] *Moses*,[6] *Moses*,[5] *Oliver*,[4] *Moses*,[3] *Stephen*,[2] *Daniel*[1]), son of David Howard[7] and Mary Jane
(Norton) Thurston, of Errol, N. H.; born there Dec. 11, 1847 ; married, in Colebrook, N. H., Oct. 26, 1874, MARY ETTA BRAGG, born
April 11, 1855, daughter of William Washington and Mary Jane (Harper) Bragg of Errol.

Mr. Thurston is a farmer and blacksmith in Errol, N. H.; associated with his brother, J. A., in the manufacture of starch.

### Their children are :

5378    Ernest Clarke,[9] b. Aug. 21, 1875.
5379    Annette Castelneau,[9] b. Oct. 28, 1877.

### 5270

CHARLES FREDERICK THURSTON[8] (*Daniel Holt*,[7] *John*,[6] *Ephraim*,[5]
*Samuel*,[4] *Robert*,[3] *Stephen*,[2] *Daniel*[1]), son of Daniel Holt[7] and Jane
Drown (Shackley) Thurston of Cambridgeport, Mass.; born there
Aug. 28, 1844 ; married, in Cambridgeport, March 15, 1866, ANNETTE

MARIA HOLDEN, born in Reading, Mass., Sept. 6, 1846 ; daughter of Cyrus Knight and Lu Fannie (Lombard) Holden of Otisfield, Me.

Mr. Thurston is a cracker manufacturer, firm of Thurston, Hall & Co., in Cambridgeport, Mass.   Has been representative to the general court, ward officer, and a member of the standing committee of the First Universalist church.   He enlisted in the 1st Massachusetts cavalry, Sept. 16, 1861, at seventeen years of age ; served through the war, and was mustered out May 29, 1865.   He was taken prisoner at the battle of Aldie, Va., June 17, 1863, sent to Libby prison ; from there to Belle Isle ; was within the enemy's lines thirty-five days, and was among the last prisoners paroled before sending them to Andersonville.   Company D, to which he belonged, was detailed as Gen. Meade's escort, and served in that capacity the last eighteen months of the war.   He was wounded at Gravelly Run, Va., at the last attack and capture of Petersburgh, Va.   After returning home, he joined the National Lancers of Boston, and is now, 1879, captain of that corps.

Their children were :

5385   Fannie Jane,[9] b. Dec. 26, 1866.
5386   Carrie Maria,[9] b. Feb. 6, 1869.
5387   Daniel Herbert,[9] b. March 10, 1873; d. March 16, 1873.          •

There are other families which no doubt belong to the descendants of Daniel, but, as the connection cannot be positively traced, are placed in the latter part of the book.

# POSTERITY OF EDWARD THURSTON.

IT gives the present compiler great pleasure to say that the work on this family, from 1647 to 1866, was most thoroughly and patiently wrought out by MR. CHARLES MYRICK THURSTON of New Rochelle, N. Y., and published in a pamphlet of seventy pages. Since that time he continued industriously to gather materials for perfecting his previous work, and to bring the records down, till the day of his sudden death, June 3, 1878. After the decease of Mr. Thurston, the result of his labors was transferred to the writer, who previously had much communication with him, to arrange for this volume. Persistent correspondence and searching of town and county records on the part of both, have resulted in bringing together a mass of facts and dates which will be valuable for future reference.

----

## First Generation.

### 5501

EDWARD THURSTON [1] was the first of the name in the Colony of Rhode Island. He must have been there some time previous to 1647, sufficient, at least, to attend to the preliminaries of his marriage, which occurred June, 1647, to ELIZABETH MOTT, daughter of Adam Mott,* and is the third on the record of the "Society of Friends," at Newport.† He is mentioned in the colonial records as a freeman in 1655; as commissioner, assistant, and deputy from Newport for many years, from 1663 to 1690. On August 26, 1686, he, with others, signed an address from the Quakers of Rhode Island, to the king. He died March 1, 1707, aged 90; she died Sept. 2, 1694, aged 67. His will, two fragments of which only remain, was made Jan. 11, 1704, and proved March 12, 1707; and on these he names his grandson Edward, the son of his son Edward; his four surviving sons, Jonathan, Daniel, Samuel and Thomas; his granddaughter, Elizabeth, the daughter of Jonathan; his sons-in-law, Weston Clarke and Ebenezer Slocum,‡ and two granddaughters named Slocum.

* Adam Mott, aged thirty-nine, from Cambridge, England, his second wife, Sarah, aged thirty-one years, four children of Adam, by a former wife, and Mary Lott, a daughter of Sarah, by a former husband, were passengers from London for New England, in the "Defence," in July, 1634. One of the children, Elizabeth, born in 1605 or 1608, became the wife of Edward Thurston.—C. M. THURSTON.

† To the Society of Friends we are indebted for a complete record of his family, and of those of his descendants "who remained faithful."

‡ Ebenezer Slocum, son of Giles and Joan Slocum, born March 25, 1650; died in Jamestown, Feb. 13, 1715, aged sixty-five.

Their children were :

5502　Sarah,[2] b. March 10, 1648.
5503　Elizabeth,[2] b. Feb., 1650.
+5504　Edward,[2] b. April 1, 1652; m. —— Jeffries.
5505·　Ellen,[2] b. March, 1655; m. 1674, George Havens, and had :
　　　5506　*George* (Havens), b. at Shetland island *[Mar]*
　　　5507　*Jonathan* (Havens), b. at Jamestown, R. I., Feb. 22, 1681.
5508　Mary,[2] b. 1657; m. Ebenezer Slocum, b. March 25, 1650, son of Giles and
　　　Joan Slocum; he d. in Jamestown, Feb. 13, 1715; she d. Nov. 16, 1732.
　　　Two granddaughters named Slocum, were mentioned in their grandfather
　　　Thurston's will, who are supposed to have been children of these :
　　　5509　*Rebecca* (Slocum), m. Aug. 29, 1704, William Burling of Flushing, L. I.
　　　5510　*Mary* (Slocum), m. Jan. 3, 1699, David Greene of Warwick, R. I.
+5511　Jonathan,[2] b. Jan. 4, 1659; m. Sarah ——.
+5512　Daniel,[2] b. April, 1661: m. Mary Easton.
5513　Rebecca,[2] b. April, 1662; m. 1st, Peter Easton; he d. Dec. 17, 1690, aged
　　　31; 2d, Nov. 25, 1691, Weston Clarke; she d. Sept. 16, 1737.　Mr.
　　　Clarke was freeman 1655, representative of Providence 1663, but re-
　　　turned to Newport.　His daughter, Elinor, by a former marriage, m. in
　　　1674, George Havens of Portsmouth, R. I.　Rebecca's children were :
　　　5514　*Rebecca* (Easton), b. July 5, 1684.
　　　5515　*Peter* (Easton), b. Nov. 11, 1685; m. 1st, Content Slocum; 2d, Ann
　　　　　Stanton; d. Dec., 1747.
　　　5516　*Ann* (Easton), b. Sept. 3, 1687; d. Nov. 23, 1690.
　　　5517　*Joshua* (Easton), b. April 27, 1689.
　　　5518　*Jeremiah* (Clarke), b. July 27, 1692; d. Sept. 3, 1756.
　　　5519　*Mary* (Clarke), b. Feb. 8, 1694.
　　　5520　*Elizabeth* (Clarke), b. Nov. 5, 1695.
　　　5521　*Weston* (Clarke), b. Aug. 25, 1697; d. June 22, 1737.
5522　John,[2] b. Dec., 1664; m. Elizabeth ——.　He was freeman May 6, 1690.
　　　She d. Oct. 7, 1690, aged 21; he d. at the house of Peter Easton, Oct.
　　　22, 1690.
5523　Content,[2] b. June, 1667.
+5524　Samuel,[2] b. Aug. 24, 1669; m. Abigail Clarke.
+5525　Thomas,[2] b. Oct. 8, 1671; m. Mehitable Mayo.

NOTE. Probably a large number of this family and their descendants were buried in the
Coddington burying-ground, Newport. Stones are still standing in memory of Elizabeth,
wife of Edward, and their sons, Daniel, Samuel, and many others.

## Second Generation.

### 5504

EDWARD THURSTON [2] of Newport (*Edward*[1]), son of Edward [1]
and Elizabeth (Mott) Thurston of Newport, R. I.; born there April
1, 1652; married, —— JEFFRIES.* He died Dec. 7, 1690, aged
38.　He was a freeman May 6, 1679.

Their children were :

+5526　Edward,[8] b. 1678; m. Elizabeth Gardner.
+5527　William,[8] b. 1680; m. Phebe Batty.

* William Jeffries was in Massachusetts in 1630, in Rhode Island in 1655, and died in Newport, 1675, aged eighty-four.　In his will he mentions his wife, Mary, his mother, J. Audry, of
Chittingly county, Sussex; his wife's brothers, John and Daniel Gould, and his children:
Mary married John Green, John, Thomas, Sarah married James Barker, Priscilla, Susanna.　One of the two last named was probably the wife of the above Edward Thurston,
and married after the date of her father's will, made in 1674.

5528  Abigail,[2] b. April 3, 1686; m. 1st, William Dyer; 2d, Capt. Job Bennett. From her will, made in Providence, May 5, 1753, but never proved, as she married after, and other writings in possession of E. W. Seabury, Esq., of New Bedford, Mass., we learn that her paternal grandfather came from England, and m. Elizabeth Mott. Her maternal grandfather was William Jeffries, who came from England, and m. Mary Gould. She d. Oct. 16, 1761. Her children, by first husband, were:

    5529  *William* (Dyer), d. Sept. 29, 1713, aged 14 months.
    5530  *Abigail* (Dyer), d. July 31, 1735, aged 21.
    5531  *Edward* (Dyer), d. April 25, 1721, aged 5.
    5532  *Priscilla* (Dyer), m. John Eastman; d. May 11, 1746, aged 28.
    5533  *John* (Dyer), d. July 16, 1737, aged 17.
    5534  *Daughter*, m. Nicholas Tillinghast.
5535  Priscilla,[2] m. April 16, 1713, Job Lawton, and had:
    5536  *George* (Lawton), b. Feb. 1, 1714.
+5537  Jonathan,[2] baptized, adult, Oct. 9, 1719; m. 1st, Phebe Holmes; 2d, Mehitable Claghorn.

## 5511

JONATHAN THURSTON[2] of Little Compton, R. I. (*Edward*[1]), brother of the preceding, and son of Edward[1] and Elizabeth (Mott) Thurston of Newport, R. I.; born there Jan. 4, 1659; married, 1678, SARAH ———. He died 1740, aged 81. His will made Aug. 22, 1735, proved in Taunton April 15, 1740.

Their children were:

+5538  Edward,[3] b. Oct. 18, 1679; m. 1st, Susanna Pearce; 2d, Sarah Carr.
5539  Elizabeth,[3] b. Nov. 29, 1682; m. Jan. 6, 1703, Jonathan Wood, and had:
    5540  *Rebecca* (Wood), b. Dec. 26, 1704.
    5541  *Bridgett* (Wood), b. June 22, 1706.
    5542  *Elizabeth* (Wood), b. Jan. 31, 1708.
    5543  *Ruth* (Wood), b. Aug. 7, 1710; d. July 13, 1766.
    5544  *Susanna* (Wood), b. June 21, 1712; d. Aug. 13, 1712.
    5545  *Jonathan* (Wood), b. July 5, 1714.
    5546  *Mary* (Wood), b. Jan. 19, 1716.
5547  Mary,[3] b. March 20, 1685; m. July 6, 1706, George Brownell, and had:
    5548  *Giles* (Brownell), b. March 1, 1707.
    5549  *Phebe* (Brownell), b. June 19, 1708.
    5550  *Mary* (Brownell), b. Nov. 9, 1709.
    5551  *George* (Brownell), b. June 21, 1711.
    5552  *Thomas* (Brownell), b. Feb. 1, 1713.
    5553  *Elizabeth* (Brownell), b. Sept. 15, 1717.
    5554  *Jonathan* (Brownell), b. March 19, 1719.
    5555  *Paul* (Brownell), b. June 12, 1721.
    5556  *Stephen* (Brownell), b. Nov. 29, 1726.
+5557  Jonathan,[3] b. July 5, 1687; m. ——— ———.
5558  Rebecca,[3] b. Nov. 28, 1689; m. May 6, 1711, Edward Richmond, and had:
    5559  *Sarah* (Richmond), b. Dec. 20, 1711.
    5560  *Mary* (Richmond), b. 1714.
    5561  *Priscilla* (Richmond), b. Feb. 27, 1718.
    5562  *Eunice* (Richmond), b. Sept. 23, 1722.
5563  Content,[3] b. Aug. 18, 1691; m. Sept. 14, 1715, Henry Wood, and had:
    5564  *Henry* (Wood), b. Nov. 17, 1716.
    5565  *William* (Wood), b. Sept. 7, 1720; d. March 9, 1724.
    5566  *Peleg* (Wood), b. March 20, 1722.
    5567  *Sarah* (Wood), b. June 4, 1726; m. July 31, 1771, James Chace.
    5568  *Rebecca* (Wood), b. Dec. 15, 1727; d. Jan., 1797.
    5569  *Thomas* (Wood), b. March 3, 1733.
5570  Sarah,[3] b. Nov. 9, 1693; m. June 26, 1712, Benjamin Sawdy.
5571  John,[3] b. July 12, 1695.
5572  Eleanor,[3] b. Nov. 26, 1696; m. ——— Peters; they had:
    5573  *Lovell* (Peters), named in will of grandfather, 1735.
5574  Hope,[3] b. Nov. 26, 1698; d. Feb., 1716; gravestone still standing in Coddington burying-ground, Newport.

5575　Abigail,[8] b. May 7, 1700; m. Oct. 2, 1729, William White.
5576　Patience,[8] b. Feb. 16, 1702; m. Feb. 21, 1723, Thomas Southworth, and
　　　　had :
　　　5577　*Rebecca* (Southworth), named in will of grandfather, 1735.
5578　Amy,[8] b. Jan. 29, 1705.
5579　Peleg,[8] b. July 8, 1706.
5580　Jeremiah,[8] b. May 8, 1710.
5581　Susanna,[8] b. Aug. 20, 1712; m. —— Carr. She was baptized in Trinity
　　　　church, Oct. 12, 1740.
5582　Joseph,[8] b. April 25, 1714; m. June 1, 1738, Mercy Burgess, daughter of
　　　　Thomas Burgess; they had :
　　　5583　*Mary*,[4] b. Dec. 2, 1741; d. in Newport, Aug. 30, 1742.
5584　Job,[8] b. July 1, 1717; m. Aug. 10, 1766, Mary Gibbs, resided in Little
　　　　Compton, R. I.; estate inventoried in Taunton, Mass., Dec. 19, 1780,
　　　　Jonathan Thurston, appraiser, his widow, administratrix; they had :
　　　5585　*Thomas*,[4] d. Sept. 30, 1767.

NOTE. Rebecca, John, Hope, Amy, Peleg and Jeremiah are not mentioned in the will,
and therefore supposed to have died before 1735.

## 5512

DANIEL THURSTON[2] of Newport, R. I. (*Edward*[1]), brother of the
preceding, and son of Edward[1] and Elizabeth (Mott) Thurston of
Newport; born there April, 1661 ; married MARY EASTON, daughter
of John and Mehitable (Gant) Easton.

His will was made July 18, 1712, in which he names all his children. Previous to his death he was administrator on the estate of his
brother John.

### Their children were :

5586　Daniel,[8] b. Sept. 25, 1687; a mariner in Newport, 1716.
5587　Elizabeth,[8] b. Jan. 14, 1689; m. Samuel Collins. She died Oct. 6, 1767 ;
　　　　they had:
　　　5588　*Samuel* (Collins), b. Feb. 24, 1712; d. March 13, 1738.
　　　5589　*Mary* (Collins), b. Oct. 3, 1713.
　　　5590　*Hannah* (Collins), b. Nov. 15, 1715.
　　　5591　*John* (Collins), b. Nov. 1, 1717.
　　　5592　*Elizabeth* (Collins), b. March 3, 1720.
　　　5593　*Rebecca* (Collins), b. May 24, 1722.
　　　5594　*Ruth* (Collins), b. July 3, 1724.
　　　5595　*Daniel* (Collins), b. Dec. 16, 1727.
5596　Mary,[8] b. March 9, 1690; m. 1st, Sept. 7, 1710, John Tompkins; 2d, be-
　　　　fore Feb. 28, 1727, Daniel Gould.
5597　John,[8] b. June 9, 1692; m. Elizabeth ——. He was a farmer in Newport,
　　　　and member of the Episcopal church. They had:
　　　5598　*Samuel*,[4] b. June 4, 1737; d. July 8, 1825. By a lengthy notice of
　　　　　him in "The Memorials of Deceased Friends," we infer he never
　　　　　married, and that he was a prominent member of that denomination
　　　　　in Newport.
5599　Edward,[8] b. Sept. 1, 1693; a mariner in Newport, 1716.
5600　Eleanor,[8] b. Jan. 18, 1694; m. —— Cranston.
+5601　Benjamin,[8] b. Mar. 25, 1697; m. 1st, Sarah Casey; 2d, Mrs. Hepzibah Smith.
5602　James,[8] b. July 15, 1698.
5603　Peter,[8] b. July 3, 1704; a sailmaker in Newport, 1733.

## 5524

SAMUEL THURSTON[2] of Newport, R. I. (*Edward*[1]), brother of the
preceding, and son of Edward[1] and Elizabeth (Mott) Thurston of
Newport; born there Aug. 24, 1669; married ABIGAIL CLARKE,

daughter of Latham and Hannah (Wilbor*) Clarke and granddaughter of Jeremiah and Frances (Latham) Clarke. She died Nov. 30, 1731, aged 56; he died Oct. 27, 1747, aged 78.

Mr. Thurston was admitted freeman May 5, 1696. Will dated May 13, 1740, and proved Nov. 2, 1747; the seal attached has a bird with wings expanded.

Their children were:

+5604 Edward,[8] b. May 26, 1696; m. Elizabeth Norton.
5605 Son,[8] b. July 18, 1698.
+5606 Samuel,[8] b. Oct. 16, 1699; m. Mary ——.
5607 Hannah,[8] b. Dec. 11, 1701; m. July 18, 1723, William Cornell; she d. Sept. 23, 1753. They had:
    5608 *Sarah* (Cornell), b. April 26, 1724; d. Sept. 7, 1730.
    5609 *Thomas* (Cornell), b. Jan. 13, 1726.
    5610 *Abigail* (Cornell), b. July 11, 1728; d. Sept. 24, 1730.
    5611 *Hannah* (Cornell), b. Nov. 22, 1730.
    5612 *Elizabeth* (Cornell), b. May 17, 1740.
+5613 Latham,[8] b. June 3, 1704; m. Mary Wanton.
+5614 Joseph,[8] b. Sept. 24, 1706; m. Abigail Pinnegar.
5615 Elizabeth,[8] b. Dec. 22, 1708; m. Jan. 16, 1729, George Cornell. They had:
    5616 *Walter* (Cornell), b. Oct. 11, 1729.
    5617 *Thomas* (Cornell), b. Sept. 22, 1731.
    5618 *Latham* (Cornell), b. Oct. 22, 1733; d. May 5, 1734.
    5619 *Gideon* (Cornell), b. Dec. 6, 1737.
    5620 *Matthew* (Cornell), b. Oct. 31, 1743.
5621 Mary,[8] b. Feb. 11, 1711; d. Oct. 28, 1733.
+5622 John,[8] b. April 10, 1713; m. Mary Coffin.
5623 Phebe,[8] b. Nov. 20, 1715; m. Jan. 6, 1742, Peleg Shearman, and had:
    5624 *Elizabeth* (Shearman), b. Feb. 21, 1744; m. Jonathan Marsh; d. Jan. 14, 1767.
    5625 *Samuel* (Shearman), b. June 16, 1749.
5626 Abigail,[8] b. Jan. 6, 1718; d. Dec. 18, 1730.
5627 Sarah,[8] b. May 16, 1720.

## 5525

THOMAS THURSTON †[2] of Freetown, Mass. (*Edward*[1]), brother of the preceding, and son of Edward[1] and Elizabeth (Mott) Thurston of Newport, R. I.; born there Oct. 8, 1671; married, first, July 23, 1695, MEHITABLE MAYO, born Jan. 6, 1669, daughter of John and Hannah (Graves) Mayo of Wrentham, Mass.; second, Jan. 29, 1712, ELIZABETH CORNELL, daughter of Stephen Cornell of Dartmouth, Mass. He died March 22, 1730; will dated March 20, 1730, son Thomas to have his Bible. His widow was living in Newport, R. I., Oct. 21, 1736.

In 1708 he was the owner of the south half of the tenth lot in Freetown, Mass. This property was conveyed by John Rogers to Edward Thurston, senior, of Newport, R. I., for sixty pounds, Oct. 3, 1702. He was grand-juryman in 1706, selectman, 1708–9, surveyor of highways, 1712–13, assessor, 1718, 1722.

His children were:

+5628 Edward,[8] b. 1696; m. Hannah Dodson.
+5629 Thomas,[8] m. —— ——.

---

*Hannah Wilbor was the daughter of Samuel and Hannah (Porter) Wilbor, and granddaughter of Samuel and Ann (Bradford) Wilbor. Hannah Porter was the daughter of John Porter. Ann Bradford was the daughter of Thomas Bradford. Frances Latham was the daughter of Lewis Latham.

† Thomas, in his will, names his brother-in-law, Peleg Tripp, who, therefore, must have married one of his sisters, either Sarah, Elizabeth, or Content.

+5630 Peleg,[3] m. 1st, Sarah Borden; 2d, Amy Richardson.
+5631 Jonathan,[3] m. Lydia Goddard.
5632 Samuel.[3]
5633 John.[3]
5634 Ruth,[3] m. —— Eddy.
5635 Elizabeth,[3] b. 1717, m. Joseph Church; d. 1798.
5636 Anne,[3] m. —— Sprague.
5637 Mehitable,[3] m. —— Joslin.
5638 Mary,[3] m. Oct. 21, 1736, John Tayer of Newport, and had:
    5639 *William* (Tayer), b. June 29, 1738.
    5640 *Mehitable* (Tayer), b. Feb. 26, 1740.
5641 Nathaniel.[3]

## Third Generation.

### 5526

Capt. Edward Thurston[3] of Newport, R. I. (*Edward,[2] Edward[1]*), eldest son of Edward and —— (Jeffries) Thurston of Newport; born there 1678; married, Jan. 16, 1699, Elizabeth Gardner, probably a sister to Joseph Gardner, who married Catherine Holmes. He died April 27, 1727; she died Sept. 24, 1754, aged 70. Her son William administered on her estate, April 5, 1755.

Capt. Thurston was chosen, May 4, 1709, commissioner, to provide all military stores for the Rhode Island colony.

Their children were:

+5642 Edward,[4] b. Sept. 8, 1702; m. Catherine Gardner.
5643 Elizabeth,[4] b. April 3, 1705; m. —— Chapman; d. May, 1739.
5644 Abigail,[4] b. Nov. 18, 1707; m. Joseph Gardner.* She was a widow May 5, 1753, and d. April 9, 1768, leaving:
    5645 *Joseph* (Gardner), named in will of Abigail Dyer.
5646 John,[4] b. May 14, 1710; d. Nov. 4, 1728.
5647 Susanna,[4] b. Aug. 2, 1714; d. Nov. 22, 1716.
5648 Grindall,[4] b. Dec. 29, 1715; lost at sea, Nov., 1748.
5649 Samuel,[4] b. April 21, 1719; lost at sea, Nov., 1748.
+5650 Gardner,[4] b. Nov. 14, 1721; m. 1st, Frances Sanford; 2d, Martha Sanford.
5651 William,[4] b. July 13, 1724; d. Feb. 13, 1775.
5652 Valentine,[4] b. Feb. 14, 1726; d. at Cape Francois, 1760.

### 5527

William Thurston[3] of Newport, R. I. (*Edward,[2] Edward[1]*), brother of the preceding, and son of Edward[2] and —— (Jeffries) Thurston of Newport; born there 1680; married, Nov. 3, 1704, Phebe Batty of Jamestown, R. I. She died Aug. 3, 1706, aged 24; he died June 21, 1717, aged 37; both buried with the Fourtane family. His estate was settled by the widow Rebecca, July 1, 1717. The three children are named in the will of their aunt Abigail Dyer.

Their children were:

5653 Priscilla,[4] m. —— Havens.
5654 Mary,[4] m. George Gardner, and had:
    5655 *Joseph* (Gardner), d. Aug. 8, 1727, aged 16 days.
    *Daughter*, d. Oct. 17, 1729.
    5656 *William Thurston* (Gardner), b. July 7, 1732.

---

* Joseph Gardner married, Nov. 30, 1673, Catherine Holmes, and had Joseph and George (Gardner), previous to his marriage with Abigail Thurston.

5657   *Abigail* (Gardner), d. Jan. 6, 1764, aged 22 years.
5658   *Mary* (Gardner), named in will of her aunt.
5659   William.[4]

## 5537

JONATHAN THURSTON[3] of Newport, R. I. (*Edward,*[2] *Edward*[1]), brother of the preceding, and son of Edward[2] and —— (Jeffries) Thurston of Newport. He was baptized Oct. 9, 1719, in Trinity church, adult; married, first, PHEBE HOLMES, sister of William [*] and John Holmes; she died March 31, 1734, aged 39. Second, Aug. 26, 1736, MEHITABLE CLAGHORN. She died Sept. 7, 1745, aged 38; he died April 13, 1749, aged 61. His will dated March 31, 1749, proved May 1, 1749.

His children, by first wife, Phebe, were:

+5660   John,[4] b. Aug. 17, 1723; m. Elizabeth Oxx.
5661   Mary,[4] b. May 2, 1725; m. William Almy; she d. July 12, 1768. His will
  was made July 29, 1749. They had:
  5662   *William* (Almy).
  5663   *Ann* (Almy), b. 1740; d. Sept. 24, 1756.
  5663½ *Phebe* (Almy).
  5664   *Elizabeth* (Almy).
  5665   *Jonathan* (Almy), b. Feb. 18, 1746; m. 1st, May 14, 1770, Elizabeth
    Hammond; she d. Feb. 18, 1783, aged 32; 2d, Jan. 20, 1796, Eliza-
    beth Perry; she d. Feb. 4, 1801, aged 38; 3d, Hope Campbell; she
    d. Sept. 4, 1804, aged 40. He had seven children and
    5666   *Jonathan Thurston* (Almy), b. Jan. 20, 1782; m. Dec. 31, 1809,
      Ann Coggeshall.
  5667   *Mary* (Almy), b. 1747; d. Jan. 3, 1755.
  5668   *Job* (Almy), b. 1749; d. May 1, 1750.
+5669   Jonathan,[4] bap. May 2, 1725; m. Ruth Scott.
5670   Peleg,[4] bap. July 16, 1727; d. Oct. 20, 1727.
+5671   William,[4] b. Oct. 7, 1728; m. Dorothy Carter.
5672   Peleg,[4] bap. Dec. 20, 1729; d. Dec. 29, 1729.
5673   Deborah,[4] bap. June 27, 1731; d. Nov. 20, 1749.

NOTE. The above five surviving children were legatees in a codicil to the will of John Holmes, made May 12, 1743, proved Dec. 5, 1748, as his cousins (or nephews and niece).

By second wife, Mehitable:

5674   Thomas,[4] bap. July 3, 1737.
5675   Phebe,[4] bap. June 22, 1740.
5676   Peleg,[4] bap. April 4, 1742; d. Aug. 16, 1742.
5677   Edward,[4] bap. Aug. 28, 1743; d. Sept. 20, 1759.
5678   Job,[4] bap. Sept. 15, 1745.

## 5538

EDWARD THURSTON[3] of Little Compton, R. I. (*Jonathan,*[2] *Edward*[1]), eldest son of Jonathan[2] and Sarah Thurston of Little Compton; born there Oct. 18, 1679; married, first, Dec. 19, 1706, SUSANNA PEARCE, daughter of George and Alice (Hart) Pearce; second, Oct. 15, 1712, SARAH CARR. His will is dated March 20, 1739, proved in Taunton, Mass., May 15, 1739; the widow executrix.

His children, by first wife, Susanna, were:

+5679   George,[4] b. Nov. 4, 1709; m. 1st, Keziah ——; 2d, —— Greene.
5680   William,[4] b. April 13, 1711; d. March 13, 1712.

---

[*] Will of William Holmes, March 23, 1713, proved April, 1720, mentions his mother Mary and five sisters, Frances Carr, Ann Peckham, Deborah Manchester, Phebe Holmes, and Mary Dyer of Kingston. Brother Nicholas Carr of Jamestown, executor.

By second wife, Sarah:

5681 Mary,[4] b. May 16, 1714; m. July 2, 1733, John Brownell.
5682 Elizabeth,[4] b. Sept. 24, 1719; m. Mar. 4, 1739, Christopher White, and had :
    5683 *Sarah* (White), b. Sept. 28, 1740.
    5684 *Thurston* (White), b. Oct., 1741.
    5685 *William* (White),
    5686 *Mary* (White), } twins, b. May 26, 1744.
    5687 *Noah* (White), b. March, 1745.
    5688 *Peregrine* (White), b. Nov. 19, 1748.
    5689 *Susanna* (White), b. Aug. 11, 1751.
    5690 *Elizabeth* (White), b. Feb. 27, 1753.
    5691 *Lucy* (White), b. Jan. 24, 1755.
5692 Ruth,[4] b. Oct. 3, 1722; m. Feb. 7, 1740, Pearce Brownell, and had :
    5693 *Pearce* (Brownell), b. 1743.
    5694 *Gideon* (Brownell), b. 1746.
    5695 *Hope* (Brownell), b. 1750.
    5696 *Susanna* (Brownell), b. 1755.
    5697 *George* (Brownell), b. July 5, 1763.
    5698 *Lois* (Brownell), b. 1765.
5699 Sarah,[4] b. July 14, 1725.
5700 Hope,[4] b. Sept. 8, 1727; m. Dec. 26, 1751, Ichabod Potter.

## 5557

JONATHAN THURSTON[3] of Little Compton, R. I. (*Jonathan*,[2] *Edward*[1]), brother of the preceding, and son of Jonathan[2] and Sarah Thurston of Little Compton ; born there July 5, 1687 ; married ———.

Their children were:

5701 Edward,[4] b. 1719.
5702 Jonathan,[4] b. 1721.
5703 Mary,[4] b. 1723.
5704 Content,[4] b. 1725.
5705 Abigail,[4] b. 1727.

## 5601

BENJAMIN THURSTON[3] of Newport, R. I. (*Daniel*,[2] *Edward*[1]), son of Daniel[2] and Mary (Easton) Thurston of Newport; born there March 25, 1697 ; married, first, SARAH CASEY, daughter of Thomas and Rebecca Casey ; she died Aug. 18, 1732, aged 28. Second, MRS. HEPZIBAH SMITH, daughter of Peleg Bunker ; her first husband was Eliphalet Smith of Nantucket. Mr. Thurston died March 14, 1750, aged 53. He owned the sloop Pelican, the first regularly equipped whaler from Rhode Island. He received a bounty from the colony on 114 barrels of oil and 200 pounds of bone, brought into Newport June 11, 1733.

His children, by first wife, Sarah, were:

5706 Sarah,[4] b. May 25, 1729; m. Oct. 14, 1751, Joseph Turner, a mechanic in Newport and an original member of the "Mechanics Society." Children:
    5707 *Hannah* (Turner), m. Seth Yates.
    5708 *Ruth* (Turner), d. single.
5709 Mary,[4] b. June 18, 1730; m. Dec. 18, 1753, Jonathan Remington.
5710 Benjamin,[4] b. May 6, 1731; m. March 30, 1752, Ann Jackson. He was lost at sea and she died July, 1793, aged 59, leaving:
    5711 *Sarah Casey*,[5] b. 1756; m. Nov. 13, 1783, Thomas Ward Bliss. He died Sept. 5, 1798, aged 37; she died May 26, 1822, aged 66. The old house in which Mr. Bliss lived, on the corner of Farewell and Marlboro streets in Newport, was one of the oldest in town, and was standing till 1876; always called the "Bliss House." They had:
        5712 *Elizabeth Ayers* (Bliss), b. Oct. 2, 1784; m. ——— Wells.

5713 *Barbara Phillips* (Bliss), b. March 14, 1786; m. —— Murphy, a shipmaster of Newport, and had three children.
5714 *Benjamin Thurston* (Bliss), b. March 20, 1788.
5715 *Sarah Thurston* (Bliss), b. Sept. 11, 1790; m. —— Stillman.
5716 *Thomas Ward* (Bliss), b. Nov. 13, 1792.
5717 *Ebenezer David* (Bliss), b. Dec. 29, 1796.

By second wife, Hepzibah :

5718 Daniel,[4] b. 1734; d. May 12, 1735.
5719 Hepzibah,[4] b. Dec. 25, 1736; m. 1st, May 16, 1754, Nicholas Townsend; 2d, Dec. 1, 1764, Nathaniel Barney.

## 5604

EDWARD THURSTON[3] of Newport, R. I. (*Samuel,*[2] *Edward*[1]), eldest son of Samuel[2] and Abigail (Clarke) Thurston of Newport; born there May 26, 1696; married, May 9, 1723, ELIZABETH NORTON, daughter of Benjamin and Avis Norton. He died Feb. 22, 1776, aged 79; she died April, 1783, aged 76. Her will was dated Nov. 6, 1781, proved May 5, 1783.

Mr. Thurston was a cooper, and was thus noticed on the record of the society of Friends : " Recorder and keeper of these records divers years, yet nevertheless, for not following the advice of Friends respecting the manumitting his slaves, was set aside from being a member of the society several years before his death. However, at the earnest request of his widow, the present recorder hath presumed to record his death, although in the strictest sense he might not have done it."

Their children were :

+5720 Samuel,[4] b. April 5, 1724; m. Eunice Anthony.
5721 Abigail,[4] b. Jan. 4, 1726; d. March 28, 1726.
+5722 Edward,[4] b. Jan. 12, 1729; m. Mary Fourtane.
+5723 Benjamin,[4] b. Nov. 20, 1732; m. Amy Sherman.

## 5606

SAMUEL THURSTON[3] of Newport, R. I. (*Samuel,*[2] *Edward*[1]), brother of the preceding, and son of Samuel[2] and Abigail (Clarke) Thurston of Newport; born there Oct. 16, 1699; married MARY ——. He died in East Greenwich, R. I., Sept. 1, 1792, aged 92 y. 11 m.

Mr. Thurston was a saddler; was a freeman May 1, 1722; was at Providence in 1772, and removed to East Greenwich in 1786. A partition of his father's estate was made Nov. 7, 1750, among his four sons, Edward, Samuel, Joseph, and John.

Child :

5724 Lydia,[4] b. March 25, 1725; m. Samuel Tompkins.

## 5613

LATHAM THURSTON[3] of Newport, R. I. (*Samuel,*[2] *Edward*[1]), brother of the preceding, and son of Samuel[2] and Abigail (Clarke) Thurston of Newport; born there June 3, 1704; married, Jan. 1, 1730, MARY WANTON, daughter of John and Mary Wanton. He was lost at sea 1737; she died Sept. 30, 1737, aged 30.

Their children were:

5725  John,[4] b. Oct. 27, 1730; drowned at Jamaica Jan. 22, 1756.
5726  Latham,[4] b. Sept. 21, 1732; death on record, no date.
5727  Abigail,[4] b. May 9, 1735; d. May 20, 1760.
+5728  Samuel,[4] b. Sept. 23, 1737; m. Mary Brett.

## 5614

JOSEPH THURSTON[3] of Newport, R. I. (*Samuel,*[2] *Edward*[1]), brother of the preceding, and son of Samuel[2] and Abigail (Clarke) Thurston of Newport; born there Sept. 24, 1706; married, April 8, 1733,
ABIGAIL PINNEGAR, daughter of William and Abigail Pinnegar. He
died in Amsterdam Jan. 6, 1758; she died March 16, 1779, aged 61.
He was a freeman May 4, 1742.

Their children were:

5729  Abigail,[4] b. July 28, 1739; d. Oct. 1, 1740.
+5730  Joseph,[4] b. June 21, 1741; m. 1st, Mary Easton; 2d, Susanna Brownell.
5731  Abigail,[4] b. Nov. 6, 1742; d. April 11, 1754.
5732  Samuel,[4] b. Dec. 20, 1745; d. Feb. 7, 1746.
+5733  William,[4] b. March 8, 1747; m. Priscilla Norman.
5734  Sarah,[4] b. Aug. 16, 1749; m. William Bell; d. Dec. 25, 1829.
5735  Edward,[4] b. April 20, 1753; m. Rebecca Bassell; was lost at sea 1779.
    They had:
      5736  *Edward,*[5] b. 1779; m. June 28, 1812, Andra Place: d. March, 1860.
        They had:
          5737  *William Bassell,*[6] b. May 3, 1814; d. June 2, 1814.
          5738  *Elisa Ann,*[c] b. Dec. 16, 1816; d. Oct. 20, 1818.
5739  Benjamin,[4] b. Sept. 24, 1754.
5740  Latham,[4] b. 1757; d. 1757.

## 5622

JOHN THURSTON[3] of Newport, R. I. (*Samuel,*[2] *Edward*[1]), brother
of the preceding, and son of Samuel[2] and Abigail (Clarke) Thurston
of Newport; born there April 10, 1713; married, Jan. 7, 1741, MARY
COFFIN.* He was a freeman May 3, 1745; died March 1, 1771.
The will of Mary Thurston was dated March 6, 1773, and proved
June 5, 1783.

Their children were:

+5741  Latham,[4] b. Oct. 20, 1748; m. 1st, Sarah Wanton; 2d, Mrs. Martha
    Coggeshall.

* Mary Coffin was the daughter of Paul and Mary (Allen)† Coffin, granddaughter of Stephen
and Mary (Bunker) Coffin, great-granddaughter of Tristram and Dionis (Stevens) Coffin, great-
great-granddaughter of Peter and Joanna (Thember) Coffyn, great-great-great-granddaughter
of Nicholas and Joan Coffyn.‡ The witnesses to this marriage were Edward Thurston
[5604], John Thurston [5680], Benjamin Thurston [5601], Hepsibah Thurston [5601], Edward
Thurston [5722], Samuel Thurston [5606], Mary Thurston [5606], Samuel Thurston [5624], Sarah
Thurston [5627], Lydia Thurston [5724], Elizabeth Thurston [5604], Phebe Thurston [5623],
Paul Coffin, brother of bride, Mary Pearce, mother of bride, Clothier Pearce, son of Mary
Pearce.
† Mary Allen was the daughter of Edward and Anne (Coleman) Allen. Anne Coleman was
the daughter of Joseph and Anne (Bunker) Coleman and granddaughter of Thomas and
Susanna Coleman. Mary Bunker and Anne Bunker were daughters of George and Jane
(Godfrey) Bunker and granddaughters of William Bunker. Dionis Stevens was the daughter
of Robert Stevens.
‡ Robert Allen Coffin was a descendant of this family, who died at Conway, Mass., 1878,
aged seventy-seven years. He was the first student registered for admission to Amherst college at its opening in 1821 and was its oldest living alumnus. He was the founder of the Warren Female Seminary of Rhode Island, author of the "History of Conway," and a work on
natural philosophy, a contributor to "Bibliotheca Sacra," and a member of the Massachusetts
legislature in 1856-57. He was the brother of the late James H. Coffin, LL.D., meteorologist
of the Smithsonian Institution and professor in Lafayette college.

5742   A son, b. April 10, 1749; d. April 13, 1749.
+5743   John,[4] b. June 12, 1750; m. Sabra Smith.
5744   Mary,[4] b. July 17, 1752; m. Nov. 18, 1771, Hezekiah Starbuck of Nan-
      tucket, Mass.   They moved to North Carolina in 1785.   They had :
    5745   *George* (Starbuck), b. April 8, 1775; m. Elizabeth Starbuck.
    5746   *Gayer* (Starbuck), b. Aug. 10, 1777.
    5747   *Clarissa* (Starbuck), b. Jan. 28, 1780; m. Reuben Mills.
    5748   *Hezekiah* (Starbuck), b. Oct. 14, 1782; m. —— Hussey.
    5749   *Jethro* (Starbuck), m. —— Mills.
    5750   *Samuel* (Starbuck), m. Asenath Hedge.
    5751   *Mary* (Starbuck), m. —— Hunt.
    5752   *John* (Starbuck).
    5753   *Rebecca* (Starbuck).
    5754   *Latham* (Starbuck).
5755   Samuel,[4] b. Oct. 8, 1755; d. June 19, 1757.
5756   Abigail,[4] b. March 10, 1760; d. Aug. 17, 1760.
5757   Hannah,[4] b. April 29, 1762; d. Nov. 11, 1762.
+5758   Samuel,[4] b. Feb. 9, 1763; m. Mary Landers.
5759   Paul,[4] b. July 16, 1769; m. Jan. 2, 1791, Sarah Hall.   He died in Mara-
      caybo, South America, Oct. 8, 1802; she died May 17, 1856, aged 85.

## 5628

EDWARD THURSTON[3] of Freetown, Mass. (*Thomas,*[2] *Edward*[1]),
eldest son of Thomas[2] and Mehitable (Mayo) Thurston of Freetown ;
born there 1696 ; married HANNAH DODSON, daughter of Jonathan
and Abigail (Gannett) Dodson of Freetown, and granddaughter of
Anthony Dodson of Scituate, Mass.   She died Sept. 15, 1778, aged
75 ; he died Nov. 3, 1783, aged 87.

### Their children were :

+5760   Edward,[4] b. Sept. 6, 1724; m. Parnold Mott.
+5761   Peleg,[4] b. Oct. 24, 1726; m. Amy Barton.
5762   Hannah,[4] b. Feb. 24, 1729; m. Aug. 27, 1752, William Mosher of Dart-
      mouth, Mass.
+5763   Thomas,[4] b. Dec. 25. 1730; m. 1st, Elizabeth Pearce; 2d, Hannah Winslow.
5764   Sarah,[4] b. Nov. 24, 1732; n.m.; d.
5765   Elizabeth,[4] b. Jan. 24, 1735; n.m.; d. April 5, 1826.
5766   Mehitable,[4] b. Feb. 28, 1737; m. 1st, Nov. 2, 1758, Francis Harrison of
      Freetown; 2d, Jan. 11, 1776, Joshua Weeks of Wellfleet, Mass.
5767   Mary,[4] b. March 9, 1740; m. 1st, Oct. 9, 1774, Joseph Terry of Freetown;
      2d, Noah Edminster of Freetown.
5768   Samuel,[4] b. March 7, 1743; n.m.; d. June 23, 1831; will dated Dec. 8,
      1828, proved Aug. 5, 1831.

## 5629

THOMAS THURSTON[3] of Tiverton, R. I. (*Thomas,*[2] *Edward*[1]), brother of the preceding, and son of Thomas[2] and Mehitable (Mayo)
Thurston of Freetown, Mass. ; married ——.

### Their children were :

5775   Mehitable,[4] b. Dec. 13, 1741.
5776   Samuel,[4] b. Aug. 21, 1743.
5777   Elizabeth,[4] b. Nov. 20, 1747.
+5778   Thomas,[4] b. Feb. 16, 1750; m. Patience Beers.
5779   Mary,[4] b. Feb. 12, 1753.

## 5630

PELEG THURSTON[3] of Newport, R. I. (*Thomas,*[2] *Edward*[1]), brother
of the preceding, and son of Thomas[2] and Mehitable (Mayo) Thurs-

ton of Freetown, Mass.; married, first, Nov. 15, 1739, SARAH BOR-
DEN, daughter of Joseph and Elizabeth Borden; she was a legatee in
the will of her brother, Thomas Borden, made Feb. 11, 1748. Sec-
ond, Oct. 3, 1765, AMY RICHARDSON, daughter of Thomas and Mary
Richardson. He died June, 1770; she died Oct. 31, 1791, aged 61.
Mr. Thurston was a dry goods merchant in New York city.

His children, by first wife, Sarah, were :

+5785  John,[4] b. June 15, 1740; m. 1st, Sarah Feke; 2d, Abigail Robinson.
 5786  Peleg,[4] b. March 13, 1742; m. Sept. 23, 1765, Mary Fryers. She died Jan.
        9, 1766; he died Oct. 25, 1770, aged 21.
 5787  Joseph,[4] b. June 20, 1744.
 5788  Bryer,[4] b. July 3, 1746; d. July 20, 1747.
 5789  Sarah,[4] b. Dec. 27, 1749; m. Dec. 3, 1776, Jonathan Easton; d. June 30,
        1817.
 5790  Elizabeth,[4] b. March 6, 1752; m. Oct. 7, 1779, Philip Robinson; d. June
        22, 1782.  They had :
   5791    William Philip (Robinson), b. June 13, 1780.
   5792    George Brown (Robinson), b. June 22, 1782.
 5793  Thomas,[4] b. June 3, 1754; d. Sept. 29, 1754.
 5794  Thomas,[4] b. Feb. 17, 1757.
                By second wife, Amy :
+5795  William Richardson,[4] b. July 11, 1766; m. 1st, Eleanor King; 2d, Mary
        Seaman; 3d, Abigail Eveinghlm.

## 5631

JONATHAN THURSTON[3] of Newport, R. I. (*Thomas,[2] Edward[1]*),
brother of the preceding, and son of Thomas[2] and Mehitable (Mayo)
Thurston of Freetown, Mass.; married LYDIA GODDARD, daughter of
Daniel and Mary Goddard. Peleg Thurston (his brother) and Lydia
Thurston (his widow) administrators on estate of Jonathan Thurston
June 1, 1763, bond given June 21, 1763, liberty to sell his real estate.
His widow married, June 30, 1763, James Chace.

Their children were :

 5800  Mehitable,[4] b. Nov., 1743; m. 1st, Dec. 1, 1763, Cornelius Coggeshall; 2d,
        Oct. 5, 1769, Daniel Wood.  She had, by first husband :
   5801    Elizabeth (Coggeshall), b. Aug. 27, 1764.
 5802  Samuel,[4] b. July 5, 1745.
 5803  Lydia,[4] b. 1749; m. June 27, 1782, Benjamin Gould; d. Dec. 10, 1785.

## Fourth Generation.

### 5642

EDWARD THURSTON[4] of Newport, R. I. (*Edward,[3] Edward,[2] Edward[1]*), eldest son of Edward[3] and Elizabeth (Gardner) Thurston of
Newport; born there Sept. 8, 1702; married CATHERINE GARDNER,
daughter of Joseph and Catherine Gardner, mentioned in will of her
uncle, John Holmes, Nov. 21, 1732, as Katherine Thurston.  He
was a ship carpenter; died Nov. 14, 1735, aged 33.

Their children were :

 5810  Susanna,[5] b. 1728; d. March 14, 1730.
 5811  Susanna,[5] b. 1730; d. May 10, 1736.
 5812  Edward,[5] b. 1732; was a Free Baptist preacher in Providence, R. I.

+5813  John,⁵ b. 1734; m. Mary Brett.
5814  Catherine,⁵ b. 1736; m. March 19, 1761, William Wilson, and had:
    5815  *John* (Wilson), bap. June 14, 1772.
    5816  *Edward Thurston* (Wilson), bap. May 2, 1774.

## 5650

REV. GARDNER THURSTON⁴ of Newport, R. I. (*Edward,*³ *Edward,*² *Edward*¹), brother of the preceding, and son of Edward³ and Elizabeth (Gardner) Thurston of Newport; born there Nov. 14, 1721; married, first, Sept. 16, 1747, FRANCES SANFORD, daughter of Joseph and Lydia Sanford; she died Sept. 7, 1759, aged 32. Second, Oct. 25, 1760, MARTHA SANFORD. She died Dec. 17, 1784, aged 52; he died Aug. 23, 1802, aged 81.

He was pastor of the second Baptist church in Newport, and was the only clergyman remaining there in 1780. Oct. 27, 1783, this church was incorporated as the "Six Principles Baptist church." He held services in Trinity church until his own church could be repaired.

Rev. Joshua Bradley of Mansfield, Ct., in the Evangelical Magazine for November, 1808, says: "Mr. Thurston was endowed with an excellent disposition and possessed a good natural constitution, with a quick and brilliant imagination. He was mild, religious, studious, and amiable in his family, easy and graceful in all his public movements. His voice was strong and melodious, and his heart all alive in the great and arduous work of the ministry. He generally wrote the heads of his sermons, the quotations from scripture, and some of the most interesting ideas, which he thought necessary for the clear illustration of his subject. These he committed to memory and but seldom had his notes before him in public. Being possessed of pleasing pulpit talents, and giving himself wholly to the work of the ministry, his hearers became so numerous that his meeting-house was twice enlarged and was well filled as long as he was able to preach, and he was favored with repeated revivals of religion among his people."

His children, by first wife, Frances, were:

5820  Sarah,⁵ b. June 29, 1748; d. Sept. 17, 1755.

By second wife, Martha:

5821  Frances,⁵ b. Oct. 1, 1769; m. July 25, 1813, Job E. Woodman; d. Oct. 1, 1834; no children.

## 5660

CAPT. JOHN THURSTON⁴ of Newport, R. I. (*Jonathan,*³ *Edward,*² *Edward*¹), eldest son of Jonathan³ and Phebe (Holmes) Thurston of Newport; born there Aug. 17, 1723; married, May 10, 1746, ELIZABETH OXX, born June 14, 1725. She died March 25, 1793, aged 68; he died Aug. 6, 1794, aged 71. Will dated July 21, 1794, proved Jan. 5, 1795. He was a sea captain, and maintained the coat of arms handed down from his fathers.

Their children were:

+5826  John,⁶ b. May 31, 1747; m. Elizabeth Jenkins.
5827  Phebe,⁶ b. April 14, 1749; m. Jan. 1, 1769, Christopher Champlin; d. in Providence, R. I., March 1, 1823. They had:

18

5828   *John Thurston* (Champlin), b. Feb. 8, 1770; bap. Feb. 23, 1770; m.
      Penelope Minturn.  He died July 24, 1830; she died suddenly at
      South Hampton, L. I., July 31, 1872, aged 80.*
5829   *Rebecca* (Champlin), b. Nov. 4, 1771; bap. Jan. 6, 1772; m. 1791,
      Stephen Dexter; d. Jan. 21, 1795.
5830   *Uriah Oliver* (Champlin), b. Dec. 24, 1772; bap. Jan. 6, 1773; m.
      Eliza S. De Peyster.
5831   *Elizabeth* (Champlin), b. Nov. 27, 1774; m. 1796, John Church; d.
      March 24, 1810.
5832   *Phebe* (Champlin), b. Oct. 20, 1776; m. 1798, Stephen Dexter.
5833   *Christopher Joseph* (Champlin), d. July, 1780.
5834   Samuel,[5] b. June 4, 1751; m. Nov. 5, 1783. Elizabeth Lawton.  He died
      Jan. 8, 1825; she died Dec. 27, 1825, aged 70; no children.
+5835   Peleg,[5] b. May 28, 1753; m. 1st, Phebe Lawton; 2d, Ruth Lawton.
+5836   Jonathan,[5] b. April 25, 1755; m. Hannah Beebe.
5837   Edward,[6] b. April 12, 175); d. July 27, 1782.

### 5669

JONATHAN THURSTON[4] of Newport, R. I. (*Jonathan,*[8] *Edward,*[2]
*Edward*[1]), brother of the preceding, and son of Jonathan[8] and Phebe
(Holmes) Thurston of Newport; born there May 2, 1725; married,
April 21, 1748, RUTH SCOTT, daughter of Joseph and Ruth (Gould)
Scott.  He died Aug. 24, 1757 ; she died Oct. 31, 1767, aged 37 ; her
will dated Jan. 25, 1765.  The stone over the grave has the family
coat of arms and this inscription:  " In memory of Jonathan Thurston, an honest, industrious, skillful merchant, whose piety and virtues
procured the love and esteem of his acquaintances."

Their children were :

+5840   Jonathan,[5] b. 1749; m. Margaret Sweet.
5841   Joseph,[6] bap. Dec. 27, 1750.
5842   Edward,[5] bap. Jan. 14, 1753; d. May 26, 1753.
5843   George,[5] bap. May 15, 1754; d. May 15, 1754.
5844   Elizabeth,[5] bap. May 28, 1756; m. 1st, Oct. 10, 1783, Capt. Richard Chil-
      cott; he died at sea August, 1786; 2d, Oct. 22, 1799, John Bours; she
      died April 15, 1804, having had:
     5845   *Mary* (Chilcot), d. Dec. 1, 1787, aged 20 m. 16 d.
5846   Deborah,[5] bap. April 5, 1757; d. Sept. 4, 1757.

### 5671

WILLIAM THURSTON[4] of Newport, R. I. (*Jonathan,*[8] *Edward,*[2] *Edward*[1]), brother of the preceding, and son of Jonathan[8] and Phebe
(Holmes) Thurston of Newport; born there Oct. 7, 1728 ; married,
Sept. 4, 1754, DOROTHY CARTER.  He was lost at sea in 1756, aged
28 ; she died Feb. 11, 1822, aged 96.

Child :

+5850   William,[5] b. Sept. 25, 1755; m. Mary Rowlong.

### 5679

GEORGE THURSTON[4] of Little Compton, R. I. (*Edward,*[8] *Jonathan.*[2]
*Edward*[1]), eldest son of Edward[8] and Susanna (Pearce) Thurston of
Little Compton, R. I.; born there Nov. 4, 1709; married, first, Dec.
1), 1729, KEZIAH —— ; second, —— GREENE.  He sold his homestead farm in Little Compton Jan. 21, 1740, to John Brown, and removed to Hopkinton.

---

*Ann Maria, widow of the late Gabriel L. Lewis, and daughter of the late John Thurston
Champlin of New York city, was buried from the residence of her son-in-law, U. A. Murdock, 313 Fifth avenue, New York.

His children, by first wife, Keziah, were:

5855 Susanna,⁵ b. Jan., 1731.
+5856 William,⁵ b. Jan. 17, 1733; m. Ruth Stetson.
5857 Hannah,⁵ b. Jan. 10, 1735; m. —— Greene.
5858 Mary,⁵ b. Aug. 27, 1737.
+5859 Edward,⁵ b. May 16, 1740; m. Thankful Main.
+5860 George,⁵ b. 1741; m. 1st, Dolly Cottrell; 2d, Mrs. Sarah Rathbun.
5861 Nabby,⁵ b. 1753; m. Nathaniel Main, b. 1751. They lived in North Ston-
    ington, Ct. She died 1825; he died 1827. They had:
    5862 *Job* (Main), m. —— Billings, and lived and died in Brooklyn, Ct. He
        was a good farmer, and the last of his life a trader.
    5863 *Gardner* (Main), m. —— Hakes; lived and died in Brooklyn; two
        children.
    5864 *Nabby* (Main), m. Thomas Thompson; lived and d. in No. Stonington.
    5865 *Adie* (Main), m. Israel P. Park; lived and died in North Stonington.
    5866 *Russell* (Main), m. Katura Chapman; lived and d. in No. Stonington.
    5867 *Clarissa* (Main), m. Ichabod Eccleston; lived and d. in No. Stonington.
    5868 *Hannah* (Main), m. —— Wheeler; lived and died in Brooklyn.
    5869 *Aruby* (Main), m. Jonathan Chapman; lived and died in Brooklyn.
    They were all farmers.

By second wife:

+5870 Gardner,⁵ b. 1760; m. Lydia Taylor.
+5871 Joseph,⁵ m. Sarah Taylor.

## 5720

SAMUEL THURSTON⁴ of Newport, R. I. (*Edward,*³ *Samuel,*² *Edward*¹), eldest son of Edward³ and Elizabeth (Norton) Thurston of
Newport; born there April 5, 1724; married, April 28, 1744, EUNICE
ANTHONY, daughter of Isaac and Mary Anthony. He died at His-
paniola April 8, 1760; she died Nov. 7, 1777, aged 56.

Their children were:

5876 Norton,⁵ b. May 29, 1745; m. May 25, 1768, Ann Greene; she died in
    Canajoharie, N. Y., 1814.
5877 Avis,⁵ b. July 10, 1747; m. Dec., 1784, Peleg Sherman.
5878 Elizabeth,⁵ b. April 10, 1749; m. Dec. 1, 1768, David Melville. She died
    Dec. 1, 1803; he died Dec. 13, 1804, aged 62. They had, all baptized in
    Trinity church, Newport:
    5879 *Lydia* (Melville), b. Aug. 3, 1769.
    5880 *Samuel Thurston* (Melville), b. 1771; d. Oct. 17, 1792.
    5881 *David* (Melville), b. March 21, 1773; m. March 4, 1812, Patience S.
        Shearman.
    5882 *Mary* (Melville), b. March 20, 1775; d. Sept. 10, 1794.
    5883 *Elizabeth* (Melville), b. Dec. 5, 1777.
    5884 *Eunice Thurston* (Melville), b. Sept. 4, 1781; d. Aug. 29, 1819.
    5885 *Sarah Anthony* (Melville), b. May 28, 1784; m. Jan. 1, 1815, John
        Clough.
    5886 *Avis* (Melville), b. 1786; d. May 22, 1792.
+5887 Samuel Isaac,⁵ b. Aug. 18, 1756; m. 1st, Mary C. Coggeshall; 2d, Mrs.
    Jane Futhey, née Rawlins.

## 5722

EDWARD THURSTON⁴ of Newport, R. I. (*Edward,*³ *Samuel,*² *Ed-
ward*¹), brother of the preceding, and son of Edward³ and Elizabeth
(Norton) Thurston of Newport; born there Jan. 12, 1729; married,
June 17, 1764, MARY FOURTANE, daughter of Daniel and Jane
(Whitfield) Fourtane. He died in New York city June, 1782; she
died May 19, 1818, aged 81.

Their children were:

5892  Edward,[5] b. March 2, 1766; n.m.; d. Oct. 8, 1826.
5893  Elizabeth Norton,[5] b. June 12, 1768; m. Aug. 1, 1808, John Bannister; d.
       Dec. 7, 1838; no children.

## 5723

BENJAMIN THURSTON [4] of Newport, R. I. (*Edward,[3] Samuel,[2] Edward[1]*), brother of the preceding, and son of Edward [3] and Elizabeth (Norton) Thurston of Newport; born there Nov. 20, 1732; married, Dec. 10, 1755, AMY SHERMAN, daughter of Job and Amy Sherman. She died Sept. 4, 1762, aged 28; he died in the West Indies Dec. 4, 1766.

Their children were:

5898  Job,[5] b. Oct. 1, 1756; m. 1st, 1787, Rachel Coleman; she died Sept. 13,
       1787, aged 23; 2d, Ruth Cartwright; no children.
5899  Elizabeth,[5] b. April 4, 1758; d. Aug. 4, 1777.
5900  Abigail,[5] b. May 30, 1760; m. Robert Thomas; removed to the state of
       New York after the revolutionary war.  They had:
   5901  *Amy* (Thomas), b. Nov. 28, 1781.
   5902  *Elizabeth* (Thomas), b. Dec. 5, 1783.
   5903  *Thurston* (Thomas), b. Dec. 30, 1786.

## 5728

SAMUEL THURSTON [4] of Newport, R. I. (*Latham,[3] Samuel,[2] Edward[1]*), son of Latham [3] and Mary (Wanton) Thurston of Newport; born there Sept. 23, 1737; married, Sept. 16, 1764, MARY BRETT. He died Sept. 23, 1771; she died April 10, 1819, aged 80.

Their children were:

+5908  John Brett,[5] b. June 11, 1765; m. Mary ——.
 5909  Latham,[5] b. July 1, 1766.

## 5730

JOSEPH THURSTON [4] of Newport, R. I. (*Joseph,[3] Samuel[2] Edward[1]*), eldest son of Joseph [3] and Abigail (Pinnegar) Thurston of Newport; born there June 21, 1741; married, first, May 27, 1773, MARY EASTON, daughter of John and Patience (Redwood) Easton; she died Nov. 10, 1777, aged 38.  Second, April 27, 1780, SUSANNA BROWNELL, daughter of Abraham and Mary Brownell.  He died Feb. 20, 1803, aged 62; she died May 14, 1841.

His children, by first wife, Mary, were:

5914  Joseph,[5] b. May 23, 1774; d. June 1, 1774.

By second wife, Susanna:

5915  Mary,[5] b. Jan. 30, 1781; d. Sept. 2, 1781.
5916  Hannah,[5] b. July 12, 1782; d. April 11, 1783.
5917  Joseph,[5] b. Oct. 24, 1783; d. Dec. 5, 1783.
+5918  Abraham,[5] b. Nov. 7, 1784; m. Martha D. Prior.
5919  Susanna,[5] b. Feb. 8, 1789; d. Aug. 4, 1789.
+5920  Joseph,[5] b. June 16, 1791; m. Letitia McBurney.
5921  Henry,[5] b. June 26, 1796; d. Sept. 1, 1797.
5922  Susanna.[5] b. Dec. 3, 1799; d. Sept. 18, 1873.
5923  Benjamin,[5] b. Jan. 22, 1801; d. Aug. 29, 1801.

## 5733

WILLIAM THURSTON[4] of Newport, R. I. (*Joseph,*[3] *Samuel,*[2] *Edward*[1]), brother of the preceding, and son of Joseph[3] and Abigail (Pinnegar) Thurston of Newport; born there March 8, 1747; married, Aug. 5, 1773, PRISCILLA NORMAN. Mr. Thurston's son William told his daughter Sarah that his father (William[4]) started for the South when the youngest child was an infant and was never heard from; supposed to have been lost at sea on the passage.

Their children were :

5928 Abigail,[5] b. Aug. 16, 1775; m. Aug. 25, 1793, James Searles; d. March 23, 1833, leaving :
   5929 *Mary Ann* (Searles), b. March 18, 1795; m. Jan. 1815, Stephen Martin; d. 1833.
   5930 *Lucia* (Searles), b. Dec. 27, 1796; m. Oct., 1824, Rufus Park; d. 1861.
   5931 *Fanny* (Searles), b. March 16, 1799; m. July 11, 1822, Calvin Clark; d. 1836.
   5932 *John M.* (Searles), b. Dec. 7, 1801 ; m. Philomelia Stoddard ; she d. 1862.
   5933 *Priscilla* (Searles), b. April 9, 1804; m. Dec. 7, 1838, Calvin Clark.
   5934 *James H.* (Searles), b. May 4, 1806; m. May 4, 1830, Martha G. Ransom; she died 1860.
   5935 *William Thurston* (Searles), b. June 27, 1808; m. 1st, 1838, Laurilla Williams; 2d, Lucinda B. White; d. 1864.
   5936 *Elizabeth Thurston* (Searles), b. Dec. 20, 1811 ; m. June, 1833, Edward B. Hawes; d. 1862.
   5937 · *Moses Thurston* (Searles), b. Feb. 9, 1814; m. 1840, Mary Ann Primmer.
   5938 *Bernard D.* (Searles), b. Aug. 22, 1815; m. Dec. 23, 1843, Sophia Harvey.
   5939 *Abigail* (Searles), b. Oct. 2, 1816; m. Jan. 9, 1838, L. N. Thomas.
+5940 Moses,[5] b. Feb. 6, 1780; m. 1st, Elizabeth Easton ; 2d, Mrs. Abigail Baker.
+5941 William,[5] b. 1782; m. Ruth C. Easton.

## 5741

LATHAM THURSTON[4] of Newport, R. I. (*John,*[3] *Samuel,*[2] *Edward*[1]), eldest son of John[3] and Mary (Coffin) Thurston of Newport; born there Oct. 20, 1748; married, first, Feb. 4, 1768, SARAH WANTON, daughter of John and Anna Wanton; she died Dec. 16, 1800, aged 58. Second, July 25, 1802, MRS. MARTHA (CAHOONE) COGGESHALL, daughter of James Cahoone. He died July 10, 1825; will dated June 27, 1825, proved Sept. 5, 1825.

Their children were :

5946 John Wanton,[5] m. 1st, Oct. 25, 1795, Nancy Anthony; she died May 10, 1796, aged 20; 2d, March 24, 1800, Mrs. Elizabeth Anthony, daughter of Gideon Cornell.
5947 Nancy R.,[5] m. Robert Babcock, and had:
   5948 *John* (Babcock).
   5949 *Latham* (Babcock).
   5950 *Sarah Ann* (Babcock).
   5951 *Wanton* (Babcock).
   5952 *Eliza* (Babcock).
   5953 *Abby* (Babcock).
   5954 *Cornelia* (Babcock).
+5955 William Wanton,[5] b. 1780; m. Sarah Jack.
5956 Mary,[5] m. Aug., 1802, John Snow; he died April 25, 1865. They had :
   5957 *William* (Snow).
   5958 *George* (Snow).
   5959 *John Wanton* (Snow).
   5960 *Mary* (Snow).

5961   Latham,⁵ m. Aug., 1802, Abby Wanton, daughter of John Wanton, and
         had *Abby*,⁶ m. —— Jennings.
5962   Sarah,⁵ b. 1785; m. July 30, 1806, George C. Tew; d. Oct. 20, 1832; had:
    5963   *George C.* (Tew), a noted phrenologist in Rhode Island and other states.
    5964   *Latham Thurston* (Tew), m. Maria T. Sterne [see no. 5971]; both
             dead; no children.

By second wife, Martha:

5965   Martha Coggeshall,⁵ m. Henry Higgins Thurston.   [see no. 6037.]

## 5743

JOHN THURSTON⁴ of Newport, R. I. ( *John*,³ *Samuel*,² *Edward*¹),
brother of the preceding, and son of John³ and Mary (Coffin) Thurston of Newport; born there June 12, 1750; married, March 11, 1789,
SABRA SMITH.* He died of yellow fever, in Newport, Aug. 12, 1819,
aged 69; she died June 26, 1822, aged 53. He was "disowned" by
the society of Friends in 1784 for "keeping slaves."

Their children were:

5970   Maria,⁵ b. Jan. 5, 1790; m. Dec. 8, 1811, John Sterne; d. Oct. 9, 1849; had:
    5971   *Maria Thurston* (Sterne), b. Sept. 11, 1812; m. Jan. 21, 1834, Latham
             Thurston Tew [see no. 5964]; d. Aug. 10, 1872; no children.
    5972   *Caroline* (Sterne), b. Feb. 6, 1815; m. June 14, 1838, Thomas B.
             Shearman. ' They had:
        5973   *John Sterne* (Shearman), b. Nov. 15, 1840; d. Dec. 2, 1840.
        5974   *Rowena* (Shearman), b March 5, 1842.
        5975   *John Sterne* (Shearman), b. April 6, 1843.
        5976   *Wanton Taber* (Shearman), b. April 26, 1846; d. July 20, 1846.
        5977   *Wanton Taber* (Shearman), b. Aug. 1, 1847.
        5978   *James Turner* (Shearman), b. Jan. 10, 1849.
        5979   *Maria Sterne* (Shearman), b. Feb. 29, 1852.
    5980   *Samuel* (Sterne), b. June 21, 1817; m. May 24, 1841, Martha J. Bur-
             dick: They had:
        5981   *Charles Thurston* (Sterne), b. June 8, 1849.
        5982   *Ella* (Sterne), b. May 17, 1853; d. Aug. 2, 1855.
        5983   *Kate* (Sterne), b. June 22, 1857; m. Grant Perry Taylor Oct., 1878.
        5984   *Sophia Eliza* (Sterne), b. July 29, 1862.
    5985   *Charles Thurston* (Sterne), b. July 14, 1819; d. Jan. 23, 1820.
    5986   *Charles Thurston* (Sterne), b. Jan. 23, 1821; d. March 5, 1822.
    5987   *Georgiana* (Sterne), b. Dec. 29, 1822; m. Aug. 6, 1843. William P.
             Swasey of Vineland, N. J.; she died, having had one child who died.
    5988   *Harriet Elizabeth* (Sterne), b. Aug. 3, 1825; m. Jan. 28, 1844, J. B.
             Swasey; d. Jan. 7, 1848; he was lost at sea on passage to Georgia.
    5989   *Martha Rosaline* (Sterne), b. April 16, 1828; d. May 11, 1846.
    5990   *Andrew Jackson* (Sterne), b. Oct. 7, 1830; d. Feb. 23, 1856.
    5991   *Louisa* (Sterne), b. July 16, 1832; d. June 29, 1857.

---

* Sabra Smith was the daughter of Elijah and Esther (Myrick) Smith, granddaughter of
Benjamin and Sarah (Way) Smith, great-granddaughter of Francis Smith, and great-great-
granddaughter of Richard Smith.
   Esther Myrick was the daughter of Elisha and Grace (Rogers) Myrick, and granddaughter
of John and Elizabeth (Trowbridge) Myrick.
   Elizabeth Trowbridge was the daughter of James and Margaret (Atherton) Trowbridge,
and granddaughter of Thomas Trowbridge.
   Margaret Atherton was the daughter of Humphrey Atherton.
   Grace Rogers was the daughter of Daniel and Grace (Williams) Rogers, granddaughter of
Samuel and Mary (Stanton) Rogers, and great-granddaughter of James and Elizabeth (Row-
land) Rogers.
   Elizabeth Rowland was the daughter of Samuel Rowland.
   Mary Stanton was the daughter of Thomas and Anne (Lord) Stanton.
   Anne Lord was the daughter of Thomas and Dorothy Lord.
   Grace Williams was the daughter of Thomas and Joanna Williams.
   Sarah Way was probably the daughter of George and Susanna (Nest) Way, granddaughter
of George and Elizabeth (Smith) Way, and great-granddaughter of Henry and Elizabeth Way.
   Elizabeth Smith was the daughter of John and Joanna Smith.
   Susanna Nest was the daughter of Joseph and Sarah (Bodington) Nest.

5992 *John* (Sterne), b. April 17, 1834; m. Dec. 20, 1855, Elizabeth R. Mumford; d. March 25, 1863.
+5993 Charles Myrick,[5] b. Feb. 23, 1792; m. Rachel Hall Pitman.
5994 Child, d. in infancy.
5995 Sophia Eliza,[5] b. Apr. 3, 1797; n.m.; an active member of the Methodist church; d. June 12, 1879.
5996 Esther Matilda,[5] b. July 25, 1800; m. Nov. 24, 1828, William Robinson Pitman, a watchmaker and jeweler, formerly in New Bedford, Mass., now living in Newport, R. I., 1879. She was an active member of the Methodist church; d. Nov. 7, 1834. They had:
   5997 *Harriet Elizabeth* (Pitman), b. Sept. 20, 1829; m. April 6, 1852, Rev. Carlos Banning, a Methodist clergyman; he graduated from the "Concord Theological Seminary," now removed to Boston and known as the "Boston University." Children:
      5998 *Matilda Thurston* (Banning), b. June 30, 1854; m. Nov. 15, 1877, Thomas W. Freeborn, and has:
         5999 *Jennie Thurston* (Freeborn), b. July 15, 1878.
      6000 *William Carlos* (Banning), b. May 17, 1860; d. Oct. 10, 1864.
      6001 *Arthur Staples* (Banning), b. June 9, 1862; d. Jan. 31, 1865.
      6002 *Edwin Thomas* (Banning), b. May 11, 1864.
      6003 *Mary Elizabeth* (Banning), b. Feb. 28, 1866.
      6004 *Alice Crocker* (Banning), b. Oct. 8, 1868.
   6005 *William Goddard* (Pitman), b. Oct. 15, 1834; m. March 14, 1864, Eugenie S. Bemis.* Mr. Pitman is a dry goods merchant in Madison, Wis.; they are members of the Episcopal church. He says: "I enlisted April, 1861, and served as sergeant in Co. K, 1st Wisconsin volunteers, during the three months' service. In August, 1862, I, with two others, recruited a company which was assigned to the 23d regiment Wisconsin volunteer infantry. I served as adjutant of the regiment until May, 1863, when I was commissioned captain of the company which I had helped to raise (Co. I); resigned in Dec., 1863, and have since followed my present occupation. Participated in one of the first skirmishes of the war, that at Falling Waters, Va., July 2, 1861, and also in the first attack on Vicksburgh, Dec., 1862, in the battle of Fort Hindman, Jan., 1863, Port Gibson, Champion Hills, Black River Bridge, May, 1863, in the siege and capture of Vicksburgh, July 4, 1863, in the siege of Jackson, July, 1863, and in the battle of Carrion Crow Bayou, Nov., 1863, besides numerous skirmishes and guerrilla chases." Children:
      6006 *Bertha Staples* (Pitman), b. Aug. 6, 1865; bap. Oct. 21, 1865.
      6007 *Jennie Matilda* (Pitman), b. Sept. 8, 1872; bap. Nov. 3, 1872.
      6008 *Annie Maria* (Pitman), b. Oct. 10, 1874; bap. Feb. 21, 1875.
6009 Harriet Smith,[5] b. Sept. 27, 1804; d. June 3, 1829.

## 5758

SAMUEL THURSTON[4] of Newport, R. I. (*John,[3] Samuel,[2] Edward[1]*), brother of the preceding, and son of John[3] and Mary (Coffin) Thurston of Newport; born there Feb. 9, 1763; married, Aug. 7, 1783, MARY LANDERS, daughter of John Landers; she died Sept. 13, 1816.

Mr. Thurston was disowned by the society of Friends in 1782, for having "shipped on a privateer."

Their children were:

6016 John,[5] b. April 21, 1784; d. May 12, 1785.
6017 John,[5] b. Jan. 12, 1786; m. Mrs. Lamphire, daughter of —— Burdick; had:
   6018 *Avis,[6]* m. —— Burdick.
   6019 *Nancy,[6]* m. —— Vanalger of Nile, Allegany county, N. Y.
   6020 *Mary.[6]*

---

* Eugenie S. Bemis was the daughter of Frederick and Sarah Jane (Swan) Bemis of Boston, Mass. Sarah Jane Swan was the daughter of Benjamin and Hannah (Shale) Swan of Salem, Mass. Hannah Shale was the daughter of Andrew (gentleman of Dublin university) and Jane (Elliott) Shale. Jane Elliott was the daughter of Capt. Benjamin and Abigail (Groves) Elliott of Beverly, Mass.
Frederick Bemis was the son of Isaac and Louisa (Jones) Bemis.

6021    Mary,[5] b. March 2, 1788; d. Sept. 12, 1810.
6022    Elizabeth Landers,[5] b. Feb. 14, 1791; m. Oct. 28, 1810, John P. Hammond, and had:
  6023    *Mary Thurston* (Hammond), b. June 9, 1811; d.
  6024    *John Henry* (Hammond), b. Oct. 19, 1812; d.
  6025    *William* (Hammond), b. April 5, 1814.
  6026    *James* (Hammond), b. Oct. 10, 1816.
  6027    *Joseph* (Hammond), b. Sept. 19, 1818.
  6028    *Elizabeth Landers* (Hammond), b. Sept. 30, 1820.
  6029    *Edward Landers* (Hammond), b. Aug. 16, 1822.
  6030    *Ann* (Hammond), b. Oct. 23, 1825.
  6031    *Sarah* (Hammond), b. Aug. 25, 1827; d.
  6032    *Sarah* (Hammond), b. Aug. 29, 1829.
  6033    *Phebe* (Hammond), b. Feb. 20, 1832.
  6034    *Laura Wood* (Hammond), b. March 16, 1836.
+6035   Samuel,[5] b. June 13, 1793; m. Elizabeth Gifford.
6036    Paul,[5] b. Feb. 20, 1796; d. Aug. 7, 1797.
+6037   Henry Higgins,[5] b. Sept. 20, 1799; m. Martha Coggeshall Thurston.

## 5760

EDWARD THURSTON[4] of Freetown, Mass. (*Edward,*[3] *Thomas,*[2] *Edward*[1]), eldest son of Edward[3] and Hannah (Dodson) Thurston of Freetown; born there Sept. 6, 1724; married PARNOLD MOTT of Dartmouth, Mass.

Their children were:
+6042   Gardner,[5] b. Feb. 15, 1761; m. Mary Terry.
6043    Parnold,[5] d. single, Dec. 27, 1814.
6044    Deborah,[5] m. Elisha Davis of Fall River, Mass.
+6045   Nathaniel S.,[5] b. May 10, 1771; m. Lavinia Davis.
6046    Hepzibah,[5] d. single 183–.

## 5761

PELEG THURSTON[4] of Troy, Mass. (*Edward,*[3] *Thomas,*[2] *Edward*[1]), brother of the preceding, and son of Edward[3] and Hannah (Dodson) Thurston of Freetown, Mass.; born there Oct. 24, 1726; married AMY BARTON of Warren, R. I.   She died Oct. 8, 1796, aged 59; he died Sept. 29, 1822, aged 95.   He was a farmer.

Their children were:
6050    Diadema,[5] b. 1752; d. single Sept. 11, 1838, aged 86.
6051    Peleg Rufus,[5] b. 1765; was a farmer; d. single Oct. 6, 1822, aged 57.
6052    James,[5] b. 1770; was a farmer; d. single April 4, 1829, aged 59; will made Feb., 1825, proved June 30, 1829.
+6053   Varnum,[5] b. 1773; m. Mary Gardner.
· 6054   Hannah,[5] m. Rufus Blossom, and had:
  6055    *Susan* (Blossom).
  6056    *Barton* (Blossom).
6057    Mary,[5] m. Benjamin Terry of Freetown, and had:
  6058    *Amy* (Terry), named in will of her uncle James Thurston, 1825; m. Ephraim Winslow, and had:
    6059    *Ephraim N.* (Winslow), chief engineer of Old Colony railroad, residing in Hyannis, Mass.
    6060    *Benjamin* (Winslow), d. in California.
    By second wife, Susan:
    6061    *Andrew J.* (Winslow).
  6062    *Louisa* (Terry), m. George Lawton, and had Job, Joanna, and Mary.
  6063    *Susan* (Terry), m. Ephraim Winslow, as his second wife.

## 5763

THOMAS THURSTON[4] of Freetown, Mass. (*Edward,*[3] *Thomas,*[2] *Edward*[1]), brother of the preceding, and son of Edward[3] and Hannah

(Dodson) Thurston of Freetown; born there Dec. 25, 1730; married, first, Jan. 1, 1756, ELIZABETH PEARCE of Swansea, Mass.; she died Jan. 12, 1794, aged 59. Second, HANNAH WINSLOW of Freetown. She died March 20, 1803, aged 79; he died June 4, 1811, aged 80.

His children, all by first wife, were:

6068 Mary,[5] b. Dec. 17, 1756; d. single May, 1799.
6069 Patience,[5] b. May 29, 1759; m. William H. Potter, and had:
    6070 *William* (Potter).
    6071 *Benjamin* (Potter).
    6072 *Ruby* (Potter).
    6073 *Elizabeth* (Potter).
6074 Elizabeth,[5] b. Dec. 8, 1760; d. single April 6, 1846.
6075 Sarah,[5] b. June 5, 1763; d. single Nov. 11, 1833; will made June 24, 1831.
6076 Joseph,[5] } twins, born } d. single Oct. 26, 1828.
+6077 Jonathan,[5] } June 25, 1765; { m. 1st, Sarah Luther; 2d, Mercy (Briggs) Hathaway.
6078 Phebe,[5] b. Dec., 1770; d. single Dec. 30, 1793.
6079 Lydia,[5] b. May 21, 1773; d. single May 24, 1794.

## 5778

THOMAS THURSTON[4] of Tiverton, R. I. (*Thomas,[3] Thomas,[2] Edward[1]*), fourth child of Thomas Thurston[3] of Tiverton; born there Feb. 16, 1750; married, Jan. 1, 1776, PATIENCE BEERS.

Their children were:

+6085 Samuel,[5] b. March 28, 1776; m. Mercy Tabor.
6086 John,[5] b. Jan. 22, 1778.
6087 Thomas,[5] b. Jan. 16, 1780.
+6088 George Howland,[5] b. May 11, 1782; m. Elizabeth Baker.

## 5785

JOHN THURSTON[4] of Newport, R. I. (*Peleg,[3] Thomas,[2] Edward[1]*), eldest son of Peleg[3] and Sarah (Borden) Thurston of Newport; born there June 15, 1740; married, first, SARAH FEKE, daughter of Robert and Eleanor Feke; second, April 23, 1772, ABIGAIL ROBINSON, daughter of William and Elizabeth Robinson. He died July 5, 1788; will dated July 2, 1788, proved Aug. 4, 1788; she died Nov., 1840, aged 87.

His children, by first wife, Sarah, were:

6093 Sarah,[5] b. Aug. 12, 1768; d. Aug. 19, 1787.

By second wife, Abigail:

+6094 John Robinson,[5] b. April 24, 1774; m. Mary Ann Bruce.
6095 Peleg,[5] b. Jan. 21, 1778; d. July 25, 1800.
6096 Eliza Wanton,[5] b. July 22, 1781; m. Nov. 25, 1808, Abraham S. Hallett; d. Nov. 11, 1809.
6097 William Robinson,[5] b. April 4, 1784; d. Feb., 1807.
6098 Philip Wanton,[5] b. Feb. 28, 1787; d. Dec. 3, 1806.

## 5795

WILLIAM RICHARDSON THURSTON[4] of Flushing, N. Y. (*Peleg,[3] Thomas,[2] Edward[1]*), brother of the preceding, and son of Peleg[3] and Sarah (Borden) Thurston of Newport, R. I.; born there July 11, 1766; married, first, ELEANOR KING; she died June 11, 1797. Second, March 8, 1815, MARY SEAMAN, daughter of Willet and Mary Seaman of New York; she died April 19, 1819. Third, July 12,

1821, ABIGAIL EVEINGHAM, daughter of Gilbert and Phebe Eveingham of New York. He died April 25, 1855.

Mr. Thurston removed to New York city when the tonnage of Newport was larger than that of New York, and engaged in the importation of cloths, and in 1846 retired to Flushing, where he died.

His children, by first wife, Eleanor, were:

6103    Eleanor,[5] b. May 21, 1797; d. Sept. 25, 1804.

By second wife, Mary:

+6104   William Richardson,[5] b. May 17, 1817; m. Jane Ridley Day.

By third wife, Abigail:

+6105   Joseph Delaplaine,[5] b. Feb. 22, 1823; m. Mary Wharton.
6106    Edward,[5] b. April 3, 1830; d. April 4, 1830.

---

## Fifth Generation.

### 5813

JOHN THURSTON [5] of Providence, R. I. (*Edward,[4] Edward,[3] Edward,[2] Edward[1]*), son of Edward [4] and Catherine (Gardner) Thurston of Newport, R. I.; born in Providence 1734; married MARY BRETT. He was a house carpenter. Both himself and wife died of small pox.

Their children were:

6110    Samuel,[6] was a captain and ship owner, and m. a widow who was the owner of three plantations in Nassau, N. P.
6111    William,[6] b. 1760; fell when young and so injured his head that he was very eccentric ever after. He used to wander about the country, staying awhile at home and with each of his brothers and sisters, calling himself "the pilgrim;" never married. He came near being pressed into the British service. The press-gang searched his father's house, and he hid in an empty cask that was floating in the water in the cellar. In 1824 he returned to Providence and lived to be quite aged.
6112    Grindell.[6]
6113    Edward.[6]
+6114   John,[6] m. Elizabeth Allen.
+6115   Daniel,[6] b. 1770; m. Prudence Crossman.
6116    Richard.[6]
6117    Freelove,[6] m. John Thurber, who owned a ropewalk in Providence.

### 5826

JOHN THURSTON [5] of Hudson, N. Y. (*Capt. John,[4] Jonathan,[3] Edward,[2] Edward[1]*), eldest son of John [4] and Elizabeth (Oxx) Thurston of Newport, R. I.; born there May 31, 1747; married, June 21, 1772, ELIZABETH JENKINS, eldest daughter of John and Prudence (Marion) Jenkins of Boston, Mass. He died Jan. 6, 1809; she died Aug. 19, 1815, aged 65.

Mr. Thurston lived for a time in Providence, R. I., and was one of thirty shareholders who formed themselves into an association in 1783 and founded the city of Hudson, N. Y., which he supposed would be the head of North river navigation. He moved to New York in the spring of 1794, going in a sloop, provisioned for the "voyage," hav-

NOTE.—Since printing the above, I have learned that this "voyage" was not from Providence to New York, but the passage up the Hudson river, from New York city to Hudson, and this makes the incident noteworthy. There is an enlargement of the Hudson river, near

ing also a cow on board. He placed the vessel under the control of his wife, and as she ordered the captain to cast anchor whenever the wind blew fresh, the "voyage" naturally occupied two weeks. He remained in New York till 1804, when he bought a beautiful farm near Hudson called Mt. Laurel, where he spent the remainder of his days.

A local paper says: "Few men have passed through the active scenes of life, and arrived at the age of this excellent man, with character so wholly unsullied; and few men have departed this life so universally lamented by those societies in which they have moved. Mr. Thurston was born in Newport, where he passed the morning of his life and arrived at its meridian. He was one of the original proprietors of the city of Hudson, and removed with his family to this place in the year 1784. Here he continued to reside for a number of years, and was active among his co-proprietors in laying the foundation of a city which he lived to behold the third in size and population in this state. He removed to New York in the year 1794. There for a long time he was engaged in extensive business, and there he invariably supported the character which he had acquired of an intelligent merchant and an honest and honorable man. Having acquired an ample fortune, in the year 1804 he concluded to retire from business and spend the remainder of his days in the enjoyment of domestic happiness and in the peaceful society of his early life. Accordingly he purchased an elegant seat near Hudson, to which he soon removed. There, in the neighborhood of the city which he had a large share in establishing, he continued to reside, surrounded by all those domestic pleasures which independence, peace of mind, and a most amiable family are sure to bestow. He was no bigot, but zealous in the cause of religion. He was ever a sincere and distinguished member and supporter of the Episcopal church in this city. That church will feel his loss sincerely; they were attached to him as a friend and a christian. Society will feel his loss deeply, for he was a friend to the poor and the industrious. His connections will long mourn for him, for they found him ever generous and just. And his afflicted family will ever remember with tender gratitude the exemplary manner with which he filled the endearing relations of husband and father."

"Mrs. Elizabeth Thurston was a woman who dignified and ornamented every station which she sustained in life. It is usual to apologize when we praise the dead, and it is to be lamented that eulogy is so often misapplied; but to those who knew Mrs. Thurston, who were acquainted with the sweetness of her disposition, her exertions of benevolence, and the ardor of her piety, no praise will be considered extravagant, no encomium unmerited. Her death is a loss to society at large, for she ornamented and improved every circle in which she moved. The dignity of her conduct, the purity of her mind, and her ceaseless walk of virtue commanded admiration and respect and irresistibly won esteem and affection. Her house was the seat of the most genuine and friendly hospitality and liberal charity. To her children she was everything by her instructions, example, and affections that the best of mothers could be. In her last distressing sickness she appeared in all the loveliness of christian resigna-

tion, in all the triumph of christian faith.  Her piety began in her youth; it increased with steady lustre, like the shining light, until the day of life was past.  It sustained in every trial, was consolation in every sorrow, and a firm support in the hour of death.

> Mild as a saint whose errors are forgiven,
> Calm as a vestal, and composed as heaven.

Her sick bed afforded a lesson never to be forgotten, and a proof of the perfection of faith in the Lord Jesus Christ not to be refuted. When her gentle spirit fled, all believed that for her to die was gain. 'Blessed are the dead that die in the Lord.' "

### Their children, born in Providence, were:

6123  John Holmes,[6] bap. May 1, 1776; d. Sept 8, 1776, in Newport.
+6124  Robert Jenkins,[6] m. Abigail Bogert.
6125  Phebe Watson,[6] b. 1783; n.m.; d. in New York Feb. 10, 1858, aged 75.

### Born in Hudson:

6126  Louis Marion,[6] of the firm of Proud & Thurston in Baltimore, Md.; n.m.; d. in Philadelphia, Pa., aged 23.
6127  John,[6] d. single in Bushwick.
6128  Eliza,[6] b. 1786; m. Ezra Reed of Mt. Laurel, N. Y.; he died 1858; she died Jan. 15, 1860, aged 74; no children.  "We extract from The New York Observer of Jan. 20, 1860, the following account of three ladies who have recently followed each other to the grave within the short space of two months: ' While the death of Mrs. Bedell and her sister, Mrs. Fanning, continues to spread sadness over a wide circle of christians, that of a third sister of the same family, Mrs. Eliza Thurston Reed, has taken place within the last week, bereaving the community, within the short space of two months, of three sisters, whose lives will be ever remembered with gratitude and emotion, as devoted to the noblest and most sacred aims of the christian religion.  We do not propose to refer again, on this occasion, to the great services rendered by Mrs. Bedell, trusting, as we do, that some of her admirers will prepare a memorial of her life; nor do we wish to expatiate upon the active solicitude for the poor which distinguished Mrs. Fanning, or upon the tender sympathies with the distressed which formed so bright a feature in the character of Mrs. Reed; but we cannot resist the temptation of pointing to the remarkable fact of the rapid manner in which the three sisters have followed each other to the grave, and to the lovely spirit which marked their transition from this to a higher sphere of existence. Their lives were devoted to the most generous thoughts and deeds which can engage the human soul, and on departing from this earth they were filled with joy at the anticipation of meeting their Saviour, whom they had so much loved and served for the last fifty years.'  The journal in which this notice appears is the organ of the Old-School Presbyterian church, but the ladies to whom it refers were members of the Protestant Episcopal church, while our journal represents the interests of Unitarians.  No higher homage could be paid to the exalted character of these ladies than this universal recognition by all denominations, while we rejoice, at the same time, that all theological differences disappear around the graves of those whose life was in true harmony with the laws of love of our Saviour, which transcend all creeds and all denominations.  Mrs. Bedell's husband was Rev. Gregory T. Bedell, for some time rector of St. Andrew's, Philadelphia, where he died in 1834.  For eloquence and benevolence he had hardly any superior in the Protestant Episcopal church; and his sermons, remarkable for simplicity and point, were published, with a memoir, by Rev. Dr. Tyng.  His son officiated for several years in the Church of the Ascension of this city, and has recently accepted the post of assistant bishop of Ohio, to the great regret of his constituents in New York, whose respect and affection he has won by his indefatigable and public-spirited exertion in behalf of the interests of the

church, and by his solicitude for the moral elevation of his parish. Mrs. Bedell, his mother, whose example must have contributed powerfully to inspire his zeal, was a lady in whom the religion by faith and that by good works were combined in a truly remarkable degree. Her life was full of incidents which attest the efficacy of the latter, while her personal influence purified the moral atmosphere wherever she went. Her sisters, Mrs. Fanning and Mrs. Reed, were, in a more narrow but not less beautiful sphere, remarkable for ·the highest christian qualities. The one could not hear of any person in need without endeavoring to alleviate his want; the other could not hear of a tale of sorrow without manifesting the deepest sympathy. To the influence of such women is the country indebted for many of its noble and redeeming characteristics. While men are more disposed to be absorbed by selfish aims, such women sow the seeds of the unselfish, beautiful, generous, and holy, and show how immense the moral and social influence of woman is, not only in the home life, but in the vast domain of humanity, which gathers fresh hopes from such select beings, whose life is a blessing and whose death is a triumph."—*A New York Journal.*

+6129 Edward Champlin,⁶ b. Nov. 9, 1790; m. Elizabeth Van Vredenberg.
+6130 Penelope.⁶ b. Dec. 29, 1792; m. Rev. Gregory Townsend Bedell.
+6131 Susan Alida,⁶ b. Nov. 29, 1793; m. Patrick Fanning.

## 5835

PELEG THURSTON⁵ of Portsmouth, R. I. (*Capt. John,⁴ Jonathan,³ Edward,² Edward¹*), brother of the preceding, and son of Capt. John⁴ and Elizabeth (Oxx) Thurston of Newport, R. I.; born there May 28, 1753; married, first, June 1, 1777, PHEBE LAWTON, daughter of Robert and Mary Lawton; she died Oct. 6, 1793, aged 41. Second, RUTH LAWTON, sister of his first wife. He died Dec. 4, 1831, aged 78; she died Oct. 28, 1836, aged 77.

He was a sea captain till he became too old, when he paid attention to farming; the farm that his son Peleg lived and died upon.

### His children, by first wife, Phebe, were:

·6136  Peleg,⁶ b. July 19, 1778; d. Oct. 3, 1781.
 6137  Elizabeth,⁶ b. June 21, 1782; m. March 17, 1805, Enos Gibbs, a farmer in Portsmouth, R. I.; d. Oct. 9, 1820. They had:
  6138  *Phebe Lawton* (Gibbs), b. Aug. 10, 1805; m. —— Thompson.
  6139  *Jonathan* (Gibbs), b. Aug. 14, 1807; d. March 6, 1820.
  6140  *Ruth* (Gibbs), b. Feb. 14, 1809.
  6141  *Enos* (Gibbs), b. Dec. 3, 1810; d. Aug. 12, 1822.
  6142  *Peleg* (Gibbs), b. March 28, 1813; d. Aug. 23, 1820.
  6143  *Rachel Stoddard* (Gibbs), b. Sept. 19, 1815; m. May 19, 1839, Samuel Lindon Ward, and had:
   6144  *Laura Underwood* (Ward), b. Feb. 29, 1840; m. Dec. 28, 1869, Thomas Williams, and had Charles Lyndon (Williams), b. Oct. 3, 1870.
   6145  *Elizabeth Gibbs* (Ward), b. Dec. 27, 1841; m. Sept. 4, 1865, Isaac N. Babbitt, and had Samuel Ward (Babbitt), b. July 1, 1866.
   6146  *Robert Gibbs* (Ward), b. March 14, 1844; d. Oct. 30, 1844.
  6147  *Robert* (Gibbs),          ⎫ twins, born ⎧ d. Feb., 1841.
  6148  *Fanny Brightman*, (Gibbs), ⎭ Dec. 10, 1819; ⎩ m. Dec. 24, 1840, Henry Sanford, and had:
   6149  *Ann Elizabeth* (Sanford), b. Feb. 14, 1842; d. Aug. 7, 1858.
   6150  *Fanny Brightman* (Sanford), b. Mar. 19, 1845; d. April 22, 1846.
   6151  *Caroline Frances* (Sanford), b. Sept. 2, 1847.
   6152  *Rachel Gibbs* (Sanford), b. March 10, 1858.
 6153  Phebe,⁶ b. Oct. 17, 1783; d. Oct. 17, 1785.
+6154  Peleg,⁶ b. Jan. 19, 1786; m. Susan Barker Lawton.
 6155  Phebe,⁶ b. April 30, 1788; d. July 4, 1788.

By second wife, Ruth:

6156 Samuel,[6] b. July 17, 1794; d. Dec. 6, 1794.
6157 Samuel,[6] b. Aug. 30. 1795; d. Sept. 6, 1796.
6158 Phebe Lawton,[6] b. Jan. 7, 1797; m. July 13, 1815, George L. Potter; d. March 18, 1871, having had:
    6159 *Mary Thurston* (Potter), b. March, 1817; d. Nov., 1820.
    6160 *Thomas G.* (Potter), b. April, 1818; m. 1845, Elizabeth H. Coggeshall.
    6161 *Ruth Lawton* (Potter), b. Dec., 1819.
    6162 *Peleg Thurston* (Potter), b. June, 1822; d. Dec., 1873, in Denton, Md.
    6163 *Mary Taylor* (Potter), b. March, 1824.
    6164 *Henry David* (Potter), b. Feb., 1826.
    6165 *George Lawton* (Potter), b. June, 1828.
    6166 *Elizabeth Lawton* (Potter), b. April, 1830.
    6167 *Phebe Thurston* (Potter), b. Jan., 1832.
    6168 *Robert Thurston* (Potter), b. Feb., 1834; m. 1858, Hannah H. Carr, and has:
        6169 *Nettie Carr* (Potter), b. April, 1864.
    6170 *Charles I.* (Potter), b. Aug., 1836; d. Feb., 1837.
+6171 John Samuel,[6] b. Sept. 26, 1799; m. Hannah Barker Lawton.
+6172 Robert Lawton,[6] b. Dec. 13, 1800; m. 1st, Eliza Stratton; 2d, Harriet Taylor.

## 5836

JONATHAN THURSTON[5] of Newport, R. I. (*Capt. John,[4] Jonathan,[3] Edward,[2] Edward[1]*), brother of the preceding, and son of Capt. John[4] and Elizabeth (Oxx) Thurston of Newport; born there April 25, 1755; married HANNAH BEEBE; she died Sept. 8, 1789, aged 41. The two children were mentioned in will of their grandfather.

Their children were:

+6175 Edward,[6] b. Oct. 29, 1778; m. 1st, Catharine Hubbard; 2d, Eliza Fairchild.
6176 Christopher,[6] b. about 1780; m. Phebe Farrington; lived in Bridgewater, N. Y.; no children.

## 5840

JONATHAN THURSTON[5] of Newport, R. I. (*Jonathan,[4] Jonathan,[3] Edward,[2] Edward[1]*), eldest son of Jonathan[4] and Ruth (Scott) Thurston of Newport; born there 1749; baptized April 23, 1749; married, June 15, 1771, MARGARET SWEET, daughter of Capt. Samuel Sweet. He died June 28, 1780; she was appointed administratrix Aug. 9, 1780.

Their children were:

6180 Ruth Scott,[6] bap. April 17, 1775; d. Dec. 24, 1794.
6181 Margaret Sweet,[6] bap. March 14, 1777; d. April 15, 1791.
6182 Jonathan,[6] had a guardian, John Cook, appointed 1785.

## 5850

WILLIAM THURSTON[5] of Newport, R. I. (*William,[4] Jonathan,[3] Edward,[2] Edward[1]*), only child of William[4] and Dorothy (Carter) Thurston of Newport; born there Sept. 25, 1755; married, Dec. 23, 1778, MARY ROWLONG. He died Sept. 6, 1794; she died Oct. 23, 1828, aged 69.

Their children were:

6187 Margaret,[6] b. April 11, 1779; m. Nov. 1, 1801, George Washington Carr, a dry goods merchant of Newport; d. July 19, 1878, aged 99. They had:
    6188 *Dolly Thurston* (Carr), b. July 27, 1802.
    6189 *Abby* (Carr), b. Dec. 18, 1803; m. Dec. 19, 1825, Thomas J. Potter, and had:
        6190 *Deborah Ann* (Potter), b. Sept. 19, 1826; m. Sept. 2, 1848, Thos. Stoddard; d. March 19, 1856, having had three children.

6191　*Thomas J.* (Potter).
6192　*George W.* (Potter), b. Jan. 16, 1835.
6193　*Margaret* (Carr), b. Sept. 17, 1805.
6194　*George Washington* (Carr), b. April 22, 1808.
6195　*Mary Ann* (Carr), b. Mar. 26, 1810; m. Oct., 1834, Isaiah Goodspeed, and had:
　　　6196　*Mary Ann* (Goodspeed), b. Dec. 19, 1835; m. July 31, 1856, James McKenzie Southwick and lives in Newport.
6197　*Caleb Arnold* (Carr), b. June 15, 1813; m. June 11, 1848, Martha Gladding, and had:
　　　6198　*Richard Arnold* (Carr), b. Nov. 12, 1849; d. April 12, 1850.
　　　6199　*George Henry* (Carr), b. Dec. 21, 1860.
　　　6200　*Theodore Orman* (Carr), b. March 30, 1868.
6201　*Thomas Thurston* (Carr), b. May 4, 1815; m. June 22, 1845, Clara Peckham; he is a grocer in Newport, deacon of the Baptist church. Children:
　　　6202　*Clara* (Carr), b. March 16, 1846; m. Sept. 22, 1868, Edwin Burdick, and had Bessie and William (Burdick).
　　　6203　*Josephene Augusta* (Carr), b. May 7, 1847; m. Dec. 18, 1871, Geo. A. Hazzard.
　　　6204　*Thomas Thurston* (Carr), b. Sept. 19, 1848.
　　　6205　*George Washington* (Carr), b. Nov. 29, 1850.
　　　6206　*Phebe Jackson* (Carr), b. Oct. 29, 1853.
　　　6207　*Mary Lever* (Carr), b. June 14, 1856.
　　　6208　*William* (Carr), b. Oct. 12, 1858.
　　　6209　*Anna* (Carr), b Nov. 21, 1861.
6210　*Sarah Rowlong* (Carr), b. April 5, 1818; m. Nov. 22, 1842, Benjamin C. Paul; he died July 15, 1851. They had:
　　　6211　*Mary Frances* (Paul), b. March 24, 1844; m. April 6, 1869, James W. Waldron.
　　　6212　*Benjamin Arnold* (Paul), b. Aug. 16, 1846; d. Sept. 16, 1863.
　　　6213　*Deborah Cleveland* (Paul), b. June 24, 1849.
6214　*John* (Carr), b. Feb. 22, 1821; m. Oct. 19, 1845, Sarah Crandall; they live in Newport and have:
　　　6215　*Martha Thurston* (Carr), b. July 20, 1850; m. Sept. 1, 1870, Stafford Bryer of Newport.
6216　*Amelia* (Carr), b. June 23, 1824; m. June 16, 1844, Whitman Peckham, and had:
　　　6217　*William* (Peckham), b. Feb. 24, 1845; d. Aug. 3, 1854.
　　　6218　*George E.* (Peckham), b. July 14, 1846.
6219　Thomas,[6] b. Sept. 28, 1780; d. Sept. 12, 1781.
+6220　Thomas,[6] b. Jan. 15, 1782; m. Martha Simpson.
+6221　William Carter,[6] b. Aug. 23, 1783; m. Patience Young.
6222　Dolly,[6] b. Aug. 10, 1785; d. Sept. 3, 1800.

## 5856

WILLIAM THURSTON [5] of Hopkinton, R. I., after of Bridgewater, N. Y. (*George,[4] Edward,[3] Jonathan,[2] Edward[1]*), eldest son of George [4] and Keziah Thurston of Little Compton, R. I.; born there Jan. 17, 1733; married RUTH STETSON. He died at Bridgewater Feb. 6, 1803; she died Oct. 20, 1820.

Mr. Thurston bought a farm in Bridgewater, and intended as soon as his business could be arranged to return and take his family there, but before he was ready to do so, was taken sick and died. The widow, with the children, went to Bridgewater to reside.

Their children were:

+6226　Rowland,[6] b. 1764; m. Freegift McKoon.
　6227　William,[6] m. Abby Church.
　6228　Thomas,[6] d. single March 19, 1820.
　6229　Nancy,[6] d. Oct. 20, 1810.

+6230   Elisha,[6] b. April 18, 1792; m. Climena Guild.
6231    Oliver.[6]
6232    Hannah.[6]
6233    Mary.[6]
6234    Ruth.[6]

## 5859

EDWARD THURSTON[5] of Springfield, N. Y. (*George*,[4] *Edward*,[3] *Jonathan*,[2] *Edward*[1]), brother of the preceding, and son of George[4] and Keziah Thurston of Hopkinton, R. I.; born there May 16, 1740; married, Oct. 31, 1764, THANKFUL MAIN, daughter of Jeremiah and Thankful Main. She died Sept. 14, 1819, aged 64; he died Nov. 24, 1819.

Mr. Thurston was a cabinet maker in Stonington, Ct., and in 1793 a farmer on Thurston Hill, in Springfield, Otsego county, N. Y. He was a member of the Baptist church.

Their children were:

+6240   Edward,[6] b. Aug. 21, 1766; m. Hannah Gardner.
+6241   Adam,[6] b. Aug. 11, 1768; m. Eunice Miner.
6242    Thankful,[6] b. Nov. 23, 1770; m. April 18, 1793, Jeremiah York, b. Jan. 14, 1765; he was a farmer in North Stonington, Ct.; enlisted in the revolutionary war and had a pension. They had:
6243        *Jeremiah* (York), b. Sept. 25, 1794; m. 1815, Catherine Pendleton. He was a farmer in Oxford, Chenango county, N. Y., a deacon in the Baptist church; d. April 24, 1873; four children.
6244        *Fanny* (York), b. Jan. 8, 1796; m. Nov. 20, 1814, Randall Main, a farmer in North Stonington, Ct.; moved to Oxford, N. Y., and in 1846 to New York city; deacon in the Baptist church. He died March 12, 1852; she died Aug. 17, 1878; three children.
6245        *Edward* (York), b. Aug. 25, 1797; graduated from Yale; practised medicine in North Stonington, Ct., and McDonough, N. Y.; m. 1825, Lydia Stratton; d. 1855; one son and five daughters.
6246        *Martin* (York), b. July 31, 1799; m. March, 1824, Abby Chapman, daughter of Benjamin Peabody; he was a trader; two children.
6247        *Electa* (York), b. July 30, 1802; n.m.; d. Oct. 27, 1853.
6248        *Randall* (York), b. May 8, 1805; d. in infancy.
6249        *Thankful* (York), b. Aug. 8, 1806; d. in infancy.
6250        *Hiram* (York), b. Aug. 8, 1808; d. in infancy.
6251        *Ruth Caroline* (York), b. Feb. 6, 1810; resides on the homestead, 1879; has been very helpful in procuring these statistics; post office address, Pendleton Hill, Ct.
6252        *Lydia* (York), b. Nov. 24, 1812; m. March, 1842, Stephen Main, a dealer in butter and cheese in New York. In 1846 moved to Staten Island, and d. Aug. 14, 1846.
6253    Lydia,[6] b. Jan. 17, 1773; m. Caleb Gardner; d. in Ohio.
+6254   Joshua,[6] b. Feb. 21, 1775; m. Betsey Greene.
6255    Daniel,[6] b. Oct. 7, 1777; m. Sabrina Baldwin; had two children who died in infancy; he died Oct. 19, 1838.
+6256   Charles,[6] b. July 2, 1780; m. Margaret Fish.
6257    Patty (or Martha),[6] b. Jan. 21, 1783; m. 1st, Thomas Williams, b. June 23, 1773, d. April 28, 1813, buried on Thurston Hill; 2d, James Stevens, b. Sept. 18, 1775, d. Dec. 10, 1856; she died Jan. 12, 1866. They lived in Pennsylvania. She had, by first husband:
6258        *Thomas* (Williams), b. March 14, 1802; d. June 6, 1803.
6259        *Patty* (or Martha) (Williams), b. Dec. 10, 1803; d. Aug. 24, 1805.
6260        *Alonzo* (Williams), b. April 12, 1806; m. Emma Stevens, b. Sept. 24, 1803.
6261        *Orlando* (Williams), b. Aug. 22, 1808; m. Marilla Nickerson, b. May 20, 1816; she d. June 29, 1865; he d. Mar. 14, 1865; five children.
6262        *Aurelius F.* (Williams), b. Aug. 20, 1810; m. Ursula Ives, b. Aug. 30, 1806; he died Oct. 14, 1857; she died April 8, 1870; five children.
6263        *Thomas* (Williams), b. Sept. 23, 1812; d. June 2, 1833.

By second husband :

6264  *Nancy* (Stevens), b. March 20, 1816; m. Daniel H. Wade, b. Sept. 26, 1803; six children.

6265  *Edward Thurston* (Stevens), b. April 16, 1818; m. 1st, Lucy Blowers, b. April 28, 1822, d. Aug. 10, 1850; 2d, Mary Ann Oakley, b. Sept. 29, 1827; twelve children.

6266  *Sarah* (Stevens), b. June 20, 1820; m. Nathan Mitchell, b. July 10, 1816; he died March 10, 1860. They had :
   6267  *Caroline A.* (Mitchell), b. Nov. 11, 1839.
   6268  *Mary J.* (Mitchell), b. July 16, 1841.
   6269  *Seth M.* (Mitchell), b. Aug. 27, 1843.
   6270  *Ida* (Mitchell), b. July 26, 1845.
   6271  *Patty R.* (Mitchell), b. June 8, 1847; d. June 12, 1850.
   6272  *Eva K.* (Mitchell), b. Oct. 17, 1849.
   6273  *Nathan J.* (Mitchell), b. Oct. 15, 1851; d. May 12, 1857.
   6274  *Agnes J.* (Mitchell), b. Sept. 9, 1853.

6275  *Ira* (Stevens), b. Oct. 10, 1822; d. Aug. 10, 1823.
6276  *Lydia M.* (Stevens), b. May 29, 1824.
6277  *Chandler* (Stevens), b. May 30, 1829; m. Lucy J. Palmiter, b. June 26, 1842; two children.

6278  Lucy,⁶ b. Oct. 3, 1785; m. Dec. 25, 1806, Jabez Sumner, b. Oct. 15, 1783; she died June 18, 1866; he died March 21, 1868. They had :

6279  *Melissa* (Sumner), b. Oct. 16, 1807; m. Jan. 18, 1827, Alfred Stevens, b. June 6. 1800; she died Feb. 28, 1869. They had :
   6280  *Oscar F.* (Stevens), b. Oct. 2, 1827.
   6281  *Albert M.* (Stevens), b. Nov. 15, 1830.
   6282  *Ann S.* (Stevens), b. Nov. 18, 1833.
   6283  *Emma M.* (Stevens), b. April 9, 1836.
   6284  *Gilbert J.* (Stevens), b. June 13, 1838.
   6285  *Nancy J.* (Stevens), b. April 26, 1840.
   6286  *Theresa M.* (Stevens), b. July 15, 1842.
   6287  *Charles S.* (Stevens), b. July 9, 1845.
   6288  *Lucy P.* (Stevens), b. Jan. 29, 1848.
   6289  *Lavinia M.* (Stevens), b. Oct. 31, 1851.

6290  *Almira* (Sumner), b. Aug. 28, 1809.
6291  *George* (Sumner), b. Sept. 1, 1811.
6292  *Nancy* (Sumner), b. July 19, 1813.
6293  *Lucy* (Sumner), b. Nov. 19, 1816.
6294  *Thankful* (Sumner), b. July 15, 1820.
6295  *Sarah* (Sumner), b. July 9, 1822.
6296  *Charles* (Sumner), b. Jan. 6, 1825.
6297  *Porter* (Sumner), b. Aug. 15, 1827.

+6298  Cyrus,⁶ b. March 9, 1788; m. Sarah Spencer.
6299  Ira,⁶ b. April 29, 1791; d. Oct. 28, 1814, buried on Thurston Hill.
6300  Calvin,⁶ b. in Springfield, N. Y., May 3, 1795; d. April 27, 1796, buried on Thurston Hill.

## 5860

GEN. GEORGE THURSTON ⁵ of Hopkinton, R. I. (*George,⁴ Edward,³ Jonathan,² Edward¹*), brother of the preceding, and son of George ⁴ and Keziah Thurston of Hopkinton; born there 1741; married, first, Feb. 22, 1766, DOLLY COTTRELL; she died Oct. 21, 1789, aged 42. Second, MRS. SARAH RATHBUN. She died Sept. 19, 1817, aged 64; he died Nov. 30, 1827, aged 86.

Mr. Thurston was a merchant, and was connected with " Sullivan's expedition " in revolutionary times.

His children, by first wife, Dolly, were :

+6305  Jeremiah,⁶ b. May 29, 1768; m. Sarah Babcock.
6306  Mary,⁶ b. Jan. 2, 1770; m. March 28, 1788, Benjamin Taylor, a hatter in Hopkinton; d. Sept. 13, 1808; no children.
+6307  Nathaniel,⁶ b. July 16, 1772; m. Mary Whitman.
6308  Fanny,⁶ b. Oct 4, 1774; m. Joseph Spicer; d. Aug. 18, 1795; no children.

19

6309   Susanna,⁶ b. July 18, 1777; d. single Feb. 9, 1847.
6310   Nancy,⁶ b. March 28, 1780; d. single June 25, 1848.
6311   George,⁶ b. April 26, 1783; d. Feb. 4, 1828.
　　　　　　By second wife, Sarah:
6312   Sarah,⁶ b. June 17, 1793; m. Aug. 29, 1813, Russell Clarke; d. Oct. 12,
　　　　　1814, leaving:
　　　6313   *Sarah Elizabeth* (Clarke), b. June 26, 1814; m. Thomas Potter Wells,
　　　　　　　b. Sept. 28, 1809, son of Thos. Robinson and Maria (Potter) Wells
　　　　　　　of Kingston. R. I.　Mr. T. P. Wells has been cashier of the Na-
　　　　　　　tional Landholders Bank since 1860; was town treasurer some years
　　　　　　　and is a member and deacon of the Congregational church.　Children:
　　　　　6314   *Thomas Clarke* (Wells), b. Sept. 26, 1832; living in Manhattan,
　　　　　　　　Kan.; no children.
　　　　　6315   *Frances Elizabeth* (Wells), b. April 16, 1834; m. Samuel J. Cross;
　　　　　　　　settled in Rochester, Pa.; he died; his widow m. Rev. John
　　　　　　　　Davis of Rochester, where they now reside.　Children:
　　　　　　6316   *Susan Thurston* (Cross), m. Hartford Perry Brown.
　　　　　　6317   *Julia Frances* (Cross), m. Benjamin Tolman Johnson of East
　　　　　　　　　Lynn, Ct.
　　　　　　6318   *Samuel Joseph* (Cross).
　　　　　　6319   *Emma* (Cross).
　　　　　　6320   *George* (Cross).
　　　　　　6321   *Thomas* (Cross).
6322   Fanny,⁶ b. March 27, 1798; m. July 11, 1826, Daniel Deshon; d. Nov. 23,
　　　　　1833, leaving:
　　　6323   *Daniel* (Deshon), d. without issue, 1875, in New London, Ct.

## 5870

GARDNER THURSTON⁵ of Hopkinton, R. I. (*George,*⁴ *Edward,*³ *Jonathan,*² *Edward*¹), brother of the preceding, and son of George⁴
and —— (Greene) Thurston of Hopkinton; born there 1760; married, March 21, 1782, LYDIA TAYLOR.　He was a cooper, and died at
North Stonington, Ct., Aug. 26. 1825; she died in Hampton, Ct,
July 23, 1834, aged 69.　Children:
+6328   Benjamin Taylor,⁶ b. Aug. 29, 1787; m. Mary Button
+6329   Robert,⁶ b. April 5, 1790; m. Eliza Hannahs.
6330   Lucy,⁶ b. July 11, 1792; m. in Hopkinton Feb. 18, 1811, Charles Chandler　•
　　　　　Button, b. Feb. 1, 1788, son of Roswell and Lydia (Spicer) Button of
　　　　　Preston, Ct.; he was a saddle and harness maker in Hampton, Wind-
　　　　　ham Co., Ct.　She d. Jan. 29, 1835; he d. May 15, 1877.　They had:
　　　6331   *Charles Chandler* (Button), b. Feb. 1, 1815; m. Nov. 27, 1838, Ruth
　　　　　　　H. Fuller of Mansfield, Ct.　He was a harness maker in Hampton.
　　　　　　　They had:
　　　　　6332   *LeRoy* (Button), b. Oct. 25, 1843.
　　　6333   *Lyndon Taylor* (Button), b. March 24, 1817; m. in Hartford, Ct., Nov.
　　　　　　　25, 1838, Sarah A. Curtis of Springfield, Mass.　He was a harness
　　　　　　　maker in Hampton, representative to the legislature, and county
　　　　　　　commissioner.　They had:
　　　　　6334   *George Curtis* (Button), b. Jan. 1, 1840; d. Nov. 1, 1841.
　　　　　6335   *William Thurston* (Button), b. Oct. 6, 1841; m. Nov. 29, 1867,
　　　　　　　　Eliza J. Spear of Meriden, Ct.; d. Feb. 2, 1868, leaving:
　　　　　　6336   *Jane Allen* (Button).
　　　　　6337   *Mary Gould* (Button), b. Oct. 28, 1842; m. Dec. 25, 1865, William
　　　　　　　　Henry Burnham of Hampton; they have:
　　　　　　6338   *George Lyndon* (Burnham), b. June 17, 1873.
　　　　　　6339   *Bertha Mary* (Burnham), b. Dec. 29, 1878.
　　　　　6340   *Worthington Bulkeley* (Button), b. May 12, 1853; m. Feb. 17, 1875,
　　　　　　　　Mary A. Utley of Hampton; they have:
　　　　　　6341   *Louie Worthington* (Button), b. June 26, 1875.
　　　6342   *William Thurston* (Button), b. July 1, 1819; d. in Hartford May 21, 1843.
　　　6343   *Worthington Bulkeley* (Button), b. May 16, 1822; m. May 10, 1848,
　　　　　　　Jane C. Allen of New London, Ct.　He is a merchant in New York
　　　　　　　city.　They have:

6344　*Harriet Cady* (Button), b. April 20, 1849.
6345　*Lucy Thurston* (Button), b. June 28. 1852; m. Jan. 22, 1877, Rev.
　　　James A. Church of Gill, Mass., and has Lucy Allen (Church),
　　　b. Oct. 25, 1877.
6346　*Henry Taintor* (Button), b. April 20, 1830; a merchant in New York
　　　city; m. there Jan., 1856, Mary Hanson; they have :
　　　6347　*Lillie* (Button). b. June, 1862.
　　　6348　*Jane* (Button), b. 1866.
6349　Lydia,[6] b. Oct. 5, 1795; m. 1st, July 29, 1821, by Rev. Matthew Stillman,
　　　Reuben Parsons; he died Oct. 3, 1832; 2d, March 31, 1834, Ebenezer
　　　Griffin of Hampton. She d. Dec. 20, 1856. She had by first husband :
　　　6350　*Frances Eveline* (Parsons), b. in Stonington, R. I., May 30, 1822; d.
　　　　　　June 2, 1822.
　　　6351　*Leander* (Parsons), b. in Stonington July 12, 1823; d. at Block Island,
　　　　　　R. I., Oct. 9, 1827.
　　　6352　*Sophia Wakefield* (Parsons), b. at Block Island, Jan. 12, 1826; m. April
　　　　　　4, 1846, Daniel C. Holt of Hampton; they had Dora (Holt), b. Jan.
　　　　　　1, 1848.
　　　6353　*Sarah Cole* (Parsons),　　　｝twins, b. in Wickford, ｝
　　　6354　*Susan Tillinghast* (Parsons), ｝ ˙ R. I., Oct. 23, 1828; ｝ m. Oct., 1847,
　　　　　　George Burnham of Hampton.
　　　6355　*Caroline* (Parsons), b. in Wickford Feb. 9, 1831.
　　　　　　By second husband :
　　　6356　*Lucy Thurston* (Griffin).
　　　6357　*Lydia Taylor* (Griffin).
+6358　Jeremiah,[6] b. Oct. 17, 1797; m. Maria Southworth.
6359　Gardner,[6] b. April 20, 1800; m. 1st, Oct. 3, 1825, Mary E. Clegg; she died
　　　Nov. 12, 1863; 2d, Nov. 7, 1867, Laura S. Wales. He was a blacksmith
　　　in Norwich, Ct., but retired many years before his death, which occurred
　　　in June, 1878. He had, by first wife:
　　　6360　*Marietta*,[7] b. June 9, 1835; d. May 22, 1868.
　　　6361　*Edward Gardner*,[7] b. Oct. 8, 1837; d. Oct. 19, 1856.
+6362　Ichabod,[6] b. Sept. 27, 1802; m. Sarah B. Spink.
+6363　William,[6] b. March 23, 1805; m. Abby Hannahs.
6364　Daniel B.,[6] b. Oct. 21, 1808; d. single Feb. 28, 1842.

## 5871

JOSEPH THURSTON [5] of Hopkinton, R. I. (*George*,[4] *Edward*,[3] *Jona-than*,[2] *Edward*[1]), brother of the preceding, and son of George [4] and
—— (Greene) Thurston of Hopkinton; married SARAH TAYLOR.
He was town constable. Children :
6370　Joseph,[6] d. young.
6371　Clarke,[6] d. in infancy.
+6372　Job,[6] m. Susanna Andrews.
+6373　John Taylor,[6] b. April 21, 1782; m. Mrs. Hannah Reynolds.
6374　Phebe,[6] m. Asa Langworthy of Hopkinton, and died leaving no children.
6375　Joseph,[6] d. single.
+6376　Peleg Grinald,[6] b. April 1, 1788; m. 1st, Roby Andrews: 2d, Ann York.
+6377　George,[6] b. Aug. 28, 1790; m. 1st, Artemissia Saunders; 2d, Mrs. Susan
　　　(Gavitt) Browning.
+6378　Clarke,[6] b. about 1791 ; m. Abby Reynolds.
6379　Sarah,[6] b. in Stonington, Ct., Aug. 6, 1793; m. Sept. 15, 1811, James Dick-
　　　inson, a farmer of Stonington, b. May 30, 1791, son of Ichabod, who was
　　　a soldier in the revolutionary war, and Lucy (Babcock), Dickinson of
　　　Westerly, R. I. She died Dec. 8, 1835. They had:
　　　6380　*Mary* (Dickinson), b. at Cornwall, Ct., Nov. 28, 1812; m. 1st, May
　　　　　　25, 1840, Elisha Pierce Dennison, a seaman, lost at sea in 1841, son
　　　　　　of Justin and Maria (Collins) Dennison of Stonington; 2d, May 23,
　　　　　　1849, Seabury Thomas, a farmer of Ledyard, Ct., son of Daniel and
　　　　　　Eunice (Baker) Thomas of Ledyard; he died Dec. 28, 1873, and
　　　　　　his widow resides at Mystic Bridge, Ct.
　　　　　　Born in Stonington :
　　　6381　*Ichabod* (Dickinson), b. Oct. 8, 1814; m. Dec. 25, 1842, Frances Mary
　　　　　　Chesboro, b. Sept. 13, 1822, daughter of Samuel C. and Sarah
　　　　　　(Robinson) Chesboro of Stonington.

6382   *Lucy Ann* (Dickinson), b. Nov. 17, 1816; m. May 20, 1839, William
       L. Peckham, a brass molder, son of William and Cynthia (Lewis)
       Peckham of North Stonington; reside in Waterford, Ct.
6383   *Phebe Thurston* (Dickinson), b., Dec. 21, 1819.
6384   *John Thurston* (Dickinson), b. June 22, 1821; a molder in New Lon-
       don, Ct.; m. April 4, 1846, Charlotte Elizabeth Baker, daughter of
       Zebadiah Comstock and Mary Waterman (Kimball) Baker of New
       London.
6385   *George Thurston* (Dickinson), b. May 4, 1823; m. Nov. 25, 1857, Julia
       Johnson Gifford, daughter of Warren and Lucy Ann (Harris) Gif-
       ford of Brooklyn, N. Y.
6386   *Susan Adelia* (Dickinson), b. Aug. 8, 1826; m. in Stonington Feb. 2,
       1845, Elisha Avery Denison, a livery stable keeper and layer of con-
       crete walks in New London, son of Elisha Williams and Fanny
       (Cheseborough) Denison of Groton, Ct.
6387   *Harriet Prew* (Dickinson), b. Dec. 31, 1830; m. Jan. 4, 1863, Thomas
       P. Smith, a mariner of New London, son of Samuel P. and Sarah
       (Latham) Smith of Groton.
+6388   Lodowick Lewis,[6] b. 1806; m. Mary Browning.

## 5887

S⹅MUEL ISAAC THURSTON [5] of Georgetown, S. C. (*Samuel*,[4] *Edward*,[3]
*Samuel*,[2] *Edward*[1]), youngest child of Samuel[4] and Eunice (Anthony)
Thurston of Newport, R. I.; born there Aug. 18, 1756; married, first,
MARY C. COGGESHALL; second, June 22, 1799, MRS. JANE FUTHEY,
née RAWLINS.   He died June 11, 1820, aged 64; she died June 3,
1841, aged 81.        His children, by first wife, Mary, were:
6393   Mary C.,[6] m. June, 1809, Richard Waterman of Providence, R. I., and had:
       6394 *Mary* (Waterman).   6395 *Ellen* (Waterman).   6396 *Emily* (Waterman).
6397   Samuel Isaac,[6] b. 1787; graduated from Brown 1807, and was a lawyer in
       Orangeburgh, S. C.; d. 1820.
                    By second wife, Jane:
6398   Jane Caroline,[6] b. April 2, 1800; m. 1824, Stephen Ford; d. June 14,1850;
       they had:
       6399   *Caroline Thurston* (Ford), b. Jan. 18, 1825; m. B. A. Coachman, liv-
              ing in Florida, 1879.
       6400   *Joseph Wragg* (Ford), b. Sept. 13, 1827; n.m.; d. on the passage to
              England, Aug., 1869.
       6401   *Robert Thurston* (Ford), b. Jan. 25, 1830; d. in Georgetown, Oct. 11,
              1854.
       6402   *Maria Rees* (Ford), m. Robert Thurston [see no. 7236].
       6403   *Samuel Isaac* (Ford), b. Feb. 28, 1834; d. Nov. 30, 1839.
       6404   *Esther Brown* (Ford), b. Nov. 7, 1835; m. W. W. Shackleford of
              Charleston, S. C.
       6405   *Margaret F.* (Ford), b. Dec. 5, 1836; n.m.
       6406   *Eliza Jane* (Ford., b. April 24, 1839.
       6407   *Emily Thurston* (Ford), b. Feb. 19, 1842; m. C. Rutledge Holmes of
              Somerville, S. C.
       6408   *George Thomas Stephen* (Ford), b. Sept. 2, 1843.
+6409   Robert,[6] b. Oct. 10, 1801 ; m. Eliza Emily North.
6410   Caroline,[6] b. June 28, 1805; d. Nov. 19, 1813.

## 5908

JOHN BRETT THURSTON [5] of Newport, R. I. (*Samuel*,[4] *Latham*,[3]
*Samuel*,[2] *Edward*[1]), eldest son of Samuel[4] and Mary (Brett) Thurston of Newport; born there June 11, 1765; married MARY ——.   He
died Oct. 21, 1799; she died Sept. 20, 1850, aged 81.   He was a
master mariner.           Children:
6415   Abigail Rowland,[6] b. July 16, 1792; m. Oct. 29, 1815, Edward Stanhope,
       a baker by trade, but a grocer in Newport; she d. July 7, 1853; they had:
       6416   *Jane Martha* (Stanhope), d. Oct. 8, 1819, aged 10 m.

6417  *William Henry* (Stanhope), d. Oct. 15, 1821, aged 1 y. 2 m. 25 d.
6418  *Jane Martha* (Stanhope), d. Jan. 18, 1822, aged 2 m. 14 d.
6419  *John Thurston* (Stanhope), m. Catherine Weaver.
6420  *Mary Thurston* (Stanhope), m. Thomas M. Hathaway.
6421  *Frederick Augustus* (Stanhope), m. Olivia Williams.
6422  *Charles Latham* (Stanhope), m. 1st, Ann Norman; 2d, Anne Adams.
6423  *William Henry* (Stanhope), b. 1825; m. Christiana E. Allen.
6424  *Abby Rowland* (Stanhope), m. John R. Hammett.
6425  *Francis* (Stanhope), m. Amelia Stevens.
6426  *Elizabeth Amelia* (Stanhope).
6427  Latham,[6] d. in Windsor, N. C., 1832, aged 37.
6428  John Dennis,[6] bap. Jan. 14, 1798; d. in Norfolk, Va.

## 5918

ABRAHAM THURSTON[5] of Newport, R. I. (*Joseph,*[4] *Joseph,*[3] *Samuel,*[2] *Edward*[1]), fourth child of Joseph[4] and Susanna (Brownell) Thurston of Newport; born there Nov. 7, 1784; married, Nov. 11, 1821, MAR-THA D. PRIOR. He died Feb. 2, 1865, aged, 80; she died Oct. 23, 1870, aged 79. He was clerk in Newport bank fourteen years, depu-ty collector of Newport twelve years; moved to Providence and was clerk in custom-house some years.       Children:

6432  Susan Brownell,[6] b. Sept. 21, 1823; d. June 4, 1826.
6433  Elizabeth Shepard,[6] n.m.; resides in Providence, R. I.
6434  Martha Dickerson,[6] b. Feb. 13, 1833; d. April 17, 1842.
6435  Joseph Lafayette,[6] foreman of a livery stable in Newport; m. Nov. 17, 1850, Eliza S. Greene; no children.
6436  William Pryor,[6] served in the 14th New York regiment in war against the rebellion; was prisoner in Annapolis, Md., where he died, Dec. 26, 1865.
6437  Christopher Ellery,[6] a printer in New York city; m. Nov. 25, 1854, Aman-da Baker; they had:      6438  *Charles,*[7] b. March 1, d. July 30, 1856.
6439  Susan Brownell,[6] n.m.; lives in Providence.

## 5920

JOSEPH THURSTON[5] of New York city (*Joseph,*[4] *Joseph,*[3] *Samuel,*[2] *Edward*[1]), brother of the preceding, and son of Joseph[4] and Susanna (Brownell) Thurston of Newport, R. I.; born there June 16, 1791; married, Dec. 27, 1858, LETITIA McBURNEY. He died Feb. 11, 1867. She married, April 23, 1868, Charles M. Fairbrother.

Mr. Thurston was a resident of South Carolina many years previ-ous to his marriage.       Child:

6441  Richard Lathers,[6] b. Sept. 1, 1859.

## 5940

MOSES THURSTON[5] of Newport, R. I. (*William,*[4] *Joseph,*[3] *Samuel,*[2] *Edward*[1]), second child of William[4] and Priscilla (Norman) Thurs-ton of Newport; born there May 6, 1780; married, first, April 30, 1807, ELIZABETH EASTON, daughter of Benjamin and Elizabeth (Gre-lea) Easton; she died Feb. 18, 1817, aged 36. Second, Oct. 6, 1822, MRS. ABIGAIL BAKER, daughter of Isaac Church. He died July 9, 1832; she died Dec. 22, 1861. He was a merchant.

His children, by first wife, Elizabeth, were:

6443  Sarah Ann,[6] b. April 13, 1809; m. March 1, 1831, George A. Gray of Sa-lem, Mass., a farmer in Middletown, R. I., since which time he has re-sided in various places, as will be seen by the places of birth of their children, and now, 1879, is in Hamilton, Butler Co., Ohio. Children:
6444  *Frederick Morland* (Gray), b. at Middletown Jan. 8, 1832; an Episco-pal clergyman; m. June 13, 1867, Augusta Van Kleeck.
6445  *Elizabeth Thurston* (Gray), b. at Middletown Feb. 21, 1833; d. May 18, 1852.

19*

6446　*John Morland* (Gray), b. at Newport Oct. 20, 1834.
6447　*Abby Tibbitts* (Gray), b. at Newport May 28, 1836; d. Sept. 29, 1837.
6448　*George Alexander* (Gray), b. at Hillsborough, Ill., July 31, 1839.
6449　*Annie* (Gray), b. at Audobon, Ill., March 3, 1841; d. Oct. 5, 1842.
6450　*William Thurston* (Gray), b. at Audobon April 21, 1843.
6451　*Wallace* (Gray), ⎱ twins, b. at Audobon ⎰ d. Sept. 6, 1847.
6452　*Rob'rt* (Gray), ⎰ 　　Feb. 4, 1845; ⎱ d. Sept. 7, 1847.
6453　*Charles Morland* (Gray), b. at Lawrenceburgh, Ind., Aug. 14, 1848; d. Dec. 27, 1853.
6454　*William Nicholson* (Gray), b. at Cincinnati, Ohio, March 12, 1852.
6455　Abby Grelea,[6] b. Jan. 18, 1811; m. Oct. 31, 1836, Henry Tibbitts, in the flour and grain business in Louisville, Ky., Audobon and Hillsborough, Ill., Lawrenceburgh, Ind., and Cincinnati, O., where he d. May 4, 1869. Chil.:
6456　*Anna* (Tibbitts), b. at Louisville Aug. 20, 1837; d. July 24, 1838.
6457　*Henry Cook* (Tibbitts), b. at Louisville Nov. 13, 1838.
6458　*William Thurston* (Tibbitts), b. at Audobon Nov. 9, 1840.
6459　*John Waterman* (Tibbitts), b. at Audobon March 25, 1842.
6460　*Abby Thurston* (Tibbitts), b. at Audobon Oct. 3, 1843.
6461　*Susan Green* (Tibbitts), b. at Hillsborough Nov. 25, 1845.
6462　*Sarah Gray* (Tibbitts), b. at Lawrenceburgh June 7, 1848; d. at Cincinnati Aug. 4, 1849.
6463　*Charles Norris* (Tibbitts), b. at Cincinnati March 2, 1852.
6464　William Bradford,[6] b. May 9, 1815; m. 1st, at New Bedford, Mass., Dec. 25, 1836, Louisa Sawyer of Cambridge, Mass.; 2d, Oct., 1875, Minerva Merrill of Indianapolis, Ind., where he has been a merchant many years. Three other children, died in infancy.

### 5941

WILLIAM THURSTON[5] of Middletown, R. I. (*William,*[4] *Joseph,*[3] *Samuel,*[2] *Edward*[1]), brother of the preceding, and youngest child of William[4] and Priscilla (Norman) Thurston of Newport, R. I.; born there 1782; married, Oct. 1, 1815, RUTH COGGESHALL EASTON, daughter of Benjamin and Elizabeth (Grelea) Easton. He died Nov. 19, 1840, aged 58; she died Feb. 2, 1864, aged 78.

Mr. Thurston was a farmer; attended the Moravian church. When he was an infant his father was supposed to have been lost at sea on a passage to the South. His mother died soon after, and he was left to the care of his great aunt, a widow named Pinnegar, a devout member of the Moravian church, and for whom he always maintained the highest regard, contributing to her support in her later years.

### Children:

6467　Benjamin Easton,[6] b. June 8, 1816; d. August, 1816.
6468　Elizabeth Easton,[6] b. Oct., 1817; n.m.; living in Newport, a devout member of the Episcopal church.
6469　Sarah,[6] b. Aug., 1819; m. April 2, 1838, Ayrault Wanton Dennis, a master mariner, sailing out of Newport for many years. He died at his residence in Middletown Feb. 13, 1862; his widow still resides there, a member of the Episcopal church. They had:
　6470　*Ayrault Wanton* (Dennis), b. Oct. 12, 1841; m. 1st, Oct. 26, 1869, Ella Mary Rutter; she died 1875; 2d, 1877, Margaret Ringgo. He is a farmer in Nebraska, not far from Omaha, a baptized member of the Episcopal church. Children, all but last one by first wife:
　6471　*Ella Mary* (Dennis), b. 1870; d. 1871.
　6472　*Darius* (Dennis), b. 1872.　　6473　*George* (Dennis), b. 1873.
　6474　*Ella Mary* (Dennis), b. 1875.　6475　*Daughter*, b. 1878.
　6476　*Darius* (Dennis), b. May 8, 1845; d. Dec. 22, 1857.
　6477　*Ella* (Dennis), b. June 7, 1849; d. Oct. 26, 1849.
　6478　*George* (Dennis), ⎱ twins, born ⎰ d. Sept. 6, 1856.
　6479　*Laura* (Dennis), ⎰ May 22, 1856; ⎱ d. Oct. 18, 1856.
6480　John Grelea,[6] b. July, 1821; d. April, 1822.
+6481　William Henry,[6] b. Feb. 4, 1823; m. Laura Casttoff.

6482 Mary Ann,[6] b. Dec. 1824; m. July, 1848, Robert P. Berry, a dentist, quite celebrated in his profession; he died Feb. 9, 1873; no children.
+6483 Benjamin Easton,[6] b. Oct., 1826; m. Mary Ann Siddall.
6484 Abby Searles,[6] b. Aug., 1828; d. June 15, 1850.

## 5955

WILLIAM WANTON THURSTON[5] of Newport and Providence, R. I. (*Latham*,[4] *John*,[3] *Samuel*,[2] *Edward*[1]), third child of Latham[4] and Sarah (Wanton) Thurston of Newport; born there 1780; married, Oct. 3, 1806, SARAH JACK, daughter of Alexander Jack. He died Feb. 20, 1846, aged 65; she died Aug. 17, 1863, aged 83.

Mr. Thurston was a hatter, and later in life a silk and woolen dyer.

Their children were :
6490 William Alexander,[6] b. 1807; d. in Mexico 1849.
6491 George Latham,[6] b. 1811; d. in infancy.
6492 Edward Henry,[6] b. Sept. 16, 1812; m. in Warren, R. I., Nov. 13, 1833, Martha T. Wood, daughter of Obed and Hannah (Covel) Wood. They had five children, four died in childhood.
6493 Elizabeth Jack,[6] m. Richard Beverley; d. June 20, 1848.
6494 Mary Jane,[6] b. July 24, 1817; m. May 30, 1850, Lewis Edwin Holmes of Providence, and had :
    6495 *Robert William* (Holmes), b. April 10, 1851.
    6496 *Carrie Elizabeth* (Holmes), b. Nov. 20, 1852; m. Aug. 8, 1867, James E. Burlinghame, and had :
        6497 *Mary Elizabeth* (Burlinghame), b. Aug. 29, 1868.
    6498 *Lewis Edwin* (Holmes), b. May 23, 1853.
    6499 *John Wanton* (Holmes), b. Nov. 26, 1854; d. Oct. 27, 1860.
    6500 *Thomas Thurston* (Holmes), b. Nov. 5, 1856.
6501 Wanton Jonas,[6] b. April 20, 1823.
6502 Thomas White.[6]

## 5993

CHARLES MYRICK THURSTON[5] of Newport, R. I., and after of New York city (*John*,[4] *John*,[3] *Samuel*,[2] *Edward*[1]), second child of John[4] and Sabra (Smith) Thurston of Newport; born there Feb. 23, 1792; married, Sept. 6, 1818, RACHEL HALL PITMAN.* He died May 6, 1844, aged 52.

---

* Rachel Hall Pitman was the daughter of Judge Thomas G. and Abigail (Hall) Pitman, g-daughter of John and Abigail (Nichols) Pitman, g-g-daughter of Benjamin and Mary Pitman, g-g-g-daughter of John and Mary (Saunders) Pitman.
Abigail Nichols was the daughter of Andrew and Abigail (Plaisted) Nichols.
Abigail Hall was the daughter of George and Elizabeth (Peckham) Hall, g-daughter of Benjamin and Abigail (Babcock) Hall, g-g-daughter of William and Mary (Brownell) Hall, g-g-g-daughter of Benjamin and Frances (Parker) Hall, and g-g-g-daughter of William and Mary Hall.
Frances Parker was the daughter of George and Frances Parker.
Mary Brownell was the daughter of George and Susannah (Pearce) Brownell, and g-daughter of Thomas and Ann Brownell.
Susannah Pearce was the daughter of Richard and Susannah (Wright) Pearce.
Susannah Wright was the daughter of George Wright.
Abigail Babcock was the daughter of George and Elizabeth (Hall) Babcock, g-daughter of John and Mary Babcock, and g-g-daughter of James and Sarah Babcock.
Elizabeth Peckham was the daughter of Peleg and Elizabeth (Coggeshall) Peckham, g-daughter of Joseph and Waite (Gould) Peckham, g-g-daughter of John and Sarah Peckham, and g-g-g-daughter of John and Mary (Clarke) Peckham.
Waite Gould was the daughter of Daniel and Waite (Coggeshall) Gould, and g-daughter of Jeremy and Priscilla (Grover) Gould.
Waite Coggeshall was the daughter of John and Mary Coggeshall.
Elizabeth Coggeshall was the daughter of Thomas and Mercy (Freeborn) Coggeshall, g-daughter of Joshua and Sarah Coggeshall, g-g-daughter of Joshua and Joan (West) Coggeshall, and g-g-g-daughter of John and Mary Coggeshall.
Mercy Freeborn was the daughter of Gideon and Mary (Boomer) Freeborn, and g-daughter of William and Mary Freeborn.
Mary Boomer was the daughter of Matthew Boomer.

Mr. Thurston was the founder and first president of the Newport Exchange bank. He removed to New York in 1840, where his widow still lives.

Their children were :

+6506 Charles Myrick,[6] b. July 11, 1819; m. Caroline Marsh.
6507 Abby Pitman,[6] b. Nov. 22, 1821; m. July 9, 1846, Richard Lathers, and had:
    6508 *Abby Caroline* (Lathers), b. March 9, 1848.
    6509 *Agnes* (Lathers), b. June 10, 1853.
    6510 *Richard* (Lathers), b. April 23, 1855.
    6511 *Emma* (Lathers), b. July 22, 1857.
    6512 *Joseph Thurston* (Lathers), b. Dec. 20, 1858; d. Aug. 4, 1859.
    6513 *Ida* (Lathers), b. March 20, 1862.
    6514 *Julia* (Lathers), b. Aug. 11, 1864.
    6515 *Edmund Griffin* (Lathers), b. March 24, 1866.
6516 Rachel Hall,[6] b. March 23, 1824; m. Dec. 12, 1843, Charles Connor Barrington, and had :
    6517 *Rachel Thurston* (Barrington), b. Oct. 4, 1844.
6518 Sophia Eliza,[6] b. Aug. 22, 1827; m. Sept. 22, 1847, Allan Melville. She died Oct. 3, 1858; he died Feb. 9, 1872, aged 48 y. 10 m. They had:
    6519 *Maria Gansevoort* (Melville), b. Feb. 18, 1849; m. June 10, 1874, William B. Moorewood.
    6520 *Florence* (Melville), b. Sept. 2, 1850.
    6521 *Catharine Gansevoort* (Melville), b. April 30, 1852.
    6522 *Julia* (Melville), b. Sept. 6, 1854; d. Dec. 26, 1854.
    6523 *Lucy* (Melville), b. June 14, 1856.
+6524 Alfred Henry,[6] b. Oct. 2, 1832; m. 1st, Eliza Strong Blunt; 2d, Mary Sullivan Bankhead.

## 6035

SAMUEL THURSTON[5] (*Samuel,*[4] *John,*[3] *Samuel,*[2] *Edward*[1]), fifth child of Samuel[4] and Mary (Landers) Thurston of Newport, R. I.; born there June 13, 1793; married ELIZABETH GIFFORD. He went to New Bedford, Mass., and after returned to Newport.

Their children were :

+6530 George,[6] b. March 29, 1815; m. 1st, Sophia Hawn; 2d, Margaret Manery.
6531 Mary,[6] b. Jan. 28, 1816; m. John Terry of Buffalo, N. Y.; no children.

## 6037

HENRY HIGGINS THURSTON[5] of Newport, R. I. (*Samuel,*[4] *John,*[3] *Samuel,*[2] *Edward*[1]), brother of the preceding, and son of Samuel[4] and Mary (Landers) Thurston of Newport; born there Sept. 20, 1799; married, Nov. 27, 1826, MARTHA COGGESHALL THURSTON, born Jan. 15, 1804 [see no. 5965], daughter of Latham and Martha C. (Cahoone) Thurston of Newport. He is a ship carpenter, and attends the Baptist church.

Children :

,+6536 George Henry,[6] b. Aug. 11, 1827; m. Ruth Esther Potter.
6537 Ann Martha,[6] b. Dec. 11, 1830; d. Jan. 5, 1850.
6538 Sarah Tew,[6] b. Sept. 28, 1832; m. Joshua Stacy; divorced; is a member of the Catholic church; no children.
6539 John Latham,[6] b. Oct. 3, 1835; m. Oct. 31, 1869, Abby Sullivan. He is a carpenter in Newport; served in the war against the rebellion, enlisting in Sept., 1861, in the 87th Connecticut regiment, Capt. John Lee, Col. Dodge; went to Alexandria and Yorktown, Va.; was sick with rheumatism, sent to hospital in Baltimore, where he was nearly two years; was not in any battle, but did some service as nurse; no children.
6540 Charles Edward,[6] b. Nov. 24, 1839; m. Jan. 2, 1861, Susan Frances Crowell of Newport. He is a carpenter in Newport; served in the 4th Rhode Island regiment during the war of the rebellion. Children :
    6541 *Charles Edward,*[7] b. Oct. 19, 1861; d. Aug. 4, 1863.

6542 *Martha Elizabeth*,[7] b. April 11, 1863; d. Sept. 9, 1864.
6543 *Emma Augusta*,[7] b. Dec. 11, 1865.
6544 James Fernandas,[6] b. Oct. 29, 1841; m. April 5, 1866, Eliza Ann Beegan. He is a carpenter in Newport; served in the war against the rebellion. He says: "June 6, 1861, I enlisted for three years in the 2d Rhode Island regiment, Capt. Charles Turner. July 21st we fought our first battle at Bull Run, lost our colonel, major, and about three hundred men. The regiment held the battle field forty-five minutes before assistance came. I was in ten other battles, the last one Antietam, which lasted eight hours. I was wounded in the leg, and lay on the battle field three days and four nights with only four apples, two of which I gave to a wounded confederate, who lay beside me and afterward refused me a drink of cold water. I crept to the woods and made me crutches, and traveled four miles to a confederate tobacco house, where I was allowed to stay for a week, when a union ambulance came along and took me to Maryland, and from there to Washington hospital. I was allowed a furlough of three months. On my return to Washington hospital I was transferred to the 9th regiment veteran reserve corps, doing garrison duty around the outskirts of Washington. The Mosby Guerrillas were working their way toward Philadelphia, and we were ordered to intercept them. We traveled for seven days behind them. Just before we reached Harrisburgh we had a skirmish, which resulted in our having nine killed and thirty wounded. From there we went to Philadelphia and back to Washington, where we were assigned to guard rebel prisoners. The greatest battle I fought in during the war was in front of Richmond, Va., seven days and seven nights continuous fighting; heavy loss of life on both sides. Part of the time we had to lie on our faces while the batteries fired over us. The cries of the wounded and dying were heart-rending." Children:
6545 *James Henry*,[7] b. Dec. 25, 1867.
6546 *John Burkinshaw*,[7] b. Aug. 22, 1874.

## 6042

GARDNER THURSTON[5] of Fall River, Mass. (*Edward*,[4] *Edward*,[3] *Thomas*,[2] *Edward*[1]), eldest child of Edward[4] and Parnold (Mott) Thurston of Freetown, Mass.; born there Feb. 15, 1761; married, March 31, 1796, MARY TERRY of Freetown. His will was dated Feb. 1, 1844, proved April 5, 1844.

Their children were:

6550 Hannah,[6] b. Feb. 2, 1797; m. Abraham Wardell of Westport, Mass.; had:
  6551 *Mary Ann* (Wardell), named in her grandfather's will.
6552 Sarah,[6] b. April 13, 1799; m. Dec. 15, 1822, Thomas E. Bliffins of Fall River, and had:
  6553 *Sybil Valentine* (Bliffins), b. June 15, 1823.
  6554 *Anson* (Bliffins), b. Feb. 7, 1826.
  6555 *Harriet Newell* (Bliffins), b. June 4, 1828; named in grandfather's will.
  6556 *David Evans* (Bliffins), b. Dec. 31, 1831.
  6557 *Thomas* (Bliffins), b. April 5, 1835; named in grandfather's will.
6558 Elizabeth,[6] b. March 1, 1801; d. single 1850.
6559 Peleg,[6] b. May 19, 1803; d. before 1844, as he is not named in will.
6560 Mary,[6] m. John Francis of Dartmouth, Mass.; d. Oct., 1843. Children:
  6561 *Julianna* (Francis).
  6562 *Susan* (Francis).
  6563 *Abraham* (Francis).
  6564 *Clarissa* (Francis).
  6565 *Peace* (Francis).
  6566 *Sylvia* (Francis).
  6567 *William* (Francis).
  6568 *James H.* (Francis).
  6569 *Barnaby* (Francis). All named in their grandfather's will.

## 6045

NATHANIEL S. THURSTON [5] of Fall River, Mass. (*Edward,*[4] *Edward,*[3] *Thomas,*[2] *Edward*[1]), brother of the preceding, and son of Edward [4] and Parnold (Mott) Thurston of Freetown, now Fall River, Mass.; born there May 10, 1771; married LAVINIA DAVIS. He died May 18, 1844; *d. farmer.*

### Their children were:

6575   Elizabeth,[6] b. April 21, 1794; m. Jan. 24, 1813, Thomas Freelove; d. May 24, 1869.
+6576   Samuel,[6] b. Dec. 17, 1797; m. Rachel Boomer.
+6577   James,[6] b. April 12, 1799; m. Ruth Waddell.
6578   Lucy,[6] b. July 23, 1803; m. (intention dated Jan. 15, 1841) Elisha Davis; d. Feb. 20, 1869.
6579   Joanna,[6] b. Dec. 2, 1806; m. Nov. 4, 1827, Brightman Terry, and had:
     6580   *Silas* (Terry), b. Sept. 1, 1835.
+6581   William,[6] b. Dec. 7, 1809; m. Eleanor Chace.
+6582   Gardner,[6] m. Elizabeth S. Moore.

## 6053

VARNUM THURSTON [5] of Fall River, Mass. (*Peleg,*[4] *Edward,*[3] *Thomas,*[2] *Edward*[1]), fourth child of Peleg [4] and Amy (Barton) Thurston of Troy, Mass.; born there 1773; married, Dec. 29, 1797, MARY GARDNER, born Feb. 8, 1780, daughter of Peleg and Lydia (Simmons) Gardner of Swansea, Mass. He died April 3, 1828, aged 55; she died July 5, 1862, aged 82. He was a cooper.

### Their children were:

+6587   Peleg Gardner,[6] b. Sept. 5, 1799; m. Susan Blossom.
6588   Amy Barton,[6] b. April 3, 1801; n.m.; d. June 10, 1826.
6589   Jonathan Gardner,[6] b. Nov. 14, 1802; d. single Feb. 16, 1846.
+6590   Edward,[6] b. Sept. 4, 1804; m. Sarah Maria Mason.
+6591   Samuel,[6] b. Dec. 27, 1806; m. Almira Boomer.
+6592   James,[6] b. Nov. 8, 1808; m. Hannah Pierce.
6593   Susan Gardner,[6] b. Dec. 11, 1810; d. Dec. 12, 1810.
+6594   Abraham Gardner,[6] b. June 21, 1813; m. Catharine Borden Allen.
+6595   Vernon,[6] b. Feb. 11, 1815; m. Abby Streeter.
6596   Mary Gardner,[6] b. Jan. 4, 1817; d. Oct. 8, 1819.
+6597   William Barton,[6] b. Nov. 8, 1818; m. Mary Ann Packard.
6598   Henry Gardner,[6] b. Sept. 8, 1820; d. single April 22, 1857.
6599   Amy Diadema,[6] b. July 29, 1824; d. single July 6, 1846.

## 6077

JONATHAN THURSTON [5] of Fall River,* Mass. (*Thomas,*[4] *Edward,*[3] *Thomas,*[2] *Edward*[1]), sixth child of Thomas [4] and Elizabeth (Pearce) Thurston of Fall River; born there June 25, 1765; married, first, in 1800, SARAH LUTHER of Swansea, Mass.; she died May 2, 1811, aged 37. Second, MERCY (BRIGGS) HATHAWAY. She died 1837; he died April 28, 1832; will dated April 20, 1832, proved June 26, 1832. Her estate was settled by John in 1837.

Mr. Thurston was a farmer, tanner, and shoemaker.

### His children, by first wife, Sarah, were:

6605   John,[6] b. Dec. 8, 1800; m. 1827, Hannah Holloway. He was a house carpenter in Fall River; d. March 17, 1873; no children.

---

* When Mr. Thurston was born this locality was known as Freetown; in 1803 Fall River was set off and incorporated; in 1804 the name was changed to Troy, and in 1834 it was changed back again to Fall River; so that he was born in Freetown, lived in Fall River, died in Troy, without change of residence, and now the same place is Fall River.

+6606 David,[6] b. July 26, 1802; m. Hannah Miller Hathaway.
  6607 Elizabeth,[6] b. Oct. 26, 1804; m. June, 1850, Gardner Davis. He died
      Dec. 11, 1876; she resides in Fall River; no children.
  6608 Ebenezer,[6] b. July 26, 1808; m. 1864, Philinda A. Chase. He was a house
      carpenter; d. June 3, 1878, in Somerset, Mass.; no children.
      By second wife, Mercy:
  6609 Sarah Luther,[6] b. Jan. 6, 1815; d. single July 31, 1834.
  6610 Warden Hathaway,[6] b. Sept. 4, 1818; d. Oct. 12, 1822.
+6611 Thomas,[6] b. Aug. 24, 1820; m. 1st, Betsey Jane Davis; 2d, Matilda Gray
      Davis.
  6612 Mary,[6] b. Sept. 12, 1822; m. Anson Blivens, a house carpenter in Fall
      River. They have:
      6613 *Helen M.* (Blivens), m. Charles Fisher, a house carpenter in Fall River.
      6614 *Frank H.* (Blivens), n.m.; a printer in Fall River.

## 6085

SAMUEL THURSTON[5] of Tiverton, R. I. (*Thomas,*[4] *Thomas,*[3] *Thomas,*[2] *Edward*[1]), eldest son of Thomas[4] and Patience (Beers) Thurston of Tiverton; born there Mar. 28, 1776; married, Nov. 23, 1800, MERCY TABOR. He died Dec. 30, 1805, aged 29. She married, second, Benjamin Manchester. Children:
  6620 Patience,[6] b. Sept. 25, 1801; m. George B. Seabury.
+6621 John,[6] b. 1803; m. Mary Ann Chase.

## 6088

GEORGE HOWLAND THURSTON[5] of Tiverton, R. I. (*Thomas,*[4] *Thomas,*[3] *Thomas,*[2] *Edward*[1]), brother of the preceding, and son of Thomas[4] and Patience (Beers) Thurston of Tiverton; born there May 11, 1782; married, Dec. 25, 1803, ELIZABETH BAKER. He died Aug. 1, 1841.
Children:
+6625 Thomas,[6] b. May 24, 1807; m. Barbara Whitford.
  6626 Lydia S.,[6] b. Dec. 29, 1809.
  6627 Mary A. S.,[6] b. May 10, 1812.
  6628 Samuel,[6] b. Sept. 20, 1814; d. Aug. 22, 1815.
  6629 Samuel,[6] b. Oct. 11, 1817.
  6630 William Baker,[6] b. June 4, 1820; d. at Charleston, S. C.
  6631 Hannah S.,[6] b. March 30, 1823.
  6632 Daniel Baker,[6] b. March 1, 1825.

## 6094

DR. JOHN ROBINSON THURSTON[5] of St. Christophers, West Indies (*John,*[4] *Peleg,*[3] *Thomas,*[2] *Edward*[1]), son of John[4] and Abigail (Robinson) Thurston of Newport, R. I.; born there April 24, 1774; married, 1799, in Aberdeen, Scotland, MARY ANN BRUCE. He died May 7, 1819; she died July 2, 1852.
  Mr. Thurston graduated from St. Andrews university, Scotland.
Children:
  6636 Eliza,[6] b. Oct., 1800; m. 1821, Abraham S. Rees, M.D., a graduate of Harvard; d. 1862. They had:
      6637 *Robert C.* (Rees), b. 1822; d. 1852.
  6638 Mary Ann,[6] b. Oct., 1803; d. 1829.
+6639 William Torrey,[6] b. July 14, 1805; m. Caroline Thurston [see no. 6967].
+6640 John Robinson,[6] b. 1807; m. Louisa Ann Adlam.
+6641 Wanton,[6] b. Dec., 1809; m. Sarah Ottey.
+6642 James,[6] b. April, 1812; m. Martha Smith.
  6643 Esther,[6] b. 1816; d. 1819.

## 6104

WILLIAM RICHARDSON THURSTON[5] of New York city (*William Richardson,*[4] *Peleg,*[3] *Thomas,*[2] *Edward*[1]), son of William Richardson[4]

and Mary (Seaman) Thurston of Flushing, N. Y.; born there May 17, 1817; married, Nov. 9, 1842, JANE RIDLEY DAY, born Feb. 23, 1820, daughter of Mahlon and Mary Day of New York. Mr. Day was a publisher of children's books, and nearly forty years ago editor of Day's Bank Reporter, which had a large circulation. Mr. Day, wife, and daughter were lost on board the steamer Arctic in 1854, as they were returning home from Europe.

Mr. Thurston has been actively engaged during his whole life in taking charge of the business matters of his family and friends.

Children :

6648 William Richardson,[5] b. Oct. 27, 1843; m. Nov. 4, 1869, Maria H. Sampson. He is an importer of drugs, firm of T. B. Merrick & Co., New York city. Children :
   6649 *William Richardson,*[7] b. Aug. 24, 1873.
   6650 *Edward Sampson,*[7] b. Aug. 8, 18-6.
6651 Mary Day,[6] b. May 31, 1846; n.m. 1879.
6652 Edward Day,[6] b. March 4, 1851; n.m. 1879; firm of Banning, Bissel & Co., importers of analine colors, New York.
6653 Anna Day,[6] b. May 4, 1857; n.m. 1879.

### 6105

JOSEPH DELAPLAINE THURSTON[5] of Bayside, L. I. (*William Richardson,*[4] *Peleg,*[3] *Thomas,*[2] *Edward*[1]), brother of the preceding, and son of William Richardson[4] and Abigail (Eveingham) Thurston of Flushing, N. Y.; born there Feb. 22, 1823; married, April 30, 1849, MARY WHARTON. She died Oct. 26, 1856; he died June 5, 1861.

Mr. Thurston graduated from Haverford college, Pa.; purchased a country place at Bayside, near Flushing, L. I., and devoted himself to farming and fruit culture. Children :

6655 Hetty Wharton,[6] b. March 1, 1850; d. Oct. 30, 1875.
6656 William Wharton.[6] b. April 25, 1852; m. Sept. 24, 1873, Ellen Marion Coppée, b. at West Point, Va., Sept. 20, 1854, daughter of Henry (LL.D., see civil and military history in "Graduates of West Point," Henry Coppée appointed from Georgia) and Julia de Witt Coppée of Bethlehem, Pa. Mr. Thurston graduated from the university of Pennsylvania 1871, and is vice-president of Bethlehem Iron Co.; a member of the society of Friends, wife and children Episcopalians. Children :
   6657 *Edward Coppée,*[7] b. Oct. 28, 1874.
   6658 *Joseph Wharton,*[7] b. Aug. 25, 1876.
   6659 *William Wharton,*[7] b. May 27, 1878.
6660 Anna Wharton,[6] b. April 23, 1854; d. Nov. 19, 1856.

### Sixth Generation.

### 6114

JOHN THURSTON[6] of Merrick South, now Freeport, L. I. (*John,*[5] *Edward,*[4] *Edward,*[3] *Edward,*[2] *Edward*[1]), son of John[5] and Mary (Brett) Thurston of Providence, R. I.; born there about 1769; married ELIZABETH ALLEN, daughter of Andrew and Mary (Tuttersaw) [of Long Island birth, but English descent] Allen of Falkirk, Scotland. Children :

6662 Nancy,[7] b. June 18, 1792; m. Oliver Dorlan; d. May 19, 1867.
6663 John,[7] } twins, d. in childhood.
6664 Fanny,[7] }
6665 Elizabeth,[7] b. Aug. 13, 1798; m. John Carman; d. Aug. 15, 1828.
+6666 George Allen,[7] b. April 3, 1802; m. Ellen Fenton.

## 6115

DANIEL THURSTON[6] of Utica, N. Y. (*John,*[5] *Edward,*[4] *Edward,*[8] *Edward,*[2] *Edward*[1]), brother of the preceding, and son of John[5] and Mary (Brett) Thurston of Providence, R. I.; born there 1770; married, 1791, PRUDENCE CROSSMAN, born in New Bedford, Mass., 1776. She died March 8, 1836; he died at his son John's, in Granby, Oswego county, N. Y., 1840.

Mr. Thurston at the age of fourteen was a waiter boy for a captain in the navy. He was afterward a baker, and kept a grocery and baker's shop in Providence; moved to Utica; was in the war of 1812; a member of the Free Baptist church in Providence, but joined the Methodist church in New York.    Children:

6669  Fanny,[7] d. at the age of five.
+6670  John,[7] b. Jan. 7, 1792; m. Hannah Tucker.

## 6124

ROBERT JENKINS THURSTON[6] of New York city (*John,*[5] *Capt. John,*[4] *Jonathan,*[8] *Edward,*[2] *Edward*[1]), second son of John[5] and Elizabeth (Jenkins) Thurston of Hudson, N. Y.; married, June 4, 1801, ABIGAIL BOGERT, born in New York city May 20, 1774. He died July 21, 1806; she died May 8, 1841, and was buried at Jamaica, L. I. He was a hardware dealer, firm of Bogert & Thurston.

Children:

6675  Eliza Ann,[7] b. July 1, 1802; n.m.; d. at Jamaica May 24, 1830.
6676  Cornelia Emmeline,[7] b. Oct. 20. 1803; m. April 3, 1828, Jesse Hoyt, son of Gould and Sarah (Reid) Hoyt of Jamaica; he was at one time collector of the port of New York. She died July 20, 1852; he died Mar. 17, 1867.  They had:
  6677  *Cornelia Thurston* (Hoyt), n.m.
  6678  *Louis Thurston* (Hoyt), m. Marie Antoinette Bogert [see no. 6692; a banker in New York.
  6679  *William H.* (Hoyt), n.m.; in business in Baltimore, Md.
  6680  *Emily Adele* (Hoyt), m. Francis A. de Wint of Fishkill on Hudson; he died.  They had five children.
  6681  *Robert Sands* (Hoyt), n.m.; d. May 16, 1879.
  6682  *Ella Carroll* (Hoyt), m. J. de Wint Whittemore of Fishkill on Hudson.
+6683  Louis Marion,[7] b. Oct. 23, 1804; m. Elizabeth Samuella Brewer.
6684  A child, b. Dec. 26, 1805; d. Feb. 15, 1806.

## 6129

EDWARD CHAMPLIN THURSTON[6] of New York city (*John,*[5] *Capt. John,*[4] *Jonathan,*[8] *Edward,*[2] *Edward*[1]), brother of the preceding, and son of John[5] and Elizabeth (Jenkins) Thurston of Hudson, N. Y.; born there Nov. 9, 1790; married ELIZABETH VAN VREDENBERG. He died about 1873, aged over 80.  He was a magistrate.

Children:

6690  Maria Louisa,[7] m. Dr. Cornelius Robert Bogert, a physician in New York city; he died 1877.  They had:
  6691  *Clinton* (Bogert), d. in infancy.
  6692  *Marie Antoinette* (Bogert), m. Louis Thurston Hoyt [see no. 6678], a banker in New York city; d. June 1, 1879, leaving two children:
    6693  *Geraldine* (Hoyt).    6694  *Aline* (Hoyt).
  6695  *Eugene Thurston* (Bogert), a broker in N. Y. city, m. Kate A. Vanderpool.
6696  Phebe Watson,[7] n.m.

## 6130

PENELOPE THURSTON[6] ( *John,*[5] *Capt. John,*[4] *Jonathan,*[3] *Edward,*[2] *Edward*[1]), sister of the preceding, and eighth child of John[5] and Elizabeth (Jenkins) Thurston of Hudson, N. Y.; born there Dec. 29, 1792; married, Oct. 29, 1816, REV. GREGORY TOWNSEND BEDELL, D.D., born Aug. 28, 1793, son of Israel and Elizabeth (Moore) Bedell of New York. Elizabeth Moore was born in New York Jan. 26, 1760, and died on Staten Island 1802; sister to the Rt. Rev. R. C. Moore, bishop of Virginia. Penelope was one of the most beautiful women of her day; her two sisters and herself were known as "*labelle famille.*" Israel Bedell was born September, 1750, died May 30, 1830. Dr. Bedell died in Philadelphia, Pa., Aug. 30, 1834; his widow died in New York city Dec. 30, 1859.

G. T. Bedell graduated from Columbia' college in 1811, and had his first charge in Hudson; from thence he went to Fayetteville, N. C., and from there to Philadelphia, where St. Andrews church was erected for him and consecrated in the spring of 1823. His ministry there was such that to this day it is recalled with loving gratitude by all who knew him. His life has been written by Rev. S. H. Tyng, D.D., of New York, and published with his sermons, which, with his hymns, musical compositions, books of devotion, etc., are still in use.

### Children:

6700  Gregory Thurston (Bedell), b. in Hudson Aug. 27, 1817; m. Oct. 7, 1845, Julia Strong, daughter of James and Aletta Strong of New York. Mr. Bedell graduated from Bristol college, Pa., 1836; was ordained in St. Andrews church, Philadelphia, July, 1840. His first parish was in Westchester, Pa.; the second was that of the Ascension church in New York, from where he was elected assistant bishop of Ohio, Rev. Dr. McIlvane being then bishop; since his death Dr. Bedell was consecrated to the office of bishop in Richmond, Va., and is now bishop of Ohio. They had three children, all died in infancy.

6701  Elizabeth (Bedell), m. Jan. 17, 1854, Frederick Augustus Benjamin, son of Col. Aaron Benjamin, of Stratford, Ct., an officer in the army during the whole of the revolutionary war. Mr. Benjamin was an importing merchant of New York (Bean, Benjamin & Co.); after retiring from business he erected a country seat in his native town, where he resides with his family for a portion of each year. He was one of the electors of Abraham Lincoln for president of the United States on his second term. Mrs. Benjamin is known extensively as a pleasant writer of religious books and articles for the press. They have:

6702  *Arthur Bedell* (Benjamin), b. Oct., 1854.

## 6131

SUSAN ALADA THURSTON[6] of New York city ( *John,*[5] *Capt. John,*[4] *Jonathan,*[3] *Edward,*[2] *Edward*[1]), sister of the preceding, and daughter of John[5] and Elizabeth (Jenkins) Thurston of Hudson, N. Y.; born there Nov. 29, 1793; married PATRICK FANNING. She died in New York Nov. 19, 1859.

### Children:

6703  Ann Eliza (Fanning), b. in Hudson Oct. 22, 1816; m. 1st, Oct. 5, 1836, John H. Boswell, a dry goods merchant in Norwich, Ct.; he died Nov. 13, 1857, aged 45; 2d, May 18, 1859, Capt. Charles L. Meech, a farmer in Preston City, Ct.; he died May 18, 1862, aged 54. She had:

6704  *John Lovett* (Boswell), b. Oct. 14, 1838.
6705  *Elizabeth Hand* (Boswell), b. Aug. 9, 1841.
6706  *Elizabeth* (Boswell), b. May 26, 1844.
6707  *Alla Thurston* (Boswell), b. May 2, 1847.

6708    *Charles Fanning* (Boswell), b. Sept. 14, 1850.
6709    Cornelia Dubois (Fanning), d.    6710    Harriet Dayton (Fanning), d.
6711    Caroline Winslow (Fanning), d.
6712    Frances Chester (Fanning), b. June 28, 1831; m. in Hudson April 23,
            1856, Rev. John A. Paddock, D.D., rector of St. Peter's church in Brook-
            lyn, N. Y., a devoted christian and faithful, sacrificing pastor. Children:
    6713    *Alada Thurston* (Paddock), b. June 25, 1858.
    6714    *Edith Flagg* (Paddock), b. Nov. 30, 1860; d.
    6715    *Lilly Bedell* (Paddock), b. Feb. 1, 1862; d.
    6716    *John Benjamin* (Paddock), b. March 18, 1864; d.
    6717    *Fanny Fanning* (Paddock), b. May 11, 1866.
    6718    *Louise Bogert* (Paddock), b. Jan. 16, 1868; d.
    6719    *Robert Lewis* (Paddock), b. Dec. 24, 1870.
    6720    *Ellie Morgan* (Paddock), b. Nov. 14, 1872.
    6721    *Florence Hubbard* (Paddock), b. March 6, 1875.
6722    Robert Slark (Fanning), b. April 22, 1835; m. 1st, Oct. 9, 1861, Elizabeth
            Paddock, sister to Rev. John A. Paddock, D.D.; 2d, Oct. 6, 1868, Ellen
            Wyckoff Mulligan; was a merchant in New York; d. Feb. 4, 1876. Chil.:
    6723    *Lizzie Flagg* (Fanning), b. Sept. 15, 1863.
    6724    *Ellen Wyckoff* (Fanning), b. Sept., 187–.
    6725    *Julia Mulligan* (Fanning), b. Feb., 1875.

## 6154

PELEG THURSTON [6] of Portsmouth, R. I. (*Peleg,*[5] *Capt. John,*[4] *Jonathan,*[3] *Edward,*[2] *Edward*[1]), fourth child of Peleg[5] and Phebe (Lawton) Thurston of Portsmouth; born in Hudson, N. Y., Jan. 19, 1786;
married, May 28, 1809, SUSAN BARKER LAWTON, daughter of Job
and Hannah Lawton. He died March 2, 1876, aged 90; she died
Aug. 23, 1879, aged 88 y. 4 m. 8 d. He was a farmer; served in the
war of 1812, and received a pension, 1875.

Children:

6726    Hannah,[7] b. Dec. 16, 1809; d. April 11, 1822.
6727    Phebe Lawton,[7] b. March 14, 1813; m. Oct. 10, 1833, Oliver Albro, a
            farmer of Portsmouth, and had:
    6728    *Hannah Barker* (Albro), b. Oct. 28, 1835; m. in Newport, R. I., Sept.
                25, 1859, Thomas Holman of Portsmouth, and had:
        6729    *Frederic William* (Holman), b. March 25, 1860.
        6730    *Fannie Lavoatta* (Holman), b. Oct. 1862.
        6731    *Hermon Thomas* (Holman), b. Oct. 29, 1866.
    6732    *Christopher Durfee* (Albro), b. Sept. 1, 1842; m. in Providence, R. I.,
                Aug. 17, 1875, Sarah Adelaide Hawkins.
    6733    *Caroline Adelia* (Albro), b. Dec. 10, 1844; m. Jan. 10, 1866, George
                Henry Breed of Geneseo, Ill., and had:
        6734    *Jennie Wilson* (Breed), b. Nov. 14, 1866.
        6735    *William Baxter* (Breed), b. Jan. 20, 1872.
        6736    *Cora Thurston* (Breed), b. Jan. 28, 1877; d. Feb. 6, 1877.
    6737    *James Albert* (Albro), b. in Middletown, R. I., Sept. 14, 1848; d. Nov.
                7, 1866.
    6738    *Franklin Thurston* (Albro), b. in Portsmouth May 6, 1854; d. Jan. 31,
                1863.
6739    Susan Lawton,[7] b. Feb. 20, 1815; m. April 11, 1842, John Clark, a boot
            and shoe manufacturer in Newport; no children,
+6740   Louis Jenkins,[7] b. March 18, 1818; m. Cynthia Ann Peckham.
+6741   Edward,[7] b. Nov. 26, 1820; m. Harriet Peckham.
6742    Robert Lawton,[7] b. Feb. 23, 1823; a farmer in Portsmouth; m. Nov. 13,
            1879, by Rev. E. M. Smith, Harriet J. Rawson of Newport.
+6743   Peleg Lawton,[7] b. June 18, 1826; m. Sarah Elizabeth Lawton.
6744    Benjamin Franklin,[7] b. April 30, 1830; d. at Placerville, Cal., Oct. 28, 1852.
+6745   Parker Hall,[7] b. March 2, 1833; m. Louisa Maria Rawson.

## 6171

JOHN SAMUEL THURSTON [6] of Providence, R. I. (*Peleg,*[5] *Capt. John,*[4]
*Jonathan,*[3] *Edward,*[2] *Edward*[1]), brother of the preceding, and son of

Peleg[4] and Ruth (Lawton) Thurston of Portsmouth, R. I.; born there Sept. 26, 1799; married, in Newport, R. I., by Rev. Michael Eddy, June 22, 1822, HANNAH BARKER LAWTON, born July 19, 1797, daughter of William and Sarah (Barker) Lawton of Portsmouth. He died Jan. 7, 1879, aged 79.

Mr. Thurston was in the navy in the war of 1812, in the vessel that took the British ship Nimrod, at Portsmouth, when thirteen years of age. He followed the sea for some years, and after became a steam engine manufacturer, at one time in company with his brother Robert Lawton; withdrew from this company to go to the West Indies to set up steam engines. He run the Spanish steamer Almandar between Havana and Matanzas, taking her to Providence once to put in a new engine. This steamer was wrecked, lying at the wharf, in the hurricane of 1844, after which he returned to Providence. He was a very active and resolute business man till about 1864, after which time he was unable to do any labor.

### Children, born in Portsmouth:

6750  Elizabeth Lawton,[7] b. Dec. 23, 1823; m. Jan. 29, 1843, Henry Gardner Luther of Swansea, Mass., a collector of bills in Providence. Children:
　　6751  *John Henry* (Luther), b. April 15, 1844.
　　6752  *William Gardner* (Luther), b. Nov. 29, 1845.
　　6753  *Elizabeth Thurston* (Luther), b Aug. 10. 1847.
　　6754  *James* (Luther), b. April 3, 1849; d. May 9, 1849.
　　6755  *James* (Luther), b. May 10, 1850; d. Aug. 4, 1851.
6756  Phebe Lawton,[7] b. Nov. 7, 1825; in Providence, n.m.
### Born in Providence:
+6757  John Babcock,[7] b. Feb. 26, 1829; m. 1st, Sophia A. Capwell; 2d, Addeline A. Wilbur.
6758  William Henry,[7] b. April 12, 1832; d. June 17, 1838.
+6759  George Stratton,[7] b. July 26, 1834; m. Jerusha W. Heath.
6760  Sarah Hart,[7] b. Sept. 23, 1836; in Providence, n.m.
6761  Ruth Hannah,[7] b. Oct. 5, 1839; m. Dec. 13, 1857, Daniel Henry Matthewson. a lapidary in Providence. Children:
　　6762  *George Snow* (Matthewson), b. April 20, 1861; d. Oct. 26, 1863.
　　6763  *Charles Henry* (Matthewson), b. Dec. 11, 1863.
　　6764  *Edwin Lawton* (Matthewson), b. Oct. 6, 1873.

## 6172

ROBERT LAWTON THURSTON[6] of Providence, R. I. (*Peleg*,[5] *Capt. John*,[4] *Jonathan*,[3] *Edward*,[2] *Edward*[1]), brother of the preceding, and youngest son of Peleg[5] and Ruth (Lawton) Thurston of Portsmouth, R. I.; born there Dec. 13, 1800; married, first, 1827, ELIZA STRATTON, daughter of Capt. John Stratton; she died July 10, 1828, aged 28. Second. Jan. 5, 1839, HARRIET TAYLOR, daughter of William and Elizabeth (Bailey) Taylor of Little Compton, R. I. He died Jan. 13, 1874.

" He * was one of the few intelligent, far seeing, and enterprising men, whose energy and capacity, a half century and more ago, developed successfully the long latent power of steam and applied it to navigation, to railroad transportation, to driving the spindle and the loom, and to the thousand purposes now so familiar to us. He developed an extraordinary talent as a mechanic at an early age, and

---

* Extract from Providence Daily Journal, Jan. 21, 1874.

Robert and Ruth (Lawton) Thurston of Portsmouth, R. I., born there

Robert L. Thurston,

immediately upon attaining his majority, commenced learning the trade of a machinist with Pelham & Walcott. Eight months later he had acquired sufficient skill to attract the attention of John Babcock, sen., a distinguished mechanic, who was then actively aiding in the introduction of cotton and woolen manufactures, and who was well known as an accomplished engineer and an inventor.

"These two mechanics completed an experimental steam engine, with its 'newly invented and most excellent' safety tubular boiler, as it would be called to-day, which was placed in a small ferry-boat designed for use near Fall River. The performance of this craft was sufficiently satisfactory to encourage the inventors to try again, and the 'Rushlight' and the 'Babcock,' subsequently built, were comparatively large craft. They created a sensation only equalled by the excitement attending the voyages of the 'Clermont' or the trial trips of John Stevens' boats.

"Subsequently to a journey to the South, to seek business and to study the country, Mr. Thurston was employed by the 'Iron Company' of Fall River, while building the old Annawan mill. John Babcock died in 1827, leaving a son John, who inherited fully his father's engineering ability, business capacity, and remarkable energy.

"Mr. Thurston came to Providence in 1830, and with young Babcock succeeded so well that in 1834 they commenced business, starting the first steam engine building establishment in New England, or, with two exceptions, in the United States. The company then formed was known as the Providence Steam Engine Company.

"Mr. Babcock's health failed and he was compelled to give up business. The firm of Robert L. Thurston & Co. was formed in 1838, and in 1845, by other changes, it became Thurston, Greene & Co. Just before this latter change a terrible boiler explosion destroyed the buildings and seriously crippled the resources of the company. The friends of the proprietors came promptly to the rescue, however, and the establishment was soon in working order again.

"A few months after the formation of the new company a fire broke out in an adjoining establishment, and communicated to their just rebuilt works, sweeping them away. Hardly was the fire fairly extinguished, however, when workmen were sent among the ruins, and preparations were made for rebuilding. Mr. Greene went to Europe to purchase new machinery; Mr. Gardner, the financier of the firm, skillfully and promptly obtained all necessary capital, and Mr. Thurston attended to the work of reconstruction. The new buildings were rapidly built, the new machinery was put in place, and work was resumed. The long machine shop then built still remains, forming a part of the large building now occupied by the successors of the old firm.

"Thurston, Greene & Co. purchased the Sickles patent for the 'drop cut-off' for steam engines, and were the first manufacturers, either in America or in Europe, who ever built a standard form of expansive steam engine. They were the pioneers in the introduction of the modern steam engine, and Mr. Thurston was accustomed to relate many anecdotes illustrating the difficulties attending the introduction of new devices, even when embodying acknowledged eco-

nomical principles and sustained by ample evidence of efficiency gathered from actual experience. To-day the whole engineering world is following in the track then beaten with so much difficulty, and but few, even in the profession, know to whom we are so greatly indebted.

"For a long time this firm, and Thurston, Gardner & Co., who succeeded them in 1854, were engaged in litigation with George H. Corliss, against whom they brought suit for infringement of the Sickles patent. This series of trials—Sickles *et al vs.* Corliss—was one of the most noted cases ever brought into court. The greatest engineers and the ablest patent lawyers of the country were engaged. Among the counsel employed were William H. Seward, Judge Curtis, Charles H. Keller, Mr. Stoughton, and our distinguished townsman, Benjamin F. Thurston; and among the experts were the brothers Renwick, Charles W. Copeland, and others well known to our citizens. After several decisions favorable to the plaintiffs, the late Judge Nelson, on a final appeal, reversed the decisions of the lower courts, and the contest came to an end, after a long and obstinate struggle, in which both parties expended a vast amount of time, talent, and money.

"During this interval Mr. Greene invented the well known 'Greene Engine,' and the manufacture was at once commenced by Thurston, Gardner & Co., and their successors, the Providence Steam Engine Company, still continue to build this, which was claimed by Mr. Thurston, and is now claimed by many engineers, to be the best of the modern steam engines.

"At the commencement of the war of the rebellion business became universally depressed, and the manufacture of steam engines almost entirely ceased. Southern debtors, of whom there was a long list on the books of the firm, very generally either failed entirely or took advantage of the unsettled state of affairs and refused to pay their notes. Mr. Thurston was getting advanced in years and his health was becoming enfeebled. His oldest son, who had been educated carefully in the college and in the workshops and drawing rooms, with a view to following the business, had accepted a commission in the Naval Engineer Corps, with the expressed intention of remaining until the end of a possibly long contest, and the younger son had chosen another branch of the profession of engineering. Discouraged at last, and in despair of retrieving his lost fortunes, he surrendered his interest, and, with no other reward for his long years of active life, of industry and enterprise, than a clear conscience, pleasant memories of benefits conferred upon others, and the reminiscences of the successful enterprises of earlier times, retired from business. At the formal dissolution of the copartnership in August, 1863, the establishment was purchased by the Providence Steam Engine Company, a new corporation, which had assumed the title of the earliest of the companies with which Mr. Thurston had been connected.

"The health of Mr. Thurston failed rapidly as soon as he attempted to give up all the business habits which had been formed during this long period, and both necessity and inclination soon drove him back into the old customs. During the succeeding ten years, and

until a few days before his death, when health permitted, he went as regularly to the shop, and took as much interest in the work going on, as if he still retained his former connection with the establishment. His health steadily failed, however, and finally an attack of pneumonia caused his death, Jan. 13, 1874, after but four days' illness. He died without either acute pain or mental disturbance, his last sleep coming upon him like slumber to a tired child.

"Throughout his life his benevolence, his uniform kindness to employes and to all with whom he came in contact, and his strong attachment to his friends, made him as universally beloved as he was widely known. In his own family and among his near relatives his kindness of heart, and the depth of affectionate feeling which distinguished his character, inspired a degree of reciprocal affection which is rarely found under most favoring circumstances. His religious sentiments were strongly colored by the beliefs of the society of Friends; but he had during the last years of his life been a regular attendant at the services of the Congregational church, of which his wife was a member."

His children, by second wife, Harriet:

+6770 Robert Henry,[7] b. Oct. 25, 1839; m. Susan Taylor Gladding.
6771 Eliza Stratton,[7] b. June 26, 1841; m. Oct. 29, 1862, William Walton Fletcher, and had:
 6772 *George Lincoln* (Fletcher), b. March 18, 1865; d. Sept. 17, 1866.
 6773 *Carrie Slates* (Fletcher), b. June 8, 1874.
+6774 Frank Taylor,[7] b. Sept. 17, 1844; m. Ida Treadwell.

## 6175

EDWARD THURSTON [6] of Brooklyn, N. Y. (*Jonathan,*[5] *Capt. John,*[4] *Jonathan,*[3] *Edward,*[2] *Edward*[1]), eldest son of Jonathan [5] and Hannah (Beebe) Thurston of Newport, R. I.; born there Oct. 29, 1778; married, first, June, 1806, CATHARINE HUBBARD of Catskill, N. Y.; second, Oct. 7, 1810, ELIZA FAIRCHILD; she died April 10, 1839; he died July 8, 1851, aged 71.

His children, by first wife, Catharine, were:

+6780 Henry C.,[7] b. March 24, 1807; m. 1st, Catharine Smith; 2d, Almira Allen Smith.

By second wife, Eliza:

+6781 Robert F.,[7] b. July 8, 1811; m. Sarah Ann Hughes.
6782 Hannah Beebe,[7] b. Nov. 15, 1813; m. March 29, 1835, Joseph S. Waring; d. July 26, 1836, having had:
 6783 *Hannah* (Waring), b. April 11, 1836; d. July 27, 1836.
6784 Mary,[7] b. Oct. 10, 1816; d. Aug. 6, 1817.
6785 Mary Eliza,[7] b. Feb., 1820; m. Jan. 28, 1847, William Davis, and had:
 6786 *Edward* (Davis), b. March 22, 1848.
 6787 *William* (Davis), b. Nov. 10, 1850.
 6788 *Harriet* (Davis), b. July 22, 1853.
 6789 *Thomas* (Davis), b. July 6, 1856.

## 6220

THOMAS THURSTON [6] of Newport, R. I. (*William,*[5] *William,*[4] *Jonathan,*[3] *Edward,*[2] *Edward*[1]), third child of William [5] and Mary (Rowlong) Thurston of Newport; born there Jan. 15, 1782; married, June 8, 1807, MARTHA SIMPSON. He died Sept. 3, 1814; she died Aug. 25, 1833, aged 48. He was a master mariner.

Their children were:

6794 Edward,[7] b. 1810; lost at sea, 1831.
+6795 Thomas,[7] b. June 23, 1812; m. Mary Buffington.
6796 Frances Ruth,[7] b. April, 1813; d. Aug. 14, 1836.

## 6221

WILLIAM CARTER THURSTON [6] of Newport, R. I. (*William,*[5] *William,*[4] *Jonathan,*[8] *Edward,*[2] *Edward*[1]), brother of the preceding, and son of William [5] and Mary (Rowlong) Thurston of Newport; born there Aug. 23, 1783; married, Sept. 25, 1805, PATIENCE YOUNG, daughter of Samuel Young. He died in Rehoboth, Mass., Nov. 2, 1876, aged 93; she died March 8, 1872, aged 89 y. 8 m.

Mr. Thurston was a cabinet maker in Newport, after engaged in trade in the South; was the oldest person in town at the time of his death; a prominent citizen, having filled many offices in his native town, and in full possession of his faculties to nearly the last. They were both members of the Methodist church. Rev. Daniel P. Leavitt says: " She adorned her christian profession by a cheerful piety and consistent life, and her end was peace."

Their children were:

+6800 William Carter,[7] b. Dec. 6, 1806; m. Mary A. Mott.
6801 James Wilcox,[7] b. 1808; lost at sea, 1831.
6802 Emily,[7] b. 1811; m. Oct. 6, 1830, William Joseph Clarke White, and had:
    6803 *Emily* (White), b. Nov., 1831; m. Edwin Anthony of Somerset, Mass., a machinist, and a member of the Methodist church.
    6804 *Edmund* (White), b. Dec., 1833; n.m.; a tailor, but now clerk in Clafflin's dry goods store, New York, 1879.
    6805 *Charles* (White), b. Feb., 1835; m. Ruth Amelia Barker; a carpenter and upholsterer in Somerset, Mass., Methodist.
    6806 *Amanda* (White), b. Nov., 1836; m. George Lovejoy, agent for the leather business in Newport, Methodist.
+6807 Thomas Jefferson,[7] b. May 26, 1813; m. Clarissa Monroe.
6808 Mary,[7] b. 1815; m. July, 1834, Caleb Wilbor Anthony, a grocer of Providence, R. I. She died April, 1866; he died April, 1876. They had:
    6809 *James T.* (Anthony), b. 1835; m. Mary E. Damon of New Bedford, Mass. He was a prominent member of the Broadway Methodist Episcopal church, and superintendent of Sunday-school at time of his death, 1868, in which office his brother Noel succeeds him. He left one daughter, Mary (Anthony).
    6810 *Julia* (Anthony), b. May, 1837; m. George Gorton, a carpenter of E. Greenwich, R. I., now live in Providence, Methodist.
    6811 *Mary* (Anthony), b. 1839; m. Horace Phillips, a machinist of Pawtucket, R. I., Methodist.
    6812 *Susan* (Anthony), b. 1841; m. 1st, Gilbert Steere of Providence; 2d, Willard U. Lansing, a clerk in Boston, Mass.
    6813 *Noel L.* (Anthony), b. May, 1848; m. Hattie Knox; a merchant in Providence, Methodist.
6814 Abby,[7] b. Dec. 17, 1817; m. Dec. 17, 1837, Pardon W. Stevens. He served many years in both branches of Newport, R. I., city government, in both branches of the state legislature, being state senator from 1858 to 1868; was lieutenant governor from 1868 three years, and revenue inspector at the time of his death, April 19, 1875. She was a member of the Unitarian church. They had:
    6815 *Frances* (Stevens), b. 1840; m. H. Augustus Kaull, a carpenter in Newport, Baptist.
    6816 *David* (Stevens), b. 1842; m. 1st, 1865, Helen F. Armington; she died April, 1866; 2d, Oct., 1876, Sarah B. Munro. He is the librarian of the People's Free Library in Newport.
    6817 *William* (Stevens), b. 1843; m. Emma Swan; in employ of the O. C. R. R. Co.

6818 *Thomas* (Stevens), b. 1845; n.m.; a carpenter, Methodist.
6819 Ann Elizabeth,[7] b. 1819; m. April, 1838, William Peabody, a carpenter of Newport; both members of the Methodist church. They had:
    6820 *Elizabeth H.* (Peabody), b. 1838; m. John Doty of Bristol, R. I.; d. Oct., 1867.
    6821 *Gertrude* (Peabody), b. 1846; n.m.
6822 John,[7] b. 1823; drowned 1825.
6823 Robert Carter,[7] b. 1824; a blacksmith, a licensed exhorter in the Methodist church; d. May 29, 1848.
6824 Caroline Matilda,[7] b. June 22, 1825; m. March 19, 1847, Rev. Daniel Atkins, b. Aug. 16, 1824, son of Paul and Kezia (Paine) Atkins of Truro, Mass., a Methodist clergyman; she died in Palmer, Mass., March 11, 1854. They had:
    6825 *William* (Atkins), b. in Gloucester, Mass., Dec. 14, 1848; a printer in Boston, Mass.; m.
    6826 *Benjamin Paine* (Atkins), b. April 21, 1851; d. in Millbury, Mass., Nov. 13, 1863.
    6827 *Daniel Thurston* (Atkins), b. in Palmer Feb. 23, 1854; d. in Newport Aug. 21, 1854.
6828 John Young,[7] b. March 25, 1828; m. April 9, 1867, Mary Elizabeth Almy, b. June 8, 1842, daughter of Geo. I. and Elizabeth H. (Freeborn) Almy of Newport. He is a shoemaker in Medfield, Mass.; she is a member of the Baptist church. They have:
    6829 *Alice Almy,*[8] b. May 12, 1873.

## 6226

ROWLAND THURSTON [6] of Bridgewater, Oneida county, N. Y. (*William,*[5] *George,*[4] *Edward,*[3] *Jonathan,*[2] *Edward*[1]), eldest son of William [5] and Ruth (Stetson) Thurston of Hopkinton, R. I.; born there 1764; married FREEGIFT McKOON. He died Mar. 21, 1814; she died Jan. 13, 1834.

Soon after his marriage they moved to Galway, Saratoga county, and after to Bridgewater, Oneida county, N. Y. He was a farmer.

### Their children were:

6835 Hannah,[7] b. in Galway Jan. 7, 1801; m. 1825, Harley Judd, a wagon maker, after a hotel keeper, and finally a farmer; she died in Chittenango, N. Y., Feb. 12, 1864. They had:
    6836 *Rowland Thurston* (Judd), b. 1826; d. in infancy.
    6837 *Mary Adele* (Judd), b. Feb. 9, 1829; m. 1848, Andrew J. French.
    6838 *Edward Ancill* (Judd), b. July, 1831; m. Cornelia Yates.
    6839 *Howell Hampton* (Judd), b. Nov., 1833; m. Myra Bond.
    6840 *Ruth Rosamond* (Judd), b. April, 1835; m. John Campbell.
    6841 *Helen Hannah* (Judd), b. Oct., 1838; m. Clark R. Wallace.
    6842 *Frances Jerusha* (Judd), b. July 27, 1841; m. 1st, Gould N. Lewis; 2d, Albert T. Van Antwerp.

### Born in Bridgewater:

6843 Mary G.,[7] b. Feb. 2, 1803; m. Howell Hollister, a saddle and harness maker in Savannah, Ga.; d. March 8, 1877; no children.
6844 Hampton C.,[7] b. Jan. 6, 1806; was in the United States army, and died single May 4, 1834, at Prairie duChien, when it was a frontier place.
+6845 Laurens Hull,[7] b. Jan. 7, 1808; m. 1st, Emera Brown; 2d, Mrs. Sarah Jane (Birdsall) Mosher.
6846 Ruth,[7] b. June 21, 1812; m. Nov. 20, 1844, Lyman Duane Brown, a lawyer of Morrisville, N. Y.; d. after seven years' sickness of paralysis, Oct. 2, 1872, having had:
    6847 *Thurston Duane* (Brown), b. Sept. 15, 1845; m. Hattie Badey; they reside in Bridgewater; one son.
    6848 *Rosamond* (Brown), b. July 22, 1847; m. Oct. 10, 1877, Herbert Palmer, a carriage maker; they live on the homestead in Bridgewater; no children.

## 6230

ELISHA THURSTON[6] of West Winfield, N. Y. (*William,*[5] *George,*[4] *Edward,*[3] *Jonathan,*[2] *Edward*[1]), brother of the preceding, and son of William[5] and Ruth (Stetson) Thurston of Bridgewater, N. Y.; born there April 18, 1792; married, Sept. 28, 1809, CLIMENA GUILD, born Oct. 18, 1794, daughter of Elijah and Anna (Eason) Guild of Bridgewater. She died April 22, 1851; he died in Wolcott, Wayne Co., N. Y.

Mr. Thurston was a farmer. The daughter wrote: "Although we cannot boast of any professional men among our ancestors, yet they were remarkable for their good looks."

Their children were:

6853  Emerancy Bixby,[7] b. Dec. 24, 1812; m. 1st, Feb. 20, 1839, George D. Foster, b. in Cazenovia, N. Y.; he was a merchant in West Winfield; in April, 1850, went to California for his health, returned and died at Butler, N. Y., June 26, 1851. 2d, at Lyons, N. Y., July 23, 1861, Walter Palmer, son of Vose and Sally (Chapin) Palmer of West Winfield, where he has a beautiful farm and large cheese factory. She died Jan. 25, 1879, having had, by first husband:

6854  *George Thurston* (Foster), b. April 3, 1840; enlisted in the 44th New York regiment from Lyons in 1863, was discharged for disability, and enlisted again in 1864 in the 98th New York. He was engaged in the dry goods business with George Strong in Lyons, before and after the war, until Oct., 1873, when he went to Detroit, Mich., with his brother-in-law, Richard Macauley; n.m.

6855  *Josephene Annette* (Foster), b. July 8, 1842; m. July 9, 1867, Richard Macauley, b. Nov. 28, 1838, son of Richard and Jane (McGuire) Macauley of Rochester, N. Y., an importer and jobber of millinery and fancy goods in Detroit, Mich.; was the first captain of Co. E, 54th regiment N. Y. S. N. G. of Rochester in the war against the rebellion; a member of the Presbyterian church in Rochester and of the Episcopal in Detroit; where he moved in 1869. Children:

6856  *George Thurston* (Macauley), b. in Rochester April 7, 1869.
6857  *Fanny Wood* (Macauley), b. in Detroit Sept. 21, 1871.
6858  *Richard Henry* (Macauley), b. March 9, 1873.
6859  *Joseph Foster* (Macauley), b. Sept. 30, 1878.
6860  *Climena Guild* (Foster), b. Oct. 31, 1845; d. at Butler Oct. 11, 1846.
+6861  Elijah Guild,[7] b. Nov. 6, 1815; m. Emeline Carman.

## 6240

EDWARD THURSTON[6] of Springfield, N. Y. (*Edward,*[5] *George,*[4] *Edward,*[3] *Jonathan,*[2] *Edward*[1]), eldest son of Edward[5] and Thankful (Main) Thurston of Springfield; born in North Stonington, Ct., Aug. 21, 1766; married, Jan. 20, 1788, HANNAH GARDNER, born 1767, daughter of Abiel Gardner of North Stonington. He died Feb. 8, 1818; she died Feb. 24, 1820, aged 53.

Mr. Thurston was a farmer on Thurston Hill, Springfield.

Their children were:

6866  Edward,[7] b. in North Stonington April 4, 1789; d. in infancy.
6867  Abiel,[7] b. 1791; killed at battle of Queenstown, N. Y., Feb. 18, 1813.
6868  Abigail,[7] b. 1795; m. Jason Butterfield; d. Jan. 20, 1836, having had:
6869  *Hannah* (Butterfield), d. young.
6870  Phylura,[7] b. Nov. 17, 1796; n.m.
6871  Matilda,[7] b. July 6, 1799; m. Rev. Hiram Hutchins; d. 1837; no children.
6872  Maria,[7] b. 1802; n.m.; d. 1826.

## 6241

ADAM THURSTON[6] of North Stonington, Ct. (*Edward,*[5] *George,*[4] *Edward,*[3] *Jonathan,*[2] *Edward*[1]), brother of the preceding, and son of

Edward[5] and Thankful (Main) Thurston of Springfield, N. Y.; born in North Stonington Aug. 11, 1768; married, Sept. 29, 1789, EUNICE MINER. She died Aug. 27, 1829, aged 59; he died Nov. 9, 1858.

Mr. Thurston was a farmer, and has resided in North Stonington, Thurston Hill, Springfield, and at time of his death in Ackron, Ohio.

Their children were:

6877    Cynthia,[7] b. June 20, 1790; d. July 15, 1790.
6878    Silas,[7] b. July 3, 1791; d. Nov. 5, 1795.
6879    Lucretia,[7] b. July 20, 1793; m. Oct. 22, 1818, Rev. Rufus Sabin, a Baptist clergyman, settled in Utica, N. Y., more recently has been a teacher in the western part of the state; she died Feb. 5, 1839. They had:
     6880   *Leander* (Sabin), b. Sept. 20, 1819.
     6881   *Elihu Putnam* (Sabin), b. Oct. 15, 1824; d. Aug. 22, 1829.
     6882   *Caroline Levina* (Sabin), b. Oct., 1830; d. Aug. 2, 1833.
+6883   Jeremiah,[7] b May 13, 1795; m. Sophia Thayer.
6884    Sophia,[7] b. April 23, 1797; d. in Ackron, Ohio, Sept. 25, 1863.
6885    Caroline,[7] b. Aug. 2, 1799; d. April 5, 1803.
6886    Harriet,[7] b. May 13, 1801; m. Feb. 13, 1822, John Cole Delamater: he was a farmer and had a fruit and flower nursery in Ackron. She died May 27, 1861; he died about 1871. They had:
     6887   *George Washington* (Delamater), b. Feb. 20, 1823; d. March 13, 1846.
     6888   *Rufus S.* (Delamater), b. May 17, 1824.
     6889   *Benjamin F.* (Delamater), b. Jan. 18, 1825; d. July 4, 1842.
     6890   *Maremus W.* (Delamater), b. Oct. 15, 1827; d. March 7, 1850.
     6891   *William M.* (Delamater), b. Dec. 2, 1829.
     6892   *Silas T.* (Delamater), b. June 9, 1834.
     6893   *Ellen M.* (Delamater), b. June 1, 1836.
     6894   *Helen S.* (Delamater), b. May 23, 1840; d. March 26, 1841.
     6895   *Alonzo* (Delamater), b. Sept. 15, 1841; d. Jan. 6, 1845.
6896    Silas,[7] b. May 30, 1804; d. May 7, 1830.
6897    Caroline,[7] b. Sept. 16, 1806; n.m.; lives in Ackron, 1879.
6898    Malvira,[7] b. Dec. 20, 1809; d. in Ackron Feb. 16, 1857.
+6899   Charles Edward,[7] b. April 6, 1812; m. Susan Sweet.
6900    Abiel,[7] b. Jan. 5, 1815; m. 1852, Maria Curtis; d. Jan. 5, 1856.

## 6254

JOSHUA THURSTON[6] of Springfield, N. Y. (*Edward,[5] George,[4] Edward,[3] Jonathan,[2] Edward[1]*), brother of the preceding, and son of Edward[5] and Thankful (Main) Thurston of Springfield; born in North Stonington, Ct., Feb. 21, 1775; married, Feb. 5, 1795, BETSEY GREENE of Coventry, R. I. She died Oct. 25, 1856, aged 80; he died April 4, 1861.

Mr. Thurston was a farmer on Thurston Hill, in Springfield; served in the war of 1812, and was in the battle of Queenstown.

Their children were:

6906    Lydia,[7] b. Feb. 17, 1796; m. Dec. 10, 1816, Abraham Fish of Otsego, N. Y.; d. July 5, 1825, having had:
     6907   *Ruth* (Fish), b. in Otsego July 18, 1818; m. June 23, 1837, Dr. Justus B. Jones, M.D., of Springfield, and had:
         6908   *Justus Fletcher* (Jones), b. July 19, 1838; m. May 10, 1860, Annie M. Beatty of Rockford, Ill.
         6909   *Wesley Whitfield* (Jones), b. April 25, 1841.
         6910   *Nathalia Malentha* (Jones), b. Jan. 15, 1843; m. Dec. 25, 1867, George S. Sandercook.
         6911   *Orbie Heading* (Jones), b. Dec. 31, 1851.
         6912   *Rossinie Beatty* (Jones), b. March 21, 1858.
     6913   *Seth* (Fish), b. in Warren, N. Y., March 7, 1820; in Chicago, Ill.
     6914   *Mark* (Fish), b. in Richfield, N. Y., Sept. 25, 1821; in Oswego, N.Y.
     6915   *Luke* (Fish), b. in Richfield Oct. 31, 1823; in Janesville, Iowa.
     6916   *Ezra* (Fish), b. in Richfield May 31, 1825; in Janesville.
+6917   Linus,[7] b. Aug. 4, 1797; m. Abby Blanchard.

6918    Eliza,[7] b. July 14, 1799; m. 1st, March 2, 1823, Richard Cotton; he died
        June 16, 1826; 2d, Dec. 9, 1833. Jacob Hope.    She had, by first husband:
    6919    *Erasmus Darwin* (Cotton), b. Mar. 6, 1824; m. Dec. 10, 1846, Cynthia
            M. Colman, and had Mary Eliza, b. Dec. 2, 1847, Richard H., b.
            July 14, 1851, Ira Jamison, b. Feb. 13, 1853, d. Jan. 24, 1857, Chas.
            Jacob, b. Nov. 3, 1856, Ira Jamison Jerome, b. 1859, d., Oliver Dar-
            win, b. July 11, 1861, James Alonzo, b. Oct. 17, 1865, and Clarence
            T. (Cotton), b. Feb. 11 1869.
    6920    *Lydia Orlando* (Cotton), b. Oct. 25, 1825.
                By second husband:
    6921    *Nancy Clarinaa* (Hope), b. Feb. 20, 1835; m. April 8, 1854, George J.
            Goodman, and had Minerva A., Phydora, and Martha L. (Goodman).
    6922    *Mary Louisa* (Hope), b. Sept. 9, 1842; m. 1st, Jan. 15, 1866, Anselm
            Thayer; 2d, Alfred McRorie.
6923    Nancy,[7] b. April 23, 1802; d. July 23, 1803; buried on Thurston Hill.
6924    Nancy,[7] b. Dec. 1, 1805; m. 1st, Jan., 1836, Charles Delamater, a farmer,
        b., m., and d. in Springfield; 2d. Oct. 20, 1844, Horace Colman.   She
        died Jan. 6, 1864.    She had, by first husband:
    6925    *Ruth Augusta* (Delamater), b. Dec. 4, 1836; d. June 1, 1852.
    6926    *Matilda M.* (Delamater), b. Oct., 1838; m. July 3, 1865. Levi Walrath,
            a farmer, residing at the homestead in Springfield.   They had:
        6927    *Libbie* (Walrath), b. Oct. 19, 1866.
+6928   Silas Rawson,[7] b. July 11, 1808; m. Nancy Hart.
6929    Irenus Greene,[7] b. Apr. 23, 1810; m. Sept., 1838, Marietta Brown of York,
        N.Y.  He lived in Perry Center, N.Y., and d. Feb. 25, 1846. They had:
    6930    *Wallace Fay*,[8] b. June, 1839; d. young.
    6931    *Irena*,[8] b. 1846; d. young.
6932    Ira Jerome,[7] b. March 3. 1813; m. 1836, Adaline Eaton of Broome Co., N.
        Y.; she died Feb., 1858.   He was a nurseryman in the suburbs of Ad-
        rian, Mich., and a balloonist; he ascended from Adrian Sept. 16, 1858,
        on the occasion of a county fair, accompanied on his trip by W. D. Ban-
        nister, also a citizen of Adrian.   They had a successful send-off and
        came down a few miles away.   As the men stepped from the basket, the
        net-work peeled off the balloon and the air-ship started to rise.   They
        both seized it, and while Bannister clutched the netting, Thurston
        grasped the silk and was lifted off his feet.   While thus hanging, the
        neck of the balloon was wrapped around his legs and feet, and he was
        thus held and carried away.   The hunt for his remains was maintained
        for weeks, and thousands of people were intensely interested.   The next
        spring his remains, watch, boots, and other relics were found in a piece
        of woods in the town of Deerfield, Mich.   Children:
    6933    *Helen*,[8] b. Jan., 1838; m. Dec. 28, 1859, Bradley Miller; d. Oct., 1860.
    6934    *Orlando*,[8] b. May, 1842; d. Sept., 1848.
+6935   Cyrus,[7] b. Aug. 13, 1815; m. 1st, Mary Ann Pickens; 2d, Mrs. Nancy M.
        Holmes.
6936    Serena,[7] b. July 20, 1817; m. 1st, April, 1842, Dea. Silas Rawson of Perry,
        Wyoming Co., N. Y.; he died June 25, 1850; 2d, Jan. 23, 1853, Alpheus
        Sylvester Simmons of Perry Center; no children.

## 6256

CHARLES THURSTON[6] of Cooperstown, N. Y. (*Edward*,[5] *George*,[4]
*Edward*,[3] *Jonathan*,[2] *Edward*[1]), brother of the preceding, and son of
Edward[5] and Thankful (Main) Thurston of Springfield, N. Y.; born
in North Stonington, Ct., July 2, 1780; married, in Springfield, Dec.
5, 1805, MARGARET FISH, born in Starkville, N. Y., Oct. 21, 1786,
daughter of John Christopher and Margaret (Deusler) Fish of Dan-
ube, N. Y.   He died Dec. 2, 1870, aged 90; she died Jan. 11, 1871.

Mr. Thurston, with some of his neighbors, left home when he was
ten years old on foot, carrying his clothes and a peck of walnut meats
in a pack, and settled as a farmer in Springfield; his father came
some years after, and the locality came to be called Thurston Hill.
He removed to Cooperstown and continued farming till 1817, when

he sold, moved into the village, and followed painting and turning. He was a good mechanic; was a Free Mason, and a Universalist. She was a member of the Baptist church. Mr. Thurston was always an ardent democrat, and a true and faithful Mason, as will be seen by the following:

"At a regular communication of Otsego lodge, No. 138, F. & A. M., held at their room on Tuesday evening, Dec. 20, 1870, the following resolutions were adopted:

"Whereas, the death of our beloved brother, Charles Thurston, has been mourned in our lodge; and whereas, we have paid the last sad rites to his memory; and whereas, we have deposited over his remains the emblem of our faith in the immortality of the soul; and whereas, during the dark days of masonry, our aged and revered brother stood a landmark of the fraternity, bearing himself a masonic pyramid among the ruins of masonry in this state, around whose base the waves of anti-masonry beat and roared in vain, and around whose summit the faithful clung with hope; and whereas, he lived to see the once despised order raising itself, Phoenix-like, from its own ashes, and its members honored and revered by the great and good of the country; and whereas, he has been cut down in the fullness of his years; therefore,

"Resolved, That we, as members of the lodge whose existence our deceased brother perpetuated, when others faltered and fell back, and whose loss we now deplore, do hereby express our heart-felt sympathy with those of his family who survive him, and mingle our tears with theirs; and that the lodge shall be draped with mourning for thirty days.

"Resolved, That a copy of these resolutions be sent to the family of the deceased, and that they be published in the village papers. Theodore S. Sayles, Jerome Fish, J. A. Lynes, committee."

### Children:

+6940 Hiram,[7] b. Dec. 25, 1806; m. Luanna Simons.

6941 Bille Randall,[7] b. April 20, 1809; m. May 16, 1837, by Rev. O. Whiston, Alvira E. Bates, youngest daughter of Charles and Charity Bates of Cooperstown; she died Oct. 12, 1837; he died Nov. 30, 1841, in North Bainbridge, N. Y., where he was just perfecting himself in the art of portrait painting.

6942 Delos,[7] b. Sept. 20, 1813; d. Jan. 22, 1816, buried on Thurston Hill.

6943 Amelia Caroline,[7] b. Aug. 21, 1817; m. Aug. 22, 1851, by Rev. George W. Gates, Edmund Shattuck, of the firm of Shattuck & Co., book binders, Hartford, Ct.; he died in New York city July 19, 1859. He was of the seventh generation of his family in this country, and in his death they became extinct. He attended the Episcopal church, and was baptized in his last sickness by Rev. Ferris Tripp, and the funeral services in New York were conducted by Rev. J. F. Young, now bishop of Florida; his remains were carried to Cooperstown, and services there by Rev. S. H. Sinnott, and by E. P. Byram, master of Otsego lodge of Free Masons.

6944 Cornelia Carey,[7] April 22, 1820; m. Feb. 2, 1858, by Rev. Lot Jones, church of the Epiphany, New York, Henry Slade Walker, son of George and Hannah (Benton) Walker of Rochester, N. Y., a compositor on the Independent, New York city. They are members of the Episcopal church, and have:

  6945 *Maria Louise* (Walker), b. Oct. 21, 1861; bap. Feb. 2, 1862, in St. John's chapel, Varick street, New York city, by Rev. Sullivan H. Weston.

6946 Celia Miranda,[7] b. Dec. 25, 1826; m. Feb. 22, 1852, Nathan Wilson Cole, b. Oct. 21, 1826, son of Nathan and Nancy Cole of Little Falls, N. Y.; he commenced dry goods business in Cooperstown in 1851, and is now, 1879, a prosperous wholesale grocer, owning his residence and doing a large business. They had:

6947 *Florence Vienna* (Cole), b. Sept. 15, 1853; d. Nov. 27, 1861.

## 6298

CYRUS THURSTON[6] of Springfield, N. Y. (*Edward,*[5] *George,*[4] *Edward,*[3] *Jonathan,*[2] *Edward*[1]), brother of the preceding, and son of Edward[5] and Thankful (Main) Thurston of Springfield; born in North Stonington, Ct., March 9, 1788; married, Feb. 12, 1809, SARAH SPENCER. He died Aug. 24, 1814. She married, second, Francis Porter, and moved to Watertown, Jefferson county, N. Y., where she died, May 3, 1874.

Mr. Thurston was a farmer on Thurston Hill, in Springfield.

### Children:

+6952 Philander,[7] b. Jan. 29, 1810; m. Jane Cleveland.
6953 Achsah,[7] b. June 1, 1812; m. April 12, 1836, Oliver Anthony, a farmer at Evans Mills, Jefferson county, N. Y., and had:
6954 *Francis Porter* (Anthony), b. Jan. 15, 1841.
6955 *Sarah Ettie* (Anthony), b. Oct. 5, 1843; d. Jan. 14, 1867.

## 6305

JEREMIAH THURSTON[6] of Hopkinton, R. I. (*George,*[5] *George,*[4] *Edward,*[3] *Jonathan,*[2] *Edward*[1]), eldest son of George[5] and Dolly (Cottrell) Thurston of Hopkinton; born there May 29, 1768; married, March 1, 1801, SARAH BABCOCK, daughter of Rowse Babcock of Westerly, R. I. He died March 21, 1830; she died Feb. 27, 1841, aged 59.

Mr. Thurston was a successful merchant and was lieutenant-governor of Rhode Island in 1816.

### Their children were:

6960 Eliza Rathbone,[7] b. Jan. 26, 1802; m. Nov. 1, 1824, Courtland Palmer, a merchant of New York city, b. in Stonington, Ct.; he commenced life as a barefooted boy; had great energy and business tact, which, united with an affable manner, enabled him to work his way up to a millionaire. She died Sept. 27, 1827; he died 1875; no children.
+6961 Benjamin Babcock,[7] b. June 29, 1804; m. 1st, Harriet Elizabeth Deshon; 2d, Frances Elizabeth Deshon.
6962 Horace,[7] b. July 21, 1806; d. Aug. 21, 1812.
6963 Mary Ann,[7] b. Jan. 7, 1809; m. Sept., 1830, Asa Potter, b. at Rhinebeck, N. Y., Oct. 13, 1802, son of Asa Potter, formerly of South Kingston, R. I., afterward of Rhinebeck, where he died. He graduated from Brown university 1824, studied law in the office of Hon. John Whipple in Providence, R. I., and afterward at Judge Gould's law school in Litchfield, Ct.; admitted to practice in Rhode Island in 1827; went to New York and was in business under the firm name of Brown, Potter & Co.; returned to Rhode Island and was secretary of state three years, 1851–3. She died Dec. 25, 1857; he died Oct. 11, 1872. They had:
6964 *Eliza Palmer* (Potter), m. her cousin, Maj. James B. M. Potter, paymaster U. S. A., stationed at San Francisco, 1879.
6965 *Sarah Thurston* (Potter), m. George T. Rice of Worcester, Mass.; d. Dec. 29, 1862, leaving one daughter.
6966 *Carrol Hagadorn* (Potter), b. Oct. 25, 1838; captain U. S. A.
6967 Caroline,[7] b. March 13, 1812; m. Mar. 15, 1832, Dr. Wm. Torry Thurston [see no. 6639].
+6968 Franklin,[7] } twins, born } m. 1st, Laura M. Hawley; 2d, Margaret Reece.
+6969 Horace,[7] } Mar. 4, 1814; } m. Caroline Louisa Quimby.

## 6307

NATHANIEL THURSTON[6] of Exeter, R. I. (*George,*[5] *George,*[4] *Edward,*[3] *Jonathan,*[2] *Edward*[1]), brother of the preceding, and son of George[5] and Dolly (Cottrell) Thurston of Hopkinton, R. I.; born there July 16, 1772; married, Feb. 12, 1795, MARY WHITMAN. He died Apr. 14, 1824; she died Apr. 22, 1859, aged 84. He was a saddler.

Their children were:

+6975 Whitman,[7] b. Oct. 22, 1795; m. Elizabeth Phillips.
6976 Deborah,[7] b. Feb. 1, 1797; m. March 12, 1815, Stephen Dexter of Exeter, and after of Oswego, N. Y. They had:
 6977 *Horace* (Dexter), b. Jan. 22, 1816; m. Martha Cotton, of Starkey, N. Y., and had Josephene and Harriette (Dexter).
 6978 *Francis B.* (Dexter), b. Oct. 26, 1817; m. April 11, 1849, Adelia Anderson of Owego, N. Y.; one child, Edwin (Dexter).
 6979 *Harriet* (Dexter), b. May 16, 1819; m. Oct. 28, 1841, Frederick Parmele. They had:
  6980 *Charles Frederick* (Parmele), b. Oct. 11, 1842.
  6981 *Stephen R.* (Parmele), b. March 31, 1844.
  6982 *Ella* (Parmele), b. July 5, 1849; d. Sept. 15, 1854.
  6983 *George D.* (Parmele), b. Feb. 12, 1854.
 6984 *Nathaniel Thurston* (Dexter), b. March 30, 1821; m. 1st, Feb. 6, 1850, Harriet Thurston [see no. 7822]; she died April 8, 1857; 2d, 1867, Sarah Farnham, and had Fanny Thurston (Dexter), b. 1869.
 6985 *Alfred* (Dexter), b. Dec. 29, 1823; d. Dec. 30, 1824.
 6986 *Anna Thurston* (Dexter), b. June 24, 1826; m. July 12, 1849, Charles L. Truman; he was killed in battle Sept. 20, 1863, leaving Asa H., b. Aug. 1, 1850, and Catherine (Truman), b. Jan. 2, 1852.
 6987 *Mary Whitman* (Dexter), b. May 26, 1828.
 6988 *Abby A.* (Dexter), b. Aug. 10, 1830; m. 1866, Theodore Coddington.
 6989 *George* (Dexter), b. Aug. 26, 1834; m. 1st, Nov. 27, 1855, Priscilla Nelson; she died Nov. 8, 1865; 2d, Sept. 12, 1866, Cornelia Bicknell. He had, by first wife, Everett (Dexter), b. Aug. 12, 1858.
6990 George N.,[7] b. July 5, 1799; m. Dec. 25, 1821, Sarah Reynolds. They lived in Exeter; he died Sept. 11, 1832. They had:
 6991 *Alfred,*[8] d. in infancy.
 6992 *Mercy Mary,*[8] d. in infancy.
 6993 *Linzey,*[8] d. in infancy.
6994 Harriet,[7] b. April 29, 1801; d. May 5, 1801.
6995 Abby A.,[7] b. June 26, 1802; m. June 17, 1821, Albert Sherman of Aurora, Ill. They had:
 6996 *Abby F.* (Sherman), m. Frederick Goodrich.
 6997 *Albert* (Sherman), m. Sarah Farnham.
 6998 *Susan* (Sherman), m. Osborn Parmele.
 6999 *Ann E.* (Sherman), m. Alonzo David.
 7000 *Maria* (Sherman), m. —— Wade.
 7001 *Emmeline* (Sherman), m. Cornelius Taylor.
 7002 *Adelaide* (Sherman), m. —— Miller.
7003 Sands,[7] d. young.
7004 Mary Ann,[7] b. Feb. 12, 1810; d. June 19, 1810.
7005 Alfred,[7] b. May 25, 1811; m. 1830, Amy Wilcox. He lived in Exeter, and died 1868. They had:
 7006 *Mary Frances,*[8] b. 1831; m. Sept. 8, 1851, Job T. Stanton of Newport, R. I.; d. Sept. 28, 1866, having had:
  7007 *Nathan F.* (Stanton), b. Jan. 31, 1856.
  7008 *Walter* (Stanton), b. Nov. 1, 1857.
7009 Edwin R.,[7] b. June 20, 1812; m. Sarah Gurley; d. in Indiana Oct. 3, 1850; no children.

## 6328

BENJAMIN TAYLOR THURSTON[6] of Norwich, Ct. (*Gardner,*[5] *George,*[4] *Edward,*[3] *Jonathan,*[2] *Edward*[1]), eldest son of Gardner[5] and Lydia (Taylor) Thurston of Hopkinton, R. I.; born there Aug. 29, 1787;

married, Nov. 28, 1811, MARY BUTTON. He died March 29, 1847;
she died Jan. 10, 1856, aged 66. Mr. Thurston was a farmer.

Their children were :

7014   Abby Hazard.[7] b. Aug. 23, 1814; m. Oct. 3, 1832, John Brown Clark, an
       extensive farmer in Norwich, but for several years past retired and liv-
       ing independently.  She died Nov. 21, 1865, having had :
       7015   *John Thurston* (Clark), b. Dec. 12, 1839.
7016   Joseph Taylor,[7] b. in Preston, Ct., Jan. 22, 1816; m. in Newark, N. J.,
       April 10, 1854, Elizabeth Sly, b. in Lisbon, Ct., May 19, 1822, daughter
       of John and Mary (Mowry) Sly of Norwich.  He was a prominent busi-
       ness man and a successful teacher in the public schools; d. Jan. 11, 1865.
       They had:
       7017   *Josephene*,[8] b. in Norwich May 28, 1855.
7018   Mary Ann,[7] b. Dec. 6, 1817; m. Dec. 31, 1836, Charles Pendleton Bennett,
       a farmer in Ohio; she d. 1875, and has a daughter residing in Warren,
       Ohio.  Children:
       7019   *Abby L.* (Bennett), b. Oct. 1, 1837.
       7020   *Lydia M.* (Bennett), b. March 8, 1845.
       7021   *Ella H.* (Bennett), b. April 4, 1850.
       7022   *Charlieana* (Bennett), b. Feb. 10, 1856.
7023   Harriet Kinney.[7] b. Feb. 4, 1820; m. Nov. 20, 1848, Francis Gates Brown,
       b. Oct. 27, 1810, son of Asahel and Lucia (Gates) Brown of Colchester,
       Ct., a farmer in Norwich.  Children:
       7024   *Frank Thurston* (Brown), b. Feb. 27, 1853; graduated from Yale 1872;
              a lawyer in Norwich.
       7025   *Charles Sumner* (Brown), b. Aug. 1, 1856; a farmer in Norwich.
       7026   *Oliver Winslow* (Brown), b. March 7, 1859; graduated from Yale 1878;
              a student at law in Norwich.
7027   Lydia Button,[7] b. Sept. 6, 1823; m. Dec. 2, 1846, Abel Rathbone, b. Mar.
       30, 1810, son of Abel and Alice (Brown) Rathbone of Colchester; he is
       a farmer in Norwich; has been state representative three sessions, school
       visitor, and justice of the peace.  Children:
       7028   *Mary Alice* (Rathbone), b. Nov. 8, 1850; m. Oct. 28, 1875, Joseph
              Clifford Hendrix, graduated from Cornell university 1873, and is fol-
              lowing the profession of journalism, residence Brooklyn, N. Y.
       7029   *John Fuller* (Rathbone), b. Aug. 30, 1852; graduated from Cornell
              university 1876; city editor of Morning Bulletin, Norwich.
       7030   *Caroline Louise* (Rathbone), b. Nov. 17, 1854; d. Dec., 1877.
       7031   *Jennie Sophia* (Rathbone), b. Sept. 8, 1863; n.m. ; resides in Norwich.
7032   Lucy Caroline,[7] b. March 8, 1825; m. Nov. 4, 1849, Leonard Hendee Ches-
       ter, a merchant in Buffalo, N. Y., b. Oct. 1, 1825, son of Joseph and
       Prudee (Tracy) Chester of Norwich; he is councilman, member of board
       of education, and vestryman in the Episcopal church.  Children:
       7033   *Carl Thurston* (Chester), b. in Norwich Aug. 1, 1853; A.B. Yale 1875,
              LL.B. Columbia 1877; a lawyer in Buffalo.
       7034   *Arthur Thurston* (Chester), b. in Norwich April 9, 1857; d. Aug. 2,
              1857.

## 6329

ROBERT THURSTON [6] of Livonia Center, N. Y. (*Gardner*,[5] *George*,[4]
*Edward*,[3] *Jonathan*,[2] *Edward*[1]), brother of the preceding, and son of
Gardner[5] and Lydia (Taylor) Thurston of Hopkinton, R. I.; born
there April 5, 1790; married, in Livonia, Nov. 25, 1825, ELIZA HAN-
NAHS, born in Bethlehem, Ct., Jan. 25, 1805, daughter of David and
Susan (Sanford) Hannahs.  Mr. Thurston was a harness maker.

Children :

+7040   George Gardner,[7] b. April 2, 1827; m. Abigail Almira Fairchild.
+7041   Henry David,[7] b. Sept. 25, 1828; m. Frances Adams.
 7042   Mary Eliza,[7] b. April 13, 1831; d. Aug. 14, 1856.

## 6358

JEREMIAH THURSTON[6] of Hartford, Ct. (*Gardner*,[5] *George*,[4] *Edward*,[3] *Jonathan*,[2] *Edward*[1]), brother of the preceding, and son of Gardner[5] and Lydia (Taylor) Thurston of Hopkinton, R. I.; born there Oct. 17, 1797; married, Oct. 9, 1822, MARIA SOUTHWORTH. He died March 8, 1852; she died Oct. 23, 1867, aged 66.

Mr. Thurston was a manufacturer in Norwich, Ct., many years; subsequently moved to Hartford.

Children:

7047　George,[7] b. Feb. 19, 1824; m. July 25, 1855, Mary F. Weir of Glastenbury,
　　　　Ct., where he resides; no children.
7048　Mary Maria,[7] b. May 1, 1825: m. Oct. 27, 1851, George Weir; no children.
7049　William,[7] b. June 14, 1828; m. July 12, 1852, Maria Gladding; d. Aug. 25,
　　　　1859, leaving:
　　　　7050　*Adia*,[8] b. Aug. 9, 1858.
7051　Charles,[7] b. July 5, 1829; m. Mar. 18, 1863, Melissa L. Evarts; no children.
7052　Elizabeth,[7] b. June 27, 1831; m. April 6, 1848, Nathaniel Taylor of Hart-
　　　　ford. They have:
　　　　7053　*George N.* (Taylor), b. Nov. 17, 1850.
7054　Jane,[7] b. June 3, 1834; m. Sept. 30, 1853, Geo. Smith; d. Nov. 23, 1861,
　　　　leaving:
　　　　7055　*Mary* (Smith), b. July 24, 1854.
+7056　Albert,[7] b. Sept. 17, 1837; m. Catharine M. Johnson.
7057　Martin,[7] b. April 6, 1839; m. Feb. 16, 1863, Honore B. Granius; they re-
　　　　side in Weathersfield, Ct.
7058　Martha A.,[7] b. Dec. 22, 1840; m. June 5, 1859, Charles Russell; d. Oct. 19,
　　　　1865, leaving:
　　　　7059　*Minnie* (Russell), b. Jan. 10, 1860.
　　　　7060　*Nellie* (Russell), b. Jan. 17, 1862.

## 6362

ICHABOD THURSTON[6] of Mount Morris, N. Y. (*Gardner*,[5] *George*,[4] *Edward*,[3] *Jonathan*,[2] *Edward*[1]), brother of the preceding, and son of Gardner[5] and Lydia (Taylor) Thurston of Hopkinton, R. I.; born there Sept. 27, 1802; married, Sept. 26, 1829, SARAH B. SPINK. He died Sept. 12, 1870; was a harness maker.

Children:

7065　William R.,[7] b. Aug. 27, 1830.
7066　Robert Henry,[7] b. Oct. 18, 1834; m. Jan. 18, 1869, Ada B. Maher of Chi-
　　　　cago, Ill.

## 6363

WILLIAM THURSTON[5] of Livonia, N. Y. (*Gardner*,[5] *George*,[4] *Edward*,[3] *Jonathan*,[2] *Edward*[1]), brother of the preceding, and son of Gardner[5] and Lydia (Taylor) Thurston of Hopkinton, R. I.; born there March 23, 1805; married, March 7, 1833, ABBY HANNAHS. He died Sept. 20, 1857; was a harness maker.

Children:

7070　Ellen Eliza,[7] b. Dec. 7, 1833; m. Oct. 16, 1855, Lemuel Gibbs, a farmer of
　　　　Litchfield, Hillsdale Co., Mich. They have:
　　　　7071　*Marietta D.* (Gibbs), b. July 22, 1865.
　　　　7072　*William Thurston* (Gibbs), b. April 19, 1867.
7073　John Barton,[7] b. Sept. 26, 1835; m. Sept. 20, 1858, Martha A. McPherson
　　　　of Livonia; is cashier of a bank. They have:
　　　　7074　*William*,[8] b. March 25, 1870.
+7075　Dudley Sullivan,[7] b. Jan. 27, 1839; m. Sarah Emily Wiggin.

## 6372

Job Thurston[6] of East Greenwich, R. I. (*Joseph,[5] George,[4] Edward,[3] Jonathan,[2] Edward[1]*), third child of Joseph[5] and Sarah (Taylor) Thurston of Hopkinton, R. I.; married, May 15, 1807, Susanna Andrews, daughter of Capt. Jonathan and Susanna Andrews of revolutionary memory of East Greenwich. He died Sept. 23, 1819; she died June 19, 1820.

Mr. Thurston was a prosperous grocer. The children were taken by their maternal grandparents. His will was proved Oct. 21, 1819.

### Children:

+7080  William Andrews,[7] b. Dec. 29, 1808; m. Una Lay Pratt.
7081  Sarah Perry,[7] b. in Newport, R. I., Aug. 27, 1810; d. in East Greenwich Jan. 24, 1829.
7082  Phebe Langworthy,[7] b. Aug. 6, 1812; m. in Coventry, R. I., Jan. 26, 1837, John Hanckins Hart, b. on Warwick Neck, R. I., May 26, 1814; went to Iowa as a farmer in 1839. She died at Pleasant Ridge, Lee Co., Iowa, May 12, 1851; he d. at Butler, DeKalb Co., Ind., Sept. 13, 1870. Children :
7083  *Jane Frances* (Hart), b. in E. Greenwich Nov. 22, 1837; graduated from Denmark academy June, 1865; m. Aug. 10, 1866, Robert C. Henry, b. Dec. 4, 1841, a lawyer of Iowa City, Iowa; he was in the army against the rebellion two years; in 1878 was chosen district judge of the eighth district of Iowa. She is a member of the Baptist church. They reside in Mount Ayer, Ringold Co., and have :
7084  *Lorin Lane* (Henry), b. April 28, 1868.
7085  *Iowa Ines* (Henry), b. Sept. 7, 1870.
7086  *Mary Mabel* (Henry), b. Aug. 24, 1872.
7087  *Jennie June* (Henry), b. July 19, 1874.
7088  *Baby* (Henry), b. Nov. 8, 1878.
7089  *Thomas Henry* (Hart), b. in East Greenwich April 4, 1839; served out three enlistments in the war against the rebellion, as private, corporal, sergeant, and veteran; m. June, 1864, Emily Hill; she died April, 1871, having had :
7090  *Susan Luna* (Hart), b. April, 1867.
7091  *Phebe* (Hart), b. Feb., 1869.
7092  *Charles* (Hart), b. July, 1870.
Born at Pleasant Ridge, Iowa :
7093  *Ray Sans* (Hart), b. Aug. 30, 1841; served three years in 1st Iowa cavalry against the rebellion; m. Oct. 7, 1878, Celia Stiles; is a farmer in Denmark, Iowa.
7094  *George A.* (Hart), b. March 26, 1843; served one year in 1st Iowa cavalry against the rebellion; is a carriage and wagon builder and blacksmith in Denmark; m. at Fort Madison, Iowa, Oct. 1, 1867, Leonora Cynthia Burton, b. at Glover, Vt., Feb. 24, 1845.  They have :
7095  *Glen Thurston* (Hart), b. Nov. 1, 1869.
7096  *Dorr* (Hart), b. May 23, 1873.
7097  *George Emmet* (Hart), b. March 28, 1875.
7098  *Nellie* (Hart), b. Sept. 14, 1878.
7099  *John Thurston* (Hart), b. Jan. 5, 1845; was in the 41st Missouri regiment, and died in hospital at St. Louis Oct. 12, 1864; a Baptist.
7100  *Ariadne* (Hart), b. Sept. 28, 1846; m. Oct. 4, 1868, Timothy Fox Whitmarsh, a farmer near Denmark, and has John, b. Nov. 24, 1869, and Ariadne (Whitmarsh), b. May 16, 1878.
7101  *Lorin* (Hart), b. March 12, 1848; served one year in the war against the rebellion, and is a farmer in Minnesota.
7102  *Lewis* (Hart), b. May 4, 1851; d. Aug. 26, 1851.
7103  Mary Greene,[7] b. Dec. 29, 1814; m. in Whitehall, Mass., Dec. 1, 1836, Rev. William Perkins Apthorp, b. in Quincy, Mass., March 23, 1806; he graduated from Yale 1829, studied at Andover two years, and graduated from Princeton 1832; preached for a Presbyterian church in Raleigh, N. C., a few months; after marriage went to Fort Madison and Denmark a

few months, and then took charge of a branch of the Mission Institute, founded by the late Dr. Nelson, at Quincy, Ill., for ten years; spent most of his life in the West till Dec., 1869, when he went to Tallahassee, Fla., where he now resides, 1879. She died at Port Byron, Ill., Dec. 15, 1852, a lovely woman of devoted piety. They had:

7104 *William Lee* (Apthorp), b. in Lee Co., Iowa, Aug. 31, 1837; graduated from Amherst 1859; enlisted in the war against the rebellion in 1861 was promoted to be a corporal, sergeant, captain of a colored company, and lieutenant-colonel. He m. at Beaufort, S. C., while in the army, Charlotte Childs, b. at Eton, Eng., Mar. 27, 1843. After the war he was stationed at St. Johns river, Fla., as Bureau agent, and after at Tampa in same capacity. From 1869 to 1877 was chief clerk in the surveyor general's office at Tallahassee, when he removed to a farm in Springfield, N. Y. Children:

7105   *Charlotte Elizabeth* (Apthorp), b. in Iowa City July 11, 1866; d. at Tampa Aug. 26, 1866.
7106   *Emma Matilda* (Apthorp), b. at Tampa Dec. 14, 1867.
7107   *George Henry* (Apthorp), b. at Staten Island, N.Y., Dec. 26, 1871.
7108   *Ellen Wentworth* (Apthorp), b. at Tallahassee Feb. 8, 1875.
7109   *Grace* (Apthorp), b. at Staten Island July 31, 1876.

Born in Adams county, Ill.:

7110 *John Perkins* (Apthorp), b. Sept. 7, 1839; graduated from Amherst 1861; taught the academy in Conway, Mass.; enlisted in the war against the rebellion, and after the war closed taught again in Massachusetts; went to Jacksonville, Fla., and taught a while, then to Tallahassee in 1871, where he was appointed county superintendent of schools and county surveyor. In 1873 was m. in Ipswich, Mass., to Ellen Osgood of Fryeburgh, Me. Children, b. in Tallahassee:

7111   *Frederick George* (Apthorp), b. Feb. 18, 1874; d. Sept. 27, 1874.
7112   *Mary* (Apthorp), b. April 3, 1877.
7113   *Annie Osgood* (Apthorp), b. Feb. 22, 1878.

7114 *George Henry* (Apthorp), b. Aug. 9, 1841; enlisted in the war against the rebellion; was 1st lieutenant in a company of colored troups, and was killed in a charge on the enemy near Decatur, Ala., Oct. 29, 1864. His captain says: "His men almost worshiped him, and he was much endeared by his companionable and christian qualities to his brother officers and to all who knew him." His body was sent home and buried at Port Byron, near his mother.

7115 *Anna Wentworth* (Apthorp), b. Nov. 19, 1843; with her father in Florida.
7116 *Mary Elizabeth* (Apthorp), b. Oct. 26, 1846; attended a course at Iowa college, Grinnell, and at Iowa university in Iowa City, where she is a teacher.

7117 Elizabeth Arnold,[7] b. Oct. 12, 1816; d. Oct. 12, 1818.
7118 Charles Job,[7] b. Sept. 9, 1818; m. April 15, 1844, Anstis Adalaid Seymour, b. Oct. 25, 1821, daughter of Dyer and Ellinor (Wilcox) Seymour of Batavia, N. Y. He is a sign and carriage painter, with no particular abiding place. They have:

7119   *Emma Jennette,*[8] b. Sept. 13, 1846; m. Henry Wilson of Chicago, Ill.

## 6373

JOHN TAYLOR THURSTON [6] of Westerly, R. I. (*Joseph,*[5] *George,*[4] *Edward,*[3] *Jonathan,*[2] *Edward*[1]), brother of the preceding, and son of Joseph [5] and Sarah (Taylor) Thurston of Hopkinton, R. I.; born there April 21, 1782; married, May 1, 1803, MRS. HANNAH REYNOLDS, widow of Amon Reynolds and daughter of Thomas Clarke of Stonington, Ct. She died April 11, 1840, aged 67; he died Dec. 26, 1860, aged 78.

Their children were:

7125 Lucetta,[7] b. March 29, 1805; m. July, 1822, John Wilcox Spicer; d. Sept. 23, 1850, having had:

7126   *Thomas P.* (Spicer), b. July 27, 1823; m. Sept., 1847, Sarah A. Gavitt.
7127   *John Thurston* (Spicer), b. Oct. 7, 1825; d. Oct. 9, 1825.

7128   *John Thurston* (Spicer), b. Sept. 3, 1827; d. July 3, 1828.
7129   *Hannah E.* (Spicer), b. May 15, 1829; m. March 29, 1867, Henry H.
       Barnes.
7130   *Harriet M.* (Spicer), b. Dec. 26, 1831; d. Sept. 23, 1847.
       Son, b. Aug. 4, d. Aug. 12, 1834.
7131   *Benjamin Reynolds* (Spicer), b. Nov. 23, 1835.
7132   *Ellen W.* (Spicer), b. May 11, 1838; d. Jan. 7, 1858.
7133   *Ann B.* (Spicer), b. Nov. 8, 1841; m. Jan. 25, 1859, John C. Lang-
       worthy; d. Oct. 11, 1861.
7134   *Joseph Thurston* (Spicer), b. Nov. 27, 1844; m. 1866, H. Maria Barber.
+7135  John Clarke,[7] b. June 26, 1808; m. Mary Leeds Miller.
7136   Hannah,[7] b. March 8, 1811; m. Oct. 19, 1835, Nelson Brown, and had:
       7137   *Sarah Babcock* (Brown), b. Jan. 7, 1837; m. Mar. 31, 1869, William G.
              Davis.
       7138   *Hannah Thurston* (Brown), b. Aug. 10, 1840; m. Aug. 17, 1864, Jud-
              son B. Slocumb.
       7139   *Albert Nelson* (Brown), b. April 8, 1843; m. Dec. 2, 1868, Elizabeth
              M. Lewis.
       7140   *Mary Elizabeth* (Brown), b. Dec. 31, 1845.

## 6376

PELEG GRINALD THURSTON[6] of Johnston, R. I. (*Joseph,[5] George,[4]
Edward,[3] Jonathan,[2] Edward[1]*), brother of the preceding, and son of
Joseph[5] and Sarah (Taylor) Thurston of Hopkinton, R. I.; born in
Westerly, R. I., April 1, 1788; married, first, June 13, 1810, ROBY
ANDREWS, sister to his brother Job's wife; she died Jan. 23, 1815.
Second, Sept. 18, 1817, ANN YORK, born Aug. 16, 1790, daughter of
William York of Westerly. He died July 12, 1862, aged 74; she
died in North Providence, R. I., April 28, 1873.

Mr. Thurston was an overseer of weaving, justice of the peace, and
member of the Baptist church.

His children, by first wife, Roby, were:

7145   Joseph,[7] b. in Warwick, R. I., Jan. 4, 1812; m. Penelope Northup; died
       from injuries received by catching his foot in some gearing, July 31, 1838;
       no children.
7146   Charles Andrews,[7] b. in East Greenwich, R. I., Dec. 29, 1813; d. April 16,
       1814.
7147   Julia Ann,[7] b. in East Greenwich June 7, 1815; d. Oct. 20, 1817.

By second wife, Ann, born in Westerly:

7148   Charles,[7] b. Dec. 7, 1819; d. Jan. 20, 1820.
+7149  Augustus York,[7] b. April 20, 1821; m. 1st, Julia Maria Angell; 2d, Lydia
       Bacon Potter.
7150   Sarah Ann,[7] b. Sept. 29, 1822; m. 1st, Jan. 3, 1847, Wm. Angell Sweet of
       Johnston, a carpenter, and deacon of the Baptist church, son of Philip
       Angell and Ruth (Angell) Sweet of Johnston; 2d, Jan. 21, 1853, Philip
       Angell Sweet, b. Sept. 5, 1816, brother of her first husband, a carpenter,
       and deacon of the Baptist church. She died in Providence, R. I., July
       23, 1873, having had:
       7151   *Alfred Franklin* (Sweet), b. Dec. 15, 1847; d. March 11, 1848.
       7152   *Ellen Medora* (Sweet), b. in No. Providence Feb. 20, 1858; m. Aug. 25,
              1874, Louis L. Inman, son of Dennis and Hannah Inman of Burrill-
              ville, R. I.
7153   Stephen York,[7] b. in Stonington, Ct., Jan. 7, 1824; m. Oct. 15, 1846, Mary
       Lapham Coe, b. Oct. 20, 1824, daughter of Alden and Lydia (Taft) Coe
       of Woonsockett, R. I. He is a machinist, and member of the Baptist
       church in Providence. She died June 26, 1873, aged 48, having had:
       7154   *Walter Alden,[8]* b. in Woonsockett April 22, 1849; d. April 8, 1864.
       7155   *Ida Frances,[8]* b. in Johnston March 9, 1857.

7156   William,[7] b. in Canterbury, Ct., June 14, 1826; d. April 25, 1827.
7157   Hannah Maria,[7] b. Oct. 9, 1827; m. June 29, 1854, John Butler Lawton, b.
       March 18, 1816, son of Isaac and Abigail (Fink) Lawton of Newport, R.
       I.; he is a ship master of North Providence.   Children:
    7158   *Charles Herbert* (Lawton), b. Aug. 13, 1858; m. Jan. 1, 1877, Ida
           Frances Wilbur.
    7159   *Adeliza* (Lawton), b. in Johnston May 29, 1864; d. Oct. 31, 1866.
7160   John Taylor,[7] b. in Griswold, Ct., Oct. 17, 1829; m. Sept. 11, 1858, Phebe
       Ann Mathewson, b. Feb. 1, 1833, daughter of Parish Mathewson of
       Johnston.   Children:
    7161   *Cora Estelle*,[8] b. July 20, 1861.
    7162   *Phebe Mathewson*,[8] b. March 24, 1868; d. April 5, 1868.
    7163   *John Howard*,[8] b. Oct. 30, 1869; d. Nov. 14, 1869.
    7164   *Gertrude Mathewson*,[8] b. Aug. 8, 1871.
7165   William C.,[7] b. at Central Falls, R. I., March 7, 1834; m. Nov. 28, 1851,
       Adeliza Jillson; resided in Providence. She died Sept. 29, 1861; he
       died Jan. 2, 1865.

## 6377

GEORGE THURSTON[6] of Charlestown, R. I. (*Joseph*,[5] *George*,[4] *Edward*,[3] *Jonathan*,[2] *Edward*[1]), brother of the preceding, and son of Joseph[5] and Sarah (Taylor) Thurston of Hopkinton, R. I.; born there Aug. 28, 1790; married, first, 1815, ARTEMISSIA SAUNDERS, born May 14, 1796, daughter of Nathan and Sarah (Taylor) Saunders of Charlestown; she died May 13, 1828.   Second, 1828, MRS. SUSAN (GAVITT) BROWNING, born June 9, 1797, daughter of Sanford and Hannah (Berry) Gavitt of Westerly, R. I.   He died June, 1838; she died Sept. 19, 1854.

Mr. Thurston was a justice of the peace and representative to the General Assembly.

His children, by first wife, Artemissia, were:

7170   Susan,[7] b. March 13, 1816; m. Nov. 20, 1833, Gordon Hazard Hoxie, b.
       March 24, 1813, son of Hazard and Chloe (Bailey) Hoxie of Charles-
       town; he was a farmer and representative to the General Assembly from
       Charlestown.   They had:
    7171   *Gordon Hazard* (Hoxie), b. April 16, 1835; d. Jan. 17, 1836.
    7172   *Mary Lee* (Hoxie), b. Jan. 30, 1837; m. June 26, 1867, Caleb H. Ben-
           nett.
    7173   *Susan Thurston* (Hoxie), b. Dec. 28, 1838; m. Nov. 12, 1861, William
           H. Kenyon.
    7174   *George Hazard* (Hoxie), b. June 20, 1842; m. Dec. 11, 1861, Mary P.
           Ward; d. in Charlestown May 10, 1876.
    7175   *Willie* (Hoxie), b. July 10, 1843; d. Sept. 29, 1843.
7176   George Perry,[7] b. Jan. 8, 1818; m. 1848, Mrs. Sarah (Clark) Baldwin of
       New York.   He was a bookkeeper in New York and died in Brooklyn,
       Ct., Nov. 9, 1849; she died Feb., 1852.   They had:
    7177   *Artemissia Saunders*,[8] b. Sept., 1849; d. June 23, 1851.
7178   Rhoda Earl,[7] d. in infancy.
7179   Rhoda Earl,[7] b. June 15, 1821; m. Jan. 14, 1841, David Mather Chapin, b.
       in Chicopee, Mass., then part of Springfield, Feb. 29, 1815, an optician
       in Springfield, deacon of the Baptist church, son of Herman and Phena
       (Chapin) Chapin.   They had:
    7180   *George Herman* (Chapin), b. in Plainfield, Ct., July 6, 1844; d. June,
           1851.
    7181   *Carrie Bard* (Chapin), b. in Brooklyn, Ct., Aug. 9, 1858.
7182   Nathan Saunders,[7] b. May 16, 1823; went to California when a young man
       and was traced till 1875, since which time nothing has been learned of
       him.
7183   Joseph,[7] d. in infancy.
7184   Matilda Saunders,[7] d. in infancy.
    21

7185  Artemissia Saunders,[7] b. March 13, 1828; m. May 30, 1848, Rev. Joseph
       Prentice Brown, a Baptist clergyman, b. Oct. 27, 1820, son of Henry and
       Lucy (Prentice) Brown of Waterford, Ct., now, 1879, located in New
       London, Ct. She d. Mar. 13, 1858, and he m. 2d, Susan Gavitt. She had :
       7186  *Jennie Eliza* (Brown), b. in Plainfield, Ct., Oct. 18, 1852.

                    By second wife, Susan :
7187  Ann Eliza,[7] b. July 10, 1829; m. Jan. 10, 1854, Rev. Oliver W. Pollard, a
       dealer in hardware and lumber in Dwight, Ill., b. March 18, 1831, son of
       Ezra Pollard of East Greenwich, R. I.; he is a Methodist clergyman,
       though not actively engaged as such now, 1879.  They had :
       7188  *Artemissia F.* (Pollard), b. in Weathersfield, Ill., Sept., 1855; m. June
              14, 1876, H. E. Dow.
7189  Sarah Jane,[7] b. March 4, 1831; m. Oct. 8, 1855, Hartwell Hooker Blanch-
       ard of North Attleborough, Mass., b. in South Cambridge, Mass., Dec. 5,
       1821, son of Isaac and Lucretia (Knight) Blanchard of Attleborough.
       Children :
       7190  *Jennie Thurston* (Blanchard), b. June 7, 1857.
       7191  *Hattie Earl* (Blanchard), b. Aug. 7, 1858.
       7192  *Nellie Louise* (Blanchard), b. Oct. 21, 1867.
7193  William Henry,[7] d. in his second year.
7194  Abigail Knowles,[7] d. in her fourth year.

## 6378

CLARKE THURSTON [6] of Hopkinton, R. I. (*Joseph,*[5] *George,*[4] *Edward,*[3] *Jonathan,*[2] *Edward*[1]), brother of the preceding, and son of
Joseph [5] and Sarah (Taylor) Thurston of Hopkinton ; born there
about 1791 ; married, Jan. 7, 1816, ABBY REYNOLDS, born in Newport, R. I., Dec. 20, 1794, daughter of Amon and Hannah (Clarke)
Reynolds. He was a machinist ; died in Providence, R. I., May 21,
1832, aged 42.

                    Children :
7200  Sarah Reynolds,[7] b. June 2, 1817; m. Sept. 7, 1835, John Deey; he died
       Sept. 25, 1854, aged 37.  They had :
       7201  *Daughter,* b. May 20, 1838; d. same day.
       7202  *William H.* (Deey), b. March 4, 1841; d. Aug. 5, 1841.
+7203  Benjamin Reynolds,[7] b. March 31, 1819; m. 1st, Elizabeth Harwood Mar-
       ble; 2d, Laura Henley; 3d, Lucy Paine.
+7204  Amon Reynolds,[7] b. Sept. 16, 1820; m. Sarah Ann Garland.
7205  Horatio Nelson,[7] b. in Phenix, R. I., Sept. 10, 1823; d. Sept. 8, 1824.
7206  Levi Wheaton,[7] b. in Phenix Oct. 29, 1824; d. July 12, 1825.
7207  Ann Frances Deshon,[7] b. in Phenix July 24, 1826; m. Dec. 2, 1847, Samuel
       Highland, an engraver of Cranston, R. I., b. Nov. 12, 1824, son of Jacob
       and Martha (Colwell) Highland of Smithfield, R. I.   Children, born in
       Providence :
       7208  *Eliza Ross* (Highland), b. June 1, 1848; m. Nov. 10, 1867, Thomas
              Leavitt Stone, and had Annie F. (Stone), b. Nov. 23, 1868.
       7209  *Edwin Clarke* (Highland),  )  twins, born  )  d. March 7, 1850.
       7210  *Edward Jacob* (Highland),  )  Jan. 15, 1850;  )  m. Mrs. Almira (Brayton)
              Arnold.
       7211  *Ada Louise* (Highland), b. Aug. 12, 1853.
                    Born in Cranston :
       7212  *Herbert Clarke* (Highland), b. Jan. 15, 1858; d. Nov. 26, 1863.
       7213  *Walter Clarence* (Highland), b. Aug. 3, 1860.
7214  William Ellery,[7] b. in Pawtucket, R. I., July 4, 1828; m. 1st, Jane Francis;
       2d, Dec. 2, 1854, Mary S. Cady; 3d, Oct. 8, 1857, Susan P. Phillips.
       He was a machinist and died in Providence Sept. 30, 1876.   Child :
       7215  *Sarah Elizabeth,*[8] b. Oct. 30, 1860; d. Feb. 5, 1865.
+7216  Ellis Burgess Pitcher,[7] b. May 15, 1830; m. Clarinda Mary Jane Briggs.
7217  Susan Caroline,[7] b. April 15, 1832; m. May 1, 1849, Willard B. Scott; had :
       7218  *Emma Caroline* (Scott), b. April 1, 1850.
       7219  *Lillian L.* (Scott), b. Nov. 12, 1854; d. Nov. 1, 1863.

## 6388

LODOWICK LEWIS THURSTON[6] of West Point, Iowa (*Joseph,*[5] *George,*[4] *Edward,*[3] *Jonathan,*[2] *Edward*[1]), brother of the preceding, and youngest child of Joseph[5] and Sarah (Taylor) Thurston of Hopkinton, R. I.; born there 1806; married MARY BROWNING. He died in West Point, Lee county, Iowa; 1857; she died July 2, 1867.

Mr. Thurston was tavern keeper, butcher, and sheriff in Wickford, R. I., till 1838, when he went to West Point on to a farm. He was a democratic representative in the Iowa legislature one term, a member of the Episcopal church, a man of high character, beloved and respected by all.

### Children:

7224 Hannah Melissa,[7] b. in Kingston, R. I., Aug. 25, 1825; m. July 22, 1844, William Rufus Stewart, jobber of glass ware, cutlery, etc., in Des Moines, Iowa, a member of the Methodist church, and a radical whig. She died in West Point June 11, 1861, having had:
   7225 *Mary Inez* (Stewart), b. Sept. 24, 1848; m. Dr. O. P. Sala of Bloomfield, Wis.; four sons.
   7226 *William Rufus* (Stewart), b. Oct. 29, 1853.
   7227 *Lewis Albert* (Stewart), b. June 10, 1855.
   7228 *Adrin Thurston* (Stewart), b. July 7, 1857.
      The three sons are all in business in Des Moines.
7229 Sarah Taylor,[7] b. 1837; m. George Washington Mason, a merchant and dealer in lumber in Eau Claire, Wis.

## 6409

ROBERT THURSTON[6] of Charleston, S. C. (*Samuel Isaac,*[5] *Samuel,*[4] *Edward,*[3] *Samuel,*[2] *Edward*[1]), son of Samuel Isaac[5] and Jane (Rawlins) Thurston of Georgetown, S. C.; born there Oct. 10, 1801; married, March, 1830, ELIZA EMILY NORTH, daughter of Dr. Edward W. North of Charleston. Mr. Thurston was a merchant; died May 18, 1841. .

### Children:

+7235 Edward North,[7] b. Aug. 5, 1831; m. 1st, Sarah Constance Chisholm; 2d, Mrs. Sophia Elizabeth (Hill) Bee.
+7236 Robert,[7] b. May 26, 1833; m. Maria Rees Ford.
7237 Emily,[7] b. Sept. 27, 1835; m. Jan., 1855, Dr. William Chardon Ravenel of Charleston, and had:
   7238 *Louis* (Ravenel), b. May 14, 1858.
   7239 *Robert Thurston* (Ravenel), b. May 16, 1860.
   7240 *Emily Chardon* (Ravenel), b. Jan. 7, 1869.
7241 John Gough,[7] b. Aug. 29, 1837; a cotton broker in Charleston; m. Eliza Jane Ford, b. April 24, 1839, daughter of Stephen and Jane Caroline (Thurston) Ford of Georgetown; they have:
   7242 *Edith Moultrie,*[8] b. Feb. 28, 1876.
7243 James,[7] b. Oct. 28, 1840; in charge of a warehouse in Baltimore, Md.; m. Mrs. Mary Jane Hollins; no children.

## 6481

WILLIAM HENRY THURSTON[6] of Newport, R. I. (*William,*[5] *William,*[4] *Joseph,*[3] *Samuel,*[2] *Edward*[1]), fifth child of William[5] and Ruth C. (Easton) Thurston of Middletown, R. I.; born there Feb. 4, 1823; married, Oct. 6, 1847, LAURA CASTTOFF, born Aug. 7, 1829, daughter of Henry and Elizabeth Moulton (Friend) Casttoff of Newport.

Mr. Thurston is a farmer.

Children:

7248 Benjamin Marshall,[7] b. July 10, 1848; m. May 27, 1875, Eliza S. Hammond; they have:

  7249 *Clarence*,[8] b. April 30, 1877.

7250 Laura Casttoff,[7] b. Oct. 25, 1849; m. June 1, 1874, William G. Peckham, jr., a lawyer; they reside in Westfield, N. Y., and have:

  7251 *Mary* (Peckham), b. Jan. 1, 1876.
  7252 *Laura* (Peckham), b. Sept. 14, 1877.

7253 William,[7] b. Nov. 27, 1851; m. Nov. 25, 1873, Hannah Briggs Weaver, b. Nov. 3, 1848, daughter of George and Frances Weaver. He is a farmer in Middletown, R. I.; they have:

  7254 *William*,[8] b. Feb. 20, 1875.
  7255 *George Weaver*,[8] b. Sept. 24, 1876.
  7256 *Francis Peckham*,[8] b. July 16, 1878.

7257 Caroline Marsh,[7] b. Jan. 14, 1855; m. Nov. 27, 1873, Daniel Peckham of Providence, R. I.

7258 Henry Casttoff,[7] b. May 29, 1857; a florist in Newport.

## 6483

BENJAMIN EASTON THURSTON [6] of Newport, R. I. (*William*,[5] *William*,[4] *Joseph*,[3] *Samuel*,[2] *Edward*[1]), brother of the preceding, and son of William [5] and Ruth C. (Easton) Thurston of Middletown, R. I.; born there October, 1826; married, Feb. 5, 1862, MARY ANN SIDDALL of Madison, Ind. He died at Delavan, Ill., June 4, 1870.

Mr. Thurston graduated from Amherst 1852. He studied with Rev. Thatcher Thayer for about one year in Newport, and then went with him to Europe, where he remained fifteen months, prosecuting his studies preparatory to college, being most of that time at Geneva. After leaving college he attempted to study for the ministry, but his health would not permit, and he associated himself with Jared Reid, jr., in opening a school for boys in Newport. Finding himself, after two years, unable to bear the confinement, he removed in the autumn of 1859 to a farm in Delavan, Ill., and remained there until May, 1868, when he went to New York as auditor in the New York, Delaware & Hudson Canal Co. In that situation he continued a year and then went to Grand Tower, Ill., as cashier in a manufacturing and coal company. He there contracted a malarial fever, which left him with chronic diarrhea, of which he died in Delavan, June 4, 1870.

Rev. T. Thayer, D.D., says of him: "There are few characters whose memory is cherished with so much affection and respect by those who knew him longest and best as Benjamin Thurston. A conscientious student, he faithfully improved his various opportunites, and entered upon life with a well-informed mind and a strong, clear judgment. His moral qualities were of the highest order. All who came in contact with him will bear record of this. His was a rare integrity. Thoroughly proved, it commanded unwavering confidence. An intense abhorrence of all show and pretence marked him from his earliest years, and his simple, truthful, loyal spirit appeared in all his intercourse. Plain in manners, loving strongly, and ever ready for kindness, he was beloved and respected in every relation of life. Descended from a Moravian ancestry, he early yielded his heart to the Saviour, and served his Master in simplicity and godly sincerity. This testimony is given by one with whom he spent a long time in closest intimacy, and who knew his worth, but it is given with the assurance that none of his large acquaintance will think it exaggerated."

Children:
7263  James Siddall,[7] b. Dec., 1862.
7264  Benjamin Easton,[7] b. April, 1864.
7265  Robert Berry,[7] b. Oct., 1865.
7266  Theodore Payne,[7] b. June, 1867.

## 6506

CHARLES MYRICK THURSTON[6] of New Rochelle, N. Y. (*Charles Myrick,*[5] *John,*[4] *John,*[3] *Samuel,*[2] *Edward*[1]), eldest son of Charles Myrick[5] and Rachel Hall (Pitman) Thurston of Newport, R. I.; born there July 11, 1819; married, April 16, 1843, CAROLINE MARSH, born Jan. 25, 1823, daughter of Col. Benjamin and Catharine (Casttoff) [formerly Guesthoff of Germany] Marsh of Newport. Mr. Marsh is a member and deacon of the Baptist church. Mr. Thurston died June 3, 1878. No children.

Mr. Thurston was a merchant in New York city; retired from business 1856, and removed to New Rochelle; was the first president of the village of New Rochelle, and has held office in Trinity (Episcopal) church, and acted in many positions of trust and public improvements in the village government. He was elected a member of the State Historical Society of Wisconsin in 1869, and was a corresponding member of the Rhode Island and several other State Historical Societies.

He was very deeply interested in the genealogy of his ancestry, and with great labor gathered and published a pamphlet of seventy pages, of the descendents of Edward Thurston of Newport, in 1868, and thus made it possible for the compiler of this volume to make the early records of these families as full and complete as found in these pages. He also assisted me very much during my three years' labor upon this work before his death, and his widow has kindly rendered very essential aid since.

A local paper says: "Suddenly, like a shaft from heaven, came the summons which called him from time to eternity, and as the sad news flew from house to house in the neighborhood and through the village, one note of sorrow arose. The silent tears coursing down the furrowed cheek mingled with the sobs of the little children, for each felt they had lost a friend. One remembered the bright smile he had given them, another the sweet tones of his rich voice as he had joined them in songs of praise; a third, some wise and gentle counsel, again helpful words of cheer, and each and all felt that to them the voice was hushed forever. What truer test of a pure and unblemished life could be offered than this universal testimony of old and young, rich and poor. There is scarcely one among us whose good influence in the community was more generally recognized and whose loss will be more sincerely mourned. Not being in active business, he found occupation in beautifying and adorning the grounds around his residence on Lather's Hill, had especially endeared himself to those around him, and when the 'silver cord was loosened' he was even then planting flowers, which will spring up and blossom long after in the places that will know him no more, as his kind words and pure life will blossom forever in the hearts of all who knew him, as one whom 'the beauty of the Lord was upon.' In the words of one of his favorite hymns, he was 'sowing the seed by the daylight

fair,' and we cannot but be sure as to what the harvest will be; for had he known the day and the hour when the swift-winged messenger cometh, he could not have been more at peace with his maker or his fellowmen."

## 6524

Dr. ALFRED HENRY THURSTON [6] of New York (*Charles Myrick,*[5] *John,*[4] *John,*[3] *Samuel,*[2] *Edward*[1]), brother of the preceding, and son of Charles Myrick [5] and Rachel Hall (Pitman) Thurston of Newport, R. I.; born there Oct. 2, 1832; married, first, April 10, 1856, ELIZA STRONG BLUNT, daughter of Nathaniel Bowditch and Lavinia Henrietta Blunt of New York city; she died in Nashville, Tenn., Sept. 8, 1862, aged 25. Second, April 25, 1864, MARY SULLIVAN BANKHEAD, daughter of James and Elizabeth Bankhead of Nashville. He died in New York Aug. 2, 1865, and his widow married, May 19, 1870, Dr. Jacob Bodine.

Dr. Thurston graduated from Columbia college 1851. He entered the medical college of New York and received a certificate of honor in 1854, and degree of doctor of medicine in 1855. He served as junior and senior walker and then as resident surgeon of the New York hospital, having been appointed in 1853. He practiced medicine in New York city, and was surgeon of the 12th regiment New York State Militia, and at the breaking out of the rebellion in 1861 served with the regiment, for three months, in defence of Washington. He was appointed surgeon of volunteers, with the rank of major, Oct. 5, 1861, receiving his commission from President Lincoln, and ordered to the army of the Cumberland. He was placed in charge of University hospital at Nashville, Tenn., March 8, 1862; was medical inspector on Major Gen. Rosecranz' staff Oct. 30, 1862; was assistant medical director of the department of the Cumberland in 1863, and medical director of the 12th army corps, Major Gen. Slocum commanding, Jan. 7, 1864. He was ordered to the army of the Potomac and stationed at Belle Plain in May, 1864, and afterward placed in charge of Grant hospital at Willets Point, New York harbor, July 5, 1864, remaining in command until the hospital was closed in June, 1865. He was appointed, June 15, 1865, "for faithful and meritorious service during the war," a lieutenant colonel of volunteers by brevet, to rank as such from March 13, 1865. He died in New York Aug. 2, 1865, of disease contracted while in the public service, aged 32 y. 10 m. He was a member of the Masonic order and of the Catholic church.

His children, by first wife, Eliza:

7270 Nathaniel Blunt,[7] b. April 12, 1857; m. Elizabeth Darrow, daughter of John and Emily Darrow, deceased, of New York city; they have:
    7271  *Charles Ward,*[8] b. Nov. 7, 1878.
7272  Helen Barrington,[7] b. May 6, 1862.

By second wife, Mary:
7273  Mary Bankhead,[7] b. March 18, 1865.

## 6530

GEORGE THURSTON [6] of St. Catherine, Canada (*Samuel,*[5] *Samuel,*[4] *John,*[3] *Samuel,*[2] *Edward*[1]), eldest son of Samuel [5] and Elizabeth (Gifford) Thurston of Newport, R. I.; born in ~~Westport,~~ Mass., March
*New Bedford*

29, 1815; married, first, Dec. 15, 1836, SOPHIA HAWN, daughter of John Hawn of Niagara, Canada; she died June 10, 1849, aged 33. Second, May 13, 1854, MARGARET MANERY, daughter of Thomas and Margaret (Givens) Manery of Kingston, Canada.

Mr. Thurston was a ship carpenter in New York with George Ficket and John Thomas of Portland, Me., in 1833; went to Niagara in 1834, came very near death from the cholera; was foreman for the Niagara Dock Company four years; went to Kingston in 1847 in employ of Kingston Marine Railway Company, in building thirty-eight vessels from eight hundred tons down; was burnt out and lost nearly everything by fire and employers; bought a farm, but did not succeed and sold at a loss, and went to St. Catherine and worked at his trade as foreman.

His children, by first wife, Sophia, born in Niagara:

7280  George,[7] b. April 26, 1838; a millwright at St. Catherine; n.m.
7281  Mary,[7] b. 1840; d. May 1, 1840.
7282  Joseph,[7] b. Oct. 2, 1842; enlisted in the army against the rebellion and was accidentally shot.
7283  John,[7] b. Nov. 14, 1844; a shipwright for Hudson Bay Co.; n.m.
7284  Julia,[7] d. Dec. 20, 1846.
7285  Minnie,[7] d. March 16, 1847.
+7286  Henry,[7] b. June 22, 1847; m. Sarah Davis.

Born in Kingston:

7287  William,[7] b. Jan. 24, 1848; m. Nov. 24, 1873, Sarah Robbs of Kingston, and had a daughter; d. June 6, 1874.
7288  Twin daughters, b. March 15, 1849; one died June, and one Aug., 1849.

By second wife, Margaret:

7289  Albert,[7] b. May 3, 1855; d. May 10, 1863.
7290  Thomas,[7] b. Dec. 26, 1856; a joiner.
7291  David,[7] b. March 1, 1859.
7292  Charles Douglass,[7] b. April 20, 1861; d. April 6, 1873.
7293  Margaret Elizabeth,[7] b. Feb. 6, 1863.
7294  James Wesley,[7] b. Sept. 27, 1865.
7295  Sophia,[7] b. Feb. 5, 1867.
7296  Christina,[7] b. Aug. 12, 1869.
7297  Herbert,[7] b. Dec. 30, 1871.

## 6536

GEORGE HENRY THURSTON[6] of Newport, R. I. (*Henry H.,[5] Samuel,[4] John,[3] Samuel,[2] Edward[1]*), eldest son of Henry H.[5] and Martha Coggeshall (Thurston) Thurston of Newport; born there Aug. 11, 1827; married, Dec. 29, 1852, RUTH ESTHER POTTER. He died Aug. 19, 1874, aged 47.

He was a carpenter, and both members of the Episcopal church.

Children:

7302  Ann Martha,[7] b. Nov. 2, 1853; m. Nov. 9, 1874, James Wheaton Lyon, mate of a vessel sailing out of Boston, and was to have been captain next voyage, but died in Salem, Mass., Feb. 17, 1877. They had:
7303  *Ruth Frances* (Lyon), b. Oct. 3, 1875; d. April 13, 1877.
7304  James Taggart,[7] b. May 3, 1857.
7305  George Henry Tew,[7] b. July 12, 1861; d. July 29, 1863.
7306  William Coggeshall,[7] b. Oct. 3, 1864.
7307  Harry Wheaton,[7] b. Dec. 27, 1872.

## 6576

SAMUEL THURSTON[6] of Fall River, Mass. (*Nathaniel S.,[5] Edward,[4] Edward,[3] Thomas,[2] Edward[1]*), second child of Nathaniel S.[5] and La-

vinia (Davis) Thurston of Fall River; born there Dec. 17, 1797; married, Feb. 18, 1821, RACHEL BOOMER; she died July 9, 1870, aged 71.

Children:

7312   Rachel Boomer,[7] b. April 20, 1822.
7313   Elizabeth,[7] b. May 21, 1824; m. Feb. 13, 1848, Benjamin A. Waddell.
7314   Amy Boomer,[7] b. July 6, 1826; m. Oct. 11, 1846, Martin Boomer.

## 6577

JAMES THURSTON [6] of Fall River, Mass. (*Nathaniel S.,[5] Edward,[4] Edward,[3] Thomas,[2] Edward[1]*), brother of the preceding, and son of Nathaniel S.[5] and Lavinia (Davis) Thurston of Fall River; born there April 12, 1799; married, March 27, 1823, RUTH WADDELL. She died Nov. 10, 1851; he was burned to death in his house, June 18, 1869.

Children:

+7320   Adam M.,[7] b. May 10, 1824; m. Lucy C. Harvey.
7321   Rachel M.,[7] b. March 25, 1826; m. 1842, Weston Gifford.
7322   Lavinia,[7] b. June 25, 1827; m. Dec. 25, 1847, William Pool.
7323   Ruth A.,[7] b. March 5, 1829; m. Dec. 27, 1848, Anthony Sherman.
7324   Mary B.,[7] b. April 30, 1831; d. Jan. 15, 1861.
7325   Hannah P.,[7] b. March 26, 1834; m. July, 1854, Benjamin Jenks; d. July 22, 1859.
7326   Elizabeth A.,[7] b. 1837; m. Dec. 5, 1858, Joseph Lawton; d. Feb. 20, 1864; no children.
7327   James H.,[7] b. June 5, 1839; m. July 21, 1861, Caroline D. Briggs, and had:
       7328   *Thomas H.,[8]* b. Aug. 8, 1862.
7329   Almira,[7] b. Sept. 12, 1841; m. March 5, 1867, Godfrey Westgate.
7330   Sylvia J.,[7] b. Dec. 9, 1843; m. Feb. 12, 1865, Thomas E. S. Cain.
7331   Benjamin S.,[7] b. Dec. 9, 1846; a laborer in Fall River; m. Oct. 8, 1867, Sarah J. Wilcox; no children.

## 6581

WILLIAM THURSTON [6] of Assonet Village, Freetown, Mass. (*Nathaniel S.,[6] Edward,[4] Edward,[3] Thomas,[2] Edward[1]*), brother of the preceding, and son of Nathaniel S.[5] and Lavinia (Davis) Thurston of Fall River, Mass.; born there Dec. 7, 1809; married, Dec. 10, 1833, ELEANOR CHACE. He died Feb. 20, 1871, aged 61.

Children:

7345   Edwin Chace,[7] b. Oct. 7, 1834; a molder in Fall River; m. Aug. 17, 1864, Sarah H. Anthony; they had:
       7346   *Cara Bell,[8]* b. July 17, 1865.
       7347   *Edward Anthony.[8]*          7348   *Ralph.[8]*
7349   George W.,[7] b. March 18, 1835; a farmer in Kansas.
7350   Palmer Chace,[7] b. Sept. 16, 1837; a molder in Providence, R. I.; m. April 24, 1864, Eliza Clark; they had:
       7351   *Ella M.,[8]* b. Sept. 8, 1867.
7352   Jason W.,[7] b. Jan. 5, 1839; a laborer in Fall River.
7353   Ruth,[7] b. Feb. 16, 1841; d. May 28, 1848.
7354   Caroline,[7] b. Dec. 20, 1843; d. Aug. 20, 1845.
7355   Phebe J.,[7] b. Dec. 10, 1847; m. Chester W. Brightman of Fall River, and had Alton C. and Ernest L. (Brightman).
7356   John,[7]   } twins, born   } a molder in Mansfield, Mass.; m. Abby Eastwood.
7357   James,[7]  } June 22, 1850; } a molder in Fall River; m. Areadna J. White; they have:          7358   *Fannie E.[8]*

## 6582

GARDNER THURSTON [6] of Fall River, Mass. (*Nathaniel S.,[5] Edward,[4] Edward,[3] Thomas,[2] Edward[1]*), brother of the preceding, and son of Nathaniel S.[5] and Lavinia (Davis) Thurston of Fall River; married, Aug. 18, 1835, ELIZABETH S. MOORE. He is a laborer.

Children:

7366 Lydia A.,[7] b. May 26, 1836; m. George Russell.
7367 Sophie W.,[7] b. April 12, 1838; m. April 21, 1857, Joseph R. Durfee.
7368 Nathaniel Gardner,[7] b. May 12, 1841; m. Nov. 24, 1863, Susan L. Anthony; is a general worker, residing in Fall River; they have:
    7369 *Harriet Amelia*,[8] b. July 21, 1865.
    7370 *Minerva Lorea*,[8] b. Aug. 15, 1867.
    7371 *Isaac Anthony*,[8] b. March 17, 1870.
7372 Harriet M.,[7] b. July 4, 1843; m. William Cook; d. May 8, 1864.
+7373 Albert Hiram,[7] b. March 31, 1845; m. Blanche Ellen Call.
7374 Jesse M.,[7] b. Jan. 24, 1847; m. Oct. 16, 1872, Ellen L. Bradley.
7375 Edward Henry,[7] b. Nov. 18, 1849.
7376 Sarah Elizabeth,[7] b. Aug. 13, 1852; m. Horace Ashley.
7377 Charles T.,[7] b. May 28, 1855.
7378 Isabel H.,[7] b. May 21, 1858.

## 6587

PELEG GARDNER THURSTON [6] of Fall River, Mass. (*Varnum*,[5] *Peleg*,[4] *Edward*,[3] *Thomas*,[2] *Edward*[1]), eldest son of Varnum [5] and Mary (Gardner) Thurston of Fall River; born there Sept. 5, 1799; married, Nov. 6, 1829, SUSAN BLOSSOM. He is a farmer.

Children:

7390 Hannah,[7] b. April 12, 1833.
7391 Peleg Rufus,[7] b. Oct. 31, 1834; m. Eliza Pratt; they had:
    7392 *Mary*,[8] d. July 5, 1862.
    7393 *Charles Fremont*,[8] b. Sept., 1863.
7394 Amy,[7] m. Dec. 1, 1860, Joseph Lake; d. July 18, 1875, leaving:
    7395 *Joseph Henry* (Lake), b. Sept. 15, 1862.
    7396 *Addie Louise* (Lake), b. March 11, 1864.
7397 John Niles,[7] b. Sept. 8, 1843.
7398 Adeline,[7] b. June 23, 1846; m. Dec. 27. 1870, Wm. H. Simmons, and had:
    7399 *William T. H.* (Simmons), b. May 3, 1873; d. May 5, 1875.

## 6590

EDWARD THURSTON [6] of Fall River, Mass. (*Varnum*,[5] *Peleg*,[4] *Edward*,[3] *Thomas*,[2] *Edward*[1]), brother of the preceding, and son of Varnum [6] and Mary (Gardner) Thurston of Fall River; born there Sept. 4, 1804; married, Feb. 28, 1828, SARAH MARIA MASON.

Mr. Thurston was a brick and stone mason and master builder, but for some years past, 1879, has devoted himself to farming.

Children:

7410 Mary Maria,[7] b. Jan. 16, 1829; m. Nov., 1850, William H. Hambly, a master builder and brick and stone mason in Fall River, and had:
    7411 *Sarah Maria* (Hambly), b. Jun. 30, 1851.
    7412 *Julia Edna* (Hambly), b. Aug. 11, 1859.
+7413 Edward Mason,[7] b. July 18, 1832; m. Mary Wilbur Gardner.
+7414 Anthony,[7] b. March 13, 1837; m. Ann Maria Whipple.
7415 John Mason,[7] b. June 18, 1848; d. Nov. 19, 1854.

## 6591

SAMUEL THURSTON [6] of Fall River, Mass. (*Varnum*,[5] *Peleg*,[4] *Edward*,[3] *Thomas*,[2] *Edward*[1]), brother of the preceding, and son of Varnum [5] and Mary (Gardner) Thurston of Fall River; born there Dec. 27, 1806; married (intention published March 5, 1837) ALMIRA BOOMER. He was a wheelwright; died Sept. 10, 1866.

One child:

+7420 James Emery,[7] b. Jan. 11, 1838; m. Melissa Gifford Peckham.

## 6592

JAMES THURSTON [6] of Somerset, Mass. (*Varnum,*[5] *Peleg,*[4] *Edward,*[3] *Thomas,*[2] *Edward*[1]), brother of the preceding, and son of Varnum[6] and Mary (Gardner) Thurston of Fall River; born there Nov. 8, 1808; married, Jan. 11, 1841, HANNAH PIERCE. He was a dealer in shell fish and garden truck; died 1877.

### Children :

7421　James William,[7] b. Nov. 12, 1843; n.m.
7422　Nathan Albert,[7] b. July 28, 1845; d. Sept. 17, 1854.
7423　Hannah Maria,[7] b. March 27, 1848; m. Oct. 25, 1870, Francis W. Wood.
7424　Amy Ann,[7] b, Feb. 20, 1851; m. Marshall Dane Watters.
7425　Abby Eliza,[7] b. March 31, 1854; m. Lyman Hartwell Taylor.
7426　Nathan Albert,[7] b. Aug. 29, 1857; n.m.

## 6594

ABRAHAM GARDNER THURSTON [6] of Fall River, Mass. (*Varnum,*[5] *Peleg,*[4] *Edward,*[3] *Thomas,*[2] *Edward*[1]), brother of the preceding, and son of Varnum[5] and Mary (Gardner) Thurston of Fall River; born there June 21, 1813; married (intentions April 4, 1840) CATHARINE BORDEN ALLEN, born Nov. 7, 1815, daughter of Abraham and Rachel (Gardner) Allen of Tiverton, R. I.

Mr. Thurston is a machinist, engaged in the manufacture of cotton and thread machinery.

### Children:

+7430　Charles Abraham Gardner,[7] b. July 23, 1841; m. Anna Moore.
7431　Rienzi Ware,[7] b. Jan. 8, 1851; m. May 24, 1876, Amy Chase Almy. He is a machinist, in company with his father in the manufacture of cotton and thread machinery in Fall River; is a vocalist of merit, possesses a fine baritone voice, and is quite a student in vocal and instrumental music.

## 6595

VERNON THURSTON [6] of Fall River, Mass. (*Varnum,*[5] *Peleg,*[4] *Edward,*[3] *Thomas,*[2] *Edward*[1]), brother of the preceding, and son of Varnum[5] and Mary (Gardner) Thurston of Fall River; born there Feb. 11, 1815; married, Oct. 27, 1848, ABBY STREETER.

Mr. Thurston and his son Alberto Gardner are proprietors of Thurston's Hotel at Fall River.

### Children :

7435　Alberto Gardner,[7] b. Sept. 10, 1849; m. Nellie Sullivan; is in company with his father in the hotel.  Children :
　　7436　*Vernon.*[8]
　　7437　*Effie.*[8]
　　7438　*Cora.*[8]
7439　LeRoy F.,[7] b. March 28, 1851; d. Aug. 25, 1853.
7440　Melissa M.,[7] b. June 9, 1854; d. Nov. 19, 1856.
7441　Effie,[7] b. Jan. 23, 1858; m. Frank Bullock of Providence, R. I.; no children.
7442　Ida May,[7] b. Aug. 7, 1860; d. Sept. 20, 1869.
7443　Eugene de Forest,[7] b. Sept. 20, 1862; d. Aug. 9, 1863.
7444　Cora,[7] b. Sept. 5, 1864.
7445　Minerva,[7] b. July 5, 1866; d. Oct. 8, 1866.

## 6597

WILLIAM BARTON THURSTON [6] of Brooklyn, N. Y. (*Varnum,*[5] *Peleg,*[4] *Edward,*[3] *Thomas,*[2] *Edward*[1]), brother of the preceding, and son of Varnum[5] and Mary (Gardner) Thurston of Fall River, Mass.; born

there Nov. 8, 1818; married, Feb. 9, 1845, MARY ANN PACKARD, daughter of Gideon and Rebecca (Packard) Packard.

Mr. Thurston is a house carpenter, but now, 1879, engaged in the manufacture of proprietary medicines (49 University place, New York). He was deacon of the Franklin street Christian church, and was superintendent and treasurer of Sunday-school for more than ten years in Fall River.

Children :

7450 Emma Packard,[7] b. Feb. 26, 1846; m. Oct. 30, 1872, Ellis Tinkham Lamberton of New York; they have :
 7451 *Mary Barton* (Lamberton), b. Aug. 26, 1873.
7452 Ida Barton,[7] b. April 19, 1849; m. Oct. 30, 1872, Charles Osborne Barker of Fall River.

Both married at same time, in the Franklin Christian church of Fall River, by Rev. S. Wright Butler.

## 6606

DAVID THURSTON[6] of Fall River, Mass. (*Jonathan,[5] Thomas,[4] Edward,[3] Thomas,[2] Edward[1]*), second son of Jonathan[5] and Sarah (Luther) Thurston of Fall River; born there July 26, 1802; married, Jan. 30, 1834, HANNAH MILLER HATHAWAY, daughter of Lloyd and Hannah Hathaway. She died Sept. 24, 1857, aged 42; he died Feb. 20, 1871.

Mr. Thurston was a house carpenter in Fall River, and his son says: "The Thurstons of this vicinity are noted as moral, industrious, and successful people; a large proportion are church members in good standing."

Only child :

7457 George Henry,[7] b. Jan. 13, 1835; m. Oct. 24, 1861, Julia Eliza Lapham, b. June 20, 1838, eldest daughter of Louis and Stella Ann Lapham of Fall River. He is a watchmaker and jeweler, 46 Bank street, Fall River. They have :
 7458 *Marion Hathaway,*[8] b. Aug. 4, 1862.

## 6611

THOMAS THURSTON[6] of Fall River, Mass. (*Jonathan,[5] Thomas,[4] Edward,[3] Thomas,[2] Edward[1]*), brother of the preceding, and son of Jonathan[5] and Mercy (Briggs) Thurston of Fall River; born there Aug. 24, 1820; married, first, Sept. 23, 1847, BETSEY JANE DAVIS, born May 25, 1827, died Oct. 13, 1853; second, April 18, 1859, MATILDA GRAY DAVIS, born May 13, 1831, both daughters of Gardner and Anne (Bennett) Davis of Fall River.

Mr. Thurston is a prosperous farmer; member and trustee of the North Christian church.

His children, by first wife, Betsey :

7463 Charles Irvine,[7] b. Aug. 15, 1848; a house carpenter; n.m.
7464 Annie Jane,[7] b. Nov. 16, 1852; n.m.

By second wife, Matilda :

7465 Arthur Willis,[7] b. Jan. 24, 1860.
7466 Carrie Bennett,[7] b. Jan. 13, 1864.
7467 Ellen Matilda,[7] b. Feb. 18, 1871.

## 6621

JOHN THURSTON[6] of Providence, R. I. (*Samuel,[5] Thomas,[4] Thomas,[3] Thomas,[2] Edward[1]*), youngest child of Samuel[5] and Mercy (Tabor) Thurston of Tiverton, R. I.; born May 6, 1803; married, Feb. 2, 1826,

MARY ANN CHASE. He died Jan. 31, 1858, aged 55; she died April 21, 1873.

Their children were:

7472   Ann Frances,[7] b. Nov. 29, 1826; d. April 17, 1844.
7473   Elizabeth,[7] b. Jan. 11, 1828; d. June 11, 1835.
+7474  George Edwin,[7] b. Sept. 17, 1830; m. 1st, Charlotte Amelia Tooker; 2d, Frances Tillotson.
7475   Mary Helen,[7] b. Aug. 16, 1834; d. April 19, 1835.
7476   Albert,[7] b. Nov. 27, 1836.

### 6625

THOMAS THURSTON[6] of Centerville, R. I. (*George Howland,[5] Thomas,[4] Thomas,[3] Thomas,[2] Edward[1]*), eldest son of George Howland[5] and Elizabeth (Baker) Thurston of Tiverton, R. I.; born there May 24, 1807; married, July 20, 1834, BARBARA WHITFORD, born July 24, 1807, daughter of John Summers and Barbara (Calvin) Whitford of Centerville. Mr. Thurston is a blacksmith.

Children:

7480   Elizabeth,[7] b. June 23, 1836; d. Oct. 9, 1861.
7481   Thomas Henry,[7] b. Feb. 18, 1839; a carpenter in Centerville; m. in Fall River, Mass., March 29, 1871, Mary Helen Whitford, b. in Coventry, R. I., June 13, 1849, daughter of James Edward and Sarah Madison (Johnson) Whitford of Warwick, R. I.; no children.

### 6639

DR. WILLIAM TORREY THURSTON[6] of ~~Woonsocket,~~ *Providence* R. I. (*John Robinson,[5] John,[4] Peleg,[3] Thomas,[2] Edward[1]*), third child of John Robinson[5] and Mary Ann (Bruce) Thurston of St. Christophers, W. I.; born there July 14, 1805; married, March 15, 1832, CAROLINE THURSTON, daughter of Jeremiah and Sarah (Babcock) Thurston of Hopkinton, R. I. [see no. 6967] *grad. in N. Y. city, and*

Mr. Thurston is admitting physician and superintendent of the Rhode Island Hospital in Providence; has been U. S. consul at St. Kitts, W. I.; spent the years 1842 and 1843 in Portland, Me.; was surgeon of the 1st Rhode Island light artillery during the war against the rebellion; member of the Episcopal church.

Children:

7486   Eliza,[7] b. June 28, 1833; m. Oct. 12, 1859, Isaac Butts of Boston, Mass., and had Annie Atwood, b. Jan. 29, 1861, Caroline Thurston, b. March 4, 1864, and Esther Thurston (Butts), b. Sept. 14, 1868.
7487   Esther Hodgson,[7] b. April 24, 1835; m. Mar. 18, 1862, Chas. H. Merriman of Providence, and had William Thurston, b. Aug. 4, 1863, d. May 9, 1868, Maria Lippitt, b. June 20, 1865, Charles Henry, b. Oct. 23, 1868, and Harold Thurston (Merriman), b. July 10, 1870.
7488   Caroline,[7] b. Aug. 6, 1836.

### 6640

JOHN ROBINSON THURSTON[6] (*John Robinson,[5] John,[4] Peleg,[3] Thomas,[2] Edward[1]*), brother of the preceding, and son of John Robinson[5] and Mary Ann (Bruce) Thurston of St. Christophers, W. I.; born there 1807; married, 1830, LOUISA ANN ADLAM of St. Christophers. He died 1860. Children:

7493   John Robinson,[7] b. 1831; d. 1862.   7494  Chas. Hodgson,[7] b. 1833; d. 1854.
7495   Mary Ann,[7] b. 1836; m. 1855, William McPhail; no children.
7496   Eliza,[7] b. 1838; d. 1839.        7497  Joseph Adlam,[7] b. 1840; d. 1840.
7498   Louisa Ann,[7] b. 1842; m. 1860, Henry Maynard; several children.
7499   Caroline,[7] b. 1844; m. 1862, John Maynard; several children.
7500   William Torrey,[7] b. 1849.

## 6641

WANTON THURSTON [6] of St. ~~Johns, N. B.~~ *Kitts N. J.* (*John Robinson,*[5] *John,*[4] *Peleg,*[3] *Thomas,*[2] *Edward*[1]), brother of the preceding, and son of John Robinson [5] and Mary Ann (Bruce) Thurston of St. Christophers, W. I.; born there Dec., 1809; married, 1841, SARAH OTTEY of St. John, ~~where~~ he lived and died, 1863, *in St. Kitts*

### Children :

+7510 James Ottey,[7] b. May, 1842; m. Susie Ackerman.
7511 Sarah,[7] b. May, 1844; m. Oct., 1868, James T. Waith, *a planter in St.*
7512 William Torrey,[7] b. May, 1846; d. Nov., 1860. *Vincent, W.J.*
7513 John Wentworth,[7] b. May, 1848.
7514 Allen Ottey,[7] b. May, 1850, *n. m., a planter in St. Kitts*
7515 Wanton,[7] b. May, 1852; d. 1868.
7516 Eliza,[7] b. May, 1854.

## 6642

JAMES THURSTON [6] of New York city (*John Robinson,*[5] *John,*[4] *Peleg,*[3] *Thomas,*[2] *Edward*[1]), brother of the preceding, and son of John Robinson [5] and Mary Ann (Bruce) Thurston of St. Christophers, W. I.; born there April, 1812; married, 1844, MARTHA SMITH, daughter of Joseph Smith of New York. He died in New York April, 1853; she died 1856.

### Children:

7518 Harriet,[7] b. 1846; d. 1848.
7519 Joseph Robinson,[7] b. 1848.
7520 James,[7] b. 1850.

## Seventh Generation.

## 6666

GEORGE ALLEN THURSTON [7] (*John,*[6] *John,*[5] *Edward,*[4] *Edward,*[3] *Edward,*[2] *Edward*[1]), only child of John [6] and Elizabeth (Allen) Thurston of Merrick South, now Freeport, L. I.; born there April 3, 1802; married ELLEN FENTON, daughter of John and Ellen (Thompson) Fenton of Perth, Scotland. He was a farmer; died Sept. 26, 1853. She resides with her son George W. in Philadelphia.

### Children:

7522 Elizabeth,[8] b. March 24, 1829; d. in infancy.
7523 John,[8] b. July 1, 1830; d. in infancy.
7524 William,[8] b. Dec. 14, 1831; d. in infancy.
7525 Ellen Thompson,[8] b. May 30, 1834; d. in infancy.
7526 George Washington,[8] b. in New York city June 13, 1842; m. Nov. 19, 1878, Eleanor Cadmus, b. Nov. 24, 1854. daughter of Frederick and Sarah (Thomas) Cadmus of Philadelphia, Pa. Mr. Thurston is a conveyancer, and notary public since 1873; member of the Reformed Dutch formerly, now of the Presbyterian church. *Child*

*7527 Miriam, b. Oct. 22, 1879*

## 6670

JOHN THURSTON [6] of Sumpter, Mich. (*Daniel,*[6] *John,*[5] *Edward,*[4] *Edward,*[3] *Edward,*[2] *Edward*[1]), son of Daniel [6] and Prudence (Cross-

man) Thurston of Providence, R. I.; born there Jan. 17, 1792; married, Feb. 27, 1812, HANNAH TUCKER, born Oct. 31, 1795. He died Feb. 11, 1868; she died 1858.

John Thurston moved with his father to Utica, N. Y.; was a baker, and kept the first baker's shop in that city in company with his father. He was drafted in the war of 1812, served three months, was taken sick and discharged. He afterward moved to Sumpter and carried on a farm; was a member of the Free Methodist church.

### Children :

7528  Eliza Ann,[8] b. Dec. 27, 1812; m. 1829, John R. Smith. b. at Sandy Lake, N.Y., Oct. 28, 1808, a farmer in W. Sumpter, Wayne Co., Mich. Children:
  7529  *Alvira Eston* (Smith), b. Nov. 20, 1831.
  7530  *Robert Almanson* (Smith), b. Aug. 19, 1833.
  7531  *Almira Brown* (Smith), b. Aug. 9, 1835.
  7532  *Calvin* (Smith), b. July 4, 1837; was in Bordan's company of sharp-shooters in war against rebellion and was shot through the left lung.
  7533  *Lucy Ann* (Smith), b. March 9, 1839.
  7534  *Morris* (Smith), b. Feb. 14, 1841; enlisted in 28th New York regiment against the rebellion and served twenty-two months.
  7535  *Lovina Elwell* (Smith), b. Nov. 14, 1843.
  7536  *Francis Leonard* (Smith), b. March 3, 1845. ·
  7537  *Caroline Victory* (Smith), b. Aug. 28, 1847.
  7538  *Cyrus* (Smith), b. April 14, 1852.
  7539  *Ruby Ann* (Smith), b. June 4, 1854.
7540  Caroline Maria,[8] b. Nov. 14, 1813; m. June 12, 1829, Capt. Charles Bennett of Fentonville, Genesee Co., Mich.; they had three children, all d.
7541  Daniel Dudley,[8] b. Dec., 1815; d. aged 22, member of Methodist church.
7542  Josiah,[8] b. in Verona, N. Y., Dec. 9, 1818; m. in Fulton, Oswego Co., N. Y., Cordelia Emeline Parker, b. in Jordan, Onondaga Co., N. Y., April 15, 1826, daughter of Salmon and Eliza (Scofield) Parker of Marion, N. Y. He is a farmer in Sumpter, Mich.; no children.
7543  John Wesley,[8] b. in Utica, N. Y., Dec. 17, 1819; m. at Oakville, Mich., Oct. 21, 1857, Adaline Tuers, b. in New York city May 8, 1836, daughter of Walter and Ann (Vanwinkle) Tuers of Newark, N. J. He is a farmer in Martinsville, Mich. They have :
  7544  *Charles Wesley*,[9] b. in Sumpter Oct. 20, 1858.
  7545  *Susan Eleanora*,[9] b. in Sumpter Nov. 16, 1860.
  7546  *Mary Caty*,[9] b. in London, Mich., Mar. 1, 1866.
7547  Frances Jane,[8] b. in Verona Dec. 13, 1821; m. in Oakville, Mich., April 16, 1848, Egbart Rice, b. in Warsaw, N. Y., Oct. 3, 1821, son of Chancey and Phebe (Giddings) Rice; he is a dry goods merchant in Dansville, Ingham Co., Mich.; a member of the common council, trustee and member of the Methodist church, and assessor of school district. Children:
  7548  *Gertrude Olivia* (Rice), b. in Ypsilanti, Mich., Feb. 16, 1849; d. Aug. 6, 1850.
  7549  *Letta Urzelia* (Rice), b. in Ypsilanti; m. Francis Marion Cobb; they live in Dansville.
  7550  *Charles Myron* (Rice), b. in Ypsilanti April 17, 1857.
  7551  *Mina Bell* (Rice), b. in Dansville June 26, 1866.
  7552  *Ella May* (Rice), b. in Dansville Nov. 11, 1867.
7553  Prudence Adeline,[8] b. in Verona Dec., 1823; m. William Lowry, a cooper in Toledo, Ohio.
7554  Alfred,[8] b. 1826; d. 1848, aged 22.
7555  Hiram,[8] b. April 17, 1828; d. aged 17 months.
7556  Lorinda,[8] m. Daniel Scofield; six children.
7557  Obadiah Kingsley,[8] b. in Granby, N. Y., Nov. 24, 1835; m. Sept. 22, 1860, Desire Roe of Hörnlyet, N. Y.; a farmer in West Sumpter, Mich. They have :
  7558  *Mary*,[9] b. Feb. 7, 1862; m. Charles Winters; they live in Belleville, Wayne Co., Mich.
  7559  *Hattie*,[9] b. Feb. 8, 1870.
7560  Lydia,[8] b. 1840; d. Sept., 1857.

## 6683

LOUIS MARION THURSTON[7] of Huntington, L. I. (*Robert Jenkins,*[6] *John,*[5] *Capt. John,*[4] *Jonathan,*[3] *Edward,*[2] *Edward*[1]), only son of Robert Jenkins[6] and Abigail (Bogert) Thurston of New York city; born there Oct. 23, 1804; married, April 19, 1836, ELIZABETH SAMUELLA BREWER.

Mr. Thurston was a broker in Wall street, New York, but latterly a farmer in Huntington.

Children, born in New York city:

7565   Robert Brewer,[8] b. Feb. 9. 1837; n.m.; d. Aug. 6, 1875.
7566   Louis Marion,[8] b. July 15, 1838; n.m.; d. in Huntington Dec. 4, 1864.

Born in Huntington:

7567   Charles Stewart,[8] b. April 28, 1846; m. in Brooklyn, L. I., Jan. 28, 1874, Alice Baker, b. March 12, 1850, daughter of John F. and Helen (Rust) Baker of Syracuse, N. Y. Mr. Thurston commenced the mercantile business in New York in 1858; became a member of the 22d regiment N. G. S. N. Y. in 1869 and was a corporal in 1878; took an active part against the riots of 1871, in which the regiment acted as guard of honor to the Orangemen, and won high commendation from all. They have:
     7568   *Louis Stewart,*[9] b. Aug. 7, 1878.
+7569   William Stewart,[8] b. April 8, 1848; m. Mary Seymour Ackerman.
7570   John Robert Rhinelander,[8] b. Sept. 19, 1851; m. June 20, 1875, at La Motte, Iowa, Laura Wilson; is a farmer in La Motte, Jackson Co., Iowa; no children.

## 6740

LOUIS JENKINS THURSTON[7] of Portsmouth, R. I. (*Peleg,*[6] *Peleg,*[5] *Capt. John,*[4] *Jonathan,*[3] *Edward,*[2] *Edward*[1]), fourth child of Peleg[6] and Susan Barker (Lawton) Thurston of Portsmouth; born there March 18, 1818; married, Jan. 25, 1838, CYNTHIA ANN PECKHAM, born Jan. 16, 1813, daughter of George and Cynthia (Barker) Peckham of Middletown, R. I. He is a farmer. *ideon*

Children:

7575   Phebe Elizabeth,[8] b. Dec. 15, 1838.
7576   Susan Lawton.[8] b. Nov. 13, 1842.
7577   Cynthia Barker,[8] b. Aug. 13, 1846; m. Nov. 15, 1877, Charles Carr, son of Job and Eleanor Carr of Portsmouth.
7578   Louis Jenkins,[8] b. March 22, 1848; d. Sept. 19, 1848.

## 6741

EDWARD THURSTON[7] of Newport, R. I. (*Peleg,*[6] *Peleg,*[5] *Capt. John,*[4] *Jonathan,*[3] *Edward,*[2] *Edward*[1]), brother of the preceding, and son of Peleg[6] and Susan Barker (Lawton) Thurston of Portsmouth, R. I.; born there Nov. 26, 1820; married, Jan. 17, 1843, HARRIET PECKHAM, daughter of Philip Peckham; he died Jan. 23, 1871, aged 50.

Mr. Thurston was drafted and served in the Dorr rebellion of Rhode Island, 1842.

Children:

7583   Harriet Newell,[8] b. Oct. 21, 1843; d. April 23, 1846.
7584   Harriet Newell,[8] b. Jan. 19, 1847.
7585   Hannah Barker,[8] b. Dec. 7, 1848.
7586   Lelia May,[8] b. Dec. 27, 1856.

## 6743

PELEG LAWTON THURSTON[7] of Portsmouth, R. I. (*Peleg,*[6] *Peleg,*[5] *Capt. John,*[4] *Jonathan,*[3] *Edward,*[2] *Edward*[1]), brother of the preced-

ing, and son of Peleg[6] and Susan Barker (Lawton) Thurston of Portsmouth; born there Jan. 18, 1826; married, in Newport, R. I., Aug. 10, 1856, SARAH ELIZABETH LAWTON, born March 17, 1836, daughter of Parker and Hannah (Sisson) Lawton of Portsmouth.

Mr. Thurston is a farmer.

Children:

7590   Parker Lawton,[8] b. Dec. 14, 1858.
7591   Sarah Ambler,[8] b. Jan. 8, 1862.
7592   Ruth Hannah,[8] b. March 6, 1864.
7593   Edward Walker,[8] b. Dec. 6, 1866.
7594   Clara May,[8] b. Jan. 24, 1874.
7595   Howard,[8] b. Aug. 17, 1876.

## 6745

PARKER HALL THURSTON[7] of Newport, R. I. (*Peleg,*[6] *Peleg,*[5] *Capt. John,*[4] *Jonathan,*[3] *Edward,*[2] *Edward*[1]), brother of the preceding, and son of Peleg[6] and Susan Barker (Lawton) Thurston of Portsmouth, R. I.; born there March 2, 1833; married, in North Attleborough, Mass., Oct. 22, 1857, LOUISA MARIA RAWSON, born in Cumberland, R. I., April 9, 1830, daughter of Otis and Mary (Barnes) Rawson of Wrentham, Mass.

Mr. Thurston is a carpenter; member of the Methodist church.

Children:

7600   Benjamin Franklin,[8] b. July 22, 1858; entered Brown university 1876; is a member of the Methodist church.
7601   Charles Rawson,[8] b. June 17, 1860; graduated with honor from the New port high school and entered Brown university 1878; is a member of the Methodist church.
7602   Mary Louisa,[8] b. Sept. 20, 1862; member of the Methodist church.
7603   Alice Carpenter,[8] b. Aug. 29, 1867.
7604   Annie Hall,[8] b. Sept. 15, 1869.

## 6757

JOHN BABCOCK THURSTON[7] of Providence, R. I. (*John Samuel,*[6] *Peleg,*[5] *Capt. John,*[4] *Jonathan,*[3] *Edward,*[2] *Edward*[1]), third child of John Samuel[6] and Hannah Barker (Lawton) Thurston of Providence; born there Feb. 26, 1829; married, first, Dec. 24, 1851, SOPHIA A. CAPWELL, daughter of John and Matilda Capwell; she died Aug. 19, 1854, aged 28. Second, Nov. 14, 1862, ADDELINE A. WILBUR, daughter of Albert S. and Annie A. Wilbur. Mr. Thurston is a photographer.

His children, by first wife Sophia:

7610   Eliza Heath,[8] b. May 22, 1853; m. Jan. 14, 1873, George Franklin Ryan, a printer for the Rumford Chemical Works in Providence. They have:
    7611   *Clarence Andrew* (Ryan), b. Feb. 28, 1874.

By second wife, Addeline:

7612   Samuel,[8] b. Feb. 6, 1864; d. Feb. 21, 1864.
7613   Marietta Wilbur,[8] b. April 6, 1865; d. July 14, 1866.
7614   Albert Greene,[8] b. Jan. 26, 1868.

## 6759

GEORGE STRATTON THURSTON[7] of Providence, R. I. (*John Samuel,*[6] *Peleg,*[5] *Capt. John,*[4] *Jonathan,*[3] *Edward,*[2] *Edward*[1]), brother of the preceding, and son of John Samuel[6] and Hannah Barker (Lawton) Thurston of Providence; born there July 26, 1834; married,

Robert H. Thurston

Sept. 25, 1854, JERUSHA W. HEATH, born April 29, 1829, daughter of Wilmarth and Mary (Humphrey) Heath of Barrington, R. I.

Mr. Thurston is a machinist and engineer; served as an engineer in the United States navy in the war against the rebellion, doing duty in the West Gulf blockading squadron.

Children, born in Providence:

7620   Wilmarth Heath,[8] b. Dec. 30, 1856; graduated from Brown 1877 and is studying law.
7621   Mary Louisa Carol,[8] b. July 12, 1859; d. Feb. 28, 1860.

Born in Barrington:

7622   George Henry,[8] b. Feb. 4, 1864.
7623   Walter Irving,[8] b. June 24, 1867.
7624   Samuel Lawton,[8] b. Oct. 25, 1869.

Born in Providence:

7625   Frederic Carter,[8] b. Oct. 31, 1871.
7626   James Humphrey,[8] b. May 20, 1873.

## 6770

ROBERT HENRY THURSTON[7] of Hoboken, N. J. (*Robert Lawton,*[6] *Peleg,*[5] *Capt. John,*[4] *Jonathan,*[8] *Edward,*[2] *Edward*[1]), eldest son of Robert Lawton[6] and Harriet (Taylor) Thurston of Providence, R. I.; born there Oct. 25, 1839; married, Oct. 5, 1865, SUSAN TAYLOR GLADDING, born June 26, 1838, daughter of Nathaniel and Susan Gladding of Providence; she died March 31, 1878.

Johnson's Universal Cyclopedia, 1878, says Mr. Thurston "was trained in the workshops of his father, and graduated from Brown university in 1859. He was engaged with the business firm of which his father was senior partner until 1861, when he entered the navy as an officer of engineers; served during the civil war on various vessels; was present at the battle of Port Royal and at the siege of Charleston; was attached to the North and South Atlantic squadrons until the close of 1865, when he was detailed as assistant professor of natural and experimental philosophy at the United States Naval Academy at Annapolis, where he also acted as lecturer on chemistry and physics. In 1870 he visited Europe, for the purpose of studying the British iron manufacturing districts, and in 1871 was appointed professor of mechanical engineering at the Stevens Institute of Technology. In this year he conducted, in behalf of a committee of the American Institute, a series of experiments on steam boilers, in which, for the first time, all losses of heat were noted, and by condensing all the steam generated, the quantity of water entrained by the steam was accurately noted. In 1873 he was appointed a member of the United States Scientific Commission to the Vienna Exhibition; served upon the international jury, edited the Report of the Commissioners (in which he published his own report on machinery and manufactures), in five volumes, 1875-6. In 1874 and subsequently he conducted, at the Stevens Institue of Technology, a series of researches on the efficiency of prime movers and machines, and upon the strength and other essential properties of the materials of construction. In 1875 he was appointed a member of the United States Commission on the causes of boiler explosions, and of the Board to test the metals used in construction. He is a member of

22

various scientific associations, in the United States, Great Britain, France, and Germany, and has written numerous papers on technical subjects, which have appeared in scientific journals in Europe and America, and has prepared articles upon similar topics for this Cyclopedia. Some of his more important papers are the following: 'On Losses of Propelling Power in the Paddle Wheel,' 1868; 'Steam Engines of the French Navy,' 1868; 'H. B. M. Iron Clad Monarch,' 1870; 'Iron Manufactures in Great Britain,' 1870; 'Experimental Steam Boiler Explosions,' 1871; 'Report on Test Trials of Steam Boilers,' 1872; 'Traction Engines and Road Locomotives,' 1871; 'Report on the Stevens Iron-clad Battery,' 1874; 'Efficiency of Furnaces Burning Wet Fuel,' 1874; 'The Mechanical Engineer, his Preparation and his Work,' 1875, and a number of papers embodying accounts of original investigations of the strength and other properties of materials of construction. Among his numerous inventions are the magnesium ribbon lamp, a magnesium-burning naval and army signal apparatus, an autographic recording testing machine, a new form of steam engine governor, an apparatus for determining the value of lubricants, etc."

To the above may be added: He was made vice-president of the American Institute of Mining Engineers in 1878; he was made vice-president of the American Association for the Advancement of Science, at Nashville, in 1877, in the absence of Professor Pickering, elected at the preceding meeting, and was regularly elected to serve again in 1878, at the St. Louis meeting of the association.

He is connected with the following and other societies:

Fellow of American Association for Advancement of Science.
   "  " New York Academy of Sciences.
Member of Franklin Institute of Pennsylvania.
   "  " American Institute of New York.
   "  " American Society of Civil Engineers.
   "  " American Institute of Mining Engineers.
   "  " Institute of Engineers and Shipbuilders of Scotland.
   "  " (Asso.) British Institution of Naval Architects.
   "  " British Institution of Civil Engineers.
   "  " Société des Ingenieurs Civils (France).
   "  " Verein Dutscher Ingenieure.
   "  " Oesterreichische Ingeineur-und-Architekten Verein.

He is a member of the—

United States Board appointed to test iron, steel, and other metals.
New Jersey State Commission to report a Plan for Encouragement of Manufactures of Ornamental and Textile Fabrics.

He is author of numerous other books, reports, and papers, which hold high rank among scientific men in this country and in Europe.

Only Child:

7630   Harriet Taylor,[8] b. Aug. 22, 1866.

## 6774

FRANK TAYLOR THURSTON[7] of Hoboken, N. J. (*Robert Lawton,*[6] *Peleg,*[5] *Capt. John,*[4] *Jonathan,*[3] *Edward,*[2] *Edward*[1]), brother of the preceding, and son of Robert Lawton[6] and Harriet (Taylor) Thurston of Providence, R. I.; born there Sept. 17, 1844; married, April 24,

1867, IDA TREADWELL, born March 12, 1848, daughter of Henry Payson and Phebe Nelson (Olney) Treadwell of Providence.

Mr. Thurston is a civil and mechanical engineer, and surveyor to the city of Hoboken. Mrs. Thurston is a lady of literary taste and ability, and writes for some of the public journals with great acceptance.

Children :

7635  Mabel Nelson,[8] b. at Providence June 3, 1869.
7636  Ernest Lawton,[8] b. at Fall River, Mass., Feb. 13, 1873.

## 6780

HENRY C. THURSTON[7] of Ashley Falls, Mass. (*Edward,*[6] *Jonathan,*[5] *Capt. John,*[4] *Jonathan,*[3] *Edward,*[2] *Edward*[1]), eldest son of Edward[6] and Catharine (Hubbard) Thurston of Brooklyn, N. Y.; born there March 24, 1807; married, first, Nov. 28, 1830, CATHARINE SMITH of Catskill, N. Y.; she died March 11, 1840, aged 32. Second, July 6, 1842, ALMIRA ALLEN SMITH of Green River, N. Y.

His children, by first wife, Catharine :

7640  Henry S.,[8] b. Jan. 18, 1832; m. April 7, 1855, Jennie Colton.
7641  Harriet,[8]  ⎰ twins, b. May 9, 1834;  d. Sept. 23, 1835.
7642  Marietta,[8] ⎱                          d. May 30, 1834.
7643  Harriet Evaline,[8] b. July 3, 1836; m. July 6, 1852, Eugene Decker, and had :
    7644  *Alice* (Decker), b. April 14, 1853.
    7645  *John* (Decker), b. Dec. 30, 1855.
    7646  *Frank* (Decker), b. Nov. 26, 1859.
    7647  *Madgie* (Decker), b. Nov. 8, 1862.
    7648  *Ina* (Decker), b. Dec. 17, 1866.

By second wife, Almira :

7649  Mary E.,[8] b. Nov. 10, 1844.
7650  Alice R.,[8] b. May 26, 1847.
7651  Esther Anna,[8] b. Oct. 23, 1849.
7652  Albert,[8] b. Jan. 8, 1853; d. March 20, 1853.
7653  William,[8] b. March 13, 1854.

## 6781

ROBERT F. THURSTON[7] of Brooklyn, N. Y. (*Edward,*[6] *Jonathan,*[5] *Capt. John,*[4] *Jonathan,*[3] *Edward,*[2] *Edward*[1]), brother of the preceding, and son of Edward[6] and Eliza (Fairchild) Thurston of Brooklyn; born there July 8, 1811; married, Feb. 14, 1843, SARAH ANN HUGHES. He is a painter.

Children :

7658  George Washington,[8] b. Dec. 23, 1843; d. Dec. 13, 1845.
7659  Robert Hugh,[8] b. Nov. 26, 1844; m. Oct. 10, 1867, Eve Elizabeth Clarke.
    They have :
    7660  *Sarah Ann,*[9] b. July 6, 1868.
7661  William Christopher,[8] b. Dec. 28, 1846; m. Oct. 16, 1867, Emma Virginia Lyon; with his father in business. Children :
    7662  *Geneveive R.,*[9] b. Sept. 5, 1868.
    7663  *William Fairchild,*[9] b. April 10, 1870.

## 6795

THOMAS THURSTON[7] of Pawtuckett, R. I. (*Thomas,*[6] *William,*[5] *William,*[4] *Jonathan,*[3] *Edward,*[2] *Edward*[1]), second son of Thomas[6] and Martha (Simpson) Thurston of Newport, R. I.; born there June 28, 1812; married, June 16, 1835, MARY BUFFINGTON, born May 10, 1816, daughter of Gardner and Mary Buffington. He is a machinist.

Children:

+7668 Thomas Edwin,[8] b. July 13, 1836; m. Ann Falkner.
7669 Martha Frances,[8] b. Dec. 2, 1837; m. Nov. 11, 1856, Walter Padelford, a
painter in Boston, Mass. They have:
7670 *Mary Lucretia* (Padelford), b. Dec. 27, 1857.

## 6800

WILLIAM CARTER THURSTON [7] of Wilmington, N. C. (*William Car-
ter,*[6] *William,*[5] *William,*[4] *Jonathan,*[3] *Edward,*[2] *Edward*[1]), eldest son
of William Carter [6] and Patience (Young) Thurston of Newport, R. I.;
born there Dec. 6, 1806; married, May 11, 1830, MARY A. MOTT.

Children:

7675 Catharine Hall,[8] b. Dec. 25, 1833; m. May 29, 1850, James Wright, and had:
7676 *Mary Elizabeth* (Wright), b. May 4, 1851.
7677 *Henry Clay* (Wright), b. Dec. 22, 1854.
7678 *William* (Wright), b. Feb. 14, 1856.
7679 William J. Young,[8] b. June 17, 1836; m. May 3, 1864, Zelpha Gulley; had:
7680 *William Carter,*[9] b. Aug. 4, 1865.
7681 *Alice L.,*[9] b. Aug. 11, 1867; d. Oct. 13, 1867.
7682 *Lula,*[9] b. Nov. 29, 1868.
7683 Laura R.,[8] b. Aug. 24, 1841; d. Oct. 16, 1857.
7684 Alice Young,[8] b. Sept. 24, 1844; m. May 13, 1869, William Frost, and had:
7685 *Alice* (Frost), b. Feb. 21, 1870.
7686 Franklin,[8] b. April 28, 1847; d. April 17, 1849.

## 6807

THOMAS JEFFERSON THURSTON [7] of Bristol, R. I. (*William Carter,*[6]
*William,*[5] *William,*[4] *Jonathan,*[3] *Edward,*[2] *Edward*[1]), brother of the
preceding, and son of William Carter [6] and Patience (Young) Thurston
of Newport, R. I.; born there May 26, 1813; married, April 30, 1843,
CLARISSA MONROE, born Aug. 9, 1820, daughter of Thomas B. and
Clarissa (Sandford) Monroe of Bristol; she died March 26, 1879.

Mr. Thurston is a trader; was many years postmaster of Bristol;
both members of the Episcopal church.

Children:

7688 Clara Elizabeth,[8] b. in Providence, R. I., Dec. 16, 1847; d. Jan. 24, 1848.

Born in Bristol:

7689 Winthrop Granville,[8] b. April 9, 1849; m. Nov. 28, 1872, Hannah Mary
Kenyon; graduated at Philadelphia, Pa., and is now in business in Bristol. They have:
7690 *Frank,*[9] b. Sept. 18, 1873.
7691 *A son.*
7692 William Thomas,[8] b. Aug. 2, 1854; m. Nov. 14, 1876, Mary Omsby.
7693 Clara Monroe,[8] b. Aug. 28, 1855.
7694 Madeline Richmond,[8] b. Feb. 14, 1864.

## 6845

LAURENS HULL THURSTON [7] of Bridgewater, N. Y. (*Rowland,*[6] *William,*[5] *George,*[4] *Edward,*[3] *Jonathan,*[2] *Edward*[1]), fourth child of Rowland [6] and Freegift (McKoon) Thurston of Bridgewater; born there
Jan. 7, 1808; married, first, Feb. 20, 1834, EMERA BROWN; second,
Feb. 3, 1859, MRS. SARAH JANE (BIRDSALL) MOSHER, born June 5,
1829, daughter of Rodger Stephens and Sabrina (Hecox) Birdsall of
Paris, Oneida county, N. Y. He died Aug. 24, 1874.

Mr. Thurston was a harness and saddle maker; member of the
Baptist church.

His children, by second wife, Sarah:

7700 Rowland Birdsall,[8] b. Dec. 23, 1860.
7701 Charles Hamton,[8] b. June 17, 1863.
7702 Mary Angeline,[8] b. April 11, 1868.

## 6861

ELIJAH GUILD THURSTON[7] of Lyons, N. Y. (*Elisha,[6] William,[5] George,[4] Edward,[3] Jonathan,[2] Edward[1]*), only son of Elisha[6] and Climena (Guild) Thurston of West Winfield, N. Y.; born there Nov. 6, 1815; married, Feb. 23, 1848, EMELINE CARMAN, born April 3, 1828, daughter of John and Catharine (Corad) Carman of Junius, N. Y. He died Nov. 8, 1857; was a dry goods merchant.

Children:

7707 John Carman,[8] b. Dec. 22, 1848; m. Oct. 16, 1872, Elizabeth Jeanette Fries, b. Aug. 27, 1851, daughter of Andrew and Catherine Fries of Lyons; moved to Medina, Orleans Co., N. Y., May, 1874; is in the grocery business. They have:
    7708  *Edna Carman,[9]* b. Nov. 10, 1875.
7709 Frank Walker,[8] b. Dec. 25, 1851; n.m.; a manufacturer of white lead and oil in Chicago, Ill., an advocate of hard money, free trade, and honest administration of public affairs; a member of the Episcopal church.

## 6883

JEREMIAH THURSTON[7] of Ackron, Ohio (*Adam,[6] Edward,[5] George,[4] Edward,[3] Jonathan,[2] Edward[1]*), fourth child of Adam[6] and Eunice (Miner) Thurston of North Stonington, Ct.; born there May 13, 1795; married, Oct. 25, 1818, SOPHIA THAYER. He died March 12, 1829, buried on Thurston Hill, Springfield, N. Y.

Children:

7715 Mary Florina,[8] b. June 12, 1821; d. April 19, 1842.
7716 Martha Lucretia,[8] b. April 13, 1823; d. March 7, 1863.
7717 Ursula Gates,[8] b. Jan. 11, 1827; d. Sept., 1856.

## 6899

CHARLES EDWARD THURSTON[7] of Ackron, Ohio (*Adam[6] Edward,[5] George,[4] Edward,[3] Jonathan,[2] Edward[1]*), brother of the preceding, and son of Adam[6] and Eunice (Miner) Thurston of North Stonington, Ct.; born there April 6, 1812; married, November, 1839, SUSAN SWEET. He died June 22, 1844.

Children:

7720 Silas,[8] b. Feb. 23, 1840; d. April 21, 1844.
7721 Joseph Warren,[8] b. Nov., 1841.

## 6917

LINUS THURSTON[7] of Springfield Center, N. Y. (*Joshua,[6] Edward,[5] George,[4] Edward,[3] Jonathan,[2] Edward[1]*), second child of Joshua[6] and Betsey (Greene) Thurston of Springfield, N. Y.; born there Aug. 4, 1797; married, Dec. 11, 1817, ABBY BLANCHARD, born at Argyle, N. Y., May 13, 1795, daughter of Elias [wounded at the battle of Bunker Hill] and Mary (Parker) Blanchard of Coventry, R. I.

Mr. Thurston was a farmer at Cincinnatus, Courtland Co., N. Y., and now on Thurston Hill, Springfield Center.

Children, born at Cincinnatus:

+7725 Elias,[8] b. Aug. 19, 1818; m. Phylinda Sitts.
+7726 Job,[8] b. Dec. 16, 1820; m. Margaret McRarie.
7727 Lydia,[8] b. July 5, 1822; m. 1st, Thomas Humphrey; 2d, Smith Bailey.

Born on Thurston Hill:

7728 John,[8] b. April 19, 1824; m. July 15, 1852, Katherine Stal; no children.
7729 Richard Cotton,[8] b. Aug. 29, 1826; m. Sept. 12, 1848, Helen M. Smith; a farmer on Thurston Hill. They had:
    7730 *Celia Ann*,[9] b. May 28, 1849.
7731 Mary,[8] b. Aug. 21, 1828; m. Nov. 17, 1850, Leander Welden, and had:
    7732 *Abby Jane* (Welden), b. June 1, 1852.
    7733 *Nettie* (Welden), b. Nov. 21, 1856.
7734 Barzille,[8] b. July 6, 1830; d. Aug. 28, 1840.
7735 Clark,[8] b. April 16, 1832; m. July, 1854, Christina Sitts, and had:
    7736 *Emily Jeanette*,[9] b. Aug. 10, 1855.
7737 Nancy,[8] b. March 21, 1834; m. Oct. 9, 1853, David A. Jackson, and had:
    7738 *Charles* (Jackson), b. April 17, 1859.
    7739 *Jennie* (Jackson), b. July 18, 1861.

## 6928

SILAS RAWSON THURSTON [7] of Hemlock Lake, Livingston Co., N.Y. (*Joshua*,[6] *Edward*,[5] *George*,[4] *Edward*,[3] *Jonathan*,[2] *Edward*[1]), brother of the preceding, and son of Joshua [6] and Betsey (Greene) Thurston of Springfield, N. Y.; born there July 11, 1808; married, Nov. 9, 1837, NANCY HART. He died September, 1872.

Children:

7744 George A.,[8] b. Sept. 4, 1838.
7745 Sarah Ann,[8] b. June 23, 1840.
7746 Charles Rawson,[8] b. Feb. 2, 1842; d. Sept. 18, 1847.
7747 Clara Jane,[8] b. Sept. 27, 1849; d. Oct. 16, 1853.
7748 William Henry,[8] b. March 16, 1858.

## 6935

CYRUS THURSTON [7] of Wellesville, N. Y. (*Joshua*,[6] *Edward*,[5] *George*,[4] *Edward*,[3] *Jonathan*,[2] *Edward*[1]), brother of the preceding, and son of Joshua [6] and Betsey (Greene) Thurston of Springfield, N. Y.; born there Aug. 13, 1815; married, first, Oct. 15, 1837, MARY ANN PICKENS, born in Otsego, N. Y., April 27, 1816, died in Perry, Wyoming Co., N. Y., May 22, 1874; second, June 24, 1877, MRS. NANCY M. HOLMES, born April 13, 1825, daughter of Thomas and Jemima Moon of Independence, Allegany Co., N. Y.

Mr. Thurston went to Perry in 1846 as a farmer and shoemaker. In 1875 sold his farm and moved to Wellesville, and since his last marriage lives on the farm his wife owned; is a member of the Baptist church.

His children, by first wife, Mary:

+7753 Lucian Edward,[8] } b. in Springfield Center { m. Theresa Melvina Stephens.
+7754 Lewis Daniel,[8] } July 30, 1839; { m. Martha Harriet Malone.
7755 Wesley Ward,[8] b. in Perry Nov. 11, 1848; m. May 11, 1871, Allie Preston, b. Sept. 23, 1851, daughter of John Eaton and Mary Ann (Miller) Preston of Howard, Steuben Co., N. Y.; no children. Mr. Thurston was a dry goods merchant in Wellesville till 1872, when he went into the fruit and variety business, and also became proprietor of a hand bakery, to which he applied steam and a patent oven. He was collector of taxes in Perry Center three consecutive years and a leader of the Methodist church choir.
7756 Adda Bell,[8] b. in Perry Jan. 26, 1860; in Wellesville, teaching, 1879; member of the Baptist church.

## 6940

HIRAM THURSTON[7] of Canton, Ohio (*Charles,[6] Edward,[5] George,[4] Edward,[3] Jonathan,[2] Edward[1]*), eldest son of Charles[6] and Margaret (Fish) Thurston of Cooperstown, N. Y.; born there Dec. 25, 1806; married, Sept. 16, 1831, LUANNA SIMONS, daughter of Charles and Margaret Simons of Utica, N. Y.

Mr. Thurston was a stereotyper and book-binder in employ as foreman of H. & E. Phinney of Cooperstown till the fire of 1846 and 1847, which destroyed their establishment, when he went to the Benthusens in Albany, N. Y., where he remained two years, removing to Buffalo, where he staid till 1858. He then removed to Canton, purchased a house and established a blank-book manufactory. A few years since he took his son Charles into partnership under the firm name of H. Thurston & Son.

Children :

7760   Hannah Isadore,[8] b. Sept. 30, 1834; m. Oct. 15, 1868, Richard T. Davis, b. in Pittsburgh, Pa.; he served one year and ten months in the 63d Pennsylvania regiment against the rebellion, and was honorably discharged for physical disability; is now an iron molder in Canton. They have :
    7761   *Luana* (Davis), b. Aug. 22, 1869.
    7762   *Carrie* (Davis), b. Feb. 22, 1871.
+7763   George Emerson,[8] b. Feb. 20, 1836; m. Lizzie Palmer.
7764   Hiram Lyman,[8] b. Oct. 15, 1837; d. Nov. 22, 1853.
7765   Deidama,[8] b. Sept. 19, 1840; d. Dec. 30, 1841.
7766   Charles Alonzo,[8] b. Oct. 10, 1843; m. Oct. 13, 1870, Louisiana Van Horne Cock, b. March 3, 1849, daughter of John S. and Elizabeth Cock. In business with his father; served in the 162d Ohio regiment in the war against the rebellion.

## 6952

PHILANDER THURSTON[7] of Black River, Jefferson county, N. Y. (*Cyrus,[6] Edward,[5] George,[4] Edward,[3] Jonathan,[2] Edward[1]*), eldest son of Cyrus[6] and Sarah (Spencer) Thurston of Springfield, N. Y.; born there Jan. 29, 1810; married, April 8, 1838, JANE CLEVELAND, born Jan. 1, 1814, daughter of Harvey and Relief (Cross) Cleveland.

Mr. Thurston has been a hotel keeper; now retired, in feeble health, 1879.

Children :

7770   Jane Ann,[8] b. June 9, 1839; m. Oct. 14, 1858, Orville Comins, a chair maker at Black River. Children :
    7771   *Martha* (Comins), b. April 4, 1860.
    7772   *Mary* (Comins), b. Nov. 18, 1861.
    7773   *Hattie* (Comins), b. April 3, 1863; d. Nov. 23, 1865.
    7774   *Jennie* (Comins), b. Aug. 12. 1864; d. Aug. 10, 1865.
    7775   *Alfred* (Comins), b. Nov. 26, 1866.
    7776   *Nettie* (Comins), b. Aug. 8, 1868.
    7777   *Maria* (Comins), b. July 14, 1870.
    7778   *Vernon Spencer* (Comins), b. Nov. 4, 1874.
7779   Martha Amelia,[8] b. Sept. 8, 1842; m. June 27, 1860, George Pettibone Oaks, a farmer in Fremont, Ohio. They have :
    7780   *George Kimble* (Oaks), b. April 8, 1861.
    7781   *Nellie* (Oaks), b. Dec. 5, 1864.
    7782   *Fanny Bell* (Oaks), b. Sept. 20, 1871.
7783   Maria Ophelia,[8] b. May 6, 1849; n.m.

## 6961

BENJAMIN BABCOCK THURSTON[7] of New London, Ct. (*Jeremiah,[6] George,[5] George,[4] Edward,[3] Jonathan,[2] Edward[1]*), second child of

Jeremiah[6] and Sarah (Babcock) Thurston of Hopkinton, R. I.; born there June 29, 1804; married, first, March 5, 1828, HARRIET ELIZA-BETH DESHON, daughter of Daniel and Sarah Deshon of New London; she died Nov. 8, 1832, aged 27. Second, March 12, 1834, FRANCES ELIZABETH DESHON, daughter of John and Fanny Deshon of New London; she died May 11, 1865.

Mr. Thurston resided in Hopkinton; was lieutenant governor of Rhode Island in 1839, and representative to the 30th, 32d, 33d, and 34th congress; was elected twenty consecutive times to the legisla-ture of Rhode Island; now, 1879, resides in New London, where he removed in 1861, and was elected to the general assembly in 1869 and 1870; is a member of the Episcopal church.

### His children, by first wife, Harriet:

+7788  Benjamin Francis,[8] b. Nov. 7, 1829; m. Cornelia Rathbone.
 7789  George Edward,[8] b. March 11, 1831; a lieutenant in revenue cutter service.

### By second wife, Frances:

 7790  Harriet Elizabeth,[8] b. Sept. 20, 1836; m. July 17, 1877, Lieut. James Mon-roe Ingalls, U. S. A.; he was in several battles in the war against the rebellion, the most prominent being that under Gen. Hooker in Chatta-nooga, called the "battle above the clouds." They have:
   7791  *Fanny Thurston* (Ingalls), b. June 20, 1878.
 7792  Fanny Robertson,[8] b. Feb. 15, 1839; n.m.
 7793  John Deshon,[8] b. Feb. 27, 1842; graduated from Brown 1862; n.m.; an attorney and counselor at law in Providence, R. I., associated with his brother, B. F. Thurston, and J. M. Ripley.

### 6968

FRANKLIN THURSTON[7] of Muscatine, Iowa (*Jeremiah,[6] George,[5] George,[4] Edward,[3] Jonathan,[2] Edward[1]*), brother of the preceding, and son of Jeremiah[6] and Sarah (Babcock) Thurston of Hopkinton, R. I.; born there March 4, 1814; married, first, at New Albany, Ind., September, 1839, LAURA M. HAWLEY, daughter of Earl Percy and Irene (Frisbie) Hawley; she died July, 1842. Second, Oct. 6, 1845, MARGARET REECE, born July 5, 1822, daughter of John and Susan (Hood) Reece of Chester county, Pa. He died May 26, 1878, sud-denly, of heart disease.

Mr. Thurston was in the boot and shoe business in company with his son-in-law, Eugene Horton Dolsen, in Muscatine; held several municipal offices; was a member of the Congregational church; thor-oughly respected by all who knew him.

### His children, by second wife, Margaret:

 7798  Edna Reece,[8] b. Sept. 29, 1846; m. Jan. 11, 1866, Eugene Horton Dolsen, b. April 24, 1838, son of John Jansen and Emily (Horton) [of the old Barnabas Horton family of Southold, L. I.] Dolsen of Orange Co., N. Y. Mr. Dolsen is in the boot and shoe trade in Muscatine. They have:
   7799  *Carrie Thurston* (Dolsen), b. Dec. 14, 1866.
   7800  *Laura May* (Dolsen), b. May 8, 1870.
   7801  *Frank Thurston* (Dolsen), b. June 15, 1872.
 7802  Laura Hawley,[8] b. June 13, 1850; m. Aug. 30, 1871, John Dudly Hopkin-son, b. July 4, 1848, son of Francis [b. in Maine Feb. 26, 1816] and Rachel Ann (Phillips) [b. in Virginia June 19, 1817] Hopkinson; he is a hat, cap, and fur dealer in Muscatine. They have:
   7803  *Nellie Thurston* (Hopkinson), b. April 4, 1878.

## 6969

DR. HORACE THURSTON[7] of Norwich, Ct. (*Jeremiah,*[6] *George,*[5] *George,*[4] *Edward,*[3] *Jonathan,*[2] *Edward*[1]), brother of the preceding, and son of Jeremiah[6] and Sarah (Babcock) Thurston of Hopkinton, R. I.; born there March 4, 1814; married, Sept. 6, 1849, CAROLINE LOUISA QUIMBY, born 1823, daughter of Amos [teacher, native of Maine] and Sarah (Boynton) Quimby of New Bedford and Boston, Mass.; she died in Norwich July 18, 1863.

Mr. Thurston graduated from Harvard medical department in 1844, and same year was admitted to the Massachusetts Medical Society; has been assistant surgeon in the army, clerk in treasury department in Washington, D. C., and is a member of the Episcopal church.

### Children:

7808   Evelyn,[8] b. Dec. 15, 1850; d. Nov. 20, 1863.
7809   Horace,[8] b. June 6, 1852; a machinist in Providence, R. I.
7810   Franklin,[8] b. Nov. 17, 1853; n.m.; d. July 29, 1875.
7811   Caroline Louisa,[8] b. Nov. 12, 1858; d. August, 1860.
7812   William Torry,[8] b. May 10, 1863; d. Sept. 12, 1863.

## 6975

WHITMAN THURSTON[7] of Exeter, R. I. (*Nathaniel,*[6] *George,*[5] *George,*[4] *Edward,*[3] *Jonathan,*[2] *Edward*[1]), eldest son of Nathaniel[6] and Mary (Whitman) Thurston of Exeter; born there Oct. 22, 1795; married, May 19, 1814, ELIZABETH PHILLIPS, daughter of Thomas and Lydia Phillips. He was a cotton manufacturer; died Jan. 22, 1847.

### Children:

+7817   Stephen Whitman,[8] b. Feb. 6, 1817; m. Abby Remington Johnson.
7818   Eliza Ann,[8] b. Jan. 6, 1819; m. Aug. 23, 1841, Benjamin Russell Briggs of Warwick, R. I.; he died in California. They had:
     7819   *Nichols Johnson* (Briggs), b. Aug. 5, 1842; d. Sept. 9, 1868, accidentally shot in Kansas; was three years in the war against the rebellion in the cavalry service.
7820   Mary Ann,[8] b. Aug. 11, 1820; n.m.
7821   Lydia,[8] b. Nov. 19, 1823; d. Sept. 22, 1824.
7822   Harriet,[8] b. Jan. 16, 1826; m. Feb. 6, 1850, Nathaniel Thurston Dexter of Owego, N. Y. [see no. 6984]; she died April 8. 1857; no children.
7823   Abby Arnold,[8]   } twins, born {   d. single Sept. 9, 1864.
7824   William Clark,[8]   } July 22, 1828; {   m. Oct. 13, 1854, Susan L. Guyton of Boston, Mass. He was in the army against the rebellion; d. in Exeter, R. I., 1872; no children.
7825   Caroline Matilda,[8] b. Feb. 12, 1831; m. 1858, Lieut. George W. Stevens and lives in Kansas; he served in the army against the rebellion, and died in Kansas, 1866, from exposure while in service. They had:
     7826   *Harriet Lydia* (Stevens), b. 1860.

## 7040

GEORGE GARDNER THURSTON[7] of Hemlock Lake, Livingston Co., N. Y. (*Robert,*[6] *Gardner,*[5] *George,*[4] *Edward,*[3] *Jonathan,*[2] *Edward*[1]), eldest son of Robert[6] and Eliza (Hannahs) Thurston of Livōnia Center, N. Y.; born there April 2, 1827; married, at Vernon Center, Oneida Co., N. Y., Sept. 14, 1853, ABIGAIL ALMIRA FAIRCHILD, born in Madison, N. Y., Dec. 29, 1833, daughter of Ashir and Abigail (Gaylord) Fairchild. Mr. Thurston is a farmer.

Children:

7830   George Robert,[8] b. Oct. 7, 1854.
7831   Charles Gaylord,[8] b. Jan. 20, 1856.
7832   Willie Henry,[8] b. Dec. 29, 1859..
7833   Freddie Nelson,[8] b. Feb. 5, 1869.
7834   Mary Eliza,[8] b. Oct. 22, 1873.

## 7041

HENRY DAVID THURSTON[7] of Livonia, N. Y. (*Robert,*[6] *Gardner,*[5] *George,*[4] *Edward,*[3] *Jonathan,*[2] *Edward*[1]), brother of the preceding, and son of Robert[6] and Eliza (Hannahs) Thurston of Livonia Center; born there Sept. 25, 1828; married, July 25, 1850, FRANCES ADAMS.

Children:

7840   Genevieve,[8] b. 1851.
7841   Eva E.,[8] b. 1853.
7842   Ella,[8]    }
7843   Emma,[8]   } twins, b. 1856.
7844   Eliza,[5] b. 1858.
7845   Frances,[8] b. 1859.

## 7056

ALBERT THURSTON[7] of Worcester, Mass. (*Jeremiah,*[6] *Gardner,*[5] *George,*[4] *Edward,*[3] *Jonathan,*[2] *Edward*[1]), seventh child of Jeremiah[6] and Maria (Southworth) Thurston of Hartford, Ct.; born in Glastenbury, Ct., Sept. 17, 1837; married, May 17, 1857, CATHARINE M. JOHNSON, born Feb. 24, 1837, daughter of Benjamin and Lucy F. (Larrabee) Johnson of Machiasport, Me.   He is a car inspector.

Children:

7850   Willie Albert,[8] b. in Orange, Mass., Feb. 15, 1858; d. in Hartford, Ct., Sept. 5, 1862.
7851   Blanche Ellen,[8] b. in East Hartford Sept. 3, 1863; d. Nov. 12, 1863.
7852   Ennes Redell,[8] b. in East Hartford June 8, 1866.
7853   William Eugene,[8] b. in Worcester Aug. 13, 1874.

## 7075

DUDLEY SULLIVAN THURSTON[7] of Rochester, N. Y. (*William,*[6] *Gardner,*[5] *George,*[4] *Edward,*[3] *Jonathan,*[2] *Edward*[1]), third child of William[6] and Abby (Hannahs) Thurston of Livonia, N. Y.; born there Jan. 27, 1839; married, in Livonia, Dec. 31, 1868, SARAH EMILY WIGGIN, born Nov. 1, 1846, daughter of Joseph and Emily (Edgel) Wiggin of Rochester.   Mr. Thurston is freight agent of the railroad.

Children:

7858   Gertrude Emily,[8] b. in Livonia Sept. 22, 1869.
7859   Mary Palmer,[8] b. in Livonia Oct. 4, 1871.
7860   Charles Gardner,[8] b. in Rochester Sept. 30, 1873.

## 7080

WILLIAM ANDREWS THURSTON[7] of Fort Madison, Iowa (*Job,*[6] *Joseph,*[5] *George,*[4] *Edward,*[3] *Jonathan,*[2] *Edward*[1]), eldest son of Job[6] and Susanna (Andrews) Thurston of East Greenwich, R. I.; born there Dec. 29, 1808; married, at Penn Yan, N. Y., Sept. 25, 1830, UNA LAY PRATT, born Aug. 27, 1805, daughter of Ebenezer and Susan (Pratt) Pratt of Deep River, Ct.   He died June 10, 1870.

Mr. Thurston moved to Mount Pleasant, Iowa, in 1838, and to

Fort Madison in 1846. He practiced law successfully; was state senator two years; member of the Baptist church, and superintendent of the Sunday-school from its organization ten years, till the autumn before his death he relinquished it from failing health. His widow resides with her brother, George A. Pratt, Norwich, Ct., 1879.

Children:

7865 Susan Andrews,[8] b. at Penn Yan July 21, 1832; d. at Pleasant Ridge, Iowa, July 31, 1846.
7866 Charles Jeremiah,[8] b. at Seneca Falls, N. Y., Nov. 13, 1834; d. Sept. 4, 1835.
7867 Charles Iowa,[8] b. at Pleasant Ridge Sept. 2, 1838; d. at Fort Madison Dec. 18, 1846.
7868 Josephene Golding,[8] b. at Pleasant Ridge June 30, 1842; d. Aug. 24, 1846.
7869 Eugene Thomas,[8] b. at Pleasant Ridge Feb. 18, 1845; d. at Fort Madison Feb. 15, 1847.
7870 Willie Eugene,[8] b. at Fort Madison Jan. 10, 1848; d. May 30, 1850.

## 7135

JOHN CLARKE THURSTON[7] of Providence, R. I. (*John Taylor,*[6] *Joseph,*[5] *George,*[4] *Edward,*[3] *Jonathan,*[2] *Edward*[1]), second child of John Taylor[6] and Hannah (Reynolds) Thurston of Westerly, R. I.; born there June 26, 1808; married, April 6, 1829, MARY LEEDS MILLER of Stonington, Ct. He died March 26, 1859; she died July 15, 1860; both buried in Westerly. He was a ship and house carpenter.

Children:

7875 Sarah Elizabeth,[8] b. March 4, 1830; m. June 13, 1853, Edwin Mervin Crombie; d. Oct. 30, 1858, leaving:
　　7876 *Everett Mervin* (Crombie), b. Aug. 28, 1857.
7877 John Taylor,[8] b. Nov. 10, 1832; d. Jan. 15, 1833.
7878 Frances Mary,[8] b. Dec. 12, 1833; m. Nov. 5, 1849, William D. Pendleton.
7879 Ann Josephene,[8] b. Nov. 20, 1836; m. at Rocky Brook, R. I., Oct. 5, 1861, Frank deVolney Sloan, b. June 8, 1839, son of David and Sophronia (Parker) Sloan of Wilton, Vt.; he is in the employ of the gas company of Providence; enlisted in the 1st Rhode Island regiment against the rebellion, also in the 8th Connecticut and served till the close of the war. She is a member of the Free Baptist church; no children.
7880 Benjamin Reynolds,[8] b. Feb. 19, 1839; m. Jan. 1, 1861, Susan F. James.
7881 Martha Babcock,[8] b. May 18, 1842; m. March 26, 1861, Samuel R. Eccleston of Providence.
7882 John Henry,[8] b. March 20, 1847; at the age of nineteen he went to sea, and the last heard of him he was in the Argentine service, So. America; supposed to be dead.
7883 Catherine Ella,[8] b. Sept. 6, 1853; d. Nov. 22, 1871.

## 7149

AUGUSTUS YORK THURSTON[7] of Providence, R. I. (*Peleg Grinald,*[6] *Joseph,*[5] *George,*[4] *Edward,*[3] *Jonathan,*[2] *Edward*[1]), fifth child of Peleg G.[6] and Ann (York) Thurston of Johnston, R. I.; born in Charlestown, R. I., April 20, 1821; married, first, Sept. 20, 1843, JULIA MARIA ANGELL, born in Foster, R. I., April 11, 1823, daughter of Abraham and Ann (Hill) Angell of Scituate, R. I.; she died Aug. 15, 1849. Second, May 15, 1851, LYDIA BACON POTTER, born Aug. 11, 1824, daughter of Edmund and Lydia Burlingame (Greene) Potter of North Providence. Mr. Thurston was a machinist.

His children, by first wife, Julia:

7888 Abby Frances,[8] b. in Scituate Aug. 11, 1849; d. Aug. 29, 1849.

By second wife, Lydia :
7889   Myron Marcellus,[8] b. in Providence July 1, 1854; d. Sept. 5, 1855.
7890   Warren Greene,[8] b. April 17, 1858.

## 7203

BENJAMIN REYNOLDS THURSTON [7] of Providence, R. I. (*Clarke,[6] Joseph,[5] George,[4] Edward,[3] Jonathan,[2] Edward [1]*), second child of Clarke [6] and Abby (Reynolds) Thurston of Hopkinton, R. I.; born there March 31, 1819; married, first, Jan. 19, 1840, ELIZABETH HARWOOD MARBLE, born Jan. 26, 1824, daughter of John and Margaret (Harwood) Marble of Providence; she died Dec. 26, 1844, aged 20. Second, Jan. 16, 1846, LAURA HENLEY, born Oct. 27, 1820, daughter of John Drury and Ann (Clark) Henley of Providence; she died in Pawtucket, R. I., Nov. 19, 1864, aged 44. Third, in Pawtucket, Oct. 5, 1865, LUCY PAINE, born March 1, 1821, daughter of Daniel and Sarah (Lyon) Paine of Woodstock, Ct. Mr. Thurston is a machinist.

His children, born in Providence, by first wife, Elizabeth :
7895    Lucinda J.,[8] b. July 31, 1841 ; d. June, 1847.
+7896   Clarke,[8] b. Oct. 24, 1842 ; m. Emma Rebecca Cornell.
7897    Abby Reynolds,[8] b. Sept. 18, 1844; d. Jan. 30, 1845.

By second wife, Laura :
7898    Benjamin,[8] b. April 3, 1847; m. 1st, April 9, 1873, Ida Janette Stevens, b. July 25, 1851, daughter of James Edwin and Melissa Durfee (Andrews) Stevens of Providence; she died in Anthony, R. I., Aug. 22, 1875; 2d, Aug. 26, 1876, Amelia Shockley Jillson, b. in New Bedford, Mass., Nov. 10, 1854, daughter of Albert and Elizabeth Sabin (Hathaway) Jillson of Providence. Mr. Thurston is a machinist in Providence. They have:
          7899   *Elizabeth Jillson,*[9] b. July 9, 1877.
+7900   Christopher Columbus,[8] b. Nov. 26, 1848; m. Josephene Briggs.
7901    Abby Ann,[8] b. May 27, 1850; m. Jan. 30, 1873, Edward Horace Spencer, b. July 9, 1847, son of Edward Horace and Sarah Ann (Rathburn) Spencer of Providence; he is an engraver in Providence. They have:
          7902   *Charles Morton* (Spencer), b. Nov. 19, 1873.
7903    Edward Taylor,[8] b. June 27, 1852; d. March 14, 1853.
7904    George William,[8] b. in Johnston, R. I., March 16, 1854.
7905    Charles,[8] b. in Johnston Feb. 25, 1861; d. same day.

## 7204

AMON REYNOLDS THURSTON [7] of Providence, R. I. (*Clarke,[6] Joseph,[5] George,[4] Edward,[3] Jonathan,[2] Edward [1]*), brother of the preceding, and son of Clarke [6] and Abby (Reynolds) Thurston of Hopkinton, R. I.; born there Sept. 16, 1820; married, June 17, 1845, SARAH ANN GARLAND, born in Boston, Mass., daughter of John and Sarah Garland. Mr. Thurston is a machinist.

Children :
+7910   Henry Amon,[8] b. May 3, 1848; m. Martha Hopkins Turner.
7911    Walter Deey,[8] b. March 30, 1852; d. April 6, 1853.
7912    Frank Clark,[8] b. June 22, 1855; m. Dec. 25, 1876, Mary Florence Moore; is a machinist in Providence. They have:
          7913   *Willard Henry,*[9] b. Dec. 2, 1877.

## 7216

ELLIS BURGESS PITCHER THURSTON [7] of Providence, R. I. (*Clarke,[6] Joseph,[5] George,[4] Edward,[3] Jonathan,[2] Edward [1]*), brother of the preceding, and son of Clarke [6] and Abby (Reynolds) Thurston of Hopkinton, R. I.; born there May 15, 1830; married, July 24, 1851,

CLARINDA MARY JANE BRIGGS, born in Arkwright, R. I., March 9, 1831, daughter of Joseph Warren and Roby Rathburn (Stone) Briggs of Providence. Mr. Thurston is a tool maker.

Children :

7918 Albert Deey,[8] b. May 11, 1853; a jeweler in Providence; n.m.
7919 Joseph Warren,[8] b. Feb. 7, 1858; d. Oct. 18, 1862.

## 7235

EDWARD NORTH THURSTON[7] of Charleston, S. C. (*Robert,[6] Samuel Isaac,[5] Samuel,[4] Edward,[8] Samuel,[2] Edward[1]*), eldest son of Robert[6] and Eliza Emily (North) Thurston of Charleston; born there Aug. 5, 1831; married, first, Feb. 15, 1855, SARAH CONSTANCE CHISHOLM, daughter of Dr. Edward N. Chisholm; she died Sept. 20, 1858. Second, May 29, 1865, MRS. SOPHIA ELIZABETH (HILL) BEE, widow of General Barnard E. Bee and daughter of Capt. James M. and Sophia (Hoffman) Hill. Capt. Hill was an officer in the United States army, born in Portsmouth, N. H., March 19, 1808, died in Baltimore, Md., Jan. 29, 1849. Mr. Thurston is a merchant.

His children, by second wife, Sophia :

7934 Edward North,[8] b. Jan. 29, 1866.
7935 Sophia Hoffman,[8] b. Oct. 7, 1868.
7936 Robert,[8] b. Aug. 19, 1870.
7937 William Ravenel[8] b. Dec. 25, 1872; d. Jan. 16, 1873.

## 7236

ROBERT THURSTON[7] of Charleston, S. C. (*Robert,[6] Samuel Isaac,[5] Samuel,[4] Edward,[8] Samuel,[2] Edward[1]*), brother of the preceding, and son of Robert[6] and Eliza Emily (North) Thurston of Charleston; born there May 26, 1833; married, Feb. 19, 1856, MARIA REES FORD [see no. 6402], born July 26, 1831, daughter of Stephen and Jane Caroline (Thurston) Ford of Georgetown, S. C. He died April 20, 1868, aged 35; she with her children removed to Atlanta, Ga., where she resided for a time; returned to Charleston and died June 6, 1877.

Mr. Thurston was a civil engineer by profession; president of the Charleston Gas Light Company at time of his death.

Children:

7942 Frederick Ford,[8] b. Jan. 8, 1857.
7943 Sarah Constance,[8] b. Aug. 16, 1859.
7944 Edward North,[8] b. Aug. 29, 1861; d. July, 1876.

## 7286

HENRY THURSTON[7] of Kingston, Canada (*George,[6] Samuel,[5] Samuel,[4] John,[8] Samuel,[2] Edward[1]*), seventh child of George[6] and Sophia (Hawn) Thurston of Kingston; born there June 22, 1847; married, at Millbrook, P. Q., Dec. 20, 1871, SARAH DAVIS, born Feb. 17, 1851, daughter of James and Jane (Lemond) Davis of Kingston. He is a machinist.

Children :

7948 Lilly Sophia,[8] b. Oct. 10, 1872.
7949 Edward Henry,[8] b. Dec. 20, 1874.

## 7320

ADAM M. THURSTON[7] of Centerville, R. I. (*James,*[6] *Nathaniel,*[5] *Edward,*[4] *Edward,*[3] *Thomas,*[2] *Edward*[1]), eldest son of James[6] and Ruth (Waddell) Thurston of Fall River, Mass.; born there July 10, 1824; married, April 2, 1848, LUCY C. HARVEY.

Children:

7954   Emma A.,[8] b. May 27, 1849.
7955   Lucy J.,[8] b. Nov. 11, 1852.
7956   Warren A.,[8] b. Jan. 20, 1862.
7957   George A.,[8] b. July 20, 1864.
7958   Charles C.,[8] b. Oct. 26, 1865; d. Aug. 10, 1866.

## 7373

ALBERT HIRAM THURSTON[7] of Freetown, Mass. (*Gardner,*[6] *Nathaniel,*[5] *Edward,*[4] *Edward,*[3] *Thomas,*[2] *Edward*[1]), son of Gardner[6] and Elizabeth S. (Moore) Thurston of Fall River, Mass.; born there Mar. 31, 1845; married, Feb. 28, 1872, BLANCHE ELLEN CALL, born in Dresden, Me., Feb. 27, 1856, daughter of James [inventor of Call's iron center-board for vessels] and Susan Jones (Clemen) Call of Boston, Mass.

Mr. Thurston is a molder by trade, but follows market gardening.

Children:

7963   Agnes Savilla,[8] b. March 15, 1873; d. May 20, 1876.
7964   Leland Walter,[8] b. Sept. 13, 1877.

## 7413

EDWARD MASON THURSTON[7] of Swansea, Mass. (*Edward,*[6] *Varnum,*[5] *Peleg,*[4] *Edward,*[3] *Thomas,*[2] *Edward*[1]), eldest son of Edward[6] and Sarah Maria (Mason) Thurston of Fall River, Mass.; born there July 18, 1832; married, May 1, 1853, MARY WILBUR GARDNER, born Oct. 16, 1833, daughter of Hiram and Mary Wilbur (Gardner) Gardner of Somerset, Mass.

Mr. Thurston is a furniture dealer in Providence, R. I., residence at Swansea; member of the Congregational church, and superintendent of Sunday-school for a number of years.

Children, born in Somerset:

7969   Hiram Edward,[8] b. Jan. 25, 1857; graduated from Amherst 1879.
7970   Mary Maria,[8] b. Feb. 9, 1858; m. July 24, 1878, Samuel Roscoe Chaffee of Providence.
7971   Janette Mason,[8] } twins, b. in Providence { d. Sept. 15, 1860.
7972   Jane Wilbur,[8]   }       July 4, 1859;   { d. Sept. 17, 1860.

## 7414

ANTHONY THURSTON[7] of Fall River, Mass. (*Edward,*[6] *Varnum,*[5] *Peleg,*[4] *Edward,*[3] *Thomas,*[2] *Edward*[1]), brother of the preceding, and son of Edward[6] and Sarah Maria (Mason) Thurston of Fall River; born there Mar. 13, 1837; married, June 1, 1858, ANN MARIA WHIPPLE, daughter of Clark Whipple of Fall River.

Mr. Thurston is highway surveyor and superintendent of streets.

Children:

7977   Frank Anthony,[8] b. March 15, 1864.
7978   John Mason,[8] b. Feb. 20, 1868.

## 7420

JAMES EMERY THURSTON[7] of Fall River, Mass. (*Samuel,*[6] *Varnum,*[5] *Peleg,*[4] *Edward,*[3] *Thomas,*[2] *Edward*[1]), only child of Samuel[6] and Almira (Boomer) Thurston of Fall River; born there Jan. 11, 1838; married, Nov. 7, 1861, MELISSA GIFFORD PECKHAM, daughter of James and Eliza Peckham. She died May 4, 1876; he died Sept. 6, 1878. He was a building mover.

Children:

7983 Mary Ellen,[8] b. Sept. 10, 1863.
7984 Henry Gardner,[8] b. Feb. 10, 1865.

## 7430

REV. CHARLES ABRAHAM GARDNER THURSTON[7] of North Raynham, Mass. (*Abraham Gardner,*[6] *Varnum,*[5] *Peleg,*[4] *Edward,*[3] *Thomas,*[2] *Edward*[1]), eldest son of Abraham Gardner[6] and Catharine Borden (Allen) Thurston of Fall River, Mass.; born there July 23, 1841; married, Dec. 5, 1872, ANNA MOORE, born July 6, 1847, daughter of John Haddock and Harriet Sprague (Wright) Moore of Barnet, Vt.

Mr. Thurston graduated from Brown 1866, and from Andover 1869; was ordained over the church in North Raynham Oct. 17, 1877; sermon by Rev. George Harris of Providence, R. I., ordaining prayer by Rev. S. H. Emery of Taunton, Mass., charge to pastor by Rev. H. D. Walker of Bridgewater, Mass., right hand by Rev. H. Morton Dexter of Taunton, address to the people by Rev. M. Blake, D.D., of Taunton.

Child:

7989 Frederick Harris,[8] b. Nov. 15, 1877.

## 7474

GEORGE EDWIN THURSTON[7] of New York (*John,*[6] *Samuel,*[5] *Thomas,*[4] *Thomas,*[3] *Thomas,*[2] *Edward*[1]), eldest son of John[6] and Mary Ann (Chase) Thurston of Providence, R. I.; born there Sept. 17, 1830; married, first, Sept. 12, 1859, CHARLOTTE AMELIA TOOKER, daughter of William C. and Mary A. Tooker; she died July 14, 1870, aged 36. Second, July 16, 1873, FRANCES TILLOTSON, daughter of J. R. and F. A. Tillotson.

His children, by first wife, Charlotte:

7994 Mary Dickinson,[8] b. Aug. 29, 1860.
7995 Edwin Chase,[8] b. Dec. 25, 1866.

By second wife, Frances:

7996 Maud Olivia,[8] b. Aug. 17, 1874.

## 7510

JAMES OTTEY THURSTON[7] of Brooklyn, N. Y. (*Wanton,*[6] *John,*[5] *John,*[4] *Peleg,*[3] *Thomas,*[2] *Edward*[1]), eldest son of Wanton[6] and Sarah (Ottey) Thurston of St. John, N. B.; born there May, 1842; married, September, 1868, SUSIE ACKERMAN.

Children:

8000 Martin Ackerman,[8] b. May, 1869.
8001 Maud Ottey,[8] b. April, 1871; d. May 9, 1873.
8002 James Ottey,[8] b. July, 1872.

## 𝔈𝔦𝔤𝔥𝔱𝔥 𝔊𝔢𝔫𝔢𝔯𝔞𝔱𝔦𝔬𝔫.

### 7569

WILLIAM STEWART THURSTON [8] of Huntington, L. I. (*Louis Marion,*[7] *Robert Jenkins,*[6] *John,*[5] *Capt. John,*[4] *Jonathan,*[3] *Edward,*[2] *Edward*[1]), fourth child of Louis Marion[6] and Elizabeth Samuella (Brewer) Thurston of Huntington; born there April 8, 1848; married, Dec. 24, 1872, MARY SEYMOUR ACKERMAN, born Oct. 15, 1852, daughter of George Bogert and Ann Aston (de Bevoise) Ackerman of Huntington.

Mr. Thurston is a farmer; a member and vestryman of the Episcopal church.

Children:

8007 William Marion,[9] b. Jan. 20, 1875.
8008 Annie de Bevoise,[9] b. July 7, 1876.
8009 Elizabeth Brewer,[9] b. Sept. 9, 1878.

### 7668

THOMAS THURSTON [8] of Pawtucket, R. I. (*Thomas,*[7] *Thomas,*[6] *William,*[5] *William,*[4] *Jonathan,*[3] *Edward,*[2] *Edward*[1]), eldest son of Thomas [7] and Mary (Buffington) Thurston of Pawtucket; born there July 13, 1836; married, Nov. 7, 1856, ANN FALKNER, daughter of John and Margaret Falkner of Pawtucket.

Mr. Thurston is a machinist; member of the Baptist church.

Children:

8014 Edwin Lafayette,[9] b. Oct. 3, 1857; student of Brown university, class of 1881.
8015 Harriet E.,[9] b. Oct. 15, 1860; d. June 24, 1863.

### 7725

ELIAS THURSTON [8] of Springfield Center, N. Y. (*Linus,*[7] *Joshua,*[6] *Edward,*[5] *George,*[4] *Edward,*[3] *Jonathan,*[2] *Edward*[1]), eldest son of Linus [7] and Abby (Blanchard) Thurston of Springfield Center; born there Aug. 19, 1818; married, July 26, 1845, PHYLINDA SITTS.

Children:

8020 Lavilla,[9] b. May 1, 1847; d. Aug. 21, 1853.
8021 George,[9] b. April 7, 1851; d. Aug. 20, 1857.
8022 Martha Ann,[9] b. July 28, 1853; m. Feb. 15, 1870, Charles Martin.
8023 Athalia,[9] b. July 10, 1856; d. Aug. 5, 1859.

### 7726

JOB THURSTON [8] of Springfield Center, N. Y. (*Linus,*[7] *Joshua,*[6] *Edward,*[5] *George,*[4] *Edward,*[3] *Jonathan,*[2] *Edward*[1]), brother of the preceding, and son of Linus [7] and Abby (Blanchard) Thurston of Springfield Center; born there Dec. 16, 1820; married, Dec. 25, 1842, MARGARET McRARIE.

Children:

+8028 Lucius,[9] b. Sept. 17, 1843; m. 1st, Armena Castle; 2d, Nancy Beach.
8029 Peter,[9] b. May 4, 1855.

## 7753

LUCIAN EDWARD THURSTON [8] of Perry, N. Y. (*Cyrus,*[7] *Joshua,*[6] *Edward,*[5] *George,*[4] *Edward,*[3] *Jonathan,*[2] *Edward*[1]), eldest son of Cyrus [7] and Mary Ann (Pickens) Thurston of Wellesville, N. Y.; born at Springfield Center, N. Y., July 30, 1839; married THERESA MELVINA STEPHENS, daughter of Alfred and Malissa (Sumner) Stephens of Bridgewater, Oneida county, N. Y. He is a member of the Presbyterian church.

Children:
8034  Bessie Ermina,[8] b. May 31, 1875.
8035  Mabel Stephens,[9] b. Jan. 26, 1878.

## 7754

LEWIS DANIEL THURSTON [8] of Perry, N. Y. (*Cyrus,*[7] *Joshua,*[6] *Edward,*[5] *George,*[4] *Edward,*[3] *Jonathan,*[2] *Edward*[1]), brother of the preceding, and son of Cyrus [7] and Mary Ann (Pickens) Thurston of Wellesville, N. Y.; born at Springfield Center, N. Y., July 30, 1839; married, in Perry, Nov. 17, 1862, MARTHA HARRIET MALONE, born in Churchill, N. Y., Oct. 22, 1840, daughter of Joseph and Mary Malone of La Grange, N. Y.

Mr. Thurston was a baker and grocer, which business he sold out in 1878, and engaged in the repairing of clothes-wringers; member of the first Baptist church. He enlisted three times in the war against the rebellion, in different branches, and was as often rejected on account of physical disability.

Children:
8039  Nellie Elizabeth,[9] b. in Perry July 18, 1864.
8040  Charles Edward,[9] b. in La Grange April 4, 1871.
8041  Luland Lewis,[9] b. in Perry June 20, 1878.

## 7763

GEORGE EMERSON THURSTON [8] (*Hiram,*[7] *Charles,*[6] *Edward,*[5] *George,*[4] *Edward,*[3] *Jonathan,*[2] *Edward*[1]), second child of Hiram [7] and Luana (Simons) Thurston of Canton, Ohio; born there Feb. 20, 1836; married, Dec. 13, 1863, LIZZIE PALMER.

Mr. Thurston was a book-binder in Massillon, Ohio; served in the war against the rebellion; since the war has been in several states.

Children:
8045  Edgar Coughlin,[9] b. Sept. 4, 1864.
8046  Walter Ecky,[9] b. April 2, 1867.
8047  Wilbert Palmer,[9] b. July 16, 1868.

## 7788

BENJAMIN FRANCIS THURSTON [8] of Providence, R. I. (*Benjamin Babcock,*[7] *Jeremiah,*[6] *George,*[5] *George,*[4] *Edward,*[3] *Jonathan,*[2] *Edward*[1]), eldest son of Benjamin Babcock [7] and Harriet Elizabeth (Deshon) Thurston of Hopkinton, R. I.; born there Nov. 1, 1829; married, May 9, 1853, CORNELIA RATHBONE, born June 30, 1830, daughter of Stephen Kilton and Sarah (Brown) Rathbone of Providence.

Mr. Thurston graduated from Brown university 1849, and is counselor at law in company with J. M. Ripley and his brother John D.;

23

has been representative in the state legislature three times and senator twice ; three times elected speaker of the popular branch ; is a member of the Episcopal church.

Children :

8052  Ella de Forest,[9] b. Oct. 9, 1857.
8053  Maurice Deshon,[9] b. Aug. 2, 1859; d. Oct. 3, 1860.
8054  Harriet Deshon,[9] b. Jan. 20, 1862.
8055  Benjamin Francis,[9] b. Dec. 30, 1870.

## 7817

STEPHEN WHITMAN THURSTON [8] of Fort Jones, Siskiyou Co., Cal. (*Whitman,*[7] *Nathaniel,*[6] *George,*[5] *George,*[4] *Edward,*[8] *Jonathan,*[2] *Edward*[1]), eldest son of Whitman[7] and Elizabeth (Phillips) Thurston of Exeter, R. I. ; born there Feb. 6, 1817 ; married, May 2, 1842, ABBY REMINGTON JOHNSON, daughter of Levi and Phebe Johnson of Warwick, R. I. ; she died Jan. 19, 1863.

Mr. Thurston is a teacher at Fort Jones. He says : • " I first left New York Feb. 28, 1852, and landed in San Francisco April 1st ; when I last returned I left Providence, R. I., March 18, 1879, and arrived in San Francisco April 3d, and at Fort Jones on the 22d."

Children :

8060  Edwin Remington,[9] b. in Warwick April 3, 1843; supposed to be on the Columbia river in Oregon, engaged in the Salmon fishery; was formerly a bookkeeper in San Francisco; n.m.
8061  Fanny,[9] b. Jan. 12, 1863; d. same day.

## 7896

CLARKE THURSTON [8] of Providence, R. I. (*Benjamin Reynolds,*[7] *Clarke,*[6] *Joseph,*[5] *George,*[4] *Edward,*[8] *Jonathan,*[2] *Edward*[1]), second child of Benjamin Reynolds[7] and Elizabeth Harwood (Marble) Thurston of Providence ; born there Oct. 24, 1842 ; married, July 10, 1865, EMMA REBECCA CORNELL, born April 4, 1828, daughter of James [member of the Massachusett legislature] and Annie (Rounds) Cornell of Swansea, Mass.

Mr. Thurston is vice-president of the Canada Screw Company in Dundas, Ontario. He enlisted in the war against the rebellion as a private in infantry, but subsequently and to the close of the war was an engineer officer in the navy, a greater part of the time on special Torpedo service in James river, at Dutch Gap, and below Richmond. He resides, 1879, in Providence.

Children :

8065  Frederic Lander,[9] b. Feb. 19, 1867.
8066  Emma Rebecca,[9] b. May 13, 1870.

## 7900

CHRISTOPHER COLUMBUS THURSTON [8] of New York city (*Benjamin Reynolds,*[7] *Clarke,*[6] *Joseph,*[5] *George,*[4] *Edward,*[8] *Jonathan*[2] *Edward*[1]), brother of the preceding, and son of Benjamin Reynolds[7] and Laura (Henley) Thurston of Providence, R. I. ; born there Nov. 26, 1848 ; married, in Brooklyn, N. Y., Oct. 20, 1870, JOSEPHENE BRIGGS, born in Pawtucket, R. I., Feb. 7, 1850, daughter of Hiram Augustus [of Europe] and Almira (Harris) Briggs. He is a clerk.

Children, born in Pawtucket:

8070   Laura Henley,[9] b. Oct. 9, 1871: d. in New York city Jan. 7, 1872.
8071   Alice Vivian,[9] b. June 16, 1875; d. in Providence Jan. 10, 1878.

## 7910

HENRY AMON THURSTON[8] of Providence, R. I. (*Amon Reynolds,[7] Clarke,[6] Joseph,[5] George,[4] Edward,[3] Jonathan,[2] Edward[1]*), eldest son of Amon Reynolds[7] and Sarah Ann (Garland) Thurston of Providence; born there May 3, 1848; married, June 29, 1870, MARTHA HOPKINS TURNER, born in Savannah, Ga., Jan. 7, 1849, daughter of Stephen Arnold and Mary Rebecca (Mackey) Turner of Providence. He is a machinist or tool maker.

Children:

8075   Arthur Richards,[9] b. June 1, 1871.
8076   Amon Reynolds,[9] b. Oct. 27, 1874.
8077   Elmer Arnold,[9] b. Dec. 3, 1877.

---

## Ninth Generation.

## 8028

LUCIUS THURSTON[9] of Springfield Center, N. Y. (*Job,[8] Linus,[7] Joshua,[6] Edward,[5] George,[4] Edward,[3] Jonathan,[2] Edward[1]*), eldest son of Job[8] and Margaret (McRarie) Thurston of Springfield Center; born there Sept. 17, 1843; married, first, Dec. 21, 1863, ARMENA CASTLE; second, Jan. 21, 1867, NANCY BEACH.

His children, by first wife, Armena:

8080   Libbie,[10] b. Jan. 24, 1864.

By second wife, Nancy:

8081   Peter,[10] b. May 21, 1868.
8082   Mary,[10] b. March 1, 1870.

# POSTERITY OF JOHN THURSTON.

THE more I have to do with the names and general characteristics of the descendants of John Thurston of Dedham, Mass., the more I am impressed with the conviction that he was from the same family if not a near relative of Daniel of Newbury, Mass. Joseph, the son of John, who went to Long Island, N. Y., has kept up the *names* remarkably, though the *characteristics* are not so marked as in the other members of the family, who settled in New England.

## First Generation.

### 8100

JOHN THURSTON,[1] a carpenter of Wrentham, Suffolk county, Eng., baptized Jan. 13, 1601, aged 36, and his wife MARGARET, aged 32, were passengers for New England in the "Mary Anne" of Yarmouth, Eng., May 10, 1637. They brought two sons with them. He was received into the church in Dedham, Mass., Jan. 12, 1643. He became a freeman May 10, 1643, and it is recorded that he attended a meeting in Dedham in November, 1644,* to provide some means of education for the youth. He had a grant of land in Dedham Feb. 16, 1643. His estate was part in Medfield, set off from Dedham in 1651. His family settled in the adjoining towns of Wrentham and Medfield except Joseph, who is supposed to have gone to Jamaica, Long Island. She died May 9, 1662 ; he died in Medfield Nov. 1, 1685.

Their children were:

+8101   Thomas,[2] bap. in Wrentham, Eng., Aug. 4, 1633; m. Sarah Thaxter.
+8102   John,[2] bap. in Wrentham Sept. 13, 1635; m. Mary Wood.
+8103   Joseph,[2] bap. in Dedham, Mass., Sept. 13, 1640; m. Anne ——.
 8104   Benjamin,[2] b. in Dedham May 8, 1640; bap. Sept. 13, 1640; m. Dec. 12, 1660, Elizabeth Walker, daughter of Robert Walker of Boston, Mass. He was a freeman May 3, 1665, one of the founders of the third or "Old South" church in Boston May 16, 1669, his wife also being an original member.† In 1675, before Philip's war, the General Court made

---

* The town of Dedham was incorporated Sept. 8, 1636; was divided and Medfield incorporated May 23, 1651; it was divided again and Wrentham incorporated Oct. 15, 1673. Wrentham was divided and a part set off and incorporated under the name of Franklin March 2, 1778, in honor of Benjamin Franklin, who, as an acknowledgement of the honor conferred, presented the town with a library, which also bears his name and is in a flourishing condition to this day, 1879.

† The records of this church have the name of Margrett Thurston in 1668.

him ensign under Capt. John Hull. His special friend, Charles Just. Small, says he died of small pox Nov. 10, 1678. They had, b. in Boston:

8105 *Mary*,³ ⎫
8106 *Eleazer*,³ ⎬ twins, b. April 24, 1662.

8107 *Mehitable*,³ b. Nov. 11, 1666.*
8108 *Mary*,³ b. Feb. 11, 1667.
8109 *John*,³ b. March 15, 1669.*
8110 Mary,² b. Jan. 8, and bap. Jan. 12, 1643; m. Dec. 27, 1660, Seth Smith.
+8111 Daniel,² b. May 5, 1646; m. Maria ——.
8112 Judith,² b. Mar. 17, bap. Mar. 29, 1648; m. Mar. 10, 1666, Jonathan Tread-way. She was received into the church in Dedham March 29, 1648.
8113 Hannah,² b. Feb. 28, 1650; m. March 12, 1668, Joseph Cheney.

NOTE. The town records of Medfield show that Deborah Thurston married Jabish Talman Nov. 18, 1665, and it seems almost certain that she was a daughter of the above John.¹

---

## Second Generation.

### 8101

THOMAS THURSTON² (*John*¹), eldest son of John¹ and Margaret Thurston of Dedham, Mass.; born in Wrentham, Eng., and baptized Aug. 4, 1633; married, "before Capt. Luther" of Dedham, Dec. 13, 1655 [county records say Nov. 10] SARAH THAXTER, daughter of Thomas Thaxter of Hingham, Mass. She died Sept. 1, 1678; he died Dec. 15, 1704 [another record says May 20, 1704].

Thomas Thurston and Thomas, jr., are on the list of names of those who came to Medfield from Dedham. Mr. Thurston was a man of much usefulness; one of the prudential committee and town clerk, 1673; the same year Thomas and John Thurston were on a committee chosen by the inhabitants of Dedham to manage the division of Wrentham from Dedham; sergeant in 1675, before Philip's war; made lieutenant in 1678; representative to the General Court in 1686, the last session before the abolition of the "good old charter," and was justice of the peace, with authority to solemnize marriages. Farnum thinks he must have been the man who received 544 votes for "assistant" in April, 1686.

Extracts from a deed of land in "Medfield, Suffolke County, Massachusetts Colonie, New England," given by Daniel Morse to Thomas Thurston, A.D. 1662, and "in the fourteenth year of the reign of our sovereign Lord Charles the Second, by the grace of God, King of England, Scotland, and France. To all Christian people to whom this present writing shall com, Daniell Morse late of Medfield, in the county of Suffolke, in the Massachusetts Colonie of New England, Husbandman, sends greeting. Know yee that the said Daniell Morse for and in consideration of one hundred pounds in hand, paid by Thomas Thurston of the said Medfield, Carpenter, which he, the

---

*The records in Boston say children of Benjamin and Elishua. They may belong to another Benjamin, but we can find no trace of any other person by that name in these early days, and conclude that they are children of Benjamin and Elizabeth, and that there is some mistake in the date of Mehitable's birth.

said Daniell Morse, doth by these presents acknowledge to have received and is therewith satisfied, hath given, granted, bargained, sold, enfeoffed, and confirmed, etc., etc., unto the said Thomas Thurston, etc., etc."

Their children were :

+8114    John,⁸ b. March 4, 1656; m. Hannah ——.
+8115    Thomas,⁸ b. Feb. 11, 1658; m. 1st, Mehitable Mason; 2d, Esther ——.
8116    Nathaniel,⁸ b. Jan. 24, 1660; d. June 2, 1661 [county record says April 2].
8117    Sarah,⁸ b. Sept. 16, 1662.
8118    Maria,⁸ b. March 17, 1665.
8119    Margaret,⁸ b. Aug. 9, 1668.
8120    Elizabeth,⁸ b. Sept. 19, 1671.
8121    Hannah,⁸ b. Aug. 4, 1674.
8122    Margaret,⁸ b. March 30, 1678.

Town record says Samuel and Margaret were mortally wounded by Indians and died Feb. 25, 1675. We find no other record of Thomas having a son Samuel.

## 8102

JOHN THURSTON² ( *John*¹), brother of the preceding, and son of John¹ and Margaret Thurston of Dedham, Mass.; born in Wrentham, Eng.; baptized Sept. 13, 1635; married, "before Ralph Wheelock," Oct. 4, 1660 [county record says Aug. 8], MARY WOOD, daughter of Nicholas Wood. He died Mar. 3, 1711–12; she died Nov. 23, 1726.

John Thurston was a resident of Medfield, Mass.; freeman May 27, 1663, one of the prudential committee 1673, representative to the General Court in 1683, town clerk 1687, and deacon in the church.

Their children were :

8123    Mary,⁸ b. Aug. 15, 1665; d. Nov. 24, 1744.
8124    Mehitable,⁸ b. July 7, 1667; m. May 27, 1690, Ebenezer Ellis.
8125    Hannah,⁸ b. Nov. 18, 1669.
8126    Bethia,⁸ b. April 30, 1672.
8127    Esther,⁸ b. Jan. 23, 1674; m. Feb. 12 1713, Jonathan Boyden [as his second wife]. b. Feb. 20, 1652, son of Thomas Boyden, who came from England 1634. aged 21, and settled in Medfield. They resided in Medfield; she died March 10, 1755. They had :
     *Silence* (Boyden), b. March 25, 1713–14; d. April 13, 1713–14.
     *Seth* (Boyden), b. March 15, 1715; d. 1775. One of the earliest settlers of Foxborough, Mass., and a prominent man there, engaged in the working of iron ore mined in that town.
8128    John,⁸ b. Sept. 27, 1677; m. Nov. 23, 1723, Sarah Pierce; she died June 23, 1746; he died Dec. 19, 1751.
8129    Benjamin,⁸ b. June 26, 1680; d. June 28, 1704.

## 8103

JOSEPH THURSTON² ( *John*¹), brother of the preceding, and son of John¹ and Margaret Thurston of Dedham, Mass.; baptized there Sept. 13, 1640; married ANNE ——. He died probably early in 1691, as his will, made July 9, 1688, was proved May 21, 1691. His wife survived him, and made her will April 28, 1715, which was proved Jan. 31, 1721, in which she mentions all their children, and gives the bulk of her property to her son Samuel. He was a member of the Presbyterian church in Jamaica, L. I.

Mr. Thurston had a lot of land granted him by the town of Jamaica Dec. 20, 1662, on condition that he would settle there. He built a house on this lot, which was still in his possession when he made his will. The records of the first Presbyterian church give his name,

Mar. 2, 1663, as one of twenty-four persons who bought and donated a house and lot to their minister, Rev. —— Walker. April 3, 1668, he was one of a church committee ; 1688 he was appointed a committee of one to procure a minister.

The records of the town and county contain the following concerning him : 1663 he bought fifteen acres of land. 1664 was elected townsman. 1675 was appointed to agree about building a saw and grist-mill for the town, and in 1677 was appointed to supervise the erection of the same. 1679 town granted him a lot of land. 1683 he sued John Freeman, a blacksmith, with whom he had placed his son Benjamin, a minor, who was to share the profits. Sept. 5, 1682 (Lord's day), his cattle broke into his neighbor's corn field; he took them out, but was sued for trespass, and the court ordered the case to referees. 1682 was sued for debt, but non-suited the plaintiff. 1683 protested against selling town lands. 1685 was executor of Thomas Foster's estate, and appointed to take care of town offices, etc. 1687 one of a committee to examine county treasurer's books. July 28, 1673, was one of a vigilance committee on account of the island being infested by pirates. The returns of Jamaica for seven years preceding 1688 show that in Joseph Thurston's family there was one marriage, eight christenings, and one death.\* The following is his will.

The last will and testament of Joseph Thurston, written this 9th day of July, in the year 1688.

I, Joseph Thurston, being aged about 52 years at this instant, and sound in mind and memory but weak and infirm of body, waiting for my change and dissolution, do make this my last will and testament, and in the name of God, Amen.

Imprimis, I commit my soul to God who gave it to be glorified by him and to glorify him to all eternity, my body I give to the dust to be decently buried in hope of a better and glorious resurrection thro' Jesus Christ my Lord and Saviour at the day of the general resurrection, Amen.

My worldly estate, after all my just and due debts shall be paid by my executors, I order and dispose as followeth, viz. :

I leave the whole of my estate in the hands of my wife that now is, viz., Anne Thurston, to be improved for the benefit, comfort, and support of my family until the children shall come of age to receive their respective portions that shall be allotted to them and for their education while in their nonage.

Furthermore. I do by this my will appropriate unto my dear and loving wife that now is one-third part of my moveable estate and stock to be at her disposal.

Moreover, I will that my wife have a settled, comfortable habitation with necessary conveniency adjoining to it, where she shall choose to be, either at the South or at the Town, that is to say, the house that is built at South or the house which we now live in, during her life or widowhood, and the home lot with the addition which lieth joining upon the north side of the said lot as far as the said lot did run westward, whilst she remains desolate.

My fifteen acre lot of meadow upon the hithermost and East Neck (so called) I will unto my three youngest sons, Daniel, Samuel, and Thomas, to be equally divided amongst them three, to each of them five acres, when and as they shall be of age to receive their portions.

The land that lieth at the rear of my home lot and is the rear of William Foster's two lots which was formerly William Smith's, I will unto my two sons, Daniel and Samuel, with my whole pasture lot opposite thereunto, lying upon the Hills, to be equally divided [to] the said Daniel and Samuel when they shall come of age to receive their portions.

The four acres I bought of Ephraim Palmer opposite unto my Homestead I will

unto my youngest son, Thomas Thurston, when he shall come of age to receive his portion and my Homestead at the decease of his mother or she remarry.

The rest of my estate in land or moveables not before mentioned and disposed of in this my will I order to be equally divided among all my children, viz. : Benjamin, Mary, Jane, Hannah, Joseph, Daniel, Samuel, and Thomas, to each of them an eighth part by equal proportion, when and as they shall come of age to receive their portion; and in case either of the said children shall die before they come of age, that then their part to be equally divided between them that shall survive.

I do also constitute and appoint my wife sole executrix of this my will, requesting my loving friends, Mr. John Pruden and Joseph Smith, Sr., as overseers to take care that this my will be duly and truly performed to all intents and purposes as near as may be to the mind of the testator.

Witness my hand, subscribed this instant the day and date about written Joseph Thurston. Signed in the presence of us, test., John Prudden, Daniel Sexton.

I do also by this my will order and fully empower my trusty and well esteemed friends, Mr. John Prudden and Joseph Smith, to appoint other overseers in their room, in case they shall be incapacitated to see this my will performed.

### Their children were :

+8130  Benjamin,[8] m. Sarah ——.
 8131  Mary,[8] } one of these m. John Foster, who received by his mother-in-law's
 8132  Jane,[8] }    will a pewter platter and a pewter basin which had been in the family for a long time.
 8133  Hannah,[8] m. —— Wright; by bequest received her mother's wardrobe. .
+8134  Joseph,[8] b. about 1670; m. Rebecca ——.
+8135  Daniel.[8]
+8136  Samuel,[8] m. Sarah ——.
 8137  Thomas,[8] m. Alice ——. May 21. 1719, was keeper of jail in Jamaica. Sept. 29, 1722, was witness in a church trial. He was a member and an officer in the Episcopal church; no children.

### 8111

DANIEL THURSTON[2] of Medfield, Mass. (*John*[1]), brother of the preceding, and son of John[1] and Margaret Thurston of Dedham, Mass.; born there May 5, and baptized May 12, 1646; married MARIA ——; she died in Medfield May 21, 1680. He was received into the church in Dedham May 20, 1645; died July 23, 1683.

### Their children were :

 8138  Daniel,[8] d. March 4, 1674.
+8139  Daniel,[8] b. Feb. 14, 1674; m. 1st, Experience Warren; 2d, Martha Allen.
 8140  Benjamin,[8] b. Feb. 17, 1678; d. March 26, 1680.

## Third Generation.

### 8114

JOHN THURSTON[8] (*Thomas*,[8] *John*[1]), eldest son of Thomas[2] and Sarah (Thaxter) Thurston of Medfield, Mass.; born Dec. 13, 1656 [county record says Jan. 4]; married HANNAH ——.

### Their children were :

+8142  David,[4] m. Mary Carey.
 8143  Sarah,[4] b. July 29, 1691; m. in Rehoboth, Mass., April 30, 1715, Thomas Rounds.
 8144  Hannah,[4] b. June 8, 1693; m. in Rehoboth May 16, 1716. John Carey.
 8145  Bethia,[4] b. May 29, 1695; m. in Rehoboth Dec. 7, 1721, Joseph Kent.
 8146  Jabez,[4] b. June 23, 1697; d. June 29, 1697.
 8147  Rebecca,[4] b. Aug. 19, 1698.
 8148  Mehitable,[4] b. June 18, 1700.
 8149  Phebe,[4] b. Dec. 4, 1702.
 8150  Jane,[4] b. Dec. 13, 1704.

## 8115

THOMAS THURSTON[3] (*Thomas,*[2] *John*[1]), brother of the preceding, and son of Thomas[2] and Sarah (Thaxter) Thurston of Medfield, Mass.; born Feb. 11, 1658 [the Boston record says Dec. 11]; married, first, July 3, 1685, MEHITABLE MASON; she died Aug. 11, 1692. Second, ESTHER ——, who was admitted to the Congregational church in Franklin, Mass., June 21, 1741. He died May 20, 1704, and his widow married, Oct. 3, 1711, Thomas Bacon.

Mr. Thurston was a soldier and held a commission as lieutenant of foot in the 8th Massachusetts regiment, and was at the battle of Lewisburgh. Medfield was a part of Dedham, a tract bought of the Indian chief Chickataubut and settled in 1635. Medfield was not settled till 1649–50. The deed was lost and Josias Wampatuck, jr., a son and heir of Josias Wampatuck, and grandson of Chickataubut, laid claim to both Dedham and Medfield, and both Dedham and Medfield renewed it. July 13, 1685, four Indians, Jonas ♀ Charles, Old [11] ♀ Ahawton, William ♀ Hahaton, and Robert Momantog, executed a deed of Medfield to Thomas Thurston and John Harding. A copy of this deed can be seen in the N. E. Genealogical Register, vol. vii., p. 301.

His children, by first wife, Mehitable, were:

8155  Méhitable,[4] b. Aug. 9, 1686.
8156  Mary,[4] b. March 16, 1688; d. March 30. 1688.
+8157  Thomas,[4] b. Nov. 2, 1689; m. Dorcas Gay.
8158  Ichabod,[4] b. Aug. 9, 1692; d. Aug. 29, 1692.

By second wife, Esther:

+8159  David,[4] b. Nov. 20, 1693; m. ——.
+8160  Daniel,[4] b. Sept. 25, 1695; m. Deborah Pond.
+8161  Luke,[4] b. April 20, 1698; m. Elizabeth ——.
8162  Esther,[4] b. June 21, 1700.
8163  Mary,[4] b. Sept. 3, 1702.

## 8130

BENJAMIN THURSTON[3] (*Joseph,*[2] *John*[1]), eldest son of Joseph[2] and Anne Thurston of Jamaica, L. I.; married SARAH ——. He died intestate about 1710.

Mr. Thurston was a blacksmith in Jamaica. In 1691 he was appointed on a committee to build a church, of which, Sept. 13, 1698, he was chosen to superintend the building. This was probably an Episcopal church, as in 1700 he was chosen vestryman. The Earl of Belmont, governor of New York, in a letter to the lords of trade, dated Oct. 21, 1698, refers to the depositions of Benjamin Thurston and his brother Daniel in an action against Col. Willet, member of the council, who was charged with piracy. Mar. 6, 1692, was chosen tax collector. In 1700 he was 1st lieutenant in the foot company of Jamaica. 1708 only one person paid a higher tax than he.

Their children were:

+8167  John,[4] b. Feb. 28, 1703-4; m. Grace, Olive, Lucretia (so entered in church book).
8168  Sarah[4] (records mutilated).
+8169  Jonathan,[4] m. Elizabeth ——.

## 8134

JOSEPH THURSTON[3] (*Joseph,*[2] *John*[1]), brother of the preceding, and son of Joseph[2] and Anne Thurston of Jamaica, L. I.; born there about 1670; married REBECCA ——.

Mr. Thurston was a blacksmith in Hempstead, L. I., having learned the trade of his brother Benjamin. He sold a piece of land in 1731.

Their children were:

8174 John,[4] m. 1735, Hannah Minthorn. The town of Hempstead granted him the "site of the old sheep pen in the town."
8175 Mary,[4] b. 1727.
8176 Elizabeth,[4] b. 1729.
8177 Joseph,[4] * b. 1734; m. Phebe ——; they had:
   8178 *Rebecca,*[5] b. 1769.
8179 Phebe,[4] b. 1743.

## 8135

DANIEL THURSTON[3] (*Joseph,*[2] *John*[1]), brother of the preceding, and son of Joseph[2] and Anne Thurston of Jamaica, L. I.; married ——.

Mr. Thurston was a blacksmith in Hempstead, L. I., having learned the trade with his brother Benjamin. Nov. 13, 1699, the town of Hempstead granted him a lot of land on condition he should settle there as the blacksmith for the town, and he remained there till he died.

Children:

+8184 Daniel.[4]
8185 Martha,[4] b. 1700; she was guardian of her sister Sarah and perhaps executor of her father's estate.
8186 Sarah,[4] b. 1717.

## 8136

SAMUEL THURSTON[3] (*Joseph,*[2] *John*[1]), brother of the preceding, and son of Joseph[2] and Anne Thurston of Jamaica, L. I.; married SARAH ——.

Mr. Thurston was a blacksmith. His will, made Sept. 5, 1721, proved Jan. 23, 1722, discloses the fact that he was the owner of three slaves, Jack, Mynche, and their child. Jack was sold to pay his master's debts and Mynche and the child remained with the family.

One child:

8190 Sarah,[4] b. 1709.

## 8139

DANIEL THURSTON[3] (*Daniel,*[2] *John*[1]), son of Daniel[2] and Maria Thurston of Medfield, Mass.; born there Feb. 14, 1674; married, first, Dec. 28, 1699, EXPERIENCE WARREN [Dedham records say Mason and married 1698]; she died Sept. 6, 1704. Second, Oct. 15, 1705, MARTHA ALLEN. He was town clerk in Medfield.

His children, by first wife, Experience, were:

+8195 Joseph,[4] b. Oct. 14, 1700; m. Dorothy ——. They lived in Westborough, *see p. 464* Mass.; he died about 1745. They had:

---

* In the records of Hempstead we find these items: "In 1750 paid Joseph Thurston four shillings for digging a grave." "1779 paid Phebe Thurston, widow, twelve shillings for digging a grave." The scarcity of men, on account of the revolutionary war, may account for this. Same record also contains this: "Jan. 12, 1779, paid Phebe Thurston, widow, eight shillings for going to a woman in the poor house."

8196  *Amariah,*[5] b. Dec. 23, 1729.
8197  *Experience,*[5] b. Dec. 27, 1731.
+8198  Daniel,[4]  } twins, born  } m. Miriam Allen.
8199  Increase,[4]  } Feb. 19, 1702; } d. May 29, 1702.

By second wife, Martha:

8200  Diana,[4] b. May 12, 1707; d. May 19, 1707.
8201  Martha,[4] b. March 23, 1709; m. Joseph Thompson of Uxbridge, Mass., and lived there.

## 8141

DANIEL THURSTON[3] married, first, MIRIAM ——; second, MARTHA —— of Medway, Mass. He died July 3, 1745.

Mr. Thurston was a farmer in Mendon and Uxbridge, Mass. Deeds show that he sold land to Joseph Sutton 1736, and to his son David 1745. I can get no clue to the parentage of Daniel, but the evidence is all in favor of the opinion that he descended from John of Dedham, and therefore give him a place in these records here.

His children, by first wife, Miriam, were:

+8206  Benjamin,[4] b. Dec. 25, 1711; m. 1st, Elizabeth ——; 2d, Dorcas Chapin.
8207  Mary,[4] b. Aug. 13, 1714; n.m.; lived in Grafton, Mass., as per receipt signed by her 1771.
8208  Daniel,[4] b. Nov. 21, 1716; settled at Read's Farm, Hampshire county, about 1740.
8209  Ebenezer,[4] b. Sept. 22, 1718; n.m.; d. in Grafton April 16, 1787.
8210  Elizabeth,[4] b. Oct. 22, 1720; living, 1752, in Uxbridge.
8211  David,[4] m. Abigail ——; d. in Uxbridge 1756 or 1757, having had :
    8212  *Lucy,*[5] b. April 28, 1745; m. about 1761 David Holman.
    8213  *Nathan,*[5] b. Nov., 1747.
8214  Calvin.[4]
8215  Moses.[4] b. Sept. 17, 1733.
8216  Lydia,[4] b. Aug. 26, 1735.

By second wife, Martha :

8217  Sarah,[4] b. April 9, 1742; d. previous to 1745.

---

## Fourth Generation.

## 8142

DAVID THURSTON[4] of Rehoboth, Mass. (*John,*[3] *Thomas,*[2] *John*[1]), son of John[3] and Hannah Thurston; married, Feb. 16, 1712–13, MARY CAREY.

Their children were:

+8222  John,[5] b. May 22, 1714; m. Saberah ——.
8223  Abigail,[5] b. July 11, 1716.
+8224  James,[5] b. Sept. 3, 1718; m. Phebe ——.
8225  David,[5] b. March 27, 1721.
8226  Mary,[5] b. June 30, 1723.

## 8157

THOMAS THURSTON[4] (*Thomas,*[3] *Thomas,*[2] *John*[1]), eldest son of Thomas[3] and Mehitable (Mason) Thurston of Medfield, Mass.; born there Nov. 2, 1689; married, in Boston, Mass., Dec. 4, 1718, DORCAS GAY. He was selectman of Wrentham, Mass., 1726 and 1735, perhaps during the intervening years; was deacon in the Congregational church.

Their children were :

8230    Mary,⁵ b. Aug. 27, 1720.
+8231   Thomas,⁵ b. Nov. 29, 1721 ; m. Mary Aldrage.
8232    Esther,⁵ b. Jan. 28. 1723.
8233    Mehitable,⁵ b. Jan. 29, 1726; d. Oct. 28, 1747.
8234    Dorcas,⁵  }
8235    Sarah,⁵    } twins, b. Aug. 28, 1728;  d. Oct., 1747.
8236    Margaret,⁵ b. Sept. 28, 1730.
8237    Elisha,⁵   }
8238    Elizabeth,⁵ } twins, b. Sept. 17, 1733.
8239    Dorcas,⁵ b. Sept. 26, 1735.
8240    Samuel,⁵ b. Oct. 13, 1738.

## 8159

DAVID THURSTON⁴ of Medway, Mass. (*Thomas,*⁸ *Thomas,*² *John*¹), brother of the preceding, and son of Thomas⁸ and Esther Thurston of Medfield, Mass. ; born there Nov. 20, 1693 ; married ———.

Children :

+8245   Nathan,⁵ m. —— Campbell.
8246    Paul,⁵ m. Hannah Rawson, b. May 25, 1761, daughter of Rev. Grindall
        and Desire (Thatcher) Rawson. Her father died in Sutton, Mass., 1795.

## 8160

DANIEL THURSTON⁴ (*Thomas,*⁸ *Thomas,*² *John*¹), brother of the preceding, and son of Thomas⁸ and Esther Thurston of Medfield, Mass; born there Sept. 25, 1695 ; married, in Boston, Mass., Feb. 11, 1719–20, DEBORAH POND, who was admitted to the Congregational church in Wrentham, Mass., March 6, 1743.

Mr. Thurston was a farmer and tavern keeper in Wrentham, now Franklin. The town records of Wrentham show that the old "Thurston Farm House," now in Franklin, has been licensed as a tavern for one hundred and sixteen years.

Their children were :

8248    Deborah,⁵ b. Sept. 21, 1720.
+8249   Daniel,⁵ b. June 1, 1722 ; m. Elizabeth Whiting.
8250    Esther,⁵ b. April 29, 1724.
+8251   David,⁵ b. May 9, 1726 ; m. ———.
8252    Elioenai,⁵ b. May 19, 1728 ; joined the church in Wrentham, now Frank-
        lin, May 28, 1748 ; m. Jonathan Whiting and moved to East Winthrop,
        Me., where he was a farmer and man of influence in the community.
        They had :
        8253    *Jonathan* (Whiting), m. 1st, Sarah Whittier ; 2d, Betsey Davies, and
                had eight children.
        8254    *Elias* (Whiting), d. May 3, 1775.
        8255    *John* (Whiting), d. Dec. 10, 1775.
        8256    *Thurston* (Whiting), b. in Franklin 1753 ; m. 1st, —— Brown of New-
                castle, Me.; 2d, Elizabeth McCobb of Newcastle. He was ordained
                July, 1776, a Congregational minister in Newcastle, dismissed Jan.,
                1782 ; settled Oct. 28, 1784, in Edgecomb, Me. ; pastor in Warren,
                Me., from 1785–1787, where he died, Feb. 28, 1829, aged 76; she
                died Sept. 29, 1834, aged 80, having had :
                8257    *John* (Whiting), b. 1781 ; m. Sept. 9, 1804, Nancy Lowell ; lived
                        in Union, Me.; d. Jan. 15, 1850.
        8258    *Mary* (Whiting).
        8259    *Susan* (Whiting).
        8260    *Joanna* (Whiting).
8261    Abijah,⁵ b. July 20, 1730; admitted to the church in Wrentham, now Frank-
        lin, April 9, 1749; graduated from Harvard 1749; preached, but not or-
        dained; d. July 8, 1750.
+8262   Joseph,⁵ b. about 1732 ; m. ———.

## 8161

LUKE THURSTON [4] of Rehoboth, Mass. (*Thomas,*[8] *Thomas,*[2] *John*[1]), brother of the preceding, and son of Thomas [8] and Esther Thurston of Medfield, Mass.; born there April 20, 1698; married ELIZABETH ——.

### Children:

8267   Hannah,[5] b. May 24, 1728.
8268   Elizabeth,[5] b. Feb. 6, 1729–30.
8269   Annie,[5] b. April 21, 1732.
8270   Luke,[6] b. Feb. 21, 1733–4; d. soon.
8271   Thomas,[5] b. July 31, 1736.
8272   Lucretia,[5] b. Aug. 27, 1737.
8273   Luke,[5] b. Sept. 17, 1739; d. soon.
8274   Margaret,[5] b. Aug. 27, 1741.
8275   George,[6] b. June 26, 1742.
8276   Luke,[5] b. Sept. 27, 1743.

## 8167

JOHN THURSTON [4] (*Benjamin,*[8] *Joseph,*[2] *John*[1]), eldest son of Benjamin [8] and Sarah Thurston of Jamaica, L. I.; born there Feb. 28, 1703–4; married GRACE, OLIVE, LUCRETIA.[*] The bill for her funeral was filed May 13, 1801.

Mr. Thurston was a blacksmith in Jamaica; voted to send deputies from Queens county to the provincial congress Nov. 7, 1775.

### Children:

+8280   John,[5] b. Feb. 28, 1728; m. Mary ——.
8281   Ruth,[6] b. Nov. 27, 1730; m. Samuel Whitehead, and had Charles and Pelatiot (Whitehead).
8282   Benjamin,[5] b. Dec. 17, 1732; n.m.; d. Jan. 16, 1805. English calendar records of New York contain this: "Oct. 17, 1763, Lieut. Gov. Calder wrote to Benjamin Thurston of Orange county and others concerning the defense of the frontier." We infer from records that he was a doctor. Feb. 7, 1776, Dr. Benjamin Thurston was appointed a lieutenant-colonel by committee of Goshen Precinct, Orange county, N. Y. His will is dated July 22, 1803, and codicil Oct. 2, 1804, by which he bequeathed his estate, which was of considerable amount, to his brothers and sisters' children, except fifty pounds, which he gave to the first Presbyterian church in Jamaica. The heirs were all to share alike, but the estate was so managed that many failed to get what was intended for them. He names in his will Hannah Thurston, m. Mr. Dobbs; Sarah, m. Elias Sickles; Mary, m. Jacob Benger; Jacob and John. Sarah is the only one we can trace.
+8283   Israel,[5] b. Dec. 6, 1734; m. Christina Pangburn.
8284   Sarah,[5] b. Aug. 16, 1737; m. Elias Sickles.
8285   Pelatiot,[5] b. Feb. 24, 1740; m. Jan. 4, 1764, Tabitha Marston.
8286   Walter,[6] b. Feb. 28, 1742; taken prisoner by British, and died in provost prison, New York, Dec. 10, 1777.
+8287   Flavel,[5] b. Nov. 15, 1744; m. ——.
8288   David,[5] b. Dec. 27, 1746.
8289   Elizabeth,[6] b. July 12, 1749; m. Aug. 6, 1770, Thomas Cornwell, and had two children.

## 8169

JONATHAN THURSTON [4] (*Benjamin,*[8] *Joseph,*[2] *John*[1]), brother of the preceding, and son of Benjamin [8] and Sarah Thurston of Jamaica, L. I.; married ELIZABETH ——. He died before his wife, as her will is on record, dated Oct. 4, 1770, proved 1774.

---

* This is according to the records, and whether these three names belong to one person, or are three different persons, we cannot tell.

### Children :

8295　Susanna,[5] m. Platt Vale.

8296　Sarah,[5] b. 1740; m. Daniel Tuthill of Southold, L. I., b. 1732, removed when a young man to Jamaica, where he died, 1822, aged 90; she died 1780. They had:

   8297　*John* (Tuthill), d. Feb. 2, 1791.

   8298　*Daniel* (Tuthill), b. June 4, 1762; m. May 17, 1785, Diana Mackrell, b. June 28, 1768. He died Feb. 20, 1803; she died July 23, 1824. They had:

      8299　*James M.* (Tuthill), twin, b. June 1, 1786; m. Mar. 8, 1808, Emma Townsend, b. May 8, 1789. He died July 14, 1865; she died March 28, 1867. They had:

         8300　*William H.* (Tuthill). b. Dec. 5, 1808; m. Aug. 6, 1843, Dorothy Platner, b. Feb. 2, 1826; is a banker in Tipton, Iowa. They have a son James William (Tuthill), b. June 7, 1853.

         8301　*John S.* (Tuthill), b. July 22, 1814.

         8302　*Hannah M.* (Tuthill), b. Dec. 28, 1816.

         8303　*Robert T.* (Tuthill), b. April 29, 1823; d.

         8304　*James H.* (Tuthill), b. July 22, 1825; d.

         8305　*Charles E.* (Tuthill), b. Aug. 22, 1831; m.

         8306　*George W.* (Tuthill), b. Dec. 18, 1833.

      8307　*William* (Tuthill), twin, b. June 1, 1786; m. Sarah Hallett; d. Dec. 10, 1827.

      8308　*Felicia* (Tuthill), b. Nov. 7, 1787; m. James B. Thurston [see no. 8626].

      8309　*Sarah* (Tuthill), b. Feb. 10, 1791; m. John K. Cowperthwaite.

      8310　*Susanna* (Tuthill), b. March 5, 1795; m. Henry K. Frost.

      8311　*Ellen G.* (Tuthill), b. April 4, 1801; m. Richard Brush of Jamaica, where they now live.

   8312　*Samuel* (Tuthill), b. Nov. 13, 1766; d. May 20, 1812.

   8313　*James* (Tuthill), d. single May 27, 1813.

   8314　*Sarah* (Tuthill), m. —— Denton.

   8315　*Joseph* (Tuthill), b. Aug. 30, 1772; d. March 24, 1832.

8316　Jonathan,[6] m. Priscilla ——. His will was dated Aug. 7, 1776, proved 1784. He voted a whig ticket in 1775 for a deputy to the provincial congress; was a member of the militia 1776, and the records show his name frequently as grantee and grantor of land. They had:

   8317　*Millicent,*[6] m. Nathan Smith.

## 8184

DANIEL THURSTON [4] (*Daniel,*[3] *Joseph,*[2] *John*[1]), eldest son of Daniel Thurston [3] of Hempstead, L. I.; married ——.

There is a record in the History of New York, vol. iii., p. 357, of a petition from Newburgh on the Hudson river, signed by Daniel Thurston and fifteen others, directed to Gov. Clinton, captain general and governer of the province of New York, dated Sept. 6, 1751, asking for the confirmation to them and their successors of the title of five hundred acres of land; and it seems quite likely to have been this Daniel, as his son James settled on the Hudson river.

### Children :

8322　Daniel,[5] b. 1737; m. Nov. 17, 1776, Eliza Carman of Hempstead; lived in Long Island city, Queens county, N. Y.

8323　John,[5] m. Jan. 26, 1778, Margaret Smith of Hempstead; moved to St. John, N. B.

+8324　William,[5] b. 1742-3; m. Phebe Rhodes.

+8325　James,[5] m. ——.

+8326　Cyrus,[5] m. ——.

## 8198

DANIEL THURSTON [4] (*Daniel,*[3] *Daniel,*[2] *John*[1]), second son of Daniel [3] and Experience (Warren) Thurston of Medfield, Mass.; born there Feb. 19, 1702; married, Oct. 27, 1732, MIRIAM ALLEN.

Mr. Thurston was a farmer in Sharon, Ct.

Children:

+8330　Increase.[5]
+8331　Daniel,[5] b. Sept. 18, 1737; m. Sarah Curtis. ·
+8332　Moses,[5] b. about 1740; m. Thankful Knapp.
+8333　Amos,[5] b. July 6, 1742; m. Mary Sweatland.

## 8206

BENJAMIN THURSTON [4] of Grafton, Mass. (*Daniel*[3]), eldest son of Daniel [3] and Miriam Thurston of Mendon, Mass.; born there Dec. 25, 1711; married, first, ELIZABETH ——; she died Feb. 12, 1768, aged 60. Second, DORCAS CHAPIN, daughter of John Chapin of Mendon. She died Aug. 19, 1792; he died in Grafton Feb. 6, 1795, aged 83 y. 32 d.

Mr. Thurston was collector of tithes and taxes for the 16th district of Massachusetts bay, under George III., for several years about 1764.

His children, by first wife, Elizabeth, were:

+8338　John,[5] b. April, 1741; m. Susanna Wheeler.
+8339　Peter,[5] b. Sept. 17, 1745; m. Elizabeth ——.
8340　Benjamin,[5] b. Jan. 2, 1748; m.; lived and died in Barre, Mass.; had:
　8341　*Adolphus,*[6] lived in Barre 1816.
8342　Levi,[5] b. July 30, 1751; m.; lived in Royalston, Mass.; several children.

---

## Fifth Generation.

### 8222

JOHN THURSTON [5] of Rehoboth, Mass. (*David,*[4] *John,*[3] *Thomas,*[2] *John*[1]), eldest son of David [4] and Mary (Carey) Thurston of Rehoboth; born there May 22, 1714; married SABERAH ——.

Children:

8347　John,[6] b. in Hingham, Mass., July 9, 1736.
8348　Job,[6] b. in Hingham Jan. 27, 1737–8.
8349　Joel,[6] b. in Rehoboth Feb. 9, 1739–40.

### 8224

JAMES THURSTON [5] of Rehoboth, Mass. (*David,*[4] *John,*[3] *Thomas,*[2] *John*[1]), brother of the preceding, and son of David [4] and Mary (Carey) Thurston of Rehoboth; born there Sept. 3, 1718; married PHEBE ——.

Children:

8354　Deborah,[6] b. Nov. 3, 1749.
8355　Obed,[6] b. Dec. 16, 1750.
8356　Mercy,[6] b. July 22, 1752.
8357　Phœbe,[6] b. Feb. 24, 1755.
8358　James,[6] b. Oct. 23, 1757.
8359　Birchy,[6] } twins, b. Sept., 1758.
8360　Silence,[6] }
8361　Mary,[6] b. Feb. 7, 1760.
8362　Huldah,[6] } twins, b. April 29, 1762.
8363　David,[6] }
8364　Susanna,[6] } twins, b. March 4, 1764.
8365　Abigail,[6] }

## 8231

THOMAS THURSTON [5] (*Thomas,*[4] *Thomas,*[3] *Thomas,*[2] *John*[1]), eldest son of Thomas [4] and Dorcas (Gay) Thurston of Wrentham, Mass.; born there or in Foxborough, Mass., Nov. 29, 1721; married MARY ALDRAGE.

Mr. Thurston went to Otisfield, Me., and received a portion of a grant of land for services in the war against Canada in 1770. He sold land in Otisfield to James Thurston of Otisfield in 1790, which must have been his son.

### Children:

+8367   David.[6] b. Oct. 14, 1755; m. Polly Spurr.
 8368   Elizabeth,[6] b. April 28, 1758.
+8369   Jacob,[6] b. May 19, 1760; m. Nancy Anna Edwards.
 8370   James,[6] b. Nov. 11, 1764; n.m.
 8371   Mehitable,[6] m. Samuel Ware of Wrentham, Mass., and lived in Groton, Mass.; sold her interest in her father's estate in Otisfield 1809.
 8372   Lydia,[6] b. Aug. 1. 1770; n.m.; sold her interest in her father's estate 1820; d. May 24, 1838.

## 8245

*N. C. A. Cutler, p. 501.*
NATHAN THURSTON [5] of Oxford, Mass. (*David,*[4] *Thomas,*[3] *Thomas,*[2] *John*[1]), son of David Thurston [4] of Medway, Mass.; married —— CAMPBELL.   He was a farmer.

### Children:

 8375   David T.,[6] b. 1810; m. twice; dropped dead in his barn Aug., 1875, aged 65; no children.
 One son and seven daughters, three of whom are living, 1879, but I could get no word from them.

## 8249

DEA. DANIEL THURSTON [5] (*Daniel,*[4] *Thomas,*[3] *Thomas,*[2] *John*[1]), eldest son of Daniel [4] and Deborah (Pond) Thurston of Wrentham, Mass.; born there June 1, 1722; married ELIZABETH WHITING.   He died June 25, 1785.

Mr. Thurston was a farmer and tavern keeper in Franklin; admitted to the Congregational church March 1, 1741, and chosen deacon July 3, 1754.

### Children:

 8385   Deborah,[6] b. Feb. 7, 1744-5; m. Nathan Fisher of Wrentham, Mass.
 8386   Mary,[6] b. July 20, 1746; m. Aquila Robbins, farmer; lived in Wardsborough, Vt.
 8387   Unity,[6] b. Jan. 7, 1747; m. Thomas Fisher and lived in Templeton, Mass.
+8388   Daniel,[6] b. Sept. 11, 1749; m. Susan Johnson.
+8389   Abijah,[6] b. July 5, 1751; m. Rachel Johnson.
 8390   Abigail,[6] b. May 6, 1754; m. Samuel Clark of Franklin.
 8391   Elizabeth,[6] b. Feb. 9, 1756; m. Seth Daniels, a farmer of Franklin.
 8392   Chloe,[6] b. May 28, 1758; hung herself when young with a skein of yarn.
 8393   Caleb,[6] b. Feb. 9, 1760; lived in Franklin; d. in the revolutionary army.
 8394   David,[6] b. April 25, 1762; d. in the revolutionary army.
 8395   Esther,[6] b. May 25, 1764; m. Joseph Kingsbury, a farmer of Millbury, Mass.
 8396   Lucretia,[6] b. Mar. 24, 1766; m. Nathan Pond, farmer; lived in Walpole, Ms.
 8397   Joseph,[6] b. Aug. 26, 1769.

A daughter died Oct. 4, 1757, aged 4; another died Feb. 5, 1770, aged 9, and a son died Sept. 13, 1775, aged 16.   It is said they had ten daughters and nine sons.

## 8251

REV. DAVID THURSTON[5] (*Daniel*,[4] *Thomas*,[3] *Thomas*,[2] *John*[1]), brother of the preceding, and son of Daniel[4] and Deborah (Pond) Thurston of Wrentham, Mass.; born there May 6, 1726; married ———. He died May 5, 1777.

Mr. Thurston joined the church in Wrentham, now Franklin, Mar. 6, 1743; graduated from the college of New Jersey, Princeton, 1751; ordained first pastor of the second Congregational church in Medway, Mass., June 23, 1752. Feb. 22, 1769, Mr. Thurston asked for a dismission from his pastoral office. "The certificates of a number of physicians showing that the prosecution of constant study and preaching is detrimental to his health, and considering his present indisposition of body, they voted that his request be granted." After his dismission he retired from the ministry, and in 1772 settled upon a farm in the town of Oxford, Mass.; subsequently removed to Auburn, and afterward to Sutton, Mass., where he died. During his ministry of seventeen years seventy-nine persons were added to the church and twenty-three "came under the bonds of the covenant" (half-way covenant).

## 8262

JOSEPH THURSTON[5] (*Daniel*,[4] *Thomas*,[3] *Thomas*,[2] *John*[1]), brother of the preceding, and son of Daniel[4] and Deborah (Pond) Thurston of Wrentham, Mass.; born there about 1732; married ———.

We can only trace one child:

+8408 Joseph,[6] b. Sept. 11, 1764; m. Polly Hubbard.

## 8280

JOHN THURSTON[5] (*John*,[4] *Benjamin*,[3] *Joseph*,[2] *John*[1]), eldest son of John[4] and Grace Thurston of Jamaica, L. I.; born there Feb. 28, 1728; married MARY ———.

Mr. Thurston was postmaster in Jamaica 1775. He voted against sending deputies to the provincial congress in 1775, and afterward recanted and voted in favor; joined a company of minute-men 1775.

Children:

+8413 William,[6] b. Feb. 11, 1754; m. ———.
8414 John,[6] b. April 27, 1759; d. in infancy.
8415 John,[6] b. Sept. 2, 1761.
8416 Benjamin.[6]

## 8283

ISRAEL THURSTON[5] (*John*,[4] *Benjamin*,[3] *Joseph*,[2] *John*[1]), brother of the preceding, and son of John[4] and Grace Thurston of Jamaica, L. I.; born there Dec. 6, 1734; married, 1759, CHRISTINA PANGBURN. He died about 1790. She afterward married ——— Taylor, and had one son. The British army went into winter quarters on his farm, and before they left destroyed every vestige of the buildings and timber on the place. They were members of the Presbyterian church in Rahway, N. J.

Children:

8421 Benjamin,[6] b. 1760; served through the revolutionary war, returned home with poor health, and died a few years after of consumption.
+8422 David,[6] b. March 20, 1762; m. Esther-Taylor.

24

+8423 Samuel,⁶ b. March 6, 1766; m. Hannah Kelley.
+8424 John,⁵ b. Jan. 11, 1768; m. Mary Mars.
+8425 Moses,⁶ b. May 9, 1770; m. 1st, Catherine Bottenhamer; 2d, Elizabeth
    Chester.
+8426 Flavel,⁶ b. 1772; m. Mary M. Bottenhamer.

## 8287

FLAVEL THURSTON⁵ (*John,*⁴ *Benjamin,*⁸ *Joseph,*² *John*¹), brother of the preceding, and son of John⁴ and Grace Thurston of Jamaica, L. I.; born there Nov. 15, 1744; married ———. He was a tailor in Rahway, N. J.; died about 1808, leaving something of an estate to his

Only son:
+8430 John Flavel,⁶ b. 1778; m. Martha Hopper.

## 8324

WILLIAM THURSTON⁵ (*Daniel,*⁴ *Daniel,*⁸ *Joseph,*² *John*¹), son of Daniel Thurston⁴ of Hempstead, L. I.; born there 1742-3; married, May 18, 1772, PHEBE RHODES. He died 1833, aged 90.

Children:
8435 John,⁶ m. and had:
    8436 *John C.*⁷
8437 James.⁶
8438 Thomas,⁶ m. and had:
    8439 *John.*⁷
    8440 *William.*⁷
    8441 *Nicholas.*⁷
    8442 *Henry.*⁷
    8443 *Samuel.*⁷
8444 Joseph.⁶

## 8325

JAMES THURSTON⁵ (*Daniel,*⁴ *Daniel,*⁸ *Joseph,*² *John*¹), brother of the preceding, and son of Daniel Thurston⁴ of Hempstead, L. I.; married and settled on the Hudson river, near Poughkeepsie, N. Y.

Child:
+8449 Ezra,⁶ m. Sally Gilbert.

## 8326

CYRUS THURSTON⁵ (*Daniel,*⁴ *Daniel,*⁸ *Joseph,*² *John*¹), brother of the preceding, and son of Daniel Thurston⁴ of Hempstead, L. I.; married ———. He was in the war of the revolution, a minute-man with the rank of captain.

Children:
+8454 Ebenezer,⁶ m. Eunice Kelsey.
8455 Israel,⁶ m.; went to Ohio in search of a farm and never returned; supposed to have been killed by Indians.
8456 Daniel.⁶

## 8330

INCREASE THURSTON⁵ (*Daniel,*⁴ *Daniel,*⁸ *Daniel,*² *John*¹), eldest son of Daniel⁴ and Miriam (Allen) Thurston of Sharon, Ct.; married —— CHAPIN.

Mr. Thurston removed to Lisle, Broome county, N. Y., before the revolutionary war, where he had a grant of land, then a wilderness. He was a member of the Baptist church.

Children:

+8459 Amos,⁶ m. ——.
8460 Reuben,⁶ killed in a mill.
Four daughters.

## 8331

DANIEL THURSTON⁵ (*Daniel,*⁴ *Daniel,*⁸ *Daniel,*² *John*¹), brother of the preceding, and son of Daniel⁴ and Miriam (Allen) Thurston of Sharon, Ct.; born there Sept. 18, 1737; married SARAH CURTISS, born November, 1744. She died March 30, 1789; he died Jan. 23, 1829, over 91 years of age.

Mr. Thurston was a farmer and lived in Danbury, Ct., in Albany county, N. Y., in Whitestown, Oneida county, N. Y., Steventown, Rensselaer county (formerly Oneida county), and in Albion, Orleans county, N. Y. He was a deacon in the Presbyterian church for over fifty years. He spent his last days with his son Caleb Curtiss Thurston in Barre, N. Y.

Children:

·8465 Miriam,⁶ b. Sept. 5, 1762; m. Ezra Lathrop; d. at Lockport, N. Y., Feb. 20, 1841.
8466 Sarah,⁶ b. Jan. 14, 1764; m. Jacob Elley; d. May 15, 1796.
+8467 Daniel,⁶ b. Feb. 13, 1766; m. Charlotte Mudge.
8468 Keziah,⁶ b. Oct. 5, 1767; m. Stephen Bailey; d. 1861.
8469 Hannah,⁶ b. May 4, 1769; m. Daniel Pratt; d. 1837.
8470 Thurza,⁶ b. Feb. 13, 1771; d. 1796.
8471 Laxanna,⁶ b. and d. 1772.
+8472 David,⁶ b. April 9, 1774; m. Margaret Phillips.
8473 Lovina,⁶ b. Feb. 27, 1776; d. April 13, 1796.
+8474 Caleb Curtiss,⁶ b. July 27, 1778; m. Thankful Bailey.
8475 Lydia,⁶ b. June 20, 1780; m. Joel Bailey; d. Sept. 29, 1841.

## 8332

MOSES THURSTON⁵ (*Daniel,*⁴ *Daniel,*⁸ *Daniel,*² *John*¹), brother of the preceding, and son of Daniel⁴ and Miriam (Allen) Thurston of Sharon, Ct.; born there about 1740; married THANKFUL KNAPP. He died about 1823, aged 83.

Mr. Thurston died in New Lisbon, Otsego county, N. Y., where he came before the revolutionary war. He was driven off by the Indians and went into Dutchess county and staid till after the war, when he returned.

Children:

+8480 David,⁶ m. Rachel Chapin.
8481 Seth.⁶
8422 Daughter.

## 8333

AMOS THURSTON⁵ (*Daniel,*⁴ *Daniel,*⁸ *Daniel,*² *John*¹), brother of the preceding, and son of Daniel⁴ and Miriam (Allen) Thurston of Sharon, Ct.; born there July 6, 1742; married MARY SWEATLAND, born April 15, 1744. He is reported to have commenced life as a farmer in Sharon, and removed to New Lisbon, N. Y., about 1800, where he died May 7, 1824; she died Dec. 14, 1826. He was a deacon of the Presbyterian church over fifty years.

Children:

+8486 Rowlen Sweatland,⁶ b. Sept. 27, 1765; m. Sally Ketchum.
8487 Sally,⁶ b. July 15, 1767.
8488 Mary,⁶ b. 1768; d. 1797.

+8489 Amos,⁶ b. Dec. 30, 1769; m. Lucy Dart.
8490 Sybel,⁶ b. Aug. 6, 1777; n.m.; d. Oct. 16, 1825.
8491 Emilie,⁶ b. March 16, 1779; m. Samuel Smith, b. in Norwalk, Ct., March 16, 1779, son of Uriah Smith. He was a farmer in New Lisbon, and deacon in the Presbyterian church. He died March 7, 1826; she died Sept. 12, 1849. They had:
    8492 *Philander* (Smith), m. and resides in Wisconsin.
    8493 *Uriah* (Smith), m. and resides in Morris, N. Y.
    8494 *Lewis* (Smith), m. and resides in Morris.
    8495 *Maria* (Smith), m. and resides in Morris.
+8496 Ira,⁶ b. Oct. 26, 1781; m. Ruth Benedict.
8497 Jerusha,⁶ b. Feb. 24, 1784; m. Seth Rowley, and had three sons and three daughters. One son:
    8498 *Josiah* (Rowley), in Norwich, Chenango county, N. Y.

### 8338

JOHN THURSTON⁵ of Grafton, Mass. (*Benjamin,⁴ Daniel⁸*), eldest son of Benjamin⁴ and Elizabeth Thurston of Grafton; born there April, 1741; married, April 30, 1765, SUSANNA WHEELER, born Oct. 14, 1746, daughter of Ebenezer Wheeler of Grafton. He died March 16, 1824; she died Nov. 5, 1835.

Mr. Thurston was a farmer, constable of Worcester county, collector, and much in town affairs. During the revolutionary war he was called out to serve his country and joined a company, but peace being declared he did not go. His wife, expecting every day he would have to go, took his gun to pieces, cleaned it, put it together again, loaded and fired it to prove that all was right, and had it ready for him in case of need. Her eldest·son, Timothy, stood by and watched carefully how she adjusted the pieces.

#### Children :

+8501 Timothy,⁶ b. July 10, 1766; m. 1st, Margaret Hill; 2d, Lucy Hayden.
8502 Elizabeth,⁶ b. Oct. 19, 1767; n.m.; d. Oct. 9, 1828.
8503 Rachel,⁶ b. Aug. 7, 1771; m. Amos Ellis, a blacksmith of Grafton, Mass. She died Oct. 2, 1820; he died March 2, 1839. They had:
    8504 *Amos* (Ellis), d. in Cherry, Pa.
    8505 *Susanna Thurston* (Ellis), b. July 2, 1789; m. April, 1806, Moses Roberts, b. in Princeton, Mass., Sept. 7, 1775, a shoe manufacturer in Grafton, and member of the Baptist church, son of John and Tabitha (Leland) Roberts of Grafton. They had:
        8506 *Julia Ann* (Roberts), b. March 8, 1809; m. Robert G. Taft; d. in Sturbridge, Mass., Dec. 25, 1863.
        8507 *Susan Ellis* (Roberts), b. Sept. 27, 1810; m. Milate Baker of Saranac Lake, N. Y.; d. March 16, 1864.
        8508 ·*Hannah Sabrina* (Roberts), b. April 27, 1813; m. Gregory S. Leland of Grafton; d. Jan. 31, 1837.
        8509 *Emeline* (Roberts), b. March 9, 1819; m. Samuel Packard, a shoe tool manufacturer in Grafton; they have :
            8510 *Joel S.* (Packard), in company with his father; m.
            8511 *Lizzie Isabel* (Packard), m. June 26, 1878, Rev. George S. Clarke, a Methodist minister, now, 1879, at Topsfield, Mass.
        8512 *Clarissa Lucretia* (Roberts), b. July 2, 1825; m. S. Brown of Uxbridge, Mass.; d. May 23, 1861.
        8513 *Moses Vespatian* (Roberts), b. Aug. 24, 1829; d. Aug. 20, 1830.
    8514 *Vespatian* (Ellis), d. in Cherry, Pa.
    8515 *Lucretia Doke* (Ellis), b. Dec. 3, 1795; m. April 3, 1817, Reuben P. Leland, a shoemaker in Grafton; they had :
        8516 *Chesselden E.* (Leland), b. April 4, 1820; d. Nov. 25, 1843.
        8517 *Hannah L.* (Leland).
    8518 *Lewis* (Ellis), b. Jan. 30, 1808; m. March 17, 1829, Ruth M. Leland, b. May 11, 1809, daughter of Eliab and Peasly (Adams) Leland of

Upton, Mass. Mr. Ellis is a boot and shoemaker in West Woodstock, Ct., a member of the Congregational church. They had :

8519    *Harriet Lucretia* (Ellis), b. in Grafton Feb. 19, 1830; d. in West
     Woodstock Nov. 19, 1849.

8520    *Ruth Louisa* (Ellis), b. in Grafton July 26, 1831; d. in Bingham-
     ton, N. Y., Feb. 28, 1854.

8521    *Henry Lewis* (Ellis), b. in Grafton Dec. 31, 1833; d. in West
     Woodstock March 14, 1858.

8522    *Chesselden Leland* (Ellis), b. in West Woodstock March 17, 1846;
     m. in Providence, R. I., March 13, 1872, Ellen F. Holbrook of
     Upton. He is a boot and shoe manufacturer in So. Brookfield,
     Mass. They have :
     8523    *Elsie L.* (Ellis), b. Jan. 4, 1876.

8524  *Hannah Fisher* (Ellis), m. Willard Converse; they had:
     8525    *Stilman* (Converse), d. in the war against the rebellion.
     8526    *Lucretia* (Converse), m. —— Batchelor of Whitinsville, Mass.

+8527  Daniel,[6] b. Nov. 7, 1775; m. Rosanna E. Ellis.

## 8339

PETER THURSTON [5] (*Benjamin,*[4] *Daniel*[3]), brother of the preceding,
and son of Benjamin [4] and Elizabeth Thurston of Grafton, Mass.;
born there Sept. 17, 1745; married ELIZABETH ——. He lived in
Grafton, and after removed with his family to Alstead, N. H., where
he died Oct. 16, 1781.

### Children :

8529   David,[6] b. Jan. 31, 1773; d. in infancy.
8530   Pardius,[6] b. Aug. 2, 1775; m. Sally Ward of Upton, Mass.; they had :
     8531    *Sally,*[7] m. Joseph Wood of Upton.
     8532    *Betsey,*[7] m. —— Rockwood of Upton.
+8533  Levi,[5] m. 1st, Priscilla Wheeler; 2d, Hannah Hayden.
8534   Betty,[6] b. Nov. 30, 1780; d. Aug. 25, 1781.

## Sixth Generation.

## 8367

DAVID THURSTON [6] (*Thomas,*[5] *Thomas,*[4] *Thomas,*[3] *Thomas,*[2] *John*[1]),
eldest son of Thomas [5] and Mary (Aldrage) Thurston of Otisfield,
Me.; born in Wrentham, Mass., Oct. 14, 1755; married, Dec. 22,
1789, POLLY SPURR, born in Dorchester, Mass., Jan. 17, 1754, daughter of Joseph and Miriam Spurr. He died March 25, 1829; she died
Feb. 11, 1829.

Mr. Thurston was a farmer in Otisfield, Me.; a man of note in
town, often holding responsible offices. She was a very influential
member of the Congregational church.

### Children :

+8540  David,[7] b. Feb. 16, 1791; m. Sybil Holden.
8541   Mary,[7] b. Feb. 16, 1793; m. May 5, 1812, Nathaniel Lamb, a farmer in
     Otisfield. He died Feb. 17, 1850, aged 71 y. 6 m.; she died Aug. 15,
     1862. They had:
     8542    *William* (Lamb), b. Dec. 28, 1813; m. May 5, 1850, Roxana Bucknam;
        they had:
        8543    *Nathaniel* (Lamb), b. May 21, 1851.

8544 *David Thurston* (Lamb), b. March 30, 1816; m. Jan. 23, 1858, Laura
Spurr; they had:
    8545 *Edwin* (Lamb), b. March 25, 1859.
8546 *Solomon Haskell* (Lamb), b. Sept. 16, 1820; d. May 3, 1878.
8547 *Mary Thurston* (Lamb), b. June 4, 1823; d. Sept. 5, 1859.
8548 *John* (Lamb), b. Nov. 7, 1825; n.m.
8549 *Joseph* (Lamb), b. Oct. 22, 1828; d. Dec. 13, 1868.
8550   Thomas,[7] b. July 17, 1795; d. young.
8551  Meredith Wyatt,[7] b. Dec. 11, 1797; m. May 8, 1823, Dea. John Hancock,
son of Elias and Mary (Mann) Hancock of Otisfield. He is a farmer,
a man of influence; was representative to the legislature three years,
and held many offices of trust in the town of Otisfield and also in Litchfield, Me., after removing there Nov. 5, 1857. He is a deacon in the
Congregational church. Children, all born in Otisfield :
8552 *Mary Mann* (Hancock), b. May 2, 1824; m. 1st, April 27, 1848, Lyman
Caswell; he died Sept. 29, 1854; 2d, Feb. 2, 1861, Oliver Waterman, and had :
    8553 *Lyman Caswell* (Waterman), b. Feb. 20, 1862.
    8554 *Clara Brown* (Waterman), b. Jan. 20, 1865.
    8555 *George Lincoln* (Waterman), b. Feb. 28, 1867.
8556 *Martha Ann* (Hancock), b. June 21, 1826; m. May 11, 1851, Samuel
Grosvenor Nutting, and had :
    8557 *Harriet Fidelia* (Nutting), b. Sept. 2, 1852.
    8558 *Edward Danforth* (Nutting), b. March 4. 1854.
8559 *Meredith Thurston* (Hancock), b. May 16, 1831; m. March 15, 1860,
Cowper Swartz Ayer, and had :
    8560 *John Cowper* (Ayer), b. May 31, 1861; d. May 29, 1863.
    8561 *Flora Hepzibah* (Ayer), b. Feb. 1, 1863.
    8562 *Thomas Herbert* (Ayer), b. June 18, 1865.
8563 *John Granville* (Hancock), b. June 22, 1834; d. May 14. 1859.
8564 *David Elias* (Hancock), b. March 29, 1837; d. Jan. 26, 1844.
8565 *Harriet Emeline* (Hancock), b. July 5, 1839; d. Jan. 27, 1844.

## 8369

JACOB THURSTON [6] (*Thomas,[5] Thomas,[4] Thomas,[3] Thomas,[2] John[1]*),
brother of the preceding, and son of Thomas [5] and Mary (Aldrage),
Thurston of Otisfield, Me.; born in Foxborough, Mass., May 19,
1769; married, in Otisfield, about 1798, NANCY ANNA EDWARDS,
born in Gilmanton, N. H., 1779.

Mr. Thurston served five years in the continental army and in the
revolutionary war. At the close of the war he went to the district of
Maine to visit an old friend by the name of Pearse, who lived in Otisfield, to avoid going into the army again. He was so much pleased
with the new country that he took up a tract of three hundred acres
of land and built a house. This was about 1789. The house is still
standing. He kept bachelor's hall for some time before his marriage.

Children :
8567  Elizabeth,[7] b. April, 1800; m. Zachariah Winship.
8568  Lydia,[7] b. Oct., 1802; m. William Hill.
8569  Mary,[7] b. July, 1804; m. Benjamin Larrabee.
8570  Thomas,[7] b. Dec., 1807; n.m.; d. 1829.
+8571  Israel,[7] b. Feb. 9, 1810; m. Sarah Hunt Edwards.
8572  Martha,[7] b. July, 1811; Aug. 13, 1838, she sold her brother Israel of Poland a lot of land in Otisfield.

## 8388

DANIEL THURSTON [6] (*Dea. Daniel,[5] Daniel,[4] Thomas,[3] Thomas,[2]
John[1]*), son of Dea. Daniel [5] and Elizabeth (Whiting) Thurston of
Franklin, Mass.; born there Sept. 11, 1749; married SUSAN JOHNSON
of Bellingham, Mass. He died Nov. 7, 1802.

Mr. Thurston was born in the old family homestead in Franklin, and finally settled on a small farm near the middle of the town, where all his children were born.

Children :

+8575  Daniel,[7] b. Feb. 22, 1783; m. Bathsheba Brintnall.
+8576  Luke,[7] b. Feb. 7, 1785; m. Olive Clark.
 8577  Paul,[7] m. Arivesta Hunt of Canton, Mass.; was a truckman in Boston, Ms.
 8578  Susan,[7] m. Willard Bullard, who kept the toll-gate on the turnpike in Dedham, Mass.
+8579  Nahum,[7] b. Jan. 24, 1792; m. Martha Rice.
+8580  Philo,[7] b. July 15, 1794; m. Julia Maria Daniels.
+8581  Johnson,[7] b. Oct. 9, 1797; m. Looe Starrett.

## 8389

ABIJAH THURSTON[6] (*Dea. Daniel,[5] Daniel,[4] Thomas,[3] Thomas,[2] John[1]*), brother of the preceding, and son of Dea. Daniel[5] and Elizabeth (Whiting) Thurston of Franklin, Mass.; born there July 5, 1751; married RACHEL JOHNSON of Bellingham, Mass. He died July 10, 1812, aged 61; she died Nov. 21, 1826, aged 72.

He was a farmer and somewhat noted tavern keeper in Franklin, succeeding his fathers for several generations in the same house. His house was known from Vermont to New Bedford and Cape Cod as a pleasant place to stop over night or over the Sabbath. He was admitted to the Congregational church April 9, 1779.

Children :

+8586  Levina,[7] b. May 30, 1775; m. Jesse Miller.
+8587  Nancy,[7] b. probably 1776; m. Thaddeus Hastings.
 8588  Deborah,[7] b. June 3, 1777; m. April, 1796, Jesse Metcalf, a farmer of Hope, Me., deacon of the Baptist church, b. in Wrentham, Mass., May, 1775, son of Moses and Mary (Hill) Metcalf. She died Jan., 1823; he died in Albion, Me.. July 4, 1856. They had:
       8589  *Thurston* (Metcalf), b. in Franklin Oct. 16, 1796.
               Born in Hope :
       8590  *Jesse* (Metcalf), b. Jan.. 1800; d. Sept., 1865.
       8591  *Cynthia* (Metcalf), b. 1801; d. March, 1861.
       8592  *Rachel* (Metcalf), b. 1803; d. Dec., 1822.
       8593  *Mary Hill* (Metcalf), b. Dec., 1804.
       8594  *Nancy Thurston* (Metcalf), b. 1806; d. Sept., 1828.
       8595  *Moses Glover* (Metcalf), b. Nov. 6, 1808.
       8596  *Erastus* (Metcalf), b. Feb. 22, 1810.
       8597  *Abijah Thurston* (Metcalf), b. March 8, 1813.
       8598  *Miranda* (Metcalf), b. and d. 1815.
       8599  *Julia Stover* (Metcalf), b. 1819.
       8600  *Aaron Gleason* (Metcalf), b. and d. 1823.
               Mrs. Deborah Thurston Metcalf in 1877 had had 52 grandchildren, 24 living, and 79 great-grandchildren, 66 living.
+8601  Caleb,[7] b. 1781; m. Lovicey French.
+8602  David,[7] b. Sept. 20, 1784; m. Miranda Ellis.
+8603  Julia,[7] b. Nov. 9, 1788; m. Asa Rockwood.
 8604  Rachel,[7] b. 1792; m. Nahum Pike, a carpenter of Westborough, Mass., and had :
       8605  *Clementina* (Pike).
       8606  *George S.* (Pike), b. March 27, 1834.
       8607  *Louisa M.* (Pike), b. May 2, 1837.
       8608  *Maria L.* (Pike).
       8609  *Joseph S.* (Pike).

## 8408

Joseph Thurston [6] ( *Joseph,* [5] *Daniel,* [4] *Thomas,* [3] *Thomas,* [2] *John* [1] ), son of Joseph Thurston [5]; born Sept. 11, 1764; married, June 6, 1793. Polly (or Mary) Hubbard, born in Leicester, Mass., March 12. 1766. She died March 3, 1804; he died Feb. 2, 1844.

Mr. Thurston was a trader and manufacturer of potash in North Brookfield, Mass., till 1804, when he failed in business, his wife died, his children were "put out," and he went away for some years, we know not where. He was a man of feeble health, greatly troubled with asthma. He lived with his son Joseph the last eleven years of his life; was a member of the Congregational church.

### Children, born in North Brookfield:

+8615 Lyman,[7] b. Jan. 16, 1794; m. 1st, Delia Atwood; 2d, Mrs. Rowena H. Pratt.
8616 Joseph,[7] b. Jan. 29, 1796; d. Aug. 8, 1796.
+8617 Joseph,[7] b. June 7, 1797; m. Lucy Bucknam Davis.
8618 Mary,[7] b. July 6, 1799; d. same day.
+8619 Daniel,[7] b. Sept. 4, 1800; m. Patty A. Ross.
8620 Mary,[7] b. Jan. 13, 1803; d. March 3, 1803.
8621 Mary Hubbard,[7] b. March, 1804; m. Jan. 12, 1831, Marvin S. Phetteplace; d. Dec. 23, 1843; no children.

## 8413

William Thurston [6] of Jamaica, L. I. ( *John,* [5] *John,* [4] *Benjamin,* [3] *Joseph,* [2] *John* [1] ), eldest son of John [5] and Mary Thurston of Jamaica; born there Feb. 11, 1754; married ――――. He joined a company of minute-men in the time of the revolutionary war, 1775.

### Child:

+8626 James B.,[7] b. about 1790; m. Felitia Tuthill.

## 8422

David Thurston [6] ( *Israel,* [5] *John,* [4] *Benjamin,* [3] *Joseph,* [2] *John* [1] ), son of Israel [5] and Christina (Pangburn) Thurston of Rahway, N. J.; born there March 20, 1762; married Esther Taylor, born Feb. 23, 1769. She died April 11, 1814; he died Oct. 22, 1843.

He lived in Northumberland county, Pa., and moved to Crawford county, near Meadville, Pa.; was much respected; served seven years in the revolutionary war, going first as a substitute for his father; was a member of the Baptist church; moved to Ohio in 1817.

### Children:

8631 Joanna,[7] b. Sept. 29, 1786; m. April 14, 1802, William Ewing, b. Aug. 16, 1780. She died Dec. 11, 1838; he died July 16, 1863. They had:
 8632 *David* (Ewing), b. Aug. 23, 1805.
 8633 *Alexander* (Ewing), b. March 26, 1808.
 8634 *Ralph* (Ewing), b. May 3, 1811.
 8635 *William* (Ewing), b. Aug. 12, 1813; d. Nov. 14, 1834.
 8636 *Jane* (Ewing), b. June 15, 1815.
 8637 *Nancy* (Ewing), b. June 16, 1817; d. 1854.
 8638 *James F.* (Ewing), b. Dec. 6, 1819.
 8639 *John* (Ewing), b. March 21, 1823; d. June 3, 1853.
 8640 *Rebecca* (Ewing), b. May 10, 1824; d. March 7, 1853.
 8641 *Joanna* (Ewing), b. April 13, 1826.
 8642 *Esther* (Ewing), b. March 26, 1828; d. Sept. 24, 1851.
 8643 *Samuel* (Ewing), b. Aug. 26, 1830.
 8644 *Josiah* (Ewing), b. April 23, 1834.

8645 Hannah,[7] b. Nov. 14, 1788; m. Abram Daniels. Her son Kingsbury lives at Clarke's Corners, Ohio.
+8646 Henry,[7] b. March 7, 1791; m. Cassandra Elliott.
+8647 Flavel,[7] b. July 16, 1793; m. Eleanor Mercer.
8648 Christiana,[7] b. Sept. 5, 1795; m. David Daniels.
+8649 David,[7] b. May 26, 1798; m. Esther Stanbrook.
8650 Nancy.[7] b. April 26, 1800; m. 1st, Feb. 10, 1819, William Radle, b. Dec. 21, 1795, d. Sept. 3, 1846; 2d, 1857, Rev. John L. Moor; he died 1861. She had, by first husband :
 8651 *David M.* (Radle), b. May 20, 1822; m. Feb. 5, 1843, Mary A. Hodge; ten children.  P. O. address Guy's Mills, Pa.
 8652 *Catherine C.* (Radle), b. Sept. 20, 1823; m. Aug. 21, 1842, Jacob B. Heming; ten children.  P. O. address Cooperstown, Pa.
 8653 *Esther F.* (Radle), b. June 7, 1826; m. Sept. 16, 1845, Vasey B. Jones; d. July 20, 1874; nine children.  P. O. address Eagleville, Ohio.
 8654 *Tabitha J.* (Radle), b. May 20, 1828; m. June 13, 1847, Luke Barlow; four children.  P. O. address Guy's Mills, Pa.
 8655 *William H.* (Radle), b. April 24, 1830; m. 1st, Sept. 28. 1856, Emily Keep; 2d, Nov. 24, 1866, Dianna F. Franklin; had nine children, five living.
 8656 *James Taylor* (Radle), b. March 12, 1832; m. Oct. 25, 1860, Rhoda Samantha Hall. He is a farmer in Richmond township, P. O. Randolph, Pa. They have :
  8657 *Gillie Mintadell* (Radle), lives in Buckskin township, Ross Co., O.
 8658 *Joanna* (Radle), b. Jan. 31, 1835; m. Dec. 26, 1858, Corydon Alderman, a farmer in Keepville, Pa., and had Sarah Dell, Orson Harry, Nancy Luany, and John Corydon (Alderman).
 8659 *Reuben A.* (Radle), b. July 27, 1838; m. Nov. 8, 1861, Melissa A. Patten; four children.  P. O. address Florid, Ill.
 8660 *Freeman Thurston* (Radle), b. Feb. 11, 1842; m. Jan. 10, 1865, Sarah A. McFadden; one child.  P. O. address Townville, Pa.
 8661 *John N.* (Radle), b. Jan. 28, 1845; m. Dec. 22, 1870, Juliette Guy; one child.  P. O. address Guy's Mills, Pa.
 Four other children, who died in infancy.
8662 Esther,[7] b. July 12, 1802; m. Rev. Volney-Jones, a minister of the United Brethren church; d. March 15, 1844.
+8663 Israel,[7] b. Nov. 12, 1804; m. Almira Smith.
+8664 Lewis Taylor,[7] b. Jan. 8, 1808; m. ——.
8665 Jennet M.,[7] b. Feb. 11, 1811; m. Lemuel Smith; at Sugar Lake, Crawford county, Pa.

## 8423

SAMUEL THURSTON[6] (*Israel,*[5] *John,*[4] *Benjamin,*[3] *Joseph,*[2] *John*[1]), brother of the preceding, and son of Israel[5] and Christina (Pangburn) Thurston of Rahway, N. J.; born there March 6, 1766; married, 1791, HANNAH KELLEY of Rahway. He died March 23, 1823; she died July 22, 1840. They were buried in Indian Creek burial grounds, Butler county, Ohio.

Mr. Thurston was a farmer; went to Sunbury, Pa., thence to Mixersville, Franklin county, Ind., in 1816, where he purchased one hundred and sixty acres of land of the government, and began to clear a farm from the native forest, and had succeeded so far as to be in comfortable circumstances when, March 23, 1823, as he was returning on Sunday from the Baptist church, of which he was a member, he was killed by an ash tree falling upon him.

### Children :

8673 Sarah,[7] b. Feb. 3, 1792; m. May 7, 1809, William Brady. He was a farmer and died 1859; she died Aug. 26, 1866.  They had :
8674 *John P.* (Brady).
8675 *Samuel* (Brady).

8676    *Rachel* (Brady).
8677    *Mary A.* (Brady), d. young.
8678    *Joseph* (Brady), a lawyer, d. 1862.
8679    *Emeline* (Brady).
8680    *Eliza* (Brady), d. young.
+8681   William,[7] b. Aug. 12, 1799; m. Sept., 1822, Mary Telfor.
8682    Anna,[7] m. Thomas Flint, for many years a justice of the peace. They had:
8683    *Sarah J.* (Flint), m. Caleb Barnum of Mixersville; has a large family.
8684    *Samuel* (Flint), d. single.
8685    *John* (Flint), d. single.
8686    *Malin* (Flint), m. and has a large family; at Contreras, Ohio.
8687    *Philer* (Flint).
8688    *Oilver* (Flint).
8689    *William* (Flint).
8690    *Mary* (Flint), m. James W. Doty.
+8691   Oliver Perry,[7] b. Oct. 21, 1802; m. Maria L. Flint.
8692    Mary,[7] b. Jan. 22, 1805; m. William Blake; they had:
8693    *Elizabeth* (Blake), m. Price Farr.
8694    *John* (Blake), m. Mary Miller.
8695    *Samuel* (Blake), m. Harriet Nutt.
8696    *Perry* (Blake), m. Mary E. Stephens.
8697    *Andrew J.* (Blake), d. aged 8.
8698    *Clarissa* (Blake), m. Abraham Jones.
8699    *Henry* (Blake), m. ———.
8700    *Jacob* (Blake), m. Anna Davis.
8701    *Julia* (Blake), m. Francis Morrical.
8702    *Sarah A.* (Blake), m. Philip Morrical.
8703    *James K.* (Blake), m. Cynthia Shultz.
8704    *Phebe* (Blake), d. aged 17.
8705    Isaac,[7] b. Nov. 27, 1806; m. Rhoda Lee, daughter of Abraham Lee, one of the original surveyors of Indiana. He was a farmer and member of the Baptist church; d. Nov. 14, 1864, and she soon after, leaving:
8706    *Abraham Lee,*[8] b. Feb. 25, 1830; m. Grizilla Thurston [see no. 9314]; a Baptist minister in Scipio, Ohio; no children.
8707    *Rhoda,*[8] b. Dec. 7, 1838; m. John Updike; d. 1871. They had:
8708    *John* (Updike).
8709    *Benjamin* (Updike).
8710    Rebecca,[7] b. Aug. 2, 1808; m. John Thurston [see no. 8734].
8711    Benjamin,[7] d. in infancy.
8712    David,[7] d. in infancy.
8713    John[7] and three others, d. in infancy.

## 8424

JOHN THURSTON[6] (*Israel,*[5] *John,*[4] *Benjamin,*[3] *Joseph,*[2] *John*[1]), brother of the preceding, and son of Israel[5] and Christina (Pangburn) Thurston of Rahway, N. J.; born there Jan. 11, 1768; married MARY MARS of Rahway, born Jan. 27, 1771. She died Nov. 19, 1813. Both are buried by an old Baptist church on Shamalkin creek, about seven miles from Danville, Pa.

Mr. Thurston was a weaver and farmer in Northumberland, Pa.

### Children :

8718    William,[7] b. Nov. 20, 1785; m. Anna Dull; was a farmer in Lawrenceburgh, Ind. He died 1814; she died 1837. They had:
8719    *Catherine,*[8] b. 1807; m. Benjamin Darland.
8720    *Martha,*[8] b. Dec. 12, 1808; m. Job Canara; he died 1863.
8721    *Abraham,*[8] b. Feb. 9, 1810; a carpenter in Camden, Ohio.  Children
8722    *Robert Grimes,*[9] b. Dec. 25, 1845; n.m.
8723    *Nancy,*[9] b. May 15, 1851; n.m.
8724    *Addison Carl,*[9] b. June 10, 1853; n.m.
8725    *John P.,*[8] b. 1811; killed in the Mexican war 1836.
8726    *Rose Ann,*[8] b. 1813; m. John Westerman.

+8727 Israel,[7] b. April 3, 1788; m. ———.
8728 Mahala,[7] b. March 17, 1790.
+8729 Moses,[7] b. June 1, 1793; m. Hannah Hankerson Parker.
8730 Christina,[7] b. April 17, 1794.
8731 Jane,[7] b. Jan. 10, 1796; m. George Haines; d. Nov. 23, 1863, in Salladasburgh, Pa.; had a large family.
8732 Martha,[7] b. Dec. 24, 1798; n.m.; lives in Danville, Pa.
8733 Mars,[7] } twins, b. April 11, 1800; d. same day.
+8734 John,[7] } m. Rebecca Thurston.
8735 Mary,[7] b. Oct. 11, 1802; m. William Pence, and never heard from after.
+8736 Levi,[7] b. Mar. 5, 1805: m. 1st, Sarah Shurr; 2d, Elizabeth Rhodes Bastress.
8737 Amelia,[7] b. May 11, 1807; m. 1st, Mahlon Kase; 2d, Alexander Mears; he died. She lives in Columbia county, Pa.
8738 Janet Ely,[7] b. Aug. 19, 1809.
8739 Cornelius,[7] b. July 9, 1811; d. aged 13.
8740 Sarah Ann,[7] twin, b. Nov. 18, 1813; m. Jacob Millham of Mooresburgh, Montour county, Pa. Children:
    8741 *Francis* (Millham), b. Dec. 25, 1842; m. Ann Maus; they reside near Mooresburgh. Pa.
    8742 *Martha Jane* (Millham), b. April 9, 1846; m. Feb., 1865, George Deebert of Schuylkill county, Pa.
    8743 *Gilbert D.* (Millham), b. July 18, 1848.
    8744 *Ruth A.* (Millham), b. Nov. 20, 1850; m. Nov., 1872, Alfred M. Robinson, a clerk near Mooresburgh.
    8745 *Sarah E.* (Millham), b. Feb. 17, 1852; m. Nov., 1873, Wm. C. Gibson.
    8746 *Israel* (Millham), b. Jan. 16, 1854.
    8747 *John W.* (Millham), b. July 4, 1855; m. Elizabeth Jane Hopples of Milton, Pa.
8748 Samuel M.,[7] twin, b. Nov. 18, 1813; m. Mary Ann Appleman, b. Nov. 5, 1816. He was a farmer; moved to Stryker, Ohio, 1849; d. Aug. 16, 1849. They had:
    8749 *Sarah Margaret,*[8] b. Oct. 11, 1837; m. Aug. 22, 1857, Elisha H. Knorr, b. June 16, 1836; she died 1865. They had:
    8750 *Samuel C.* (Knorr), b. Sept. 24, 1858; d. Oct. 18, 1865.
    8751 *Mathias* (Knorr), b. Aug. 6, 1864; d. Nov. 7, 1864.
    8752 *William* (Knorr), b. Dec. 19, 1865; d. Feb. 23, 1866.
    8753 *Joanna Catherine,*[8] b. July 9, 1839; m. 1st, William Camp, and had Mary (Camp); 2d, James Yuber of Burr Oak, Mich., and had Charles (Yuber).
    8754 *Mathias,*[8] b. Sept. 15, 1841; m. Feb. 4. 1864, Sarah Boyers, b. April 17, 1845. He is a farmer near Stryker; enlisted Aug. 15, 1861, in the 38th Ohio regiment infantry; with Gen. Schoeff in all his campaigns in Kentucky; at Camp Wild Cat, where the rebel general, Zollicoffer, was routed, followed him on to Loudon and Mill Springs, where he was killed; then in the 14th army corps under Gen. Rosecrans, with Gen. Thomas as division commander, in the battles of Stone River, Murfreesborough, Tenn., Pittsburgh Landing and Corinth, Miss., Perrysville, Ky., Chickamauga and Chattanooga, Tenn.; saw the battle at Lookout Mountain, Gen. Howard fighting above the clouds, and next day participated in the storming of Mission Ridge, where he received the only wound he had during the war; re-enlisted Dec. 11, 1863, as a veteran at Chattanooga, and was at the siege of Atlanta, Ga., and the battle of Boonesborough, Tenn.; with Sherman in his march to the sea, to Raleigh, N. C., where Johnston surrendered; marched to Richmond. and Washington at the grand review of the army; thence to Louisville, Ky., where he was mustered out; thence to Cleveland, Ohio, where he was discharged July 25, 1865, having served nearly four years. Child:
        8755 *Florrie,*[9] b. July 25, 1867.
    8756 *John,*[8] b. Jan. 1, 1844; d. Feb. 21, 1864.
    8757 *George Washington,*[8] b. Jan. 18, 1846; d. in infancy.
    8758 *Samuel Levi,*[8] b. May 15, 1848; d. Oct. 10, 1865.
    8759 *Harriet Elizabeth,*[8] b. March 12, 1850; m. Elisha H. Knorr, and had George, Elmer, and Cora L. (Knorr).

## 8425

MOSES THURSTON[6] (*Israel,[5] John,[4] Benjamin,[3] Joseph,[2] John[1]*), brother of the preceding, and son of Israel[5] and Christina (Pangburn) Thurston of Rahway, N. J.; born there May 9, 1770; married, first, CATHERINE BOTTENHAMER, born April 18, 1778, died July 12, 1819; second, ELIZABETH CHESTER.  He died Sept. 22, 1848.

Mr. Thurston was a weaver; went to Rushton, Northumberland county, Pa.; was a Baptist.

His children, by first wife, Catherine, were:

+8764  William,[7] b. May 25, 1795; m. Margaret Campbell.
8765  Elizabeth,[7] b. Aug. 4, 1796; m. Sept. 19, 1819, Stephen Kelley; d. Jan. 29, 1853.
8766  James,[7] b. Sept. 5, 1801; n.m.; a shoemaker; d. Feb. 7, 1827.
+8767  Asa,[7]      } twins, born { m. 1st, Susan Jordan; 2d, Sarah Heller.
8768  Samuel,[7]  } July 24, 1803; } m. —— Persing; no children; a shoemaker; d. March 29, 1870, at Augusta, Pa.
+8769  Sylvanus,[7] b. Feb. 9, 1806.
+8770  Israel,[7] b. Dec. 18, 1808; m. Abigail Persing.
8771  Rebecca,[7] b. Jan. 4, 1810; m. Jacob Yarda; d. 1869.
8772  Mary,[7] b. Feb. 28, 1812; m. George Persing; d. Oct. 4, 1862.
+8773  Mathias,[7] b. May 18, 1814; m. Eliza Jane Summerville.

## 8426

FLAVEL THURSTON[6] (*Israel,[5] John,[4] Benjamin,[3] Joseph,[2] John[1]*), brother of the preceding, and son of Israel[5] and Christina (Pangburn) Thurston of Rahway, N. J.; born there 1772; married, Jan. 14, 1794, MARY MAGDALENE BOTTENHAMER, born in Northumberland county, Pa., March 13, 1776.  She died Dec. 25, 1838; he died April 13, 1853.

Mr. Thurston was a weaver in Franklin county, Ind., from 1822 till 1848, when he went to Shelby county and lived with his children.

### Children:

+8779  Peter,[7] m. Sarah Matlock.
8780  Jane,[7] m. James Quick and had Edward, Nancy, and James (Quick) and two others.
+8781  Moses.[7]
+8782  John,[7] m. 1st, Catherine Baker; 2d, Isabel ——.
+8783  Samuel,[7] m. Rebecca Ketchman.
+8784  Lewis,[7] b. Jan. 1, 1806; m. Martha Burch.
+8785  Jesse,[7] b. April 1. 1808; m. Harriet Updike.
+8786  Enos,[7] m. Mary J. Babbs.
+8787  David,[7] b. Nov. 11, 1811; m. Lourinda Laing.
8788  Jacob.[7]
+8789  Levi,[7] b. March 24, 1820; m. Clarissa Jane Updike.

## 8430

JOHN FLAVEL THURSTON[6] (*Flavel,[5] John,[4] Benjamin,[3] Joseph,[2] John[1]*), only son of Flavel Thurston[5] of Rahway, N. J.; born there 1778; married, in New York city, March 28, 1800, MARTHA HOPPER, born Aug. 18, 1778.  He died 1818; she died April 12, 1865, and was buried in the Hopper burying grounds at Long Branch, N. Y.

Mr. Thurston was a mason in Rahway.  He spent the winters in Savannah, Ga., and died there.

### Children:

8794  John Hopper,[7] b. July 6, 1801; d. Aug. 19, 1803.
8795  Edgar Mandelbert,[7] b. June 13, 1804; m. 1st, Mary Elizabeth Rusher; she

died 1835; 2d, May 17, 1837, Jane Doty Chivvis, b. Sept. 17, 1811, daughter of Cornelius and Mary H. I. (Doty) Chivvis. He is a shipbuilder in Brooklyn, N. Y., residence 221 Bedford avenue; no children.
+8796 Abraham Hopper,[7] b. Oct., 1809; m. Mrs. Matilda (Anthony) Freeman.

## 8449

EZRA THURSTON[6] (*James,[5] Daniel,[4] Daniel,[3] Joseph,[2] John[1]*), son of James Thurston[5] of near Poughkeepsie, N. Y.; married, in Hartford, Ct., SALLY GILBERT. They lived in Dutchess county, N. Y., 1776. One son was bound out to a clergyman in Dutchess county, and no further knowledge of Mr. Thurston has been found.

Children:
+8800 Eli,[7] b. June 28, 1777; m. Margaret Coons.
8801 Ezra,[7] m. Phebe Hurd Wentworth; d. in Schenectady, N. Y.

## 8454

EBENEZER THURSTON[6] (*Cyrus,[5] Daniel,[4] Daniel,[3] Joseph,[2] John[1]*), son of Cyrus Thurston[5]; married EUNICE KELSEY.

Children:
+8802 Azor,[7] b. Feb. 22, 1799; m. Elebedy Smith.
+8803 Ebenezer,[7] b. 1801; m. Hannah Albro.
8804 Lyman.[7]
8805 Hermes.[7]
8806 Anna.[7]
8807 Eliza.[7]
8808 Child.

## 8459

AMOS THURSTON[6] (*Increase,[5] Daniel,[4] Daniel,[3] Daniel,[2] John[1]*), eldest son of Increase[5] and —— (Chapin) Thurston of Lisle, N. Y.

Children:
8809 Amos,[7] m. and had *Corsanus*[8] and *Increase.*[8]
+8810 Elisha,[7] m. Lovicey Sweet.

## 8467

DANIEL THURSTON[6] (*Daniel,[5] Daniel,[4] Daniel,[3] Daniel,[2] John[1]*), son of Daniel[5] and Sarah (Curtiss) Thurston formerly of Sharon, Ct.; born Feb. 13, 1766; married CHARLOTTE MUDGE. He died Nov. 29, 1824.

Mr. Thurston was a farmer in Verona, Oneida county, N. Y. They were members of Rev. Israel Barnard's church, meeting in a barn where the roosters, cows, and calves aided in the music. The girls wore homespun dresses and shoes tied with leather strings. In 1820 they moved to Busti, Chautauqua county, N. Y.

### Children, born in Verona:
8811 Sarah,[7] m. Morehouse Abott of West Moreland, and died 1806.
8812 L—— A.,[7] b. Aug. 18, 1803; m. —— Clement, a farmer and foundry man in Medina, N. Y. They had the care of her mother in her last days, and after her death his own father, mother, a sister with four children (two of them blind), rendered helpless by the death of her husband, were thrown upon them for support, which so drew upon their resources that he sold his foundry, moved his family to Albion, and went to California in April, 1850. At first he was not successful, but after going to Mariposa he accumulated quite a sum of money; sold in 1865 and started for home, was robbed and supposed to have been murdered. Mrs. Clement has been in the Home of the Friendless, Rochester, N. Y., for the last eight years, and has a vigorous mind and a warm heart.

## 8472

DAVID THURSTON[6] (*Daniel,[5] Daniel,[4] Daniel,[3] Daniel,[2] John[1]*),
brother of the preceding, and son of Daniel[6] and Sarah (Curtiss)
Thurston formerly of Sharon, Ct.; born April 9, 1774; married, 1795,
MARGARET PHILLIPS, born in Brunswick, Rensselaer county, N. Y.
She died in Whitestown, Oneida county, N. Y., 1824, aged 48; he
died in Albion, Orleans county, N. Y., March 23, 1829.

Mr. Thurston was a farmer in Whitestown. He was in an artillery
regiment in the war of 1812. Soon after his wife's death he removed
to Albion.

### Children, born in Whitestown :

8813   William,[7] d. many years ago, aged 30.
8814   Betsey,[7] b. April 18, 1800; m. Feb. 11, 1819, Martin Cavana, b. Feb. 3,
           1797, son of Peter Cavana of Utica, N. Y. He was a farmer in Marcy,
           Oneida county, N. Y.; d. Nov. 9, 1866, leaving a farm to each of his
           sons. Children:
       8815   *Edward* (Cavana), b. March 2, 1820.
       8816   *James* (Cavana), b. Feb. 26, 1823.
       8817   *Martin P.* (Cavana), b. June 26. 1827.
       8818   *William* (Cavana). b. March 3, 1829.
       8819   *Cornelia* (Cavana), b. July 25, 1831.
       8820   *Caroline* (Cavana), b. July 25, 1835.
       8821   *Charlotte* (Cavana), b. July 11, 1837.
8822   Lovina,[7] b. April 30, 1802; m. May 1, 1823, in Barre, N. Y., Leonard War-
           ner, b. May 23, 1799, son of Elijah Warner of Phelps, Ontario county,
           N. Y. He was a farmer in Albion; d. July 18, 1847. Children:
       8823   *Elizabeth* (Warner), b. April 20, 1824; d. May 31, 1876.
       8824   *Nelson* (Warner), b. March 2, 1826.
       8825   *Elijah* (Warner), b. Nov. 27, 1828.
       8826   *Mary Ann* (Warner), b. Sept. 24, 1830.
       8827   *William* (Warner), b. Nov. 26, 1832.
       8828   *Chester* (Warner), b. Oct. 28. 1834.
       8829   *Jeanette* (Warner), b. Aug. 18, 1837.
       8830   *Cornelia* (Warner), b. March 23, 1839.
       8831   *Morris* (Warner), b. Sept. 18. 1841.
+8832   David,[7] b. July 24, 1811; m. Sophia Curtis.
8833   Olive,[7] m. Alonzo Loomis of Albion.
8834   Jonas,[7] d. leaving a widow and three children.
8835   Henry,[7] lives in Canada; has children in Cleveland, Ohio.

## 8474

CALEB CURTISS THURSTON[6] of Barre, N. Y. (*Daniel,[5] Daniel,[4] Daniel,[3] Daniel,[2] John[1]*), brother of the preceding, and son of Daniel[6]
and Sarah (Curtiss) Thurston formerly of Sharon, Ct.; born in
Stephentown, N. Y., July 27, 1778; married, 1803, THANKFUL BAILEY,
born Jan. 27, 1786. She died April 4, 1858; he died June 30, 1867.

Mr. Thurston was a farmer in Westmoreland, Oneida county, N. Y.,
and in the spring of 1814 moved to Barre as a pioneer. In 1852 he
sold his farm there and moved to Albion, N. Y., and he and his wife
lived with their youngest daughter till their death. They were both
members of the Presbyterian church.

### Children :

8840   Sophronia,[7] b. Dec. 6, 1803; m. Orlando Rogers, b. 1801. They had :
       8841   *Edson B.* (Rogers), b. July 27, 1823.
       8842   *Urban Clark* (Rogers), b. Dec. 6, 1831.
       8843   *Lewis Berfam* (Rogers), b. Sept. 10, 1833.

8844 Joel Curtiss,[7] b. Jan. 9, 1806; m. Nov., 1835, Miranda Seymour. He was a merchant, member of the Presbyterian church; d. Dec. 5, 1843.
+8845 Stephen Bailey,[7] b. Jan. 3, 1808; m. Juliana Williams.
+8846 Urban Clark,[7] b. Sept. 8, 1810; m. 1st, Mary Wrisley; 2d, Caroline P. Howland; 3d, Louise Catherine Olds.
8847 Thankful,[7] b. Nov. 4, 1813; m. 1st, July, 1835, John Parker; 2d, Oct. 8, 1838, Asa Howard, b. Sept. 24, 1804. She is a member of the Presbyterian church. She had, by second husband:
8848 *Ellen S.* (Howard), b. Sept. 8, 1845.
8849 Lydia,[7] b. in Barre Sept. 8, 1817; m. April 16, 1840, Harlow W. Lee, b. Aug. 26, 1817. She is a member of the Presbyterian church. They had:
8850 *Henry W.* (Lee), b. Dec. 24, 1842.

## 8480

DAVID THURSTON[6] of Mexico, Otsego county, N. Y. (*Moses,*[5] *Daniel,*[4] *Daniel,*[3] *Daniel,*[2] *John*[1]), son of Moses[5] and Thankful (Knapp) Thurston of New Lisbon, N. Y.; married RACHEL CHAPIN.

Mr. Thurston was a farmer in New Lisbon, and afterward in Mexico, where they both died.

### Children:

+8855 Peter,[7] b. Jan. 31, 1795; m. Anna Kelsey.
8856 Lucinda,[7] m. —— Valentine; d. 1879.
8857 Tamor,[7] m. —— Jennings.
8858 Lucia,[7] m. —— Hutchings; d. 1874.
8859 Rachel,[7] m. —— Johnson; d. 1876.

## 8486

ROWLEN SWEATLAND THURSTON[6] (*Amos,*[5] *Daniel,*[4] *Daniel,*[3] *Daniel,*[2] *John*[1]), eldest son of Amos[5] and Mary (Sweatland) Thurston of Sharon, Ct.; born there Sept. 27, 1765; married SALLY KETCHUM.

Mr. Thurston was a farmer in Sharon, and afterward moved to Marshall, Calhoun county, Mich., where they both died.

### Child:

8864 Jesse,[7] m. 1st, Sally Thurston [see no. 8887]; she died March 22, 1827; 2d, Altha Ketchum. He was a farmer in New Lisbon, Otsego county, N. Y. He had, by first wife, Sally:
    8865 *Susan,*[8] went to Wisconsin.
    8866 *George,*[8] n.m.; d. about 1850.
    8867 *Jane,*[8] m. and lived in Michigan.
        By second wife, Altha:
    8868 *Milly,*[8] m. —— Smith, and had Uria, Maria, and Lewis (Smith).
    8869 *Jerusha,*[8] m. —— Rowley, and had:
        8870 *Mary* (Rowley).
        8871 *Reuben* (Rowley), P. O. Bainbridge, Chenango county, N. Y.
        8872 *Roderick* (Rowley), P. O. Guilford, Chenango county, N. Y.
        8873 *Harriet* (Rowley). m. Leonard Aylesworth.
        8874 *Josiah* (Rowley), P. O. Norwich, Chenango county, N. Y.
        8875 *Rosefa* (Rowley), m. Reave Guile.
    8876 *Ira,*[8] m. and had:
        8877 *Chester.*[9]
        8878 *Curtis.*[9]
        8879 *Joel,*[9] P. O. Nobleville, New Lisbon, N. Y.
        8880 *Elijah,*[9] Morris, Otsego county, N. Y.
        8881 *Polly.*[9]
        8882 *Olive.*[9]

## 8489

AMOS THURSTON[6] (*Amos,[5] Daniel,[4] Daniel,[3] Daniel,[2] John[1]*), brother of the preceding, and son of Amos[5] and Mary (Sweatland) Thurston of Sharon, Ct.; born there Dec. 30, 1769; married, November, 1796, LUCY DART, born in New Lisbon, Otsego county, N. Y., Jan. 9, 1780. He died July 21, 1852; she died Aug. 24, 1868.

Mr. Thurston was a farmer in Norwich, Chenango county, N. Y.; member of the Presbyterian church.

### Children :

+8886   Allen,[7] b. Oct. 27, 1797; m. Lucy Wakely.
 8887   Sally,[7] b. Jan. 9, 1799; m. Jesse Thurston [see no. 8864].
+8888   Gaines,[7] b. Dec. 1, 1800; m. Margaret Hasbrook.
 8889   Washington,[7] b. June 2, 1802; d. Nov. 2, 1815.
 8890   Lucinia,[7] b. April 7, 1806; d. March 5, 1833.
 8891   Mary,[7] b. April 17, 1808; m. Potter Gardner; he died.  They had :
   8892   *Washington* (Gardner), m. Eveline Brown, b. and d. in Butternut, N.Y.
   8893   *Andrew* (Gardner), m. —— Angel; d. near Panola Station, Woodford county, Ill.
   8894   *William Henry* (Gardner), m. in Norwich, N.Y., Mary Esther French, daughter of James French.
   8895   *Amanda* (Gardner), m. —— Newman of East Lynn, Vermilion Co., Ill.
   8896   *Orlando* (Gardner). m. Almeda Barrett of Gilbertsville, Butternut, Otsego county, N. Y.
+8897   William,[7] b. Dec. 18, 1809; m. Olive Draper.

## 8496

IRA THURSTON[6] of New Lisbon, N. Y. (*Amos,[5] Daniel,[4] Daniel,[3] Daniel,[2] John[1]*), brother of the preceding, and son of Amos[5] and Mary (Sweatland) Thurston of Sharon, Ct.; born there Oct. 26, 1781; married RUTH BENEDICT, born Dec. 23, 1784, daughter of Abraham Benedict of Norwalk, Ct.  She died Nov. 24, 1837; he died Jan. 22, 1853.

Mr. Thurston was a farmer in New Lisbon, an early advocate of anti-slavery, and voted for it when it was very unpopular to do so.

### Children, all born in New Lisbon :

+8903   Chester,[7] b. April 29, 1807; m. Margaret Pattengill.
 8904   Rowland,[7] b. July 1, 1808; d. Dec. 15, 1808.
+8905   Curtis,[7] b. Sept. 10, 1809; m. Julia Ann Spaulding.
+8906   Joel,[7] b. July 28, 1811; m. Eliza Ann Gregory.
 8907   Elijah N.,[7] b. Feb. 2, 1813; m. 1st, at Mt. Upton, N. Y., Jan. 24, 1836, Sally Maria Terry, b. July 4, 1817, daughter of Isaac and Sally (Roberts) Terry of Butternut, N. Y.: she died Dec. 4, 1875, aged 58 y. 5 m.; 2d, Dec. 26, 1876, Sarah Ann Haynes, b. Feb. 7, 1826, daughter of Samuel and Olive Haynes of Morris, N. Y.  Mr Thurston is a farmer in Morris.  Child :
   8908   *Abijah Hoit,*[8] d. aged five years.
 8909   Eleazer,[7] b. July 6, 1814; d. April, 1815.
 8910   Doctor Sweatland,[7] b. Jan. 19, 1816; d. Nov. 28, 1816.
 8911   Polly,[7] b. Aug. 25, 1817; n.m.; d. 1871.
 8912   Lydia,[7] b. March 30, 1819; d. May 9, 1820.
 8913   Olive,[7] b. May 10, 1822; m. Valorous Thurston, supposed to be a descendant of Increase Thurston, no. 8330; they live near Traverse City, Mich., and have Myron, Josephene, Agnes, and Leona.
 8914   Perlina,[7] b. March 11, 1824; d. Sept. 15, 1840.

## 8501

TIMOTHY THURSTON⁶ (*John,⁵ Benjamin,⁴ Daniel³*), eldest son of John⁵ and Susanna (Wheeler) Thurston of Grafton, Mass.; born there July 10, 1766; married, first, Nov. 9, 1787, Peggy or MARGARET HILLS; she died Dec. 13, 1794, aged 29 y. 4 d. Second, Jan. 10, 1796, LUCY HAYDEN, daughter of Moses and Mercy (Stone) Hayden of Grafton. He died Feb. 16, 1848.

Mr. Thurston went to Orange, Vt., in 1803 as a farmer. He was an intelligent man, and was honored by his fellow citizens with many offices of trust; was representative to the legislature in 1810 and 1811.

His children, by first wife, Margaret, were:

8920   John H.,⁷ was in the army who went against the enemy at the invasion of Plattsburgh, N. Y., Sept., 1814; m. Susan Thompson; went to Attica, N. Y.; had three children.
8921   Chloe,⁷ m. Ira Call; d. in Woodstock, Vt., having had:
     8922   *Norman* (Call).
     8923   *Vierone* (Call).
8924   Infant, d. with its mother at birth.

By second wife, Lucy, born in Grafton:
+8925   Moses Hayden,⁷ b. 1797; m. Charlotte Fifield.
8926   Lucinda,⁷ b. 1799; m. Josiah Cutler; had four sons and three daughters; d. in Hopkinton, N. H., 1860.
8927   Calvin,⁷ } twins, b. 1801; d. in Orange, Vt., 1805.
8928   Darius,⁷ }    m. Margaret ——; three children; died 1843 in Portsmouth, Ohio.
8929   Philander,⁷ b. 1803; d. 1822, in Montpelier, Vt.

Born in Orange:
8930   Selusia,⁷ b. 1805; d. 1807.
8931   Margaret,⁷ b. 1807; m. Cassius Bartlett; d. in Croyden, N. H., 1860, aged 53, having had:
     8932   *Henry* (Bartlett).
     8933   *Daniel* (Bartlett).
     8934   *Ann* (Bartlett).
     8935   *Warren* (Bartlett).
     8936   *Lucy* (Bartlett).
+8937   Daniel Sylvester,⁷ b. 1809; m. 1st, Matilda Benjamin; 2d, Ruth Town.
+8938   Elisha Madison,⁷ b. March 24, 1810; m. Angeline Robinson Montgomery.
8939   George Washington,⁷ b. 1814; m. in Lowell, Mass., April 7, 1846, Eliza Ann Dutton, b. in Vassalborough, Me., Feb. 26, 1822. He was a machinist. went to Uxbridge, Mass., in 1850, where he died April 4, 1856. They had:
     8940   *George Olendo,*⁸ b. Dec. 30, 1855; n.m.; is a wood turner in East Boston, Mass.
8941   Lucy M.,⁷ b. Feb., 1815; m. in Holliston, Mass., March 27, 1853, Hiram Nichols of Southborough, Mass., where she died Jan. 4, 1859, having had:
     8942   *Florence Clinton* (Nichols), b. June 8, 1854; n.m.
8943   Susan,⁷ b. 1817; n.m.; d. in Croyden, N. H., 1859.
8944   Anna Teresa,⁷ b. Jan. 28, 1819; n.m.; resides now in Montpelier, Vt., but is quite feeble in health.

## 8527

DANIEL THURSTON⁶ of Grafton, Mass. (*John,⁵ Benjamin,⁴ Daniel³*), brother of the preceding, and son of John⁵ and Susanna (Wheeler) Thurston of Grafton; born there Nov. 7, 1775; married, Oct. 3, 1799, ROSANNA E. ELLIS, born 1779, daughter of Amos Ellis of Bellingham, Mass. He died Aug. 22, 1825; she died June 28, 1849.

Mr. Thurston was an extensive farmer on George Hill, Grafton.

Children :

8948  Melinda Darling,[7] b. Aug. 16, 1800; d. May 14, 1816.
8949  Sylvester Hill,[7] b. May 22, 1802; d. Sept. 4, 1803.
8950  John Ellis.[7] b. Feb. 21, 1804; n.m.; d. Sept. 28, 1828.
8951  Caroline Warren,[7] b. Feb. 7, 1806; m. Levi B. Fisher; d. Jan. 9, 1830, having had :
    8952  *Levi Warren* (Fisher), b. Dec. 24, 1829; served in the Mexican war and died in Jefferson barracks, Mo., leaving a wife and child.
+8953  Calvin Sylvester,[7] b. April 7, 1808; m. Eliza Jencks Coe.
8954  Susanna Wheeler,[7] b. July 8, 1810; m. Feb. 11, 1830, Lawson Munyan, a farmer of Grafton; d. Jan. 7, 1845, having had :
    8955  *Lydia Caroline* (Munyan), d. in infancy.
    8956  *Warren Lawson* (Munyan), d. in Colorado 1878; three children.
    8957  *Daniel Marcelius* (Munyan), b. March, 1835; m. and lives in So. Framingham, Mass.
    8958  *Caroline Susan* (Munyan), b. Sept., 1837; m. 1855, Emerson Batchelder of Upton, Mass., a shoe manufacturer in Brewer, Me.
+8959  William Harrison,[7] b. March 19, 1813; m. Julia A. Bigelow.
+8960  Daniel Clarendon,[7] b. March 14, 1816; m. Lois K. Taft.
8961  Hannah Hill,[7] b. Sept. 22, 1821; m. July 2, 1850, in Worcester, Mass., David Rufus Grosvenor, b. April 25, 1806, son of David Hall and Pattie (Newton) Grosvenor of Paxton, Mass., a carpenter and builder of Petersham, Mass. They lived in Petersham and Worcester till spring of 1856, when they removed to Kalamazoo, Mich., where they lived till Nov., 1863; then at Cranbury Station, N. J., on a farm, and 1868 to Trenton, N. J.; Oct., 1879, moved to Worcester, Mass.; he was deacon of the Congregational church in Petersham, and was connected with the Presbyterian church in Trenton. They had :
    8962  *A son*, b. in Petersham July 20, 1851; d. July 22, 1851.
    8963  *Cyrus Pitt* (Grosvenor), b. in Worcester Sept. 19, 1855.
    8964  *Carrie Lydia* (Grosvenor), b. in Kalamazoo April 28, 1858; d. at Cranbury April 21, 1865.
+8965  Jonathan Vespasian,[7] b. April 14, 1824; m. Polly S. Burr.

## 8533

LEVI THURSTON [6] (*Peter,[5] Benjamin,[4] Daniel[3]*), son of Peter [6] and Elizabeth Thurston of Grafton, Mass.; married, first, April 14, 1773, PRISCILLA WHEELER, born June 1, 1755, died March 12, 1791; second, July 13, 1794, HANNAH HAYDEN.

The family removed to Alstead, N. H., and after to Sutton, Mass.

His children, by first wife, Priscilla, were :

8970  Priscilla,[7] b. Feb. 24, 1775; d. Sept. 24, 1775.
8971  Polly,[7] b. Jan. 19, 1777; d. Jan. 17, 1778.
8972  Reconcile,[7] b. April 3, 1779.
8973  Levi,[7] b. March 25, 1781.
8974  Mary,[7] b. June 16, 1783.
8975  Peter,[7] b. April 22, 1785.
8976  Benjamin,[7] b. May 8, 1789.

## Seventh Generation.

### 8540

DAVID THURSTON [7] (*David,[6] Thomas,[5] Thomas,[4] Thomas,[3] Thomas,[2] John[1]*), eldest son of David [6] and Polly (Spurr) Thurston of Otisfield, Me.; born there Feb. 16, 1791; married, Jan. 13, 1825, SYBIL HOLDEN, born June 14, 1803. He died Dec. 31, 1846, aged 55 y. 10 m. 15 d.; she died Feb. 27, 1856, aged 52 y. 8 m. 13 d.

Mr. Thurston was a farmer in Otisfield.

Children :
+8980  Abel Moors,⁸ b. Aug. 31, 1825; m. Araminta Jane Pitts.
 8981  Martha Ann,⁸ b. March 24, 1827; m. Oct. 27, 1850, Lyman Nutting Kimball, b. Feb. 16, 1823, son of Aaron and Phebe (Chadbourne) Kimball, of Bridgton, Me., a carpenter and joiner in Portland, Me.   Children :
   8982  *Ella Augusta* (Kimball), b. April 25, 1852; m. Walter North Gourlay, a machinist in Philadelphia, Pa.
   8983  *Georgia Etta* (Kimball), b. June 28, 1854.
   8984  *Lyman Edwin* (Kimball), b. Jan. 5, 1856; clerk in Denver, Col.
   8985  *Frederick Aaron* (Kimball), b. Sept. 5, 1859.
   8986  *Charles Westley* (Kimball), b. Jan. 6, 1866.
 8987  John Holden,⁸ b. Feb. 7, 1829; n.m.; farmer in Otisfield.
 8988  Charlotte Holden,⁸ b. July 28, 1831; m. in Casco, Me., April 25, 1857, Cyrus K. Holden, b. May 22, 1819, son of Roland and Dorcas (Plummer) Holden of Otisfield, a farmer at York Center, Iowa county, Iowa; town treasurer, collector, and constable.   Children:
   8989  *Charles Lewis* (Holden), b. Oct. 30, 1862.
   8990  *Ezra Cyrus* (Holden), b. Jan. 16, 1865.
   8991  *David Roland* (Holden), b. Jan. 25, 1867.
 8992  Abigail Frances,⁸ b. July 14, 1833; m. in Saco, Me., July 4, 1852, James Dorrance Hatch, b. Feb. 21, 1824, son of Elijah and Hannah (Cousens) Hatch of Lyman, Me., a farmer in Lyman, P. O. address South Waterborough, Me.; both members of the Baptist church. She died Aug. 12, 1864, having had :
   8993  *Elizabeth Loredo* (Hatch), b. in Otisfield Feb. 16, 1857; member Free Baptist church.
   8994  *James David* (Hatch), b. in Lyman Aug. 7, 1863; d. July 31, 1864.
 8995  Sybil Holden,⁸ b. Jan. 12, 1836: n.m.; d. March 24, 1867.
 8996  Syrene Wight,⁸ b. Sept. 13, 1839; m. in Portland, Me., March 4, 1860, Benjamin Bailey Walton, b. Oct. 11, 1838, son of Charles and Sarah (Bailey) Walton of Paris, Me., a farmer in York Center, Iowa. Children, b. in Cape Elizabeth, Me. :
   8997  *Hattie Benena* (Walton), b. Nov. 6, 1861.
   8998  *George Meed* (Walton), b. July 13, 1863.
   8999  *Simeon* (Walton), b. April 12, 1866.
   9000  *Sada Alice* (Walton), b. March 25, 1869.
   9001  *Charles Franklin* (Walton), b. in Troy, Iowa, Feb. 10, 1873.
+9002  David William Porter,⁸ b. Feb. 9, 1843; m. Emily Wight.
 9003  Amelia Knight,⁸ b. Oct. 7, 1845; m. July 4, 1863, John L. Holt, b. Jan. 26, 1842, son of John L. and Lucinda C. (Leach) Holt of Bethel, Me., a carpenter in Peabody, Mass., member Universalist church; no children.

## 8571

ISRAEL THURSTON ⁷ ( *Jacob,*⁶ *Thomas,*⁶ *Thomas,*⁴ *Thomas,*³ *Thomas,*² *John* ¹ ), son of Jacob ⁶ and Nancy Anna (Edwards) Thurston of Otisfield, Me.; born there Feb. 9, 1810; married SARAH HUNT EDWARDS, born May 20, 1818, daughter of George Edwards of Casco, Me. She died in Casco May 29, 1848; he died in Poland Oct. 16, 1865.

They were Free Baptists; lived in Otisfield on his grandfather's farm for several years, when he moved to Casco.

Children, born in Otisfield :
 9004  Thomas Jefferson,⁸ b. Dec. 20, 1835; a mechanic in Camden, N. J.; belongs to the Universalist church; n.m.
+9005  Francis Alman,⁸ b Oct. 19, 1837; m. Laura A. Pierce.
 9006  Charles Franklin,⁸ b. Feb. 26, 1839; Free Baptist; killed on the railroad near Mechanic Falls, Me., in 1854.

Born in Casco:
 9007  Rosella,⁸ b. Dec. 7, 1841.
 9008  Ellen Margaret,⁸ b. March 22, 1843; m. Albert M. Pattee, b. Feb. 2, 1840, son of Amos and Arvilla (Swan) Pattee of Mercer, Me., a farmer; had :
   9009  *Agnes G.* (Pattee), b. May 23, 1871.

9010   *Frank E.* (Pattee), b. March 22, 1874.
9011   Jacob,[8] b. April 16, 1845. Though not of age he entered the army against the rebellion in the 32d Maine regiment; was under fire twenty-eight days in the battles of the Wilderness, showing himself a perfect hero. and was at last wounded at Cold Harbor, Va., and was carried as far home as Augusta, Me., where he died, and was buried in the family lot at McGuire Hill, Poland.

## 8575

DANIEL THURSTON[7] (*Daniel,[6] Dea. Daniel,[5] Daniel,[4] Thomas,[3] Thomas,[2] John[1]*), eldest son of Daniel[6] and Susan (Johnson) Thurston of Franklin, Mass.; born there Feb. 22, 1783; married, Feb. 5, 1805, BATHSHEBA BRINTNALL of Attleborough, Mass. He died Nov. 13, 1844.

Mr. Thurston was a farmer and shoemaker in Franklin; had twelve children, five died quite young.

### Children:

9012   Eliza Maria,[8] b. May 7, 1810; m. John Robertson, the first carpet weaver in this country. She d. June 20, 1872; he d. before 1877; no children.
9013   Daniel Brintnall,[8] b. April 5, 1812; m. Sarah Smith of Shelburne, Mass.; was a carpet dyer; d. in Tariffville, Ct., 1850. Children:
9014   *Jennett Wright,[9]* b. July 23, 1834; m. May 1, 1856, Robert Boyl of Southwick, Mass., and had John R. and Elizabeth (Boyl).
9015   *Eliza Jane.[9]* b. April, 1836; m. April 6, 1859, James Birrit of Bridgeport, Ct.; d. Sept. 6, 1859.
9016   *George Brintnall,[9]* b. Feb. 17, 1840; m. June 15, 1865, Jane Clark of Bloomfield, Ct. He is a railroad engineer, residing in Hartford, Ct.; two children.
9017   *Bathsheba Abigail,[9]* b. Nov. 17, 1843; m. Frank M. Auliff, a traveling salesman, residing in Southwick; two children.
9018   Gilbert Rodney,[8] b. April 10, 1814; m. Oct. 8, 1837, Mary Jane Follett. b. in Wrentham, Mass., Aug. 22, 1815, daughter of Benjamin and Catura (Hayden) Follett of Attleborough; is a carpenter in Sheldonville, Mass.; no children.
9019   George Newell,[8] b. Oct. 1, 1818; m. and lives in New Orleans.
9020   Alfred Lafayette,[8] b. Dec. 12, 1822; m. 1st, Jan. 20, 1851, Sarah Jemima Catlin Smith, b. Jan. 17, 1811, daughter of Samuel and Abigail (DeWolf) Smith of Tariffville, where he is a hotel keeper and farmer; selectman of Simsbury twenty-five years, member of the legislature 1861, and justice of the peace. She died Jan. 2, 1878, and he m. 2d, Feb. 9, 1879, Hannah Bill Burr of Fish Creek, Wis.; no children.
9021   Lewis,[8] b. May 12, 1827; member 10th Connecticut volunteers in the war against the rebellion; d. of disease contracted in the army Nov. 7, 1864.
9022   Louisa Marion,[8] b. Oct. 8, 1829; m. Edson D. Hammond of New York city; d. Oct. 23, 1872. Children:
9023   *Amelia* (Hammond), m. Harry Coles of New York city; live there.
9024   *Annie* (Hammond), m. George Southwick of New York city; live there.
9025   *Frank* (Hammond), is on board a U. S. man-of-war.

## 8576

LUKE THURSTON[7] (*Daniel,[6] Dea. Daniel,[5] Daniel,[4] Thomas,[3] Thomas,[2] John[1]*), brother of the preceding, and son of Daniel[6] and Susan (Johnson) Thurston of Franklin, Mass.; born there Feb. 7, 1785; married, December, 1810, OLIVE CLARK, born June 25, 1785, daughter of Samuel and Esther (Jones) Clark of Franklin.

Mr. Thurston was a farmer in Walpole, N. H.; member of the Christian church.

### Children:

9026   Esther,[8] b. Oct. 10, 1811; m. 1st, March 13, 1851, Samuel Clark Underwood; he died Nov. 4, 1868; 2d, Dec. 17, 1873, Dr. Willard Witt of Newfane, N. Y. They reside, 1879, in Westminster, Vt.; no children.

9027 Willard Clark,[8] b. Jan. 29, 1815; n.m.; was a justice of the peace, and worked on his father's farm; d. April 10, 1853.
9028 Emeline,[8] b. Oct. 31, 1818; m. Nov., 1832, Henry Jackson Watkins; had:
    9029 *Emily Ann* (Watkins), b. April 9, 1844.
    9030 *Albert Henry* (Watkins), b. May 22, 1848.
    9031 *Hattie Elizabeth* (Watkins), b. Feb. 22, 1859.
9032 Harriet,[8] b. Dec. 24, 1821; n.m.; d. July 13, 1865.
+9033 Eliza Ann,[8] b. May 30, 1825; m. Eri Richardson.

## 8579

NAHUM THURSTON[7] (*Daniel*,[6] *Dea. Daniel*,[5] *Daniel*,[4] *Thomas*,[8] *Thomas*,[2] *John*[1]), brother of the preceding, and son of Daniel[6] and Susan (Johnson) Thurston of Franklin, Mass.; born there Jan. 24, 1792; married, April 1, 1819, MARTHA RICE, born Nov. 25, 1788, daughter of Jonathan and Anna (Belknap) Rice of Natick, Mass. She died Dec. 5, 1861; he died Jan. 11, 1867.

Mr. Thurston was a farmer in Union, Me.; school agent in 1834.

Children:

9034 John,[8] } twins, b. April 22, 1822; d. May 3, 1822.
9035 Joseph,[8] }                       d. May 12, 1822.
+9036 Nahum,[8] b. June 2, 1824; m. Ann Elizabeth Cole.
9037 Martha Ann,[8] b. June 19, 1826; m. in Newburyport, Mass., Sept. 12, 1853, Augustus Amos Barrett, b. in Ashby, Mass., May 7, 1823. He is a mechanic; worked in Lawrence machine shop ten years; lived in Ashby fourteen years, and now, 1879, live in Fitchburgh, Mass. Mrs. Barrett has taken great interest in this genealogy, and has rendered very essential service in collecting names and dates among her own connections, and also with the descendants of Daniel who reside in and around Fitchburgh. Children:
    9038 *Augusta Angenette* (Barrett), b. Oct. 16, 1855; d. in Lawrence April 4, 1865.
    9039 *Albion Roscoe* (Barrett), b. Dec. 14, 1858; d. in Lawrence Aug. 15, 1860.
    9040 *Florence Marion* (Barrett), b. May 18, 1861; d in Lawrence Apr. 5, 1865.
    9041 *Isabella Thurston* (Barrett), b. Nov. 13, 1864.
+9042 Caroline Antinette,[8] b. Jan. 2, 1829; m. Stillman Nye.

## 8580

PHILO THURSTON[7] (*Daniel*,[6] *Dea. Daniel*,[5] *Daniel*,[4] *Thomas*,[8] *Thomas*,[2] *John*[1]), brother of the preceding, and son of Daniel[6] and Susan (Johnson) Thurston of Franklin, Mass.; born there July 15, 1794; married, Feb. 19, 1818, JULIA MARIA DANIELS, born Aug. 4, 1798, daughter of Joseph and Susan (Fisher) Daniels of Franklin. She died Dec. 20, 1869; he died May 2, 1877.

Mr. Thurston enlisted in the war of 1812, served three months in Fort Warren, Boston harbor, and elsewhere. They came to Union, Me., April 1, 1818, and settled on a farm. He was an officer of the militia, and at one time having in a quiet way done his part at the muster-farce, he was the only officer in town whom the field officers had not had difficulty with. And being the only recognized officer, he maintained that it was unreasonable to require him to organize the three or four hundred men in Union in the state of things then existing, and would not move in the matter. He joined the Free Masons in 1820, and continued with them in good standing, and a much respected member till his death.

## Children:

+9043 Philo,[8] b. Sept. 22, 1819; m. Olive Robbins.
9044 Hiram Abiff,[8] b. June 23, 1821; d. May 28, 1829.
+9045 Albert,[8] b. July 13, 1824; m. Lavinia A. Hawes.
+9046 Nathaniel Emmons,[8] b. Nov. 12, 1826; m. Sarah Hills.
9047 Joseph Daniels,[8] b. July 12, 1830; d. Oct. 8, 1853.
9048 Harlous Whiting,[8] b. March 19, 1837; m. 1st, Mrs. Nye of Union; 2d, in Bangor, Me., Nov. 12, 1868, Laura C. Nickerson, b. Aug. 30, 1838, daughter of T. R. and Jane (Eames) Nickerson of Swanville, Me. Mr. Thurston is a builder, residing in Everett, Mass.; no children.
9049 Darwin Daniels,[8] b. April 13, 1843; d. June 11, 1861.

### 8581

JOHNSON THURSTON [7] (*Daniel,*[6] *Dea. Daniel,*[5] *Daniel,*[4] *Thomas,*[3] *Thomas,*[2] *John*[1]), brother of the preceding, and son of Daniel [6] and Susan (Johnson) Thurston of Franklin, Mass.; born there Oct. 9, 1797; married LOOE STARRETT, born in Warren, Me., 1804. He died in Appleton, Me., Oct. 18, 1874.

Mr. Thurston came to Maine in 1825, and bought a farm in Appleton, where he resided. He was one of the selectmen, a justice of the peace for fourteen years, and for thirty-eight years a member of the Free Baptist church.

### Children:

+9054 William Johnson,[8] b. Jan. 22, 1826; m. 1st, Martha Russ; 2d, Martha Jane Philbrook.
9055 Susan Frances,[8] b. Sept. 20, 1828; m. John Leonard; two sons.
9056 Sarah Josephene,[8] b. May 8, 1831; m. in Rockland, Me., March 20, 1866, John Mears, born April 18, 1825, son of Rev. George Z. and Abigail (Wentworth) Mears of Washington, Me. Mr. Mears married first, June 6, 1850, Roxcy M. Miller, daughter of Dea. Rufus Miller of Appleton. He went to California, his wife died Sept. 18, 1862, and he returned to Appleton in 1864, and married Miss Sarah Josephene Thurston. Their post-office address is North Union, Me. He is a farmer and lumberman. They have:
9057 *Frank Willis* (Mears), b. Sept. 9, 1868.
9058 Charles Hammond,[8] b. Aug. 13, 1834; m. Margaret Jackson.
+9059 Milton,[8] b. Jan. 19, 1837; m. Caroline S. Perkins.
9060 John Stevens,[8] b. March 13, 1839; d. Sept., 1842.
9061 Martha Caroline [8] b. Feb. 23, 1843; d. May 20, 1866.
+9062 Albert Llewellyn,[8] } twins, born } m. Emily Jane Jackson.
9063 Irene Luella,[8] } Feb. 23, 1847; } m. July 2, 1872, George King Carpenter of South Lawrence, Mass., a carpenter by trade.

### 8586

LEVINA THURSTON [7] (*Abijah,*[6] *Dea. Daniel,*[5] *Daniel,*[4] *Thomas,*[3] *Thomas,*[2] *John*[1]), daughter of Abijah [6] and Rachel (Johnson) Thurston of Franklin, Mass.; born there May 3, 1775; married, Dec. 19, 1793, JESSE MILLER, born Oct. 1, 1772, son of Dea. Joseph and Thankful (Gilmore) Miller of Franklin.

Mr. Miller was a farmer. They were both members of the Baptist church in Sheldonville, Mass., formerly West Wrentham.

### Children:

9064 Rufus (Miller), b. Nov. 17, 1794; m. April 6, 1818, Lena Metcalf, b. Feb. 10, 1791, daughter of Nathan and Patty Metcalf of Franklin. He was a farmer in Appleton, Me.; deacon * of the Free Baptist church for thirty-five years; d. June 27, 1861. They had:

* Dea. Rufus Miller went to Appleton before any roads were made, marking his way by spotted trees, built a log house and lived in it six months while he was building a frame house, where his widow now lives with her son, Jesse Richardson Miller.

9065 *Olive Maria* (Miller), b. Jan. 13, 1819; m. Mar. 7, 1837, Carlton Johnson; d. Sept. 4, 1838.
9066 *Rachel Levina* (Miller), b. Jan. 12, 1822; m. Jan. 10, 1848, J. B. Mitchell; d. April 4, 1877.
9667 *Julia Ann* (Miller), b. Feb. 29, 1824; m. Feb. 19, 1846, Hollis Knowlton; d. March 31, 1861.
9068 *Sarah Luce* (Miller), b. March 19, 1826; m. June 6, 1849, J. M. Hart; d. Jan. 27, 1850.
9069 *Roxy Metcalf* (Miller), b. July 20, 1829; m. June 6, 1850, John Mears; d. Sept. 18, 1862.
9070 *Albert* (Miller), b. July 11, 1831; m. Feb. 11, 1856, Celia J. McCurdy; she died April 25, 1875.
9071 *Gilmore* (Miller), b. Sept. 11, 1833; m. Feb. 19, 1857, Eliza J. Evans.
9072 *Jesse Richardson* (Miller). b. April 25, 1836; m. Feb. 6, 1858, Louisa S. Bartlett.
9073 Abijah Thurston (Miller), b. July 9, 1796,
9074 Jesse (Miller), b. July 9, 1798; d. Nov. 18, 1799.
9075 Hannah Fales (Miller), b. Sept. 16, 1799; m. April 25, 1822, Nathan Rockwood, b. Jan. 9, 1798, a farmer in Franklin, son of Timothy and Sarah Rockwood of Franklin. He died suddenly Oct. 26, 1874; she after long suffering June 9, 1876. They had two sons and one daughter who died in infancy, and
9076 *Sarah Jane* (Rockwood). b. June 9, 1832.
9077 Joseph (Miller), b. Nov. 12, 1800; deacon of Baptist church, Norfolk, Mass.
9078 Elkanah (Miller), b. Aug. 14, 1802.
9079 Levina (Miller), b. Jan. 22, 1805.
9080 Nancy (Miller), } twins, born } m. Herman Blake.
9081 Sally (Miller), } Nov. 28, 1807; } m. Robert Blake, brother of above, deacon of Congregational church at Woonsocket Falls, R. I.
9082 Rachel Johnson (Miller), b. May 17, 1809; m. Sept. 18, 1828, Daniel Merrill Hancock, b. Dec. 28, 1807. They had :
9083 *Reuben Merrill* (Hancock), b. July 9, 1829; d. Sept. 14, 1830.
9084 *Rachel Miranda* (Hancock), b. Aug. 14, 1833; m. Oct. 13, 1852, Warren Rhodes, b. Jan. 1, 1829, and had:
9085 *Stillman Merrill* (Rhodes), b. Sept. 15, 1854.
9086 *Cora Charlotte* (Rhodes), b. Aug. 17, 1858.
9087 *Nancy Levina* (Hancock), b. Sept. 8, 1835; m. Oct. 11, 1854, A. Fenner Hawkins, b. Oct. 28, 1833, and had:
9088 *Mary Idella* (Hawkins), b. Aug. 3, 1855; m. June 1, 1874, Frank E. Barney, b. Sept. 26, 1852, and had:
9089 *Grace Plimpton* (Barney), b. Aug. 31, 1875.
9090 *Eugene Augustus* (Hawkins), b. Nov. 13, 1857.
9091 *Daniel Fenner* (Hawkins), b. Feb. 26. 1861.
9092 *Daniel Merrill* (Hancock), b. Dec. 27, 1838; m. Aug. 2, 1863, Lucretia R. Barber, b. March 17, 1840, and had:
9093 *Lyman Barber* (Hancock), b. Oct. 6, 1865.
9094 *Nellie Marion* (Hancock), b. Jan. 5, 1869.
9095 *Charlotte Miller* (Hancock), b. April 19, 1844.
9096 *Harriet Eldora* (Hancock), b. Aug. 18, 1850.
+9097 Jesse (Miller), b. Aug. 20, 1811; m. 1st, Susan R. Rhoades; 2d, Susan W. Waltze.
9098 Gilmore (Miller), b. Oct. 17, 1817.
+9099 Charlotte (Miller), b. Aug. 20, 1819; m. Willard Whiting.

## 8587

NANCY THURSTON [7] (*Abijah,* [6] *Dea. Daniel,* [5] *Daniel,* [4] *Thomas,* [3] *Thomas,* [2] *John* [1]), sister of the preceding, and daughter of Abijah [6] and Rachel (Johnson) Thurston of Franklin, Mass.; born there probably 1776; married, April 19, 1800, THADDEUS HASTINGS, born Sept. 10, 1769, son of Thaddeus and Mary (Stratton) Hastings of Lexington, Mass. She died Jan. 7, 1805; he died Feb. 11, 1841.

Mr. Hastings was a farmer in South Hope, Me., justice of the peace, and selectman for nineteen years.

Children :

9100  Erwin (Hastings), b. July 4, 1801; m. Jan. 30, 1831, Elizabeth Walker,
      daughter of Amos and Judith (Bailey) Walker of Union, Me.  Children:
9101  *Amos W.* (Hastings), b. May 11, 1832; m. March, 1856, Susan Sedg-
      wick of Adamsville, Ohio, where he is a teacher.  Children:
  9102  *Florence* (Hastings), b. Dec. 13, 1858.
  9103  *Eugenia* (Hastings), b. May, 1860; d. Aug., 1861.
  9104  *Nellie* (Hastings), b. Sept. 14, 1862.
9105  *Thaddeus* (Hastings), b. May 18, 1835; a farmer in Hope, Me.; m. 1st,  ·
      Mary A. Fish; she died Feb. 4, 1871; 2d, Jan. 1, 1872, Martha
      Boggs.  He had, by first wife, Mary:
  9106  *Lillie E.* (Hastings), b. May 15, 1861; d. March 18, 1862.
  9107  *Everett S.* (Hastings), b. March 9, 1863.
  9108  *Carrie Walker* (Hastings), b. June 26, 1868.
    By second wife, Martha:
  9109  *Edwin C.* (Hastings), b. Oct. 27, 1873.
  9110  *Emma A.* (Hastings), b. Oct. 19, 1875.
9111  *Nancy Thurston* (Hastings), b. Nov. 18, 1837; m. Aug. 22, 1863, Ed-
      win Davis; he died at South Hope March 7, 1869; they had:
  9112  *Fannie L.* (Davis), b. March 11, 1867.
9113  *Emily E.* (Hastings), b. Jan. 18, 1841; d. May 15, 1857.
9114  *Edmund Bailey* (Hastings), twin, b. April 26, 1845; m. Feb. 17, 1870,
      Jerusha Blackington of Rockland Me., where he is a merchant.
      They have:
  9115  *Albert Mills* (Hastings), b. 1872.
9116  *Sarah M.* (Hastings), twin, b. April 26, 1845; m. Nov. 22, 1863, Minot
      D. Hewett, a mechanic.  Children:
  9117  *George E.* (Hewett), b. May 18, 1865.
  9118  *Arthur L.* (Hewett), b. March 20, 1867.
  9119  *Florence M.* (Hewett), b. Oct. 18, 1876.
9120  Julia (Hastings), b. Jan. 6, 1805; m. May 22, 1843, George Fogler, a farm-
      er of Hope, and had :
  9121  *Mary Frances* (Fogler), b. Feb. 26, 1849.

## 8601

CALEB THURSTON [7] (*Abijah,*[6] *Dea. Daniel,*[5] *Daniel,*[4] *Thomas,*[3]
*Thomas,*[2] *John* [1]), brother of the preceding, and son of Abijah [6] and
Rachel (Johnson) Thurston of Franklin, Mass.; born there 1781;
married LOVICEY FRENCH, born 1778.  He died Sept. 12, 1840, aged
59; she died July 13, 1843, aged 65.

Mr. Thurston succeeded his fathers, for several generations, in
the tavern in Franklin which was so noted all over that part of the
country.  He was a colonel of militia; represented his town in the
legislature several times, town treasurer twenty-five years in succession, and selectman more than that length of time.  She was admitted
to the Congregational church in Franklin May 27, 1810, and he Sept.
29, 1811.

Children :

9122  Paulina French,[8] b. 1803; m. John Phillips Nye, a farmer in New Brain ·
      tree, Mass., b. 1789, son of William and Eunice Nye; she died Feb. 14,
      1857.  They had:
  9123  *Caleb Thurston* (Nye), b. Nov. 8, 1818.
  9124  *William* (Nye), b. 1820.
  9125  *James Arnold* (Nye), b. 1823.
  9126  *Susan* (Nye), b. 1826.
  9127  *John Harrington* (Nye), b. 1832.
  9128  *Nathan* (Nye), b. 1834.
9129  Julia,[8] b. Sept. 28, 1807; d. Sept. 28, 1822.
9130  Harriet,[8] b. March 6, 1809; d. Aug. 9, 1810.
9131  Harriet Sophronia,[8] b. Feb. 21, 1812; d. April 12, 1816.

9132 Charlotte Lovicey,⁸ b. Sept. 24, 1814; d. Oct. 29, 1815.
9133 Abigail,⁸ b. April 27, 1817; m. by Rev. Elam Smalley, pastor Congregational church in Franklin, May 18, 1835, David Ely, a trader in Humphrey, N. Y., b. in Harwinton, Ct., March 29, 1811. She died Sept. 21,
1867. They had:
    9134 *Julia Thurston* (Ely), b. Sept. 2, 1840; m. at Cuba, N. Y., Feb. 18,
    1861, George Peter Learn, b. Dec. 17, 1836; he is a farmer in Hum-
    phrey Center, N. Y. They have:
        9135 *William Edwin* (Learn), b. May 9, 1863.
    9136 *Sarah Jane* (Ely), b. May 27, 1845; m. in 1868, Alphonso Oristes
    Winters, a farmer in Franklinville, N. Y., b. in Portville, N. Y.,
    Feb. 23, 1841; no children.
9137 Maria,⁸ b. June 22, 1822; d. Nov. 12, 1822.

## 8602

DAVID THURSTON⁷ (*Abijah,⁶ Dea. Daniel,⁵ Daniel,⁴ Thomas,³
Thomas,² John¹*), brother of the preceding, and son of Abijah⁶ and
Rachel (Johnson) Thurston of Franklin, Mass.; born there Sept. 20,
1784; married. Sept. 5, 1809, MIRANDA ELLIS, born Dec. 8, 1786,
daughter of Timothy and Sarah (Richardson) Ellis of Franklin,
Mass. He died July 25, 1811. She married, second, April 17, 1832,
Jemotis Pond, and died in Holliston, Mass., Aug. 15, 1870.
Mr. Thurston was a farmer.

### One child:

9140 Nancy,⁸ b. March 18, 1811; m. Nov. 29, 1832, Stephen Metcalf, b. in Bellingham, Mass., June 8, 1802, son of Stephen and Olive (Burr) Metcalf.
He died Nov. 4, 1875; was a merchant in Holliston, where his widow
still resides, 1879. Children:
    9141 *Nancy Maranda* (Metcalf), b. May 24, 1834; m. Feb. 13, 1856, Ed-
    mund F. Pond of Franklin, a merchant in Philadelphia, Pa., and has:
        9142 *Annie Frances* (Pond), b. in Medway, Mass., Oct. 21, 1857.
    9143 *Stephen George* (Metcalf), b. Sept. 4, 1835; m. June 7, 1864, Adeline
    Trowbridge of Framingham, Mass. He was a merchant; d. Oct.
    24, 1868. Child:
        9144 *Irene* (Metcalf), b. in Framingham Feb. 16, 1867.
    9145 *Julia Ann* (Metcalf), b. Jan. 6, 1839; m. Oct. 8, 1874, Dr. A. J. John-
    son of Cambridge, Ill. They resided in Holliston; he d. Jan. 30, 1875.
    9146 *Mary Jane* (Metcalf), b. Oct. 3, 1841; d. Aug. 30, 1842.
    9147 *David Waldo* (Metcalf), b. July 1, 1846; m. June 16, 1869, Emma M.
    Clark of Portland, Me.

## 8603

JULIA THURSTON⁷ (*Abijah,⁶ Dea. Daniel,⁵ Daniel,⁴ Thomas,³
Thomas,² John¹*), sister of the preceding, and daughter of Abijah⁶
and Rachel (Johnson) Thurston of Franklin, Mass.; born there Nov.
9, 1788; married, Nov. 26, 1812, ASA ROCKWOOD, born March 25,
1787, son of Timothy and Sarah (Phillips) Rockwood. She died
April 5, 1857; he died Aug. 29, 1870.
Mr. Rockwood was a merchant in Franklin, keeping a country
store for over forty years. He was also a pioneer in the manufacture
of straw bonnets.

### Children:

9150 Erastus (Rockwood), b. Aug. 17, 1813; a trader in Franklin, chairman of
selectmen six years, and justice of the peace; m. 1st, Nov. 27, 1834,
Mary Ann Daniels, daughter of Joel and Philena (Smith) Daniels; she
died April 7, 1842; 2d, April 2, 1845, Louisa Morse, daughter of Isaac
Morse of Natick, Mass. He died Mar. 7, 1864. He had, by first wife:
    9151 *Erastus D.* (Rockwood), b. April 7, 1837.

9152  *Edmund J.* (Rockwood), b. April 2, 1842.
By second wife:
9153  *Louisa Mary* (Rockwood), b. Feb. 3, 1846; d. 1863.
9154  *Eugene Morse* (Rockwood), b. Dec., 1848.
9155  *Elmer* (Rockwood), b. Dec., 1853; d. 1862.
9156  Asa Phillips (Rockwood), } twins, born } d. Aug. 11, 1821.
9157  Julia Ann (Rockwood), } Jan. 24, 1818; } d. Aug. 28, 1836.
9158  Abijah Thurston (Rockwood), b. March 24, 1820; a straw bonnet bleacher in Franklin; m. Aug. 20, 1843, Sarah Maria Peck, b. in Cumberland, R. I., daughter of William Peck of Franklin. He d. Dec. 1, 1874. Children:
9159  James (Rockwood), b. Nov. 6, 1821; d. April 7, 1822.
9160  *Lucius Osborn* (Rockwood), b. Jan. 15, 1847.
9161  *Julia Etta* (Rockwood), b. July, 1849.
9162  *Frank Ernest* (Rockwood), b. Dec. 20, 1853.
9163  Susan Bailey (Rockwood), b. March 17, 1824; m. May 27, 1853, Francis Baylies Ray, a manufacturer in Franklin, b. in Mendon, Mass., May 15, 1823, son of Joseph and Lydia (Paine) Ray of Franklin; they are both members of the Congregational church, and have:
9164  *William Erancis* (Ray), b. March 2, 1854.
9165  William (Rockwood), b. Jan. 16, 1827; a grocer in Franklin. He has rendered much service in perfecting the records of this family and that of the early settlers of the Thurston name in that region; has been selectman, overseer of the poor, and justice of the peace; m. Dec. 29, 1858, Laura Matilda Blake, b. Nov. 12, 1828, daughter of Ira and Laura (Mory) Blake of Franklin. Both are members of the Congregational church. They have:
9166  *Elbert William* (Rockwood), b. July 4, 1860.
9167  *Bradley Mortimer* (Rockwood), b. May 24, 1862.
9168  *Julius Thurston* (Rockwood), b. May 21, 1866.

## 8615

LYMAN THURSTON [7] (*Joseph,*[6] *Joseph,*[5] *Daniel,*[4] *Thomas,*[3] *Thomas,*[2] *John*[1]), eldest son of Joseph[6] and Polly (Hubbard) Thurston of North Brookfield, Mass.; born there Jan. 16, 1794; married, first, May 4, 1823, DELIA ATWOOD MAYO of Brewer, Me.; she died Oct. 19, 1846. Second, Aug. 4, 1850, MRS. ROWENA H. PRATT; she died May 19, 1857. He died Dec. 30, 1872, aged 78 y. 11 m. 15 d.

Mr. Thurston learned the printers' art in Brookfield, and, says the Cambridge Chronicle, "carried on the business for many years in Boston and Cambridge, and many are the printers who received their first knowledge of the art under his direction. He was one of the proprietors of the Chronicle for about four years, from 1859 to 1863, when he retired from business. He was a man highly respected by all who knew him, and they will learn of his death with sorrow and regret."

He had no children, but adopted a niece of his first wife, Delia Atwood, born in Brewster, Mass., now living, 1877, in Boston, Dorchester district. By act of the legislature the name of Thurston was added to her name.

Child:
9170  Delia Atwood, b. Jan. 14, 1822.

## 8617

JOSEPH THURSTON [7] (*Joseph,*[6] *Joseph,*[5] *Daniel,*[4] *Thomas,*[3] *Thomas,*[2] *John*[1]), brother of the preceding, and son of Joseph[6] and Polly (Hubbard) Thurston of North Brookfield, Mass.; born there June 7, 1797; married, June 25, 1823, LUCY BUCKNAM DAVIS, daughter of

Dea. David and Patty (Howe) Davis of Paxton, Mass. He died Oct. 30, 1857, aged 60.

Mr. Thurston was a farmer; lived in Leicester, Mass., a while, afterward with his uncle J. Hubbard in Paxton, of whose farm he came into possession by taking care of his uncle and aunt during their lives. About 1851 he sold his farm and bought real estate in Worcester, Mass., where he lived till his death; his widow resides there, 1879, with her son-in-law, Ezra Kent.

Children, born in Leicester:

9175   Mary Elizabeth,[8] b. May 12, 1824; d. June 21, 1826.
+9176   Abigail Brown,[8] b. April 4, 1827; m. Ezra Kent.

Born in Paxton:

+9177   Jonathan Hubbard,[8] b. Oct. 11, 1829; m. Maria L. Whittemore.
+9178   Lyman Davis,[8] b. Sept. 8, 1832; m. 1st, Hannah S. Lyon; 2d, Mary E. Denny.
9179   Martha Howe,[8] b. Nov. 28, 1834; m. April 4, 1855, Hasky Wight; d. March 10, 1856.
9180   Sarah Ideal,[8] b. Feb. 28, 1840; d. Jan. 24, 1845.
9181   Joseph Harrison,[8] b. March 21, 1842; d. Jan. 2, 1845.

## 8619

DANIEL THURSTON[7] (*Joseph,*[6] *Joseph,*[5] *Daniel,*[4] *Thomas,*[3] *Thomas,*[2] *John*[1]), brother of the preceding, and son of Joseph[6] and Polly (Hubbard) Thurston of North Brookfield, Mass.; born there Sept. 4, 1800; married, Dec. 5, 1822, PATTY ALLEN ROSS, born Sept. 9, 1805, daughter of Levi and Eliza (Carruth) Ross. He died Nov. 29, 1862, aged 62; she died June 21, 1877.

Mr. Thurston was a boot maker; afterward bought a farm and carried it on a number of years, when he sold it, moved to West Brookfield, built a house, and lived there till his death.

Children:

9185   Harriet Hubbard,[8] b. April 8, 1826; m. Oct. 2, 1844, George Crowell of West Brookfield; he died May 10, 1870; four daughters.
+9186   Levi Sherman,[8] b. Aug. 5, 1828; m. Esther Keep.
9187   Mary Eliza,[8] b. March 27, 1830; d. Nov. 26, 1839.

## 8626

JAMES B. THURSTON[7] (*William,*[6] *John,*[5] *John,*[4] *Benjamin,*[3] *Joseph,*[2] *John*[1]), son of William Thurston[6]; born about 1790; married, July 4, 1813, FELICIA TUTHILL [see no. 8308], born Nov. 7, 1787. He died in 1871. For many years he was in the custom house in New York city.

Children:

9190   Abbie Ann,[8] m. Charles Miner; they live in Brooklyn or New York city.
9191   Charles F.,[8] was a physician in Englewood, N. J., and it is thought removed to Brooklyn or New York city.

## 8646

HENRY THURSTON[7] (*David,*[6] *Israel,*[5] *John,*[4] *Benjamin,*[3] *Joseph,*[2] *John*[1]), eldest son of David[6] and Esther (Taylor) Thurston of Meadville, Pa.; born there March 7, 1791; married, Sept. 3, 1819, CASSANDRA ELLIOTT, born in Washington county, Pa., Aug. 6, 1800, daughter of Mark and Mary (Atwood) Elliott of Maryland. He died Dec. 24, 1868, aged 77.

Mr. Thurston went to Ohio in 1817, and settled in Jacobsburgh, Belmont county, in 1819, as a school teacher and tavern keeper. He was a justice of the peace twenty years; would have enlisted in the war of 1812 but for having his arm put out of joint. They were both members of the Methodist church. She is living, 1879, remarkably smart, eyesight so good as to enable her to sew fine cambric with ease.

Children, all born in Jacobsburgh:

9196    Nancy Radle,[8] b. July 27, 1820; m. Nov. 25, 1841, Thomas Moore Shotwell, b. in Harrisville, Harrison county, Ohio, Sept. 16, 1817, a retired gentleman of Antioch, Monroe county, Ohio. Children:

     9197   *Susan Amanda* (Shotwell), b. in Woodville, Ohio, Jan. 18, 1843; m. June 21, 1860, Richard Thomas Chaney, a merchant of Barnesville, Ohio; four children. He served two years and a half against the rebellion, in the 116th Ohio regiment, as lieutenant and captain, when his health failed and he resigned; both Methodists.

     9198   *Emily Anne* (Shotwell), b. Dec. 7, 1845; d. Jan. 13, 1846.

     9199   *Henry Alden* (Shotwell), b. Oct. 4, 1850; d. Sept. 26, 1854.

9200    Lavina F.,[8] b. Jan. 16, 1822; d. Sept. 19, 1832.

+9201   David Stanton,[8] b. Dec. 22, 1823; m. Jane White Lingo.

9202    Rachel Amanda,[8] b. Aug. 29, 1827; d. Sept. 22, 1829.

9203    Mary Isabel,[8] b. May 21, 1832; m. Nov. 15, 1849, Thomas Jefferson Rowles, b. Jan. 5, 1827, a blacksmith. Children:

     9204   *Thurston Henry* (Rowles), b. Oct. 12, 1850; m. Nov. 16, 1875, Mary Brice; a school teacher; one daughter.

     9205   *Sarah Amanda* (Rowles), b. May 4, 1852; m. Dec. 30, 1869, George Brice, a farmer; they have William and Dallas (Brice).

     9206   *David Tyson* (Rowles), b. June 25, 1854; a teacher.

     9207   *William Thomas* (Rowles), b. May 23, 1856; a teacher.

     9208   *Alverda Cassandra* (Rowles), b. May 16, 1858.

     9209   *Mary Radle* (Rowles), b. Aug. 7, 1860.

     9210   *Lizzie Jane* (Rowles), b. July 6, 1863.

     9211   *Hattie Roland* (Rowles), b. Jan. 31, 1866.

     9212   *James Elihu* (Rowles), b. June 3, 1870; d. March 13, 1877.

     9213   *Charles Nathan* (Rowles), b. March 2, 1873.

9214    William Henry,[8] b. April 2, 1840; d. Oct. 8, 1845.

## 8647

FLAVEL THURSTON [7] (*David,*[6] *Israel,*[5] *John,*[4] *Benjamin,*[3] *Joseph,*[2] *John*[1]), brother of the preceding, and son of David[6] and Esther (Taylor) Thurston of Meadville, Pa.; born there July 18, 1793; married ELEANOR MERCER, born Aug. 12, 1800. He died Oct. 1, 1852.

Mr. Thurston was a farmer in Sheffield, Ill. He was a thorough disbeliever in American slavery, and prayed and labored against it.

Children:

9219    Mary Ann,[8] b. 1821; m. Charles Watts, who came from London, Eng., in 1844 and d. in 1869. P. O. Netawaka, Jackson Co., Kansas. They had:

     9220   *Mary Ellen* (Watts), in Princeton, Ill.

     9221   *Alfred, Rev.* (Watts), in Netawaka.

+9222   Edward M.,[8] b. Sept. 29, 1824; m. 1st, Mary ——; 2d, Sarah ——.

9223    Hester B.,[8] b. 1827; m. Thomas Taylor, who came from England; they live in Wyanet, Bureau county, Ill., and have:

     9224   *Joseph* (Taylor), b. 1860.

     9225   *Ida* (Taylor), b. 1866.

9226    Rebecca,[8] b. 1829; m. 1853, Stephen Young of New York. He died 1861; she died 1866. They had:

     9227   *Orange* (Young), b. 1854.

     9228   *Mary* (Young), b. 1858.

+9229   David,[8] b. 1832; m. Eleanor ——.

+9230   John Flavel,[8] b. 1834; m. Mary Smith.

9231    Lorin Isabel,[8] b. 1838; lived in Sheffield, Ill., 1873; n.m.

## 8649

DAVID THURSTON [7] (*David*,[6] *Israel*,[5] *John*,[4] *Benjamin*,[3] *Joseph*,[2] *John*[1]), brother of the preceding, and son of David [6] and Esther (Taylor) Thurston of Meadville, Pa.; born there May 26, 1798; married, first, July 10, 1823, ESTHER STANBROOK; she died May 10, 1836. Second, Aug. 18, 1837, ABIGAIL SPRING, born May 1, 1813. Mr. Thurston was a farmer in Black Ash, Crawford county, Pa.

His children, by first wife, Esther:

+9235   Henry,[8] b. Dec. 23, 1834; m. 1st, Angeline Strayer; 2d, Adelia Dickerson.

By second wife, Abigail:

9236   Mary Esther,[8] b. July 3, 1838; m. Samuel Ford, Lineville, Pa.
+9237   Ephraim Edgar,[8] b. May 5, 1840; m. Sarah Frances Jones.
9238   James S.,[8] b. March 25, 1842; d. Oct. 24, 1854.
9239   Naomi Janet,[8] b. Dec. 23, 1845; m. James Braymer of Black Ash.
9240   David S.,[8] b. Dec. 20, 1847; d. Oct. 7, 1854.
9241   William M.,[8] b. Oct. 3, 1850; d. Oct. 10, 1854.

## 8663

ISRAEL THURSTON [7] (*David*,[6] *Israel*,[5] *John*,[4] *Benjamin*,[3] *Joseph*,[2] *John*[1]), brother of the preceding, and son of David [6] and Esther (Taylor) Thurston of Meadville, Pa.; born there Nov. 12, 1804; married, first, March 27, 1831, ALMIRA SMITH, born Feb. 8, 1811, died Oct. 13, 1841; second, Jan. 26, 1843, JOANNA PHILLIPS. He died Sept. 20, 1872; she died Feb. 26, 1874. Mr. Thurston was a farmer at Mead Corners, Crawford Co., Pa.

His children, by first wife, Almira:

9245   William H.,[8] b. Jan. 26, 1832; m. 1st, Sept. 27, 1860, Lauretta A. Griffith, b. Oct. 29, 1839, d. Feb. 24, 1870; 2d, Dec. 26, 1871, Mary M. Bartlett, d. Feb. 5, 1875. He is a merchant in Hebron, Minn.; had, by first wife:
     9246   *David Israel*,[9] b. July 21, 1861; d. Jan. 5, 1864.
     9247   *Wilber Harken*,[9] b. Feb. 9, 1863.
     9248   *Junius Floyd*,[9] b. Dec. 26, 1867.
9249   Lemuel Smith,[8] b. Feb. 5, 1834; m. Nov. 7, 1858, Ellen A. Bartlett. He lived in Hebron, Minn., and died April 5, 1865. They had:
     9250   *Clarence Odell*,[9] b. and d. 1859.
     9251   *Carroll Smith*,[9] b. 1861.
     9252   *John Fred*,[9] b. 1862; d. 1863.
     9253   *Henry Llewellyn*,[9] b. 1865.
9254   David R.,[8] b. March 6, 1836; m. Sept. 28, 1860, Mary Childs. They lived in Princeton, Ill.; he died 1864. They had:
     9255   *Israel Eugene*,[9] d. 1861.
     9256   *Jessie Elizabeth*,[9] d.
9257   Sarah Jenkins,[8] b. May 1, 1838; d. June 13, 1839.
9258   John F.,[8] b. June 23, 1840; killed in battle before Richmond, Va., June, 1862.

By second wife, Joanna:

9259   Lydia C.,[8] b. Nov. 25, 1843; m. March 24, 1864, Ansel Oakes of Mead Corners, Pa.; he died Aug., 1867. They had:
     9260   *Elizabeth J.* (Oakes), b. Oct., 1865.
     9261   *Altia N.* (Oakes), b. April, 1867.
9262   Israel,[8] b. March 16, 1845; d. Jan. 4, 1849.
9263   Ahab Keller,[8] b. Dec. 25, 1846; m. Feb. 19, 1871, Myra F. Gleason, b. July 24, 1854. They live at Mead Corners, and have:
     9264   *Lida J.*,[9] b. Jan. 30, 1873.
     9265   *Henrietta*,[9] b. April 15, 1874.
9266   Jeremiah,[8] b. March 3, 1853; n.m.; at Mead Corners.

## 8664

LEWIS TAYLOR THURSTON [7] (*David*,[6] *Israel*,[5] *John*,[4] *Benjamin*,[3] *Joseph*,[2] *John*[1]), brother of the preceding, and son of David [6] and

Esther (Taylor) Thurston of Meadville, Pa.; born there Jan. 8, 1808; married ———. He died Feb. 22, 1870.

Children :

9270   Emeline,[8] b. Feb. 15, 1833; m. Nov., 1850, Thomas Sturgis; d. Sept. 24, 1863. He is at Ovid Center, Mich. Children:
 9271   *Charles* (Sturgis). b. April 6, 1857.
 9272   *Emma* (Sturgis), b. Oct., 1858.
 9273·  *Flavilla* (Sturgis), b. Jan., 1860.
9274   Samuel S.,[8] b. Sept. 23, 1834; m. Feb. 3, 1859, ———. He is a brewer in Meadville. They have :
 9275   *Alice*,[9] b. Aug. 6, 1861.
9276   Flavilla,[8] b. May 15, 1836; m. William Quay of Thurston House, Meadville.
9277   David Floyd,[8] b. Sept. 27, 1839.

## 8681

WILLIAM THURSTON[7] (*Samuel*,[6] *Israel*,[5] *John*,[4] *Benjamin*,[8] *Joseph*,[2] *John*[1]), son of Samuel[6] and Hannah (Kelley) Thurston of Mixersville, Ind.; born Aug. 12, 1799; married, September, 1822, MARY TELFOR, daughter of Alexander and Nancy (Thatcher) Telfor. He died May 12, 1835, and she married James Walden of Darrtown, Butler county, Ohio. Mr. Thurston was a farmer in Mixersville.

Children :

+9282   Samuel David,[8] b. July 20, 1823; m. 1st, Jannet Retherford; 2d, Mrs. Mary Ellen Robinson.
9283   Angeline,[8] b. Jan. 13, 1825.
9284   Mary Jane,[8] b. July 23, 1826.

## 8691

OLIVER PERRY THURSTON[7] (*Samuel*,[6] *Israel*,[5] *John*,[4] *Benjamin*,[8] *Joseph*,[2] *John*[1]), brother of the preceding, and son of Samuel[6] and Hannah (Kelley) Thurston of Mixersville, Ind.; born Oct. 21, 1802; married, Nov. 11, 1824, MARIA L. FLINT. He died May 22, 1865; she died June 18, 1870.

Mr. Thurston was a farmer in Mixersville, and they were both consistent members of the old school Baptist church.

Children :

9289   Sarah Ann,[8] b. Dec. 7, 1825; m. Robert Spears; in Alexandria, Ind.
+9290   John Flint,[8] b. May 28, 1828; m. Margaret Morris.
9291   Elizabeth,[8] b. May 20, 1830; m. Walter Brady; in Mixersville.
+9292   Samuel,[8] b. Jan. 4, 1833; m. Nancy ———.
9293   William,[8] b. April 25, 1835; d. May 8, 1835.
9294   Dorcas,[8] b. May 9, 1836; d. 1853.
+9295   Joseph H.,[8] b. Oct. 22, 1838; m. Mary E. Welsh.
9296   Benjamin K.,[8] b. June 17, 1841; m. Jan. 1, 1867, Sarah J. Gray, b. Aug. 8, 1847, daughter of David and Elizabeth Gray. He was a saddle and harness maker, but is now a farmer in Contreras, Ohio. They had a daughter, b. and d. Nov. 12, 1867, and
 9297   *Frank H.*,[9] b. Jan. 8, 1869.
9298   Maria Fonissa,[8] b. Nov. 20. 1843; m. William Brady; in Riley, Ohio.
9299   George R.,[8] b. May 14, 1846; m. March 21, 1867, Almira Allen; they have :
 9300   *Ida Elizabeth*,[9] b. Aug. 19, 1868.
9301   Oliver Perry,[8] b. Dec. 17, 1849; d. Aug., 1851.

## 8727

ISRAEL THURSTON[7] (*John*,[6] *Israel*,[5] *John*,[4] *Benjamin*,[8] *Joseph*,[2] *John*[1]), son of John[6] and Mary (Mars) Thurston of Northumberland, Pa.; born there April 3, 1788; married, 1809, NANCY ELY, born 1789. Mr. Thurston was a farmer at Wiley Station, Ohio.

Children:

+9305   Caleb,[8] b. June 15, 1811; m. 1st, Hannah Vanzant; 2d, Mary Buckingham.
9306   Hester,[8] b. Jan. 5, 1813; m. Charles Stoll.
9307   Catherine,[8] b. April 10, 1819; m. Ziber Vanzant.
9308   Maria,[8] b. March 10, 1821; m. William Linn.
9309   Joshua E.,[8] b. March 24, 1823; m. May 7, 1846, Catherine Applegate, b. Feb. 2, 1823. He enlisted in the army against the rebellion from Dry Ridge, Ohio, in 1864, and not long afterward disappeared and has not been heard from since. They had:
     9310   *Ida Lutrena*,[9] b. Nov. 10, 1847.
     9311   *Emma Jane*,[9] b. Jan. 3, 1854.
9312   Susanna,[8] b. Nov. 17, 1824; m. D. M. Deams.
9313   Elizabeth,[8] b. Jan. 8, 1828; m. James Hiatt.
9314   Grizilla H.,[8] b. May 18, 1830; m. Rev. Abraham Thurston [see no. 8706].

## 8729

MOSES THURSTON[7] (*John*,[6] *Israel*,[5] *John*,[4] *Benjamin*,[3] *Joseph*,[2] *John*[1]), brother of the preceding, and son of John[6] and Mary (Mars) Thurston of Northumberland, Pa.; born there June 1, 1793; married, July 29, 1815, at Crosswicks, N. J., HANNAH PARKER, born April 17, 1791, daughter of William and Catharine (Hankerson) Parker of Groveville, N. J. He died in Rahway, N. J., July 30, 1821, and she married Amasa Allen; he died and she married C. Gregg. She died in Perry, Wyoming county, N. Y., April 9, 1861.

Mr. Thurston was a worker in a cotton factory in Germantown, N. J.; a member of the Methodist church.

His children were:

9319   Catharine Ann,[8] b. April 7, 1816; m. 1st, in Covington, N. Y., Nov. 12, 1834, Willard Shaw, b. in Vermont Sept. 4, 1813, d. in Jonesville, Mich., June 28, 1870; 2d, Asa Fuller, a farmer in Charlotte, Eaton Co., Mich. She had, by first husband:
     9320   *Lydia Ann* (Shaw), b. Aug. 24, 1835.
     9321   *Elizabeth* (Shaw), b. March 5, 1838.
     9322   *Mary Eliza* (Shaw), b. Feb. 8, 1840.
     9323   *Martha Lavilla* (Shaw), b. Dec. 7, 1844.
     9324   *Frances Augusta* (Shaw), b. April 18, 1849.
     9325   *Helen Maria* (Shaw), b. Aug. 16, 1853.
9326   Eliza Vanshaik,[8] b. July 23, 1817; m. in Moscow, N. Y., Aug. 14, 1844, Daniel Porter, a contractor, who died in Danville, N. Y., Nov. 3, 1863. She resides in Thorold, Ontario. They had:
     9327   *Richard Hankerson* (Porter), b. March 28, 1846.
     9328   *Catherine Hannah* (Porter), b. June 18, 1853.
9329   John Jackson,[8] b. June 4, 1819; d. July 15, 1821.
9330   Deborah Maria,[8] b. June 16, 1821; m. 1st, March 23, 1842, Nahum W. Thayer, a ship carpenter of Niagara, N. Y.; he was killed Sept. 16, 1856, at the raising of an electioneering flag-staff in the canvass for President Buchanan; 2d, March 19, 1857, William Lewin, a house joiner, b. in Douglass, Isle of Man, Dec. 13, 1803. They resided in Buffalo, N. Y.; he died July 22, 1878, aged 75.

## 8734

ELDER JOHN THURSTON[7] (*John*,[6] *Israel*,[5] *John*,[4] *Benjamin*,[3] *Joseph*,[2] *John*[1]), brother of the preceding, and son of John[6] and Mary (Mars) Thurston of Northumberland, Pa.; born there April 11, 1800; married, March 9, 1826, REBECCA THURSTON, his cousin [see no. 8710], born Aug. 2, 1808, daughter of Samuel and Hannah (Kelley) Thurston of Mixersville, Ind. [see no. 8423]. She died Oct. 27, 1876.

Mr. Thurston is a Baptist minister and farmer; he invented in 1847-8 an improvement in fanning mills which has considerable notoriety.

### Children:

9335   Mary,[8] b. April 9, 1827; m. Feb. 11, 1844, Samuel Montgomery.
9336   Hannah,[8] b. July 6, 1828; m. Feb., 1854, Thomas Boen; d. Jan., 1855.
9337   Israel,[8] b. Jan. 3, 1830; m. May 7, 1857, Margaret E. McAllister, b. Jan.
       13, 1839. He lived in Mixersville, enlisted against the rebellion, and
       was killed in battle June 22, 1863; she died 1862. They had:

   9338   *John M.*,[9] b. May 12, 1858.
   9339   *Lewella,*[9]  } twins, b. May 30, 1860; d. Aug. 11, 1862.
   9340   *Estella,*[9]  }                        d June 9, 1860.
9341   Elizabeth,[8] b. Oct. 2, 1831; d. Jan. 20, 1844.
9342   Isaac,[8] b. April 24, 1833; m. April 15, 1853, Rebecca Riner, b. May 16,
       1839, daughter of Peter and Margaret (Kelley) Riner. He is a farmer
       in Elmwood, Ill. Children:

   9343   *John Leoria,*[9] b. Aug. 2, 1859.
   9344   *Israel Peter,*[9] b. Nov. 3, 1862.
   9345   *Francis Elmer,*[9] b. June 12, 1868.
   9346   *Albert Ricardo,*[9] b. Feb. 9, 1872.
9347   Sarah,[8] b. June 7, 1835.
9348   Rachel,[8] b. Aug. 18, 1838; m. John Wesley Riner.
9349   Hester Ann,[8] b. Jan. 21, 1840.
9350   Emeline,[8] b. Jan. 29, 1842.
9351   Maria,[8] b. July 28, 1844.
9352   Rebecca Jane,[8] b. Jan. 9, 1847.

### 8736

LEVI THURSTON[7] (*John,*[6] *Israel,*[5] *John,*[4] *Benjamin,*[3] *Joseph,*[2] *John*[1]),
brother of the preceding, and son of John[6] and Mary (Mars) Thurs-
ton of Northumberland, Pa.; born there Mar. 5, 1805; married, first,
Dec. 4, 1827, SARAH SHURR; she died Nov. 26, 1834.  Second, June
2, 1836, ELIZABETH RHODES BASTRESS of Poolsgrove, Pa.

Mr. Thurston was a shoemaker at Jersey Shore, Lycoming county,
Pa., till his second marriage, when he moved to Mt. Gilead, Ohio,
where he is the oldest man in the boot, shoe, and leather business.

### His children, by first wife, Sarah:

9357   William,[8] b. Oct. 13, 1828; d. Oct. 21, 1830.
9358   Michael,[8] b. Feb. 11, 1830; d. April 13, 1834.
9359   James Caldwell,[8] b. May 15, 1832; d. Dec. 13, 1834.
9360   Sarah Rachel,[8] b. Nov. 23, 1834; was adopted by her aunt, Rachel Orr;
       fell heir to $40,000 on the death of her adopted parents, and m. Harry
       Reeder, Esq.; they reside in Watsontown, Northumberland county, Pa.

### By second wife, Elizabeth:

9361   Charity Ann,[8] b. March 5, 1837; d. Aug. 10, 1840.
9362   Sophia Jane,[8] b. Nov. 2, 1838; m. Osceo Germain; they reside in Martins-
       ville, Clarke county, Ill.
9363   Solomon Clinton,[8] b. March 30, 1840; d. Aug. 28, 1842.
9364   David Clark,[8] b. March 11, 1843; enlisted April 26, 1861, in the 20th Ohio
       regiment, and participated in all the battles of the army of the Cumber-
       land, served through the entire war, and won a commission of first lieu-
       tenant for bravery and honor.  April, 1866, went to Kansas as a pioneer
       in North township, near city of Parsons, Labette county; m. 1st, May 21,
       1868, Sarah Elizabeth Barnes, b. 1841, d. Feb. 18, 1869; 2d, April 16,
       1871, Christena Frances Biley, d. June 11, 1877; 3d, July 14, 1878, Re-
       becca A. Chapman, b. 1854.  He had, by second wife:

   9365   *Levi Harrison,*[9] b. July 20, 1872.
   9366   *Edward Everet,*[9] b. Nov. 1, 1873.
   9367   *Alfred Albert,*[9] b. June 10, 1875.
9368   Levi Judson,[8] d. young.
9369   John Wesley,[8] b. March 6, 1845; enlisted in the army of the Potomac; is
       in company with his father in Mt. Gilead; has been a member of the
       city council and of the Methodist church; m. Aug. 27, 1872, Aleti Ruha-
       ma Shaw, b. Feb. 23, 1843, daughter of John and Nancy (McDonough)
       Shaw of Mt. Gilead; no children.

9370 Charles Stott,[8] b. Feb. 7, 1846, a shoemaker and lumberman; enlisted in the 136th and 187th Ohio regiments in the army against the rebellion; m. Sept. 28, 1873, Elizabeth Elleanore Thurston [see no. 10,091], daughter of Daniel Marvin and Emily (Ford) Thurston. They reside in Parsons, Kansas, and have:
    9371 *Charles Worthington*,[9] b. Sept. 28, 1874.
9372 Elmira Eleanora,[8] b. March 13, 1848; m. Isaac M. de Witt; they reside near Mt. Gilead.
9373 Mary Ellen,[8] b. Dec. 3, 1851; d. Mar. 26, 1869; very beautiful in character.
9374 George Tucker Stone,[8] b. March 8, 1855: in the employ of his father and brother.

## 8764

WILLIAM THURSTON[7] (*Moses,[6] Israel,[5] John,[4] Benjamin,[3] Joseph,[2] John[1]*), eldest son of Moses[6] and Catherine (Bottenhamer) Thurston of Sunbury, Pa.; born there May 25, 1795; married, Oct. 31, 1819, MARGARET CAMPBELL.

### Children:

9379 George,[8] m. —— Sickles.
9380 Cattrenn,[8] m. Dora Newkirk.
9381 Elizabeth,[8] m. —— Mowery.
9382 Andrew Jackson.[8]
9383 Lucretia Ann.[8]
9384 Thomas.[8]
9385 Tucker,[8] and three others.

## 8767

ASA THURSTON[7] (*Moses,[6] Israel,[5] John,[4] Benjamin,[3] Joseph,[2] John[1]*), brother of the preceding, and son of Moses[6] and Catherine (Bottenhamer) Thurston of Sunbury, Pa.; born there July 24, 1803; married, first, SUSAN JORDAN; second, SARAH HELLER, born 1810. He was a farmer in Sunbury; died at Elmira, N. Y., Oct. 25, 1849.

### Children:

9390 Israel.[8]
9391 Catherine,[8] b. 1830; m. 1st, 1851, S. G. Bowman; 2d, 1874, E. H. Bellnedge.
9392 Moses W.,[8] b. 1835; m. 1856, Helen C. Strader, b. 1838; they live in Watkins, Schuyler county, N. Y., and have:
    9393 *Oakley B.*,[9] b. 1857.
    9394 *George S.*,[9] b. 1860.
9395 Michle H.,[8] b. 1838; m. 1867, Jennie Nush, b. 1843; a grocer in Sunbury. They have:
    9396 *Helen*,[9] b. 1870.
    9397 *Mary*,[9] b. 1872.
9398 William K.,[8] b. 1841; m. 1866, Kit Randall, b. 1844; they have:
    9399 *Lewella*,[9] b. 1869.
9400 Reuben M.,[8] b. 1843; m. 1868, Maria Beker, b. 1844; they have:
    9401 *Henry*,[9] b. in Sunbury 1871.

## 8769

SYLVANUS THURSTON[7] (*Moses,[6] Israel,[5] John,[4] Benjamin,[3] Joseph,[2] John[1]*), brother of the preceding, and son of Moses[6] and Catherine (Bottenhamer) Thurston of Sunbury, Pa.; born there Feb. 9, 1806; married ————. He was a farmer in Scipio, Ind.

### Children:

9407 Sylvanus Welden.[8]
9408 Eli.[8]
9409 Rebecca,[8] m. —— Renn.
9410 Louisa,[8] m. Samuel Robbins; he died.

26

## 8770

ISRAEL THURSTON[7] (*Moses,*[6] *Israel,*[5] *John,*[4] *Benjamin,*[3] *Joseph,*[2] *John*[1]), brother of the preceding, and son of Moses[6] and Catherine (Bottenhamer) Thurston of Sunbury, Pa.; born there Dec. 18, 1809; married, Aug. 15, 1835, ABIGAIL PERSING, born Feb. 11, 1817, daughter of William and Margaret (Dimmick) Persing of Shamokin, Pa.

Mr. Thurston is a blacksmith in Rushtown, Pa., where he and his family are highly esteemed.

Children:

9415  Embly,[8] b. at Hickory Corners, Pa., Dec. 27, 1835.
9416  William Henry,[8] b. at Sunbury March 11, 1838.
9417  Elizabeth,[8] b. March 30, 1840; m. Philip Arison.
9418  Silas,[8] b. in Sunbury June 27, 1842.
9419  Reuben Wasen,[8] b. in Sunbury July 24, 1845.
9420  Caroline Whirl,[8] b. in Trevorton, Pa., May 18, 1848.
9421  Mary Amanda,[8] b. Sept. 22, 1851; m. D. F. Wagner.
9422  Elias Persing,[8] b. in Lower Augusta, Pa., Jan. 23, 1855; n.m., 1878, blacksmith in Rushtown.
9423  Isaac,[8] b. in Lower Augusta July 23, 1857; n.m., 1878, blacksmith in Rushtown.
9424  Louisa Catherine,[8] b. in Rushtown Sept. 30, 1860.

## 8773

MATHIAS THURSTON[7] (*Moses,*[6] *Israel,*[5] *John,*[4] *Benjamin,*[3] *Joseph,*[2] *John*[1]), brother of the preceding, and son of Moses[6] and Catherine (Bottenhamer) Thurston of Sunbury, Pa.; born there May 18, 1814; married, Jan. 4, 1843, ELIZA JANE SUMMERVILLE.

Mr. Thurston is a boot and shoe manufacturer in Fairfield Center, Ind., where he carries on the business quite extensively.

Children:

9429  William James,[8] b. Oct. 18, 1843.
9430  Elma Catherine,[8] b. July 24, 1845.
9431  Indiana Malicia,[8] b. Dec. 18, 1847.
9432  Benjamin Burton,[8] b. Jan. 16, 1850.
9433  John Wesley,[8] b. April 18, 1852.
9434  Mary Eliza,[8] b. Oct. 14, 1857.

## 8779

PETER THURSTON[7] (*Flavel,*[6] *Israel,*[5] *John,*[4] *Benjamin,*[3] *Joseph,*[2] *John*[1]), eldest son of Flavel[6] and Mary M. (Bottenhamer) Thurston of Shelbyville, Ind.; married SARAH MATLOCK.

Mr. Thurston is a farmer in Shelbyville; member of Baptist church.

Children:

9439  Catherine,[8] m. Harrison Updike.
9440  Jane,[8] m. William McDonal.
9441  Jacob.[8]
9442  Lucinda,[8] m. —— Snow.
9443  John.[8]
9444  Harriet,[8] m. Joseph Roe.
9445  Ellen,[8] m. John Hemphill.
9446  Wesley.[8]

## 8781

MOSES THURSTON[7] (*Flavel,*[6] *Israel,*[5] *John,*[4] *Benjamin,*[3] *Joseph,*[2] *John*[1]), brother of the preceding, and son of Flavel[6] and Mary M. (Bottenhamer) Thurston of Shelbyville, Ind.; married MARTHA WILLET. He is dead; she resides in Indianapolis, Ind.

Mr. Thurston was a farmer in Shelbyville.

Children :

9449   Catherine Ann,[8] m. Walter Baker, internal revenue collector in Brookville,
       Franklin county, Ind.
9450   Samuel.[8]
9451   Joab,[8] d. young.
9452   Jane,[8] m. Adam Updike of Shelbyville.
9453   Mary,[8] m. William Kelso.
9454   Lucretia,[8] d.
9455   Ellen,[8] m. Samuel Thurston, her cousin [see no. 9479]; he was killed in the
       war against the rebellion.
9456   Lurinda,[8] d. young.
9457   Thomas,[8] d. in the army in the war against the rebellion.
9458   Martha.[8]

## 8782

JOHN THURSTON [7] (*Flavel,*[6] *Israel,*[5] *John,*[4] *Benjamin,*[3] *Joseph,*[2] *John*[1]), brother of the preceding, and son of Flavel [6] and Mary M. (Bottenhamer) Thurston of Shelbyville, Ind. ; married, first, CATHERINE BAKER of Northumberland, Pa. ; second, ISABEL ——; she lives at Shelbyville.

Mr. Thurston was a blacksmith. In 1840 went to Franklin county, Ind., and from thence to Shelbyville, where for many years he owned and worked a farm.

Children :

9463   Caroline,[8] m. William Crosby; he died.
9464   Sophia,[8] m. William Snider.
9465   John,[8] m. Matilda ——.
9466   Mary Ann,[8] m. John McKee; she died.
9467   Eliza,[8] m. John McKee.
9468   Emma,[8] m. Samuel Reason; she died.
9469   Ellen,[8] m. —— Kiswell.
9470   Louisa,[8] m. Samuel Reason, her deceased sister's husband.
       Three others by last wife.

## 8783

SAMUEL THURSTON [7] (*Flavel,*[6] *Israel,*[5] *John,*[4] *Benjamin,*[3] *Joseph,*[2] *John*[1]), brother of the preceding, and son of Flavel [6] and Mary M. (Bottenhamer) Thurston of Shelbyville, Ind.; married REBECCA KETCHMAN. He was a farmer in Shelbyville.

Children :

9475   John.[8]
9476   Priscilla Jane.[8]
9477   William Flavel,[8] killed in the war against the rebellion.
9478   Benjamin.[8]
9479   Samuel,[8] m. his cousin, Ellen Thurston [see no. 9455], and was killed in
       the war against the rebellion.
9480   Christopher Columbus.[8]
9481   Rebecca.[8]
9482   Moses.[8]

## 8784

LEWIS THURSTON [7] (*Flavel,*[6] *Israel,*[5] *John,*[4] *Benjamin,*[3] *Joseph,*[2] *John*[1]), brother of the preceding, and son of Flavel [6] and Mary M. (Bottenhamer) Thurston of Shelbyville, Ind. ; born Jan. 1, 1806 ; married, Nov. 15, 1830, MARTHA BURCH, daughter of William and Mary Burch of Franklin county, Ind.

Mr. Thurston is a farmer in Forest Hill, Ind. They began life with nothing, but now, by hard work and economy, they own a splendid large farm with all the comforts of good living ; most of their children are settled near by.

Children:

9487 Elizabeth,[8] b. Aug. 14, 1831.
9488 Charles,[8] b. Feb. 14, 1834.
9489 Mary,[8] b. Aug. 31, 1836.
• 9490 William,[8] b. Nov. 19, 1838.
9491 Enos,[8] b. July 4, 1840; m. Mary Louvena Thurston [see no. 9533].
9492 Sarah,[8] b. Nov. 19, 1843.
9493 Benjamin,[8] b. Jan. 26, 1846.
9494 Thomas,[8] b. Dec. 19, 1848.
9495 Emma,[8] b. May 28, 1850.
9496 Morgan,[8] b..Jan. 24, 1853.

## 8785

JESSE THURSTON[7] (*Flavel,[6] Israel,[5] John,[4] Benjamin,[8] Joseph,[2] John[1]*), brother of the preceding, and son of Flavel[6] and Mary M. (Bottenhamer) Thurston of Shelbyville, Ind.; born in Northumberland county, Pa., April 1, 1808; married, in Franklin county, Ind., July 27, 1829, HARRIET UPDIKE, born Oct. 18, 1802, daughter of Elijah and Elizabeth (Snook) Updike of Northumberland county.

Mr. Thurston was a farmer in Franklin county, Ind., till 1844, when they removed to seven miles west of Shelbyville.

Children, born in Franklin county:

9500 Sarah,[8] b. Nov. 3, 1832; d. June 2, 1836.
9501 Joab Howell,[8] b. April 15, 1834.
9502 Isaiah Updike,[8] b. July 27, 1835; d. June 6, 1836.
9503 Mary Elizabeth,[8] b. July 13, 1837; m. William Belangee of Shelbyville.
9504 Elijah Wilton,[8] b. Feb. 15, 1839.
9505 James Lawrence,[8] b. March 22, 1841.
9506 Harvey Nelson,[8] b. Jan. 16, 1843.

Born in Shelbyville:

9507 David,[8] b. Dec. 12, 1844; d. March 27, 1870.
9508 Andrew Jackson,[8] b. Jan. 30, 1847; d. May 3, 1850.
9509 Levi,[8] b. Jan. 11, 1849.
9510 Henry,[8] b. April 8, 1851.
9511 John Sampson,[8] b. May 3, 1853.
9512 Delcina Arabella,[8] b. June 20, 1855; m. George Pierson of Shelbyville.
9513 Ezekiel Theodore,[8] } twins, b. Sept. 2, 1858.
9514 Dedama Ann,[8] }

## 8786

ENOS THURSTON[7] (*Flavel,[6] Israel,[5] John,[4] Benjamin,[8] Joseph,[2] John[1]*), brother of the preceding, and son of Flavel[6] and Mary M. (Bottenhamer) Thurston of Shelbyville, Ind.; married MARY J. BABBS; she is dead. He is a farmer in Champaign, Ill.; an invalid.

Children:

9519 Mary Elizabeth,[8] m.
9520 Anna,[8] d. in childhood.
9521 James Henry.[8]
9522 Jane.[8]
9523 William.[8]
9524 Eliza.[8]
9525 Charles.[8]
9526 Anna.[8]
Two others.

## 8787

DAVID THURSTON[7] (*Flavel,[6] Israel,[5] John,[4] Benjamin,[8] Joseph,[2] John[1]*), brother of the preceding, and son of Flavel[6] and Mary M. (Bottenhamer) Thurston of Shelbyville, Ind.; born in Northumber-

land county, Pa., Nov. 11, 1811; married, July 1, 1838, LURINDA LAING, born Aug. 29, 1822, daughter of John and Sarah (Tucker) Laing of Shelbyville.

Mr. Thurston moved to Franklin county, Ind., 1820, thence to Johnson county, Ind., 1844, then 1845 to Hendrick's plantation, Ind.; is a farmer, the happy owner of a first-class farm of nearly six hundred acres in Shelbyville; a member of the Missionary Baptist church.

Children:

9530　John Laing,[8] b. June 17, 1839; d. June 9, 1840.
9531　Mary Elizabeth,[8] b. Nov. 13, 1841; d. Oct. 12, 1844.
9532　Frozzie,[8] b. Jan. 20, 1844; d. Aug. 4, 1849.
9533　Mary Louvena,[8] b. March 14, 1846; m. Enos Thurston [see no. 9491].
9534　Martha Jane,[8] b. Feb. 7, 1848; d. June 19, 1850.
+9535　Arthur Jefferson,[8] b. April 11, 1849; m. Mary Jane Hackney.
9536　Emma,[8] b. Oct. 12, 1851; m. Sept. 16, 1869, John Clark, b. Feb. 19, 1847, son of John and Susan (Webb) Clark; he was a miller, but now a farmer in Muncie, Delavan county, Ind. They are Episcopalians. Children:
　　9537　*William Angus* (Clark), b. in Johnson county, Ind., June 30, 1870.
　　9538　*John Talbot* (Clark), b. in Johnson county Sept. 5, 1871.
　　9539　*Lucy Emma* (Clark), b. in Delavan county Sept. 29, 1873.
9540　Maude,[8] b. Dec. 6, 1853; d. Oct. 3, 1854.
9541　Winfield Scott,[8] b. July 16, 1855.
9542　Abner,[8] b. Feb. 24, 1858.
9543　Firman Franklin,[8] b. July 28, 1861.
9544　George McClellan,[8] b. Aug. 19, 1864.

## 8789

LEVI THURSTON [7] (*Flavel,[6] Israel,[5] John,[4] Benjamin,[3] Joseph,[2] John[1]*), brother of the preceding, and son of Flavel [6] and Mary M. (Bottenhamer) Thurston of Shelbyville, Ind.; born March 24, 1820; married, June 15, 1848, CLARISSA JANE UPDIKE, born in Franklin county, Ind., Feb. 14, 1827, daughter of Elijah and Elizabeth (Snook) Updike.

Mr. Thurston is a farmer in Shelbyville; member of Baptist church.

Children:

9549　Adin,[8] b. Oct. 2, 1850; m. Nov. 1, 1874, Alice Susanna Campbell, b. in Cincinnati, Ohio, June 30, 1854; they live in Shelby Co., Ind., and have:
　　9550　*Daisy Olive,*[9] b. Aug. 27, 1875.
　　9551　*Gordon Herford,*[9] b. Feb. 16, 1876.
9552　Nancy Lavina,[8] b. Oct. 7, 1852; m. Oct. 7, 1874, Hampton Bryam Yelton, b. in Campbell county, Ky., June 24, 1851, a farmer; they have:
　　9553　*Earnest Ithamar* (Yelton).
9554　Aaron Elsbuary,[8] b. March 24, 1855.
9555　Isaiah,[8] b. Nov. 27, 1856.
9556　Tuella,[8] b. Sept. 2, 1860.

## 8796

ABRAHAM HOPPER THURSTON [7] (*John Flavel,[6] Flavel,[5] John,[4] Benjamin,[3] Joseph,[2] John[1]*), son of John Flavel [6] and Martha (Hopper) Thurston of Rahway, N. J.; born there October, 1809; married, Jan. 19, 1845, MRS. MATILDA (ANTHONY) FREEMAN, daughter of Franklin Anthony of Franklin county, Tenn. He died Oct. 4, 1860.

Mr. Thurston settled as a hatter in Huntsville, Ala., about 1838.

Children:

9560　Edgar Mandelbert,[8] b. Jan. 18, 1846; a merchant.
9561　Jennie Bell,[8] b. Feb. 13, 1850; graduated from the Huntsville female college; m. May 25, 1870, Jason A. White of New York city. They have:
　　9562　*Mabel Rose* (White), b. March 26, 1871.

9563    Theodore Anthony,[8] b. Oct. 4, 1852; a merchant.
9564    Mattie Hopper,[8] graduated from the Huntsville female college.
9565    Walter Alonzo,[8] entered West Point Military Academy in 1875, graduated
        in June, 1879, and has entered the United States army.

## 8800

ELI THURSTON[7] (*Ezra,[6] James,[5] Daniel,[4] Daniel,[3] Joseph,[2] John[1]*),
son of Ezra[6] and Sally (Gilbert) Thurston of Dutchess county, N. Y.;
born there June 28, 1777; married, 1804, MARGARET COONS of Livingston manor, and moved to Chenango county, N. Y.

### Children :

9569   Lucinda,[8] b. Sept. 4, 1804; m. 1832, Joel Soper of North Norwich, N. Y.
+9570  Alfred,[8] b. April 20, 1806; m. Emily O. Pike.
9571   Eli,[8] b. April 21, 1808; m. 1838, Louisa Tracy, b. 1818. He died 1855;
       she died 1856; had eight children, only two living.
9572   Sally,[8] b. March 2, 1809; m. Jan. 20, 1833, Mark Lowell, and had seven
       children; he died 1847 in Bowling Green, Ohio.
9573   Louisa,[8] b. July 4, 1812; m. June 4, 1831, Mark Lowell; d. July 4, 1831.
9574   Simeon,[8] b. Dec. 24, 1813; d. young.
9575   Fanny,[8] b. Jan. 8, 1816; m. 1837, Jacob Stauper and moved to Missouri;
       d. 1840.
9576   John Hermon,[8] b. June 27, 1817; m. 1847, Melissa Main; moved to Bow-
       ling Green; had eight children, all dead but *Sidney[9]* and *Louisa L.[9]*
+9577  Daniel,[8] b. Feb. 1. 1820; m. —— Jackman.
9578   Lorenzo,[8] b. July 16, 1823; m. in Indiana; went to some place in Iowa.

## 8802

AZOR THURSTON[7] (*Ebenezer,[6] Cyrus,[5] Daniel,[4] Daniel,[3] Joseph,[2]
John[1]*), son of Ebenezer[6] and Eunice (Kelsey) Thurston; born Feb.
22, 1799; married, June 15, 1824, ELEBEDY SMITH, born in Oxford,
Butler county, Ohio. He died Jan. 20, 1849, and his widow married
Joseph de Puey.

Mr. Thurston removed from Pennsylvania about 1830 to Oxford,
Ohio, and settled on a farm. He was offered the land where Sandusky city now stands very cheap, but considered it worthless and
did not buy.

### Children :

+9583  Cyrus,[8] b. Aug. 14, 1825; m. Hannah Boone Woolverton.
9584   Albert,[8] b. Jan. 28, 1829; d. June 17, 1858.
9585   Iuna,[8] b. June 19, 1837; d. Sept. 5, 1848.
+9586  Asher,[8] b. Mar. 4, 1839; m. 1st, Mahala Montross; 2d, Mary Jane Norton.
9587   Adnah.[8] b. March 13, 1844; m. 1st, at Sandusky, Erie county, Ohio, Dec.
       28, 1864, Nancy A. Gallaway; she died Nov. 6, 1873; 2d, Nov. 18, 1875,
       Frances Gertrude Hatmaker, b. July 31, 1856, daughter of Andrew and
       M. (Mitchell) Hatmaker of Bloomingville, Erie county. He is a farmer
       at Four Corners, Huron county, O.; had, by first wife :
9588    *Amy Philena,[9]* b. Nov. 3, 1865.
9589    *Berton E.,[9]* b. Sept. 4, 1871.
                        By second wife :
9590    *Andrew Delos,[9]* b. Jan. 7, 1877.

## 8803

EBENEZER THURSTON[7] (*Ebenezer,[6] Cyrus,[5] Daniel,[4] Daniel,[3] Joseph,[2]
John[1]*), brother of the preceding, and son of Ebenezer[6] and Eunice
(Kelsey) Thurston; born near Genesee valley, N. Y., Feb. 18, 1801;
married HANNAH ALBRO.

Mr. Thurston was a farmer in Scott, La Grange county, Ind.

### Children:

9592 Elizabeth,[8] b. in Luzerne county, Pa., Jan., 1823; m.; d. 1855.
+9593 Daniel Marvin,[8] b. Aug. 13, 1825; m. 1st, Lovina Allen; 2d, Emily Ford.
9594 Mary,[8] b. 1827; d. 1842.
9595 Mahala,[8] b. 1832; m.
9596 Eunice,[8] b. 1834.
9597 Caroline,[8] b. 1836.
9598 Thomas Jefferson,[8] b. in Erie Co., O., 1838; engaged in selling machinery.
9599 Ebenezer,[8] b. 1840; m.; a painter in Scott.
9600 Hiram,[8] m.; a miner in Colorado.

## 8810

ELISHA THURSTON[7] (*Amos,*[6] *Increase,*[5] *Daniel,*[4] *Daniel,*[3] *Daniel,*[2] *John*[1]), son of Amos Thurston[6]; married LOVICEY SWEET of Morris, N. Y. He was a mason in Morris.

### Children:

9601 Valorous,[8] a farmer.
9602 Albertus,[8] a Methodist preacher.
9603 Wesley,[8] a mason.
9604 Elijah,[8] a carpenter.
9605 Laura,[8] m. —— Bancroft.
9606 Lorindy,[8] m. —— Write.
9607 Triphena,[8] m. —— Short.
9608 Helen,[8] m. —— Short.
9609 Eliza,[8] m. —— Thomas.

## 8832

DAVID THURSTON[7] of Newton, Ohio (*David,*[6] *Daniel,*[5] *Daniel,*[4] *Daniel,*[3] *Daniel,*[2] *John*[1]), son of David[6] and Margaret (Phillips) Thurston of Whitestown, Oneida county, N. Y.; born there July 24, 1811; married, Oct. 10, 1830, SOPHIA CURTIS, born Feb. 14, 1813, daughter of Comfort and Catherine Curtis of Sodus, Wayne county, N. Y.

Mr. Thurston removed with his father, about 1825, to Albion, Orleans county, N. Y. Two or three years after marriage he removed to Newton, Ohio. He was sometimes engaged in clearing land and speculating, and being a good mechanic, he occupied some of his time in building. He had delicate health, the country in Ohio was new and sickly, and he died of consumption Feb. 10, 1844. He was a man of great energy and good business qualities, and if his health had been good would undoubtedly have been a man of wealth and position. He was a member of the Presbyterian church. His wife, in accordance with the advice of her husband just before his death, moved back to Albion in 1844. This was before the day of railroads and was no small undertaking, with five small children, all sick at the time. She now resides at Knowlesville, Orleans county, N. Y., 1879.

### Children:

9610 Catherine,[8] b. in Albion Aug. 23, 1832; thrown upon her own resources after the death of her father, she prepared for teaching and taught four years, till 1852, when she m. Josiah Page. They removed to California in 1869 and returned in 1871 to Albion, where she died. She was a conscientious christian of the Adventist faith. Children:
9611 *Velma* (Page).
9612 *Frank* (Page), m. and in San Francisco, Cal.
9613 *Helen* (Page), in Washington, D. C.
9614 *Leonard* (Page), in Hillsdale county, Mich.
9615 *Walter* (Page).
9616 *Fred* (Page).

9617 Savilla Loomis,[8] b. in Albion July 25, 1834: m. Nov. 5, 1857, Alphonzo
St. Clair, eldest son of Charles and Elmina St. Clair of Albion; he was
killed by the fall of a tree Feb. 22, 1865, aged 30. The widow and son
reside in Knowlesville 1879. Child:
  9618 *Frank Alphonzo* (St. Clair), b. July 21, 1861.

Born in Ohio:
+9619 William Henry,[8] b. Sept. 1, 1836; m. 1st, Mary Van Alstyne; 2d, Elizabeth Hooper.
+9620 Alonzo Loomis,[8] b. July 15, 1838; m. Phebe Flansburg.
+9621 James Hamilton,[8] b. Nov. 6, 1840; m. Eleanor J. Field.
  9622 Margaret,[8] b. Nov. 11, 1843; d. April 12, 1844.

## 8845

STEPHEN BAILEY THURSTON[7] (*Caleb Curtiss,[6] Daniel,[5] Daniel,[4]
Daniel,[3] Daniel,[2] John[1]*), son of Caleb Curtiss[6] and Thankful (Bailey)
Thurston of Barre, N. Y.; born in Westmoreland, N. Y., June 3,
1808; married, June 11, 1832, JULIANA WILLIAMS, born April 5, 1812.

Mr. Thurston was a farmer in Albion. Orleans county, N. Y.; has
been town assessor for nine years; retired, and was killed by the cars
at Albion depot Sept. 29, 1879.

Children:
  9623 Mary Jane,[8] b. Oct. 10, 1832; m. April 3, 1873, Alphonso Gillett, b. April
26, 1836; member of the Presbyterian church.
  9624 Joel Curtiss,[8] b. April 29, 1834; supposed to have been drowned in Feather
river, Cal., July 10, 1860.
+9625 Horace Fitch,[8] b. April 4, 1836; m. 1st, Mary Frances Kingsley; 2d,
Mary L. Goodwin.
  9626 William Stephen Bailey,[8] b. Oct. 6, 1837; m. Feb. 1, 1865, Sophia Harriet
Murray, b. Sept. 13, 1841. He is a farmer on the homestead in Albion.
Children:
  9627 *Burton Reed,[9]* b. Oct. 27, 1868.
  9628 *William Murray,[9]* b. Nov. 29, 1872.
  9629 Daniel Allen,[8] b. Nov. 9, 1841; m. Nov., 1865, Vietta Celestia Bragg, b.
Feb. 16, 1848. He is a farmer in Carlton, N. Y. They have:
  9630 *John Bragg,[9]* b. Sept. 1, 1868.

## 8846

URBAN CLARK THURSTON[7] of Albion, N. Y. (*Caleb Curtiss,[6] Daniel,[5]
Daniel,[4] Daniel,[3] Daniel,[2] John[1]*), brother of the preceding, and son of
Caleb Curtiss[6] and Thankful (Bailey) Thurston of Barre, N. Y.; born
in Westmoreland, N. Y., Sept. 8, 1810; married, first, Dec. 26, 1832,
MARY WRISLEY of Barre, born Feb. 17, 1813; second, April 22, 1847,
CAROLINE P. HOWLAND, born July 19, 1826; third, April 18, 1858,
LOUISE CATHERINE OLDS of Westport, N. Y., born Nov. 23, 1824.

Mr. Thurston was a farmer in Albion till 1852, when he went into
the forwarding business.

His children, by first wife, Mary:
  9634 Caleb Curtiss,[8] b. March 13, 1835; d. Dec. 10, 1857.
  9635 Jason Wrisley,[8] b. Dec. 18, 1845; d. Sept. 23, 1867.

By third wife, Louise:
  9636 Charles Howland,[8] b. Sept. 28, 1861.

## 8855

PETER THURSTON[7] (*David,[6] Moses,[5] Daniel,[4] Daniel,[3] Daniel,[2]
John[1]*), son of David[6] and Rachel (Chapin) Thurston of Mexico,
N. Y.; born in New Lisbon, N. Y., Jan. 31, 1795; married, January,

1821, ANNA KELSEY, born in New Lisbon Aug. 28, 1799. She died at Grand Marsh, Adams county, Wis., Jan. 5, 1856.

Mr. Thurston is a farmer in Garden City, Blue Earth county, Minn.; a member of the Baptist church.

Children :

+9640    Ellis David,[8] b. in Pittsfield, N. Y., Nov. 10, 1821.

Born in New Lisbon :

9641    Esther,[8] b. Jan. 1, 1823; m. 1844, Rev. Rodney S. Rose; d. Oct., 1859.
+9642    Jesse Moses,[8] b. May 14, 1825; m. Ann ——.
9643    Charles Edwin,[8] b. Dec. 15, 1826; m. 1852, Sarah Ballard. He sailed from New York city for the Sandwich Islands and after a six months' voyage arrived at San Francisco, Cal. He lived in that state a few years and died at Lower Lake, Cal., 1867; no children.
9644    Phebe,[8] b. Feb., 1832; m. 1854, Lucius Terry, a farmer in Garden City.
9645    Albert Peter,[8] b. Aug., 1837; m. ; was a surgeon in the war against the rebellion, and died from exposure and fatigue at the battle of Pittsburgh Landing, at Keokuk, Ill., Aug. 3, 1862. He had one child, but I can learn nothing from him.

## 8886

ALLEN THURSTON[7] (*Amos,[6] Amos,[5] Daniel,[4] Daniel,[3] Daniel,[2] John[1]*), eldest son of Amos[6] and Lucy (Dart) Thurston of Norwich, Chenango county, N. Y.; born there Oct. 27, 1797 ; married LUCY WAKELY, born Oct. 12, 1799. He died Aug. 22, 1851 ; she died June 26, 1868.

Mr. Thurston was a farmer in Preston, Wayne county, Pa.

Children :

9646    Maria Jane,[8] b. 1818; m. Samuel Scott Breed; he is dead and she resides in Bloomington, Grant county, Wis.
9647    David,[8] b. 1822; m. 1846, Sarah Jane Hine; enlisted from Wisconsin in the war against the rebellion and served three years, returned to his family and moved to Harvey county, Kansas.
9648    Armena,[8] b. 1827; m. 1846, John Hine, a farmer in Preston, b. 1819; had :
     9649   *Marion* (Hine), b. 1848.
     9650   *Nettie* (Hine), b. 1852.
9651    Lucy Ann,[8] b. 1829; m. 1848, Abel Reynolds. They lived in Pennsylvania for a while, then moved to Bloomington, Wis. He was drafted for the war against the rebellion, died, and was buried in a soldier's grave.
9652    Henry Allen,[8] b. 1835; m. Christana Drown; in 1862 he enlisted in the war against the rebellion; after some months of service was taken sick, died in the hospital at Fortress Monroe, and was buried there; a christian; one child. His widow m. —— Knapp and resides in Starrucca, Wayne county, Pa.

## 8888

GAINES THURSTON[7] (*Amos,[6] Amos,[5] Daniel,[4] Daniel,[3] Daniel,[2] John[1]*), brother of the preceding, and son of Amos[6] and Lucy (Dart) Thurston of Norwich, Chenango Co., N. Y.; born in New Lisbon, N. Y., Dec. 1, 1800 ; married, Oct. 1, 1823, MARGARET HASBROOK, born in Washington, Dutchess Co., N. Y., Mar. 29, 1803, daughter of Benjamin Daniel and Hannah (Green) Hasbrook of Pleasant Valley, Dutchess Co.

Mr. Thurston is a retired farmer, residing in New Lisbon, N. Y.; member of the Episcopal church.

Children :

9653    James,[8] b. Nov. 3, 1824; m. Oct. 8, 1850, Caroline M. Hanford of Starrucca, Wayne county, Pa.; in New Lisbon.
9654    Hannah,[8] b. Aug. 9, 1826; m. April 21, 1867, Daniel Teal of Oneida Castle, Oneida county, N. Y.
9655    Adeline,[8] b. Sept. 3, 1829; d. Aug. 26, 1849.
+9656    Alfred,[8] b. Oct. 10, 1843; m. Mary Adelia Hawkins.

## 8897

WILLIAM THURSTON[7] (*Amos,*[6] *Amos,*[5] *Daniel,*[4] *Daniel,*[3] *Daniel,*[2] *John*[1]), brother of the preceding, and son of Amos[6] and Lucy (Dart) Thurston of Norwich, Chenango county, N. Y.; born in New Lisbon, N. Y., Dec. 18, 1809; married, Nov. 8, 1831, OLIVIA DRAPER, born July 5, 1806, daughter of Benjamin and Olive (Pettingall) Draper of Butternuts [afterward called Morris] Otsego county, N. Y. She died Sept. 21, 1879; Rev. M. L. S. Haynes of Norwich preached the funeral sermon.

Mr. Thurston is a farmer; lived in Butternuts, and after that in Norwich; member of the Baptist church.

Children, all born in Norwich:

9658    Marion Letitia,[8] b. Sept. 22, 1832; m. Oct. 16, 1851, Levi Haynes, a farmer in Norwich; both members of the Baptist church. Mrs. Haynes says she "pieced a quilt before she was five years old and at the age of ten went to a show and had a ride on an elephant." Children:

9659    *George Byron* (Haynes), b. Dec. 13, 1857; joined the Baptist church at fourteen years of age.
9660    *Ella May* (Haynes), b. Nov. 15, 1863.
9661    *William Levi* (Haynes), b. July 4, 1867.
+9662   William Jason,[8] b. Nov. 13, 1834; m. Harriet Amelia Hunt.
9663    Edwin Curtis,[8] b. April 17, 1838; d. March 6, 1840.
9664    Amos Draper,[8] b. Dec. 21, 1840; d. Dec. 9, 1842.
9665    Helen Adelia,[8] b. Sept. 22, 1844; m. James Briggs of Norwich; member of the Baptist church. They have:

9666    *Howard William* (Briggs), b. Feb. 4, 1874.
9667    Melona Araminta,[8] b. Feb. 21, 1848; m. Oct. 20, 1868, Edwin Lewis Graves, b. Dec. 30, 1846; he is a farmer in New Berlin, P. O. address Norwich, member of the Congregational church. They have:

9668    *Merton Edwin* (Graves), b. Nov. 14, 1877..

## 8903

CHESTER THURSTON[7] (*Ira,*[6] *Amos,*[5] *Daniel,*[4] *Daniel,*[3] *Daniel,*[2] *John*[1]), eldest son of Ira[6] and Ruth (Benedict) Thurston of New Lisbon, N. Y.; born there April 29, 1807; married, Dec. 27, 1838, MARGARET PATTENGILL, born Sept. 29, 1818, daughter of Samuel and Elizabeth (Ackley) Pattengill of Laurens, Otsego county, N. Y. He died May 17, 1850; she died at Mt. Vision, N. Y., Oct. 10, 1877.

Mr. Thurston was a farmer in New Lisbon and in Laurens; member of the Presbyterian church.

Children:

9673    Mary Elizabeth,[8] b. in New Lisbon March 13, 1840; n.m.; a dressmaker in Mt. Vision.
9674    Samuel Dexter,[8] b. in Virgil, Cortland county, N. Y., Aug. 17, 1844; m. Feb. 11, 1868, Caroline Elizabeth Hubbard, daughter of George and Julia (Smith) Hubbard) of Hartwick, Otsego county, N. Y. He is a carpenter, farmer, and egg dealer in Mt. Vision; a member of the Methodist church. They have:

9675    *Chester Dexter,*[9] b. Sept. 11, 1871.
9676    Charles Torrey,[8] b. in Virgil May 10, 1846; m. 1st, Helen Hall; 2d, Libbie Bowdich; served in the war against the rebellion in the 152d New York regiment. He is a farmer in Norwich, N. Y.; has, by second wife:

9677    *Charles.*[9]
9678    Ada Leona,[9] b. at Laurens Sept. 19, 1849; d. March 9, 1852.

## 8905

REV. CURTIS THURSTON[7] (*Ira,*[6] *Amos,*[5] *Daniel,*[4] *Daniel,*[3] *Daniel,*[2] *John*[1]), brother of the preceding, and son of Ira[6] and Ruth (Bene-

dict) Thurston of New Lisbon, Otsego county, N. Y.; born there Sept. 10, 1809; married, April 15, 1846, JULIA ANN SPAULDING. He died suddenly of heart disease Sept. 22, 1872.

Mr. Thurston graduated from Union college in 1837, while Rev. Dr. Nott was president; studied theology in Auburn, N. Y., under Drs. Richards and Mills; was principal of Syracuse academy for a while; went to Athens, Pa., and preached for the Old and New School Presbyterians, and was installed there February, 1841; remained there till 1848, when the two societies united and he retired, after which he was not settled but preached as occasion offered.

### Children:

+9680   William Owen,[8] b. Oct. 21, 1847; m. Mary E. Allen.
9681   Joseph Spaulding,[8] b. March 9, 1850; m. Nov. 10, 1875, Hattie Allen; is
     a farmer on the homestead in Athens, Pa. They have:
     9682   *John Spaulding*,[9] b. March 16, 1879.
9683   John Curtis,[8] b. March 24, 1852; n.m.; living in Elmira, N. Y.

### 8906

JOEL THURSTON[7] (*Ira*,[6] *Moses*,[5] *Daniel*,[4] *Daniel*,[3] *Daniel*,[2] *John*[1]), brother of the preceding, and son of Ira[6] and Ruth (Benedict) Thurston of New Lisbon, N. Y.; born there July 28, 1811; married ELIZA ANN GREGORY. He is a wagon maker by trade, but occupying himself as a farmer in New Lisbon.

### Children:

9692   Henry Egbert,[8] b. 1841; d. 1863.
9693   Julius E.,[8] b. 1843; m. Lucy S. Duroe; farmer in New Lisbon. Children:
     9694   *Maria*,[9] b. 1874.
     9695   *Joel Ernest*,[9] b. 1876.
9696   Mary Ann,[8] b. 1847; m. C. R. Duroe of Norwich, N. Y. Children:
     9697   *Vernon* (Duroe), b. 1873.
     9698   *Addison* (Duroe), b. 1874.
     9699   *Mary Ann* (Duroe), b. 1877.
9700   Pliny S.,[8] b. 1852; m. Fanny Cole; a farmer in Mt. Vision, N. Y.
9701   Child            } twins, b. 1857; d. in infancy.
9702   Clarence G.,[8]   } twins, b. 1857; a merchant in Cooperstown, N. Y.
9703   Frances Jane,[8] b. 1862.
9704   Laura Eliza,[8] b. 1865.

### 8925

MOSES HAYDEN THURSTON[7] (*Timothy*,[6] *John*,[5] *Benjamin*,[4] *Daniel*[3]), son of Timothy[6] and Lucy (Hayden) Thurston of Orange, Vt.; born in Grafton, Mass., 1797; married CHARLOTTE FIFIELD. He died at Charlestown, N. H., 1860, aged 63.

### Children:

9709   George Washington,[8] b. in Wheelock, Vt., July 23, 1826; m. Dec. 14, 1847,
     Lucretia Gould, b. Dec. 14, 1824, daughter of William and Clarissa
     (Damon) Gould of Springfield, Vt. He is, 1879, a dealer in fresh and
     salt meats in Windsor, Vt.; was the first constable in Windsor; member
     of the Congregational church; no children.
9710   Sarah Fifield,[8] b. June 18, 1833; m. Charles Artemas Witt, b. Oct. 26,
     1830, son of Willard and Lydia (Harvey) Witt, a carpenter of Drews-
     ville, N. H. Children:
     9711   *George Moses* (Witt), b. in Keene, N. H., Dec. 25, 1857.
     9712   *Charles Willard* (Witt), b. in Drewsville Sept. 22, 1859; d. 1868.
     9713   *Della Grace* (Witt), b. in Charlestown, N. H., March 24, 1863.
9714   Orpha,[8] b. Nov. 14, 1835; m. April 4, 1858, Otis Walker, b. Jan. 14, 1814,
     a farmer in Langdon, N. H. He died Oct. 17, 1870; she resides in Al-
     stead, N. H. They had:

9715  *Ellery Otis* (Walker), b. Nov. 1, 1860.
9716  *Etta M.* (Walker), b. Oct. 3, 1863.

## 8937

DANIEL SYLVESTER THURSTON[7] ( *Timothy,*[6] *John,*[5] *Benjamin,*[4] *Daniel*[3]), brother of the preceding, and son of Timothy[6] and Lucy (Hayden) Thurston of Orange, Vt.; born there 1809; married, first, MATILDA BENJAMIN of Berlin, Vt.; she died in 1845. Second, in 1846, MRS. RUTH TOWN, widow of Josiah Town and daughter of John and Ruth (Hopkins) Mellen.

Mr. Thurston was a farmer, tanner and currier of the firm of Thurston, Keith, Peck & Co., of Montpelier, Vt. He was a town and school officer, and was nominated for the legislature by the Free Soil party, but declined to be a candidate; was a member of the Methodist church. He moved to Madison, and from thence to Beaver Dam, Wis. During the war of the rebellion he volunteered in the 1st Wisconsin regiment and received a lieutenant's commission, and afterward was in the 1st Wisconsin cavalry, in which he served nine months, contracted a disease of the lungs, was discharged, but lived only three days after reaching his home, dying April 9, 1863. He was a stern advocate of every good cause, and a successful business man.

His children, by first wife, Matilda, all born in Montpelier:

+9720  Angelia Louisa French,[8] b. Dec. 4, 1837; m. 1st, Frank Kilgore; 2d, David Newman.
9721  Caroline Gertrude,[8] b. 1840; m. Lorenzo H. Dow, who served through the war of the rebellion in the 1st Wisconsin infantry without a scratch; is now, 1877, clerk in a hotel in Portage City, Wis.; no children.
9722  Carrie Langdon,[8] b. 1842; m. Elijah J. Fisher of Chicago, Ill. She studied elocution and taught in the normal school at Englewood, Ill., and died suddenly just as she was entering upon a three months' engagement as an elocutionist. Her husband is an inn-keeper in Chicago; three children.
9723  Matilda,[8] b. 1844; m. —— Bailey, connected with a railroad in Kansas City, Mo.

By second wife, Ruth:

+9724  John Mellen,[8] b. Aug. 21, 1847; m. Martha L. Poland.
9725  Ruth Mellen,[8] b. Dec. 4, 1849; d. March 29, 1867.

## 8938

HON. ELISHA MADISON THURSTON[7] ( *Timothy,*[6] *John,*[5] *Benjamin,*[4] *Daniel*[3]), brother of the preceding, and son of Timothy[6] and Lucy (Hayden) Thurston of Orange, Vt.; born there March 24, 1810; married, August, 1843, ANGELINE ROBINSON MONTGOMERY, born July 20, 1826, daughter of John and Jane (Burton) Montgomery of Cushing, Me. She died Oct. 5, 1858; he died March 17, 1859.

Mr. Thurston lived at home on the farm till nineteen years of age; studied for the ministry in Newton high school and at South Reading academy, and graduated from Colby in 1838, at which time he delivered the Salutatory, and Danford Thomas the Valedictory. From 1838 to 1844 he was principal of the Charleston (Me.) academy; was representative to the state legislature 1844, sick nearly a year, and in 1846 and 1847 member of the state senate, where "he endeavored to secure a general state revision of the common school system, which by his earnest and persevering efforts was finally carried into effect."

From 1850 to 1853, three years, he was secretary of the Maine Board of Education, still residing at Charleston. After 1852 he was laid aside from business by sickness. Oct. 6, 1854, he went to Missouri and Kansas, and shared in all the "troubles" of that region and period, being an active worker in the cause of freedom. In the autumn of 1857 he disposed of his property in Maine and removed his family to Manhattan, Kansas, where he practised law, having an extensive business, and at the time of his death was mayor of the city. His children were educated in Kansas for teachers, which profession they now follow, 1878.

Children, born in Charleston:

9730 Emma Leoline,[8] b. Jan. 28, 1848.
9731 Margaret Ann,[8] b. Feb. 14, 1850; d. 1860.
9732 Ella Adelaide,[8] b. 1852; d. in Topeka. Kansas, 1860.
9733 Annie Montgomery,[8] b. 1854; d. in infancy.
9734 Nettie Florence,[8] b. May 17, 1856.

## 8953

CALVIN SYLVESTER THURSTON[7] (*Daniel,[6] John,[5] Benjamin,[4] Daniel[3]*), son of Daniel[6] and Rosanna (Ellis) Thurston of Grafton, Mass.; born there April 7, 1808; married, in Upton, Mass., May 24, 1830, ELIZA JENCKS COE, born in Little Compton, R. I., May 1, 1809, daughter of Isaac and Sarah (Weaver) Coe of Westford, Ct. She died Sept. 29, 1876.

Mr. Thurston is a farmer in Grafton, 1879; has been selectman and held other town offices.

Children:

+9739 John Coe,[8] b. June 20, 1832; m. Cordelia Walker.
+9740 Isaac Daniel,[8] b. March 21, 1834; m. Laura Anna Boyd.
+9741 Edward Harrison,[8] b. April 24, 1836; m. Adelaide Lucretia Gould.
9742 Albert Sylvester,[8] b. April 29, 1838; d. Sept. 5, 1838.
9743 Eliza Melinda,[8] b. Jan. 13, 1842; d. Oct. 27, 1844.

## 8959

WILLIAM HARRISON THURSTON[7] of Oxford, Mass. (*Daniel,[6] John,[5] Benjamin,[4] Daniel[3]*), brother of the preceding, and son of Daniel[6] and Rosanna (Ellis) Thurston of Grafton, Mass.; born there March 19, 1813; married, Nov. 30, 1839, JULIA AUGUSTA BIGELOW, born June 21, 1820, daughter of William H. and Sarah Fisk (Gibbs) Bigelow of Webster, Mass.

Mr. Thurston was a manufacturer of boots and shoes, but is now retired from business; has been selectman, trustee and steward in the Methodist church.

Children:

9748 William Henry Harrison,[8] b. Dec. 25, 1840; m. Aug. 18, 1865. Mary Augusta Lackey, daughter of Albert Lackey. He is a shoe manufacturer and dealer in Oxford.
9749 Eugene,[8] b. April 2, 1858; d. April 5, 1864.

## 8960

DANIEL CLARENDON THURSTON[7] (*Daniel,[6] John,[5] Benjamin,[4] Daniel[3]*), brother of the preceding, and son of Daniel[6] and Rosanna (Ellis) Thurston of Grafton, Mass.; born there March 14, 1816; married, Sept. 28, 1842, LOIS K. TAFT of Upton, Mass. At the time of

his death, Jan. 6, 1868, he was proprietor of dining rooms in Worcester, Mass. After his death his sons carried on the business about five years.

Children :

9754 Frank Eugene,[8] b. Aug. 26, 1845; m. April 12, 1868, Maria H. White of Petersham, Mass. He is in company with E. J. Putnam, they being proprietors of dining rooms at Worcester. Children :
    9755 *Nellie*,[9] b. Oct. 24, 1870.
    9756 *Gertrude*,[9] b. March 14, 1873.
9757 Fred Judson,[8] b. June 22, 1849; m. Sept. 12, 1872, Carrie W. McFarland of Worcester; they have :
    9758 *Louie Clarendon*,[9] b. Nov. 1, 1874.
    9759 *Robby Judson*,[9] b. Oct. 22, 1876.
    9760 *Carrie Lois*,[9] b. Jan. 25, 1879.

## 8965

JONATHAN VESPASIAN THURSTON[7] (*Daniel*,[6] *John*,[5] *Benjamin*,[4] *Daniel*[3]), brother of the preceding, and son of Daniel[6] and Rosanna (Ellis) Thurston of Grafton, Mass.; born there April 14, 1824; married, Feb. 20, 1844, POLLY S. BURR, daughter of Asa Burr of Bellingham, Mass.

Mr. Thurston is a produce and commission merchant in West Washington market, New York city, firm of Thurston & Moore. His residence is in Jersey City, N. J.

Children :

9765 Stephen Clinton,[8] b. Feb. 3, 1845; m. Nov., 1866, Sarah C. Gough of Jersey City. They had :
    9766 *Fred*.[9]
    9767 *Bertie*.[9]
9768 Lilla Josephine,[8] b. June 20, 1847; m. June 23, 1869, A. Augustus Smyth of Jersey City. They had :
    9769 *Clinton Augustus* (Smyth).
    9770 *Frank* (Smyth), b. 1873.
9771 Clarence,[8] b. 1851; d. 1853.
9772 Louis Vespasian,[8] b. Aug. 8, 1854; m. Nov., 1877, ———.

## Eighth Generation.

### 8980

ABEL MOORS THURSTON[8] of Harrison, Me. (*David*,[7] *David*,[6] *Thomas*,[5] *Thomas*,[4] *Thomas*,[3] *Thomas*,[2] *John*[1]), eldest son of David[7] and Sybil (Holden) Thurston of Otisfield, Me.; born there Aug. 31, 1825; married, Dec. 28, 1871, ARAMINTA JANE PITTS, born Dec. 7, 1846, daughter of Daniel and Rachel Pitts of Magalloway Grant, N. H. He is a farmer.

Children :

9777 David,[9] b. April 15, 1873.
9778 Sybil,[9] b. July 26, 1874.
9779 John Leaon,[9] b. June 30, 1877.
9780 Daniel Willis,[9] b. Sept. 10, 1878.

## 9002

DAVID WILLIAM PORTER THURSTON [8] of Nebraska (*David,*[7] *David,*[6] *Thomas,*[5] *Thomas,*[4] *Thomas,*[3] *Thomas,*[2] *John*[1]), brother of the preceding, and son of David[7] and Sybil (Holden) Thurston of Otisfield, Me.; born there Feb. 9, 1843; married, May 1, 1866, EMILY WIGHT, daughter of Benjamin Wight of Otisfield.

Mr. Thurston was a farmer in Iowa, and about 1878 went to Eight Mile Grove, Cass county, Nebraska. He served in the 5th Maine regiment in the war against the rebellion.

### Children:

9785 Isabel,[9] b. July 15, 1869.
9786 John Holden,[9] b. March 21, 1871.
9787 Benjamin Wight,[9] b. June 5, 1873.
9788 Charles Wight,[9] b. Sept. 21, 1875.
9789 Syrena Walton,[9] b. Feb. 26, 1878.

## 9005

FRANCIS ALMAN THURSTON [8] (*Israel,*[7] *Jacob,*[6] *Thomas,*[5] *Thomas,*[4] *Thomas,*[3] *Thomas,*[2] *John*[1]), second son of Israel[7] and Sarah Hunt (Edwards) Thurston of Otisfield, Me.;.born there Oct. 19, 1837; married, in Mercer, Me., July 3, 1864, LAURA A. PIERCE, born in Otisfield, Me., in 1844, daughter of Calvin and Julia Ann (Swan) Pierce of Solon, Me.

Mr. Thurston is a master mechanic in the Little Androscoggin Water Power Company at Auburn, Me., 1877; belongs to the Universalist denomination and his wife is a Congregationalist.

### Children, born in Lewiston, Me.:

9792 Marion Frances.[9] b. Nov. 12, 1865.
9793 Herbert Russell,[9] b. March 24, 1869.

## 9033

ELIZA ANN THURSTON [8] (*Luke,*[7] *Daniel,*[6] *Dea. Daniel,*[5] *Daniel,*[4] *Thomas,*[3] *Thomas,*[2] *John*[1]), daughter of Luke[7] and Olive (Clark) Thurston of Walpole, N. H.; born there May 30, 1825; married, Jan. 13, 1853, ERI RICHARDSON, born April 6, 1825, son of Barzilla and Lydia (Foster) Richardson of Keene, N. H.

Mr. Richardson was wood contractor on the I. C. & L. R. R.; is a justice of the peace, school director, and member of the Baptist church in Delhi, Hamilton county, Ohio, 1877.

### Children:

9794 Gratia Ann (Richardson). b. in Troy, N. H., March 22, 1855; graduated from the Hughes high school in Cincinnati, Ohio, 1874, and from the normal school 1875.
9795 Alice Olive (Richardson), b. at Hazel Green, Delaware county, Iowa, Aug. 29. 1857; graduated from Hughes high school 1877.
9796 Leslie Thurston (Richardson), b. at Hazel Green Feb. 14, 1859; graduated from Hughes high school 1876, has since attended Cincinnati university.
9797 Eva Lydia (Richardson), b. at St. Paul, Ind., Nov. 10, 1862.
9798 Gertrude Agnes (Richardson), b. at Harrison, Ohio, Nov. 9, 1864.
9799 Dora Belle (Richardson), b. at Delhi, Ohio, Oct. 12, 1867.

## 9036

NAHUM THURSTON [8] (*Nahum,*[7] *Daniel,*[6] *Dea. Daniel,*[5] *Daniel,*[4] *Thomas,*[3] *Thomas,*[2] *John*[1]), son of Nahum[7] and Martha (Rice)

Thurston of Union, Me.; born there June 2, 1824; married, Oct. 6, 1847, ANN ELIZABETH COLE, born in Hope, Me., Oct. 20, 1824, daughter of Joseph and Abigail Cole of Union. Joseph Cole was born in Medfield, Mass., and died in 1849. Abigail Cole was born in Framingham, Mass., and died March, 1873.

Mr. Thurston is a farmer in Union; has held the office of constable eight years, county sheriff twelve years, and United States deputy marshal five years.

### Children, born in Union:

9804 Ella Manerva,[9] b. April 22, 1849; m. Oct. 5, 1871, Alanson Coggan, son of William Coggan of Union; they have:
9805   *Ada Athelda* (Coggan),  } twins, b. May 12, 1873.
9806   *Ida Aleda* (Coggan),  }
+9807 Frank Warren,[9] b. Dec. 2, 1850.
9808 Ethel Erastus,[9] b. Feb. 6, 1852; a lumberman in Nevada county, Cal.
9809 Leroy Augustus,[9] b. Oct. 28, 1853; a lumberman, has a ranch in Cherokee; his post-office address is Patterson, Nevada county, Cal.; m. Mar., 1877, Emma Hawley of North Columbia, Cal. Mrs. Thurston is a lady of literary taste and writes for the papers.
9810 Ida Carrie,[9] b. April 8, 1856.
9811 Willie La Forest,[9] b. Oct. 18, 1859; a lumberman in Nevada county.

## 9042

CAROLINE ANTINETTE THURSTON [8] (*Nahum,*[7] *Daniel,*[6] *Dea. Daniel,*[5] *Daniel,*[4] *Thomas,*[3] *Thomas,*[2] *John*[1]), sister of the preceding, and daughter of Nahum [7] and Martha (Rice) Thurston of Union, Me.; born there Jan. 2, 1829; married, Nov. 29, 1850, STILLMAN NYE, born April 30, 1822, son of Stillman and Mary (Sargus) Nye.

Mr. Nye is a farmer and butcher in Union.

### Children, all born in Union:

9816 Emily Caroline (Nye), b. Sept. 22, 1855; d. Nov. 30, 1869.
9817 Abbie Florence (Nye), b. Nov. 19, 1856.
9818 Frank Everett (Nye), b. Dec. 20, 1857; d. Dec. 2, 1860.
9819 Martha Elizabeth (Nye), b. March 26, 1859; d. Aug. 11, 1860.
9820 Nellie May (Nye), b. Jan. 9, 1862.

## 9043

PHILO THURSTON [8] (*Philo,*[7] *Daniel,*[6] *Dea. Daniel,*[5] *Daniel,*[4] *Thomas,*[3] *Thomas,*[2] *John*[1]), eldest son of Philo [7] and Julia Maria (Daniels) Thurston of Union, Me.; born there Sept. 22, 1819; married, Jan. 11, 1844, OLIVE ROBBINS, daughter of David and Lydia (Maxey) Robbins of Union.

Mr. Thurston is an iron founder and machinist in Rockland, Me., where he has lived since 1853. He has been in city council two years and alderman seven years.

### Child, born in Union:

9825 Willis E.,[9] b. Oct. 19, 1849; d. March 21, 1862.

## 9045

REV. ALBERT THURSTON [8] (*Philo,*[7] *Daniel,*[6] *Dea. Daniel,*[5] *Daniel,*[4] *Thomas,*[3] *Thomas,*[2] *John*[1]), brother of the preceding, and son of Philo [7] and Julia Maria (Daniels) Thurston of Union, Me.; born there

July 19, 1824; married, April 9, 1848, LAVINIA ANTHONY HAWES, born in Appleton, Me., July 20, 1825, daughter of Otis and Elsie (Davis) Hawes of Union.

Mr. Thurston was a farmer, and traveling preacher in the Methodist church till the last two years of his life, when he was a local preacher in Union, and died there Jan. 20, 1869. He was on the school committee in 1848.

Children:

9827 Charles Albert,[9] b. Feb. 20, 1849; d. Dec. 27, 1850.
9828 Irville Clinton,[9] b. June 14, 1850; m. Clara Ella Larrabee, b. in Freedom, Me., March, 1850, daughter of Sewall and Mary Jane (Larrabee) Larrabee of Frankfort, Me. He is a machinist by trade, worked in Lawrence, Mass., six years, till 1874, when he returned to Union and went into the manufacture of caskets and coffins with his brother Joseph D.
9829 Julia Lavinia,[9] b. Jan. 30, 1852; d. Jan. 29, 1865.
9830 Charles Albert,[9] b. April 2, 1854; m. Oct. 30, 1875, Adelia Perry, b. Mar. 31, 1857, daughter of Thomas Abner and Margaret Orinda (Norwood) Perry of Rockland, Me. He is a truckman in Union. They have:
    9831 Wilber Charlie,[10] b. Aug. 8, 1876.
9832 Joseph Daniels,[9] b. Oct. 17, 1855; n m. He carried on the farm with his brother Charles Albert till 1872, when he went to Augusta, Me., and learned cabinet making with his uncle, I. C. Hovey. In 1874 returned to Union and went into business with his brother Irville C. in the manufacture of caskets and coffins.
9833 Willie,[9] b. Dec. 16, 1856; d. Dec. 20, 1856.

## 9046

NATHANIEL EMMONS THURSTON [8] (*Philo,[7] Daniel,[6] Dea. Daniel,[5] Daniel,[4] Thomas,[3] Thomas,[2] John[1]*), brother of the preceding, and son of Philo[7] and Julia Maria (Daniels) Thurston of Union, Me.; born there Nov. 12, 1826; married, June 17, 1851, SARAH HILLS, born March 24, 1830, daughter of Samuel and Sarah B. (Rogers) Hills of Union. Samuel Hills was born in Danville, N. H., and Sarah B. Rogers was born in Marshfield, Mass.

Mr. Thurston says he is a "farmer and an independent man, belonging to no church or society whatever," residing in Union.

Children:

9837 Herbert Melville,[9] b. Jan. 8, 1853; m. in Everett, Mass., Dec. 25, 1875, Martha Emery Fall, b. in Lebanon, Me., Nov. 1, 1855, daughter of Sylvester and Catherine (Hanscom) Fall of Chelsea, Mass. He is proprietor of Thurston's Express, running between Everett and Boston; residence Everett. They have:
    9838 Maud Adele.[10] b. Jan. 10, 1877.
9839 Joseph Daniels,[9] b. Sept. 25, 1854; d. Oct. 19, 1854.
9840 Arthur Roberts,[9] b. Aug. 12, 1856; d. Jan. 18, 1865.
9841 Flora Emma,[9] b. April 9, 1859; d. March 4, 1861.
9842 Ralph.[9] b. Jan. 5, 1861.
9843 Carl Walton,[9] b. Nov. 23, 1863.
9844 George,[9] b. Aug. 2, 1866.
9845 Julia Maria,[9] b. Nov. 13, 1869.
9846 Philo,[9] b. Sept. 3, 1871.

## 9054

WILLIAM JOHNSON THURSTON [8] (*Johnson,[7] Daniel,[6] Dea. Daniel,[5] Daniel,[4] Thomas,[3] Thomas,[2] John[1]*), son of Johnson[7] and Loee (Starrett) Thurston of Appleton, Me.; born there Jan. 22, 1826; married, first, Nov. 12, 1851, MARTHA RUSS, born in Washington, Me., March 12, 1829, daughter of William and Nancy (Cunningham) Russ of

27

Belfast, Me.; she died Aug. 23, 1860. Second, March 22, 1861, MARTHA JANE PHILBRICK, born May 23, 1833, daughter of Walter and Rachel (Walton) Philbrick of Rockland, Me.

Mr. Thurston is a cooper in Rockland. He enlisted in the army against the rebellion and served in the 28th Maine regiment as an orderly sergeant; member of Rockland city council from 1869 to 1873, and a representative in the legislature in 1873.

His children, by second wife, Martha Jane:

9850 Flora Evelyn,[9] b. Oct. 6, 1862.
9851 William Philbrick,[9] b. Oct. 17, 1864.
9852 Clinton Augustus,[9] b. Sept. 23. 1866.
9853 Walter Johnson,[9] b. Nov. 23, 1869; d. Dec. 12, 1869.
9854 Walter Ernest,[9] b. Sept. 25, 1873; d. Sept. 26, 1874.
9855 Frank,[9] b. Aug. 3, 1876.

## 9059

MILTON THURSTON [8] (*Johnson*,[7] *Daniel*,[6] *Dea. Daniel*,[5] *Daniel*,[4] *Thomas*,[3] *Thomas*,[2] *John*[1]), brother of the preceding, and son of Johnson[7] and Loee (Starrett) Thurston of Appleton, Me.; born there Jan. 19, 1837; married, Dec. 22, 1866, at Gloucester, Mass., CAROLINE STONE PERKINS, born July 25, 1844, daughter of Christopher Gore and Catherine (Stone) Perkins of Kennebunkport, Me.

Mr. Thurston is a farmer and cooper in Appleton; served in the late rebellion, and received a medal of honor from congress.

Children:

9860 Nellie Loee,[9] b. in Kennebunkport Nov. 16, 1868.
9861 Hattie Dickens,[9] b. in Gloucester, Mass., March 19, 1871.
9862 George Carpenter,[9] b. in Appleton Feb. 22, 1873.
9863 Carrie Lillian,[9] b. in Appleton Nov. 21, 1876.
9864 Alice Gertrude,[9] b. June 29, 1879.

## 9062

ALBERT LLEWELLYN THURSTON [8] (*Johnson*,[7] *Daniel*,[6] *Dea. Daniel*,[5] *Daniel*,[4] *Thomas*,[3] *Thomas*,[2] *John*[1]), brother of the preceding, and son of Johnson[7] and Loee (Starrett) Thurston of Appleton, Me.; born there Feb. 23, 1847; married, Dec. 1, 1872, EMILY JANE JACKSON, born Aug. 26, 1851, daughter of Greenleaf and Betsey (Jackson) Jackson of Naples, Me. He is a cooper in Appleton.

Child, born in Appleton:

9868 Albert Leon,[9] b. Nov. 21, 1874.

## 9097

JESSE MILLER (*Levina Thurston*,[7] *Abijah*,[6] *Dea. Daniel*,[5] *Daniel*,[4] *Thomas*,[3] *Thomas*,[2] *John*[1]), son of Jesse and Levina (Thurston) Miller of Sheldonville, Mass.; born there Aug. 20, 1811; married, first, April 2, 1834, SUSAN R. RHOADES, daughter of Aaron and Sally (Hawkins) Rhoades of Wrentham, Mass.; she died Jan. 7, 1870. Second, Dec. 26, 1870, SUSAN W. WALTZE of Augusta, Me.

Mr. Miller was a manufacturer of proprietary medicines in Providence, R. I., till Jan. 1, 1877, when they removed their manufactory to Boston, Mass., nearly opposite the Norfolk House, Roxbury dis-

trict. Two sons associated with him in this business are Lyman G. and Bradford T., under the firm name of Dr. J. Miller & Sons & Co. His residence is Sheldonville, where he has been a deacon of the Baptist church for thirty-eight years.

His children, all by first wife :

9870 Mary Eliza (Miller), b. Sept., 1836; m. 1856, Daniel L. Willard, and had two sons, died young. She died Sept. 28, 1863; he died Aug. 22, 1864.
9871 Susan Josephine (Miller), b. Aug. 20, 1841; m. Aug. 27, 1865, Benjamin Collins, and had :
    9872 *Benjamin Miller* (Collins), b. July 6, 1866.
9873 Lyman Gilmore (Miller), b. Sept. 29, 1845; m. April 24, 1865, Gertrude E. Page. He is in business with his father and lives in Boston. They have :
    9874 *Anna S.* (Miller), b. Oct. 12, 1867.
    9875 *Nellie* (Miller), b. Oct. 16, 1869.
    9876 *Mabel Maud* (Miller), b. June 25, 1871.
9877 Bradford Thurston (Miller), b. Sept. 27, 1850; m. Jan. 1, 1871, Helen Foster Norton. He is in company with his father and brother, and lives in Attleborough, Mass. They have :
    9878 *Jessie May* (Miller), b. Sept. 12, 1873.

## 9099

CHARLOTTE MILLER (*Levina Thurston,[7] Abijah,[6] Dea. Daniel,[5] Daniel,[4] Thomas,[3] Thomas,[2] John[1]*), sister of the preceding, and daughter of Jesse and Levina (Thurston) Miller of Sheldonville, Mass.; born there Aug. 20, 1819; married, Nov. 15, 1838, WILLARD CLARK WHITING. She died June 7, 1843. Mr. Whiting married, second, 1848, Sarah O. Hancock of Wrentham, Mass., and adopted a daughter, Anna Olivia Whiting, born Dec. 9, 1846, who married Daniel Bennett of Wrentham and had Willard Francis (Bennett), born Sept. 4, 1874, died Nov. 26, 1876; Alice Bradford (Bennett), born Nov. 25, 1876.

Mr. Whiting is a farmer in South Franklin, Mass. In 1856 he was chosen deacon of the Congregational church there, which office he now holds, 1879.

Children :

9880 Daniel Willard (Whiting), b. Oct. 12, 1839. He enlisted Oct. 30, 1861, in the 23d Massachusetts regiment and served during the war of the rebellion; m. 1st, Nov. 19, 1863, Abby Sophia Summer of Foxborough, Mass.; she died Feb. 19, 1865; 2d, Nov. 19, 1876, Estelle N. Briggs of Franklin. Children :
    9881 *Florence Levina* (Whiting), b. Jan. 14, 1864; d. same day.
    9882 *Mertievara Almira* (Whiting), b. March 3, 1877.
9883 Eunice Levina (Whiting), b. Aug. 19, 1841; d. in infancy.
9884 Gilmore Miller (Whiting), b. May 25, 1843; d. in infancy.

## 9176

ABIGAIL BROWN THURSTON[8] (*Joseph,[7] Joseph,[6] Joseph,[5] Daniel,[4] Thomas,[3] Thomas,[2] John[1]*), daughter of Joseph[7] and Lucy Bucknam (Davis) Thurston of Worcester, Mass.; born in Leicester, Mass., April 4, 1827; married, in Paxton, Mass., Oct. 4, 1843, EZRA KENT, born July 8, 1818, son of Ezra and Eusebia (Southwick) Kent, of Wallingford, Vt.

Mr. Kent's father died Feb. 3, 1818, and after two years his mother took him with three other children to Worcester to her sister's, Abigail Southwick, where her father and mother lived, they being old

people and past labor, and she died Nov. 9, 1820, leaving him in the care of this aunt, where he remained till he was eight years old, when he went on to a farm in Paxton and worked till he was eighteen. In 1851 he went to Worcester; worked in a stable about two years, then learned the trade of shoemaking; was on the Worcester police off and on for nearly three years. In 1859 purchased a team and has since been driving a baggage and express wagon.

Children:

9888 Joseph Harrison (Kent), b. in Paxton June 8, 1847; killed on the railroad Nov. 8, 1864, aged 17.
9889 Ada Flora (Kent), b. in Worcester Oct. 26, 1855; m. in Worcester Oct. 21, 1873, Lewis C. Batson, b. in New Castle, N. H., Dec. 20, 1842, a machinist. They have:
9890 *Frankie Lewis* (Batson), b. May 7, 1877.

### 9177

JONATHAN HUBBARD THURSTON [8] (*Joseph,*[7] *Joseph,*[6] *Joseph,*[5] *Daniel,*[4] *Thomas,*[3] *Thomas,*[2] *John*[1]), brother of the preceding, and son of Joseph[7] and Lucy Bucknam (Davis) Thurston of Worcester, Mass.; born in Paxton, Mass., Oct. 11, 1829; married, April 10, 1851, MARIA LOUISA WHITTEMORE, born in Charlton, Mass., daughter of Charles and Mary (Parker) Whittemore of Leicester, Mass. Mr. Whittemore died Dec. 16, 1873.

Mr. Thurston was a merchant and selectman of Leicester, Mass. He went to Passaic city, N. J., where he was a deacon in the North Reformed church and city councilman. He left there and is now, 1877, in Lincoln, Sussex county, Del., and member of the Presbyterian church iu Milford, Del.

Children:

9894 Effie Gertrude,[9] b. in Leicester Sept. 6, 1855.
9895 Inez May,[9] b. in New York city Feb. 10, 1864.
9896 Mabel Louise,[9] b. in Passaic city Sept. 30, 1869.

### 9178

DEA. LYMAN DAVIS THURSTON [8] (*Joseph,*[7] *Joseph,*[6] *Joseph,*[5] *Daniel,*[4] *Thomas,*[3] *Thomas,*[2] *John*[1]), brother of the preceding, and son of Joseph[7] and Lucy Bucknam (Davis) Thurston of Worcester, Mass.; born in Paxton, Mass., Sept. 8, 1832; married, first, March 15, 1854, HANNAH SMITH LYON; she died May 1, 1864, aged 31 y. 3 m. 21 d. Second, Sept. 21, 1865, MARY ELIZABETH DENNY, born March 22, 1834, daughter of Joseph Addison and Mary (Davis) Denny of Leicester, Mass. Mr. Denny died 1875; his ancestors came from Coombs, England, and he visited the old homestead in 1874 and found it still in the hands of the Denny family.

Mr. Thurston is a merchant in Leicester; has been postmaster since 1861; elected town clerk March, 1879; deacon of the first Congregational church.

His children, by first wife, Hannah:

9900 Newbirt Augustus,[9] b. May 21, 1855; d. Sept. 2, 1855.
9901 Joseph Lyman,[9] b. May 23, 1859; d. May 24, 1864.

By second wife, Mary:

9902 Carrie Louise,[9] b. March 21, 1869.
9903 Mary Davis,[9] b. Sept. 16, 1872.

## 9186

LEVI SHERMAN THURSTON[8] (*Daniel,*[7] *Joseph,*[6] *Joseph,*[5] *Daniel,*[4] *Thomas,*[3] *Thomas,*[2] *John*[1]), son of Daniel[7] and Patty Allen (Ross) Thurston of West Brookfield, Mass.; born there Aug. 5, 1828; married, April 8, 1851, ESTHER KEEP, born April 8, 1829, daughter of William E. and Polly (Wood) Keep of Oakham, Mass.

Mr. Thurston is a farmer and milkman, a deacon in the Congregational church in North Brookfield, Mass.

### Children:

9907 Daniel Sherman,[9] b. Nov. 7, 1853; a grocer in West Brookfield, firm of Thurston & Sibley; m. April 15. 1875, Thankful Hobbs. They had:
    9908 *Arthur Hobbs,*[10] b. March 14, 1877; d. Aug. 27, 1877.
9909 Edward Eaton,[9] b. Dec. 13, 1860.

## 9201

DR. DAVID STANTON THURSTON[8] (*Henry,*[7] *David,*[6] *Israel,*[5] *John,*[4] *Benjamin,*[3] *Joseph,*[2] *John*[1]), son of Henry[7] and Cassandra (Elliott) Thurston of Jacobsburgh, Belmont county, Ohio; born there Dec. 22, 1823; married, April 23, 1846, JANE WHITE LINGO, born in Barnesville, Belmont county, Ohio, Nov. 24, 1827, daughter of Gideon and Mary (Boyd) Lingo.

Mr. Thurston was a school teacher from the age of eighteen for eighteen years, during which time he studied medicine. In 1859 he moved to St. Clairsville, the county seat of Belmont county, and served for four years as sheriff. In 1863 he moved to Newark, Licking county, Ohio, and opened a drug store, in company with J. W. Collins, under the firm name of Collins & Thurston, where he is, 1879.

### Children, born in Jacobsburgh:

9914 William Henry,[9] b. Jan. 28, 1847; m. June 21, 1869, Augusta McCrum, b. Feb. 9, 1847; no children.
9915 Elizabeth Josephene,[9] b. June 29, 1849; d. Sept. 18, 1849.
9916 Mary Cassandra,[9] b. Dec. 30. 1850.
9917 Frank Albert,[9] b. Jan. 18, 1855.
9918 Emma Jane,[9] b. April 27, 1857; d. Dec. 20, 1857.
9919 James Milton,[9] b. Nov. 9, 1859.

## 9222

EDWARD M. THURSTON[8] (*Flavel,*[7] *David,*[6] *Israel,*[5] *John,*[4] *Benjamin,*[3] *Joseph,*[2] *John*[1]), eldest son of Flavel[7] and Eleanor (Mercer) Thurston of Sheffield, Ill.; born Sept. 29, 1824; married, first, MARY ——; second, SARAH ——. He is a real estate broker in Davenport, Iowa.

### Children:

9924 William F.,[9] b. Sept. 18, 1852.
9925 Cory A.,[9] b. Aug. 26, 1859.

## 9229

DAVID THURSTON[8] (*Flavel,*[7] *David,*[6] *Israel,*[5] *John,*[4] *Benjamin,*[3] *Joseph,*[2] *John*[1]), brother of the preceding, and son of Flavel[7] and Eleanor (Mercer) Thurston of Sheffield, Ill.; born 1832; married ELEANOR ——. He is a farmer in Sheffield.

Children :

9930   Mary Jane,[9] b. 1858.
9931   Wilson,[9] b. 1860.
9932   Delkar,[9] b. 1864.
9933   Henry,[9] b. 1869.
9934   Emily,[9] b. 1872.

## 9230

JOHN FLAVEL THURSTON [8] (*Flavel,*[7] *David,*[6] *Israel,*[5] *John,*[4] *Benjamin,*[3] *Joseph,*[2] *John*[1]), brother of the preceding, and son of Flavel[7] and Eleanor (Mercer) Thurston of Sheffield, Ill.; born in Belmont county, Ohio, Feb. 12, 1834; married, July 4, 1857, MARY SMITH, born at Princeton, Ill., Dec. 13, 1840, daughter of Noahdiah and Rebecca (Patten) Smith.

Mr. Thurston is a farmer in Manlius, Bureau county, Ill.; is a member of the Wesleyan Methodist church, of which he is clerk, and is school director.

Children :

9939   Edwin Rebecca,[9] b. March 20, 1861.
9940   Nelly Arloa,[9] b. Aug. 26, 1862.
9941   Loren Elzea,[9] b. Jan. 21, 1867.
9942   Clara Adelia,[9] b. Jan. 26, 1869.
9943   Caroline Amelia,[9] b. Feb. 27, 1871.
9944   Etta May,[9] } twins, b. July 27, 1873.
9945   Elmer Day,[9] }

## 9235

HENRY THURSTON [8] (*David,*[7] *David,*[6] *Israel,*[5] *John,*[4] *Benjamin,*[3] *Joseph,*[2] *John*[1]), eldest son of David[7] and Esther (Stanbrook) Thurston of Black Ash, Pa.; born in Crawford county, Pa., Dec. 23, 1824; married, first, March 12, 1848, ANGELINE STRAYER, born in Crawford county March 6, 1830, died Sept. 1, 1856; second, July 16, 1857, ADELIA DICKERSON, born in Crawford county Nov. 25, 1829.

Mr. Thurston is a carpenter in Corry, Erie county, Pa.

His children, by first wife, Angeline :

9950   Allen,[9] b. Jan. 7, 1849; d. Sept. 4, 1850.
9951   Flora,[9] b. Jan. 2, 1851; m. Wilson Reynolds, a barber in Knoxville, Steuben county, N.Y. They have Maud, William, Fred and George (Reynolds).
9952   Hattie,[9] m. Emery Mayer, a cooper in Cochranton, Crawford county, Pa.; no children.
9953   Crawford,[9] b. Oct. 30, 1852; m. Elah Snapp; is a butcher in Spartansburgh, Crawford county, Pa. They have:
    9954   *Maud Crawford.*[10]
9955   David,[9] b. April 11, 1854; d. March 21, 1857.
9956   Angeline Esther,[9] b. July 25, 1856.

By second wife, Adelia :

9957   Asena,[9] b. Jan. 16, 1859.
9958   Joseph Ellsworth,[9] b. Dec. 8, 1861; a telegraph operator, living with his parents.
9959   Wave,[9] b. March 19, 1865.
9960   Mack,[9] b. March 19, 1867; d. Aug. 22, 1867.
9961   Alena,[9] b. Oct. 3, 1869.
9962   Harry,[9] b. July 17, 1875.

## 9237

EPHRAIM EDGAR THURSTON [8] (*David,*[7] *David,*[6] *Israel,*[5] *John,*[4] *Benjamin,*[3] *Joseph,*[2] *John*[1]), brother of the preceding, and son of David[7]

and Abigail (Spring) Thurston of Black Ash, Pa.; born in Crawford county, Pa., May 5, 1840; married, Feb. 13, 1868, SARAH FRANCES JONES, born April 20, 1851.

Mr. Thurston is a farmer at Wilson's Mills, Venango county, Pa.

Children :

9964   William David,[9] b. Dec. 11, 1868.
9965   Mary Abigail,[9] b. Jan. 28, 1872.

## 9282

SAMUEL DAVID THURSTON [8] (*William,*[7] *Samuel,*[6] *Israel,*[5] *John,*[4] *Benjamin,*[3] *Joseph,*[2] *John*[1]), son of William[7] and Mary (Telfor) Thurston of Mixersville, Ind.; born there July 20, 1823; married, first, Oct. 9, 1850, JANNET RETHERFORD, born Feb. 7, 1828, daughter of William and Phebe (Long) Retherford; she died Oct. 20, 1859. Second, April 24, 1862, MRS. MARY ELLEN (ROBINSON) FORD, born Feb. 12, 1831, daughter of John and Ann (Young) Robinson of Camden, Ohio.

Mr. Thurston is a merchant tailor and dealer in gents' furnishing goods; has been treasurer of Camden nine years and treasurer of the Masonic lodge for ten years, and has for some years been collecting matter for the genealogy of his ancestors, which has been a very great aid in preparing this branch of it.

His children, by first wife, Jannet:

9970   Angeline Isabella,[9] b. Oct. 17, 1851; m. Sept. 6, 1871, Isaac Shafer, b. Jan. 25, 1848, a farmer in Sardinia, Ind.   Children:
   9971   *Melvin Warren* (Shafer), b. Jan. 20, 1872; d. Aug. 27, 1875.
   9972   *Gurtha Alveno* (Shafer), b. Sept. 28, 1873.
   9973   *Alma Rosella* (Shafer), b. March 25, 1875.
   9974   *Minnie Leizetta* (Shafer), b. June 10, 1877.
9975   Marthy Deetta,[9] b. Feb. 13, 1853; d. Jan. 7, 1866.
9976   Mary Phebe Philena,[9] b. July 10, 1856; d. Sept. 8, 1857.
9977   William Alexandrew,[9] b. July 8, 1858; d. Aug. 7, 1867.

By second wife, Mary:

9978   Harry Hayworth,[9] b. Sept. 10, 1864; d. Jan. 11, 1865.
9979   Oliver Warren,[9] b. July 1, 1867; d. Feb. 10, 1870.
9980   Samuel Ellwood,[9] b. March 20, 1871.

## 9290

JOHN FLINT THURSTON [8] (*Oliver Perry,*[7] *Samuel,*[6] *Israel,*[5] *John,*[4] *Benjamin,*[3] *Joseph,*[2] *John*[1]), eldest son of Oliver Perry[7] and Maria L. (Flint) Thurston of Mixersville, Ind.; born there May 28, 1828; married, Sept. 7, 1852, MARGARET MORRIS, born Sept. 24, 1832, daughter of Enoch and Nancy Morris.

Mr. Thurston is a farmer and stock raiser in Summitville, Madison county, Ind.

Children:

9985   Mary Maria,[9] b. Aug. 10, 1853; m. James Henry Woollen, a farmer in Summitville and dealer in grain, cattle, and hogs for shipping. Children:
   9986   *Ella Bell* (Woollen), b. Oct. 20, 1870.
   9987   *Maggie Viola* (Woollen), b. Oct. 20, 1872.
   9988   *John* (Woollen), b. Nov. 8, 1874.
   9989   *Errick Gilbert* (Woollen), b. March 24, 1876.

9990　Enoch Palmer,⁹ b, Oct. 4, 1854; m. Joanna Runyan; is a farmer and has:
　　9991　*Dory Bell*,¹⁰ b. July 3, 1877.
9992　Nancy Bell,⁹ b. Oct. 19, 1858; m. Joseph Henry Howard, a merchant.
9993　Robert Oliver Perry,⁹ b. March 19, 1861.
9994　George Franklin,⁹ b. Jan. 16, 1864.
9995　Francis Clement,⁹ b. July 2, 1871; d.
9996　Orah Walter,⁹ b. Feb. 18, 1876.

## 9292

SAMUEL THURSTON⁸ (*Oliver Perry*,⁷ *Samuel*,⁶ *Israel*,⁵ *John*,⁴ *Benjamin*,⁸ *Joseph*,² *John*¹), brother of the preceding, and son of Oliver Perry⁷ and Maria L. (Flint) Thurston of Mixersville, Ind.; born there Jan. 4, 1833; married NANCY ——, born Nov. 30, 1838.
　Mr. Thurston is a farmer in Alexandria, Madison county, Ind.

Children:

10,000　Oliver D.,⁹ b. Jan. 30, 1861; d. Jan. 5, 1874.
10,001　Ida M.,⁹ b. Jan. 28, 1865.
10,002　Maria E.,⁹ b. Jan. 22, 1869.
10,003　John W.,⁹ b. Aug. 15, 1871.

## 9295

JOSEPH HUMPHREY THURSTON⁸ (*Oliver Perry*,⁷ *Samuel*,⁶ *Israel*,⁵ *John*,⁴ *Benjamin*,⁸ *Joseph*,² *John*¹), brother of the preceding, and son of Oliver Perry⁷ and Maria L. (Flint) Thurston of Mixersville, Ind.; born there Oct. 22, 1838; married, Oct. 18, 1860, MARY ELIZABETH WELSH, born March 24, 1841.
　Mr. Thurston is a farmer in Summitville, Madison county, Ind.

Children:

10,008　Martha Alice,⁹ b. Sept. 19, 1862.
10,009　John Franklin Perry,⁹ b. Oct. 3, 1865.
10,010　Joseph Elmere,⁹ b. April 11, 1868.
10,011　Walter Brady Scott,⁹ b. Jan. 18, 1871.
10,012　Harvey Allen,⁹ b. March 5, 1875.
10,013　Owen Edwin,⁹ b..Sept. 24, 1879.

## 9305

CALEB THURSTON⁸ (*Israel*,⁷ *John*,⁶ *Israel*,⁵ *John*,⁴ *Benjamin*,⁸ *Joseph*,² *John*¹), eldest son of Israel⁷ and Nancy (Ely) Thurston of Wiley Station, Ohio; born there June 15, 1811; married, first, Sept. 27, 1837, HANNAH VANZANT, born Aug. 26, 1817, daughter of James and Hannah Vanzant; second, June 13, 1858, MARY BUCKINGHAM.
　Mr. Thurston is a carpenter by trade, but for many years has turned his attention to farming at Wiley Station, where he is regarded as a first-class farmer and valuable citizen.

Children:

10,016　Edmond M.,⁹ b. Nov. 12, 1838; m. May 26, 1862, Ellen Peirce. He is
　　　engaged in railroad business in Chicago, Ill. Children:
　　10,017　*Adda*.¹⁰
　　10,018　*Carrie*.¹⁰
　　10,019　*Harry*.¹⁰
　　10,020　*Maud*.¹⁰
10,021　Alvin N.,⁹ b. Sept. 29, 1840; m. Dec. 24, 1866, Lydia Town.. He is en-
　　　gaged in railroad business in Chicago; was in the 5th Ohio cavalry
　　　three years during the war against the rebellion. Children:
　　10,022　*George L.*¹⁰
　　10,023　*Lee W.*¹⁰
　　10,024　*Franklin*.¹⁰

10,025 Almira C.,[9] b. Oct. 22, 1841; m. June 9, 1861, Milton Brawley, a farmer in Darke county, Ohio, b. Feb. 8, 1838. They have :
 10,026 *Charles Caleb* (Brawley), b. May 14, 1862.
 10,027 *Thomas Grant* (Brawley), b. April 13, 1864.
 10,028 *Anna Mary* (Brawley), b. Nov. 5, 1865.
10,029 Urmina Ann,[9] b. Dec. 19, 1842; m. Sept. 30, 1860, Milton M. Buckingham. They have :
 10,030 *Florence Permelia* (Buckingham), b. Aug. 21, 1861.
 10,031 *William Newton* (Buckingham), b. Jan. 25, 1864.
10,032 Maria Frances,[9] b. June 1, 1844; m. Nov. 3, 1864, Charles W. Martin, b. May 10, 1844. They have :
 10,033 *William L.* (Martin), b. July 12, 1870.
 10,034 *Oliver May* (Martin), b. June 12, 1873.
 10,035 *Franklin* (Martin).
10,036 Lyman C.,[9] b. Nov. 26, 1845; m. Aug. 8, 1867, Emma J. Keltner, b. March 21, 1851. He is a farmer in Indiana. They have :
 10,037 *Jerre,*[10] b. May 2, 1868.
 10,038 *Anna Mary,*[10] b. Jan. 16, 1871.
 10,039 *Ida M.*[10]
 10,040 *Dorsey E.*[10]
 10,041 *Iven C.*[10]
10,042 Joshua C.,[9] b. Aug. 13, 1850; a teamster, residing at New Paris, Ohio; m. March 15, 1873, Elizabeth A. Swain, b. Feb. 18, 1854. They have :
 10,043 *William.*[10]
10,044 Oliver H. P.,[9] b. Dec. 4, 1851; a hackman.
10,045 James W. M.,[9] b. April 7, 1854; a farmer at Preble Corner, Ohio; m. Dec. 18, 1877, Sarah E. Miles.
10,046 George W.,[9] b. Nov. 5, 1855; a farmer in Darke county, Ohio.

## 9535

ARTHUR JEFFERSON THURSTON[8] (*David,*[7] *Flavel,*[6] *Israel,*[5] *John,*[4] *Benjamin,*[3] *Joseph,*[2] *John*[1]), son of David[7] and Lurinda (Laing) Thurston of Shelbyville, Ind.; born there April 11, 1849; married, in Johnson county, Ind., May 9, 1875, MARY JANE HACKNEY, born in Edinburgh, Ind., Dec. 12, 1858, daughter of William B. and Elizabeth Jane (Richardson) Hackney.

Mr. Thurston prepared himself for teaching in the Franklin college, 1869–70, which profession he followed till 1877, when he engaged in the sale of agricultural implements, in all of which he has been quite successful. He is a member of the Missionary Baptist church in Shelbyville.

Child :

10,048 Walter Scott,[9] b. Jan. 2, 1878.

## 9570

ALFRED THURSTON[8] (*Eli,*[7] *Ezra,*[6] *James,*[5] *Daniel,*[4] *Daniel,*[3] *Joseph,*[2] *John*[1]), son of Eli[7] and Margaret (Coons) Thurston of Chenango county, N. Y.; born there April 20, 1806; married, in Smyrna, N. Y., Feb. 14, 1834, EMILY O. PIKE, born in Plymouth, N. Y., Oct. 25, 1814.

Mr. Thurston removed to Bowling Green, Wood county, Ohio, in 1835, when it was a wilderness, infested with wolves, Indians, and ignorant people. He is a land owner and broker, and they are members of the Presbyterian church.

Children :

+10,050 Alvan A.,[9] b. March 27, 1836; m. Amelia Clough.
+10,051 Wesley S.,[9] b. June 10, 1838; m. Martha J. Gorrell.
+10,052 Theron Alfred Earl,[9] b. Oct. 1, 1846; m. Edna Pool.

10,053   Roland Stanley,[9] b. Feb. 27, 1852; n.m.; went into the army against the
         rebellion as a drummer when thirteen years of age, and was at Peters-
         burgh when fifteen miles of fatigue trenches were dug in one night.
10,054   Georgiana Udora,[9] b. March 6, 1856; n.m.; is a teacher of vocal and
         instrumental music in Toledo, Ohio, and sings in the choir of the Pres-
         byterian church.

## 9577

DANIEL THURSTON [8] (*Eli,*[7] *Ezra,*[6] *James,*[5] *Daniel,*[4] *Daniel,*[3] *Joseph,*[2]
*John*[1]), brother of the preceding, and son of Eli[7] and Margaret
(Coons) Thurston of Chenango county, N. Y.; born there Feb. 1,
1820; married, in Indiana, —— JACKMAN. He was killed in a well.

Child:

10,059   Calvin H.[9]

## 9583

CYRUS THURSTON [8] (*Azor,*[7] *Ebenezer,*[6] *Cyrus,*[5] *Daniel,*[4] *Daniel,*[3] *Joseph,*[2] *John*[1]), son of Azor[7] and Elebedy (Smith) Thurston of Oxford, Ohio; born in Luzerne county, Pa., Aug. 14, 1825; married,
June 8, 1848, HANNAH BOONE WOOLVERTON, born in Shamokin, Pa.,
daughter of Jonathan and Ann (Boone) Woolverton of Groton, Erie
county, Ohio.

Mr. Thurston is a farmer in Galien, Berrien county, Mich. He is
township superintendent of schools and a member of the Latter Day
Saints church.

Children:

10,064   Selina,[9] b. at Oxford July 4, 1849; m. Aug. 12, 1872, Maurice Herbert
         Baum; d. at Gibson's Station, Lake county, Ind., July 6, 1874.
10,065   Albert Vastine,[9] b. in La Grange county, Ind., Sept. 18, 1852; m. at New
         Buffalo, Berrien county, Mich., July 4, 1873, Ella Johnson. They re-
         side in Galien and have:
         10,066   *Elmar,*[10] b. July 5, 1876.
10,067   Flora Alice,[9] b. March 21, 1855; d. June 3, 1857.
10,068   Elizabeth,[9] b. in Galien Sept. 27, 1856; m. May 11, 1876, Maurice Her-
         bert Baum, agent and operator for the M. C. R. R. at Three Oaks,
         Berrien county, Mich. They have:
         10,069   *Lina Allah* (Baum), b. June 19, 1877.
10,070   Ida Belle,[9] b. in Oxford March 9, 1858.
10,071   Allah,[9] b. in Galien Sept. 3, 1860; d. June 22, 1863.
10,072   Moroni,[9] b. in Galien March 10, 1862; d. March 30, 1863.
10,073   Cyrus Milton,[9] b. in Galien April 15, 1865.
10,074   Jennie Lillian,[9] b. in Galien Nov. 10, 1868.

## 9586

ASHER THURSTON [8] (*Azor,*[7] *Ebenezer,*[6] *Cyrus,*[5] *Daniel,*[4] *Daniel,*[3] *Joseph,*[2] *John*[1]), brother of the preceding, and son of Azor[7] and Elebedy (Smith) Thurston of Oxford, Ohio; born there March 4, 1839;
married, first, Sept. 17, 1857, MAHALA MONTROSS, born Sept. 6, 1835,
daughter of Elijah and Abby (Hedstal) Montross of Bowman's Creek,
Pa.; she died May 17, 1874. Second, Dec. 22, 1875, MARY JANE
NORTON, born Oct. 16, 1849, daughter of Galen and Martha (Paine)
Norton of South Toledo, Ohio.

Mr. Thurston is a farmer in Grand Rapids, Wood county, Ohio,
where he went when the country was new.

His children, by first wife, Mahala:

10,080   Ella,⁹ b. in Erie county, Ohio, May 12, 1859.
10,081   Azor.⁹ b. Jan. 6, 1861.
10,082   Willard.⁹ b. Dec. 14, 1865; d. Oct. 17, 1866.
10,083   Myrtie Blanch,⁹ b. July 10, 1870; d. Jan. 19, 1871.

## 9593

DANIEL MARVIN THURSTON⁸ (*Ebenezer,*⁷ *Ebenezer,*⁶ *Cyrus,*⁵ *Daniel,*⁴ *Daniel,*³ *Joseph,*² *John* ¹), eldest son of Ebenezer⁷ and Hannah (Albro) Thurston of Scott, La Grange county, Ind.; born in Wilkesbarre, Luzerne county, Pa., Aug. 13, 1825; married, first, 1847, LOVINA ALLEN, born Nov. 20, 1828, died Dec. 10, 1850; second, October, 1851, EMILY FORD, born Oct. 14, 1827, daughter of Edward and Eleanor (Jenks) Ford.

Mr. Thurston was a farmer in Indiana; in 1859 sold and moved to South Missouri, where he bought a farm in 1861, since which he has become a farmer and stock raiser at Walnut Grove Farm, six miles west of Parsons, Labette county, Kansas; is a deacon in the Baptist church; was born with a vail over his face, and has visions corresponding, as he thinks, to those of John the revelator.

His children, by first wife, Lovina:

10,088   Frances Adaline,⁹ b. in Ohio Dec. 7, 1848; m. Lewis Krager, a farmer in Bynumville, Chariton county, Mo.; two children.
10,089   Hannah Lovina,⁹ b. in Ohio July 16, 1850; m. Aaron Reed, a farmer in Scott.

By second wife, Emily:

+10,090   Daniel Edward,⁹ b. May 12, 1852; m. Isadora Forestina Stowe.
10,091   Elizabeth Eleanora,⁹ b. in Indiana Sept. 20, 1854; m. Charles Stott Thurston [see no. 9370].
10,092   Clara Jane,⁹ b. Feb. 8, 1856; m. Worthington Meixwell, a lumber merchant in Parsons, Kansas; they have:
      10,093   *John Lewis* (Meixwell).
10,094   Cyrus Ebenezer,⁹ b. Aug. 17, 1858; a farmer in Parsons.
10,095   Mary Emily,⁹ b. in Iowa June 5, 1861.
10,096   Calvin Marvin,⁹ b. Sept. 25, 1863.
10,097   George Washington,⁹ b. Oct. 10, 1865.
10,098   Alice Caroline,⁹ b. Oct. 28, 1868.
10,099   William Ford,⁹ b. in Kansas July 11, 1871; killed by kick of a mule Feb. 12, 1876.
10,100   William Ford,⁹ b. Feb. 12, 1877.

## 9619

WILLIAM HENRY THURSTON⁸ of Milwaukee, Wis. (*David,*⁷ *David,*⁶ *Daniel,*⁵ *Daniel,*⁴ *Daniel,*³ *Daniel,*² *John* ¹), third child and eldest son of David⁷ and Sophia (Curtis) Thurston of Newton, Ohio; born there Sept. 1, 1836; married, first, Jan. 1, 1856, MARY VAN ALSTYNE, eldest daughter of Lawrence Van Alstyne of Oakland county, Mich.; he separated from her Oct. 3, 1863. Second, ELIZABETH HARGER.

Mr. Thurston is engaged in oyster packing, having a large packing establishment in Maryland, from which he supplies a great portion of the retail trade of the North West, having his headquarters for distribution in Milwaukee, Wis. He moved from Ohio to Albion, N. Y., thence to Farmington, Oakland county, Mich., thence to Kenosha, Wis., and thence to Milwaukee, where he now resides. He is a member of the Methodist church.

His children, by first wife, Mary:

10,105 Clara,[9] b. in Michigan Nov. 13, 1858.
10,106 Infant, b. and d. in 1859.
10,107 Harry,[9] b. in Michigan Dec., 1860; d. 1874.

## 9620

ALONZO LOOMIS THURSTON [8] of Knowlesville, Orleans county, N. Y. (*David,*[7] *David,*[6] *Daniel,*[5] *Daniel,*[4] *Daniel,*[3] *Daniel,*[2] *John*[1]), brother of the preceding, and son of David[7] and Sophia (Curtis) Thurston of Newton, Ohio; born there July 15, 1838; married, February, 1863, PHEBE FLANSBURG, born at Fort Plain, Montgomery county, N. Y., Jan. 7, 1844, daughter of Charles Flansburg of Eagle Harbor, Orleans county, N. Y. Mr. Thurston is a butcher.

Children :

10,112 Catharine Jane,[9] b. Nov. 19. 1863; d. March 20, 1868.
10,113 Smith,[9] b. Oct. 7, 1865; d. Oct. 14, 1865.
10,114 Hattie Sophia,[9] b. Oct. 7, 1866.
10,115 William Fenn,[9] b. Jan. 16, 1870; d. Jan. 24, 1873.
10,116 Nellie Saville,[9] b. Sept. 25, 1872.
10,117 Alice Maud,[9] b. March 12, 1875.
10,118 Jessie Frances,[9] b. Oct. 15, 1877.

## 9621

JAMES HAMILTON THURSTON [8] of Jamestown, Chautauqua county, N. Y. (*David,*[7] *David,*[6] *Daniel,*[5] *Daniel,*[4] *Daniel,*[3] *Daniel,*[2] *John*[1]), brother of the preceding, and son of David[7] and Sophia (Curtis) Thurston of Newton, Ohio; born there Nov. 6, 1840; married, Sept. 9, 1869, ELEANOR JANE FIELD, born Sept. 9, 1850, only daughter of George Warren and Mary (Kane) Field of New York city. Mr. Field is superintendent of Third avenue railroad.

Mr. Thurston, at the age of thirteen, started out to support and educate himself. He was in Barre, Orleans county, N. Y., Flint, Genesee county, Mich., in 1856, and in Farmington, Oakland county, Mich., 1859; studied dentistry and in 1863 commenced to practice in Titusville, Pa. In 1868 removed to Jamestown, N. Y., where he became acquainted with his future wife. In 1877 sold out a fine practice and engaged in producing oil in the Bradford oil region, Pa., still residing in Jamestown. When his wife was ten years of age she went with her uncle, who was United States Minister to that country under President Lincoln, to Guatamala, Central America, and remained three years with him. She attended school in a convent (the only school in existence there). In 1863 she returned to New York and entered the ladies seminary in Brattleborough, Vt., where she remained till 1867.

Children:

10,123 George Hamilton,[9] b. July 5, 1870; d. July 31, 1872.
10,124 Wallace David,[9] b. Dec. 11, 1875.

## 9625

HORACE FITCH THURSTON [8] of Albion, N. Y. (*Stephen Bailey,*[7] *Caleb Curtiss,*[6] *Daniel,*[5] *Daniel,*[4] *Daniel,*[3] *Daniel,*[2] *John*[1]), son of Stephen Bailey[7] and Juliana (Williams) Thurston of Albion; born there April

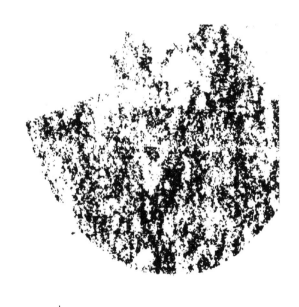

4, 1836; married, first, Jan. 22, 1861, MARY FRANCES KINGSLEY, born May 27, 1841; second, Sept. 15, 1875, MARY L. GOODWIN, born Oct. 31, 1853. He is a farmer, member of the Baptist church.

His children, by first wife, Mary:

10,129    Willie Grant,[9] b. July 12, 1864; d. Jan. 20, 1865.
10,130    Stephen Bradford,[9] b. April 17, 1866.
10,131    Millard Fitch,[9] b. April 23, 1871.

By second wife, Mary:

10,132    Nellie Louise,[9] b. Dec. 22, 1877.

## 9640

ELLIS DAVID THURSTON[8] (*Peter,[7] David,[6] Moses,[5] Daniel,[4] Daniel,[3] Daniel,[2] John[1]*), eldest child of Peter[7] and Anna (Kelsey) Thurston of Garden City, Blue Earth county, Minn.; born in Pittsfield, N. Y., Nov. 10, 1821; married, Aug. 2, 1846, ELEANOR AUGUSTA LYNCH, born in Bainbridge, N. Y., Aug. 28, 1823, daughter of Walter and Linda (Smith) Lynch of Morris, N. Y.

Mr. Thurston is a Methodist Episcopal clergyman, residing in West Dryden, Tompkins county, N. Y.

Children:

10,137    Ellis N.,[9] b. in Richmondville, N. Y., Nov. 24, 1847; d. Dec. 26, 1847.
10,138    Mary Amelia,[9] b. in South New Berlin, N. Y., Feb. 2, 1849; d. in Guilford, N. Y., Aug. 5, 1862.
10,139    Sarah Elizabeth,[9] b. in Coventry, N. Y., May 14, 1850; n.m.
10,140    Rosamond,[9] b. in Bainbridge June 26, 1852; n.m.
10,141    Ellen Julia,[9] b. in Guilford May 13, 1862; d. Sept. 10, 1862.
10,142    Lewis Powell,[9] b. in New Berlin July 10, 1865.

## 9642

JESSE MOSES THURSTON[8] (*Peter,[7] David,[6] Moses,[5] Daniel,[4] Daniel,[3] Daniel,[2] John[1]*), brother of the preceding, and son of Peter[7] and Anna (Kelsey) Thurston of Garden City, Minn.; born in New Lisbon, N. Y., May 14, 1825; married, 1855, ANN ——.

Mr. Thurston is a Baptist clergyman at Redwood Falls, Redwood county, Minn.

Children:

10,147    Lucius.[9]
10,148    Irving.[9]
10,149    Anne E.[9]

## 9656

ALFRED THURSTON[8] (*Gaines,[7] Amos,[6] Amos,[5] Daniel,[4] Daniel,[3] Daniel,[2] John[1]*), son of Gaines[7] and Margaret (Hasbrook) Thurston of New Lisbon, N. Y.; born there Oct. 10, 1843; married, in West Burlington, N. Y., July 24, 1870, MARY ADELIA HAWKINS, born in Pittsfield, N. Y., July 28, 1847, daughter of Emery S. and Lydia (Tory) Hawkins of New Berlin, Chenango county, N. Y.

Mr. Thurston is a commercial traveler, residing in New Lisbon. In 1869–1871 was connected with the firm of Moore & Thurston, general merchandise, in Morris, Otsego county, N. Y. In 1872 sold his interest to his partner, Nathaniel Moore, who failed in about two years, subjecting Mr. Thurston and his father to a heavy loss. He is a member of the Episcopal church.

Children:

10,154   Mary Adeline,⁹ b. May 5, 1871.
10,155   Anna Elizabeth,⁹ b. April 15, 1873.
10,156   James Edward,⁹ b. April 9, 1877.

## 9662

WILLIAM JASON THURSTON ⁸ (*William*,⁷ *Amos*,⁶ *Amos*,⁵ *Daniel*,⁴ *Daniel*,³ *Daniel*,² *John*¹), second child of William ⁷ and Olivia (Draper) Thurston of Norwich, Chenango county, N. Y.; born there Nov. 13, 1834; married, Jan. 18, 1855. HARRIET AMELIA HUNT, born Oct. 9, 1834, daughter of Warren and Esther (Turner) Hunt of Norwich.

Mr. Thurston was a farmer in Pharsalia, Chenango county, N. Y., and now, 1879, in Monroe, Platte county, Neb. He enlisted in the 114th New York regiment against the rebellion. " I served two years, was in the first Fredericksburgh fight under Burnside ; was not strong enough to endure the hardships of army life and was sent to the hospital at Annapolis Junction, where I remained six months,very sick of fever a portion of the time. After the fever left me I was helpless as an infant ; my limbs were like sticks, perfectly useless for more than a year. I finally got better so as to walk without help, but never recovered the full use of myself." He has a pension. They are both members of the Congregational church.

Children:

10,160   Herbert Marelle,⁹ b. in Pharsalia May 29, 1856; m. Oct. 12, 1877, Cynthia A. Jones; they have :
    10,161   *Harriet Amelia*,¹⁰ b. in Monroe July 19 1878.
10,162   Cora Olivia,⁹ b. in Pharsalia April 23, 1858; m. Feb. 23, 1876, William A. Routson; they have :
    10,163   *Howard William* (Routson), b. March 23, 1877.
    10,164   *Daughter*, b. Aug., 1879.
10,165   Harriet Adelaide,⁹ b. in Pharsalia Dec. 27, 1859.
10,166   Ina May,⁹ b. in Norwich June 20, 1866.
10,167   Carrie Esther,⁹ b. in Norwich July 30, 1868.
10,168   Mary Malona,⁹ b. in Norwich Dec. 22, 1871.
10,169   Ida Emogene,⁹ b. in Monroe April 10, 1877; d. Sept. 28, 1877.
10,170   Edwin Jason,⁹ b. in Monroe May 12, 1878.

## 9680

WILLIAM OWEN THURSTON ⁸ (*Rev. Curtis*,⁷ *Ira*,⁶ *Amos*,⁵ *Daniel*,⁴ *Daniel*,³ *Daniel*,² *John*¹), eldest son of Rev. Curtis ⁷ and Julia Ann (Spaulding) Thurston of Athens, Pa.; born there Oct. 21, 1847; married, Jan. 29, 1870, MARY E. ALLEN. He went to Texas; a farmer.

Children:

10,175   Charles Curtis,⁹ b. Sept. 8, 1872.
10,176   Prentice Spaulding.⁹ b. June 5, 1874.
10,177   William Edward,⁹ b. April 8, 1877.

## 9720

ANGELIA LOUISA FRENCH THURSTON ⁸ (*Daniel Sylvester*,⁷ *Timothy*,⁶ *John*,⁵ *Benjamin*,⁴ *Daniel*³), eldest child of Daniel Sylvester and Matilda (Benjamin) Thurston of Montpelier, Vt.; born there Dec. 4, 1837; married, first, FRANK KILGORE, whose father was a Methodist

minister; he died eight months after marriage. Second, Aug. 25, 1859, DAVID NEWMAN, born in New York city.

Mr. Newman lived a year in Cincinnati, Ohio, fifteen years at Beaver Dam, Wis., and for the past five years in Lincoln, Neb., in the dry goods business. He has been fifteen years superintendent of Sunday-school in the Methodist Episcopal church, Grand Worthy Chief Templar in Wisconsin, and Grand Worthy Patriarch.

Mrs. Newman has quite a literary taste and is a lady of great enthusiasm in the work of the Woman's Foreign Missionary Society of the Methodist church, of which she has been state secretary for five years, often speaking on the platform, and is associate editor of the "Heathen Woman's Friend," published at Boston, Mass.

Children:

10,182    Cora Fanny (Newman), b. Nov. 30, 1860.
10,183    Henry Byron (Newman), b. April 10, 1863.

## 9724

JOHN MELLEN THURSTON[8] of Omaha, Neb. (*Daniel Sylvester,*[7] *Timothy,*[6] *John,*[5] *Benjamin,*[4] *Daniel*[3]), brother of the preceding, and son of Daniel Sylvester[7] and Ruth (Town) Thurston of Montpelier, Vt.; born there Aug. 21, 1847; married, in Omaha, Dec. 25, 1872, MARTHA L. POLAND, born at Montpelier May 12, 1848, daughter of Luther and Clara M. (Bennett) Poland of Salt Lake City, Utah.

Mr. Thurston, although a native of Vermont, was transplanted to the West at an early age. His father, a man of limited means, could not afford him the facilities for a higher education, but he managed to overcome these obstacles by working on the farm in the summer and pursuing his studies during the winter. Thus he was enabled to complete a collegiate course, graduating from Wayland (Wis.) university at the age of twenty. Admitted to the bar at twenty-one, he located at Omaha in 1869. He was alderman in 1872, 1873; representative in the legislature 1875, 1876; city attorney of Omaha 1874–1877. While in the legislature he was chairman of the judiciary committee. In 1875 he was nominated for district judge, but was defeated by a very small majority, mostly on account of his youthfulness. July 1, 1877, he accepted the position of first assistant attorney of the Union Pacific railroad.

One child:

10,188    Charles Poland,[9] b. Feb. 7, 1874.

## 9739

JOHN COE THURSTON[8] of Grafton, Mass. (*Calvin Sylvester,*[7] *Daniel,*[6] *John,*[5] *Benjamin,*[4] *Daniel*[3]), eldest son of Calvin Sylvester[7] and Eliza Jencks (Coe) Thurston of Grafton; born there June 20, 1832; married, Mar. 9, 1859, CORDELIA WALKER, born Nov. 24, 1835, daughter of Chester William and Nancy (Claflin) Walker of Upton, Mass.

Mr. Thurston lived for a while in Montreal, Canada, and during the centennial exhibition in Philadelphia in 1876 was agent for the "Pneumatic Fire Extinguisher," having his stand in the Canadian department. He enlisted in the war against the rebellion in the 13th

Massachusetts regiment July 29, 1861, as a musician under Col. Samuel H. Leonard, and was in active service till August, 1862, and was honorably discharged from the hospital in Alexandria, Va., Nov. 19, 1862. In 1877 he went on to his father's farm in Grafton.

Children :

10,193   Wilbur Herbert,[9] b. March 9, 1860.
10,194   Mabel Grace,[9] b. March 26, 1862.
10,195   Sarah Miranda,[9] b. Dec. 27, 1863.
10,196   Lizzie Ada,[9] b. Feb. 2, 1866.
10,197   Susie Arabella,[9] b. Jan. 9, 1868.

## 9740

ISAAC DANIEL THURSTON [8] (*Calvin Sylvester,*[7] *Daniel,*[6] *John,*[5] *Benjamin,*[4] *Daniel*[3]), brother of the preceding, and son of Calvin Sylvester[7] and Eliza Jencks (Coe) Thurston of Grafton, Mass.; born there March 21, 1834; married, Sept. 5, 1858, LAURA ANNA BOYD, born Nov. 11, 1839, daughter of James and Anna (Hitchcock) Boyd of Marlborough, Mass.

Mr. Thurston is a wholesale boot and shoe manufacturer in Lachine, Canada, Province of Quebec.

Children:

10,202   Alice Melinda,[9] b. in Grafton Nov. 18, 1859.
10,203   Florence Boyd,[9] b. in Marlborough Oct. 27, 1862.
10,204   Charles Edward,[9] b. in Montreal Oct. 1, 1865.
10,205   Rosanna Edith,[9] b. in Montreal Jan. 3, 1868.
10,206   Arthur Frederick,[9] b. in Montreal May 17, 1871; d. July 28, 1871.
10,207   Ernest Coe,[9] b. in Montreal June 4, 1873.
10,208   Amy Frances,[9] b. in Montreal Dec. 5, 1875; d. in Lachine Dec. 20, 1876.
10,209   Clinton Salsbury,[9] b. in Lachine March 28, 1879.

## 9741

EDWARD HARRISON THURSTON [8] of Ottawa, Canada (*Calvin Sylvester,*[7] *Daniel,*[6] *John,*[5] *Benjamin,*[4] *Daniel*[3]), brother of the preceding, and son of Calvin Sylvester[7] and Eliza Jencks (Coe) Thurston of Grafton, Mass.; born there April 24, 1836; married, in Marlborough, Mass., May 11, 1867, ADELAIDE LUCRETIA GOOLD, born in Lancaster, Mass., Nov. 18, 1847, daughter of James Edward and Harriet (Hapgood) Goold of Natick, Mass.

Mr. Thurston went to Kansas at the age of twenty-one; was with John Brown at the battle of Ossawatomie, and with Jim Lane at the battle of Black Jack, and in nearly all the engagments between the border ruffians and the advocates of freedom in Kansas on the free side. After all the troubles were settled and Kansas made a free state, he returned to the east and settled in Marlborough, in the manufacture of boots and shoes. He paid $1500 for a substitute in the war against the rebellion, and about $300 a month in tax on his business to help carry on the war. Removed to Canada about ten years ago, in the same business, and attained some notoriety as the inventor of " an improved method of cutting boot and shoe uppers," patented 1875; also, " Thurston's patent seamless balmoral," patented 1879.

Child :

10,214   Lola Edna Pearl,[9] b. April 4, 1879.

## Ninth Generation.

### 9807

FRANK WARREN THURSTON[9] (*Nahum,*[8] *Nahum,*[7] *Daniel,*[6] *Dea. Daniel,*[5] *Daniel,*[4] *Thomas,*[3] *Thomas,*[2] *John*[1]), eldest son of Nahum[8] and Ann Elizabeth (Cole) Thurston of Union, Me.; born there Dec. 2, 1850; married, Jan. 23, 1879, EMMA WELLS of Brookdale, Rice county, Kansas.

Mr. Thurston is an enterprising man, the inventor of a patent ironing machine, for ironing and polishing shirts, collars, and cuffs, which he claims will iron and polish at the same time twenty shirts per hour.

### 10,050

ALVAN A. THURSTON[9] (*Alfred,*[8] *Eli,*[7] *Ezra,*[6] *James,*[5] *Daniel,*[4] *Daniel,*[3] *Joseph,*[2] *John*[1]), son of Alfred[8] and Emily O. (Pike) Thurston of Bowling Green, Wood county, Ohio; born there March 27, 1836; married, 1852, AMELIA CLOUGH.

Mr. Thurston is a merchant in Bowling Green; both are members of the Presbyterian church. Child:

10,219  Frank.[10]

### 10,051

WESLEY S. THURSTON[9] (*Alfred,*[8] *Eli,*[7] *Ezra,*[6] *James,*[5] *Daniel,*[4] *Daniel,*[3] *Joseph,*[2] *John*[1]), brother of the preceding, and son of Alfred[8] and Emily O. (Pike) Thurston of Bowling Green, Ohio; born there June 10, 1838; married, 1867, HATTIE J. GORRELL.

Mr. Thurston is a lawyer in Toledo, Ohio, under the firm name of Bissell, Thurston & Co. He enlisted in the 111th Ohio regiment against the rebellion; served three years as a corporal, rising to a captaincy. Children:

10,224  Jessie.[10]  10,225  William.[10]  10,226  Alice.[10]  10,227  Martha.[10]
10,228  Wesley.[10]

### 10,052

THERON ALFRED EARL THURSTON[9] (*Alfred,*[8] *Eli,*[7] *Ezra,*[6] *James,*[5] *Daniel,*[4] *Daniel,*[3] *Joseph,*[2] *John*[1]), brother of the preceding, and son of Alfred[8] and Emily O. (Pike) Thurston of Bowling Green, Ohio; born there Oct. 1, 1846; married, 1865, EDNA POOL.

Mr. Thurston is a brick and tile maker in Bowling Green. He enlisted in the navy against the rebellion, on the ship Ino, and served to the close of the war. Both members of the Presbyterian church. Children:

10,233  Nellie,[10] b. Oct. 2, 1872.  10,234  Dora,[10] b. Dec. 27, 1877.

### 10,090

DANIEL EDWARD THURSTON[9] (*Daniel Marvin,*[8] *Ebenezer,*[7] *Ebenezer,*[6] *Cyrus,*[5] *Daniel,*[4] *Daniel,*[3] *Joseph,*[2] *John*[1]), eldest son of Daniel Marvin[8] and Emily (Ford) Thurston of Parsons, Kansas; born in Sandusky City, Ohio, May 12, 1852; married, on summit Santa Cruz mountains, Santa Clara county, Cal., Dec. 17, 1875, ISADORA FORESTINA STOWE, born in Waupun, Wis., Dec. 7, 1845, daughter of Isaac Mars and Salina (Storey) Stowe of Santa Clara county.

Mr. Thurston is a lumber sawyer in Santa Cruz, Santa Cruz county, Cal., a member of the Baptist church. Child:

10,239  Albert Grant,[10] b. Oct. 14, 1877.

28

# POSTERITY OF MOSES THURSTON.

Moses Thurston of Hollis, N. H., we feel quite persuaded was a descendant of Daniel of Newbury, Mass., notwithstanding some of the later generations think otherwise. We have had a large correspondence upon the subject and have noted down the points made by some of them, and leave the subject for future development.

## First Generation.

### 10,250

Moses Thurston[1] of Hollis, born 1721; married, first, Hannah Sewall; second, Dec. 18, 1777, Catherine Emerson,* born Dec. 20, 1718, sister to Rev. Daniel Emerson, the first pastor of the Congregational church in Hollis. Moses Thurston died of apoplexy, while leading in prayer at a religious meeting, April 6, 1800, aged 79, and was buried in Hollis, as appears by his grave-stone in the Central Hollis burying ground.

Mr. Thurston was a hatter; deacon in the Congregational church. He enlisted June 19, 1775, two days after the battle of Bunker Hill, in Capt. Reuben Dow's company. He enlisted again, June, 1777, in Capt. Daniel Emerson's company, raised for the defence of Ticonderoga. Hon. Samuel T. Worcester of Nashua, N. H., the historian of Hollis, informed me of the above facts in a letter dated April 1, 1879, and says, "none of the name or family have lived in Hollis since my remembrance." He also furnished me the names and dates of birth of the first six children.

There is a tradition in the family that Moses moved to Cohoes, N. Y., and came back to stay with his son Moses before he died, but I think this is unfounded. I get from three reliable sources the manner of his death, all of whom agree, but one says he died in Hollis and another that he died in Westminster. I am satisfied from all I can gather from the descendants knowing most about it, that he lived and died in Hollis. It was also said by another that he was translated, as Elijah the prophet was, and that his mantle fell upon his son Moses, who was a very devoted christian and deacon in the church at Westminster, Mass.

There is also a tradition that this Moses came from Canterbury in

England, with two or three brothers, and that there were five generations back of him by the name of Moses, who were distinguished for their piety, and that some of them settled in Cohoes, N. Y. Miss Mary L. Chadwick of Jeffersonville, Vt., a great-granddaughter of Moses, says she has often heard her grandmother tell of going on horseback, sometimes two on one horse, the one behind on a pillion, to Cohoes to see her relatives. They carried their food in saddle-bags, thrown across the back of the horses, and their clothing in a round valise strapped on to the back of the saddle. It may be these "relatives" were connected with *her* father, Chadwick, which under the circumstances seems to me more probable.

Rev. Joseph Fuller of Vershire, Vt., a grandson of Moses Thurston, seems to have more positive knowledge of the *place* where Moses Thurston came from to Hollis than any other of the descendants I have found. He says in a letter dated June 25, 1879, "When Mr. Crocker married one of his [Moses] daughters, my mother visited them and spent some time with them. She also spent some eighteen months with an uncle of hers in Newburyport, Mass. She said of them, 'they were grand folks.' Grandfather Moses Thurston used to visit us before my remembrance, but who his father was I never knew. . . . . This only I know, that my mother had kind, rich, and genteel kinsfolks by the name of Thurston in Newburyport. . . . She was in Newburyport when about eighteen. . . . Pepperell, Mass., joins Hollis, and I remember hearing mother say that the farm on which they lived was on the line between the two towns—partly in Pepperell and partly in Hollis. The house stood in Pepperell and the family record dates her birth in Pepperell; but they always attended church in Hollis and I presume their town relations were with Hollis." All this confirms me in the opinion that Moses was descended from Daniel Thurston of Newbury.

Dea. Richard Thurston [no. 38] of Rowley, Mass., owned land in Hollis and several deeds are upon record from him to various persons in Hollis, but none that we can discover to Moses Thurston.

His children were :

10,251 Hannah,[2] b. Sept. 10, 1744; m. John Wheeler; moved first to "Lake Memphremagog," then to Ohio. They had :
    10,252 *Laura* (Wheeler), m. —— Bean.
    10,253 *Annie* (Wheeler).
    10,254 *Jack* (Wheeler).
    10,255 *Ralph* (Wheeler).
    10,256 *Wilder* (Wheeler).
    10,257 *Crowell* (Wheeler).
    10,258 *Royal Tyler* (Wheeler), became a lawyer and went to Austin, Texas, where he was afterward made judge of the supreme court of Texas; was residing at Galveston in 1856-7.
+10,259 Moses,[2] b. July 9, 1746; m. Esther Bigelow.
10,260 Shuah,[2] b. July 15, 1748; m. Benjamin Crocker, Esq., of Newburyport, a rope maker and owner of a farm in North Haverhill, N. H., where he lived and died. They had :
    10,261 *Edward* (Crocker).
10,262 Gilman,[2] b. July 19, 1750.
10,263 Mary,[2] b. July 24, 1752; m. Rev. —— Spofford, a Presbyterian minister.
10,264 Lydia,[2] b. July 6, 1756; m. —— Johnson.
+10,265 Chloe,[2] b. 1758; m. Stephen Runnells.
+10,266 Peter,[2] b. Dec. 10, 1761; m. 1st, Eunice Chadwick; 2d, Mrs. Hannah Wheeler.

10,267  Phebe,[2] b. in Pepperell, Mass., Feb. 14, 1765; m. at Newbury, Vt., by
        Rev. Jacob Wood, Oct. 7, 1788, Rev. Stephen Fuller, b. in North
        Mansfield, Ct., Dec. 3, 1756. He graduated from Dartmouth 1786,
        studied theology with Rev. Asa Burton, D.D., at Thetford, Vt., and was
        ordained pastor of the Congregational church in Vershire, Vt., Sept.
        3, 1788, Dr. Burton preaching the sermon. He remained pastor there
        about thirty years, till his death, which occurred at the house of his
        brother, Dr. Fuller of New Haven, Vt., April 12, 1816; she died Oct.
        29, 1856. They were both buried in Vershire. He was a man of good
        talents, a deep thinker, a close reasoner, thoroughly orthodox in belief,
        a faithful pastor, and an earnest and impressive preacher. He aimed
        not at elegance of style, or at popularity in any way, but to preach the
        pure gospel in the most impressive manner he possibly could, realizing
        his entire dependence upon God for success. He was distinguished
        for making himself understood and the force of his appeals felt. He
        labored amidst many discouragements, but not in vain. His labors
        abroad were highly appreciated. Several of his sermons were pub-
        lished. Under his instruction, several young men received their theo-
        logical training and became highly esteemed preachers of the gospel.
        Children :

    10,268  *Henry* (Fuller), b. Aug. 11, 1789; became a Congregational minis-
           ter and settled in Smithtown, L. I.; m. March, 1818, Maria
           Buffet of Smithtown, and had Amanda Buffet, Hannah Maria,
           William Henry, and Edward Thurston (Fuller).

    10,269  *Stephen Hopkins* (Fuller), b. April 20, 1791; became a physician
           and settled in Hadley, Mass.; after went with his uncle Peter to
           Ohio; m. Susan Seymour of Hadley, and had Robert, Lydia,
           Mary Ann, George McKeen, Joseph, and Stephen (Fuller).

    10,270  *Sewall* (Fuller), b. June 18, 1793; a farmer in Vershire; m. So-
           phronia Jones of Vershire, and had Cyrus, Roxana, Lydia, Se-
           rena McKeen, Stephen, and Samuel (Fuller).

    10,271  *Phebe* (Fuller), b. Dec. 18, 1794; m. June 3, 1816, Rev. Silas Mc-
           Keen, a Congregational clergyman in Bradford, Vt. She died
           Nov. 30, 1820, having had Marrianne Serena (McKeen). m. Rev.
           Charles Duren, a Congregational clergyman, and died in West
           Charleston, Vt., March 24, 1845. Rev. Charles Duren is now,
           1879, acting pastor of the Congregational churches in Granby
           and Victory, Essex county, Vt. Julia (McKeen), d. in Belfast,
           Me., June 9, 1841.

    10,272  *Lucy* (Fuller), b. Feb. 15, 1797; n.m.; d. June 6, 1875.

    10,273  *Lydia* (Fuller), b. Dec. 22, 1798; n.m.; d. May 8, 1821.

    10,274  *Edwin* (Fuller), b. Dec. 3, 1800; a farmer in Fairlee, Vt., residing
           1879 in Bradford; m. Wealthy Clark of Bradford, and had Su-
           san, Joseph, Edward Payson, Hannah Maria, Dan Blodgett
           [killed in battle], and Albert (Fuller).

    10,275  *Edward Crocker* (Fuller), b. Jan. 16, 1803; graduated from Wil-
           liams college 1826, became a Congregational minister in Pier-
           mont, N. H.; m. Rebecca Mathison of New York city. He
           died and his children reside in New York and Brooklyn. They
           had Joseph Edwin, Robert, Phebe, Sarah, Cornelia, Julia, Mar-
           garet, Edward, Ketha, and Rebecca (Fuller).

    10,276  *David Thurston* (Fuller), b. Jan. 18, 1805; graduated from Wil-
           liams college 1826, became a lawyer, and settled in Delaware,
           Ohio; m. Catharine Shephard of Jamaica, W. I.; he d. They
           had Sarah Josephene, David, Edward, and Geo. Sebring (Fuller).

    10,277  *Joseph* (Fuller), b. Dec. 18, 1806; graduated at Middlebury, Vt.,
           1827, and from Andover 1830; ordained over the Congregation-
           al church in Kennebunk, Me., Sept. 3, 1830, Rev. Bennett Ty-
           ler, D.D., of Portland, Me., preached; dismissed July, 1834;
           settled in Brimfield, Mass., March, 1835, dismissed July, 1837;
           settled in Ridgefield, Ct., Feb. 28, 1838, dismissed May 17, 1842,
           and stated supply in Vershire from 1853–1860, where he now re-
           sides on the homestead, 1879; n.m.

10,278  Joseph,[2] m. Polly Melvin of Cambridge, Vt.; went to Canada, and
        nothing is known of him save that he died at Colchester, Vt., many
        years ago.

## Second Generation.

### 10,259

DEA. MOSES THURSTON [2] (*Moses* [1]), second child of Moses [1] and Hannah (Sewall) Thurston of Hollis, N. H.; born there July 9, 1746 (another authority says born June 7, 1744, but more probably the July 9, 1746 is right); married, April 22, 1768, ESTHER BIGELOW, born April 22, 1744. He died June 29, 1809; she died Oct. 24, 1831.

Mr. Thurston was a hatter in Westminster, Mass., excepting a few years in Hollis, N. H. He was quite a successful business man; a minute-man in the revolutionary war; a deacon of the Congregational church, which he loved with a great love; a zealous and elevated christian. He was noted for a retentive memory. When quite young he was boarding in a family where the minister also boarded. One Sunday morning, while the family were at breakfast, he took the sermon from the table where the minister had been writing it and read it through hastily, went to the table and said he thought he should not attend church, as he would not hear anything new if he went. The minister protested, and said the sermon he was going to preach was a new one that he had never delivered. Moses said there was nothing in it that he did not know already, and further, that he could repeat every word of it. They doubted and he was requested to repeat it, which he did much to the amazement of all who heard him.

Their children, born in Westminster except as noted, were:

+10,285  Lydia,[3] b. April 4, 1769; m. Enoch Carleton.
+10,286  Gilman,[3] b. Feb. 15, 1771; m. Azubah Gillett.
+10,287  Sarah,[3] b. June 10, 1773; m. John Parker Wiswall.
+10,288  Mary,[3] b. in Hollis June 9, 1775; m. David Chadwick.
+10,289  Hannah,[3] b. in Hollis June 3, 1777; m. Peter Chadwick.
+10,290  Moses,[3] b. June 18, 1780; m. Hannah Bolton.
+10,291  Esther,[3] b. Aug. 17, 1782; m. 1st, Francis Weatherby; 2d, Rufus Thurston.
+10,292  Lucy,[3] b. Oct. 12, 1784; m. Luther Weatherby.
 10,293  Nancy,[3] b. Jan. 12, 1787; d. March 1, 1796.
 10,294  Catharine,[3] b. Dec. 6, 1789; m. 1811, James Tottingham; moved to Pittsford, Vt., where they resided till he died, March 12, 1843; she sold and moved to Cambridge, Vt., and lived with her friends till she died, Oct. 15, 1868; no children.

### 10,265

CHLOE THURSTON [2] (*Moses* [1]), sister of the preceding, and daughter of Moses [1] and Hannah (Sewall) Thurston of Hollis, N. H.; born there 1758; married, 1782, STEPHEN RUNNELLS, born July 3, 1754, son of Ebenezer and Abigail (Sollis) Runnells of Haverhill, Mass. He died suddenly July 22, 1798; she died Dec. 13, 1807.

Mr. Runnells was a "minute-man" in Capt. James Sawyer's company 1775, and among the eight months' men raised just after the battle of Lexington; was at the battle of Bunker Hill. He was six years in the revolutionary war, a sergeant, and at the surrender of Burgoyne. He was a blacksmith, like his father, and in 1777 changed his residence to Hollis. Here he became affianced to Miss Chloe Thurston, and being absent as a soldier, used to send his wages to

her, which she faithfully kept, notwithstanding the depreciation of its value, so that when she came to buy her furniture she was obliged to pay seven dollars for a white cream pitcher, and for other things in a like proportion. In 1789 they moved to Vershire, Vt., where her brother-in-law, Rev. Stephen Fuller, was settled. He "had a loving disposition and great muscular powers." She afterward moved to Fletcher, Vt., but finally settled on the wild lands owned by her husband in Topsham, Vt., where she died.

### Their children, born in Hollis, were:

10,300  Stephen (Runnells), b. 1783; d. by scalding at the age of thirteen months.

10,301  Mary Crocker (Runnells), b. Aug. 4, 1784; m. 1st, Moses Melvin of Cambridge Vt.; 2d, William Elmer of Orange, Vt.; she died June 8, 1863; twelve children.

10,302  Stephen (Runnells), b. Sept. 1, 1785; m. Jane Brown of Cambridge, Vt. In the spring of 1819 he moved to McKean township, Licking county, Ohio, as a pioneer, built a log cabin, and moved into it the third day without chinking, flooring, or chimney. Small timbers of split bass wood were afterward used for a floor. He planted two acres of corn among the logs; had to go thirty miles to mill. Their salt was brought forty miles and cost five dollars per bushel. The clothing they carried with them had to be substituted by buckskin. In 1821 and 1822 they could get but twenty-five cents per bushel for wheat after carrying it forty miles and taking pay in unbleached cotton cloth at fifty cents per yard. The building of the Ohio canal brought them relief and their circumstances began to amend. He was an enterprising christian man, devoted to the cause of education and the advancement of the settlement. He died Oct. 30, 1844; thirteen children.

10,303  Chloe (Runnells),  }  twins, born  }  d. in Fletcher Aug. 29, 1804.
10,304  Hannah (Runnells),  }  Dec. 10, 1787;  }  d. in Topsham 1808.

### Born in Vershire:

10,305  Moses Thurston (Runnells), b. March 5, 1790; m. 1st, Adaline Willey of Jericho, Vt.; 2d, Caroline Stearns of Jaffrey, N. H., a former pupil of his in Cambridge, b. in Waltham, Mass., Nov. 25, 1797, being the seventh generation from Isaac Stearns of Watertown, Mass. He was a teacher and afterward a merchant and leading man in Cambridge; d. Oct. 5, 1831; one son, a Methodist clergyman.

10,306  Sarah (Runnells), b. June 14, 1793; m. William Cox, a farmer in Vershire; removed to West Fairlee, Vt., where she still resides; thirteen children.

10,307  Sollis (Runnells),  }  twins, born  }  m. Mary D. Parker of Chelsea, Vt.;
10,308  Sewall (Runnells).  }  April 5, 1797;  }  first located as a merchant in Cambridge, and in 1853 removed to Sigourney, Iowa, and he still resides in that neighborhood; ten children. Sewall Runnells m. 1st, Malinda Willey; settled, as a farmer, first in Ohio and then in Calumet county, Wis. He is now residing in Grovesville, Wis., where he married Mrs. Viann Walker; two children by first wife.

## 10,266

PETER THURSTON [2] (*Moses* [1]), brother of the preceding, and son of Moses [1] and Hannah (Sewall) Thurston of Hollis, N. H.; born there Dec. 10, 1761; married, first [published in Boxford, Mass., April 22, 1787, Peter Thurston as from Fairfax, Vt.] EUNICE CHADWICK of Haverhill, Mass.; second, MRS. HANNAH WHEELER, née BUTLER of Fairfax, who had several children by her first husband, one of whom was Almon Wheeler, the father of William Almon Wheeler of New York city, the vice-president of the United States 1879. Peter Thurston died at the house of his son Johnson in Centerburgh, Knox coun-

ty, Ohio, October, 1827, and was buried in Granville, Ohio. His widow died at the same place, May 23, 1866, aged 97, and was buried in the family cemetery of her son Johnson in Centerburgh.

Mr. Thurston was a remarkably strong and tough man, with double teeth all round both jaws. He was always cheerful and very agreeable to his friends, and was the champion of all his region at "pulling sticks," a game in vogue in those days to test the strength. Many experiences and tests of his strength and endurance are told by his children. He was, withal, a great and successful hunter and trapper, paying for his farm in Vermont by these means. Moose, deer, beaver, sable, marten, otter, and other game were plenty there. He was in the battle of Lexington. Was once taken prisoner by the Indians and with others carried to Montreal, kept some three weeks, when he made his escape and found his way back to Vermont, on foot, to a place since called Fletcher, which attracted his attention by the fertility of the soil, then a wilderness with only a few white settlers at long distances and no roads. He marked the trees and went on to Haverhill, where he married, and took his wife, with such effects as they could carry on horseback, and started for Vermont. They arrived in course of time, with no way-marks for much of the distance save the spotted trees. He erected a log-cabin, laid out his farm, began work with a will, and soon made the place attractive, so that several of their friends and relatives came and settled in that place, in Fairfax, and in Cambridge.

His descendants tell this curious incident in his life. He was told that if he would bite a live adder his teeth would never ache or decay. So on his journey from Montreal to Vermont he found adders swimming in a pond, caught one and bit it. The result was, his mouth was very sore and his teeth became loose. A friendly Indian squaw made him some tea and prepared a wash for his mouth from leaves and roots, which soon relieved him. His teeth never troubled him and remained perfectly sound till his death.

He lived in Fletcher till after his first wife's death, and in April, 1813, during the last war with England, he sold his place to his son Rufus, gave Edward a portion near by, and removed to Granville, Licking county, Ohio, with the rest of his family, his sister Wheeler, Samuel Chadwick, and several others. They fitted up long wagons, covered them with a coarse cloth manufactured by themselves, and attached two horses to each; supplied them with bedding, so they could be used for camping in nights, and with cooking utensils for baking bread and cooking game and fish, which they found in abundance on the way. These operations, together with fording streams, encounters with copperhead and rattle snakes, which were numerous, rendered the journey lively and often exciting. There were but few settlers on the route, and no hotels, making it necessary to camp out most every night during the two months it required for the journey. When they arrived at Buffalo, N. Y., the place had been burnt by the British and all the people fled. Some years after he returned home to visit his brother Moses and other friends, and reported they were well pleased with their Ohio home, but advised his brother, who asked him if he had better sell out and go too, that as long as he was doing well in

Massachusetts he had better stay there. They were both members and he a deacon in the Baptist church. She joined the Methodist church in Ohio.

Mrs. Thurston was a woman of great energy, endurance, bright intellect, and social culture; having remarkably uniform good health, a sound and strong physical body, which, together with similar qualities in her husband, produced a wonderfully healthy, vigorous, and hardy family of children. She would weave fourteen yards of cloth a day after she was sixty years of age.

His children, by first wife, Eunice:

+10,313  Edward,[8] m. Betsey Page.
+10,314  Rufus,[8] b. 1789; m. Mrs. Esther Weatherby [see no. 10,291].
+10,315  Peter,[8] b. 1800; m. Elizabeth Jackson.

By second wife, Hannah:

+10,316  Johnson,[8] b. Oct. 20, 1803; m. Julia Everett.
+10,317  George Washington,[8] } twins, born } m. Charlotte Jackson.
+10,318  Thomas Jefferson,[8] } Feb. 12, 1805; } m. 1st Rosetta Bull; 2d, Elizabeth Smith.
+10,319  Reuben Harris,[8] b. Dec. 11, 1806; m. Mary Brooks.
 10,320  Jane,[8]     } twins, born { d. aged 1 y. 6 m.
 10,321  Caroline,[8] } Aug., 1807; } she was refined in manners and an excellent teacher; m. 1839, Henry Charter of Michigan; d. at the birth of her first child.
 10,322  Maria[8] (formerly Siata, changed to Maria), b. April, 1809; m. 1828, Orren Chipman of Licking county, Ohio, afterward removed to Richmond, Washington county, Iowa. She was a lady of natural literary gifts and quite a poet. Children:
     10,323  *Virgil* (Chipman).
     10,324  *Maria* (Chipman).
 10,325  Cordelia,[8] b. 1810; m. 1829, Calvin Woods, a merchant and farmer in Homer, Ohio; she died near Homer, Licking county 1860, and he m. second, Sarah Thurston Campbell [see no. 10,518]. Children:
     10,326  *Ann* (Woods).
     10,327  *Sophina* (Woods).
     10,328  *Maria* (Woods).
     10,329  *Calvin Imri* (Woods).
     10,330  *Rose* (Woods).
     10,331  *Clarence* (Woods).

---

### Third Generation.

### 10,285

LYDIA THURSTON [8] (*Moses,[2] Moses[1]*), eldest child of Moses[2] and Esther (Bigelow) Thurston of Westminster, Mass.; born there April 4, 1769; married, March, 1805, ENOCH CARLETON, ESQ., born Sept. 15, 1763, son of Dea. Oliver Carleton of Amherst, N. H. Enoch Carleton married as his first wife, Feb. 2, 1790, Hannah Peabody, born July 1, 1768; she died Dec. 12, 1804, having had Enoch (Carleton), born March 20, 1791; George (Carleton), born Aug. 7, 1793; after which the family moved to Cambridge, Vt., and she had Hannah (Carleton), born April 16, 1795; Stephen Peabody (Carleton), born May 30, 1797. Enoch Carleton married for his third wife Mrs. Powell of Richford, Vt., and had one son by her. Mr. Carleton was a

shoemaker in Cambridge and after in Richford; a soldier in the revolutionary war; representative to the legislature two terms while in Cambridge. He died July 1, 1845. Lydia Thurston Carleton, his second wife, died Oct. 20, 1832, having had four children, three of whom died in infancy and

10,335   Caroline (Carleton), b. Nov. 16, 1807; m. March 7, 1824, Alden Sears, b. in Weathersfield, Vt., Aug. 6, 1797, a merchant two or three years in Cambridge, when he removed to Richford; representative to the legislature in 1844, 1845, 1846. He died in Columbia, Cal., March 2, 1858; she died in Salem, Oregon, Jan. 17, 1877. They had, born in Richford:

    10,336   *Louisa* (Sears), b. Jan. 17, 1825; d. 1838.
    10,337   *Elvira* (Sears), b. April, 1827; d. 1830.
    10,338   *Lucy T.* (Sears), b. April 4, 1830; m. Judge E. E. White of Columbia, Cal., and had Nelly Sears (White), b. Oct., 1863, and Edwin (White), b. 1866.
    10,339   *Malcome* (Sears), b. April 4, 1832.
    10,340   *Ellen A.* (Sears), b. April 22, 1835; m. June 29, 1856, Rev. John Henry Brodt, b. in Troy, N. Y., June 2, 1827. Mr. Brodt was a man of pronounced individuality, and one not easily classified, being possessed of striking and somewhat diverse characteristics, though he was by no means an eccentric. He was a guileless man; possessed great boldness of spirit, which neither a mob of California ruffians armed to the teeth, during the days of the vigilance committee, nor the manifest displeasure of more polite sinners, could deter from manly utterances in behalf of truth, righteousness, and innocence. He was pre-eminently a disciple of the Master. He was a warm-hearted, generous, and loyal friend. He could not be biased by any subtle misrepresentations. He scented a slanderer instantly and gave him no quarter. He was educated at the Troy polytechnic institute, Williams college, and Union theological seminary. He spent the first twelve years of his ministry in California, going there in 1854, where as a preacher, teacher, editor, and an active citizen, during those stirring times, he exerted a controlling and molding influence. Returning to New York, he became pastor of the Brick Presbyterian church in Dansville for two years, and was subsequently settled in New York and Brooklyn, until compelled by illness to relinquish the work of an active pastor. He died Sept. 8, 1875. As a preacher Mr. Brodt was a natural orator, had a strong bass voice, and was distinguished by uncommon clearness of conception and directness of speech. There was never any mistaking his meaning. His convictions of truth were very strongly held, earnestly declared, and often with such exceeding power of illustration as to leave his thoughts indelibly impressed upon the minds of his hearers. Children: Carrie A. (Brodt), b. in San Francisco, Cal., April 13, 1857; John Ingold (Brodt), b. in Petaluma, Cal., Jan. 30, 1859, d. in Marysville, Cal., Jan. 30, 1861; Edwin Elwell (Brodt), b. in Petaluma Feb. 8, 1862, d. in Marysville Dec. 28, 1863; Henry Prewden (Brodt), b. in Marysville Feb. 1, 1863; Ellen Reno (Brodt), b. in San Francisco May 17, 1865; Charles Hawley (Brodt), b. in Salem, N. Y., Oct. 25, 1867; Daisie Louise (Brodt), b. in New York city Sept. 29, 1869; Philip Ernest (Brodt), b. in Brooklyn, N. Y., June 21, 1871; Alfred Randolph (Brodt), b. in Dansville, N. Y., Dec. 18, 1873, d. Aug. 23, 1874.

  10,341   *Charles T.* (Sears), b. Oct. 27, 1838.
  10,342   *George C.* (Sears), b. April 5, 1840.
  10,343   *Homer A.* (Sears), b. May 10, 1843.

## 10,286

GILMAN THURSTON [8] (*Moses,*[2] *Moses*[1]), brother of the preceding, and son of Moses [2] and Esther (Bigelow) Thurston of Westminster, Mass.;

born there Feb. 15, 1771; married Azubah Gillett of Fitchburgh, Mass. He was a hatter in Westminster and Lunenburgh, Mass.; died June 14, 1851.

Children :

10,348  Merriam Waters Thurston,[4] b. in Westminster Nov. 24, 1798; d. Aug. 8, 1800.
10,349  Merriam Waters Thurston,[4] b. in Westminster March 2, 1801.
10,350  Nancy More,[4] b in Lunenburgh, May 4, 1803.
10,351  Charles Gilman,[4] b. in Lunenburgh April 19, 1805.
10,352  Azubah,[4] b. in Lunenburgh Jan. 23, 1807.
10,353  Julianna,[4] b. in Westminster April 22, 1809.
10,354  Fanny Gillett,[4] b. in Westminster April 15, 1811.
10,355  Marietta,[4] b. in Westminster April 1, 1813.
10,356  John Gillett,[4] b. May 21; d. May 28, 1815.
10,357  Adah Maria,[4] b. Oct. 18, 1817.

## 10,287

Sarah Thurston[3] (*Moses*,[2] *Moses*[1]), sister of the preceding, and daughter of Moses[2] and Esther (Bigelow) Thurston of Westminster, Mass.; born there June 10, 1773; married John Parker Wiswall of Westminster. He had three sons and a daughter by a former marriage. He died in Troy, N. Y., April 6, 1828; she died Jan. 8, 1862.

Mr. Wiswall moved to Burlington, Vt., during the war of 1812, while it was a place of rendezvous for the soldiers. He was pretty outspoken in his opinions and made himself obnoxious to the soldiers, who set fire to his house and burned it to the ground. By the assistance of neighbors, they and some of their household effects were saved from the flames. They fled to Cambridge, Vt., remained till the close of the war, when they returned to Burlington and remained a few years, moved to Middlebury, Vt., and thence to Troy, N. Y., and purchased a farm. Shortly after this he built a shop and began the manufacture of knife handles and other implements from bone, but was not successful financially. He was very ingenious, and in after years succeeded better in this business, so that he left something at his decease for his family. His family remained in Troy till all the children but Mary Ann were married, when she and her mother, with Mr. and Mrs. Parmer went to Embarrass, Waupaca county, Wis., where Mrs. Wiswall died. She was a devoted christian woman; "held strongly to the golden rule."

Children :

10,359  Jonas (Wiswall), b. out of wedlock, May 29, 1794.
10,360  Elvira (Wiswall), b. in Westminster 1806; m. John Parke Parmer of Rome, N. Y., a farmer till he moved to Embarrass, where he was a merchant and postmaster.
10,361  Moses Thurston (Wiswall), m. and had four children. Two of his sons served in the war against the rebellion, and one was taken prisoner at Harper's Ferry and paroled. Mr. Wiswall was an Adventist in religion and afterward a Spiritualist.
10,362  Sarah Jane (Wiswall), b. in Burlington Jan. 1, 1815; m. Hiram Pearse of Troy; he died.
10,363  Mary Ann (Wiswall), n.m.

## 10,288

Mary Thurston[3] (*Moses*,[2] *Moses*[1]), sister of the preceding, and daughter of Moses[2] and Esther (Bigelow) Thurston of Westminster, Mass.; born in Hollis, N. H., June 9, 1775; married, May, 1794,

DAVID CHADWICK, born March 11, 1775. She died instantly of apoplexy June 1, 1844; he died Jan. 11, 1850.

Mr. Chadwick was a carpenter and joiner. They lived with her uncle Peter for a year after marriage, and then moved to Cambridge, Vt., where he purchased a farm of virgin soil, and went into a loghouse, with stone fireplace and oven, and chimney made of sticks and clay. He had very little beside his tools and a few articles of household furniture to commence with. He was a good mechanic and fitted up a shop to work in winters, where he made sleighs. Mary's mother was a tailoress and taught her the same trade, and also how to spin, weave, and do housework. They were both industrious, energetic, and prosperous, and soon had a good farm, house, and other pleasant surroundings. He was a captain in the war of 1812, but did not serve long, as there were plenty of volunteers and his presence seemed to be needed at home.

### Children :

10,368    Alonzo (Chadwick), b. in Fletcher, Vt., Dec. 1, 1796; m. April 3, 1824, Samantha Melvin. He was a farmer in Cambridge till June, 1833, when he went to Cleveland, Ohio, into a chair factory. He was a Congregationalist; d. Oct. 19, 1833; one son.

10,369    Rosamond (Chadwick), b. in Cambridge Oct. 7, 1798; m. Dec. 5, 1816, Enoch Carleton, b. in Amherst, N. H., Mar. 20, 1791, moved to Cambridge 1794. He was a shoe manufacturer and later in life a farmer in Cambridge; was high sheriff several years; a deist, but a man of high moral principle and remarkably sympathetic, always ready to befriend any one in need. As an officer it was once his duty to take a poor debtor, whose family were entirely dependent on him for daily support, to St. Albans jail. He arrived back in the evening and found an enthusiastic meeting in progress in the church under the charge of Rev. John Truer. He stated the case of the poor debtor, raised the money, paid it over to the demandant, went back to St. Albans and brought the poor man back to his family before sunrise next morning, traveling about eighty miles to do this favor to the poor man. Children :

10,370    *Rosamond* (Carleton), b. Sept. 5, 1817; d March 24, 1847.
10,371    *George* (Carleton), b. Feb. 5, 1819; d. March 26, 1863.
10,372    *Lewis P.* (Carleton), b. July 11, 1822; d. Jan. 19, 1823.
10,373    *Lewis Parker* (Carleton), b. May 26, 1824.
10,374    *Mary Chadwick* (Carleton), b. Nov. 15, 1826; d. May 25, 1847.
10,375    *David Chadwick* (Carleton), b. Jan. 27, 1829.
10,376    *Hannah Peabody* (Carleton), b. Jan. 17, 1831; d. April 3, 1864.
10,377    *Alonzo Chadwick* (Carleton), b. July 27, 1834.
10,378    *Franklin Benjamin* (Carleton), b. May 16, 1837; d. Mar. 12, 1877.
10,379    *Caroline Sears* (Carleton), b. Jan. 1, 1840; d. May 1, 1864.
10,380    *Louisa* (Carleton), b. Aug., 1842; d. March 2, 1878.

10,381    Almira (Chadwick), b. Nov. 2, 1800; m. Willard Griswold, b. in Springfield, Vt., April 13, 1778. They had, born in Cambridge :

10,382    *Harrison* (Griswold), b. May 7, 1824; m. Marion Safford of Fairfax. Vt. He was a merchant, now a traveling agent, of Lacross, Wis.; a Baptist. They had Adelia (Griswold).

10,383    *David Chadwick* (Griswold), twin, b. June 7, 1826; m. Mary Ann Chadwick; is a wheelwright and farmer; four children, one son in college.

10,384    *Adelia Almira* (Griswold), twin, b. June 7, 1826; m. 1st, Earl Smilie, b in Cambridge July, 1816, a merchant, Episcopalian in sentiment, d. Sept. 4, 1855; 2d, Oct. 14, 1867, Joel M. Wilcox. She had two children by each husband.

10,385    *Willard Henry* (Griswold), b. March 1, 1831; m. March 31, 1858, Marion Heath. He is town clerk and notary. She is a member of the Congregational church; one child, d. in infancy.

10,386    *Cornelius* (Griswold), b. May 8, 1833; a farmer in Montana.

10,387   *Caroline Matilda* (Griswold), b. June 16, 1835; m. Osgood McFarland of Waterville, Vt.; moved to St. Paul, Minn.

10,388   *Mary Chadwick* (Griswold), b. March 10, 1838; m. 1st, Martin Jackson, a merchant in Eau Clare, Wis., a Baptist; four children; 2d, M. Oscar Jackson of Eau Clare; one child.

10,389   *Alonzo Chadwick* (Griswold), b. Sept. 22, 1841; m. Helen L. Brown of Bakersfield, Vt.; is a telegraph operator and depot agent at Cambridge Junction; three children.

10,390   *Lucius Hoyt* (Griswold), b. May 19, 1844; d. May 9, 1851.

10,391   Mary Louise (Chadwick), b. March 11, 1804; n.m.; resides in Jeffersonville, Vt., and has furnished much material concerning these families for this work.

10,392   Christopher Columbus (Chadwick), twin, b. March 14, 1814; m. Oct. 17, 1839, Electa Lemira Hawley. He was a machinist and farmer, and later in life judge of probate for Lamoille county, Vt.; d. Dec. 22, 1875. Children:

10,393   *Helen Mary* (Chadwick), b. Aug. 3, 1841; m. Aug. 9, 1875, Birney Fullington of Johnson, Vt., a traveling salesman.

10,394   *Harrietta Elizabeth* (Chadwick), b. Oct. 31, 1844; she was engaged to John Woodard of Burlington, Vt., son of Rev. John Woodard. He had enlisted in the war against the rebellion, had received a furlough and come home to rest and recruit, and she was taken suddenly very sick when he was summoned to return to his regiment again. He asked her what he should do. She replied, cheerfully, "Go and do your duty, the separation will be short." He returned to his regiment and was gallantly leading his command in the battle of Boonesborough when he fell, mortally wounded. His father, who was chaplain of the regiment, took his remains to Hagerstown for burial and marked the grave. They were afterward removed to Cambridge and placed beside those of his spouse, who had died May 31, 1863. An interesting incident occurred as he was fighting Mosby, the guerilla. He was shot in the arm and his horse was shot and fell over him so he could not extricate himself, though he had his pistol in his hand and could use it. He fired at but did not hit Mosby, who saw his situation and came and relieved him, and said he had fought so bravely he deserved his life and paroled him, for which he received the sincere thanks of Woodard.

10,395   Christia Columbia (Chadwick), twin, b. March 14, 1814; m. Nov. 24, 1833, Julius Hoyt Bostwick of Jericho, Vt., b. Sept. 10, 1837; one son:

10,396   *Lucius Hoyt* (Bostwick), enlisted in the war against the rebellion. When the call for volunteers was made, he attended a public meeting and proposed to go himself, and not only refused the bounty, but offered to give fifty dollars to be divided between the first five who should enlist after him. He was a man of frail constitution, and more than twenty stepped forward and said he should not go; they would go in his stead. No persuasions, however, could deter him from going. He entered the 13th Vermont regiment, was promoted to lieutenant, then to captain. He was brave, cheerful, amiable, and beloved by all, but the service was too severe for him and he died June 6, 1863. His remains were brought home and buried in Montpelier, Vt.

10,397   *Mary Chadwick* (Bostwick), b. in Jericho Sept. 17, 1835; m. Samuel Walton, a book-binder in Montpelier. She is a member of the Episcopal church.

## 10,289

HANNAH THURSTON [8] (*Moses*,[2] *Moses* [1]), sister of the preceding, and daughter of Moses [2] and Esther (Bigelow) Thurston of Westminster, Mass.; born in Hollis, N. H., June 3, 1777; married, September, 1797, PETER CHADWICK, born in Guilford, Vt., Sept. 11, 1775. He fell from the staging of a house he was building and received injuries from which he died in a few hours, May 26, 1846; she died April 30, 1857.

Mr. Chadwick was a carpenter, joiner, and later in life a farmer in Cambridge Center, Vt.

Children:

10,400    Elias (Chadwick), b. June 26, 1800; m. July 6, 1830, Maria Melvin of Cambridge, b. Dec., 1800; she died March 22, 1874. He was a carpenter, and afterward a tavern keeper in Cambridge Center, but living, 1879, in Jeffersonville, Vt., with his youngest daughter. They had:

     10,401    *Harriet R.* (Chadwick), b. July 19, 1834; m. April 10, 1851, George W. Phelps of Burlington, Vt.

     10,402    *James Madison* (Chadwick), b. Oct. 3, 1836; m. Oct. 30, 1865, Harriet Ayers of Bakersfield, Vt.

     10,403    *Mary Ann* (Chadwick), b. Oct. 5, 1838; m. Dec. 25, 1857, David Griswold of Cambridge.

     10,404    *Horace Alexander* (Chadwick), b. Aug. 3, 1844; m. May 10, 1871, Mary F. McHerhany of Washington, Vt.

10,405    Harriet (Chadwick), b. May 13, 1802; d. Sept. 4, 1807.

10,406    Gilman (Chadwick), b. June 28, 1804; d. by being scalded June 14, 1808.

10,407    Enos (Chadwick),     } twins. b. Oct. 9, 1806; d. Sept. 1, 1807.

10,408    Edward (Chadwick), }                d. Sept. 7, 1807.

10,409    Rufus (Chadwick), b. July 1, 1808; d. Feb. 10, 1812.

10,410    Gilman F. (Chadwick), b. March 23, 1811.

10,411    Horace (Chadwick), b. June 20, 1813.

10,412    Almon (Chadwick), b. Nov. 20, 1815; m. Mrs. Louise Melvin; lives in Underhill, Vt.; three children.

10,413    William Harrison (Chadwick), b. Aug. 22, 1818.

10,414    John (Chadwick), b. Jan. 6, 1821; fell from a bridge his father and brother Elias were building over the Lamoille river, April 7, 1831, and was carried under the ice and drowned. This family seemed to have had a natural bent to accidents. This John accidentally shot his mother with a gun, but did not kill her.

## 10,290

MOSES THURSTON [3] (*Moses,*[2] *Moses*[1]), brother of the preceding, and son of Moses[2] and Esther (Bigelow) Thurston of Westminster, Mass.; born there June 18, 1780; married, Dec. 12, 1806, HANNAH BOLTON, born June 26, 1783, daughter of Aaron and Dorcas (Winchap) Bolton. Mr. Bolton was captain in the revolutionary war. Moses Thurston died July 29, 1854; she died May 3, 1865.

Mr. Thurston moved to Cambridge, Vt., in 1815; was a farmer; member of the Congregational church. His mother spent her last days with him.

Children, born in Westminster:

10,420    Fidelia,[4] b. Nov. 10, 1807; m. Oct. 21, 1828, Henry William Sabin; d. Nov. 18, 1872. They had seven children, two died in infancy:

     10,421    *Charles Thurston* (Sabin), a farmer and civil engineer in Montpelier, Vt.; m. Emily McFarland; they have:

         10,422    *Fanny Thurston* (Sabin).

         10,423    *Laura McFarland* (Sabin).

         10,424    *Jessie* (Sabin).

     10,425    *Helen Matilda* (Sabin), m. Charles Turner, a merchant in Cambridge; two sons, live in Montpelier.

     10,426    *Harvey Durkee* (Sabin), a machinist in St. Albans, Vt.; m.; three sons.

     10,427    *James Thurston* (Sabin), m. Mary Waite of Cambridge; is secretary in Mutual Insurance Co. of Montpelier. They have one son and one daughter.

     10,428    *Kate* (Sabin), m. Freeman D. Gilman, a farmer in N. H.; two sons.

10,429    Nancy Bolton,[4] b. Sept. 28, 1809; m. July 24, 1828, Otis Bennett; he died May 12, 1847. In June, 1834, Mr. Bennett purchased land in Grand Detour, Ogle county, Ill., on Rock river, built a log-house, and com-

menced a farm. June 4, 1835, his wife, with three children between the ages of six years and eighteen months, started for their new home, and arrived there July 4, travel worn and weary. The Winnebago and Pottawatomy Indians were still living there, and remained for over a year after she arrived, greatly disturbing her peace of mind, though they never actually proved unfriendly. Several times, when her husband was away from home, she suffered untold anxiety for fear of them; and several times it was only a providence of God that protected her and her children from them, when under the influence of liquor, which occasionally they would get, notwithstanding it was against the law for any one to sell it to an indian. Sickness and death came to them, and no physician or friend to alleviate their sickness or sympathize with their loss. She is a member of the Congregational church. Children:

10,430   *James* (Bennett), b. June 8, 1829; m. Lucy Jane Dunsha; is a farmer and large land owner in York, Ill.; deacon in the Baptist church. Children :

    10,431   *Heber Amasa* (Bennett), b. Aug. 27; 1852; d. Aug. 21, 1872.
    10,432   *Francis Wayland* (Bennett), b. May 24, 1859.
    10,433   *Robert Dunsha* (Bennett), b. Sept. 14, 1862.
    All members of the Baptist church.

10,434   *Moses Thurston* (Bennett), b. Nov. 14, 1831; m. Matilda Tracy; is a Methodist minister and farmer in Waterville, Marshall county, Kansas. Children :

    10,435   *Miriam Alice* (Bennett).
    10,436   *Jennie Eva* (Bennett).
    10,437   *James Thurston* (Bennett).
    10,438   *Harrison* (Bennett).
    10,439   *Alfred* (Bennett).
    10,440   *Loannia* (Bennett).
    10,441   *Nancy* (Bennett).
    10,442   *Delia* (Bennett).
    10,443   *Albert* (Bennett). All members of the Methodist church.

10,444   *Nancy Fidelia* (Bennett), b. Nov. 16, 1833; d. Nov. 31, 1835.
+10,445   Moses,[4] b. Oct. 2, 1811; m. Mrs. Eliza (Chaffin) Flagg.
10,446   Matilda Bolton,[4] b. Oct. 19, 1813; m. June 29, 1842, Earl Smilie, a merchant in Cambridge; d. Sept. 28, 1844, having had:

    10,447   *Melville Earl* (Smilie), m. Ellen Pinea; is a lawyer in Montpelier; one son.

Born in Cambridge :

+10,448   James Tottingham,[4] b. Feb. 18, 1818; m. 1st, Fanny Witherell; 2d, Mrs. Jane Currier.
10,449   David Chadwick,[4] b. July 19, 1821; m. Freelove Carey; was a merchant (hardware and kitchen furniture) in Worcester, Mass.; member of the Congregational church; d. Sept. 19, 1863; no children.

## 10,291, 10,314

ESTHER THURSTON[3] (*Moses,*[2] *Moses*[1]), sister of the preceding, and daughter of Moses[2] and Esther (Bigelow) Thurston of Westminster, Mass.; born there Aug. 17, 1782; married, first, 1805, FRANCIS WEATHERBY, a shoemaker in Westminster. They were both Congregationalists. They moved to Fletcher, Vt., in 1815, and he died May 9, 1816. Second, RUFUS THURSTON [see no. 10,314], born 1789, son of Peter Thurston. She died July, 1860.

Mr. Rufus Thurston was a farmer in Fletcher on the homestead. He afterward sold and moved to Cambridge, Vt. He died at Saratoga springs, N. Y., Sept. 12, 1856, aged 67.

Her children, by first husband, Weatherby, all born in Westminster :

    10,455   Catherine Thurston (Weatherby), b. 1806; d. 1873.
    10,456   Alonzo (Weatherby), d. in Cambridge Nov. 18, 1845, aged 37.
    10,457   Moses Thurston (Weatherby), d. in Cambridge Oct., 1834.

10,458  Francis (Weatherby), d. in Fletcher.
10,459  Esther Bigelow (Weatherby), m. Feb. 7, 1843, Amariah J. Wheelock, b.
        in Eden.Vt., May 7, 1807, a carpenter, joiner, and farmer in Cambridge.
        They had :
    10,460  *Maria* (Wheelock), b. May 25, 1845; m. George Saxby, a hotel
            keeper in Johnson, Vt.
    10,461  *Lucius A.* (Wheelock), b. June 13, 1847; m. Jan. 1, 1879, Alvira J.
            Thomas of Cambridge; is a carpenter, joiner, mason, and farmer.
    By second husband, Thurston, several children died in infancy, and :
10,462  Adelia,[4] m. 1st, Edwin Melvin, who lived with his father-in-law in Cam-
        bridge, and died about 1858, having had one child; 2d, Ira Rickard,
        by whom she had three children. She separated from him and re-
        sumed her former name of Melvin. Children :
    10,463  *George* (Melvin), a merchant in Cambridge Center, Vt.
    10,464  *Rufus* (Melvin), d. in infancy.
    10,465  *Fanny* (Melvin), d. in infancy.
    10,466  *Addie* (Melvin), b. Feb. 14, 1865.

## 10,292

Lucy Thurston[8] (*Moses,*[2] *Moses*[1]), sister of the preceding, and
daughter of Moses[2] and Esther (Bigelow) Thurston of Westminster,
Mass.; born there Oct. 12, 1784; married, Oct. 11, 1804, Luther
Weatherby, born in Haverhill, Mass., Sept. 4, 1782. He was a
farmer in Westminster; drowned at High Gate springs, Vt., April 8,
1819; she died in Cambridge, Vt., April 11, 1870.

### Children :

10,467  Farewell (Weatherby), b. Oct. 5, 1805; m. 1st, Feb. 23, 1830, Mary G.
        Page of Cambridge, Vt., b. Nov. 7, 1809, d. Oct. 18, 1841; 2d, Mary
        Antonette Marcy of Berkshire, Vt., b. July 8, 1809, d. Feb. 21, 1846;
        3d, May 15, 1849, Pauline Bailey of Fletcher,Vt. He had, by first wife :
    10,468  *Homer Farewell* (Weatherby), b. April 2, 1837; m. Catherine
            Holmes of Michigan; she died Aug. 13, 1879, aged 40.
    By third wife :
    10,469  *Charles* (Weatherby), b. 1852.
    10,470  *Henry* (Weatherby), b. Oct., 1855.
10,471  Mary Ann (Weatherby), b. in St. Albans, Vt., April 2, 1811; m. Feb. 20,
        1834, Norman Atwood, b. Sept. 11, 1809. They had :
    10,472  *Levi* (Atwood), b. Nov. 9, 1834; m. March 19, 1863, Cynthia Jones,
            b. April 29, 1837. They had :
        10,473  *Norman Nathan* (Atwood), b. Aug. 2, 1865.
        10,474  *Lillian* (Atwood), b. Nov. 2, 1868.
    10,475  *Oscar* (Atwood), b. Aug. 5, 1842; graduated from Burlington uni-
            versity and is superintendent in the institute in Rutland,Vt.
    10,476  *Charlotte* (Atwood), b. Oct. 15, 1844; m. Robert McFarland, a
            merchant and member of the legislature.

## 10,313

Edward Thurston[8] (*Peter,*[2] *Moses*[1]), eldest son of Peter[2] and
Eunice (Chadwick) Thurston of Fletcher, Vt.; married Betsey Page
of Fairfax, Vt. He was a farmer in Fletcher till after his wife died,
soon after his youngest child was born, when he sold his farm and
went into other business. After his children were married they all
went to Baltimore, Md., where he married a second wife and died
about 1846 or 1847.

### His children, all by first wife, born in Fletcher :

10,480  Eunice,[4] m. —— Gould.
10,481  Clarissa,[4] m. —— Robinson, a photographer. She died and he m. a sec-
        ond time and lived in Cincinnati, Ohio, and Covington, Ky. She had:

10,482   *Clarissa* (Robinson).
10,483   *Gertrude* (Robinson).
10,484   Phineas,[4] was proprietor of the Fountain hotel in Baltimore and after a
a hotel keeper in Philadelphia.   He acquired a competence through
the decision of a land suit in favor of his father.   His religion was " to
be governed by reason and to do good."

## 10,315

PETER THURSTON[3] (*Peter,*[2] *Moses*[1]), brother of the preceding, and
son of Peter[2] and Eunice (Chadwick) Thurston of Fletcher, Vt.;
born there 1800; married ELIZABETH JACKSON, born in New York
March 27, 1801, of Granville, Licking county, Ohio, where Mr. Thurston went with his parents in 1813.   He was a farmer, a pleasantly
disposed though not a very strong man.   He died August, 1836; his
widow resides in Ceresco, Blue Earth county, Minn., 1879.

Children:

10,489   Cordelia.[4]
10,490   Mary.[4]
10,491   Rufus.[4]
10,492   Elizabeth.[4]
10,493   Charlotte.[4]
10,494   Sarah.[4]
+10,495   Charles,[4] b. Feb. 23, 1833; m. Joanna Dilley.

## 10,316

JOHNSON THURSTON[3] of Centerburgh, Knox county, Ohio (*Peter,*[2]
*Moses*[1]), brother of the preceding, and son of Peter[2] and Hannah
(Wheeler) Thurston of Fletcher, Vt.; born there Oct. 20, 1803; mar-
ried, Feb. 22, 1824, JULIA EVERETT, born July 15, 1808, daughter of
Samuel and Annis Agnes (Battles) Everett of Granby, Ct.   He died
on a farm in Lebanon, Ill., Dec. 7, 1858; his remains were carried to
Centerburgh and deposited in his family cemetery.

Mr. Thurston went to Granville, Ohio, with his father.   His son
says: " He had a rugged constitution, fine black hair, hazel eyes,
ruddy complexion; when full grown was five feet ten inches high, and
at fifty weighed two hundred pounds.   Though not having the facilities for acquiring a classical education, he learned rapidly and with
great judgment grasped the leading topics of the day and foretold
their conclusion; was a great reasoner, philosopher, theologian, and
lawyer, though he followed none of these professions.

" He was captain of a military company in Homer, Licking county,
Ohio, and afterward major of a regiment.   He was popular as a commander, and genial and engaging in conversation.   He drew about
him and enjoyed much company, and entertained them with new
and important ideas in the most simple and easy manner.   He employed many who were out of work, usually with profit to both."

He possessed great physical strength and unflinching courage.
His brother says: " He could handle as many men as could get
around him.   Fifteen men attacked him on a steamboat and the first
blow with his fist knocked three of them down, and he cleared and
piled the most of them.   At another time he was attacked in a barber's shop by a man who said he had a grudge against him and believed he would settle it then, and went for him.   Johnson caught

him by the seat of his pants and threw him over his shoulder out of the door and over the sidewalk into the street."

"He joined the Methodist Episcopal church when young, and when turned out of it by the Rev. Mr. McMann, without a trial, he joined the Methodist Protestant church, and before his death became a free thinker. He was an advocate of open doors to love feasts and class-meetings.

"He was one of the first in Licking county who advocated the ,abolition of slavery, and contended zealously for it in Ohio, Virginia, and Missouri during the border ruffian war between Kansas and Missouri, and up to the time of the war of the rebellion, spending time and money freely to advance the cause, when it was unpopular and often dangerous to do so." He held frequent meetings, and was once "mobbed and egged." We give a few incidents of his experiences during these times, as given by his son.

"About 1840 a small, delicately framed man from Cincinnati had an appointment to lecture against slavery in Hartford, Licking county. A mob, having several guns and other weapons, had the lecturer in custody, intending to tar and feather him and ride him on a rail. Mr. Thurston discovered this, and having two single shooters gave one to his brother-in-law, Reuel Everett, drove in his sleigh near to the place, made his way into the crowd and demanded the prisoner to be given up to him, which was done. He took the lecturer into his sleigh and drove away. Some of the mob fired at them as they were leaving the town, but without effect. That evening a meeting was held at Lock, five miles and a half from Hartford, and after an address by the lecturer an anti slavery society of forty members was formed.

"During the slavery agitation along the borders of Kansas and Missouri, Mr. Thurston, with his horse and buggy, and five others had paid their fare on the 'Polar Star' steamer from St. Louis to St. Joseph, Mo., and were put off at Lexington for speaking their sentiments upon the subject of slavery. His clothes were torn and his buggy broken, but notwithstanding he arrived in St. Joseph before the boat. He obtained a written protest from forty of the passengers against the conduct of the captain and crew, served legal process upon the owners at Weston, Mo., obtained judgment and his executor collected $110. He explained the destructive influence of slavery upon free labor, and altogether produced a revolution of sentiment against slavery in that slaveholding district."

He was outspoken in his opposition to intemperance and the use of tobacco. B. T. Vail of Morrow county, Ohio, says: "At a hotel, after supper, the boarders and travelers were taking a smoke. Mr. Thurston told them if they would throw away their cigars he would sing them a song. One or two consented, and while he was singing 'the sweeper in high life,' the cigars were all thrown away and some of the smokers promised never to smoke again." He offered his eldest son $100 to promise never to smoke another cigar. The son refused the money, but does not smoke.

Mr. Thurston had a farm of fourteen hundred acres in Centerburgh, well stocked and worked. He was also a large dealer in stock

29

and real estate, and became quite wealthy. Mrs. Thurston joined the Methodist church before her marriage ; went with her husband to the Methodist Protestant church, but has since joined the Congregational church in Centerburgh, where she resides, 1879, and her good influence and benevolence are felt in a wide circle. She is a lady of medium size, mentally and physically strong; and still enjoys tolerable health.

### Children :

+10,500 Elihu,[4] b. Dec. 4, 1824; m. Martha Cowgill.
  10,501 Eunice,[4] b. June 30, 1826; d. Sept. 10, 1827.
  10,502 Eunice Hilfa,[4] b. in Homer, Ohio, April 1, 1828; m. near Lock, Ohio, April 1, 1846, Albert Webster; divorced, name restored by law; resides in Chicago, Ill. Children:
      10,503 *Glessner* (Webster), committed suicide while on a vist to his uncle Orlin, when twenty-one years of age, from depression of spirits.
      10,504 *Arista* (Webster), m. Jerome Lambrite of Chicago ; divorced; is now the fashion writer for the Chicago Times.
  10,505 Lucy,[4] b. Feb. 1, 1830; d. Oct. 6, 1832.
+10,506 Orlin,[4] b. March 12, 1834; m. Mary R. Weaver.
  10,507 Lucy,[4] b. Oct. 17, 1841; graduated from Sloan's academy in Mt. Vernon, Ohio; m. Jan. 12, 1869, Edwin Buckingham Robbins, b. near Quincy, Ill., Mar. 1, 1835, son of Smith and Emily (Doane) Robbins of Columbus, Ohio. He was a wholesale merchant in New York city, but now in Columbus ; both members of the Congregational church. Children :
      10,508 *Edwin Thurston* (Robbins), b. in Brooklyn, N. Y., Feb. 17, 1871.
      10,509 *George Arthur* (Robbins), b. in Columbus Jan. 4, 1878.
  10,510 Susan,[4] b. Sept. 13, 1843; a brilliant lady; graduated from the female seminary in Washington, Pa., an accomplished organist and pianist; is a member of the Episcopal church; m. Feb. 27, 1866, Cary Cooper, b. in Lexington, Ohio, Sept. 22, 1847, son of Hugh and Elizabeth Cooper; he went to Oskaloosa, Mahaska county, Iowa, when seventeen years of age and engaged in the hardware business, and now has a foundry and machine shop. Children :
      10,511 *Maude Thurston* (Cooper), b. Dec. 28, 1869.
      10,512 *Bessie Dean* (Cooper), b. Dec. 27, 1875.

### 10,317

GEORGE WASHINGTON THURSTON [8] (*Peter,*[2] *Moses* [1]), brother of the preceding, and son of Peter [3] and Hannah (Wheeler) Thurston of Fletcher, Vt.; born there Feb. 12, 1805; married, May 20, 1832, CHARLOTTE JACKSON, sister to his brother Peter's wife. He died June 30, 1835. His widow married, second, John Hanawalt; he died 1867, having had eight children, three only now living. Married, third, Carlton Belt; he died 1875, and she is living with her daughter, Mrs. Wood, in Marshalltown, Marshall county, Iowa, vigorous in mind and body, 1879.

Mr. Thurston was small in stature, but strong and active; came to Ohio with his parents and lived with them till his marriage, when he purchased a farm two miles from New Haven, Huron county, Ohio. He built the canal aqueduct over the north fork of the Licking river at Newark, Ohio. He was a member of the Methodist church.

### Children :

  10,513 Mary Elizabeth,[4] b. Aug. 24, 1834; m. 1st, Sept. 3, 1851, John Tannahill Hanawalt; he purchased a farm one mile west of Westerville, Franklin county, Ohio. In 1856 they moved to Camanche, Clinton county, Iowa; he died, and his widow and children returned to Westerville, and in the fall of 1859 she m. 2d, Selah Sammis. She died June, 1869. Her children, by first husband:

10,514 *George Washington* (Hanawalt), b. Aug., 1852; a farmer six miles south of Columbus, Ohio; m. Dec., 1878, Annie Ferris.

10,515 *Emma Elizabeth* (Hanawalt), b. Oct., 1854; m. May 13, 1877, Russell Bigelow, a farmer one mile from Center Village, Delaware county, Ohio.

By second husband:

10,516 *Lovet Taft* (Sammis), b. fall of 1860; d. aged 1 y. 6 m.

10,517 *Charlotte* (Sammis), b. 1862.

They are all intelligent, accomplished, and in every way worthy citizens, republicans in politics, radical on temperance, educated at the Otterline university in western Ohio, members of the Methodist church.

10,518 Sarah Rosetta,⁴ b. March 3, 1836; "five feet three inches high, weight 115 pounds, mental motive temperament;" m. 1st, Sept. 18, 1855, Insley Campbell, a farmer three miles east of Utica, Licking county, Ohio, on the farm where he was born, Aug. 15, 1829; he died Nov. 20, 1859, after which the widow purchased a place in the village of Chatham, Licking county, six miles from Newark, where her mother lived. In the fall of 1864 she purchased a farm and moved to it. Sept. 5, 1865, m. 2d, Calvin Woods [whose first wife was Cordelia Thurston, see no. 10,325] and moved to Marshalltown, Marshall county, Iowa, where he was engaged in mercantile business till he died, August, 1873. She had:

10,519 *Ensley Gilmore Denison* (Campbell), b. July 12, 1856; took a commercial course of study in Iowa city; m. Feb. 16, 1876, Julia Pesk of Iowa city; went into mercantile business in Marshalltown. In Sept., 1878, removed to Waukegan, Lake county, Ill., where he is pursuing the same business. "In temperament vital mental, five feet ten inches high, weight 200 pounds, blue grey eyes, brown hair, and fair complexion; favors both father and mother."

10,520 *Sarah Alice* (Campbell), b. May 13, 1858; d. May 30, 1870; intelligent, interesting, mature beyond her years, and a member of the Baptist church.

10,521 *Daughter*, b. Nov. 29, 1872; d. Aug., 1873.

## 10,318

THOMAS JEFFERSON THURSTON³ (*Peter,² Moses¹*), brother of the preceding, and son of Peter³ and Hannah (Butler) Thurston of Fletcher, Vt.; born there Feb. 12, 1805; married, first, in Granville, Ohio, March 28, 1828, ROSETTA BULL, born April 25, 1809, daughter of Smith and Sarah (Burr) Bull of Manchester, Vt. [The family moved to Ohio in 1813.] Second, at Salt Lake city, Utah, Nov. 18, 1855, ELIZABETH SMITH, born Feb. 27, 1835, daughter of John and Mary (Johnson) Smith of Lancaster, England.

Mr. Thurston was a "straight, medium-sized man, with fine auburn hair, fair skin, large mental development; much accustomed to argumentative reasoning, expressed by a clear, ringing voice; when a boy a very fast runner." He went to Ohio with his parents when eight years of age, and tells this incident concerning the journey. They met a company of our soldiers taking English prisoners to Flat Bush and heard his father say to one of them, "you have got into the land of liberty," and the prisoners replied, "it is no land of liberty for us." After his first marriage they moved to a farm which he had previously purchased in New Haven, Huron county, Ohio, taking his wife's family connections with him. He remained there several years, gave his farm to his brother George Washington, and moved to a half section of land he had purchased in Seneca county, Indian Reservation. It was very heavily timbered. He

cleared a hundred acres and built a house thirty-two by eighteen feet, of poplar logs, the average size of which was two feet in diameter. The logs were hewed to eight inches in thickness, and six logs, laid one above the other, furnished the required height for the walls, making a story and a half house. Timber was so plenty the butts of the trees only were used for building. He also built a barn, boarded and shingled, doing nearly all the work himself. In 1845 he sold this place for $2,300 in cash and $1,000 in teams and wagons, in which he moved to Nauvoo, Ill., where he spent the winter. In the spring of 1846 he went three hundred and twenty-five miles to Council Bluffs, Iowa, and spent that winter. In the spring of 1847 started for Salt Lake city, arrived in October, spent the winter in his wagons, and in 1848 built an adobe house in the sixth ward. He took up a farm of seventy or eighty acres in Centerville, Davis county, Utah, twelve miles from the city. He made the first boat ever put into Salt Lake. The crickets ate up all the corn and other cereals he planted the first year; he found himself in sore distress and was compelled to sell his last yoke of cattle to furnish food for his family. A company of gold-seekers came along, and seeing his boat hired him to carry them across Weber and Bear rivers. Their teams were worn out and some of the company had exhausted their means, but he carried them just the same. They proved to be generous, and left many things for him, partly because they could not haul them. In 1849 he built upon his farm in Centerville and raised a good crop. He made a road into Weber valley, which was a hard job, and moved his family to their new home, which, by hard labor and natural advantages, he has made one of the most desirable places in the county.

Mr. Thurston was a very successful hunter, as was his father before him, and he says: "I hunted some for a pastime. Now hunting is a science and requires a firm and steady nerve, and a knowledge of the traits of the animals one is hunting. One day I went out and killed four deer. The news spread, and the next day thirty or forty men turned out to hunt and killed two fawns that could not get away. Two of the men were after two deer, one passed me and I killed it. They killed no more that winter; gave it up completely discouraged. I killed that winter thirty-three, the next winter forty, and the next thirty-three. I readily sold the venison for five cents per pound, and at the same time pork sold for $1.50 per one hundred pounds." He tells several stories about his hunting excursions, and one severe conflict with a deer that he caught by the horns after he became enraged by a shot that did not enter a vital part and showed fight; how he held him as in a vice while a lad that was with him dispatched him with a knife. He says: "I went to market with a forty-three gallon barrel of cider, sold it, and was asked how we could get it out. I said I guessed we could manage it some way. Two men rolled the barrel to the back end of the wagon. I took hold of it and carried it more than twenty feet and set it down on its end. I was a chopper also and had no peer."

The differences between the Mormons and the general government in 1857 and 1858 caused the sending of an army there, when the entire population packed up, Mr. Thurston among the rest, and went

south some seventy-five miles to Spanish Fork; but the people compromised with the government and they returned. Mr. Thurston says he got back to his farm in season to harvest three hundred bushels of wheat from eight or ten acres where no wheat was sown and had not been watered or cared for; "volunteer wheat," he calls it.

He embraced the Mormon religion and was, he says, "acting bishop for Mormon people for the whole county of Morgan for many years. I am at present [1879] president of the high council for Morgan county, stake of Zion, and have been for some years. The high council consists of twelve men, high priests, a quorum to sit in judgment to try all cases in dispute, the highest tribunal in the stake of Morgan county from which an appeal can be taken to the first presidency of the whole church." His present residence is Littleton, Morgan county, Utah.

His children, by first wife, Rosetta, born in New Haven, Ohio:

10,525　Harriet Elizabeth,[4] b. Jan. 7, 1829; m. 1st, July 3, 1851, William Washington Potter, b. in the state of New York Jan. 9, 1809; was killed by the Indians Oct., 1853, at the same time that Lieut. Gunnison was killed, while acting as pilot for an exploring expedition of the United States, under command of Col. Steptoe, in San Pete county, Utah. In commemoration of the murder of Gunnison, the place has been established as a town and named Gunnison. Mr. Potter was a farmer in Manti, San Pete county, and a member of the Mormon church. He was a very energetic and courageous man, carried the mail, and had made fifteen successful trips through the same part of the country, notwithstanding the Indians were hostile and it was very dangerous traveling. At the time they were killed a division arose in their camp and a majority determined, against Mr. Potter's earnest protestation, to camp one night in a beautiful grove of trees, where they were surrounded by the Indians and all killed but two. Mrs. Potter was well educated, a great student of history both ancient and modern, and was the author of many very creditable productions in poetry and prose. She taught school nearly eight years before marriage and during her widowhood, and kept the post-office at Morgan city till near the time of her death. She m. 2d, Jan. 10, 1862, Daniel Williams, a merchant and farmer in Morgan city, b. in Monmouthshire, Eng., May 23, 1822, son of Daniel and Maria (Rawlins) Williams. He had been previously married and had five children; was not connected with any church. She had one child by first husband:

10,526　*Thomas Jefferson Thurston* (Potter), b. in Centerville, Utah, April 18, 1853; n.m.; connected with the Mormon church; was killed by falling upon a saw, while bearing off lumber, at a saw-mill in Kanab, Kane county, Utah, Nov. 30, 1873.

+10,527　George Washington,[4] b. Nov. 1, 1830; m. Sarah Lucina Snow.

+10,528　Smith Butler,[4] b. Jan. 4, 1833; m. Mary Gom.

10,529　Sarah Ann,[4] b. May 20, 1835; m. 1st, Dec. 15, 1853, Rev. Jedediah Morgan Grant, b. in Windsor, Broome county, N. Y., Feb. 21, 1816, son of Joshua and Thalia Grant. He was brigadier general in the Nauvoo Legion, the first mayor of Salt Lake City, speaker of the house of representatives in the Utah Representative Assembly, counselor to Brigham Young at the time of his death, minister to the Latter Day Saints, and held many other offices. He had married three wives previous to this marriage and had six children; two of his wives and three of his children were living when he married Sarah Ann. She married, 1857, the brother of her first husband, George Davis Grant, who was general of militia, held many offices of trust, and was much respected; was a particular friend of Joseph Smith, the Mormon prophet. They all resided in Salt Lake City. He died March 27, 1864. She was again married, to John Frederick Snedaker, b. in Pennsylvania, a farmer in Big Cottonwood, Salt Lake county, Utah. He is priest of a branch of the church of Latter Day Saints, justice of the peace, and president of a quorum of seventies. She had, by first husband:

10,530   *George Smith* (Grant), b. April 27, 1855; graduated from the university of Deseret. He is a farmer in West Jordan, Salt Lake county, an elder in the Mormon church, and is now, 1879, on a mission to England, laboring in the London Conference. He married, Jan. 1, 1877. Louisa Matilda Morgan, b. in Salt Lake City Nov. 16, 1857, daughter of Edward and Louisa Morgan of Big Cottonwood; she died Aug. 26, 1877.

By second husband :

10,531   *Sarah Helen* (Grant), b. in Bountiful, Davis county, Utah, Oct. 27, 1859; d. Oct. 6, 1860.

By third husband :

10,532   *Charles Alma* (Snedaker), b. Jan. 10, 1865; d. Dec. 19, 1869.
10,533   *Rosetta Alice* (Snedaker), b. April 26, 1866; d. Oct. 11, 1867.
10,534   *Lauria Elizabeth* (Snedaker), b. July 5, 1868; d. Sept. 20, 1868.
10,535   *Minnie Janett* (Snedaker), b. Nov. 13, 1870; d. May 25, 1871.
10,536   *Rosalia Vilate* (Snedaker), b. Oct. 22, 1873.
10,537   *Willard Jefferson* (Snedaker), } twins, born } d. Sept. 30, 1878.
10,538   *Jedediah Lewy* (Snedaker),  } Nov. 4, 1876; }
10,539   Hannah Maria,[4] b. May 18, 1837; d. Oct. 3, 1838.
10,540   Reuben Johnson,[4] b. Oct. 9, 1839; d. at Salt Lake City Sept. 22, 1858.
10,541   Julia Rosetta,[4] b. Nov. 21, 1841; m. 1st, in Salt Lake City, Jan. 15, 1856, Joseph Bates Noble, b. in New York state 1809, a farmer in Bountiful, member of the Mormon church. By reason of gross ill-treatment from her husband, she was divorced May, 1864. She m. 2d, Feb. 1, 1865, Jacob Arthurs, b. in Ireland, son of Jacob and Sarah Arthurs; he was a sawyer in Hardscrabble Kanyon, Utah. She had, by first husband :

10,542   *Rozetta Josephene* (Noble), b. in Salt Lake City Mar. 13, 1857; m. in Salt Lake City Nov. 15, 1875, William Joseph Spendlove, a farmer in Littleton, Morgan county, Utah, member of the Mormon church, b. Dec. 17, 1853, son of Joseph and Harriet (Paine) Spendlove of Sutterworth, Leicestershire, England. Children :
    10,543   *Mary Josephene* (Spendlove), b. Aug. 5, 1877.
    10,544   *William Orson* (Spendlove), b. Feb. 15, 1879.
10,545   *Harriet* (Noble), b. in Salt Lake City Feb. 10, 1860; m. in Salt Lake city, July 6, 1874, Andrew Jackson Walton, b. May 12, 1835, son of Arthur and Martha (Walton) Walton of Mexico, Me., a machinist in Ogden City, Utah, an ordained elder in the Mormon church. Arthur Walton went with his family to Utah in 1851, and with his son Andrew J. constructed the first threshing machine made in Utah. He was born June 1, 1802 and died in Logan City June 9, 1878; his wife was born in Canada 1802 and died 1853.
10,546   *Sarah Maria* (Noble), b. in Milton, Morgan county, May 6, 1863; m. in Park City, Utah, Dec. 25, 1876, Edward Mull, b. in Ohio, a miner in Park City; has been a soldier in the United States army; member of the Mormon church. They had Franklin (Mull), b. Oct. 30, 1877, d. next day.
10,547   *Charles* (Noble), b. in Bountiful April 20, 1864; d. July 27, 1877.

By second husband, born in Hardscrabble :

10,548   *Elizabeth* (Arthurs), b. Feb. 2, 1867; d. June 22, 1870.
10,549   *Henry* (Arthurs), b. Dec. 9, 1869.
10,550   *James Edward* (Arthurs), b. Feb. 22, 1872.
10,551   *Lizzie Helen* (Arthurs), b. in Salt Lake City May 20, 1874.
10,552   *Thomas* (Arthurs), b. in Park City Aug. 20, 1876.
10,553   *Peter Franklin* (Arthurs), b. in Milton April 15, d. April 27, 1878.
10,554   Caroline Rozalia,[4] b. Jan. 3, 1843; m. in Salt Lake City, Oct. 15, 1864, John James Fry, a brewer in Ogden City, Weber county, Utah, an ordained elder in the Mormon church, b. Aug. 7, 1838, son of John James and Ann (Tumor) Fry of Portsmouth, Eng. Children, born in Salt Lake City :
    10,555   *Caroline Rozalia* (Fry), b. Aug. 1, 1865; d. Oct. 21, 1866.
    10,556   *John James* (Fry), b. Jan. 10, 1867.
    10,557   *Rozetta Ann* (Fry), b. Oct. 12, 1868; d. Sept. 27, 1869.
    10,558   *Sarah Jane* (Fry), b. June 10, 1870.

Born in Ogden City:
10,559  *Mary Cordelia* (Fry), b. Feb. 18, 1872; d. Oct. 21, 1875.
10,560  *Fanny Josephene* (Fry), b. Sept. 15, 1873.
10,561  *William Alonso* (Fry), b. July 10, 1875.
10,562  *Clara* (Fry), b. Aug. 20, 1877.
10,563  Huldah Cordelia,[4] b. in Van Buren county, Iowa, June 1, 1846; m. Willard G. Smith of Salt Lake City.
10,564  Thomas Jefferson,[4] b. in Salt Lake City Dec. 13, 1848; was shot without provocation by John Olson, in Morgan county, Aug. 20, 1870.
10,565  Peter Franklin,[4] b. in Salt Lake City June 24, 1851, a farmer in Milton, Morgan county, an ordained elder in the Mormon church; m. Oct. 3, 1871, Mary Ann Spendlove, b. Oct. 22, 1855, daughter of Joseph and Harriet (Paine) Spendlove of Sutterworth, Eng.  Children:
10,566  *Harriet,*[5] b. Sept. 14, 1872.
10,567  *Rozetta,*[5] b. July 11, 1874.
10,568  *Mary Ann,*[5] b. Dec. 25, 1875.
10,569  *Joseph Franklin,*[5] b. in Prattville, Sevier county, Utah, Feb. 23, 1878; d. April 14, 1878.
10,570  *Jefferson Smith,*[5] b. in Milton July 13, 1879.

By second wife, Elizabeth, born in Centerville:
10,571  Rozetta,[4] b. Oct. 25, 1856.
10,572  Elizabeth,[4] b. March 17, 1857.

Born in Morgansville, Utah:
10,573  John,[4] b. Dec. 14, 1859.
10,574  Clara,[4] b. Sept. 17, 1861.
10,575  Mary,[4] b. July 22, 1863.
10,576  William Henry,[4] b. Nov. 15, 1865.  This boy is quite remarkable for his memory.  When two years old he could talk very plainly and was much interested in a primer having pictures of four birds in it, and under each bird three stanzas of poetry.  He brought this primer to his father and asked him to read the poetry to him, which he did, and at the boy's request read it over to him several times, when the youngster took the book and went away.  The next day he repeated the whole twelve stanzas to his mother, and then to his father, correctly.
10,577  Frederick,[4] b. Sept. 29, 1867.
10,578  Jedediah Morgan,[4] b. Sept. 1, 1869.
10,579  Edward,[4] b. Aug. 12, 1871; d. Aug. 23, 1871.
10,580  Leah Helen,[4] b. Sept. 6, 1872.
10,581  Rebecca,[4] b. Aug. 7, 1875.
10,582  Le Roy,[4] b. June 7, 1877.
10,583  Harris,[4] b. May 7, 1879.

## 10,319

REUBEN HARRIS THURSTON[3] (*Peter,*[2] *Moses*[1]), brother of the preceding, and son of Peter[2] and Hannah (Wheeler) Thurston of Fletcher, Vt.; born there Dec. 11, 1806; married, in Granville, Licking county, Ohio, March 15, 1827, MARY MORSE BROOKS, born June 12, 1803, daughter of Nathan and Sarah (Morse) Brooks of Underhill, Chittenden county, Vt.  She died May 11, 1876.

Mr. Thurston is a farmer in Garden City, Blue Earth county, Minn.  In religion a free thinker; having a fertile mind, he writes essays and poems upon religious and moral subjects, discrediting the bible as a revelation, but holding to the great first cause, God, as revealed in nature only.  He always advocates morality, "and is a most genial gentleman, a man of good judgment and taste;" takes a deep interest in the history of the Thurstons in this country.

Children:
+10,589  Irvin Harris,[4] b. Jan. 11, 1828; m. 1st, Fredonia Case; 2d, Lydia Ellen Dunham; 3d, Mary Frances Gerry.

10,590    Sarah Hannah,[4] twin, b. in Granville April 26, 1829; m. April 25, 1847,
Henry Clinton Cowgill, b. March 27, 1823, son of George and Eliza
(Dunham) Cowgill of Delaware county, Ohio, a farmer and stock dealer in Albion, Marshall county, Iowa, justice of the peace. Mrs. Cowgill says : " So far as I know, there never has been a drunkard among
my own or husband's relations, and in my own family there are none
who use tobacco. Our labors have secured a moderate competency;
the prophet's prayer has been answered to us, 'Give me neither poverty nor riches.'"    Children:

10,591    *George Thurston* (Cowgill), b. Oct. 28, 1848; county superintendent of schools, Grundy Center, Grundy county, Iowa.

10,592    *Henry Ernest* (Cowgill), b. Dec. 2, 1851; d. Oct. 16, 1874.

10,593    *Frank Brooks* (Cowgill), b. June 2, 1856; graduated from Iowa
State university 1879, valedictorian.

10,594    *Rosa* (Cowgill), b. Feb. 28, 1858; in Iowa State university, class of
1881.

10,595    *Nellie May* (Cowgill), b. July 6, 1863.

10,596    Mary Eliza,[4] twin, b. April 26, 1829; m. 1st, Dr. George S. Eaton of
Delaware, Ohio; divorced 1862; 2d, Florentine Everett Snow of St.
Paul, Minn., formerly of Boston, Mass. The names of her children
by first husband were changed by act of the legislature to Snow. She
is a strong, active, and cheerful lady of merit a good singer. Children:

10,597    *Son*, d. aged one year.

10,598    *Lilla* (Snow), m. William Kindred of Fargo, Cass county, Dakota
territory.

10,599    *Rose* (Snow), m. Robert Harrison of St. Louis, Mo.

10,600    *Georgiana* (Snow), m. George Allen of St. Paul.

10,601    *Stella* (Snow), n.m.

10,602    Rose Lucia,[4] b. in Granville April 29, 1831; m. at Delaware, 1852, Brig.
Gen. James Heaton Baker, b. in Butler county, Ohio, son of Henry
and Mary (Heaton) Baker. He was secretary of state in Ohio and
also in Minnesota, commissioner of pensions under President Grant,
register of consolidated land office at Boonville, Mo., surveyor general
of Minnesota, and brigadier general in the war against the rebellion.
He has retired from business and resides in Mankato, Blue Earth
county, Minn. She was an accomplished lady and genial companion.
Children :

10,603    *Arthur Heaton* (Baker), m. Elizabeth Towles of Boston; is a clerk
in the post-office department at Washington, D. C.; two children.

10,604    *Henry Edgar* (Baker), n.m.; a lawyer in Mankato.

+10,605    Cyrus Brooks,[4] b. Jan. 21, 1834; m. Mary Harrison.

10,606    Caroline Matilda,[4] b. May 14, 1837; m. in Iowa, June, 1856, Sherman E.
Finch, a graduate of a commercial college in Cincinnati, Ohio, a merchant and farmer, and has been sheriff of Blue Earth county. She died
in Mankato Dec. 31, 1867; six children.

10,607    Otho,[4] b. Nov. 12, 1842; d. 1843.

+10,608    Frank,[4] b. Sept. 22, 1844; m. Julia Marvin.

+10,609    Charles Edgar,[4] b. Dec. 31, 1849; m. Ida Barton.

## Fourth Generation.

### 10,445

MOSES THURSTON [4] of Holden, Mass. (*Moses,[3] Moses,[2] Moses [1]*), son
of Moses [3] and Hannah (Bolton) Thurston of Cambridge, Vt.; born
in Westminster, Mass., Oct. 2, 1811; married, 1840, MRS. ELIZA
CHAFFIN FLAGG of Holden. He died of hydrophobia, induced by
an injury from a mad steer, June 12, 1854.

Mr. Thurston was a hunter and trapper with the famous John

Brown (now, 1877, 92 years old), who explored what is called "the John Brown track" in western New York. He was with him seven years previous to coming to Holden in 1839, where he was a farmer and stone-mason.

Children :

+10,614   Lyman Flagg,⁵ b. Dec. 25. 1841; m. Alice Gertrude Swett.
10,615   George Washington,⁵ b. Dec. 20, 1843; enlisted in the 57th Massachusetts regiment, and was killed in his first engagement, the first battle of the Wilderness, May 9, 1864.
10,616   Alvin Eugene,⁵ b. Jan. 28. 1847; a foreman builder, in the employ of Norcross Brothers of Worcester, Mass. ; n.m.
10,617   Matilda Bolton,⁵ b. May 25, 1849; m. Frank St. George and lives in Oxford, Mass. ; one daughter.
10,618   Mary Freelove,⁵ b. Jan. 31, 1851; d. Oct. 29, 1864.

## 10,448

JAMES TOTTINGHAM THURSTON⁴ ( *Moses,*³ *Moses,*² *Moses*¹), brother of the preceding, and son of Moses³ and Hannah (Bolton) Thurston of Cambridge, Vt. ; born there Feb. 19, 1818 ; married, first, Feb. 14, 1843, FANNY WITHERELL, born Sept. 22, 1822, daughter of Elijah and Lucretia (Bailey) Witherell; she died 1865. Second, MRS. JANE CURRIER, widow of J. Q. Currier. He died June 14, 1878, aged 60 y. 4 m.

Mr. Thurston was president of the Vermont Mutual Fire Insurance Company of Montpelier, the largest corporation of the kind in New England, and had held nearly all town offices. He was a prominent man in Vermont, perhaps as widely and personally known as any man in the state. Although connected with nearly every public measure there for many years, he avoided notoriety and declined office, although it often sought him. An eminently practical man, a fluent speaker, and some of his terse sentences were widely quoted in the time of the war of the rebellion.

He had, by first wife :

+10,623   John Baldwin,⁵ b. Feb. 10, 1849; m. Lucy Fiske.

## 10,495

CHARLES THURSTON⁴ (*Peter,*³ *Peter,*² *Moses*¹), son of Peter³ and Elizabeth (Jackson) Thurston of Granville, Licking county, Ohio; born there Feb. 23, 1833 ; married, in Nekama, Wis., Nov. 27, 1854, JOANNA DILLEY, born in Allegany county, N.Y., Nov. 11, 1838, daughter of John and Mary (Barker) Dilley of Garden City, Blue Earth county, Minn.

Mr. Thurston is a farmer and manufacturer of a scrofula medicine, for which he claims power to render cures certain. He has been a member of the Baptist church. He says they were pioneers in Minnesota, and experienced all the trials and hardships from Indians and a new country, usual to pioneer life, for twenty-five years ; have aimed to give a right direction to the character of the people.

Children :

10,628   Mary E.,⁵ b. Oct. 17, 1856; m. June 2, 1875, Thomas L. Rogers, a miller, living in Vernon Center, Blue Earth county, Minn.   They have:
10,629   *Charles* (Rogers), b. Feb. 29, 1876.
10,630   *Jessie* (Rogers), b. Dec. 10, 1877.

10,631  Lizzie,⁵ b. May 30, 1858; m. in Lyra, Ohio, March 19, 1878, Dorsal G.
        Willard, a farmer in Redwood Falls, Redwood county, Minn.  Child:
        10,632  *Ray* (Willard), b. March 6, 1879.
10,633  Charles E.,⁵ b. April 7, 1860; d. March 31, 1864.
10,634  Johnson D.,⁵ b. April 9, 1866.

## 10,500

ELIHU THURSTON⁴ ( *Johnson,*⁸ *Peter,*² *Moses*¹), eldest son of John-
son⁸ and Julia (Everett) Thurston of Centerburgh, Ohio; born in
Granville, Ohio, Dec. 4, 1824; married, in Delaware, Ohio, June 21,
1849, MARTHA COWGILL, born Oct. 25, 1826, daughter of Daniel
Morris [son of George, son of George Cowgill, who came to this
country with William Penn and settled in Pennsylvania] and Nancy
(Finley) Cowgill of Brown township, Delaware county, Ohio.

Mr. Thurston inherited a tough constitution, strong and active.
Before arriving at majority he had mastered, at home, the common
branches of study and phrenology.  He attended the Wesleyan university at Delaware one year, where he studied latin grammar, algebra,
and geometry.  He settled in Peru township, Morrow county, Ohio,
upon a farm, where he resided [except from 1859–1862, while settling
his father's estate, he was at St. Joseph, Mo.] till June, 1874, when
he sold his five hundred and sixty-six acres of land and removed to
Kalida, Putnam county, Ohio, where he has three hundred acres of
land, which he expects to make "one of the most attractive and pro-
ductive places in the world."  He has engaged more or less in raising and trading stock, cattle, mules, hogs, and sheep.  During all
this time he has been a student, and mastered "common law,"
though, for want of time, has never practiced law.  He is a strong
advocate for temperance, not using any intoxicating beverages, tea,
coffee, or tobacco, and proved by his ability to win foot races in 1867
the advantage one who abstains has over those who use these stimu-
lants.  "July, 1867, at the fair grounds in Mt. Gilead, Ohio, with
seven other contestants, he won the race and received the prize of
ten dollars.  The same year, at Berea, Ohio, he challenged any who
drank tea or coffee twice a day to run with him.  Several of the students accepted and were easily beaten, which resulted in the selection
of a better quality of food and drink."  In 1878 he was silenced by
the bogus Murphy organization of Kalida, for reporting in their local
paper, which he was editing, the drunkenness of the Roman Catholic
priesthood and some of their membership.  Eighteen voted to rescind
the silencing resolution, but that was not a majority.

He is a member of the Christian church, sometimes called "New
Light;" is a man of liberal views, and has written and published his
faith in a pamphlet entitled, "How does the blood of the Innocent
suffice for and effect the regeneration of the guilty."  Mrs. Thurston
is a cheerful lady, member of the Methodist church, and writes:
"Our sons neither drink tea, coffee, whiskey, beer, nor smoke or
chew tobacco; neither do their father nor myself."

Children, born in Peru township:
10,637  Norman,⁵ b. Aug. 20, 1850; m. Feb. 13, 1873, Ida Peet, b. April 16,
        1852, daughter of William and Penelope (Halley) Peet of Delaware,
        Ohio.  He graduated from Sharp's Commercial college, Delaware,
        and is a farmer of much intelligence and enterprise at Pleasant Point,
        Paulding county, Ohio.  They have:

10,631  Lizzie

Faithfully Yours
Eli: W. Thurston

10,638   *Flora,*[6] b. Dec. 17, 1875.
10,639   *Lester,*[6] b. June 15, 1877.
10,640   David Morris,[5] b. Aug. 27, 1852; a man of nervous, sanguine temperament, red hair and hazel eyes; left home at nineteen and worked at
making farm machinery in Columbus, Ohio; while there attended the
medical college; graduated from the medical college in Cincinnati, O.,
1875; studied with Drs. Welch and Hess of Delaware; m. Agnes
Hess, daughter of Dr. Hess; had a son who soon died, and his wife
left him and sued for a divorce. He practiced medicine a while in
Deavertown, Morgan county, Ohio, and is now in Hartford, Croton
post-office. Licking county, Ohio, where he has a profitable business.
10,641   Johnson,[5] b. July 20, 1858; spent two years in Baldwin university, Berea,
Ohio; is now teaching, 1879, expecting to return to college and finish
his studies.

## 10,506

ORLIN THURSTON[4] (*Johnson,*[3] *Peter,*[2] *Moses*[1]), brother of the preceding, and son of Johnson[3] and Julia (Everett) Thurston of Centerburgh, Ohio; born in Homer, Ohio, March 12, 1834; married,
June 23, 1858, MARY R. WEAVER of Mt. Vernon, Ohio.

Mr. Thurston, when twelve years old, was herding cattle with his
father on the prairies of Illinois; graduated from the Delaware college, Ohio; studied law with Gen. George Morgan in Mt. Vernon,
where he was admitted to the bar. He took a steam saw-mill and
went to Humboldt, Kansas, where he has practiced law, farmed it extensively, attained a fortune and a reputation; is a prominent man in
the democratic party and a man of influence in the community. He
was colonel of a Kansas regiment during the war against the rebellion; was burned out twice by the confederates.

One child:

10,642   Orlin,[5] b. 1862; is studying in the Roman Catholic university at St.
Louis, Mo.

## 10,527

GEORGE WASHINGTON THURSTON[4] (*Thomas Jefferson,*[3] *Peter,*[2]
*Moses*[1]), son of Thomas Jefferson[3] and Rosetta (Bull) Thurston of
Littleton, Morgan county, Utah; born in New Haven, Huron county,
Ohio, Nov. 1, 1830; married, in Salt Lake City, March 28, 1858,
SARAH LUCINA SNOW, born in Chester county, Pa., Jan. 21, 1841,
daughter of Erastus [one of the twelve apostles of the Mormon
church] and Artemissia (Beaman) Snow of St. George, Washington
county, Utah.

Mr. Thurston is engaged, 1879, in raising poultry and in bee culture
in Santa Anna, Los Angeles county, Cal. He was brought up under
the influence and education of Mormonism; is by nature conscientious, sympathetic, and earnest in his opposition to all shams, tyranny,
and selfish avarice. He was commissioned by Brigham Young and
sent as a missionary to England, where he remained nearly four years,
paying his passage each way and supporting himself; receiving no
pecuniary support from the authorities that sent him. He received
much abuse and reproach, and bore it with fortitude and with somewhat of pride, in the belief that he was laboring for the cause of God.
After his return to Utah, seeing so much corruption, self-seeking, and
the demand for "unconditional obedience to the priesthood, whether
right or wrong," led him to reject the Mormon religion altogether and
leave its communion. He says he believes in God as revealed in his

works; a God of justice, mercy, and love. He has been in various enterprises in different places in Utah since his mission ended, but with little success pecuniarily, owing more to the anguish occasioned by the loss of their child, who was stolen by the Indians, which almost unmanned him, and the changes of location, than to any lack of enterprise or industry, which traits were both a second nature to him. He says: "We have lived where we now are nearly eight years; very much longer than we have ever staid in one place before." He has sent us a number of poems of his composition, but we cannot insert more than the following acrostic to his mother, "one of the best women that ever lived."

Round the strong tree the ivy twines
Or clambers o'er the rocky wall,
Zealous some firm support to gain
Ere its frail, helpless form shall fall;
Thus fondly through my helpless years
To thee, dear mother, did I cling,
And found a firm support in thee;

True shelter 'neath thy dove-like wing.
How beamed thine eye, undimmed by years;
Unseamed by age, how bloomed thy cheek;
Rows of rich pearl thy lips disclosed,
Soft smiling or when moved to speak;
Truth love, and virtue, polished gems
Of priceless worth, adorned thy mind,
Not truest gold, from Ophir's strand,

By mortal e'er was more refined.

Years have sped by on time's fleet wing,

Yet years have left no blight behind,
Or aught diminished from the light,
Unsullied, beaming from thy mind;
Round thee the leaves of autumn fall,

Softly the frosts of age descend.
O! glad would I sustain thee now,
Now gladly truest succor lend.

Gladly each tender thought and word,
Each gentle, kindly act return;
Or twine my arms in filial love
Round thee whose love doth quenchless burn;
Gently as infant should'st thou rest,
Enfolded fondly to my breast.

Children:

10,643  George Washington,[5] b. May 9, 1859.
10,644  Erastus Jefferson,[5] b. Oct. 7, 1860; d. Jan. 26, 1864.
10,645  Sarah Lucina,[5] b. May 26, 1862.
10,646  Artemissia,[5] b. Nov. 12, 1863.
10,647  Rozetta,[6] b. Nov. 1, 1865; carried off by the Indians in 1868, and never heard from since.
10,648  Lafayette,[6] b. March 23, 1867.
10,649  Joseph Smith,[5] b. Nov. 26, 1868.
10,650  Joan Alice,[6] b. Sept. 2, 1871.
10,651  Hulda Cordelia,[6] b. July 4, 1873.
10,652  Benjamin Franklin,[6] b. Nov. 14, 1874.
10,653  Harriet Elizabeth,[6] b. March 8, 1876.
10,654  Annie Mariah,[5] b. Dec. 28, 1877.
10,655  Charlotte Frances,[6] b. Oct. 14, 1879.

## 10,528

REV. SMITH BUTLER THURSTON [4] (*Thomas Jefferson*,[3] *Peter*,[2] *Moses*[1]), brother of the preceding, and son of Thomas Jefferson [3] and Rosetta (Bull) Thurston of Littleton, Morgan county, Utah; born in New Haven, Huron county, Ohio, Jan. 4, 1833; married, in Salt Lake City, Nov. 2, 1861, MARY GOM, born in Solihill, Warwickshire, Eng., daughter of Owen and Elizabeth (Howard) Gom of Virginia City, Kane county, Utah. She died in Cedar City, Iron county, Utah, Feb. 22, 1873.

Mr. Thurston is a trader and farmer, 1879, in Prattville, Sevier county, Utah. He says: "I am a minister of what I truly believe to be the gospel of Christ, church of Jesus Christ of Latter Day Saints." He was sent by Brigham Young as a missionary to the Sandwich Islands in 1853, and returned in July, 1857, bearing all his expenses without aid from those by whom he was sent, showing a devotion to the cause which bespeaks sincerity and love for the work. He is quite a poet and sends some lines commendatory of these genealogical labors, which modesty forbids the compiler to publish.

Children:

10,656  Mary Loeza,⁶ b. in Salt Lake City Dec. 6, 1862.
10,657  Smith Butler,⁶ b. in Salt Lake City Aug. 15, 1865.
10,658  Sarah Elizabeth,⁶ b. in Salt Lake City Dec. 2, d. Dec. 8, 1866.
10,659  Catherine Rozetta,⁶ b. in Salt Lake City Nov. 30, 1867.
10,660  Alice Mary,⁵ b in Salt Lake City Oct. 28, 1869; d. July 30, 1870.
10,661  Anna Sophia,⁵ b. in Virginia City June 15, d. June 30, 1871.
10,662  Caroline Cordelia,⁶ b. in Cedar City Feb. 11, 1873.

## 10,589

IRVIN HARRIS THURSTON⁴ (*Reuben Harris*,³ *Peter*,² *Moses*¹), eldest son of Reuben Harris⁸ and Mary (Brooks) Thurston of Garden City, Blue Earth county, Minn.; born Jan. 11, 1828; married, first, Feb. 11, 1849, FREDONIA CASE of Liberty township, Delaware county, Ohio; she died November, 1851, leaving a son, who soon died. Second, 1855, LYDIA ELLEN DUNHAM, born in Salem, Henry county, Iowa, Feb. 15, 1836; she died July 29, 1869. Third, Nov. 21, 1870, MARY FRANCES GERRY of Garden City.

Mr. Thurston studied medicine with Drs. Hill and Williams of Delaware, Ohio; attended a six months' course of lectures at Starling Medical college, Columbus, Ohio, in 1853–4; spent a year in traveling in different states, practicing some in operative surgery, and looking for a place to locate. In the fall of 1855 settled in Salem, Iowa. In the spring of 1857 moved to Garden City, took a claim and worked it and practiced his profession till the war of the rebellion broke out. In 1862 joined the army under a commission of first assistant surgeon to the 8th Minnesota regiment, and was promoted to surgeon 1865.

His children, born in Garden City, by second wife, Lydia Ellen:

10,663  Minnie Ellen,⁶ b. May 18, 1857.
10,664  Cora Baker,⁶ b. June 15, 1859; d. March 2, 1861.
10,665  Nettie,⁶ b. April 3, 1861.
10,666  Julia Marvin,⁵ b. Aug. 12, 1865.
10,667  Arabel,⁵ b. Jan. 5, 1868.

By third wife, Mary Frances:

10,668  Reuben Harris,⁶ b. May 7, 1872.
10,669  Rose Elfin,⁶ b. Feb. 2, 1874.
10,670  Winfred Otho,⁵ b. Jan. 15, 1876; d. March 22, 1876.

## 10,605

CYRUS BROOKS THURSTON⁴ (*Reuben Harris*,³ *Peter*,² *Moses*¹), brother of the preceding, and son of Reuben Harris⁸ and Mary (Brooks) Thurston of Garden City, Blue Earth county, Minn.; born in Granville, Ohio, Jan. 21, 1834; married, March 21, 1857, MARY HARRISON, born in Columbus, Ohio, Dec. 7, 1836, a relative of President Harrison.

Mr. Thurston graduated from a commercial college in Cincinnati, Ohio in 1854; has been in mercantile business mainly, but now is manufacturers' general agent for agricultural implements and carriages, at No. 18 West Third street, St. Paul, Minn. His business is very large, extending through the North West and into the British Possessions. During the fair week at St. Paul in 1878 his sales amounted to about $30,000. He is a member of the Chamber of Commerce and of the Presbyterian church.

Children :

10,675  William Harrison,⁵ b. Dec. 7, 1857.
10,676  Mary,⁵ } twins, b. April 27, 1861.
10,677  Nellie.⁵ }
10,678  Cyrus Harrison,⁵ b. Oct., 1868: d. Jan., 1870.
10,679  Harry Harrison,⁵ b. Nov. 22, 1873; d. July 13, 1878.

## 10,608

FRANK THURSTON ⁴ (*Reuben Harris,*³ *Peter,*² *Moses* ¹), brother of the preceding, and son of Reuben Harris ³ and Mary (Brooks) Thurston of Garden City, Blue Earth county, Minn.; born in Delaware, Ohio, Sept. 22, 1844; married, Jan. 11, 1865, JULIA MARVIN, born in St. Lawrence county, N. Y., Feb. 18, 1850.

Mr. Thurston is a farmer in Garden City.

Children :

10,684  Jessie Marvin,⁵ b. July 7, 1867.
10,685  Jennie.⁵ b. June 11, 1870.
10,686  Rose B.,⁵ b. May 2, 1872; d. June 5, 1872.
10,687  Mary,⁵ b. Sept. 9, 1878.

## 10,609

CHARLES EDGAR THURSTON ⁴ (*Reuben Harris,*³ *Peter,*² *Moses* ¹), brother of the preceding, and son of Reuben Harris ³ and Mary (Brooks) Thurston of Garden City, Blue Earth county, Minn.; born in Delaware, Ohio, Dec. 31, 1849; married, July 2, 1872, IDA FLORA BARTON, born June 23, 1854.

Mr. Thurston is a United States surveyor and farmer in Garden City. In religion, a free thinker.

Children :

10,692  Cye Arthur,⁵ b. April 28, 1873.
10,693  Charles,⁵ b. May 12, 1877.
10,694  Raymond Heaton,⁵ b. Feb. 15, 1879.

## Fifth Generation.

### 10,614

LYMAN FLAGG THURSTON ⁵ (*Moses,*⁴ *Moses,*³ *Moses,*² *Moses* ¹), eldest son of Moses ⁴ and Eliza (Chaffin) Thurston of Holden, Mass.; born there Dec. 25, 1841; married, Jan. 3, 1871, ALICE GERTRUDE SWETT, born Jan. 7, 1850, daughter of Samuel Doyne and Martha Page (Floyd) Swett of Worcester, Mass.

Mr. Thurston is a builder and carpenter in Worcester. He says: "When a boy twenty years old I was in the field with my uncle and some other men, mowing, where I could hear the drums beating to call in volunteers (this was after the first battle of Bull Run). It awoke my patriotism. I had just complained to my uncle that my scythe did not hang well. He said, 'No, it never hangs well, you are always complaining;' whereupon, hanging the scythe upon the limb of an apple tree, with the remark, 'It hangs well there,' I went and enlisted in the 21st Massachusetts regiment in July, 1861; fought in

the battles of Roanoke Island. N. C.; Newburn, N. C., Feb. 1, 2, 3, 1862; Camden, N. C.; 2d Bull Run, Va., Aug. 30, 1862; Chantilla, Va., Sept. 1, 1862; South Mountain, Md., Sept. 14, 1862; Antietam, Md., Sept. 15, 16, 17, 1862; Fredericksburgh, Va., Dec. 13, 1862; Blue Springs, Tenn., Oct. 10, 1863; Campbell's Station, Tenn., Nov. 16, 1863; Siege of Knoxville. Having then served two years and seven months, I re-enlisted at Blaine Cross Roads, Eastern Tenn., and served until the close of the war in 1865; was wrecked in the Burnside expedition off Hatteras and fought in the battles of the Wilderness, Spottsylvania Court House, Cold Harbor, Bethel Church, and in front of Petersburgh; was wounded there on the 28th of July, 1864, and narrowly escaped being taken prisoner.

"After being honorably discharged from the army, at the close of the war, I served three years at my trade. In the spring of 1869 I and my brother, Alvin Eugene Thurston, went west. Our first stopping place was Kansas City, Mo. Leaving him there, I started with a party bound for Black Canion, Arizona. When west of the Rocky mountains, near Salt Lake City, we were attacked by the Indians, and the man riding next me was killed and several were wounded, so that we were obliged to abandon our journey. I then returned to Worcester and settled down to my trade, and soon commenced business for myself, as builder and contractor, in which I have been quite successful."

One child:

10,699    Corinna Swett,[6] b. July 27, 1872.

## 10,623

JOHN BALDWIN THURSTON [5] (*James Tottingham,*[4] *Moses,*[3] *Moses,*[2] *Moses*[1]), only son of James Tottingham[4] and Fanny (Witherell) Thurston of Montpelier, Vt.; born there Feb. 10, 1849; married, Nov. 28, 1872, LUCY FISKE, born July 28, 1849, daughter of B. G. and A. M. Fiske; she died Sept. 29, 1877, aged 28 y. 2 m.

Mr. Thurston graduated from Amherst in 1870, and is in the insurance business in Montpelier; has been superintendent of public schools for the past two years. He has in his possession a cane of English brier, tradition says, "cut in England by the younger of the two brothers before leaving there for this country;" but how far back in the generation he does not know. It may be an *uncertain* tradition about the two brothers. We are unable to trace back further than Moses Thurston of Hollis, N. H., as seen on page 434.

Children:

10,704    Harrison Bingham,[6] b. Sept. 12, 1873.
10,705    Robert Fiske,[b] b. Sept. 12, 1877.

30

[See page 362, no. 8195.]
Since printing the foregoing pages, I have found the connection of
Joseph with his ancestry and give it here.

## 8195

JOSEPH THURSTON[4] of Westborough, Mass. (*Daniel,*[3] *Daniel,*[2]
*John*[1]), eldest son of Daniel[3] and Experience (Warren) Thurston of
Medfield, Mass.; born there Oct. 14, 1700; married DOROTHY FRIZ-
ZELL. He died 1745.

Mr. Thurston owned a small farm in the extreme south part of the
town, which remained in the name till the death of Samuel Thurston
in 1839, since which time the name is extinct in Westborough. They
were admitted to the church in Westborough by letter Nov. 8, 1741;
his letter from Medfield, and hers from Marlborough, Mass.

### Children :

10,710   Amariah,[5] b. Jan. 17, 1734; killed in French and Indian war Jan. 28, 1761.
10,711   Dorothy,[5] b. Jan. 26, 1735; d. Nov. 11, 1828.
10,712   Experience,[5] d. Dec. 11, 1750, aged about 14.
10,713   Joseph,[5] b. Dec. 29, 1739; m. Thankful Woods and moved to Spencer or
         Leicester, Mass.
+10,714   Samuel,[5] b. Feb. 1, 1744; m. 1st, Sarah Townsend; 2d, Sarah Harrington.
10,715   Zeruah,[5] m. Roger Bruce of North Brookfield, Mass.; intention entered
         April 18, 1761.

## 10,714

SAMUEL THURSTON[5] (*Joseph,*[4] *Daniel,*[3] *Daniel,*[2] *John*[1]), son of
Joseph and Dorothy (Frizzell) Thurston of Westborough, Mass.;
born there Feb. 1, 1744; married, first, Oct. 15, 1765, SARAH TOWN-
SEND of Westborough; she died Sept. 12, 1766. Second, July 16,
1770, SARAH HARRINGTON of Westborough. He was a farmer in
Westborough; died Sept. 11, 1810.

### His children, by first wife, Sarah :

10,720   Sarah,[6] b. Sept. 5, 1766; m. May 31, 1798, Asa Keyes, b. Sept. 21, 1768,
         son of Thomas and Mary (Temple) Keyes of West Royalston, Mass.
         She died Feb. 26, 1807; he died Dec. 27, 1850. Mr. Keyes was a
         farmer in Sterling, Mass.  They had:
   10,721   *Sarah* (Keyes), b. July 15, 1801; d. Dec. 12, 1830.
   10,722   *Mary* (Keyes), b. April 25, 1803; d. April 18, 1836.
   10,723   *Asa* (Keyes), b. Sept. 17, 1805; m. 1st, April 10, 1833, in West
            Boynton, Mass., Lucy W. Hubbard, daughter of Eli and Mehit-
            able (Haskell) Hubbard of Holden, Mass., b. May 29, 1807, d.
            Sept. 6, 1846; 2d, May 19, 1847, Martha Johnson, daughter of
            Joseph and Charlotte Johnson of Southborough, Mass., b. Apr.
            16, 1805, d. Feb. 25, 1867. He had, all but last one by first wife :
      10,724   *Charles B.* (Keyes), b. Jan. 24, 1834; enlisted in the 53d reg.
               Mass. vol. and died at Brashear City, La., May 23, 1863.
      10,725   *Mary* (Keyes), b. Jan. 21, 1837; d. Dec. 21, 1844.
      10,726   *Martha J.* (Keyes), b. Oct. 9, 1838.
      10,727   *Susan M.* (Keyes), b. March 23, 1842; d. March 11, 1843.
      10,728   *Mary F.* (Keyes), b. Oct. 24, 1845; m. Everett Kendall of
               Worcester.
      10,729   *George H.* (Keyes), b. Aug. 30, 1848.

10,730   *Lucy* (Keyes), b. Jan. 25, 1807; m. Oct. 30, 1827, Welcome W. Johnson, b. Aug. 26, 1804, son of Caleb and Mary (Hartwell) Johnson of Nahant, Mass. ; he was a merchant in Nahant. Children:
  10,731   *Asa Keyes* (Johnson), b. Oct. 26, 1828; d. Oct. 1, 1829.
  10,732   *Sarah E.* (Johnson), b. Aug. 31, 1830; m. B. B. Hawkes and lives in Buffalo, N. Y.
  10,733   *Caleb Thurston* (Johnson), b. Aug. 2, 1832; d. Jan. 22, 1833.
  10,734   *Caleb W.* (Johnson), b. April 26, 1834; m. Julia Connor and lives in San Francisco, Cal.
  10,735   *Martin Keyes* (Johnson), b. Aug. 16, 1836; d. Nov. 15, 1840.
  10,736   *Rev. Charles Thurston* (Johnson), b. Oct. 16, 1838; m. Elizabeth S. Edson.
  10,737   *Herbert E.* (Johnson), b. Nov. 24, 1840; m. Cynthia Ann Taylor and lives in Walla Walla, Washington territory.
  10,738   *Edwin W.* (Johnson), b. Feb. 28, 1843; m. Mary T. Crandall and lives in Nahant.
  10,739   *Harriet L.* (Johnson), b. April 26, 1845; d. Aug. 28, 1848.
  10,740   *Frederic Keyes* (Johnson), b. Feb., 1848; d. Sept. 21, 1851.

By second wife, Sarah :

+10,741   Samuel,[6] b. March 5, 1771; m. 1st, Sarah Knowlton; 2d, Sophia Miles; 3d, Rachel Bullard.
 10,742   Elizabeth,[6] b. Dec. 3, 1772; m. 1st, March, 1807, Robert Knowlton; 2d, Oct., 1819, Josiah Bush. She died Feb. 8, 1860, aged 87.
+10,743   Joseph,[6] b. Feb. 12, 1775; m. Lucy Goodwin.
+10,744   Eli,[6] b. May 3, 1777; m. Frances Burrill.
 10,745   Hannah,[6] b. Dec. 7, 1779; d. aged 11 or 12 years.
 10,746   Lydia,[6] b. June 26, 1782; m. —— Brigham; d. Sept. 22, 1851, leaving :
    10,747   *Sarah Elizabeth* (Brigham), b. Dec. 15, 1815; m. May 14, 1850, Jonathan Gleason, a florist, and had :
      10,748   *Jennie Estelle* (Gleason), b. Aug. 21, 1850.
      10,749   *Mary* (Gleason), b. March 18, 1855; d. Sept. 22, 1855.
 10,750   Benjamin,[6] b. May 15, 1785; d. March 9, 1811.

## 10,741

SAMUEL THURSTON [6] (*Samuel*,[5] *Joseph*,[4] *Daniel*,[3] *Daniel*,[2] *John*[1]), son of Samuel [5] and Sarah (Harrington) Thurston of Westborough, Mass.; born there March 5, 1771; married, first, June 24, 1802, SARAH KNOWLTON of Shrewsbury, Mass.; she died Dec. 22, 1815. Second, July 10, 1816, SOPHIA MILES of Shrewsbury; she died April 10, 1817. Third, Feb. 14, 1818, RACHEL BULLARD of Medway, Mass. He died Sept. 3, 1839; his widow died March 7, 1854.

His children, all by first wife, Sarah :

10,755   Harriet,[7] b. Feb. 9, 1804; m. May 27, 1825, Corning Fairbanks, a machinist of Grafton, Mass. Children :
  10,756   *Sarah Melinda* (Fairbanks), b. Nov. 27, 1825; m. Feb. 22, 1845, William Trowbridge; two children.
  10,757   *Angeline Harriet* (Fairbanks), b. Dec. 27, 1827.
  10,758   *Lucy Elizabeth* (Fairbanks), b. March 24, 1830; m. May 25, 1858, Charles Draper Stone; three children.
  10,759   *Henry George* (Fairbanks), b. April 16, 1832; m. Susan A. Smith; d. Sept. 3, 1865; seven children, six died in infancy.
  10,760   *Lyman Edward* (Fairbanks), b. April 3, 1834; d. June 3, 1852.
  10,761   *Charles A.* (Fairbanks), b. July 29, 1836; m. Eliza Fairbanks of Worcester, Mass.; two children.
  10,762   *Jane Sophia* (Fairbanks), b. Feb. 20, 1839; m. Dec. 28, 1859, Geo. T. Newton; no children.
  10,763   *Eli Thurston* (Fairbanks), b. Dec. 26, 1841; d. May 25, 1842.
  10,764   *Benjamin Nourse* (Fairbanks), b. Oct. 20, 1843; m. Nov. 1, 1865, Louisa Bigelow; five children.

10,765  *Caroline Maria* (Fairbanks), b. Sept. 18, 1845; d. March 20, 1866.
10,766  *Emeline Amelia* (Fairbanks), b. Jan. 11, 1848; d. Sept. 3, 1870.
10,767  Melinda,[7] b. May 17, 1805; d. July 12, 1830.
10,768  Hannah Augusta,[7] b. Nov. 22, 1806; m. 1830, Jonathan Daniels, a farmer
in Middleton, N. H.; d. May 22, 1843, having had :
   10,769  *Estus Hamilton* (Daniels), b. Sept. 13, 1832; d. April 12, 1834.
   10,770  *Helen Maria* (Daniels), b. June 5, 1834; m. Dec. 6, 1863, William
G. Chandler, a boot and shoe dealer in New Bedford, Mass.
10,771  Lucy,[7] b. Feb. 3, 1809; m. May 1, 1833, Solomon Hall, a blacksmith in
Worcester, Mass.  She died Aug. 23, 1840; he died May 6, 1859,
leaving :
   10,772  *Emily Amanda* (Hall), b. March 7, 1835; m. Aug. 17, 1862, Frederic W. Boswell, a truckman, and had :
      10,773  *Wilber Frederic* (Boswell), b. in Worcester May 22, 1863.
      10,774  *Arthur Henry* (Boswell), b. Nov. 29, 1867.
   10,775  *Samuel Thurston* (Hall), b. June 18, 1840; d. April 24, 1865.
10,776  Maria,[7] b. Jan. 9, 1811; n.m.; lives in Shrewsbury.
10,777  Julia,[7] b. April 22, 1813; m. Dec. 8, 1869, Alonzo O. Farr, a farmer of
Shrewsbury; no children.

## 10,743

JOSEPH THURSTON[6] (*Samuel*,[5] *Joseph*,[4] *Daniel*,[3] *Daniel*,[2] *John*[1]),
brother of the preceding, and son of Samuel[5] and Sarah (Harrington)
Thurston of Westborough, Mass.; born there Feb. 12, 1775; married
LUCY GOODWIN, born Dec. 12, 1782, daughter of John and Esther
Goodwin of Cambridge, Mass.  She died in Framingham, Mass., May
24, 1823; he died in Brookfield, Mass., Jan. 29, 1847.

Mr. Thurston was engaged in the provision business in Roxbury,
Mass., until disabled by rheumatism; lived in Framingham, Fayville,
and Brookfield, Mass.

### Children :

10,780  Lucy,[7] b. Feb. 17, 1807; d. in infancy.
10,781  Lucy,[7] b. Nov. 10, 1808; m. at Troy, N. Y., Nov. 24, 1834, Cyrus Warren, b. Aug. 17, 1808, son of Nathaniel and Lydia Warren of Buck-
field, Me.  He was a shoe manufacturer in Troy, N.Y., where he died
Nov. 11, 1835; she resided in Boston, Mass., till July, 1878, when she
went to Brookfield, Mass.; no children.
10,782  Joseph,[7] b. June 11, 1811; a tailor in Boston; m. Sarah Augusta Sherburne, daughter of Joseph and Sarah Sherburne of Boston, where he
died, May 6, 1848; no children.
10,783  Thomas Palmer,[7] b. Dec. 29, 1813; n.m.; d. in Boston July 22, 1835.
10,784  Jane,[7] b. Nov. 29, 1815; m. Henry Daniel Fales son of Daniel and
Mary Fales of Shrewsbury, Mass.  He was a boot manufacturer and
dealer in Chicago, Ill., in firm of Fargo, Fales & Co.; now resides in
West Brookfield, Mass.  Children :
   10,785  *Charlotte* (Fales), b. in Southborough, Mass., Dec. 25, 1837.
   10,786  *Lucy* (Fales), b. in Brookfield June 8, 1840.
   10,787  *Daniel* (Fales), b. in Brookfield May 25, 1846; d. Aug. 14, 1846.
   10,788  *Sophia Warren* (Fales), b. in Brookfield Sept. 25, 1847.
10,789  Eliza,[7] b. in Fayville, Mass., Oct. 30, 1817; m. Jan. 1, 1846. John Blair, a
stone-mason in Fayville, son of William and Abigail (Palmer) Blair of
Peterborough. N. H., a member of the Universalist church.  They had :
   10,790  *Abbie Eliza* (Blair), b. Dec. 8, 1846; m. Sept. 24, 1872, George
Lyman Herrick; d. Feb. 8, 1874.
   10,791  *Emilie Augusta* (Blair), b. June 4, 1848.
10,792  Samuel,[7] b. June 5, 1821; m. Alice ——.  He was a shoemaker in Leicester, Mass.; enlisted in the 25th Massachusetts regiment for the war
against the rebellion, served three years, was wounded, came home on
a furlough, returned, re-enlisted in March, and was killed in battle
at Drury's Bluff, Va., May 16, 1864; no children.

## 10,744

ELI THURSTON [6] (*Samuel,*[5] *Joseph,*[4] *Daniel,*[3] *Daniel,*[2] *John* [1]), brother of the preceding, and son of Samuel [5] and Sarah (Harrington) Thurston of Westborough, Mass.; born there May 3, 1777; married, April 27, 1806, FRANCES BURRILL of Roxbury, Mass. He was in the cattle business in Brighton and Roxbury; was in the war of 1812, and in 1813 moved to Jamaica Plain, Mass., where he died, Oct. 28, 1817; she died in Chelsea, Mass., July 2, 1874.

### Children:

10,795   Frances,[7] d. aged two years.
+10,796   Eli,[7] b. in Brighton June 14, 1808; m. 1st, Martha Caroline Sanford; 2d, Julia Ann Sessions.
+10,797   George Burrill,[7] b. in Brighton Dec. 8. 1809; m 1st, Sarah Jane Sleeper; 2d, Patience Rogers Buffum; 3d, Mrs. Elizabeth (Kent) Cridland.
+10,798   Edwin,[7] b. in Roxbury Nov. 2, 1812; m. Sarah Lincoln Humphrey.

## 10,796

REV. ELI THURSTON [7] (*Eli,*[6] *Samuel,*[5] *Joseph,*[4] *Daniel,*[3] *Daniel,*[2] *John* [1]), son of Eli [6] and Frances (Burrill) Thurston of Brighton, Mass.; born there June 14, 1808; married, first, in Wrentham, Mass., June 20, 1838, MARTHA CAROLINE SANFORD, born in Newark in 1816 or 1817, daughter of Philo and Martha (Druice) Sanford of Newark, Wrentham, Mass., Hallowell, Me., and Boston, Mass.; she died at Fall River, Mass., Nov. 7, 1852. Second, Jan. 24, 1854, JULIA ANN SESSIONS, born 1818, daughter of Samuel and Hannah Sessions of Westminster, Vt. He died Dec. 19, 1869.

When about five years old his parents removed to Jamaica Plain, Mass., where his father died in 1817. This broke up the family, and Eli went to live with a godly uncle in Westborough, Mass. At seventeen he went to Millbury, Mass., to learn the trade of a gunsmith. He was converted in his twentieth year and immediately commenced studying for the ministry. He fitted for college at Day's academy, Wrentham, graduated at Amherst in 1834, spent the following year at Andover, and the next two years with Rev. Jacob Ide, D.D., of West Medway, Mass. He was approbated to preach by the Mendon Association Aug. 16, 1836, and was ordained over the Congregational church in Hallowell, Me., Jan. 3, 1838; dismissed July, 1848, and installed over the Central church in Fall River, Mass., March 21, 1849, where he remained till his death. The degree of D.D. was conferred upon him by his Alma Mater in 1866.

In theology Dr. Thurston was ranked and avowed himself as a Hopkinsian Calvinist, holding that moral agency, both divine and human, consists in volition, and that sin consists in sinning. In this theory he held all the doctrines of religion clear and consistent. His sermons were all constructed on the basis of this theology, which gave to them no small part of their instructiveness and power of holding the attention. They, every one, had some positive pith to them.

As a preacher, he was specially remarkable for the distinct and lucid statement of his theme, the directness and cogency of his arguments, the clearness and nicety of his illustrations, and the Anglo-Saxon directness with which he carried his message home to his hearers.

In his various relations, as pastor, citizen, etc., he was positive, faithful, and entirely affable. The poor and the afflicted families especially loved him. On moral questions he was a decided and strong champion, earnest for pilgrim moralities as well as principles. He was of course ready always to advocate the cause of freedom, temperance, and the Sabbath. So earnest was he that, whenever any moral interest became involved in political movements, he entered personally into the caucus and upon the platform to advocate what he regarded the right. In all respects he was a strong soldier of the Lord, not to be frightened or cajoled from his convictions of duty, and when he died the whole city and community were stirred with deep grief at their irreparable loss.

An interesting incident, illustrative of his bold and plain spoken words, came under our notice. When he was pastor of the church in Hallowell and Rev. David Thurston was pastor of the church in Winthrop, the subject of slavery was deeply agitating the public mind. Strong partizanship was manifested in many of the congregations of New England, and Winthrop was much divided on this question. The pastor at Winthrop was ill and unable to preach on a certain Thanksgiving day. He made arrangement to have Mr. Eli Thurston of Hallowell, ten miles distant, preach for him as soon as he could after preaching for his own people in the morning. The people knew of the arrangement, and all seemed to be pleased. The pro-slavery party thought they would manage it so that no anti-slavery person should speak to the minister, so as to influence him in the selection of a subject, previous to the service. To this end one of them rode a half mile out of town, met Mr. Thurston and took him to his house for refreshments, then to the church, and saw him enter the desk without speaking to a single anti-slavery person. Great satisfaction was felt that their plans had been so successful. After the preliminary services, the first words of his address were, "The dark and damning sin of slavery." These persons were compelled, as a matter of etiquette to one to whom they had shown so much attention, to remain and hear a thorough and powerful anti-slavery address, when they would have been very glad to have left the house.

The compiler of this volume had an intimate acquaintance with the subject of this sketch and felt the affection of a child toward him, as his influence, more than that of any other person, led him to Christ.

His children, by first wife, Martha, born at Hallowell:

10,800    Philo Sanford,[5] b. 1840; d. March 17, 1876.
10,801    Anna Hamilton,[5] b. 1843; m. Feb. 21, 1871. George Hill Buck, b. May 31, 1843, son of David Hill and Mary (Low) Buck of Bucksport, Me. He is in the lumber business in Chelsea, Mass., in company with his brother, Theodore Hastings Buck, under the firm name of T. H. Buck & Co. He enlisted in the 40th Massachusetts regiment against the rebellion and served three years; was member of the common council in Chelsea 1875-6-7, and alderman 1878. They have:
10,802        *David Chace* (Buck), b. May 25, 1873.
10,803    Edwin Ingersoll,[5] b. 1845; d. in infancy.

By second wife, Julia, born at Fall River:

10,804    Thatcher Thayer,[5] b. 1857.
10,805    Caroline Sanford,[5] b. 1859.

## 10,797

GEORGE BURRILL THURSTON[7] (*Eli,*[6] *Samuel,*[5] *Joseph,*[4] *Daniel,*[3] *Daniel,*[2] *John*[1]), brother of the preceding, and son of Eli[6] and Frances (Burrill) Thurston of Brighton, Mass.; born there Dec. 8, 1809; married, first, Oct. 21, 1838, SARAH JANE SLEEPER of Boston, Mass.; she died May 7, 1846, aged 36, and was buried in Lynn, Mass. Second, PATIENCE ROGERS BUFFUM, daughter of Jonathan and Lydia (Stacy) Buffum of North Berwick, Me.; she died Dec. 6, 1860. Third, MRS. ELIZABETH KENT CRIDLAND, born in Brackwell, Eng., daughter of William and Mary A. (Rose) Kent of London, Eng.

Mr. Thurston is a carriage and harness manufacturer, doing business in East Boston, Mass., under the firm name of Thurston & Strong, residing in Chelsea, Mass.; made a visit, with his wife, to England, 1879.

His children, by first wife, Sarah:

10,810 Sarah Elizabeth,[8] b. Aug. 2, 1840; m. May 5, 1865, Theodore Hastings Buck, son of David Hill and Mary (Low) Buck of Bucksport, Me. He is in the lumber business in Chelsea, in company with his brother, George Hill Buck; served two years in the war against the rebellion in the 40th Massachusetts regiment, and was wounded at the battle of Olustee, Fla. She died Sept. 28, 1877.

By second wife, Patience:

10,811 Albert Buffum,[8] b. July 4, 1852; n.m.; in dry goods business, living with his parents.

## 10,798

EDWIN THURSTON[7] (*Eli,*[6] *Samuel,*[5] *Joseph,*[4] *Daniel,*[3] *Daniel,*[2] *John*[1]), brother of the preceding, and son of Eli[6] and Frances (Burrill) Thurston of Jamaica Plain, Mass.; born in Roxbury, Mass., Nov. 2, 1812; married, Sept. 14, 1841, SARAH LINCOLN HUMPHREY, born Mar. 26, 1824, daughter of George and Catherine Humphrey of Boston, Mass.

Mr. Thurston was a machinist and railroad engineer; went to Cincinnati, Ohio, in the fall of 1854; moved his family there in the spring of 1855; was engineer on the Little Miami railroad until the spring of 1858, when he moved to Covington, Ky., and was master mechanic of the Kentucky Central railroad until the 20th of April, 1865, when he was instantly killed on the railroad, near Falmouth, Ky., while superintending the removal of a wreck. Mr. Thurston was a man who loved knowledge and studied a great deal, thus acquiring a good education. He was a strong union man during the war of the rebellion and did everything in his power for the comfort and good of the union soldiers. He was very much beloved and highly respected in society and by his employes. His death was considered a public calamity, and his funeral was attended by a large concourse of people; a special train of cars was run from Lexington, Ky., to bring those who wished to attend. Mrs. Thurston and her eldest daughters are members of the Episcopal church.

Children:

10,815 Frances Josephene,[8] b. in Boston Dec. 15, 1842; d. Jan. 12, 1843.
10,816 Georgietta,[8] b. in Boston April 9, 1844; a teacher in Covington.
10,817 Charles Edwin,[8] b. in Boston Aug. 11, 1846; d. Aug. 9, 1852.
10,818 Frances Catherine,[8] b. in South Braintree, Mass., Oct. 27, 1850; a teacher.
10,819 Harriet Emery,[8] b. in South Braintree Oct. 25, 1853; d. in Covington Sept. 20, 1858.

10,820   Edwin,[8] b. in Cincinnati Sept. 20, 1856; a railroad engineer; n.m.
10,821   Esther Maria,[8] b. in Covington Sept. 15, 1858; d. March 29, 1861.
10,822   William Hunt,[8] b. in Covington July 25, 1862; d. Nov. 26, 1865.
10,823   Carrie May,[8] b. in Covington April 6, 1865.

---

Probably descendants of Daniel Thurston of Newbury, Mass.

## 10,825

SAMUEL THURSTON, married ANN FOSTER; lived in Guilford, N. H.

10,826   Miles Thurston, brother of Samuel, had nine sisters, lived and died in
         Guilford, N. H.
+10,827  Mary, probably sister to Samuel and Miles, m. Isaac Runnells.

Children of Samuel and Ann (Foster) Thurston:

+10,828  Miles, b. Dec. 13, 1821; m. Eliza Ricker.
10,829   Samuel, lived in Gloucester, Mass.

## 10,827

MARY THURSTON of Guilford, N. H., probably one of the sisters
of the preceding; married, 1798, ISAAC RUNNELLS, born 1771, son of
Isaac and Anna (Ham) Runnells of Barrington, N. H. He was a
farmer in Gilmanton and Guilford (now Laconia Village), N. H. She
died 1815. He married twice after, had five other children, and died
at his daughter's, Mrs. Buzzell, Jan. 14, 1864.

### Children:

10,830   Isaac (Runnells), b. June 2, 1799; a farmer in Gilmanton, Loudon, N. H.,
         Bennington, Vt., and Warrensville, Ill.; m. 1st, Mehitable P. Sargent
         of Loudon; 2d, Mrs. Anna Vaughn; five children.
10,831   Lydia (Runnells), b. Jan. 14, 1801; m. 1842, Levi Lovett of Laconia, N.
         H. She was deaf and dumb, but enabled to lead a very useful life.
10,832   Polly (Runnells), b. April 26, 1803; m. 1826, Samuel Brown, a farmer in
         Gilmanton and Northfield, N. H.; d. Aug. 2, 1837; five children.
10,833   Samuel (Runnells), b. 1805; d. young.
10,834   Josiah (Runnells), b. 1806; killed by mill logs, aged 8.
10,835   Betsey (Runnells), b. Oct. 3, 1808; m. 1833, Elias Smith Buzzell, a farm-
         er in Sanbornton, N. H.; seven children.
10,836   Lucinda (Runnells), b. 1810; killed by mill logs with her brother.
10,837   John (Runnells), b. April 15, 1814; m. 1st, 1831, Sally Gilman of San-
         bornton; 2d, 1839, Artimesia Stewart Witcher of Northfield; resided
         in Northfield and Sanbornton till 1869, then removed to Canterbury,
         N. H.; eleven children.

## 10,828

MILES THURSTON (*Samuel*), son of Samuel and Ann (Foster)
Thurston of Guilford, N. H.; born there Dec. 13, 1821; married, Feb.
13, 1843, ELIZA RICKER, born in Dover, N. H., Feb. 11, 1824, daughter of James Shores and Eliza (Whitten) Ricker of Alton, N. H.

Mr. Thurston is a farmer in Lynnfield Center, Mass., and a member of the Methodist church. Previous to taking up his present residence, he lived in Alton and Tamworth, N. H., and in Peabody, Mass.

### Children, born in Alton:

10,840   Eliza Jane, b. Sept. 18, 1845; m. 1st, Sept. 18, 1861, Caleb Augustus Web-
         ster of Peabody, her parents residing there at the time. He enlisted in
         the army against the rebellion in August, 1862, took the swamp fever,
         came home sick in June, 1863, and died a few days after. She removed
         to Lynnfield Center with her parents, and m. 2d, Jan. 1, 1868, Robert
         Sweetser Henfield, a farmer. She had, by first husband:
10,841   *Daniel Augustus* (Webster), b. in Peabody March 30, 1862.

By second husband:
10,842  *Joseph Stillman* (Henfield), b. Nov. 8, 1868.
10,843  *Ethel Perkins* (Henfield), b. June 12, 1876.
10,844  James Melvin, b. April 22, 1847; m. Aug. 1, 1868. Lydia Jane Sayward.
He was a wheelwright, residing in Woburn, Mass., and after in Peabody, where he died suddenly Aug. 27, 1878.  They had:
   10,845  *Lillian Elma*, b. Aug. 7, 1869; d. Aug. 18, 1869.
+10,846  John Langdon, b. Jan. 26, 1850; m. Carrie Matilda Henfield.
10,847  Eliza Melvina, b. Sept. 25, 1852; m. April 4, 1877, James Louis Tucker, a farmer in Lynnfield Center.
10,848  Daniel Lander, b. Nov. 6, 1854; d. Aug. 13, 1855.
10,849  Caroline Maria, b. in Tamworth Sept. 17, 1856; d. Sept. 23, 1858.
10,850  Carrie Helen, b. in Peabody Oct. 16, 1861.

## 10,846

JOHN LANGDON THURSTON (*Miles, Samuel*), son of Miles and Eliza (Ricker) Thurston of Lynnfield Center, Mass.; born at Alton, N. H., Jan. 26, 1850; married, May 2, 1870, CARRIE MATILDA HENFIELD, born Nov. 23, 1848, daughter of Joseph and Elizabeth Green (Sweetser) Henfield of Lynnfield Center, Mass.

Mr. Thurston is collector in San Francisco, Cal.; a member of the Congregational church.  Before going to California, he was conductor on trains running out of Boston, living in Danvers, Lynn, Mass., and Portsmouth, N. H.

Child:

10,855  Edwin Langdon, b. in Danvers March 5, 1871.

## 10,859

STEPHEN THURSTON of Deerfield, N. H., had a son, 10,860.

## 10,860

EDWARD THURSTON, son of Stephen, born in Deerfield, N. H.; married DELIA WALLACE.

Children:
+10,861  Stephen, b. March, 1795; m. Mary Mead.
+10,862  William Wallace, b. May 13, 1810; m. Lydia Johnson.

## 10,861

STEPHEN THURSTON (*Edward, Stephen*), son of Edward and Delia (Wallace) Thurston of Deerfield, N. H.; born there March, 1795; married, in Newbury, Vt., MARY MEAD.  She died in Hanover, N. H., 1852; he died in Haverhill, N. H., Feb. 22, 1877.

Mr. Thurston was a mechanic in Lebanon, N. H.; was in the French and Indian war, experiencing many hardships, living many days on roots and horse flesh; was a member of the Methodist church.

Children:
10,865  Louisa, b. in Newbury, Vt.; d. 1863.
+10,866  George Washington, b. in Newbury Dec. 23, 1825; m. Polly Ann Coburn.
10,867  Mary Jane, b. in Lebanon, N. H., May, 1827; lives with the Shakers in Enfield, N. H.
10,868  Fanny, b. in Canaan, N. H., 1829; m. 1st, 1860, John Martin of New York; he enlisted in the war against the rebellion, as a musician, and died in the army; 2d, —— Sargent; live in Hanover; a son, d. young.

## 10,862

WILLIAM WALLACE THURSTON (*Edward, Stephen*), brother of the preceding, and son of Edward and Delia (Wallace) Thurston of Deerfield, N. H.; born there May 13, 1810; married, April 2, 1829, LYDIA JOHNSON, born Feb. 26, 1809, daughter of Moses and Betsey (Weber) Johnson of Enfield, N. H.

Mr. Thurston is a farmer in West Braintree; was a sergeant in the state militia.

Children, born in Norwich, Vt.:

| | | |
|---|---|---|
| 10,873 | Charles, in West Randolph, Vt. |
| +10,874 | Aulendo Decelle, b. Feb. 7, 1833; m. Jennie M. Derby. |
| 10,875 | Susan Blanchard, b. April 1, d. April 5, 1836. |
| 10,876 | Adelaide, b. July 19, 1841; m. Mar. 27, 1863, Phineas Campbell of West Braintree. |
| 10,877 | Sylvester, b. April 18, 1843; m. April 26, 1863, Betsey Pratt; d. in North Randolph, N. H., June 21, 1871. |
| 10,878 | Orra, b. Jan. 20. 1845; m. April 19, 1863. Almon Pratt of West Braintree. |
| 10,879 | Francely, b. Nov. 24, 1847; d. Aug. 7, 1850. |

## 10,866

GEORGE WASHINGTON THURSTON (*Stephen, Edward, Stephen*), son of Stephen and Mary (Mead) Thurston of Lebanon, N. H.; born in Newbury, Vt., Dec. 23, 1825; married, at Enfield Center, N. H., Mar. 6, 1864, POLLY ANN COBURN, born Feb. 3, 1834, daughter of Seth and Deborah (Parker) Coburn of Pittsfield, Vt.; she died Oct. 12, 1878.

Mr. Thurston is a mechanic in Lebanon; member Methodist church.

Child:

10,884   Elmer George, b. in Enfield Dec. 31, 1864; d. in Lebanon Oct. 22, 1875.

## 10,874

AULENDO DECELLE THURSTON (*William Wallace, Edward, Stephen*), son of William Wallace and Lydia (Johnson) Thurston of West Braintree, Vt.; born in Norwich, Vt., Feb. 7, 1833; married, in Manchester, N. H., April 5, 1856, JENNIE M. DERBY, daughter of Elihu and Hannah (Clark) Derby of Canaan, N. H.

Mr. Thurston is a cabinet maker and merchant in Lebanon, N. H.; member of the Methodist church.

Child:

10,889   Arthur Bertie, b. in Hartford. Vt., Sept. 29, 1858; studied medicine with Dr. Currier, and entered Dartmouth Aug., 1878.

## 10,894

FRANCIS THURSTON, born in Portsmouth, N. H.; married HARRIET TYRRELL. He was a carpenter; was in the war of 1812 and wounded at the battle of Lundy's Lane. He died in Canada 1870.

Child:

+10,895   Arba Oscar, b. May 10, 1839; m. Hattie Serena Olney.

## 10,895

ARBA OSCAR THURSTON of Detroit, Mich. (*Francis*), son of Francis and Harriet (Tyrrell) Thurston of Canada West; born there May 10,

1839; married, in Pontiac, Mich., Nov. 3, 1866, HATTIE SERENA OL-NEY, born in Gouverneur, St. Lawrence county, N. Y., Jan. 7, 1847, daughter of Sanford Pool and Sarah Ann (Mix) Olney of Detroit.

Mr. Thurston is a carpenter. He was in the army against the rebellion four years and eight months; in the 34th Illinois regiment, the 19th U. S. infantry, and the 4th regiment veteran volunteers, Hancock's veteran corps; was in the battles of Shiloh, Tenn., Corinth, Miss., Perryville and Frankfort, Ky., Hood's Gap and Chickamauga, Tenn., where he was taken prisoner and confined in Libby prison two months, in Danville, Va., four months, and Andersonville, Ga., six months and two days. He acted as commissary clerk and sergeant-major, and after the war was clerk in the war department at Washington and at Gen. Ord's headquarters in Detroit, and in quartermaster's department in Columbus, Ohio, for two years; has been town clerk in Taylor, Ogle county, Ill.

Children:

10,899  Frank Webster, b. Jan. 19, 1868; d. April 19, 1874.
10,900  Albert Irving, b. Dec. 24, 1870.
10,901  Edwin Arthur, b. April 3, 1873.
10,902  Frank Clifton, b. Feb. 21, 1875.

---

Descended from Edward Thurston of Newport, R. I., probably.

## 10,907

JABEZ THURSTON of Cranston, R. I., married SARAH McLEOD.

Children:

10,908  George Omri, b. March 27, 1829; m. Mary Abby Bailey and had:
    10,909  *Charles Edwin*, b. June 4, 1855.
    10,910  *Ellen Frances*, b. Jan. 4, 1857.
10,911  Elbridge Kimball, b. 1839.
10,912  Caroline Elizabeth, b. 1842.
10,913  George Kimball, b. 1849.
    Three others, d. in childhood.

---

## 10,918

NORTEN THURSTON. Children:

+10,919  Daniel Green, m. Fanny Thayer.
10,920  Benjamin.
10,921  Samuel.
10,922  Isaac.

## 10,919

DANIEL GREEN THURSTON (*Norten*), married FANNY THAYER.

Mr. Thurston was a potter, justice of the peace, and class leader in the Methodist church. He died in Eden township, Licking county, Ohio, 1843; she died in Eden 1860. They came to Ohio with their private conveyance in 1810, and endured all the hardships incident to pioneer life, often having to leave their homes to avoid the Indians.

## Children:

10,923  Harriet, m. 1st, —— Monroe; 2d, 1831, John Loofborough, both physicians; she died 1834, having had:
    10,924  *Lucy Ann* (Monroe).
    10,925  *William* (Monroe).
10,926  Mary, b. March 3, 1800; m. Israel Wood and had:
    10,927  *Priscilla* (Wood).
    10,928  *Elizabeth* (Wood).
    10,929  *Rachel* (Wood).
    10,930  *Fanny* (Wood).
    10,931  *Daniel* (Wood).
    10,932  *Rhoda* (Wood).
    10,933  *Eunice* (Wood).
    10,934  *Jonathan* (Wood).
    10,935  *Sarah* (Wood).
    10,936  *Beulah* (Wood).
+10,937  Joseph, b. 1802; m. Charlotte Loofborough.
10,938  Betsey, b. 1804; m. Dec., 1819, Ralph Longwell, a soldier in the war of 1812. They had:
    10,939  *Martha E.* (Longwell), m. B. F. Loofborough, clerk of Delaware county; two children.
    10,940  *Nancy L.* (Longwell), m. Miller Abrams, blacksmith; four children.
    10,941  *Harriet M.* (Longwell), m. Wesley Abrams, farmer; seven children.
    10,942  *Mary W.* (Longwell), m. Hon. J. R. Hubble; seven children.
    10,943  *Albert Green* (Longwell), sergeant in the war against the rebellion; m. 1859, Cordelia S. Eaton; two children.
    10,944  *Lydia Sevas* (Longwell), m. Morris Clay, carpenter; four children.
    10,945  *Esther L.* (Longwell), m. Willis Myers, blacksmith; two children.
    10,946  *Fanny S.* (Longwell), m. Hiram Hipple, a farmer; one child.
    10,947  *Phebe S.* (Longwell), m. John C. Greary, a lawyer; two children.
    10,948  *Norten Thurston* (Longwell), a soldier in the war against the rebellion; m. 1867, Ella E. Hyde; two children.
    10,949  *Helen Sarah* (Longwell), m. 1867, James P. McKay, a molder; two children.
    10,950  *Charles* (Longwell).
    10,951  *Millie B.* (Longwell), m. 1868, W. S. Coyner; four children.
    10,952  *Charlotte Hough* (Longwell), m. 1872, George N. States, a farmer; two children.
10,953  Sarah, b. 1809; m. 1st, Lyman Thrall; 2d, Alexander Thrall, a brother of first husband. She had:
    10,954  *Idelia* (Thrall).
    10,955  *Almira* (Thrall).
    10,956  *Wesley* (Thrall).
    10,957  *Timothy* (Thrall).
    10,958  *Fanny* (Thrall).
    10,959  *Homer* (Thrall).
10,960  Phebe, b. 1813, a Spiritualist; m. 1831, William Kimball Thrall, a house joiner in Berlin township, Delaware county, Ohio. They had:
    10,961  *Octavia Bernice* (Thrall), b. April 25, 1841; m. 1865, Tilden Scott, and has Harry S., William Tilden, and Louie Belle (Scott), in Eden township, Licking county.
10,962  Eunice, b. 1815; m. Nathan Herrendeen and had:
    10,963  *Orrison* (Herredeen).
    10,964  *Martha Huldah* (Herrendeen).
    10,965  *Norton* (Herrendeen).
    10,966  *Irvin* (Herrendeen).
    10,967  *Samuel* (Herrendeen).
    10,968  *Morris* (Herrendeen).
10,969  Norten, b. 1817; m. Rebecca Jones; they had:
    10,970  *Daniel Green.*
    10,971  *Annette.*
    10,972  *Fanny.*
    10,973  *William.*
    10,974  *Olive.*
    10,975  *Charles.*

+10,976  Vinal, b. May 19, 1819; m. Ann L. Plant.
 10,977  Nancy, b. 1821; m. Isaac Seward and had:
    10,978  *Fanny* (Seward).
    10,979  *Harriet* (Seward).
 10,980  Fanny, b. 1823; m. Henry Walker and had:
    10,981  *Ruth* (Walker).
    10,982  *John* (Walker).
    10,983  *Margaret* (Walker).
    10,984  *Octavius* (Walker).
    10,985  *Mary* (Walker).
 10,986  Barbary Triphosa, b. 1825; m. William Livingston and had:
    10,987  *Martha* (Livingston).
    10,988  *William* (Livingston).
    10,989  *Daniel* (Livingston).
    10,990  *Francis* (Livingston).
    10,991  *George* (Livingston).
    10,992  *Alice* (Livingston).
    10,993  *Harvey* (Livingston).

## 10,937

JOSEPH THURSTON (*Daniel Green, Norten*), son of Daniel Green and Fanny (Thayer) Thurston of Eden, Licking county, Ohio; born 1802; married CHARLOTTE LOOFBOROUGH.

Children:

 10,995  Wilson.
 10,996  Maria.
 10,997  Alfred.
 10,998  Louisa.
 10,999  Lucretia.
 11,000  Elmore.
 11,001  Jerusha.
 11,002  Adell.
 11,003  Clara.

## 10,976

VINAL THURSTON of Bennington, Morrow county, Ohio (*Daniel Green, Norten*), brother of the preceding, and son of Daniel Green and Fanny (Thayer) Thurston of Eden, Licking county, Ohio; born May 19, 1819; married, in Berkshire, Delaware county, O., July 1, 1839, ANN L. PLANT, born in Leicestershire, Eng., June 22, 1821.

Children:

+11,004  Charles G., b. May 4, 1840; m. Mary Morehouse.
 11,005  Custer.
 11,006  Joseph.

## 11,004

CHARLES G. THURSTON of Deshler, Henry county, Ohio (*Vinal, Daniel Green, Norten*), son of Vinal and Ann L. (Plant) Thurston of Bennington, Ohio; born in Berkshire, Ohio, May 4, 1840; married, Nov. 9, 1867, MARY MOREHOUSE, born Aug. 20, 1844, daughter of Charles and L. (Aldrich) Morehouse of Bennington.

Mr. Thurston is a farmer. He was in the 20th Ohio regiment in the war against the rebellion and came near starving in the Andersonville prison. He has been trustee of the township two years, and is a member of the Methodist church.

Children:

 11,007  Charles D., b. in Berkshire Aug. 25, 1868.
 11,008  Estella, b. in Deshler Nov. 13, 1873.
 11,009  Vinal, b. in Deshler Sept. 24, 1877.

## 11,010

JOSEPH THURSTON of Fishkill, N. Y.

**11,011** SAMUEL THURSTON, brother of Joseph.

**11,012** JEMIMA THURSTON, sister of Joseph and Samuel.

One of Joseph's descendants says: "They came to this country from England shortly before the revolutionary war. Joseph purchased a large part of Dutchess county, N. Y., and settled in Fishkill. Samuel and Jemima purchased Staten Island and Jamaica on Long Island; lived, died, and were buried on Staten Island."

Children of Joseph, born in Fishkill:

11,013 Jemima, b. Jan. 2, 1751; m. Nov. 2, 1774, Benjamin Bloom, a farmer in Fishkill, member of the Dutch church. He died March 4, 1817; she died Oct. 18, 1837. They had:

    11,014 *Joseph* (Bloom), b. Nov. 6, 1776; d. 1777.
    11,015 *Abraham* (Bloom), b. Dec. 3, 1779; d. 1800.
    11,016 *Jacob* (Bloom), b. Feb. 9, 1781; d. 1782.
    11,017 *Phebe* (Bloom), b. Mar. 13, 1785; m. —— Van Siclen; d. 1818; had:
        11,018 *Caroline* (Van Siclen), who resides in Flatbush, N. Y., and gave me these facts.

11,019 Montross. It is said he traveled from New York city, on horseback, with important government papers, to Albany, on the west side of Hudson river, when it was a wilderness, for which service he received a grant of land on Long Island, but never appropriated it to himself; lived in Pleasant Valley, Dutchess county, N. Y. Children:

    11,020 *Samuel*, a lawyer, who settled his grandfather's estate.
    11,021 *Hannah*, m. —— Thorn.

11,022 Rachel, m. —— Hanson, lived in East Greenbush, Renselaer county, N. Y., and had a granddaughter, Julia (Coon).

+11,023 Thomas, b. Dec. 2, 1767; m. Catherine Ter Ross.
+11,024 Jacob, m. Martha Valentine.

## 11,023

THOMAS THURSTON of La Grangeville, N.Y. (*Joseph*), son of Joseph Thurston of La Grangeville, Dutchess county, N. Y.; born in Fishkill, N. Y., Dec. 2, 1767; married, 1786, CATHERINE TER ROSS, born April 10, 1765. He died Sept. 16, 1824; she died Aug. 29, 1833.

Mr. Thurston was a farmer, and member of the Dutch Reformed church, of which Rev. Thomas Dewitt, D.D., was pastor. He was tall, slender, pale, had dark brown hair and a grave countenance. She was short and slender, a light brunette. Her wedding dress was a blue tint of white satin damask, such as is now used for window curtains, gored so as to fit the form without plait or gather, a full over dress or tunic of linen lawn finely embroidered, white satin slippers with pointed toes and very high heels. During the pleasant jesting after the marriage ceremony, he raised his arm to a horizontal position and it just rested on her head, and he said, "You see I can shelter and protect her." Her granddaughter, Mrs. Minerva Thurston Chalker, has a book containing the Psalms of David set to music, and the hymns of the Reformed Dutch church, together with the articles of faith, heavily bound with heavy silver clasps and chains, which she has been told her grandmother carried to church by the chains over her arm.

Children:

+11,027 Samuel Thomas, b. March 18, 1787; m. Ruth Rowe.
+11,028 Isaac, } twins, born { m. Rebecca Rosekrans.
  11,029 Ann, } Mar. 29, 1790; { m. 1st, Baltus Overacker; 2d, John Van Vleit; both farmers and most respectable men; no children.

11,030 Peter, b. March 9, 1793; m. Eliza Jewell; was a carpenter and afterward a farmer in La Grangeville; several children who died young, and
11,031   *Joseph*, n.m.
11,032   *Sarah*, m. —— Jewell and had one daughter.
11,033 Sarah, b. May 7, 1797; m. Benjamin Pollock of Fishkill; he was an architect in New York city till a short time before his death, he had retired and settled in his native town; no children.
11,034 Joseph, b. Aug. 17, 1804; killed by being thrown from a carriage Feb. 14, 1824.

## 11,024

JACOB THURSTON of Schenectady, N. Y. (*Joseph*), brother of the preceding, and youngest child of Joseph Thurston of La Grangeville, Dutchess county, N. Y.; born in Fishkill, N. Y.; married MARTHA VALENTINE of New York, from one of the best old families.

Mr. Thurston went to Schenectady before marriage and established himself there in the watch and jewelry trade, in which he did a large and lucrative business. He was the second postmaster in the city, which office he held till his death. A relative writes: "There were six daughters; their home was for many years an attractive place to many students of Union college, and commencement week was a bright week to lots of us cousins when we were young. They were remarkable for their devotion to one another and especially to their mother, as long as she lived. Aunt Martha was very beautiful, very gentle in manner, and very sweet in disposition, and was beautiful in old age, and as lovely in every respect as when young; but she in character was like the beautiful vine clinging to the sturdy oak, and needed the devotion of her daughters, which was lavishly given. We used to say Aunt Martha sits a queen among her daughters, as they would all gather around her chair, and it was a beautiful picture. They have had access to the best old families in Schenectady, and have a great deal of family pride. Uncle Jacob was highly esteemed in the community and was devoted to his wife and daughters."

### Children:

11,040 Abby.
11,041 Martha, m. Elisha L. Freeman, a paint and oil merchant in Schenectady; had two sons, lawyers, one in Schenectady and one in New York city.
11,042 Charlotte, b. about 1809.
11,043 Matilda.
11,044 Louisa.
11,045 Rachel Hanson, n.m.; lives in Schenectady, the last of the family.
11,046 Jemima. Three of these daughters have taught select schools of their own separate establishing.

## 11,027

SAMUEL THOMAS THURSTON of La Grangeville, Dutchess county N. Y. (*Thomas, Joseph*), eldest son of Thomas and Catherine Ter (Ross) Thurston of La Grangeville; born there March 18, 1787; married, 1814, RUTH ROWE, born April 14, 1788. She died May 7, 1867; he died June 4, 1874.

Mr. Thurston was a farmer; an earnest, exemplary, and sympathizing christian, and for some years a deacon of the Congregational church in Fairport, N. Y., of which himself and wife were members.

### Children:

11,050   Peter Samuel, b. July 17, 1816; m. Sept. 15, 1841, Mary Ann Wilbur of Macedon, N. Y. He was a farmer till 1850, when he engaged in the produce and commission business, in which he was quite successful till 1857 he met with reverses, but still continued the business with moderate success till his death, Feb. 28, 1869. They had:

        11,051   *Helen Louisa*, m. June 24, 1876, Jesse Halsey of Macedon.

11,052   Phebe Ann, b. July 7, 1818; d. July 24, 1818.

11,053   John Summerfield, b. May 20, 1823.

11,054   Sarah Elizabeth, b. March 23, 1826; m. Sept. 18, 1844, Albert Alison Wilbur, a miller in Macedon. In 1859 he sold his flouring mill and removed to Council Bluffs, Iowa. They have:

        11,055   *Daughter*, m. Charles Waite of Council Bluffs.

11,056   Mary Emma, b. Dec. 24, 1831; m. May 18, 1852, William E. Willets of Macedon; he has been in the dry goods and grocery business, and in 1864 moved to Hillsdale, Mich., where he is in the staple and fancy goods business. They have:

        11,057   *Helen Maria* (Willets), b. Jan. 16, 1854; m. Aug. 12, 1874, Benjamin B. Fisher of Hillsdale.

        11,058   *William Thurston* (Willets), b. Aug. 11, 1861.

## 11,028

ISAAC THURSTON (*Thomas, Joseph*), brother of the preceding, and son of Thomas and Catherine Ter ( Ross) Thurston of La Grangeville, Dutchess county, N. Y.; born there March 29, 1790; married, Jan. 30, 1817, REBECCA ROSEKRANS, daughter of John Menaman and Maria (Hix) Rosekrans of Fishkill, N. Y. He died in Macedon, Wayne county, N. Y., Aug. 22, 1842; she died at Lambertville, N. J., Dec. 28, 1876.

. Mr. Thurston was a tanner, currier, and shoemaker at Farmer's Landing, a mile below New Hamburgh, N. Y., on the Hudson river; an important landing sixty years ago. He sent his shoes to New York city to market by sailing vessels, there being no steamboat or railroad then. He was a member of the Presbyterian church, and held responsible offices in both church and town.

### Children:

11,063   Minerva, b. April 20, 1818; m. May 23, 1844, Rev. Richard A. Chalker of Saybrook, Ct. He entered Middletown Wesleyan university 1836, but was compelled to leave before finishing his course, by loss of health. He afterward graduated from Union theological seminary of New York 1840, and became a Methodist clergyman, resident in Rondout, N. Y., well and favorably known in the New York and New Jersey conferences. He labored uninterruptedly till 1878, when he asked release for a year's rest. They both wear their years lightly; there is not a silver thread among her dark locks and but few in his. She says: " Our home we call ' Sunny Wild,' where we have a beautiful view of mountain, valley, river, and sky as ever Nature gave to mortal. For three generations I know we need not blush for our record; excellent moral character, strong. practical common sense, just dealing and kindness to all—the bad as well as the good—is the summing up of their record." They had:

        11,064   *Abraham Pollock* (Chalker), b. Sept. 21, 1845; graduated from Pennington (N. J.) seminary 1864, from Princeton 1868, and from Philadelphia Medical college 1870, and three months afterward commenced practice in Rondout, residing with his parents; n.m.

11,065   Marvin, b. July 4, 1820; a young man of rare excellence; d. Oct. 8. 1843. " Between him and his father was a remarkable oneness and attachment. None knew him but to love; none named him but to praise."

11,066  Ann Maria, b. Sept. 12, 1822; m. Nov. 10, 1840, Peter Reed, a farmer, son of Dr. Aaron Reed of Athens, N. Y.; d. Mar. 2, 1874, having had :
    11,067  *Henry Hobart* (Reed), b. Oct. 30, 1841; m. March 13, 1867, Annie Dietrich of Rochester, N. Y.; they have:
        11,068  *Kittie May* (Reed), b. Feb. 16, 1868.
        11,069  *Jerome Dietrich* (Reed), b. Oct. 3, 1870.
        11,070  *Genevieve* (Reed), b. April 19, 1873.
        11,071  *Harry W.* (Reed), b. Sept. 3, 1875.
    11,072  *Marvin Thurston* (Reed), b. Aug. 15, 1843; n.m.; in New York city.
11,073  A daughter, b. Sept. 19, d. Sept. 20, 1824.

---

## 11,078

THOMAS THURSTON, born in Staffordshire, Eng., 1758, where his father, William Thurston, was a weaver and member of the Episcopal church.   Thomas came to Boston about 1780, and married there SUSANNA ALLEN, settled in Smithfield, R. I., and in 1792 went to Lyndon, Caledonia county, Vt., then almost a wilderness, bought a farm in the woods, and became a successful farmer.   He was said to have been a man of great moral worth and unusual energy of character.   He died 1815 ; she died in the family of her son Joseph, in Niagara county, N. Y., 1833.

Children :

+11,079  William, b. in Smithfield 1782; m. Thirza Lockling.
+11,080  Joseph, b. about 1784.
 11,081  Richard.

## 11,079

WILLIAM THURSTON (*Thomas*), son of Thomas and Susanna (Allen) Thurston of Lyndon, Vt.; born in Smithfield, R. I., 1782; married, about 1804, THIRZA LOCKLING, daughter of Jonathan Lockling of Lyndon.   Mr. Thurston was a farmer in Lyndon, and in 1816 moved to Ilion, Herkimer county, N. Y.; was a member of the Methodist church.   She died 1862 ; a lady of excellent character, of more than ordinary intellectual endowment, a member of the Methodist church.   He died in St. Ansgar, Iowa, Jan. 25, 1867, aged 85.   He lived a quiet life, esteemed by his neighbors, and maintained his religious integrity to the last.

Child :

+11,085  Thomas William, b. Feb. 5, 1815; m. Mary Brown Faville.

## 11,080

JOSEPH THURSTON of Armada, Mich. (*Thomas*), brother of the preceding, and son of Thomas and Susanna (Allen) Thurston of Lyndon, Vt.; born in Smithfield, R. I., about 1784; married ———, and lived in Batavia, N. Y., and in Armada, Mich.

Child :

+11,090  James Gilbert, m. Lucy Ann Hough.

## 11,085

REV. THOMAS WILLIAM THURSTON (*William, Thomas*), son of William and Thirza (Lockling) Thurston of Lyndon, Vt.; born there Feb. 5, 1815 ; married, 1842, MARY BROWN FAVILLE, born Feb. 2,

31

1821, daughter of Thomas and Betsey (West) Faville of Manheim, Herkimer county, N. Y.

Mr. Thurston intended to make law his profession and devoted three years to its study; but then, believing it to be his duty to preach the gospel, he joined the Black River Methodist Episcopal Conference of New York and preached thirteen years under its direction, with good success. In 1858 he went to Iowa and preached four years in the Upper Iowa Methodist Conference. In 1863 his eldest son entered the Union army in the war against the rebellion, which rendered it necessary for him to be at home more, so he located upon a farm in St. Ansgar, Mitchell county, Iowa, and carried it on, preaching as occasion offered, sustaining the relation of "located elder" to the conference. He has been supervisor of schools, justice of the peace, and has held several civil offices of trust.

Children :

+11,095  Charles Parker, b. Aug. 30, 1844; m. Harriet Rebecca Dodge.
11,096  Mary Louise, b. in Trenton, N. Y., April 24, 1848; m. 1869, William E. Morehouse of Otranto, Mitchell county, Iowa.
11,097  William Dwight, b. in Wilmurt, N. Y., Jan. 3, 1850; a blacksmith in St. Ansgar.
11,098  Evangeline St. Clair, b. in Bombay. N. Y., Jan. 6, 1854; m. 1872, Arthur Turney, a farmer in St. Ansgar; they have :
    11,099  *Carlton Cyrus* (Turney), b. Oct. 27, 1874.
11,100  Thomas Faville, b. in Osage, Iowa, Oct. 29, 1858.
11,101  Frank Lochlan, b. in St. Ansgar April 4, 1861.
11,102  Laura Bessie, b. Dec. 25, 1864.

**11,090**

JAMES GILBERT THURSTON of Armada, Mich. (*Joseph, Thomas*), son of Joseph Thurston of Armada; born in Batavia, N. Y.; married LUCY ANN HOUGH. He came from Batavia with his father to Armada.

Child :

+11,106  James Orson, b. Oct. 24, 1846; m. Eliza Officer.

**11,095**

CHARLES PARKER THURSTON (*Rev. Thomas William, William, Thomas*), eldest son of Rev. Thomas William and Mary Brown (Faville) Thurston of St. Ansgar, Iowa; born in Schuyler, Herkimer county, N. Y., Aug. 30, 1844; married, May 24, 1866, HARRIET REBECCA DODGE, born in New Portage, Summit county, Ohio, Jan. 21, 1844, daughter of Horace Kingsbury and Lorinda M. (Willard) Dodge of Newburgh, Mitchell county, Iowa..

Mr. Thurston is a farmer in Northwood, Worth county, Iowa. He was in the employ of the United States government from November, 1862, doing duty as express messenger at St. Louis and clerk in quartermaster's office at Pilot Knob, Mo. Enlisted Oct. 10, 1863, at St. Ansgar in the 9th Iowa cavalry; was with the regiment at St. Louis and Rolla, Mo., went to Duvall's Bluff, Ark., doing guard duty for a year on the railroad from Duvall's Bluff to Little Rock; was detailed as postmaster to the regiment, taken sick, went to Jefferson Barracks, then to Keokuk, Iowa, was detailed as baker in the Seventh street hospital, and was discharged at Davenport, by general order, June 21, 1865; a justice of the peace and member of the Methodist church.

Children:

11,110 Frederick William, b. at Spirit Lake, Iowa, May 4, 1867.
11,111 Thirza Locklan, b. at St. Ansgar Dec. 16, 1869; d. Sept. 14, 1870.
11,112 Horace Dodge, b. at St. Ansgar July 21, 1871.
11,113 Hattie May, b. at Northwood May 1, 1873.
11,114 Edith Maria, b. at Northwood Feb. 23, 1876.
11,115 Charles Parker, b. at Northwood Dec. 2, 1877.

## 11,106

JAMES ORSON THURSTON of Almont, Lapeer county, Mich. (*James Gilbert, Joseph, Thomas*), son of James Gilbert and Lucy Ann (Hough) Thurston of Almont; born in Armada, Mich., Oct. 24, 1846; married, in Bruce, Mich., Dec. 25, 1867, ELIZA OFFICER, born in New York Nov. 7, 1846, daughter of Alexander and Emeline E. (Austin) Officer of Almont. Mr. Thurston is a druggist and town clerk.

Children:

11,120 Lucy E., b. in Addison, Mich., Aug. 18, 1869.
11,121 Mary E., b. in Addison Sept. 14, 1871.
11,122 Hervey, b. in Almont Jan. 20, 1877.

## 11,127

PETER THURSTON of London, Eng., married MARTHA ——. He died in London January, 1817, aged 80.

Children:

+11,128 Peter, b. Aug. 21, 1767; m. Sarah Baldwin.
+11,129 Joshua, b. Feb. 6, 1775; m. 1st, Mary ——; 2d, ——.

## 11,128

PETER THURSTON (*Peter*), eldest son of Peter and Martha Thurston of London, Eng.; born there Aug. 21, 1767; came to New York city October, 1794; married, Oct. 25, 1796, SARAH BALDWIN, daughter of Kipps Baldwin of Newark, N. J., who also came from England with his family in 1794.

Mr. Thurston was a Baptist minister, pastor of the First Baptist church in Newark, and afterward of the Baptist church in Catskill, N. Y. He died in New York city February, 1847; she died in New York city November, 1805.

Children:

+11,134 Nathaniel, b. Oct. 12, 1797; m. Ann Ketcham.
11,135 Joseph, b. July 2, 1799; d. May 14, 1806.
+11,136 Henry, b. Dec. 26, 1801; m. Margaret Ann ——.
11,137 Peter Kipps, b. March 13, 1804; m. ——; d. several years ago, leaving:
  11,138 *Henry*, m. and lives in Connecticut; several children.
  11,139 *Charles B.*, m. and lives in Jersey City, N. J.; no children.
  11,140 *Matilda*, m. Theodore Gray; no children living.

## 11,129

JOSHUA THURSTON (*Peter*), brother of the preceding, and son of Peter and Martha Thurston of London, Eng.; born there Feb. 6, 1775; married, first, MARY ——; came to this country in 1815, bringing his wife and four children; married again, in New York, 1819.

Mr. Thurston was a piano manufacturer in New York city, residing

in Brooklyn, N. Y., where he died, 1854. His will was dated June 9, 1849, proved May 19, 1854; executors, Nathaniel Thurston of New York, John H. Williams, and J. H. Robert Haus.

### His children, by first wife:

11,145  Ann, b. 1795; n.m.; d. 1868.
11,146  Martha, b. 1798; n.m.; d. 1817.
11,147  Elizabeth, m. 1st, ———; 2d, Thomas E. Baker; d. 1849, without issue.
11,148  Jasper Scambler, m. Fanny Durando, daughter of P. M. P. Durando; He died 1866, leaving:
    11,149  *Sarah Elizabeth*, b. 1831; m. Hanford Nichols; live at Black Rock, Fairfield county, Ct.; several children.
    11,150  *Joshua*, b. 1833; m. lately, 1879.

### By second wife:

11,151  Martha, b. 1821; m. 1st, Alfred N. Brewer; he died 1863; 2d, Charles Howard, deceased; she died 1871; she had, by first husband:
    11,152  *Alfred F.* (Brewer), living in New York.
11,153  Mary, m. George F. Brandt, deceased; she died 1850; no children.

## 11,134

NATHANIEL THURSTON (*Peter, Peter*), eldest son of Peter and Sarah (Baldwin) Thurston of New York city; born there Oct. 12, 1797; married, April 15, 1821, ANN KETCHAM, born Sept. 26, 1794, daughter of Solomon Ketcham of Howell township, Monmouth county, N. J. She died in New York city Feb. 10, 1876.

### Children, all born in New York city.

11,158  George Hobdey, b Mar. 25, 1822; m. Hannah Frances Hawkins, daughter of Mills Hawkins of Lakeland, Long Island, where they are now living with their four children:
    11,159  *Jeannie.*
    11,160  *George.*
    11,161  *Thomas.*
    11,162  *Lillie.*  All young and unmarried.
11,163  Sarah Baldwin, b. July 30, 1823; m. Oct. 23, 1850, Thomas E. Baker, now deceased.  Children:
    11,164  *Annie* (Baker), b. July 23, 1851; m. Oct. 23, 1877, Israel F. R. Dissosway; they live on Staten Island; one son.
    11,165  *Mary Elizabeth* (Baker), b. Mar. 17. 1858; n.m.; in New York city.
11,166  William Ketcham, b. Nov. 17, 1824; d. Dec. 7, 1829.
11,167  David, b. Jan. 1, 1826; m. Charlotte Augusta Purdy, daughter of Hackaliah Purdy; they live in New York city and have:
    11,168  *Lottie.*
    11,169  *David.*  Both young and unmarried Dec., 1879.
11,170  Mary Cooper, b. March 2, 1827; n.m.; d. March 4, 1862.
11,171•  Elizabeth, b. July 12, 1828; d. May 26, 1841.
11,172  Thomas L., b. Oct. 16, 1830; twice married, both wives dead; he died Dec. 13, 1864; no children living.
11,173  Joseph, b. June 17, 1832; n.m.; d. Aug. 28, 1854.
11,174  Solomon, b. Sept. 13, 1834; d. April 6, 1839.
11,175  Nathaniel, b. Sept. 8, 1836; m. Phebe E. Hatt, daughter of Rev. George Hatt; they have:
    11,176  *Sophie*, b. about 1866.
11,177  Alfred, b. June 5, 1838; m. Catharine Snow; they have:
    11,178  *Mary.*
    11,179  *Catharine.*
    11,180  *Fanny.*
    11,181  *Alfred.*  All young and unmarried Dec., 1879.

## 11,136

HENRY THURSTON (*Peter, Peter*), brother of the preceding, and son of Peter and Sarah (Baldwin) Thurston of New York city; born there Dec. 26, 1801; married MARGARET ANN ———.

Mr. Thurston lived in Brooklyn, N. Y. He died Dec. 25, 1855; will dated Nov. 3, 1855; executors, wife, brother Nathaniel, and friend John F. Sampson of Brooklyn.

Children:

11,186　Wallace Henry; m. ———; one child, an infant, 1879.
11,187　Emma Cornelia, m. Albert Holbrook; one child, an infant, 1879.

## 11,194

WILLIAM THURSTON (*William*), son of William and Hester (Wightwick) Thurston of Hamstreet, Kent, Eng.; born there Mar. 31, 1819; married at High Halden, Kent, Eng., ESTHER ANN CARPENTER, born March 19, 1825, daughter of James and Elizabeth (Weller) Carpenter of Frittenden, Kent, Eng.

Mr. Thurston is a painter in Syracuse, N. Y.; had four brothers and two sisters, all in England except one brother, Wightwick Thurston, who lives in Argyle, La Fayette county, Wis.

Children:

11,195　William, b Jan. 19, 1846; m. July 6, 1862; d. June 11, 1869, leaving:
　　　11,196　*Douglass*.
11,197　Esther Ann, b. May 16, 1848; m. Nov. 25. 1870, John C. Golding.
11,198　Mary Elizabeth, b. Oct. 10, 1850; m. Sept. 20, 1871, Walter Addison Scuyler.

## 11,200

——— THURSTON, married ——— TINGEY. He was captain of a vessel belonging in England, trading with the West Indies, and died of the fever (supposed yellow fever) on one of the voyages. His widow married again, and her brother, Capt. Tingey, brought the two children to this country, and himself sailed out of Philadelphia in the East India trade, taking Robert with him, who after became a master of a vessel. When the revolutionary war broke out Capt. Tingey joined the navy of this country and afterward became commodore, and was in command of the navy yard in Washington when it was destroyed by the British.

Children:

+11,201　Robert, m. Elizabeth Eldredge.
11,202　Susanna.

## 11,201

ROBERT THURSTON married ELIZABETH ELDREDGE, born April 1, 1781, daughter of Capt. Phineas Eldredge of Philadelphia, who commanded the privateer " Fair America." She died Jan. 28, 1855.

Children:

11,205　Jane, b. Feb. 22, 1805; living.
11,206　Susanna, b. April 22, 1808; m. Dr. Barry of Washington, D. C.; he was a surgeon in the navy and died in service. They had:
　　　11,207　*Richard* (Barry), m.; in St. Louis, Mo.
　　　11,208　*Susanna* (Barry), n.m.; in St. Louis.
11,209　Phineas Eldredge, b. Aug. 27. 1810; d. of yellow fever in Havana, Cuba, on the brig Caroline, of which his father was master, Dec. 15, 1824, and was buried there.
+11,210　Robert, b. Oct. 3, 1814; m. Emma Dewees.

## 11,210

ROBERT THURSTON (*Robert*), son of Robert and Elizabeth (Eldredge) Thurston of Philadelphia, Pa.; born there Oct. 3, 1814; married. by Rev. Mr. Coleman of Trinity church, June 17, 1838, EMMA DEWEES, adopted daughter of Spencer and Mary Ann (Valance) Dewees of Philadelphia.

Children:

11,215    Emma, b. March 11, 1839; d.
11,216    Spencer Dewees, b. Nov. 19, 1841; chief engineer of the steamship Norfolk.
11,217    Robert, b. Sept. 23, 1844; d. of cholera on board the steamship Montivedio, in the harbor of Rosario, Argentine Republic, South America, Jan. 5, 1868, and was buried there.
11,218    Phineas Eldredge, b. April 23, 1848; now chief engineer of the steamship Rattlesnake of Philadelphia.

## 11,220

ROBERT THRUSTON of Bristol, Eng., in the reign of Queen Elizabeth, motto "*Esse quam videri*," crest a stork, had a grandson John, who came to America.

## 11,221

JOHN THRUSTON, grandson of Robert, of Bristol, Eng., came to Gloucester, Gloucester county, Va. Children:

11,222    Charles Mynn, who married and had:
     11,223   *Buckner*, a judge in Washington, D. C., who had a daughter who m. Capt. Powell, U. S. N.
     11,224   *Mrs. Dandridge.*
     11,225   *Mrs. Fauntleroy.*
     11,226   *Mrs. Powell*, whose son was Capt. Powell above.
11,227    John.
11,228    Robert. who had:
     11,229   *Mrs. Thornton*, the mother of
         11,230   *Lieut. Col. John Thruston* (Thornton) and four other children.
11,231    Mrs. Mallery.
11,232    Frances, m. Col. William Hubard of Charlotte, Va., and had:
     11,233   *Dr. James Thruston* (Hubard) of Buckingham, Va. Children:
         11,234   *Hon. E. W.* (Hubard), who had:
             11,235   *Willie* (Hubard).
             11,236   *Susan* (Hubard).
             11,237   *E. W.* (Hubard).
             11,238   *John E.* (Hubard).
         11,239   *Robert Thruston* (Hubard), who had:
             11,240   *James L.* (Hubard).
             11,241   *Wm. B.* (Hubard).
             11,242   *Robert Thruston* (Hubard), a lawyer, who had two sons and two daughters, and who communicated these facts concerning his Thurston ancestry.
         11,243   *Edward* (Hubard).
         11,244   *Louisa* (Hubard), m. —— Randolph.
         11,245   *Bolling* (Hubard).
         11,246   *P. A.* (Hubard).

## 11,250

EMANUEL JONES THURSTON of Millwood, Gloucester county, Va., married CATHARINE PENDLETON COOKE.

Child:

11,251 John Mynn, b. Jan. 11, 1825; is a farmer at Warehouse, Gloucester county, Va.; m. Oct. 9, 1850, Mary Ann Virginia Robins, b. at Point Lookout, Gloucester county, Va., July 5, 1829, daughter of Thomas Coleman [of " The Globe"] and Amelia (Armistead) Robins of Gloucester county. They have:

    11,252 *Amelia*, b. Aug. 29, 1856.
    11,253 *William Pendleton*, b. Sept. 17, 1859.
    11,254 *Mary Washington*, b. Feb. 22, 1864.
    11,255 *Ellen Coleman*, b. May 22, 1871.

## 11,260

ARMISTAD THURSTON of King and Queen county, Va. He had a sister who married —— Brown.

Children of Armistad:

    11,261 Lemuel, m. in Richmond, Va., went to Huntsville, Ala., thence to Little Rock, Ark., where he died.
+11,262 Armistad.
    11,263 John.
    11,264 Daniel.

## 11,262

ARMISTAD THURSTON (*Armistad*), son of Armistad Thurston, married in Goochland county, Va., went to Newmarket, seventeen miles north of Huntsville, Ala., where he died, 1842 or 1843.

Child:

11,265 William S., went to Richmond, Va., 1858, and has resided there since, 733 Brook avenue.

## 11,266

AZARIAH THURSTON, a ship-master of Northampton county, Va., lost at sea.

**11,267** JAMES THURSTON, brother of Azariah, married in Northampton county, Va., had two children, all dead.

Children of Azariah:

11,268 James B., lives in Matthews county, Va., m. and had :
    11,269 *James P.*, a ship-master; says he thinks his grandfather and brother came from Maine.
    11,270 *William B.*, a bookkeeper in Baltimore, Md.
    11,271 *Charles E.*, a seaman.
    11,272 *Azariah E.*, a seaman.
    11,273 *Melvin T.*
11,274 William H., lives in New York.
11,275 Edgar, d.
11,276 Sarah E., lives in Matthews county, Va.

## 11,277

WILLIAM THURSTON, son of Thomas, born near Clear Spring, Md., Feb. 2, 1823; married, March 25, 1850, JENNIE BARTLESON, born in Philadelphia, Pa., May 14, 1831, daughter of Elijah [architect and builder] and Esther Gesner (Whitecar) Bartleson of Berkeley county,

West Va.   He died Feb. 9, 1868.   She married, second, Oct. 3, 1876, Zerobabel Mentzer.

Mr. Thurston was a carpenter in Hagerstown, Washington county, Md., member of the Lutheran church.

Children :

11,278   Calvin Beesley, b. in Virginia Jan. 5, 1851, a brick layer in Hagerstown ; m. and has :

    11,279   *Thomas Edward*, b. Jan. 13, 1877.

Born in Hagerstown :

11,280   Thomas Claggette, b. Aug. 18, 1852; m. 1872; divorced by mutual consent 1878; no children; is special correspondent of the Times, Kansas City, Mo.   He says: "I left home at fifteen and have been in the west ever since; learned the printers' trade; was editor and proprietor of Platte City, Mo., Advocate (democratic) 1876 and 1877; was shot while running this paper; killed my adversary, by shooting him through the heart, after I had been shot through the head; have been city editor of Leavenworth Times.   Since 1877 have been connected with Kansas City Times, editorially and traveling correspondent.   When the Missouri legislature is not in session travel as correspondent through new and old Mexico, Missouri, Colorado, Texas, Arizona, Nebraska, Kansas, Indian Territory, and part of Iowa."

11,281   Elijah Bartleson, b. July 29, 1854; d. Aug. 18, 1856.
11,282   Edward Dorsey, b. Jan. 14, 1857; farmer near Harrisburgh City, Pa.
11,283   Charles William, b. June 20, 1859; in shoe factory.
11,284   McClellan, b. Sept. 9, 1861; on farm near Harrisburgh.
11,285   Robert Joseph, b. Jan. 13, 1864; works with a butcher.
11,286   Albert, b. March 25, 1867.

---

**11,287**   BENJAMIN THURSTON, born in Berkeley county, W. Va.
**11,288**   JAMES THURSTON, brother of Benjamin, born in W. Va.

### 11,290

WILLIAM THURSTON, brother of Benjamin and James, born in Berkeley county, W. Va., Jan. 31, 1772; married ELIZABETH ——, born April 21, 1776.   He died April 10, and she died April 21, 1843.

Mr. Thurston moved to Ohio; was a miller in Greenfield, Highland county, on the Little Miami river, twenty-six miles from Cincinnati. He emigrated from Wheeling, Va., on a flat boat in 1811 and landed at Cincinnati when there were but few houses there.   Of his two brothers, one authority says John, and another says Benjamin, went to North Bend, Ohio, and James to near Cincinnati in 1809; he had three half brothers who remained in Virginia.

Children :

11,291   George Washington.
11,292   Andrew Jackson.
11,293   Henry.
+11,294   William Hauk, b. May 2, 1801; m. Delila Miller.
11,295   Rachel.
11,296   Margaret.
11,297   Sarah.
11,298   Eliza.

### 11,294

WILLIAM HAUK THURSTON ( *William* ), son of William and Elizabeth Thurston of Berkeley county, West Va.; born there May 2, 1801 ;

married, Sept. 13, 1827, DELILA MILLER, born June 28, 1808. He died in Greenfield, Ohio, May 21, 1873; she died Sept. 8, 1875.

Mr. Thurston was a miller; went with his father to the Little Miami river, Ohio, in 1811; in 1846 to Clarksville, Ohio; in 1849 to Wilmington, Ohio; in 1855 to Madison, Ohio; in 1860 to New Holland, Ohio; in 1862 to Washington, Ohio; in 1867 to Greenfield, O., having been in all these places engaged in the milling business.

They were both members of the church, and it is said in an obituary notice of Mrs. Delila Thurston: "Peacefully and happily they journeyed arm in arm through forty-six years of life's pilgrimage, enjoying more of life's comforts, pleasures, and happiness than is common. The mother of eleven children, nine of whom lived to maturity, always endeavoring to bring them up in the fear of the Lord. Eight of them are living to-day, 1877, respected in the community where they live."

### Children :

11,299  William Henry Harrison, b. Aug. 4, 1828; d. Nov. 1, 1836.

11,300  Jacob Harner, b. in Deerfield, Warren county, Ohio, Dec. 4. 1829; m. Aug. 12. 1852, Rachel Ann Wolary, b. March 6, 1833, daughter of Michael and Elizabeth (Mears) Wolary of Wilmington, Clinton county, Ohio. He is a physician in Athens, Ohio; graduated from the Physio-medical college at Cincinnati in 1873; no children

11,301  John Ferris, b. Nov. 6, 1831; m. Jan. 18, 1855, Lydia A. Peters. He is a miller. Children :

    11.302  *Charles Harner*. b. Sept. 6. 1855.

    11,303  *Emily Bell*, b. May 25, 1858.

    11.304  *Calvin L.*, b. Jan. 16, 1861.

    11.305  *Jodney*, b. Sept. 19, 1863.

11,306  Sarah Catherine, b. Dec. 22, 1833; d. March 24, 1857.

11,307  George Washington, b. Nov. 6, 1836; m. May 20, 1869. Elizabeth Wilson; no children. He owns a mill in Greenfield, Highland county, Ohio; was in the war against the rebellion.

11,308  David Miller, b. March 10, 1839; m. Sept. 12, 1861, Mary Jane Deek. He is chief engineer of the fire department at Washington, Fayette county, Ohio. Children :

    11,309  *Clara Bell*. b. Jan. 18, 1863.

    11,310  *William Marshall*, b. Feb. 8, 1865.

    11.311  *Rowena*, b. May 10, 1867.

    11,312  *Martha B.*, b. June 17, 1868.

    11,313  *Eli*, b. Sept. 5, 1870.

    11,314  *Harry Elmer*, b. Nov. 23, 1871.

    11,315  *Ada Bernice*, b. June 7, 1874.

    11,316  *James Wilfred*. b. Feb. 27, 1876.

11,317  Joseph Marshall, b. July 2, 1841; m. Oct. 19, 1869, Ida Elliott and has one child, *Eva*. He is a physician in Hagerstown, Ind.; graduated at at the Physio-medical college at Cincinnati in 1866, and was appointed professor of physiology and anatomy in the Physio-medical college at Indianapolis, Ind., in 1875; was in the war against the rebellion.

11,318  James Morrow, b. Oct. 8, 1844; m. Dec. 13, 1864, Susan Frances White. He is engineer on the Mobile railroad and lives at Dresden, Muskingum county, Ohio. Children :

    11,319  *John Cessney*, b. Nov. 3, 1865.

    11,320  *Ida Bell*, b. June 22, 1867.

    11,321  *Herbert*, b. March 11, 1871.

11,322  Martha Steveson, b. Oct. 8, 1846; m. Nov. 28, 1867, W. C. Brant; four children.

11,323  Eli Hadley, b. Sept. 11, 1848; m. Aug. 17, 1870, Nana McDay. He is a physician in Jacksonburgh, Wayne county, Ind.; graduated at Physiomedical college in 1870. Children :

    11,324  *Helena Florence*, b. Aug. 21, 1871.

    11,325  *Thomas P.*, b. July 28, 1874.

## . 11,330

RICHARD THURSTON of Washington, D. C., born in the upper part of Spottsylvania county, Va., April, 1810, son of William Toliver and Millie Thurston of King William county, Va.; married, 1830, ELLEN HENDERSON, born 1815, daughter of Jacob and Clara Henderson of Orange county, Va.

Mr. Thurston says his brothers Henry and Paris died in Virginia, Toliver and wife were sold to western states, Plummer and wife were sold to another place. He is a boot and shoemaker; says his second master was Toliver Powell, for whom he worked twelve years.

Children:
11,331   James H., b. 1832; d. in Orange county during the war.
11,332   Harriet Ann, b. 1839; d. in Washington 1876.
11,333   Jane Elizabeth, b. 1841; d. in New York 1870.
11,334   Millard Ann, b. 1843; d. in Washington 1875.
11,335   Jacob Toliver, b. 1844; m. and lives in Washington; four children.
11,336   Mary Eliza, b. 1849; lives in Washington; n.m.

---

Probably descendants of Edward Thurston of Newport, R. I.

## 11,338

MATHEW THURSTON of Ithica, N. Y., married ELIZA JANE STEVENS.

Children:
11,339   Maggie Augusta, m. and lives in Providence, R. I.
+11,340  John J., b. Sept. 18, 1838; m. Mary Augusta Wood.

## 11,340

JOHN J. THURSTON, son of Mathew and Eliza Jane (Stevens) Thurston of Ithica, N. Y.; born there Sept. 18, 1838; married, in Jersey City, N. J., April 17, 1865, MARY AUGUSTA WOOD, born May 30, 1841, daughter of James and Kate (Wood) Wood of Newark, N. J.

Mr. Thurston is a painter in Jersey City.

Children, all born in Jersey City:
11,341   Tillie May, b. Feb. 11, 1867.
11,342   George Stevens, b. Oct. 20, 1868.
11,343   Maggie Jane, b. June 2, 1871; d. Jan. 4, 1874.
11,344   Mary Eliza, b. May 25, 1876.

---

Probably descendants of John Thurston of Dedham, Mass.

## 11,350

DANIEL THURSTON, married FRANCES ——. He was a farmer and moved to Delaware, Delaware county, Ohio, about 1820.

Children:
+11,351  Samuel, b. Jan. 18, 1807; m. Prudence Bearss.
11,352   Phebe, m. —— Thrall and lives in Killbourne, Delaware county, Ohio.

## 11,351

SAMUEL THURSTON (*Daniel*), son of Daniel and Frances Thurston of Delaware, Ohio; born Jan. 18, 1807; married, Nov. 18, 1830,

PRUDENCE BEARSS, born May, 1810, daughter of Joshua B. [born June 18, 1775] and Ruth (Knapp) Bearss. He died June 20, 1847; she died May 21, 1861.

Mr. Thurston was a farmer and settled in Laketon, Wabash county, Ind., in 1835, one of the first white families in that vicinity.

### Children:

11,357    Samuel Wesley, b. Aug. 4, 1832; in Red Oak, Iowa.
+11,358   William Kilbourn. b. May 5, 1834; m Mary H. Culbertson.
+11,359   Daniel Bearss, b. Feb. 5, 1837; m. Nancy Schuler.
11,360    Mary Frances, b. Dec. 22, 1838; m. Oct., 1862, Jacob Schuler of Wabash, Ind.
11,361    Laura Caroline. b. Jan. 7, 1841 ; m. Sept., 1867, T. E. Brown of Red Oak.
11,362    Clement, b. May 3, 1843; d 1844.
11,363    Prudence Philena, b. Aug. 31, 1847; m. Oct., 1871, Robert McLaughlin of Red Oak.

## 11,358

WILLIAM KILBOURN THURSTON (*Samuel, Daniel*), son of Samuel and Prudence (Bearss) Thurston of Laketon, Wabash county, Ind.; born in Marion county, Ohio, May 5, 1834; married, Nov. 21, 1855, MARY H. CULBERTSON of Matamoras, Ind. She died Feb. 5, 1874.

Mr. Thurston is a druggist, bookseller, and jeweler in Wabash, Ind., firm of Gordon & Thurston, and is a member of and ruling elder in the Presbyterian church.

### Children:

11,368    Clara Prudence, b. Oct. 20, 1856; m. Dec. 19, 1876, James D. Conner jr. They have :
     11,369   *Annis* (Conner), b. Nov. 13, 1878.
11,370    Annie Laura, b. June 4, 1858; m. April 14, 1879, Rev. Charles Little, b. Dec. 1, 1845. graduated from Marietta, Ohio, June 26. 1867, and from Lane theological seminary 1872; installed pastor of the Presbyterian church in Wabash April 29, 1873.
11,371    Georgia E., b. March 20, 1860.
11,372    Florence Bell, b. June 2, 1862.
11,373    Margaret Ross, b. July 30, 1864.
11,374    Lena Blanche, b. July 4, 1868.
11,375    Nerva Rose, b. Jan. 11, 1871.

## 11,359

DANIEL BEARSS THURSTON (*Samuel, Daniel*), brother of the preceding, and son of Samuel and Prudence (Bearss) Thurston of Laketon, Wabash county, Ind.; born there Feb. 5, 1837; married, April 19. 1862, NANCY SCHULER, born Jan. 28, 1840, daughter of Robert and Betsey (Reusz) Schuler of Wabash, Ind.

Mr. Thurston is a druggist and stationer in Blue Earth City, Faribault county, Minn. He is a member of the Methodist church, of which he is treasurer, steward, and superintendent of the Sunday-school. He served as delegate to the United States Christian Commission, at Harpers Ferry and Winchester, Va.

### Children:

11,380    Nellie May, b. in Wabash March 5, 1864.
11,381    Annie Dell. b. in Blue Earth City Feb. 7, 1866.
11,382    Mary Bell, b. in Blue Earth City May 23, 1867.
11,383    Laura Brown, b. in Blue Earth City Dec. 15, 1872.

## 11,388

DR. JAMES THURSTON of Chester, Vt.   Children:

+11,389  David, m. Alice Johnson.
+11,390  James.

## 11,389

DAVID THURSTON of Jay, N. Y. (*Dr. James*), married ALICE JOHN-SON : both died in Jay.

Mr. Thurston was a farmer in Dublin, N. H., and Chester, Vt., till 1827, when he moved to Jay, where he was a manufacturer of willow baskets.   Their children were all Baptists but one.

### Children:

11,396  Susanna, m. 1st, Joshua Whitney; 2d, Ira Boynton; both farmers of Jay.
11,397  Alice, b. in Dublin, N. H., Dec. 5, 1794; m. in Chester, Vt., by Rev.
         Aaron Lelon, Feb. 5, 1818, Ephraim Boynton, a farmer in Jay, b. in
         Weathersfield, Vt., April 7, 1793; he died in Grand Chute, Outagamie
         county, Wis.   Children:
    11,398  *Sarah* (Boynton), b. Nov. 24, 1818; m. Bela B. Murch of Appleton,
            Wis.
    11,399  *Obed* (Boynton), b. Oct. 7, 1822; served in the war against the re-
            bellion and d. in Sedgwick hospital, New Orleans, April 8, 1864,
            of wounds received in an attack on Spanish fort.
    11,400  *Caroline* (Boynton), b. Sept. 12, 1824; m. Samuel Mitchell, a farm-
            er in Depere, Brown county, Wis.
    11,401  *Lestina* (Boynton), b. Aug. 31, 1827; m. —— Bowman, a farmer in
            Spencer, Clay county, Iowa.
    11,402  *Nelson* (Boynton), b. Feb. 3, 1830; a farmer in Kansas Center,
            Rice county, Kansas.
    11,403  *Boardman Judson* (Boynton), b. March 20, 1833; graduated from
            Kalamazoo college; became a minister; d. in Mich. Aug. 12, 1870.
    11,404  *Myra Ann Amelia* (Boynton), b. Feb. 18, 1835; m. —— Goodale,
            a farmer in Potsdam, N. Y.
+11,405  Obed, b. Feb. 3, 1797; m. Sally Bigelow.
11,406  Charlotte, m. John Otis, a farmer in Jay, where he died.   They had :
    11,407  *Leland* (Otis), in Jay, upper village.

## 11,390

JAMES THURSTON (*Dr. James*), brother of the preceding, and son of Dr. James Thurston of Chester, Vt.

### Children:

11,411  John, in Rhode Island.
11,412  Ebenezer, out west.

## 11,405

OBED THURSTON (*David, Dr. James*), son of David and Alice (Johnson) Thurston of Jay, N. Y.; born in Dublin, N. H., Feb. 3, 1797 ; married, Jan. 26, 1828, SALLY BIGELOW, born in Winchendon, Mass., June 29, 1804.   He died 1851.

Mr. Thurston was a farmer in Baltimore, Vt., but moved to Ludlow, Vt., a short time before he died.   His widow married Parker Petti-grew, who died, and she lives in Ludlow.

### Children:

+11,417  Wales Bigelow, b. July 29, 1836; m. Julia Carol Jones.
11,418  Arabella Emergene, b. Nov. 17, 1848; n.m.

## 11,417

WALES BIGELOW THURSTON (*Obed, David, Dr. James*), son of Obed and Sally (Bigelow) Thurston of Baltimore, Vt.; born there July 29, 1836; married, Oct. 7, 1869, JULIA CAROL JONES, born Aug. 12, 1847. Mr. Thurston is a manufacturer of alcohol, cologne, and refined spirits in St. Louis, Mo., under firm name of W. B. Thurston & Co.

Children :

11,424   Royal Church, b. Dec. 27, 1870.
11,425   Wales Bigelow, b. July 29, 1872.
11,426   Maria Louise, b. Oct. 26, 1873.
11,427   Lawrence Jones, b. Feb. 8, 1875; d. Aug. 11, 1875.
11,428   Julian M., b. Aug. 7, 1879.

## 11,429

JOHN THURSTON of Chester, Vt., born at Providence, R. I., Nov. 14, 1759; married, in Chester, Sept. 9, 1790, LYDIA FLETCHER, born March 2, 1769. She died Jan. 25, 1842; he died May 10, 1847.

Mr. Thurston was a farmer; served three years and nine months in the revolutionary war, after which he purchased a farm in Chester, going on horseback, the roads then permitting no other means of travel; cleared a farm in the wilderness upon which he lived till his death, May 10, 1847.     Children:

11,430   Abigail, b. Aug. 15, 1791; d. 1794.
11,431   Mehitable, b. July 21, 1792; m. Apr. 2, 1815. James Field, a farmer of
    Chester, Vt., b. Mar., 1789; he d. July 8, 1850. Mrs. Field moved to
    Dell Prairie, Adams Co., Wis., with her youngest son, with whom she
    still lives, 1880.   Children b. in Chester:
        11,432   *Abigail* (Field), b. Jan. 29, 1816; m. Dec. 19, 1843, John W. Horton
            of Chester, later of Dell Prairie, where she d. Dec. 17, 1857.
        11,433   *Elisabeth*(Field),b. Apr. 25, 1819; m. June 6, 1848,Warren T. Atch-
            erson of Chester, later of Dell Prairie, where she d. Feb. 4, 1878.
        11,434   *Henry A.* (Field), b. March 26, 1821; m. Feb. 7, 1850, Olive Thurs-
            ton of Heuvelton, N. Y. [see no. 11, 460].  He was a farmer in
            Chester till 1855, when he moved to Dell Prairie, post-office ad-
            dress, Kilbourn City, Wis.
11,435   Abigail Willard, b. July 29, 1794; m. Joseph Field of Ludlow, Vt.; died
    Feb. 8, 1879.  They had:
        11,436   *Joseph* (Field), in Heuvelton, N. Y.     11,437   *William* (Field).
        11,438   *Abigail* (Field).                        11,439   *Serepta* (Field).
+11,440   William, b. March 17, 1796; m. Philena Burroughs.
+11,441   John, b. March 9. 1798; m. Polly Greely.
11,442   Lydia, b. March 18, 1800; m. Samuel Greely; both dead.   They had :
        11,443   *John* (Greely), in Heuvelton.
        11,444   *Lydia* (Greely).                          11,445   *Angeline* (Greely).
11,446   Ira, b. April 2, 1802; d. Oct., 1804.
+11,447   Daniel, b. Oct. 10, 1804; m. Mary Porter.
11,448   Mary, b. Dec. 22, 1806; m. Andrew Mead; d. June 16, 1868; no children.
11,449   Elizabeth, b. Mar. 24, 1809; m. Herod Pierce of Albany, Vt.; she died
    June 20, 1865, having had:           11,450   *Ira* (Pierce).
+11,451   Welcome, b. Dec. 21, 1814; m. Mariah Harriet Field.

## 11,440

WILLIAM THURSTON of Heuvelton, St. Lawrence county, N. Y. (*John*), son of John and Lydia (Fletcher) Thurston of Chester, Vt.; born there May 17, 1796; married, Oct. 30, 1824, PHILENA BURROUGHS, daughter of David Burroughs of Brattleborough, Vt.

Mr. Thurston left Chester in 1819 and settled in Heuvelton as a

hotel keeper and farmer, where he has lived excepting two years in California, during the gold excitement there ; now retired.

### Children :

11,453   Socrates Sherman, b. Feb. 10, 1825; n.m.; proprietor of the Academy of Music, Chicago, Ill.
11,454   David Burroughs, b. Oct. 8, 1829; m. Mary E. Griffin [see p. 598].
11,455   George Guest, b. Oct. 28, 1834; n.m.; graduated from Union college in 1860; a grocer in Heuvelton.

## 11,441

JOHN THURSTON ( *John*), brother of the preceding, and son of John and Lydia (Fletcher) Thurston of Chester, Vt. ; born there March 9, 1798 ; married, Oct., 1822, POLLY GREELY, born Aug. 30, 1803, in Andover, Vt. ; she died Nov. 9, 1878.   He died Aug. 22, 1878.
Mr. Thurston was a farmer in Heuvelton, N. Y.          Children :

11,456   Ira, b. in Chester, Vt., Oct. 23, 1823; a farmer near Heuvelton, 1880.
11,457   Lorenzo, b. in Heuvelton Oct. 27, 1825; d. June 17, 1842.
11,460   Olive, b. Oct. 23, 1827; m. Henry A. Field of Chester [see no. 11,434], later of Dell Prairie, Wis.
11,459   Mehitable, b. June 3, 1830; d. Dec. 8, 1838.
11,461   Mary, b. Aug. 6, 1832; m. April 6, 1862.
11,461*a*  Rosana, b. Jan. 14, 1835; d. June 14, 1842.
11,461*b*  Charles S., b. April 13, 1837; d. June 6, 1842.
11,461*c*  William H., b. July 6, 1839; d. June 22, 1842.
11,462   Elizabeth, b. Nov. 24, 1841; m. May 22, 1867.
11,463   Lydia F., b. April 13, 1844; m. Feb. 18, 1867, A. C. Ketcham of Adams county, Wis., later of Brookfield, Linn county, Mo.
11,464   Ellen E., b. Jan. 12, 1846; m. Oct. 23, 1879, John Ross of Heuvelton.

## 11,447

DANIEL THURSTON (*John*), brother of the preceding, and son of John and Lydia (Fletcher) Thurston of Chester, Vt.; born there Oct. 10, 1804; married MARY PORTER, born in Langdon, N. H.   He died Nov. 13, 1871.   Mr. Thurston was a bridge builder and farmer in Barton, Vt.; went west about 1848, and about 1865 settled in Brookfield, Linn Co., Mo.          Children :

11,465   William Sherman, b. in Barton April 11, 1833; m. in Holyoke, Mass., Feb. 4, 1860, Agnes Kearney, b. Dec. 15, 1837, daughter of Morris and Sophia (Odell) Kearney of Eastport, Me.   He is a teamster in Springfield, Mass.   Children :
  11,466   *Carrie Agnes*, b. Oct. 5, 1861.
  11,467   *Flora Lorinda*, b. Nov. 29, 1867.
  11,468   *Eddie Sherman*, b. Aug. 10, 1869.
11,469   Jane, n.m.; in Brookfield.

## 11,451

WELCOME THURSTON (*John*), brother of the preceding, and son of John and Lydia (Fletcher) Thurston of Chester, Vt.; born there Dec. 21, 1814; married, Sept. 23, 1837, MARIAH HARRIET FIELD, born Oct. 13, 1814, daughter of Robert Wescott and Lydia (Field) [same name but not related] Field of Chester.   Mr. Thurston is a farmer in Mendota, La Salle county, Ill., to which place he moved in 1853.

### Children :

11,470   Robert Field, b. in Chester July 18, 1838; n.m.; a farmer in Lincoln, Neb.
11,471   Alfred John, b. in Chester May 17, 1841; a farmer in Mendota; m. Dec. 31, 1875, Malvina Ann Wood, b. in Westfield, Bureau county, Ill., daughter of Edgar Maxwell and Elizabeth (Wenham) Wood of Sheboygan Falls, Sheboygan county, Wis.; no children.

## CORRECTIONS AND ADDITIONS.

Page 30, no. 27, 3d line, Lydia Seaver, b. Dec. 5, 1684. daughter of Thomas and Demaris (Bailey) Seaver of Rowley. Daniel Thurston died March 10, 1720, and his widow married, Nov. 23, 1725, Stephen Jewett, as his third wife; she died Sept. 7, 1754. It is said she was the widow of Robert Rogers when she married Daniel Thurston.

Page 31, in connection with foot note. The above lot [lot 2, letter D] was deeded in 1772 by John and Benjamin Thurston [nos. 84, 88] to Lieut. Samuel Merrill, one of the first settlers in Buxton, Me.

Lot 4 was drawn on the right of Nathaniel Emerson by John and Benjamin Thurston.
Lot 1 was drawn on the right of Daniel Thurston by John and Benjamin Thurston.
Lot 15 was drawn on the right of Daniel Thurston by Daniel Thurston, no. 27.
Lot 5 was drawn on the right of Daniel Thurston by John L. Hancock.
Lot 12 was drawn on the right of Nathaniel Emerson by John Thurston.

Page 43, no. 317, read, m. 1770, Col. Joseph Hilton. b. June 13, 1747, a large land owner, farmer, and manufacturer of oil from flax seed, of Deerfield, N. H. She died May 15, 1813. No. 321, Mehitable Hilton, b. Aug. 16, 1790; m. April 4, 1810, Capt. David Haines, who commanded a company of artillery at Portsmouth, N. H. No. 322 m. —— Butler and moved to Maine. No. 323 went to Maine. No. 324 lived in Deerfield. No. 325 went to Maine. No. 328 graduated from Dartmouth and died in Deerfield.

Page 49, no. 488, Eunice (Jewett), m. Joshua Noyes, a farmer in Byfield, Mass.; had:
490 Phebe Thurston (Noyes), m. Samuel Thurston, no. 11,525.
491 Rev. Randall (Noyes), d. in Atkinson, Me.
Page 54, no. 572 [see no. 551].
Page 56, no. 671 [see no. 2128].
Page 58, no. 732. All we know is he lived in Windsor, Me.
Page 67, no. 1056, Ruth m. Feb. 2, 1802.
Page 123, no. 2128 [see no. 671].

### Page 126, no. 2215.

CALEB THURSTON[6] ( *Caleb,*[5] *Caleb,*[4] *Abner,*[3] *James,*[2] *Daniel*[1]), son of Caleb[5] and Anne (Wiggins) Thurston of Exeter, N. H. ; married JANE ——, born in Peterborough, N. H. They are supposed to have lived in Maine. She died in Boston, Mass., Aug. 4, 1875, aged 73 y. 8 m., as per city record of deaths.

### Children:

2220  John.[7]
2221  Moses,[7] m. Betsey Filer: said to be living, 1879, in Exeter, N. H. Their son Charles Filer says his father left his mother in Canada when he was six years old and his brother one year old. He heard from him by way of his uncle John, some years after, who reported he had married in Utica, N. Y., and had three children. Moses told his brother John that his first wife was dead and he had put his son Charles Filer out to live. Charles says he was put out to live, and when he was sixteen years of age his mother heard that her husband was married, and she married, although he opposed it all he could. Children of Moses and Betsey :
  2222  *Charles Filer,*[8] b. in Stanstead, Lower Canada, Nov. 8, 1827; went to Philadelphia, Pa., when he was twenty-one and m. March 3, 1852, Elizabeth Shuster, b. Jan. 27, 1835, daughter of Samuel and Ann (Mervine) Shuster of Philadelphia. He went to California in 1861 and did pretty well in business; his family came to him in 1868, did not like California, and returned to Philadelphia after five weeks. In 1869 he went to his family intending to stay, but was not contented and returned to San Francisco; began to speculate in stocks and lost all he had made. His children are with him, 1879, all occupied in stage and carriage driving. Children, b. in Philadelphia :
    2223  *Charles Filer,*[9] b. Dec. 12, 1852.
    2224  *George Washington,*[9] b. Nov. 19, 1854.
    2225  *Adelaide,*[9] b. May 8, 1857.
    2226  *Sallie,*[9] b. March 3, 1859.
    2227  *Bessie,*[9] b. in California March 13, d. April 16, 1877.
2228  *A son,*[8] b. 1832.

### Page 134¾, no. 2561.

### Children of Betsey Thurston, who married Caleb Tillson.

11,476  Mary (Tillson), b. April 27, 1804; m. —— Newberry about 1852 or 1853;
d. April 20, 1853; no children.

11,477  Stephen (Tillson), b. May 20, 1806; d. April 23, 1808.

11,478  Elizabeth (Tillson), b. Aug. 1, 1808; m. Oct. 8, 1829, James Colwell Mellen, a stone-mason of Prescott, Mass., b. July 12, 1807, son of Jonathan
Mellen.  Children:

    11,479  Caroline Elizabeth (Mellen), b. in Enfield, Mass., June 10, 1830; d.
at Redding Ridge, Ct., May 7, 1870.

    11,480  Zebina Tillson (Mellen), b. in Prescott March 6, 1832; a stone-ma-
son; m. May 11, 1856, Sarah C. Burr, b. May 5, 1835, daughter
of Walter and Eunice (Bradley) Burr.  He died Jan. 25, 1873.
They had, b. at Redding Ridge:  Ella T., b. Nov. 16, 1857, Charles
B., b. Feb. 16, 1859, Emma C., b. Aug. 6, 1860, Jennie, b. March
31, 1865, Franklin C., b. June 10, 1869, and John Z. (Mellen), b.
Sept. 21, 1872.

    11,481  Almira Jane (Mellen), b. in Prescott Feb. 9, 1834; m. June 3, 1856,
Peter P. Keeler.  She died April 24, 1870.  They had, born at
Redding Ridge:  Oscar Hibbard, b. Dec. 1, 1857, Jessie Almira,
b. April 8, 1862, and Mary Elizabeth (Keeler), b. Nov. 27, 1864.

    11,482  James Colister (Mellen), b. in Weston, Ct., Feb. 24, 1847; a stone-
mason; m. about 1869, Emeline Whitehead of Redding.  They
live in South Hadley, Mass., and have Nettie Theresa, Archie
Colister, and Minnie Caroline (Mellen).

    11,483  Daniel Webster (Mellen), b. at Redding Ridge April 15, 1851; a ma-
son; m. at New Haven, Ct., Nov. 4, 1875, Sarah Emma Josephine
Stebbins, b. May 30, 1853, daughter of Franklin Stebbins.  They
have Franklin Stebbins (Mellen), b. Jan. 8, 1878.

11,484  Caleb (Tillson), b. April 29, 1810; m. April 29, 1846, Esther Dean Stone,
b. in Enfield Sept. 6, 1805.  He is a farmer in Enfield.  They had:

    11,485  Elzina Elizabeth (Tillson), b. Dec. 31, 1849; m. about 1864, Oscar
Fitzgerald Winslow; they live in Enfield.  Children:  Frederic
Eugene, b. July 22, 1867, Rose B., b. Jan. 11, 1870, and Berty
(Winslow), b. Jan. 13, d. July 25, 1872.

11,486  Elmira (Tillson), b. April 11, 1812; n.m.; d. of brain fever, Oct. 23, 1836,
in Hadley, Mass., where he was a student in the Hopkins academy; was
buried in Enfield.

11,487  Thomas Thurston (Tillson), b. May 10, 1814; m. March 11, 1841, Sarah
Ballard, b. Feb., 1814.  He was a house carpenter near Princeton, Bureau county, Ill., when last heard from, some years ago, and had a family.

11,488  Zebina (Tillson), b. May 28, 1816; m. 1840, Mercy Edwards; lived a few
years in Ware village, Mass., and a short time on the old homestead in
Enfield, and then removed to Shutesbury, Mass., bought a small farm,
and has lived there since, working a considerable part of his time in
neighboring towns at carpenter and joiner work.  They are members of
the Congregational church.  Children:

    11,489  George William (Tillson), b. Nov. 7, 1840; m. Lucy Cooly of North
Hadley, Mass.  They have George Dwight, Henry Edwards, Ben-
ager English, and Eva Adelia (Tillson).

    11,490  Nellie Elizabeth (Tillson), b. April 25, 1842; m. Nathaniel Belcher
of Boston, Mass..  They have Carrie Edith (Belcher).

    11,491  Susan Almira (Tillson), b. Aug. 8, 1843; m. Lysander Chaffin of
Hatfield, Mass.  They have Sarah Emma, Arthur L., Laura, Rosa,
Edgar, and Lorin (Chaffin).

    11,492  Mary (Tillson), b. March 17, 1845; m. George Wheeler of Boston;
no children, 1879.

    11,493  Hattie M. (Tillson), b. Oct. 8, 1846; m. Charles Stetson of New Sa-
lem, Mass.; no children, 1879.

    11,494  Henry D. (Tillson), b. Oct. 11, 1848; m. Nellie Boyder of Pelham,
Mass.  They have Albert Henry, Charles Sanford, Homer Lewis,
and John David (Tillson).

11,495 Sadie Emma (Tillson), b. Oct. 17, 1853; m. Charles Woodworth of Watertown, Mass. They have Charles Townsen (Woodworth).

11,496 Adella (Tillson), b. April 3, 1859; n.m. Aug., 1879.

11,497 James (Tillson), b. Nov. 17, 1818; m. Nov., 1840, Elzina Ruth Stebbins, b. March 1, 1815, daughter of Dan and Sally Stebbins of North Chester, Mass. Mr. Tillson learned the machinist trade in Stafford, Ct., April 13, 1836,—April 13, 1839. He lived the six years following in Chicopee Falls village, Cabotville, and Lowell, Mass., Nashua and Manchester, N. H., Athol and Worcester, Mass. From Worcester he removed to Elmira, Chemung county, N. Y., where he now resides, 1879. He has always been actively interested in every project that would more thoroughly educate and elevate the people, believing if the whole people were highly educated, the public interests would be promoted through a more moral, intelligent, and happy people, that it would be safe to trust with all matters of human concern. The only public offices he has held are those of school trustee and commissioner of the city board of education, serving in each position several years; was the first to make a successful move for organizing the free graded schools of Elmira with its free academy, which is the pride of the city. Children :

11,498 James Lafayette (Tillson), b. in Manchester July 29, 1842; d. in Elmira Dec. 28, 1856.

11,499 Caroline Elizabeth (Tillson), b. in Athol Oct. 18, 1843; m. April 4, 1868 ———, and had Charlie Lafayette ———, b. March 5, 1869; this was an unfortunate union, and they separated after living together about a year. She is a school teacher.

11,500 Adelaide Elzina (Tillson), b. in Elmira Oct. 8, 1845; n.m.; lives with her parents.

11,501 Malinda Rowena (Tillson), b. in Elmira Feb. 28, 1847; m. April 4, 1868, Francis Marion Weaver, b. in Erin Center, Chemung county, N. Y., June 10, 1843. They live in Manton, Wexford county, Mich., are members of the Methodist church, and he is one of the stewards. He has been justice of the peace and sheriff of the county; is now farming. They have Jay Tillson (Weaver), b. July 25, 1879.

11.502 Immogene (Tillson), b. in Elmira Nov. 18, 1854; d. Feb. 24, 1863.

11,503 John Charles Fremont (Tillson), b. in Elmira May 26, 1856; graduated at the Elmira free academy in 1874, and at the United States military academy at West Point June 13, 1878, with the honor of a high standing in his class; is now, 1879, second lieutenant in the 5th regiment of infantry, United States army, located with General Miles at Fort Keogh, Montana territory.

11,504 Susan Maria (Tillson), b. March 15, 1821; m. Dec. 21, 1850, William Newberry; he is dead, and his widow lives on the old homestead in Enfield. They had George William (Newberry), b. April 1, 1852; m. Oct. 28, 1875, Lizzie M. Davis of Northfield, Mass., and have George Warren (Newberry), b. Sept. 7, 1876.

11,505 George Sumner (Tillson), b. March 18, 1823; n.m.; d. Feb. 3, 1867. He lived in Princeton, Bureau county, Ill., from 1837 to 1846; worked at digging wells, farming, and sometimes at carpenter work. In the early spring of 1847 he went on a whaling voyage for a little more than two years; during the voyage he was taken with the rheumatism, which produced a curvature of the spine, and he was a great sufferer the rest of his days. He united with the Congregational church and died firm in the faith of that organization, at the old Tillson homestead, the home of his sister Susan, who tenderly nursed him during his last illness.

Page 67, no. 1052, Enoch m. Martha ———; she d. May 5, 1835, aged 62. Children :

1065 Eliza.[6] b. April 11, 1795.

1066 John,[6] b. Oct. 26, 1796.

1067 Stephen,[6] b. July 31, 1801; was a smart, capable, and thrifty business man in Newburyport in 1845; afterward removed to California, became intemperate and died there.

## Page 134¾, no. 2581.

SAMUEL THURSTON[6] of Epping, N. H. (*Samuel,*[5] *Samuel,*[4] *Robert,*[3]

32

*Stephen,*[2] *Daniel*[1]), eldest son of Samuel[6] and Elizabeth (Gilman) Thurston of Epping; born there; married ELIZABETH BROWN of Salisbury, N. H. He died in Monmouth, Me., 1795; she spent the last years of her life at her son Gilman's in Monmouth, and died 1825.

Children, all born in Epping:

+11,510 Nathaniel,[7] b. 1775; m. 1st, Mary Fogg; 2d, Abigail Frances Starbord; 3d, Nancy Rose.

11,511 Gilman,[7] b. 1778; a farmer in Monmouth; m. at the age of 55, Betsey Starks; d. 1843; no children.

11,512 Ezekiel[7] [see page 130, no. 924]. It seems probable that they are the same person, but how to account for the different reports about his parentage I am at a loss.

11,513 Samuel,[7] killed in war.

11,514 Dolly,[7] m. Henry Pike, a farmer in Middleton, N. H.; both dead; no children.

11,515 Betsey,[7] n.m.; lived with her mother and went to Monmouth with her; d. 1843 in Gardiner, Me.

11,516 Nancy,[7] m. John Pike, brother to Dolly's husband, a farmer in Cornish, Me. They had:

    11,517 *Job* (Pike).
    11,518 *John* (Pike), a minister in New Hampshire.
    11,519 *Simeon* (Pike).

## 11,510

NATHANIEL THURSTON[7] (*Samuel,*[6] *Samuel,*[5] *Samuel,*[4] *Robert,*[3] *Stephen,*[2] *Daniel*[1]), son of Samuel[6] and Elizabeth (Brown) Thurston of Epping, N. H.; born there 1775; married, first, MARY FOGG of Epping; she died 1810. Second, ABIGAIL FRANCES STARBORD of Hartland, Me.; third, Oct. 20, 1822, NANCY ROSE of Waterville, Me. He died Jan. 9, 1834, aged 59, in Bangor, Me., where his widow still resides, 1880.

Mr. Thurston went to Hartland, Me., in 1807, when it was a wilderness; was a member of the Methodist church.

Children, by first wife, Mary:

+11,525 Samuel,[8] b. May 1, 1798; m. 1st, Phebe Thurston Noyes; 2d, Susan Richardson Thompson.

11,526 Nancy,[8] b. Oct. 2, 1802: m. 1st, Philemon Ware, a farmer of Monmouth, Me.; 2d, Dr. Jacob Stafford, a physician in Gardiner, Me.; 8 children.

By second wife, Abigail:

11,527 Nathaniel,[8] b. April 5, 1811; a wheelwright in Nantucket, Mass., but followed the sea in the whale fishery business; d. 1879.

+11,528 Gilman,[8] b. Mar. 16, 1812; m. 1st, Clarissa E. Gilman; 2d, Nancy Frost.

+11,529 Benjamin Franklin,[8] b. Jan. 7, 1819; m. Mary Ann Clark.

11,530 Abigail Frances,[8] } twins, born { d. in Boston, Mass., Aug. 5, 1856.

+11,531 William,[8] } April 11, 1822; { m. 1st, Clara Pike; 2d, Elizabeth Jane (Tucker) Holt.

By third wife, Nancy:

11,532 Elizabeth Brown,[8] b. Sept. 28, 1823; m. Aug. 8, 1841, John F. Libbey. Children:

    11,533 *Helen Augusta* (Libbey), b. May 26, 1842; m. June 6, 1859, Samuel Gibson of Bangor. Children:

        11,534 *Arthur Callis* (Gibson), b. April 18, 1860; now in Bowdoin college.
        11,535 *Eva Lucretia* (Gibson), b. Dec. 9, 1861.
        11,536 *Alice Louise* (Gibson), b. Jan. 14, 1863.

    11,537 *Charles Henry* (Libbey), b. Jan. 25, 1844; served in the war against the rebellion three years; n.m.; resides in Bangor.

    11,538 *Elizabeth Frances* (Libbey), b. May 26, 1849; m. Aug. 5, 1874, Charles Sargent of Bangor. Children:

        11,539 *Grace* (Sargent), b. 1874.
        11,540 *Walter* (Sargent), b. 1877.

11,541 Josephene,[8] } twins, born { m. James Kirkpatrick of Bangor.
11,542 Octavia,[8] } Nov. 4, 1827; { m. Henry Temple; now live in St. Paul, Minn.
11,543 John Rose,[8] b. March 24, 1831; served in the war against the rebellion three years, in the 2d Maine cavalry; d. in Bangor July 4, 1875.

## 11,525

SAMUEL THURSTON [8] (*Nathaniel*,[7] *Samuel*,[6] *Samuel*,[5] *Samuel*,[4] *Robert*,[3] *Stephen*,[2] *Daniel*[1]), eldest son of Nathaniel[7] and Mary (Fogg) Thurston of Hartland, Me.; born in Epping, N. H., March 5, 1798; married, first, 1821, PHEBE THURSTON NOYES, daughter of Joshua and Eunice (Jewett) Noyes of Byfield, Mass.; she died 1862. Eunice Jewett [see page 49, no. 488] the daughter of Rev. David and Phebe (Thurston) Jewett of Rowley, Mass., Candia, N. H., and Winthrop, Me. Second, 1862, SUSAN RICHARDSON THOMPSON, daughter of Daniel P. Thompson, Esq., of Woburn, Mass.

Mr. Thurston, when thirteen years of age, went to live with his uncle Gilman Thurston of Monmouth, Me. After marriage he went to Gardiner, Me., and engaged in lumbering and farming. In 1837 was lumbering some one hundred miles above Bangor, family residing in Bangor. In 1845 moved to Woburn Center, Mass., in the leather business till within a few years. He was an ordained deacon in the Free Baptist church, but on moving to Woburn they both joined the Congregational church.

Children, by first wife, Phebe:
11,548 Harriet Adams,[9] b. May 4, 1823; m. Aug. 8, 1845. Charles Henry Blaisdell, a carpenter of Amesbury, Mass., now residing in Woburn. Children:
    11,549 *Charles T.* (Blaisdell), enlisted in the war against the rebellion; d. March 13, 1865, in the Foster General hospital at Newbern, N. C., from wounds received in the battle of Kinston, N. C.
    11,550 *Harriet* (Blaisdell).
    11,551 *Daniel* (Blaisdell), d. in infancy.
    11,552 *Phebe* (Blaisdell).
    11,553 *Louisa* (Blaisdell).
11,554 Mary Elizabeth,[9] b. Sept. 7, 1842; an invalid; n.m.

## 11,528

GILMAN THURSTON [8] (*Nathaniel*,[7] *Samuel*,[6] *Samuel*,[5] *Samuel*,[4] *Robert*,[3] *Stephen*,[2] *Daniel*[1]), brother of the preceding, and son of Nathaniel[7] and Abigail Frances (Starbord) Thurston of Hartland, Me.; born there March 16, 1812; married, first, April 3, 1838, CLARISSA ELMINA GILMAN, born Mar. 7, 1807; she died July 27, 1868. Second, NANCY FROST, born May 7, 1813. He is a farmer in Monmouth, Me.

Children, by first wife, Clarissa:
11,560 Sarah Han,[9] b. Feb. 14, 1839; d. Aug. 12, 1852.
11,561 John Gilman,[9] b. Oct. 25, 1841; a hatter in San Francisco, Cal.; n.m.
11,562 Augusta Ann,[9] } twins, born } d. Jan. 25, 1847.
11,563 Augustus Arthur,[9] } Oct. 3, 1845; { d. Aug. 8, 1846.

## 11,529

BENJAMIN FRANKLIN THURSTON [8] (*Nathaniel*,[7] *Samuel*,[8] *Samuel*,[5] *Samuel*,[4] *Robert*,[3] *Stephen*,[2] *Daniel*[1]), brother of the preceding, and son of Nathaniel[7] and Abigail Frances (Starbord) Thurston of Hartland, Me.; born there Jan. 7, 1819; married, Jan. 19, 1840, MARY ANN CLARK, born in Lebanon, Me., Nov. 16, 1815. He was a truckman in Bangor, Me.; died Sept. 24, 1854.

### Children, all born in Bangor:

11,568  Georgianna,[9] b. Sept. 9, 1843; d. Sept. 11, 1850.
11,569  Henrietta,[9] b. Sept. 29, 1844; d. Aug. 30, 1846.
11,570  Henrietta,[9] b. June 14, 1847; m. by Rev. Sewall Tenney, in Ellsworth, Me., Dec. 9, 1868, Thomas Henry Dodge, a barber in Bangor, b. in Sedgwick, Me., April 18, 1846, son of Thomas and Sophronia Ann (Hamlin) Dodge; both members of the Congregational church.   Children:
   11,571  *Minnie Etta* (Dodge), b. Oct. 13, 1869.
   11,572  *Albert Henry* (Dodge), b. Sept. 1, 1871.
   11,573  *Freddie Gaston* (Dodge), b. Oct. 10, 1875.
11,574  Frank,[9] b. Aug. 7, 1848; a painter in Bangor; m. 1st, Dec. 12, 1869, Hattie Tiler, b. in Amherst, Me., May 5, 1850, d. May 9, 1871; 2d, 1872, Rose Ellen Shaw, b. in Chatham, N. H., Jan. 19, 1853.  Children:
   11,575  *Frank Wesley*,[10] b. Nov. 3, 1873.
   11,576  *Cora Estelle*,[10] b. Dec. 28, 1874.
   11,577  *Flora Belle*,[10] } twins, b. Oct. 28, 1879.
   11,578  *Freddie Nelson*,[10] }
11,579  George Henry,[9] b. March 30, 1850; a silver plater in Bangor; d. Sept. 21, 1874.
11,580  Georgianna,[9] b. May 27, 1852; d. Oct. 1, 1853.
11,581  Abbie ·Frances,[9] b. Aug. 29, 1853; m. July 16, 1871, Richard Bickford Coombs, a barber in Bangor, b. in Vinalhaven, Me., Jan. 28, 1850. Chil.:
   11,582  *Ida May* (Coombs), b. May 8, 1873.
   11,583  *Herbert Leslie* (Coombs), b. April 6, 1879.

## 11,531

WILLIAM THURSTON [8] (*Nathaniel*,[7] *Samuel*,[6] *Samuel*,[5] *Samuel*,[4] *Robert*,[3] *Stephen*,[2] *Daniel*[1]), brother of the preceding, and son of Nathaniel [7] and Abigail Frances (Starbord) Thurston of Hartland, Me.; born there April 11, 1822; married, first, April 23, 1843, CLARA PIKE of Wellington, Me.; she died Jan. 9, 1861.   Second, June 26, 1864, MRS. ELIZABETH JANE (TUCKER) HOLT of Dexter, Me.

Mr. Thurston is a farmer in Dexter; was drafted for the war against the rebellion in 1864 and paid $1,000 for a substitute.   His mother died when he was three hours old, and at seven months he was given to Rev. William Knowles of Wellington, pastor of a sect of christians called Hamiltonians, since called The Christian Band.

### Children, by first wife, Clara:

11,588  Mary Ann,[9] b. March 26, 1844: m. Aug. 24, 1865, Roscoe Greene Winslow, a painter in Dexter, named for Roscoe G. Greene of Portland, secretary of the state of Maine 1831.   He enlisted 1864 as a bugler, and served to the end of the war, in the 6th Maine battery, commanded by Edwin B. Dow of Portland, and Samuel Thurston of Portland first lieutenant.   They adopted:
   11,589  *Arthur Melvin* (Winslow), b. May 1, 1879.
11,590  Martha Maria,[9] b. March 19, 1846; m. April 2, 1864, Francis Warren Ladd of Mt. Vernon, Me., a stone-mason in Brockton, Mass ; he enlisted in the war against the rebellion in Brockton sharpshooters, taken prisoner at Gettysburgh, and furloughed home.   Children:
   11,591  *Lilly May* (Ladd), b. July 15, 1867.
   11,592  *Freddie Warren* (Ladd), b. Oct. 9, 1871.
   11,593  *George* (Ladd), b. Aug. 17, 1877.
   11,594  *Nellie* (Ladd), b. Aug. 18, 1878.
11,595  Carrie Elizabeth,[9] b. Jan. 24, 1848; running a sewing machine for Tappan & Kelly, Haverhill, Mass.
11,596  Charles William,[9] b. May 9, 1850; a lumberman in Michigan.
11,597  George Henry,[9] b. July 24, 1852; a farmer in Ripley, Me.; m. Jan. 1, 1872, Cordelia Puffer of Dexter.  Children:
   11,598  *William*,[10] b. Jan. 1, 1873.
   11,599  *Gertrude*,[10] b. April 13, 1877.

11,600   Abbie Frances,[9] b. Nov. 13, 1854; at work in a factory in Lawrence, Mass.; m. Oscar Froosdell of Boston, Mass.
11,601   Julia Etta,[9] b. Sept. 30, 1856; with her sister Abbie in Lawrence.
11,602   Melvin Leslie,[9] b. Feb. 8, 1859; with his brother Charles in Michigan.

By second wife, Elizabeth:

11,603   Alice Bellteena,[9] b. Aug. 11, 1865.
11,604   Jennie Estelle,[9] b. Oct. 13, 1869.
11,605   Maud Louisa,[9] b. April 13, 1872.

Page 141, no. 2885, they had Clara, b. in Boston, Mass., July 6, 1860.
Page 143. no. 2951, line 4. read (Hutchinson) McKenzie of Mt. Desert, Me.
Page 163, no. 3128, m. in Boston, Mass., May 26, 1850, Harriet Sherman.
Page 183, no. 3446, m. Nov., 1879, Carmelita A. Taylor.
Page 184, no. 1714. We were informed by what we supposed to be good authority that the subject of no. 1714 derived his name direct from the martyr John Rogers of England, and after considerable correspondence obtained the following facts; but the Rev. J. R. T. of this notice has upset the whole of this interesting story by saying his John came from his father and his Rogers from Rogers Lawrence, his grandfather. We insert this item to preserve the facts about the martyrs Rogers and Cranmer, and to show how easily history may be made entirely wrong, with the best endeavors to make it right. The martyr John Rogers was burnt at the stake Feb. 4, 1555. His portrait was brought to this country in 1636, and was presented to the American Antiquarian Society of Worcester, Mass., by Rev. William Bentley, D.D., of Salem, Mass., and can be seen at their rooms now. John Rogers of Dedham, Eng., a great-grandson of the martyr, had a son Nathaniel, who came to this country in 1636 and settled in Ipswich, Mass., and it was through this family that the above portrait came to this country. There is a bible now in the same rooms in Worcester, once owned by Archbishop Thomas Cranmer, who was burnt at the stake March 21, 1556, supposed to have been brought over by Nathaniel Rogers above, and is valued at $1,500. It is quite natural to suppose that a descendant of a martyr should feel an interest in possessing a sacred relic of another martyr so prominent as Cranmer.

Since the first part of this book was printed I received from a daughter of Rev. James Thurston the following concerning this bible and the Rogers and Peabody families: "This bible was in the possession of Thomas Carter of Lunenburgh, Mass., who received it from Gen. Nathaniel Peabody of Exeter, N. H. It was transmitted through the Boxford family. It is thought to be the edition of John Cawood, printed in 1549."

---

The ROGERS FAMILY.
I. JOHN ROGERS, the martyr, burnt at the stake Feb. 4, 1555.
II. —— ROGERS, son of the martyr.
III. JOHN ROGERS of Dedham, England.
IV. NATHANIEL ROGERS of Ipswich, Mass., second son of John, born about 1598, while his father was minister of Haveril, Eng ; came from England in 1636. Children: John; Nathaniel, no children; Samuel. m. Nov. 13, 1661, Sarah Wade of Ipswich, had children, and died Dec. 21, 1693; Timothy, lived some time in Ipswich, nothing known of his family; Ezekiel, had Nathaniel, Ezekiel, Timothy, and Samuel; a daughter.
V. —— ROGERS, son of Nathaniel, as supposed; possibly Samuel or Timothy.
VI. JEREMIAH ROGERS of Salem, Mass., died 1729.
VII. REV. JOHN ROGERS, second minister of Boxford, Mass., born in Salem; graduated at Harvard 1705; ordained 1709; dismissed 1748; moved to Leominster, Mass , and died there Aug. 14, 1755; his widow died Dec. 23, 1757.
VIII. REV. JOHN ROGERS of Leominster, born in Boxford Sept., 1712; married, 1750, seven years after his settlement, Relief Prentice, daughter of Rev. John Prentice of Lancaster, Mass. Seven children. One of his descendants in Leominster in 1848, a great-grandchild, daughter of Rufus Kendall. A brother and two sisters married in Leominster and resided there during a part of Mr. Rogers' ministry. For character of Mr. Rogers see Dr. Bancroft's Half Century Sermon, Whitney's Hist. of Wor. Co. (Leominster), Eccles. Hist. Sterling in Wor. Mag., Aug., 1826.
VIII. SUSANNA ROGERS, eldest daughter of Rev. John Rogers of Boxford, married Dr. Jacob Peabody of Leominster; nine children.

The PEABODY FAMILY.
I. LIEUT. FRANCIS PEABODY of St. Albans, Hertfordshire, Eng., born 1614, came to New England in the ship Planter, Nicholas Travice master, in 1635. See 'Gleanings' for N. E. History," Mass. Hist. Coll., 3d series, vol. viii. page 253. He married Mary Foster, daughter of Reginald Foster or Forster, whose family is honorably mentioned in the "Lay of the Last Minstrel " and in "Marmion." Fourteen children.
II. JACOB PEABODY, twelfth child of Francis, born July 29, 1664; married, Jan. 12, 1686, Abigail Towne; died Nov. 24, 1689; three children. [For other chil. see foot note next page.]

Page 194, no. 3787, n.m., a clerk in Boston, Mass.; enlisted in the war against the rebellion in the 1st and 10th Maine regiments, and was wounded in battle.

Page 194, no. 3789, a ship broker in Boston, firm of William H. Kinsman & Co.; m. Oct. 6, 1864, Josephene A. Parker of Boston; no children living.

Page 194, no. 3790, m. July 8, 1867, Calvin Warren, a fancy goods dealer in Biddeford, Me.; a farmer in Denmark, Me., 1879. He enlisted in the 1st Maine cavalry in the war against the rebellion.

Page 199, no. 3927; they have a son, 3929 Roscoe Edwin (Prescott), b. Aug. 1, 1878.

Page 205, no. 4074 [see no. 5017]. No. 2346. line 3, Elias Hurd.

Page 207, no. 4113, Mrs. Augustus E. Carr, says: "In regard to my mother [no. 4103] there is perhaps no one great thing to record, for her life was made up of beautiful littles. Married at the age of sixteen, the mother of fifteen children, with all the perplexities and inconveniences that limited means and a life of toil would bring, she was never known to wear other than a cheerful face, and her morning smile and greeting to all is remembered as a household benediction. Her word was law, and the christian precept of love and kindness was lived out in her life at home and in the community where she dwelt. In my recollection there were times when she had but one calico dress suitable to appear before company in, and on one occasion company came on washing day, before the dress was brought from the laundry. Some of the older girls entertained the guests, while others ironed the garment, attired their mother, and in her best cap and sweetest smile of welcome she entered the room and performed in a queenly manner the part of hostess, obliging her guests to admit afterward, 'the best visit we ever had.' She lived to see more prosperous days, her husband having nearly paid up for two fine farms. And when told that she must die she said, 'I would be glad to live to see the final payment made, but the Lord's will be done,' and in her last hours her prayer was, 'Wash me, make me pure, let me go to Jesus.' A more devoted wife and mother never lived, and in heaven we believe that she awaits the coming of our feet."

Page 208, no. 4162, m. 1st, Elsie Emeline Locklin of Farmington, Me.; 2d, Oct. 9, etc.

Page 244, no. 4102. Moses Thurston, says a daughter, "was an orphan boy. At the age of seven bound out to a wealthy, aristocratic uncle, who gave him the benefit of a common school education for three months in a year till the age of sixteen, and held him for the remaining time in unceasing bondage to toil and privation. At the age of twenty-one he was sent out into the world penniless, without books, and with but few clothes. For four consecutive years he labored six months in a year and spent the remaining time and his earnings in study. At the age of twenty-six he married (settling in Hartford, Vt.) and began the work of securing a competency for his family. Six years later he purchased a two hundred acre wood lot in the town of Northfield, Vt., felled trees sufficient to erect a small house and barn, and in midwinter, with his wife and three little ones, left his pleasant home and began pioneer life. With indomitable will and perseverance timber was cleared away, large fields of wheat and herds-grass raised, payments met, a new and commodious house erected, two barns, and the necessary appendages for a large stock. Having freed himself from debt, this house was exchanged for a fine village farm, where began a more earnest work for the education of his children, it being the desire of his life that 'they should have a better bringing up than his had been or hers.' At the age of forty-two he was called from earth, but the work of toil and love that was begun in·unison was carried out by a loving mother, whose devotion was unceasing and whose 'children arise up and call her blessed, her husband also and he praiseth her.' One of the pleasantest recollections of my father was the calling us around him on Sabbath afternoon and reading us bible stories. There was always a place for me on his knee, and he seldom came to the house without saying, 'I hope my little girl is trying to be good.' No doubt he had his faults and his failings, but his children live only in his virtues."

Page 250, line 3, read Eaton instead of Errol. No. 5166, Annette Castelnear. No. 5168, Mottier.

---

III. JACOB PEABODY, born Nov. 9, 1689; married, April 30, 1712, Rebecca Baker; died July 24, 1749; eight children.

IV. DR. JACOB PEABODY, born Feb. 18, 1713; married, 1st, Feb. 18, 1735, Susanna Rogers, daughter of Rev. John Rogers minister of Boxford; died 1758; nine children.

V. THOMAS PEABODY; born Dec. 6, 1746; married, March 23, 1769, Elizabeth Shaw; died Nov. 20. 1777; two children.

VI. ELIZABETH PEABODY, born Aug. 16, 1774; married, Oct. 9, 1791, James Thurston [see page 124, no. 719]; died Oct. 15, 1845; nine children.

Page 275, no. 5876, on page 473, no. 10,918, are further facts.

Page 283, line 4, for farm read place.

Page 296, no. 6507, Richard Lathers is not in business, and resides alternately in Pittsfield, Mass., and New Rochelle, N. Y., having a very extensive and elegant residence in each place. No. 6516, C. C. Barrington is not living 1879; was a wholesale and retail dry goods merchant in Philadelphia, Pa. No. 6518, Allen Melville is not living 1879; was a lawyer in New York city. No. 6519, W. B. Moorewood resides in Elizabeth, N. J. They had Allen Melville (Moorewood), b. Oct. 31, 1876.

Page 310, no. 6869, died a natural death. No. 6870 resides in Springfield, N. Y., a very intellectual and vigorous lady for one of her age, Nov., 1879.

Page 310, no. 6871, was married July 6, 1832. Hiram Hutchins, D.D., graduated from Madison university, N. Y.; is a Baptist clergyman, has labored in Richfield, N. Y., Norristown, Pa., Boston, Mass., and has just completed his twentieth year with the Bedford Avenue Baptist church in Brooklyn, N. Y. No children by this marriage. He married again and has several children.

Page 318, no. 7103, for Whitehall read Whitinsville.

Page 327, no. 7280, died May 15, 1877. Nos. 7284 and 7285 should be stricken out. No. 7291 is in college. No. 7293 died April 10, 1876.

Page 341, no. 6861, line 5, for Corad read Cosad.

Page 346, no. 7056, line 4, read Catherine McKeller; line 5, Lucy Foster.

Page 351, no. 7420, line 5, read Joseph and Eliza (Chase) Peckham. Next line, building mover and wheelwright.

Page 362, no. 8195, see Appendix, page 464, for descendants of Joseph.

Page 364, no. 8246, read Paul[6] m. May 25, 1761, Hannah Rawson, who died Mar. 31, 1816, in Ware, Mass.

## Page 368, no. 8245.

NATHAN THURSTON[5] (*David*,[4] *Thomas*,[3] *Thomas*,[2] *John*[1]), eldest child of David Thurston[4] of Medway, Mass.; born there 1764; married [intention Nov. 3, 1786] SALLY CAMPBELL, born June 19, 1769, daughter of Alexander Campbell. He died in Oxford, Mass., March 17, 1817, aged 53.

Mr. Thurston was a farmer, living in Westminster, Rockingham, and Putney, Vt., and in Oxford, Mass.

### Children:

+11,610   Alexander Campbell,[6] b. in Westminster Aug. 7, 1788; m. Polly Eddy.

11,611   Sally,[6] b. in Rockingham May 11, 1790; m. Oct. 11, 1810, Joel Eddy.

11,612   Susan,[6] b. in Putney Sept. 18, 1792; m. Dec. 24, 1812, Jonas Ward of Ashburnham, Mass.

Born in Oxford:

11,613   Mary,[6] b. June 30, 1794; m. Nov. 19, 1812, John Griggs of Sutton, Mass.

11,614   Nathaniel,[6] b. April 12, 1796; d. Aug. 27, 1803.

11,615   Hannah Rawson,[6] b. April 5, 1798; m. Nov. 9, 1820, Ira Trask of Millbury, Mass.

11,616   Fanny Hawkins,[6] b. March 2, 1800; m. Dec., 1821, Alfred Torrey of Woodstock, Ct.

11,617   Miranda Pond,[6] b. May 16, 1801; d. July 12, 1801.

11,618   Emily Stearns,[6] b. Sept. 20, 1802; d. Aug. 22, 1803.

11,619   Patty Davis,[6] b. Sept. 11, 1804; m. May 31, 1824, Henry P. Howe of Millbury, Mass.

11,620   Catharine Pratt,[6] b. Nov. 29, 1805.

8375   David Thatcher,[6] b. Jan. 16, 1810; twice married; was a farmer in Oxford; dropped dead in his barn Aug., 1875; no children.

## 11,610

ALEXANDER CAMPBELL THURSTON[6] (*Nathan*,[5] *David*,[4] *Thomas*,[3] *Thomas*,[2] *John*[1]), eldest son of Nathan[5] and Sally (Campbell) Thurston of Westminster, Vt.; born there Aug. 7, 1788; married, March 16, 1815, POLLY EDDY of Oxford, Mass.

## Children:

11,625   William Eddy,[7] b. Sept. 6, 1816; m. June 30, 1842, Louisa Ann Abbe of
Dalton, Mass.  Children :
   11,626   *John Alexander*,[8] b. Sept. 23, 1843.
   11,627   *James Franklin*,[8] b. Aug. 17, 1845.
   11,628   *Josephine Louisa*,[8] b. May 9, 1847.
   11,629   *Abby Jane*,[8] b. April 6, 1850.
11,630   Nathan,[7] b. Sept. 28, 1818; d. Nov. 21, 1824.
11,631   Levi Eaton,[7] b. June 29, 1821 ; m. April 8, 1846, Martha Matilda Newton of Troy, N. H.  They lived in Ware, Mass., and had :
   11,632   *May Elizabeth*,[8] b. Jan. 9, 1847.
   11,633   *Martha Ann*,[8] b. Oct. 6, 1848.
11,634   Mary Miriam,[7] b. March 2, 1825; m. April 29, 1844, Henry Allen Baker
of Charlton, Mass.; he is a trader in Douglass, Mass.  Children :
   11,635   *Estes Eugene* (Baker), b. July 5, 1845.
   11,636   *Caroline Adelia* (Baker), b. Feb. 14, 1847.
   11,637   *Willard Alexander* (Baker), b. Feb. 15, 1849.
11,638   Alexander,[7] b. Aug. 13, 1828; d. Dec. 31, 1830.
11,639   Sally Campbell,[7] b. July 26, 1830; m. April 27, 1848, George Bridgford,
a machinist of Fisherville, Ct., and had :
   11,640   *George* (Bridgford), b. Feb. 23, 1849.
   11,641   *Anna C.* (Bridgford), b. May 3, 1850.
11,642   Henry,[7] b. Jan. 19, 1833.

### Page 381, no. 8454.

EBENEZER THURSTON [6] (*Cyrus*,[5] *Daniel*,[4] *Daniel*,[3] *Joseph*,[2] *John*[1]),
married, in the state of New York, 1791, EUNICE KELSEY, and in
1815 moved to Eaton, Luzerne county, Pa., where he was a farmer,
and school teacher winters.  She died there 1834, and he died a few
years after at his daughter's in Bradford county, Pa.  They were both
members of the Baptist church.  Their children were all members of
the Baptist and Methodist churches, an industrious, thrifty family ; the
daughters each had the wheel and loom soon after they were married.

## Children:

11,647   Margaret,[7] tall, slim, dark complexion; m. in New York, John Wilson, a
farmer of means in Eaton, where they moved in 1814 or 1815.  She
died about 1849.
11,648   Dorcas,[7] } twins, born } m. in New York, William Hall, a farmer in
11,649   Anna,[7] { Feb. 16, 1794; { Bradford county, Pa., where she died.
Anna, dark complexion, slim form, m. 1st, in Delaware county, N. Y.,
Sept. 1, 1814, Isaac Birdsill, b. 1783, a chair maker and wheelwright.
In 1817 they moved to Eaton, and in 1833 to Sherman, Huron county,
Ohio, where he died, 1836.  She moved to Franklin county, Ohio, in
1837 and m. 2d, 1859, John Smothers of Genoa, Delaware county, O.,
where he died, 1868.  The widow then went to reside with her daughter Electa and died in Williams county, Ohio, March 21, 1877.  They
were members of the Methodist church.  Children, by first husband :
   11,650   *Sarah* (Birdsill), b. in Delaware county July 6, 1815; m. July 4,
1838, Joseph Brown, a cooper and farmer at Hastings, Mills
county, Iowa ; she is a member of the Methodist church.
   11,651   *Electa* (Birdsill), b. in Delaware county Feb. 5, 1817; m. Oct. 27,
1838, Ira Paine, a farmer in Sherman ; 1870 moved to Bryan,
Williams county, Ohio ; both members of the Disciples church.
     Born in Eaton :
   11,652   *Elizabeth* (Birdsill), b. July 16, 1819; m. 1838, Henry Smothers, a
farmer in Franklin Co., O. ; he d. 1872, and she resides in Harlem, Delaware Co., O., 1880; both members Methodist church.
   11,653   *Isaac* (Birdsill), b. Dec. 16, 1822; a carpenter and farmer ; m. 1848,
Harriet Frazell; moved to Adams county, Ill., the same year,
and 1876 to Sunshine, Boulder county, Colorado; was in the war
against the rebellion three years; a member of the Methodist
church; she died 1868.

11,654   *Fanny* (Birdsill), b. May 8, 1824; n.m.; lives with her sister Electa.

11,655   *Cynthia* (Birdsill), b. April 2, 1827; d. in Sherman Aug. 30, 1848.

11,656   *Lyman* (Birdsill), b. Jan. 14, 1830; a mechanic; went to California about 1853, and has not been heard from for twenty years; was a member of the Methodist church.

11,657   *Ebenezer* (Birdsill), b. Jan. 1, 1833; went to Colorado in 1851; m. 1877, Sarah Strock; is a farmer and carpenter in Pella, Boulder county, Col.; served in war against rebellion three or four years.

11,658   Hannah,[7] m. in Luzerne county, Pa., 1816, George Leger, a farmer near Philadelphia, Pa.

11,659   Victorina,[7] dark complexion, m. in Luzerne county, 1827, Isaac Garrison, a farmer in Pennsylvania; d. in Franklin county, Ohio, 1843.

11,660   Electa,[7] } d. at age of nine years.

11,661   Eliza,[7] } m. in Luzerne Co., 1834, James Mead, farmer; d. in Lucas Co., O. Azor[7] and Ebenezer,[7] see page 406, nos. 8802 and 8803.

11,662   Lyman,[7] tall, slim, dark complexion, a farmer and basket maker near Kingston, Luzerne county; m. Amy Albro; d. in Bradford county, Pa. Children:

| | | |
|---|---|---|
| 11,663  *Anson.*[8] | 11,664  *Henry.*[8] | 11,665  *Joseph.*[8] |
| 11,666  *Russell.*[8] | 11,667  *Lydia.*[8] | 11,668  *Jane.*[8] |

11,669   Hermes,[7] light complexion, medium height, a farmer; n.m.; d. in Margaretta, Erie county, Ohio, 1843.

Page 381, no. 8459, Amos Thurston m. Louisa ——; d. in Morris, N. Y., aged 94.

Page 386, no. 8956, Warren Lawson (Munyan), b. in Grafton, Mass., Oct. 29, 1832; m. Lizzie B. Wesson of Grafton; was a boot and shoe manufacturer and dealer; d. in Colorado Dec. 20, 1877, and was buried there. Children:

8956*a*   Charles (Munyan).

8956*b*   Fred. (Munyan).

8956*c*   Harry Warren (Munyan), b. May 15, 1863.

8956*d*   Carrie (Munyan), b. March, 1866; d.

8956*e*   Laura Louise (Munyan), b. Feb. 16, 1868.

8956*f*   Hattie Sophia (Munyan), b. May 10, 1876.

Page 386, no. 8961, Rufus Grosvenor by a previous marriage had three sons and three daughters; one daughter died 1877. L. Dwight (Grosvenor), the eldest son, is an architect in Jackson, Mich., George S. (Grosvenor) is a lawyer in Trenton, N. J., and R. Henry (Grosvenor) is a lawyer in Kalamazoo, Mich.

Page 390, no. 8586, for Lovina read Vina; she died Aug. 21, 1837; her husband died Sept. 14, 1845. No. 9064, for Lena read Sena.

Page 395, no. 9185. Children of Harriet H. and George Crowell:

9185*a*   Edward Sherman (Crowell), b. July 24, 1846; d. Sept. 28, 1846.

9185*b*   Mary Eliza (Crowell), b. March 10, 1848; m. Allen Jones, a mechanic of West Brookfield, Mass.; d. Aug. 6, 1877.

9185*c*   Ella Frances (Crowell), b. Jan. 19, 1854; m. George B. Sanford, a mechanic of West Brookfield.

9185*d*   Charles Fowler (Crowell), b. Oct. 13, 1857; d. Dec. 11, 1857.

9185*e*   Harriet Ross (Crowell), b. Jan. 26, 1860.

9185*f*   Carrie Estelle (Crowell), b. March 22, 1869.

Page 397, no. 8649, line 4, for Stanbrook read Stainbrook. No. 9245, William Henry. No. 9254, David Radle, b. March 16, was a teacher. Mary Childs, b. Dec. 14, 1842. He died Oct. 17.

Page 397, no. 9255, Israel Eugene, b. Aug. 21, d. Dec. 11, 1861.

Page 397, no. 9256, Jessie Elizabeth, b. May 9, 1863; d. Nov. 23, 1865.

Page 398, no. 8681, line 4, for Alexander read Alexandrew. No. 9289, Robert Spears was a Baptist minister, P. O., Ioka, Keokuk county, Iowa. No. 9299, George R. is a farmer in Summitville, Ind.

Page 401, no. 8767, line 3, July 27; line 4, second, March 13, 1829, Sarah Heller, born Aug. 31, 1810, daughter of Michael and Catherine Heller of Elmira, N. Y. Asa Thurston was a shoemaker in Elmira. She still lives there, 1880. Children:

9391   Catherine,[8] b. Jan. 8, 1831; m. 1st, Feb. 1, 1851, Sergeant Jasper Bowman, b. Feb. 1, 1829, d. in Elmira Feb. 28, 1864; 2d, in Elmira, Jan. 1, 1874, Edward H. Bettridge, b. in England. Children:

9391*a*   Alice E. (Bowman), b. Dec. 13, 1851.

9391*b*   William Newton (Bowman), b. Jan. 16, 1853.

9391*c*   Clara Agnes (Bowman), b. Feb. 12, 1855; m. in Elmira, James Easton, M.D.; they have Frank (Easton), b. July 7, 1879.

9391d  Lillie S. (Bowman), b. June 22. 1859.
9391e  Helen Eliza (Bowman), b. April 16, 1862; d. in infancy.
9391f  Albert H. (Bettridge), b. May 29, 1875.
9391g  Abraham S.,[8] b. Aug. 4. 1833; d. in infancy.
9392  Moses W.,[8] b. Feb. 8. 1835; m. Dec. 15, 1856, Helen C. Strader.
9395  Michael Heller,[8] b. Feb. 28, 1838; m. 1867, Jennie Neish; is a carriage builder in Elmira.
9398  William K.,[8] b. Jan. 19; is a house carpenter in Elmira.
9400  Reuben M.,[8] b. Dec. 16. 1843; m. 1868, Maria Riker, b. 1844, daughter of Abraham Riker. Children:
    9402  Clarence,[9] d. in infancy.
Page 406, no. 9589, read Barton Eugene.
Page 406, last line, add, Ebenezer Thurston was a tall, dark complexioned, good, honest man, living in White Pigeon, St. Joseph county, Mich.

## Page 407, no. 8810.

ELISHA THURSTON [7] (*Amos,*[6] *Increase,*[5] *Daniel,*[4] *Daniel,*[3] *Daniel,*[2] *John*[1]), son of Amos[6] and Louisa Thurston of Lisle, N. Y.; born there 1798; married, 1816, LOVISA SWEET of New Berlin, N. Y., born 1800.  He died April, 1874; she died 1875.

Mr. Thurston was a mason in Morris, Otsego county, N. Y.; was noted for his industry and strict integrity; joined the Baptist church when quite young and was a faithful and honored member till his death.

Children:

11,675  Louisa,[8] d. in youth.
11,676  Laura,[8] m. Leroy Bancroft of Milwaukee, Wis ; d. 1859, leaving 4 children.
+11,677  Valorous Fernando,[8] b. April 20, 1822; m. Olive Thurston [see no. 8913].
11,678  Amos Orlando,[8] d. in youth.
11,679  Maria Saphfena,[8] b. in North New Berlin, Otsego county, N. Y., Dec. 19, 1827; m. 1st, Dec. 19, 1848, Timothy Short, a farmer in Morris, N. Y., d. March 10, 1861; 2d, Oct. 11, 1862, Benjamin Franklin Genung; he d. Oct. 28, 1873, and she resides in Flint, Genesee Co., Mich. Children:
    11,680  *Helen Maria* (Short), b. in Hartwick. Otsego Co., Jan. 13, 1850.
    11,681  *Mary Miranda* (Short), b. in Maryland, Otsego Co., Dec. 1, 1851.
    11,682  *Cyrus Marvin* (Short), b. in Morris Jan. 9, 1854.
    11,683  *Esther Melissa* (Short), b. in Hartwick March 11, 1857.
    11,684  *Emma Parmelia* (Short), b. in Otsego Aug. 24, 1860.
    11,685  *Emily* (Genung), b. in Morris Sept. 24, 1863.
11,686  Lorinda Dimis,[8] b. May 2, 1829; m. May 26, 1849, John Calvin Wright, a mechanic in New Berlin, b. May 26. 1825. She died 1860; he resides at Troy Mills, Linn county, Iowa. Children:
    11,687  *Silas Ambrose* (Wright), b. Jan. 10, 1852.
    11,688  *Ernest Elisha* (Wright). b. Jan. 17, 1854.
    11,689  *Ellis Stanley* (Wright). b. June 29, 1859.
11,690  Helen Emily,[8] b. July 2, 1831; m. March 2, 1850. Calvin Short, a farmer and hop grower in Oneonta, Otsego county, N. Y.  He died April 6, 1872. and she is a dressmaker in Colliersville, N. Y.  Children:
    11,691  *Roseltha Lorinda* (Short), b. July 28, 1850; m Aug. 12, 1872, Myron Vanhuron, a lawyer in Davenport, Delaware county, N. Y., an invalid 1879. Children:
        11,692  *John E.* (Vanhuron). d.     11,693  *Minnie* (Vanhuron), d.
    11,694  *Charles Calvin* (Short), b. June 22, 1852; m. Feb. 15, 1874, Mary Elizabeth King of Cooperstown, N. Y.; is a farmer in South Amboy, N. J.
    11,695  *Venilla Angeleta* (Short), b. Oct. 25, 1854; m. Dec. 25, 1870, James Winn, a farmer in Coventry, Chenango Co., N. Y.; they have:
        11,696  *Ida Angelia* (Winn), b. March 2, 1877.
    11,697  *Ida Diva* (Short), b. July 15, 1862; d. May 12, 1871.
    11,698  *Russell Henry* (Short). b. Oct. 6. 1867; d. March 18, 1868.
    11,699  *Grace Estella* (Short), b. March 19, d. March 21, 1872.
+11,700  Albertus Elisha,[8] b. Dec. 15, 1833; m. 1st, Lydia M. Marble; 2d, Eliza Ann Bulson.

+11,701    Daniel Wesley,[8] b. Sept. 6, 1834; m. Lucy Jane Davis.
 11,702    Melissa.[8]
+11,703    Elijah,[8] } twins, born } m. Ellen Maria Henderson.
 11,704    Eliza,[8] } Nov. 14, 1839; } m. 1856, Alexander Thomas, a mason in Morris. Children:
     11,705   *Esther Elizabeth* (Thomas), m. 1877, Newell Chase of Morris.
     11,706   *Willard Orville* (Thomas).
     11,707   *Clara Lovisa* (Thomas), m. 1878, Wm. Benjamin of Morris; have:
        11,708   *Alice May* (Benjamin).
     11,709   *Mertie R.* (Thomas).
     11,710   *Mary Louie* (Thomas).
     11,711   *Earl Alexander* (Thomas).
     11,712   *Susan Grace* (Thomas).
     11,713   *E. Eliza* (Thomas).

Page 407, no. 9601.

## 11,677

VALOROUS FERNANDO THURSTON [8] (*Elisha,*[7] *Amos,*[6] *Increase,*[5] *Daniel,*[4] *Daniel,*[3] *Daniel,*[2] *John*[1]), son of Elisha[7] and Lovisa (Sweet) Thurston of Morris, N. Y.; born in Lisle, Chenango county, N. Y., April 20, 1822; married, Mar. 10, 1845, OLIVE THURSTON, born May 10, 1822, daughter of Ira and Ruth (Benedict) Thurston of New Lisbon, N. Y. [see no. 8913]. She died July 1, 1874, in Platte, Benzie county, Mich.

Mr. Thurston is a farmer and job contractor in Frankfort, Benzie county, Mich. He is justice of the peace, supervisor, and state road commissioner; member of the Methodist church, and was licensed as a local preacher Oct. 24, 1857.

### Children:

11,718   Myron Ervin,[9] b. in Burlington, Otsego county, N. Y., Feb. 4, 1846; m. in Elmira, N. Y., Nov. 6, 1870, Jane M. Burnett; is a merchant in Platte; no children.
11,719   Agnes Ruth,[9] b. in Oxford, Chenango Co., N. Y., Aug. 16, 1852; m. in Platte, Jan. 4, 1871, Jeboam Carter, an engineer in Frankfort. Children:
     11,720   *Lulu Olive* (Carter), b. in Platte Jan. 19, 1872.
     11,721   *Grace Aldyth* (Carter), b. in Frankfort Aug. 14, 1878.
11,722   Ella Josephene,[9] b. in Oxford June 7, 1854; m. April 16, 1871, Byron Hare Dart, a farmer in Lake, Mich. Children:
     11,723   *Pearl* (Dart), b. June 9, 1873.
     11,724   *Raymond Hays* (Dart), b. May 8, 1875.
11,725   Frances Leona,[9] b. in Washington, Sauk county, Wis., Nov. 12, 1862; m. July 17, 1879, Wm. Mulford Carter, a farmer in Frankfort; no children.

Page 407, no. 9602.

## 11,700

ALBERTUS ELISHA THURSTON [8] (*Elisha,*[7] *Amos,*[6] *Increase,*[5] *Daniel,*[4] *Daniel,*[3] *Daniel,*[2] *John*[1]), brother of the preceding, and son of Elisha[7] and Lovisa (Sweet) Thurston of Morris, Otsego county, N. Y.; born there Dec. 15, 1833; married, first, Oct. 15, 1851, LYDIA M. MARBLE of Morris; she died July, 1852. Second, in Williamstown, N. Y., Oct. 30, 1852, ELIZA ANN BULSON, born June 25, 1835, daughter of William K. and Ann (Clover) Bulson of Milford, N. Y.

Mr. Thurston is a painter, grainer, and paper-hanger in Colliersville, Otsego county, N. Y.; a local preacher in the Methodist church.

### Children, by first wife, Lydia:

11,730   Ambrose Dewane,[9] b. July 15, 1852; a lawyer in Waterloo, Iowa.

By second wife, Eliza :

11,731    Mary Elizabeth,[9] b. Oct. 15, 1853; m. 1871, William Andrew Cooke of Morris, a harness maker in W. Oneonta, Otsego Co., N. Y. Children:

11,732    *Adin Lull* (Cooke), b. Sept. 1, 1872.
11,733    *Harvey Jay* (Cooke), b. June 1, 1874.
11,734    *Gracie Eliza* (Cooke), b. May 18, 1878.

11,735    Eldorous Elijah,[9] b. June 16, 1856; is telegraph operator and ticket clerk at Cooperstown Junction, N. Y.
11,736    William Valorous,[9] b. April 24, 1858; a farmer in Colliersville.

Page 407, no. 9603.

## 11,701

DANIEL WESLEY THURSTON[8] (*Elisha,*[7] *Amos,*[6] *Increase,*[5] *Daniel,*[4] *Daniel,*[3] *Daniel,*[2] *John*[1]), brother of the preceding, and son of Elisha[7] and Lovisa (Sweet) Thurston of Morris, Otsego county, N. Y.; born there Sept. 6, 1834; married, Sept., 1859, LUCY JANE DAVIS. He was a mason in Morris; died Dec. 13, 1874.

### Children :

11,740    Arlina May,[9] b. May 13, 1860; m. Oct. 31, 1877, William Shove, a farmer of Mt. Vision, N. Y.
11,741    Lorinda Ellen,[9] b. Dec. 25, 1862; m. Oct. 17, 1878, Eugene Cook, a farmer of Morris. They have :
11,742    *Cora Emeline* (Cook), b. Nov. 1, 1879.
11,743    John Wesley,[9] b. 1866; d. in infancy.
11,744    Adrien Eugene,[9] b. Nov. 6, 1871.

Page 407, no. 9604.

## 11,703

ELIJAH THURSTON[8] (*Elisha,*[7] *Amos,*[6] *Increase,*[5] *Daniel,*[4] *Daniel,*[3] *Daniel,*[2] *John*[1]), brother of the preceding, and son of Elisha[7] and Lovisa (Sweet) Thurston of Morris, Otsego county, N. Y.; born there Nov. 14, 1839; married, in Milford, Otsego county, N. Y., ELLEN MARIA HENDERSON, born Dec. 2, 1842, daughter of Cyril and Mary M. (Hamilton) Henderson of Morris.

Mr. Thurston is a carpenter in Morris; enlisted in the 152d New York regiment, served three years, was in twenty-two engagements, and had his right arm broken twice ; received a pension.

### Child :

11,750    Atson Cyril,[9] b. July 30, 1870.

Page 407, no. 8832, line 4, read Sophia Curtis, b. in Spafford, Onondaga Co., N. Y.
Page 408, no. 9619, read Elizabeth Harger.
Page 408, no. 8845, lines 3 and 4, read January instead of June.

Page 409, no. 9647.

DAVID THURSTON[8] (*Allen,*[7] *Amos,*[6] *Amos,*[5] *Daniel,*[4] *Daniel,*[3] *Daniel,*[2] *John*[1]), son of Allen[7] and Lucy (Wakely) Thurston of Preston, Pa.; born in New Lisbon, Otsego county, N. Y., May 12, 1822; married, May 12, 1847, SARAH JANE HINE, born March 6, 1829, daughter of Merrit and Catherine (Belcher) Hine of Hine's Corners, Wayne county, Pa.

Mr. Thurston is a farmer; went to Hine's Corners in 1842. In 1854 moved with his family to Grant county, Wis., then an undeveloped country. In 1862 he enlisted in the war against the rebellion and served through the war, being engaged in the battles of Prairie

Grove, Mo., siege of Vicksburgh, and Fort Morgan. In 1872 he moved to Alta, Harvey county, Kansas, then an unbroken prairie, where he has succeeded, in the face of many difficulties, including the grasshopper raid, when famine stared every one in that region in the face, in securing a beautiful home in the midst of a beautiful and fertile country, where he is now enjoying the results of an industrious and laborious life. They are both members and he a steward of the Methodist church.

### Children:

11,755    Charlotte Sylphronda,[9] b. March 24, 1848; m. —— Lord of Alta.

11,756    Francis Hezekiah,[9] } twins, born } in River View, Rice Co., Kansas.
11,757    Franklin Belmire,[9] }   Feb. 1, 1850; } d. May 5, 1850.

11,758    Henry Jackson,[9] b. May 1, 1853; a farmer in Rice county, Kansas; n.m.

11,759    Corrinnia Catherine,[9] b. Aug. 21, 1855; m. —— Gibbs of Lancaster, Wis.

11,760    Elizabeth Jane,[9] b. Jan. 28, 1856; m. and lives with her parents; joined the Methodist church Nov. 25, 1877.

11,761    Lucy Ella,[9] b. April 22, 1858.

11,762    Mary Josephene,[9] b. Sept. 1, 1859; m. —— Peirce of Halstead, Harvey county, Kansas.

11,763    Edgar Byron.[9] b. Aug. 1, 1860; d. July 5, 1863.

11,764    Merrit Lorenzo,[9] b. July 30, 1862; d. Sept. 5, 1862.

11,765    Gertrude Jenette,[9] b Aug. 12, 1866; d. May 2, 1869.

11,766    David Allen,[9] b. Jan. 29, 1870.

Page 410, no. 8897, line 7, read 1878.

Page 410, no. 9658, b. in Butternut; all the rest born in Norwich.

Page 410, no. 9674, line 2. read Feb. 12, 1868, Caroline Elizabeth Hubbard, born Sept. 14, 1849, daughter of George Washington and Julia Ann (Smith) Hubbard of Hartwick.

Page 410, no. 9676, read m. 1st, Nov. 24, 1870, Helen L. Hall, daughter of Thomas W. and Sarah A. (Wescott) Hall, d. June 26, 1876; 2d, March 21, 1877, Libbie Delaphene Bowdish, daughter of Philander and Augusta (Gorham) Bowdish. Children:

9677   Lucius Earl,[9] b. July 25, 1878.    9677a   Ira M.,[9] b. March 15, 1879.

Page 413, no. 8959, line 4, read October. No. 9749, read Albert Eugene.[8]

Page 414, no. 9757, is clerk in the Atlantic House in Worcester, Mass.

Page 414. no. 9765, is with his father in West Washington market, New York. No. 9769, b. Sept., 1870. No. 9770, b. Aug. 31, 1874. No. 9772, is with his father in West Washington market, m. Helen Wynkoop of Bergen, N. J., and has:

9773   Helen,[9] b. Sept., 1878.

Page 418, line 1, read d. Aug. 23, 1859. No. 9853, d. Dec. 7. No. 9855, Irving Frank.

Page 418, no. 9059, line 8, read late rebellion in the 27th Maine nine months; their time expired before the battle of Gettysburgh. The troops were all taken from Washington, and they were invited to stop and defend the city. About three hundred stopped and Congress gave each of them a bronze medal.

Page 418, no. 9861, read Katie instead of Hattie.

Page 422, no. 9235, line 2, read Stainbrook; line 3, b. in Mead township; line 6, Dickson, b. in Woodcock township 1827. Add to the next line, has charge of buildings, bridges, and trestle-work on the Chautauqua Lake and Pittsburgh railroad.

Page 422, no. 9951, Florence,[9] b. Jan. 2, 1851; m. Feb. 9, 1870, Wilson G. Reynolds of Shamburgh, Venango county, Pa., b. in Troupsburgh, Steuben county, N. Y., Jan. 3, 1845; he is a hairdresser in Knoxville, Tioga county, Pa. Children, b. in Oil City, Venango county, Pa.:

9946   Maud (Reynolds), b. April 29, 1871.

9947   William (Reynolds), b. Feb. 9, 1873.

9948   Frederick (Reynolds), b. Dec. 5, 1875.

9949   George (Reynolds), b. Feb. 22, 1879.

9953   Crawford,[9] b. Oct. 30, 1852; m. Oct. 30, 1873, Ella Arelia Snapp, b. Aug. 4, 1854; is a butcher in Spartansburgh, Crawford Co., Pa.; no children.

9956   Angeline Esther[9] (now called Hattie), b. July 25, 1856; m. Nov. 6, 1874, Emery L. Mayer, b. Nov. 25, 1854, a cooper in Cochranton, Crawford county, Pa. They have:

9954   Maud (Mayer), b. Sept. 19, 1875.

Page 423, line 3, read Irons instead of Jones. Add to line 4. served in the war against the rebellion; post-office address is Black Ash, Crawford county, Pa. Add to his children.

9966 Orpha J.,[9] b. Jan. 27, 1875.
9967 Stanley,[9] b. May 2, 1877.
9968 Alta,[9] b. Sept. 24, 1879.

Page 423, no. 9985, m. Sept. 19, 1869, J. H. Woollen, b. May 8, 1843. No. 9988, John William. No. 9989, Enoch instead of Errich.

Page 424. no. 9990. J. Runyan, b. Dec. 9, 1855. No. 9991, b. July 21. No. 9992, m. Sept. 12, 1878, a merchant and farmer near Summitville, Ind. No. 9995, d. Aug., 1872.

Page 424, no. 9292, line 4, read m. Dec. 28. 1859, Nancy Elizabeth McGilvery. No. 10,000, Oliver Daniel. No. 10,001, Ida May. No. 10,002, Maria Elizabeth. No. 10,003, John William.

Page 426, no. 10,071, d. Jan. 23. No. 10,072, b. October, d. 1864.

Page 429, no. 9640, line 8, add 1879, in Mill Port, Chemung county, N. Y. No. 10,137, Ellis W. No. 10,141, b. 1861.

Page 431, after no. 10,188, add 10,189 Frank Mellen,[9] b. Aug. 4, 1877.

Page 432, no. 9740. line 8, add doing business in Montreal. No. 10,205, b. Jan. 6.

Page 436, no. 10,268, line 2. after L. I., add he afterward settled in No. Stamford, Ct., over the Congregational church, and continued twenty-five years its pastor.

Page 448, no. 10,315. line 3, m. 1822, b. in Oneida county, daughter of John and Jemima (Denison) Jackson.

Page 448, no. 10,489, Cordelia,[4] b. 1823; m. 1st, 1838, A. H. French, a tanner in Ohio, Wisconsin, Smith county, Kansas. and in Lucas county, Iowa, where he died, 1869; 2d, 1878, B. C. Robinson of Smith county, Kansas. She is a member of the Methodist church. Children:

   10,489a Henry (French), b. 1840.
   10,489b Charles A. (French), b. 1842.
   10,489c Alvaro (French), b. 1844.
   10,489d Rufus (French), b. 1847.
   10,489e Mary E. (French), b. 1849; d. in Lucas county, Iowa, 1861.

10,491 Rufus,[4] b. 1826; m. 1855. Esther Sharratt, a teacher of Fond du Lac Co., Wis.; in 1856 they moved to Minnesota; he is a member of the Methodist church. Children:

   10,491a Francis,[5] b. Oct. 11, 1856.
   10,491b Sherman Harvey,[5] b. May 6, 1863.
   10,491c Mary Elizabeth,[5] b. Jan. 1, 1867.

10,490 Mary,[4] b. 1828; m. 1846, Rev. William Ross, a Methodist clergyman; she was a member of the Methodist church, d. in Chatham, O., 1846.

10,493 Charlotte.[4] b. 1830; m. Rev. William Ross, after her sister's death; he d. at Shelbyville, Tenn., of cholera. She was a member of the Methodist church. Children:

   10,493a Sarah (Ross). a graduate, d. same time her father did, of cholera.
   10,493b James (Ross).
   10,493c Mattie (Ross), graduate of Columbus, Ohio.

10,494 Sarah,[4] b. 1832; teacher; m. 1853, Nathan Carral of Winnebago Co.,Wis.

10,492 Elizabeth,[4] b. 1837; a teacher, member of Methodist church; m. 1857, George Rice of Mankato, Minn.; d. July 10, 1858, leaving:

   10,492a George (Rice), b. July 4, 1858.

Page 455, no. 10,563, Huldah Cordelia m. in Salt Lake City, Utah, April 15, 1865, Willard Gilbert Smith, b. in Amherst, Lorain county, Ohio, May 9, 1827, son of Warren and Amanda (Barrs) Smith, a farmer in Littleton, Morgan county, Utah; is probate judge and president of Morgan stake of Zion, in the church of Jesus Christ of Latter Day Saints. His father was killed by a mob in the Hanns Mill massacre, Missouri. Children:

   10,563a Cordelia Rozetta (Smith), b. Sept. 11, 1866.
   10,563b Amanda Caroline (Smith), b. April 3, 1868.
   10,563c Willard Gilbert (Smith), b. Sept. 8, 1870.
   10,563d David Franklin (Smith), b. July 29, 1872.
   10,563e Deseretta (Smith), b. April 13, 1874.
   10,563f Georgianna (Smith), b. May 5, 1876.
   10 563g Sarah (Smith), b. Jan. 25, 1878.

Page 473. no. 10,918, should be Norton, son of Samuel, p. 275, no. 5720.

Page 486, no. 11,280, after last time, add Jan. 1, 1880, he shot and killed W. W. Embry, his associate in publishing a Sunday paper in Leavenworth, Kansas.

Page 491, no. 11,431, read m. April 2, 1815. James Field, a farmer of Chester,Vt., b. March, 1789, d. July 8, 1850. Mrs. Field moved to Dell Prairie, Adams county, Wis., with her son, with whom she still lives, 1880.  Children, b. in Chester :

11,432  Abigail (Field), b Jan. 29, 1816; m. Dec. 19, 1843, John W. Horton of Chester, later of Dell Prairie, where she died Dec. 17, 1857.

11,433  Elizabeth (Field), b. Apr. 25, 1819; m. June 6, 1848, Warren T. Atcherson of Chester, later of Dell Prairie, where she d. Feb. 4, 1878.

11,434  Henry A. (Field), b. March 26, 1821; m. Feb. 7, 1850, Olive Thurston of Heuvelton. N. Y. [see no. 11,460].  He was a farmer in Chester till 1855. when he moved to Dell Prairie, post-office address Kilbourn City, Wis.

Page 491, no. 11,446, d. Oct., 1804.  No. 11,449, Elizabeth, d. June 20, 1865.

Page 492, no. 11,441, line 3, m. Oct., 1822, Polly Greeley, b. in Andover, Vt., Aug. 30, 1803.  He was a farmer in Heuvelton, N. Y., where he died, Aug. 22, 1878; she died Nov. 9, 1878.  Children, instead of as printed on page 492, read :

11,456  Ira, b. in Chester, Vt., Oct. 23, 1823; a farmer near Heuvelton, 1880.
11,457  Lorenzo, b. in Heuvelton Oct. 27, 1825; d. June 17, 1842.
11,460  Olive, b. Oct. 23, 1827; m. Henry A. Field of Chester [see no. 11,434], later of Dell Prairie, Wis.
11,459  Mehitable, b. June 3, 1830; d. Dec. 8, 1838.
11,461  Mary, b. Aug. 6, 1832; m. April 6, 1862.
11,461a  Rosana, b. Jan. 14, 1835; d. June 14, 1842.
11,461b  Charles S., b. April 13, 1837; d. June 6, 1842.
11,461c  William H, b. July 6, 1839; d. June 22, 1842.
11,462  Elizabeth, b. Nov. 24, 1841; m. May 22, 1867.
11,463  Lydia F., b. April 13, 1844; m. Feb. 18, 1867, A. C. Ketcham of Adams county, Wis., later of Brookfield, Linn county, Mo.
11,464  Ellen E., b. Jan. 12, 1846; m. Oct. 23, 1879, John Ross of Heuvelton.

Page 493, no. 2228. read George Almore, b. in Barnstead, L. C., Feb., 1833; m. and has four children; lives in Cambridge, Mass.

Page 493, no. 2227a, Fred,[9] b. Sept. 17, 1879, son of Charles Filer.

The following five persons united to deed land to Thomas Piper of Stratham, N. H., in 1749, and therefore are supposed to be brothers and sisters.

11,771  Moses Thurston of Andover.
11,772  Samuel Thurston, gentleman, of Epping, a parish in Exeter, deeded land 1748 and 1757; his estate was settled 1765.
11,773  Ichabod Thurston of Exeter.
11,774  Joseph Thurston of Stratham.
11,775  Elizabeth Thurston m. —— Mason of Stratham.

---

11,780  George H. Thurston, b. in Boston, m. Sarah A. ——, b. in Newbury, Mass.  Children :
11,781  Son, b. April 26, 1854, on Foundry street.
11,782  Son, b. April 15, 1855.
11,783  Sarah H., b. Oct. 27, 1856 (the record says daughter of George H. and Sarah L. of Newburyport).
11,784  George J., teamster in Boston, b. 1830, son of Noah and Ruby of Springfield, Me.; m. 1st, Emma W. of Tremont, Me.: 2d, in Boston, Aug. 4, 1872, Olive Pillsbury of Boston, formerly of Lewiston, Me.  Child:
11,785  Waldo W., b. March 3, 1861; d. 1862.
11,786  Caleb A. of Boston, aged 25, salesman, b. in Boston, son of George H. and Sarah L. ; m. Emma A. Glynn of Boston, aged 25. b. in Lawrence, Mass., daughter of Jacob W. and Lucy F. Glynn.  They had :
11,787  George H., b. Aug., 1829; d. by being scalded June 11, 1831.
11,788  Ellen Frances, b. Sept., 1834; d. July 7, 1837.
11,789  Joseph, b. in Boston, m. Mary Elizabeth ——, b. in Biddeford, Me.  Child :
11,790  Alvinza B., b. Sept. 19, 1857; m. 1st, in Boston, April 18, 1877, Josephene L. Hovey, b. 1859, daughter of Eben W. and Sarah E. Hovey of Charlestown, Mass.; 2d, Feb. 22, 1879, Frances Ellis of Boston, b. in Rockport, daughter of Henry S. and Frances Ellis.

## 11,791

SARAH (or SALLY) THURSTON, born about 1776; married in Gilmanton, N. H., where most of her married life was spent, Hubbard Thompson, one of a large family, originally of Durham, but living chiefly in Holderness, N. H. The family tradition is that she was from "down country," in the neighborhood of Portsmouth, Durham, or Exeter. She died in Danville, Vt., two weeks after the birth of her daughter, Sept. 5, 1811, aged 35.    Children :

11,792   Hubbard (Thompson), d. 1835, leaving a wife and daughter in Ohio.
11,793   Elizabeth (Thompson), m. —— Curtis; d. in Vermontville, Mich., 1867, leaving a son and daughter.
11,794   Sarah (Thompson), m. —— Wait; d. in Pine Hill, N. Y., 1876, leaving a son, Thompson (Wait).
11,795   Lorenzo (Thompson), d. in Center, Wis., 1860, leaving Mary, Thurston, and Alice (Thompson).
11,796   Hannah Thurston (Thompson), m. Harvey Brace; d. in Janesville, Wis., Nov. 4, 1864, aged 43. They had M. B., Sarah Minerva, F. Helen, Marshall P., Calista E., Amanda H., and Harriet E. (Brace).


11,797   John Thurston of Gilmanton had a daughter Lucy, b. May or Nov. 19, 1789; m. Feb. 3, 1814, Samuel Sanborn, b. Dec. 5, 1784, son of Theophilus Sanborn, and had Julia Ann, Samuel, and Lucy (Sanborn).
11,798   Samuel Thurston of Gilmanton m. April 11, 1775, Elizabeth Moulton, daughter of Robert Moulton, who came from Rye and settled in Gilmanton 1775.
11,799   Samuel Thurston settled in Gilmanton 1791.
11,800   Samuel Thurston died in Gilmanton 1822, aged 54.
11,801   Ambrose Thurston enlisted in the revolutionary war April 1, 1777, for three years, from Gilmanton.
11,802   James Thurston of Gilmanton was paid Nov. 17, 1762, £63 2s 6d for iron work for the grist-mill.
11,803   John Thurston d. suddenly in the field while mowing, July 1, 1828, in Gilmanton.
11,804   Daniel Thurston of Gilmanton had a son who hung himself, aged 16.
11,805   William H. Thurston of Raymond, N. H., m. Sarah Ann B. Maloon, b. Feb. 19, 1831; enlisted in Co. B, 11th N. H. regiment Aug. 28, 1862, mustered out June 4, 1865.

## 11,806

EBENEZER THURSTON of Hopkinton, N. H., son of —— (said to have been a college student) and Merriam (Judkins) Thurston; married, in Concord, N. H., Dec. 16, 1799, MARY MERRILL of Hopkinton. He was taxed in Hopkinton from 1806 to 1813; enlisted in the war of 1812, was wounded at the battle of Plattsburgh, and died from the effects of the wound. She died 1860.

### Children :

11,807   True, d. at Cape Cod.
11,808   Benjamin, d. in Boston, probably same as no. 11,953.
11,809   Lucinda, d. in Concord, N. H., young.
11,810   Hannah, d. in Boscawen, N. H., about 1872.
11,811   Merriam, m. Moses Putney of Hopkinton; moved to Illinois and both died there.                         11,812   Juda.


11,813   Caroline E. Thurston of South Wolfborough, N. H., b. July 28, 1831; m. Oct. 11, 1857, James S. Wentworth, b. Nov. 22, 1836, son of John and Abigail (Gerrish) Wentworth. They live in West Lebanon, Me.  Children :
    11,814   Walter E. (Wentworth), b. Dec. 9, 1859.
    11,815   Eugene Forest (Wentworth), b. Oct. 23, 1861.
    11,816   Evan P. (Wentworth), b. Feb. 23, 1867.
        Daughter, b. June 6, 1872.

## Page 33, no. 84.

JOHN THURSTON [4] ( *John,*[3] *Daniel,*[2] *Daniel*[1]), son of John [3] and Dorothy (Woodman) Thurston of Newbury, Mass.; born there 1744; married EUNICE DOLE.

### Children not on page 33:

+11,820   Enoch,[5] b. Sept. 30. 1770; m. Martha Jaques.
11,821   Mehitable,[5] m. Enoch Plummer, a farmer in Newbury.
11,822   Elizabeth,[5] m. James Kilborn of Boscawen, N. H.
11,823   Ednah,[5] m. William Dole of Newbury.
11,824   Judith,[5] m. Edmund Dole, a cabinet maker of Bangor, Me.

## Page 33, no. 88.

BENJAMIN THURSTON [4] ( *John,*[3] *Daniel,*[2] *Daniel*[1]), brother of the preceding, and son of John [3] and Dorothy (Woodman) Thurston of Newbury, Mass.; born there 1746; married, Jan. 20, 1785, JANE KNIGHT, daughter of James Knight of Newbury. He died Dec. 11, 1807; she died April 8, 1820, aged 65, both buried in Newbury Old-town. He was assessor in Newbury 1807.

### Children not given on page 33:

+11,830   John,[5] b. Aug. 12, 1787; m. Nancy Baker.
11,831   Benjamin,[5] who went west, and finally died in New Orleans.

## 11,820

ENOCH THURSTON [5] ( *John,*[4] *John,*[3] *Daniel,*[2] *Daniel*[1]), son of John [4] and Eunice (Dole) Thurston; born Sept. 30, 1770; married MARTHA JAQUES, born July 5, 1772. He died June 13, 1805.

### Children:

11,835   Elizabeth,[6] b. April 11, 1795; m. June 11, 1822, Anthony Perkins. Child:
    11,836   *Martha* (Perkins), b. March 26, 1823; m. Nov. 7, 1843, Elbridge Dole of Bangor. Me.; d. Oct. 30, 1849, leaving:
    11,837   *Thaddeus P.* (Dole), now in Bangor.
    11,838   *Frederick N.* (Dole), now in California.
    11,839   *Martha E.* (Dole), m. Oct., 1872, Richard Jaques, and died without issue June, 1874.
11,840   John,[6] b. Oct. 26, 1796; d. of ship fever Aug. 26, 1819.
11,841   Martha,[6] b. April 4, 1799; m. Dec. 14, 1826, Abel Lunt. Children:
    11,842   *John Thurston* (Lunt), b. 1828; d. 1850.
    11,843   *Martha E.* (Lunt), b. Aug. 23, 1830; m. July 8, 1852, Hiram P. Mackintosh. Children:
        11,844   *Willis A.* (Mackintosh), b. Apr. 8, 1856, a druggist in Boston.
        11,845   *Hiram P.* (Mackintosh), b. Nov. 11, 1860, a bookkeeper in Newburyport.
        11,846   *Frederick L.* (Mackintosh), b. Feb. 23, 1867.
    11,847   *Ann Brown* (Lunt), b. Feb. 11, 1833; d. June 26, 1845.
11,848   Stephen,[6] b. July 31, 1801; m. March 28, 1832, Harriet Perkins. She died June 24, 1839; he died in California Sept. 9, 1859. Children:
    11,849   *Mary Perkins,*[7] b. Feb. 19, 1833; d. May 5, 1839.
    11,850   *Caroline E.,*[7] afterward went by the name of Caroline Perkins, b. Feb. 7, 1835; m. Fred B. Dodge; they live in Toledo, Ohio.
11,851   Mary,[6] b. Sept. 6, 1803; m. Nov. 11, 1847, Philip Lord of Newburyport, as his second wife; no children by this marriage.

## 11,830

DR. JOHN THURSTON [5] (*Benjamin,*[4] *John,*[3] *Daniel,*[2] *Daniel*[1]), eldest son of Benjamin [4] and Jane (Knight) Thurston of Newbury, Mass.; born there Aug. 12, 1787; married NANCY BAKER. He died in New-

33

buryport Dec. 10, 1835; she died at Mrs. Baker's, a relative, in Brunswick, Me., Sept. 16, 1855, aged 64.

Mr. Thurston graduated from Harvard 1807, received M.D. at Dartmouth 1818; no children.

---

## 11,855

SHUAH THURSTON of Epping, N. H., born Feb. 8, 1748; married, Dec. 14, 1769, ANDREW FREESE, born Oct. 1, 1747, son of Jacob Freese of Epping, born Oct. 10, 1716, died April 20, 1780. Andrew went to Deerfield, N. H., Oct. 19, 1773, and died Oct. 19, 1814.

### Children:

11,856  Sarah (Freese), b. Oct. 11, 1771; d. Oct. 27, 1772.
11,857  Sarah (Freese), b. May 23, 1774; m. Isaiah Langley of Andover, and had
      Dudley F. (Langley), who went to St. Paul, Minn.; she d. Feb. 6. 1853.
11,858  Anne (Freese), b. Aug. 7, 1776; m. James Tucker of Deerfield, and had
      Charles, Harriet, Dudley F., Eliza, Franklin G., and John T. (Tucker);
      d. Aug. 27, 1849.
11,859  Jacob (Freese), b. Oct. 29, 1778; m. Eunice James, and had :
      11,860  Andrew (Freese). m. Sally T. Jenness.
      11,861  Benjamin James (Freese), m. 1st, Sally Merrill; 2d, Jones Canfield.
11,862  Gordon (Freese), b. May 26, 1781.
11,863  Dudley (Freese), b. Oct. 16, 1787.

---

## 11,864

—— THURSTON lived in Royalstown, Mass., 1834. Children:

+11,865  David, b. March 13, 1795; m. Anna Crocker Bacon.
11,866  Benjamin, m. ——; d. many years ago at Ottawa, Ill.; several children.
11,867  Nizolla.

## 11,865

DAVID THURSTON, born, probably at Royalston, Mass., March 13, 1795; married, July 23, 1821, ANNA CROCKER BACON, born in Barnstable, Mass., June 17, 1795. He died in Wheeling, Va., Mar. 31, 1844; she died at Newport, Pa., July, 1870.

Mr. Thurston was an auctioneer in Portland, Me. 1835-6 moved to Baltimore, Md. They were members of the first Baptist church in Portland.

### Children:

+11,868  George Henry, b. Aug. 3, 1822; m. Mary Curry Lewis.
      Five children d. in infancy.
11,869  Francis Edward, b. Aug. 12, 1830; m. Mary Heston of Philadelphia,
      Pa., and had eight children, five living, 1880.

## 11,868

GEORGE HENRY THURSTON, eldest son of David and Anna Crocker (Bacon) Thurston of Portland, Me.; born there Aug. 3, 1822; married Sept. 9, 1852, by Rev. Mr. Lyman, now bishop of California, MARY CURRY LEWIS, daughter of Richard and Elizabeth (Walters) Lewis of Baltimore; Elizabeth Walters was a native of Pittsburgh.

Mr. Thurston was engaged in mercantile pursuits from 1838—1843; from 1843—1853 in newspaper business; from 1853—1865 publishing the Pittsburgh city directory; from 1865—1872 president of the Pacific and Atlantic Telegraph Co. During the war was secretary of the "committee of public safety of Allegheny county;" for several

years president of the Pittsburgh board of trade and vice-president of the national board; for the past seven years chairman of the executive committee of the board of commissioners for the improvement of the Ohio river and its tributaries; residence Pittsburgh, Pa.: is not now engaged in any business. They are members of the Episcopal church.

### Children:

11,870 Paul, b. Feb. 28, 1854; d. April 19, 1863.
11,871 Anna Lucy, b. Dec. 6, 1855; in Vassar college 1874.
11,872 Alice Maud, b. Aug. 2, 1858; graduated from the Bishop Benmone Institute, Pittsburgh, 1878.
11,873 George Pitt, b. Oct. 6, 1861; d. April 12, 1863.
11,874 Mary Elizabeth, b. July 29, 1864.
11,875 Georgia Henry, b. Aug. 28, 1871.

Page 498, no. 11,531, dropped dead in the woods Jan. 30, 1880.

### BAPTISMS OF THURSTONS FROM ROWLEY, MASS., CHURCH RECORDS.

Daniel [no. 27], Aug. 3, 1690; Hannah [no. 45], Nov. 18, 1694; Dorcas [no. 46], Dec. 27, 1696; Mehitabel [no. 39], Joseph [no. 40], Benjamin [no. 41], Feb. 5, 1698-9; Abner [no. 47], April 30, 1699; Abigail [no. 42], Oct. 27, 1700; Hannah [no. 43], Feb. 28, 1702-3; Benjamin [no. 44], Aug. 27, 1705; Thomas [no. 69], Nov. 25, 1716; Sarah [no. 70], May 17, 1719.
Joseph Thurston owned y$^e$ coven$^t$ ffeb$^{ry}$ 5, 1698-9. Dan$^{ll}$ Thurston & 's wife owned y$^e$ coven$^t$ Nov. 25, 1716.

From city and town records, and other sources, we obtained the following names of Thurstons, which we cannot trace, and are not in the previous pages. Being alphabetically arranged, these names do not appear in the index.

### BIRTHS.

11.887 Alice Maria, in Boston, Mass., Oct. 30, 1866, daughter of Richard of England and Mary A. of Ireland.
11.888 Arabella Jennette, in Charlestown, Mass., Dec. 28, 1852, daughter of Andrew and Anna. Her father was born in Ireland.
11.889 Charles A., in Charlestown, Mass., March 31, 1849, son of Andrew and Amelia.
11.890 John, son of —— Thurston of Exeter, N. H., m. Elizabeth Folsom, b. about 1715, dau. of John and Hannah (Gilman) Folsom of Exeter; at time of death of her father had:
11.891 John, named in his will.
11.892 Lucy, in Roxbury. Mass., Feb. 17, 1807, dau. of Joseph, d. Jan. 15, 1808.
11.893 Lucy, dau. of Joseph and Lucy, Nov. 10, 1808.
11.894 Joseph, son of Joseph and Lucy, June 11, 1811.

11.895 Thomas Palmer, son of Joseph and Lucy, Dec. 29, 1813.
11.896 Margaret Aurelia, in Roxbury, Mass., Feb. 10, 1863, dau. of Wm. P. and Elizabeth.
11.897 Paluma, in Deerfield, N. H., daughter of John and Hannah (Smith) Thurston.
11.898 Penelope, in Wrentham. Mass., Nov. 29, 1711, daught-r of Peter and Abigail.
11.899 Samuel and i edee of Wrentham had:
  11,900 Betty, Dec., 1769.
  11,901 Abijah, Aug. 25, 1770.
  11,902 Pedee (dau.), May 14, 1772.
  11,903 Susan, April 24, 1774.
  11,904 Royal, May 10, 1778.
11.905 Sarah, in Portland, Me., Mar. 17, 1728, daughter of Daniel and M——, who are said to have gone to Grafton, Mass.

### MARRIAGES.

11.910 Abigail, colored, in Charlestown, Mass., to John Moseley June 19, 1812.
11.911 Abner, in Charlestown, Mass., to Mary Huntoon Jan., 1823.
11.912 Andrew, inten. in Charlestown, Mass., to Amelia S. Nay Dec. 27, 1847.
11.913 Arminta, to Hiram Holt, 1823, of Whitestown, N. Y., b. April 11, 1794.
11.914 Caleb, in Boston, to John Sargent Dec. 2, 1823.
11.915 Catherine, to James Galeway Sept. 19, 1775.
11.916 Catherine S., in Boston, to —— 1858.
11.917 Charl-s C., inten. in Boston Jan. 13, in Charlestown, to Mary A. Hastings Feb. 18, 1849.
11.918 Charlotte, in Deerfield, N. H., to Zebulon Durgin Aug. 2, 1827.

11.919 Daniel of Cambridge, Mass., to Mary Stedman, dau. of Robert Stedman, and had Daniel. b. April 11, 1676, and soon removed from town.
11.920 Daniel, Dea., of Bedford, N. H., to Sally Abbott May 2, 1777.
11.921 Daniel of Rehoboth, Mass , to Hannah Miller Dec 6, 1681. They had:
  11.922 Sarah, b. Dec. 2, 1683; m. May 12, 1714, Thomas Bowen.
11.923 Daniel, in Boston, to Mary M. Laird April 25, 1833.
11.924 Daniel of Salem, Mass., to Mary Stacy of Marbl-head, Mass., Sept. 29, 1805.
11.925 David of Bridgewater, Mass., to Mercy Carey April 23, 1713.
11.926 David, in Charlestown, Mass., to Ann C. Beacon of Barnstable, Mass., Jan. 26, 1821.

11,927 David, 1st in Rehoboth, Mass., to Hannah Carpenter Nov. 18, 1725 ; 2d, in Rehoboth, to Patience Carpenter Sept. 10, 1745.

11,928 Deborah, in Medfield, Mass., to Jabish Talman Nov. 18, 1665.

11,929 Deborah, in Deerfield N. H., to Benj. Noyes, both of Nottingham, N. H., June 2, 1829.

11,930 Dolly, in Dorchester, Mass., 1811, to —.

11,931 Elihu, in Oxford, Mass., to Deborah Stevens of Worcester, Mass., Aug. 14, 1776.

11,932 Elizabeth V., aged 18, of Boston, b. in Seekonk, Mass., dau. of Geo. W. and Mary E., in Boston, to Mark Davis, R. R. trackman of Boston, b. in Bangor, Me., son of Mark and Hannah Davis, June 10, 1878.

11,933 Emily W., b. in Tremont, Me., dau. of Benj. and Eliza, intention in Charlestown, Mass., to Wm. S. Battis, aged 40, July 1, 1873.

11,934 Emma A. of Boston, aged 32, b. in Union, Me., dau. of Thomas C. and Mary J. (Nye), 2d mar., in Boston, May 27, 1874, to Joseph T. Brown, b. in Harmony, Me.

11,935 Esther, in Rowley, Mass., to Joseph Leland of Sherborn, Mass.

11,936 Ezra of Pawlet, Vt., to Mary Wentworth, and had a dau. who m. — Gould.

11,937 Fanny, in Charlestown, Mass., to Joseph Steadman Nov. 2, 1814.

11,938 Frances, in Charlestown, Mass., to James Coolidge Jan. 14, 1824.

11,939 George of Newbury, Mass., to — Thurlow and d. Jan. 1. 1713.

11,940 Grace to Jacob Dayton of Southold, N. Y., Nov. 24, 1714.

11,941 Hannah, widow, in Boston, to Thomas Lord July 28, 1652.

11,942 Hannah, in Charlestown, Mass., to John Hamilton Sept. 2 1824.

11,943 Helen A. of Cambridge, Mass., aged 31, b. in Boston, dau. of Caleb and Jane, in Boston, to Geo. T. Terry of Boston, trader, b. in Limington, Me , son of John and Abigail Terry, June 12 1878.

11,944 James to Deborah Tarr of Bristol, Me.

11,945 Jane, in Rehoboth, Mass., to Stephen Carpenter April 2, 1744.

11,946 John to Hannah Carey, both of Kittery, Me., Aug. 15, 1688.

11,947 John, in Boston, to Sarah Pierce, Nov. 18, 1722.

11,948 John, in Boston, to Susan Hartford Dec. 18, 1848.

11,949 John, cutter, in Boston, son of Moses and Phebe of Freedom, Me., to Mary D. Tarbox of Milton, Me., Aug. 15, 1868.

11,950 John to his cousin Lois of Deer Isle, Me.

11,951 John of Hempstead, L. I., to Milicen Smith Jan. 3, 1772.

11,952 John H., in Gilsum, N. H., to Susan Thomson Sept. 26, 1816, both of Orange, Vt.

11,953 Joseph, in Charlestown, Mass., to Betsey Johnson Feb. 2, 1810.

11,954 Leland, in Charlestown, to Margaret L. Hutchins April 4, 1827.

11,955 Louisa, in Charlestown, to John L. Leighton Aug. 17, 1844.

11,956 Louisa, in Dorchester. Mass., to Elnathan Cushing March 4, 1827.

11,957 Lovitt, in N. York, as per records Ref. Dutch ch. to Catherine Dobbs Oct. 22 1763.

11,958 Lucretia to Francis Welber May 8, 1782.

11,959 Lydia of Rowley, Mass., to John Sargent of Newbury, Mass., July 5, 1748.

11,960 Lydia, in Rowley, to Dea. Wm. Fisk Jan. 6, 1743-4.

11,961 Malinda of Exeter, N. H., to John G. Johnson of Newburyport. Mass . Sept. 7, 1857.

11,962 Margaret, in Rehoboth, Mass., to Dan Carpenter Dec. 12, 1710.

11,963 Margaret, in Portland, Me., to Jason H. Shaw Jan. 9, 1853.

11,964 Margaret D., in Charlestown, Mass., to Thomas E. Stutson Sept. 14, 1824.

11,965 Martha of Hempstead, L. I., to Oliver Valentine 1728.

11,966 Mary, in Bradford, Mass., to James Chadwick March 5, 1752.

11,967 Mary Ann, in Charlestown, Mass., to James Fanew June 1, 1820.

11,968 Mary A. of Lowell, Mass., intention in Charlestown, to Benj. Larrabee Mar. 5, 1843.

11,969 Mary F. of Lancaster, Mass., aged 21, dau. of Silas, to Charles H. Fay of Boston May 30, 1855.

11,970 Nancy M., intention in Charlestown, to George W. Horne of Wolfborough, N. H., about 1845.

11,971 Nathaniel, in Exeter, N. H., to Sarah York May 13, 1832.

11,972 Phebe to Willard Walker of Royalston, Mass., and had Delina (Walker), m. April 21, 1858, Dea. Wm. L. Lamb, b. in Worcester, Mass., descendant of Thos. Lamb of England.

11,973 Pomp, colored, intention in Boston Nov. 2, in Charlestown, Mass., by Rev. Thos. Paul, to Mary White Dec. 18. 1816.

11,974 Pomp, colored, in Charlestown, to Patty Turner, colored, of Boston Nov. 4, 1821.

11,975 Rebecca to Geo. Thurlow of Newbury, Mass., Nov. 4, 1791.

11,976 Rook to Susan Butler about 1800; he d. and she m. 2d, Samuel Edgerly and lived in Limerick, Me.

11,977 Ruth of Stratham, N. H., in R wley, ass., to Nathaniel Wiggin of Maine.

11,978 Sally to Hubbard Thompson of Gilmanton, N. H., 1810.

11,979 Sarah, in Rehoboth, Mass., to John Carpenter Sept. 12. 1717.

11,980 Sarah, in Rehoboth, to Thomas Bowen May 12, 1714.

11,981 Sarah J. of Providence, R. I., in Charlestown, Mass , to Henry Y. Graham of Boston July 5, 1836.

11,982 Susan W., aged 22, b. in Freedom, Me., dau. of Henry and Drusilla, to Henry S Foster, clerk in Boston, aged 23, son of Homer and Mary J. Foster, intention July 1, 1871.

11,983 Susanna to Henry Putnam of Deer Isle, Me.

11,984 Susanna Mrs. of Oxford, Mass., to Dr. Daniel Fisk Nov. 10, 1772.

11,985 Thomas to Clarissa Stickney Mar., 1816.

11,986 Thomas, in the neighborhood of Rochester, N. H., to Mary Hurd: he d. and she m. David Hartford Wentworth, b. Apr. 7. 1817.

11,987 Vashty, in Charlestown, to Luther Gates Feb. 10, 1824.

11,988 Waldo W., b. Mar. 3, 1861, son of Geo. J. of Springfield, Me., in Boston, to Emily W. of Tremont, Me.

11,989 William, mariner, aged 27, b. in England, son of James and Eliza, in Boston, to Catherine Parker, formerly of England, Sept. 18, 1863.

11,990 William E., machinist, of Boston, b. in Pawtucket, R. I., son of Charles and Abby, in Boston, to Elizabeth Chappel of Boston May 13. 1867.

11,991 William H., intention in Charlestown, Mass., to Sarah F. Caldwell Oct. 14, 1848.

11,992 William H. H., manufacturer of Oxford, Mass , son of William H. of Oxford, in Boston, to Mary A. Lackey of Boston, formerly of Salem, Mass., Aug. 18, 1865.

11,993 — Thurston, b. Jan., 1793, to Lydia Gould and d. April 13, 1839.

## DEATHS.

12,000 Almira A. in Boston Aug., 1845, dau. of Zebulon.

12,001 Arthur in Boston Feb. 1, 1874, infant son of Charles A. of Portland, Me.

12,002 Augusta R. in Boston May 19. 1878.

12,003 Benjamin of intemperance in house of industry, Boston. Feb. 24, 1842, aged 34.

12,004 Charles A. in Boston June 1, 1877, aged 65, ship-master, son of James and Sarah of Scarborough, Me.

12,005 Donald in Boston Sept. 3. 1862, a mariner, son of Nathan, b. in Lexington, Mass.

12,006 Eliza Ann in Hempstead, L. I., May 30, 1770. aged 28.

12 007 Frederick W. in Portland, Me., son of John K., Mar. 29, 1862. aged 8 y. 3 m., buried in Rockport, Me.

12,008 Gilman A. in Portland, Me., Sept. 15, 1860, aged 1 y. 1 m.

12,009 Hannah M. Mrs. in Portland, Me., July 24, 1854, aged 83.

12,010 Henry L. in Boston May 11, 1842, aged 11 mos., son of Leonard M., buried at Great Falls, N. H.

12,011 Infant son of Prescott and Frances in Boston April 9, 1859.

12,012 Jerusha in Boston Dec. 20, 1870, wife of George. b. in Eastham. Mass.

12,013 John in Rehoboth, Mass., Nov. 24, 1711.

12,014 Joseph's child in Roxbury, Mass., Jan. 16. 1808.

12,015 Joseph W. at soldiers home in Boston Aug. 12. 1868, b. in Northampton, Mass.

12,016 Joshua Terry, drowned at Lewiston Falls. Me., Sept. 7, 1847, aged 25, buried in Portland, Me.

12,017 Martha, colored, in Boston 1868, aged 72, wife of Pomfrey, b. in Plymouth, dau. of Pinto of Africa.

12,018 Mehitable in Boston Sept. 11, 1716.

12,019 Nathaniel S. in Portland, Me., Oct. 12, 1853, son of John.

12,020 Phebe at lunatic hospital in Boston Mar. 18, 1863. wife of Saul of Boscawen, N.H.

12,021 Samuel in Boston almshouse Nov.4,1808.

12,022 Samuel in Exeter. N. H., June 25,1751, son of Samuel and Elizabeth.

12,023 Sarah B., single, in Boston Aug. 19, 1823, aged 20.

12,024 Sarah F. in Charlestown, Mass., Mar. 27, 1853. daughter of James and Lucy.

12,025 Son of Samuel in Portland, Me., Jan. 10. 1846.

12,026 Sylvina H. Mrs. in Boston Nov. 28, 1876, b. in France, wife of Richard M., b. in Damariscotta, Me.

Deaths in Stratham, N. H., kept by a private citizen, no town records, gravestones destroyed and burying place plowed up.

1742, Nov. 27, Moses Thurston's child.
" Dec. 31, " " "
1743, May 23, " " young child.
1748, Nov. 28, " " wife.
" Dec. 12, " " young child.
1749. Nov. 15, Stephen " child.
1754, Oct. 29. John " wife.
1755, Jan. 15, " " child.
1756. Oct. 12, Moses "
1757, Nov. 29, Abner " child.
1758, June 24, Mary " child, died at Enoch Merrill's.
1759, Mar. 5, John " 1st twin.
" Mar. 18, " " 2d twin.
" Mar. 27. " " child.
1761, July 2. Stephen Thurston jr.'s child.
1782, Nov. 27. " "
1787, Oct. 4. John " child.
" July. Robert " d. down east.
1796. July 30, John " child.
1801, Feb. 19, widow Phebe Thurston.
We are not sure who any of these were therefore cannot tell whether we have the record or not.

## MISCELLANEOUS.

### The dates denote the time when in places named.

12,030 A——, mason in Topsham, Vt., 1878.

12,031 Albert A., Buffalo, N. Y., 1876.

12,032 Alexander, San Francisco, Cal., 1876.

12,033 Allen O., milk, New York, 1879.

12,034 Alonzo, Great Falls, N. H., 1876.

12,035 Alonzo H., Chicago, Ill . 1876.

12, 36 Amos B., Nashua, N. H , 1879.

12,037 Ann M., Albany, N. Y., 1876.

12,038 Ansel, Brownfield, Me., 1879.

12,039 August, milliner, Farmington, N. H., 1871.

12,040 Benjamin of Kingston, joining Exeter, N. H., deeds land 1777.

12,041 Benjamin of Concord, N. H., master of arts, buys land of Foster of Canterbury 1779 deeds land to John of Stratham, N. H., 1781.

12,042 Benjamin, near New London, Ct., Dec. 29, 1778—Jan. 30. 1779.

12 043 Benjamin, joined church in Westborough, Mass., 1829.

12,044 Benjamin, midshipman, Madison, Ind., 1879.

12 045 Benjamin of Dutchess Co., N. Y., 1776.

12 046 Benjamin of Goshen, N. Y., 1776.

12,047 Benjamin, Chicago, Ill., 1876.

12,048 Benjamin F., printer, New York, 1879.

12,049 B. E., merchant, Laconia, N. H., 1878.

12,050 B. F., French polish, Boston, 1879.

12,051 Caleb (H. Emery & Co.), Boston, 1860.

12,052 Catherine, widow, New York, 1879.

12,053 Catherine, widow of John, N. Y., 1879.

12,054 Catherine, Queen Co., rec. New York, had guardian Aug. 28, 1812.

12,055 Charles, merchant, West Randolph, Vt., 1878.

12,056 Charles, Washington, D. C , 1876.

12,057 Charles, Clinton, Mass., 1876.

12,058 Charles, San Francisco, Cal., 1876.

12,059 Charles, Toledo, Ohio, 1876.

12,060 Charles B., secretary, New York, 1879.

12,061 Charles B., Bergen, N. J., 1876.

12,062 Charles E., Concord, N. H., 1876.

12,063 Charles F., Brooklyn, N. Y., 1876.

12,064 Charles J., dentist, East Greenwich, R. I., 1871.

12,065 Christian, San Francisco, Cal., 1876.

12,066 C. W., merchant, Dover, N. H., 1879.

12,067 Daniel of Exeter, N. H., bought land 1734.

.2,068 Daniel F., Grand Rapids, Mich., 1876.

12,069 David, lawyer, New York, 1879.

12.070 Dorcas, milliner, Poland, Me., buys land 1861.

12,071 D. E., Patchin, Santa Clara Co., Cal., 1875.

12,072 Ebenezer H., Chicago, Ill., 1876.

12,073 Edward D., dyes, New York, 1879.

12,074 Edward W., Syracuse, N. Y., 1876.

12,075 Edwin M., Chelsea, Mass., 1876.

12,076 Eli, Columbus, Ohio. 1877.

12,077 Eliza, Brownfie'd, Me., 1879.

12,078   Eliza, in Vassar college, Poughkeepsie, N. Y., 1874.
12,079   Eliza B., widow of Robert P., Brooklyn, N. Y., 1879.
12,080   Elmer Q., Chicago, Ill., 1876.
12,081   Eugene, Quincy, Ill., 1875.
12,082   E. H., physician, Chicago, Ill., 1879.
12,083   E. M., Chicago, Ill., 1876.
12,084   E. T., San Francisco, Cal., 1876.
12,085   Frank, Houlton, Me., 1879.
12,086   Frank G., Portsmouth, N. H., 1879.
12,087   Frank N., Brooklyn, N. Y., 1876.
12,088   Fred. A., Great Falls, N. H., 1876.
12,089   F., painter, Bangor, Me., 1879.
12,090   F. S., Boston, Mass., 1879.
12,091   F. W., French polish, Boston, 1879.
12,092   George, Queens Co., N. Y., grantor and grantee of land about 1780.
12,093   George, San Francisco, Cal., 1876.
12,094   George, Toledo, Ohio, 1876.
12,095   George A., tinsmith, Brooklyn, N. Y., 1879.
12,096   George D., bookkeeper, Brooklyn,1879.
12,097   George H., Hudson, N. Y., 1876.
12,098   George I., Brooklyn, N. Y., 1876.
12,099   George J., clerk in Boston, 1860.
12,100   George P., San Francisco, Cal., 1876.
12,101   George S.,       "          "          "
12,102   Goodman, Oct., 1637, at a division of meadow lands by Salem, Mass., authorities had three acres set off to him.
12,103   Harrison, Chicago, Ill., 1876.
12,104   Harrison F., tinman, Center Bartlett, N. H., 1879; moved from Porter, Me., 1876.
12,105   Harrison H., Concord, N. H., 1876.
12,106   Henry C., merchant, Ashley Falls, Sheffield, Mass., 1871.
12,107   Herbert S., Rumford Point, Me., 1878.
12,108   Horace J., San Francisco, Cal., 1876.
12,109   H. T., clothier, Leominster, Mass., 1871.
12,110   James, Chicago, Ill., 1876.
12,111   James E., Brooklyn, N. Y., 1876.
12,112   James F., Pittsfield, Mass., 1876.
12,113   James O., Newark, N. J., 1876.
12,114   Janet Miss, Boston, 1860.
12,115   Joel, in Dutchess Co., N. Y., 1775.
12,116   John, New Market, N. H., 1746.
12,117   John of Exeter N. H., bought land 1733.
12,118   John Rev., Methodist, Barton Landing, Vt., 1871.
12,119   John of Portsmouth. N. H., was deputy 1776, and lieutenant 1778, Jan. 1.
12,120   John, b. May 1, 1643, made freeman 1663 at Black Point, Casco Bay, Me.
12,121   John, Albany, N. Y., 1876.
12,122   John Colby, Tomah, Wis.
12,123   John G., Chicago, Ill., 1876.
12,124   John L., San Francisco, Cal., 1876.
12,125   John M., Poughkeepsie, N. Y., 1876.
12,126   John M., Syracuse, N. Y., 1876.
12,127   John M., Utica, N. Y., 1876.
12,128   John P., liquors, New York, 1879.
12,129   Jonathan of Epping, N. H., perhaps no. 145, sold land 1789.
12,130   Joseph, Boston, 1860.
12,131   Joseph, Custar, Wood Co., Ohio, 1879.
12,132   Joseph, Columbus, Ohio, 1877.
12,133   Joseph, Dutchess Co., N. Y., 1775.
12,134   J., Newport Center, Vt., 1877.

12,135   J. H., physician, Athens, Ohio, 1877.
12,136   J. H., Chicago, Ill., 1876.
12,137   J. Morris, postmaster 1862 in East Fairfield, Columbus Co., Ohio.
12,138   Kimball of Exeter, N. H., had a child died April 5, 1841.
12,139   Leonard, Toledo, Ohio, 1876.
12,140   Lewis, Chicago, Ill., 1876.
12,141   Lewis V., merchant, New York, 1879.
12,142   Lorenzo of Poland, Me., sold land to George F. of Poland 1853.
12,143   Louisa, widow of Carnaby D., fancy goods, New York, 1879.
12,144   Louisa, Brooklyn, N. Y., 1876.
12,145   L., grocer, Barre, Vt., 1871.
12,146   Margaret, wid. of Chas., N. York, 1879.
12,147   Martha, joined the church in Westborough, Mass., 1825.
12,148   Martin, Utica, N. Y., 1876.
12,149   Mary, in Queens Co., N. Y., record, guardian appointed Aug. 28, 1812.
12,150   Moses, New Market, N. H., 1746.
12,151   Nathaniel, New York, 1879.
12,152   Nelson, Washington, D. C., 1879.
12,153   Norton, Bennington, Ohio, 1879.
12,154   Nowell F., messenger, Brooklyn, 1879.
12,155   Oliver, Exeter, N. H., July 25, 1788.
12,156   Prescott, Boston, 1860.
12,157   P. Sanford., clerk, Boston, 1860.
12,158   Richard K., manager New York, 1879.
12,159   Robert of Stratham, N. H.
12,160   Robert H., actor in New York, 1879.
12,161   Robert H., Chicago, Ill., 1876.
12,162   Robert L.,       "          "          "
12,163   Samuel, Hempstead, N. Y., 1780.
12,164   Samuel R., Chicago Ill., 1876.
12,165   Stephen, taxed in Raymond, N. H., 1770—1778.
12,166   Stephen, New Market, N. H., 1776.
12,167   Susie A., Tiskilwa, Bureau Co., Ill.
12,168   Thaddeus, Brownfield, Me., 1879.
12,169   Thomas, b. 1649; swore allegiance in Hampton, Mass., 1678; provost martial 1681; made a deed of land to Timothy Hilliard Dec. 20, 1681, recorded in Exeter, N. H.
12,170   Thomas, piano mover, New York, 1879.
12,171   Thomas L., Chicago, Ill., 1876.
12,172   Thurston, Twombly & Co., spool manufacturers, Alton, N. H., 1871.
12,173   Thurston & Harrison, cotton brokers, Baltimore, Md., burnt out Jan. 1880, loss $100,000.
12,174   Thurston & Stevens, stable, Winsor, Vt., 1871.
12,175   Wallace H., Brooklyn, N. Y., 1876.
12,176   Walter.      "          "          "
12,177   Walter, New Market, N. H., 1879.
12,178   Wilbur, Dover, N. H., 1876.
12,179   William, Buffalo, N. Y., 1876.
12,180   William, Hempstead, N. Y., 1780.
12,181   William C., express in New York, 1879.
12,182   William H., b. in Nottingham, N. H., living in Raymond, N. H., 1878.
12,183   William H., in business in Boston, 1860.
12,184   William H., New York, 1879.
12,185   William H., Cleveland, Ohio, 1876.
12,186   William P., in business in Boston, 1860.
12,187   W. H., Boston, 1879.

# INDEX.

DESCENDANTS OF DANIEL THURSTON BEARING THE NAME OF THURSTON.

The figures before each name denote the year of birth; the figures after the name denote the consecutive number which runs through the entire volume. The interrogation mark (?) shows uncertainty as to the date.

| Year | Name | No. |
|---|---|---|
| 1833 | Francis Henry | 4003 |
| 1839 | Francis Warren | 3147 |
| 1860 | Frank | 4697 |
| 1870 | Frank | 4782 |
| 1869 | Frank | 4880 |
| 1848 | Frank | 11,574 |
| 1858 | Frank Alston | 5296 |
| 1852 | Frank Benjamin | 4480 |
| 1877 | Frank Freeman | 4542 |
| 1876 | Frank Hale | 5353 |
| 1848 | Frank L. | 3183 |
| 1862 | Frank Melvin | 5149 |
| 1865 | Frank Watson | 4795 |
| 1878 | Frank Wesley | 11,575 |
| 1869 | Franklin | 3689 |
| 1850 | Franklin | 4274 |
| 1834 | Franklin Alden | 3781 |
| 1847 | Franklin Hinckley | 1793 |
| 1836 | Franklin Josiah | 2365 |
| 1861 | Franklin Marston | 3989 |
| 1815 | Franklin Robinson | 1513 |
| 1856 | Franklin Waldo | 4518 |
| 1872 | Fred | 4405 |
| 1859 | Fred Alston | 4531 |
| 1860 | Fred Howard | 4991 |
| 1871 | Fred W. | 5230 |
| 1857 | Fred Walter | 4434 |
| 1879 | Freddie Nelson | 11,578 |
| 1865 | Frederic Harlow | 1803 |
| 1808 | Frederick George | 2902 |
| 1853 | Frederick Gilman | 3099 |
| 1863 | Frederick Lewis | 5150 |
| 1854 | Frederick William | 8508 |
| 1864 | Frederick William | 3363 |
| 1815 | Freeman Dexter | 2648 |
| 1849 | Freeman Elijah | 4586 |

**G**

| Year | Name | No. |
|---|---|---|
| 1760 | Gates | 756 |
| 1865 | General Wellington | 5019 |
| 1797 | George | 1224 |
| 1814 | George | 2528 |
|  | George | 2919 |
|  | George | 8532 |
| 1876 | George | 4843 |
| 1852 | George Abel | 4752 |
| 1842 | George Boothby | 4987 |
|  | George Breed | 4713 |
| 1861 | George Carpenter | 3497 |
| 1837 | George Carter | 4236 |
| 1863 | George E. | 4395 |
| 1868 | George E. | 5287 |
| 1835 | George Elward | 3682 |
|  | George Elbridge | 5087 |
| 1860 | George Everett | 4878 |
| 1817 | George Fickett | 3816 |
| 1848 | George Francis | 8286 |
| 1869 | George Frank | 5111 |
| 1838 | George Franklin | 3196 |
| 1839 | George Greeley | 4967 |
| 1845 | George Henry | 1792 |
| 1838 | George Henry | 3787 |
| 1846 | George Henry | 8970 |
| 1873 | George Henry | 3980 |
| 1850 | George Henry | 11,579 |
| 1852 | George Henry | 11,597 |
| 1855 | George Humphrey | 4773 |
| 1849 | George Kimball | 5040 |
| 1877 | George Kimball | 5042 |
| 1874 | George Lawrence | 1789 |
| 1831 | George Lee | 4001 |
| 1801 | George Peter | 2317 |
| 1849 | George Pierce | 3408 |
| 1859 | George Quincey | 5143 |
| 1849 | George Roswell | 3151 |
| 1867 | George Sheldon | 3095 |
| 1831 | George Soule | 3891 |
| 1841 | George W. | 4401 |
| 1816 | George Waldo | 1442 |
| 1810 | George Washington | 2031 |
| 1854 | George Washington | 2224 |

| Year | Name | No. |
|---|---|---|
| 1832 | George Washington | 4158 |
| 1856 | George Washington | 5211 |
| 1836 | George William | 1868 |
| 1854 | Georgia Anna | 5197 |
| 1855 | Georgia Emma | 4159 |
| 1875 | Georgia Eva | 3771 |
| 857 | Georgia Lou Emma | 5072 |
| 1843 | Georgianna | 11,568 |
| 1812 | Georgianna | 11,580 |
| 1857 | Georgie Adah | 5240 |
| 1877 | Gertrude | 11,599 |
| 1877 | Gertrude Addie | 5814 |
| 1716 | Gideon | 68 |
| 1841 | Gilbert Remick | 4667 |
| 1811 | Gilman | 2250 |
| 1821 | Gilman | 2898 |
|  | Gilman | 2584 |
| 1838 | Gilman | 3962 |
| 1819 | Gilman | 4212 |
| 1827 | Gilman | 4221 |
| 1778 | Gilman | 11,511 |
| 1812 | Gilman | 11,528 |
| 1792 | Ginnet | 421 |
| 1869 | Grace | 4853 |
| 1862 | Grace | 4901 |
| 1864 | Grace Carpenter | 3488 |
| 1850 | Granville True | 3981 |
| 1865 | Guy Linley | 5174 |

**H**

| Year | Name | No. |
|---|---|---|
| 1657 | Hannah | 2 |
| 1698 | Hannah | 82 |
| 1703 | Hannah | 43 |
| 1694 | Hannah | 45 |
| 1740? | Hannah | 83 |
| 1741? | Hannah | 176 |
| 1738 | Hannah | 158 |
| 1744 | Hannah | 161 |
|  | Hannah | 218 |
| 1749? | Hannah | 858 |
| 1774? | Hannah | 511 |
| 1801 | Hannah | 548 |
| 1773 | Hannah | 599 |
| 1765 | Hannah | 742 |
| 1774 | Hannah | 862 |
|  | Hannah | 953 |
| 1803 | Hannah | 981 |
|  | Hannah | 1039 |
| 1811 | Hannah | 1229 |
| 1781 | Hannah | 1344 |
| 1818 | Hannah | 1475 |
| 1837 | Hannah | 1755 |
|  | Hannah | 2096 |
|  | Hannah | 2238 |
| 1812 | Hannah | 2647 |
| 1852 | Hannah Adelaide | 4615 |
| 1819 | Hannah Ann | 2018 |
| 1836 | Hannah Ann | 3637 |
| 1788 | Hannah Ardway | 2385 |
| 1842 | Hannah D. | 4402 |
| 1831 | Hannah Descomb | 2884 |
| 1826 | Hannah Dutch | 4316 |
| 1862 | Hannah E. | 5343 |
| 1831 | Hannah Eliza | 8914 |
| 1823 | Hannah Jane | 2139 |
| 1850 | Hannah Jane | 5043 |
| 1812 | Hannah Lewis | 2510 |
| 1814 | Hannah Lomantha | 4128 |
| 1849 | Hannah Louisa | 4549 |
| 1809 | Hannah Merrill | 3805 |
| 1909 | Hannah Wallace | 2636 |
| 1848 | Harriet | 3647 |
| 1823 | Harriet Adams | 11,548 |
| 1829 | Harriet Ann | 1648 |
| 1847 | Harriet Chapman | 3285 |
| 1874 | Harriet Elizabeth | 3370 |
| 1829 | Harriet Elizabeth | 4000 |
| 1852 | Harriet Ellen | 3202 |
| 1858 | Harriet Ellen | 3744 |
| 1844 | Harriet Ellen | 4475 |
| 1857 | Harriet Elvira | 5106 |

| Year | Name | No. |
|---|---|---|
| 1871 | Harriet Emily | 5158 |
| 1862 | Harriet Emma | 5200 |
| 1849 | Harriet Emma | 5274 |
| 1823 | Harriet How | 4508 |
|  | Harrison | 2642 |
| 1840 | Harrison Franklin | 4376 |
| 1854 | Harry Darling | 3446 |
| 1872 | Harry David | 1788 |
| 1879 | Harry Dodge | 3116 |
| 1866 | Harry Lee | 4992 |
| 1806 | Hartley | 1511 |
| 1802 | Hartwell | 1468 |
| 1830 | Harvey | 9068 |
| 1742 | Hattie | 350 |
| 1856 | Hattie Edda | 5127 |
| 1868 | Hattie Maria | 4625 |
| 1832 | Hattie Newell | 2527 |
| 1877 | Helen | 3459 |
| 1864 | Helen A. | 4634 |
| 1855 | Helen Augusta | 4691 |
| 1860 | Helen Foster | 3447 |
| 1860 | Helen Goodale | 4783 |
| 1842 | Helen Jane | 4904 |
| 1842 | Helen Jane Elizabeth | 5296 |
| 1860 | Helen Maria | 1692 |
| 1845 | Helen Maria | 3180 |
| 1852 | Helen Stacy | 2953 |
|  | Helpy | 1033 |
| 1843 | Henrietta | 3790 |
| 1844 | Henrietta | 11,549 |
| 1847 | Henrietta | 11,570 |
| 1843 | Henrietta Butler | 4784 |
| 1839 | Henrietta Maria | 1756 |
| 1836 | Henrietta Maria | 3736 |
| 1804 | Henrietta Peabody | 2196 |
| 1808 | Henry | 2141 |
| 1792 | Henry | 2294 |
| 1805 | Henry | 2491 |
| 1853 | Henry | 3510 |
| 1832 | Henry | 3776 |
| 1854 | Henry | 3792 |
| 1853 | Henry Bartels | 8363 |
| 1841 | Henry Clark | 4558 |
| 1839 | Henry Elliott | 5033 |
| 1848 | Henry Irving | 5118 |
| 1866 | Henry Lynden | 3367 |
| 1836 | Henry Martin | 1694 |
| 1846 | Henry Melville | 4750 |
| 1805 | Henry Rice | 3802 |
| 1844 | Henry S. | 3134 |
| 1823 | Henry Warren Lyman | 2824 |
| 1845 | Henry William | 3735 |
| 1818 | Henry Winchester | 2951 |
| 1861 | Henry Winfred | 5368 |
| 1752? | Hepzibah | 376 |
| 1771 | Hepzibah | 411 |
| 1849 | Herbert | 5058 |
| 1853 | Herbert Elon | 5367 |
| 1862 | Herbert Elroy | 4950 |
| 1875 | Herbert Melvin | 5313 |
| 1820 | Hiram | 3877 |
| 1829 | Hiram | 4070 |
| 1828 | Hiram Leonard | 4515 |
| 1859 | Hiram Leonard | 4519 |
| 1834 | Hiram Richardson | 5017 |
| 1867 | Hiram Sargent | 3684 |
| 1842 | Horace Livermore | 2369 |
| 1841 | Horace Page | 1697 |
| 1859 | Howard Forrist | 5172 |
| 1870 | Howard Lewis | 4854 |
| 1800 | Hubbard | 1467 |
| 1813 | Huldah | 4078 |
| 1812 | Huldah Spaulding | 4120 |

**I**

| Year | Name | No. |
|---|---|---|
| 1731? | Ichabod | 210 |
| 1867 | Ida | 4268 |
| 1864 | Ida Adelaide | 5320 |
| 1856 | Ida Ann | 4609 |

| | | | | | | | | | |
|---|---|---|---|---|---|---|---|---|---|
| 1878 | Leroy | 5283 | 1801 | Mahala | 1870 | | Mary | 2214 |
| 1751 | Levi | 198 | 1817 | Mahala | 2064 | 1791 | Mary | 2329 |
| 1770 | Levi | 427 | 1813 | Malvina | 1478 | 1798 | Mary | 2433 |
| | Levi | 2645 | | Malvina | 2665 | 1855 | Mary | 2651 |
| 1802 | Levi Moody | 2245 | 1855 | Marcia M. | 3019 | | Mary | 2649 |
| 1834 | Levi Moody | 3960 | 1830 | Margaret | 1713 | 1810 | Mary | 4140 |
| 1840 | Levi Pool | 1869 | | Margaret | 2567 | 1835 | Mary | 4226 |
| 1841 | Lewis | 3552 | 1850 | Margaret | 3742 | 1807 | Mary | 4478 |
| 1846 | Lewis | 3555 | 1825 | Margaret | 4350 | 1803 | Mary | 11,851 |
| 1839 | Lewis Lincoln | 4283 | 18.9 | Margaret Aurelia | 3996 | 1839 | Mary Abigail | 3661 |
| 1869 | Lilla Belle | 4173 | 1845 | Margaret Helen | 4710 | 1847 | Mary Adelaide | 4674 |
| 1858 | Lilla Emma | 4442 | 1837 | Margaret Knights | 4227 | 18:3 | Mary Almeda | 1445 |
| 1870 | Lillia Adelaide | 5321 | 1862 | Margaret Mead | 3454 | 1832 | Mary Ann | 2100 |
| 1870 | Lillian B. | 5024 | 1829 | Margaretta | 4222 | 1816 | Mary Ann | 2507 |
| 1859 | Lillian Isaphene | 4877 | 1838 | Margery A. | 1887 | 1836 | Mary Ann | 3766 |
| 1870 | Lillie Ellen | 4631 | 1867 | Margetta | 4840 | 1842 | Mary Ann | 4377 |
| 1849 | Lillie Maria | 4770 | 1803 | Maria | 1374 | | Mary Ann | 4593 |
| 1861 | Lilly Arabella | 5173 | 1797 | Maria | 1462 | 1826 | Mary Ann | 4660 |
| 1870 | Lilly May | 2870 | | Maria | 1467 | 1844 | Mary Ann | 11,588 |
| 1866 | Linda May | 5298 | 1804 | Maria | 1980 | 1858 | Mary Anna | 4533 |
| 1864 | Lizzie Bell | 48 9 | | Maria | 2338 | 1859 | Mary Augusta | 5199 |
| 1876 | Lizzie Mabel | 5800 | 1824 | Maria | 4150 | 1809 | Mary Bartlett | 2774 |
| 1857 | Lizzie Odell | 3987 | 1845 | Maria | 5054 | 1823 | Mary Brown | 1846 |
| 1858 | Loren Andrews | 4731 | 1843 | Maria Buck | 1816 | 1851 | Mary Brown | 3299 |
| 1816 | Lorenda Holt | 4505 | 1844 | Maria Hutchins | 4425 | 1804 | Mary Carr | 991 |
| 1840 | Lorenzo Dow | 4903 | 1858 | Maria Stetson | 8411 | 1836 | Mary Catharine | 3027 |
| 1833 | Lorenzo E. | c4481 | 1866 | Marilla | 8569 | 1806 | Mary Colman | 1628 |
| 1847 | Lorenzo Goldsbury | 3201 | 1828 | Marilla | 4481 | 1838 | Mary Colman | 1814 |
| 1815 | Lorenzo Swett | 3815 | 1844 | Marion Emogene | 8189 | 1827 | Mary Delia | 1630 |
| 1877 | Lottie Alice | 3740 | 1863 | Mariou Percy | 8397 | 1839 | Mary E. | 3132 |
| 1869 | Lottie Elizabeth | 8737 | 1699 | Martua | 84 | 1859 | Mary E. | 5284 |
| 1869 | Lottie Eugene | 4982 | 1737 | Martha | 144 | 1823 | Mary Edgecomb | 3861 |
| | Louie | 3625 | 1765 | Martha | 682 | 1852 | Mary Elizabeth | 1448 |
| 1857 | Louis Buchanan | 4990 | 1801 | Martha | 1396 | 1843 | Mary Elizabeth | 1696 |
| 1800 | Louisa | 1502 | 1794 | Martha | 1415 | 1883 | Mary Elizabeth | 3067 |
| 1807 | Louisa | 2628 | | Martha | 1864 | 1821 | Mary Elizabeth | 3069 |
| 1351 | Louisa | 3671 | | Martha | 1892 | 1865 | Mary Elizabeth | 3094 |
| 1855 | Louisa Bartels | 3364 | | Martha | 2095 | 1832 | Mary Elizabeth | 4837 |
| 1875 | Louisa Doratha | 4431 | | Martha | 2145 | 1831 | Mary Elizabeth | 4527 |
| 1877 | Louise | 5000 | 1808 | Martha | 2449 | 1851 | Mary Elizabeth | 4771 |
| 1842 | Louise Milliscent | 4053 | 1801 | Martha | 2459 | 1859 | Mary Elizabeth | 5001 |
| 1785? | Lovis | 649 | 1799 | Martha | 11.841 | 1842 | Mary Elizabeth | 11,'54 |
| 1820 | Lucetta | 4085 | 1813 | Martha Ann | 2292 | 1842 | Mary Ell n | 3694 |
| 1856 | Lucia Frances | 3843 | 1872 | Martha Antoinette | 4306 | 18:1 | Mary Ellen | 4276 |
| 1808 | Lucia Maria | 2806 | 1797 | Martha Bridges | 13.18 | 1846 | Mary Ellen | 4415 |
| 1805 | Lu inda | 1627 | 1828 | Martha Bridges | 2937 | 1866 | Mary Ellen | 5345 |
| 1840 | Lucinda | 2889 | 1838 | Martha Ellen | 2368 | 1846 | Mary Emma | 4638 |
| 1842 | Lucius Hurlbert | 5021 | 183 | Martha Elvira | 4331 | 1865 | Mary Emma | 5048 |
| 1825 | Lucretia | 4572 | 1840 | Martha F. | 4398 | 1867 | Mary Etta | 4161 |
| 1848 | Lucretia Ellen | 8741 | 1822 | Martha Fickett | 3818 | 1842 | Mary F. | 3563 |
| | Lucy | 1054 | 1834 | Martha J. | 3131 | 1853 | Mary Fuller | 3558 |
| | Lucy | 1872 | 1835 | Martha Jane | 2826 | 1874 | Mary Fuller | 4855 |
| | Lucy | 2144 | 1846 | Martha Jane | 2892 | 1824 | Mary Greenleaf | 4010 |
| 1791 | Lucy | 2155 | 1868 | Martha Lenora | 4850 | 1830 | Mary Herrick | 2523 |
| 1803 | Lucy | 3801 | 1846 | Martha Maria | 11,5 0 | 1818 | Mary Holt | 4506 |
| 1810 | Lucy | 3825 | 1807 | Martha Wood | 3028 | 1831 | Mary Howe | 2961 |
| 1850 | Lucy Adaline | 4983 | | Martin | 4359 | 1878 | Mary Ina | 5224 |
| 1845 | Lucy E. | 8563 | 1857 | Martin Daniel | 5045 | 1857 | Mary Isabella | 2954 |
| 1823 | Lucy Goodale | 2979 | 1694 | Mary | 30 | | Mary J. | 2832 |
| | Lucy J. | 4071 | 1716 | Mary | 53 | 1814 | Mary Jane | 1934 |
| 1840 | Lucy Redington | 1815 | 1737 | Mary | 81 | 18:4 | Mary Jane | 2275 |
| 1820 | Lurena Carlton | 2823 | 1732 | Mary | 141 | 1820 | Mary Jane | 4223 |
| 1698 | Lydia | 33 | 1734 | Mary | 156 | 1842 | Mary Jane | 4272 |
| 1730 | Lydia | 140 | 1746 | Mary | 85: | 1853 | Mary Jane | 4450 |
| 1759 | Lydia | 292 | 1761 | Mary | 4:0 | 1827 | Mary Jane | 4895 |
| 1774 | Lydia | 412 | 1792 | Mary | 542 | 1840 | Mary L. | 2890 |
| | Lydia | 1055 | 1757 | Mary | 715 | 1851 | Mary Lavina | 5169 |
| 1810 | Lydia | 2182 | 1767 | Mary | 815 | 18:9 | Mary Louise | 5326 |
| | Lydia | 3624 | 1770 | Mary | 1089 | 1810 | Mary Lovering | 4119 |
| 1812 | Lydia Elizabeth | 2998 | 1792 | Mary | 1174 | 1835 | Mary Luvinna | 4188 |
| 1850 | Lydia Estelle Eudora | c4481 | 1806 | Mary | 1227 | 1815 | Mary Maria | 2999 |
| 1854 | Lydia May | 3984 | 1801 | Mary | 1395 | 1866 | Mary Olive | 3528 |
| 1874 | Lydia Maybelle | 3966 | 1817 | Mary | 1643 | 1840 | Mary Parmelee | 3343 |
| 1804 | Lydia Parsons | 604 | 1835 | Mary | 175 | 1833 | Mary Perkins | 11,849 |
| 1847 | Lyman Cummings | 3150 | | Mary | 1949 | 1840 | Mary Pool | 4703 |
| 1837 | Lysander | 4497 | 1798 | Mary | 1984 | 1808 | Mary Stacy | 2950 |
| | **M** | | 1804 | Mary | 1999 | 1858 | Mary Victoria | 4830 |
| 1870 | Mabel | 3685 | 1782 | Mary | 2151 | 1800 | Mary Walker | 1316 |
| 1873 | Mabel Isadore | 4535 | 1813 | Mary | 2188 | 1809 | Matilda | 2081 |
| | | | 1792 | Mary | 2194 | 1850 | Mattier Lafayette | 5168 |

| | | | | | | | | |
|---|---|---|---|---|---|---|---|---|
| 1782 | Sally | 1123 | 1844 | Sarah Frances | 4905 | 1850 | Susan Webster | 4608 |
| 1795 | Sally | 1218 | 1840 | Sarah Frances | 5264 | 1769 | Susanna | 403 |
| 1783 | Sally | 1384 | 1822 | Sarah French | 2515 | | Susanna | 2568 |
| | Sally | 1896 | 1808 | Sarah Frost | 4103 | 1836 | Susanna B. | 3961 |
| | Sally | 1916 | 1823 | Sarah Greenough | 3070 | 1763 | Susannah | 293 |
| 1796 | Sally . | 2128 | 1839 | Sarah Hun | 11,560 | 1768 | Susannah | 500 |
| 1807 | Sally | 2181 | | Sarah Jane | 4360 | 1798 | Susannah Osgood | 1410 |
| | Sally | 2421 | 1860 | Sarah Jane | 5214 | 1798 | Sylvania | 1367 |
| 1801 | Sally | 2448 | | Sarah Jane Wiggin | 720 | | | |
| 1812 | Sally | 2460 | 1819 | Sarah Maria | 3990 | | **T** | |
| | Sally | 4065 | 1859 | Sarah Minnie | 4987 | | Tenney | 2353 |
| 1819 | Sally | 4312 | 1812 | Sarah Robbins | 3593 | 1835 | Thaddeus Henry | 4372 |
| 1812 | Sally Fickett | 3814 | 1827 | Sarai Cushion | 2875 | 1838 | Theodore | 3242 |
| | Sampson | 2350 | | Serena | 3665 | 1718? | Thomas | 69 |
| 1817 | Sampson | 4147 | 1842 | Serena | 3662 | 1756? | Thomas | 384 |
| 1727 | Samuel | 139 | 1885 | Sherman Horace | 3583 | 1752 | Thomas | 686 |
| | Samuel | 261 | 1858 | Sidney Lane | 3580 | | Thomas | 946 |
| 1775 | Samuel | 429 | 1757 | Silas | 291 | | Thomas | 1009 |
| 1798 | Samuel | 543 | 1758 | Silas | 899 | 1782 | Thomas | 1343 |
| | Samuel | 1007 | 1804 | Simeon Lovering | 4100 | 1822 | Thomas | 2065 |
| | Samuel | 1020 | 1877 | Simon Harvey | 5257 | 1790 | Thomas | 2154 |
| 1791 | Samuel | 1414 | 1819 | Snell | 3876 | 1789 | Thomas | 2562 |
| 1825 | Samuel | 1647 | 1783 | Solomon | 648 | 1828 | Thomas | 3810 |
| | Samuel | 1873 | | Solomon | 952 | 1809 | Thomas | 3804 |
| | Samuel | 2299 | 1804 | Solomon | 2080 | 1824 | Thomas | 4247 |
| | Samuel | 253 | 1811 | Solomon | 2094 | 1811 | Thomas | 4481 |
| 1820 | Samuel | 2641 | | Solomon | 3621 | 1825 | Thomas Boutelle | 3017 |
| 1850 | Samuel | 3755 | 1908 | Solomon Hutchins | 2508 | 1836 | Thomas Gairdner | 2982 |
| 1834 | Samuel | 4225 | 1849 | Sophia Louisa | 4193 | 1810 | Thomas Gates | 2300 |
| 1782? | Samuel | 11,513 | | Sophronia | 2097 | 1833 | Thomas Hobbs | 4263 |
| 1793 | Samuel | 11,525 | 1817 | Sophronia | 4245 | 1848 | Thomas Jefferson | b4481 |
| 1809 | Samuel A. | 3034 | 1851 | Sophronia Baker | 4939 | 1861 | Thomas Lincoln | 4264 |
| | Samuel D. | 2656 | 1674 | Stephen | 12 | 1816 | Thomas Peabody | 2203 |
| 1822 | Samuel David | 1660 | 1704 | Stephen | 36 | 1742 | Timothy | 216 |
| 1775 | Samuel Davis | 640 | 1720 | Stephen | 55 | 1814 | Triphena T. | 4177 |
| 1802 | Samuel Davis | 603 | 1715 | Stephen | 85 | 1836 | True Remick | 4063 |
| 1845 | Samuel Davis | 1870 | 1733 | Stephen | 155 | 1777 | Trueworthy | 734 |
| 1845 | Samuel Hovey | 4604 | 1736? | Stephen | 232 | 1819 | Trueworthy | 2253 |
| 1825 | Samuel Redington | 1690 | 1750 | Stephen | 278 | | | |
| 1853 | Samuel Richard | 3410 | 1760 | Stephen | 306 | | **U** | |
| 1816 | Samuel Royal | 2252 | 1759? | Stephen | 386 | 1819 | Uzziel | 4184 |
| 1847 | Samuel Royal | 3975 | 1783 | Stephen | 441 | | | |
| 1875 | Samuel Royal | 3976 | 1770 | Stephen | 501 | | **V** | |
| 1843 | Samuel Stokes | 4805 | 1797 | Stephen | 546 | 1838 | Vallorous | 4632 |
| 1064 | Saran | 6 | 1776? | Stephen | 645 | 1810 | Valorous Morris | |
| 1706 | Sarah | 37 | 1801 | Stephen | 1067 | | Tillotson | 2807 |
| 1719 | Sarah | 70 | 1781 | Stephen | 1120 | 1806 | Volney | 2805 |
| 1793 | Sarah | 90 | 1802 | Stephen | 1226 | | | |
| 1731 | Sarah | 122 | 1796 | Stephen | 2612 | | **W** | |
| 1734 | Sarah | 123 | | Stephen | 2850 | 1855 | Wallace | 4872 |
| 1725 | Sarah | 138 | 1829 | Stephen | 2883 | | Wallace | 5089 |
| 1748 | Sarah | 164 | 1825 | Stephen | 3609 | 1860 | Walter Lawrence | 8453 |
| 1726 | Sarah | 177 | 1801 | Stephen | 11,548 | 1876 | Walter Merrill | 5329 |
| 1731? | Sarah | 231 | 1841 | Stephen Atwell | 4539 | 1874 | Walter S. | 6025 |
| 1747 | Sarah | 276 | 1829 | Stephen Augustus | 1747 | | Warren | 3042 |
| | Sarah | 279 | 1824 | Stephen Daniel | 4315 | 1875 | Warren | 3692 |
| 1752 | Sarah | 817 | 1853 | Stephen Laroy | 5258 | 1852 | Warren Violin | 4885 |
| 1796 | Sarah | 545 | 1832 | Stephen Rollo | 1749 | 1855 | Watson | 3660 |
| 1751 | Sarah | 589 | 1821 | Stillman | h4481 | 1816 | Wesson | 1491 |
| 1769 | Sarah | 735 | 1754? | Suah | 687 | 1805 | Wilbert | 4839 |
| | Sarah | 1078 | 1836 | Sumner Cummings | 4899 | 1806 | Wilder Stoddard | 2302 |
| 1783 | Sarah | 1251 | 1735? | Susan | 212 | 1826 | Willard | 4151 |
| 1786 | Sarah | 1500 | 1789? | Susan | 654 | 1841 | Willard Nelson | 1696 |
| 1809 | Sarah | 2054 | 1793 | Susan | 1302 | 1866 | Willard S. | 3687 |
| 1809 | Sarah | 2089 | 1757 | Susan | 1388 | 1864 | Willard Sylvester | 5073 |
| 1780 | Sarah | 2150 | | Susan | 1971 | 1742 | William | 183 |
| 1792 | Sarah | 2882 | 1802 | Susan | 3988 | 1807 | William | 551 |
| 1799 | Sarah | 2478 | | Susan | 3927 | 1783 | William | 591 |
| 1817 | Sarah | 4084 | 1844 | Susan | 8663 | 1782 | William | 594 |
| 1822 | Sarah | 4243 | 1816 | Susan | f4481 | 1778 | William | 646 |
| 1799 | Sarah Ann | 2314 | 1857 | Susan Abby | 5259 | 1767 | William | 668 |
| 1825 | Sarah Ann | 4254 | 1826 | Susan Abigail | 3002 | 1772 | William | 720 |
| 1851 | Sarah Ann | 4314 | 1843 | Susan Alice | 3733 | | William | 729 |
| 1835 | Sarah Ann | 4348 | 1847 | Susan C. | 3773 | 1777 | William | 950 |
| 1867 | Sarah Ann | 5220 | 1822 | Susan F. | 2084 | 1786 | William | 1173 |
| 1821 | Sarah Ann Card | 4213 | 1815 | Susan Jackman | 2785 | 1838 | William | 1715 |
| 1835 | Sarah Augusta | 4934 | 1820 | Susan Maria | 4486 | 1847 | William | 1918 |
| 1836 | Sarah Buck | 1754 | 1850 | Susan Spear | 4693 | 1816 | William | 1867 |
| 1836 | Sarah Eaton | 3916 | 1805 | Susan Sproul | 2046 | 1811 | William | 1884 |
| 1855 | Sarah Fannie | 4760 | 1848 | Susan Vyrene | 4388 | 1802 | William | 2029 |
| | | | | | | | William | 2109 |
| | | | | | | 1802 | William | 2135 |

## DESCENDANTS OF DANIEL THURSTON BEARING OTHER NAMES.

**BATTLES**
1846 Abby Foster 3038
1837 Albert Gannett 3031
1839 Charles P. 8032
1833 David Warren 8.29
1835 George Thurston 8030

**BEAG.**
1871 Charles M. 8851
1869 Florence A. 8850
1873 Jane G. 8852

**BELCHER—APP.**
Carrie Edith 11,490

**BENFIELD**
1871 Clara 4738
1869 Eric Rex 4737
1874 Ida 4739
1868 Lilly 4736

**BENSON**
1850 Hannah 2861

**BICKFORD**
1865 Charles Wilmot 4239

**BLAISDELL**
Charles T. 11,549
Daniel 11,551
Harriet 11,550
Louisa 11 553
Phebe 11,552

**BLAKE**
Ann 2631
Ellen 2634
Henry Clay 2630
Louisa 2632
Mary 2635
Samuel 2633

**BLANCHARD**
1855 Alice Benson 1745
1852 Lucy Nichols 1744
1857 Maria Woodbury 1746

**BLODGET**
1855 Albert Morrill 3440
1864 Annie Maltby 3444
1890 Benjamin Pond 3442
1857 Charlotte Ripley 3138
1822 Elizabeth 1674
1876 Frederick Swazey 8445
1831 George 1677
1836 George Howard 1679
1862 George Redington 3443
1864 Grace Howard 3441
1825 Henry 1675
1854 Henry 3437
1827 John 1676
1853 Julia Case 3139
1819 Mary Thurston 1672
1820 Sarah Ann 1673
1879 Sarah Elizabeth a3445
1834 William Stephen 1678

**BOWRING**
1877 Harriet Cornelia 8249

**BRADSTREET**
Lydia 674

**BROOKS**
1864 Bell 1595
1852 Edwin 1595
1850 Emma 1595
1873 Ida 1596

**BROWN**
1796 Aaron 2168
1826 Caroline 2164
1873 Eleanora A. 2167
1833 George H. 2167

1792 Hannah 2161
1791 Mary 2160
1830 Sewall 2166
1794 Suah 2162
1829 Suah 2165

**BRYANT**
1878 Almon 4298
1876 Clara 4896
1854 Emma 4292
1862 Etta 4295
1858 Frank 4291
1871 Herman 4297
1857 Laura A. 4293
1860 Mary 4294

**BUCK**
1847 Albert Redington 3464
1859 Augustus Walker 3480
1878 Belle Pearson a3476
1856 Carl Darling 3186
1866 Carrie Maria 3484
1837 Charlotte Elizabeth 1782
1829 Edward 1729
1827 Frank 1728
1855 Frank Swazey 3469
1862 Fred 3482
1857 George Alfred 3479
1832 Hannah Thurston 1730
1853 Harriet Elizabeth 3468
1851 Harry Hill 3467
1850 James Herbert 3481
1854 Jennie Nelson 3478
1825 John Albert 1727
1878 John Dudley 3465
1857 Joseph 3470
1860 Julia Florence 3475
1868 Kitty Clover 3485
1861 Lizzie Lane 3472
1864 Lizzie Rice 3483
1890 Lottie Linwood 3471
1853 Lucilla Pierce 3477
1824 Maria 1726
1849 Maria 3466
1835 Sarah Emeline 1731
1849 Waldo Pierce 3474
1865 Walter Darling 3473
1851 Willis Frank 3476

**BULLEN**
1805 Hannah 787
1809 Henry Martin 739
1810 Laura 740
1807 Paulina 738
1812 Samuel 741

**BURRAGE**
1874 Champlin 3047
1860 Charles Albert 3046
1840 Edwin Augustus 3049
1837 Henry Sweetser 3047
1857 Henry Thompson 3046
1834 Thomas Fairbanks 8.46
1875 Thomas Jayne 3047
1859 William Edwin 3046
1888 William Upton 3048

**CAMERON**
1849 Charles 2071
1861 Emma 2076
1863 Freddie 2077
1858 John 2078
1846 Mahala 2069
1851 Melissa Alice 2072
1866 Moses Nickerson 2078
1848 Sarah Alice 2070
1855 Thomas Thurston 2074
1857 William 2075

**CAMPBELL**
1878 Eda Maude 5105
1872 Frank Arthur 5102
1874 William Henry 5103

**CANNEY**
1878 Etta Belle 4534

**CARLETON.**
1848 Abby E. 3060
1790 Benjamin 287
1785 David 284
1846 Eliza 3059
1787 Hannah 285
1794 John 289
1788 Miner 286
1792 Paul Thurston 288
1796 Tappan 290
1850 William Abel 3061

**CASWELL**
1840 Charles Melvin 2994
1852 Ellen Maria 2997
1849 Emma Etta Mindwell 2996
1848 Herbert Eugene 2995
1854 Lottie Elizabeth 2998

**CHAFFEE**
1875 Charles Francis 4182
Charles William 4181
1832 Elvira Clarissa 4178
Emily 4179
Esther Emily 4180

**CHAPMAN**
1840 Abbie L. 3305
1807 Abigail 3301
1853 Adelaide Josephene 3330
1817 Albion Perry 3317
1873 Alger Baldwin 3306
1858 Alice Greenwood 4825
1828 Amanda 3335
1858 Annie Grace 3332
1878 Arthur B. 4176
1853 Augustine Washington 3322
1849 Augustus Faulkner 3313
1851 Clarence Eugene 3339
1850 Ebenezer Eames 3320
1831 Fordyce 3336
1836 Fordyce Granville 3303
1850 Fordyce Granville 3328
1858 George Albion 3334
1809 George Granville 3308
1844 George T. 3310
1851 Hannah Prince 3321
1826 Hannibal Greenwood 3 34
1872 Hannibal Hamlin 3307
1845 Hannibal Hamlin 3311
1813 Harriet 3315
1857 Harriet Amanda 3331
1822 Jarvis 3327
1815 Joseph Greenwood 3316
1848 Lamartine T. 3312
1866 Laura Appleton 4826
1819 Leander Thurston 3313
1845 Leander Thurston 3325
1876 Marion Eliza 3309
1811 Mary 3314
1847 Pauline Kimball 3319
1838 Sarah Elizabeth 3304
1856 Sophronia Hazen 3323
1824 Timothy Appleton 3333
1862 Timothy Hannibal 3326
1876 William 1610
1841 William Chalmers 3306

| | | |
|---|---|---|
| 1826 | Edmund Bostwick | 889 |
| | Edwin Upton | 3055 |
| 1840 | Hattie Adoresta | 895 |
| | Henry Clifford | 3055 |
| 1819 | James Harvey | 885 |
| 1824 | John Thurston | 888 |
| 1834 | Lorena Allen | 893 |
| 1882 | Louisa Rebecca | 892 |
| | Martha Gertrude | 3055 |
| | Nelson O. | 3055 |
| 1821 | Palmira Leach | 886 |
| 1823 | Sally | 887 |
| 1838 | William Henry | 894 |

**CUTLER**

| | | |
|---|---|---|
| 1°56 | Addie Ellen | 5013 |
| 1858 | Edna Carrie | 5014 |
| 1850 | Fayette Tower | 5011 |
| 1858 | Flora Emma | 5012 |

**DAILEY**

| | | |
|---|---|---|
| 1830 | Amanda Malvina | 4141 |
| 1833 | Julietta Walker | 4142 |

**DANIELS**

| | | |
|---|---|---|
| 1848 | Mary Ellen | 2746 |

**DAVIS**

| | | |
|---|---|---|
| | Anna Isadore | 1119 |
| | George Henry | 4505 |
| | George Ransom | 1119 |
| | Sarah Keziah | 1119 |
| | William | 593 |

**DAY**

| | | |
|---|---|---|
| 1875 | Annie Gertrude | 3561 |
| 1861 | Emma C. | 4400 |
| 1848 | Eva | c4402 |
| 1872 | Frank Sawyer | 3559 |
| 1870 | Grace | d4402 |
| 1874 | Mabel Dennison | 3560 |
| 1860 | Mary E. | a4402 |
| 1863 | Melvina | b4402 |
| 1859 | Sumner C. | 4399 |

**DEAN**

| | | |
|---|---|---|
| 1874 | Carrol Edward | 1578 |
| 1863 | Chester Colman | 1574 |
| 1834 | Clarissa Thurston | 1587 |
| 1875 | Edwin Leroy | 4196 |
| 1869 | Elmore Williams | 1577 |
| 1864 | James Sumner | 1575 |
| 1880 | James William | 1573 |
| 1872 | Minora May | 4195 |
| 1832 | Sarah Colman | 1580 |
| 1876 | Susan Clara | 1579 |
| 1877 | Walter Harrison | 4197 |
| 1867 | William Allen | 1576 |
| 1868 | William Denison | 4194 |

**DEANE**

| | | |
|---|---|---|
| 1853 | Ada | 3381 |
| 1868 | Alice Harriet | 3382 |
| 1850 | Sarah Shepard | 3380 |

**DEARBORN**

| | | |
|---|---|---|
| 1842 | Henry | 3991 |
| 1847 | Sarah Ellen | 3992 |

**DELA**

| | | |
|---|---|---|
| 1844 | Lewis | 2401 |

**DEMERITT**

| | | |
|---|---|---|
| 1852 | Edgar Frank | 4382 |

**DEXTER**

| | | |
|---|---|---|
| | Abigail | 2698 |
| 1806 | Alonzo | 2716 |
| 1869 | Alston B. | 2618 |
| | Amanda F. | 2688 |
| 1808 | Amasa | 2708 |
| | Arianna | 2734 |
| 1816 | Betsey | 2780 |

| | | |
|---|---|---|
| 1864 | Carrie A. | 2621 |
| | Charles | 2728 |
| | Charles | 2728 |
| 1812 | Charles S. | 2727 |
| 1851 | Clara E. | 2680 |
| 1864 | Daniel | 2683 |
| | Drusilla | 2700 |
| | Ellen | 2705 |
| | Emeline Trufant | 2684 |
| 1837 | Emily | 2704 |
| | Emma Jane | 2717 |
| 1874 | Ernest | 2622 |
| | Everett | 2719 |
| 1877 | Everett Elwood | 26?8 |
| 1798 | Freeman | 2695 |
| 1856 | George | 2681 |
| 1857 | George A. | 2616 |
| 1839 | George Monroe | 2706 |
| | George W. | 2721 |
| 1808 | Gideon | 2720 |
| 1810 | Hannah | 2724 |
| | Harrison | 2679 |
| 1861 | Hattie E. | 2617 |
| | Ira L. T. | 2619 |
| 1797 | Irving | 2694 |
| | Isaiah | 2614 |
| | Julia | 2696 |
| | Lemuel | 2722 |
| 1806 | Louisa | 2712 |
| | Lucilla | 2708 |
| | Lucy Ann | 2718 |
| 1804 | Mary | 2711 |
| | Mary E. | 2624 |
| | Mary Jane | 2609 |
| 1814 | Meribah | 2729 |
| 1795 | Nathaniel | 2678 |
| 1860 | Nathaniel G. | 2682 |
| | Reuel | 2701 |
| | Roansa | 2735 |
| | Samuel | 2697 |
| 1856 | Sarah | 2615 |
| | Scott | 2710 |
| | Stephen Alston | 2736 |
| 1819 | Stephen T. | 2733 |
| 1800 | Sumner | 2702 |
| 1851 | Wesley | 2707 |
| | Wilbor | 2709 |
| 1860 | Willard M. | 2620 |

**DINSMORE**

| | | |
|---|---|---|
| 1862 | Frank Thurston | 1561 |
| 1857 | George S. | 1559 |
| 1874 | Louis | 1563 |
| 1860 | Lucy Colman | 1560 |
| 1863 | Robert | 1562 |

**DOBLE**

| | | |
|---|---|---|
| | Gracie | 2876 |

**DODGE**

| | | |
|---|---|---|
| 1871 | Albert Henry | 11,572 |
| 1875 | Freddie Gaston | 11,573 |
| 1869 | Minnie Etta | 11 571 |

**DOLE**

| | | |
|---|---|---|
| | Frederick N. | 11,838 |
| | Martha E. | 11,839 |
| | Thaddeus P. | 11,837 |

**DORT**

| | | |
|---|---|---|
| | Ausian Mansfield | 1506 |
| | Hattie Maria | 1504 |
| | Helen Laura | 1505 |
| 1828 | Joseph Hartley | 1507 |
| 1831 | Mary Louisa | 1508 |
| 1819 | Sarah French | 1503 |

**DOYLE**

| | | |
|---|---|---|
| | Abraham | 664 |
| | Felix | 665 |
| | Martha | 666 |
| | Sally | 667 |
| | William | 663 |

**DURANT**

| | | |
|---|---|---|
| 1857 | Freddie Martin | 3024 |
| 1855 | George Henry | 3023 |
| 1862 | Walter | 3025 |
| 1862 | Willie | 3026 |

**DURGIN**

| | | |
|---|---|---|
| 1856 | Alonzo | 4353 |
| 1866 | Alonzo Edwin | 4356 |
| 1859 | Edwin | 4354 |
| 1862 | Emma Jane | 4355 |
| 1852 | Martha Francenia | 4352 |

**EASTON**

| | | |
|---|---|---|
| 1879 | Frank (p. 503) | c9391 |

**ELLIOT**

| | | |
|---|---|---|
| 1809 | Elijah Parish | 524 |
| 1817 | Matthew Pearson | 525 |

**ELLIS**

| | | |
|---|---|---|
| 1860 | Abbie Ann | 4261 |
| 1849 | Amanda Jane | 4258 |
| 1855 | Charles Sumner | 4260 |
| | Clara Spofford | 1306 |
| | Clara Thurston | 1307 |
| 1852 | Ellen Frances | 4259 |
| | George | 1304 |
| | Julia Ann | 1305 |
| | Susan | 1303 |
| 1868 | Thomas | 4262 |

**ESTABROOK**

| | | |
|---|---|---|
| 1798 | Alvan | 2799 |
| 1800 | John | 2800 |
| 1809 | Joseph | 2804 |
| 1797 | Porter | 2798 |
| 1807 | Porter | 2803 |
| 1805 | Theoda | 2802 |

**FALES**

| | | |
|---|---|---|
| 1847 | Mary | 8347 |
| 1843 | Nathaniel | 3345 |
| 1845 | Sarah Ozetta | 8846 |

**FARRAR**

| | | |
|---|---|---|
| 1854 | Alexis Walter | 2525 |
| 1865 | Alice Eugenia | b2526 |
| 1862 | Estella Etta | a2526 |
| 1852 | Grace Greenwood | 2524 |
| 1861 | Lauriston Everett | 2526 |
| 1868 | Liston Alverdo | c2526 |

**FARWELL**

| | | |
|---|---|---|
| 1780 | Abel | 372 |
| 1774 | Abram | 370 |
| 1818 | Asa Thurston | 1860 |
| | Curtis | 330 |
| 1843 | Edward P. | 1862 |
| 1825 | Elizabeth Hannah | 1846 |
| 1831 | Elizabeth Mersilvia | 1347 |
| 1812 | Hannah | 1857 |
| 1770 | Hepzibah | 368 |
| 1846 | Jane Todd | 1853 |
| 1833 | John A. | 1848 |
| 1803 | John Thurston | 1845 |
| 1787 | Joseph | 375 |
| 1777 | Josiah | 371 |
| 1784 | Levi | 374 |
| 1807 | Lydia Elizabeth Thurston | 1855 |
| 1838 | Maria Thurston | 1350 |
| 1840 | Mary Jane | 1351 |
| 1816 | Matilda B. | 1389 |
| 1820 | Mebitable W. | 1351 |
| 1782 | Merriam | 373 |
| 1772 | Samuel | 369 |
| 1814 | Sarah | 1358 |
| 1836 | Sarah C. | 1349 |
| 1805 | Stephen Thurston | 1354 |
| 1809 | Thomas Thurston | 1356 |

**HIGGINS**

| 1866 | Freddie Eugene | 2888 |
|---|---|---|

**HILL**

| 1844 | Henry Newell | 4487 |
| 1854 | James Thurston | 4491 |
| 1851 | Jane Eliza | 4490 |
| 1846 | Jason Abbott | 4488 |
| 1850 | Susan Ellen | 4489 |

**HILTON**

| | Betsey | 818 |
| | Daniel | 325 |
| 1818 | Hannah | 820 |
| | Joseph | 824 |
| | Mehitable | 821 |
| | Nathaniel | 827 |
| 1772 | Sally | 819 |
| | Stephen | 823 |
| | Theodore | 326 |
| | Winthrop | 828 |

**HINCKS**

| 1872 | Annie Hart | 3429 |
| 1979 | Annie Perry | 3427 |
| 1869 | Edward Baldwin | 3423 |
| 1-44 | Edward Young | 3426 |
| 1846 | Enoch Pond | 3428 |
| 1875 | Henry Winslow | 3430 |
| 1856 | Jane Isabel | 3432 |
| 1849 | John Howard | 3431 |
| 1879 | Percy Thurston | a3431 |
| 1875 | Robert Stanley | 3425 |
| 1841 | William Bliss | 3422 |
| 1870 | William Thurston | 3424 |

**HOBART**

| 1826 | Daniel Franklin | 1180 |
| 1821 | Elizabeth | 1177 |
| 1829 | George Fargo | 1182 |
| 1831 | Hannah Wright | 1183 |
| 1818 | Huldah | 1175 |
| 1833 | Joel Williams | 1184 |
| 1824 | Martha Jane | 1179 |
| 1822 | Mary | 1178 |
| 1828 | Sextus | 1181 |
| 1319 | Warren | 1176 |

**HODGDON**

| 1860 | Charlie Merrill | 3932 |
| 1835 | George Morey | 3931 |
| 1832 | Hiram | 3930 |
| 1838 | Sarah Eaton | 3933 |

**HOLBROOK**

| | Abbie Jane | 2864 |
| | Cyrus Delmont | 2863 |

**HOPKINSON**

| 1806 | Deborah Thurston | 750 |
| 1800 | Dolly Scribner | 747 |
| 1799 | Hannah | 746 |
| 1804 | Harriet | 749 |
| 1797? | Joseph | 745 |
| 1807 | Lucy Dana | 751 |
| 1795 | Noyes | 744 |
| 1798? | Samuel | 743 |
| 1802 | Sarah Thurston | 748 |

**HORNE**

| 1850 | Charles Albert | 2534 |
| 1845 | Charles William | 2532 |
| 1847 | Fanny Sarah | 2533 |
| 1852 | George Allen | 2535 |
| 1843 | Georgianna Emma | 2531 |
| 1841 | Gustavus Henry | 2530 |
| 1855 | John Edwin | 2536 |
| 1861 | Susan Alice | 2537 |

**HOUSE**

| 1871 | Elwood Horace | 4557 |

**HOYER**

| 1876 | Francis | 1609 |
| 1876 | Martin | 1609 |

**HUBBARD**

| 1878 | Alice Jeanette | 5268 |
| 1875 | Amy Louise | 5269 |

**HUMPHREY**

| 1871 | Mary | 3394 |

**HUNTOON**

| 1858 | Albert | 846 |
| 1789 | Ariel | 840 |
| 1851 | Ariel Augustus | 838 |
| 1816 | Augustus Pingry | 844 |
| 1813 | Eudosia Dorothy | 843 |
| 1800 | Harvey | 852 |
| 1848 | Ira McLaughlin | 856 |
| 1847 | Lemira Janett | 857 |
| 1851 | Mary | 845 |
| 1839 | Mary Augusta | 849 |
| | Ora Morse | 855 |
| 1809 | Parmenas | 841 |
| 1836 | Ransom | 854 |
| 1810 | Ransom | 860 |
| 1794 | Reuel | 851 |
| 1832 | Reuel | 838 |
| 1805 | Roxana | 859 |
| 1811 | Sylvanus | 842 |
| 1791 | Tryphena | 850 |
| 1847 | Tryphena Ruth | 847 |
| 1882 | William Philo | 848 |

**HUNTRESS**

| 1849 | Albert Bridge | 2772 |
| 1842 | Charles Walker | 2769 |
| 1840 | Clara Ann | 2768 |
| 1846 | Francis Edson | 2771 |
| 1844 | George Hervey | 2770 |
| 1838 | John Emery | 2767 |
| 1827 | William Augustus | 2766 |

**HURD**

| 1786 | Anna | 782 |
| 1787 | Asenath | 783 |
| 1788 | Lydia | 781 |
| 1795 | Lydia | 788 |
| 1796 | Lydia | 790 |
| 1790 | Parmenas | 786 |
| 1801 | Paulina | 791 |
| 1798 | Ruel | 789 |
| 1789 | Samuel | 785 |
| 1792 | Samuel | 787 |

**INGRAHAM**

| 1865 | Annie Belle | 2107 |
| | Benjamin | 1264 |
| | Caroline | 1268 |
| | Caroline | 1285 |
| | Charles | 1287 |
| 1857 | Edwin | 2102 |
| 1807 | Elizabeth Thurston | 1262 |
| 1868 | Enos Eugene | 2106 |
| | Henry | 1264 |
| 1805 | James Milk | 1261 |
| 1861 | Job Washburn | 2105 |
| | John Phillips Thurston | 1266 |
| 1809 | Joseph Holt | 1268 |
| | Josephene | 1268 |
| | Julia | 1268 |
| | Louisa | 1263 |
| 1855 | Nancy Jeannette | 2101 |
| 1872 | Ralph | 2103 |
| 1858 | Sarah | 2103 |
| | Sargent | 1268 |
| | William | 1264 |

**IRVING**

| 1854 | Edson E. | 2690 |
| | Emma | 2698½ |

| 1856 | Flora | 2691 |
| 1862 | Frank | 2689 |
| 1861 | Minnie | 2693 |
| 1858 | William | 2692 |

**JEWETT**

| 1851 | Ansel | 2855 |
| | David | 486 |
| 1855 | Emma Jessie | 2857 |
| | Eunice | 488 |
| 18 7 | Frank Rowley | 2858 |
| | Henry C. | 473 |
| 1864 | Howard Leslie | 2859 |
| | John | 489 |
| 1847 | Marcellus | 2853 |
| | Mary | 474 |
| 1849 | Maxie | 2854 |
| | Phebe | 485 |
| | Sarah | 487 |
| 1853 | Sumner | 2856 |

**JONES**

| 1877 | Ada Helen | 2650 |

**JORDAN**

| 1835 | John Henry | a4478 |

**KEELER—APP.**

| 1862 | Jessie Almira | 11,481 |
| 1864 | Mary Elizabeth | 11,481 |
| 1857 | Oscar Hibbard | 11,481 |

**KELLEY**

| 1867 | Grace Gertrude | 5267 |

**KELSEY**

| 1866 | Alice Cornelia | 1584 |
| 1862 | Archibald Rodell | 1583 |
| 1870 | Clara Dean | 1585 |
| 1858 | Frank Chester | 1582 |
| 1854 | James Munroe | 1581 |
| 1873 | Sarah Malvina | 1586 |

**KENNISON**

| | Asenath | 2434 |
| | Daniel | 2435 |
| | Elmon | 2444 |
| | Henry | 2442 |
| | Isaac | 2437 |
| | Ivory | 2436 |
| | John | 2440 |
| | Mary | 2443 |
| | Melvina | 2439 |
| | Oliver | 2441 |
| | Susan | 2438 |

**KILBORN**

| 1742 | Daniel | 71 |

**KIMBALL**

| | Benjamin | 1288 |
| | Eliza | 1284 |
| | Ellen | 1286 |
| | Leonard | 1287 |
| | Thurston | 1285 |

**KIMBLE**

| 1859 | Ellen M. | 1611 |
| 1867 | Fanny Colman | 1609 |
| 1874 | Flora May | 1611 |
| 1871 | Frank S. | 1611 |
| 1861 | John E. | 1611 |
| 1877 | Lucy | 1611 |
| 1856 | Mary L. | 1610 |
| 1864 | William Colman | 1611 |

**KING**

| | Alburtus Rice | 2685 |
| | Emogene Crowell | 2687 |
| | Eva Arletta | 2686 |

**NOBLE**

| | | |
|---|---|---|
| 1864 | Walter Herbert | 4581 |

**NOURSE**

| | | |
|---|---|---|
| 1848 | Mary Susan | 993 |
| 1832 | Nathaniel Thurston | 992 |
| 1847 | Sarah Elizabeth | 994 |

**NOYES**

| | | |
|---|---|---|
| 1801 | Edna Adams | 1098 |
| 1799 | Elizabeth Wyatt | 1092 |
| 1832 | Huldah | 4578 |
| 1795 | James | 1090 |
| 1797 | Jane | 1091 |
| | Judith Stickney | 1094 |
| 1806 | Nicholas Moody | 1095 |
| | Phebe Thurston | 490 app. |
| | Rev. Randall | 491 app. |

**NUTE**

| | | |
|---|---|---|
| 1878 | Lillian Alice | 5210 |

**NUTTING**

| | | |
|---|---|---|
| 1842 | Ann Jane Morrill | 2845 |
| 1846 | Frank Thurston | 2846 |
| 1838 | Horatio Nelson | 2843 |
| 1848 | Jerome Jewett | 2847 |
| 1840 | Marcellus Albert | 2844 |
| 1852 | Mary Elizabeth | 2848 |

**OSBORNE**

| | | |
|---|---|---|
| 1804 | Abram | 382 |
| 1794 | Ephraim | 380 |
| 1787 | Hepzibah B. | 377 |
| 1792 | John | 379 |
| 1790 | Lydia K. | 378 |
| 1801 | Miriam | 381 |

**OSGOOD**

| | | |
|---|---|---|
| 1852 | Benjamin Binney | 3075 |
| 1846 | Clara Call | 3071 |
| 1864 | Edward Tufts | 3081 |
| 1854 | Emily Call | 3077 |
| 1857 | Frederick Huntington | 3078 |
| 1847 | George | 3072 |
| 1851 | John Gardner | 3074 |
| 1861 | Mary Florence | 3080 |
| 1853 | Samuel Call | 3076 |
| 1859 | Walter Griffith | 3079 |
| 1849 | William Thurston | 3073 |

**PALMER**

| | | |
|---|---|---|
| | Aaron | 2725 |
| | Mary E. | 2725 |

**PARKER**

| | | |
|---|---|---|
| 1875 | George Gilman | 1329 |
| 1877 | Herbert Chandler | 1330 |

**PAUL**

| | | |
|---|---|---|
| 1845 | Dealbea Osca | 2247 |
| 1849 | William | 2248 |

**PEABODY**

| | | |
|---|---|---|
| 1865 | Ada Louise | 3269 |
| 1871 | Francis Richardson | 3272 |
| 1866 | Henry Asa | 3270 |
| 1864 | Mary Gertrude | 3268 |
| 1869 | William Welcome | 3271 |

**PEARSON**

| | | |
|---|---|---|
| 1689 | Abigail | 18 |
| 1706? | Bartholomew | 26 |
| 1690 | Benjamin | 19 |
| | Charles | 1819 |
| 1832 | Charles S. | 1321 |
| 1684 | Daniel | 16 |
| 1796? | Daniel | 504 |
| | Daniel | 1819 |
| 1830 | Daniel Thurston | 1820 |

| | | |
|---|---|---|
| 1702 | David | 24 |
| 1780 | Elizabeth | 526 |
| | Gertrude | 1818 |
| | Grace | 1819 |
| 1681 | Hannah | 14 |
| 1785 | Hannah | 531 |
| | Harriet | 506 |
| | Henry | 505 |
| | Henry | 509 |
| | Ida | 1318 |
| 1694 | Jedediah | 21 |
| 1791 | John | 582 |
| 1699 | Jonathan | 28 |
| 1822 | Laburton | 1318 |
| | Louisa | 5 3 |
| | Louise | 1819 |
| 1794 | Luther | 503 |
| 1833 | Martha A. C. | 1328 |
| 1834 | Mary Thurston | 1822 |
| 1695 | Mehitable | 22 |
| 1783 | mehitable | 527 |
| | Nydra | 1819 |
| 1704 | Oliver | 25 |
| 1682 | Phebe | 15 |
| | Phebe | 503 |
| | Richard | 506 |
| 1687 | Ruth | 17 |
| 1776 | Ruth | 522 |
| | Samuel | 507 |
| 1691 | Sarah | 20 |
| | Sarah | 508 |
| 1778 | Sarah | 523 |
| 1820 | Sarah W. | 1317 |
| | Susan | 508 |
| 1798? | William | 505 |
| | William | 506 |
| | William | 1819 |
| 1825 | William Henry | 1819 |

**PERKINS**

| | | |
|---|---|---|
| 1823 | Martha | 11,836 |

**PHELPS**

| | | |
|---|---|---|
| 1837 | Edward Douglass | 8940 |

**PHILBRICK**

| | | |
|---|---|---|
| 1806 | Anna McKenstry | 867 |
| 1794 | Betsey Eliza | 863 |
| 1811 | Diah | 868 |
| 1798 | Dorothy | 865 |
| 1816 | Emily Bingham | 869 |
| 1801 | Lua | 866 |
| 1796 | Samuel | 864 |

**PHILBROOK**

| | | |
|---|---|---|
| 1854 | Charles | 3349 |
| 1856 | Ella | 3350 |
| 1846 | Francis Thurston | 3347 |
| 1859 | Harriet | 6351 |
| 1848 | William Thomas | 3848 |

**PHILLIPS**

| | | |
|---|---|---|
| | Ivers | 1886 |
| | Sally | 1385 |

**PIERCE**

| | | |
|---|---|---|
| 1851 | Harvey Thomas | 2061 |
| 1846 | Hollis Loring | 2059 |
| 1849 | Ida Ella | 2060 |
| 1870 | James Wilson | 5275 |
| 1844 | Mahale Thurston | 2058 |
| 1841 | Susan Elizabeth | 2057 |
| 1839 | Thomas Warren | 2056 |

**PIKE**

| | | |
|---|---|---|
| | Job | 11,517 |
| | John | 11,518 |
| | Simon | 11,519 |

**POND**

| | | |
|---|---|---|
| 1844 | Mary Bliss | 3421 |

**PRESCOTT**

| | | |
|---|---|---|
| 1873 | Roscoe Edwin (p. 500) | 3929 |

**PUTNAM**

| | | |
|---|---|---|
| | Ann Maria | 3068 |
| | Charles Benjamin | 3053 |
| | Daniel Cowdin | 3068 |
| | Frank Porter | 3053 |
| | Frederic Adams | 3053 |
| | James Edward | 3053 |
| | Thomas Farrington | 3053 |
| | Walter Herbert | 3053 |
| | William Sweetser | 3053 |

**RAND**

| | | |
|---|---|---|
| 1828 | Charles Henry | 2297 |
| 1831 | Ellen Elizabeth | 2298 |

**RAYMOND**

| | | |
|---|---|---|
| 1845 | Luman | 3008 |
| 1845 | Lyman | 3004 |
| 1849 | Mary Abbie | 3005 |

**REED**

| | | |
|---|---|---|
| 1871 | Helen | 3832 |
| 1862 | Ida M. | 3831 |

**RICH**

| | | |
|---|---|---|
| | Allura | 2715 |
| | David | 2731 |
| | John L. | 2714 |
| | Louisa | 2732 |

**RICHARDS**

| | | |
|---|---|---|
| 1878 | Effie Jane | 4455 |
| 1876 | Ernest Irving | 4454 |
| 1875 | Harry Wilbur | 4451 |
| 1878 | Rosetta Mary | 4452 |

**RICHARDSON**

| | | |
|---|---|---|
| 1829 | Amos Thurston | 2000 |
| | Clara | 2004 |
| 1877 | Frank Linden | 3215 |
| | Frederick | 2002 |
| 1887 | Henry Brown | 3263 |
| 1876 | John | 3266 |
| 1883 | John Francis | 3261 |
| 1887 | Mabel Wolcott | 3262 |
| | Mary Ann | 2003 |
| 1841 | Mary Elizabeth | 3267 |
| 1878 | Mary Wolcott | 3965 |
| 1871 | Thomas Farrar | 3264 |
| | William | 2601 |

**RING**

| | | |
|---|---|---|
| | Abijah | 306 |
| | Daniel | 313 |
| | Iphaliah | 309 |
| | Rebecca | 310 |
| | Sally | 311 |
| | Stephen | 312 |

**ROBARDS**

| | | |
|---|---|---|
| 1831 | Esther | 2126 |
| 1828 | George | 2123 |
| 1824 | Henry | 2134 |
| 1827 | Laura | 2125 |
| 1821 | Lucy | 2122 |
| 1817 | Mary | 2121 |
| 1836 | William | 2127 |

**ROGERS**

| | | |
|---|---|---|
| | Hester Ann | 1603 |
| | Mary Jane | 1603 |
| 1872 | Stephen Thurston | 1753 |
| 1868 | William Thurston | 1752 |

**ROUNDY**

| | | |
|---|---|---|
| 1872 | Nellie Lillian | 3208 |

**RUNDLETT**

| | | |
|---|---|---|
| 1870 | Maud Noble | 4585 |

**RUSSELL**

| | | |
|---|---|---|
| 1831 | Ellen | 2049 |
| 1851 | Hannah | 2052 |
| 1841 | Mahala | 2051 |
| 1-37 | Margaret Ann | 2050 |
| 1845 | Mary Elizabeth | 2057 |
| 1829 | Rachel Ann | 2048 |

## PERSONS WHO HAVE MARRIED DESCENDANTS OF DANIEL THURSTON OF NEWBURY.

The dates at left of names denote the time of marriage, when known; the number at end of name, the number of the person married.

35

| | | | | | | |
|---|---|---|---|---|---|---|
| 1807 | Upton Joseph | 1888 | | Welch Henry | 611 | 1852 Willis Wm. Wallace 4188 |
| 1807 | Upton Mehitable | 884 | 1841 | Welch Jeremy Paul | 4087 | 1877 Wills George 1589 |

**V**

| | | |
|---|---|---|
| | Varney Elizabeth | 4477 |
| | Verrill John | 1950 |
| 1842 | Vining Sally | 4148 |
| 1866 | Vose Amelia F. | 8044 |

**W**

| | | |
|---|---|---|
| | Wadleigh George A. | 3713 |
| | Walbridge John | 4170 |
| 1871 | Walker Alman | 4654 |
| 1868 | Walker Augustus Hall | 1698 |
| | Walker David | 1800 |
| 1771 | Walker Edward | 125 |
| 1771 | Walker Dea. Richard | 852 |
| | Walton Edward | 1597 |
| 1871 | Waltz Granville Otis | 4616 |
| 1828 | Ward Charles | 1930 |
| 1845 | Ward Erastus | 2451 |
| 1846 | Wardwell A. E. | 1119 |
| 1866 | Wardwell James | 4560 |
| | Ware Philemon | 11,526 |
| 1815 | Warren Aurelia | 2294 |
| 1874 | Warren Bernice Babbidge | 4860 |
| 1867 | Warren Calvin (p. 500) | 8790 |
| 1874 | Warren Leander D. | 8902 |
| | Warren Martin V. | 1995 |
| 1872 | Warren Nora | 5011 |
| 1784 | Warren Thomas | 65 |
| 1846 | Waterhouse Hannah Gorham | 8816 |
| 1854 | Waterhouse Sarah E. | 8878 |
| 1858 | Waters Mary Louisa | 1647 |
| 1828 | Watson Hale | 2449 |
| 1807 | Watson Ithamar | 1126 |
| | Weatherspoon Mrs. Ella A. (Carver) | 8774 |
| | Weatherspoon Jas. | 2096 |
| 1868 | Weaver Francis Marion | 11,501 |
| 1856 | Webb Martha Jane | 4899 |
| 1780 | Webster Betsey | 368 |
| | Webster Frank P. | 8773 |
| | Webster James | 527 |
| | Webster Joseph | 62 |
| 1858 | Webster Martha Thurston | 8930 |
| | Webster Mary | 8621 |
| | Webster Sullivan | 1962 |
| | Webster Thomas | 860 |
| | Wedgwood Drusilla | 2491 |

| | | |
|---|---|---|
| | Welch Lydia | 2493 |
| 1846 | Welch Rachel Fisher | 2253 |
| | Weld Charles | 2889 |
| | Weld Esther | 2883 |
| | Wells Amasa | 812 |
| 1839 | Wells George W. | 803 |
| 1846 | Wells Homer | 805 |
| 1846 | Wells John T. | 876 |
| 1837 | Wescott Lydia C. | 4481 |
| 1814 | West Mary | 2298 |
| 1864 | Weston Isaac Franklin | 4668 |
| 1869 | Weston Sophia R. | 4665 |
| | Wetherbee Benj. | 1887 |
| 1846 | Wheeler Allison | 2930 |
| 1871 | Wheeler John | 4023 |
| | Wheeler Otis H. | 4146 |
| 1872 | Whiffin Fred Jas. | 1193 |
| | Whipple Josiah | 2884 |
| | Whitcomb Parmenas | 790 |
| 1868 | White Addie Milici | 8715 |
| | White George A. | 4632 |
| 1854 | Whitehead Alonzo | 807 |
| 1869 | Whitehead Em'line | 11,482 |
| 1871 | Whitmarsh Carrie A. | 8975 |
| 1851 | Whitney Charles Robinson | 8861 |
| 1786 | Whitney Eunice | 143 |
| 1859 | Whitney Mary Baldwin | 4001 |
| 1852 | Whitten Elisha Merritt | 2057 |
| 1846 | Whitten Hannah Hubbard | 4815 |
| 1861 | Whittier Rev. Chas. | 1756 |
| 1825 | Whorf William | 1929 |
| | Wight Persis | 1444 |
| 1784 | Wiggin Betsey | 306 |
| | Wiggin Betsey | 985 |
| 1860 | Wiggin Geo. Wash'n | 986 |
| 1856 | Wiggin Jennie | 2508 |
| | Wiggin Jonathan | 72 |
| 1850 | Wiggin Mary | 1135 |
| | Wiggin Mrs. Phebe | 50 |
| | Wiggin Simon | 718 |
| | Wiggin — | 815 |
| 1799 | Wiggins Anne | 781 |
| | Wilbur — | 5081 |
| 1348 | Wiley Betsey M. | 2351 |
| | Wilkinson Ambrose | 4850 |
| 1868 | Williams Emma J. | 1612 |
| 1866 | Williams Frank T. | 4674 |
| | Williams — | 504 |
| 1848 | Willis Louisa C. | 3052 |

| | | |
|---|---|---|
| | Wills Orris | 2611 |
| 1819 | Wilmarth Philander | 1590 |
| | Wilson Henry | 1305 |
| | Wilson James | 3624 |
| | Wing Rufus | 2704 |
| 1782 | Wingate Jane | 61 |
| 1862 | Winship Susan Matilda | 4238 |
| 1864 | Winslow Julia C. | 1808 |
| 1864 | Winslow Oscar Fitzgerald | 11,485 |
| 1865 | Winslow Roscoe Greene | 11,588 |
| | Winn William | 1896 |
| 1874 | Winnie Jacob Percy | 4790 |
| | Witham Leonard O. | 4573 |
| | Witham — | 2232 |
| | Withee Leslie | 4468 |
| 1869 | Wonson Wm. Lamson | 2746 |
| 1858 | Wood Ann Eliza | 809 |
| 1855 | Wood Charles | 1698 |
| | Wood Clara | 1844 |
| 1782 | Wood Esther | 835 |
| 1844 | Wood Harriet | 802 |
| | Wood Lucy | 60 |
| | Wood P. M. B. | 2805 |
| 1787 | Wood Polly | 778 |
| 1797 | Wood Polly | 861 |
| | Wood Sarah | 67 |
| 1850 | Wood Sarah | 1444 |
| 1874 | Woodard Dennison J. | 3856 |
| 1707 | Woodbury Elizabeth | 8 |
| | Woodfall John | 607 |
| 1732 | Woodman Dorothy | 29 |
| 1854 | Woodruff Mary Jane | 3062 |
| 1830 | Woodward Lucy | 2716 |
| 1809 | Woodward Sarah | 1151 |
| 1867 | Woodward W. A. | 1530 |
| | Woodworth Chas. | 11,495 |
| 1826 | Worcester Hannah | 501 |
| 1829 | Works Jane | 4070 |
| | Wright Abbie | 2109 |
| 1877 | Wright Ethelinda | 4190 |
| 1853 | Wright Orville | 1557 |

**Y**

| | | |
|---|---|---|
| | York Edwin | 1862 |
| | York Mary Jane | 1962 |
| 1849 | Young David | 2482 |
| 1873 | Young Hugh | 1661 |
| | Young Lewis | 4298 |
| 1843 | Young William H. | 2815 |

Page 248, no. 5127, Hattie Edda Thurston m. Feb. 12, 1880, by Rev. J. C. Clark of the Methodist church, assisted by Rev. Asa Dalton of the Episcopal church, Portland, Me., Herbert Grignon Starr, b. July 17, 1855, son of George Herbert [British vice consul] and Ellen (Goodwin) Starr of Portland. They both graduated from the Portland high school in 1874. He went to sea in the merchant service and was twice shipwrecked. His friends persuaded him to leave the sea, and he went to Ohio in the railroad service, and in 1878 formed a copartnership with Ed. S. Everett formerly of Portland, and is now engaged in the druggist and apothecary business in Wellington, Ohio, under the firm name of Everett & Starr.

# DESCENDANTS OF EDWARD THURSTON,

## BEARING THE NAME OF THURSTON.

| No. | Name | Ref. |
|---|---|---|
| 1617 | Edward | 5501 |
| 1652 | Edward | 5504 |
| 1678 | Edward | 5526 |
| 1679 | Edward | 5538 |
| 1698 | Edward | 5599 |
| 1696 | Edward | 5604 |
| 1696 | Edward | 5629 |
| 1702 | Edward | 5642 |
| 1748 | Edward | 5677 |
| 1719 | Edward | 5701 |
| 1729 | Edward | 5722 |
| 1758 | Edward | 5735 |
| 1779 | Edward | 5736 |
| 1724 | Edward | 5760 |
| 1782 | Edward | 5812 |
| 1759 | Edward | 5837 |
| 1753 | Edward | 5842 |
| 1756 | Edward | 5844 |
| 1740 | Edward | 5859 |
| 1766 | Edward | 5892 |
| 1830 | Edward | 6106 |
|  | Edward | 6113 |
| 1778 | Edward | 6175 |
| 1766 | Edward | 6240 |
| 1804 | Edward | 6590 |
| 1820 | Edward | 6741 |
| 1810 | Edward | 6794 |
| 1789 | Edward | 6866 |
|  | Edward Anthony | 7347 |
| 1790 | Edward Champlin | 6129 |
| 1874 | Edward Coppée | 6657 |
| 1851 | Edward Day | 6652 |
| 1837 | Edward Gardner | 6361 |
| 1812 | Edward Henry | 6492 |
| 1849 | Edward Henry | 7375 |
| 1874 | Edward Henry | 7949 |
| 1832 | Edward Mason | 7418 |
| 1831 | Edward North | 7285 |
| 1866 | Edward North | 7934 |
| 1861 | Edward North | 7944 |
| 1876 | Edward Sampson | 6630 |
| 1852 | Edward Taylor | 7903 |
| 1866 | Edward Walker | 7593 |
| 1834 | Edwin Chace | 7845 |
| 1966 | Edwin Chace | 7995 |
| 1857 | Edwin Lafayette | 8014 |
| 1812 | Edwin R. | 7009 |
| 1848 | Edwin Remington | 8061 |
|  | Effie | 7487 |
| 1853 | Effie | 7441 |
| 1696 | Eleanor | 5572 |
| 1694 | Eleanor | 5600 |
| 1797 | Eleanor | 6108 |
| 1818 | Elias | 7725 |
| 1815 | Elijah Guild | 6861 |
| 1792 | Elisha | 6230 |
| 1781 | Eliza | 6096 |
| 1786 | Eliza | 6128 |
| 1800 | Eliza | 6636 |
| 1799 | Eliza | 6918 |
| 1833 | Eliza | 7486 |
| 1839 | Eliza | 7496 |
| 1854 | Eliza | 7616 |
| 1858 | Eliza | 7844 |
| 1816 | Eliza Ann | 5738 |
| 1802 | Eliza Ann | 6675 |
| 1812 | Eliza Ann | 7528 |
| 1819 | Eliza Ann | 7818 |
| 1853 | Eliza Heath | 7610 |
| 1802 | Eliza Rathbone | 6960 |
| 1841 | Eliza Stratton | 6771 |
| 1650 | Elizabeth | 5503 |
| 1682 | Elizabeth | 5539 |
| 1689 | Elizabeth | 5587 |
| 1708 | Elizabeth | 5615 |
| 1717 | Elizabeth | 5636 |
| 1706 | Elizabeth | 5643 |
| 1719 | Elizabeth | 5682 |
| 1735 | Elizabeth | 5765 |
| 1747 | Elizabeth | 5777 |
| 1752 | Elizabeth | 5790 |
| 1749 | Elizabeth | 5878 |
| 1758 | Elizabeth | 5899 |
| 1790 | Elizabeth | 6074 |
| 1782 | Elizabeth | 6137 |
| 1801 | Elizabeth | 6558 |
| 1794 | Elizabeth | 6575 |
| 1804 | Elizabeth | 6607 |
| 1796 | Elizabeth | 6665 |
| 1881 | Elizabeth | 7052 |
| 1824 | Elizabeth | 7313 |
| 1828 | Elizabeth | 7473 |
| 1836 | Elizabeth | 7480 |
| 1829 | Elizabeth | 7522 |
| 1837 | Elizabeth A. | 7326 |
| 1816 | Elizabeth Arnold | 7117 |
| 1878 | Elizabeth Brewer | 8009 |
| 1817 | Elizabeth Easton | 6468 |
|  | Elizabeth Jack | 6498 |
| 1877 | Elizabeth Jillson | 7899 |
| 1791 | Elizabeth Landers | 6022 |
| 1823 | Elizabeth Lawton | 6750 |
| 1768 | Elizabeth Norton | 5898 |
|  | Elizabeth Shepard | 6433 |
| 1856 | Ella | 7842 |
| 1857 | Ella de Forest | 8052 |
| 1857 | Ella M. | 7351 |
| 1655 | Ellen | 5505 |
| 1833 | Ellen Eliza | 7070 |
| 1871 | Ellen Matilda | 7467 |
| 1834 | Ellen Thompson | 7525 |
| 1830 | Ellis Burgess Pitcher | 7216 |
| 1877 | Elmer Arnold | 8077 |
| 1812 | Emerancy Bixby | 6858 |
| 1811 | Emily | 6802 |
| 1835 | Emily | 7237 |
| 1865 | Emily Jeanette | 7786 |
| 1849 | Emma | 7843 |
| 1865 | Emma A. | 7964 |
| 1865 | Emma Augusta | 6543 |
| 1846 | Emma Jennette | 7119 |
| 1846 | Emma Packard | 7450 |
| 1870 | Emma Rebecca | 8066 |
| 1866 | Ennes Bedell | 7852 |
| 1873 | Ernest Lawton | 7636 |
| 1816 | Esther | 6643 |
| 1849 | Esther Anna | 7651 |
| 1835 | Esther Hodgson | 7487 |
| 1800 | Esther Matilda | 5996 |
| 1862 | Eugene de Forest | 7443 |
| 1845 | Eugene Thomas | 7869 |
| 1853 | Eva E. | 7841 |
| 1850 | Evelyn | 7808 |

**F**

| No. | Name | Ref. |
|---|---|---|
|  | Fannie E. | 7358 |
| 1774 | Fanny | 6308 |
| 1796 | Fanny | 6322 |
|  | Fanny | 6664 |
|  | Fanny | 6669 |
| 1863 | Fanny | 8061 |
| 1839 | Fanny Robertson | 7792 |
| 1859 | Frances | 5821 |
| 1821 | Frances | 7845 |
| 1833 | Frances Jane | 7547 |
| 1813 | Frances Mary | 7878 |
| 1878 | Frances Ruth | 6796 |
|  | Francis Peckham | 7256 |
|  | Frank | 7690 |
| 1864 | Frank Anthony | 7977 |
| 1855 | Frank Clark | 7912 |
| 1844 | Frank Taylor | 6774 |
| 1851 | Frank Walker | 7709 |
| 1814 | Franklin | 6968 |
| 1847 | Franklin | 7686 |
| 1858 | Franklin | 7810 |
| 1869 | Freddie Nelson | 7833 |
| 1871 | Frederic Carter | 7625 |
| 1867 | Frederic Lander | 8065 |
| 1857 | Frederick Ford | 7942 |
| 1877 | Frederick Harris | 7939 |
|  | Freelove | 6117 |

**G**

| No. | Name | Ref. |
|---|---|---|
| 1721 | Gardner | 5650 |
| 1760 | Gardner | 5870 |
| 1761 | Gardner | 6042 |
| 1800 | Gardner | 6359 |
|  | Gardner | 6562 |
| 1851 | Genevieve | 7340 |
| 1868 | Genevieve R. | 7662 |
| 1709 | George | 5679 |
| 1754 | George | 5843 |
| 1741 | George | 5960 |
| 1788 | George | 6311 |
| 1790 | George | 6377 |
| 1815 | George | 6530 |
| 1824 | George | 7047 |
| 1838 | George | 7290 |
| 1851 | George | 8021 |
| 1838 | George A. | 7744 |
| 1864 | George A. | 7957 |
| 1802 | George Allen | 6696 |
| 1831 | George Edward | 7789 |
| 1830 | George Edwin | 7744 |
| 1836 | George Emerson | 7762 |
| 1827 | George Gardner | 7040 |
| 1827 | George Henry | 6536 |
| 1835 | George Henry | 7457 |
| 1864 | George Henry | 7622 |
| 1861 | George Henry Tew | 7375 |
| 1782 | George Howland | 6088 |
| 1811 | George Latham | 6491 |
| 1799 | George N. | 6990 |
| 1818 | George Perry | 7176 |
| 1854 | George Robert | 7890 |
| 1834 | George Stratton | 6759 |
| 1835 | George W. | 7849 |
| 1842 | George Washington | 7526 |
| 1848 | George Washington | 7655 |
| 1876 | George Weaver | 7265 |
| 1854 | George William | 7904 |
| 1869 | Gertrude Emily | 7858 |
| 1871 | Gertrude Mathewson | 7164 |
| 1715 | Grindall | 5648 |
|  | Grindell | 6112 |

**H**

| No. | Name | Ref. |
|---|---|---|
| 1806 | Hampton C. | 6844 |
| 1701 | Hannah | 5607 |
| 1762 | Hannah | 5757 |
| 1729 | Hannah | 5762 |
| 1735 | Hannah | 5857 |
| 1782 | Hannah | 5916 |
|  | Hannah | 6064 |
|  | Hannah | 6232 |
| 1797 | Hannah | 6550 |
| 1823 | Hannah | 6631 |
| 1809 | Hannah | 6726 |
| 1801 | Hannah | 6835 |
| 1811 | Hannah | 7186 |
| 1823 | Hannah | 7390 |
| 1848 | Hannah Barker | 7586 |
| 1813 | Hannah Beebe | 6752 |
| 1834 | Hannah Isadore | 7760 |
| 1827 | Hannah Maria | 7157 |
| 1848 | Hannah Maria | 7428 |
| 1825 | Hannah Melissa | 7224 |
| 1834 | Hannah P. | 7396 |
| 1801 | Harriet | 6586 |
| 1801 | Harriet | 6994 |
| 1846 | Harriet | 7518 |
| 1832 | Harriet | 7641 |
| 1836 | Harriet | 7332 |
| 1855 | Harriet Amelia | 7399 |
| 1862 | Harriet Deshon | 8054 |
| 1860 | Harriet E. | 8415 |
| 1896 | Harriet Elizabeth | 7730 |

| Year | Name | No. |
|---|---|---|
| 1836 | Harriet Evaline | 7643 |
| 1820 | Harriet Kinney | 7023 |
| 1843 | Harriet M. | 7872 |
| 1848 | Harriet Newell | 7583 |
| 1847 | Harriet Newell | 7584 |
| 1804 | Harriet Smith | 6009 |
| 1866 | Harriet Taylor | 7630 |
| 1872 | Harry Wheaton | 7307 |
| 1870 | Hattie | 7559 |
| 1838 | Helen | 6933 |
| 1862 | Helen Barrington | 7272 |
| 1796 | Henry | 5921 |
| 1847 | Henry | 7296 |
| 1848 | Henry Amon | 7910 |
| 1807 | Henry C. | 6780 |
| 1857 | Henry Casttoff | 7258 |
| 1828 | Henry David | 7041 |
| 1820 | Henry Gardner | 6567 |
| 1865 | Henry Gardner | 7984 |
| 1799 | Henry Higgins | 6037 |
| 1832 | Henry S. | 7640 |
| 1736 | Hepzibah | 5719 |
|  | Hepzibah | 6046 |
| 1871 | Herbert | 7297 |
| 1850 | Hetty Wharton | 6655 |
| 1806 | Hiram | 6940 |
| 1828 | Hiram | 7555 |
| 1857 | Hiram Edward | 7969 |
| 1837 | Hiram Lyman | 7764 |
| 1696 | Hope | 5574 |
| 1727 | Hope | 5700 |
| 1806 | Horace | 6962 |
| 1814 | Horace | 6969 |
| 1852 | Horace | 7809 |
| 1823 | Horatio Nelson | 7205 |
| 1876 | Howard | 7595 |

**I**

| Year | Name | No. |
|---|---|---|
| 1802 | Ichabod | 6362 |
| 1849 | Ida Barton | 7452 |
| 1857 | Ida Frances | 7155 |
| 1860 | Ida May | 7442 |
| 1791 | Ira | 6299 |
| 1813 | Ira Jerome | 6982 |
| 1846 | Irena | 6981 |
| 1808 | Irenus Greene | 6929 |
| 1870 | Isaac Anthony | 7371 |
| 1858 | Isabel | 7318 |

**J**

| Year | Name | No. |
|---|---|---|
| 1698 | James | 5802 |
| 1770 | James | 6052 |
| 1799 | James | 6577 |
| 1808 | James | 6592 |
| 1812 | James | 6642 |
| 1840 | James | 7248 |
| 1850 | James | 7357 |
| 1850 | James | 7520 |
| 1838 | James Emery | 7420 |
| 1841 | James Fernandas | 6544 |
| 1839 | James H. | 7327 |
| 1867 | James Henry | 6545 |
| 1873 | James Humphrey | 7626 |
| 1842 | James Ottey | 7510 |
| 1872 | James Ottey | 8002 |
| 1862 | James Siddall | 7263 |
| 1857 | James Taggart | 7304 |
| 1865 | James Wesley | 7294 |
| 1808 | James Wilcox | 6801 |
| 1843 | James William | 7421 |
| 1834 | Jane | 7064 |
| 1839 | Jane Ann | 7770 |
| 1800 | Jane Caroline | 6398 |
| 1859 | Jane Wilbur | 7972 |
| 1859 | Janette Mason | 7971 |
| 1839 | Jason W. | 7352 |
| 1710 | Jeremiah | 5580 |
| 1798 | Jeremiah | 6305 |
| 1797 | Jeremiah | 6358 |
| 1796 | Jeremiah | 6883 |
| 1847 | Jesse M. | 7874 |
| 1806 | Joanna | 6579 |
| 1717 | Job | 5584 |
| 1745 | Job | 5678 |
| 1756 | Job | 5896 |
|  | Job | 6372 |
| 1820 | Job | 7726 |
| 1664 | John | 5522 |
| 1696 | John | 5571 |
| 1692 | John | 5597 |
| 1718 | John | 5622 |
|  | John | 5638 |
| 1710 | John | 56·6 |
| 1728 | John | 5660 |
| 1780 | John | 5725 |
| 1750 | John | 5743 |
| 1740 | John | 5785 |
| 1784 | John | 5813 |
| 1747 | John | 5826 |
| 1784 | John | 6016 |
| 1786 | John | 6017 |
| 1778 | John | 6086 |
|  | John | 6114 |
|  | John | 6127 |
| 1800 | John | 6606 |
| 1808 | John | 6621 |
|  | John | 6663 |
| 1792 | John | 6670 |
| 1828 | John | 6822 |
| 1844 | John | 7283 |
| 1850 | John | 7356 |
| 1830 | John | 7528 |
| 1824 | John | 7728 |
| 1829 | John Babcock | 6757 |
| 1835 | John Barton | 7673 |
| 1765 | John Brett | 5908 |
| 1874 | John Burkinshaw | 6546 |
| 1848 | John Carman | 7707 |
| 1808 | John Clark | 7135 |
| 1798 | John Dennis | 6428 |
| 1842 | John Desbon | 7793 |
| 1837 | John Gough | 7241 |
| 1821 | John Grelea | 6480 |
| 1847 | John Henry | 7882 |
| 1776 | John Holmes | 6123 |
| 1869 | John Howard | 7163 |
| 1835 | John Latham | 6539 |
| 1848 | John Mason | 7415 |
| 1868 | John Mason | 7978 |
| 1848 | John Niles | 7397 |
| 1851 | John Robert Rhinelander | 7570 |
| 1774 | John Robinson | 6094 |
| 1807 | John Robinson | 6640 |
| 1862 | John Robinson | 7493 |
| 1790 | John Samuel | 6171 |
|  | John Taylor | 6373 |
| 1829 | John Taylor | 7160 |
|  | John Taylor | 7877 |
| 1795 | John Wanton | 5946 |
|  | John Wentworth | 7518 |
| 1819 | John Wesley | 7543 |
| 1828 | John Young | 6828 |
| 1659 | Jonathan | 5511 |
|  | Jonathan | 5537 |
|  | Jonathan | 5557 |
|  | Jonathan | 5631 |
| 1687 | Jonathan | 5669 |
| 1725 | Jonathan | 5702 |
| 1721 | Jonathan | 5826 |
| 1749 | Jonathan | 5840 |
|  | Jonathan | 6077 |
|  | Jonathan | 6182 |
| 1802 | Jorathan Gardner | 6589 |
| 1714 | Joseph | 5582 |
| 1706 | Joseph | 5614 |
| 1741 | Joseph | 5730 |
| 1744 | Joseph | 5787 |
| 1750 | Joseph | 5841 |
|  | Joseph | 5871 |
| 1774 | Joseph | 5914 |
| 1791 | Joseph | 5920 |
| 1765 | Joseph | 6076 |
|  | Joseph | 6875 |
| 1812 | Joseph | 7145 |
|  | Joseph | 7188 |
| 1842 | Joseph | 7282 |
| 1840 | Joseph Adlam | 7497 |
| 1828 | Joseph Delaplaine | 6105 |
|  | Joseph Lafayette | 6435 |
| 1848 | Joseph Robinson | 7519 |
| 1816 | Joseph Taylor | 7016 |
| 1841 | Joseph Warren | 7721 |
| 1858 | Joseph Warren | 7919 |
| 1876 | Joseph Wharton | 6658 |
| 1855 | Josephene | 7017 |
| 1842 | Josephene Golding | 7868 |
| 1725 | Joshua | 6254 |
| 1818 | Josiah | 7542 |
| 1846 | Julia | 7284 |
| 1815 | Julia Ann | 7147 |

**L**

| Year | Name | No. |
|---|---|---|
| 1704 | Latham | 5613 |
| 1733 | Latham | 5726 |
| 1757 | Latham | 5740 |
| 1748 | Latham | 5741 |
| 1766 | Latham | 5909 |
| 1802 | Latham | 5961 |
| 1796 | Latham | 6427 |
| 1849 | Laura Casttoff | 7250 |
| 1850 | Laura Hawley | 7802 |
| 1871 | Laura Henley | 8170 |
| 1841 | Laura R. | 7683 |
| 1808 | Laurens Hull | 6845 |
| 1847 | Lavilla | 8020 |
| 1827 | Lavinia | 7822 |
| 1877 | Leland Walter | 7964 |
| 1856 | Lelia May | 7586 |
| 1851 | Leroy F. | 7489 |
| 1824 | Levi Wheaton | 7206 |
| 1839 | Lewis Daniel | 7754 |
| 1864 | Libbie | 8080 |
| 1872 | Lilly Sophia | 7948 |
| 1797 | Linus | 6917 |
|  | Linzey | 6993 |
| 1806 | Lodowick Lewis | 6388 |
|  | Lorinda | 7556 |
| 1818 | Louis Jenkins | 6740 |
| 1848 | Louis Jenkins | 7578 |
|  | Louis Marion | 6126 |
| 1804 | Louis Marion | 6683 |
| 1838 | Louis Marion | 7566 |
| 1878 | Louis Stewart | 7558 |
| 1842 | Louisa Ann | 7498 |
| 1805 | Lucetta | 7125 |
| 1839 | Lucian Edward | 7753 |
| 1841 | Lucinda J. | 7896 |
| 1848 | Lucius | 8028 |
| 1798 | Lucretia | 6879 |
| 1785 | Lucy | 6278 |
| 1792 | Lucy | 6330 |
| 1808 | Lucy | 6578 |
| 1825 | Lucy Caroline | 7082 |
| 1852 | Lucy J. | 7955 |
| 1878 | Luland Lewis | 8041 |
| 1868 | Lulu | 7682 |
| 1725 | Lydia | 5724 |
| 1749 | Lydia | 5803 |
| 1773 | Lydia | 6079 |
| 1778 | Lydia | 6253 |
| 1795 | Lydia | 6349 |
| 1796 | Lydia | 6906 |
| 1840 | Lydia | 7560 |
| 1822 | Lydia | 7727 |
| 1828 | Lydia | 7821 |
| 1836 | Lydia | 7366 |
| 1823 | Lydia Button | 7027 |
| 1809 | Lydia S. | 6026 |

**M**

| | | |
|---|---|---|
| 1869 | Mabel Nelson | 7685 |
| 1878 | Mabel Stephens | 8035 |
| 1864 | Madeline Richmond | 7694 |
| 1809 | Malvira | 6898 |
| 1779 | Margaret | 6187 |
| 1777 | Margaret Sweet | 6181 |
| 1865 | Margetta Wilbur | 7618 |
| 1790 | Maria | 5970 |
| 1802 | Maria | 6872 |
| | Maria Louisa | 6688 |
| 1849 | Maria Ophelia | 7788 |
| 1835 | Marietta | 6860 |
| 1834 | Marietta | 7642 |
| 1862 | Marion Hathaway | 7458 |
| 1840 | Martha A. | 7068 |
| 1842 | Martha Amelia | 7779 |
| 1858 | Martha Ann | 8022 |
| 1842 | Martha Babcock | 7881 |
| | Martha Coggeshall | 5965 |
| 1833 | Martha Dickerson | 6434 |
| 1863 | Martha Elizabeth | 6542 |
| 1837 | Martha Frances | 7669 |
| 1823 | Martha Lucretia | 7716 |
| 1839 | Martin | 7057 |
| 1869 | Martin Ackerman | 8000 |
| 1657 | Mary | 5508 |
| 1685 | Mary | 5547 |
| 1741 | Mary | 5583 |
| 1690 | Mary | 5596 |
| 1711 | Mary | 5621 |
| 1736 | Mary | 5638 |
| | Mary | 5654 |
| 1725 | Mary | 5661 |
| 1714 | Mary | 5681 |
| 1728 | Mary | 5703 |
| 1780 | Mary | 5709 |
| 1752 | Mary | 5744 |
| 1740 | Mary | 5767 |
| 1753 | Mary | 5779 |
| 1737 | Mary | 5858 |
| 1781 | Mary | 5915 |
| 1802 | Mary | 5956 |
| | Mary | 6020 |
| 1788 | Mary | 6021 |
| | Mary | 6057 |
| 1756 | Mary | 6068 |
| | Mary | 6283 |
| 1770 | Mary | 6306 |
| 1816 | Mary | 6531 |
| | Mary | 6560 |
| 1822 | Mary | 6612 |
| 1812 | Mary | 6627 |
| 1816 | Mary | 6784 |
| 1815 | Mary | 6808 |
| 1840 | Mary | 7281 |
| 1862 | Mary | 7392 |
| 1862 | Mary | 7558 |
| 1828 | Mary | 7781 |
| 1870 | Mary | 8082 |
| 1868 | Mary Angeline | 7702 |
| 1824 | Mary Ann | 6482 |
| 1808 | Mary Ann | 6638 |
| 1809 | Mary Ann | 6963 |
| 1810 | Mary Ann | 7004 |
| 1817 | Mary Ann | 7018 |
| 1836 | Mary Ann | 7496 |
| 1820 | Mary Ann | 7820 |
| 1831 | Mary B. | 7824 |
| 1865 | Mary Bankhead | 7273 |
| 1809 | Mary C. | 6898 |
| 1866 | Mary Caty | 7546 |
| 1846 | Mary Day | 6651 |
| 1860 | Mary Dickinson | 7994 |
| 1844 | Mary E. | 7649 |
| 1834 | Mary Ellen | 7475 |
| 1868 | Mary Ellen | 7983 |
| 1820 | Mary Eliza | 6785 |
| 1881 | Mary Eliza | 7042 |
| 1878 | Mary Eliza | 7834 |
| 1821 | Mary Florina | 7715 |
| 1831 | Mary Frances | 7006 |
| 1808 | Mary G. | 6843 |
| 1817 | Mary Gardner | 6596 |
| 1814 | Mary Greene | 7103 |
| 1817 | Mary Jane | 6494 |
| 1862 | Mary Louisa | 7602 |
| 1859 | Mary Louisa Carroll | 7621 |
| 1825 | Mary Maria | 7048 |
| 1829 | Mary Maria | 7410 |
| 1858 | Mary Maria | 7970 |
| 1871 | Mary Palmer | 7859 |
| 1799 | Matilda | 6871 |
| | Matilda Saunders | 7184 |
| 1874 | Maud Olivia | 7996 |
| 1871 | Maud Ottey | 8001 |
| 1859 | Maurice Deshon | 8053 |
| | Mehitable | 5637 |
| 1787 | Mehitable | 5766 |
| 1741 | Mehitable | 5775 |
| 1748 | Mehitable | 5800 |
| 1854 | Melissa M. | 7440 |
| | Mercy Mary | 6992 |
| 1866 | Minerva | 7445 |
| 1867 | Minerva Lorea | 7370 |
| 1847 | Minnie | 7285 |
| 1879 | Miriam | 7527 |
| 1780 | Moses | 5940 |
| 1854 | Myron Marcellus | 7889 |

**N**

| | | |
|---|---|---|
| 1758 | Nabby | 5861 |
| | Nancy | 6019 |
| 1810 | Nancy | 6229 |
| 1780 | Nancy | 6310 |
| 1792 | Nancy | 6662 |
| 1805 | Nancy | 6924 |
| 1834 | Nancy | 7737 |
| | Nancy R. | 5947 |
| 1845 | Nathan Albert | 7422 |
| 1857 | Nathan Albert | 7426 |
| 1828 | Nathan Saunders | 7182 |
| | Nathaniel | 5641 |
| 1772 | Nathaniel | 6307 |
| 1857 | Nathaniel Blunt | 7270 |
| 1841 | Nathaniel Gardner | 7368 |
| 1771 | Nathaniel S. | 6045 |
| 1864 | Nellie Elizabeth | 8089 |
| 1745 | Norton | 5876 |

**O**

| | | |
|---|---|---|
| 1835 | Obadiah Kingsley | 7557 |
| | Oliver | 6231 |
| 1842 | Orlando | 6984 |

**P**

| | | |
|---|---|---|
| 1837 | Palmer Chace | 7350 |
| 1833 | Parker Hall | 6745 |
| 1858 | Parker Lawton | 7590 |
| 1814 | Parnold | 6043 |
| 1702 | Patience | 5576 |
| 1759 | Patience | 6069 |
| 1801 | Patience | 6620 |
| 1783 | Patty | 6257 |
| 1769 | Paul | 5759 |
| 1796 | Paul | 6036 |
| 1706 | Peleg | 5579 |
| | Peleg | 5680 |
| 1727 | Peleg | 5670 |
| 1729 | Peleg | 5672 |
| 1742 | Peleg | 5676 |
| 1726 | Peleg | 5761 |
| 1742 | Peleg | 5786 |
| 1758 | Peleg | 5835 |
| 1765 | Peleg | 6051 |
| 1778 | Peleg | 6095 |
| 1778 | Peleg | 6136 |
| 1778 | Peleg | 6154 |
| 1808 | Peleg | 6569 |
| 1799 | Peleg Gardner | 6587 |
| 1788 | Peleg Grinald | 6376 |
| 1826 | Peleg Lawton | 6743 |
| 1834 | Peleg Rufus | 7391 |
| 1792 | Penelope | 6130 |
| 1704 | Peter | 5603 |
| 1855 | Peter | 8029 |
| 1868 | Peter | 8061 |
| 1715 | Phebe | 5623 |
| 1740 | Phebe | 5675 |
| 1749 | Phebe | 5827 |
| 1770 | Phebe | 6078 |
| 1788 | Phebe | 6153 |
| 1788 | Phebe | 6155 |
| | Phebe | 6374 |
| 1888 | Phebe Elizabeth | 7575 |
| 1847 | Phebe J. | 7855 |
| 1812 | Phebe Langworthy | 7082 |
| 1797 | Phebe Lawton | 6158 |
| 1818 | Phebe Lawton | 6727 |
| 1825 | Phebe Lawton | 6756 |
| 1868 | Phebe Mathewson | 7162 |
| 1788 | Phebe Watson | 6125 |
| | Phebe Watson | 6696 |
| 1810 | Philander | 6952 |
| 17x7 | Philip Wanton | 6096 |
| 1796 | Phylura | 6870 |
| 1713 | Priscilla | 5536 |
| | Priscilla | 5663 |
| 1828 | Prudence Adeline | 7553 |

**R**

| | | |
|---|---|---|
| 1822 | Rachel Boomer | 7312 |
| 1824 | Rachel Hall | 6516 |
| 1826 | Rachel M. | 7321 |
| | Ralph | 7848 |
| 1662 | Rebecca | 5513 |
| 1689 | Rebecca | 5558 |
| 1821 | Rhoda Earl | 7179 |
| | Richard | 6116 |
| 1826 | Richard Cotton | 7729 |
| 1859 | Richard Lathers | 6441 |
| 1851 | Rienzi Ware | 7431 |
| 1790 | Robert | 6329 |
| 1901 | Robert | 6409 |
| 1838 | Robert | 7296 |
| 1870 | Robert | 7896 |
| 1865 | Robert Berry | 7295 |
| 1837 | Robert Brewer | 7555 |
| 1824 | Robert Carter | 6823 |
| 1811 | Robert F. | 6781 |
| 1839 | Robert Henry | 6770 |
| 1834 | Robert Henry | 7096 |
| 1844 | Robert Hugh | 7659 |
| | Robert Jenkins | 6124 |
| 1800 | Robert Lawton | 6172 |
| 1823 | Robert Lawton | 6742 |
| 1764 | Rowland | 6326 |
| 1860 | Rowland Birdsall | 7700 |
| | Ruth | 5634 |
| 1722 | Ruth | 5692 |
| | Ruth | 6234 |
| 1812 | Ruth | 6346 |
| 1841 | Ruth | 7853 |
| 1829 | Ruth A. | 7328 |
| 1839 | Ruth Hannah | 6761 |
| 1864 | Ruth Hannah | 7592 |
| 1775 | Ruth Scott | 6180 |

**S**

| | | |
|---|---|---|
| 1669 | Samuel | 5524 |
| 1737 | Samuel | 5596 |
| 1699 | Samuel | 5606 |
| | Samuel | 5632 |
| | Samuel | 5649 |
| 1719 | Samuel | 5720 |
| 1724 | Samuel | 5728 |
| 1737 | Samuel | 5732 |
| 1745 | Samuel | 5755 |
| 1755 | Samuel | 5758 |
| 1763 | Samuel | 5763 |
| 1743 | Samuel | 5763 |

| | | | | | | | | | |
|---|---|---|---|---|---|---|---|---|---|
| 1743 | Samuel | 5776 | 1882 | Susan Andrews | 7865 | | William | 5659 |
| 1745 | Samuel | 5802 | 1828 | Susan Brownell | 6439 | 1728 | William | 5671 |
| 1751 | Samuel | 5834 | 1832 | Susan Caroline | 7217 | 1711 | William | 5680 |
| 1793 | Samuel | 6035 | 1860 | Susan Eleanora | 7545 | 1747 | William | 5733 |
| 1776 | Samuel | 6085 | 1810 | Susan Gardner | 6593 | 1755 | William | 5850 |
| | Samuel | 6110 | 1815 | Susan Lawton | 6739 | 1783 | William | 5856 |
| 1705 | Samuel | 6157 | 1842 | Susan Lawton | 7576 | 1782 | William | 5941 |
| 1797 | Samuel | 6576 | 1712 | Susanna | 5581 | 1760 | William | 6111 |
| 1806 | Samuel | 6591 | 1714 | Susanna | 5647 | | William | 6227 |
| 1817 | Samuel | 6629 | 1728 | Susanna | 5810 | 1805 | William | 6368 |
| 1864 | Samuel | 7612 | 1728 | Susanna | 5811 | 1809 | William | 6581 |
| 1756 | Samuel Isaac | 5887 | 1731 | Susanna | 5855 | 1828 | William | 7049 |
| 1787 | Samuel Isaac | 6397 | 1799 | Susanna | 5922 | 1870 | William | 7074 |
| 1869 | Samuel Lawton | 7624 | 1777 | Susanna | 6309 | 1826 | William | 7156 |
| | Sands | 7008 | 1843 | Sylvia J. | 7830 | 1851 | William | 7258 |
| 1648 | Sarah | 5502 | | | | 1875 | William | 7254 |
| 1698 | Sarah | 5570 | | **T** | | 1848 | William | 7287 |
| 1720 | Sarah | 5627 | 1770 | Thankful | 6242 | 1831 | William | 7524 |
| 1725 | Sarah | 5699 | 1867 | Theodore Payne | 7266 | 1854 | William | 7653 |
| 1729 | Sarah | 5706 | 1671 | Thomas | 5525 | 1858 | William Albert | 7850 |
| 1749 | Sarah | 5734 | 1767 | Thomas | 5586 | 1807 | William Alexander | 6490 |
| 1732 | Sarah | 5764 | | Thomas | 5629 | 1808 | William Andrews | 7080 |
| 1749 | Sarah | 5789 | 1737 | Thomas | 5674 | 1820 | William Baker | 6630 |
| 1748 | Sarah | 5820 | 1730 | Thomas | 5763 | 1818 | William Barton | 6597 |
| 1785 | Sarah | 5962 | 1750 | Thomas | 5778 | 1814 | William Bassell | 5737 |
| 1763 | Sarah | 6075 | 1757 | Thomas | 5794 | 1815 | William Bradford | 6464 |
| 1768 | Sarah | 6093 | 1780 | Thomas | 6087 | 1834 | William C. | 7165 |
| 1793 | Sarah | 6312 | 1782 | Thomas | 6220 | 1788 | William Carter | 6231 |
| 1793 | Sarah | 6379 | | Thomas | 6228 | 1806 | William Carter | 6300 |
| 1819 | Sarah | 6469 | 1820 | Thomas | 6611 | 1865 | William Carter | 7680 |
| 1799 | Sarah | 6552 | 1807 | Thomas | 6625 | 1846 | William Christopher | 7681 |
| 1844 | Sarah | 7511 | 1812 | Thomas | 6795 | 1828 | William Clark | 7894 |
| 1862 | Sarah Ambler | 7591 | 1856 | Thomas | 7290 | 1864 | William Coggeshall | 7806 |
| 1809 | Sarah Ann | 6443 | 1836 | Thomas Edwin | 7668 | 1828 | William Ellery | 7214 |
| 1822 | Sarah Ann | 7150 | 1862 | Thomas H. | 7828 | 1874 | William Eugene | 7853 |
| 1868 | Sarah Ann | 7660 | 1839 | Thomas Henry | 7481 | 1870 | William Fairchild | 7663 |
| 1840 | Sarah Ann | 7745 | 1813 | Thomas Jefferson | 6807 | 1823 | William Henry | 6481 |
| 1756 | Sarah Casey | 5711 | | Thomas White | 6502 | 1832 | William Henry | 6758 |
| 1859 | Sarah Constance | 7943 | | | | | William Henry | 7192 |
| 1860 | Sarah Elizabeth | 7215 | | **U** | | 1858 | William Henry | 7748 |
| 1852 | Sarah Elizabeth | 7376 | 1827 | Ursula Gates | 7717 | 1836 | William J. Young | 7679 |
| 1830 | Sarah Elizabeth | 7875 | | **V** | | 1875 | William Marion | 8007 |
| 1836 | Sarah Hart | 6760 | 1726 | Valentine | 5652 | | William Pryor | 6436 |
| 1831 | Sarah Jane | 7189 | 1799 | Varnum | 6053 | 1830 | William R. | 7065 |
| 1815 | Sarah Luther | 6609 | 1815 | Vernon | 6595 | 1872 | William Ravenel | 7937 |
| 1810 | Sarah Perry | 7081 | | Vernon | 7436 | 1766 | William Richardson | 5795 |
| 1817 | Sarah Reynolds | 7200 | | **W** | | 1817 | William Richardson | 6104 |
| 1837 | Sarah Taylor | 7229 | 1889 | Wallace Fay | 6930 | 1843 | William Richardson | 6648 |
| 1832 | Sarah Tew | 6588 | 1849 | Walter Alden | 7154 | 1873 | William Richardson | 6649 |
| 1817 | Serene | 6936 | 1852 | Walter Deey | 7911 | 1784 | William Robinson | 6097 |
| 1791 | Silas | 6878 | 1867 | Walter Ecky | 8046 | 1848 | William Stewart | 7569 |
| 1804 | Silas | 6896 | 1867 | Walter Irving | 7623 | 1854 | William Thomas | 7692 |
| 1840 | Silas | 7720 | 1809 | Wanton | 6641 | 1805 | William Torrey | 6639 |
| 1808 | Silas Rawson | 6928 | 1852 | Wanton | 7515 | 1849 | William Torrey | 7500 |
| 1797 | Sophia | 6884 | 1823 | Wauton Jones | 6501 | 1846 | William Torrey | 7512 |
| 1867 | Sophia | 7295 | 1818 | Warden Hathaway | 6611 | 1868 | William Torrey | 7812 |
| 1797 | Sophia Eliza | 6095 | 1862 | Warren A. | 7956 | 1780 | William Wanton | 5955 |
| 1827 | Sophia Eliza | 6518 | 1858 | Warren Greene | 7890 | 1852 | William Wharton | 6656 |
| 1868 | Sophia Hoffman | 7955 | 1848 | Wesley Ward | 7755 | 1878 | William Wharton | 6659 |
| 1838 | Sophie W. | 7367 | 1795 | Whitman | 6975 | 1848 | Willie Eugene | 7870 |
| 1817 | Stephen Whitman | 7817 | 1868 | Wilbert Palmer | 8047 | 1859 | Willie Henry | 7882 |
| 1824 | Stephen York | 7553 | 1877 | Willard Henry | 7918 | 1856 | Wilmarth Heath | 7620 |
| 1816 | Susan | 7170 | 1680 | William | 5527 | 1849 | Winthrop Granville | 7689 |
| 1793 | Susan Alida | 6131 | 1724 | William | 5651 | | | |

---

## DESCENDANTS OF EDWARD THURSTON BEARING OTHER NAMES.

**ALBRO**

| | | |
|---|---|---|
| 1844 | Caroline Adelia | 6738 |
| 1842 | Christopher Durfee | 6732 |
| 1854 | Franklin Thurston | 6738 |
| 1835 | Hannah Barker | 6728 |
| 1848 | James Albert | 6737 |

**ALMY**

| | | |
|---|---|---|
| 1740 | Ann | 5663 |
| 1744? | Elizabeth | 5664 |
| 1749 | Job | 5668 |
| 1746 | Jonathan | 5665 |
| 1782 | Jonathan Thurston | 5666 |

| | | |
|---|---|---|
| 1747 | Mary | 5667 |
| 1742? | Phebe | 5668½ |
| 1788? | William | 5662 |

**ANTHONY**

| | | |
|---|---|---|
| 1841 | Francis Porter | 6964 |
| 1885 | James T. | 6809 |
| 1887 | Julia | 6810 |
| | Mary | 6809 |
| 1839 | Mary | 6811 |
| 1848 | Noel L. | 6813 |
| 1843 | Sarah Kttle | 6965 |
| 1841 | Susan | 6812 |

**APTHORP**

| | | |
|---|---|---|
| 1848 | Anna Wentworth | 7115 |
| 1878 | Annie Osgood | 7113 |
| 1866 | Charlotte Elizabeth | 7105 |
| 1875 | Ellen Wentworth | 7108 |
| 1867 | Emma Matilda | 7106 |
| 1874 | Frederick George | 7111 |
| 1871 | George Henry | 7107 |
| 1841 | George Henry | 7114 |
| 1876 | Grace | 7109 |
| 1889 | John Perkins | 7110 |
| 1877 | Mary | 7112 |

1846 Mary Elizabeth 7116
1837 William Lee 7104

**ATKINS**

1851 Benjamin Paine 6326
1854 Daniel Thurston 6327
1848 William 6825

**BABBITT**

1866 Samuel Ward 6145

**BABCOCK**

Abby 5953
Cornelia 5954
Eliza 5952
John 5948
Latham 5949
Sarah Ann 5950
Wanton 5951

**BANNING**

1868 Alice Crocker 6004
1862 Arthur Staples 6001
1864 Edwin Thomas 6002
1866 Mary Elizabeth 6003
1854 Matilda Thurston 5998
1860 William Carlos 6000

**BARRINGTON**

1844 Rachel Thurston 6517

**BEDELL**

1819? Elizabeth 6701
1817 Gregory Thurston 6700

**BENJAMIN**

1854 Arthur Bedell 6702

**BENNETT**

1837 Abby L. 7019
1856 Charlieana 7022
1850 Ella H. 7021
1845 Lydia M. 7020

**BLANCHARD**

18?8 Hattie Earl 7191
1857 Jennie Thurston 7190
1867 Nellie Louise 7192

**BLIFFINS**

1826 Anson 6554
1831 David Evans 6556
1828 Harriet Newell 6555
1823 Sybil Valentine 6558
1835 Thomas 6557

**BLISS**

1786 Barbara Phillips 5713
1788 Benjamin Thurston 5714
1796 Ebenezer David 5717
1784 Elizabeth Ayers 5712
1790 Sarah Thurston 5715
1792 Thomas Ward 5716

**BLIVENS**

Frank 6614
Helen 6613

**BLOSSOM**

Barton 6056
Susan 6055

**BOGERT**

Clinton 6691
Eugene Thurston 6695
Maria Antoinette 6692

**BOSWELL**

1847 Alla Thurston 6707
1850 Charles Fanning 6708
1844 Elizabeth 6706
1841 Elizabeth Hand 6705
1888 John Lovett 6704

**BREED**

1877 Cora Thurston 6736
1866 Jennie Wilson 6784
1872 William Baxter 6735

**BRIGGS**

1842 Nichols Johnson 7819

**BRIGHTMAN**

Alton C. 7355
Ernest L. 7355

**BROWN**

1843 Albert Nelson 7139
1856 Charles Sumner 7025
1853 Frank Thurston 7024
1840 Hannah Thurston 7138
1852 Jennie Eliza 7186
1845 Mary Elizabeth 7140
1859 Oliver Winslow 7026
1847 Rosamond 6848
1837 Sarah Babcock 7187
1845 Thurston Duane 6847

**BROWNELL**

1717 Elizabeth 5553
1711 George 5551
1753 George 5697
1746 Gideon 5694
1707 Giles 5548
1750 Hope 5695
1719 Jonathan 5554
1765 Lois 5698
1709 Mary 5550
1721 Paul 5555
1748 Pearce 5698
1708 Phebe 5549
1726 Stephen 5556
1755 Susanna 5696
1713 Thomas 5552

**BURDICK**

Bessie 6202
William 6202

**BURLINGAME**

1868 Mary Elizabeth 6497

**BURNHAM**

1878 Bertha Mary 6339
1873 George Lyndon 6338

**BUTTERFIELD**

Hannah 6869

**BUTTON**

1815 Charles Chandler 6331
1840 George Curtis 6384
1849 Harriet Cady 6344
1880 Henry Taintor 6346
1866 Jane 6348
Jane Allen 6336
1843 LeRoy 6332
1862 Lillie 6347
1876 Louie Worthington 6341
1852 Lucy Thurston 6345
1817 Lyndon Taylor 6333
1842 Mary Gould 6337
1841 William Thurston 6335
1819 William Thurston 6342
1858 Werthington Bulkeley 6340
1822 Worthington Bulkeley 6343

**BUTTS**

1861 Annie Atwood 7486
1864 Caroline Thurston 7486
1868 Esther Thurston 7486

**CARR**

1808 Abby 6189
1824 Amelia 6216

1861 Anna 6209
1813 Caleb Arnold 6197
1846 Clara 6202
1802 Dolly Thurston 6188
1860 George Henry 6199
1808 George Washington 6194
1850 George Washington 6206
1821 John 6214
1847 Josephene Augusta 6203
1805 Margaret 6196
1850 Martha Thurston 6215
1810 Mary Ann 6195
1856 Mary Lever 6207
1853 Phebe Jackson 6206
1849 Richard Arnold 6198
1818 Sarah Rowlong 6210
1858 Theodore Orman 6200
1815 Thomas Thurston 6201
1848 Thomas Thurston 6204
1858 William 6208

**CHAMPLIN**

1780 Christopher Joseph 5833
1774 Elizabeth 5831
1770 John Thurston 5828
1776 Phebe 5832
1771 Rebecca 5829
1772 Uriah Oliver 5830

**CHAPIN**

1858 Carrie Bard 7181
1844 George Herman 7180

**CHESTER**

1857 Arthur Thurston 7084
1853 Carl Thurston 7082

**CHILCOT**

1787 Mary 5845

**CHURCH**

1877 Lucy Allen 6345

**CLARK**

1839 John Thurston 7015

**CLARKE**

1814 Sarah Elizabeth 6318

**COGGESHALL**

1764 Elizabeth 5801

**COLE**

1853 Florence Vienna 6947

**COLLINS**

1727 Daniel 5595
1720 Elizabeth 5594
1715 Hannah 5590
1717 John 5591
1718 Mary 5593
1722 Rebecca 5592
1724 Ruth 5594
1712 Samuel 5588

**COMINS**

1866 Alfred 7775
1863 Hattie 7773
1864 Jennie 7774
1870 Maria 7777
1860 Martha 7771
1861 Mary 7772
1868 Nettie 7776
1874 Vernon Spencer 7778

**CORNELL**

1728 Abigail 5610
1740 Elizabeth 5612
1737 Gideon 5619
1730 Hannah 5611
1733 Latham 5618
1748 Matthew 5620
1724 Sarah 5606
1725 Thomas 5609
1731 Thomas 5617
1729 Walter 561

**HAVENS**

| | George | 5506 |
|---|---|---|
| 1681 | Jonathan | 5507 |

**HENRY**

| 1878 | Baby | 7083 |
|---|---|---|
| 1870 | Iowa Ines | 7085 |
| 1874 | Jennie June | 7087 |
| 1868 | Lorin Lane | 7084 |
| 1872 | Mary Mabel | 7086 |

**HIGHLAND**

| 1858 | Ada Louise | 7211 |
|---|---|---|
| 1850 | Edward Jacob | 7210 |
| 1850 | Edwin Clarke | 7209 |
| 1848 | Eliza Ross | 7208 |
| 1858 | Herbert Clarke | 7212 |
| 1860 | Walter Clarence | 7213 |

**HOLMAN**

| 1862 | Fannie Lavoatia | 6730 |
|---|---|---|
| 1860 | Frederic William | 6729 |
| 1866 | Hermon Thomas | 6731 |

**HOLMES**

| 1852 | Carrie Elizabeth | 6496 |
|---|---|---|
| 1854 | John Wanton | 6499 |
| 1858 | Lewis Edwin | 6498 |
| 1851 | Robert William | 6495 |
| 1856 | Thomas Thurston | 6500 |

**HOLT**

| 1848 | Dora | 6352 |
|---|---|---|

**HOPE**

| 1842 | Mary Louisa | 6922 |
|---|---|---|
| 1835 | Nancy Clarinda | 6921 |

**HOPKINSON**

| 1878 | Nellie Thurston | 7808 |
|---|---|---|

**HOXIE**

| 1842 | George Hazard | 7174 |
|---|---|---|
| 1835 | Gordan Hazard | 7171 |
| 1837 | Mary Lee | 7172 |
| 1838 | Susan Thurston | 7173 |
| 1843 | Willie | 7175 |

**HOYT**

| | Aline | 6694 |
|---|---|---|
| | Cornelia Thurston | 6677 |
| | Ella Carroll | 6682 |
| | Emily Adele | 6680 |
| | Geraldine | 6693 |
| | Lewis Thurston | 6678 |
| | Robert Sands | 6681 |
| | William | 6679 |

**INGALLS**

| 1878 | Fanny Thurston | 7791 |
|---|---|---|

**JACKSON**

| 1859 | Charles | 7738 |
|---|---|---|
| 1861 | Jennie | 7739 |

**JONES**

| 1838 | Justus Fletcher | 6908 |
|---|---|---|
| 1843 | Nathalia Malentha | 6910 |
| 1861 | Orbie Heading | 6911 |
| 1858 | Rossinie Beatty | 6912 |
| 1841 | Wesley Whitfield | 6909 |

**JUDD**

| 1831 | Edward Ancill | 6838 |
|---|---|---|
| 1841 | Frances Jerusha | 6842 |
| 1838 | Helen Hannah | 6841 |
| 1833 | Howell Hampton | 6889 |
| 1829 | Mary Adele | 6887 |
| 1826 | Rowland Thurston | 6836 |
| 1835 | Ruth Rosamond | 6840 |

**LAKE**

| 1864 | Addie Louise | 7396 |
|---|---|---|
| 1862 | Joseph Henry | 7395 |

**LAMBERTON**

| 1878 | Mary Barton | 7451 |
|---|---|---|

**LATHERS**

| 1848 | Abby Caroline | 6508 |
|---|---|---|
| 1858 | Agnes | 6509 |
| 1866 | Edmund Griffin | 6515 |
| 1857 | Emma | 6511 |
| 1862 | Ida | 6513 |
| 1858 | Joseph Thurston | 6512 |
| 1864 | Julia | 6514 |
| 1855 | Richard | 6510 |

**LAWTON**

| 1864 | Adeliza | 7159 |
|---|---|---|
| 1858 | Charles Herbert | 7158 |
| 1714 | George | 5546 |
| | Joanna | 6062 |
| | Job | 6062 |
| | Mary | 6062 |

**LUTHER**

| 1847 | Elizabeth Thurston | 6753 |
|---|---|---|
| 1849 | James | 6754 |
| 1850 | James | 6755 |
| 1844 | John Henry | 6751 |
| 1845 | William Gardner | 6752 |

**LYON**

| 1875 | Ruth Frances | 7303 |
|---|---|---|

**MACAULEY**

| 1871 | Fanny Wood | 6857 |
|---|---|---|
| 1869 | George Thurston | 6856 |
| 1878 | Joseph Foster | 6859 |
| 1878 | Richard Henry | 6858 |

**MAIN**

| | Adie | 5865 |
|---|---|---|
| | Aruby | 5889 |
| | Clarissa | 5867 |
| | Gardner | 5963 |
| | Hannah | 5864 |
| | Job | 5862 |
| | Nabby | 5864 |
| | Russell | 5866 |

**MATTHEWSON**

| 1863 | Charles Henry | 6763 |
|---|---|---|
| 1873 | Edwin Lawton | 6764 |
| 1861 | George Snow | 6762 |

**MELVILLE**

| 1786 | Avis | 5886 |
|---|---|---|
| 1852 | Catharine Gansevoort | 6521 |
| 1778 | David | 5881 |
| 1777 | Elizabeth | 5883 |
| 1781 | Eunice Thurston | 5884 |
| 1850 | Florence | 6520 |
| 1854 | Julia | 6522 |
| 1856 | Lucy | 6523 |
| 1769 | Lydia | 5879 |
| 1849 | Maria Gansevoort | 6519 |
| 1775 | Mary | 5882 |
| 1771 | Samuel Thurston | 5880 |
| 1784 | Sarah Anthony | 5885 |

**MERRIMAN**

| 1868 | Charles Henry | 7487 |
|---|---|---|
| 1870 | Harold Thurston | 7487 |
| 1865 | Maria Lippitt | 7487 |
| 1863 | William Thurston | 7487 |

**MITCHELL**

| 1858 | Agnes J. | 6274 |
|---|---|---|
| 1839 | Caroline A. | 6267 |
| 1849 | Eva K. | 6272 |
| 1845 | Ida | 6270 |
| 1841 | Mary J. | 6268 |
| 1851 | Nathan J. | 6273 |
| 1847 | Patty R. | 6271 |
| 1843 | Beth M. | 6269 |

**MOOREWOOD**

| 1876 | Allen Melville (p. 501) | 6519 |
|---|---|---|

**OAKS**

| 1871 | Fanny Bell | 7782 |
|---|---|---|
| 1861 | George Kimble | 7780 |
| 1864 | Nellie | 7781 |

**PADDOCK**

| 1858 | Alada Thurston | 6713 |
|---|---|---|
| 1860 | Edith Flagg | 6714 |
| 1872 | Ellie Morgan | 6720 |
| 1866 | Fanny Fanning | 6717 |
| 1875 | Florence Hubbard | 6721 |
| 1864 | John Benjamin | 6716 |
| 1862 | Lilly Bedell | 6715 |
| 1868 | Louise Bogert | 6718 |
| 1870 | Robert Lewis | 6719 |

**PADELFORD**

| 1857 | Mary Lucretia | 7670 |
|---|---|---|

**PARMELE**

| 1842 | Charles Frederick | 6980 |
|---|---|---|
| 1849 | Ella | 6982 |
| 1854 | George D. | 6983 |
| 1844 | Stephen R. | 6981 |

**PARSONS**

| 1831 | Caroline | 6355 |
|---|---|---|
| 1822 | Frances Emeline | 6380 |
| 1813 | Leander | 6351 |
| 1853 | Sarah Cole | 6353 |
| 1826 | Sophia Wakefield | 6352 |
| 1848 | Susan Tillinghast | 6354 |

**PAUL**

| 1846 | Benjamin Arnold | 6212 |
|---|---|---|
| 1849 | Deborah Cleveland | 6213 |
| 1844 | Mary Frances | 6211 |

**PEABODY**

| 1838 | Elizabeth H. | 6820 |
|---|---|---|
| 1846 | Gertrude | 6821 |

**PECKHAM**

| 1846 | George E. | 6218 |
|---|---|---|
| 1877 | Laura | 7252 |
| 1876 | Mary | 7251 |
| 1845 | William | 6217 |

**PETERS**

| | Lovell | 5573 |
|---|---|---|

**PITMAN**

| 1874 | Annie Maria | 6008 |
|---|---|---|
| 1865 | Bertha Staples | 6006 |
| 1829 | Harriet Elizabeth | 5997 |
| 1872 | Jennie Matilda | 6007 |
| 1834 | William Goddard | 6005 |

**POLLARD**

| 1855 | Artemissia F. | 7188 |
|---|---|---|

**POTTER**

| | Benjamin | 6071 |
|---|---|---|
| | Carrol Hagadorn | 6966 |
| 1836 | Charles I. | 6170 |
| 1826 | Deborah Ann | 6190 |
| | Eliza Palmer | 6964 |
| | Elizabeth | 6073 |
| 1830 | Elizabeth Lawton | 6166 |
| 1828 | George Lawton | 6165 |
| | George W. | 6192 |
| 1826 | Henry David | 6164 |
| 1824 | Mary Taylor | 6163 |
| 1817 | Mary Thurston | 6159 |
| 1864 | Nettie Carr | 6169 |
| 1822 | Peleg Thurston | 6162 |
| 1832 | Phebe Thurston | 6167 |

37

**THOMAS**

| 1781 | Amy | 5901 |
| 1783 | Elizabeth | 5902 |
| 1786 | Thurston | 5903 |

**TIBBITTS**

| 1843 | Abby Thurston | 6460 |
| 1687 | Anna | 6456 |
| 1852 | Charles Norris | 6463 |
| 1833 | Henry Cook | 6457 |
| 1842 | John Waterman | 6459 |
| 1848 | Sarah Gray | 6462 |
| 1845 | Susan Green | 6461 |
| 1840 | William Thurston | 6458 |

**TRUMAN**

| 1850 | Asa H. | 6986 |
| 1852 | Catherine | 6986 |

**TURNER**

| | Hannah | 5707 |
| | Ruth | 5708 |

**WALKER**

| 1861 | Mary Louise | 6945 |

**WALRATH**

| 1866 | Libbie | 6927 |

**WARD**

| 1841 | Elizabeth Gibbs | 6145 |
| 1840 | Laura Underwood | 6144 |
| 1844 | Robert Gibbs | 6146 |

**WARDELL**

| | Mary Ann | 6551 |

**WARING**

| 1836 | Hannah | 6783 |

**WATERMAN**

| | Ellen | 6895 |
| | Emily | 6896 |
| | Mary | 6894 |

**WELDEN**

| 1872 | Abbie Jane | 7782 |
| 1856 | Nettie | 7783 |

**WELLS**

| 1834 | Frances Elizabeth | 6315 |
| 1832 | Thomas Clarke | 6314 |

**WHITE**

| 1836 | Amanda | 6806 |
| 1835 | Charles | 6805 |
| 1838 | Edmund | 6804 |
| 1753 | Elizabeth | 5690 |
| 1831 | Emily | 6803 |
| 1756 | Lucy | 5691 |
| 1744 | Mary | 5686 |
| 1745 | Noah | 5687 |
| 1748 | Peregrine | 5688 |
| 1740 | Sarah | 5683 |
| 1751 | Susanna | 5689 |
| 1741 | Thurston | 5684 |
| 1744 | William | 5685 |

**WHITMARSH**

| 1878 | Ariadne | 7100 |
| 1869 | John | 7100 |

**WILLIAMS**

| 1806 | Alonzo | 6260 |
| 1810 | Aurelius F. | 6262 |
| 1870 | Charles Lyndon | 6144 |
| 1808 | Orlando | 6261 |
| 1803 | Patty | 6259 |
| 1802 | Thomas | 6258 |
| 1812 | Thomas | 6263 |

**WILSON**

| 1774 | Edward Thurston | 5816 |
| 1772 | John | 5815 |

**WINSLOW**

| | Andrew J. | 6061 |
| | Benjamin | 6060 |
| | Ephraim N. | 6059 |

**WOOD**

| 1706 | Bridget | 5541 |
| 1708 | Elizabeth | 5542 |
| 1716 | Henry | 5564 |
| 1714 | Jonathan | 5545 |
| 1716 | Mary | 5546 |
| 1722 | Peleg | 5506 |
| 1704 | Rebecca | 5540 |
| 1727 | Rebecca | 5563 |
| 1710 | Ruth | 5543 |
| 1726 | Sarah | 5567 |
| 1712 | Susanna | 5544 |
| 1733 | Thomas | 5562 |
| 1720 | William | 5565 |

**WRIGHT**

| 1854 | Henry Clay | 7677 |
| 1851 | Mary Elizabeth | 7676 |
| 1856 | William | 7678 |

**YORK**

| 1797 | Edward | 6245 |
| 1802 | Electa | 6247 |
| 1796 | Fanny | 6244 |
| 1808 | Hiram | 6 50 |
| 1794 | Jeremiah | 6243 |
| 1812 | Lydia | 6262 |
| 1799 | Martin | 6246 |
| 1805 | Randall | 6248 |
| 1810 | Ruth Caroli·ie | 6251 |
| 1806 | Thankful | 6249 |

## PERSONS WHO HAVE MARRIED DESCENDANTS OF EDWARD THURSTON.

**A**

| 1872 | Ackerman Mary Seymour | 7569 |
| 1868 | Ackerman Susie | 7510 |
| | Adams Anne | 6422 |
| 1850 | Adams Frances | 7041 |
| 1830 | Adlam Louisa Ann | 6640 |
| 1838 | Albro Oliver | 6727 |
| 1840 | Allen Catharine Borden | 6594 |
| | Allen Christiana E. | 6423 |
| | Allen Elizabeth | 6114 |
| 1848 | Allen Jane C. | 6343 |
| 1876 | Almy Amy Chase | 7481 |
| 1867 | Almy Mary Elizab'th | 6828 |
| | Almy William | 5661 |
| 1849 | Anderson Adelia | 6978 |
| 1810 | Andrews Roby | 6876 |
| 1807 | Andrews Susanna | 6873 |
| 1843 | Angell Julia Maria | 7149 |
| 1884 | Anthony Caleb Wilbor | 6808 |
| | Anthony Edwin | 6808 |
| 1800 | Anthony Mrs. Elizabeth (Cornell) | 5946 |
| 1744 | Anthony Eunice | 5720 |
| 1795 | Anthony Nancy | 5946 |
| 1836 | Anthony Oliver | 6953 |
| 1854 | Anthony Sarah H. | 7845 |
| 1863 | Anthony Susan L. | 7868 |
| | Antwerp Albert T. | 6842 |
| 1886 | Apthorp Rev. Wm. Perkins | 7108 |

| 1865 | Armington Helen F. | 6816 |
| | Arnold Mrs. Almira (Brayton) | 7210 |
| | Ashley Horace | 7876 |
| 1847 | Atkins Rev. Daniel | 6824 |

**B**

| 1865 | Babbitt Isaac N. | 6145 |
| | Babcock Robert | 5947 |
| 1801 | Babcock Sarah | 6305 |
| | Badey Hattie | 6847 |
| | Bailey Smith | 7727 |
| 1822 | Baker Mrs. Abigail | 5940 |
| 1874 | Baker Alice | 7567 |
| 1854 | Baker Amanda | 6437 |
| 1872 | Baker Chas. Osborne | 7452 |
| 1846 | Baker Charlotte Elizabeth | 6384 |
| 1808 | Baker Elizabeth | 6088 |
| | Baldwin Sabrina | 6255 |
| 1848 | Baldwin Mrs. Sarah (Clark) | 7176 |
| 1864 | Bankhead Mary Sullivan | 6524 |
| 1852 | Banning Rev. Carlos | 5997 |
| 1808 | Bannister John | 5898 |
| 1866 | Barber H. Maria | 7134 |
| | Barker Ruth Amelia | 6905 |
| 1867 | Barnes Henry H. | 7129 |
| 1764 | Barney Nathaniel | 5719 |
| 1843 | Barrington Charles Connor | 6516 |
| | Barton Amy | 5761 |
| | Bassell Rebecca | 5735 |

| 1837 | Bates Alvira E. | 6941 |
| 1704 | Batty Phebe | 5527 |
| 1867 | Beach Nancy | 8028 |
| 1860 | Beatty Annie M. | 6908 |
| | Bebee Hannah | 5836 |
| 1816 | Bedell Rev. Gregory Townsend, D.D. | 6180 |
| 1865 | Bee Mrs. Sophia Elizabeth (Hill) | 7235 |
| 1866 | Beegan Eliza Ann | 6544 |
| 1776 | Beers Patience | 5778 |
| | Bell William | 5734 |
| 1864 | Bemis Eugenie S. | 6005 |
| 1851 | Benjamin Frederick Augustus | 6701 |
| 1867 | Bennett Caleb H. | 7172 |
| 1829 | Bennett Capt. Chas. | 7540 |
| 1836 | Bennett Chas. Pendleton | 7017 |
| | Bennett Capt. Job | 5536 |
| 1848 | Berry Robert P. | 6482 |
| | Beverley Richard | 6498 |
| 1866 | Bicknell Cornelia | 6989 |
| | Billings —— | 5862 |
| 1859 | Birdsall Sarah Jane | 6845 |
| 1817 | Blanchard Abby | 6917 |
| 1855 | Blanchard Hartwell Hooker | 7189 |
| 1822 | Bliffins Thomas E. | 6552 |
| 1788 | Bliss Thomas Ward | 5711 |
| | Blivens Anson | 6612 |
| | Blossom Rufus | 6054 |
| 1829 | Blossom Susan | 6537 |
| | Blowers Lucy | 6265 |

| | T | | | | U | | | | | |
|---|---|---|---|---|---|---|---|---|---|---|
| 1800 | Tabor Mercy | 6085 | 1875 | Utley Mary A. | 6840 | | White Areadna J. | 7357 |
| 1736 | Tayer John | 5688 | | **V** | | 1789 | White Christopher | 5682 |
| 1788 | Taylor Benjamin | 6306 | | Vanalger —— | 6019 | | White Lucinda B. | 5685 |
| | Taylor Cornelius | 7001 | | Vanderpool Kate A. | 6695 | 1729 | White William | 5575 |
| | Taylor Grant Perry | 5983 | 1867 | Van Kleeck Augusta | 6444 | 1830 | White Wm. Joseph | |
| 1839 | Taylor Harriet | 6172 | | Van Vredenberg | | | Clarke | 6802 |
| 1782 | Taylor Lydia | 5870 | | Elizabeth | 6129 | 1834 | Whitford Barbara | 6625 |
| | Taylor Lyman Hart- | | | **W** | | 1871 | Whitford Mary Helen | 7481 |
| | well | 7426 | 1848 | Waddell Benj. A. | 7313 | 1795 | Whitman Mary | 6307 |
| 1848 | Taylor Nathaniel | 7052 | 1828 | Waddell Ruth | 6577 | 1868 | Whitmarsh Timothy | |
| | Taylor Sarah | 5871 | | Wade Daniel H. | 6264 | | Fox | 7100 |
| | Terry Benjamin | 6057 | | Wade —— | 7000 | | Whittemore J. de | |
| 1827 | Terry Brightman | 6579 | 1868 | Waith James T. | 7511 | | Wint | 6682 |
| | Terry John | 6581 | 1869 | Waldron James W. | 6211 | 1868 | Wiggin Sarah Emily | 7075 |
| 1774 | Terry Joseph | 5767 | 1847 | Wales Laura S | 6359 | 1802 | Wilbur Addeline A. | 6751 |
| 1796 | Terry Mary | 6042 | 1858 | Walker Henry Slade | 6944 | 1877 | Wilbur Ida Frances | 7158 |
| 1806 | Tew George C. | 5962 | | Wallace Clark E. | 6841 | | Wilcox Amy | 7006 |
| 1834 | Tew Latham Thurs- | | 1865 | Walrath Levi | 6926 | 1867 | Wilcox Sarah Jane | 7331 |
| | ton | 5971 | | Walters Marshal | | 1838 | Williams Laurilla | 5925 |
| 1866 | Thayer Anslem | 6922 | | Dane | 7424 | | Williams Olive | 6421 |
| 1818 | Thayer Sophia | 6888 | 1780 | Wanton Mary | 5613 | 1869 | Williams Thomas | 6144 |
| 1838 | Thomas L. N. | 5939 | 1768 | Wanton Sarah | 5741 | | Williams Thomas | 6257 |
| | Thomas Robert | 5900 | 1861 | Ward Mary P. | 7174 | | Wilson Henry | 7119 |
| 1849 | Thomas Seabury | 6380 | 1889 | Ward Sam'l Lindon | 6143 | 1875 | Wilson Laura | 7570 |
| | Thompson Thomas | 5864 | | Wardell Abraham | 6550 | 1761 | Wilson William | 5814 |
| | Thompson —— | 6183 | 1885 | Waring Joseph S. | 6782 | 1802 | Winslow Abby | 5961 |
| | Thurber John | 6117 | 1809 | Waterman Richard | 6398 | | Winslow Ephraim | 6656 |
| 1836 | Tibbitts Henry | 6455 | | Weaver Catherine | 6419 | | Winslow Hannah | 5762 |
| | Tillinghast Nicholas | 5534 | 1878 | Weaver Hannah | | | Wint Francis A. de | 6680 |
| 1873 | Tillotson Frances | 7474 | | Briggs | 7253 | | Winters Charles | 7558 |
| 1710 | Tompkins John | 5596 | | Weeks Joshua | 5766 | 1769 | Wood Daniel | 5890 |
| | Tompkins Samuel | 5724 | 1851 | Weir George | 7048 | 1870 | Wood Francis W. | 7428 |
| 1859 | Tooker Charlotte | | 1855 | Weir Mary F. | 7047 | 1715 | Wood Henry | 5568 |
| | Amelia | 7474 | 1850 | Welden Leander | 7731 | 1703 | Wood Jonathan | 5558 |
| 1754 | Townsend Nicholas | 5719 | | Wells Thos. Potter | 6813 | 1833 | Wood Martha T. | 6491 |
| 1867 | Treadwell Ida | 6774 | | Wells —— | 5712 | 1814 | Woodman Job E. | 5721 |
| 1849 | Truman Charles L. | 6986 | 1867 | Westgate Godfrey | 7329 | 1850 | Wright James | 7675 |
| 1812 | Tucker Hannah | 6670 | 1849 | Wharton Mary | 6105 | | **Y** | |
| 1857 | Tuers Adaline | 7543 | | Wheeler —— | 5868 | | Yates Cornelia | 6838 |
| 1751 | Turner Joseph | 5706 | 1858 | Whipple Ann Maria | 7414 | | Yates Seth | 5707 |
| 1870 | Turner Martha Hop- | | | | | 1817 | York Ann | 5376 |
| | kins | 7910 | | | | 1793 | York Jeremiah | 6242 |
| | | | | | | 1805 | Young Patience | 5221 |

### Further records from Rowley, Mass.

### 12,190

BENJAMIN and SARAH THURSTON, according to the church records of Rowley, had seven children baptized there. I can get no clue to the parentage of this Benjamin. Gage, in his History of Rowley, says there was a Benjamin Thurston in Richard Thurston's "alarm list;" and also this, "1778 the parish voted to build a new school-house near where Benjamin Thurston's house stood." So there surely must have been such a person, of whom I have no previous record.

### Children of Benjamin and Sarah Thurston.

12,191   David, bap. July 4, 1736. It is not impossible that this David is the same as no. 143, on pp. 36 and 47, as from later developments, I have serious doubts of his being the son of Jonathan, as given there. The date of David's birth, as given on page 47, was obtained from a letter giving the day of his death, and his age in years, months and days, by reckoning back from that data, and may not be perfectly accurate. It was customary in those times to have children baptized when but a few days old. The year of birth is given the same in both cases, and the days vary but very little, not more than I have had from members of the same family concerning the date of birth of their own parents.

12,192   Sarah, bap. Oct. 22, 1738.
12,193   Mehitable, bap. March 29, 1740.
12,194   Esther, bap. May 15, 1743.
12,195   Hannah, bap. June 23, 1745.
12,196   Abigail, bap. Jan. 3, 1747.
12,197   Lois, bap. March 4, 1749.

# DESCENDANTS OF JOHN THURSTON,

## BEARING THE NAME OF THURSTON.

### A

| | | |
|---|---|---|
| 1845 | Aaron Elsbuary | 9554 |
| | Abbie Ann | 9190 |
| 1850 | Abby Jane | 11.629 |
| 1825 | Abel Moors | 8940 |
| 1716 | Abigail | 8223 |
| 1764 | Abigail | 8365 |
| 1754 | Abigail | 8890 |
| 1817 | Abigail | 9133 |
| 1827 | Abigail Brown | 9176 |
| 1833 | Abigail Frances | 8992 |
| 1780 | Abijah | 8261 |
| 1751 | Abijah | 8389 |
| | Abijah Hoit | 8908 |
| 1858 | Abner | 9642 |
| 1810 | Abraham | 8721 |
| 1809 | Abraham Hopper | 8796 |
| 1830 | Abraham Lee | 8706 |
| 1833 | Abraham S. | g9391 |
| 1849 | Ada Leona | 9678 |
| | Adda | 10,017 |
| 1858 | Addison Carl | 8724 |
| 1829 | Adeline | 9655 |
| 1850 | Adin | 9549 |
| 1844 | Adnah | 9687 |
| | Adolphus | 8341 |
| 1871 | Adrien Eugene | 11,744 |
| | Agnes | 8913 |
| 1852 | Agnes Ruth | 11,719 |
| 1846 | Ahab Keller | 9263 |
| 1824 | Albert | 9045 |
| 1829 | Albert | 9584 |
| 1852 | Albert Buffum | 10,811 |
| 1858 | Albert Eugene | 9749 |
| 1877 | Albert Grant | 10,289 |
| 1874 | Albert Leon | 9865 |
| 1847 | Albert Llewellyn | 9062 |
| 1837 | Albert Peter | 9645 |
| 1872 | Albert Ricardo | 9346 |
| 1838 | Albert Sylvester | 9742 |
| 1852 | Albert Vastine | 10,065 |
| | Albertus | 9602 |
| 1833 | Albertus Elisha | 11,700 |
| 1869 | Alena | 9961 |
| 1828 | Alexander | 11,638 |
| 1788 | Alex. Campbell | 11,610 |
| 1806 | Alfred | 9570 |
| 1843 | Alfred | 9656 |
| 1875 | Alfred Albert | 9367 |
| 1822 | Alfred Lafayette | 9020 |
| 1861 | Alice | 9275 |
| 1859 | Alice | 10,202 |
| | Alice | 10,223 |
| 1868 | Alice Caroline | 10,098 |
| 1879 | Alice Gertrude | 9864 |
| 1875 | Alice Maud | 10,117 |
| 1860 | Allah | 10,071 |
| 1797 | Allen | 8886 |
| 1849 | Allen | 9950 |
| 1841 | Almira C. | 10,025 |
| 1838 | Alonzo Loomis | 9620 |
| 1819 | Alta (p. 508) | 9968 |
| 1836 | Alvan A. | 10,060 |
| 1840 | Alvin N. | 10,021 |
| 1729 | Amariah | 8196 |
| 1734 | Amariah | 10,710 |
| 1852 | Ambrose Dewane | 11,780 |
| 1807 | Amelia | 8737 |
| 1845 | Amelia Knight | 9003 |
| 1742 | Amos | 8333 |
| | Amos | 8459 |
| 1769 | Amos | 8489 |
| | Amos | 8809 |
| 1840 | Amos Draper | 9664 |

| | | |
|---|---|---|
| | Amos Orlando | 11,678 |
| 1875 | Amy Frances | 10,208 |
| 1865 | Amy Philena | 9589 |
| 1877 | Andrew Delos | 9690 |
| | Andrew Jackson | 9382 |
| 1847 | Andrew Jackson | 9508 |
| 1837 | Angella Louisa | |
| | French | 9720 |
| 1825 | Angeline | 9288 |
| 1856 | Angeline Esther | 9956 |
| 1851 | Angeline Isabella | 9970 |
| | Anna | 8682 |
| | Anna | 8806 |
| | Anna | 9526 |
| 1794 | Anna | 11,649 |
| 1873 | Anna Elizabeth | 10,155 |
| 1843 | Anna Hamilton | 10,8 ·1 |
| 1871 | Anna Mary | 10,038 |
| 1819 | Anna Teresa | 8944 |
| 1782 | Annie | 8269 |
| | Annie E. | 10,149 |
| 1854 | Annie Montgomery | 9733 |
| | Anson | 11,668 |
| 1860 | Arlina May | 11,740 |
| 1827 | Armena | 9648 |
| | Arthur Frederick | 10,206 |
| 1877 | Arthur Hobbs | 9908 |
| 1849 | Arthur Jefferson | 9585 |
| 1856 | Arthur Roberts | 9640 |
| 1843 | Asa | 8767 |
| 1859 | Asena | 9957 |
| 1889 | Asher | 9586 |
| 1870 | Atson Cyril | 11,150 |
| 1799 | Azor | 8862 |
| 1861 | Azor | 10,081 |

### B

| | | |
|---|---|---|
| 1871 | Barton Eugene | 9589 |
| 1843 | Bathsheba Abigail | 9017 |
| 1640 | Benjamin | 8104 |
| 1680 | Benjamin | 8129 |
| | Benjamin | 8130 |
| 1678 | Benjamin | 8140 |
| 1711 | Benjamin | 8206 |
| 1782 | Benjamin | 8282 |
| 1748 | Benjamin | 8340 |
| | Benjamin | 8416 |
| 1760 | Benjamin | 8421 |
| | Benjamin | 8711 |
| 1789 | Benjamin | 8976 |
| | Benjamin | 9478 |
| 1846 | Benjamin | 9498 |
| 1873 | Benjamin | 9787 |
| 1785 | Benjamin | 10,750 |
| 1850 | Benjamin Burton | 9432 |
| 1841 | Benjamin K. | 9296 |
| | Bertie | 9767 |
| 1672 | Bethia | 8126 |
| 1695 | Bethia | 8145 |
| | Betsey | 8682 |
| 1800 | Betsey | 8814 |
| 1780 | Betty | 8584 |
| 1758 | Birchy | 8359 |
| 1868 | Burton Reed | 9627 |

### C

| | | |
|---|---|---|
| 1760 | Caleb | 8393 |
| 1781 | Caleb | 8601 |
| 1811 | Caleb | 9205 |
| 1778 | Caleb Curtiss | 8474 |
| 1835 | Caleb Curtiss | 9684 |
| | Calvin | 8214 |
| 1801 | Calvin | 8927 |
| | Calvin H. | 10,059 |

| | | |
|---|---|---|
| 1863 | Calvin Marvin | 10,096 |
| 1808 | Calvin Sylvester | 8963 |
| 1863 | Carl Walton | 9848 |
| | Caroline | 9463 |
| | Caroline | 9597 |
| 1836 | Caroline Amelia | 9943 |
| 1871 | Caroline Annette | 9042 |
| 1829 | Caroline Gertrude | 9721 |
| 1840 | Caroline Sanford | 10,805 |
| 1859 | Caroline Warren | 8961 |
| 1806 | Caroline Whirl | 9420 |
| 1848 | Carrie | 10,018 |
| | Carrie Esther | 10,167 |
| 1868 | Carrie Langdon | 9722 |
| 1842 | Carrie Lillian | 9848 |
| 1876 | Carrie Lois | 9760 |
| 1879 | Carrie Louise | 9902 |
| 1869 | Carrie May | 10,323 |
| 1865 | Carroll Smith | 9251 |
| 1861 | Catharine Jane | 10,112 |
| 1863 | Catharine Pratt | 11,620 |
| 1806 | Catherine | 8719 |
| 1807 | Catherine | 9307 |
| 1819 | Catherine | 9391 |
| 1830 | Catherine | 9439 |
| | Catherine | 9610 |
| 1832 | Catherine Ann | 9319 |
| 1816 | Catherine Ann | 9449 |
| | Cattrenn | 9880 |
| 1837 | Charity Ann | 9361 |
| 1884 | Charles | 9488 |
| | Charles | 9525 |
| | Charles | 9677 |
| 1849 | Charles Albert | 9627 |
| 1854 | Charles Albert | 9830 |
| 1872 | Charles Curtis | 10,175 |
| 1865 | Charles Edward | 10,204 |
| 1826 | Charles Edwin | 9643 |
| 1846 | Charles Edwin | 10,817 |
| | Charles F. | 9191 |
| 1839 | Charles Franklin | 9006 |
| 1834 | Charles Hammond | 9058 |
| 1861 | Charles Howland | 9636 |
| 1874 | Charles Poland | 10,188 |
| 1846 | Charles Stott | 9370 |
| 1846 | Charles Torrey | 9676 |
| 1875 | Charles Wight | 9788 |
| 1874 | Chas. Worthington | 9371 |
| 1831 | Charlotte Holden | 8988 |
| 1814 | Charlotte Lovicey | 9132 |
| 1848 | Charlotte Syl- | |
| | phronda | 11,755 |
| | Chester | 8877 |
| 1807 | Chester | 8908 |
| 1871 | Chester Dexter | 9675 |
| 1758 | Chloe | 8392 |
| | Chloe | 8921 |
| 1795 | Christiana | 8648 |
| 1794 | Christiana | 8730 |
| | Christopher Colum- | |
| | bus | 9480 |
| 1858 | Clara | 10,105 |
| 1869 | Clara Adelia | 9942 |
| 1858 | Clara Jane | 10,092 |
| | Clarence | 9402 |
| 1853 | Clarence | 9771 |
| 1857 | Clarence G. | 9702 |
| 1854 | Clarence Odell | 9250 |
| 1866 | Clinton Augustus | 9852 |
| 1879 | Clinton Salsbury | 10,209 |
| | Cora Olivia | 10,162 |
| 1811 | Cornelius | 8739 |
| 1855 | Corrinnia Cath- | |
| | erine | 11,759 |

|      | Corsanus | 8309 |
|------|----------|------|
| 1559 | Cory A. | 9925 |
| 1852 | Crawford | 9958 |
|      | Curtis | 8878 |
| 1809 | Curtis | 8906 |
|      | Cyrus | 8326 |
| 1825 | Cyrus | 9588 |
| 1858 | Cyrus Ebenezer | 10,094 |
| 1865 | Cyrus Milton | 10,078 |

**D**

| 1875 | Daisey Olive | 9550 |
|------|--------------|------|
| 1646 | Daniel | 8111 |
|      | Daniel | 8185 |
| 1674 | Daniel | 8189 |
| 1695 | Daniel | 8160 |
|      | Daniel | 8184 |
| 1702 | Daniel | 8196 |
| 1716 | Daniel | 8208 |
| 1722 | Daniel | 8249 |
| 1737 | Daniel | 8322 |
| 1737 | Daniel | 8331 |
| 1749 | Daniel | 8388 |
|      | Daniel | 8456 |
| 1766 | Daniel | 8467 |
| 1775 | Daniel | 8527 |
| 1783 | Daniel | 8575 |
| 1800 | Daniel | 8619 |
| 1820 | Daniel | 9577 |
| 1841 | Daniel Allen | 9629 |
| 1812 | Daniel Brintnall | 9013 |
| 1816 | Daniel Clarendon | 8960 |
| 1852 | Daniel Edward | 10,090 |
| 1825 | Daniel Marvin | 9593 |
| 1853 | Daniel Sherman | 9907 |
| 1809 | Daniel Sylvester | 8937 |
| 1834 | Daniel Wesley | 11,701 |
| 1878 | Daniel Willis | 9780 |
| 1801 | Darius | 8928 |
| 1843 | Darwin Daniels | 9049 |
|      | David | 8142 |
| 1698 | David | 8159 |
|      | David | 8211 |
| 1721 | David | 8225 |
| 1728 | David | 8251 |
| 1746 | David | 8288 |
| 1782 | David | 8363 |
| 1755 | David | 8367 |
| 1762 | David | 8394 |
| 1762 | David | 8422 |
| 1774 | David | 8472 |
|      | David | 8480 |
| 1773 | David | 8529 |
| 1791 | David | 8540 |
| 1784 | David | 8602 |
| 1796 | David | 8649 |
|      | David | 8712 |
| 1811 | David | 8787 |
| 1811 | David | 8832 |
| 1832 | David | 9229 |
| 1844 | David | 9507 |
| 1822 | David | 9647 |
| 1878 | David | 9777 |
| 1854 | David | 9955 |
| 1870 | David Allen | 11,766 |
| 1843 | David Clark | 9364 |
| 1839 | David Floyd | 9277 |
| 1861 | David Israel | 9246 |
| 1836 | David Radle | 9264 |
| 1847 | David S. | 9240 |
| 1828 | David Stanton | 9201 |
| 1810 | David Thatcher | 8375 |
| 1843 | David Wm. Porter | 9002 |
| 1665 | Deborah (note) | 8113 |
| 1720 | Deborah | 8248 |
| 1749 | Deborah | 8854 |
| 1744 | Deborah | 8385 |
| 1777 | Deborah | 8558 |
| 1821 | Deborah Maria | 9330 |
| 1858 | Dedama Ann | 9614 |

| 1855 | Delcina Arabella | 9512 |
|------|------------------|------|
| 1822 | Della Atwood | 9170 |
| 1864 | Delkar | 9932 |
| 1707 | Diana | 8200 |
| 1816 | Doctor Sweatland | 8910 |
| 1877 | Dora | 10,234 |
| 1728 | Dorcas | 8284 |
| 1735 | Dorcas | 8289 |
| 1836 | Dorcas | 9294 |
| 1794 | Dorcas | 11,648 |
| 1735 | Dorothy | 10,711 |
|      | Dorney E. | 10,040 |
|      | Dory Bell | 9991 |

**E**

| 1718 | Ebenezer | 8209 |
|------|----------|------|
|      | Ebenezer | 8454 |
| 1801 | Ebenezer | 8803 |
| 1840 | Ebenezer | 9599 |
| 1860 | Edgar Byron | 11,763 |
| 1804 | Edgar Mandelbert | 8796 |
| 1846 | Edgar Mandelbert | 9560 |
| 1888 | Edmond M. | 10,016 |
| 1800 | Edward Eaton | 9909 |
| 1373 | Edward Everett | 9366 |
| 1836 | Edward Harrison | 9741 |
| 1824 | Edward M. | 9222 |
| 1812 | Edwin | 10,798 |
| 1856 | Edwin | 10,820 |
| 1838 | Edwin Curtis | 9663 |
| 1845 | Edwin Ingersol | 10,808 |
| 1878 | Edwin Jason | 10,170 |
| 1861 | Edwin Rebecca | 9939 |
| 1855 | Effie Gertrude | 9894 |
| 1856 | Eldorous Elijah | 11,735 |
| 1662 | Eleazer | 8106 |
| 1814 | Eleazer | 8909 |
|      | Electa | 11,660 |
| 1777 | Eli | 8800 |
|      | Eli | 9408 |
| 1808 | Eli | 9671 |
| 1777 | Eli | 10,744 |
| 1808 | Eli | 10,796 |
| 1845 | Elias Persing | 9422 |
|      | Elijah | 8880 |
|      | Elijah | 9604 |
| 1839 | Elijah | 11,708 |
| 1813 | Elijah N. | 8907 |
| 1839 | Elijah Wilton | 9504 |
| 1728 | Elioenai | 8252 |
| 1738 | Elisha | 8237 |
|      | Elisha | 8810 |
| 1810 | Elisha Madison | 8933 |
|      | Eliza | 8807 |
|      | Eliza | 9467 |
|      | Eliza | 9524 |
|      | Eliza | 9609 |
| 1817 | Eliza | 10,789 |
|      | Eliza | 11,661 |
| 1839 | Eliza | 11,704 |
| 1825 | Eliza Ann | 9033 |
| 1836 | Eliza Jane | 9015 |
| 1810 | Eliza Maria | 9012 |
| 1842 | Eliza Melinda | 9748 |
| 1817 | Eliza Vanshalk | 9326 |
| 1671 | Elizabeth | 8120 |
| 1796 | Elizabeth | 8165 |
| 1729 | Elizabeth | 8176 |
| 1720 | Elizabeth | 8210 |
| 1733 | Elizabeth | 8238 |
| 1729 | Elizabeth | 8268 |
| 1749 | Elizabeth | 8289 |
| 1758 | Elizabeth | 8368 |
| 1756 | Elizabeth | 8391 |
| 1767 | Elizabeth | 8502 |
| 1800 | Elizabeth | 8567 |
| 1830 | Elizabeth | 9291 |
| 1828 | Elizabeth | 9313 |
| 1831 | Elizabeth | 9341 |
|      | Elizabeth | 9381 |

| 1840 | Elizabeth | 9417 |
|------|-----------|------|
| 1831 | Elizabeth | 9487 |
| 1832 | Elizabeth | 9592 |
| 1856 | Elizabeth | 10,088 |
| 1772 | Elizabeth | 10,742 |
| 1854 | Elizabeth Eleanora | 10,091 |
| 1856 | Elizabeth Jane | 11,760 |
| 1849 | Elizab'th Jos. phene | 9915 |
| 1859 | Ella | 10,080 |
| 1852 | Ella Adelaide | 9732 |
| 1854 | Ella Josephene | 11,722 |
| 1849 | Ella Manerva | 9604 |
|      | Ellen | 9445 |
|      | Ellen | 9455 |
|      | Ellen | 9469 |
| 1962 | Ellen Julia | 10,141 |
| 1843 | Ellen Margaret | 9006 |
| 1821 | Ellis David | 9640 |
| 1847 | Ellis W. | 10,137 |
| 1876 | Elmar | 10,088 |
| 1878 | Elmer Day | 9945 |
| 1848 | Elmira Eleanora | 9372 |
| 1845 | Elna Catherine | 9430 |
| 1835 | Embly | 9415 |
| 1818 | Emeline | 9028 |
| 1838 | Emeline | 9270 |
| 1842 | Emeline | 9350 |
| 1779 | Emilie | 8491 |
| 1872 | Emily | 9964 |
| 1802 | Emily Stearns | 11,618 |
|      | Emma | 9466 |
| 1850 | Emma | 9496 |
| 1851 | Emma | 9586 |
| 1854 | Emma Jane | 9811 |
| 1857 | Emma Jane | 9918 |
| 1848 | Emma Leoline | 9730 |
| 1854 | Enoch Palmer | 9990 |
|      | Enos | 8786 |
| 1840 | Enos | 9491 |
| 1840 | Ephraim Edgar | 9237 |
| 1873 | Ernest Coe | 10,207 |
| 1860 | Estella | 9840 |
| 1674 | Esther | 8127 |
| 1700 | Esther | 8162 |
| 1723 | Esther | 8322 |
| 1724 | Esther | 8250 |
| 1764 | Esther | 8395 |
| 1802 | Esther | 8682 |
| 1811 | Esther | 9036 |
| 1823 | Esther | 9641 |
| 1858 | Esther Maria | 10,831 |
| 1852 | Ethel Erastus | 9806 |
| 1878 | Etta May | 9944 |
| 1834 | Eunice | 9596 |
| 1731 | Experience | 8197 |
| 1750 | Experience | 10,712 |
| 1858 | Ezekiel Theodore | 9513 |
|      | Ezra | 8449 |
|      | Ezra | 8801 |

**F**

| 1816 | Fanny | 9575 |
|------|-------|------|
| 1800 | Fanny Hawkins | 11,616 |
| 1861 | Firman Franklin, | 9643 |
| 1744 | Flavel | 8237 |
| 1772 | Flavel | 8426 |
| 1798 | Flavel | 8647 |
| 1836 | Flavilla | 9276 |
| 1855 | Flora Alice | 10,067 |
| 1859 | Flora Emma | 9641 |
| 1862 | Flora Evelyn | 9650 |
| 1851 | Florence | 9951 |
| 1862 | Florence Boyd | 10,203 |
| 1837 | Florrie | 8755 |
| 1807 | Frances | 10,795 |
| 1858 | Frances Adalene | 10,088 |
| 1850 | Frances Catherine | 10,818 |
| 1862 | Frances Jane | 9708 |
| 1842 | Frances Josephene | 10,815 |

38

John 9475
1843 John Alexander 11,626
1868 John Bragg 9630
John C. 8436
1832 John Coe 9739
1852 John Curtis 9683
1804 John Ellis 8950
1840 John F. 9258
1778 John Flavel 8430
1834 John Flavel 9230
1828 John Flint 9290
1865 John Franklin Perry 10,009
1862 John Fred 9252
John H. 8920
1817 John Hermon 9576
1829 John Holden 8957
1871 John Holden 9786
1801 John Hopper 8794
1819 John Jackson 9829
1839 John Laing 9630
1877 John Leason 9779
1859 John Leoria 9343
1858 John M. 9838
1847 John Mellen 9724
1811 John P. 8725
1833 John Sampson 9511
1879 John Spaulding 9682
1809 John Stevens 9060
1845 John Wesley 9869
1852 John Wesley 9433
1866 John Wesley 11,748
1871 John William 10,003
1797 Johnson 8761
Jonas 8834
Jonathan 8169
Jonathan 8816
1829 Jonathan Hubbard 9177
1824 Jonathan Vespatian 8965
1640 Joseph 8103
1670 Joseph 8134
1734 Joseph 8177
1700 Joseph 8195
1732 Joseph 8262
1769 Joseph 8397
1764 Joseph 8408
Joseph 8444
1797 Joseph 8617
1822 Joseph 9035
1739 Joseph 10,713
1775 Joseph 10,748
1811 Joseph 10,782
Joseph 11,665
1830 Joseph Daniels 9047
1855 Joseph Daniels 9832
1854 Joseph Daniels 9839
1861 Joseph Ellsworth 9958
1868 Joseph Elmere 10,010
1838 Joseph H. 9296
1842 Joseph Harrison 9181
1859 Joseph Lyman 9901
1850 Joseph Spaulding 9681
Josephene 8913
1847 Josephene Louisa 11,628
1850 Joshua C. 10,042
1828 Joshua E. 9809
1648 Judith 8112
1788 Julia 8603
1807 Julia 9129
1813 Julia 10,777
1852 Julia Lavinia 9829
1869 Julia Maria 9845
1845 Julius E. 9693
1837 Juna 9685
1867 Junius Floyd 9248

### K
1871 Katie Dickins 9661
1767 Keziah 8468

### L
1808 L. A. 8612
Laura 9605
Laura 11,676
1865 Laura Eliza 9704
1822 Lavina F. 9200
1772 Lazanna 8471
Lee W. 10,023
1834 Lemuel Smith 9249
Leona 8913
1853 Leroy Augustus 9809
1860 Lewella 9339
1751 Levi 8342
Levi 8583
1805 Levi 8736
1820 Levi 8789
1781 Levi 8973
1849 Levi 9509
1821 Levi Eaton 11,631
Levi Harrison 9366
Levi Judson 9368
1828 Levi Sherman 9186
1806 Lewis 8784
Lewis 9021
1865 Lewis Powell 10,142
1808 Lewis Taylor 8864
1873 Lida J. 9264
1847 Lilla Josephene 9768
1866 Lizzie Ada 10,196
1879 Lola Edna 10,214
1867 Loren Elzea 9941
1838 Loren Isabel 9231
1823 Lorenzo 9678
Lorinda 9606
1829 Lorinda Dimis 11,686
1862 Lorinda Ellen 11,741
1854 Louie Clarendon 9758
Louis Vespatian 9772
Louisa 9110
1812 Louisa 9470
Louisa 9573
Louisa 11,675
1860 Louisa Catherine 9424
Louisa L. 9676
1829 Louisa Marion 9022
1776 Lovina 8478
1802 Lovina 8622
Lucia 8858
Lucinda 8856
1799 Lucinda 8926
Lucinda 9442
1804 Lucinda 9569
Lucinia 8890
Lucius 10,147
1878 Lucius Earl (p. 507) 9677
1737 Lucretia 8272
1766 Lucretia 8396
Lucretia 9454
Lucretia Ann 9683
1745 Lucy 8212
1809 Lucy 10,771
1808 Lucy 10,781
1827 Lucy Ann 9651
1858 Lucy Ella 11,761
1815 Lucy M. 8941
1869 Luella 9899
1696 Luke 8161
1733 Luke 8270
1789 Luke 8273
1743 Luke 8376
1785 Luke 8676
Lurinda 9456
1735 Lydia 8216
1770 Lydia 8372
1780 Lydia 8475
1802 Lydia 8568
1817 Lydia 8849
1819 Lydia 8912
1782 Lydia 10,746
Lydia 11,667

1843 Lydia C. 9259
1794 Lyman 8615
Lyman 8804
Lyman 11,662
1845 Lyman C. 10,026
1832 Lyman Davis 9178

### M
Mabel Grace 10,194
1869 Mabel Louise 9896
1867 Mack 9960
1790 Mahala 8728
1882 Mahala 9595
1668 Margaret 8119
1678 Margaret 8122
1780 Margaret 8226
1741 Margaret 8274
1807 Margaret 8931
1843 Margaret 9622
Margaret 11,647
1850 Margaret Ann 9781
1665 Maria 8118
1822 Maria 9137
1821 Maria 9296
1844 Maria 9351
1874 Maria 9694
1811 Maria 10,776
1869 Maria Elizabeth 10,002
1843 Maria Fonissa 9298
1844 Maria Frances 10,052
1818 Maria Jane 9646
1827 Maria Saphena 11,679
1865 Marion Frances 9792
1822 Marion Letitia 9658
1800 Mars 3733
1811 Martha 8185
1709 Martha 8201
1811 Martha 8573
1906 Martha 8730
1798 Martha 8732
Martha 9458
Martha 10,227
1862 Martha Alice 10,006
1827 Martha Ann 8961
1826 Martha Ann 9037
1848 Martha Ann 11,633
1848 Martha Caroline 9061
1853 Martha Deetta 9975
1831 Martha Howe 9179
1848 Martha Jane 9534
1662 Mary 8105
1667 Mary 8106
1643 Mary 8110
1665 Mary 8123
Mary 8131
1688 Mary 8156
1702 Mary 8163
1727 Mary 8175
1714 Mary 8207
1723 Mary 8236
1720 Mary 8289
1760 Mary 8361
1746 Mary 8366
1797 Mary 8488
1793 Mary 8541
1804 Mary 8560
1805 Mary 8693
1802 Mary 8736
1812 Mary 8772
1808 Mary 8891
1788 Mary 8974
1827 Mary 9035
1872 Mary 9697
Mary 9458
1836 Mary 9489
1827 Mary 9504
1794 Mary 11,613
1872 Mary Abigail 9665
1871 Mary Adeline 10,154
1851 Mary Amanda 9421

| | | | | | | | | |
|---|---|---|---|---|---|---|---|---|
| 1865 | Smith | 10,113 | 1838 | Thomas Jefferson | 9598 | 1809 | William | 8897 |
| 1840 | Solomon Clinton | 9368 | 1818 | Thomas Palmer | 10,783 | 1835 | William | 9298 |
| | Sophia | 9464 | 1771 | Thursa | 8470 | 1828 | William | 9357 |
| 1838 | Sophia Jane | 9662 | 1766 | Timothy | 8501 | 1838 | William | 9490 |
| 1803 | Sophronia | 8840 | | Triphena | 9607 | | William | 9522 |
| | Susan | 8678 | | Tucker | 9385 | | William | 10,043 |
| | Susan | 8865 | 1860 | Tuella | 9556 | | William | 10,235 |
| 1817 | Susan | 8943 | | | | 1858 | William Alexander drew | 9977 |
| 1792 | Susan | 11,612 | | **U** | | | | |
| 1828 | Su-an Frances | 9055 | 1747 | Unity | 8387 | 1868 | William David | 9964 |
| | Susanna | 8296 | 1810 | Urban Clark | 8346 | 1816 | William Eddy | 11,625 |
| 1764 | Susanna | 8364 | 1842 | Urmina Ann | 10,029 | 1877 | William Edward | 10,177 |
| 1822 | Susanna | 9812 | | | | 1852 | William F. | 9934 |
| 1810 | Susanna Wheeler | 8964 | | **V** | | 1870 | William Fenn | 10,115 |
| 1868 | Susie Arabella | 10,197 | | Valorous | 9601 | | William Flavel | 9477 |
| 1877 | Stanley (p. 508) | 9967 | 1822 | Valorous Fernando | 11,677 | 1871 | William Ford | 10,099 |
| 1808 | Stephen Bailey | 8845 | | Victorina | 11,659 | 1877 | William Ford | 10,100 |
| 1866 | Stephen Bradford | 10,130 | 1775 | Vina | 8586 | 1813 | William Harrison | 8969 |
| 1845 | Stephen Clinton | 9765 | | | | 1840 | William Henry | 9214 |
| 1777 | Sybil | 8490 | | **W** | | 1832 | William Henry | 9945 |
| 1874 | Sybil | 9778 | 1875 | Wallace David | 10,124 | 1838 | William Henry | 9416 |
| 1836 | Sybil Holden | 8995 | 1842 | Walter | 8286 | 1836 | William Henry | 9619 |
| 1806 | Sylvanus | 8769 | | Walter Alonzo | 9565 | 1847 | William Henry | 9914 |
| | Sylvanus Welden | 9407 | 1871 | Walter Brady Scott | 10,011 | 1840 | William Henry Harrison | 9748 |
| 1802 | Sylvester Hill | 8949 | 1873 | Walter Ernest | 9854 | 1862 | William Hunt | 10,822 |
| 1878 | Syrena Walton | 9789 | 1869 | Walter Johnson | 9853 | 1843 | William James | 9429 |
| | | | 1878 | Walter Scott | 10.048 | 1634 | William Jason | 9687 |
| | **T** | | 1802 | Washington | 8889 | 1826 | William Johnson | 9054 |
| | Tamor | 8857 | 1865 | Wave | 9959 | 1841 | William K. | 9399 |
| 1818 | Thankful | 8847 | | Wesley | 9446 | 1850 | William M. | 9241 |
| 1867 | Thatcher Thayer | 10,804 | | Wesley | 9608 | 1872 | William Murray | 9628 |
| 1852 | Theodore Anthony | 9563 | | Wesley | 10.228 | 1847 | William Owen | 9680 |
| 1846 | TheronAlfred Earl | 10,052 | 1838 | Wesley S. | 10,051 | 1864 | William Philbrick | 9851 |
| 1683? | Thomas | 8101 | 1863 | Wilber Harken | 9247 | 1887 | William Stephen Bailey | 9626 |
| 1658 | Thomas | 8115 | 1876 | Wilbur Charlie | 9831 | 1858 | William Valorous | 11,736 |
| | Thomas | 8187 | 1860 | Wilbur Herbert | 10,193 | 1856 | Willie | 9632 |
| 1689 | Thomas | 8157 | 1865 | Willard | 10,082 | 1864 | Willie Grant | 10,129 |
| 1721 | Thomas | 8231 | 1815 | Willard Clark | 9027 | 1859 | Willie La Forest | 9811 |
| 1786 | Thomas | 8271 | 1742 | William | 8324 | 1849 | Willis E. | 9826 |
| | Thomas | 8438 | 1754 | William | 8413 | 1860 | Wilson | 9981 |
| 1795 | Thomas | 8550 | | William | 8440 | 1855 | Winfield Scott | 9541 |
| 1807 | Thomas | 8570 | 1799 | William | 8681 | | | |
| | Thomas | 9384 | 1785 | William | 8718 | | **Z** | |
| | Thomas | 9457 | 1795 | William | 8764 | 1761 | Zeruiah | 10,715 |
| 1848 | Thomas | 9494 | | William | 8813 | | | |
| 1885 | Thomas Jefferson | 9004 | | | | | | |

## DESCENDANTS OF JOHN THURSTON BEARING OTHER NAMES.

| | **ALDERMAN** | | | **BASTON** | | | Elizabeth | 8698 |
|---|---|---|---|---|---|---|---|---|
| | John Corydon | 8658 | 1877 | Frankie Lewis | 9890 | | Henry | 8699 |
| | Nancy Luany | *658 | | | | | Jacob | 8700 |
| | Orson Harry | 8658 | | **BAUM** | | | James K. | 8703 |
| | Sarah Dell | 8658 | 1877 | Lina Allah | 10,069 | | John | 8694 |
| | | | | | | | Julia | 8701 |
| | **AYER** | | | **BENJAMIN** | | | Perry | 8696 |
| 1863 | Flora Hepzibah | 8561 | | Alice May | 11,708 | | Phebe | 8704 |
| 1861 | John Cowper | 8560 | | | | | Samuel | 8695 |
| 1865 | Thomas Herbert | 8562 | | **BETTRIDGE** | | | Sarah A. | 8702 |
| | | | 1875 | Albert H. | f9891 | | | |
| | **BAKER** | | | | | | **BOSWELL** | |
| 1847 | Caroline Adelia | 11,636 | | **BIRDSILL** | | 1867 | Arthur Henry | 10,774 |
| 1845 | Estes Eugene | 11,635 | 1827 | Cynthia | 11,655 | 1863 | Wilber Frederic | 10,773 |
| 1849 | Willard Alexand'r | 11.637 | 1833 | Ebenezer | 11,657 | | | |
| | | | 1817 | Electa | 11,651 | | **BOWMAN** | |
| | **BARNEY** | | 1819 | Elizabeth | 11,652 | 1851 | Alice E. | a9891 |
| 1875 | Grace Plimpton | 9089 | 1824 | Fanny | 11,664 | 1855 | Clara Agnes | c9891 |
| | | | 1822 | Isaac | 11,653 | 1862 | Helen Eliza | e9891 |
| | **BARRETT** | | 1830 | Lyman | 11,656 | 1859 | Lillie S. | d9891 |
| 1858 | Albion Roscoe | 9089 | 1815 | Sarah | 11,650 | 1858 | William Newton | b9891 |
| 1855 | Augusta Angenette | 9088 | | | | | | |
| 1861 | Florence Marion | 9040 | | **BLAIR** | | | **BOYDEN** | |
| 1864 | Isabella Thurston | 9041 | 1846 | Abbie Eliza | 10,790 | 1715 | Seth | 8127 |
| | | | 1848 | Emilie Augusta | 10,791 | 1718 | Silence | 8127 |
| | **BARTLETT** | | | | | | | |
| | Ann | 8984 | | **BLAKE** | | | **BOYL** | |
| | Daniel | 8988 | | Andrew J. | 8697 | | Elizabeth | 9114 |
| | Henry | 8982 | | Clarissa | 8698 | | John R. | 9114 |
| | Lucy | 8986 | | | | | | |
| | Warren | 8985 | | | | | | |

**HINE**

| | | |
|---|---|---|
| 1848 | Marion | 9649 |
| 1852 | Nettie | 9650 |

**HOLDEN**

| | | |
|---|---|---|
| 1862 | Charles Lewis | 8989 |
| 1867 | David Roland | 8991 |
| 1865 | Ezra Cyrus | 8990 |

**HOWARD**

| | | |
|---|---|---|
| 1845 | Ellen S. | 8848 |

**JOHNSON**

| | | |
|---|---|---|
| 1828 | Asa Keyes | 10,781 |
| 1832 | Caleb Thurston | 10,733 |
| 1834 | Caleb W. | 10,734 |
| 1838 | Rev. Charles Thurston | •10,786 |
| 1843 | Edwin W. | 10 738 |
| 1848 | Frederic Keyes | 10,740 |
| 1845 | Harriet L. | 10,739 |
| 1840 | Herbert E. | 10,737 |
| 1836 | Martin Keyes | 10,735 |
| 1830 | Sarah E. | 10,782 |

**KENT**

| | | |
|---|---|---|
| 1855 | Ada Flora | 9889 |
| 1847 | Joseph Harrison | 9888 |

**KEYES**

| | | |
|---|---|---|
| 1805 | Asa | 10,723 |
| 1834 | Charles B. | 10,724 |
| 1848 | George H. | 10,729 |
| 1807 | Lucy | 10,730 |
| 1838 | Martha J. | 10,726 |
| 1808 | Mary | 10,722 |
| 1837 | Mary | 10,725 |
| 1845 | Mary F. | 10,728 |
| 1801 | Sarah | 10,721 |
| 1842 | Susan M. | 10,727 |

**KIMBALL**

| | | |
|---|---|---|
| 1866 | Charles Westley | 8986 |
| 1852 | Ella Augusta | 8982 |
| 1859 | Frederick Aaron | 8985 |
| 1854 | Georgia Etta | 8983 |
| 1856 | Lyman Edwin | 8984 |

**KNORR**

| | | |
|---|---|---|
| | Cora L. | 8759 |
| | Elmer | 8759 |
| | George | 8759 |
| 1864 | Mathias | 8751 |
| 1858 | Samuel C. | 8750 |
| 1865 | William | 8752 |

**LAMB**

| | | |
|---|---|---|
| 1816 | David Thurston | 8544 |
| 1859 | Edwin | 8545 |
| 1825 | John | 8548 |
| 1828 | Joseph | 8549 |
| 1823 | Mary Thurston | 8547 |
| 1851 | Nathaniel | 8543 |
| 1820 | Solomon Haskell | 8546 |
| 1813 | William | 8542 |

**LEARN**

| | | |
|---|---|---|
| 1863 | William Edwin | 9135 |

**LEE**

| | | |
|---|---|---|
| 1842 | Henry W. | 8850 |

**LELAND**

| | | |
|---|---|---|
| 1820 | Chesselden E. | 8516 |
| | Hannah L. | 8517 |

**MARTIN**

| | | |
|---|---|---|
| | Franklin | 10,035 |
| 1873 | Oliver May | 10,034 |
| 1870 | William L. | 10,033 |

**MAYER**

| | | |
|---|---|---|
| 1875 | Maud (p. 507) | 9954 |

**MEARS**

| | | |
|---|---|---|
| 1868 | Frank Willis | 9057 |

**MEIXWELL**

| | | |
|---|---|---|
| | John Lewis | 10,093 |

**METCALF**

| | | |
|---|---|---|
| 1823 | Aaron Gleason | 8600 |
| 1813 | Abijah Thurston | 8597 |
| 1801 | Cynthia | 8591 |
| 1846 | David Waldo | 9147 |
| 1810 | Erastus | 8596 |
| 1867 | Irene | 9144 |
| 1840 | Jesse | 8590 |
| 1839 | Julia Ann | 9145 |
| 1819 | Julia Stover | 8599 |
| 1804 | Mary Hill | 8593 |
| 1841 | Mary Jane | 9146 |
| 1815 | Miranda | 8598 |
| 1808 | Moses Glover | 8595 |
| 1834 | Nancy Maranda | 9141 |
| 1806 | Nancy Thurston | 8594 |
| 1803 | Rachel | 8592 |
| 1835 | Stephen George | 9143 |
| 1796 | Thurston | 8589 |

**MILLER**

| | | |
|---|---|---|
| 1796 | Abijah Thurston | 9073 |
| 1831 | Albert | 9070 |
| 1867 | Anna S. | 9874 |
| 1850 | Bradford Thurston | 9877 |
| 1819 | Charlotte | 9099 |
| 1802 | Elkanah | 9078 |
| 1833 | Gilmore | 9071 |
| 1817 | Gilmore | 9098 |
| 1799 | Hannah Fales | 9075 |
| 1798 | Jesse | 9074 |
| 1811 | Jesse | 9097 |
| 1836 | Jesse Richardson | 9072 |
| 1873 | Jessie May | 9878 |
| 1800 | Joseph | 9077 |
| 1824 | Julia Ann | 9667 |
| 1805 | Levina | 9079 |
| 1845 | Lyman Gilmore | 9873 |
| 1871 | Mabel Maud | 9876 |
| 1836 | Mary Eliza | 9870 |
| 1807 | Nancy | 9080 |
| 1869 | Nellie | 9875 |
| 1819 | Olive Maria | 9065 |
| 1809 | Rachel Johnson | 9082 |
| 1822 | Rachel Levina | 9066 |
| 1829 | Roxy Metcalf | 9069 |
| 1794 | Rufus | 9064 |
| 1807 | Sally | 9081 |
| 1826 | Sarah Luce | 9068 |
| 1841 | Susan Josephine | 9871 |

**MILLHAM**

| | | |
|---|---|---|
| 1842 | Francis | 8741 |
| 1848 | Gilbert D. | 8743 |
| 1854 | Israel | 8746 |
| 1855 | John W. | 8747 |
| 1846 | Martha Jane | 8742 |
| 1850 | Ruth A. | 8744 |
| 1852 | Sarah E. | 8745 |

**MUNYAN**

| | | |
|---|---|---|
| 1837 | Caroline Susan | 8953 |
| 1866 | Carrie | d8956 |
| | Charles | a3956 |
| 1835 | Daniel Marcellus | 8957 |
| | Fred. | b8956 |
| 1868 | Harry | c8956 |
| 1876 | Hattie Sophia | f8956 |
| 1868 | Laura Louise | e8956 |
| | Lydia Caroline | 8955 |
| 1882 | Warren Lawson | 8956 |

**NEWMAN**

| | | |
|---|---|---|
| 1860 | Cora Fanny | 10,182 |
| 1868 | Henry Byron | 10,183 |

**NICHOLS**

| | | |
|---|---|---|
| 1854 | Florence Clinton | 8942 |

**NUTTING**

| | | |
|---|---|---|
| 1854 | Edward Danforth | 8553 |
| 1852 | Harriet Fidelia | 8557 |

**NYE**

| | | |
|---|---|---|
| 1856 | Abbie Florence | 9817 |
| 1818 | Caleb Thurston | 9123 |
| 1855 | Emily Caroline | 9616 |
| 1857 | Frank Everett | 9618 |
| 1828 | James Arnold | 9125 |
| 1832 | John Harrington | 9127 |
| 1859 | Martha Elizabeth | 9619 |
| 1834 | Nathan | 9126 |
| 1862 | Nellie May | 9890 |
| 1826 | Susan | 9126 |
| 1820 | William | 9124 |

**OAKES**

| | | |
|---|---|---|
| 1867 | Altia N. | 9`61 |
| 1865 | Elizabeth J. | 92:0 |

**PACKARD**

| | | |
|---|---|---|
| | Joel S. | 8510 |
| | Lizzie Isabel | 8511 |

**PAGE**

| | | |
|---|---|---|
| | Frank | 9612 |
| | Fred | 9616 |
| | Helen | 9613 |
| | Leonard | 9614 |
| | Velma | 9611 |
| | Walter | 9615 |

**PATTEE**

| | | |
|---|---|---|
| 1871 | Agnes G. | 9009 |
| 1874 | Frank E. | 9010 |

**PIKE**

| | | |
|---|---|---|
| | Clementina | 8805 |
| 1834 | George S. | 8806 |
| | Joseph S. | 8809 |
| 1837 | Louisa M. | 8607 |
| | Maria L. | 8808 |

**POND**

| | | |
|---|---|---|
| 1857 | Annie Frances | 9142 |

**PORTER**

| | | |
|---|---|---|
| 1853 | Catherine Hannah | 9828 |
| 1846 | Richard Hankerson | 9827 |

**QUICK**

| | | |
|---|---|---|
| | Edward | 8780 |
| | James | 8780 |
| | Nancy | 8780 |

**RADLE**

| | | |
|---|---|---|
| 1823 | Catherine C. | 8652 |
| 1822 | David M. | 8651 |
| 1926 | Esther F. | 8653 |
| 1842 | Freeman Thurston | 8660 |
| | Gillie mintadell | 8657 |
| 1832 | James Taylor | 8656 |
| 1835 | Joanna | 8658 |
| 1845 | John N. | 8661 |
| 1838 | Reuben A. | 8659 |
| 1828 | Tabitha J. | 8654 |
| 1830 | William H. | 8655 |

**RAY**

| | | |
|---|---|---|
| 1854 | William Francis | 9154 |

**REYNOLDS (p. 507)**

| | | |
|---|---|---|
| 1875 | Frederick | 9945 |
| 1879 | George | 9949 |
| 1871 | Maud | 9946 |
| 1873 | William | 9947 |

## PERSONS WHO HAVE MARRIED DESCENDANTS OF JOHN THURSTON.

**A**

| | | |
|---|---|---|
| 1842 | Abbe Louisa Ann | 11,625 |
| | Abott Morehouse | 8811 |
| | Albro Amy | 11,862 |
| | Albro Hannah | 8803 |
| 1858 | Alderman Corydon | 8658 |
| | Aldrage Mary | 8231 |
| 1867 | Allen Almira | 9299 |
| 1875 | Allen Hattie | 9681 |
| 1847 | Allen Lovina | 9593 |
| 1705 | Allen Martha | 8139 |
| 1870 | Allen Mary E. | 9680 |
| 1782 | Allen Miriam | 8198 |
| 1856 | Alstyne Mary Van | 9619 |
| | Angell — | 8893 |
| 1845 | Anthony Matilda | 8796 |
| 1846 | Applegate Catherine | 9809 |
| | Appleman Mary Ann | 8748 |
| | Arison Philip | 9417 |
| | Auliff Frank M. | 9017 |
| 1860 | Ayer Cowper Swartz | 8559 |
| | Aylesworth Leonard | 8878 |

**B**

| | | |
|---|---|---|
| | Babbe Mary J. | 8786 |
| | Bailey Joel | 8475 |
| | Bailey Stephen | 8468 |
| 1808 | Bailey Thankful | 8474 |
| | Bailey — | 9728 |
| | Baker Catherine | 8782 |
| 1844 | Baker Henry Allen | 11,684 |
| | Baker Milate | 8507 |
| | Baker Walter | 9449 |
| | Balangee William | 9603 |
| 1852 | Ballard Sarah | 9643 |
| | Bancroft Leroy | 11,676 |
| | Bancroft — | 9605 |
| 1863 | Barber Lucretia R. | 9092 |
| 1847 | Barlow Luke | 8654 |
| 1868 | Barnes Sarah Eliz'th | 9364 |
| 1874 | Barney Frank E. | 9088 |
| | Barnum Caleb | 8683 |
| | Barrett Almeda | 8896 |
| 1853 | Barrett Amos Augustus | 9087 |
| | Bartlett Cassius | 8931 |
| 1858 | Bartlett Ellen A. | 9249 |
| 1868 | Bartlett Louisa S. | 9072 |
| 1871 | Bartlett Mary M. | 9245 |
| 1838 | Bastress Elizabeth Rhodes | 8736 |
| 1855 | Batchelder Emerson | 8958 |
| | Batchelor — | 8526 |
| 1873 | Batson Lewis C. | 9889 |
| 1872 | Baum Maurice Herbert | 10,064, 10,068 |
| 1868 | Beker Maria | 9400 |
| | Benedict Ruth | 8496 |
| | Benger Jacob | 8282 |
| | Benjamin Matilda | 8937 |
| 1878 | Benjamin William | 11,707 |
| 1874 | Bettridge Edward H. | 9391 |
| 1839 | Bigelow Julia Augusia | 8959 |
| 1865 | Bigelow Louisa | 10,764 |
| 1871 | Biley Christena Frances | 9364 |
| 1814 | Birdsill Isaac | 11,649 |
| 1859 | Birrit James | 9015 |
| 1870 | Blackington Jerusha | 9114 |
| 1846 | Blair John | 10,789 |
| | Blake Herman | 9080 |
| 1858 | Blake Laura Matilda | 9165 |
| | Blake Robert | 9081 |
| | Blake William | 8692 |
| 1854 | Boen Thomas | 9836 |
| 1872 | Boggs Martha | 9105 |

| | | |
|---|---|---|
| 1862 | Roswell Fred'k W. | 10,772 |
| | Bottenhamer Catherine | 8425 |
| 1794 | Bottenhamer Mary Magdelene | 8426 |
| | Bowdich Delaphene Libbie | 9676 |
| 1851 | Bowman Sergeant Jasper (p. 503) | 9391 |
| 1858 | Boyd Laura Ann | 9740 |
| 1718 | Boyden Jonathan | 8127 |
| 1863 | Boyers Sarah | 8754 |
| 1856 | Boyl Robert | 9014 |
| | Brady Walter | 9291 |
| 1809 | Brady William | 8673 |
| | Brady William | 9298 |
| 1865 | Bragg Vietta Celestia | 9629 |
| 1861 | Brawley Milton | 10,025 |
| | Braymer James | 9239 |
| | Breed Samuel Scott | 9646 |
| 1869 | Brice George | 9205 |
| 1875 | Brice Mary | 92.4 |
| 1848 | Bridgford George | 11,689 |
| 1876 | Briggs Estelle N. | 9380 |
| | Briggs James | 9665 |
| | Brigham — | 10,746 |
| 1805 | Brintnall Bathsheba | 8575 |
| | Brown Emeline | 8892 |
| 1888 | Brown Joseph | 11,650 |
| | Brown S. | 8512 |
| | Brown — | 8256 |
| 1761 | Bruce Roger | 10.715 |
| | Brush Richard | 8811 |
| 1871 | Buck George Hill | 10,801 |
| 1865 | Buck Theodore Hastings | 10,810 |
| 1858 | Buckingham Mary | 9305 |
| 1860 | Buckingham Milton M. | 10,029 |
| 1850 | Bucknam Roxana | 8542 |
| | Buffum Patience Rogers | 10,797 |
| 1818 | Bullard Rachel | 10,741 |
| | Bullard Willard | 8578 |
| 1852 | Bulson Eliza Ann | 11,700 |
| 1830 | Burch Martha | 8754 |
| 1870 | Burnett Jane M. | 11,718 |
| 1879 | Burr Hannah Bill | 9020 |
| 1844 | Burr Polly S. | 8965 |
| 1806 | Burrell Frances | 10,744 |
| 1819 | Bush Josiah | 10,742 |

**C**

| | | |
|---|---|---|
| | Camp William | 8753 |
| 1874 | Campbell Alice Susanna | 9549 |
| 1819 | Campbell Margaret | 8764 |
| 1786 | Campbell Sally (p. 501) | 8245 |
| | Canara Job | 8720 |
| 1716 | Carey John | 8144 |
| 1718 | Carey Mary | 8142 |
| 1776 | Carman Eliza | 8322 |
| 1672 | Carpenter Geo. King | 9068 |
| 1871 | Carter Jeboam | 11,719 |
| 1879 | Carter Wm. Mulford | 11,725 |
| 1848 | Caswell Lyman | 8552 |
| 1819 | Cavana Martin | 8814 |
| 1863 | Chandler Wm. G. | 10,770 |
| 1860 | Chaney Richard Thomas | 9197 |
| | Chapin Dorcas | 8206 |
| | Chapin Rachel | 8480 |
| | Chapin — | 8330 |
| 1878 | Chapman Rebecca A. | 9364 |
| 1877 | Chase Newell | 11,705 |
| 1668 | Cheney Joseph | 8118 |

| | | |
|---|---|---|
| | Chester Elizabeth | 8425 |
| 1860 | Childs Mary | 9254 |
| | Chivvis Jane Doty | 8795 |
| 1869 | Clark Emma M. | 9147 |
| 1865 | Clark Jane | 9016 |
| 1869 | Clark John | 9536 |
| 1810 | Clark Olive | 8576 |
| | Clark Samuel | 8890 |
| 1878 | Clarke Rev. Geo. S. | 8511 |
| | Clement — | 8812 |
| 1852 | Clough Amelia | 10,050 |
| 1890 | Coe Eliza Jencks | 8958 |
| 1871 | Coggan Alaneon | 9904 |
| 1847 | Cole Ann Elizabeth | 9036 |
| | Cole Fanny | 9700 |
| | Coles Harry | 9023 |
| 1865 | Collins Benjamin | 9871 |
| | Connor Julia | 10,734 |
| | Converse Willard | 8594 |
| 1878 | Cooke Eugene | 11,741 |
| 1871 | Cooke Wm. Andrew | 11,731 |
| 1804 | Coons Margaret | 8800 |
| 1770 | Cornwell Thomas | 8289 |
| | Cowperthwaite John K. | 8309 |
| | Crandall Mary T. | 10,738 |
| | Cridland Mrs. Elizabeth (Kent) | 10,797 |
| | Crosby William | 9468 |
| 1844 | Crowell George | 9135 |
| 1850 | Curtis Sophia | 8882 |
| | Curtiss Sarah | 8331 |
| | Cutler Josiah | 8926 |

**D**

| | | |
|---|---|---|
| | Daniels Abram | 8645 |
| | Daniels David | 8648 |
| 1830 | Daniels Jonathan | 10,767 |
| 1818 | Daniels Julia Maria | 8580 |
| 1834 | Daniels Mary Ann | 9150 |
| | Daniels Seth | 8391 |
| | Darland Benjamin | 8719 |
| 1871 | Dart Byron Hare | 11,723 |
| 1796 | Dart Lucy | 8489 |
| | Davies Betsey | 8253 |
| | Davis Anna | 8700 |
| 1863 | Davis Edwin | 9111 |
| 1823 | Davis Lucy Bucknam | 8617 |
| 1859 | Davis Lucy Jane | 11,701 |
| | Deams D. M. | 9812 |
| 1865 | Deebert George | 8253 |
| 1865 | Denny Mary Eliza'th | 9173 |
| | Denton — | 8314 |
| | De Witt Isaac M. | 9372 |
| 1857 | Dickerson Adelia | 9236 |
| | Dobbs — | 8282 |
| | Doty James W. | 8690 |
| | Doty Jane | 8795 |
| | Dow Lorenzo H. | 9721 |
| 1881 | Draper Olivia | 8897 |
| | Drown Christana | 9652 |
| | Dull Anna | 8718 |
| | Duroe C. R. | 9696 |
| | Duroe Lucy S. | 9668 |
| 1846 | Dutton Eliza Ann | 8939 |

**E**

| | | |
|---|---|---|
| | Easton Jas. (p. 503) | c9891 |
| 1810 | Eddy Joel | 11,611 |
| 1815 | Eddy Polly | 11,610 |
| | Edson Elizabeth S. | 10,736 |
| 1796 | Edwards Nancy Anna | 8969 |
| | Edwards Sarah Hunt | 8671 |
| | Elley Jacob | 8691 |
| 1819 | Elliott Cassandra | 8646 |
| | Ellis Amos | 8503 |
| 1690 | Ellis Ebenezer | 8124 |

39

# DESCENDANTS OF MOSES THURSTON,

## AND MISCELLANEOUS, BEARING THE NAME OF THURSTON.

**S**

| | Name | No. |
|---|---|---|
| | Samuel | 10,825 |
| | Samuel | 10,829 |
| | Samuel | 10,921 |
| | Samuel | 11,011 |
| | Samuel | 11,020 |
| 1807 | Samuel | 11,351 |
| | Samuel | 11,772 |
| | Samuel | 11,798 |
| | Samuel | 11,799 |
| | Samuel | 11,800 |
| 1786 | Samuel (end of index) | 12.202 |
| 1787 | Samuel Thomas | 11,027 |
| 1832 | Samuel Wesley | 11,367 |
| 1778 | Sarah | 10,287 |
| 1832 | Sarah | 10,494 |
| 1843 | Sarah | 10,510 |
| 1809 | Sarah | 10,958 |
| | Sarah | 11,032 |
| 1797 | Sarah | 11,033 |
| | Sarah | 11,297 |
| 1776? | Sarah or Sally | 11,791 |
| 1788 | Sarah (p. 556) | 12,192 |
| | Sarah (end of index) | 12.200 |
| 1835 | Sarah Ann | 10,529 |
| 1823 | Sarah Baldwin | 11,163 |
| 1838 | Sarah Catherine | 11,306 |
| | Sarah E. | 11,276 |
| 1866 | Sarah Elizabeth | 10,658 |
| 1826 | Sarah Elizabeth | 11,054 |
| 1831 | Sarah Elizabeth | 11,149 |
| 1856 | Sarah H. | 11,783 |
| 1829 | Sarah Hannah | 10,590 |
| 1862 | Sarah Lucina | 10,645 |
| 1836 | Sarah Rosetta | 10,518 |

| | Name | No. |
|---|---|---|
| 1825 | Sherman | 11,453 |
| 1863 | Sherman Harvey | b10,491 |
| 1748 | Shuah | 10,260 |
| 1748 | Shuah | 11.855 |
| 1833 | Smith Butler | 10,528 |
| 1865 | Smith Butler | 10,657 |
| 1834 | Solomon | 11.174 |
| 1854 | Son | 11.781 |
| 1855 | Son | 11,782 |
| 1866 | Sophie | 11.176 |
| 1841 | Spencer Dewees | 11.216 |
| | Stephen | 10 859 |
| 1795 | Stephen | 10,861 |
| 1858 | Susan Blanchard | 10,875 |
| | Susanna | 11,202 |
| 1808 | Susanna | 11.206 |
| | Susanna | 11.396 |
| 1843 | Sylvester | 10,577 |

**T**

| | Name | No. |
|---|---|---|
| 1869 | Thirza Locklan | 11,111 |
| 1767 | Thomas | 11,023 |
| 1758 | Thomas | 11.078 |
| | Thomas | 11.161 |
| 1852 | Thomas Claggett | 11,280 |
| 1877 | Thomas Edward | 11,279 |
| 1858 | Thomas Faville | 11,100 |
| 1805 | Thomas Jefferson | 10,318 |
| 1848 | Thomas Jefferson | 10,564 |
| 1880 | Thomas L. | 11,172 |
| 1874 | Thomas P. | 11,325 |
| 1815 | Thomas William | 11,085 |
| 1867 | Tillie May | 11,341 |
| | True | 11,807 |

**V**

| | Name | No. |
|---|---|---|
| 1819 | Vinal | 10,976 |
| 1877 | Vinal | 11,009 |

**W**

| | Name | No. |
|---|---|---|
| 1861 | Waldo W. | 11,795 |
| 1836 | Wales Bigelow | 11,417 |
| 1872 | Wales Bigelow | 11,425 |
| | Wallace Henry | 11,186 |
| 1878 | Walter David (end of index) | 12,255 |
| 1814 | Welcome | 11,451 |
| | Wightwick | 11,194 |
| | William | 10,973 |
| 1782 | William | 11,079 |
| 1319 | William | 11,194 |
| 1846 | William | 11,195 |
| 1823 | William | 11,377 |
| 1772 | William | 11,290 |
| 1796 | William | 11,440 |
| | William B. | 11,370 |
| 1850 | William Dwight | 11,097 |
| | William H. | 11,274 |
| 1839 | Wm. H. (p. 509) | c11,461 |
| | William H. | 11,805 |
| 1857 | William Harrison | 10,675 |
| 1801 | William Hauk | 11,294 |
| 1865 | William Henry | 10,576 |
| 1828 | William Henry Harrison | 12,299 |
| 1824 | William Ketcham | 11,166 |
| 1834 | William Kilbourn | 11,358 |
| 1865 | William Marshall | 11,310 |
| 1859 | Wm. Pendleton | 11,253 |
| | William S. | 11,265 |
| 1833 | William Sherman | 11,465 |
| 1810 | William Wallace | 10,862 |
| | Wilson | 10,995 |
| 1876 | Winfred Otho | 10,670 |

## DESCENDANTS OF MOSES THURSTON AND MISCELLANEOUS BEARING OTHER NAMES.

**ARTHURS**

| | Name | No. |
|---|---|---|
| 1867 | Elizabeth | 10 548 |
| 1869 | Henry | 10,549 |
| 1872 | James Edward | 10,550 |
| 1874 | Lizzie Helen | 10,551 |
| 1878 | Peter Franklin | 10,553 |
| 1876 | Thomas | 10,552 |

**ATWOOD**

| | Name | No. |
|---|---|---|
| 1844 | Charlotte | 10,476 |
| 1834 | Levi | 10,472 |
| 1868 | Lillian | 10,474 |
| 1865 | Norman Nathan | 10,473 |
| 1842 | Oscar | 10,475 |

**BADGLEY (end of index)**

| Name | No. |
|---|---|
| Calvert Jerome | 12,216 |
| Catherine | 12,213 |
| Charles | 12,221 |
| Eliphalet Ackerman | 12,217 |
| Emma | 12,223 |
| Flora | 12,219 |
| Geo. Washington | 12,215 |
| Mary Elizabeth | 12,214 |
| Minerva | 12,220 |
| William Edmund | 12,218 |

**BAKER**

| | Name | No. |
|---|---|---|
| 1851 | Annie | 11,164 |
| | Arthur Heaton | 10,603 |
| | Henry Edgar | 10,604 |
| 1858 | Mary Elizabeth | 11,165 |

**BARRY**

| Name | No. |
|---|---|
| Richard | 11,207 |
| Susanna | 11,208 |

**BENNETT**

| | Name | No. |
|---|---|---|
| | Albert | 10,448 |
| | Alfred | 10,439 |
| | Delia | 10,442 |
| 1859 | Francis Wayland | 10,432 |
| | Harrison | 10,438 |
| 1852 | Heber Amasa | 10,431 |
| 1829 | James | 10,430 |
| | James Thurston | 10,487 |
| | Jennie Eva | 10,436 |
| | Loanua | 10,440 |
| | Miriam Alice | 10,435 |
| 1831 | Moses Thurston | 10,434 |
| | Nancy | 10,441 |
| 1833 | Nancy Fidelia | 10,444 |
| 1862 | Robert Dunsha | 10,433 |

**BLOOM**

| | Name | No. |
|---|---|---|
| 1779 | Abraham | 11,015 |
| 1781 | Jacob | 11,016 |
| 1776 | Joseph | 11,014 |
| 1785 | Phebe | 11,017 |

**BOSTWICK**

| | Name | No. |
|---|---|---|
| | Lucius Hoyt | 10,396 |
| 1835 | Mary Chadwick | 10,397 |

**BOYNTON**

| | Name | No. |
|---|---|---|
| 1833 | Boardman Judson | 11,403 |
| 1824 | Caroline | 11,400 |
| 1827 | Lestina | 11,401 |
| 1835 | Myra Ann Amelia | 11,404 |
| 1830 | Nelson | 11,402 |
| 1822 | Obed | 11,399 |
| 1818 | Sarah | 11,398 |

**BRACE**

| Name | No. |
|---|---|
| Amanda H. | 11,796 |
| Callista E. | 11,796 |
| F. Helen | 11,796 |
| Harriet E. | 11,796 |
| M. B. | 11,796 |
| Marshal P. | 11,796 |
| Sarah Minerva | 11,796 |

**BREWER**

| Name | No. |
|---|---|
| Alfred F. | 11,152 |

**BRODT**

| | Name | No. |
|---|---|---|
| 1873 | Alfred Randolph | 10,340 |
| 1857 | Carrie A. | 10,340 |
| 1867 | Charles Hawley | 10,340 |
| 1869 | Daisie Louise | 10,340 |
| 1862 | Edwin Elwell | 10,340 |
| 1865 | Ellen Reno | 10,340 |
| 1863 | Henry Prewden | 10,340 |
| 1869 | John Ingold | 10,340 |
| 1871 | Philip Ernest | 10,340 |

**CAMPBELL**

| | Name | No. |
|---|---|---|
| 1856 | Ensley Gilmore Denison | 10,519 |
| 1858 | Sarah Alice | 10,520 |

**CARLETON**

| | Name | No. |
|---|---|---|
| 1834 | Alonzo Chadwick | 10,377 |
| 1807 | Caroline | 10,835 |
| 1840 | Caroline Sears | 10,379 |
| 1329 | David Chadwick | 10,375 |
| 1837 | Franklin Benjamin | 10 878 |
| 1819 | George | 10,371 |
| 1831 | Hannah Peabody | 10,876 |

## PERSONS WHO HAVE MARRIED DESCENDANTS OF MOSES THURSTON· AND MISCELLANEOUS.

## NAMES OF PERSONS INCIDENTALLY MENTIONED.

The figures on the left denote the time when spoken of and those on the right the page upon which the name appears.

41

584                THURSTON GENEALOGIES.

| | | |
|---|---|---|
| 1835 Smith John 451 | 1844 Strang Sam'l Bartow 288 | 1740 Tilison William 134½ |
| 1844 Smith Joseph 838 | 1827 Stratton Capt. John 304 | 1781 Tilton Daniel 57 |
| 1857 Smith Joseph 453 | 1882 Strong Daniel 248 | 1760 Tilton Capt. Jacob 69 |
| 1840 Smith Noahdiah 422 | 1865 Strong George 810 | Tingey Capt. 482 |
| Smith Richard 278 | 1845 Strong James 802 | 1859 Tooker William C. 351 |
| 1811 Smith Samuel 388 | 1679 Strong Elder John 75 | 1805 Toombs Rev. S. 96 |
| 1867 Smith Rev. Samuel F. 200 | 1805 Strong Rev. Jonathan 96 | 1797 Tooms Rev. Samuel 52 |
| 1853 Smith Samuel P. 292 | 1679 Strong Mary 75 | 1819 Towle Stephen 252 |
| 1882 Smith Thomas 188 | 1878 Strong —— 469 | Town Josiah 412 |
| 1779 Smith Uriah .872 | 1873 Strout Stuart A. 172 | Town Salem 172 |
| 1827 Smith Warren 508 | 1819 Sturgis —— 151 | 1851 Trafton Charles 253 |
| 1870 Smyth Rev. Newman 180 | 1787 Sullivan Gen. John | 1636 Travice Capt Nicholas 499 |
| 1812 Snell William 216 | 59, 289 | 1848 Tresdwell Henry |
| 1858 Snow Erastus 459 | 1807 Summers John 332 | Payson 389 |
| 1856 Snow Henry Jacob 259 | 18.5 Sutherland Rev. —— 95 | 1859 Tripp Rev. Ferris 313 |
| 1820 Snow Martin 225 | Sutton Joseph 363 | 1790 Tripp Peleg 265 |
| 1814 Snow Richard 247 | 1642 Swain Richard 171 | Trowbridge James 278 |
| 1813 Sodus Comfort 407 | Swan Benjamin 279 | Trowbridge Thomas 275 |
| 1858 Soper Elisha 185 | 1847 Sweet Philip Angell 320 | True Dr. N. T. 175 |
| Southgate William S. 194 | 1771 Sweet Capt. Samuel 286 | 1820 ?Truer Rev. John 443 |
| 1826 Southworth Dr.Ablah 176 | 1778 Sweetser Jacob 128 | 1824 Tucker Jonathan 210 |
| 1850 Southworth Charles | 1850 Swett Samuel Doyne 462 | 1857 Tuers Walter 384 |
| Upham Shepard 177 | 185 Sylvester Jas.Whitton 258 | 1849 Turner Stephen Ar- |
| 1857 Southworth Edw. 177, 235 | 1831 Sylvester Maj. John 246 | nold 365 |
| 1842 Southworth Edward | 1827 Sylvester Joseph 286 | 1757 Tush Maj. Thomas 58 |
| Wells 177 | 1635 Symonds Rose 83 | 1849 Twitchell Col. Eli 174 |
| 1859 Southworth Mary | 1635 Symonds Samuel 33 | 1830 Tyler Rev. Bennett 436 |
| Woodbury 177 | | 1828 Tyng S. H.. D.D. 284, 392 |
| 1847 Southworth Mase | **T** | |
| Shepard 177 | 1844 Talkington Samuel 241 | **U** |
| 1861 Southworth Thomas | 1846 Tappan Benj. D.D. 178,181 | 1802 Updike Elijah 405 |
| Shepard 177 | 1887 Tappan Rev. Dan'l D. 99 | 1807 Upton John 159 |
| 1852 Southworth Wells 177 | 1797 Tappan David, D.D. 52 | |
| 1852 Sparhawk Noah 179 | 1879 Tappan & Kelly 498 | **V** |
| 1828 Spear James 227 | 1792 Tarr Benjamin 122 | Vail B. T. 449 |
| 1847 Spencer Edw. Horace 348 | 1837 Taylor Davis 191 | 1837 Vanzant James 424 |
| 1787 Spencer Joseph 128 | 1818 Taylor Eleazar 2.8 | Veehten Rev. Jacob |
| 1853 Spendlove Joseph 454, 465 | 1604 Taylor Mary 36 | Van 90 |
| 1822 Spofford Dr. Amos 76 | Taylor Rev. Townsend | Victoria Queen 257 |
| 1782?Spofford Eleazer 38 | Elijah 156 | |
| 1729 Spofford William 27 | 1604 Taylor William 36 | **W** |
| 1796 Spring Rev. Samuel, | 1839 Taylor William 304 | 1777 Wait Capt. 56 |
| D.D. 52, 81, 82, 183 | Taylor —— 369 | 1840 Walden Capt. Green 248 |
| 1746 Spring Solomon 85 | 1812 Teague Joseph 86 | 1837 Walden James 898 |
| 1854 Spurling Gen. A. P. 221 | Teguer Bishop 17 | 1864 Walker Adelaide 249 |
| 1754 Spurr Joseph 873 | 1822 Telfor Alexandrew 898 | 1831 Walker Amos 392 |
| 1837 Stackpole David 113 | 1809 Temple Zeruiah 87 | 1835 Walker Chester Wm. 431 |
| 1620 Standish Hannah 89 | 1704 Tenney Ann 88 | 1853 Walker George 513 |
| 1799 Standish Dea. Josiah 167 | 1805 Tenney Rev. Caleb | 1871 Walker Haskel 225, 226 |
| 1620 Standish Capt. Miles | Jewett 96 | 1877 Walker Rev. H. D. 351 |
| 89, 167 | 1868 Tenney Rev. Sewall 498 | 1663 Walker Rev. Mr. 359 |
| 1652 Stanley Christopher 21 | 1805 Tenney Capt. Wm. 95, 96 | 1660 Walker Robert 354 |
| 1832 Stantenburgh Her- | 1819 Tenoee William 151 | 1677 Walker Sarah 26 |
| man 598 | 1817 Terry Isaac 884 | 1665?Walker Shubael 37 |
| Stanton Thomas 278 | 1655 Thaxter Thomas 857 | 1843 Wallace Gen. Lew 231 |
| 1834 Starkey Benjamin 164 | 1852 Thayer Thatcher, D.D. 324 | 1845 Waltman A. C. 113 |
| 1890 Starr Geo. Herbert 542 | 1838 Thomas Danford 412 | 1839 Walton Arthur 454 |
| 1857 St. Clair Charles 408 | 849 Thomas Daniel 292 | 1839 Walton Charles 887 |
| Stearns Isaac 438 | 1862 Thomas Gen. 879 | 1850 Waltz Samuel Otis 224 |
| 1815 Stebbins Dan 495 | 1833 Thomas John 327 | 1650 Wampatuck Josias 381 |
| 1875 Stebbins Franklin 494 | 1825 Thomas Vial 283 | 1780 Wanton John 266 |
| 1839 Stephens Alfred 853 | 1862 Thompson Daniel P. 497 | 1768 Wanton John 277 |
| 1853 Steptoe Col. 453 | 1805 Thompson Ignatius 95 | 1802 Wanton John 278 |
| 1798 Stetson Mr. 179 | Thor, son of Odin 17 | Ward Judge 125 |
| 1871 Stevens Edwin A. 337 | 1780?Thoreau 77 | 1799 Warner Elijah 882 |
| 1857 Stevens James Edwin 848 | 1751 Thurlo 81 | 1858 Warren Benjamin F. 236 |
| Stevens John 805 | 1182 Thurstan, archbishop 18 | 1794 Warren James 202 |
| Stevens Robert 271 | 1877 Thurston F. H. 17 | 1834 Warren Nathaniel 466 |
| 1878 Stewart Rev. S. J. 157,158 | Thurston Keith, Peck | 1850 Warren Wm, D.D. 186 |
| 1821 Stillman Rev. Mat- | & Co. 412 | 1850 Washington George 186 |
| thew 291 | 1805 Tibbetts John 237 | 1829 Waterhouse John P. 242 |
| 1831 Stinson Joseph C. 237 | 1878 Tillotson J. R. 351 | Waterhouse Samuel 283 |
| 1800?Stockbridge Benjamin 55 | 1775 Tillson Cephas 134½ | 1858 Waters Cornelius 175 |
| 1834 Stokes Jeremiah 132 | Tillson Edmund 184½ | 1834 Watson Caleb 69 |
| 1870 Stone Samuel F. 113 | 1750 Tillson Ichabod 184½ | 1795 Watson Daniel 131 |
| 1871 Storey Chas. William 184 | 1771 Tillson Jonah 134½ | Way George 273 |
| 1865 Storrs Richard S , D.D.178 | 1778 Tillson Moses 184½ | Way Henry 278 |
| 1854 Stoughton —— 306 | 1700 Tillson Stephen 184½ | 1848 Weaver George 324 |
| 1845 Stowe Isaac Mars 483 | 1747 Tillson Stephen 184½ | 1815 Webster Daniel 104, 126 |
| 1775 Strang Major 288 | 1773 Tillson Stephen 134½ | 1805 Webster Ezekiel 96 |

## MISCELLANEOUS ITEMS OF INTEREST.

7

Page 46, no. 137, Dea. John Thurston had three children not named there:
365*a* Jonathan,[6] bap. Nov. 25, 1744.
366*a* Sarah,[5] b. June 8, bap. June 12, 1748.
367*a* Miriam,[6] bap. April 19, 1752.
Page 80, no. 385, b. Feb. 20, bap. Feb. 27, 1757.
Page 81, no. 386, bap. July 17, 1763.
Page 364, no. 8342, Levi is very likely same as —— Thurston, p. 512, no. 11,864.
Page 446, no. 10,314, Rufus Thurston b. Oct. 18.
Page 447, no. 10,313, Edward Thurston b. March 9, 1788.
Page 468, no. 10,801, m. Feb. 15; line 2, read Mary Low (Bradley) Buck.

Page 476, no. 10,010. Since I commenced printing the index, I have received the following names, which it is very evident belong to the same family as given on page 476, though the authorities sending the two lists do not agree as to the name of the father of these children, one calling him Joseph, and the other Thomas; one saying, also, that the immediate ancestor came from England, and the one who furnished the following record that Thomas came from Rhode Island.

## 10,010½

THOMAS THURSTON married —— MONTROSS; moved to Fishkill, Dutchess county, N. Y., from Rhode Island in 1740.

### Children:

11,013 Jemima, b. Jan. 2, 1751; m. George Bloom, another informant says Benjamin Bloom (see p. 476).
+11,019 John Montross (see p. 476, no. 11,019), b. 1753; m. 1st, —— Ackerman; 2d, Jemima Rosenkrans; 3d, Susan Van Wagner; 4th, Phebe Wiley.
+11,023 Thomas, b. Dec. 2, 1767; m. Catherine Ter Ross (see p. 476).
+11,024 Jacob, m. Martha Valentine (see p. 477).
11,022 Rachel, m. Stephen Hanson (see p. 476).
11,025 Mary, m. John Rowland.
11,026 Sarah, m. Mynard Cooper.

## 11,019

JOHN MONTROSS THURSTON, eldest son of Thomas and —— (Montross) Thurston of Fishkill, Dutchess county, N. Y.; born there 1753; married, first, —— ACKERMAN; second, JEMIMA ROSENKRANS; third, SUSAN VAN WAGNER; fourth, PHEBE WILEY. He died 1834.

Mr. Thurston was a farmer; settled in Pleasant Valley, Dutchess county, N. Y., in 1770. He was assembly man in the legislature from 1801 to 1804 inclusive. During this time there was a law passed, giving to one man the monopoly of sturgeon fishing in the Hudson river. Mr. Thurston was opposed to all monopolies and strenuously opposed this measure. He was a devoted member and deacon many years of the Salt Point Baptist church.

### Children, by first wife:

12,200 Sarah, m. 1st, Garrett Adriance.
12,201 Joseph, n.m., d. aged 36.

#### By second wife:

+12,202 Samuel Montross, b. Nov. 18, 1786; m. 1st, Hannah Ackerman; 2d, Catherine Ackerman; 3d, Mary Kimley.
12,203 Hannah, m. Benjamin Lathin.
12,204 Jane, m. Edgar Thorne, a lawyer in Poughkeepsie, N. Y.; d. June 2, 1828. Children:
12,205 *Samuel Thurston* (Thorne).
12,206 *Jane* (Thorne).

## 12,202

SAMUEL MONTROSS THURSTON (*John Montross, Thomas*), son of John Montross and Jemima (Rosenkrans) Thurston of Pleasant Valley, Dutchess county, N. Y.; born there Nov. 18, 1786; married, first, by Rev. John Hotchkin of Green Bush, N. Y., Feb. 18, 1813, HANNAH ACKERMAN; she died Dec. 19, 1814. Second, by Rev. John Dewitt, May 2, 1816, CATHERINE ACKERMAN, sister to his first wife. Third, MARY KIMLEY of Camillus, N. Y., two weeks before his death, which occurred Jan. 17, 1856.

Mr. Thurston succeeded his father as a farmer on the homestead in Pleasant Valley. He was a surveyor, also, and laid out many of the towns in Dutchess county and some of the streets in Poughkeepsie; was assembly man in 1823. He was quite a noted business man and was chosen executor of estates far and near, great confidence being placed in his judgment and capacity. These trusts never suffered in his hands. Mr. Thurston was a man of stately form, not a particle bent even in age. He was a well educated gentleman, a great singer, led the choir for a number of years in the Salt Point Baptist church, of which he was a member and deacon.

"Mrs. C. A. Thurston," says a daughter-in-law, "was a devoted christian woman, member of the same church with her husband. Very retiring in her manners, her whole life was spent in self-sacrificing labors for the good of her husband, her children, and the church. The last words she uttered were prayer for her two sons, John and Platt, the only children out of the fold of Christ, and for the church she so dearly loved."

Children, by first wife:

12,210  Hannah Ackerman, b. Dec. 19, 1814; m. Harry P. Wooley and d. without issue Oct. 21, 1850.

By second wife:

+12,211  Jasper Ackerman, b. March 31, 1817; m. Mary Allen Wood.

12,212  Jemima, b. Feb. 8, 1819; m. Nov. 27, 1839, William Edmund Badgley, formerly a farmer in the town of Poughkeepsie, now retired from business; he is a member of the Presbyterian church in Pleasant Valley; she is a member of the Baptist church in Poughkeepsie. Children:

12,213  *Catherine* (Badgley), d. in infancy.

12,214  *Mary Elizabeth* (Badgley), b. Jan. 9, 1842; m. March 27, 1867, Edward I. Van Wagner, a farmer in Newburgh, Orange county, N. Y. They have Ida P., b. July 31, 1868, Albert, b. Sept. 7, 1870, and Edna (Van Wagner), b. April 28, 1872.

12,215  *George Washington* (Badgley), b. May 5, 1843; m. March 25, 1868, Mary V. Tomlison; a farmer in Clinton, N. Y.; no children.

12,216  *Calvert Jerome* (Badgley), b. Nov. 14, 1844; m. Oct. 28, 1868, Isabelle Peck; is a milk dealer in the town of Poughkeepsie. They have Edith Isabelle, b. Jan. 22, 1873, Charles E., b. March 16, 1874, and Arthur J. (Badgley), b. March 9, 1879.

12,217  *Eliphalet Ackerman* (Badgley), b. Feb. 14, 1846; m. Nov. 15, 1872, Mary C. Doty; is a farmer in Poughkeepsie. They have Willie E. (Badgley), b. Aug. 29, 1873.

12,218  *William Edmund* (Badgley), b. June 25, 1848; m. Jan. 14, 1874, Augusta Corliss; he is a farmer in Poughkeepsie. They have George C. (Badgley), b. Aug. 30, 1876.

12,219  *Flora* (Badgley), d. young.

12,220  *Minerva* (Badgley), d. aged 18, at Armenia seminary, where she was a student.

12,221  *Charles* (Badgley), b. June 6, 1855; n.m.; lives at home and is an extensive milk dealer.

12,222　*Emma J.* (Badgley), b. Sept. 25, 1860; n.m.; lives at home.
+12,223　John Montross, b. Feb. 19, 1821; m. Rebecca A. Bishop.
12,224　Elizabeth, b. May 15, 1823; m. Gerauld Underwood, a farmer in Pleasant Valley; she was a member Baptist ch.; d. Oct., 1870. Children:
　　12,225　*Julia* (Underwood), n.m.
　　12,226　*Jane* (Underwood), m. Theodore Horton.
　　12,227　*Susan* (Underwood), m. William Sheldon.
　　12,228　*Emma* (Underwood), d. young.
　　12,229　*Samuel M.* (Underwood), n.m.
+12,230　Platt, b. July 23, 1827; m. 1st, Mary Jane Champlain; 2d, Ann Stantenburgh.
12,231　Jane, b. May 18, 1829; m. Nathan Hollister of Burnt Hills, Saratoga county, N. Y.; d. 1849, aged 20. Children:
　　12,232　*Alfred* (Hollister), b. 1847; m.
　　12,233　*Katie* (Hollister), b. 1849; m. —— Hibbard; in New York city.
+12,234　Eliphalet Ackerman, b. June 17, 1831; m. Clara Turner Killey.

## 12,211

JASPER ACKERMAN THURSTON (*Samuel Montross, John Montross, Thomas*), eldest son of Samuel Montross and Catherine (Ackerman) Thurston of Pleasant Valley, Dutchess county, N. Y.; born there Mar. 31, 1817; married MARY ALLEN WOOD. He died Oct. 8, 1863.

Mrs. Thurston resides with her daughter in New York city; is an exemplary member of the Baptist church and devotes much time to church and benevolent objects; is one of the managers of the Baptist Old Ladies Home in New York.

### Children:

12,240　Elizabeth, m. Flavius J. Allen. When quite young he went from Maine to New York city; was a long time clerk in A. T. Stewart's dry goods store; afterward he was a partner in a large clothing store under the firm name of Von Keller & Allen, and is now proprietor of the Astor House in New York city.
12,241　Henry W., d. young.

## 12,223

JOHN MONTROSS THURSTON (*Samuel Montross, John Montross, Thomas*), brother of the preceding, and son of Samuel Montross and Catherine (Ackerman) Thurston of Pleasant Valley, Dutchess county, N. Y.; born there Feb. 19, 1821; married, March 17, 1847, REBECCA A. BISHOP, born Dec. 17, 1824. daughter of Rev. Titus Bishop of Olive, Ulster county, N. Y., a Baptist clergyman.

Mr. Thurston is not in any business at present, has always been a farmer; lives in Poughkeepsie, N. Y. Mrs. Thurston joined the Baptist church at the age of eighteen. She has been doing mission work for the last ten years; is engaged in the work of the Woman's Christian Temperance Union, and is corresponding secretary of the Poughkeepsie W. C. T. U. and recording secretary of the Dutchess county W. C. T. U.

### Children:

12,245　Mary Catherine, b. in South Danby, Tompkins county, N. Y., May 26, 1854; graduated from the Poughkeepsie high school in 1872, and is teaching in the city schools. She was converted when eleven years of age; is a member of the Baptist church.
12,246　Jasper Ackerman, b. in the town of Eden, Fond du Lac county, Wis., Apr. 29, 1857; d. Dec. 21, 1857.
12,247　Eliza T. (adopted), graduated from Vassar 1874; has taught in Louisville, Ky., three years, in Bethel Female college, Ky., one year, in Stamford, Ct., and now, 1880, is in Richmond Female seminary, Va.; is a member of the Baptist church.

## 12,230

PLATT THURSTON (*Samuel Montross, John Montross, Thomas*), brother of the preceding, and son of Samuel Montross and Catherine (Ackerman) Thurston of Pleasant Valley, Dutchess county, N. Y.; born there July 23, 1827; married, first, Sept. 26, 1854, MARY JANE CHAMPLAIN, born June 1, 1836, daughter of Henry Champlain of Rhinebeck, N. Y.; she died Feb. 15, 1860. Second, Feb. 19, 1862, ANN STANTENBURGH, born July 14, 1832, daughter of Herman Stantenburgh of Esopus, Ulster county, N. Y.

Mr. Thurston is in the freighting business in Hyde Park village, N.Y.

### Children, by first wife:

12,250   Nathan Hollister, b. July 13, 1856; n.m.; at Cedar Rapids, Iowa.
12,251   Arthur, b. March 9, 1859; d. June 29, 1860.
                    By second wife:
12,252   Herman Stantenburgh, b. March 1, 1866.
12,253   Hattie Scott, b. Jan. 27, 1868.
12,254   Mary Elizabeth, b. March 28, 1870.
12,255   Walter David, b. Jan. 12, 1873.

## 12,234

ELIPHALET ACKERMAN THURSTON (*Samuel Montross, John Montross, Thomas*), brother of the preceding, and son of Samuel Montross and Catherine (Ackerman) Thurston of Pleasant Valley, Dutchess county, N. Y.; born there June 17, 1831; married, March 21, 1854, CLARA TURNER KILLEY, born Sept. 14, 1834, daughter of Egbert Killey, who was editor of the Poughkeepsie Telegraph for twenty-five years, and died some years since.

Mr. Thurston went into the Poughkeepsie bank as bookkeeper at the age of seventeen, and by faithful attention to his duties was promoted to be teller in the Manufacturers and Mechanics bank in Williamsburgh, Brooklyn, N. Y., which position he filled satisfactorily for several years, when he was made cashier of the National bank at Green Point, N. Y. He died March 14, 1872, and his widow is living in Poughkeepsie, N. Y., 1880.

### Children, all born in Williamsburgh:

12,260   Edgar, b. April 12, 1855; d. in infancy.
12,261   Ada, b. Oct. 16, 1856; in Vassar, class of 1880.
12,262   Jennie, b. Oct, 17, 1859; student in New York Normal college.
12,263   Alfred Henry, b. April 11, 1870.

Page 491, no. 11,440, line 3, read Philena Burroughs, daughter of David Burroughs of Brattleborough, Vt.

Page 492, no. 11,454. David Burroughs Thurston m. Sept. 27, 1853, Mary Elizabeth Griffin, b. March 11, 1832, daughter of Nathan Ford and Mary Griffin. Mr. Thurston was in the boot, shoe, harness, and tanning business in Heuvelton till 1870, when he sold and went to West Point, Cuming county, Neb., where he "lives on his rents;" is "a liberalist in belief, considers nature all." Children:

12,268   Horace Murdock, b. Aug. 9, 1854; n.m.; fire ins. agent in Chicago, Ill.
12,269   Mary Louise. b. Mar. 31, 1859; m. Aug. 21, 1878, Fred Robert Kittle, the first child born in Fremont, Dodge Co., Neb., where they reside.
12,270   Ella Philena, b. Dec. 18, 1863.
12,271   Anna Laura, b. Oct. 12, 1865.
12,272   David Burroughs, b. Feb. 18, 1871.

Page 512, no. 11,864, very likely is Levi, found on p. 364, no. 8342.

**29**    ᴐ

CPSIA information can be obtained
at www.ICGtesting.com
Printed in the USA
LVHW081352240321
682328LV00002B/15

9 781296 565275